KT-488-400

Psychology

PSYCHOLOGY

Saul Kassin

WILLIAMS COLLEGE

Houghton Mifflin Company   **Boston**   **Toronto**

Geneva, Illinois   Palo Alto   Princeton, New Jersey

I dedicate this book to Betty Kassin, my mother.

Sponsoring Editor: Rebecca Dudley
Senior Associate Editor: Jane Knetzger
Editorial Assistant: Dana Arnaboldi
Senior Project Editor: Janet Young
Editorial Assistant: Marybeth Griffin
Production/Design Coordinator: Carol Merrigan
Senior Manufacturing Coordinator: Priscilla Bailey
Marketing Manager: Pamela Shaffer

Cover photograph by Scott Morgan, Inc.
Cover design by Harold Burch/Harold Burch Design, NYC

Anatomical art by Hans & Cassady, Inc.

Illustrations by Stephen Moore

All other art by Illustrious, Inc.

All part opening photos (pp. 35, 169, 327, 445, 555, and 683): "Bow Tie #1," © 1991 by Nancy Crow. Hand-dyed cottons, 47 1/2" wide x 44 1/2" high. Photo by J. Kevin Fitz-simons.

Chapter opening photos: p. vi (top), p. 1: © Richard Pasley/Stock Boston. p. vi (bottom), p. 37: © Scott Camazine/Photo Researchers. p. vii (top), p. 79: © Lennart Nilsson, *Behold Man*, Little, Brown and Company. p. vii (bottom), p. 131: © Charles Gupton/Tony Stone Images. p. viii (top), p. 171: © Andy Sacks/Tony Stone Images. p. viii (bottom), p. 209: © Forest McMullin/Black Star. p. ix (top), p. 253: © David Joel/Tony Stone Images. p. ix (bottom), p. 293: © Bob Martin/AllSport/Vandystadt/Photo Researchers. p. x (top), p. 329: © Esbin-Anderson/The Image Works. p. x (bottom), p. 369: © Lawrence Migdale/Stock Boston. p. xi (top), p. 407: © Chris Cheadle/Tony Stone Images. p. xi (bottom), p. 447: © Bob Daemmrich. p. xii (top), p. 481: © Paul Conklin/PhotoEdit. p. xii (bottom), p. 515: © Robert Fox/Impact Visuals. p. xiii (top), p. 557: © Ann Purcell/Photo Researchers. p. xiii (bottom), p. 601: © Esbin-Anderson/The Image Works. p. xiv (top), p. 645: © Bruce Ayres/Tony Stone Images. p. xv, p. 685: © David Madison/Tony Stone Images.

(Credits continue following appendix.)

Printed in the U.S.A.

Library of Congress Catalog Card Number: 94-76518

ISBN: Student Copy 0-395-52681-7

Complimentary Examination Copy 0-395-71717-5

23456789-VH-98 97 96 95

Brief Contents

Contents

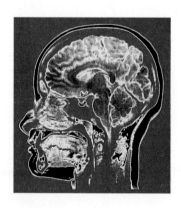

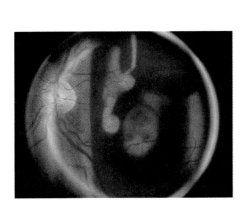

PART II   COGNITIVE AND AFFECTIVE PROCESSES

7.   Thought and Language

8.   Emotion

PART III   HUMAN DEVELOPMENT

9. Infancy and Childhood

10. Adolescence and Adulthood

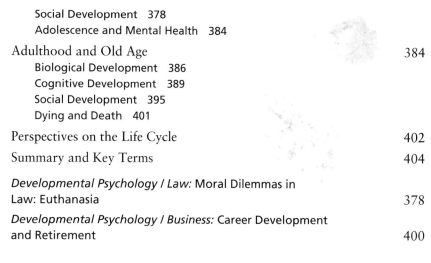

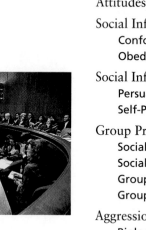

PART V   CLINICAL PSYCHOLOGY   554

15. Personality   556

PART VI   PUTTING THE PIECES TOGETHER   682

18.   Health and Well-Being   684

Preface

Some of my best friends are psychologists. They all have different interests, but they're all excited about the field and the contributions that are being made. In my own department alone, I have one colleague who is testing the treatment effects of a new drug on Alzheimer's disease, another who studies memory without awareness, a third who studies the use of language and pretend play in young children, a fourth who analyzes the process of psychotherapy, and a fifth who looks at social influences on voter perceptions of political candidates. Others in my department study stereotypes and prejudice, the structure of personality, children's use of defense mechanisms, the effects of alcohol on the developing fetus, and the role of impulsiveness in human decision-making. My own research is focused on social and cognitive aspects of the psychology of evidence and jury decision-making. As you can see, psychology is a remarkably diverse and exciting discipline.

I have three goals in writing this textbook. The first is to spark in students the passion that psychologists have for their work. Toward this end, I have tried to write a book that is not only "readable," but warm, personal, engaging, intelligent, and newsy. I have not ducked the hot and sticky issues. The ethics of animal research, the biological roots of homosexuality, and the recovery of repressed childhood memories are just a few of the controversies that I have confronted head-on by reviewing available research. I have also made it a point to illustrate the principles of psychology with vivid events from the worlds of sports, entertainment, literature, medicine, law, politics, and current events. I never, ever resort to "John and Mary in the dorm" hypotheticals to illustrate a point—it's just not necessary. The examples I use reflect my conviction (held, I believe, by too few textbook writers) that students have a deep and vested interest in a world that extends past the borders of the college campus.

My second goal is to teach students that psychology is not a mere laundry list of names, dates, theories, terms, and results, but an active and dynamic process of discovery—and that the state of our knowledge evolves over time. Every psychology textbook author seeks to present the discipline as a science. Indeed, many authors devote a whole second chapter to the topic of research methods and then insert critical thinking exercises within subsequent chapters. I have taken a somewhat more integrated approach. Since research methods are central to psychology's identity and development, this topic is introduced fully and comprehensively in Chapter 1, along with the field itself. In learning about research methods ranging from the use of case studies to experiments and meta-analysis, students are encouraged to think of science as a process that is both slow and steady, as well as dynamic.

As for critical thinking, I have always been skeptical of the exercises inserted into many current textbooks. An author cannot invoke critical thinking in students the way a parent spoonfeeds a baby. Rather, critical thinking is a frame of mind, an attitude that emerges naturally in response to information perceived to be personally relevant. I have thus made it a point to describe key experiments in vivid detail, often casting the reader into the role of a subject or experimenter, and often posing rhetorical questions about the results and implications.

My third goal is to demonstrate to students that basic and applied research are seamlessly connected enterprises. There are many, many specific domains of application in psychology. I have chosen to present five of these areas—health, education, business, law, and the environment—systematically throughout the text. These areas are featured in special, high-interest boxes on such topics as subliminal advertising, right-brain education, the insanity defense, gambling, behavioral treatments of headaches, repressed childhood memories, and jury decision-making.

ORGANIZATION AND COVERAGE

In writing a comprehensive, mainstream textbook, I sought to provide a broad organizational framework that makes sense to students—and to instructors. This book is divided into five major parts in a manner that captures the way many psychologists identify themselves within the profession. In order of their presentation, these parts—and the chapters they contain—represent *biological* psychology (behavioral neuroscience, sensation and perception, and consciousness), *cognitive* psychology (learning, memory, thought and language, and emotion), *developmental* psychology (infancy and childhood, adolescence and adulthood, and intelligence), *social* psychology (social perception, social influence, and human diversity), and *clinical* psychology (personality, psychological disorders, and treatment).

Individual instructors may disagree about the best way to organize the discipline within these five areas. For example, intelligence could be presented in the cognitive section, but I chose to place this chapter in the section on development in order to highlight the nature-nurture debate and the intimate link between intelligence testing and education. Similarly, the chapter on personality could be grouped under social psychology, but instead I use it to introduce the question of stability versus the capacity for change, an inquiry that is vital to the clinical enterprise. Indeed, most approaches to personality—from psychoanalysis to cognitive social learning theory—have direct implications for our understanding of psychopathology and prescribed methods of treatment.

Perhaps the most notable departure from the organizational norm is the absence of a specific chapter on motivation. In all my years of teaching psychology, I never quite understood the logic of grouping topics as unrelated as self-actualization and the physiology of hunger under a single banner. Motivation is basic to all areas of psychology and is treated as such in this text. Another curious strategy, common in today's texts, is to combine the topics of motivation and emotion. The literature on emotion, however, is now so extensive that it merits (and, in this book, has received) its own separate chapter. For instructors searching for the coverage of familiar material on motivation, here is a list of topics and the chapters in which they can be found:

- hunger and thirst (behavioral neuroscience, pp. 59–60)
- sleep and waking (consciousness, pp. 136–146)
- drugs and addiction (consciousness, pp. 160–165)
- instinct theories (learning, pp. 172–173)
- opponent process theory (emotion, pp. 316–318)
- intrinsic-extrinsic motivation (intelligence, pp. 425–426)
- sexual behavior (social perception, pp. 472–479)
- sexual orientation (human diversity, pp. 549–552)
- need for achievement (personality, p. 571)
- Maslow's hierarchy (personality, pp. 584–586)
- sensation seeking (personality, pp. 594–595)

From one area to the next, this book is remarkably up to date: close to half the references in many of the chapters are from the 1990s. Rather than adhere to a textbook "formula" that may have outlived its usefulness, I have taken a fresh look at the latest developments in each and every chapter. To be sure, I have tried to strike a balance between classics from psychology's historical warehouse and new studies hot off the presses. But my main goal is to describe the state of psychology *today*—and to do so in a way that is responsible. As in any textbook, the scholarship must be presented as accurately as possible. Therefore I rely almost exclusively on research reported in high-quality refereed journals. My review of the current literature led to coverage of numerous topics, such as the following, that are unique to this text or presented in a novel way:

- meta-analysis (Chapter 1)
- split-brain research (Chapter 2)
- psychology and the immune system (Chapters 1 and 18)
- extrasensory perception (Chapter 3)
- implicit memory (Chapter 6)
- unintentional plagiarism (Chapter 6)
- unconscious transference in eyewitness testimony (Chapter 6)
- autobiographical memory (Chapter 6)
- animal language (Chapter 7)
- cognitive heuristics in gambling (Chapter 7)
- the psychological impact of sexist language (Chapter 7)
- the cultural context of emotion (Chapter 8)
- happiness and life satisfaction (Chapter 8)
- seasonal affective disorder (Chapter 8)
- the newborn infant (Chapter 9)
- the child witness (Chapter 9)
- euthanasia as a moral dilemma in law (Chapter 10)
- adolescence and mental health (Chapter 10)
- the educational implications of intelligence testing (Chapter 11)
- practical intelligence (Chapter 11)
- the sociobiology of mate selection (Chapter 12)
- women and minorities in the workplace (Chapter 13)
- acculturation and acculturative stress (Chapter 14)
- racism in America (Chapter 14)
- comorbidity (Chapter 16)

- repressed childhood memories (Chapter 17)
- self-awareness and self-deception (Chapter 18)
- realities, illusions, and mental health (Chapter 18)

SPECIAL FEATURES

Determined to write a gimmick-free textbook, I have tried to weave distinctive features through the pages without a great deal of fanfare. This approach should help students see psychology's theories, research, and applications as unified and integrated. I would thus like to draw your attention to the following features:

- *"The Big Picture."* In distinguishing the subfields of psychology represented in the five parts of the book, I discuss how each centers on a basic and underlying question about human nature: How do the body and mind interact? (biological); Are human beings rational or irrational? (cognitive); What are the relative influences of nature and nurture? (developmental); Can situations overpower individuals? (social); and To what extent do people have the capacity for change? (clinical). Each question is introduced in the first chapter of each part with an opening section entitled "The Big Picture." Helping to provide a cohesive framework for the material in each subfield, these questions continually surface throughout the chapters.

- *Prediction Studies.* To introduce students to each area and to get them thinking about these underlying questions in operational terms, each "Big Picture" section contains an extensive account of a classic or recent study in which the student is cast in the role of subject or experimenter. After reading about the procedures, students are asked to predict the results. I have been using this technique in the classroom for many years, and have found that after students become personally committed to a prediction, they sit at the edge of their seats, eager to know what happened. Then when the outcome is revealed, they think long and hard about the study—particularly when the results contradict their predictions. Now, *that's* critical thinking.

- *Intersection Boxes.* In addition to dividing this book into the subfields of biological, cognitive, developmental, social, and clinical psychology, I have identified five major domains of application: health, education, business (including industrial-organizational and consumer psychology), law, and environment (including human factors research). The result is a two-dimensional, 5 x 5 matrix of intersections between basic and applied psychology. Throughout the text, areas of research representing each of the 25 cells of the matrix are highlighted in special boxes. For example, there is a biological environment box on being left-handed in a right-handed world, a cognitive law box on eyewitness testimony, a developmental health box on drugs and the fetus, a social business box on women in the workplace, and a clinical education box on attention deficit hyperactivity disorder. A complete listing of topics is presented on p. 14.

- *Coverage of Human Diversity.* Psychologists have always been fascinated by differences—between cultures, racial and ethnic groups within cultures, men and women, gays and straights. As we approach the twenty-first century, this topic is generating a great deal of scientific interest and controversy. Diversity is addressed, as appropriate, throughout this text. Similarities and differences are thus noted in perception, emotion, reasoning, intelligence, development, social behavior, the structure of personality, and psychopathology. To bring together some of the most important work in this area, I have also written a chapter entitled "Human Diversity," which examines such topics as stereotyping and prejudice, racism in America, gender differences, sexual orientation, and the cultural differences between East and West. As this chapter reveals, everyone is basically the same—yet no two people are alike.

- *A Capstone Chapter.* All introductory psychology texts that I've seen end on whatever happens to be the final word of the last substantive chapter. Typically, no effort is made to integrate the material or to provide students with a sense of closure. In a feature unique to this text, a closing "capstone" chapter brings together the various areas of psychology on an important and hot topic that is dear to everyone's heart: health and well-being. Following a brief discussion of "mind over matter," this chapter presents the latest research on the self, the health implications of self-awareness and self-deception, the processes of stress and coping, and the exciting new work in the area of psychoneuroimmunology. As noted in this final chapter, "The mind is a powerful tool. The more we know about how to use it, the better off we'll be. "

- *Pedagogical Aids.* In addition to the features just described, the following pedagogical devices are included:

- Chapter outline at the start of each chapter
- Narrative summary at the end of each chapter
- Key terms boldfaced in the text, defined in the margin, italicized in the chapter summary, and reprinted in a glossary at the end of the book
- Numerous tables, figures, photographs, hands-on exercises, cartoons, and quotations carefully selected to illustrate important principles
- Detailed subject and author indexes and a complete list of references cited in the text

ANCILLARIES

An extensive, high-quality package of teaching and learning supplements accompanies the text. Helpful annotated chapter outlines in the *Instructor's Resource Manual* coordinate all components of the package by showing which are relevant to each subsection of the text.

The *Instructor's Resource Manual,* prepared by Mark Garrison of Kentucky State University, provides for each chapter a set of learning objectives that are repeated in the *Test Bank* and *Study Guide;* a lecture outline that is annotated to coordinate all available teaching materials and activities; lecture resources, discussion topics; classroom activities; student projects; recommended readings; and recommended videos and films. A wealth of handouts to go with the many activities in the chapters are gathered at the end of the manual. The complete *Instructor's Resource Manual* is available on disk as well as in a three-ring binder.

The *Test Bank,* prepared by Grace Galliano of Kennesaw State College, contains three thousand multiple-choice questions, well over half of which test the student's ability to apply, not just recall, facts and concepts. The key for each question provides the correct answer and corresponding page in the text, the cognitive type, the relevant learning objective, and whether the question covers material on a box from the text. The *Test Bank* is available in print and on disk. The computerized *Test Bank* allows the instructor to add, edit, and scramble questions with ease and includes a number of other useful functions. On-line testing and gradebook options are also available.

The *Study Guide,* also prepared by Grace Galliano of Kennesaw State College, enables students to check their mastery of the material in the text, to practice taking multiple-choice questions of both the factual and the applied type, and to practice essay writing and critical thinking. Following sections on becoming a critical thinker and an active reader, each chapter includes learning objectives, a detailed outline of key concepts, a fill-in guided review organized by learning objective, two practice multiple-choice tests with an answer key that usefully discusses why the incorrect choices are wrong, and one or two synthetic critical thinking assignments. The *Study Guide* is availiable in print for student purchase and on disk for distribution by the instructor.

Psychabilities, designed by Sarah Ransdell of New College, University of South Florida, comprises fifteen interactive computer activities for use as a presentation tool in the classroom or for use by the individual student in the lab or at home. The exercises provide simulations of psychology experiments and demonstrations of psychological phenomena. Each module includes an introduction describing the content covered by the activity, the activity itself, a set of multiple-choice questions, and a list of key terms.

A comprehensive set of Transparencies for overhead projection covers material drawn from both within and outside the text.

"The Psychology Show" Videodisc and Instructor's Guide (also available on videocassette), a one-hour program, features motion segments, animation, and still images to illustrate concepts in introductory psychology. Some segments are designed to be provocative and stimulate class discussion, while others illustrate important biological or clinical functions that would be difficult to observe in the classroom. The footage, most of which is unavailable elsewhere, includes some classic experiments by Piaget and Milgram.

Under the Houghton Mifflin Multimedia and Film Rental Policies, a wide variety of videos are available. Contact your sales representative for information.

ACKNOWLEDGMENTS

In 1989, Mike DeRocco—then Houghton Mifflin's sponsoring editor for psychology—planted in my mind the idea of writing this textbook. Now, after five long years, I want to thank him for his support and encouragement. I also want to thank Becky Dudley, who stepped in for Mike and immediately adopted this book as her own.

I am indebted to many others on the Houghton Mifflin staff for their commitment to excellence. I particularly want to thank Jane Knetzger, my developmental editor, who worked on everything from the first draft of my first chapter to the final draft of my last chapter—and oversaw the entire project. Nobody knows this book better than Jane does, and she deserves a great deal of the credit for what's right about it. I want to thank Charlotte Miller, Ann Schroeder, and Janet Young for their many contributions to the artwork, photography, and other aspects of production. I also want to thank Grace Galliano of Kennesaw State College for writing the *Test Bank* and *Study Guide* that accompany this book, and Mark Garrison of Kentucky State University for his work on the *Instructor's Manual.*

I could never have written this textbook without the many, many thoughtful and scholarly reviews provided by colleagues at other institutions. I am indebted to Richard Lewis of Pomona College for his help on early drafts of the neuroscience and consciousness chapters; to Charles Collyer of the University of Rhode Island for his help on the sensation and perception chapter; and to Paul Whitney of Washington State University for his assistance in the area of thought and language. I am also deeply grateful to Cindy Kennedy of Sinclair Community College, who provided thoughtful, comprehensive, critical reviews of all chapters.

Through the various stages of this project, a total of eighty-six additional consultants contributed many comments, corrections, references, examples, and alternative points of view, which helped make me a better author and this a better book. For their expertise and generosity, I thank:

Lewis R. Aiken, *Pepperdine University*

Tony Albiniak, *University of South Carolina—Coastal Carolina College*

Larry M. Anderson, *Kwantlen College*

Viginia Andreoli Mathie, *James Madison University*

James R. Averill, *University of Massachusetts—Amherst*

Gregory F. Ball, *Johns Hopkins University*

Marie Banich, *University of Illinois at Urbana-Champaign*

Patricia Barker, *Schenectady Community College*

Carol M. Batt, *Sacred Heart University*

Robert C. Beck, *Wake Forest University*

Charles Blaich, *Wabash College*

Marc Bornstein, *National Institute of Child Health and Human Development*

John J. Boswell, *University of Missouri—St. Louis*

Jack H. Brennecke, *Mt. San Antonio College*

Robert C. Brown, *Georgia State University*

Danuta Bukatko, *College of the Holy Cross*

David W. Carroll, *University of Wisconsin—Superior*

John L. Caruso, *University of Massachusetts—Dartmouth*

John C. Cavanaugh, *University of Delaware*

John S. Childers, *East Carolina University*

Larry Christensen, *Texas A&M University*

Charles E. Collyer, *University of Rhode Island*

John Colombo, *University of Kansas*

Joseph G. Cunningham, *Brandeis University*

Robin DiMatteo, *University of California—Riverside*

V. Mark Durand, *State University of New York—Albany*

Robert A. Emmons, *University of California—Davis*

Martha Ewing, *Collin County Community College*

Morton P. Friedman, *University of California—Los Angeles*

Mauricio Gaborit, *Saint Louis University*

William Peter Gaeddert, *State University of New York—Plattsburgh*

Grace Galliano, *Kennesaw State College*

Rod Gillis, *University of Miami*

David Goldstein, *Duke University*

Mary Alice Gordon, *Southern Methodist University*

Robert L. Gossette, *Hofstra University*

Peter Gram, *Pensacola Junior College*

Richard A. Griggs, *University of Florida*

Jim Hail, *McLennan Community College*

Lynn Halpern, *Brandeis University*

Elaine Hatfield, *University of Hawaii—Honolulu*

John C. Jahnke, *Miami University*

Patricia A. Jarvis, *Illinois State University*

John Jonides, *University of Michigan—Ann Arbor*

Cindy Kennedy, *Sinclair Community College*

Frederick L. Kitterle, *Stephen F. Austin State University*

Stephen B. Klein, *Mississippi State University*

Mike Knight, *University of Central Oklahoma*

Richard S. Lehman, *Franklin & Marshall College*

Paul E. Levy, *University of Akron*

Robert M. Levy, *Indiana State University*

Dan Lipscomb, *Collin County Community College*

Mark Marschark, *University of North Carolina—Greensboro*

Louis D. Matzel, *State University of New Jersey—Rutgers*

Joan K. McDermott, *Towson State University*

David McDonald, *University of Missouri—Columbia*

Susanne W. McKenzie, *Dawson College*

Steven E. Meier, *University of Idaho*

Rick Mitchell, *Hartford Community College*

Steven O. Moldin, *Washington University School of Medicine*

Timothy H. Monk, *University of Pittsburgh School of Medicine*

Douglas Moore, *Temple University*

James H. Nelson, *Parkland College*

Michael Numan, *Boston College*

Richard Panman, *State University of New York—New Paltz*

Fred Patrizi, *East Central University*

David G. Payne, *State University of New York—Binghamton*

Roger D. Phillips, *Lehigh University*

Cornelius P. Rea, *Douglas College*

Judith C. Reiff, *University of Georgia*

Daniel Rosenbaum, *Detroit College of Business*

Laurie Rotando, *Westchester Community College*

Timothy A. Salthouse, *Georgia Institute of Technology*

Edwin A. Schwartz, *College of San Mateo*

Barry D. Smith, *University of Maryland—College Park*

William P. Smotherman, *Binghamton University*

Patricia N. Taylor, *Sumter Area Technical College*

David G. Thomas, *Oklahoma State University*

Arthur Tomie, *State University of New Jersey—Rutgers*

Lori R. Van Wallendael, *University of North Carolina—Charlotte*

Scott R. Vrana, *Purdue University—West Lafayette*

Paul J. Wellman, *Texas A&M University*

Bernard E. Whitley, Jr., *Ball State University*

Gordon Whitman, *Sandhills Community College*

Gail M. Williamson, *University of Georgia*

Sharon B. Zeitlin, *University of Toronto—Scarborough*

Betty Zimmerberg-Glick, *Williams College*

Last but not least, I am grateful to friends, co-workers, and my family, who had to tolerate my absences and occasional fits of emotion. I have but one message for Carol, Briana, Marc, my parents, sisters, grandmother, cousins, uncles, aunts, nephews, nieces, in-laws, and long-lost friends: "It's good to be back."

About the Author

Saul Kassin is Professor of Psychology at Williams College in Williamstown, Massachusetts. Born and raised in New York City, he graduated from Brooklyn College. After receiving his Ph.D. in 1978 from the University of Connecticut, he spent one year at the University of Kansas and two at Purdue University. In 1984–85, he was awarded a U.S. Supreme Court Judicial Fellowship, and in 1985–86 he worked in the Psychology-Law Program at Stanford University.

Kassin is coauthor of *Social Psychology* (now in its 2nd edition) and *The American Jury on Trial: Psychological Perspectives.* He has authored or edited five other books and has written numerous articles on attribution theory, social-cognitive development, and applications of psychology to the law. He has also served on the editorial boards of several major journals.

Away from work, Kassin manages a Little League baseball team. He enjoys quiet nights at home with the family, and has an insatiable appetite for sports, politics, rock 'n' roll, computer games, and ethnic food.

Psychology

Chapter 1

Introducing Psychology and Its Methods

As you prepare for the challenges of the twenty-first century, there are many directions you can take. In the future, as in the past, it will be essential to come equipped with the most basic tools of literacy: reading, writing, and arithmetic, an awareness of geography, some sense of history, and some knowledge of general science. Knowing a second or third language would be nice, too. You may be especially intrigued by the world of high technology. Fast personal computers equipped with high-resolution monitors, modems, and CD-ROM players, communications satellites that orbit the globe, FAX machines that transmit images thousands of miles in a matter of seconds, recent advances in genetic engineering, and the use of laser beams to repair delicate tissue—these are just a few of the jewels found in this brave new world.

But tomorrow, as well as yesterday and today, the key to success will be understanding people: yourself, your parents, romantic partners, friends, adversaries, teachers, coworkers, business associates, political leaders, and others. The questions we often ask about what makes people tick are numerous. How do we make important life decisions? Can people accurately bring back memories repressed from childhood? Can hypnosis be used to break the smoking habit? What motivates us to work hard or slack off, or to pursue one career instead of another? Why are some men and women homosexual and others heterosexual in orientation? Why do we fall in or out of love? Why do some teenagers get so depressed they commit suicide, and what can be done to prevent it? Why do we dream during sleep? What is intelligence, and how can it be brought out in our children? Why do some people age more gracefully than others? Can therapy for the mind be used to heal the body? Why do some athletes choke under pressure? What causes prejudice, and why is it so widespread? Why do nations go to war, or make peace? If you find these questions interesting and important, and if you think the answers should be sought in a serious manner, then psychology should be part of your future.

WHAT IS PSYCHOLOGY?

Psychology is the scientific study of behavior and the mind. If you dissect this definition, you'll see that it contains three elements. First is that psychology is a *scientific* enterprise. At an intuitive level, everyone is a psychologist—you, me, Ann Landers, the bartender who listens to one drunken sob story after another, the philosopher who reflects on the human condition, the minister who dispenses spiritual advice, the salesperson trying to close a deal, and the novelist who paints exquisite verbal portraits of fictional characters (see Table 1.1). Unlike those who rely on personal experience, however, psychologists employ systematic, objective methods of observation.

The second key element in the definition of psychology is that it is the study of behavior. The term *behavior* refers to any activity that can be observed, recorded, and measured. It may be as simple as the blink of an eye and as complex as making the decision to get married. Third, psychology is the study of the *mind*. For many years, researchers flinched at the mere use of the term. It was like talking about spirits or souls, or a ghost in the hu-

"Maybe you love too much."

Each of us has intuitive theories about people and their behavior. [Drawing by Cline; © 1993 The New Yorker Magazine, Inc.]

■ **psychology** The scientific study of behavior and the mind.

Table 1.1

How much do you already know about mind and behavior? Read the following statements and indicate whether you think each one is *true* or *false*. To see how well you did, the answers can be found on p. 4 and are explained elsewhere in this text. (Chapter numbers appear in parentheses.)

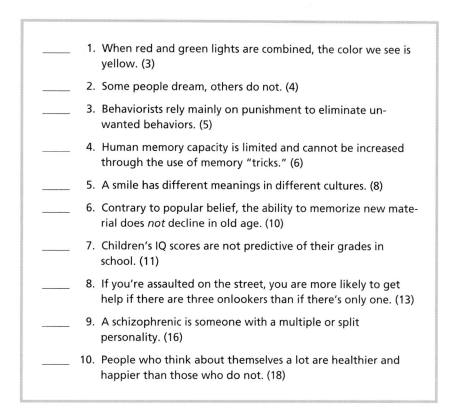

_____ 1. When red and green lights are combined, the color we see is yellow. (3)

_____ 2. Some people dream, others do not. (4)

_____ 3. Behaviorists rely mainly on punishment to eliminate unwanted behaviors. (5)

_____ 4. Human memory capacity is limited and cannot be increased through the use of memory "tricks." (6)

_____ 5. A smile has different meanings in different cultures. (8)

_____ 6. Contrary to popular belief, the ability to memorize new material does *not* decline in old age. (10)

_____ 7. Children's IQ scores are not predictive of their grades in school. (11)

_____ 8. If you're assaulted on the street, you are more likely to get help if there are three onlookers than if there's only one. (13)

_____ 9. A schizophrenic is someone with a multiple or split personality. (16)

_____ 10. People who think about themselves a lot are healthier and happier than those who do not. (18)

man machine. Today, the "mind" refers to all conscious and unconscious mental states. These states cannot actually be seen, but psychologists try to infer them from observable behavior.

Historical Roots

It has been said of psychology that it has a long past but a short history. This statement is true. The Greek philosopher Socrates (470–399 B.C.) and his followers, Plato and Aristotle, wrote extensively about human nature. They wrote about pleasure and pain, the five senses, imagination, desire, and other aspects of the "psyche." They also speculated about whether human beings were inherently good or evil, rational or irrational, and capable of free will or controlled by outside forces. At about the same time, Hippocrates (460–377 B.C.), the father of modern medicine, referred to the human brain as an "interpreter of consciousness." Years later, Roman physician Galen (130–200 A.D.) theorized that every individual is born with one of four personality types or "temperaments."

Many other men and women planted more recent seeds as well. French mathematician and philosopher René Descartes (1596–1650) theorized that the body is a physical structure, that the mind is a spiritual entity, and that the two interact through a tiny structure in the brain. This position, known as **dualism**, implied that although the body could be studied scientifically, the mind, the product of a willful "soul," could not. Thomas Hobbes (1588–1679) disagreed. He and other English philosophers argued

■ **dualism** The assumption that the body and mind are separate, though perhaps interacting, entities.

Answers to Common-Sense Psychology Quiz: All ten statements are false.

Wilhelm Wundt

■ **introspection** Wundt's method of having trained observers report on their conscious, moment-to-moment reactions.

that the entire human experience, including our conscious thoughts and feelings, are physical processes emanating from the brain—and, therefore, are subject to study.

Psychology also has its origins in physiology (a branch of biology that deals with living organisms) and medicine. In the nineteenth century, physiologists began studying the brain and other psychologically relevant structures. For example, Hermann von Helmholtz (1821–1894) studied sensory receptors in the eye and ear, and Gustav Fechner (1801–1887) developed a technique to measure subjective perceptions by varying physical sensations. Within the medical community, there were two notable developments. German psychiatrist Emil Kraeplin (1885–1926) wrote an influential textbook in which he likened mental disorders to physical illness and devised the first comprehensive system for classifying the various disorders. And in Paris, neurologist Jean Charcot (1825–1893) discovered that patients suffering from nervous disorders could sometimes be cured through hypnosis, a psychological form of intervention. From philosophy to physiology and medicine, psychology is deeply rooted in the past (Hilgard, 1987; Watson & Evans, 1991).

Pioneers in the Study of Mind   Historians tell us that modern experimental psychology was born in 1879, in Germany, at the University of Leipzig. It was there that physiologist *Wilhelm Wundt* (1832–1920) founded the first laboratory ever dedicated to the scientific study of the mind. At the time, there were no courses because the discipline on its own did not exist. Yet many students from Europe and the United States were drawn to his laboratory, producing the first generation of scholars ever to call themselves psychologists. In this group were G. Stanley Hall (who in 1892 founded the American Psychological Association [APA], with twenty-six members), James McKeen Cattell (a pioneer in the study of individual differences), and Hugo Munsterberg (among the first to apply psychology to industry and law). Overall, one hundred and eighty-six students were awarded doctoral degrees under Wundt's supervision, including thirty-three from the United States (Benjamin et al., 1992). Over the course of his career, Wundt published fifty-four thousand pages of material, edited psychology's first journal, and wrote its first book. His goal, as stated in the book's preface, was ambitious: "to mark out a new domain of science."

Wundt's approach to the study of mind was a far cry from the "armchair speculation" of the philosophers of his time. He used methods of intensive **introspection** in which trained observers would report on their moment-to-moment reactions to tones, visual displays, and other stimuli that were presented to them. In this way, Wundt studied attention span, reaction time, color vision, time perception, and other topics. In one study, for example, he had an observer look at a block of twelve letters for a fraction of a second and immediately report as many as he could remember. Six seemed to be his limit. What would happen if the number of letters in the array were varied? How would others do if given the same task? By recruiting people to serve as subjects, varying stimulus conditions, and demanding that all observations be repeated, Wundt was laying the foundation for today's psychology experiment.

In the United States, this budding new field was hearing a second voice.

That voice belonged to *William James* (1842–1910)—a graduate of medical school who went on to become a professor at Harvard University. In 1875, James (whose brother Henry was the famous novelist) offered his first course in psychology. He was very different from Wundt—but also influential. While Wundt was establishing psychology as a rigorous new laboratory science, James was arousing interest in the subject matter through rich ideas and eloquent prose. Those who studied with James described him as an "artist" (Leary, 1992). This group included G. Stanley Hall (who had also worked with Wundt), Mary Whiton Calkins (a memory researcher who became the first female president of the American Psychological Association), and Edward Thorndike (known for his work on animal learning).

In 1890 James published a brilliant two-volume text entitled *Principles of Psychology,* and in 1892 he followed this with a condensed version. In twenty-eight chapters, James wrote about habit, the stream of consciousness, individuality, the link between the mind and body, emotions, the self, and other deep and challenging topics. The original text was referred to as "James"; the brief version was nicknamed "Jimmy." For American psychology students of many generations, at least one of these was required reading. Now, more than a hundred years later, psychologists continue to cite these classics. The brief version can still be found in the paperback section of many bookstores.

A third prominent leader of the new psychology was *Sigmund Freud* (1856–1939), a Viennese neurologist. Quite far removed from the laboratory, Freud was developing a very different approach to psychology through clinical practice. After graduating from medical school, he saw patients who seemed to be suffering from certain ailments but had nothing physically wrong with them. These patients were not consciously faking, and they could often be "cured" under hypnosis. Based on these observations, Freud formulated psychoanalysis—a theory of personality, a form of psychotherapy, and one of the most influential schools of thought in modern history. Freud and his early followers (most notably, Carl Jung and Alfred Adler) left a permanent mark on psychology.

Freud (1900) introduced his theory in *The Interpretation of Dreams,* the first of twenty-four books he would write. In sharp contrast to Wundt and James, who were defining psychology as the study of conscious experience, Freud argued that people are driven largely by *un*conscious forces. Indeed, he likened the human mind to an iceberg: the small tip that floats on the water is the conscious part, and the vast region submerged beneath the surface is the unconscious. Based on this assumption, Freud and his followers developed therapy techniques and personality tests that were designed to penetrate this hidden but truly important part of the human mind (see Chapter 15).

Despite the differences in their approaches, Wundt, James, and Freud were the pioneers of modern psychology. Indeed, they were recently ranked by twenty-nine prominent historians as the first, second, and third most important psychologists of all time (Korn et al., 1991). As we'll see later, there are many others who also helped shape this new discipline. In 1885, German philosopher *Hermann Ebbinghaus* published the results of many classic experiments on memory and forgetting, using himself as a subject. In 1905, French psychologist *Alfred Binet* devised the first major intelligence

William James

Sigmund Freud

test in order to assess the academic potential of schoolchildren in Paris. And in 1912, *Max Wertheimer* discovered that people see two stationary lights flashing in succession as a single light moving back and forth. This illusion of apparent motion paved the way for Gestalt psychology, a theoretical approach based on the idea that what people perceive is greater than the sum of isolated sensations. In the emergence of psychology as the study of mental processes, there were many heroes (see Table 1.2).

Table 1.2

Pioneers of Modern Psychology

Wilhelm Wundt	Establishes the first psychology laboratory at the University of Leipzig, Germany (1879)
William James	At Harvard University, publishes *The Principles of Psychology* (1890)
Sigmund Freud	In Vienna, introduces psychoanalysis in *The Interpretation of Dreams* (1900)
Hermann Ebbinghaus	In Germany, conducts classic first experiments on memory and forgetting (1885)
G. Stanley Hall	Founds the American Psychological Association (1892)
Edward Thorndike	In the United States, reports on the first experiments on animal learning (1898)
Alfred Binet	Develops the first modern intelligence test for assessing schoolchildren in Paris (1905)
Mary Whiton Calkins	Becomes the first female president of the American Psychological Association (1905)
Ivan Pavlov	A Russian physiologist, discovers classical conditioning in research with dogs (1906)
Max Wertheimer	Discovers the illusion of apparent movement, which launches Gestalt psychology (1912)
John Watson	Defines psychology as the study of behavior, sparks behaviorism in the United States (1913)

The Behaviorist Alternative   The first generation of psychologists were just beginning to explore conscious and unconscious mental processes when they were struck by controversy about the direction they were taking. Can a science really be based on introspective reports of subjective experience? Should understanding how the mind works be the goal of this new science? There were those who did not think so.

In 1898, *Edward Thorndike* conducted a series of experiments on "animal intelligence." In one study, he put cats into a cage, put food outside a door, and timed how long it took for them to learn how to escape. After several trials, Thorndike found that by repeating behaviors that "worked," the cats became quicker with practice. Then in 1906, Russian physiologist *Ivan Pavlov* made another discovery. Pavlov was studying the digestive system in dogs by putting food in their mouths and measuring the flow of saliva. After repeated testing, he found that the dogs would salivate in anticipation, before the food was in the mouth. At first, Pavlov saw this "psychic secretion" as a nuisance. But soon he realized what it revealed: that a very basic form of learning had taken place.

Interesting. But what do puzzle-solving cats and salivating dogs have to do with psychology? Indeed, what's the relevance to people of any animal research? To answer these questions, *John Watson* (1913)—an American psychologist who had experimented with dogs, cats, monkeys, frogs, fish, rats, and chickens—redefined psychology as the study of observable behavior, not of the invisible and elusive mind. Said Watson, "Psychology as the behaviorist views it is a purely objective experimental branch of natural science. Its theoretical goal is the prediction and control of behavior" (p. 158). Sensations, thoughts, feelings, and motivations may fuel speculation for the curious philosopher, but if it can't be seen, then it has no place in psychology. Psychoanalysis, barked Watson, was "voodooism" (1927, p. 502). As for using animals, Watson—like others who were influenced by Darwin's theory of evolution—saw no reason to believe that the principles of behavior would be any different from one species to the next.

American psychologists were immediately drawn to the hard-boiled approach of **behaviorism.** The behaviorist's research goals were clear: vary a *stimulus* in the environment and observe the organism's *response.* There were no fuzzy ideas about mental processes inside the head, just stimulus-response connections. It was all neat, clean, and objective. Watson himself was forced out of academic psychology in 1920 when it became public that he was having an affair with his research assistant. He divorced his wife, married the assistant, and was fired as a result of the scandal (Watson went into advertising, where he applied the new principles of conditioning and became a leading figure in the industry). But behaviorism was alive and well. Psychology was defined as the scientific study of behavior, and animal labs were springing up all over the country.

Behaviorism had many proponents and was popular for many years. After Watson, another leader emerged: *B. F. Skinner*, the psychologist who coined the term *reinforcement*, invented an apparatus for use in testing animals, and demonstrated in numerous experiments with rats and pigeons that behavior is controlled by the reward and punishment contingencies in the environment. Skinner first reported on his experiments in 1938. Later, he and others used his findings to modify behavior in the workplace, the classroom, the clinic, and other settings. To the day he died, Skinner (1990) maintained that psychology could never be a science of mind.

The "Cognitive Revolution"   Behaviorism dominated psychology in the United States from the 1920s through the 1960s. Ultimately, however, psychologists were unwilling to limit their scope to the study of observable behavior. There was too much happening inside the organism that was interesting and hard to ignore. Physiology researchers were locating new pathways in the brain that regulate thoughts, feelings, and behavior. Animal researchers were finding that inborn biological instincts often interfere with learning. Child development researchers were noticing that children pass through a series of cognitive stages in the way they think about the world. Those interested in social relations were finding that our interactions with people are influenced by the way we perceive and interpret their

■ **behaviorism** A school of thought that defines psychology as the scientific study of observable behavior.

■ **cognition** A general term that refers to mental processes such as thinking, knowing, and remembering.

actions. Those experimenting with psychoanalysis were coming to appreciate more and more the role of unconscious motivation. And psychologists who called themselves humanists argued that people strive not only for reward but to achieve "self-actualization," a higher state of fulfillment. There were many, many voices in the wilderness waiting to be heard.

The most dramatic change that took place in psychology was (and still is) the "cognitive revolution." The term **cognition** refers to the mental processes that intervene between a stimulus and response—including images, memories, expectations, and abstract concepts. At least in the United States, the cognitive psychologies of Wundt and James were swept under the proverbial rug for years with the rise of behaviorism. The subject matter was considered "soft" and nonscientific. Then the pendulum swung back—and cognitive psychology re-emerged, stronger than ever. Looking back, many researchers view the cognitive revolution as sudden and dramatic (Sperry, 1993); others argue that the change was gradual rather than abrupt (Leahey, 1992). Either way, many eminent psychologists admit that they were stunned by the power and dominance of this new perspective (Boneau, 1992).

What rekindled this interest in mental processes? One source of inspiration was the invention of the *computer*. Designed for information-processing purposes, computers provided a new and intriguing model of the human mind. The computer receives input in the form of symbols, converts the symbols into a special code, stores the information, and then retrieves it from memory as needed. The hardware was likened to the brain, and its programs provided a step-by-step flow-chart model of how information about a stimulus is processed to produce a response. Computers were at the cutting edge of science, so the metaphor was readily accepted (Neisser, 1967; Newell et al., 1958).

A second source of inspiration came from the work of Swiss psychologist *Jean Piaget*. Beginning in the 1920s, Piaget studied the way children think. He developed various tasks that revealed how children of various ages reason about people, objects, time, nature, morality, and other aspects of the world. From dozens of studies described in his more than forty books, Piaget theorized that from infancy to adolescence, all children advance through a series of cognitive stages. Behaviorism or not, Piaget had a large following in Europe, and his work—which was being translated into English in the 1950s and 1960s—was ultimately deemed too important to ignore.

The cognitive revolution was also fueled by developments in the study of language. B. F. Skinner (1957) had argued that the laws of learning control the acquisition of language in much the same way they control the bar-pressing response of a rat. However, linguist *Noam Chomsky* (1959) was quick to charge that such an account was naive. Chomsky noted that children all over the world start to speak at roughly the same age and proceed at roughly the same rate without explicit training or reinforcement. Indeed, he argued convincingly that our capacity for language is innate and that specialized cognitive structures are "hardwired" into the human brain as a result of evolution. Chomsky's theory dealt a serious blow to behaviorism and stimulated a great deal of interest in psycholinguistics—a topic that has played a key role in the cognitive revolution.

Today, very few psychologists identify themselves as strict behaviorists. Free to probe beneath the surface, they have made some interesting discoveries. We now know, for example, that people all over the world smile when they're happy, that a memory can be altered by misinformation, that our opinions of one another are biased by first impressions, that intelligence, creativity, and personality are partly inherited, that drugs can be used to treat mental disorders, and more. Behaviorism has had a profound, lasting, and positive impact on psychology, but our horizons have expanded in exciting ways.

Expansion of Psychology's Horizons   One hundred years ago, psychology was in its infancy. Since that time, it has grown up and is taller, wider, and stronger than it used to be (see Figure 1.1). Psychology has developed in three important ways. First, there are more specialized areas of **basic research** than in the past. The goals of basic research are to test theories, study processes, discover general principles, and build a factual foundation of knowledge for the field. There are many subfields of psychology, and each focuses on mind and behavior from a different angle. To provide a comprehensive and balanced look at these perspectives, this textbook is divided into five major parts: biological, cognitive, developmental, social, and clinical.

Figure 1.1

Growth of Psychology

As measured by the number of articles published annually, psychology has flourished over the years—and is currently in the midst of an enormous growth spurt.

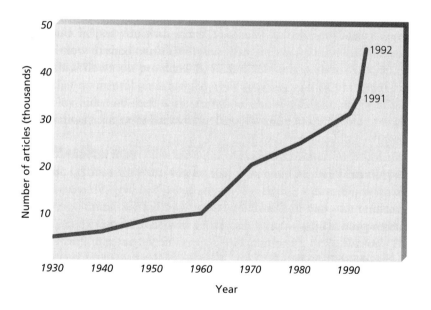

Second, psychology has expanded in the area of **applied research.** Although some psychologists believe that the discipline should remain a pure and basic lab science, others seek to study people in real-world settings and use the results to solve practical problems. There are numerous specific areas of applied research—such as religion, the military, politics, engineering, and sports. In this text, five major areas of application are systematically presented within each part. These areas are health, education, business, law, and the environment.

Third, psychology has become strengthened over the years by refining its *research methods*. Human beings are very complex and difficult to study. As individuals, we differ in our biological makeup, gender, age, experience, and cultural background. The way we behave in one setting may differ

■ **basic research** "Pure science" research that tests theories and builds a foundation of knowledge.

■ **applied research** Research that aims to solve practical human problems.

from the way we behave in another. The inner workings of the mind can never be "seen." In fact, we often lack insight into ourselves. To meet these challenges, researchers use controlled interviews, IQ tests, questionnaires that measure attitudes and personality, mazes, inkblots, optical illusions, shock-generating devices, computerized perception tasks, brain scans and sophisticated instruments that record inner physiological states. Most important, as we'll soon see, psychology stands on the shoulders of the scientific method.

Basic Areas of Specialization

Psychology is a highly specialized discipline. To provide a comprehensive look at the various subfields, this text is divided into five broad areas of interest, each centering on an important question concerning human nature, as follows:

Part I
How do the body and mind interact?

1. *Biological Psychology:* What is the link between the body and the mind? Are these distinct parts of the human being, or are they one and the same, intimately connected in important ways? Inspired by this classic philosophical debate, we consider first the subfield that focuses on the biological roots of experience. There is not just one biological approach, however, but many. *Ethologists* observe fish, birds, insects, primates, and other animal species in their natural habitat. *Sociobiologists* theorize about the evolutionary origins of aggression, altruism, and other social behaviors. *Behavioral geneticists* seek to estimate the extent to which different human characteristics are inherited. And *neuropsychologists* study the links between behavior and the brain, nervous system, hormones, and sensory organs. If you are interested at all in anatomy, Alzheimer's disease, color vision, sleep and dreams, hypnosis, meditation, or mind-altering drugs, you'll find answers in Part I of this book. Biological perspectives also appear in other chapters.

Part II
Are people rational or irrational?

2. *Cognitive Psychology:* Are human beings rational or irrational? Competent or incompetent? Among cognitive psychologists, who study the mental processes involved in learning, memory, thought, language, and emotion, these questions have sparked many debates. As we'll see, both sides are correct—some of the time. The specific topics studied in this area are suggested by such additional questions as, How do people learn by association? How and where in the brain are memories stored? Can a blow to the head really cause amnesia? Does language limit thought? Are joy, anger, pride, and shame similarly felt by people all over the world, or does each culture have its own set of emotions? Cognitive psychology is presented in Part II of this text. It's important to realize, however, that all psychologists share an interest in cognitive processes.

Part III
What are the relative influences of nature and nurture?

3. *Developmental Psychology:* Are you programmed by nature, or is your fate molded by nurturing forces in the environment? There has always been a tension in psychology between researchers who focus on innate genetic dispositions and those who study the influences of learning, culture, families, peers, and the environment. This "nature-nurture" debate

Psychology is a diverse discipline. Its interests range from the human brain and nervous system (left) to social behavior in crowds (right).

surfaces often in the study of development. Rather than take "snapshots," developmental psychologists focus on *change*. By comparing people of different ages and by tracking individuals over time, they try to understand how people grow, mature, and evolve over the life span. Some specialize in prenatal development, infants, children, or adolescents. Others study adults, the elderly, or the process of dying. If you want to know more about the effects of alcohol on the fetus, a baby's first smile, the strained relations between teens and parents, the midlife crisis, or old age, or if you want to know more about intelligence and education, you'll find what you're looking for in Part III of this text.

Part IV
Can situations overpower the individual?

4. *Social Psychology:* Do you ever behave in ways that are profoundly "out of character" just to suit the situation you're in? Could you be coaxed into doing something distasteful, even harmful to yourself or others? Drawn together by the belief that situations have the power to overwhelm even the best of us, social psychologists focus on the influence of other people on the individual. Human beings are social creatures who need each other, sometimes desperately. By observing people in carefully staged social situations, these researchers study the way we perceive, interact with, and influence one another. Specific topics include stereotypes and prejudice, attraction, close relationships, attitudes and persuasion, obedience, leadership, and behavior in social and cultural groups. These topics are discussed in Part IV.

Part V
Do people have the capacity for change?

5. *Clinical Psychology:* Is your personality set in stone, for better or worse? Are individuals who are troubled doomed to remain so, or do we have a capacity for change and renewal—helped along, perhaps, by psychotherapy, counseling, or medical intervention? Armed with hope and a desire to help people in need of change, clinical psychology is the largest branch of the discipline. Working in hospitals, community mental health centers, and private practice, *clinical psychologists* seek to diagnose, understand, and treat serious mental disorders. In addition, *counseling psycho logists* provide marriage, family, career, and guidance counseling to people with less severe problems. If you are curious about a personality test you once took, if you are interested in anxiety, schizophrenia, or depression, or if you want to know more about different psychotherapies and the drugs prescribed in the treatment of various disorders, be patient. Part V of this text is for you.

Practical Applications

Many Olympic teams hire sports psychologists to help their athletes. Corporations, advertising agencies, law firms, and school systems hire psychologists for research and consulting purposes. And psychologists teach in schools of medicine, law, business, and education. Like other basic sciences, psychology has strayed from the laboratories of the ivory tower into the real world. The secret is out.

The application of psychology, or any other science for that matter, raises hard questions concerning values, professional ethics, and social responsibility. For example, should research be suppressed if it yields socially sensitive results? It's easy to assert that we must seek the truth regardless of where it may lead, but what about the policy implications? Should one compare intelligence-test scores of different racial and ethnic minority groups? Then, if some groups score lower than others, should the disparity be reported? What about studies suggesting that the testimony of young children—so often essential to the prosecution of child sex abusers—is not reliable? Additional questions confront those who seek to apply psychology. Is it ethical to dispense mental health advice on TV or over the radio? Should psychologists use their scientific credentials to promote drug company products, or lobby for abortion rights, gun control, and other political causes? Should psychologists testify as experts in trials involving the insanity defense? Working in a discipline that addresses many delicate topics, psychologists face several important questions.

To illustrate some of the intersections between basic and applied psychology, each part of this text presents five domains of application: health, education, business, law, and the environment.

1. *Health:* Psychology is applied in many ways to the study of health and medicine. How does stress affect the body, and what coping mechanisms are most adaptive? Is it healthier to have an accurate perception of reality or a bias toward optimism? Are people with certain types of personalities prone to disease? Why do cancer patients live longer if they are socially connected than if they are alone and isolated? Answers to these questions appear throughout the text, and are the focus of the final chapter.

2. *Education:* In a 1993 paper entitled *Adult Literacy in America,* the U.S. Department of Education estimated that 90 million American adults are incompetent at practical life tasks such as reading a bus schedule and computing the cost of carpeting a room. Clearly, psychology has a lot to say about education—about IQ tests, creativity, bilingualism, the effects of reward on a child's motivation to learn, ways to improve memory, and so on. Researchers are finding answers to these practical questions.

3. *Business:* There are two ways in which psychology is applied to business. *Industrial/organizational (I/O) psychology* focuses on human behavior in the workplace and other organizations. I/O researchers study the processes of personnel selection, training, and evaluation; leadership; and worker motivation, satisfaction, and productivity. In contrast, *consumer psychology* is the study of behavior in the marketplace. Researchers in this area study consumer attitudes, advertising, gambling, and economic decision making. Indeed, psychology's involvements in the world of business are numerous.

"There are no such things as applied sciences, only applications of science."

LOUIS PASTEUR

4. *Law:* Many psychologists are at work in the legal system consulting with attorneys, testifying in court, counseling prisoners, teaching in law schools, and conducting research on justice-related issues. This area is lively and often controversial. Those studying psychology and the law are involved in a range of topics, including jury selection and decision making, eyewitness testimony, lie-detector tests, procedural justice, the death penalty, and the insanity defense.

5. *The Environment:* Why are some cities healthier to live in than others? Can the architectural design of a building affect the crime rate? As these and other questions illustrate, *environmental psychologists* study the relations between people and their physical environment—including the effects of street noise, heat, privacy, and population density. In a related field, *human factors psychologists* help design appliances, furniture, tools, and other human-made aspects of the environment to maximize comfort and convenience.

To summarize, psychology has expanded its horizons both in the study of basic processes and in the domains of application. In the coming chapters, each of the five basic areas will be discussed—and in each of these areas, instances of the five applications will be highlighted in special boxes. As shown in the matrix presented in Table 1.3 (p. 14), this two-dimensional growth has given rise to some exciting new research connections.

SCIENTIFIC METHODS

It happens all the time. I'll see a report on the evening news, or a magazine story, or an advertisement for a new product, and I'll react with a mixture of curiosity and skepticism. For example, I heard there's a new cure for baldness, that adults can retrieve hidden memories from early childhood, that students can raise SAT scores 150 points by taking a test-preparation course, that a full moon triggers bizarre behavior, that workaholics drive themselves to an early grave, that pornography incites rape, that girls start talking before boys do, and that watching TV lowers a child's IQ. Some of these claims are true, others are false. My reaction, however, is always the same: "Hmm. Interesting," I'll say to myself. "But prove it!"

Many of us are drawn to psychology because people are fascinating and the subject matter is important. What unifies psychology as a discipline, however, is its commitment to the scientific approach. The aim in science is an aim that should be modeled by everyone: *critical thinking*. It's a skill, and it's also an attitude. The goal is to generate creative ideas and entertain these ideas with an open mind—but, at the same time, to be cautious, to demand that all claims be tested, and to scrutinize the results. The "art" in science is to achieve a balance between these competing objectives. It's great to be creative, but not intellectually sloppy. Similarly, it's important to be critical, even skeptical, but not close-minded. The key to thinking like a psychologist is learning how to walk these fine lines. And that means knowing something about our methods of research.

The first important step in the research enterprise is to formulate a hypothesis to be tested. You may not realize it, but you have many intuitive theories on psychological matters. Everyone does. When I was choosing a graduate school, I had to decide whether to go out of town to the best

"At the heart of science is an essential tension between two seemingly contradictory attitudes—an openness to new ideas, no matter how bizarre or counterintuitive they may be, and the most ruthless skeptical scrutiny of all ideas, old and new."

CARL SAGAN

Basic Subfields of Psychology

	Biological Psychology	Cognitive Psychology	Developmental Psychology	Social Psychology	Clinical Psychology
Health	▪ Night Work, Sleep, and Health (p. 144)	▪ Self-Help Through Operant Conditioning (p. 198) ▪ The Pursuit of Happiness (p. 320)	▪ Drugs and the Fetus (p. 342)	▪ Promoting Health Through the Arousal of Fear (p. 494)	▪ The Behavioral Treatment of Headaches (p. 660)
Education	▪ Right-Brain Education: Science or Science Fiction? (p. 74)	▪ Ways to Improve Your Memory (p. 246)	▪ Cultural Literacy: A Key to Success? (p. 418)	▪ Using Schools to Combat Racism (p. 534)	▪ Attention Deficit Hyperactivity Disorder (p. 608)
Business	▪ Subliminal Persuasion (p. 138)	▪ Gambling: Irrational Thinking in the Casino (p. 272)	▪ Career Development and Retirement (p. 400)	▪ Minorities in the Workplace (p. 532) ▪ Women in the Workplace (p. 546)	▪ Using Personality Tests in Personnel Selection (p. 590)
Law	▪ Can Hypnosis Enhance Eyewitness Testimony? (p. 156)	▪ Eyewitness Identification (p. 242)	▪ The Child Witness: Competent to Testify? (p. 354) ▪ Moral Dilemmas in Law: Euthanasia (p. 378)	▪ Social Perception Biases and the Jury (p. 462) ▪ Sexism: Taking the Case to Court (p. 476)	▪ The Insanity Defense (p. 640) ▪ Putting Repressed Memories on Trial (p. 654)
Environment	▪ Lefties in a Right-Handed World (p. 66) ▪ Noise and Your Hearing (p. 100)	▪ Weather and Emotion: Seasonal Affective Disorder (p. 316)	▪ The Physical Setting of a Classroom (p. 440)	▪ Population Density, Architecture, and Social Behavior (p. 498)	▪ Type A and B Cities: The Pace of Life and Death (p. 578)

Areas of Applied Research

Table 1.3

Intersections of Basic and Applied Research

The topics highlighted in boxes throughout this text demonstrate the exciting interaction between the five basic subfields of psychology and five areas of practical application. These connections are also explored in the body of the chapters.

"All the world is a laboratory to the inquiring mind."

MARTIN H. FISHER

■ **theory** An organized set of principles that describes, predicts, and explains some phenomenon.

■ **hypothesis** A specific testable prediction, often derived from a theory.

possible program—which meant leaving behind a girlfriend. What should I do? What effect would distance have on our relationship? One friend was certain he knew the answer: "Absence makes the heart grow fonder." Those words of encouragement made sense to me—until a second friend said with equal certainty, "Out of sight, out of mind." Just what I needed. Two contradictory theories, both derived from common sense.

Psychological theories are more formal than the hunches we come up with in everyday conversation. A **theory** is an organized set of principles that describes, predicts, and explains some phenomenon. One can derive a theory from logic, a world event, a personal experience or observation, another theory, a research finding, or an accidental discovery. Some theories are broad and encompassing, others account for only a thin slice of behavior. Some are simple, others contain a large number of interrelated propositions. In all cases, a theory should provide specific testable predictions, or **hypotheses**, about the relation between two or more variables. Researchers can then test these hypotheses to evaluate the theory as a whole.

There is no magical formula for determining how to test a hypothesis. In fact, as we'll see, studies can vary along at least three dimensions: (1) the setting in which observations are made, (2) the ways in which psychological variables are measured, and (3) the types of conclusions that can be drawn. Let's separately examine each of these dimensions.

Research Settings

There are two types of settings in which people can be studied. Sometimes, data are collected in a laboratory, usually located at a university, so that the environment can be regulated and the subject carefully observed. *Laboratory research* offers control, precision, and an opportunity to keep conditions uniform for different subjects. For example, bringing volunteers into a sleep lab enables the psychologist to monitor their eye movements and brain-wave activity, record the exact time they fall asleep, and get dream reports the moment they awaken. Likewise, bringing a parent and child into a special playroom equipped with hand-picked toys, two-way mirrors, and a hidden camera and microphone enables the psychologist to record every word uttered and analyze every nuance of their interaction.

Laboratory research is common in science. NASA physicists construct special chambers to simulate weightlessness in space, chemists generate chemical reactions in the test tube, botanists study plant growth in the greenhouse, meteorologists use wind tunnels to mimic atmospheric conditions, and zoologists observe animals in captivity. To study the way juries make decisions, I recruit people to serve on mock juries so I can videotape and analyze the deliberation process. In order to make certain observations, then, psychologists often find it necessary to simulate the events in a laboratory. There is, however, a drawback. Can someone sleep normally in a strange bed with metal electrodes pasted to the scalp? Will a parent and child interact in the playroom the way they do at home? Do mock juries reach verdicts the same way real juries do? Possibly not. The laboratory is an artificial world and may elicit atypical behavior.

The alternative is *field research* conducted in real-world locations. The psychologist interested in sleep and dreams may have subjects report back

There are two types of research settings. In a laboratory study, behavior is observed in a controlled environment—such as a playroom (left). In field studies, people are observed in real-world settings—such as singles bars (right).

periodically on their experiences. The parent and child could be visited in their own home. And jurors could be questioned about their decision-making process after a trial is over. The setting chosen depends on the behavior to be measured. Indeed, psychologists have observed people in city streets, classrooms, factories, offices, restaurants, bars, dormitories, prisons, subways, elevators, and even the public restroom. To understand behavior in real-world settings, there is just no substitute for field research. Unfortunately, the researcher "out there" cannot control what happens to subjects or measure with precision all aspects of their experience. Thus, the most fruitful approach is to use both laboratory and field settings.

Psychological Measurements

Regardless of where observations are made, there are many different types of measures that can be taken. These fall into three categories: self-reports, behavioral observations, and archival records. These three types of observations, and the advantages and disadvantages of each, are summarized in Table 1.4.

Self-Reports   One way to assess a person's thoughts, feelings, or behavior is to go right to the source and ask. This is the method of **self-report**. Through live interviews, or in questionnaires, people are asked to report on past behavior, intentions for future behavior, or perceptions, beliefs, attitudes, and emotions. Using true-false statements, checklists, multiple-choice items, and rating scales, self-reports are quick and easy to get. Unfortunately, the information can be inaccurate and misleading.

There are two problems with self-reports. First, people sometimes distort their responses in order to present themselves in a favorable light. It's hard to get anyone to admit to their failures, mistakes, and shortcomings. Studies show, for example, that people overestimate their own contribution to a joint effort (Ross & Sicoly, 1979), report after the occurrence of an event that they knew all along it would happen (Hawkins & Hastie, 1990), cover up feelings of prejudice (Crosby et al., 1980), and overestimate the accuracy of their own predictions (Dunning et al., 1990). A second problem with self-reports is that even when respondents try to be accurate, their ability to do so often is limited. Long ago, Freud noted that people block

■ **self-report** A method of observation that involves asking people to describe their own thoughts, feelings, or behavior.

Table 1.4

Three Ways to "Observe" People

Method	Description	Advantages	Disadvantages
Self-reports	Ask people to report on themselves in interviews, surveys, or questionnaires.	People can reveal inner states that cannot be "seen" by others.	People distort self-reports to present themselves in a favorable light. People are not always aware of their own inner states.
Behavioral observations	Observe behavior firsthand, openly or covertly, sometimes using special tasks or instruments.	Behavior can be measured objectively.	Inner states can only be inferred from behavior, not actually seen. People may behave differently if they know they are being observed.
Archival records	Observe behavior secondhand, using available records of past activities.	The behavior occurs without the biasing presence of an observer.	Records of past activities are not always complete or accurate.

certain thoughts and wishes from awareness. And studies show that people often lack insight into the causes of their own behavior (Nisbett & Wilson, 1977). In a surprising illustration of the limits of self-reports, Stanley Coren (1993), an expert on left-handedness, notes that when he asks people if they're right- or left-handed, 7 percent answer incorrectly. "One man who confidently reported that he was a right-hander, when tested to see which hand he used to throw a ball, aim a dart, cut with scissors, and the like, performed every single action with his left hand. His only detectable right-handed activity was writing" (p. 34).

Self-report measures are common in psychology, sometimes even essential. As you read through this book, however, you'll see that researchers often go out of their way to collect data in other, less direct ways. Now you know the reason: the source is not always the best source.

Behavioral Observations   It is said that actions speak louder than words—and many psychologists would agree. The major alternative to self-reports is first-hand *behavioral observation*. To animal researchers, the

Behavioral observation is critical to psychology. In this experiment, a four-month-old baby is tested to see if she knows that an object in motion will not stop in midair.

pressing of a bar, the running of a maze, and the consumption of food pellets are important behaviors. To those who study infants, sucking, smiling, crying, moving the eyes, and turning the head are significant sources of information. As for those who study adults, psychologically relevant behaviors range from the blink of an eye to the choice of a career. Even changes in internal states can be monitored through the use of special instruments. Heart rate, breathing, blood pressure, eye movements, brain waves, reflexes, hormone levels, contraction of facial muscles, and white blood cell activity are among the physiological measures frequently used in the study of behavior.

Behavioral observation plays a particularly important role in the study of subjective experience. One cannot crawl under a subject's skin and see what's on his or her mind. But we can try to infer various internal states from behavior. It is usually (though not always) safe to assume, for example, that recognition reveals the presence of a memory, that solving difficult problems reveals intelligence, that a spontaneous smile signals joy, and that the person who breaks into a cold sweat and runs at the sight of a snake has a fear of snakes.

Archival Records   A third way to collect information about people is to look at "archival" records of past activities instead of ongoing behavior. Archival measures used in psychology include medical records, literacy rates, crime rates, newspaper stories, sports statistics, photographs, consumer purchases, absenteeism rates at work, birth rates, marriages, and divorce. An advantage of this method is that by observing behavior secondhand, researchers can be sure they did not influence subjects by their presence. An obvious limitation is that existing records of human activity are not always complete or detailed enough to be useful.

Archival measures are particularly valuable for examining cultural or historical trends. For example, Coren (1993) wanted to know if right-handedness was always dominant among humans (today, roughly 90 percent of the population is right-handed). So he went through a collection of art books and analyzed 1,180 drawings, paintings, and engravings that depicted an individual using a tool or a weapon. The drawings ranged from Stone Age sketches dated 15,000 B.C. to paintings from the year 1950 A.D. Yet Coren found that 90 percent of all characters were portrayed as right-handers—and that this percentage was the same thousands of years ago as in the twentieth century.

Research Designs

Regardless of how and where the information is obtained, researchers use **statistics** to summarize and analyze the results. In some cases, statistical tests are used simply to *describe* what happened in terms of averages, percentages, frequencies, and other quantitative measures. In other cases, analyses are used to test *inferences* about people in general and their behavior. More about the use of statistics in psychological research is presented in the Appendix of this book. For now, it is important to note that the types of conclusions that are drawn are limited by the way a study is designed. In particular, three types of research are used: descriptive studies, correlational studies, and experiments.

Descriptive Research   The first purpose of research is simply to *describe* a person, group, or psychological phenomenon through systematic observation. This goal can be achieved through case studies, surveys, and naturalistic observations.

Case Studies   Every now and then, it is useful to study one or more individuals in great detail. Information about a person can be obtained in a number of ways, including interviews, tests, questionnaires, first-hand observation, and biographical material such as diaries and letters written. **Case studies** are conducted in the hope that an in-depth look at one individual will reveal something important about people in general. The problem is, case studies are time consuming and limited in their generality. To the extent that a subject is atypical, the results may say little about the rest of us.

Nevertheless, case studies have played an important role in psychology. Sigmund Freud based his theory of personality on a handful of patients. Behaviorist John Watson used a case study to try to debunk psychoanalysis. Swiss psychologist Jean Piaget formulated a theory of intellectual development, at first by questioning his own children. Neuroscientists gain insights into the workings of the brain by testing patients who have suffered brain damage. Cognitive psychologists learn about memory from rare individuals who can retain enormous amounts of information. Psycholinguists study language development by recording the speech utterances of their own children over time. Intelligence researchers learn about human intellectual powers by studying child prodigies, chess masters, and other gifted individuals. Social psychologists pick up clues about leadership by analyzing biographies of great leaders. And clinical psychologists refine the techniques of psychotherapy through their shared experiences with individual patients.

■ **statistics** A branch of mathematics that is used for analyzing research data.

■ **case studies** A type of research that involves making in-depth observations of individual persons.

■ **survey** A research method that involves interviewing or giving questionnaires to a large number of people.

■ **random sample** A method of selection in which everyone in a population has an equal chance of being chosen.

When an individual comes along who is exceptional in some way, or when a psychological hypothesis can be answered only through systematic, long-term observation, the case study provides a valuable starting point.

Surveys   In contrast to the in-depth study of one person, **surveys** describe an entire population by looking at many cases. In a survey—which can be conducted in person, over the phone, or through the mail—people are asked various questions about themselves. Surveys have become very popular in recent years, as people are asked to report on their sexual practices, the TV shows they watch, the consumer products they own, the candidates they intend to vote for, and their opinions on hot social and political issues. Surveys tell us that 10 to 20 percent of Americans refrain from sex before marriage (Janus & Janus, 1993), that 95 percent believe in God (Harris, 1987), that 49 percent daydream about being rich (Roper Reports, 1989), and that 75 percent report that they're happy (Myers, 1993). In case you've been wondering, 37 percent of women and 18 percent of men squeeze the toothpaste tube from the bottom (Weiss, 1991).

All kidding aside, surveys are sometimes necessary for the purpose of describing psychological states that are difficult to observe directly. For example, this method is an important tool in *epidemiology*—the study of the distribution of illness in a population. How many children are awakened by nightmares? What percentage of college students are plagued by test anxiety? How common are depression, alcoholism, and suicide? These kinds of questions are vital for determining the extent of a problem and knowing how to allocate health care resources. Surveys are also useful for describing sexual practices. With AIDS spreading at an alarming rate, it's important to know how sexually active people are, whether they use condoms, and whether some segments of the population are more at risk than others. Today, surveys are so common, and the results have such significant implications, that the method (which, after all, relies on self-report) should be carefully scrutinized. Two factors are particularly important: who the respondents are and how the questions are asked.

To describe a group, any group—males, females, college students, red-heads, homeowners, Americans, or registered voters—researchers select a subset of individuals. The entire group is called the *population;* the subset of those questioned constitutes a *sample.* For a survey to be accurate, the sample must be similar to or "representative" of the population on key characteristics such as sex, race, age, region, cultural background, and income. Short of questioning everyone in the population, the best way to ensure representativeness is to use a **random sample,** a method of selection in which everyone has an equal chance of being chosen. Survey researchers usually pick names arbitrarily from a phone book or some other list. This seems like a reasonable strategy (and the larger the sample, the smaller the margin of error), but no sample is perfect. Not everyone has a telephone, some people have unlisted numbers, and some people who are called may not be home or may refuse to participate. In the 1948 U.S. presidential election, pollsters nationwide predicted that Thomas Dewey would defeat Harry Truman by a wide margin. Truman, of course, won. The problem? Most polls were conducted by phone—and at the time, more Republicans than Democrats had phones. For a sample to accurately reflect its parent population, it must be selected in a manner that is random, not biased.

In 1948, newspapers announced before all the votes had been counted that Dewey defeated Truman for president. As Truman basked in his victory, pollsters came to realize that their pre-election predictions were based on non-random samples of voters. Most polls were conducted by phone—and more Republicans than Democrats had phones.

■ **naturalistic observation** The observation of behavior as it occurs naturally in real-world settings.

■ **correlation** A statistical measure of the extent to which two variables are associated.

Naturalistic observation is a common method of descriptive research. For many years, Jane Goodall has observed chimpanzees in the wild.

A second factor to consider is the wording of questions and the context in which they are asked (Tourangeau et al., 1991). There are numerous examples to illustrate the point: (1) When subjects were asked about "assisting the poor," only 23 percent said too much money was being spent. When asked about "welfare," however, 52 percent gave this response (*Time*, 1988). (2) When subjects estimated how often in the past three months they dined in a restaurant, the average was 20. When asked about different types of restaurants—such as Chinese or Mexican—their estimated total was 26 (Schwarz, 1990). (3) Subjects who were asked if "People should have the freedom to express their opinions publicly" were more likely to say *yes* after answering a question about the Catholic Church than after a question about the American Nazi Party (Ottati et al., 1989). (4) Eighty-eight percent of subjects thought condoms were effective in stopping AIDS when condoms were said to have a "95 percent success rate." Only 42 percent were as optimistic when condoms were said to have a "5 percent failure rate" (Linville et al., 1992).

Naturalistic Observations   A third descriptive approach is to observe behavior as it occurs in real life. **Naturalistic observations** are common in anthropology, in which field workers seek to describe a culture by living within it for long periods of time. Psychologists use this method as well, to study parents and their children, corporate executives, factory workers, psychiatric patients, nursing home residents, and others.

Naturalistic observation is particularly common among ethologists, who study the behavior of animals in their natural habitat. For example, Jane Goodall spent more than thirty years watching chimpanzees in African jungles (Goodall, 1986; Peterson & Goodall, 1993). She observed their social structure, courting rituals, struggles for dominance, and child-rearing practices. She also saw the chimps strip leaves from twigs and use the twigs to fish termites out of nests, a finding that disproved the widely held assumption that only humans are capable of making tools. In other research, Dorothy Cheney and Robert Seyfarth (1990) spent thirteen years observing vervet monkeys in Kenya, and discovered that these monkeys behave as if they know the kinship bonds within their group, use deception to outsmart rivals, and use vocal calls in ways that are more sophisticated than was previously expected. To truly understand primates, and perhaps their similarities to humans, one has to observe their behavior in the wild—not captive in a zoo or laboratory.

Correlational Studies   Description is a nice first step, but science demands much more. A second goal is to find connections, or "correlations," between variables so that one factor can be used to predict another. Correlational research is reported in psychology, and in the news, with remarkable frequency. Here are a few simple examples: The more violence children watch on TV, the more aggressive they are. Men with high levels of testosterone are prone to crime and violence. College graduates earn more money than nongraduates. The more optimistic people are, the less often they get sick. Adults who exercise regularly live longer than those who are less active. People who are shy have fewer friends than those who are outgoing.

A **correlation** is a statistical measure of the extent to which two factors are associated. Expressed in numerical terms, *correlation coefficients* range from $+1$ to -1. A *positive* correlation exists when the two variables increase or decrease together, in the same direction. The link between TV violence and aggression is positive; more of one means more of the other. So are the correlations between testosterone and aggression, education and income, exercise and longevity. In contrast, a *negative* correlation exists when an increase in one variable is accompanied by a decrease in the other, and vice versa. The link between optimism and illness is in a negative direction, as is the one between shyness and friendships.

Correlation coefficients vary not only in direction but also in strength. The higher a correlation is, regardless of whether it is positive or negative, the stronger the link is between variables. Correlations that are very low, near zero, indicate that two variables are independent. Contrary to popular opinion, research shows, for example, that there is no correlation between phases of the moon and criminal activity, between an eyewitness's confidence and accuracy, or between intelligence test scores in infancy and adulthood. In short, full moons, confident witnesses, and infant test scores cannot be used to predict crime, accuracy, or adult IQ (see Figure 1.2).

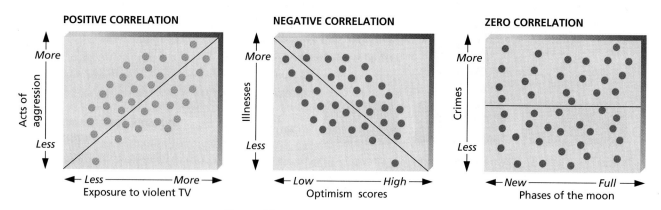

Figure 1.2

Visualizing Correlations

"Scatterplots" provide a graphic representation of the observed relationship between two variables. The following graphs illustrate a positive correlation (left), a negative correlation (center), and a zero correlation (right). Each point locates the position of a single subject on the two variables. The solid straight lines show what the correlations would look like if they were perfect.

Correlational studies serve an important function: based on existing associations, researchers can use one variable (or more) to make *predictions* about another variable. Before interpreting correlations, however, two important limitations should always guide the cautious scientist. First, correlations between psychological variables are seldom perfect. Human beings are complex and their behavior is multi-determined. If you know a boy who spends twenty hours a week watching war movies, professional wrestling, or MTV's controversial heavy-metal cartoon, *Beavis and Butt-Head*, you might predict that he gets into fights at school. But the positive correlation between TV violence exposure and aggressiveness is far from perfect, and you may well be wrong. Similarly, not every optimist is healthy, and not every college graduate brings home a hefty paycheck. Unless a correlation is close to 1, it can be used only to make general statements of probability, not predictions about specific individuals.

■ **experiment** A type of research in which the investigator varies some factors, keeps others constant, and measures the effects on randomly assigned subjects.

There is also a limit to the types of conclusions that can be drawn from correlational evidence. It's tempting to assume that because one variable predicts another, the first must have caused the second. Not true. This interpretation is an error frequently committed by lay people, college students, the news media, and sometimes even researchers themselves. Think about the correlations described earlier. Now, admit it: Didn't you assume that exposure to TV violence *causes* aggression, that testosterone fuels violence, that a college diploma brings financial reward, that optimism fosters health, that exercise prolongs life, and that shyness inhibits friendships? Regardless of how intuitive or accurate these conclusions may be, there's a cardinal rule of statistics that you should not violate: *correlation does not prove causation.*

It's important to know and understand this rule. It does not mean that correlated variables are never causally related, only that the link may or may not be causal. Think again about our examples, and you'll see there are other ways to interpret these correlations. Sure, it's possible that TV violence (X) triggers aggression (Y). But based solely on the observation that these two variables go hand in hand, it's also possible that the causal arrow points in the opposite direction—that children who are aggressive (Y) are naturally drawn to violent shows (X). Or perhaps both variables are caused by a third factor (Z), such as the absence of involved parents at home.

Reconsider our other examples, and you'll further appreciate the point. Perhaps people become optimistic *because* they are healthy, or are shy *because* they lack friends. As for the fact that college graduates earn more money than nongraduates, being smart or coming from an upper-middle-class family (Z) may propel a student through college (X) and lead to financial success (Y). In a similar vein, maybe adults who exercise regularly live longer because they also tend to smoke less, drink less, and eat healthier food (see Figure 1.3).

Experiments   Correlation allows prediction, but to *explain* a relationship between variables, one needs a more exacting method of research: the scientific experiment. In an **experiment**, the psychologist seeks to establish

Figure 1.3

Explaining Correlations

There are three possible ways to explain the association between two variables, X and Y. Look at the examples below and consider possible alternatives (Z refers to extraneous variables).

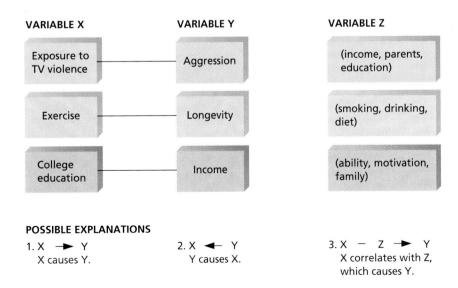

VARIABLE X   VARIABLE Y   VARIABLE Z

Exposure to TV violence —— Aggression   (income, parents, education)

Exercise —— Longevity   (smoking, drinking, diet)

College education —— Income   (ability, motivation, family)

POSSIBLE EXPLANATIONS

1. X ➡ Y
   X causes Y.

2. X ⬅ Y
   Y causes X.

3. X — Z ➡ Y
   X correlates with Z, which causes Y.

■ **independent variable** Any variable that the researcher manipulates in an experiment (the proposed cause).

■ **dependent variable** A variable that is being measured in an experiment (the dependent variable is the proposed effect).

■ **experimental group** Any condition of an experiment in which subjects are exposed to the independent variable.

■ **control group** The condition of an experiment in which subjects are not exposed to the independent variable.

causal connections by actively controlling the variables in a situation and measuring the subject's behavior. The factor an experimenter manipulates (the proposed cause) is called the **independent variable,** so named because it can be varied on its own, "independent" of any other factors. The behavior that is being measured (the proposed effect) is called the **dependent variable,** because it is said to "depend" on the experimental situation. If you were to test the hypothesis that exposure to TV violence causes aggression, TV violence would be the independent variable, aggression the dependent variable.

The purpose of an experiment is to focus like a laser beam on a causal hypothesis—by manipulating the independent variable, keeping other aspects of the situation constant, and observing behavior. A true experiment contains two essential ingredients. The first is control over the independent variable and use of a comparison group. Second is the random assignment of subjects to conditions. By means of these ingredients, differences in behavior can logically be traced back to the independent variable (see Figure 1.4).

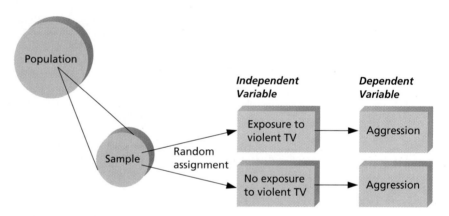

Figure 1.4   **Basic Model of an Experiment**

To test the hypothesis that TV violence triggers aggression, researchers select a subset of the population, randomly assign these subjects to an experimental (exposure) or control (no exposure) group, and measure subsequent behavior.

Control and Comparison   I heard a report on the radio recently that half of all couples who live together before marriage ultimately get divorced. "Wow, that's high," I said to a friend. "I wonder why." Then it hit me. "Wait a second. Isn't there a 50 percent divorce rate in the United States?"

In order to evaluate the significance of a number, you have to ask the question "Compared to what?" In its most basic form, a typical experiment compares subjects who are exposed to the independent variable with others, similarly treated, who are not. Subjects who receive the treatment make up the **experimental group;** the others constitute the **control group.** To the extent that the two groups differ in behavior, that difference can then be attributed, with varying degrees of certainty, to the independent variable. The key is to *vary one factor, keep other aspects of the situation constant, and measure the effect.* To test the hypothesis that TV violence triggers aggression, for example, researchers bring children into the laboratory, show

■ **random assignment** The procedure whereby subjects are assigned to conditions of an experiment in an arbitrary manner.

■ **replication** The process of repeating a study to see if the findings are reliable enough to be duplicated.

rock'em-sock'em films to half of them (the others would watch nonviolent films or else nothing at all), and measure subsequent aggression in a laboratory or field setting (Wood et al., 1991).

The comparison between an experimental and control group provides the building blocks for more complex experiments. There are three ways to expand upon this basic two-group design. The first is to create more than two levels of the independent variable. Instead of comparing the presence and absence of TV violence, for example, one might form three groups by varying the amount or "dosage" of exposure (high, medium, low). Second, researchers can manipulate more than one independent variable in the same experiment. For example, they might vary not only the amount of exposure but also the context in which the violence is portrayed (cartoons, films, or sports). The separate and joint effects of these variables can then be evaluated. The third way to increase the complexity of an experiment is to use more than one dependent variable, or to measure the dependent variable on more than one occasion. In our example, aggression could be measured both before and after subjects watch TV.

Random Assignment The second ingredient of an experiment is that subjects be assigned to conditions in an arbitrary manner. **Random assignment** ensures that all participants in a study have an equal chance of being put in an experimental or control group. If I were to show *Beavis and Butt-Head* to children in one school and *Mary Poppins* to those in another school, it would later be impossible to know whether observed differences in aggression were produced by this exposure, or whether they reflect differences that exist between the schools. Similarly, if I were to let children pick their own condition ("Would you rather see *Beavis and Butt-Head* or *Mary Poppins*?"), observed differences might mean only that those who chose the violent show were more aggressive to begin with.

By flipping a coin to determine which children in a sample are in the experimental and control groups, a researcher can neutralize individual differences. Assuming that enough subjects are recruited, the two conditions would contain roughly equal numbers of male and female children as well as rich and poor, active and passive, and bright and dull. To similarly evaluate the health benefits of exercise, one might recruit volunteers and assign half of them randomly to take part in an experimental aerobics program. Chances are, both the exercise and no-exercise groups would have an equal mixture of men, women, smokers, health-food eaters, couch potatoes, and so on. Then if exercisers turn out to be healthier, the reason would be clear.

"No amount of experimentation can ever prove me right; a single experiment can prove me wrong."

ALBERT EINSTEIN

Literature Reviews Seeking to describe, predict, and explain psychological phenomena, researchers use a diverse assortment of investigative tools, including individual case studies, large-scale surveys, naturalistic observations, correlational studies, and experiments in laboratory and field settings. Yet there is a humbling lesson in this scientific enterprise: it is that knowledge accumulates slowly, in increments, one small step at a time. There are no "critical" experiments, and no single study can literally "prove" a hypothesis.

Sure, there are exciting new discoveries destined to become research classics. But each raises questions, the most important being: Will a finding replicate? **Replication** is an essential property of science. It refers to the

■ **generalizability** The extent to which a finding applies to a broad range of subject populations and circumstances.

■ **meta-analysis** A set of statistical procedures used to review a body of evidence by combining the results of individual studies.

process of conducting a second, nearly identical study to see if the initial findings can be repeated. If the result does not replicate, the cautious scientist concludes that it may not be reliable enough to pursue further. If the result does replicate, which means it is consistent enough to stand the test of time, then attention shifts to a second key question, that of **generalizability**: Is a finding limited to one narrow set of conditions, or does it apply across a broad range of circumstances? Just how generalizable is the result? Suppose I find that TV violence causes aggression. Would the result be the same if the study is conducted in another culture, or if children of a different age group are used? What if subjects are shown different materials, or if aggression is measured in a different way? Once replication is achieved, the next step is to establish the boundaries of the phenomenon. As with fine wine, good science takes time.

As science demands replication and generalizability, it is often difficult to make sense of the growing bodies of evidence. One study may show that exposure to TV violence causes aggression in children, another study may produce contradictory or ambiguous results. Why the disparity? Sometimes many studies are needed before clear patterns begin to emerge. There are two ways to discern these patterns. One is to conduct a *narrative review* of the literature by noting the strengths or weaknesses of various studies, making comparisons, and arguing for certain conclusions. The other—in contrast to the interpretive, somewhat impressionistic style of narrative reviews—is to use a newly developed quantitative method of review known as **meta-analysis**. Meta-analysis is a set of statistical procedures that is used to review a body of evidence by combining the data and results from different studies (Cook et al., 1992; Rosenthal, 1991; Schmidt, 1992). By "meta-analyzing" previous *studies* the way researchers "analyze" individual *subjects*, reviewers can often draw precise conclusions concerning the strength and breadth of support for a hypothesis. Many of the conclusions drawn in this textbook were informed by the narrative reviews and meta-analyses published by others.

To summarize, advances in psychological knowledge are made through "primary" research in the form of descriptive studies, correlational studies, and experiments. As the data from these efforts accumulate in the published literature, patterns begin to emerge. These patterns are revealed in narrative reviews and statistical meta-analyses. The various tools of discovery discussed here are summarized in Table 1.5.

Ethical Dilemmas

All professions must wrestle with ethical questions, and psychology is no exception. Regardless of whether a psychologist teaches for a living, administers tests, offers counseling and psychotherapy, conducts research, writes books, consults with the media or professionals in other areas, or testifies to Congress or in the courts, ethical dilemmas abound (Kendler, 1993; Pope & Vetter, 1992). For the scientists of psychology, questions arise most often concerning the use and treatment of research subjects.

Ethics Considerations in Human Research   When I took introductory psychology in my first year of college, I signed up for all sorts of experiments. In one, other students and I were preparing to fill out questionnaires when

Table 1.5

The Tools of Discovery

Method	Purpose
Descriptive research	To *describe* the thoughts, feelings, and behaviors of an individual or group using case studies, surveys, and naturalistic observations
Correlational studies	To uncover links, or "correlations," between variables so that one factor can be used to *predict* another
Experiments	To test hypotheses about cause and effect in order to establish that one factor can *cause* another
Literature reviews	To *summarize* an existing body of research in a narrative review or a statistical meta-analysis of studies previously conducted

our experimenter—a young female graduate student—was mugged by an intruder, right there in front of us, in the classroom! Soon after the commotion subsided, a security officer walked in and asked us to describe what happened and to pick the culprit from a set of photographs. Apparently, the crime was staged and we were subjects in a study of eyewitness testimony. Years later, I came to realize that this experiment was a classic. It was an awesome experience.

That same semester, I spent an hour trying to memorize 100 strings of letters (I still see them in my dreams: *PTVPS, PVV, TSSSXS*), only to be tested afterward for whether I had discerned the rules that were used to generate these items (I didn't even know there were rules). The session was harmless but boring. Then three years later, I heard more about the research (the task was designed to simulate the way people learn grammar, by mere exposure) and was so intrigued by it (people seem to "learn" the grammar without even realizing there is one) that I seized upon an opportunity to serve as experimenter. That experience was my *real* introduction to psychology.

I was also in a third experiment I'll never forget. I was given an IQ test containing SAT-like analogies and math questions—and was told afterward that my score was very low, in the 25th percentile. I don't remember exactly how badly I felt, but after I left and walked down the hall, I was approached by a student conducting a survey. Would I answer some questions? Not being in the mood, I said no. Suddenly my experimenter reappeared to tell me that there was no survey and that the feedback I was given earlier had been false. The purpose was to see if having a positive or negative experience in one situation (some subjects were told they scored high on the IQ test) influences whether people are willing to help someone in an unrelated situation (the student with the survey).

My encounters as a psychology subject were, I think, pretty typical. In most experiments, subjects fill out questionnaires; work on learning, problem-solving, perception, or memory tasks; or interact socially with other subjects. Physiological functions may be recorded, responses may be made on a computer keyboard, or behavior may be videotaped. Some experiments are interesting and fun, others are tedious and relatively boring.

■ **deception** A research procedure used to mislead subjects about the true purposes of a study.

■ **informed consent** The ethical requirement that prospective subjects be given enough information to permit them to decide freely whether or not to participate in a study.

Most psychology experiments are inoffensive. But sometimes subjects are asked personal questions, or stressed, saddened, or put into a bad mood, or deceived about the true purposes of the experiment. Witnessing a crime and being told I had failed an IQ test were upsetting experiences. Trying to memorize letter strings was not. In all cases, I was misled about what was being tested.

What ethical issues are raised by research involving human subjects, and how are these issues resolved? There are three specific concerns: the subject's right to privacy, the possible harm or discomfort caused by experimental procedures, and the use of **deception**. To address these concerns, researchers follow guidelines established by professional organizations, university ethics committees, and granting agencies. For example, the American Psychological Association (1992) urges its members to (1) tell prospective subjects what they will encounter so they can give their **informed consent** to participate, (2) instruct subjects that they're free to withdraw from the experiment at any time, (3) minimize all harm and discomfort, (4) keep the data obtained from subjects confidential, and (5) if deception is necessary, "debrief" subjects afterward by fully explaining the research.

The principles contained in these guidelines are important, and all investigators are responsible for the well-being of those who participate in their research. Some psychologists argue that these rules should be followed without exception. Others point out that many important issues could not then be investigated. In practice, ethical decisions are seldom clearcut. For example, informed consent is necessary, and everyone agrees that deception is undesirable, but it's often impossible to test a hypothesis on a fully informed subject. Think about my experiences. If I knew in advance I would witness a staged crime, if I knew I was supposed to look for patterns while memorizing letters, and if I knew that the IQ test I took was phony, I would have behaved in ways that were unnatural, not spontaneous. As a compromise, therefore, many researchers describe to subjects the procedures they may encounter, but withhold complete disclosure of the key variables and hypothesis until later, when subjects are debriefed.

Other types of judgment calls also must be made from time to time. For example, is it ethical to put subjects under stress—perhaps by presenting impossible problems to solve, or showing a pornographic film, or sharing the negative results of a test they took, or leading them to think temporarily that they inflicted harm on another person? Is it ethical to study pain tolerance, or to ask subjects to recount a traumatic episode? When the polio vaccine was tested in 1954, two million children were selected for study, but many received a placebo (a dummy medication that contains no active ingredients) instead of the real vaccine. Was that ethical? Similarly, is it ethical for psychologists testing a new remedy for anxiety to randomly assign half the subjects to a no-treatment control group? In making these kinds of decisions, researchers weigh the costs to the subject against the benefits to science and humanity. In weighing these outcomes, however, there is widespread disagreement among psychologists of differing values (Kimmel, 1991; Rosnow et al., 1993).

Ethics Considerations in Animal Research   When Charles Darwin (1859) presented his theory of evolution in *The Origin of Species*, he set the stage for the use of animals in research. Human beings, said Darwin, are biologically related to other creatures on the planet. Hence, the study of animals has relevance for understanding people. Does it ever. Over the years, psychology has made great strides using animals to study the brain and nervous system, vision and other senses, learning, reasoning, social behavior, psychological disorders, and the impact of various drugs. Mice, rats, rabbits, cats, dogs, apes, monkeys, and even birds, fish, insects, and sea slugs have proved valuable in this endeavor.

There are three reasons for using animals in research: to learn more about certain kinds of animals, to evaluate the cross-species generality of the principles of behavior, and to examine variables that cannot ethically be imposed on human subjects. Many years ago, medical researchers noted a correlation between cigarette smoking and lung cancer, but they could not determine if there was a causal link by forcing randomly selected people to smoke. Similarly, psychologists cannot inject human subjects with steroids in order to test the hypothesis that testosterone fuels aggression. For questions such as these, animal research is the only alternative.

Is it ethical to experiment on animals? Many animal rights activists say no—and are vocal in their opposition (Langley, 1989). A few years ago, at a psychology convention in Washington, D.C., I saw a hundred or so demonstrators waving posters depicting mutilated dogs and cats. Their claim was that research animals are routinely shocked senseless, starved to death, locked in isolation chambers, and injected with painful mind-altering drugs. Animals are entitled to the same rights as humans, they say, and besides, the research is trivial. On a number of occasions, militants have broken into laboratories, vandalized the equipment and records, and stolen experimental animals. In one incident, the words *ANIMAL KILLER* were spray-painted in black across the garage door of a National Institutes of Health researcher.

To understand how psychologists respond to these charges, it helps to know what the animal rights groups stand for. Everyone, including those in

Laboratory experiments using rats and other animals are important in psychology, as in medicine. However, animal rights activists believe that it is not ethical to use animals for research purposes.

the research community, consider themselves to be advocates for animal *welfare*—and support the establishment of shelters for lost pets, inoculation programs, the prevention of cruelty to animals, and the protection of endangered species (Johnson, 1990). Indeed, researchers argue that although food deprivation, mild shock, drugs, and surgery are often performed, the allegations of mistreatment are grossly exaggerated. Thus when Caroline Coile and Neil Miller (1984) analyzed 608 animal research articles published in the preceding five years, they found that these allegations were not supported in a single instance.

As formalized in the American Psychological Association's Code of Ethics (1992), researchers have a moral obligation to treat animals humanely and minimize their pain and suffering. However, many researchers and activists part company over the issue of animal *rights*. In the eyes of most activists, killing chickens for food, cows for leather, insects to save crops, or rats for research purposes are all acts of murder because humans and other animals should be treated equally. A poster held up at an animal rights march scorned the Amish use of horses to plow cornfields as a form of animal exploitation. In a recent survey of more than four hundred activists, a majority said they were strict vegetarians, did not use leather products, and placed an equal or greater value on nonhuman life. Overall, 85 percent endorsed the statement, "If it were up to me, I would eliminate all research using animals"—and 60 percent favored laboratory break-ins to achieve that goal (Plous, 1991). According to one researcher, "The animal rights movement is not about achieving humane treatment for animals. It is about ending all human uses of animals" (Johnson, 1990).

Psychologists and medical researchers defend their practices by pointing to the many ways in which their work has helped to improve the quality of life (Miller, 1985). Animal studies were instrumental in the development of a rabies vaccine, in organ transplants, and in understanding cancer, diabetes, and other diseases. Animal studies help in the treatment of anxiety, depression, and other mental disorders, and shed light on what is currently known about neuromuscular disorders, visual defects, Alzheimer's disease, mental retardation, headaches, high blood pressure, obesity, alcoholism, aggression, and the effects of stress on the immune system. Should animals be sacrificed to spare, prolong, or enhance the quality of human life? Should scientists probing the genetic roots of schizophrenia or seeking a cure for AIDS use mice to test experimental drugs? Animal activists say no, researchers say yes. Indeed, psychologist Neil Miller (1985) argues that it would be cruel and immoral *not* to use animals to solve these problems.

PSYCHOLOGY TODAY

Before psychology became established in science, it was popularly associated with astrology, numerology, dream analysis, graphology, and psychic experiences. In fact, the phenomena of "parapsychology" continue to fascinate people. Yet you are in no way influenced by the movements of planets and stars (I'm a Taurus and, yes, sometimes I'm stubborn, but who isn't?); your personality cannot be assessed by the size of your nose, the bumps on your head, or the way you curve your "S" when you write; and nobody can predict the future by analyzing your dreams or reading the palm of your

■ **cross-cultural research** A body of studies designed to compare and contrast people of different cultures.

hand. The problem with these claims is that despite their widespread appeal (according to a 1989 Gallup poll, more Americans believe in ESP than in evolution), and despite thousands of experiments, there is not a shred of convincing empirical support for them (Marks, 1986).

Grounded in the older disciplines of philosophy, biology, and medicine, and firmly rooted in the conviction that mind and behavior can be studied using scientific methods, psychology has made enormous progress. From the first subject to be tested in Wundt's original Leipzig laboratory, to the first patient to lie on Freud's couch, to the first psychologist ever to work in an applied setting, to the barrage of new discoveries concerning the links among mind, body, and health, we have come a long, long way.

Although psychologists study basic processes, we often touch upon some of the most important and socially sensitive topics of our generation. The similarities and differences between men and women, cultural diversity, AIDS, homosexuality, marriage and divorce, sex abuse, rape, brainwashing, abortion, adoption, the Scholastic Aptitude Tests (SATs), dieting, lie-detector tests, and the effects of drugs are among the topics currently being addressed. If you're interested in the possibility of a future career in psychology, refer to the list of major subfields (what we do) and employment settings (where we do it) presented in Figure 1.5.

Psychology has grown by leaps and bounds. For example, more and more psychologists are now conducting **cross-cultural research** in an effort to evaluate the global generality of their theories and to compare people who have lived very different lives. Cross-cultural studies tell us if all children start to walk and talk at the same age, if the smile is a universal expression of joy, or if depression is a worldwide affliction. Studies like these are discussed throughout this text, then highlighted in Chapter 14, on human diversity.

There are also more men and women in the field than ever before, more Blacks, Asians, Hispanics, and other minorities, more journals and articles being published, and more topics being studied. The American Psychological Association now has 73,000 members and 48 divisions—each dedicated

Figure 1.5

Psychology as a Profession

A census taken in 1983 indicates there are well over 100,000 psychological personnel in the United States. This graphic shows what these psychologists do for a living (their fields of specialization, left) and where they do it (employment settings, right) (Stapp et al., 1983).

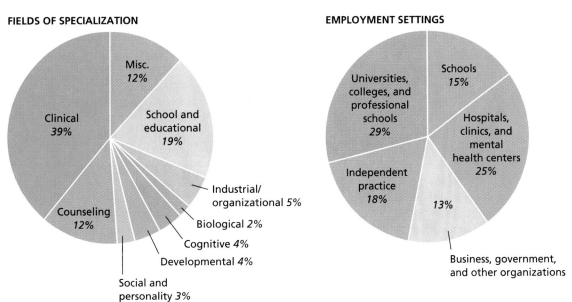

FIELDS OF SPECIALIZATION

Misc. 12%
Clinical 39%
School and educational 19%
Counseling 12%
Industrial/organizational 5%
Biological 2%
Cognitive 4%
Developmental 4%
Social and personality 3%

EMPLOYMENT SETTINGS

Universities, colleges, and professional schools 29%
Schools 15%
Hospitals, clinics, and mental health centers 25%
Independent practice 18%
13%
Business, government, and other organizations

"In this field, Dudley, you miss a few hours and you're no longer on the cutting edge."

[Harris/Cartoonists & Writers Syndicate]

to a particular aspect of the discipline (there were only 56,000 members and 38 divisions in the year 1980). In addition, a group of scientists recently established a rival organization dedicated solely to basic research (the APA addresses the concerns of practicing clinical and counseling psychologists as well). This new organization, which was founded in 1989, is called the American Psychological Society, or APS. Already it has 14,000 members. In many ways it's clear that psychology is firing on all cylinders.

There are so many new advances in theory, technology, and research, and so many new areas of specialization, that it is impossible to cover all of psychology in a single textbook. It is also important to realize that because psychology is a dynamic discipline, our knowledge evolves somewhat over time. To be sure, at least some of the conclusions drawn in this book may differ from those appearing in textbooks of the 1980s—and some may require further revision in the year 2000. To the extent possible, I have tried to stay up-to-date in order to present to you the state of psychology *today*.

As described earlier, this book is divided into five major parts, each containing three or four chapters. The five parts are as follows: (1) the biological roots of experience (with chapters on behavioral neuroscience, sensation and perception, and states of consciousness), (2) cognitive and affective processes (learning, memory, thought and language, and emotion), (3) human development (infancy and childhood, adolescence and adulthood, and intelligence), (4) social psychology (social perception, social influence, and human diversity), and (5) clinical psychology (personality, psychological disorders, and treatment). Drawing on each of these areas, we then close with a "capstone" chapter on some of the exciting new discoveries in the psychology of health and well-being. As you'll see in that final chapter, "the mind is a powerful tool. The more we know about how to use it, the better off we'll be."

SUMMARY AND KEY TERMS

In tomorrow's world, the key to success in life will be the same as it is today: understanding people. Psychology is a serious means of pursuing this understanding.

What Is Psychology?

Psychology can be defined as the scientific study of behavior and the mind.

Historical Roots

Psychology's origins can be traced to ancient Greek philosophers and physicians. During the Renaissance, René Descartes developed *dualism*, a theory that the mind is spiritual and the body physical. This theory implied that the mind could not be studied scientifically. English philosophers such as Thomas Hobbes disagreed, arguing that thoughts and feelings are physical processes.

Modern experimental psychology began in 1879 when Wilhelm Wundt established his laboratory in Germany. Wundt and

his students used the method of intensive *introspection*, in which trained observers described their reactions to stimuli. Meanwhile, in the United States, William James wrote his classic *Principles of Psychology;* and in Vienna, Sigmund Freud began to develop psychoanalysis to examine the unconscious mind.

The emerging discipline faced a major controversy: Should psychologists speculate about the invisible mind, as Freud and Wundt did, or should they confine themselves to observable behavior? *Behaviorism,* as defined by John Watson, held that psychology should concentrate on what can be seen and measured. Studying the way organisms respond to stimuli, behaviorists such as B. F. Skinner refused to speculate about mental processes.

Behaviorism dominated American psychology from the 1920s through the 1960s. At that point the focus shifted to *cognition,* the mental processes that intervene between a stimulus and response. The computer, which offers a model of the human mind, helped inspire this "cognitive revolution." So did the child development theories of Jean Piaget and the linguistic studies of Noam Chomsky.

Since its early days, psychology has expanded considerably. It now includes specialized areas of both *basic research* and *applied research,* and it relies on sophisticated research methods.

Basic Areas of Specialization

The main parts of this textbook reflect broad subfields in basic research. Each of them explores a fundamental question: (1) the biological subfield focuses on the links between the mind and body; (2) the cognitive subfield considers whether human beings are essentially rational or irrational; (3) developmental psychology tackles the nature-nurture controversy; (4) social psychology considers the extent to which social situations can overpower an individual's character and beliefs; and (5) clinical psychology, which includes psychotherapy and counseling, deals with the basic question of whether individuals can truly change their behavior.

Practical Applications

Throughout this text, the five main subfields of basic research are linked to five important areas of applied psychology—health, education, business, law, and the environment—to demonstrate psychology's many real-world implications.

Scientific Methods

Connecting all the strands of modern psychology is an emphasis on critical thinking and the scientific method. A psychological *theory*—an organized set of principles that describes, predicts, and explains a phenomenon—provides specific testable propositions, known as *hypotheses.* But psychological studies vary in terms of their settings, their ways of measuring variables, and the types of conclusions that the research is designed to reach.

Research Settings

There are two basic types of research setting: laboratory research, valuable for its control and precision; and field research, conducted in a real-world environment.

Psychological Measurements

Self-reports are interviews or questionnaires in which people report on their own thoughts, feelings, or behavior. These are easy to administer but sometimes misleading. The major alternative is direct behavioral observation. Archival records, such as medical files and public documents, constitute another source of information.

Research Designs

No matter how the information is collected, researchers use *statistics* to analyze it and draw conclusions. The types of conclusions they reach depend on the research design.

In descriptive studies the goal is simply to describe a person, group, or phenomenon. *Case studies* collect detailed information about a particular person. *Surveys,* in contrast, use interviews or questionnaires to assemble information about an entire population. To make a survey as accurate as possible, researchers generally rely on a *random sample,* so that each individual in the group has an equal chance of being chosen. Another type of descriptive study, *naturalistic observation,* involves the measurement of behavior in its natural setting.

When description is not enough, researchers often employ correlational studies. A *correlation* is a statistical measure of the extent to which two factors are associated. In numerical terms, correlation coefficients range from $+1$ to -1. Researchers use correlational studies to make predictions about one variable based on what they know about another variable. Correlation, however, does not prove causation.

To study causal links, researchers turn to the scientific *experiment,* in which the investigator manipulates the *independent variable* (the proposed cause) and measures the *dependent variable* (the proposed effect). Then the researcher compares the *experimental group* of subjects to a *control group* that was not exposed to the independent variable. An effective experiment requires *random assignment* of subjects, so that each participant has an equal chance of being in either group.

Finally, psychological research often includes reviews of the existing literature. By summarizing the current state of knowledge, literature reviews can help resolve the questions of *replication* (Would a new study produce the same results?) and *generalizability* (Is a finding limited to a narrow set of conditions?). Some reviews are narrative reviews. In other cases, psychologists use *meta-analysis,* a sophisticated set of statistical review procedures.

Ethical Dilemmas

Like other professions, psychology faces ethical questions, particularly about the use and treatment of research subjects. For human subjects, concerns include the subject's right to privacy, the harm or discomfort that may be caused by experimental procedures, and the use of *deception.* Research guidelines stress the need to obtain the *informed consent* of participants, let them know they can withdraw at any time, minimize harm and discomfort, keep data confidential, and debrief the subjects afterward. When the experimental subjects are animals, researchers must treat them humanely and minimize their pain and suffering.

Psychology Today

Because of the richness of psychological research and its many applications, there are more people in psychology today than ever before, and their work touches on such vital social topics as cultural diversity, sexuality, abortion, and drugs. Increasingly, too, *cross-cultural research* is helping psychologists determine whether their findings can apply throughout the world.

PART I

What is the link between the body and the mind? Inspired by this classic philosophical debate, Part I focuses on the biological roots of experience. Chapter 2 on *behavioral neuroscience* begins with an overview of the brain and nervous system, describing their structures and functions, exciting new developments in research in this area, and the tools used to conduct this research. Chapter 3 examines the processes of *sensation and perception,* and includes such topics as vision, hearing, and other senses; perceptual abilities and illusions; and extrasensory perception. Chapter 4 examines *consciousness,* and includes discussions of attentional processes, sleep and dreams, hypnosis, and psychoactive or "mind-altering" drugs. The material in these chapters provides a solid biological foundation for the scientific study of mind and behavior.

BIOLOGICAL ROOTS
OF EXPERIENCE

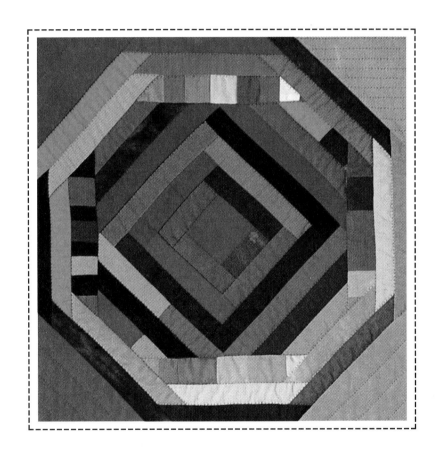

Chapter 2

Behavioral Neuroscience

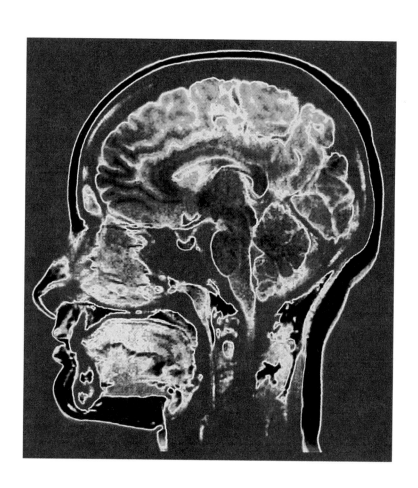

At twenty-five years of age, Phineas Gage was a supervisor for the Rutland & Burlington Railroad in Vermont. He was bright, well liked, and energetic. On the afternoon of September 13, 1848, Gage and his co-workers were blasting rock to pave the way for new railroad tracks. To do this, they drilled holes in the rock and packed the holes with gunpowder and sand using a three-foot-long rod called a "tamping iron." All of a sudden, a spark ignited the powder, causing an explosion that propelled the rod upward like a missile. As shown in Figure 2.1, the rod (which was an inch and a quarter in diameter) pierced Gage's left cheek, exited the front-top part of his skull, flew fifty feet into the air, and landed in a pile of dirt, covered with blood.

Gage's body was catapulted backward to the ground, where he began to shake uncontrollably. To everyone's amazement, he was still alive. Minutes later, he was sitting up, moving about, and talking to the people around him. Doctors soon stopped the bleeding, cleaned out the loose bits of bone and brain tissue, and packed the wound. Within a few months, Gage was back at work. He showed no loss of intellectual ability. But the front part of his brain, the area known as the *frontal lobes*, was badly damaged. As a result, the normally soft-spoken, controlled, and considerate young man had become irritable, demanding, and unrestrained—and at times he engaged in gross profanity. According to his doctor, the change in his personality was so profound that his friends said he was "no longer Gage." To complete the sad story: Gage lost his job, traveled with P. T. Barnum, and exhibited his skull and tamping iron at circuses all over the country. Twelve years after the accident, at the age of thirty-seven, he died (Harlow, 1868; Macmillan, 1986).

Psychologists now know that the frontal lobes are involved in planning, setting goals, and inhibiting impulses (Fuster, 1989). But the case of Phineas Gage told us much more. It told us that the human brain and nervous system are not a single or simple entity, but an integrated "system" consisting of different specialized parts. And it told us that the links between the brain, the mind, and behavior can be revealed by the effects of damage to specific structures. These points set the stage as we begin to explore the biological roots of the human experience. As we'll see, all aspects of our existence—every sight, sound, taste, and smell, every twitch, every movement, every feeling of pleasure or pain, all our dreams, learned associations, memories, thoughts, and emotions, and even our personalities and social interactions—are biological events. The subfield of psychology that focuses on the links between the brain, mind, and behavior is called **behavioral neuroscience.**

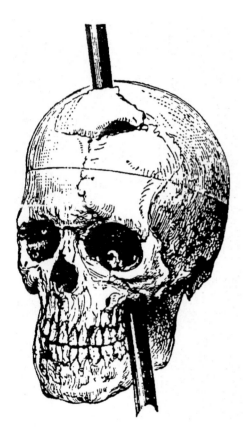

Figure 2.1

Phineas Gage's Skull and the Tamping Iron That Penetrated It

■ **behavioral neuroscience** The subfield of psychology that studies the links among the brain, nervous system, mind, and behavior.

THE BIG PICTURE

Before we explore the nervous system, let's step back for a moment and examine an old and profound philosophical question: What is the relationship between the body and the mind? On one side of the debate, René Descartes (1596–1650) and others have argued that body and mind are interacting but separate entities (dualism). On the other side, Thomas

Hobbes (1588–1679) and others have argued that the body and mind are one, a single physical entity (monism).

To some extent, dualism has dominated the way we think about the human experience. If you have a headache, heart disease, or a seizure, you would visit a doctor and seek a medical cure. But if you're sad or anxious, if you cry a lot, or if you're afraid to leave the house, you would seek psychological treatment from a counselor or therapist. Physicians heal the body, psychologists the mind. Sure, everyone agrees that the two influence each other in some way. But what is the nature of this interaction, and how extensive is it? One nineteenth-century theorist likened the mind's influence on the body to "the steam-whistle which accompanies the work of a locomotive engine, but cannot influence its machinery." Now, however, many psychologists believe that "mind and body have their hands so deep in each other's pockets it's hard to tell whose car keys are whose" (Barasch, 1993).

Although dualist notions persist, psychologists no longer make sharp distinctions. As we'll see in later chapters, human biological and psychological processes are intertwined and inseparable: change one, and you change the other, too. Brain surgery, drugs, and other medical interventions thus alter the mind. Similarly, stress, relaxation, and other psychological factors can profoundly affect the body. This seamlessness is a recurring theme in psychology and provides a solid foundation for studying the biological roots of behavior. It also sets the stage for a new way of thinking about health and medicine. To illustrate this point, imagine that you are a subject in the following experiment.

What's Your Prediction?

THE SITUATION

This time you really outdid yourself. You're one of 420 volunteers in a medical experiment for which you agreed to risk exposure to a common cold virus. You'll be reimbursed for travel expenses and for nine days will receive free room and board in the clinic. So you pack your bags, check in, and sign an informed-consent statement.

The first two days are hectic. First you're given a complete medical examination, including a blood test. Then you fill out a stack of questionnaires. You answer questions about your mood, personality, health practices, and recent stressful experiences (such as a death in the family, pressures at work, or the breakup of a relationship). Then it happens. To simulate the person-to-person transmission of a virus, an attendant exposes you to a solution using nasal drops. If you're lucky, you were randomly assigned to the control group and receive only a saline solution. If not, you're in an experimental group and receive a low dose of a cold virus. You don't know it, but these exposures tend to produce illness rates of between 20 and 60 percent.

You are now quarantined in a large apartment for seven days—alone or with one or two roommates. Every day, you're examined by a nurse who takes your temperature, extracts a mucus sample, and looks for signs of a cold: sneezing, watery eyes, stuffy nose, hoarseness, sore throat, and cough (the nurse also keeps track of the number of tissues you use). Basically, the researchers are interested in two results: Are you infected (is there a virus in your system), and do you have a cold (as judged by the various symptoms)? What you don't realize is that the researchers are trying to see if there is a link between the stress in your life and illness.

MAKE A PREDICTION

Based on the questionnaires initially filled out, you and others are classified as having a high or low level of stress. Does this psychological factor make a person more or less vulnerable to viral infection? Among those who are infected, does recent life stress elevate the risk of catching a cold? All subjects were healthy at the start of the project—and not a single saline control subject developed a cold. Among those exposed to the virus, however, 82 percent became infected, and 46 percent caught a cold, symptoms and all. A virus is a virus, and there is no escape. But were the rates significantly different among the high- and low-stress groups? What do you think?

Were high-stress subjects more likely to become infected?

YES   NO

Were high-stress subjects more likely to catch a cold?

YES   NO

THE RESULTS

In 1985, the prestigious *New England Journal of Medicine* published a study that failed to find a significant link between psychological factors and medical outcomes. In an accompanying note, the journal's editor took the opportunity to scoff at the notion that a person's mental state can affect physical health. Six years later, Sheldon Cohen and his colleagues (1991) published the aforementioned study in the same *New England Journal of Medicine*—marking a "turning point in medical acceptance of a mind/body connection" (Kiecolt-Glaser & Glaser, 1993).

The results of this study were convincing. Life stress was uncorrelated with the rate of infection. Among those exposed to a virus, 85 percent of the high-stress subjects and 81 percent of the low-stress subjects became infected. Among those who were infected, however, high-stress subjects (53 percent) were more likely to catch a cold than were low-stress subjects (40 percent). In fact, when subjects who had been housed with infected roommates were eliminated from the analysis (because of the risk that they had been re-exposed), the high-stress subjects (45 percent) were still more likely than their low-stress counterparts (28 percent) to catch a cold. Apparently, once infected, people whose lives are filled with stress are particularly vulnerable to illness.

WHAT DOES IT ALL MEAN?

This study reveals that there is a correlation between life stress and susceptibility to illness. Correlations do not prove causality, however, so one cannot conclude from this study alone that stress *per se* has this ef-

■ **psychoneuroimmunology (PNI)** A subfield that examines the interactions among psychological factors, the nervous system, and the immune system.

■ **central nervous system (CNS)** The network of nerves contained within the brain and spinal cord.

■ **peripheral nervous system (PNS)** The network of nerves that radiate from the central nervous system to the rest of the body. The PNS comprises the somatic and autonomic nervous systems.

■ **somatic nervous system** The branch of the peripheral nervous system that transmits signals from the sensory organs to the CNS, and from the CNS to the skeletal muscles.

■ **autonomic nervous system** The branch of the peripheral nervous system that connects the CNS to the involuntary muscles, organs, and glands.

fect. However, other researchers are finding that stress compromises the immune system, the body's first line of defense against illness. Studies show that the activity of the immune system's white blood cells can be temporarily diminished in subjects who are randomly exposed to a mildly stressful laboratory experience—such as a difficult task, a gruesome film, the recollection of bad memories, loud noise, or a bad social interaction (Kiecolt-Glaser et al., 1992).

This research has profound implications. Until recently, psychological and medical researchers alike believed that the human brain and immune system were separate and noninteracting. Not so. We now know that the organs of the immune system are richly endowed with nerve fibers, providing a direct pipeline to the brain—and that psychological factors, such as stress, play an important role. The result is a new field that focuses on the seamless interplay of mental and physical health. This new field is called **psychoneuroimmunology (PNI)**: *psycho* for mind, *neuro* for the nervous system, and *immunology* for the immune system (Ader et al., 1991). Later in this book, we'll see that PNI is generating a great deal of excitement. To build the necessary foundation for this area, and for the rest of psychology, we begin with an overview of the nervous system.

OVERVIEW OF THE NERVOUS SYSTEM

It weighs only three pounds and, with its gnarled mass of cells, feels like a lump of jelly and looks like an oversized, wrinkled gray walnut. It sounds gross, but the human *brain* is an extraordinary organ—capable of great feats and more complex than any computer. It is one of those "miracles" of life that inspire philosophers and scientists alike. Perhaps that is why the U.S. Congress declared the 1990s to be the "decade of the brain."

The human brain is part of the *nervous system*, an elaborate electrochemical communication network that connects the brain and spinal cord to all sensory organs, muscles, and glands. The nervous system is divided into two parts: central and peripheral. The **central nervous system (CNS)** consists of the brain and the spinal cord. The spinal cord is a long column of neural tissue surrounded by a ring of bone that runs from the lower back up to the base of the skull (basically, it is a transmission cable filled with nerve fibers). The **peripheral nervous system (PNS)** consists of all the nerves that radiate from the CNS to the rest of the body—from the top of your head to your fingers, toes, and skin.

The peripheral nervous system is further divided into two components: somatic and autonomic. The nerves of the **somatic nervous system** transmit signals (such as sights, sounds, tastes, smells, and feelings of pain) from the sensory organs and skin to the CNS. They also relay motor commands from the CNS to the skeletal muscles of the arms and legs, thus directing the body's *voluntary* movements. The nerves in the **autonomic nervous system** connect the CNS to all the smooth *involuntary* muscles and organs (such as the heart, stomach, and liver) and to the body's many glands, which secrete hormones. As the term *autonomic* implies, this system regulates internal states such as heartbeat, blood pressure, body temperature,

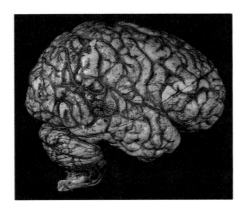

A lateral view of the human brain.

■ **sympathetic nervous system** The division of the autonomic nervous system that heightens arousal and energizes the body for action.

■ **parasympathetic nervous system** The division of the autonomic nervous system that reduces arousal and restores the body to its pre-energized state.

■ **neurons** Nerve cells that serve as the building blocks of the nervous system.

■ **sensory neurons** Neurons that send signals from the senses, skin, muscles, and internal organs to the central nervous system.

■ **motor neurons** Motion-producing neurons that transmit commands from the central nervous system to the muscles, glands, and organs.

■ **interneuron** Central nervous system neurons that connect sensory inputs and motor outputs.

digestion, hormone levels, and glucose levels, automatically. As we'll see later in this book, however, people can learn to use yoga and other techniques to exert some control over these bodily functions.

The autonomic nervous system has two parts: sympathetic and parasympathetic. The functions served by these subsystems might well be likened to "war and peace," or "spend and save." The **sympathetic** division energizes the body for action. In times of stress, it directs the adrenal glands, which rest atop the kidneys, to secrete more of the hormones epinephrine and norepinephrine (otherwise called adrenaline and noradrenaline)—thereby increasing the heart rate and heightening physiological arousal. The pupils dilate to let in more light, breathing speeds up to bring in more oxygen, and perspiration increases to cool down the body. When action is no longer necessary, as when stress subsides, the **parasympathetic** division takes over and restores the body to its pre-energized state. The heart stops racing, the pupils contract, breathing slows down, and energy is conserved. The levels of epinephrine and norepinephrine in the bloodstream slowly diminish, and the body relaxes, cools down, and returns to normal. As we'll see in Chapter 8, these systems play a vital role in the experience of emotion.

To summarize, the brain is a member of the nervous system, which has two parts, central and peripheral. The CNS contains the brain and spinal cord. The PNS is divided into the somatic (voluntary) and autonomic (involuntary) systems. In turn, the autonomic system contains both sympathetic (arousing) and parasympathetic (calming) divisions. This overview is presented in Figure 2.2.

THE NEURON

Now that we have drawn a sketch of the nervous system, let's fill in the textures and fine details. We begin with the tiny but numerous building blocks and the electrical and chemical impulses that fire throughout the body. In humans and other animals, the nervous system consists of two main types of cells: nerve cells and glial cells. Playing the lead role are the nerve cells, or **neurons**. Neurons send and receive information throughout the body in the form of electrochemical signals. There are three types of neurons. **Sensory neurons** send signals from the senses, skin, muscles, and internal organs to the CNS. When you see an awesome sunset, scrape your knee, or enjoy the flavor of a gourmet meal, messages fire from the eyes, knee, and taste buds; these messages are then relayed up to the brain. **Motor** (motion-producing) **neurons** transmit commands the other way around—from the CNS to the muscles, glands, and organs. Once the sunset, injured knee, and delicious food "register," you and your body act accordingly. Finally, **interneurons** serve as neural connectors within the central nervous system. Among their functions is that of linking input signals from the sensory neurons to output signals from the motor neurons.

No one knows for sure how many neurons there are in a brain, but researchers estimate that the number is between 100 and 200 billion—more than the number of stars in our galaxy. To give you an idea of how much that is, consider this: if you were to count one neuron every second, it would take you up to six thousand years to count them all. Even more

"Living threads more numerous than stars frame the universe of my mind."

DANIEL P. KIMBLE (1988)

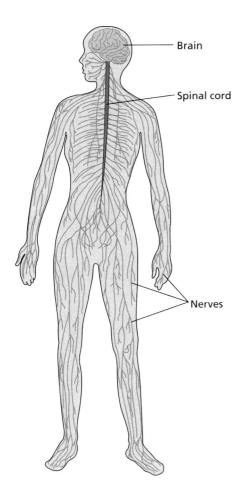

Figure 2.2

Divisions of the Human Nervous System

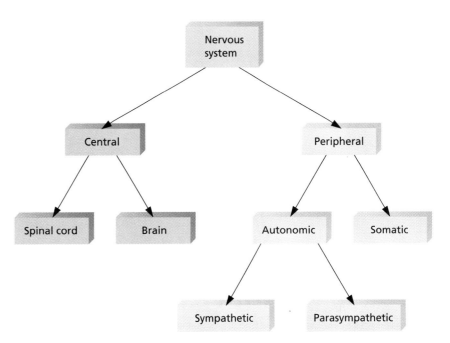

mind-boggling is the fact that each neuron is linked to more than a thousand other neurons, thus providing each of us with literally trillions of connections among the neurons in the brain.

The nervous system also has a supporting cast of smaller cells called **glial cells,** or neuroglia. The word *neuroglia* is derived from the Latin and Greek words meaning "nerve glue." These cells are so named because they provide structural support, insulation, and nutrients to the neurons, thereby "gluing" the system together. They also play a role in the development and repair of neurons and the speed of the neural signals throughout the system. Glial cells are much smaller than the neurons they support. But because they outnumber neurons ten to one, they constitute about half of the brain's total mass (Nicholls et al., 1992).

To see how neurons work together within the nervous system, let's trace the neural pathway of a simple **reflex,** defined as an automatic response to external sensory stimulation. If you've ever had a medical checkup, you are probably familiar with the "knee jerk" reflex. Using a rubber mallet, the doctor taps your patellar tendon, located just below the knee, and this causes your leg to kick forward. You don't have to think about it: the reaction is immediate, and there's nothing you can do to stop it. The tap triggers the kick automatically. How? As shown in Figure 2.3, the knee stretches your thigh muscle, which sends a sensory signal to the spinal cord, which sends a motor signal right back to the thigh muscle. Tap, kick! This two-step chain of events takes only 50 milliseconds because it does not involve higher mental processes in the brain. Reflexes like this are very adaptive. When your hand touches a hot iron or the thorn of a rose bush, a sensory neuron sends a quick message to the spinal cord, which activates a motor neuron and causes you to pull your hand away. The entire reaction takes place in the spinal cord—before you and your brain feel the pain, and before too much damage is done.

In the case of more complex forms of behavior—driving, working on a math problem, playing a musical instrument, talking to a friend, or reading

■ **glial cells** Nervous system cells that provide structural support, insulation, and nutrients to the neurons.

■ **reflex** An inborn automatic response to a sensory stimulus.

A. THE KNEE-JERK REFLEX

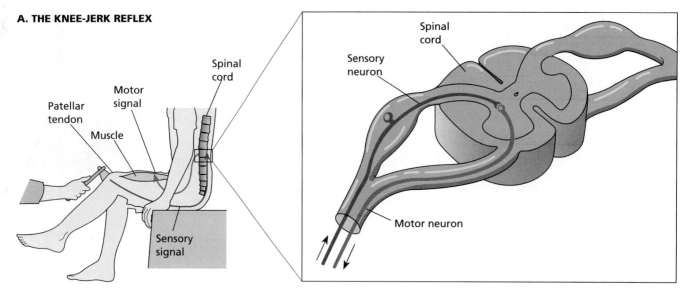

B. THE WITHDRAWAL REFLEX

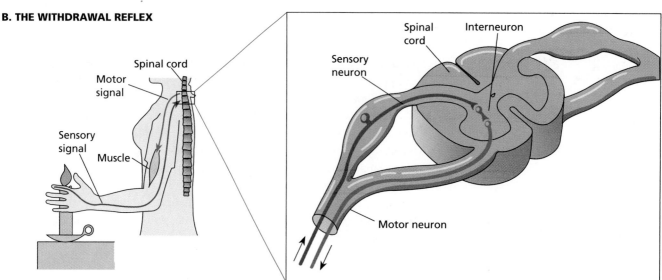

Figure 2.3

(a) The Knee-Jerk Reflex

A tap on the knee sends a sensory signal to the spinal cord, which sends a motor signal back to the muscle. Tap, kick!

(b) The Withdrawal Reflex

Touch a hot object, and your hand will immediately pull away. In this case, sensory and motor neurons are linked by an interneuron.

this sentence, more extensive activity is needed than is possible within the spinal cord. Sensory inputs travel toward the spinal cord (via the somatic nervous system), but they are then forwarded to the brain and "processed" before a behavioral "decision" is reached. This decision is sent back down through the spinal cord and out to the muscles, resulting in behavior. Most of the behaviors that interest psychologists are of this sort.

Structure of the Neuron

The neuron is a lot like other cells in the body. It is surrounded by a membrane and has a nucleus that contains genetic material. What makes the neuron so special is its ability to communicate. Indeed, everything that we do and all that we know depend on the transfer of signals from one neuron to another.

It's hard to describe the dimensions of a "typical" neuron because these cells come in hundreds of different shapes and sizes—depending on their

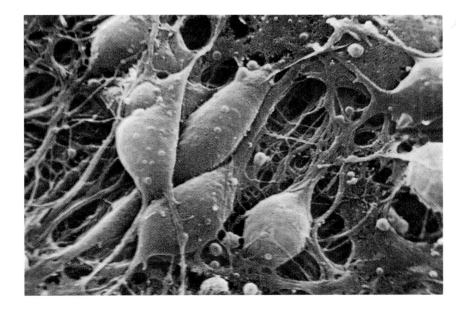

As shown, neurons are nerve cells that transmit electrochemical signals throughout the body.

specific function. But the various neurons do have certain structural features in common. As illustrated in Figure 2.4, every neuron has a roundish **soma,** or cell body, which stores the nucleus of the cell and maintains a chemical balance. Connected to the cell body are two types of branched fibers or tentacles. The **dendrites** (derived from the Greek word for "tree") *receive* impulses from sensory organs or other neurons. The more dendrites there are, the more information can be received. The **axon** (so named because of its axle-like shape) *sends* the impulse through the neuron to other neurons. Some axons are short and stubby; others are several feet long and slender (some run from the spine down to the muscles of your big toe). At the end of each axon are branches with knob-like tips called *axon terminals.* As we'll see, these tips contain vital chemical substances to be released

Figure 2.4   Structure of the Neuron

Every neuron consists of a soma, or cell body, and two types of branched fibers. Dendrites receive electrical impulses from sensory organs or other neurons, and the axon relays these impulses to other neurons or muscles. As shown, many axons are insulated with myelin sheath, a layer of fatty cells that speeds the movement of the impulses.

■ **soma** The cell body of a neuron.

■ **dendrites** Extensions from the cell body of a neuron that receive incoming impulses.

■ **axon** Extension of the cell body of a neuron that sends impulses to other neurons.

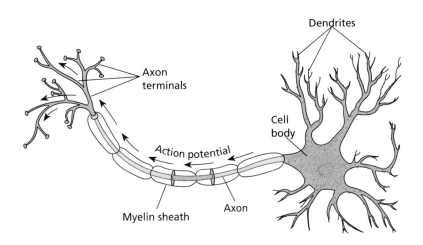

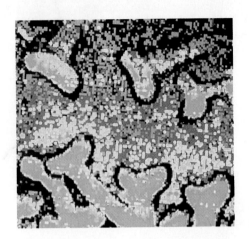

Microscopic photograph of the knob-like axon terminals.

onto other cells. Many axons are also covered with **myelin sheath**, a shiny white layer of fatty cells that is tightly wrapped around the axon to insulate it. This insulation helps to speed up the movement of electrical impulses. To summarize, neural signals travel from the dendrites, through the soma, down the axon, and into the axon terminals.

The Neuron in Action

To understand how messages are transmitted from the axon of one neuron to the dendrites of another, you need to know that these messages occur in the form of electrical impulses. So, here is a quick lesson in the electricity of the nervous system.

Every neuron is covered by a membrane, a semipermeable skin that permits some chemicals to pass through more easily than others. Dissolved in fluid on both sides of the membrane are electrically charged particles called *ions*. Three kinds of ions are present: sodium (*positively* charged ions that do not pass through the membrane easily, so are concentrated *outside* the cell), potassium (positively charged ions that cross easily and are concentrated inside the cell), and *negatively* charged ions that are trapped permanently *inside* the cell). When a neuron is at rest, the inside of the cell has a negative charge relative to the outside, making it a store of potential energy—like a tiny battery.

When the dendrites of a neuron are stimulated, usually by other neurons, this delicate balance is suddenly altered. The semipermeable membrane breaks down, permitting the positively charged sodium ions outside the cell to rush in. For an instant, the charge inside the cell becomes less negative and, as a result, may trigger an **action potential**—a quick burst of electrical energy that surges through the axon like a spark along a trail of gunpowder. Depending on the neuron, most impulses travel at speeds ranging from 2 miles an hour up to 200 miles an hour—faster than a car, but three million times slower than the speed of electric current passing through a wire. At top speed, then, it takes an action potential one-hundredth of a second to run along an axon from the spinal cord to a muscle in the finger or toe. Then, after an impulse has passed, the positive ions inside the cell are pumped back to the outside of the membrane. The neuron returns to its resting state—and is once again ready for action.

The stimulation of a neuron does not always trigger the firing of an electrical impulse. At any given moment, a neuron may be receiving signals on its dendrites from very few or from hundreds, even thousands, of other neurons. Whether the neuron fires depends on the sum total of signals impinging upon it. Only if the combined signals exceed a certain minimum intensity, or *threshold*, does the neuron's membrane break down and begin to transmit an electrical impulse. If it does not, then nothing changes. In other words, the action potential is an *all or none response*. Either it fires or it does not. This effect is like the shooting of a gun. If you squeeze the trigger past a certain point (the threshold), bang! If not, nothing is fired. You can't half-shoot, and you can't vary the intensity of the shot. It's also like turning on a lamp. Unless you have a special dimmer switch, the light is either on or off.

The firing of an electrical impulse is as quick as the blink of an eye, but it has profound significance. Information in the nervous system is made up of action potentials. Every thought you have, every dream, every emotion,

■ **myelin sheath** A layer of fatty cells that is tightly wrapped around the axon to insulate it and speed the movement of electrical impulses.

■ **action potential** An electrical impulse that surges through an axon, caused by an influx of positive ions in the neuron.

■ **synapse** The junction between the axon terminal of one neuron and the dendrites of another.

■ **neurotransmitters** Chemical messengers in the nervous system that transmit information by crossing the synapse from one neuron to another.

every action you take and every decision you make is coded in the form of action potentials. For behavioral neuroscientists, cracking the action potential code is a key to understanding the language of the nervous system and unlocking new discoveries about the biology of our minds and behavior.

How Neurons Communicate

Imagine that you are watching a neural impulse racing from the dendrites (the starting line), through the cell body, and down the axon. What happens when the signal reaches the axon terminals? How does it then get to the dendrites of the next neuron? The transmission of messages through the nervous system is like a relay race. So when the impulse reaches the end of one cell, it passes the electrochemical baton to the next cell, or to a muscle or gland. How is this accomplished? Scientists used to think that the branching axons and dendrites of adjacent neurons always touched, thus enabling impulses to travel seamlessly, the way an electrical current crosses two extension cords that are plugged together. We now know that this is not the main way it works—and that there is a narrow gap between neurons that is roughly a millionth of an inch wide. This gap is called a **synapse,** from the Greek word meaning "point of contact." The question is, How does the impulse cross this synaptic gap to the next neuron?

The answer has to do with **neurotransmitters.** When an electrical impulse reaches the knob-like axon terminal, it forces the release of chemical messengers called neurotransmitters—so named because they aid in the *transmission* of information from one *neuron* to another. These chemical substances are manufactured by the neuron and stored in tiny round packets called *synaptic vesicles.* Upon their release, the neurotransmitters squirt across the synapse and bind to specialized *receptors* on the dendrites of the receiving neuron. There are different types of neurotransmitters. Some will

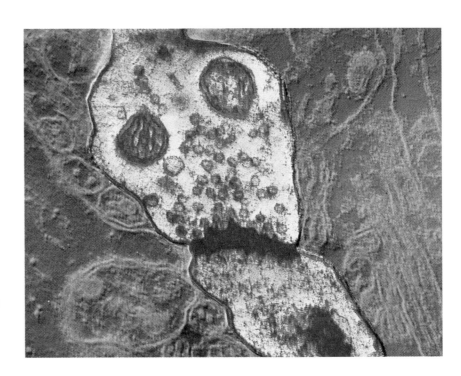

Micrograph of neurotransmitters in synaptic vesicles (top) squirting across the synaptic gap (center) to a receiving neuron (bottom).

excite ("fire") an action potential in the next neuron, while others will *inhibit* ("restrain the firing of") the next action potential. It's a truly remarkable process. There are different neurotransmitters and different types of receptors—and each has its own shape. This fact is significant, because a neurotransmitter binds snugly only to certain receptors the way a key fits only one lock. The entire electrochemical process is illustrated in Figure 2.5.

Figure 2.5

How Neurons Communicate

When an impulse reaches the axon terminal, it forces the release of neurotransmitters, which are stored in tiny vesicles. These chemicals squirt across the synaptic gap and bind to special receptors on the receiving neuron. There are different neurotransmitters. Each fits only certain receptors the way a key fits only one lock.

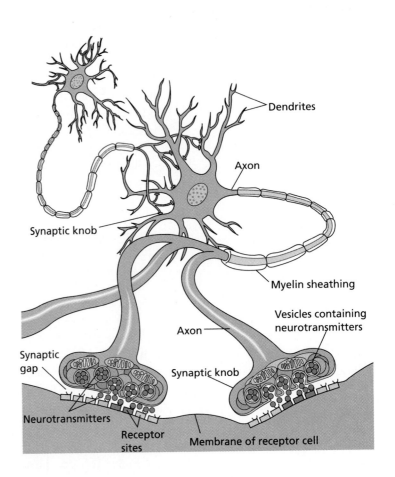

Dendrites

Axon

Synaptic knob

Myelin sheathing

Vesicles containing neurotransmitters

Axon

Synaptic knob

Synaptic gap

Neurotransmitters

Receptor sites

Membrane of receptor cell

Neurotransmitters

Anxiety, feelings of calm, sadness and depression, pain and relief, memory disorders, drowsiness, hallucinations, paralysis, tremors and seizures, all have something in common: a link to the activity of neurotransmitters. Neuroscientists used to think that just a few substances were involved in neural transmission. But thanks to recent technological advances, some of which will be discussed later, we now know that the human nervous system is a prolific chemical factory. To date, researchers have identified more than fifty neurotransmitters—and have further suggested the possibility of up to three hundred in all. Indeed, the most recent, and surprising, discovery was the identification of the gases nitric oxide and carbon monoxide as neurotransmitters (Snyder, 1992; Verma et al., 1993).

The activities of certain neurotransmitters—where in the body they're produced, their effects on mind and behavior, and their responsiveness to drugs—are well understood (see Table 2.1). The first substance identified as a neurotransmitter was **acetylcholine (ACh)**, which is found throughout

■ **acetylcholine (ACh)** A neurotransmitter found throughout the nervous system that links the motor neurons and muscles.

Table 2.1

The nervous system produces dozens of neurotransmitters. These are some of the more important ones. Also noted are their functions and the chapters in which they are discussed.

Neurotransmitter	Function	Chapter
Acetylcholine	Links motor neurons and muscles. Also facilitates learning and memory. Alzheimer's patients have an undersupply of ACh.	6
Dopamine	Concentrated in the brain, it is linked to muscle activity. A shortage can cause Parkinson's disease; an excess of dopamine receptors is linked to key symptoms of schizophrenia.	16, 17
Endorphins	Distributed throughout the CNS, these natural opiates relieve pain.	3
Norepinephrine	Widely distributed in the CNS, it increases arousal. Too much may produce a manic state; too little may lead to depression.	16, 17
Serotonin	Produced in the brain, it lowers activity level and causes sleep. An excess is linked to depression.	4, 16, 17
GABA (gamma aminobutyric acid)	Produced in the brain, it lowers arousal and reduces anxiety. It is the main inhibitory neurotransmitter in the nervous system.	17

the nervous system and is particularly concentrated in the parts of the brain that control motor behavior. ACh is the chemical key that links the motor neurons and muscles. Thus, it is released whenever you walk, talk, ride a bike, throw a ball, or take a breath. So, what would happen if you somehow blocked the release of all ACh in the system? Think about the link that would be severed, and you'll have the answer. Curare—a poison that some South American Indians put on their hunting arrows—blocks the ACh receptors and causes complete paralysis of the skeletal muscles. And what about the opposite condition? What would happen if you were to flood the synapses between motor neurons and muscles with ACh? The toxic bite of a black widow spider does just that, resulting in violent muscle contractions, sometimes even death. ACh may also play a role in the formation of new memories. As we will see in Chapter 6, people who have been struck by *Alzheimer's disease*, a degenerative disorder that destroys memory, have abnormally low levels of ACh.

In contrast to ACh, which has an excitatory effect on the muscles, the neurotransmitter **dopamine** has an inhibitory effect. Thus, *Parkinson's disease*—a motor disorder characterized by hand tremors, stooped posture, and a loss of control over voluntary movements—is caused by the death of neurons that produce dopamine. People with this disease can thus be treated with L-dopa, a substance that the body converts into dopamine, thereby replenishing the supply (as we'll see later, another promising new

■ **dopamine** A neurotransmitter that functions as an inhibitor and is involved in the control of voluntary movements.

Intense exercise triggers the release of endorphins—which may account for the "runner's high" sensation experienced by many long-distance runners.

approach is to implant healthy tissue containing dopamine into the brains of Parkinsonian patients). Researchers have also found that many *schizophrenia* patients have an oversupply of dopamine receptors in the brain (Resnick, 1992)—and that the symptoms can often be treated with drugs that block the activity of dopamine (see Chapters 16 and 17).

Another exciting discovery is that the brain produces it own morphine, a pain killer. Several years ago, Candace Pert and Solomon Snyder (1973) injected laboratory animals with morphine, a powerful and addictive painkilling drug derived from opium. To their surprise, they found that the morphine binded to certain receptors in the brain the way neurotransmitters do. This discovery is only mildly interesting, you may think. But wait. Why would the brain have receptors for a chemical produced outside the body? If there's a special receptor for morphine, doesn't it mean that the brain produces its own morphine-like substance? The answer is yes—and the neurotransmitter is called an **endorphin** (from the words *endogenous*, which means internal, and *morphine*). Researchers soon found that endorphins and their receptors, and other similar substances, are distributed throughout the central nervous system (Hughes et al., 1975).

What triggers the release of endorphins? Sensations of pain and discomfort. For example, the exhilarating "runner's high" so often described by long-distance runners might be caused by the release of endorphins (Farrell et al., 1982). So might the pain-relieving effects of acupuncture, the traditional Chinese medical procedure in which needles are inserted into certain parts of the body (He, 1987). Still other researchers have suggested that the release of endorphins is triggered by physical injury, and by the labor pains that precede childbirth (Akil, 1982). Although the causes and effects of endorphins are not yet clearly understood, it does appear that the human body comes equipped with a natural, built-in pharmacy for pain relief.

THE BRAIN

Encased in a hard protective skull, the brain is the crown jewel of the nervous system. It weighs only three pounds and constitutes only 1/45th of the human body's average weight. But, as we saw earlier, it contains billions of neurons and trillions of synaptic connections. For those interested only in anatomy, it was easy to determine the physical *structure* of the brain by dissecting the brains removed from dead animals, and from humans who had donated their bodies to science. But for behavioral neuroscientists, the task is far more challenging: to determine the *functions* of the living brain, and thus to understand its links to the way we think, feel, and behave.

■ **endorphin** A morphine-like neurotransmitter that is produced in the brain and linked to pain control and pleasure.

■ **phrenology** The pseudoscientific theory that psychological characteristics are revealed by bumps on the skull.

Tools of Behavioral Neuroscience

Before the term *neuroscience* had ever been uttered, Viennese physician Franz Gall (1758–1828) founded **phrenology**, the pseudoscientific theory that psychological characteristics are revealed by bumps on the skull. (Apparently, as a young boy, Gall "noticed" that his friends who had the best memories also had protruding, large eyes.) In believing that speech, math ability, aggression, and other characteristics are "localized" in certain regions of the brain, Gall was on the right track (see Figure 2.6). However, in using bumps on the skull to find these links, he was very much on the wrong track.

To fully understand and evaluate what researchers currently know about the brain, it helps to be aware of *how* they arrive at that knowledge—the methods they use, and why. Thanks in part to advances in technology, today's behavioral neuroscientists are like explorers on a new frontier. As we'll see, four types of research methods are used: clinical case studies, experimental interventions, electrical recordings, and imaging techniques.

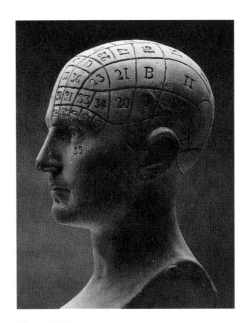

Figure 2.6
Phrenology

In the nineteenth century, Franz Gall tried to map the human brain by measuring bumps on the skull.

Clinical Case Studies   One approach is the clinical case study, in which researchers observe people with brain damage resulting from tumors, diseases, head injuries, or exposure to toxic substances. In the case of Phineas Gage, massive damage to the frontal lobes was followed by changes in his personality (specifically, an inability to control impulses), yet his intellectual abilities remained the same as before. Thus, this case suggested that the frontal lobes are involved in the control of behavior. Other case studies, too, have proved invaluable. In best sellers such as *Awakenings* (1983) and *The Man Who Mistook His Wife for a Hat* (1985), for example, neurologist Oliver Sacks tells colorful and provocative stories about brain-damaged patients who exhibited specific deficits in speech, memory, motor behavior, sleep, and even their self-concept.

Clinical evidence is tantalizing, and often enlightening, but it cannot provide the sole basis for behavioral neuroscience. One drawback is that when part of the brain is damaged, nearby neurons sometimes sprout new branches—and other structures sometimes pick up the slack. These forms of compensation are wonderfully adaptive, but they may mask the effects of damage. Another drawback is that natural injuries are seldom localized, so the resulting deficit may not really be traceable to a single structure. In the case of Phineas Gage, for example, the skull was pierced by a long rod that was over an inch in diameter—hardly a surgical incision.

Experimental Interventions   A second common method is to "invade" the brain through an experimental *intervention* and then to measure the effects on behavior. One technique, often used by animal researchers, is to purposely disable, or *lesion*, a part of the brain by surgically destroying it. Often this is done by anesthetizing the animal, implanting an electrode into a specific site in the brain, and passing a high-voltage current through it to burn the tissue. A second technique is to administer *drugs* that are suspected of having effects on neurotransmitters and other activity in the brain. Over the years, the effects of many substances on the brain and behavior have been tested in this manner—substances including alcohol, caffeine, adrenaline, and the sex hormones testosterone and androgen.

A third form of intervention is through *electrical brain stimulation*. In these studies, a microelectrode is inserted in the brain and a mild electrical current is used to "activate" the neurons in a particular site. Most of these experiments are conducted with animals, but on occasion clues are derived from human brain-surgery patients. Since no two brains are exactly alike, brain surgeons often must "map" the patient's brain so they don't accidentally destroy key functions. Toward this end, the patient is given a local anesthetic and kept awake for the procedure. While treating epilepsy patients, for example, neurosurgeon Wilder Penfield stimulated different areas along the surface of the brain and found that, depending on the region he stimulated, the patients would report visual images, tingling sensations, muscular twitches, and other reactions (Penfield & Roberts, 1959).

Electrical Recordings   The most exciting advances in behavioral neuroscience arise from techniques that are not "invasive" to the human subject. In 1929, German psychiatrist Hans Burger invented a machine that could detect, amplify, and record "waves" of electrical activity in the brain using metal electrodes pasted to the surface of the scalp. The instrument is called an **electroencephalograph (EEG)**, and the information it provides is in the form of line tracings called *brain waves* (see Figure 2.7).

Figure 2.7

The EEG

Through electrodes on a subject's scalp, the electroencephalogram records electrical activity in the brain and displays the output in line tracings called brain waves. Varying in their frequency (cycles per second) and amplitude (voltage), EEG patterns differ according to a person's mental state.

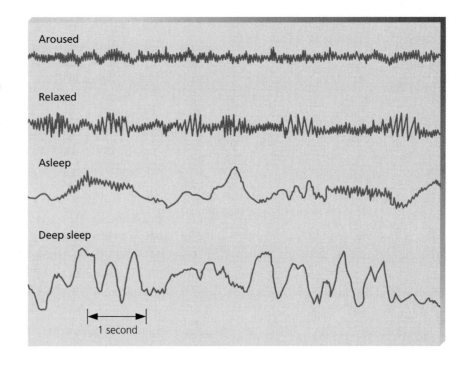

As we'll see in later chapters, researchers using the EEG have found that brain waves differ depending on whether a person is excited, relaxed, pensive, drowsy, or asleep. It's also used for diagnosing brain damage and various neurological disorders. For example, people with epilepsy have seizures because a certain portion of the brain is overexcitable and prone to fire in a wild manner—which sets off electrical spikes, or "explosions." The EEG may even be useful for diagnosing pathological conditions such as depression and alcoholism (John et al., 1988). There are limits, however, to what EEG recordings can tell us. The problem is that the EEG merely summarizes all the electrical activity of billions of neurons firing along the brain's surface. Thus, as one group of researchers put it, "we are like blind men trying to understand the workings of a factory by listening outside the

■ **electroencephalograph** (EEG) An instrument used to measure electrical activity in the brain through electrodes placed on the scalp.

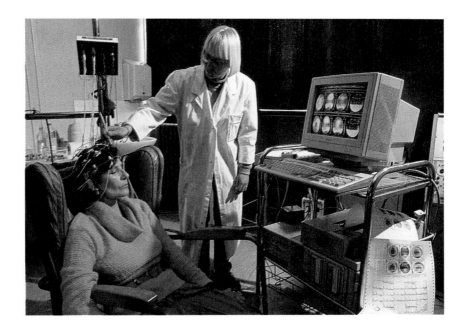

An electroencephalograph records waves of electrical activity in the brain. Here it is being used to test for Alzheimer's disease.

walls" (quoted by Hassett, 1978). For greater precision, then, researchers sometimes use microelectrodes with tips so small that they can record the activity of a single cell.

Brain-Imaging Techniques   When people think about the wonders of high technology, what comes to mind are global communication satellites and giant-sized telescopes that can spy on the distant galaxies of the universe. But recent advances in technology have also enabled us to turn the scientific eye on ourselves, to inner recesses of the human brain never previously seen. Designed to provide visual images of the live human brain, without ever having to lift a scalpel, this new technology uses computers to combine thousands of still "snapshots" into models of the brain in action. There are three basic imaging techniques, all popularly known by their initials: CAT scan, PET scan, and MRI.

The **computerized axial tomograph (CAT) scan** is a computer-enhanced x-ray of the brain. In this technique, x-ray beams are passed through the head at 1-degree intervals over a 180-degree arc, and a computer is used to convert this information into an image that depicts a horizontal slice of the brain. CAT scans are invaluable for diagnosing tumors and strokes and for identifying brain abnormalities in people suffering from schizophrenia and other psychological disorders.

A second revolutionary imaging technique, one that can be used to map the activity of the brain over time, is the **positron emission tomograph (PET) scan.** Based on the fact that glucose supplies the brain with energy, the level of activity in a given region of the brain can be measured by the amount of glucose that it burns. After a tiny amount of radioactive glucose is injected into the brain, the scanner measures the amount of this substance as it is consumed in different regions. The results are then fed to a computer, which produces an enhanced color picture (Martin et al., 1991). Can the PET scan spy on our thought processes? In a way, yes. Look at Figure 2.8, and you'll see the PET scans of a person with his eyes and ears

■ **(computerized axial tomograph) CAT scan** A series of x-rays taken from different angles and converted by computer into an image that depicts a horizontal slice of brain.

■ **(positron emission tomograph) PET scan** A visual display of brain activity, as measured by the amount of glucose being used.

Figure 2.8

PET Scans

After radioactive glucose has been injected into the brain, a scanner measures how much glucose is consumed in different regions. The results are displayed in a computer-enhanced picture in which hotter colors (red, orange, yellow) indicate more activity. In these images, visual areas of the brain "lit up" when the subject's eyes were open, as did auditory areas when the subject's ears were stimulated with sound.

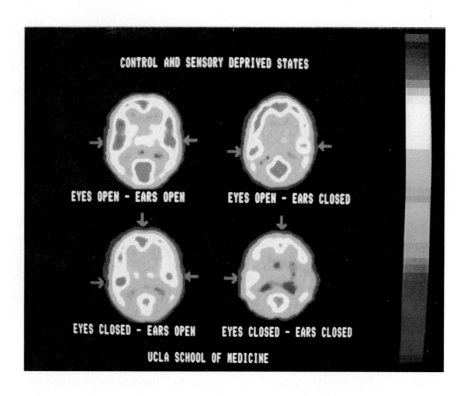

CONTROL AND SENSORY DEPRIVED STATES

EYES OPEN - EARS OPEN   EYES OPEN - EARS CLOSED

EYES CLOSED - EARS OPEN   EYES CLOSED - EARS CLOSED

UCLA SCHOOL OF MEDICINE

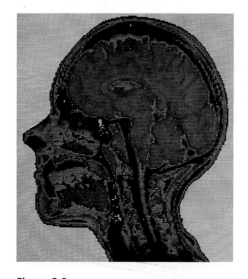

Figure 2.9

The MRI

Magnetic resonance imaging yields the best resolution for visualizing brain structures.

■ **magnetic resonance imaging (MRI)** A brain-scanning technique that uses magnetic fields and radio waves to produce clear, three-dimensional images.

open or closed. Research also shows that PET scans often distinguish among different types of psychological disorders (Andreasen, 1988). In these scans, the hot colors (red, orange and yellow) indicate more activity, while the cool colors (violet, blue, and green) mean less activity.

A "new and improved" imaging technique is **magnetic resonance imaging (MRI)**. This technique is similar to the CAT scan, but instead of using an x-ray, it passes the subject's head through a strong but harmless magnetic field to align the brain's atoms. A quick pulse of radio waves is then used to disorient the atoms, which give off detectable signals as they return to normal. More sensitive than a CAT scan, the MRI produces images with better resolution and, if necessary, moving pictures of the brain (see Figure 2.9). This new technology is generating tremendous excitement. Indeed, researchers are now saying, "This is the wonder technique we've all been waiting for" and calling it "the most exciting thing to happen in the realm of cognitive neuroscience in my lifetime" (Blakeslee, 1993). Does the brain respond differently to music than to words? Is there something different about the brain of an artist, or a physicist? Thanks to the MRI and other new imaging technologies, there are many new frontiers to explore and new discoveries on the horizon (Raichle, 1994).

Regions of the Brain

The human brain is a unique product of evolution—in some ways similar to the brains of "lower" animals, in other ways different. Salmon, caribou, and migrating birds have navigational abilities unparalleled in our own species. Dogs, cats, and many other mammals have senses of hearing and smell that are downright superhuman. Yet no other animal on the planet can solve problems, think about itself and the future, or communicate as

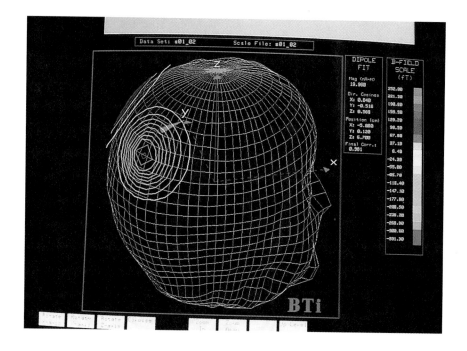

Brain imaging technology is advancing at a rapid rate. This particular image is derived from SQUID (superconducting quantum interference device), a system that can detect the tiny changes in magnetic fields that accompany the firing of neurons.

we do. As we'll see, these relative strengths and weaknesses can be traced to the unique structure of the human brain.

Although the brain is a single organ containing interconnected pathways of nerve fibers, neuroscientists find that there are really three mini-brains rolled into one. The *brainstem* is the old "inner core" that rests atop the spinal cord and regulates primitive life-support functions such as breathing, heartbeat, and muscle movements. Surrounding the brainstem, the *limbic system* provides an increased capacity for motivation, emotional responses, and basic forms of learning and memory. And in the *cerebral cortex*, which features the wrinkled outer layer of the brain, "higher" mental processes enable more complex forms of learning, memory, thought, and language. The cerebral cortex is the last part to develop—both within the individual and in the species as a whole (see Figure 2.10).

Figure 2.10

The Human Brain

There are three main regions of the human brain. The *brainstem* is the old "inner core" that controls life support functions. The *limbic system* regulates motivation, emotion, and basic forms of learning and memory. The *cerebral cortex,* which features the wrinkled outer layer of the brain, controls "higher" mental processes that enhance learning, memory, thought, and language.

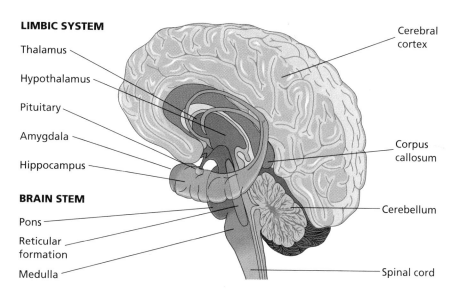

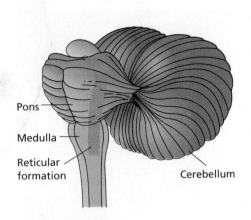

Figure 2.11

The Brainstem

The brainstem is the most primitive structure of the brain. Resting atop the spinal cord, it contains the medulla, pons, and reticular formation, and is attached to the cerebellum.

■ **brainstem** The inner core of the brain that connects to the spinal cord and contains the medulla, pons, and reticular formation.

■ **medulla** A brainstem structure that controls vital involuntary functions.

■ **pons** A portion of the brainstem that plays a role in sleep and arousal.

■ **reticular formation** A group of nerve cells in the brainstem that help to control sleep, arousal, and attention.

■ **cerebellum** A primitive brainstem structure that controls balance and coordinates complex voluntary movements.

■ **limbic system** A set of loosely connected structures in the brain that help to regulate motivation, emotion, and memory.

■ **thalamus** A limbic structure that relays neural messages between the senses and areas of the cerebral cortex.

The Brainstem   As the spinal cord enters the skull, it enlarges into the **brainstem**, a primitive inner core. As illustrated in Figure 2.11, the brainstem contains three key structures: the medulla, the pons, and the reticular formation. Located just above the spinal cord, the **medulla** controls our most vital, involuntary functions—swallowing, breathing, heart rate, and muscle control. As we'll soon see, it's also a "crossover" point where nerves from one side of the brain connect to the opposite side of the body. There's nothing particularly exotic about the medulla, but if it were severed, blood pressure would drop to zero, breathing would stop, and death would soon follow. Just above the medulla is a bulbous structure called the **pons** (meaning "bridge"), which helps to connect the lower and higher regions of the brain. The pons also has neurons that play a role in sleep and arousal. Damage to this area can put a person into a coma. Finally, the **reticular formation** is a net-like group of nerve cells and axons that project throughout the brain and help to control sleep, arousal, and attention. It is here that sensory information is filtered in or out of our consciousness.

Also attached to the back of the brainstem is the **cerebellum**, which means "little brain." Look again at Figure 2.11, and you'll see that the cerebellum resembles a miniature brain within the brain, wrinkles and all. This structure is one of the oldest in the nervous system and is highly developed in fish, birds, and lower mammals. It plays a role in learning and memory, but its primary function (like that of certain other structures distributed throughout the brain) is balance and the coordination of voluntary movements (Thach et al., 1992). Damage to the cerebellum makes it difficult to coordinate movements such as walking, kicking, typing, or throwing a ball. The reason that drunken drivers can't pass the roadside test administered by the police ("close your eyes, put out your arms, and touch your nose with the index finger") is that alcohol affects the cerebellum.

The Limbic System   Continuing upward from the brainstem is a ring of loosely connected structures collectively known as the **limbic system**. Just above the inner core, yet surrounded by the cerebral cortex, the limbic system is a mini-brain on the borders of "reason" (the term itself comes from the Latin word *limbus*, which means border or edge). Separating the old and the new, the primitive and the sophisticated, the lower and higher functions, the limbic system contains several structures that play a role in the regulation of motivation, emotion, and memory. Brain researchers disagree as to which ones qualify as "limbic" and whether they really form a unified "system." Still, the key structures here include the thalamus, the amygdala, the hippocampus, and the hypothalamus (see Figure 2.12).

The Thalamus   Directly atop the brainstem, and buried like the pit inside a peach, is the **thalamus** ("inner chamber"). The thalamus is a sensory relay station that directs neural traffic between the senses and the cerebral cortex. Input from what you see, hear, taste, and touch is received in the thalamus and then sent for processing to the appropriate region of the cortex. For example, there's a special nucleus located in the thalamus that receives visual input from the optic nerve behind the eye and sends the information to the visual cortex. It's interesting that the sense of smell completely bypasses the thalamus because it has its own private relay station that directs input from the nose to the *olfactory bulb*, which sits near areas that control

Figure 2.12

The Limbic System

Just above the inner core, yet surrounded by the cerebral cortex, the limbic system plays a role in motivation, emotion, and memory. As shown, this system is composed of many structures, including the thalamus, amygdala, hippocampus, and hypothalamus.

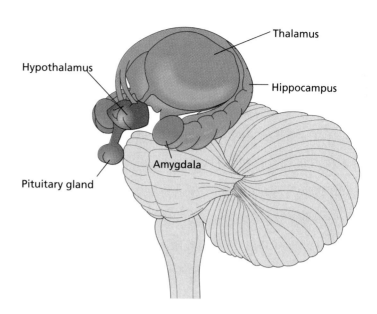

emotion. This may explain why perfume, meat sizzling on the grill, freshly cut grass, and other scents often arouse powerful emotions in us.

The Amygdala The **amygdala** is an almond-shaped bulge that has been called an "aggression center." This phrase oversimplifies both the functions of the amygdala and the biological roots of aggression. But there is a link, and experiments have shown that stimulation of the amygdala can produce anger and violence, as well as fear and anxiety (Davis, 1992).

In 1937, psychologist Heinrich Kluver and neurosurgeon Paul Bucy found that lesions of the amygdala calmed ferocious rhesus monkeys. Later experiments on other wild animals revealed the same mellowing effect. Can amygdala lesions be used to treat people who are uncontrollably violent? In one case, Julia, a twenty-one-year-old woman, had suffered from epilepsy since childhood. Every now and then, she would have seizures accompanied by fits of rage, temper tantrums, and violent outbursts. Julia was dangerous to herself and others. Four times she tried to commit suicide, and in one incident she plunged a dinner knife into the chest of a woman who had accidentally bumped into her. Julia's father called neurosurgeon Vernon Mark for help. Mark implanted electrodes in Julia's brain to record electrical activity and detected abnormal discharges in the amygdala. Next he tried electrical stimulation. In most sites, nothing happened. But activating the amygdala triggered explosive attacks. At one point, Mark stimulated the amygdala while Julia was playing the guitar. Suddenly she stopped, stared into space, and smashed the guitar against the wall, just missing the doctor's head. Mark treated Julia by destroying part of her amygdala, and her fits of rage eventually subsided (Mark & Ervin, 1970). Clearly, there is a relationship between the amygdala and aggression. We'll see in Chapter 17, however, that the use of *psychosurgery*—operating on the brain to alter behavior—raises profound ethical questions (Valenstein, 1986).

Artist Craig Smith, who has epilepsy, portrays his own seizure in this painting.

■ **amygdala** A limbic structure that controls fear, anger, and aggression.

■ **hippocampus** A limbic structure that plays a key role in the formation of new memories.

The Hippocampus The largest structure in the limbic system is the **hippocampus**, which is Greek for "seahorse," whose shape it roughly resembles. Research reveals that the hippocampus plays a key role in the formation of new memories. In rats, monkeys, and other animals, hippocampal lesions cause deficits in memory. In fact, when this structure is removed from black-capped chickadees—food-storing birds that have an unusually large hippocampus, compared to nonstoring birds—they lose the natural ability to recover the food they had previously stored (Sherry, 1992). In humans, brain scans reveal that the hippocampal area is shrunken in people with severe memory loss, even though surrounding areas of the brain are intact (Squire, 1992). As we'll see in Chapter 6, long-term memories are not necessarily stored in the hippocampus, but they may well be formed there.

The Hypothalamus   At the base of the brain, there is a tiny yet extraordinary limbic structure called the **hypothalamus** (which means "below the thalamus"). The hypothalamus is the size of a kidney bean, weighs only about half an ounce, and constitutes less than 1 percent of the brain's total volume. Yet it regulates the body's temperature and the activities of the autonomic nervous system, triggers the release of hormones into the bloodstream, helps regulate basic emotions such as fear and rage, is involved in basic drives such as hunger, thirst, sleep, and sex, and is home to one of the brain's "pleasure centers" (an area that is highly rewarding when stimulated). If you had to sacrifice an ounce of brain tissue, you wouldn't want to take it from the hypothalamus. As they say, good things come in small packages.

Before continuing on our tour of the brain, let's stop for a moment and zoom in on the control that the hypothalamus exerts over two important maintenance functions: the release of hormones, and hunger and eating.

The Hypothalamus and Endocrine System   The **endocrine system** is a collection of ductless glands that regulate many aspects of growth, sexuality, reproduction, metabolism, and behavior by secreting chemical messengers called **hormones** (the word *hormone* means "set in motion"). The hormones secreted from endocrine glands are a lot like neurotransmitters. In fact, some chemical substances, such as norepinephrine and endorphin, serve in both capacities. But whereas neurons secrete neurotransmitters into synapses, hormones are secreted into the bloodstream, which then carries them to "target organs" throughout the body. Compared to the speedy transmission of impulses through the nervous system, hormonal messages may take several seconds, hours, or even days to take effect. Once they do, however, their effects are often long lasting. Dozens of hormones are produced by the body. Some of the major glands, along with their locations and their functions, are illustrated in Figure 2.13.

The hypothalamus controls the endocrine system through the **pituitary gland**, a pea-sized gland that sits below it at the base of the brain. Upon command from the hypothalamus, the pituitary releases a hormone that stimulates the production of hormones in other endocrine glands. In turn, many hormones flow from the bloodstream back to the brain—which signals to the hypothalamus that more or less additional secretion is needed. There is thus a critical "feedback loop" between the brain and the endocrine system in which the hypothalamus regulates the release of hormones the way a thermostat maintains the temperature of a room. If you set a thermostat at 70 degrees and the temperature dips below that level, the heat comes on until the room tops 70 degrees, at which point it shuts it-

■ **hypothalamus** A tiny limbic structure in the brain that helps regulate the autonomic nervous system, endocrine glands, emotions, and basic drives.

■ **endocrine system** A collection of ductless glands that regulate aspects of growth, reproduction, metabolism, and behavior by secreting hormones.

■ **hormones** Chemical messengers secreted from endocrine glands, into the bloodstream, to various organs throughout the body.

■ **pituitary gland** A tiny gland in the brain that regulates growth and stimulates hormones in other endocrine glands at the command of the hypothalamus.

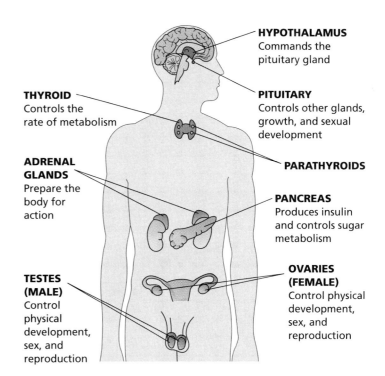

Figure 2.13

Major Endocrine Glands

Taking commands from the hypothalamus, the glands of the endocrine system regulate growth, reproduction, metabolism, and behavior by secreting hormones into the bloodstream. These hormones are carried to certain "target organs" throughout the body.

self off. Similarly, if a hormone drops below a certain level, the hypothalamus signals the pituitary and other glands that more is needed. Then once the hormone levels are sufficient, the hypothalamus signals the pituitary to stop the additional release of hormones. In this interaction between the brain and endocrine system, the hypothalamus serves as the command center.

The Hypothalamus, Hunger, and Eating   The hypothalamus also regulates certain basic biological drives, including hunger—a sensation that triggers the search for and consumption of food. Common sense notions about hunger are often incorrect. Sometimes, after working nonstop for a few hours, I'll hold my stomach, feel the growling, and just know that I'm hungry. On empty. Time to eat. Breakfast, lunch, dinner, a morning coffee break, an early afternoon snack, even a late-night raid on the refrigerator are part of the routine. At other times, after a big meal, I'll put my hand over my stomach, feel bloated and stuffed, and complain that I'm full. Time to stop. It's as if sensations from the belly were sending "eat" and "don't eat" messages to the brain. But is this the way it works?

The biological mechanisms underlying hunger are numerous and complex. Early researchers focused on "peripheral" (outside the central nervous system) cues that triggered hunger. In an initial experiment, researcher A. L. Washburn, working with Walter Cannon, swallowed a long tube attached to a balloon—which was partially inflated and specially designed to rest in his stomach. Whenever the stomach contracted, the balloon compressed. At the same time, Washburn pressed a key whenever he felt hungry. Using this device, and then testing other subjects, Cannon and Washburn (1912) found a link between stomach contractions and reports of hunger. In fact, the subjects reported feeling hungry at the height of the contractions, not at the beginning—suggesting that the contractions had caused the hunger and not the other way around (see Figure 2.14).

Figure 2.14

Cannon and Washburn's Hunger Experiment

In this study, subjects swallowed a balloon, which rested in the stomach. Recorded (A) is the volume of the balloon (B) over time, in minutes (C), and subjects pressed a key whenever they felt hungry (D). Subjects reported feeling hungry at the height of their stomach contractions.

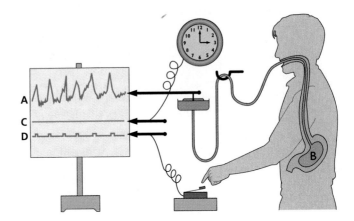

There may be a correlation between stomach contractions and hunger, but additional observations soon discredited the theory. The fatal blow came when studies revealed that people continue to feel hungry even after their cancerous or ulcerated stomachs have been surgically removed. As a result, researchers turned their focus on "central" nervous system factors. According to this view, the brain monitors glucose (which provides energy) and other nutrients in the bloodstream the way it monitors hormone levels. When glucose drops below a certain level, called a *set point*, we get hungry and eat. When glucose levels exceed the set point, we feel satiated and stop eating. Here is where the hypothalamus comes in.

Although different regions of the brain are involved, two distinct areas of the hypothalamus play an important role. But what are the mechanisms involved? Many years ago, researchers thought of the *lateral hypothalamus* (LH) as a "hunger center": when its neurons are stimulated, an animal will eat, and eat, and eat—even if it's full. When the LH is destroyed, the animal will not eat and will even starve to death unless it is force-fed (Anand & Brobeck, 1951; Teitelbaum & Epstein, 1962). At the same time, researchers thought of the *ventromedial hypothalamus* (VH) as a "satiation center": when it's stimulated, an animal will not eat, even if it has been deprived of food. When this area is destroyed, the rat will eat more often than usual, consume larger quantities, and eventually triple its own weight (Hetherington & Ranson, 1942; Wyrwicka & Dobrzecka, 1960).

At first, these results suggested that the hypothalamus monitors blood glucose levels and has something like an on-off switch for eating (Stellar, 1954). But more recent studies show that the mechanism is much more complicated. It turns out, for example, that certain nerves form a tract that runs from the brainstem up through the lateral hypothalamus—and that these nerves are somehow involved. In fact, such areas may be part of a general motor-activation system that, when stimulated, tells the organism to "do something!" This general command results in eating if food is present, drinking if water is present, or running around if neither food nor water is present (Berridge et al., 1989). Research also shows that many other factors control hunger and eating as well—including the taste of food, the time of day, hormonal activity in the intestines, and so on. In short, the hypothalamus is part of an extensive system that regulates hunger and eating (Logue, 1991; Stricker, 1990).

■ **cerebral cortex** The outermost covering of the brain, largely responsible for higher-order mental processes.

The Cerebral Cortex   The **cerebral cortex** is the outermost covering of the brain. Its name is derived from the words *cerebrum* (which is Latin for "brain") and *cortex* (which means "bark"). It is the newest product of evolution, overlaid upon the older structures. If you were to examine the cerebral cortex of various species, you would see that the more complex the animal, the bigger the cerebral cortex is relative to the rest of the brain. You would also notice that in complex animals, the cortex is wrinkled rather than smooth, and lined with ridges and valleys. This wrinkling allows more tissue to fit compactly inside the skull (much like crumpling up a piece of paper allows one to squeeze it into a small space). As shown in Figure 2.15, the cerebral cortex is virtually absent in fish, reptiles, and birds, present in mammals (particularly so in primates, dolphins, and whales), and the most highly developed in humans. In volume, it constitutes 80 percent of the human brain (Kolb & Whishaw, 1990). Whenever you read, write, count, speak, reflect on the past, think about the future, plot your next move on the chessboard, go up for the basket, or daydream about being rich and famous, neurons are firing by the billions—in the cerebral cortex.

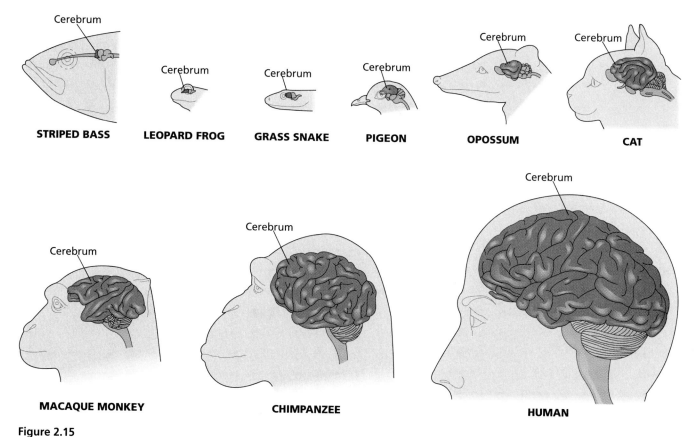

Figure 2.15

The Cerebral Cortex in Animals

From fish and birds to mammals, primates, and humans, there is an increase in the relative size and wrinkling of the cerebral cortex (Hubel, 1979).

The cortex is divided into left and right *hemispheres*, and each hemisphere is further divided along deep grooves, which are called *fissures*, into four sections called *lobes*. These are the *frontal* (in front, just behind the forehead), *temporal* (at the temple, above the ear), *parietal* (in the back, at the top of the skull), and *occipital* (in the back, at the base of the skull) lobes. These lobes describe the anatomy of the cerebral cortex, but most psychologists prefer to divide the regions of the brain according to their

Figure 2.16

The Cerebral Cortex

The cortex is divided along deep grooves, or fissures, into four lobes. Within these lobes, areas are further distinguished by their functions. These include the sensory areas (visual, auditory and somatosensory), the motor area, the association areas, and two special areas found in the left hemisphere, where language is processed and produced.

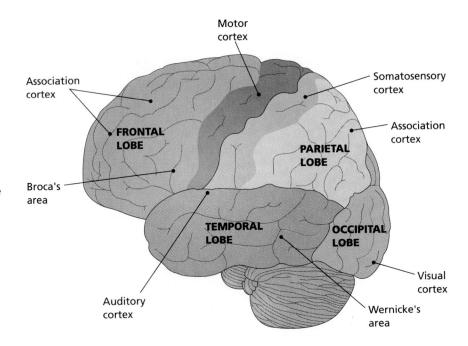

functions. As shown in Figure 2.16, the functional regions include the *sensory areas* of the cortex, the *motor* cortex, the *association* cortex, and two special areas where *language* is processed and produced.

Sensory and Motor Areas   While operating on his hundreds of epilepsy patients, Wilder Penfield (1947) stimulated exposed parts of the cortex with a tiny electric probe and thereby "mapped" the human cortex. One of Penfield's discoveries was that certain areas specialize in receiving sensory information. When he touched the occipital lobe in the back of the brain, patients would "see" flickering lights, colors, stars, spots, wheels, and other visual displays. This area is the primary *visual cortex*—and damage to it can leave a person blind. Or, damage to a specific region may result in a more specific visual deficit. For example, Oliver Sacks (1985) tells a story about a patient who suffered occipital lobe damage. As this patient searched for his hat while preparing to leave Sacks's office, he grabbed his wife's head and tried to lift it. Suffering from "visual agnosia"—an inability to recognize familiar objects—this patient had apparently mistaken his own wife for a hat.

Penfield discovered other sensory areas in the cortex as well. When he stimulated a small area of the temporal lobe, now called the *auditory cortex*, the patients would "hear" doorbells, engines, and other sounds. Indeed, damage in this area can cause deafness. And when he stimulated a narrow strip in the parietal lobe, the **somatosensory cortex**, they would "feel" a tingling of the leg, hand, cheek, or some other part of the body. In general, the more sensitive to touch a body part is, the larger is the cortical area devoted to it (see Figure 2.17).

Mirroring the somatosensory cortex is another narrow strip that specializes in the control of motor functions. Once again, much of what is currently known came from Penfield's work. Stimulating different parts of this strip triggered movement in different parts of the body. Stimulate the top, and a leg would twitch; stimulate the bottom, and the tongue or jaw would

■ **somatosensory cortex** The area of the cortex that receives sensory information from the touch receptors in the skin.

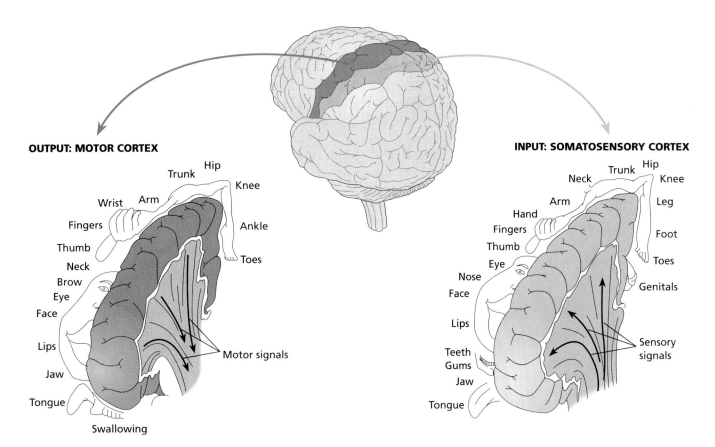

OUTPUT: MOTOR CORTEX

INPUT: SOMATOSENSORY CORTEX

Figure 2.17

The Somatosensory and Motor Areas

Each part of the body is represented in the somatosensory (right) and motor (left) cortex. Note that the amount of tissue devoted to a body part does not correspond to its actual size. Rather, more area is devoted to parts that are most sensitive to touch (such as the lips) and in need of fine motor control (such as the thumbs).

■ **motor cortex** The area of the cortex that sends impulses to voluntary muscles.

■ **association cortex** Areas of the cortex that communicate with the sensory and motor areas and house the brain's higher mental processes.

move. All six hundred muscles of the human body were represented in what is now called the **motor cortex**. As in the somatosensory cortex, the greater the need for precise control over a body part, the larger is its area in the motor cortex. Thus, Figure 2.17 shows more surface area devoted to the face, hands, and fingers than to the arms and legs.

Association Areas The cerebral cortex does more than just process sensory information and direct motor responses. There are also vast areas that collectively make up the **association cortex**. These areas communicate with both the sensory and motor areas and house the brain's higher mental processes. Electrical stimulation of these sites does not elicit specific sensations or motor twitches in specific parts of the body, so it's hard to pin these areas down. But damage to the association cortex can have devastating results. In the frontal lobes, such damage can change someone's personality, as in the case of Phineas Gage. In other association areas, damage can impair specific kinds of memories, distort our spatial awareness, or cause odd speech deficits. For the most part, our ability to adapt to life's demands through learning, memory, and thought processes is spread throughout the regions of the cortex. But language—a complex activity for which humans, and in some ways only humans, are uniquely prepared—is different. Carved within the cortex are two special areas dedicated to language.

Language Areas Look back at Figure 2.16, and you'll see that there are two specially marked regions of the cortex. One controls the production of speech; the other, comprehension. In 1861, French physician Paul Broca observed that people who have incurred damage in an area of the frontal

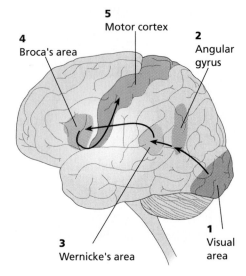

Figure 2.18

Language Processing

Although different regions specialize in certain functions, the brain operates as an integrated system. The "simple" act of speaking a written word, for example, requires a coordinated effort of the eyes, the visual cortex, the angular gyrus, Wernicke's area, Broca's area, and the motor cortex.

"I felt a cleavage in my mind
As if my brain had split;
I tried to match it, seam by seam
But could not make them fit."

EMILY DICKINSON

■ **Broca's area** A region in the left hemisphere of the brain that directs the muscle movements in the production of speech.

■ **Wernicke's area** A region in the left hemisphere of the brain that is involved in the comprehension of language.

lobe of the left hemisphere lose the ability to form words to *produce* fluent speech. The words sputter out slowly, and what is said is often not grammatical ("Buy milk store"). This region of the brain is called **Broca's area** (Schiller, 1992). A few years later, German neurologist Karl Wernicke (1874) found that people with damage to part of the left temporal lobe lose their ability to *comprehend* speech. As you might expect, this region is called **Wernicke's area**. In short, people with language disorders, or *aphasias*, demonstrate that there are at least two distinct cortical centers for language. People with Broca's aphasia comprehend speech but have trouble producing it. Those with Wernicke's aphasia can speak, but their comprehension is impaired. Interestingly, these two areas are connected by a neural pathway, thus forming part of a language circuit within the brain (Geschwind, 1979).

Before concluding our overview of the cortex, let's stop for a moment and ponder the contention that different functions, or behaviors, are "localized" in certain areas. As noted earlier, Penfield was able to pinpoint or "map" various locations in the cortex that house sensory and motor functions. However, it is important not to overstate the case for localization. It's clear that different cortical regions *specialize* in certain functions, but it's also clear that the healthy brain operates as an *integrated* system. This point is illustrated by the role of the brain in language, whereby different cortical areas are activated depending on whether a word is spoken, written, or presented in music, or even whether it is a verb or a noun (Caramazza & Hillis, 1991). Consider what it takes simply to repeat the written word *ball*. From the eyes, the stimulus must travel for processing to the visual cortex. The input must then pass through the angular gyrus to be recoded, to Wernicke's area to be understood, and then to Broca's area, where signals are sent to the motor cortex, which drives the muscles of your lips, tongue, and larynx so that you can repeat the word (see Figure 2.18). As in an orchestra, it takes the coordinated work of many instruments to make music.

The Split Brain

Before the first psychology laboratory was founded, in 1879, scientists interested in the nervous system, and intrigued by the relationship between the body and mind, debated an old question concerning the brain. The "traditional" view was that the left and right hemispheres were symmetrical, mirror images of each other. Just as the body has two eyes, two ears, two legs, and two hands, the brain has two identical hemispheres. The symmetry argument seemed self-evident. If you open up a skull, you'll see that the brain looks just like the two halves of a walnut packed together inside a shell. To the naked eye, it's like looking at a three-dimensional inkblot.

Others argued that things are not always as they seem on the surface. Portrait artists know fully well that the human face is not perfectly symmetrical—for example, one eye may be larger than the other, or one cheek may have a dimple that the other does not. The same asymmetry is true of the brain. As we saw, Broca (1861) and Wernicke (1874) both found key language centers only in the left hemisphere. From the start, this finding gave rise to the notion that the left hemisphere is "dominant" (Jackson, 1958)—a notion also used to explain why most people are right-handed. Indeed, nearly all right-handers and a majority of left-handers process language mainly in the left hemisphere (see box p.66). It also suggested that the two hemispheres may be specialized for different functions. Carrying this idea a giant step further, German physicist Gustav Fechner (1860) proposed that each side of the brain has its own mind. If your brain could be divided in half, he speculated, you would have two separate streams of consciousness. What a fascinating concept for an experiment. At the time, Fechner had no idea that such an experiment would one day come to pass.

Split-Brain Studies   For people with severe epilepsy, seizures are the brain's equivalent of thunder and lightning storms. A seizure usually starts in one small area, but it quickly spreads across the brain from one side to the other. The experience can be terrifying, and at times life-threatening. In the past, neurosurgeons tried to control the problem by removing the over-active area, but these operations had only limited success. To prevent the seizures from spreading, a more radical approach was needed. The goal was to separate the two hemispheres. The method was to cut the **corpus callosum**, a four-inch-long, quarter-inch-thick bundle consisting of millions of white nerve fibers that join the two hemispheres (see Figure 2.19). This **split-brain** surgery often eliminates epileptic seizures, as hoped. But are there psychological side effects? Was Fechner right in proposing that a split brain, in which the link between the two hemispheres is severed, contains two minds?

Before we examine the effects of split-brain surgery, it's important to know more about the divisions of labor within the brain. Specifically, the *left hemisphere* receives sensory input from, and sends motor commands to, the right side of the body (hands, legs, arms, and so on), whereas the *right hemisphere* communicates with the left side of the body. Processing visual and auditory input is somewhat more complex. Both eyes send information to both hemispheres, but images in the right half of the visual field are sent to the left hemisphere, and images in the left half of the visual field are sent to the right hemisphere. In other words, if you're looking straight ahead at someone, images on the left are sent by both eyes to the right hemisphere, and images on the right are sent by both eyes to the left hemisphere (see Figure 2.20). Auditory inputs are also sent to both hemispheres, but sounds received in one ear register in the opposite hemisphere first.

If your brain is intact, then this odd crossover arrangement poses no problem because information received by each hemisphere is quickly sent to the other side through the corpus callosum. By sharing information in this manner, the two sides of the brain work as a team. But what happens when the neuron-filled highway connecting the hemispheres is severed?

In 1963, two neurosurgeons, Philip Vogel and Joseph Bogen, described the case of a forty-eight-year-old man who had severe epileptic seizures following a head injury. A split-brain operation was performed (the corpus callosum was cut), and it was successful. As for side effects, the man's behavior, like that of other split-brain patients, seemed normal (tests generally show that perceptual abilities, memory, intelligence, and personality are unaffected). But when researchers probe further beneath surface appearances, some unusual effects are revealed (Iaccino, 1993; Nebes, 1990; Springer & Deutsch, 1989).

Roger Sperry (who, in 1981, was awarded a Nobel Prize), Michael Gazzaniga (his student), and others have helped bring this picture into focus

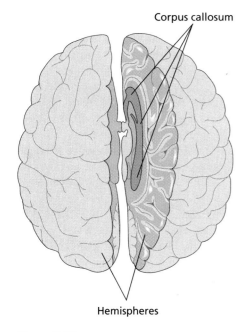

Corpus callosum

Hemispheres

Figure 2.19

The Corpus Callosum

Containing millions of nerve fibers, the corpus callosum joins the left and right hemispheres.

■ **corpus callosum** A bundle of nerve fibers that connects the left and right hemispheres.

■ **split brain** A surgically produced condition in which the corpus callosum is severed, thus cutting the link between the left and right hemispheres of the brain.

BIOLOGICAL PSYCHOLOGY   Environment

Lefties in a Right-Handed World

When Bill Clinton, George Bush, and Ross Perot faced each other in the 1992 presidential election, they had something else in common: all are left-handers.

With which hand do you write or draw? Which hand do you use to throw a ball? In which hand do you hold your toothbrush, or a knife, or a hammer? In which hand do you hold a match to strike it? And which hand removes the top card when you're dealing from a deck? In short, are you predominantly right-handed or left-handed?

Roughly 90 percent of the human population is right-handed. This percentage (though somewhat higher among women and lower among men) is highly consistent over time and place. Using art history books, Stanley Coren (1993) analyzed 1,180 drawings, paintings, and engravings that depicted someone using a tool or weapon. He found that 90 percent of all the human characters portrayed were right-handers, and that this was as true thousands of years ago as it is today. In fact, archaeological records of prehistoric stone tools yield fossil evidence for right-handedness as far back as two or three million years ago—long before the evolution of *Homo sapiens* (Corballis, 1989). This asymmetry is not the product of culture, either. Studies across different cultures show that right-hand predominance is universal, and that most thumb-sucking fetuses suck the right thumb rather than the left (Hepper et al., 1990). It's interesting that a similar preference is not found in cats, rats, mice, or monkeys (Annett, 1985; MacNeilage et al., 1987). It's also interesting that even though nine out of ten humans are right-handed, only eight out of ten show a preference for the right foot, seven out of ten for the right eye, and six out of ten for the right ear (Coren, 1993).

Lefties, righties, what's the difference? Does it really matter? It might. Research shows that left-handers are more likely to emerge as gifted athletes, mathematicians, and artists. But they're also more likely to have allergies, insomnia, reading disabilities, and certain other disorders. Investi-

gating the links between cerebral lateralization and behavior, Clare Porac and Stanley Coren (1981) surveyed 5,147 men and women of all ages in the United States and Canada. Much to their surprise, the percentage of left-handers in the population showed a steady decline across the life span. As illustrated at right, 15 percent of the ten-year-olds were left-handed, compared to only 5 percent of the fifty-year-olds and less than 1 percent of the eighty-year-olds. By age eighty-five, right-handers outnumbered left-handers by two hundred to one. Other researchers have more recently replicated this puzzling finding (Halpern & Coren, 1993). For some reason, the population of lefties dwindles with age. The question for the psychologist detective is, Why?

There are two possible explanations. One is the *longevity hypothesis*, which states that left-handers simply have a shorter life span. In support of this hypothesis, Coren and Halpern (1991) examined 987 death certificates and found that the average age of death was higher for right-handers than for left-handers. Other researchers have argued that this disparity is small. Instead, they propose the *modification hypothesis*, which states that the number of left-handers diminishes with age because many natural lefties switch to the right hand—due, perhaps, to pressures from parents, teachers, or an environment that is far better suited to right-handedness. According to Lauren Harris (1993), modification is the more plausible explanation. Indeed, a new study reveals that the decline in left-handedness is matched by an increased number of right-handers who say they had switched when they were younger (Hugdahl et al., 1993).

Researchers may disagree about the reason that left-handers do not appear in the elderly population, but they agree completely that the physical environment is designed more for the comfort and safety of right-handers. Scissors and pruning shears have handles shaped so that one hole is angled correctly for the right thumb and the other hole is for the other fingers of the right hand. In schools, spiral notebooks, chairs with built-in desktops on the right, and even rulers are designed for use with the right hand. In the workplace, com-

through an ingenious series of studies. Involving split-brain patients, the basic procedure was to present information to one hemisphere or the other, and then to measure what the subject "knew" by testing each hemisphere separately.

In one study, Sperry (1968) asked a female patient, identified as N.G., to stare at a black dot in the center of a screen. Then, for only a fraction of a second, he flashed a picture of a spoon either to the right or to the left of

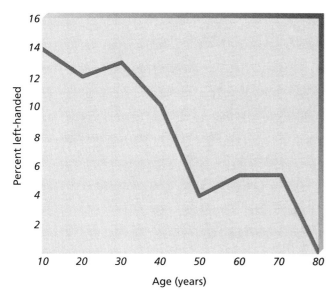

Left-Handedness Across the Life Span
In a study of 5,147 individuals, the percentage of left-handers in the sample declined with age (Coren, 1993).

swerving the car into traffic rather than to the right side of the road. Consistent with this speculation, Coren finds that traffic accidents in general are less frequent in the United Kingdom and Ireland, where motorists drive on the left side of the road, than in other European countries.

Can anything be done to improve safety conditions for the average left-hander? Yes. Coren (1993) argues that the physical environment can be made more "user friendly." Tool grips can be designed for lefties at no extra cost, on-off and safety switches can be placed on both sides of an instrument, and left-handed kitchen utensils, power tools, school supplies, and office equipment can all be mass-produced. Many ambidextrous items can also be manufactured—such as soup ladles with two pouring lips, knives with serrated edges on both sides of the blade, tools with finger grooves that can accommodate either hand, and instrument panels with controls that are centered. Environmental solutions would be easy to implement. The problem is that the right-handed majority does not sufficiently recognize that the problem exists.

puter keyboards, portable power saws, drills, and certain other types of heavy machinery create problems as well. Indeed, on-off and safety switches are almost always on the right side for quick use in an emergency. It's no wonder, says Coren (1993), that lefties are so often stereotyped as "clumsy" and "awkward." (See figure at right.)

These inconveniences are like booby traps and may prove hazardous to the health of all left-handers. For example, Coren asked nearly two thousand college students to fill out a handedness questionnaire and to report on any accidents they had experienced in the past two years. Responses showed that left-handers were 89 percent more likely to have accident-related injuries requiring medical attention—in sports, at work, at home, using tools, and, most of all, driving a car. Why is driving so risky? Coren notes that driving on the right side of the road puts the steering wheel on the left and the gear shifting on the right, a design that favors right-handers. What's more, he finds that when startled (which causes us to put our hands up to protect the body), lefties are more likely to raise the right hand higher than the left. In a driving emergency, this reflexive response could cause them to veer left,

RIGHT-HANDER   **LEFT-HANDER**

Right-Handed Objects
Many common items are designed for right-handers. As shown, left-handers have to hold their hands in an awkward position while using a manual can opener, and stand dangerously close to the blade while using a portable power saw (Coren, 1993).

the dot and asked, "What do you see?" The result was fascinating. When the image was shown in the right visual field, and thus sent to the left hemisphere, N.G. was quick to reply that she saw a spoon. But when the image was presented on the left side, and sent to the right hemisphere, she could not say what she saw. Why? As noted earlier, speech is controlled by the left hemisphere. If an image in the right side of the brain cannot cross over to the left side, then the person cannot transform what is seen into words.

Figure 2.20

Visual Processing

Both eyes send information to both hemispheres, but images in the right half of the visual field are sent to the left hemisphere, and images in the left half of the visual field are sent to the right hemisphere. Each image is instantly sent to the other side through the corpus callosum.

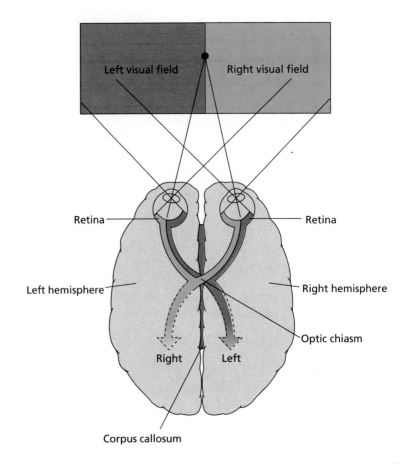

Figure 2.21

Split-Brain Experiment

When the image of a spoon was projected to the right hemisphere, the split-brain patient could not say what she saw. Yet when she felt various objects with her left hand, she selected the spoon. The right side knew all along that it saw the spoon, but only the left side could say so (Sperry, 1968).

But wait. How do we know that N.G. actually saw the spoon? Maybe the right hemisphere is just stupid. To probe further, Sperry asked N.G. to reach behind a screen and feel an assortment of objects, such as a pencil, an eraser, a key, and a piece of paper. "Which of these did you see before?" Easy. Touching the objects with her left hand (which sent the sensations to the right hemisphere), she selected the spoon. The right side knew all along it had seen a spoon, but only the left side could say so (see Figure 2.21).

In a second similar study, Gazzaniga (1967) had split-brain patients stare at a black dot and flashed the word *teacup* on the screen. The letters *tea*

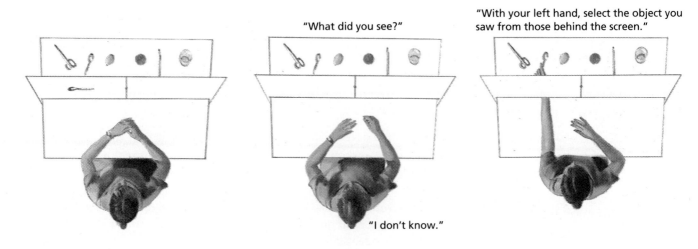

were presented to the left visual field (the right hemisphere), and *cup* was presented to the right visual field (the left hemisphere). If you were the subject—and if your corpus callosum was intact—you would see the full word, *teacup*. But the split-brain patients reported seeing only *cup*, the portion of the word that was flashed to the left hemisphere. Again, how do we know they actually saw the second part of the word? When told to choose between the two parts by pointing with the left hand, they pointed to *tea*, the letters sent to the right hemisphere. As in the spoon study, each hemisphere was in touch with only half of the total input. Under normal circumstances, stimuli reaching both hemishperes are blended to form a unified experience. Disconnected, each hemisphere has a mind of its own.

In a third study, Jerre Levy and others (1972) took pictures of various faces, cut them vertically in half, and pasted different right and left halves together. These composite photographs were then presented rapidly on slides. As in other studies, subjects stared at a center dot so that half of the image fell on either side. Look at the stimulus presented in Figure 2.22.

A

B
"Whom did you see?"

"It was the child."

C
"Point to the person you saw."

Figure 2.22

Another Split-Brain Experiment

Split-brain subjects stared at a dot and viewed a composite of two faces (A). When asked what they saw, subjects chose the child—the image sent to the verbal left hemisphere (B). But when subjects pointed to the face with the left hand, they chose the woman with glasses—whose image was received by the right hemisphere (C) (Levy et al., 1968).

When asked what they saw, subjects *said* it was a child. Because they were forced to respond in words, the left hemisphere dominated, causing them to name the image in the right visual field. But when subjects were told to point to the face with the left hand, they *pointed* to the woman wearing glasses, whose image was projected on the left side. Remarkably, split-brain patients did not seem to know that the composite face was unusual.

Split-brain patients exhibit so much "disconnection" in laboratory tests that one wonders how they manage to get along in their everyday affairs. To be sure, some instances of bizarre behavior have been observed. One patient had trouble dressing because he would pull his pants up with one hand and pull them down with the other. Another couldn't decide what to wear one morning because she would pick one item of clothing from the closet with her right hand and a different item with her left hand. In instances like these, one hand literally does not know what the other is doing.

Although there are plenty of stories like these to be told, disconnection experiences are not all that common. Why not? One possibility is that some input reaches both hemispheres through "subcortical" (below the cortex) structures that remain connected after the corpus callosum is cut. Justine Sergent (1990) recently explored this issue. In a split-brain study, she flashed pictures of celebrities to the left or right hemisphere and asked a series of probing questions. At one point, for example, she presented a picture of Robert Redford to the patient's right hemisphere and asked, "Is this a man or a woman?" The patient responded, "I am not sure . . . a man." Let's eavesdrop on part of the interview:

Q: Does this man look familiar to you?
A: I think so.

Q: Where have you seen him?
A: I don't know.

Q: What does he do for a living?
A: Is he a movie actor? . . . Yes, an actor.

Q: What kind of character does he play?
A: A playboy.

Q: What do you mean?
A: He is quite handsome, don't you think?

Q: How do you know he is handsome?
A: Well, I know.

Q: Can you picture him? Can you describe his face?
A: No, I can't say what he looks like but I think he's handsome.

Q: Can you recall some movies of his you saw?
A: I know I have seen him play, but I can't tell any movie.

Q: Do you know his name?
A: No.

Q: Do you have any idea?
A: No.

Now notice what happened when the same picture was presented to the patient's left hemisphere.

Q: Did I show this face before?
A: No.

Q: Does he look like the one you just saw?
A: No. I don't know.

Q: Do you know who he is?
A: Yes. He is quite handsome too . . . Robert Redford.

These scripts are typical of the split-brain syndrome: the patient's left hemisphere could not identify or describe Robert Redford's picture when it was presented in the left visual field. And when it appeared in the right visual field, the patient did not know that she had seen it before. But notice that even though she could not identify the picture through the left hemisphere, she knew, somehow, that it depicted a handsome male actor. Sergent speculates that the disconnection in split-brain patients is only partial, not complete—and that some information may have slipped into the left hemisphere through subcortical structures.

■ **cerebral lateralization** The tendency for each hemisphere of the brain to specialize in different functions.

Cerebral Lateralization Split-brain research has generated tremendous excitement in behavioral neuroscience. When the corpus callosum is severed, input to one hemisphere is trapped, unable to pass to the other side. As a result, neither hemisphere knows what the other is doing. But what about the day-to-day operations of a normal and healthy brain, corpus callosum and all? We know that speech is usually located in the left hemisphere, but are other functions similarly **lateralized**? Does one side or the other control math, or music, or the ability to recognize faces?

Several different methods are used to determine if there are hemispheric differences in the "connected" brain. One method is to compare people with damage to the right or left hemisphere. A second method is to present various tasks and then measure activity in both sides of the brain using EEG recordings, measures of cerebral blood flow, or imaging techniques. To the extent that a given task is processed in one hemisphere more than in the other, that hemisphere should be relatively more active. A third method is to present a stimulus to either the right or left hemisphere and measure the speed with which subjects act on the information. If the input has to be relayed through the corpus callosum to the other side, it will take the subject up to 20 milliseconds longer to make a response. A fourth method is to briefly sedate the right or left hemisphere and then test for disruptive effects.

Using an array of tools, researchers have uncovered many strands of evidence for hemispheric lateralization in the human brain (Iaccino, 1993; Springer & Deutsch, 1989). As we saw, the left hemisphere largely controls verbal activities—including reading, writing, speaking, and other aspects of language. It has long been known that damage to Broca's and Wernicke's areas, which reside in the left hemisphere, produces various types of aphasias, or speech disorders. Studies also show that people recognize words, letters, and other verbal stimuli faster when these stimuli are sent directly to the left hemisphere. Deaf people also seem to rely on the left hemisphere more than the right for reading sign language (Corina et al., 1992). Finally, PET scans show that different regions of the left hemisphere (and some areas of the right hemisphere as well) "light up" depending on whether subjects are listening to words that are spoken (hearing), reading words on a screen (seeing), saying words aloud (speaking), or coming up with related words (thinking). A sample PET scan appears in Figure 2.23 (Peterson & Fiez, 1993).

Whereas the left hemisphere is a verbal specialist, there is converging evidence that the right hemisphere plays a vital role in nonverbal activities such as visual-spatial tasks, music, and face recognition. Clinical case studies illustrate this point. Gazzaniga (1985) instructed a split-brain patient to draw a cube, and found that he produced a better drawing with the left hand than with the right—even though he was right-handed. He then asked the patient to match a printed design using colored blocks. When the patient used his left hand to manipulate the blocks, he matched the design easily. But when told to use his right hand, he struggled so much that his left hand kept trying to intervene.

Other case studies reveal that various nonverbal deficits—such as an impaired ability to recognize faces—are more likely to result from damage to the right hemisphere than from damage to the left. For example, right-hemisphere damage may cause people to lose their sense of direction while driving, get lost in their own homes, or have trouble locating items in a

Figure 2.23

The Talking Left Hemisphere

PET scans show that a single word activated different left-hemisphere areas depending on whether it was heard, seen, spoken, or thought about. Notice that these "lit-up" areas are in the visual cortex, auditory cortex, Broca's area, and frontal lobes, respectively.

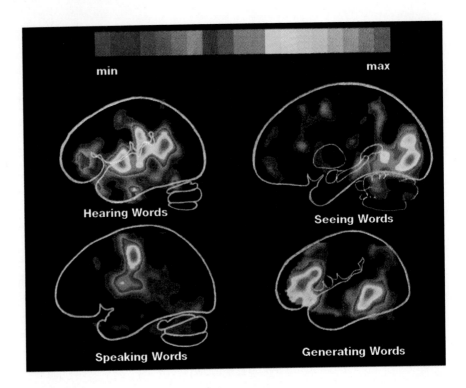

Figure 2.24

Neglect Syndrome

A patient with a stroke in the right hemisphere was asked to copy model pictures. As with many neglect patients, he almost completely overlooked the left side of each drawing.

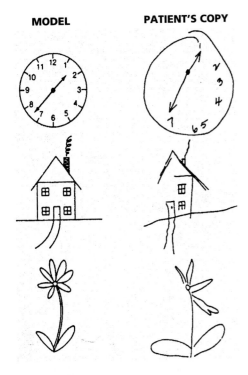

familiar supermarket (Newcombe & Ratcliff, 1990). In some cases, right-hemisphere damage caused by a stroke or accident triggers a disruption of spatial awareness called "neglect." People with *neglect syndrome* lose all awareness of the left side of space, including the left side of their own bodies. As a result, they may comb their hair only on the right side of the head, shave only the right side of the face, or eat food only if it's on the right side of the plate (see Figure 2.24). Finally, laboratory studies show that people are usually faster at locating dots, drawing three-dimensional objects, and recognizing faces when the material is presented to the right hemisphere than when it is presented to the left (Bradshaw & Nettleton, 1981).

There is no simple way to summarize all the research on hemispheric differences. The evidence clearly suggests that there is specialization, with the left side more verbal and the right side more spatial. But some researchers now believe that the key difference between hemispheres is not in *what* kind of input is processed, but in *how* that input is processed. In essence, a good deal of research suggests that the left hemisphere processes information in an analytical, piecemeal style—as in word analogies, arithmetic, and logical problem solving, and that the right hemisphere processes information in a more global, holistic style—as used in music, art, and various forms of creative expression (Ornstein, 1978). Either way, it's important not to overstate the case for lateralization, since neither hemisphere has exclusive control over functions. Indeed, both sides of the brain are capable of processing various kinds of information (Efron, 1990).

One Mind, or Two?   Let us now step back for a moment, and reflect on the big picture: Does splitting the brain in half produce two separate minds, as Fechner had proposed? From the start, Sperry (1966) argued that severing the corpus callosum leaves the split-brain patient with two separate minds, and that "what is experienced in the right hemisphere seems to lie entirely outside the realm of experience of the left hemisphere". Sir John Eccles (1965), who won a Nobel prize in physiology, disagreed. According to Eccles, the right hemisphere cannot think without the speech capabilities of the left side.

Clearly, the research supports Sperry's claim. At one point, researchers encountered a split-brain patient, known as P.S., who had the unique ability to communicate with the right hemisphere by arranging Scrabble letters with the left hand in response to questions. To put the dual-mind hypothesis to the test, Joseph Ledoux and his colleagues (1977) separately questioned each hemisphere—and found that the two sides often disagreed. For example, when P.S. was asked what job he would like, his left hemisphere said he wanted to be a "draftsman," but his right hemisphere spelled out "automobile racer"!

Although split-brain patients seem to have two independent streams of consciousness, it's important to keep in mind that their behavior is reasonably well integrated. It's also important to be cautious in generalizing to individuals whose brains are intact. The fact that our right and left hemispheres are specialized in no way implies that they function independently. Through the corpus callosum, information between the hemispheres is exchanged with such speed that we enjoy a seamless, well-synchronized experience. (See box, p. 74, for the educational implications of split-brain studies).

FUTURE PROSPECTS: REPAIRING THE DAMAGED BRAIN

The human brain is a remarkable organ. Encased in a hard, protective skull, it has more neurons than there are stars in our galaxy and is more complex than any computer. But, alas, we are mortal and our brains are fallible. Strokes, head injuries, diseases that strike at the core of the nervous system, exposure to toxic substances, and addictions to alcohol and other drugs are among the possible causes of brain damage. The possible effects include paralysis; motor disorders; a loss of sensory capabilities, consciousness, memory, or language; blunted emotion; and a host of psychological disorders.

One of the sad realities of brain damage is its permanence. If you get an ulcer, or break a finger, or scrape your knee, new cells will be produced to heal the wound. But the brain does not have this capacity to completely repair itself. Once a neuron is damaged, it is forever disabled. And once the brain is developed, it does not produce more neurons. Yet every now and then, we hear stories about "miraculous" recoveries from brain damage. What makes this possible is that neurons have an adaptive capacity to compensate for loss by strengthening old synaptic connections and sprouting new axons and dendrites to form new connections. Also, healthy brain tissue will sometimes pick up lost functions. Thus, children who have substantial damage to the left hemisphere early in life can still learn to speak, and adults who suffer strokes are often able to recover their speech and motor abilities.

Is it possible to further restore the brain through medical intervention? For the millions of people each year who are struck by Parkinson's disease, Alzheimer's disease, and other degenerative nerve disorders, can the

Right-Brain Education: Science or Science Fiction?

I recently read a magazine article that advised parents to have their children tested to see whether they're "right-brained" or "left-brained" thinkers, so that teachers can customize their lessons and methods to suit each child's style. Similar claims are often made about people in different occupations. Do artists use the right hemisphere more than lawyers do? What about chemists and poets? Are there hemispheric differences between cultures? And what about commercial products such as books, tapes, and seminars that are designed to unleash your "untapped" brain resources? If you browse through the shelves of your local bookstore, you will see paperback titles such as *Whole-Brain Thinking, Educating the Right Brain,* and *The Other Side of the Mind.* So, what advice is contained in these books? What are the educational implications of the split-brain studies discussed in this chapter?

Research indicates that the left hemisphere largely controls verbal skills (such as reading, writing, arithmetic, and logical problem solving), while the right hemisphere plays a major role in various nonverbal activities (such as spatial tasks, music, art, and face recognition). Based on these findings, Robert Ornstein (1972) argued that westerners use only the left side of the brain and neglect the "intuitive" right side. Some educators went on to complain that American schools, because they focused on reading, writing, and arithmetic, did not enable children to develop their right-brain potential in visualization, music, art, and other forms of creative expression.

This view inspired educational reformists critical of a conventional curriculum that relies heavily on reading, speaking, listening, and writing. The proposed alternatives vary. They include increased exposure to music and art; a greater use of

■ **neural graft** A technique of transplanting healthy tissue from the nervous system of one animal into that of another.

damaged brain be repaired? As wild and fanciful as the idea may seem, researchers have been busy trying to transplant healthy tissue from the central nervous system of one animal into that of another—in a surgical procedure called a **neural graft**. Using amphibians and fish, researchers long ago demonstrated that it was possible to transplant neurons in cold-blooded animals. In a classic series of experiments conducted in the 1940s, Sperry transplanted the eyeballs in frogs and found that these grafts formed new pathways to the brain and restored vision. Would neural grafting work as well in warm-blooded mammals? To find out, a team of researchers destroyed a dopamine-producing area of the brainstem called the *substantia nigra* in laboratory rats. As anticipated, the lack of dopamine caused severe tremors and other symptoms that mimicked Parkinson's disease. Next, they implanted healthy tissue from the brains of rat fetuses. The result: After four weeks, there was a 70 percent decline in symptoms (Perlow et al., 1979). In later experiments involving rats, mice, and primates, researchers successfully used neural grafting in other regions of the brain also to reverse learning deficits, spatial deficits, alcohol-induced memory loss, and age-related sexual impotence (Kimble, 1990).

News from animal laboratories is encouraging. But is it possible to use brain grafts in treating people who suffer from degenerative nerve disorders? In March 1982, a male Parkinson's patient in Stockholm, Sweden, agreed to serve as a human guinea pig. Barely able to move without medication, he underwent an experimental operation. The neurosurgeons removed part of his adrenal gland, which produces dopamine, and injected the tissue directly into his brain (Parkinson's disease results from a shortage of dopamine). But the result was disappointing. The patient showed some

drawings, charts, and other illustrative material; and right-brain mental exercises such as mirror drawing, charades, fantasy, meditation, and photography. In a book entitled *Drawing on the Right Side of the Brain,* for example, art teacher Betty Edwards (1979) claims that although the right hemisphere has the ability to draw, many people find it difficult to copy familiar scenes or objects because they tend to label and analyze the material. To reduce this interference from the left hemisphere, she recommends that students view the pictures to be copied upside down so the pictures cannot be recognized and labeled. According to Edwards, this exercise improves the quality of the drawings that are rendered.

Although discussions of right-brain education have sparked excitement, there is little scientific evidence to support this application of the split-brain research (Hellige, 1990; Springer & Deutsch, 1989). Lauren Harris (1988) points to two related problems. First, this application is based on the incorrect assumption that various functions are completely localized within the right and left hemispheres. In reality, of course, both hemispheres are involved at least to some extent in language, music, art, and other mental activities. Indeed, except in split-brain patients, information between the two hemispheres flows quickly through the corpus callosum.

Second, the call for right-brain education springs from the complaint that schools do not sufficiently encourage children to use the right hemisphere—and that this lack of exercise prevents them from realizing their full potential in various domains. Granted, the school curriculum may be flawed, and perhaps a greater emphasis should be placed on music, the visual arts, and other "nonacademic" subjects. As Harris (1988) warns, however, "educators who are displeased with the educational curriculum should present the case for change on its own merits and not seek to win scientific respectability for their arguments by dressing them in neuropsychological jargon" (p. 226). The concern here is that the call for right-brain education is founded on an exaggerated and overly simplistic view of the brain. In short, as two researchers put it, "the duplex house that Sperry built grew into the K mart of brain science" (Hooper & Teresi, 1986, p. 223).

minor improvement during the first couple of weeks, but he soon reverted to his presurgery state (Backlund et al., 1985). Undiscouraged, others pursued the use of brain grafts with Parkinson's patients with varying degrees of success. In 1987, a group of Mexican researchers stirred up a good deal of excitement when they reported that transplanted dopamine-producing tissue produced remarkable improvement in two patients (Madrazo et al., 1987). Additional clinical studies were then conducted. The results were not nearly as dramatic, but they did reveal at least a modest improvement in many patients (Sladek & Shoulson, 1988). To date, the most encouraging news comes from Sweden, where researchers implanted tissue from human fetuses and found that all patients exhibited improvement (Lindvall et al., 1990).

As we approach the twenty-first century, neuroscientists are poised at the edge of an exciting new frontier: using fetal tissue to repair the damaged brain. As with many scientific discoveries, however, controversy surrounds progress. Is it *ethical* to use medical procedures that generate a need for fetal tissue? It's doubtful that anyone would object to using miscarried fetuses to save lives, but what about the use of aborted fetuses? Would such use encourage women to conceive children and have abortions in order to help an ailing family member, or to make a profit? As neural grafting becomes more effective, this debate is sure to heat up (Hoffer & Olson, 1991). Another question concerns whether the procedure is ready for use with human beings. Some researchers "call for patience rather than patients" (Sladek & Shoulson, 1988). Yet others are eager to consider the clinical possibilities of using neural grafting to treat people suffering from various disorders (Bjorklund, 1991).

The human brain and nervous system remains one of the great frontiers in science. From the nervous system's trillions of tiny building blocks, consisting of axons, dendrites, synapses, neurotransmitters, and glial cells, to the structures of the brainstem, limbic system, and cerebral cortex, there is a solid biological foundation for the study of mind and behavior. The goal, as we'll see in later chapters, is to understand the links between the body and psychological processes—processes that range far and wide, from visual perception and mind-altering drugs to moral development, social aggression, and the benefits of psychotherapy.

SUMMARY AND KEY TERMS

Phineas Gage's dramatic brain injury showed that the human brain and nervous system form a complex, integrated system—the concern of *behavioral neuroscience.*

The Big Picture

Although we generally think about everyday experience dualistically—as if the mind and body were distinct entities—psychologists now view the mind and body as inseparable. Experiments indicate, for example, that stress compromises the immune system and correlates with the likelihood of catching a cold. The new field of *psychoneuroimmunology (PNI)* focuses on this connection between mental and physical health.

Overview of the Nervous System

The human nervous system has two basic parts. The *central nervous system (CNS)* includes the brain and the spinal cord. The *peripheral nervous system (PNS)* consists of the nerves that radiate from the CNS to the rest of the body.

The PNS is further divided into two components. The *somatic nervous system* transmits signals from the sensory organs and skin to the CNS. It also relays motor commands from the CNS to the skeletal muscles, thus governing the body's voluntary movements. The *autonomic nervous system,* in contrast, connects the CNS to the involuntary muscles, organs, and glands, thereby regulating internal functions such as heartbeat and temperature.

The autonomic nervous system itself has two parts. Through the hormones epinephrine and norepinephrine, the *sympathetic nervous system* energizes the body for action. The *parasympathetic nervous system* returns the body to its normal state.

The Neuron

Neurons, or nerve cells, send and receive information throughout the nervous system. *Sensory neurons* transmit information from the senses, skin, muscles, and internal organs to the CNS. *Motor neurons* send commands from the CNS to the muscles, glands, and organs. *Interneurons* serve as connectors within the

CNS. *Glial cells* help support, insulate, and nourish the neurons. A simple *reflex* like the knee jerk—an automatic response to a sensory stimulus—illustrates the amazing speed of neural signals.

Structure of the Neuron

Each neuron has a rounded body, called the *soma,* and two types of branched fibers: *dendrites* that receive impulses and an *axon* that sends impulses through its terminals. Many axons are covered with *myelin sheath,* a fatty insulating layer that speeds impulses.

The Neuron in Action

A neuron transmits messages by means of an electrical process. When the dendrites receive signals of sufficient strength, the cell's membrane breaks down. Positively charged sodium ions rush in, altering the charge inside such that a burst of electrical energy known as an *action potential* surges through the axon.

How Neurons Communicate

To transmit a signal across the *synapse,* the tiny gap between two neurons, the sending neuron releases chemical *neurotransmitters* from vesicles in its axon terminals. These chemicals bind to receptors on the dendrites of the receiving neuron. There are many neurotransmitters, and each fits only certain receptors.

Neurotransmitters

Acetylcholine (ACh) is a neurotransmitter that links motor neurons and muscles. ACh has an excitatory effect. *Dopamine,* in contrast, inhibits the muscles and helps control voluntary movements. Alzheimer's disease, Parkinson's disease, and schizophrenia have all been linked to problems with these chemical messengers. Other neurotransmitters called *endorphins* serve as the body's own pain relievers.

The Brain

The basic anatomy of the brain has long been known, but behavioral neuroscientists face the more difficult task of understanding how it functions.

Tools of Behavioral Neuroscience

Although *phrenology* was erroneous in linking psychological characteristics to bumps on the skull, it correctly supposed that characteristics are localized in particular parts of the brain. Today, neuroscientists use four methods to study brain functions: (1) Clinical case studies of people with brain damage provide some help in linking parts of the brain to specific functions. (2) Through experimental interventions, researchers "invade" the brain and measure the effects. These interventions can involve surgery (on animals), drugs, or electrical brain stimulation. (3) Electrical recordings such as the *electroencephalograph* (EEG) gather information without invading the brain. (4) New brain-imaging techniques create computerized models of the brain. The *computerized axial tomograph* (CAT) *scan* uses x-rays to depict a horizontal slice of the human brain. The *positron emission tomograph* (PET) *scan* produces a color picture showing the amounts of glucose consumed in different brain regions. And *magnetic resonance imaging* (MRI) employs a magnetic field and radio waves to create high-resolution images.

Regions of the Brain

The brain consists of three main parts: the brainstem, the limbic system, and the cerebral cortex. Each of these comprises several important structures.

The *brainstem* is the inner core. It contains the *medulla,* which controls vital involuntary functions such as breathing; the *pons,* involved in sleep and arousal; and the *reticular formation,* a net-like group of cells that filter sensory information and help control sleep, arousal, and attention. Nearby is the *cerebellum,* which plays an important role in balance and coordination.

Above the brainstem is the *limbic system,* which helps govern motivation, emotion, and memory. It includes the *thalamus,* a relay station for sensory information; the *amygdala,* linked to fear, anger, and aggression; the *hippocampus,* which performs a key function in memory formation; and the *hypothalamus,* which helps regulate the autonomic nervous system, emotions, and basic drives.

The hypothalamus plays a critical role in controlling the *endocrine system,* a collection of ductless glands that release *hormones* into the bloodstream. The hypothalamus prompts the *pituitary gland* to release a hormone that stimulates the production of hormones in other endocrine glands. These hormones then affect the activity of organs throughout the body. The mechanism for controlling hunger and other basic drives is less well understood, but it involves similarly complex interactions between the hypothalamus and other regions of the body.

The outermost 80 percent of the brain, the wrinkled *cerebral cortex,* controls higher-order mental processes. Anatomically it consists of two hemispheres and four lobes. Psychologists generally divide it into areas based on function: (1) The sensory areas specialize in receiving sensory information. For example, the *somatosensory cortex* receives information from the touch receptors in the skin. (2) The *motor cortex* controls the voluntary muscles. (3) The *association cortex* areas communicate with the sensory and motor areas and house the higher mental processes. (4) Within the association cortex, two areas specialize in language. *Broca's area* directs the production of speech, and *Wernicke's area* is involved in language comprehension.

The Split Brain

Researchers have investigated Fechner's idea that each side of the brain has its own mind. The studies rely on the fact that the left hemisphere communicates with the right side of the body, and the right hemisphere with the left side. The hemispheres are connected by, and share information through, the *corpus callosum.* Experiments with *split-brain* patients, in whom the corpus callosum has been severed, show that each hemisphere has a somewhat different version of experience.

Other research has tried to determine which functions are *lateralized,* or controlled by a single side of the brain. The key language centers are in the left hemisphere. The right hemisphere plays a crucial role in nonverbal functions such as spatial recognition. But the most important distinction may be the style of processing. The left hemisphere seems to rely on analytical processing, while the right hemisphere is more global and holistic.

Overall, research supports the notion that the two hemispheres, when their links are cut, produce separate streams of consciousness. But in the healthy brain the hemispheres exchange information so quickly that our experience is a seamless whole.

Future Prospects: Repairing the Damaged Brain

Advances in understanding the brain have led to attempts at brain repair. With the *neural graft* procedure, researchers have transplanted brain tissue from one animal to another in an effort to reduce deficits in brain function. In human beings the results have not been dramatic. The greatest hope may lie in transplantation of fetal tissue, a highly controversial procedure.

Chapter 3

Sensation and Perception

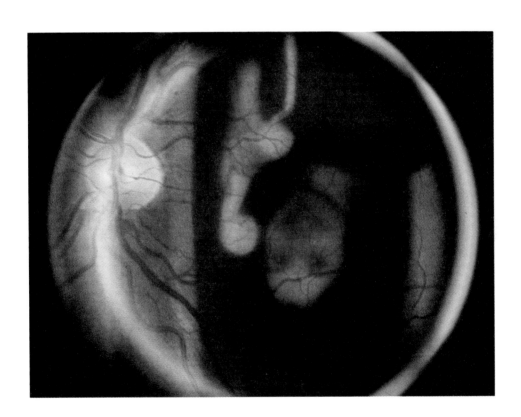

"How sense-luscious the world is."

DIANE ACKERMAN

Before you were born, you spent nine months floating in a warm, wet, mostly dark sack of fluid. You swished around a bit from all the movement, and you could hear the drum-like beat of your mother's heart, but none of this quite prepared you for the sensations that later make life so worth living. The thunderous noise of ocean waves crashing into the shore, the floury aroma that surrounds your nose in a bakery, the haunting vision of a bright full moon against the black night sky, the colors of a rainbow splashed over a canvas, the rich sweet flavor of chocolate ice cream sliding down a cold throat, and the warm tingly feeling inside that comes with a lover's embrace: the world out there has lots to offer, and our sensory systems bring some of it into the brain with radar-like sensitivity.

In this chapter, we will examine the psychology of *sensation* and *perception*. These terms are used to describe different stages in the process by which we acquire information about the world. In **sensation**, raw physical energy is absorbed by our eyes, ears, and other sensory receptors. Through the process of **transduction**, this energy is converted into neural signals that are sent to the brain. In **perception**, these signals are then selected, organized, and interpreted (see Figure 3.1).

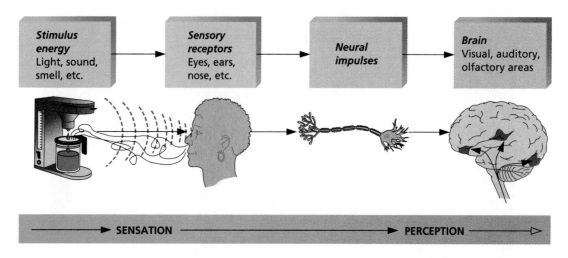

Figure 3.1

Processes of Sensation and Perception

■ **sensation** The set of processes by which our sense organs receive information from the environment.

■ **transduction** The process by which physical energy is converted into sensory neural impulses.

■ **perception** The set of processes by which people select, organize, and interpret sensations.

Psychologists used to treat sensation and perception as separate. Sensation was considered a strictly physiological process involving the various sense organs, receptors, neural pathways, and regions of the brain. Perception was considered a purely psychological process by which we derive meaning from these sensations. In this view, the body supplied the raw material, and then the mind made sense of that material. We now know, however, that in this continuous stream of events, there is no bright line dividing sensation and perception. As we'll see, the interaction between body and mind is seamless. There are different processes at work, however, so psychologists still find it useful to make the distinction.

THE STORY OF VIRGIL: A CASE STUDY

This distinction comes to life in a poignant story told by neurologist Oliver Sacks (1993). The story was about Virgil, a fifty-year-old Oklahoma man who was blind since the age of six. Based on the fact that Virgil could see light and faint shadows, a local ophthalmologist suggested that it might be possible to restore his eyesight through surgery. Starting with the right eye, the doctor removed a thick cataract that blanketed the retina, inserted a new lens implant, and bandaged the eye for twenty-four hours. The next day, the bandage was removed. It was the moment of truth. But Virgil did not cry out with joy or react in any other way. Instead, he stared blankly at the surgeon, silent and bewildered. As Sacks put it, "The dramatic moment stayed vacant, grew longer, sagged." Was the operation a success? Could Virgil see? In a manner of speaking, yes. He said he could detect light, forms, movement, and color, all mixed up in a confusing and cluttered blur. But only when the doctor started to speak did Virgil realize that he was staring at a face. His retina was alive and well, but his brain could not make sense of the information. There was sensation, but no perception.

Even as the weeks passed, Virgil remained disoriented. In the supermarket, he was overwhelmed, even stressed, by all the visual stimulation—the bright lights, the shelves lined with cans and jars, the fruits and vegetables, and the people wheeling carts up and down the aisles. "Everything ran together," he said. Virgil could not identify by sight common objects such as chairs and tables that he recognized easily by touching. He also lacked the ability to perceive depth. He was confused by shadows, often coming to a stop and trying to step over one. Yet he saw a staircase as a flat surface of parallel and crossing lines rather than as a three-dimensional solid object. Movement posed additional problems. He would recognize his dog one moment, but then wonder if it was the same animal when he saw it from a different angle.

For reasons that are unclear, Virgil suddenly became ill, collapsed, and almost died. He had a respiratory illness and needed a constant supply of oxygen. By the time he returned home from the hospital, he had to carry an oxygen tank wherever he went. Unable to work, Virgil lost his job, his house, and, once again, his eyesight. Extensive tests showed that there was no response to light whatsoever—and no electrical activity in the visual cortex. He was totally blind. But perhaps all was not lost. As Sacks (1993) put it, "Now, at last, Virgil is allowed not to see, allowed to escape from the glaring, confusing world of sight and space, and to return to his own true being, the touch world that has been his home for almost fifty years" (p. 73).

This chapter will begin with the study of sensation, the raw material that transforms the brain into a mind. We will examine the physiology of vision, hearing, smell, taste, touch, and other sensory systems. Then we will examine the psychological processes of perception that enable us to comprehend and interpret this raw material. As we'll see, the world "out there" comes to us through an interaction of physical energy, the body, and the mind.

MEASURING THE SENSORY EXPERIENCE

Light, vibration, odor-filled molecules, cold winds, warm breezes, and the collision of bodies. Whatever the stimulus, the first generation of psychologists, including Wilhelm Wundt and his predecessors, raised the most basic of questions: How does physical energy become a psychological experience?

How much light is necessary to see? Can you hear a pin drop, or detect minute variations in pitch well enough to tune a musical instrument? How different must two wines be for a wine taster to tell them apart? Inspired by the work of Gustav Fechner (1860), questions of this nature gave birth to **psychophysics**, psychology's first subfield.

The key to psychophysics is measurement. Because sensation is subjective, it cannot be measured using objective instruments the way you would assess height, weight, or time. There are no yardsticks, or scales, or stopwatches—only the subject and his or her self-report. New procedures thus had to be devised to maximize the accuracy of these reports (Bolanowski & Gescheider, 1991; Gescheider, 1985). Much of the material discussed in this chapter was derived from these psychophysical procedures.

Absolute Thresholds

What is the minimum amount of light that can be seen, the weakest vibration that can be heard, or the faintest odor that can be smelled? How much sugar needs to be added to a food for it to taste sweeter? What is the slightest amount of skin pressure that can be felt? Just how sensitive are our sensory systems? Researchers interested in a sensation begin by trying to determine our **absolute threshold**, the minimum level of stimulation that an organism can detect.

There are different ways to derive an absolute threshold. One method is simply to ask a subject to adjust the intensity of a stimulus until it is barely detectable. In a second method, the experimenter gradually increases the intensity level and asks the subject from one trial to the next if he or she detects the stimulus. A third method is to vary the stimulus presentation randomly, again checking with the subject on each trial. Over the years, research has shown that absolute thresholds are not "absolute." There is no single point on the intensity scale at which people suddenly detect a stimulus. Rather, the detection rates increase gradually. Psychophysics researchers thus define the absolute threshold as the point at which a stimulus can be detected 50 percent of the time. Defined in this way, some of our absolute thresholds are highly impressive (see Table 3.1).

Signal-Detection Theory

Imagine you're a subject in a classical psychophysics experiment. You're sitting in a darkened room staring at a blank wall, and the experimenter presents a series of flashes varying in brightness. Did you see it? What about the next one? On some trials, the flashes are clear, well above threshold, so you say "yes." On other trials, however, you're just not sure. The experimenter is waiting for a response, so what do you say? Confronted with this dilemma, some subjects prefer to say "yes" (when in doubt, go for it). Others, more cautious, say "no" (unless it's clear, don't go out on a limb). These tendencies to respond "yes" and "no" in uncertain situations are called *response biases*—and they have little to do with sensation. The problem for the researcher, then, is that responses are influenced not only by the strength of the signal but also by background factors such as a subject's personality, motivation, and expectations.

■ **psychophysics** The study of the relationship between physical stimulation and subjective sensations.

■ **absolute threshold** The smallest amount of stimulation that can be detected.

Table 3.1

Some Absolute Thresholds

Sensory system	Absolute threshold
Vision	A lit candle 30 miles away on a dark, clear night
Hearing	The tick of a watch 20 feet away in total quiet
Smell	One drop of perfume dispersed throughout a 6-room apartment
Taste	One teaspoon of sugar in 2 gallons of water
Touch	The wing of a bee falling on your cheek from a height of 1 centimeter

Enter signal-detection theory. Based on the assumption that performance is jointly determined by the strength of the signal and the subject's response criterion (that is, by his or her willingness to say "yes" rather than "no"), **signal-detection theory** gave rise to a more sophisticated method. On some trials, a weak stimulus is presented. On others, no stimulus is presented. By comparing a subject's "hit" versus "miss" rate on stimulus trials to his or her tendency to commit "false alarms" by saying "yes" in blank trials, the researcher can mathematically separate the subject's detection performance from the response bias (Green & Swets, 1966). The method of establishing absolute thresholds was based on the assumption that a threshold is determined solely by the stimulus. But signal-detection theory recognizes that response biases are also at work. This approach provides the psychologist with a valuable tool for analyzing why air-traffic controllers are so quick to detect danger signals on the radar screen, why overeager witnesses identify innocent suspects in police lineups, or why doctors overdiagnose certain diseases from available test results (Swets, 1992).

Difference Thresholds

Sensory capacities are measured not only by our ability to detect low levels of stimulation but also by the extent to which we can detect subtle differences. This ability is determined by asking subjects to compare the brightness of two light bulbs, the loudness of two tones, the weight of two blocks, and so on. Given one stimulus, the subject is asked to adjust the level of another stimulus so that the two are the same. Or subjects are given two stimuli and asked to report whether they are the same or different. Either way, it is possible to pinpoint the smallest change in stimulation that subjects can detect 50 percent of the time. This point is called the difference threshold, or **just-noticeable difference (JND)**.

While measuring difference thresholds, Ernst Weber (1834) quickly noticed that JNDs increase with the size or intensity of the stimulus—and that the magnitude of a JND is a constant *proportion* of the original stimulus. This general principle is known as **Weber's law**. To illustrate, the JND for weight is 1/50, or 2 percent. In other words, if you lift a 50-ounce object, and then a 51-ounce object, you will probably notice that the second one is heavier than the first. However, you would not feel a difference between one object that weighs 50 pounds and another that weighs 50 pounds, 1

■ **signal-detection theory** The theory that detecting a stimulus is jointly determined by the signal and the subject's response criterion.

■ **just-noticeable difference (JND)** The smallest amount of change in a stimulus that can be detected.

■ **Weber's law** The principle that the just-noticeable difference of a stimulus is a constant proportion, despite variations in intensity.

Tuning a piano requires a heightened ability to detect subtle differences among tones.

ounce. Again, there is an absolute difference of 1 ounce; but a JND of 2 percent means that if your reference point is a 50-pound object, you would not detect a difference unless the second object was equal to or greater than 51 pounds. Except at the extremes, Weber's law provides a good estimate of our difference thresholds. It can also be applied to other senses—though each has a different threshold (for example, the JND is 2 percent for brightness, 10 percent for loudness, and 20 percent for the taste of salt).

SENSATION

"From a swirling sea of energies, each sense selects its own."

DANIEL P. KIMBLE (1988)

Back in school, I was taught that there are five senses: vision, hearing, taste, smell, and touch. This notion can be traced to Aristotle (384–322 B.C.). Even today, people who believe in "extrasensory" perception, or ESP, often call it the "sixth sense." In fact, there are more than five sensory modalities. Vision has two subsystems, one for daylight and one for nighttime conditions. The chemical senses of taste and smell are easily distinguished, but touch is really a mix of several skin senses—including pressure, pain, warmth, and cold. We also have a keen sense of balance, and of the position and movement of body parts. Combined, these various systems bring in a steady stream of information from the world around us.

Vision

You and I are visual creatures. How many times have you said, "Show me." "I'll believe it when I see it." "I saw it with my own eyes." "Out of sight, out of mind." "See?" "My eyes are playing tricks on me." As with other aspects of human anatomy, our visual system is a brilliantly molded product of evolution. The earliest forms of life could "see" in the sea through faint patches of membrane that were sensitive to light. They could tell brightness from dark, even turn in the direction of the light source. As for shapes, textures, motion, and color—these features could be detected only later, by more advanced forms of life (Land & Fernald, 1992).

Light   Every sensory system uses physical energy as its source of stimulation. The stimulus input for vision is light—a form of energy known as electromagnetic radiation that travels through empty space in oscillating waves. As illustrated in Figure 3.2, what we see as light comes from a narrow band in the spectrum of electromagnetic radiation. All matter gives off

Figure 3.2

The Electromagnetic Spectrum

The human eye is sensitive to only a narrow band of electromagnetic radiation. As shown, visible wavelengths range from 380 to 760 nanometers.

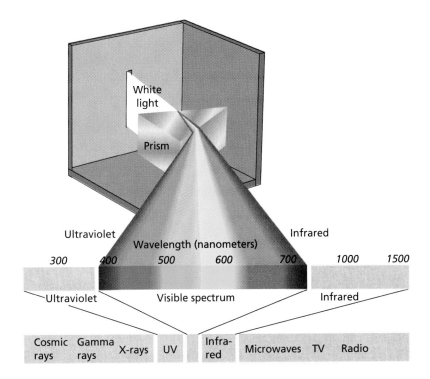

electromagnetic radiation of different wavelengths (a wavelength is measured by the distance between waves). The sun and other stars give off radiation that includes light. So do fires and electric lamps. Visible wavelengths range from about 380 to 760 nanometers (a nanometer is one billionth of a meter). Thus, some waves (such as x-rays, ultraviolet rays, and gamma rays) are too short for us to see and fall below our visible range. Others (such as infrared rays, TV signals, radio waves, and radar) are too long for us to see, so they exceed our visible range. In both cases, the wavelengths are invisible to the human eye. Other organisms have sensory capabilities that are different from ours. For example, most insects can see shorter wavelengths in the ultraviolet spectrum, and most fish and reptiles can see longer wavelengths in the infrared spectrum.

The *length* of a light wave determines its hue, or perceived *color*. To the human eye, white light is made up of all visible wavelengths combined. Short wavelengths look bluish, medium wavelengths look greenish, and long wavelengths look reddish. The picturesque colors of the visible wavelengths can be seen in a rainbow, or in the spectrum of colors produced

■ **cornea** The clear outer membrane that bends light so that it is sharply focused in the eye.

when white light passes through a glass prism. A second property of light is its intensity or *amplitude*, as measured by the height of the peaks in the wave. Whereas wavelength determines color, amplitude determines *brightness*. The higher the amplitude, the brighter the light appears to be. A third physical property of light is its *purity*, as measured by the number of wavelengths that make up the light. Purity influences the *saturation*, or richness, of colors. The fewer wavelengths there are in a light (the purer it is), the richer or more saturated is the color. A pure red light made up of only a narrow band of wavelengths would give off a rich fire-engine or tomato-like color. In contrast, white light—which contains all visible wavelengths—is completely unsaturated and lacking in color.

The Visual System   Light waves provide the stimulus input for vision, but what is actually seen depends on the capabilities of the visual system that's in place. Accordingly, different species see the world in different ways. Eagles can spot a tiny field mouse moving in the grass a mile away. Owls have binocular-like eyes that enable them to see prey in the dark of night. Cows and sheep have eyes on the sides of their heads so they can spot predators sneaking up from behind. And bees can judge the angle at which light strikes the eye, so they know the sun's position in the sky—even on an overcast day. Nature provides us with visual systems uniquely suited to our ways of life.

The Eye   The fantastic journey of neural impulses through the human visual system begins with the eye—an extension of the brain and the most exposed part of the central nervous system. Lying in a protective bony socket within the skull, the eye transforms, or transduces, light waves into electrochemical neural impulses. The major structures of the human eye are presented in Figure 3.3.

Light rays from the outside world first pass through the **cornea**, a clear, curved membrane, or "window." The cornea bends light so that it is sharply focused within the eye. Abnormalities in the shape of the cornea

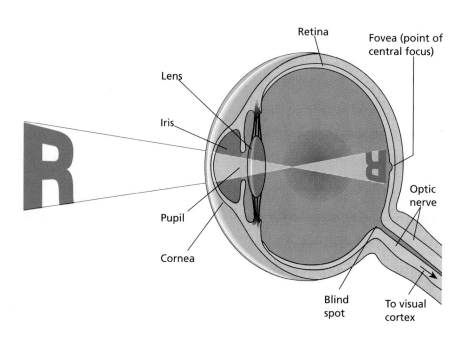

Figure 3.3

Structures of the Human Eye

iris The ring of muscle tissue that gives eyes their color and controls the size of the pupil.

pupil The small round hole in the iris of the eye through which light passes.

lens A transparent structure in the eye that focuses light on the retina.

accommodation The visual process by which lenses become rounded for viewing nearby objects and flatter for viewing remote objects.

retina The rear multilayered part of the eye where rods and cones convert light into neural impulses.

Figure 3.4

The Retina

The back wall of the retina has three major layers containing 130 million photoreceptor cells. The light-sensitive rods are concentrated in the sides of the retina, and the color-sensitive cones are clustered in the center.

cause astigmatism, usually experienced as a selective blurring of parts of the image at a particular orientation, such as horizontal. Next, there is the ring-shaped **iris**, which gives the eye its color. The iris is a muscle that is controlled by the autonomic nervous system. Its function is to regulate the size of the **pupil**—the small, round hole in the iris through which light passes. The iris causes the pupil to dilate (enlarge) under dim viewing conditions to let in more light, and to contract (shrink) under brightness to let in less light.

Behind the pupil, light continues through the **lens**, another transparent structure whose function is to fine-tune the focusing of the light. The lens brings an image into focus by changing its shape, in a process called **accommodation**. Specifically, the lens becomes more rounded for focusing on nearby objects and flatter for more distant objects (the cornea, which has a fixed shape, cannot make these adjustments for different distances). With age, the lens loses much of its elasticity and keeps the flatter shape appropriate for viewing at a distance. As a result, many middle-aged people start to need glasses for reading, or bifocals with a near-vision portion in the lower part of the glass.

Filling the central part of the eyeball is a clear jelly-like substance called the *vitreous humor*. Light passes through this fluid before it reaches the retina. The **retina** is a multilayered screen of cells that lines the back inside surface of the eyeball. It is one of the most fascinating tissues in the body—both because of its function, which is to transform patterns of light into images that the brain can use, and because of its structure, which illustrates many basic principles of neural organization (see Figure 3.4). In an odd

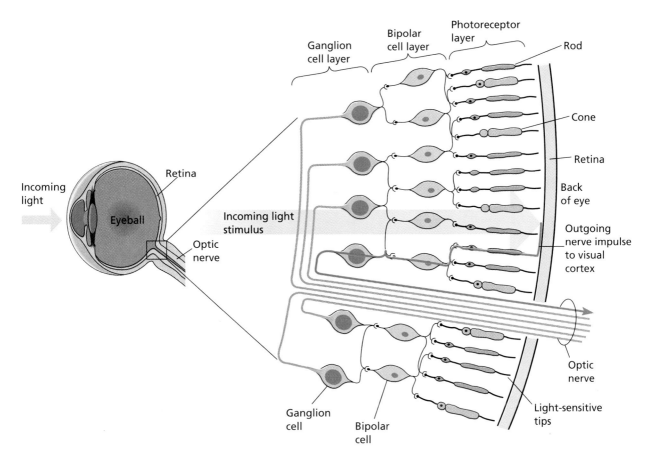

■ **rods** Rod-shaped photoreceptor cells in the retina that are highly sensitive to light.

■ **cones** Cone-shaped photoreceptor cells in the retina that are sensitive to color.

■ **fovea** The center of the retina, where cones are clustered.

twist of nature, the image projected on the retina is upside down. That is, light from the top part of the visual field stimulates photoreceptor cells in the bottom part of the retina, and vice versa.

The retina has aptly been called an extension of the brain (Gregory, 1990). It has several relatively transparent layers and contains 130 million *photoreceptor cells* that convert light energy into neural activity. The bottom layer, closest to the back of the eyeball, is lined with two specialized types of nerve cells called rods and cones (again, see Figure 3.4). The **rods** are long, thin, cylindrical cells that are highly sensitive to light. They are concentrated in the sides of the retina and are responsible for black-and-white vision in dim light. Under impossibly ideal conditions, rods have the capacity to detect the light produced by one ten-billionth of a watt. On a perfectly clear, pitch-dark night, that's like seeing the light of a match struck thirty miles away! **Cones** are shorter, thicker, more tapered cells that are sensitive to color under high levels of illumination. Cones are densely clustered in the **fovea**, the pinhead-sized center of the retina. The fovea contains only cones, but the ratio of rods to cones increases in the outer edges of the retina.

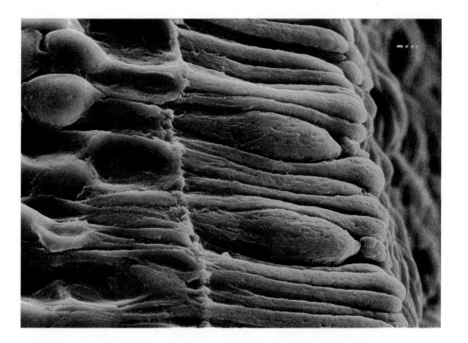

Magnified approximately 14,000 times, this photo shows how light-sensitive rods and color-sensitive cones line the back wall of the retina.

In owls and other nocturnal (active only at night) animals, the retina contains only rods. Thus, they can see at night but their vision is in black-and-white. In chipmunks, pigeons, and other diurnal (active only during the day) animals, the retina contains only cones. Thus, they are virtually blind at night. In animals that are active both day and night, the retina has a mixture of rods and cones. For example, the human retina has about 120 million rods and 6 million cones, enabling us to see colors under normal lighting and to make out forms under low levels of illumination. Individuals whose retinas contain no rods suffer from night blindness; those without cones lack all color vision.

Often, we need to adjust to radical changes in illumination. It's happened to me, and I'm sure it has happened to you, too. You step inside a darkened

■ **dark adaptation** A process of adjustment by which the eyes become more sensitive to light in a dark environment.

■ **light adaptation** The process of adjustment by which the eyes become less sensitive to light in a bright environment.

■ **optic nerve** The pathway that carries visual information from the eyeball to the brain.

■ **blind spot** A part of the retina through which the optic nerve passes. Lacking rods and cones, this spot is not responsive to light.

Figure 3.5

How to Find Your Blind Spot

The optic nerve area has no rods or cones, so it is "blind." To find your blind spot, hold this book at arm's length, cover your left eye and stare at the left button with your right eye. Now slowly move the book toward you until the right button disappears. To test your left eye, simply reverse the procedure.

movie theater on a sunny day. As you start walking down the aisle, however, you have to put your arms out and inch slowly forward, stumbling around as if you were blind. After a few minutes, you can see again. This common experience illustrates **dark adaptation**, the process by which eyes become more sensitive to light in a dark environment. It takes about thirty minutes for you to fully adapt to the dark—at which point the eyes are ten thousand times more sensitive. It also takes time to adjust to bright light. When you emerge from a movie theater during the day, everything seems so "washed out" that you have to squint initially to keep out the glare. This is an instance of **light adaptation**, the process by which our eyes become less sensitive to light under high levels of illumination.

When light strikes the rods and cones, it sparks a chain of events within a network of interconnected neurons that results in vision. Rods and cones contain *photopigments*, chemicals that break down in response to light, thus triggering neural impulses. These impulses activate *bipolar cells*, which, in turn, activate nearby *ganglion cells*. The axons of the ganglion cells form the **optic nerve**, a pathway that carries visual information from each eyeball to the brain. The area where the optic nerve enters the eye has no rods or cones, only axons. So, each eye has a **blind spot**. You don't normally notice it because your eyes are always moving, but the blind spot can be located through a simple exercise (see Figure 3.5).

Psychologists used to think that electrical impulses were delivered from the retina to the brain, as on an assembly line. It was as if there was a simple division of labor, whereby retinal neurons "received" sensory information and passed it along on a conveyer belt to the visual cortex for perceptual "processing." We now know that the mechanisms of vision are more complex. Ultimately, signals from 130 million rods and cones are funneled through a mere 1 million axons in the optic nerve. Think for a moment about these numbers, and you'll realize what they mean: that the bipolar and ganglion cells must be integrating and compressing signals from multiple receptors. The retina is a "smart" optical instrument. Not only does it receive light, but it also processes visual information.

Any ganglion cell that represents a cluster of neighboring rods and cones receives input from a sizable portion of the retina. This region is called a *receptive field*. By recording the activity of individual ganglion cells, researchers have found that there are many different types of receptive fields (Kuffler, 1953). The most common are circular "center-surround" fields in which light falling in the center has the opposite effect of light in the surrounding area. Some cells are activated by light in the center and inhibited by light in the surrounding area (center-on cells), while others work the opposite way, inhibited by light in the center and activated by light in the surrounding area (center-off cells). This arrangement makes the human eye particularly attuned to brightness-and-darkness contrasts in the visual field—contrasts that indicate corners, edges, and borders. There's an old joke about an art dealer who tries to sell a blank canvas. "What is it?" asks the prospective buyer. "A white cow in a snowstorm" says the dealer. Funny or not, this joke clearly underestimates our visual acuity. A white cow would differ in brightness from white snow, and its body would differ in texture, thus forming a subtle but discernable outline against the background.

Visual Pathways   Axon fibers of ganglion cells form the optic nerve, which is the first part of the visual pathway that links each eyeball to the brain. The two optic nerves meet at the *optic chiasm*, where axons from the inside half of each eye cross over to the opposite half of the brain. This arrangement means that the left visual field of both eyes is projected to the right side of the brain, while the right visual field of both eyes is projected to the left side of the brain. After reaching the optic chiasm, the nerve fibers travel along two tracts, through the *thalamus*, the relay station where sensory signals are directed to appropriate areas of the *visual cortex*. Located in the back of the brain, the visual cortex is the main information-processing center for visual information (see Figure 3.6).

Figure 3.6

Visual Pathways

From both eyes, the optic nerves meet at the optic chiasm, where the signals cross to the opposite half of the brain. The nerve fibers travel in two tracks through the thalamus, where they are directed to the visual cortex.

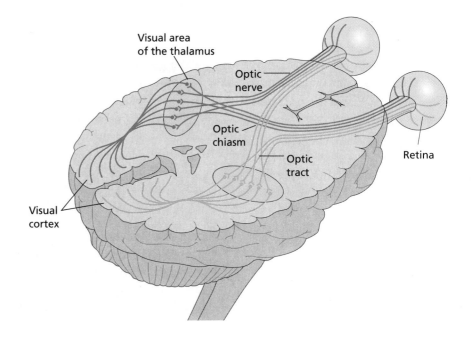

The Visual Cortex   Once information from the ganglion cells reaches the visual cortex, it is processed by *feature detectors*—neurons that are sensitive only to certain aspects of a visual image. This phenomenon was first revealed by David Hubel and Torsten Wiesel (1962), who implanted microelectrodes in the visual cortexes of cats (and later monkeys), projected different types of visual stimuli on a screen, and measured the electrical activity of single cells. Do different neurons specialize in certain types of information? If so, the goal was to map or "decode" the visual cortex (see Figure 3.7).

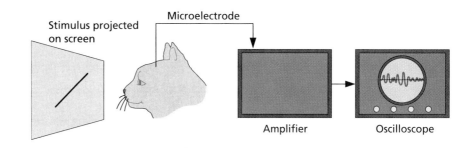

Figure 3.7

Hubel and Wiesel's Apparatus

Hubel and Wiesel implanted microelectrodes in a cat's visual cortex, projected visual stimuli, and measured single-cell activity. These signals were amplified and displayed on an oscilloscope.

In 1981, Hubel and Wiesel were awarded a Nobel prize for their work. In a painstaking series of studies, they discovered that three types of neurons service the visual cortex, and that each type has its own specialists at work (Hubel & Wiesel, 1979; Hubel, 1988). *Simple cells* are activated by highly particular images. For example, some simple cells fire in response to a vertical line in the middle of the screen, but not to a line that is off-center or tilted at a different angle. Other simple cells fire in response to horizontal lines, wider lines, or lines tilted at a 45-degree angle. It's that specific. *Complex cells* receive input from many simple cells, and although they specialize in certain types of images, they react to those images anywhere in the receptive field—center, bottom, side, and so on. Finally, *hypercomplex cells* receive input from complex cells and respond to stimulus patterns. If one simple cell is activated by "/," a second by "\," and a third by "-," the hypercomplex cell might react to a combination of these features, as in the letter "A." When you consider the complexity of words, faces, three-dimensional objects, landscapes, skylines, and other images that enrich our lives, it's no wonder that the visual cortex is tightly packed with over 100 million neurons.

In the years since Hubel and Wiesel discovered feature detectors in the visual cortex, others have identified neurons that fire only in response to certain features. Research shows that the color, form, movement, and depth of a visual stimulus are all processed separately (Livingstone & Hubel, 1988), and that damage to certain areas of the visual cortex produces very specific deficits—such as a complete or partial loss of color vision, impairments in face recognition, or an inability to see stationary or moving objects (Zeki, 1992). Certain areas of the visual cortex also specialize in patterns, or configurations. For example, experiments with monkeys indicate that some cells in the visual cortex are activated by the image of a hand (Gross et al., 1972), others fire in response to faces (Bayliss et al., 1985), and still others react only to movement in an upward or downward direction (Logothetis & Schall, 1989). It seems that the visual system is uniquely prepared to detect biologically adaptive types of visual stimulation.

Color Vision   Ruby red apples. Yellow taxi cabs. Lush green grass. Navy blue uniforms. Shiny copper pennies. Fertile brown soil. Juicy orange oranges. Purple mountains at sunset. Many animals see the world in black and white, or in pale shades (including the bull, which is supposedly enraged by the sight of a matador's bright red cape). For human beings, however, color is a vital part of the visual experience. It is also linked in interesting ways to emotion. Thus, sadness feels blue, anger makes us see red, death is mourned in black, and jealousy brings a visit from the green-eyed monster.

People think that color is an objective property of objects. In fact, it is a property of organisms. When sunlight shines on a red rose, only the long red rays in the spectrum are reflected into our eyes. All other wavelengths are absorbed into the flower's surface. (If no wavelengths were absorbed, the rose would appear white.) Ironically, then, the rose holds everything but red. Most people can discriminate among two hundred different colors and thousands of different shades. How do we do it? There are two major theories of color vision: the trichromatic theory and the opponent-process theory (Boynton, 1988).

Early in the nineteenth century, physiologists Thomas Young (1802) and Hermann von Helmholtz (1852) argued that the human eye is receptive to three primary colors—red, blue, and green—and that all other colors are derived from combinations of these primaries. By recording the neural responses of individual cones to different wavelengths of light, twentieth-century researchers later confirmed the Young-Helmholtz **trichromatic theory** (Schnapf et al., 1987; Wald, 1964). Specifically, there are three types of cones, each having a different photochemical that produces a particular response to light. One type fires most when struck by short wavelengths, so it picks up the color blue. The second type is most sensitive to the middle wavelengths, for the color green. The third type is most sensitive to long wavelengths, for the color red. In short, blue cones, green cones, and red cones serve as the building blocks for color vision. Other colors in the eye's "palette" are produced by the different combinations of cones. Activate both red and green cones, for example, and you will see the color yellow. Activate all three types of cones, and white is produced (see Figure 3.8). This, by the way, is what happens on a color TV screen—where pictures are formed from tiny red, green, and blue dots (hence the name "Trinitron" given by the Sony Corporation to its color TVs).

German physiologist Ewald Hering (1878) was not completely satisfied with the trichromatic theory. As he saw it, yellow was a primary color, not a derivative of red and green. He also noticed that certain color combinations just don't seem to exist. A mix of red and blue gives rise to varying shades of purple, but what is reddish green? Another puzzling phenomenon that didn't fit was the occurrence of negative **afterimages**. An afterimage is a sensation that persists after prolonged exposure to a stimulus. Stare at the image presented in Figure 3.9 for sixty seconds and in good lighting. Then look at a blank white sheet of paper. What do you see? In situations such as this one, staring at a green image leaves a red afterimage, yellow leaves a trace of blue, and black leaves white.

Putting the pieces together, Hering proposed the **opponent-process theory** of color vision. According to this theory, there are three types of visual receptors, and each is sensitive to a pair of complementary or "opponent" colors. One type reacts to the colors blue and yellow, a second type detects red and green, and a third type detects variations in brightness ranging from black to white. The color wheel presented in Figure 3.10 illustrates how these primary colors and their "companions" line up on nearly opposite sides of the circle. Notice that red and green are opponent colors, as are blue and yellow. Within each pair of red-green, blue-yellow, and black-white receptors, some parts fire more to one color whereas other parts react to its opposite. That's why we never see bluish yellow or reddish green, but we might see bluish green and reddish yellow. While seeing one color at a

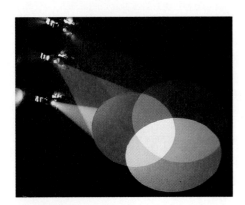

Figure 3.8

Trichromatic Theory

As shown, any color can be produced by mixing blue, green, and red light waves. When all three colors are combined, white is produced.

■ **trichromatic theory** A theory of color vision stating that the retina contains three types of color receptors—for red, blue, and green—and that these combine to produce all other colors.

■ **afterimage** A visual sensation that persists after prolonged exposure and removal of a stimulus.

■ **opponent-process theory** The theory that color vision is derived from three pairs of opposing receptors. The opponent colors are blue and yellow, red and green, and black and white.

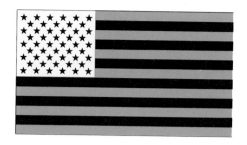

Figure 3.9

Afterimages

Stare at this flag for 60 seconds, then look at a white sheet of paper. According to the opponent-process theory, you should see a negative afterimage that converts green to red, yellow to blue, and black to white. If you don't see an afterimage right away, blink and look again.

specific spot on the retina, you cannot also see its opposite on the same spot (Shapley, 1990).

The opponent-process theory can explain two aspects of color vision that its predecessor theory could not. First, it explains afterimages. Staring at the green stripes in Figure 3.9 causes the green-seeing cells to fire. Then, when the green color is removed from view, these parts of the cells become temporarily fatigued, leaving only the red parts to fire normally (Vimal et al., 1987). This process tips the neural balance to red, producing a brief "rebound" effect (staring at yellow and black triggers a similar rebounding of blue and white).

Second, opponent-process theory can explain color blindness, a genetic disorder (Nathans et al., 1986). In actuality, very few people are color "blind"—that is, very few people see the world only in black, white, and shades of gray. Rather, color-deficient people tend to confuse certain colors. The most common problem, particularly among men, is red-green color blindness, in which there is an inability to distinguish between red and green because both appear gray (how ironic that these are the universal traffic colors for stop and go!). Though very rare, a second form of color blindness is the inability to distinguish between—you guessed it, blue and yellow (see Figure 3.11).

For many years, researchers debated the relative merits of the trichromatic and opponent-process theories of color vision. As often happens in

Figure 3.10

The Color Wheel

As shown, opponent colors are directly across from each other in the circle (red is across from green, blue is across from yellow). The numbers on the spokes are wavelengths, expressed in nanometers.

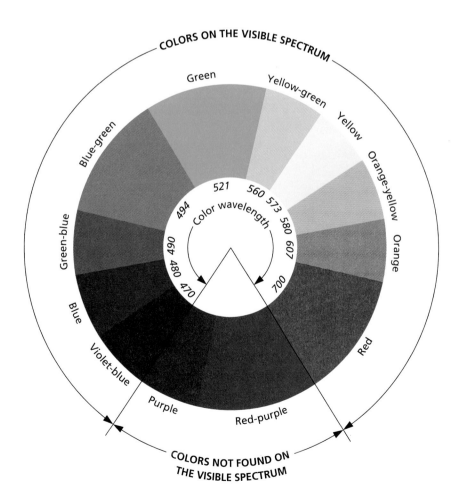

Figure 3.11

Test of Color Deficiency

In items like these, people with red-green color blindness have difficulty perceiving the numbers embedded in the pattern.

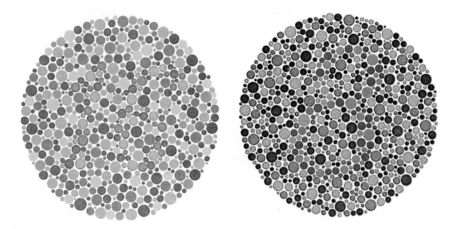

either-or debates, it now appears that both theories are correct—and that both are necessary to fully understand the way we sense color. The human retina contains red, blue, and green cones, as suggested by the trichromatic theory. But in the thalamus—where these signals are sent en route to the visual cortex—single-cell recordings reveal that neurons operate in accordance with the opponent-process theory. That is, some cells are excited by red and inhibited by green, and vice versa. Other cells react to blue and yellow (DeValois & DeValois, 1975). Color vision is thus a complex two-step process (Coren & Ward, 1989).

Hearing

If you had to suffer one fate, to be blind or deaf, which would you choose? It's a morbid question, I know. Ask around, however, and you'll find that most people would rather lose their hearing than their eyesight. Yet Helen Keller, like many others who are both blind and deaf, wrote that deafness was by far the greater handicap.

It's easy to take the sounds of everyday life for granted—and, indeed, we often say that "silence is golden." But auditory sensations surround us, and inform us. The chatter of voices, the clanging of dinner dishes, music throbbing from stereo speakers, birds chirping, babies crying, dogs barking, horns honking, a creaking old floor breaking the silence of night, the trickling of water over pebbles, the whisper of a secret, the crunching of potato chips, the sound of a figure skater's blade scraping the ice, the steady hum of a fluorescent lamp, the crack of a wooden bat against a baseball, the clinking of champagne glasses on New Year's Eve, audiences cheering, the screeching of a train roaring into the station, the snap-crackle-pop of breakfast cereal, and the one I've become the most accustomed to—the woodpecker-like tapping of fingers on a computer keyboard. These are just some of the sounds of life. But what is sound, and how do we hear it?

audition The sense of hearing.

Sound Waves   Every sensation is born of energy. For vision, or seeing, the stimulus is light. For **audition**, or hearing, the stimulus is sound. As in light, sound travels in waves. Physically, sound is *vibration*, a pattern of rapid wave-like movement in molecules of air. First, something has to move—an engine, vocal cords, violin strings. The movement jolts the surrounding molecules of air, and these collide with other air molecules. As in the ocean, sound ripples in waves that ebb and flow in all directions. It loses energy from one ripple to the next, however, which is the reason sound fades at a distance. Sound travels through air at 750 miles per hour—far slower than the speed of light, which is 186,000 miles per second. That's why, in thunderstorms, you see lightning before you hear the accompanying thunder.

As with light, sound waves can be distinguished by three major properties. The first is wavelength, or *frequency*. As molecules of air push outward from a source, they expand and compress in cycles. Frequency, measured by the number of cycles completed per second, is expressed as hertz (Hz). One cycle per second equals one Hz. Subjectively, the frequency of a sound wave determines its *pitch*. The higher the frequency, the higher the pitch. Humans can hear frequencies ranging from about 20 Hz to 20,000 Hz—in music, the equivalent of almost ten octaves. Homing pigeons and elephants can hear lower frequencies. Bats, dogs, and dolphins hear at higher frequencies (dogs can hear at 50,000 Hz, which is why a "silent" dog whistle is not silent to a dog). Most of the sounds we need to hear, and certainly those we enjoy hearing, are well within this capacity (the lowest note on a piano is 27.5 Hz, the highest note is 4,180 Hz, and the voices of conversation range from 200 to 800 Hz). When all frequencies of the sound spectrum are combined, they produce a hissing sound. This hissing is called **white noise**—named by analogy to the white light that results from the combination of all wavelengths in the visible light spectrum.

The second property of sound is *amplitude*. Amplitude refers to the intensity, or height, of each sound wave. Psychologically, the amplitude of a wave determines its *loudness*. The greater the amplitude, the louder the sound. We may not be able to hear a pin drop, but our ears are responsive to a remarkably wide range of amplitudes. Indeed, the loudest sound we can tolerate without pain is billions of times greater in amplitude than the softest sound we can hear! For variations within this range, amplitude is measured in decibels (dB). The box on pp. 100–101 provides examples of the loudness of various sounds at different dB levels. As you look at the figure, note that dB levels of over 120 are painful, and can cause permanent damage to the ears (Henry, 1984).

A third property of sound is purity, or *complexity*. Strike a tuning fork, and you will produce something rare: a pure tone consisting of a single frequency of vibration. In reality, most sounds are complex mixtures of waves of different frequencies. Speech, music, the ringing of a bell, and the breaking of a window are just a few common examples (Bregman, 1990; Krumhansl, 1991). Psychologically, the complexity of a sound determines its *timbre*, or tonal quality. Play the same note at the same loudness on a piano, trumpet, saxophone, tuba, and violin, and what you'll hear are differences in timbre.

■ **white noise** A hissing sound that results from a combination of all frequencies of the sound spectrum.

The Auditory System Philosophers like to ponder the age-old question "If a tree falls in a forest, but no one is around to hear it, does it make a sound?" This really is a profound question. We know that the fall of a tree sends waves of molecules blasting through the air, but we also know that without an auditory system to catch these molecules—well, you make the

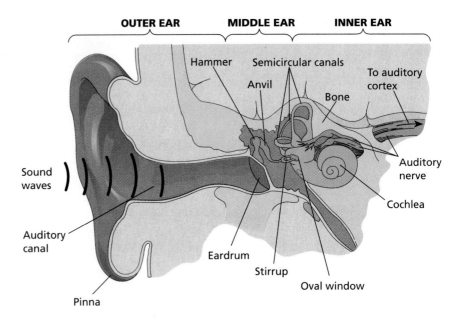

OUTER EAR   MIDDLE EAR   INNER EAR

Figure 3.12

The Human Ear

As shown, the process of hearing begins in the three-part (outer, middle, and inner) structure of the ear. From the auditory nerve, signals are relayed to the auditory cortex.

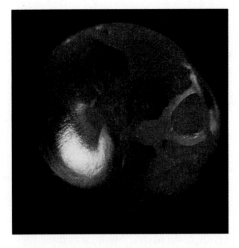

In this photograph of the middle ear, you can see the eardrum (left), hammer (top), anvil (center), and stirrup (right).

call. As in vision, hearing requires that energy be detected, converted into neural impulses, and relayed to the brain. As shown in Figure 3.12, this complex process begins in the three-part (outer, middle, and inner) structure of the human ear.

Sound waves are collected in the outer ear, beginning with the fleshy *pinna*. Some animals, such as dogs, cats, and deer, can wiggle this structure like a radar dish to maximize the reception of sound (humans cannot). The sound waves are then funneled through the auditory canal to the *eardrum*, a tightly stretched membrane that separates the outer and middle portions of the ear. The eardrum vibrates back and forth to the waves, thereby setting into motion a series of tiny connecting bones in the middle ear—the hammer, the anvil, and the stirrup (for you trivia fans, these are the three smallest bones in the body). This middle-ear activity amplifies sound by a factor of 30. The last of these bones, the stirrup, then vibrates against a soft inner-ear membrane called the oval window. This, in turn, vibrates the fluid that fills the canals of the *cochlea,* a snail-shaped tube—and the resulting motion presses the *basilar membrane,* which brushes up against about a million sensitive hair cells (Hudspeth, 1985). These hair cells bend, exciting fibers in the *auditory nerve*—a bundle of 35,000 axons that link to auditory centers of the brain (Teas, 1989).

To summarize, the "plumbing" and "wiring" that turn sound waves into meaningful input are fairly intricate. Air collected in the outer ear is transformed first into a salt-watery fluid, and then into electrical impulses in the inner ear. From the auditory nerve, signals then cross to the other side of the brain. Next, they get routed to the thalamus, where they're relayed to areas of the auditory cortex. Once there, the signals are processed by cells that specialize in either high, middle, or low frequencies of sound.

Hearing Abilities   Hearing is not one sensory ability, but many. People can detect sound, understand spoken language, and appreciate the acoustical qualities of music. Everyone with normal hearing can distinguish between sounds that are loud and soft, or between those produced by horns and string instruments (Coren & Ward, 1989). And although fewer than one in a thousand people have "absolute pitch" (an ability to identify a musical note as middle C, F-sharp, or B-flat), we can all make judgments of "relative pitch"—enabling us to know, for example, that a child's voice is higher than a man's (Takeuchi & Hulse, 1993). In many ways, our auditory competence is impressive.

One particularly adaptive aspect of normal hearing that we take for granted is **auditory localization**—the ability to tell the *direction* a sound is coming from. Localization is needed to determine if the blaring siren you hear is coming from behind you on the road, or if approaching footsteps are coming from your left or your right. This skill was vital to our primitive ancestors and is a matter of life and death to all animals of prey.

Unless you're being fooled by the visual manipulations of a ventriloquist, it's usually easy to tell if a sound is coming from your left or your right. Have you ever heard children in a swimming pool screaming "Marco— Polo—Marco—Polo"? Most kids love the game, and most adults trying to enjoy a relaxing day at the pool find it irritating. Basically, it's a game of tag in which one player, with eyes closed, screams "Marco," prompting the others to reply by yelling "Polo." The first player then tries to find the others by tracking their voices. The key skill here is auditory localization, and children of all ages are good at it. In fact, if you stand to the left or right of an infant and shake a rattle, it will often turn its head in your direction, as if locating the source (see Chapter 9).

What makes auditory localization possible is that we hear in stereo, using two ears spaced about six inches apart. If you're at a noisy gathering and someone on your left calls your name, your left ear receives the signal before the right ear does (it's closer to the source) and more intensely (your head is a barrier to the more distant ear). The six inches of brain tissue and skull that separate your ears may seem too little to matter, but our auditory system is sensitive. The brain can detect small differences in timing and intensity between the two ears—and then use these differences to localize the source (Middlebrooks & Green, 1991). This process is shown in Figure 3.13.

Auditory localization is not always so easy. If you're at a noisy gathering and someone directly behind you calls your name, both ears will receive the input at the same time and at the same intensity. What then? Lacking physical cues to locate the source, you will turn your head as though it were a radar dish in an effort to produce controlled differences in the timing and intensity of the signals to the two ears. The objective in such circumstances is to "fine-tune" the reception of information.

Hearing Disabilities   It's natural to take your sensory competence for granted—until you don't have it. In fact, millions of people have hearing impairments that range from a partial loss to profound deafness. There are two kinds of hearing impairment. The symptoms are the same, but the causes and treatment are very different. One type is **conduction deafness,** in which damage to the eardrum or to the bones in the middle ear diminishes their ability to conduct sound waves. Fortunately, hearing can be partially restored through surgery or by means of a hearing aid that amplifies sound waves—provided that the inner-ear structures are intact. A far more serious problem is **nerve deafness,** in which there is inner-ear damage to the

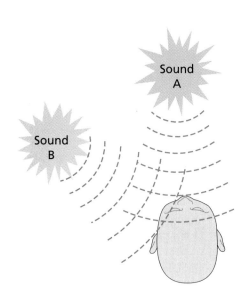

Figure 3.13

Auditory Localization

The brain is able to detect small differences in the timing and intensity of sound between the two ears—and can use these differences to localize the source.

■ **auditory localization** The ability to judge the direction a sound is coming from.

■ **conduction deafness** Hearing loss caused by damage to the eardrum or bones in the middle ear.

■ **nerve deafness** Hearing loss caused by damage to the structures of the inner ear.

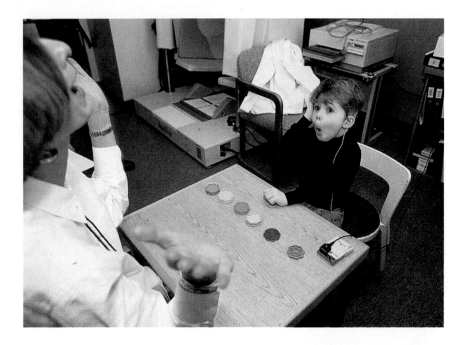

With the help of a surgical implant that stimulates the auditory nerve, this four-year-old boy—who has been deaf since birth—is hearing sound for the first time in his life.

cochlea, hair cells, or auditory nerve. Once neural tissue is destroyed, it cannot be repaired or replaced—and conventional hearing aids do not help. Nerve deafness can be caused by certain diseases, by biological changes due to old age, or by exposure to intensely loud noises (see box, p. 100).

Conventional hearing aids cannot restore hearing in nerve deafness, and researchers are uncertain as to whether it will ever be possible to regenerate damaged auditory hair cells in humans (Corwin & Cotanche, 1988; Warchol et al., 1993). But researchers are now developing artificial cochlea implants, or "bionic ears." Intended for people with damaged hair cells, this device has a tiny microphone in the outer ear that sends sound to a miniature electrode implanted in the cochlea. This electrode stimulates the auditory nerve—and an impulse is fired to the brain. Cochlea implants may enable many people who are profoundly deaf to detect the presence of sound, perhaps for the first time. Granted, the sensations produced by these devices are crude. A patient can detect changes in volume and pitch, but cannot distinguish between different words (Mulder et al., 1992; Townsend et al., 1987). Still, this development is a promising one.

Other Senses

Psychologists know more about seeing and hearing than about other sensory systems, but these other systems are just as essential to the adaptive human package. You can't see or hear the heat of a fire, the sting of a bee, the stench of a gas leak, or the bitter taste of a poisonous plant. Nor can you see or hear the sensuous pleasures of a scent-filled rose, a creamy Swiss chocolate, or a soothing massage. To get along, human beings have developed the ability to detect, process, and integrate information from many sources.

Thanks to their acute sense of smell, trained dogs can sniff out tiny leaks in underground pipelines that carry oil, gas, and chemicals.

Smell   Dogs are known for their ability to sniff out faint scents, and to track down animals, criminals, and illegal drugs over time and long distances. In a contest of smelling ability, we would have little to brag about compared to our canine buddies—who may have the keenest noses in the whole animal kingdom (Marshall & Moulton, 1981). But our own sense of smell, the product of the body's **olfactory system,** is more sensitive than you may realize—and more important.

All smells have a chemical origin (Bartoshuck & Beauchamp, 1994). Depending on their molecular structure, substances emit odor-causing molecules into the air. Some objects, such as glass and metal, have no smell (any scent these objects may emit comes from impurities on the surface). Others, like the musk oil extracted from animal sweat glands, produce overpowering odors. By breathing through the nose and mouth, we inhale these airborne odorant molecules—which dissolve and become trapped by *olfactory receptors* in the moist yellow lining of the upper nasal passages just above the roof of the mouth. There are about 10 million of these hair-like receptors in the human nose (the average dog has 200 million!). Once activated, they trigger an action potential in the *olfactory nerve* (Firestein & Werblin, 1989). This nerve connects the nose to the *olfactory bulb,* a bean-sized organ that distributes information throughout the cortex and to the nearby limbic-system structures that control memory and emotion. Interestingly, smell is the only sensation that is not routed to the cortex through the thalamus. The olfactory bulb is its own private relay station (see Figure 3.14).

Unlike other animals, humans do not need a sense of smell to mark their territory, signal danger, establish dominance hierarchies, or attract a mate. Furthermore, as language does not provide an adequate supply of olfaction

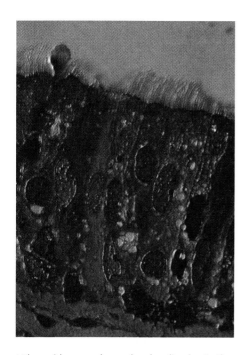

When airborne odor molecules dissolve in the nose, they are trapped by the hair-like olfactory receptors shown in this picture.

Figure 3.14

The Olfactory System

Once in the nose, odorant molecules are trapped by olfactory receptors. These receptors send signals through the olfactory nerve to the olfactory bulb, which communicates with various parts of the brain.

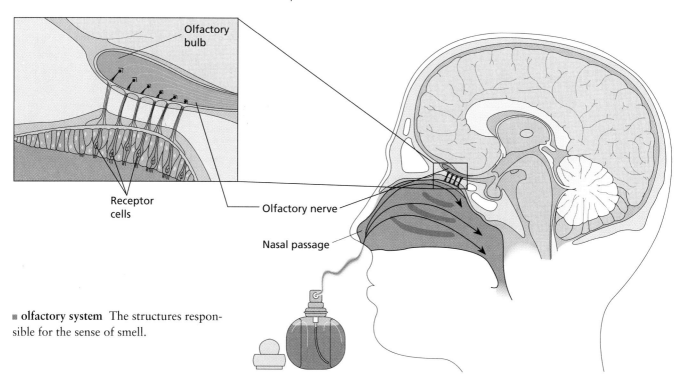

Olfactory bulb

Receptor cells

Olfactory nerve

Nasal passage

■ **olfactory system** The structures responsible for the sense of smell.

BIOLOGICAL PSYCHOLOGY   Environment

Noise and Your Hearing

When I was a teenager, my parents would warn me that the constant blaring of my stereo and the Grateful Dead marathons I went to would "hurt my ears." "Parents," I muttered to myself. "What do they know?" Sure, my ears would be ringing after a rock concert, and sure, voices would seem muffled for a while, but my ears were back to normal the next day. Or were they?

It is estimated that 28 million Americans—more than 10 percent of the population—suffer serious hearing loss. Often this hearing loss is due to exposure to loud noise, and often the victims are adolescents and children. Indeed, researchers are now convinced that exposure to intense noise can cause such violent vibrations in the inner ear that it can damage hair cells and permanently impair hearing. When does "sound" become "noise"? When does "loud" become "too loud"? The amplitude of a sound, which determines its loudness to the human ear, is measured in decibels (dB). To fully understand this scale, it's important to know that loudness doubles with every increase of 10 dBs. (An increase from 0 to 100 dBs thus produces a 10-billion-fold increase in loudness!) Constant daily exposure to sounds over 85 decibels (heavy street traffic, jackhammers, subways, and machinery) can,

over time, flatten the inner-ear hair cells and cause a gradual loss of hearing. Even a brief assault by an ear-shattering sound that exceeds 140 dBs (a gunshot, explosion, or rocket launch) can tear the delicate inner-ear tissues and cause permanent hearing loss. Look again at the figure, and you'll see that danger to the ear is all around us.

Most current research addresses the occupational hazards of noise in factories, airports, construction sites, and other work settings. But there's also a lot of concern about exposures to amplified music vibrating from huge speakers. Spend two hours at a rock concert, or turn the stereo volume up to full blast, and you're listening to 110 or 120 dBs—and putting your ears at risk (West & Evans, 1990). In fact, many experts claim that if your Walkman can be heard by someone near you, then you are damaging your ears. And the loss can be irreversible. Peter Townshend of the "Who" and Jeff Baxter of the "Doobie Brothers" are just two of several rock musicians who are now partially deaf. According to audiologist Dean Garstecki, director of a hearing impairment program, "We've got 21-year-olds walking around with hearing loss patterns of people 40 years their senior" (Toufexis, 1991).

Much of the noise that surrounds us is unavoidable. But

"Smells are surer than sounds or sights to make your heartstrings crack."

RUDYARD KIPLING

words, it's hard for people to describe smells (Richardson & Zucco, 1989). Yet the millions of olfactory receptors in the nose do enable us to distinguish among 10,000 different odors (Buck & Axel, 1991)—including the proposed "primary" odors of vinegar, roses, mint, rotten egg, mothballs, dry-cleaning fluid, and musk oil (Amoore et al., 1964). Many smells have powerful effects on people all over the world. (Perhaps that's why so much money is spent on deodorants, mint-flavored mouthwashes, pine- and lemon-scented air fresheners, herbal shampoos, and perfumes.) The olfactory bulbs are closely linked to the limbic system, so it is not that surprising that familiar smells—a whiff of cologne, a musty attic, or holiday food cooking in the oven—often bring on a rush of memories and emotions (Engen, 1982).

Our sense of smell is influenced by many factors. To begin with, individuals differ in their sensitivity. Helen Keller, who had a prodigious olfactory sense, wrote that she could often smell storms brewing. At the other end of the spectrum, some people suffer from *anosmia*, or "odor blindness." A serious head injury, viral infection, or toxic exposure can cause someone to lose all sense of smell permanently. But far more common are the millions of people who are unable to smell certain odors.

For reasons yet unknown, women outperform men at identifying odors (Doty et al., 1985). Odor sensitivity also changes with age. Young babies

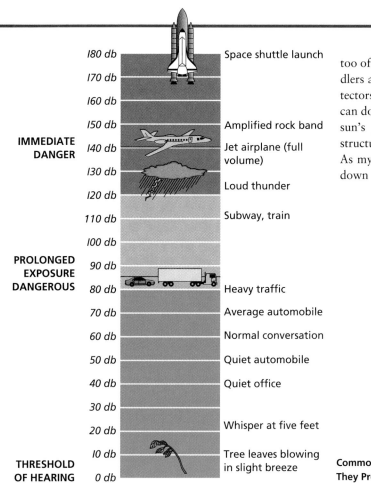

	180 db — Space shuttle launch
	170 db
	160 db
	150 db — Amplified rock band
IMMEDIATE DANGER	140 db — Jet airplane (full volume)
	130 db — Loud thunder
	120 db
	110 db — Subway, train
	100 db
PROLONGED EXPOSURE DANGEROUS	90 db
	80 db — Heavy traffic
	70 db — Average automobile
	60 db — Normal conversation
	50 db — Quiet automobile
	40 db — Quiet office
	30 db
	20 db — Whisper at five feet
	10 db — Tree leaves blowing in slight breeze
THRESHOLD OF HEARING	0 db

Common Sounds and the Amounts of Noise They Produce, in Decibels

too often people don't realize how harmful it is. Baggage handlers and others who work on airport runways wear ear protectors, which can muffle noise by about 35 dBs. Each of us can do the same if necessary. Just as you wouldn't stare at the sun's penetrating rays, you should not expose the delicate structures of your ears to piercing, high-volume sound waves. As my parents used to say, "Can't you just turn the volume down a little?"

cannot talk, but they do respond nonverbally to odor. Put a swab of honey under a baby's nose, and you may well see a smile. Put a swab of rotten egg under the nose, and the baby will grimace (Steiner, 1979). Even at the tender age of two weeks, nursing infants are more attracted to their own mothers' body odor than to that of other women (Cernoch & Porter, 1985). Among adults, olfactory sensitivity peaks in middle age and declines as people reach their seventies and eighties. This developmental trend was revealed in a *National Geographic* survey of 1.42 million people who responded to a scratch-and-sniff odor recognition test (Gilbert & Wysocki, 1987).

Smell is a primitive sense—yet so successful, suggests Diane Ackerman (1990), "that in time the small lump of olfactory tissue atop the nerve cord grew into a brain" (p. 20). Given this view, it's hardly surprising that researchers have tried to identify pheromones in human beings. **Pheromones** are chemicals secreted by animals that transmit signals to others, usually of the same species. Ants, bees, termites, and other insects secrete chemicals that attract mates and "release" other behaviors. Many mammals are also sexually excited by scent; for example, a female dog in heat sends neighboring male dogs into a state of frenzy. Are humans similarly aroused? If so, could the scent be manufactured and bottled? For perfumists, the potential is easy to imagine.

■ **pheromones** Chemicals secreted by animals that transmit signals to others, usually of the same species.

Smells can influence us in subtle but interesting ways. [Harris/Cartoonists & Writers Syndicate]

It may seem hard to believe, but if you slice an apple and an onion into small cubes, hold your nose, and conduct a blind taste test, you'll have trouble telling the two foods apart.

■ **gustatory system** The structures responsible for the sense of taste.

Studies show that people can recognize others by their body odor. In this research, various subjects would shower using the same soap and then wear a T-shirt for at least twenty-four hours. After the shirts were collected, subjects would sniff them and try to identify the wearer. The result: College students can usually recognize their own shirts, mothers can pick out the shirts worn by their own children, and people in general can discriminate by odor between the shirts worn by men and women (Russell, 1976). Is there any evidence for a *sexual* attractant in humans? Some perfumes currently found in stores contain *alpha androstenol*, a sexual pheromone secreted by male pigs (and also found in human underarm secretions). To date, there's not enough evidence one way or the other to draw a firm conclusion. We do know, however, that human sexuality is too complex to be chemically "controlled" by scent.

Taste   Taste is a product of the body's **gustatory system** (Simon & Roper, 1993). Like smell, it is a chemical sensation. Put a morsel of food or a squirt of drink in the mouth, and it will come into contact with clusters of receptor cells called *taste buds*. There are about ten thousand hair-like taste buds in the mouth. Some cling to the roof and back of the throat, but most line the trenches and bumps on the surface of the tongue. Within each taste bud, about fifty cells absorb the chemical molecules of food and drink—and trigger neural impulses that are routed to the thalamus and cortex. These cells are replaced every week, so if you burn your tongue on hot soup, the damage to your receptors will be repaired. The number of taste buds that dot the tongue diminishes with age. Children have more taste buds than adults do—which may explain why children are often so picky about eating "grown-up" foods. The more taste buds there are on your tongue, the more sensitive you are to various tastes (Miller & Reedy, 1990).

There are four primary tastes: sweet, salty, sour, and bitter. Each taste bud, and each region of the tongue, is more sensitive to one of these tastes than to the others. The taste buds at the tip are most responsive to sweet-tasting molecules; bitterness is detected in the back, sourness on the sides; and the receptors for saltiness are spread all over, but can be found mostly in the front and on the sides. A droplet of sugar will thus satisfy your sweet tooth most if you apply it to the tip of your tongue, where there is an abundance of sweet-sensitive receptors, while the mouth-puckering effects of lemon are greater when put on the sides than in the center (see Figure 3.15).

The *flavor* of a food is determined not only by its taste but by other factors as well. You may have noticed that after you've brushed your teeth in the morning, orange juice tastes bitter. And after you've eaten artichokes, water tastes sweet. The chemical residues from the substance already eaten mix with what you're eating to produce a new taste sensation. Temperature, texture, and appearance are also important factors, which is why no one likes warm soda or soggy potato chips, and why great chefs prepare dishes for the eye as well as for the palate. By far the most important determinant of flavor is odor. When I have a cold, and my nose is all stuffed up, I lose my appetite. For me, there is just no joy to chewing on food without flavor. Indeed, research shows that people lose their ability to identify common flavors—such as chocolate, vanilla, coffee, wine, and even onion and garlic—when they're prevented from smelling the food (Mozell et al., 1969).

(A) TASTE REGIONS OF THE TONGUE

Bitter
Sour
Salty
Sweet

(B) TASTE BUD

Taste pore
Hair
Supporting cell
Nerve fibers
Gustatory cell

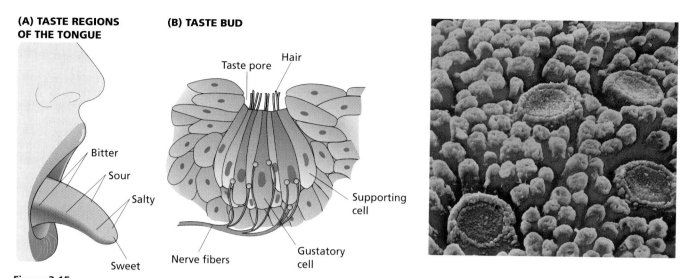

Figure 3.15

Taste Buds

Magnified 75 times, this photograph is of the surface of a human tongue. As shown, the taste buds are located in the large round areas called papillae.

Touch   Every organism has a sense of touch. Sea snails withdraw their gills at the slightest pressure. Sponges sense an intruder by feeling the water around them quiver. As for humans, often feeling is believing. Put up a "wet paint" sign, and you'll find, paradoxically, that it seems to invite touching rather than to inhibit it. Tactile sensations are unique in many ways. To begin with, touch is the only sensation with receptors that are not localized in a single region of the body. We need eyes to see, ears to hear, a nose to smell, and a tongue to taste. But the organ of touch, and the site of its sensory receptors, is *skin*.

Skin is by far the largest organ of the body. It covers two square yards and weighs six to ten pounds. It is multilayered, waterproof, elastic, and filled with hair follicles, sweat-gland ducts, and nerve endings that connect to the central nervous system (see Figure 3.16). When you consider all the

Figure 3.16

The Skin

This cross-sectional diagram illustrates the various types of nerve endings beneath the surface of the skin that connect to the central nervous system.

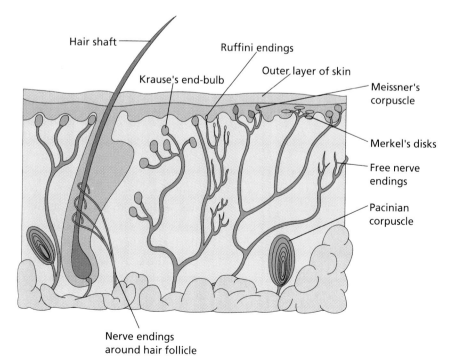

Hair shaft
Ruffini endings
Krause's end-bulb
Outer layer of skin
Meissner's corpuscle
Merkel's disks
Free nerve endings
Pacinian corpuscle
Nerve endings around hair follicle

sensations that emanate from your skin—feeling hot, cold, wet, dry, sore, itchy, scratchy, sticky, gooey, greasy, tingly, numb, and sharp pain—you can see that touch involves not one sensory system but many (Heller & Schiff, 1991).

The sensations of touch are vital for survival. Without it, you would not know that you're in danger of becoming frostbitten, or burned; you would not know if you've been stung by a bee; you would be unable to swallow food. When other sensory systems fail, touch takes on even more importance. All of us can feel the distinctions between leather, sandpaper, brick, cork, velvet, and other textures (Hollins et al., 1993). But for Virgil, the blind man whose eyesight was temporarily restored, shapes and textures are particularly important for recognizing objects. When passed a bowl of fruit, he could easily tell the difference between a slick plum, a soft fuzzy peach, a smooth nectarine, and a rough dimpled orange. He was even able to "see" through the disguise of an artificial wax pear that had fooled everyone else. "It's a candle," he said at once, "shaped like a bell or a pear" (Sacks, 1993, p. 72).

It's important to distinguish between passive and active touch. In passive touch, a person's skin is contacted by another object, as when a cat rubs up against your leg. In active touch, it is the person who initiates the contact, as when you pet your cat. Psychologically, the effects are different. For example, James Gibson (1962) tested subjects for their ability to identify shapes from cookie cutters shaped like stars, triangles, circles, and so on. When the objects were pressed lightly onto the hand (passive), they were identified correctly 29 percent of the time. When the subjects actively explored the shapes with their fingers, the accuracy rate increased to 95 percent. Active touch is what allows Virgil to feel the differences among plums, peaches, oranges, and nectarines. It is also the key to *Braille*, the alphanumeric system that allows many blind people to read. Braille letters and numbers consist of coded patterns of raised dots on a page that readers scan with their fingertips (see photo). Some Braille readers can achieve a reading rate as high as 200 words per minute—which is remarkable considering that the average rate among sighted readers is 250 words per minute (Foulke, 1991).

Most psychologists agree that the sense of touch consists of four basic types of sensations: pressure, warmth, cold, and pain. Researchers initially thought that there was a separate receptor in the skin for each of these four sensations, but it now appears that only *pressure* sensations have unique and specialized nerve endings dispersed throughout the body. One of the most striking aspects of touch is that sensitivity to pressure or vibration is different from one part of the body to another. To determine the thresholds for touch (how much force it takes before a subject reports a feeling), researchers would apply a thin rod or wire to different areas of skin, and vary the pressure (Weinstein, 1968). Figure 3.17 shows that the hands, fingers, and face are the most sensitive areas, while the calves, thighs, and arms are the least sensitive. In all cases, pressure causes the nerve endings to fire messages through the spinal cord, brainstem, and thalamus en route to the somatosensory cortex (Cholewiak & Collins, 1991).

Temperature   Normal human body temperature is 98.6 degrees Fahrenheit, or 37 degrees Celsius (temperatures at the surface of the skin are

Using Braille, blind people learn to read by running their fingers over coded patterns of raised dots.

Figure 3.17

Sensitivity to Touch

Thresholds for touch are estimated by applying varying degrees of pressure to the skin (a lower threshold means greater sensitivity). Below are the average thresholds for male subjects (the relative values for females are similar but slightly lower overall). The genital areas, which are likely to contain the lowest thresholds, were not tested. [From S. Weinstein, "Intensive and Extensive Aspects of Tactile Sensitivity as a Function of Body Part, Sex, and Laterality." In D. R. Kenshalo (Ed.), The Skin Senses (pp. 195–218), 1968. Courtesy of Charles C. Thomas, Publisher, Springfield Illinois.]

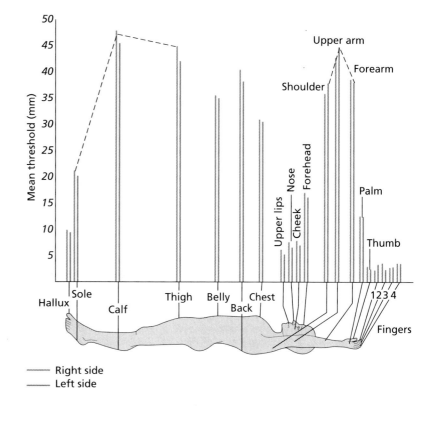

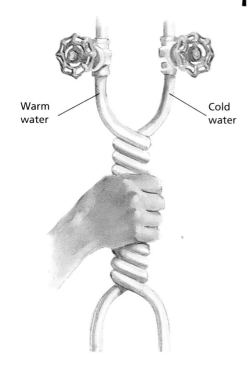

Figure 3.18

The Heat Grill

When people grasp two braided pipes—one with cold water running through it, the other with warm water—the sensation is "very hot."

slightly lower). There are two striking facts about the sensation of temperature. First is that it's largely *relative* to your current state. To demonstrate, fill three buckets with tap water—one cold, the second hot, and the third at room temperature. Place your right hand into the cold water and your left hand into the hot water, and leave them there for a minute. Then place both hands together into the third bucket. You can probably predict the amusing result: both hands are now in the same water, yet your right hand feels warm and your left hand feels cool. If you ever took the plunge into a cold pool or eased yourself into a hot tub, you know that the sensations are triggered by temperatures that are well above or below your own current "adaptation level" (Hensel, 1981).

The second fact about temperature is that there are really two separate sensory systems—one for signaling warmth, the other for signaling cold. Early studies showed that some spots on the skin respond more to warming, and others more to cooling (Dallenbach, 1927). "Hot" is a particularly intriguing sensation in that it is triggered when the warm and cold spots are simultaneously stimulated. Thus, when people grasp two braided pipes—one with cold water running through it, the other with warm water—they will pull away, complaining that the device is literally too hot to handle (see Figure 3.18). Apparently, the brain interprets the dual firing of both types of temperature receptors as being caused by a burning hot stimulus.

Pain   Pain is a dentist's drill boring through a tooth. Pain is stepping on a thumbtack. Pain is a pulled muscle, a splitting headache, a backache, sunburn blisters, and leg cramps. Ouch! Whatever the source, people are understandably motivated to avoid and escape from pain. Yet pain is crucial to survival because it serves as a red flag, a warning system that signals

A few weeks before the 1994 Olympics, figure skater Nancy Kerrigan was clubbed in the knee. The sensation was quickly relayed to the spinal cord and brain, causing her to wince in pain and grab her leg. Kerrigan went on to win a silver medal.

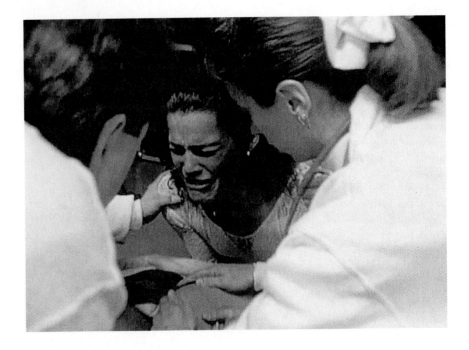

When asked by his dentist, "Where does it hurt?" philosopher Bertrand Russell replied: "In my mind, of course."

■ **gate-control theory** The theory that the spinal cord contains a neurological "gate" that blocks pain signals from the brain when flooded by competing signals.

danger and the risk of tissue damage. Life without pain may sound great, but it would be a life that is not likely to last very long. The case of a seven-year-old girl named Sarah illustrates the point. Born with a congenital indifference to pain, she often injures herself without realizing it. As a result, her body is scarred by burns, cuts, scrapes, and bruises (Restak, 1988).

Pain is a subjective, emotionally charged sensation. No single stimulus triggers pain the way that light does vision, no nerve endings in the skin are specially dedicated to pain over other sensations, and people with similar injuries often experience different degrees of pain. Clearly, the conditions that lead us to report pain include not only the threat of bodily harm but also culture, personality, expectations, and other factors. Theories of pain must take all of these factors into account (Fernandez & Turk, 1992).

Gate-control theory.   If you have a sore leg muscle, or if you scrape your knee, nerve endings in the skin send messages to the spinal cord through one of two types of nerve fibers. Dull, chronic aches and pains—as in a sore muscle—are carried to the spinal cord by "slow" thin nerve fibers that also respond to nonpainful touch. Sharp, acute, piercing sensations—as when you scrape your knee—are relayed through "fast" myelinated fibers. In short, an express lane to the spinal cord is reserved for acute, emergency-like sensations. But how are these signals then sent from the spinal cord to the brain? And can they be blocked when the pain is too intense to bear?

In answer to these questions, Ronald Melzack and Patrick Wall (1965) proposed the **gate-control theory** of pain. According to this theory, the nervous system can process only a limited number of sensory signals at once. When the system is full, a neural "gate" in the spinal cord either blocks or allows the upward passage of additional signals to the brain (the gate is not an actual structure but a pattern of inhibitory neural activity). Research shows that although Melzack and Wall were wrong about the physiological details of their theory, they were right about the key point—that pain signals to the brain can be blocked (Jessell & Kelly, 1991).

This theory has a valuable practical implication: that you can partially shut the gate on pain by creating competing sensations. If you fall and hurt your knee, rubbing it hard will send new impulses into the spinal cord— and inhibit other pain signals. That's one reason it often helps to put ice on a bruise or to scratch the skin near a mosquito bite. For chronic pain, such interventions as deep massage, electrical stimulation, and acupuncture may provide temporary relief in the same way. It seems paradoxical, but as the theory correctly suggests, you can ease the pain by causing additional pain.

What's nice about gate-control theory is the idea that our sensory system enables us to partially regulate how much pain we have to endure. To further help matters, our bodies send in reinforcements in the form of *endorphins*, neurotransmitters that are distributed throughout the central nervous system and are released in response to pain or discomfort (see Chapter 2). Studies show that endorphin-rich areas are also involved in the "gating" of pain signals—and that pain can be reduced by electrically stimulating these areas (Watkins & Mayer, 1982; Barbaro, 1988).

Psychological control. One psychological approach people often use is to block the pain from awareness. Just try not to think about it, okay? This advice sounds great, but beware: the strategy can backfire. Research shows that the more we try to suppress a particular thought, the more readily that thought pops to mind. Try not to think about the itch you're not supposed to scratch, and the harder you try, the less likely you are to succeed (Wegner, 1989).

Fortunately, there is a happy solution: focused self-distraction (McCaul & Malott, 1984). In a study of pain tolerance, Delia Cioffi and James Holloway (1993) had subjects put one hand into a bucket of ice-cold water and keep it there until they could no longer bear it. One group was instructed to avoid thinking about the sensations in the hand (suppression), while a second group was told to form a vivid mental picture of their room at home (distraction). Regardless of which strategy was used, most subjects kept their hand in the water for a little over two minutes. Afterward, however, subjects who had coped through suppression were slower to recover from the pain than those who had used distraction. To manage the effects of intense physical discomfort, you'd do better to focus on something specific ("think about the layout of your room") than try to suppress the thought ("don't think about the ice-cold water"). In prepared-childbirth classes, women are encouraged to cope with labor pains by staring at a "focal point" (it could be a key chain, a wall hanging, a door knob, or anything else) and concentrating on special breathing techniques. As we'll see in Chapter 4, hypnosis can also be used to combat pain, in part through a refocusing of attention. Mind over sensation.

Coordination The five traditional senses and their subdivisions are vital adaptive mechanisms, but by themselves they do not enable us to regulate sensory input through movement. To bend, lean, stretch, climb, turn the head, maintain an upright posture, and run from danger, we need to sense the parts of our bodies as well as our orientation in space. The **kinesthetic system** monitors the positions of various body parts in relation to each other. Just as vision comes to us through sensory receptors in the eye, coordination of movement is provided by receptors in the joints, tendons, and

■ **kinesthetic system** The set of structures distributed throughout the body that give us a sense of position and movement of body parts.

Fencing requires quickness, agility, and the coordination of movements provided by the kinesthetic system.

muscles. These receptors are linked to motor areas of the brain. Without this system, an acrobat could not turn somersaults and cartwheels. Nor could gymnasts, dancers, and athletes perform their feats of bodily magic. Nor, for that matter, could you and I walk upright, deliver a firm handshake, aim food into our mouths, or touch our noses with the tip of the index finger.

A related sensory mechanism is provided by the **vestibular system**, which monitors head tilt and location in space. Situated in the inner ear, this system has two parts: (1) the *semicircular canals*, three fluid-filled tubes that are set at right angles to one another, and (2) two *vestibular sacs*, which are also filled with fluid. Whenever you move about, the movement rotates and tilts your head, causing the fluid to slosh back and forth, which pushes tiny hair cells. In turn, these hair cells send impulses to the cerebellum, which signals from moment to moment whether you are sitting, lying down, or standing on your head. The vestibular system provides us with the sense of *equilibrium*, or balance. But sometimes this delicate sense is disrupted by an excess of fluid, or by certain types of motion. The result may be car sickness, sea sickness, or the dizzying aftereffects of twirling in circles (Howard, 1986).

Sensation: Keeping the Signals Straight

In a world filled with lights and colors, voices and musical tones, smells and tastes, and feelings of cold, warmth, pressure, pain, and other sensations, our sensory ability seems marvelously adaptive. How do we bring in so much information without becoming overwhelmed? With neural impulses flooding the brain from an array of different receptors throughout the body, it's amazing that we don't get our signals crossed. Why is it that we see light and hear sound rather than the other way around?

In a rare condition known as *synesthesia* ("joining the senses"), some people say they experience sensory "crossovers"—and thus report that bright lights are loud, that the sound of a jazz trumpet is hot, that colors

■ **vestibular system** The set of inner ear and brain structures that give us a sense of equilibrium.

■ **reversible figure** A drawing that one can perceive in different ways by reversing figure and ground.

Figure 3.19

Reversible Figures

What do you see—a young woman or an older woman? A rabbit or a duck? Visual input can be perceived in different ways.

An early version of this drawing was entitled "My wife and my mother-in-law" [From Wright, Edmond (1992): "The Original of E.G. Boring's 'Young Girl/Mother-in-law' drawing and its relation to the pattern of a joke", from *Perception,* volume 21, pages 273–275, figure 1. Reprinted by permission of Pion Limited, London and the author.]

"It may take a magician to pull a rabbit out of a hat, but we all possess sufficient magic to pull a duck out of a rabbit" (Shepard, 1990).

can be felt through touch, or that they can "taste the sound of raindrops" (Cytowic, 1989; Stein & Meredith, 1993). Although fascinating cases have been described, as in Richard Cytowic's (1993) book entitled *The Man Who Tasted Shapes,* the phenomenon is very rare. As a general rule, our sensory systems do not cross. After all, different receptors are sensitive only to certain types of energy and stimulate only certain nerve pathways to the brain. Rods are responsive to light, not sound, and they transmit impulses through the optic nerve, not the auditory nerve. There are some exceptions—as when pressing on a closed eyelid stimulates the optic nerve and causes you to "see" a flash of light—but each sensory system operates independent of the others (Martin, 1991).

There are two other aspects of sensation that enable us to respond to volumes of information without confusion. First, all of our sensory systems are designed to detect novelty, contrast, and change—not sameness. After constant exposure to a stimulus, sensation fades. This decline in sensitivity is known as *sensory adaptation.* We saw earlier that the eyes gradually adapt to bright light and darkness. The same is true of other senses. After a while, you simply get used to the new contact lenses in your eyes, the new watchband on your wrist, the noise level at work, the coldness of winter, or the musty odor in the hallway of your apartment. Indeed, by adapting to repeated stimulation, you are free to detect important changes in the environment.

A second adaptive mechanism is *selective attention.* As we will discover in Chapter 4, people can choose to focus on some sensory input and block out the rest. This selective attention enables us to pick out a face or a voice in a crowded room, or to find distractions from pain and discomfort. Parents thus can hear their baby cry over the sounds of a TV, traders on the floor of the stock exchange can hear orders to buy and sell amidst all the noise, and commuters in a city can spot yellow cabs in the street through all the commotion of rush-hour traffic. People are not passive sensation-recording devices. We have a way of "zooming in" on sensations that are personally important.

PERCEPTION

Our sensory systems convert physical energy from a multitude of sources into neural signals that are transmitted to the brain. But we do not see inverted retinal images, hear the bending and swaying of hair cells in the cochlea, or smell the absorption of odorant molecules in the nose. These and other sensations must be further processed to make sense. Perception is not just a "copying" process, and the brain does more than just serve as a sensory Xerox machine. As perceivers, we must select, organize, and interpret input from the world in ways that are adaptive. Putting the sensory pieces together is a "constructive" mental process.

To illustrate this point, look at the picture in Figure 3.19. What do you see? When I first saw it, I didn't hesitate to say it was an elegant young woman. Then I read the caption, which revealed that the picture is a **reversible figure** that could also be seen as an "old hag." Huh? I stared and stared, but I just could not see it. All of a sudden, I did a double take. There

■ **Gestalt psychology** A school of thought rooted in the idea that the whole (perception) is greater than the sum of its parts (sensation).

it was! The lines and shading had not changed, yet now I saw the woman's chin as a nose. I took another look a few minutes later, and once again all I could see was a young woman. The point is, visual input can be processed in different ways. The sensation may be the same, but the perception can vary.

When Virgil's eyesight was restored at the age of fifty, he was able to detect lights, shadows, colors, shapes, and textures, but he could not separate one figure from another or identify common objects just by looking at them. In busy settings such as a supermarket, he was so overwhelmed by sensory information that "everything ran together." In this section, we examine the ways in which the brain organizes and interprets sensory input. As in much of the research, we will focus on *visual* perception.

Perceptual Organization

In 1912, Max Wertheimer discovered that people perceive two stationary lights flashing in rapid succession as a single light moving back and forth. This illusion of apparent motion paved the way for **Gestalt psychology**—a school of thought arising in Germany that was founded on the premise that the whole (perception) is greater than the sum of its parts (sensation). The word *gestalt* is German for "pattern" or "whole," and gestalt psychologists believed that we have an inborn tendency to construct meaningful perceptions from fragments of sensory input. A classic example is the way people listen to music. A melody has a form that is different from the individual notes that make it up. So if the melody is transposed to another key, even if that means changing every note, listeners would still recognize the music because the form of the melody would be the same. The perception of music is based on a gestalt, not on a particular set of notes (Koffka, 1935; Kohler, 1947; Rock & Palmer, 1990).

Figure and Ground   The first gestalt principle of perceptual organization is that people automatically focus on some objects in the perceptual field to the exclusion of others. What we focus on is called the *figure*. Everything else fades into the *ground*. A teacher in front of a blackboard, an airplane in the sky, the printed black words on this page, the neon light that burns bright on a dark highway, a scream in the night, and the lead singer's voice in a rock band—all are common figures and grounds. Gestalt psychologists were quick to point out that these perceptions are in the eyes of the beholder—but also that people are prone to "figurize" objects that are novel, different, intense, loud, and moving rather than still. As in the reversible figure shown earlier, however, the image in Figure 3.20 illustrates that you can mentally flip-flop the figure and ground from one moment to the next. It is as if each of us is shining a spotlight on a portion of the sensory field— and can move that spotlight if necessary.

Gestalt Laws of Grouping   Another principle of perceptual organization is that we tend to group collections of shapes, sizes, colors, and other features into perceptual wholes. These natural grouping tendencies are not arbitrary; on the contrary, they follow rules like those illustrated in Figure 3.21. The gestalt psychologists have maintained that these tendencies are inborn, and they may have been right. Research shows that even infants

Figure 3.20

Figure and Ground

Depending on whether you see the white or black areas as figural, this drawing may be perceived as a vase or as two people facing each other.

"group" stimulus objects in the predicted ways (Kellman & Spelke, 1983; Quinn et al., 1993; Van Giffen & Haith, 1984).

Proximity. The closer objects are to one another, the more likely they are to be perceived as a unit. The lines in Figure 3.21(a) are thus seen as rows rather than as columns because they are nearer to one another horizontally than vertically.

Similarity. Objects that are similar in shape, size, color, or any other feature tend to be grouped together. The dots in Figure 3.21(b) form perceptual columns rather than rows because of similarities in color.

Figure 3.21

Gestalt Laws of Grouping

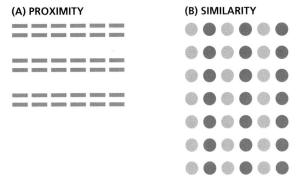

(A) PROXIMITY

(B) SIMILARITY

Continuity. People perceive the contours of straight and curved lines as continuous flowing patterns. In Figure 3.21(c), we see points 1 and 2 as belonging to one line, and points 3 and 4 as belonging to another. The same pattern could be seen as two V-shapes, but instead we perceive two smooth lines that form a cross in the center.

Closure. When there are gaps in a pattern that resembles a familiar form, as in Figure 3.21(d), people mentally "close" the gaps and perceive the object as a whole. This tendency enables us to recognize imperfect representations in hand drawings, written material, and so on.

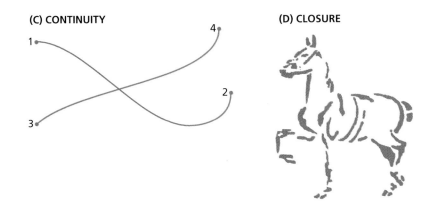

(C) CONTINUITY

(D) CLOSURE

Common fate. Extending upon the static grouping principles of proximity and similarity, we find that objects moving together in the same direction, or sharing a "common fate," are perceived as belonging to a single group. Examples include marching bands, schools of fish, flocks of birds, and sports fans sending the "wave" around a stadium.

By blending into the lily, this white-lipped green tree frog is concealed from predators by a natural form of camouflage.

The principles of gestalt psychology describe how people transform raw visual input—lights, shadows, lines, points, shapes, and colors—into meaningful displays. Indeed, the same principles explain the confusion that results when figures are concealed from view through camouflage. But what happens to our perception of an object when its retinal image changes from one moment to the next? How do we know that objects have depth when the images projected on the retina are flat and two-dimensional? How are interpretations of input influenced by characteristics of the perceiver? As we'll see, we are highly adept, yet often fooled, by disparities between sensation and perception.

Perceptual Constancies

Unlike a camera or microphone stationed on a tripod, the human perceiver is active and mobile. And unlike the portrait or landscape hanging on a wall, many of the objects of our perception are likewise active and mobile. As the perceiver and perceived move about, the image projected on the retina may change in size, shape, brightness, color, and other properties. But this is not a problem. Thanks to *perceptual constancies*, perceptions remain stable despite radical changes in sensory input.

Size Constancy   Size constancy is the tendency to view an object as constant despite changes in the size of its image on the retina. You've noticed this phenomenon countless times. You'll be watching from the ground as an airplane pokes its nose through a cloud to descend for a landing. Or a friend will walk away and eventually fade into the distance. Close your eyes and construct these moving pictures. As the plane approaches, its image looms larger and larger. And as your friend walks away, the image gets smaller. If you didn't know better, these changing sensations might lead you to think that the airplane was growing and that your friend was shrinking right before your eyes (see Figure 3.22).

But we do know better—for two reasons. One has to do with experience and familiarity. You know that airplanes are bigger than people and that people are bigger than insects, so your perceptions are stable despite variations in retinal image size. Distance cues provide a second source of information. As objects move around in space, we perceive the change in distance and adjust our size perceptions accordingly. In other words, we know that the closer an object is, the larger the image it casts on the retina, so we make a perceptual adjustment. This skill is so basic that it can be observed in infants, shortly after birth. To demonstrate, Alan Slater and his colleagues (1990) presented newborns in a maternity ward with a large or small black-and-white block. After they became familiarized to it, they were shown either the same block at a different distance or a different sized (larger or smaller) block. Did the babies recognize the familiar block when distance was varied? Infants are visually attracted to novel objects, so the researchers recorded their eye movements as the blocks were shown. The result: They spent more time looking at a new block than at an old block presented at a different distance. Through size constancy, they "recognized" the original blocks despite the change in distance.

The capacity for size constancy may be present in infancy, but cultural experience also plays a role. In 1961, anthropologist Colin Turnbull stud-

■ **size constancy** The tendency to view an object as constant in size despite changes in the size of the retinal image.

Figure 3.22

Size Constancy

Note how these women appear to be the same size even though their images shrink with distance.

ied Pygmies who lived in a densely wooded central African forest. At one point, he took a native named Kenge for a Jeep ride out of the forest. It was Kenge's first trip away from home—and he was disoriented. Standing on a mountain overlooking miles and miles of open plain, Kenge saw buffaloes and thought they were insects. Then he saw a fishing boat in the middle of a lake and thought it was a floating piece of wood. The problem? Turnbull came to realize that "in the forest the range of vision is so limited that there is no great need to make an automatic allowance for distance when judging size" (1961, p. 252). As for the rest of us, the perceived link between size and distance makes us vulnerable to some striking illusions (see Figure 3.23).

Shape Constancy   Also important is **shape constancy**, the tendency to see an object as retaining its form despite changes in its orientation. Take a coin, hold it up at eye level so that the "head" side faces you, and it will reveal a circular appearance. Rotate it 45 degrees, and it casts an elliptical, egg-shaped image on the retina. Turn it another 45 degrees, and it looks like a straight line. These changes in orientation are dramatic, yet you still perceive the coin as a flat, circular object (see Figure 3.24). As with size, shape constancy is inborn. But it may require visual experience. That is why Virgil found it difficult to recognize moving objects—including his own pet dog—when seen from another angle of view (Sacks, 1993).

Depth and Dimension

Perceptual constancies enable us to identify objects despite changes in sensory input. But there's another problem: How do we know that objects in three-dimensional space have depth, and how do we perceive distance,

■ **shape constancy** The tendency to see an object as retaining its form despite changes in orientation.

Figure 3.23

Size Constancy Illusions

With images of the same size, the one that seems farther away is seen as larger. In this sketch, the size difference is just an illusion.

Adelbert Ames designed this room to distort perceptions of size. The room seems rectangular, which makes the two figures look equally distant. But the right corner is closer to the peephole (and has a lower ceiling) than the left. The person on the right is thus perceived as bigger because distance cues are masked.

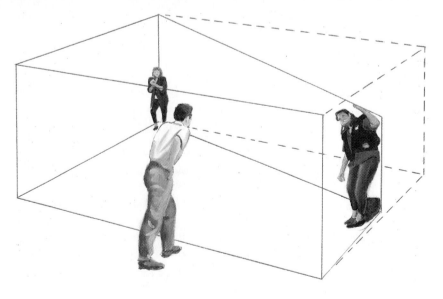

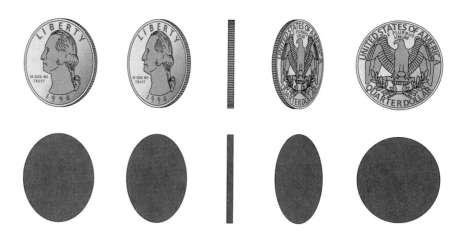

Figure 3.24

Shape Constancy

People see objects as retaining their form despite changes in their orientation.

when images projected on each retina are flat and two-dimensional? Two types of information are used in **depth perception**: binocular cues and monocular cues.

Binocular Depth Cues   Horses, cows, and other prey have eyes on the sides of their heads, so they can use peripheral vision to see predators sneaking up from behind. By contrast, lions, owls, and other predators have eyes squarely at the front of their heads, an arrangement that maximizes depth perception and enables them to track their prey. Look into the mirror, and you'll see that human eyes are the eyes of a predator. Thus we are provided with binocular (two-eyed) vision, which in turn allows us to use two binocular depth cues: convergence and binocular disparity.

Convergence refers to the fact that the eyes turn in toward the nose or "converge" as an object gets closer, and move outward or "diverge" to focus on objects farther away. Hold your finger up at arm's length and slowly move it toward your nose. As you refocus, you can actually feel your eye muscles contracting. This signals the brain about the object's distance from the eyes. The second cue is **binocular disparity**. With our eyes set about 2-1/2 inches apart on the face, each retina receives a slightly different image of the world. To demonstrate, hold your finger about four inches from your nose and shut your right eye. Then shut only your left eye and look at the finger. Right. Left. As you switch back and forth, you'll see that each eye picks up the image from a slightly different vantage point. Now hold up your finger farther away—say, at arm's length—and repeat the routine. This time you'll see less image-shifting. The reason: Binocular disparity decreases with distance. Special neurons located in the visual cortex use this retinal information to "calculate" depth, distance, and dimensionality (Mustillo, 1985).

If two eyes combine to give us a three-dimensional look at the world, can flat pictures do the same? In the nineteenth century, British physicist Charles Wheatstone invented the stereoscope, an optical instrument that brought two-dimensional pictures to life. To create a 3-D illusion, Wheatstone photographed a scene twice, using two cameras spaced inches apart. He then mounted both pictures side by side on the device, using mirrors to overlap the images. Today, the same technique underlies the "Viewmaster"—a children's toy that shows 3-D scenes through double-view cardboard slides.

■ **depth perception** The use of visual cues to estimate the depth and distance of objects.

■ **convergence** A binocular cue for depth perception involving the turning inward of the eyes as an object gets closer.

■ **binocular disparity** A binocular cue for depth perception whereby the closer an object is to a perceiver, the more different the image is in each retina.

■ **monocular depth cues** Distance cues, such as linear perspective, that enable us to perceive depth with one eye.

Monocular Depth Cues Binocular depth cues are useful at short distances. But for objects that are farther away, convergence and binocular disparity are uninformative. At such times, we can utilize **monocular depth cues,** which enable us to perceive depth, quite literally with one eye closed. These are cues that many artists use to bring a flat canvas to life. What are they? Look at the pictures accompanying each description, and see for yourself.

Relative image size: We saw earlier that as the distance of an object increases, the size of its retinal image shrinks—and vice versa. Object size can thus be used to judge depth.

Texture gradient: As a collection of objects recedes into the horizon, they appear to be spaced more closely together, which makes the surface texture appear to become denser.

Relative image size.

Texture gradient.

Linear perspective: With distance, the parallel contours of highways, rivers, railroad tracks, and other row-like structures perceptually converge—and eventually reach a vanishing point. The more the lines converge, the greater the perceived distance.

Linear perspective.

[Cartoon by John Chase.]

Interposition: As most objects are not transparent, those nearer to us will partly or completely block our view of more distant objects. This overlap provides a quick and easy way to judge relative distances.

Atmospheric perspective: The air contains a haze of dust particles and moisture that blurs images at a distance. This blurring, or "atmospheric perspective," makes duller and less detailed objects appear farther away.

Interposition.

Atmospheric perspective.

Relative elevation: Below the horizon line, objects that are lower in our field of vision are seen as nearer than those that are higher. Above the horizon line, however, objects that are lower are perceived as farther away.

Relative elevation.

Motion parallax: As we move forward or backward, objects in the environment appear to move as well (anyone who has looked out the window of a moving car knows this). But the nature of this perceived movement depends on distance. Compared to what we're gazing at, closer objects seem to speed by in the opposite direction, while remote objects appear to move more slowly and in the same direction. Relative distances are thus revealed by the speed and direction of apparent movement.

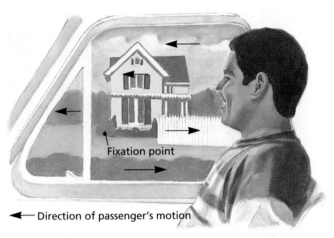

Fixation point

◄— Direction of passenger's motion

Motion parallax.

Familiarity: Experience provides familiar reference points for judging distance. We know the approximate size of houses, people, cars, and other objects, and this knowledge helps us judge their distance. In fact, the presence of a familiar object in a scene helps us judge the sizes and distances of everything around it.

Origins of Depth Perception   With normal vision, interpreting the layout of objects in an environment is easy, and requires no conscious thought or effort. Why is depth perception so easy? Clearly, a rich array of depth cues are available to one or both eyes—especially when we're moving about (Gibson, 1979). But how do we know how to interpret these cues? Assuming you're not a visual artist or mathematician, how do *you* so easily interpret angles of convergence, linear perspective, texture gradients, relative elevations, and other "geometric" types of information? How do you know that railroad tracks are parallel, even though they seem to converge? You may think that this is an odd question because, well, "you just know." But were you born with this skill, or did you learn it from experience?

Perceptual Experience   The average person has an enormous amount of experience with depth perception. Is this experience necessary? Case studies of blind people who had their eyesight surgically restored during adulthood suggest that experience is critical to depth perception. Sacks (1993) noted that Virgil sometimes stepped over shadows so he would not trip, or failed to step up on a staircase that, for all he knew, was a flat surface consisting

■ visual cliff An apparatus used to test depth perception in infants and animals.

of parallel and crossing lines. Richard Gregory (1990) studied a similar patient by the name of S.B., and described his perception of depth as "peculiar." At one point, S.B. thought he could touch the ground below his hospital window with his feet—even though his window was on the fourth floor.

Cross-cultural evidence also highlights the importance of perceptual experience and learning. We saw earlier that when a Pygmy named Kenge was taken from his dense forest home to the open plain, he saw distant buffaloes as insects and a large boat as a floating log. Similarly, researchers have found that in cultures where people seldom see three-dimensional representations in artwork, subjects have difficulty judging relative distance from pictures (Deregowski, 1989). Look at the sketches in Figure 3.25. Which animal would you say is closer to the hunter, the elephant or the antelope? Using monocular depth cues, you probably chose the antelope. But among Bantu natives in Africa, many subjects selected the elephant, which is physically closer on the page (Hudson, 1960).

Figure 3.25

Culture and Perception

Which animal is closer to the hunter? In cultures where people have little exposure to three-dimensional representations, many subjects chose the elephant, which is physically closer on the page.

Depth Perception as Inborn   Experience may seem necessary, but studies of infants suggest otherwise. Infants cannot tell us what they see, so Eleanor Gibson and Richard Walk (1960) devised the **visual cliff**, a clever nonverbal test of depth perception. As shown in Figure 3.26, the apparatus consists of a glass-covered table top, with a shallow one-inch drop on one end and a steep "cliff" on the other end. Infants ranging in age from six to

Figure 3.26

The Visual Cliff

This apparatus is used to test depth perception in infants and animals.

■ **perceptual set** The effects of prior experience and expectations on interpretations of sensory input.

fourteen months were placed in the middle of the table, and their mothers tried to lure them into crawling to one side or the other. The entire surface was covered by sturdy transparent glass, so there was no real danger. The result: At six months old, the babies would crawl to their mothers at the shallow end. But despite all the calling, clapping, waving, and encouragement, most babies did not crawl out over the cliff. Clearly, they had perceived the steepness of the drop.

Does the visual cliff experiment prove that depth perception is innate? Not necessarily, argued critics. Perceptual learning begins at birth, so by the tender age of six months an infant has already experienced well over a thousand waking hours—and lots of perceptual practice. What about babies younger than six months old? They're not able to crawl, but their bodies can communicate to an observant researcher. Accordingly, Joseph Campos and his colleagues (1970) moved two-month-old infants from one side of the glass top to the other, and found that the infants exhibited a change in heart rate when placed over the deep side but not over the shallow side. These infants were too young to fear the situation as you and I would, but they did "notice" the difference. Indeed, additional studies have shown that most newborn lambs, chicks, ducklings, pigs, cats, rats, and other animals that can walk the day they're born also avoid the deep end of the visual cliff (Walk, 1981).

Is depth perception innate, or is it the product of visual experience? As the pieces of the puzzle have come together, it seems that both factors are at work. Using binocular cues—and, later, monocular cues—infants are capable of perceiving depth and dimension. But early experience is necessary for this capability to emerge. Thus, newborn rats and cats that are initially reared in a dark laboratory step over the visual cliff when first tested—and formerly blind humans have trouble making judgments of depth when their eyesight is surgically restored. As the saying goes, you have to "use it or lose it."

Perceptual Set

At any given moment, your interpretation of sensory input can be influenced by prior experiences and expectations, which create a **perceptual set**. To illustrate, look at Figure 3.27. The middle drawings in this series are ambiguous: they can be seen as either a man's face or the figure of a kneeling young woman. Which do you see? As it turns out, interpretations are biased by prior experience. Subjects who were first shown the drawing on the far left saw the middle pictures as a man's face, while those who were first shown the drawing on the far right saw the same pictures as a woman's figure (Fisher, 1968). This finding highlights an important point about perception: at times, we see what we expect to see.

Figure 3.27

Perceptual Set

What you see in the middle drawings depends on the order in which you look at the pictures. Subjects who start at the far left see the drawings in the middle as a man's face; those who start at the far right see a woman's figure.

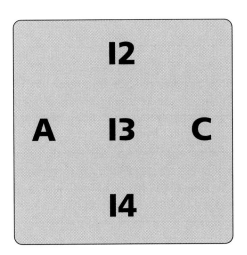

Figure 3.28

Context Effects

Indicating the effects of context on perception, people see the middle item as *B* or *13* depending on whether it is surrounded by letters or numbers.

Sometimes perception is influenced not only by what we *expect* to see but by what we *want* to see. [Drawing by Stevenson; © 1991 The New Yorker Magazine, Inc.]

Perceptual sets are established not only by past experience but also by the context in which a stimulus is perceived. In Figure 3.28, for example, the same physical pattern of black and white is used for the letter *B* as for the number *13*. Look closely and you'll see that the *B* and the *13* are physically identical. Which of the two you "see" thus depends on whether the surrounding context consists of letters or numbers. The same phenomenon may also influence our perceptions of others. For example, subjects examined photographs of people, each with a neutral expression on his face. When the target person was supposedly being threatened by a vicious dog, subjects saw his facial expression as fearful; when told that he had just won money in a TV game show, subjects interpreted the very *same* expression as a sign of happiness (Trope, 1986).

By leading us to see what we expect to see, perceptual sets can lead us astray. Imagine that you're looking at a slide that is completely out of focus. Gradually, it is focused enough so that the image becomes less blurry. At each step, the experimenter asks, Can you recognize the picture? The response you're likely to make is interesting. Subjects have more trouble identifying the picture if they watch the gradual focusing procedure than if they simply view the final image. In trying to interpret the initially blurry image, subjects exposed to gradual focusing formed perceptual sets that later interfered with their ability to "see straight" once presented with improved evidence (Bruner & Potter, 1964). Similarly, people are slower to identify common objects such as toothbrushes and fire hydrants when such objects are presented "out of context" (Biederman, 1987).

The World of Illusions

"The eye, or really the mind behind the eye, can be tricked into interpretive flips or mental somersaults."

ROGER N. SHEPARD

The brain's capacity to transform sensations into accurate perceptions of reality is impressive. Without conscious thought, effort, or instruction, we often manage to perceive size, shape, depth, and other properties in an accurate manner. But the mind also plays tricks on us. Magicians, ventriloquists, and artists count on it. So do perception psychologists. Over the

■ **perceptual illusions** Patterns of sensory input that give rise to misperceptions.

years, researchers have learned a good deal about how people perceive the world by probing the systematic ways in which we *mis*perceive the world. **Perceptual illusions** are all around us (Block & Yuker, 1989; Wade, 1990). A few examples illustrate the point.

■ A puddle glistens on the highway in front of you. It seems about a mile away. But as you drive, the road stays dry and the wet spot remains out of reach. There is no puddle, of course, just a "mirage"—an illusion caused by a layer of hot air sitting below cooler air and casting a reflection from the sky onto the road.

■ Baseball players claim that many pitchers throw a "rising fastball." But the laws of physics state that this is impossible. So why do players insist that they can see the fastball rise? Apparently, it's an illusion that occurs when the batter underestimates the speed of a fast pitch (Bahill & Karnavas, 1993).

■ If you've ever driven through St. Louis, then you've seen the towering Gateway Arch. Look at the picture of it below. Is the arch taller than it is wide? Most people say yes—and this illustrates the common "horizontal-vertical illusion." In fact, the height and width of the Gateway Arch are both 630 feet.

The horizontal-vertical illusion can be seen in the St. Louis Gateway Arch and in the perpendicular lines in the drawing to the right.

What's interesting about perceptual illusions is that they often stem from the overapplication of rules that normally serve us well. Look at the two vertical lines with the arrowed tips in Figure 3.29. Which is longer? Most people see the line on the right as slightly longer than the one on the left.

Figure 3.29

The Müller-Lyer Illusion

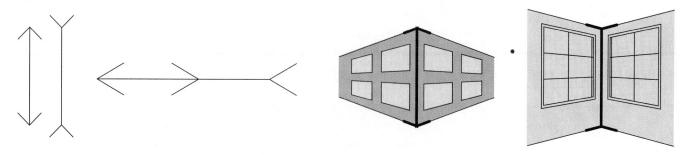

■ **Müller-Lyer illusion** An illusion in which the perceived length of a line is altered by the position of other lines that enclose it.

■ **Ponzo illusion** An illusion in which the perceived length of a line is affected by linear perspective cues.

Measure them, however, and you'll see that they are of the same length. Now compare the two sides of the horizontal line. Again, which is longer? Most people see these lines as equal. Wrong. In this case, the line on the left is longer than the one on the right. As devised by Franz Müller-Lyer (1889), these comparisons illustrate the classic **Müller-Lyer illusion**.

Why is the Müller-Lyer illusion so compelling? There are several possible explanations (Nijhawan, 1991). One is that the arrowed tips trick us into overapplying linear-perspective depth cues and the principle of size constancy. As also shown in Figure 3.29, the vertical configuration on the left side resembles the near outside corner of a room or building, while that on the right resembles a far inside corner. Since both lines cast equal-sized retinal images, we assume that the farther one must be larger. Part of the problem, then, is that people mistakenly apply a rational rule of three-dimensional depth perception—that distance decreases image size—to a flat two-dimensional figure (Gregory, 1990).

Look at the horizontal lines in Figure 3.30, and you'll see a second illusion. The tendency of most people to view the horizontal line on top as longer than the one on the bottom is called the **Ponzo illusion**. Can you see

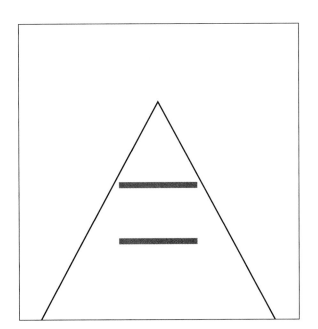

Figure 3.30

The Ponzo Illusion

why this misperception is so common? Think again about depth perception, and you may notice that the linear perspective that provides the context for these lines makes the top one seem farther away. As in the Müller-Lyer illusion, the two lines cast the same-sized retinal image, so the one that seems more distant is perceived to be larger. In fact, the more depth-perception cues there are in the background, the stronger is the illusion (Leibowitz et al., 1969). Consistent with this explanation is the fact that people from certain African tribes who live in rural "noncarpentered" environments—without right angles, corners, squares, and hard edges—are less likely to be fooled by the Müller-Lyer and Ponzo illusions (Deregowski, 1989; Segall et al., 1966).

■ **moon illusion** The tendency for people to see the moon as larger when it's low on the horizon than when it's overhead.

A third illusion that seems to stem from depth-related cues is the most spectacular but also the most puzzling. Have you ever noticed how a full moon looks much larger when it's low over the horizon than when it's high in the sky? The moon is the moon, of course. It does not change in size or in its distance from the earth. So, what causes this **moon illusion?**

Throughout history, scholars have tried to understand this phenomenon. Then, in 1962, Lloyd Kaufman and Irvin Rock brought it to the attention of perception psychologists, stimulating numerous theories and explanations. Some psychologists claimed that the increased perceived size is caused by buildings, trees, and other earth-bound depth cues that make the moon seem farther away and thus trick us into "seeing" a larger object. Indeed, if you peer at the low moon through a tube, apart from surrounding cues, it will appear smaller. But others have found that people sometimes perceive the horizon moon as closer, not more distant (Coren & Aks, 1990), that the illusion cannot be recreated when the target object is a star rather than the moon (Reed & Krupinski, 1992), and that the illusion persists even when the moon is projected at different angles without depth cues, as in the total darkness of an indoor planetarium (Suzuki, 1991). To this day, the moon illusion remains a perceptual mystery (Hershenson, 1989).

The moon illusion. Viewed low over the San Francisco skyline (left), the moon seems larger than when it is higher in the sky (right).

EXTRASENSORY PERCEPTION

Every New Year's Eve, "psychics" make predictions for the year to come. From political fortunes to natural disasters, the soothsayers among us claim they can see the future the way you and I see the sun rise and set. Can they really? With varying degrees of accuracy, scientists make predictions all the time. Astronomers tell us when we will see the next solar eclipse, economists forecast inflation rates, and meteorologists warn us about upcoming

■ **parapsychology** The study of ESP and other claims that cannot be explained by existing principles of science.

storms. But there's a difference between these forms of prediction and psychic fortune-telling. Scientists base their predictions on sensory input, whereas psychics claim to have *extrasensory perception,* or *ESP*—an ability to perceive in the absence of ordinary sensory information.

Psychologists as a group have long been skeptical, if not downright cynical, about these claims. Indeed, this entire chapter is dedicated to the proposition that perception is the product of *physical* energy received by *sensory* receptors and interpreted by the *brain.* Yet pollsters consistently find that over half of all Americans believe in ESP—more than the number who believe in evolution! So, what is the basis for this belief? Are there people who can read your mind, levitate or move objects without contact, have "out of body" experiences, communicate with ghosts, see the future in dreams, or identify serial killers for the police? In order to evaluate the evidence, we must first make some distinctions.

The Case for ESP

The claims vary far and wide, but **parapsychologists**—who study psychic phenomena through case studies and experiments—distinguish among three types of extrasensory power (Broughton, 1991). The first is *telepathy,* or mind-to-mind communication, an ability to receive thoughts transmitted by another person without the usual sensory contact. The second type is *clairvoyance,* the ability to perceive remote events via "extra" sensory channels or contact with another person. The third type is *precognition,* the ability to see future events, also without direct contact with another person. Whatever the details, these phenomena are all thought to involve the same power: perception without sensation (some psychics also claim to have *telekinesis,* the ability to move objects or influence events without material contact).

These are the claims. Why, then, are there so many believers? And what's the evidence? According to Thomas Gilovich (1991), the reason for widespread public acceptance of ESP is that the evidence "seems" overwhelming. Stage magicians, TV psychics, paperbacks that generate millions of dollars from tales of the occult, coincidences that supposedly defy explanation, and the friend who has a premonition come true, all conspire to leave the impression that where there's smoke, there must be fire. So, where's the fire?

In the 1930s, Duke University professor J. B. Rhine sought for the first time to document ESP through rigorous laboratory experiments. Considered by many to be the founder of parapsychology, Rhine devised a special set of ESP cards, each designated by a distinct, easy-to-recall symbol on one side (see Figure 3.31). Subjects were asked to guess the symbol on each card, and the number of "hits" was compared to "chance" performance (for 25 cards, subjects can be expected by pure guesswork to make 5 correct responses). This procedure was used to test telepathy (a "sender" looked at the cards and the subject tried to read his or her mind), clairvoyance (the cards were placed face down), and precognition (the subject predicted the sequence of cards before the deck was shuffled). In many hours of painstaking research, Rhine obtained close to 100,000 responses from various subjects. Then, in 1934, he reported the results: using a 25-card

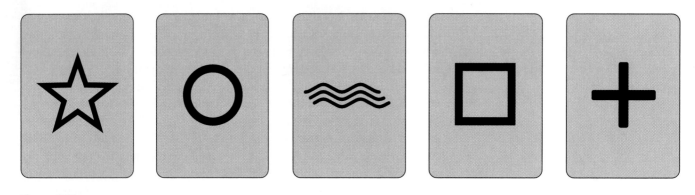

Figure 3.31

ESP Cards

As devised by Rhine (1934), these five arbitrary symbols have been used in hundreds of ESP experiments.

deck, subjects averaged 7.1 correct identifications—a statistically significant, and large, improvement over pure chance performance. The skeptics were baffled. Had they been too close-minded, like those who laughed at Galileo, Edison, and the Wright brothers, or like those who once used the term *impossible* to describe space travel and the splitting of the atom?

The Case Against ESP

In many ways, Rhine's (1934) studies were like so much of parapsychology's history—promising high points, inevitably followed by disappointment. Researchers scrutinized Rhine's methods and found that many subjects had been allowed to handle the cards, which made it possible to cheat; that the cards could be identified by warped edges, spots, and other physical marks; and that faint images of the symbols could be seen when held up to light. Worst of all, Rhine's most impressive subject could not replicate his performance for outside experimenters.

Over the years, hundreds of additional experiments were performed. Some provided what seemed to be clear and compelling "evidence" of psychic powers. But typically the findings obtained in one laboratory could not be reproduced in another. And often hoaxes were exposed. If you've ever watched a live stage psychic, you know how compelling the performance can be. Some mind readers have associates who circulate through a crowd before the show and spy on conversations, picking up personal information that can later be used. Another strategy is to use "multiple outs," which are statements that apply to almost anyone ("sometimes you are shy, yet at other times you're outgoing"). A third strategy is the "one-ahead" ploy in which audience members submit questions in sealed envelopes to be "read" without opening. Secretly, the psychic opens one envelope and memorizes its contents. Then he or she begins the performance by holding up and "reading" a second envelope. In fact, the first remembered message is recited. He or she then opens the second envelope, supposedly to confirm the prediction, and uses its contents to "read" a third envelope. This procedure can be repeated indefinitely, with the psychic always one step ahead of the mystified audience.

It's important to realize that many parapsychologists are exacting in their methods and honorably motivated to seek the truth. But it's also important to realize that many so-called psychics are frauds who use magic and illusion. In 1974, physician Andrew Weil investigated an Israeli psychic named

Uri Geller, who claimed that he could bend metal without touching it, start broken watches, and guess the contents of sealed envelopes. Apparently true to his word, Geller was able to perform these remarkable feats and convinced Weil of his psychic powers. Then Weil met James Randi, a famous magician. Amazingly, Randi duplicated many of Geller's feats—through trickery. Illustrating the power of perceptual sets, Weil marveled at how the mind (in this case, his own) "can impose its own interpretations on perceptions" and "see what it expects to see."

The Continuing Controversy

So, what are we to conclude? Some forms of ESP, such as the ability to "will" the movement of objects, openly defy the laws of physics. But many parapsychologists argue for the possibility that people can receive messages from others through a sensory medium that simply has yet to be identified—and they point to rigorous new studies as evidence of this phenomenon (Broughton, 1991).

Today, ESP researchers use the "Ganzfield Procedure" in which a "receiver" relaxes in a reclining chair in a soundproof chamber. A red floodlight is shined at the eyes, which are covered by ping-pong ball halves. Headphones placed over the ears play continuous white noise. In a separate room, a "sender" spends thirty minutes concentrating on a visual stimulus—it could be a drawing, photograph, or film. In the meantime, receivers talk aloud about what they are thinking. Afterward, they are given four stimuli and asked to rate the extent to which each one matches their earlier thoughts. Despite their lack of access to any sensory information, the receivers in these studies are reported to have achieved a 32 percent "hit" rate—which is statistically higher than the 25 percent expected by chance (Bem & Honorton, 1994).

Do these new studies prove that ESP exists? It depends on who you ask. Some critics point out that parapsychological research methods are still flawed in important ways, so they take a wait-and-see attitude (Hyman, 1994). Others, less patient, say that enough is enough. Reviews of the literature, they insist, have consistently shown that, despite thousands of studies, there is no sound empirical support, nor is there a single individual who can demonstrate ESP powers to independent investigators (Marks, 1986). Chairing a committee that spent two years studying ESP for the U.S. Army, John Swets concluded that "the committee finds no scientific justification from research conducted over a period of 130 years for the existence of para-psychological phenomena" (Swets & Bjork, 1990). So, what are we to conclude? What do *you* think? The one safe prediction I can make is that we have not heard the last of this perennial debate.

SUMMARY AND KEY TERMS

Through *sensation* we absorb raw energy with our sense organs. *Transduction* converts this energy into neural signals to the brain, and then we select, organize, and interpret the signals through *perception*. Sensation and perception are interconnected. But as the story of Virgil demonstrates, they involve different processes.

Measuring the Sensory Experience

Psychophysics uses special measuring procedures to study the link between physical stimuli and the sensations they arouse.

Absolute Thresholds

The *absolute threshold* is the smallest amount of stimulation an organism can detect. In research terms, this is the level at which a stimulus can be detected 50 percent of the time.

Signal-Detection Theory

The original work on absolute thresholds assumed that the stimulus alone determined the threshold. But *signal-detection theory* has led to a more sophisticated type of measurement that takes the subject's response bias into account.

Difference Thresholds

Researchers also measure the ability to detect differences between two levels of a stimulus. The smallest detectable change is called the difference threshold, or *just-noticeable difference* (*JND*). According to *Weber's law*, the JND is a constant proportion of the stimulus, so it increases as the stimulus increases.

Sensation

Humans have a number of distinct sensory modalities—more than the five senses that people commonly assume we possess.

Vision

The light we see is only a small band in the spectrum of electromagnetic radiation. The physical properties of light waves—wavelength, amplitude, and purity—correspond to our sensations of color, brightness, and saturation.

The human eye translates light waves into neural impulses. Light first passes through the *cornea,* which bends the light to focus it. Behind the cornea, the ring-shaped *iris* controls the size of the *pupil,* the hole through which light enters the eye. The *lens* then continues the task of focusing the light, becoming rounder for nearby objects and flatter for remote ones—a process called *accommodation.* After passing through the vitreous humor, the light hits the *retina,* a multilayered screen of photoreceptor cells. The *rods* in the retina are responsible for black-and-white vision in dim surroundings. The *cones,* which provide for color vision, are concentrated in the *fovea,* the center of the retina. With its millions of photoreceptors, the eye can adjust to lighting changes through both *dark adaptation* and *light adaptation.*

The rods and cones stimulate bipolar and ganglion cells that intergrate the information they receive and pass it on to the *optic nerve,* composed of the axon fibers of the ganglion cells. Since the area where the optic nerve enters the eye has no rods or cones, each eye has a *blind spot.*

The two optic nerves meet at the optic chiasm, where the axons split up so that fibers from inside half of each eye cross to the opposite side of the brain. The fibers travel through the thalamus to the brain's visual cortex. There the image is processed by specialized neurons called feature detectors.

There are two theories of color vision. According to the *trichromatic theory,* the human eye has three types of cones, sensitive to red, green, and blue, respectively. However, this theory cannot explain *afterimages,* the visual sensations that linger after prolonged exposure to a stimulus. The *opponent-process theory* also assumes the existence of three types of photoreceptors, but it contends that each kind responds to a pair of "opponent" colors. Recent research suggests that both theories are correct. The retina contains the types of cones described by the trichromatic theory, but neurons in the thalamus operate in accordance with the opponent-process theory.

Hearing

The stimulus for *audition,* or hearing, is sound—vibrations in air molecules caused by movement of an object. Our sensations of pitch, loudness, and timbre derive from the frequency, amplitude, and complexity of sound waves. *White noise* is the hissing sound we hear when all frequencies of the sound spectrum are combined.

Collected by the outer ear, sound waves travel through the auditory canal to vibrate the eardrum. The vibration then continues through the bones in the middle ear, the oval window of the inner ear, the fluid of the cochlea, and the basilar membrane, which excites hair cells that activate the auditory nerve. As with visual impulses, signals cross to the opposite side of the brain and pass through the thalamus before reaching the auditory cortex.

The remarkable faculties of human hearing include *auditory localization,* our ability to judge a sound's direction. Hearing impairments may involve *conduction deafness* (damage to the eardrum or middle-ear bones) or *nerve deafness* (damage to the inner ear).

Other Senses

Our sense of smell derives from the *olfactory system.* Odor-causing molecules dissolve and become trapped by receptors in the upper nasal passages, triggering the olfactory nerve. Instead of passing through the thalamus like other sensory information, the impulse goes to the olfactory bulb, which distributes the information to the cerebral cortex and to limbic structures. Because of this connection to the limbic system, smells often produce strong emotions. In fact, researchers are investigating whether humans secrete *pheromones,* chemicals that transmit signals to other humans.

Like smell, taste is a chemical sensation. The *gustatory system* begins with taste buds in the mouth, which absorb molecules in food or drink and trigger neural impulses to the thalamus and cortex. Each taste bud is most sensitive to one of the four primary tastes: sweet, salty, sour, and bitter. The flavor of food, however, depends on other factors as well, especially odor.

Touch is based in the skin, the body's largest organ. Touch actually involves many sensory systems, including the sensations of pressure, warmth, cold, and pain. Active touch, as used by Braille readers, produces much more information than passive touch.

Temperature is a sensation with two unusual aspects: it is generally relative to a person's current state, and it entails two separate sensory systems—one for signaling warmth, the other for signaling cold.

Pain is a subjective sensation with no single stimulus. The *gate-control theory* suggest that pain signals to the brain can be blocked when they become too intense. This theory explains why pain can often be eased by a competing sensation. Endorphins, the body's natural pain relievers, also help control pain, as does the psychological technique of distraction.

Our sense of coordination derives from the *kinesthetic system*. Receptors in the joints, tendons, and muscles, linked to motor areas of the brain, help us register the body's position and movements. Similarly, the *vestibular system* includes structures in the inner ear that monitor the head's tilt and location in space, giving us our sense of equilibrium.

Sensation: Keeping the Signals Straight

In the welter of sensations that confront us, three factors help us keep our signals straight. First, the different senses have different receptors. Second, our senses detect novelty rather than sameness; because of sensory adaptation, our sensitivity declines when a stimulus remains constant. Finally, selective attention allows us to focus on one input and to block out the rest.

Perception

Perception is not just a "copying" process. As a simple *reversible figure* demonstrates, perception involves selecting, organizing, and interpreting sensory information.

Perceptual Organization

Based on the idea that the whole (perception) is greater than the sum of its parts (sensation), *gestalt psychology* studies the way we construct meaningful perceptions. In any perceptual field, we focus on the figure and let the rest fade into the ground. We also group features into perceptual wholes according to rules of proximity, similarity, continuity, closure, and common fate.

Perceptual Constancies

Although sensory inputs are always changing, perceptual constancies keep our perceptions stable. Because of *size constancy*, we see an object as retaining its size even when its retinal image grows or diminishes. And because of *shape constancy*, we see an object's form as remaining the same when its orientation varies.

Depth and Dimension

Through *depth perception* we use two-dimensional visual information to perceive distances in three-dimensional space. One binocular depth cue is *convergence*, the turning inward of the eyes when objects get closer. Another cue is *binocular disparity*, the difference in retinal image between the two eyes. The closer the object is, the greater the disparity. There are also many *monocular depth cues*, including relative image size, linear perspective, and motion parallax.

Case studies of blind people whose eyesight was restored, as well as cross-cultural evidence, suggest that we need experience to interpret depth cues correctly. But experiments with the *visual cliff* indicate that some depth perception is inborn.

Perceptual Set

Our prior experiences and expectations often create a *perceptual set* that leads us to see what we expect to see.

The World of Illusions

Despite the brain's astonishing feats of perception, it falls prey to *perceptual illusions*. In the *Müller-Lyer illusion*, the perceived length of a line is changed by the position of other lines that enclose it. The *Ponzo illusion* makes the length of two equal lines seem different if they appear to be at different distances. And in the *moon illusion*, the full moon looks larger when it's close to the horizon.

Extrasensory Perception

More than half of all Americans believe in extrasensory perception (ESP). But can anyone perceive in the absence of sensory input?

The Case for ESP

Parapsychologists distinguish three types of extrasensory power: telepathy, clairvoyance, and precognition. Rhine's experiments suggested that all three types exist.

The Case Against ESP

Critics pointed out flaws in Rhine's methods, and similar problems were revealed by later experiments. Findings could not be reproduced, and hoaxes were exposed.

The Continuing Controversy

The debate about ESP continues. The Ganzfield Procedure has produced new evidence for ESP, but some critics still criticize the methods. As yet, there is no sound empirical support for the existence of ESP.

Chapter 4

Consciousness

Have you ever been offered "a penny for your thoughts"? As strange as it sounds, it's not always that easy to respond. From one moment to the next, there is an endless stream of new sights and sounds to absorb, new odors, internal sensations pressing for attention, thoughts, daydreams, and memories that pop to mind, problems that need to be solved, and other intrusions on what we call consciousness.

When psychology was born as a discipline, it was defined primarily as the study of consciousness. Wilhelm Wundt trained subjects to report on their own moment-to-moment reactions to tones, visual displays, and other stimulus cues. William James wrote extensively about the functions and contents of "normal waking consciousness," and Sigmund Freud argued that people are driven by *un*conscious forces that stir beneath the surface. Despite this initial interest, however, the rise of behaviorism led many researchers to focus on observable behavior, not the mind. It wasn't until the decline of behaviorism that interest in consciousness returned. Equipped with electrical recording devices, brain imaging techniques, computers, and cognitive tests, researchers made important new discoveries about attention, sleep and dreams, hypnosis, and mind-altering drugs.

ATTENTIONAL PROCESSES

The term **consciousness** has many different meanings (Baruss, 1987), but most psychologists define it in terms of **attention**—a state of awareness consisting of the sensations, thoughts, and feelings that one is focused on at a given moment. As implied by this definition, consciousness has a limited capacity. Whether you are mentally focused on a memory, a conversation, a foul odor, this sentence, a daydream, or your growling stomach, consciousness is like a spotlight. It can shift rapidly from one stimulus to another, but it can shine on only one stimulus at a time. Try to "free-associate" into a tape recorder some time, and you'll find yourself mentally straying in what William James (1890) called the "stream of consciousness."

Consciousness may be limited and the mind may wander, but three important and adaptive processes are at work. First, attention is selective—so, to some extent, we can control consciousness the way we control the channels of a television set. Second, for tasks that require little conscious effort, we can divide our attention and simultaneously engage in more than one activity. Third, even when conscious of one stimulus, we are also capable of reacting to other stimuli—which suggests that we can process information outside of awareness. As we'll see, these features enable us to widen, narrow, and move the spotlight of consciousness as needed.

Selective Attention

Picture this scene in your mind. You're standing at a cocktail party with a drink in one hand and a drumstick in the other. There's music playing in the background, as well as the chatter of voices. You're in the middle of a conversation when, suddenly, you hear two people talking about someone you know. Can you tune into the gossip and still carry on a conversation? How easy is it to selectively attend to one stimulus among many?

■ **consciousness** An awareness of the sensations, thoughts, and feelings that one is attending to at a given moment.

■ **attention** A state of awareness consisting of the sensations, thoughts, and feelings that one is focused on at a given moment.

■ **cocktail party effect** The ability to attend selectively to one person's speech in the midst of competing conversations.

■ **selective attention** The ability to focus awareness on a single stimulus to the exclusion of other stimuli, as in the cocktail party effect.

In a classic test of this **cocktail party effect**, Colin Cherry (1953) presented subjects wearing headphones with two different messages, played simultaneously, one to each ear. In this *dichotic listening* task, the subjects were told to "shadow"—that is, to follow and repeat aloud—only one of the two messages. Could they do it? Yes, especially when the competing messages were different—as when one featured the voice of a man and the other the voice of a woman. But what happened to the message that subjects had filtered out? Afterward, subjects could not recall any of it. Even when they were interrupted during the presentation and asked to repeat the unshadowed message, their ability to do so was limited. Through a process of **selective attention**, people can zoom in on one auditory stimulus, but then they lose track of competing auditory stimuli (see Figure 4.1).

Figure 4.1

Visual Shadowing

The following passage contains two messages—one in red ink, the other in blue. Read only the red-ink message aloud as quickly as possible. Now without looking back, write down all the blue-ink words you can remember. The result? As in dichotic listening studies, you probably did not recall many nonshadowed words—even though the same words appeared over and over again.

In performing an experiment like this one on man attention car it house is boy critically hat important shoe that candy the old material horse that tree is pen being phone read cow by book the hot subject tape for pin the stand relevant view task sky be red cohesive man and car grammatically house complete boy but hat without shoe either candy being horse so tree easy pen that phone full cow attention book is hot not tape required pin in stand order view to sky read red it nor too difficult

Figure 4.2

Selective Attention

Shown here are drawings of the two videotapes (left and center) and the resulting superimposed image (right). As in the dichotic listening experiments, subjects who were focused on the basketball players did not see the hand-slappers, and vice versa (Neisser & Becklen, 1975).

To examine selective attention in another sensory modality, Ulric Neisser and Robert Becklen (1975) devised a visual analog of the cocktail party effect. They showed subjects two videotapes, one superimposed over the other. One tape showed three people passing a basketball, and the other showed two people playing a hand-slapping game (see Figure 4.2). The subjects' task was to keep track of one game or the other. The result: As in the shadowing study, subjects could attend to only one stimulus at a time.

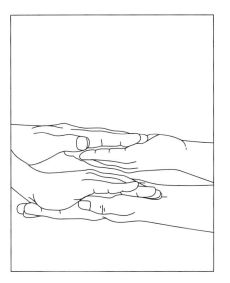

■ **divided attention** The ability to distribute one's attention and simultaneously engage in two or more activities.

In fact, the filtering process was so complete that out of twenty-four subjects who were focused on the basketball players, all but one failed to notice that the hand slappers had stopped their game at one point to shake hands! When the experimenter later replayed this segment, these subjects were shocked at what they had missed. This result shows that information may be entered into or excluded from consciousness through a process of selective attention.

Divided Attention

Consciousness may be limited, but the filtering process does not immediately block out all extraneous information. In dichotic listening experiments, for example, most subjects manage to hear the mention of their own names (Moray, 1959), sexually explicit words (Nielson & Sarason, 1981), or words that were associated with electric shock (Dawson & Schell, 1982) —even when these stimuli are spoken in the unshadowed ear. So is it possible, despite our selective tendencies, to divide attention among competing stimuli? Can you simultaneously watch TV and read a book, or else drive a car, listen to the radio, and carry on a conversation? It depends on how much conscious effort is needed for the various tasks (Damos, 1992).

Think about driving. When first learning to drive, you had to concentrate on how to operate the steering wheel, accelerator, brake, clutch, and gears, on how to monitor traffic and watch for pedestrians, signs, and lights. At that point, driving was so *effortful* an activity that even the radio was distracting. As you gained more experience behind the wheel, however, driving became an *automatic* process that did not require high levels of effort or awareness, or your undivided attention. As a result, you can now drive, listen, and talk all at the same time (Logan, 1992; Schneider & Shiffrin, 1977; Treisman et al., 1992).

The distinction between effortful and automatic processing explains how people are able to exhibit **divided attention** when at least one competing task is "on automatic." It's easy to walk, talk, and chew gum simultaneously, but for most of us it is difficult to play chess while watching TV. To demonstrate the automatic nature of highly practiced activities, look at the patches of color in Figure 4.3. Beginning in the top left-hand column, try to name all the colors as fast as you can—and time yourself. Ready, set, go! That was easy, right? Now look at the list of color-printed words, and this time name the colors of the ink in which each word is printed. Again, do it as fast as you can and time yourself.

Figure 4.3

The Stroop Test

Beginning in the top left-hand corner, name each color as fast as you can.

Beginning in the top left-hand corner, name the color of ink in which each word is printed as fast as you can.

If you followed these instructions, then you have just taken the **Stroop test**, which was devised in 1935 by John Stroop. As for the result, you probably found that the second task was much more difficult than the first and took almost twice as long. When Stroop first presented subjects with one hundred items, he found that the first task took an average of 63 seconds, and the second took 110 seconds—a 74 percent slowdown in performance time. I took this test as an undergraduate and thought it would be easy. Then I repeatedly paused, stammered, and got all tongue-tied, and had to admit that the words, which contradicted the colors, kept getting in the way. Researchers have now used the Stroop test in more than seven hundred experiments, and they continue to debate the reasons for the effect (MacLeod, 1991). However, one conclusion is clear: experienced readers process word meanings automatically, without effort or awareness. It just happens. And since the test words contradict the colors (when they don't, performance is quicker), reading interferes with the color-naming task.

Influence Without Awareness

Whereas Wundt and James were focused on conscious processes, Sigmund Freud theorized that people are driven more by *un*conscious forces. Freud argued that there are three levels of awareness in the human mind: (1) *conscious* sensations, thoughts, and feelings that are currently in the spotlight, (2) *preconscious* material that is temporarily out of awareness but is easy to bring to mind, and (3) an *unconscious* reservoir of material that is suppressed, banned from awareness. According to Freud, then, people are influenced by material that resides outside of awareness. Was he right?

For years, many researchers were skeptical of this claim. But an outpouring of new studies brought unconscious processes to the forefront of modern psychology. These studies suggest that people can be influenced by **subliminal messages**—information that is presented so faintly or so rapidly that it is perceived "below" our threshold of awareness (Bornstein & Pittman, 1992). Let's consider some examples to illustrate the point.

1. *Mere exposure:* Research shows that the more often you see a stimulus—whether it's a word, an object, a melody, or a face—the more you come to like it (Zajonc, 1968). Must you be aware of the prior exposures for this effect to occur? Not necessarily. In one study, subjects were shown a series of geometrical objects, each for only a millisecond—which is too quick to register in awareness. Yet when they were later asked about these and other items, the pattern of responses was consistent: Do you like this item? Yes. Have you ever seen it before? No. This result demonstrates influence without awareness (Kuntz-Wilson & Zajonc, 1980; Bornstein, 1992).

2. *Priming:* Have you ever noticed that once a novel word slips into conversation, it gets repeated over and over again? If so, then you have observed *priming*, the tendency for a recently presented concept to "prime" responses to a subsequent "target" question. Thus, when subjects are asked to decide if the letters *d-o-c-t-o-r* form a word, they are quicker to respond "yes" if the previous item was *n-u-r-s-e* than if it was *a-p-p-l-e* (Meyer & Schvaneveldt, 1971). What if the prime word is presented subliminally, below our threshold of awareness? As shown in

Can you juggle and ride a unicycle at the same time? When you learn a task so well that the process becomes automatic, it is possible to divide your attention and engage simultaneously in more than one activity.

■ **Stroop test** A color-naming task that demonstrates the automatic nature of highly practiced activities such as reading.

■ **subliminal message** A stimulus that is presented below the threshold for awareness.

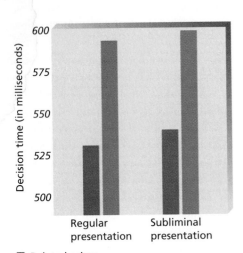

Figure 4.4

Subliminal Priming

Subjects took less time to decide if a target item was an actual word after exposure to a related prime word (left). This priming effect also occurred when the first words were subliminally presented (right). This result demonstrates influence without awareness (Marcel, 1983).

■ **prosopagnosia** A condition stemming from damage to the temporal lobes of the brain that disrupts the ability to recognize familiar faces.

■ **blindsight** A condition caused by damage to the visual cortex of the brain in which a person encodes visual information without awareness.

Figure 4.4, the result is the same—even when the prime word is presented so quickly that subjects could detect only a flash of light (Marcel, 1983; Merikle & Reingold, 1992).

3. *Prosopagnosia:* Influence without awareness can also be seen in people with **prosopagnosia**—a condition, often resulting from damage to the temporal lobes, whereby the affected persons can no longer recognize family members, friends, celebrities, and other familiar faces—including their own. Or can they? Research shows that even though prosopagnosics cannot identify known faces, they exhibit unique patterns of eye movements, electrical activity in the brain, and increased autonomic arousal when presented with faces that are familiar rather than unfamiliar (Renault et al., 1989; Tranel & Damasio, 1985). And when asked to determine if two faces are the same or different, they make judgments more quickly when one of the faces is familiar (Young & DeHann, 1992). In short, prosopagnosics exhibit glimmers of "recognition"—they just don't realize it. We will revisit this phenomenon, and others like it, in Chapter 6.

4. *Blindsight:* Another rare condition is **blindsight**, a form of vision without awareness. When people suffer damage that is limited to the primary visual cortex, optic nerve fibers from the eyes may still be connected to other regions of the brain that process visual information. In such cases, the patient is consciously blind, yet able to locate and reach for objects, identify colors in flashing lights, and track moving objects (Cowey & Stoerig, 1991; Weiskrantz, 1986). Thus the person can react to certain visual cues without awareness. As noted, people may be conscious of one stimulus, yet also react to other stimuli—and process information outside of awareness.

Although consciousness is limited by selective attention, people are able to perform certain tasks automatically and have the capacity to react to stimuli that are not "in the spotlight." This ability to simultaneously process information from many sources, and to do so outside of awareness, is adaptive. But can this ability be used against us? Are there limits to influence without awareness, or are we at the mercy of subliminal messages designed to shape our beliefs, tastes, attitudes, and behavior? Can teenagers be provoked into violence by subliminal rock-music lyrics? Many people believe that subliminal messages are more powerful than ordinary "supraliminal" (above-threshold) messages because they bypass our conscious defenses. Is this fear well founded? The answer is provided by recent research on the so-called hidden persuaders (see box on p. 138).

Consciousness is not a single, all-or-nothing state of mind. Rather, it is a continuum that ranges from an alert waking state to varying depths of sleep, dreams, hypnosis, and the "altered" states that are produced by psychoactive drugs. We will examine each of these conditions, beginning with sleep and dreams.

SLEEP AND DREAMS

It may start with a deep yawn. Then the eyelids begin to fall. Then your head drops and you get that drowsy sense of calm before nodding off, tun-

■ **biological rhythm** A periodic, more or less regular fluctuation in a biological organism.

■ **circadian rhythm** A biological cycle, such as sleeping and waking, that occurs approximately every twenty-four hours.

ing out, and calling it a day. For most people, falling asleep is a pleasurable experience. Why? What is sleep? Why do we need to have it? And what about dreams—what purposes do they serve, and what if anything do they mean?

The average person spends about eight hours a day sleeping and ninety minutes dreaming. Given an average life expectancy of seventy-five years, that amounts to about twenty-five years of sleep and five years of dreaming in a lifetime. Yet until recently, we knew very little about this important aspect of our lives. Shakespeare once referred to sleep as "the death of each day's life." Others, too, think of sleep as a state of complete dormancy. They are wrong. As we'll see, the sleeping brain is humming with activity (Carskadon, 1993).

The Sleep-Wake Cycle

Many birds migrate south for the winter. Bears and raccoons hibernate. Certain plants open their leaves during the day and close them at night— even if kept in a dark closet. As biological organisms, humans are also sensitive to seasonal changes, the twenty-eight-day lunar cycle, the twenty-four-hour day, and the ninety-minute activity-rest cycle that is linked to variations in alertness and daydreaming. These and other regular fluctuations are forms of **biological rhythms** (Aschoff, 1981).

From a psychological standpoint, there is one particularly important internal clock: Every twenty-four hours, we undergo a single sleep-wake cycle. We refer to this cycle, and to others that take roughly a day to complete, as a **circadian rhythm**. Humans tend to be most active and alert during the middle of the day, when body temperature peaks; and least active and alert at night, when body temperature drops to its low point. The circadian rhythm is also evident in fluctuations in blood pressure, pulse rate, blood sugar level, potassium level, growth hormone secretions, cell growth, and other physiological functions.

We are all influenced by the circadian rhythm, but everyone's inner clock is set somewhat differently. Think about yourself. Are you a morning person or a night person? An early bird or an owl? If you had a choice, would you rather wake up at 6, 8, or 10 o'clock in the morning? Would you prefer to go to bed at 10, 12, or 2 o'clock at night? How alert are you when you first climb out of bed? How easy is it for you to work late into the night? Questions like these can be used to determine your circadian rhythm (Smith et al., 1989). As it turns out, only 10 percent of the population are extreme in their preference. Most of us fall somewhere in the middle and, by necessity, adapt to the schedules that our responsibilities dictate.

Is the circadian rhythm *endogenous* (that is, set by an inner clock), or is the human body responsive to patterns of light and darkness? Ask Stefania Follini, a young Italian interior designer. In January 1989, she descended into a plexiglass bunker buried in a cave in New Mexico. Sealed off from sunlight, outside noises, changes in temperature, schedules, and clocks, she lived alone in this underground home for 131 days—a "free-running" period of time that allowed her body to establish its own rhythm. Her only link to the world was a personal computer. When Follini emerged from her isolation in May, she thought it was only March. Her "day" had extended

"Larks see owls as lazy, owls see larks as party poopers."

RICHARD M. COLEMAN

BIOLOGICAL PSYCHOLOGY   Business

Subliminal Persuasion

In 1957, Vance Packard published *The Hidden Persuaders,* an exposé of Madison Avenue. As the book climbed to the top of the bestseller list, it awakened in the public a deep fear of being manipulated by forces that could not be seen or heard. What had Packard uncovered? In the 1950s, amid growing fears of communism, McCarthyism, and the birth of rock 'n' roll, a group of advertisers reported that they used *subliminal advertising*—the presentation of commercial messages below the level of conscious awareness. It started in a drive-in movie theater in New Jersey, where the words *Drink Coca-Cola* and *Eat popcorn* were flashed on the screen during the film for 1/3,000th of a second. Although the audience never noticed the message, Coke sales were said to have increased 18 percent and popcorn sales 58 percent over a six-week period of intermissions (Brean, 1958).

This incident was followed by many others. A Seattle radio station presented sub-audible antitelevision messages during its programs ("TV is a bore"), department stores played music tapes over public-address systems that contained sub-audible antitheft statements ("If you steal, you'll get caught"), and advertisers embedded faint sexual images in visual ads to heighten the appeal of their products. Subliminal messages in rock music recordings have also raised concern. In one recent case, the families of two young men who had committed suicide blamed the British rock group Judas Priest for subliminal lyrics that promoted satanism and suicide on their *Stained Glass* album (National Law Journal, 1990). Clearly, many people believe in the power of hidden persuaders.

Can subliminal advertising really influence us without our awareness? At the time of the New Jersey movie theater scandal, research on the topic was so sketchy, and the public so outraged by the sinister implications, that the matter was dropped like a hot potato. But today there is renewed interest, new research developments, and continued controversy. In what has become a multimillion-dollar industry, companies sell self-help tapes that play soft music or nature sounds and

Stefani Follini emerges into daylight after 131 days in an underground plexiglass bunker in New Mexico.

also contain fleeting messages designed to help listeners relax, lose weight, stop smoking, make friends, raise self-esteem, and improve their sex lives.

Can subliminal messages really get us to drink Coke, eat popcorn, or purchase a particular product? And what about all the subliminal self-help tapes for which consumers pay $29.95 apiece? In 1982, Timothy Moore reviewed the existing research and concluded that "what you see is what you get"—nothing, "complete scams." Moore may have been right. The original Coke-and-popcorn study was never published—and may have been just a publicity stunt, a hoax. So, is there any solid evidence of this covert form of influence?

In a well-controlled experiment, Anthony Greenwald and his colleagues (1991) had subjects listen for five weeks to a music tape that contained a hidden message designed either to improve memory or to raise self-esteem. For half the subjects, the tapes were correctly labeled; for the others, the labels were reversed. Subjects were tested both before and after the five-week period. They were also questioned afterward on their beliefs concerning the tapes. Try to predict the results. Did subjects think they were helped by the tapes? Did they actually improve? There were two key results. First, test scores on objective measures of memory and self-esteem were not any higher after exposure to the tapes than before. Second, subjects perceived an improvement in their memory or self-esteem—depending on which label was on the tape, not on which message the tape actually contained. Other research has shown that subliminal weight-loss tapes are similarly ineffective (Merikle & Skanes, 1992). In short, consumers may believe in the power of hidden messages, but subliminal self-help tapes do not have therapeutic value.

At this point you may be wondering, Why is there strong evidence for influence without awareness (as in mere exposure, priming, prosopagnosia, and blindsight)—but no evidence for subliminal persuasion? There seems to be a contradiction here. If you think about the differences, however, you'll see that this contradiction is more apparent than real. In the studies of influence without awareness, subliminal exposures have a short-term effect on simple laboratory judgments. But in subliminal persuasion, these simple exposures are supposed to have longer-term effects on consumer needs, purchases, suicide, and other complex behaviors. Many psychologists now believe that although a great deal of information can be simultaneously processed at an unconscious level, this processing is "analytically limited" (Greenwald, 1992).

to twenty-five hours, then to forty-eight. As time went on, she would sleep and wake up later and later. She stopped menstruating, ate fewer meals, and lost seventeen pounds.

Other volunteers have similarly been isolated for extended periods of time. Some individuals naturally settled into a "short" day, but most free-ran on a longer cycle that averaged twenty-five hours. With each successive cycle, these subjects tended to go to sleep a little later, and to wake up a little later (see Figure 4.5). Body temperature and hormone levels tended to follow the same rhythm. Like Follini, they drifted toward a longer day—and then underestimated the amount of time they had been isolated. Upon their re-exposure to sunlight, the subjects readjusted their biological clocks.

So where is this timing device? Animal experiments have shown that the circadian rhythm is controlled by a cluster of neurons in the *suprachiasmatic nucleus (SCN)* of the hypothalamus (Takahashi & Zatz, 1982; Ralph et al., 1990). How does the SCN function? You may recall from Chapter 3 that light passing through the eye is converted to neural signals and sent to the brain through the optic nerve. Apparently, some of these optic nerve axons—and the information they convey about light—are diverted to the SCN (Moore, 1982).

The circadian rhythm is synchronized like a fine watch by interactions between environmental cues and the brain. But what happens when one's rhythm is disrupted? One common source of disruption is air travel—specifically, flying across time zones—which throws your body out

Figure 4.5

The Inner Clock

When people are placed in a "free-running" environment, isolated from all day and night cues, they typically drift toward a twenty-five-hour "day." With each cycle, subjects sleep and wake up a little later.

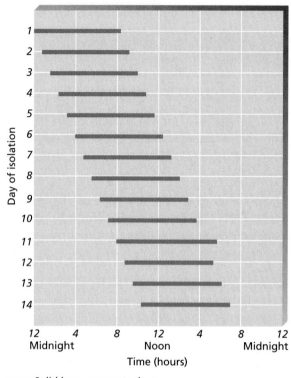

Solid bar represents sleep

of sync with the new time of day and causes you to sleep at the wrong time. If you've ever flown from one coast to the other, or overseas, then you may have suffered *jet lag*, a condition that makes you feel tired, sluggish, and grumpy. Most people find it easier to fly west, which lengthens the day, than to fly east, which shortens it. Since the body naturally drifts to a longer day, this makes sense. Flying westward goes "with the flow" rather than against it. Consistent with this analysis, research shows that long-distance travel within the same time zone does not cause jet lag (Coleman, 1986).

Recent research provides behavioral tips for the weary long-distance traveler. If you plan to travel east—say, from Los Angeles to New York—you can facilitate the adjustment process by sleeping earlier than normal before you leave so that you more closely "fit" the light-dark cycle of the new time zone. As soon as you board the plane, set your watch to your destination's time zone and eat and sleep accordingly. Based on studies indicating that bright light exposure at night speeds the resetting of the inner clock, researchers also advise that, upon arrival, you spend the first day outdoors (Czeisler et al., 1989).

The Stages of Sleep

Just as activity levels follow a rhythm, so too does sleep. Every night, humans cycle through five distinct stages of sleep. Much of what we know about these stages first came to light in the 1950s, thanks to the pioneering

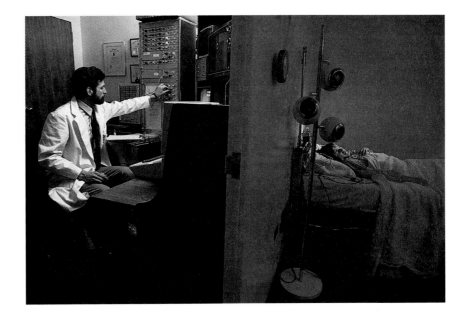

As shown, a subject spends the night in the "bedroom" of a sleep lab (right), while an experimenter in an adjacent room records brain-wave activity, eye movements, muscle tension, and other physiological functions (left).

collaborative work of Nathaniel Kleitman, Eugene Aserinksy, and William Dement.

To appreciate how these discoveries were made, imagine that you're a subject in a sleep study. As you enter the sleep lab, you meet an experimenter who gives you some questionnaires to fill out, prepares you for the experience, and takes you to a carpeted, tastefully decorated, soundproof "bedroom." Electrodes are then taped to your scalp to record brain-wave activity, near your eyes to measure eye movements, and under the neck and chin to record muscle tension (see Figure 4.6). Other devices may also be used to measure breathing, heart rate, and even genital arousal. The pillow is fluffy, the bed is okay, and the blanket is warm. But you know you're being watched and you can feel the electrodes and wires on your skin, so you wonder how you'll ever manage to fall asleep. The experimenter reassures you that it may take a couple of nights to adapt to the situation.

Presleep   The experimenter departs, shuts off the lights, and leaves you alone. As you try to settle down, EEG recordings reveal that all is well (see Figure 4.7). Typical of a person who is awake and alert, your EEG shows

Figure 4.6

Measuring Sleep

In sleep laboratories, researchers record brain-wave activity, eye movements, and muscle tension by taping electrodes to the scalp, near the eyes, and elsewhere on the face (Dement, 1978).

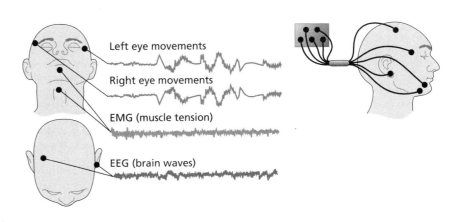

PRESLEEP

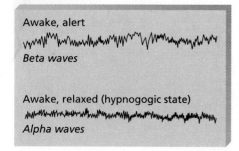

NON-REM

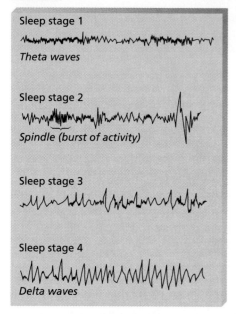

REM

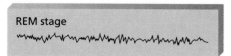

Figure 4.7

The Stages of Sleep

As recorded by the EEG, brain waves get larger and slower as sleep deepens from stages 1 to 4. You can see that REM sleep waves closely resemble those of the presleep state.

short, quick *beta waves*. This pattern indicates that different parts of your brain are producing small bursts of electrical activity at different times—a sure sign of mental activity. Your eyes move rapidly up and down and from side to side, and there is tension in many of your muscles.

Stages 1–4   You start to become drowsy. Your breathing slows down, your mind stops racing, your muscles relax, your eyes move less, and EEG recordings show a slower, more synchronized pattern of *alpha waves*. For a minute or two, you drift into a "hypnogogic state" in which you may imagine seeing flashes of color or light, and perhaps jerk your leg abruptly as you sense yourself falling. You are entering stage 1 sleep. Electrical activity in the brain slows down some more—and *theta waves* dominate the EEG. Your breathing becomes more regular, your heart rate slows, and your blood pressure drops. This is a period of very light sleep. No one makes a sound or calls your name, however, so you do not wake up.

After about ten minutes in stage 1 sleep, your EEG pattern shows waves that are even slower and larger. As you slip into stage 2 sleep, you become progressively more relaxed, the rolling eye movements stop, and you become less easily disturbed. On the EEG, stage 2 is marked by periodic short bursts of activity called *sleep spindles*. If the experimenter in the next room makes a noise, your brain will register a response—but you probably would not wake up.

After about twenty minutes in stage 2, you fall into the deepest stages of sleep. Stages 3 and 4 are hard to distinguish because they differ only in degree. Both are marked by the appearance of very slow, large *delta waves*, which last for about thirty minutes. At this point, you are "out like a light" or "sleeping like a rock." If the phone rings, you may not hear it. If you do answer the call, you'll sound dazed and confused. It is during the very deep sleep of stages 3 and 4 when young children may wet the bed, or when you may walk or talk in your sleep. It's this stage that Mark Twain had in mind when he said, "There ain't no way to find out why a snorer can't hear himself snore." Yet, in keeping with the adaptive and selective nature of our attention, certain noises will penetrate consciousness. New parents may be oblivious to the sounds of traffic outside, for example, but they're quick to hear the baby cry.

REM Sleep   After an hour of deepening sleep, something odd happens—something that was first discovered in Kleitman's lab (Aserinksy & Kleitman, 1953; Dement & Kleitman, 1957; Kleitman, 1963). Rather than maintain your deep sleep, you begin to cycle backward to stage 3, then to stage 2. But instead of returning to stage 1, you enter a new fifth stage marked by two dramatic types of changes. On the one hand, the EEG reveals a surge of short, high-frequency beta waves like those found when you were awake. Also indicating an increased level of activity, blood flow to the brain increases, your breathing and pulse rates speed up, and your genitals become aroused—even without sexual thoughts or dreams. On the other hand, you have lost skeletal muscle tone throughout the body. In fact, your arms, legs, and trunk are so totally relaxed that, except for an occasional twitch, you are completely paralyzed. You're also hard to awaken at this stage. This odd combination—of being internally active but externally immobile—has led some researchers to refer to it as *paradoxical sleep*.

The most prominent change occurs in the eyes. The eyelids are shut, but

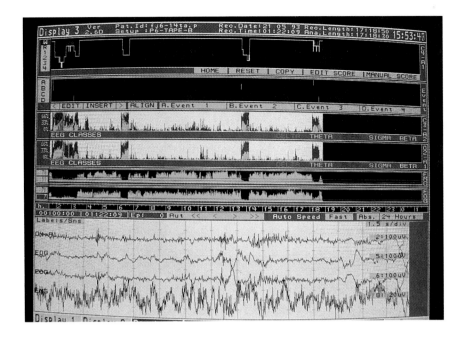

Computer readout of a subject's EEG activity (and other processes) during sleep.

underneath, your eyeballs are darting frantically back and forth as if you were watching a world-class ping-pong match. These *rapid eye movements* are so pronounced that this stage has been named **REM sleep**—and it is contrasted with stages 1–4, which are lumped together as non-REM or **NREM sleep**. What makes rapid eye movements so special is what they betray about the state of your mind. When experimenters awaken sleeping subjects during non-REM stages, the subjects report on dreams 14 percent of the time. But when subjects are awakened during REM, they report on dreams 78 percent of the time—and that includes those subjects who came into the lab saying they don't ever dream (Dement, 1978). Compared to the fleeting thoughts and images reported during stages 1–4, REM dreams are more visual, vivid, detailed, and storylike. In the mind's late-night theater, the production of dreams can be seen in the resurgence of activity in the eyes and brain.

From the time you fall asleep, it takes about ninety minutes to complete a cycle. The contrasts within this cycle are striking. Richard Coleman (1986) describes NREM sleep as "an idling brain in a moveable body" and REM as "an active brain in a paralyzed body." In a full night's sleep, you are likely to recycle through the stages four to six times. The first time through the cycle, you spend only about ten minutes in REM sleep. As the night wears on, however, you spend less time in the deeper NREM periods and more time in REM sleep. During the last hour before you awaken in the morning, the REM period is thirty to sixty minutes long. This explains why people are so often in the midst of a dream when the mechanical tyrant we call an alarm clock rings. The sleep cycles, and the progression of stages within each cycle, are illustrated in Figure 4.8.

Why Sleep?

Since humans spend a third of their lives in this state, it's natural to wonder, Why do we sleep? When we are tired, the urge to doze is overwhelming

■ **REM sleep** The rapid-eye-movement stage of sleep associated with dreaming.

■ **NREM sleep** The stages of sleep not accompanied by rapid eye movements.

BIOLOGICAL PSYCHOLOGY   Health

Night Work, Sleep, and Health

We humans are diurnal creatures—active during the day and asleep at night. Thus we like to work from 9 to 5 and then play, sleep, and awaken to the light of a new day. Yet an estimated 20 percent of all Americans—including emergency-room doctors and nurses, fire-fighters, police officers, telephone operators, security guards, factory workers, interstate truckers, and power-plant operators—are forced to work late night shifts. The question is, What is the effect? Do people adapt over time to shift work, and other late-night activity, or does it compromise their health and safety?

Both biological and social clocks set the body for activity during the daytime and sleep at night, so many shift workers must struggle to stay alert. People who choose night work fare better than those who are assigned on a rotating shift basis (Barton, 1994). Still, surveys reveal that shift workers in general get fewer hours of sleep per week than day workers, complain that their sleep is significantly disrupted, and report being drowsy on the job. Often they blame their lack of sleep

on environmental stimuli such as ringing phones, crying babies, honking horns, and other daytime noises. But part of the problem, too, is that the body's internal alarm clock tries to awaken the day sleeper. Either way, the adverse effects can be seen at work. In a survey of a thousand train drivers, 70 percent admitted to having dozed off at the wheel at least once and 11 percent said they do so on most night shifts. These reports are confirmed by studies in which EEG activity in train drivers was monitored. Those who operated trains in the middle of the night often took quick, two- to three-second microsleeps, which may interfere with job performance and increase the risk of accident (Carskadon, 1993).

The National Highway Transportation Safety Administration estimates that up to 200,000 traffic accidents a year are sleep related—and that 20 percent of all drivers have dozed off at least once while behind the wheel. To avoid rush-hour traffic, interstate truckers often drive late at night. The result: Due to drowsiness, truck drivers are 16 times more likely to have an accident between 4 A.M. and 6 A.M. than during the

Figure 4.8

A Typical Night's Sleep

People pass through four to six 90-minute sleep cycles per night. Progressively more time is spent in REM sleep and progressively less is spent in the deeper stages.

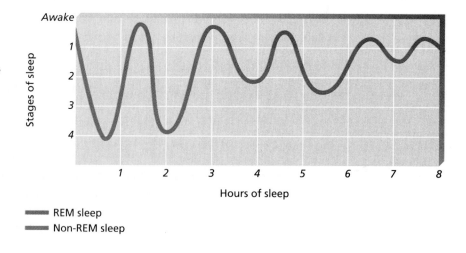

and very hard to fight, regardless of what we are doing or where we are. And if we are still tired when the alarm clock rings, we may shut it off, clutch our pillows to our ears, or pretend we didn't hear it—even if we have a schedule to keep. Our need for sleep is powerful and irresistible. But why?

One way to investigate this question is to deprive people of sleep and see what happens. I pulled a few "all-nighters" when I was younger and

To avoid traffic, many truckers drive at night. Due to drowsiness, however, they are more likely to have an accident between 4 and 6 A.M. than during daytime hours.

daytime hours (Chollar, 1989). Similarly disturbing are the stories told by medical interns and residents, many of whom have worked 120-hour work weeks, including 36 hours at a stretch. According to David Dinges, "Human error causes between 60 percent and 90 percent of all workplace accidents . . . and inadequate sleep is a major factor in human error" (quoted in Toufexis, 1990, pp. 78–79).

Can anything be done to lessen the dangers that are posed by shift work and the corresponding decline in alertness and job performance at night? Richard Coleman (1986) recommends that when rotating shifts are necessary, managers should maximize the number of days between shift changes (for example, adjustment is easier in three-week cycles than in one-week cycles) and assign workers to successively later shifts rather than earlier shifts (a person who is rotated from the 4 P.M. shift to the midnight shift will adjust more quickly than one who is rotated in the opposite direction, from midnight to 4 P.M.). Charles Czeisler and his colleagues (1990) have also found that the realignment of the circadian rhythm can be speeded up by exposing shift workers to bright, daytime levels of light in the workplace and to eight hours of total darkness at home during the day. Within a week, the body's biological clock can thus be reset and the health risks of night work reduced.

"burned the midnight oil." You may have done so as well, but probably not for periods of time that are long enough to push the limits. A unique opportunity to observe the effects of sleep deprivation presented itself in New York City, in 1959. As part of a fund-raising drive, disc jockey Peter Tripp forced himself to stay awake and on the air for 200 hours. By the fifth day, Tripp's speech was slurred—and he was hallucinating and showing signs of paranoia (he believed that "enemies" were trying to drug his coffee). It seemed that sleep was essential to his mental health. But after sleeping for 13 hours, Tripp had completely recovered.

A second highly publicized case came about in 1965, when seventeen-year-old Randy Gardner sought fame in the *Guinness Book of World Records*. As part of a high school science project, and with the help of friends, Gardner stayed awake for 264 hours—that's 11 straight days, a world record (which was later broken). When it was over, he held a news conference, during which he said "it's just mind over matter." He then slept for 15 hours, woke up feeling fine, and resumed his normal schedule. Follow-up tests confirmed that Gardner had suffered no long-term ill effects (Dement, 1978).

On the basis of these episodes and numerous studies, sleep researchers have concluded that sleep deprivation leads people to become weary and irritable, and to lose their concentration, their attention, and their drive to perform at simple tasks. But these effects are overcome after just a single night's rest. Does this mean that sleep is unnecessary? No. It turns out that sleep-deprived subjects—including disc jockey Peter Tripp—occasionally nod off for two- or three-second intervals. These "microsleeps," which show up on EEG tracings, make it nearly impossible to achieve a state of complete deprivation (Webb, 1992).

There are two types of explanations for why we must sleep (Hobson, 1989). One comes from *restoration theory*, which states that sleep recharges the battery, enabling us to recover from the day's physical, cognitive, and emotional demands. This explanation is consistent with the experience of feeling run-down as the day wears on, and refreshed after a good night's sleep. It also receives support from the finding that prolonged sleep deprivation in laboratory rats often results in death (Rechtschaffen et al., 1983). There must be more to sleep than restoration, however, because sleep-deprived humans recover fully from the experience. In addition, there is little evidence to suggest that people sleep more than usual after an active, high-energy day (Horne & Minard, 1985).

A second type of explanation comes from *circadian theory*, which focuses on the evolutionary significance of sleep (Hobson, 1989). According to this view, sleep is a neural mechanism that evolves over time so that animals can conserve energy and minimize their exposure to predators when they're not foraging for food or seeking a mate. Circadian theory is consistent with species-specific differences in sleep patterns. As shown in Figure 4.9, animals that sleep the longest find food easily and are well hidden from predators while sleeping. In contrast, animals that sleep the shortest

Figure 4.9

Daily Hours of Sleep: Cross-Species Comparisons

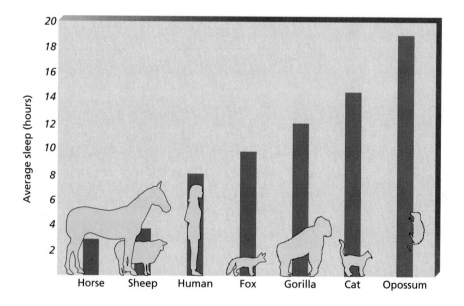

amount of time spend more hours foraging and can defend themselves only by running away. Seen from this perspective, humans sleep at night because we're not very well adapted to searching for food in the dark or protecting ourselves from nocturnal predators (Allison & Cicchetti, 1976).

The question of why we sleep is still something of a mystery. Although the restoration and circadian theories do not contradict one another, the evidence for each is slim. Still, many researchers currently believe that both mechanisms may be at work (Borbely, 1986; Webb, 1992).

Dreams

Between the ages of twelve and eighteen, I had an odd recurring dream. At eye level, I would be looking across a straight, smooth, waxed wood surface. Then from a distance, a silver ball would start to roll toward me. It started slowly at first, but picked up speed as it came closer. As the ball rolled toward my nose, a voice inside it would repeat my name—and get louder as the ball got closer. I could never understand why the ball rolled, since, as the dreamer, I "knew" that the surface was perfectly horizontal. But roll it did, and I would always wake up just as the ball was about to hit my nose. Though not a scary dream, it had a haunting quality. Like most people, I wondered, "What does it mean?"

Dreams have always fascinated people. Eight thousand years ago, the Assyrians believed that dreams were messages sent from evil spirits. The Egyptians believed they were messages sent by the gods. The Eskimos of Hudson Bay and the Pantani of Malaysia believe that one's soul leaves the body during sleep and enters another world. Among the Kurdish and Zulu, dreaming of adultery is an offense, and if you dream of receiving a gift, you must compensate the gift-giver in waking life (Webb, 1992). In Western cultures, we assume that dreams, if properly analyzed, tell us something about the dreamer's past, present, or future. But what are dreams, why do we have them, and what if anything do they mean?

The Nature of Dreams   Dreams are less puzzling now than they were before the 1953 discovery of REM sleep. Psychologists used to believe that the mind was idling in sleep and that dreaming was a rare, and therefore significant, event. But then EEG recordings revealed that the sleeping human brain is active and that everyone dreams, without exception—several times a night. We now know that dreams are electrochemical events involving the brainstem and areas of the cortex, and that the eyes flutter back and forth. What more is known about this mysterious state of consciousness, a state in which the mind is active but the sleeper is immobilized and hard to awaken?

Researchers now believe that REM sleep, and the dreaming that accompanies it, is biologically adaptive. This belief arises from three sources of evidence. The first is that all mammals have REM sleep (some birds do too, but reptiles, amphibians, and fish do not). Second, the amount of REM sleep is greatest early in life, while the brain is developing (Hobson, 1989). Among premature infants, 60 to 80 percent of all sleep time is spent in the REM stage. That number drops to 50 percent in full-term newborns, 30 percent at six months of age, and 25 percent at two years of age, before leveling off at 20 percent in early childhood and then diminishing later in life. Third, when subjects are deprived of REM sleep one night, they exhibit a "rebound effect" by taking extra REM time the next night (Brunner et al., 1990).

Is there a link between a sleeper's eye movements and dreams? This is a tricky question. Research shows that the longer a REM episode is, the more words an awakened subject uses to describe the dream—and the more elaborate the story. Similarly, the more active the brain is during REM, the more eventful are the dreams that are later reported. However, patterns of eye movements do not seem to correspond to the images and actions of a dream—as when we follow characters in a film (Chase & Morales, 1983).

"Dreaming permits each and every one of us to be quietly and safely insane every night of our lives."

CHARLES FISHER

"From the conservative assumptions of three REM periods per night and two dream stories within each period there is a resultant 150,000 dreams per person over a life span of 70 years."

WILSE B. WEBB

■ **lucid dreaming** A semiconscious dream state in which a sleeper is aware that he or she is dreaming.

The Contents of Dreams   What do people dream about? What do *you* dream about? Over the years, analyses of dream content have shown that certain themes seem to arise with remarkable frequency. The three most commonly reported dreams are of falling, being chased or attacked, and trying repeatedly to do something but failing. Also common are dreams of flying, being unprepared or late for a big event, rejection, and appearing naked in public (Stark, 1984). Cataloging more than 10,000 dream reports, Calvin Hall and Robert Van de Castle (1966) found that 64 percent were associated with sadness, fear, or anger, while only 18 percent were happy or exciting. Acts of aggression outnumbered acts of friendship by more than two to one. Twenty-nine percent of all dreams were in color, 10 percent involved strangers, and only 1 percent involved having sex.

What influences the contents of your dreams? There are two documented sources. One is the concerns of daily life. If you're struggling financially, if you've had a death in the family, or if you're studying for a big exam or are involved in an exciting new relationship, these issues may well slip into your dreams—and provide an opportunity for creative problem solving (Cartwright, 1978). External stimuli are a second possible source of influence. Have you ever heard the radio alarm go off but slept through the music and dreamed you were at a concert? William Dement (1978) sprayed water on subjects' hands during REM sleep, awakened them a short time later, and found that 42 percent, far more than normal, reported dreaming of rainfalls, leaking roofs, swimming pools, and the like. Similarly, 56 percent incorporated into their dreams the taped sounds of dogs, trains, bells, and other stimuli.

For some dreamers, there is a third source of influence that, in some ways, is the most interesting. Have you ever had the odd sensation of dreaming—and knowing that you were in a dream? This "half in–half out" state of consciousness is called **lucid dreaming**. Relatively few people have lucid dreams, but the ability has been documented—and it can be developed. In some studies, for example, sleepers are trained to signal the onset of a dream by moving their eyes and clenching their fists. As both actors and observers, lucid dreamers can even use the power of suggestion to *control* the contents and outcomes of their own dreams. In this manner, lucid dreaming can be used to resolve conflicts and tame nightmare's monsters (LaBerge, 1992).

Our dreams may be influenced by inner concerns and external stimuli, and even by our own will. But often our dreams have a bizarre, magical quality—whereby time seems to stand still or speed forward, shadowy figures appear and vanish on cue, or we fall into bottomless pits, fly like Superman, and float in defiance of gravity. How can these qualities be explained? And what do they tell us about why we dream? No one really knows for sure, but there are two major theories.

Freud's Interpretation   In 1900, Sigmund Freud published a classic book entitled *The Interpretation of Dreams*. According to Freud, people are unconsciously motivated to satisfy sexual and aggressive urges. These ideas are too threatening to express or even to recognize, so we keep them from awareness through the use of defense mechanisms. So far, so good. During sleep, however, our defensive guard is down, and the pent-up drives can no longer be suppressed. It would be psychologically shattering to come face

■ **manifest content** According to Freud, the conscious dream content that is remembered in the morning.

■ **latent content** According to Freud, the unconscious, censored meaning of a dream.

■ **activation-synthesis theory** The theory that dreams result from the brain's attempt to make sense of random neural signals that fire during sleep.

to face with our deepest, darkest urges. Such realizations would also disrupt our sleep. The solution: We construct dreams that express the fulfillment of these drives—but in ways that are too indirect and confusing to recognize. In short, the dream we remember in the morning is a disguised, scrambled expression of our unconscious wishes. The drive is fulfilled, but in such a way that the psyche—and sleep—are protected.

With his theory of psychoanalysis to guide him (see Chapter 15), Freud saw dreams as a "royal road" to the unconscious. He called the dream we remember in the morning the **manifest content**. The underlying thoughts, urges, conflicts, and needs that give rise to that dream constitute its **latent content**. According to Freud, the only way to uncover this unconscious latent material (which, after all, is the "true meaning") is to decode the dream and the symbols that disguise it. In the language of dreams, said Freud, kings and queens symbolize parents, small animals symbolize children, a house symbolizes the human body, and flying is the mental equivalent of having sex.

Activation-Synthesis Theory Freud's theory is hard to prove or disprove, and many psychologists worry that it encourages us to "overinterpret" dreams. Recent theories take a different, more neuropsychological approach. The most important of these is the **activation-synthesis theory** of J. Allan Hobson and Robert McCarley (1977), which was later revised by Hobson (1988). According to this two-process theory, random neural signals firing in the brainstem spread up to the cortex (activation). Drawing on past experiences stored in memory, the brain then constructs images and stories in an effort to make sense out of these random signals (synthesis).

Research shows that dreams of flying are very common. This "flying carpet" image was created by a man who reports his dreams through drawing.

Both Freud's account and activation-synthesis theory agree that the dream's manifest content is not meaningful. But they differ in two respects. The first concerns the interpretation of the manifest content. For Freud, the mind constructs bizarre dreams to disguise its true meaning from the dreamer. For Hobson and McCarley, the brain constructs bizarre dreams because it has only limited information and operates on short notice. In other words, "the manifest content is the dream. There is no other dream" (Hobson, 1988, p. 258). The second key difference concerns the significance attached to the so-called latent content. Freud believed that dreams spring from deep unconscious wishes. Hobson and McCarley argue that dreams are the incidental by-product of neural overactivity. At this point,

"I wouldn't be too concerned with this dream. Sometimes a 35-foot-tall singing pirate juggling bowling balls is just a 35-foot-tall singing pirate juggling bowling balls."

[© Joe Dator and The Cartoon Bank, Inc.]

[© 1994 Liz Haberfeld and The Cartoon Bank, Inc.]

there is not enough research to declare a winner between these approaches. What has become clear, however, is that the mind is remarkably active during sleep.

Sleep Disturbances

At some point in life, nearly everyone suffers from a sleep-related problem. You lie in bed, tossing and turning, brooding over something that happened or worrying about something that might. Or you keep nodding off in class, or at work, or in other embarrassing situations. Or you leap up in a cold sweat, with your heart pounding, from a realistic and terrifying nightmare. There are three types of disturbances: sleeping too little (insomnia), sleeping too much (hypersomnia), and disturbed or troubled sleep (parasomnia).

Insomnia   The sleep disturbance known as **insomnia** is characterized by a recurring inability to fall asleep, stay asleep, or get the amount of sleep needed to function during the day. Very few of us adhere to the daily "ideal" of eight hours for work, eight for play, and eight for sleep. On the contrary, people differ in the amount of sleep they want. Some are at their most alert after five or six hours a night, while others need nine or ten hours to get along. How much time is sufficient thus depends on the person.

Thirty percent of the population complain of insomnia—and half of these people consider the problem to be serious (American Psychiatric Association, 1994). It's not that easy to know when someone has insomnia based on self-report, however. In a study that illustrates this point, Mary Carskadon brought 122 insomniacs into the laboratory and compared their perceptions to EEG measures of sleep. The next morning, the subjects estimated that it took them an hour to fall asleep and that they slept for 4 ½

"It is extremely rare to find an animal with insomnia. . . . Insomnia is a human disorder."

RICHARD M. COLEMAN

■ **insomnia** An inability to fall asleep, stay asleep, or get the amount of sleep needed to function during the day.

hours. But EEG tracings revealed that it took them only 15 minutes to fall asleep—and that they slept for 6½ hours. Apparently, more than 10 percent of all complaints are from "pseudo-insomniacs" who sleep normally but don't realize it (Kelly, 1991).

Among people who do have trouble falling or staying asleep, insomnia is not a disease but a symptom that has many causes. Studies show that psychiatric patients get less sleep than do people without mental disorders (Benca et al., 1992). Medical ailments, pain, life stresses, depression, jet lag, shifting work schedules, old age, and alcohol and drug abuse are also linked to insomnia. In some cases, the only "problem" is that people think they should sleep eight hours a night, so they go to bed before they're really tired. The use of medications poses a particularly ironic danger. Over-the-counter sleeping pills such as Sominex and Sleep-eze are not effective. Prescription drugs will, at first, put an insomniac to sleep and prevent rude awakenings during the night. But these sedatives will also inhibit certain stages of sleep, and cause restlessness after the drug is terminated—if it is terminated. The habit of popping sleeping pills can be addictive and should be avoided. Experts agree that people can overcome the problem instead by altering their behavior. Some helpful tips are presented in Table 4.1.

> *"The only thing wrong with insomniacs is that they don't get enough sleep."*
>
> W. C. FIELDS

Table 4.1

How to Overcome Insomnia

- Record how much sleep you *actually* get in a night , and set that total as a goal. If you sleep four or five hours, aim for a four-hour schedule.
- Do not take naps during the day.
- Avoid all alcohol, caffeine, and cigarettes within five hours of bedtime; avoid exercise within two hours of bedtime; relax.
- Make sure the bedroom is completely dark when you go to bed. When you awaken, turn on the lights and raise the shades.
- Keep a rigid schedule. Get into bed at 1 A.M., not earlier. Set the alarm for 5 A.M.—and get out of bed no matter what.
- If you're awake but relaxed, stay in bed.
- If you're awake and anxious, get out of bed and return when you are sleepy. Keep the alarm set, and get up when it rings.
- If you stick to this schedule, you should see results in three to five weeks. If you want, you can then add thirty to sixty minutes to your schedule.
- Rest assured that you can get by on less sleep than you want, and that a temporary loss of sleep will not cause harm.

Hypersomnia Much less common but far more dangerous are the sleep disturbances of "hypersomnia," or too much sleep. The most profound problem of this type is **narcolepsy**, a disorder that is characterized by sudden, irresistible attacks of drowsiness and sleep during the day (Mahowald & Schenck, 1989).

A narcolepsy attack may strike without warning at any time—playing basketball, eating a meal, having a conversation, working in an office, or having sex. The attack lasts from five to thirty minutes and plunges its victim into REM sleep. The narcoleptic's jaw will sag, the head will fall forward, the arms will drop, and the knees will buckle. This collapse is often accompanied by the hypnogogic hallucinations that usher in the onset of

■ **narcolepsy** A sleep disorder characterized by irresistible and sudden attacks of REM sleep during the day.

sleep. Narcolepsy can be life-threatening. In one study, 40 percent of the narcoleptics who were questioned admitted they had fallen asleep while driving. To some extent, the problem can be minimized by avoiding potentially dangerous activities and taking stimulant drugs (Siegel et al., 1991).

Parasomnias   For some people, falling asleep at night and staying awake during the day are not a problem—but too often their sleep is disturbed. There are several possible sources of disruption. *Nightmares* are vivid, anxiety-provoking dreams that occur during REM sleep. More common among children than adults, nightmares are a "problem" only if they persist for long periods of time. Nightmares are not dangerous, except in cases of *REM sleep behavior disorder*, a rare condition in which the skeletal muscles do not become paralyzed during REM sleep. People with this disorder thus have the mobility to act on their nightmares, and often do so in violent ways. Indeed, 85 percent of sufferers have injured themselves and 44 percent have hurt their bed partners, sometimes seriously (Mahowald & Schenck, 1989).

There are also NREM sleep disruptions. In *night terrors*, the person jolts abruptly from a deep sleep, in a state of panic, and gives off a loud, blood-curdling scream. Like nightmares, this problem is more common among children than adults. It's also more frightening, particularly for others in the household. Since it occurs during NREM sleep, however, the night terror victim will usually not recall a dream and by morning will have forgotten the whole episode. Another NREM experience is *sleepwalking*, in which the sleeper quietly sits up, climbs out of bed, and walks about with eyes open and a blank expression. Sleepwalkers may start slowly, but soon they are going to the bathroom, dressing, eating, and opening doors. They are prone to accidents such as falling down stairs, so it is safer to gently awaken a sleepwalker than to allow the person to wander about. People used to think that sleepwalkers were acting out dreams. But that's not the case. These episodes occur early in the night, during the deep, slow-wave stages of sleep. Sometimes sleepwalkers will wake up and be disoriented, but most often they just go back to bed. As with night terror victims, sleepwalkers seldom recall their travels in the morning. This finding reinforces the point that the brain is active even during sleep—and that consciousness is complex and multilayered (Kelly, 1991).

[© 1994 Liz Haberfeld and The Cartoon Bank, Inc.]

HYPNOSIS

About twenty years ago, Ernest Hilgard was demonstrating hypnosis in his psychology class. The student who volunteered to serve as a subject happened to be blind, so Hilgard hypnotized him and said that on the count of three he would become deaf—and stay that way until touched on the right shoulder. One, two, three! Hilgard then proceeded to bang blocks together and fire a starter's pistol that made everyone else leap from their seats. But the subject did not respond. His classmates shouted out questions and taunted him, but still he did not respond. Then a hand went up. A student wanted to know if any part of the subject knew what was happening since, after all, there was nothing really wrong with his ears.

It was a fascinating question. Hilgard said to the subject, "Perhaps there is some part of your mind that is hearing my voice and processing the information. If there is, I should like the index finger of your right hand to rise as a sign that this is the case." To everyone's surprise, even Hilgard's, the young man raised his finger! Then he said, "Please restore my hearing so that you can tell me what you did." Hilgard put his hand on the subject's shoulder and asked, "Can you hear me now?" The subject did. "I remember your telling me that I would be deaf at the count of three and could have my hearing restored when you placed your hand on my shoulder. Then everything was quiet for a while. It was a little boring just sitting here so I busied myself with a statistical problem that I had been working on. I was still doing that when I felt my finger lift; that is what I want you to explain to me."

Next, Hilgard asked to speak with "that part of your mind that listened to me before, while you were hypnotically deaf." "Do you remember what happened?" The subject remembered it all. "After you counted to make me deaf, you made some noises as if banging blocks together behind my head. Members of the class asked me some questions to which I did not respond. Then one of them asked if I might really be hearing, and you told me to raise my finger if I did. This part of me responded by raising my finger, so it's all clear now." Hilgard lifted his hand from the subject's arm to restore the "normal" hypnotic state and said, "Please tell me what happened in the last few minutes." The subject responded, "You said . . . some part of me would talk to you. Did I talk?" The young man was assured that he would later recall everything that happened, and the session was terminated (Hilgard, 1992).

Hilgard called the aware part of the subject's mind a "hidden observer." This concept is controversial—and, as we'll see, it has far-reaching implications for the study of consciousness. But first things first. What is hypnosis, how is this state induced, and what are its effects?

The Seeds of Controversy

Hypnosis is a heightened state of suggestibility induced by systematic attention-focusing procedures. In one form or another, hypnosis has probably been around for centuries. But the earliest known reference to it is traced to Franz Anton Mesmer (1734–1815), a Viennese physician. Mesmer believed that illness was caused by an imbalance of magnetic fluids in the body—and could be cured by restoring the proper balance. Working in Paris, he would pass his hands across the patient's body and wave a magnetic wand over the infected area. Many patients would descend into a trance, and then awaken feeling better. The medical community, however, viewed this treatment with skepticism, and in 1784 a French commission chaired by Benjamin Franklin found that there was no scientific basis for the "animal magnetism" theory, only "mere imagination." Mesmer was labeled a quack and run out of town. When he died, he was penniless. To this day, however, we acknowledge his work whenever we describe ourselves as "mesmerized."

In the nineteenth century, the trance-like state Mesmer had created was called "hypnotism," from the Greek word for sleep. From that point on,

■ **hypnosis** A heightened state of suggestibility induced by systematic attention-focusing procedures.

hypnosis has had a rocky relationship with science. On the one hand, stage hypnotists who swing pocket watches back and forth, and try to make audience members cluck like chickens, lead people to associate hypnosis with parlor games, carnivals, and magic acts. On the other hand, psychoanalysis originated with Freud's use of hypnosis to treat patients with various nervous disorders. And today, many health care specialists use hypnosis with some success to control pain and help patients break bad habits. For researchers interested in consciousness, hypnosis is a useful and provocative phenomenon—one that is still not completely understood (Rhue et al., 1993).

The Hypnotic Induction

Hypnosis consists of two stages: an *induction*, which guides the subject into a pliable, suggestible frame of mind; and then a specific suggestion. The induction process is not like casting a spell. There are no magical words or incantations to be uttered, and there is no single technique. But there is one essential ingredient: a focusing of *attention*.

Speaking in a slow, soft, repetitive voice, the hypnotist asks the subject to concentrate on something. It can be anything. Hypnotists used to have subjects stare at a flame, or a shiny object, or a swinging pendulum, but a spot on the wall will work just as well. So will the subject's imagination. "Imagine that you're lying on a quiet beach. You are so warm and relaxed on the soft white sand, under the sun. You're very tired, and your eyes are closed. You can hear the ocean waves crashing on the shore . . . and the sea gulls flying overhead. And you can smell the warm salted air. It's so sunny. Your skin is so warm. And you're so relaxed. Your eyes are growing tired. Very tired. Your eyelids are getting heavy. Heavy. They're starting to close." Whatever technique is used, the purpose is to help the subject tune out all distractions and focus his or her mental spotlight.

Once the subject is in a state of "relaxed alertness," he or she is ripe for stage 2, *suggestion*. The hypnotist may begin with a quick test by suggest-

Hypnosis is important in the history of psychology and has profound implications for our understanding of consciousness. As shown here, hypnosis is also performed at carnivals for entertainment purposes.

ing that "your eyes are closed . . . and your eyelids are shut so tight that you cannot open them no matter how hard you try." Sure enough, the subject's eyes remain closed. At that point, the subject is ready for more. The hypnotist may note that the subject's arm is filling with air like a balloon, and feeling lighter and lighter—and rising in the air. The subject does not know why, but the arm rises, as if being pulled up on a string. The hypnotist may even invite the subject to enjoy the scent of "perfume"—and watch as he or she inhales the fumes from a jar of ammonia. After the subject has "passed" the preliminary tests, any additional suggestions depend on the reasons for the hypnosis. Thus, a subject may be encouraged to block out pain, recall a traumatic past event, forget a past event, or break a bad habit when the session is over.

Hypnotic Responsiveness

Contrary to popular belief, you cannot be hypnotized against your will. Nobody can. People also differ. Several years ago, Hilgard (1965) developed the Stanford Hypnotic Susceptibility Scale (SHSS), a twelve-item behavioral test that measures **hypnotic susceptibility**, or responsiveness, to hypnosis. In this test, a brief induction is followed by suggestions for the subject to close his or her eyes, sway back and forth, stiffen an arm, lower a hand, see an imaginary person, and so on. Consistently, Hilgard has found that 10 percent are highly susceptible to hypnosis, as indicated by a nearly perfect score on the twelve items. At the other extreme, 10 percent are invulnerable to hypnosis, as indicated by a very low score on the test. With an average test score of six, most of us follow some hypnotic suggestions but not others (Hilgard, 1982).

Why are some people more susceptible to hypnosis than others? Research has shown that college students who scored high or low in the early 1960s obtained similar scores when they were retested twenty-five years later (Piccione et al., 1989). Clearly, there are stable personality differences between highs and lows. The question is, How are these differences to be interpreted? It is interesting to me that in discussions of hypnosis, some students often seem overeager if not proud to surmise that they are too "independent" or too "strong-willed" to be hypnotized. But research shows that hypnotic responsiveness is not a sign of weakness—and that high scorers are not generally more conforming, compliant, or obedient. But they are more open to experience, have more vivid imaginations, and have an ability to become deeply absorbed in books, movies, and other activities (J. Hilgard, 1979; Nadon et al., 1991). High scorers also have a more sustained attention span and a greater ability to filter out distractions (Crawford et al., 1993).

The Myths and Realities

■ **hypnotic susceptibility** The characteristic extent to which an individual is responsive to hypnosis.

Can a hypnotist make you strip naked in front of an audience, clap your hands together, and bark like a seal? Popular portrayals of hypnosis are sometimes accurate, but often they are not. Based on the results of controlled research, let us examine the effects of hypnosis and try to separate the myths from the realities.

Can Hypnosis Enhance Eyewitness Testimony?

In 1976, in Chowchilla, California, a busload of twenty-six schoolchildren and their driver were abducted at gunpoint by three masked kidnappers and held for ransom in an underground tomb. Somehow, they managed to escape. The driver, who had tried to memorize the license plate number of the van the kidnappers had used, could not recall the number. He was then hypnotized by the police and mentally sent back to the scene of the crime. All of a sudden, he blurted out all but one digit of the license plate—which led to the arrest and later conviction of the abductors (Smith, 1983).

This case and others like it raise an intriguing question: Can hypnosis be used to refresh a witness's memory? Many police officers seem to think so, and use hypnosis to help eyewitnesses recall details of violent crimes they seem to have forgotten. In one popular technique, devised by Martin Reiser (1980), subjects under hypnosis are asked to imagine that they are calmly watching a TV documentary about the event to be recalled, and that they can rewind it, stop it, play it back, slow it down, speed it up, zoom in for close-ups, and turn the sound volume up or down to improve hearing. Using this technique, police investigators have made some fantastic claims about the memory-enhancing power of hypnosis (Reiser & Nielson, 1980).

The success stories are fascinating, but serious questions remain. When a hypnotized witness reports a memory, how do we know that the report is accurate? And if the recollection is later corroborated, how do we know that it was retrieved because of the hypnosis? To answer these questions, researchers have conducted experiments in which subjects witness a staged event, report on their memory, and try to recall additional details—either under hypnosis or in a normal waking state. Consistently, these studies have shown that although people report more and more information with repeated testing, they also inadvertently produce false "memories" (Dywan & Bowers, 1983; Dinges et al., 1992). After hypnosis, witnesses are also more confident about the accuracy of their recollections, yet they are unable to separate the actual memories from those produced under hypnosis (Sheehan & Tilden, 1983).

Another disturbing outcome of hypnosis is that it places the witness in a state of heightened suggestibility. For example, Peter Sheehan and his colleagues (1991) showed 168 subjects

---

Coercion   As noted earlier, people cannot be hypnotized against their will. But once under hypnosis, can subjects be coerced into committing acts that violate their conscience? Are they at the mercy of a skilled hypnotist? For the sake of those who stand to benefit from the therapeutic uses of hypnosis, one would hope not. In response to the idea that the subject is under the hypnotist's control, Karen Olness (1993), a pediatrician and hypnotherapist, says, "Nonsense. All hypnosis is self-hypnosis" (p. 280). Many psychologists share this view. And as a general rule, hypnotized subjects will reject immoral commands, knowing fully well that they are in control.

But there is evidence to suggest that hypnotic coercion can lead people to shed inhibitions. In one experiment, Martin Orne and Frederick Evans (1965) convinced hypnotized subjects to throw what they thought to be nitric acid into a research assistant's face. To see if this result proved that hypnosis can overpower the will, Orne and Evans told a second group of subjects only to pretend they were hypnotized, issued the same command, and found that they too threw the "acid." As we'll see in Part IV of this book, on social psychology, these disturbing results may say more about obedience to authority than about hypnosis.

Pain Relief   "On the operating table, I put myself into a deeply relaxed state. I then concentrated on a favorite memory: living on a farm as a child.

a videotape of a staged bank robbery. In it, a man enters a bank, waves a pistol, warns the tellers not to press an alarm, orders them to put the money on the counter, puts the money in a bag, and runs out. Subjects were immediately questioned about the incident. Half the subjects were then hypnotized; the others were not. Moments later, everyone was requestioned by an examiner who "suggested" that the robber wore a mask over his face, which he did not. The hypnotized subjects were then dehypnotized, and everyone was questioned again, this time by a new examiner. So, did anyone "recall" the robber wearing a mask? If so, how often did this occur? As illustrated in the accompanying figure, the results were striking—and sobering. Subjects were far more likely to incorporate the false suggestion into memory when they were under hypnosis, and this was particularly true of those who had high or medium scores on a test of a hypnotic susceptibility. Among the most vulnerable of subjects—those who were highly responsive and exposed to a hypnotic suggestion—false memories were created 63 percent of the time.

Today, some states will allow witnesses to testify about memories brought out under hypnosis. In light of recent research findings, however, a majority of American courts have reasonably decided to ban or at least limit the testimony of witnesses who had earlier been hypnotized (Scheflin & Shapiro, 1989).

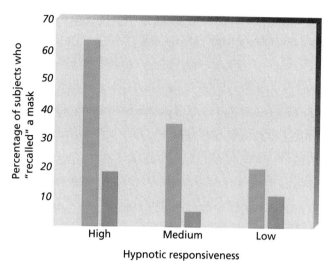

Hypnosis and the Suggestible Eyewitness

After seeing a staged crime, subjects were questioned in a hypnotized or waking state by an examiner who suggested that the culprit had worn a mask. Under hypnosis, many subjects—particularly those of high responsiveness—later incorporated this false suggestion into memory.

In my mind, I felt what it was like to lie on the grass, gaze up at the heavens, and see a bit of the barn out of the corner of my eye. As the surgeon cut into the base of my thumb, I reassured him that I felt no pain. . . . Although I was perfectly aware that I was undergoing surgery, I just wasn't very interested in it." This story, as described by Karen Olness (1993, p. 277), embodies one of the real benefits of hypnosis: to act as a psychological anesthetic.

In the classic test of this hypothesis, Hilgard and his colleagues (1975) instructed two groups of subjects to immerse one hand in a tank of ice water for almost a minute. Every ten seconds, they rated how much pain they felt on a 0-to-10-point scale. In one group, the subjects were hypnotized and given the suggestion that they would feel no pain. In the second group, there was no hypnosis and no suggestion. The result: Hypnotized subjects reported less pain than did the controls. We'll return to this study shortly to see what it implies about consciousness. What it implies about pain, however, is clear. New studies continue to show that for people who are high in hypnotic responsiveness, hypnosis reduces pain through the power of suggestion (Miller & Bowers, 1993). Clearly, not everyone can be hypnotized, and not all who are hypnotized will gain relief from pain. But for some, hypnosis is what it takes to cope with dental work, childbirth, and the chronic pain of headaches, backaches, and arthritis (Kihlstrom, 1985).

■ **posthypnotic suggestion** A suggestion made to a hypnosis subject to be carried out *after* the induction session is over.

■ **posthypnotic amnesia** A reported tendency for hypnosis subjects to forget events that occurred during the induction.

■ **hypermnesia** A term referring to the unsubstantiated claim that hypnosis can be used to facilitate the retrieval of past memories.

■ **state theories** Theories that maintain that hypnosis induces a unique "altered" state of consciousness.

■ **nonstate theories** Theories that view hypnosis as an ordinary state of consciousness.

■ **dissociation** A division of consciousness that permits one part of the mind to operate independent of another part.

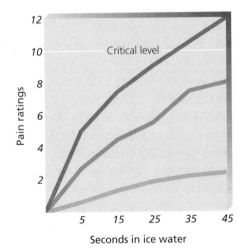

Figure 4.10

Hypnosis, Pain, and the "Hidden Observer"

Subjects immersed a hand in ice water and rated the pain they felt. Those under hypnosis reported less pain than did controls. But by pressing a key, they also indicated that some part of them—a "hidden observer"—was aware of the pain (Hilgard et al., 1975).

Posthypnotic Suggestion   In the situations described thus far, the subject acts upon the hypnotist's suggestions during the session. In a procedure known as **posthypnotic suggestion**, the subject carries out the hypnotist's suggestion *after* the session is terminated. You've probably seen this procedure depicted on TV shows. With a snap of the finger, the subject would emerge from his or her "trance" and reflexively perform a specific behavior in response to a preset cue. In reality, posthypnotic suggestion lacks dramatic flair. But the technique has been used effectively to help people stop smoking, drinking, or overeating. It can also help speed the healing of warts and other skin conditions that are affected by psychological factors—though positive suggestions made without hypnosis have the same therapeutic effect (Spanos et al., 1988).

Memory Enhancement   As in Hilgard's classroom demonstration, hypnosis subjects very often exhibit **posthypnotic amnesia**, an inability to recall events that occurred during the session. It's important to note that these memories have not been permanently erased. In response to a prearranged signal ("When I snap my fingers you'll recall everything that took place"), subjects can usually retrieve the lost events. At the other end of the hypnosis-memory spectrum, many hypnotists claim that the highly focused and relaxed state of mind produced by hypnosis *enhances* memory—a phenomenon known as **hypermnesia**. This claim has its roots in psychoanalysis—as Freud reported that hypnotized patients sometimes relived repressed traumas from childhood—and has resurfaced in a rash of recent cases in which hypnosis was used to dredge up buried memories of child sex abuse (Loftus, 1993). This use of hypnosis within the legal system has come under scrutiny (see box p.156).

Is Hypnosis an "Altered" State?

From the time Mesmer first used hypnotism to treat medical ailments, there has been widespread interest in the phenomenon. Freud used hypnosis to unlock the unconscious. Others have used it to relieve pain, to treat obesity, smoking, and other problems, to uncover repressed memories, and to entertain audiences around the world. Using hypnosis (including self-hypnosis) is easy. The tougher question is, What is it? Does hypnosis produce an out-of-the-ordinary, trance-like, "altered" state of consciousness?

Psychologists are divided on this question. Some say yes, others say no. In general, **state theories** maintain that hypnosis induces a unique state of consciousness and that people are more responsive to suggestion while in hypnosis than in other states (Hilgard, 1986; Bowers, 1976). In contrast, **nonstate theories** generally maintain that hypnosis is not a distinct physiological state and that hypnosis phenomena can be produced through relaxation, role playing, positive expectations, or the power of suggestion—without a hypnotic induction (Barber, 1969; Lynn et al., 1990; Spanos, 1986; Wagstaff, 1981).

State Theories   According to Ernest Hilgard (1986), hypnosis produces a state of **dissociation**—a division of consciousness in which one part of the person operates independently of another. To some extent, dissociation is a common experience—as when you drive somewhere, only to realize afterward that you "spaced out" and do not recall the route you took or the traffic signals you obeyed. One part of you drove, while another part daydreamed about fame and fortune. In many people, says Hilgard, hypnosis produces a similar split in which one part of the mind goes along with hypnotic suggestions, while the other part—a "hidden observer"—knows what's happening but does not participate.

To illustrate this concept, let's return to the pain-tolerance experiment described earlier (Hilgard et al., 1975). This was the study in which subjects immersed a hand in ice water and periodically rated how much pain they were in. Look at Figure 4.10, and you'll see that subjects reported far less pain when they were hypnotized to "feel no pain" than when they were not. In fact, compared to control subjects, who reached a pain level of 10 within twenty-five seconds, the average pain rating of hypnotized subjects never exceeded a 2 on the scale. In a fascinating variation on this experiment, the *hypnotized* subjects were told to press a key with their free hand if "some part" of them was in pain. Look once more at Figure 4.11, and you'll see what happened. Even though the hypnotized subjects reported low pain levels, their "hidden observer" was passively aware of the pain. Since these subjects reported two different experiences at once, the hypnosis must have put them in an altered state of consciousness. Well, perhaps.

Nonstate Theories   The skeptics differ in their emphasis, but all agree that the impressive effects of hypnosis stem from the power of social influence, not from a trance-like state of altered consciousness. Perhaps highly responsive subjects are motivated to comply. Or perhaps they become so absorbed by the situation that they get caught up in their role the way dramatic actors often do. In support of the nonstate view, research shows that control subjects in the waking state often exhibit the same remarkable behaviors—when they are sufficiently motivated and believe they can succeed. Thus, pain tolerance in the ice water test can be increased without the hypnotic induction (Spanos & Katsanis, 1989).

It's important to realize that most nonstate theorists do not believe that hypnosis subjects consciously fake their compliance with hypnotic suggestions. Is it possible to test this hypothesis? Yes. If subjects are merely playing along, they might respond to suggestions in the hypnotist's presence—but not in his or her absence. In fact, however, the hypnotic effects carry over. For example, Irving Kirsch and his colleagues (1989) hypnotized highly responsive subjects but instructed low-responsive subjects to simulate hypnosis. The hypnotic test was twice administered over a tape recorder—once in front of the examiner, and once when the subject was left alone. As shown in Figure 4.11, the results were clear: in front of the examiner, both hypnotized subjects and simulators complied equally with suggestions. But in the alone condition, a hidden camera revealed that subjects who were under hypnosis continued to respond to the test suggestions even while the simulators did not (in some cases, the simulators actually opened their eyes and read a magazine!). Additional studies have replicated this result (Spanos et al., 1993) and indicated that hypnotized subjects are not faking the experience (Kinnunen et al., 1994). Hypnosis may be less than an altered state, but it is more than mere compliance.

At this point, there are two ways to view hypnosis—and these need not be exclusive of one another. It is possible, if not likely, that highly responsive individuals experience an altered state of consciousness. When college

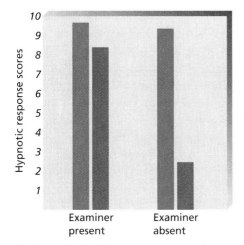

Figure 4.11

Hypnosis: More Than Mere Compliance

Subjects who were hypnotized or told to simulate hypnosis were twice given a tape-recorded hypnotic induction—once in the presence of the examiner, and once alone. As shown, both groups followed the suggestions in front of the examiner (left). Hypnotized subjects, but not simulators, continued to do so even when alone (right) (Kirsch et al., 1989).

students were interviewed about their performance in a campus-wide hypnotism show, 28 percent of those who participated thought the hypnotist had complete control over their behavior and that they could not resist the suggestions (Crawford et al., 1992). Also, new evidence suggests that people who are highly responsive to hypnosis exhibit increases in right-hemisphere brain activity during hypnosis (McCormack & Gruzelier, 1993). At the same time, it seems clear that there are others who succumb to hypnosis and comply with suggestions without an altered state of consciousness—thus explaining why the subject's expectations, motivations, and rapport with the hypnotist play an important role (Sarbin, 1992). In short, there may be two roads, both leading to the treasure.

PSYCHOACTIVE DRUGS

Throughout history, people in all parts of the world have sought new ways to achieve altered states of consciousness. Dancing, chanting, twirling in circles, repetitive prayer, yoga, meditation, ritualized fasting, sensory isolation, and intoxicants such as opium, alcohol, marijuana, and cocaine are just a few examples. The historical and cross-cultural consistency of these behaviors is so compelling that some researchers believe there is an inborn human need to experience altered states of mind (Siegel, 1989; Weil & Rosen, 1993).

Alcohol, probably the first "mind-altering" substance used by humans, goes back about 10,000 years. Opium was used 6,000 years ago, and hallucinogenic mushrooms and weeds go back about 4,000 years (Palfai & Jankiewicz, 1991). More recently, Native Americans smoked tobacco as a goodwill offering. South Pacific islanders drink kava, a calming drink that is made from dried roots. And Europeans celebrate special occasions with wine and champagne. Instances of drug use can even be found among animals, as baboons eat tobacco, rabbits eat intoxicating mushrooms, and elephants seek out fermented fruit.

People have used psychoactive drugs throughout history. In this Egyptian painting, dated 1350 B.C., the man on the left is sipping beer through a cane.

People all over the world behave in ways that alter states of consciousness. As shown, college football players do relaxation exercises, Haitian men and women dance in a ritual voodoo ceremony, and Chinese girls sip wine through a bamboo straw.

■ **psychoactive drug** A chemical that alters perceptions, thoughts, moods, or behavior.

■ **physical dependence** A physiological addiction in which a drug is needed to prevent symptoms of withdrawal.

■ **psychological dependence** A condition in which drugs are needed to maintain a sense of well-being or relief from negative emotions.

■ **sedatives** A class of depressant drugs that slow down activity in the central nervous system (e.g., alcohol, barbiturates).

A quick but often dangerous way to alter consciousness is to use a **psychoactive drug**, a chemical that influences perceptions, moods, thoughts, or behavior. Depending on where in the world you are, a psychoactive substance may be legal or illegal. In most countries, caffeine, tobacco, alcohol, tranquilizers, and sleeping pills are legal, while marijuana, cocaine, crack, heroin, and LSD are not. As in our ancient past, humans are also in hot pursuit of the perfect "aphrodisiac"—a drug that will enhance sexual desire, pleasure, and performance (Rosen & Ashton, 1993).

Psychoactive drugs can become physically or psychologically addictive. **Physical dependence** is a physiological state in which continued drug use is needed to satisfy an intense craving and prevent the dreaded onset of *withdrawal* symptoms such as shaking, sweating, and vomiting. Continued use of psychoactive drugs also produces *tolerance*, a condition in which larger and larger doses are needed to experience the same effect. Even without a physical addiction, people can also develop a **psychological dependence**, in which continued drug use is needed to maintain a sense of well-being. As described in the coming pages and summarized in Table 4.2, there are four classes of psychoactive drugs: sedatives, stimulants, hallucinogens, and opiates. The drugs most commonly used by people eighteen to twenty-five years old in the United States are presented in Figure 4.12.

Sedatives

Sedatives, or depressants, slow down activity in the central nervous system and produce calmness, drowsiness, and, in large doses, a loss of consciousness. The most commonly used sedatives are alcohol, barbiturates, and benzodiazepines. The last two are used for anesthetic purposes and in the treatment of anxiety and insomnia. As a rule, these drugs are highly addictive (Winger et al., 1992).

Alcohol is one of the most widely used drugs in the world. Regardless of whether it comes out of a six-pack, a bottle of fine wine, or a glass of whiskey, gin, or vodka, alcohol is something of a paradox. It's known as a

Table 4.2

Psychoactive Drugs

Type	Substance	Range of effects
Sedatives	alcohol barbiturates benzodiazepines	Slowdown of body functions, relaxation, drowsiness, possibly depression and loss of consciousness
Stimulants	caffeine nicotine amphetamines cocaine	Speed up of body functions, alertness, energy, elation, jitteriness, loss of appetite
Hallucinogens	LSD marijuana	Heightened sensory awareness, distorted perceptions of time and space, hallucinations
Opiates	Heroin Morphine Codeine	Suppressed pain, depressed neural activity, relaxation, drowsiness, euphoria

"First you take a drink, then the drink takes a drink, then the drink takes you."

F. SCOTT FITZGERALD

"Drunkenness reveals what soberness conceals."

ENGLISH PROVERB

party drug that lifts spirits and lowers inhibitions, yet it has a sedative, depressant effect on the body. The symptoms include decreased visual acuity; diminished attention; lowered sensitivity to taste, smell, and pain; slowed reaction times; a loss of balance; slurred speech; and lowered performance on intelligence tests. Alcohol hastens the onset of sleep (as do most depressants) but does not increase the overall amount of time one sleeps in a night. In fact, it suppresses REM sleep—which has a disruptive effect once the alcohol wears off.

Anyone who has had a few drinks knows that alcohol alters awareness and behavior. As we'll elaborate on later, alcohol has two effects in this regard. First, people often drown their sorrows in a bottle to escape from fail-

Figure 4.12

The Five Most Commonly Used Drugs

Shown here are the percentages of people eighteen to twenty-five years old who have tried and regularly use various drugs—not for medical purposes (National Household Survey of Drug Abuse, 1991).

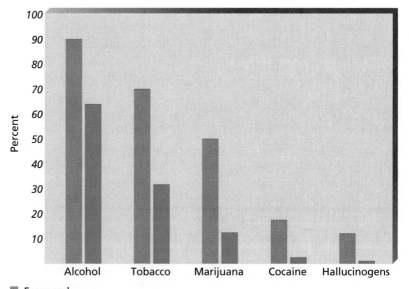

■ Ever used
■ Regularly use

Alcohol is one of the most widely used drugs in the world. Inside and outside this London pub, it is known as a social party drug.

ure and its harsh implications for their self-esteem. Many of us expect alcohol to provide this type of "relief" (Leigh & Stacy, 1993). Second, people take more risks when drunk than when sober. Part of the problem is that alcohol leads us to become short-sighted about the consequences of our actions—thus evoking a state of "drunken excess" (Steele & Josephs, 1990). Statistics consistently link drinking to highway fatalities, murders, stabbings, child abuse, and other acts of crime and violence. In laboratory experiments, subjects are more aggressive when given alcohol to drink than when given a nonalcoholic beverage (Bushman & Cooper, 1990).

Barbiturates are sedatives used in the treatment of epilepsy, anxiety, and insomnia (Lickey & Gordon, 1991). The behavioral effects of barbiturates are similar to those of alcohol, such as drowsiness, slowness, and decreased performance on perceptual and cognitive tasks. In large doses, barbiturates also serve as an anesthetic, providing significant relief from pain. However, they tend to cause hangovers after the effects wear off. Barbiturates are among the most abused of drugs. They are also addictive. Tolerance to barbiturates develops rapidly, and withdrawal symptoms are unpleasant. Mixing alcohol with barbiturates is particularly dangerous.

Benzodiazepines, or tranquilizers, are a class of drugs often used in the treatment of anxiety and insomnia. Valium and Librium are among the most common "downers." Taken in pill form, they have a calming and relaxing effect and put people to sleep—usually for the entire night. Benzodiazepines are much safer than barbiturates. For many, they have become the sedatives of choice (see Chapter 17).

Stimulants

Stimulants excite the central nervous system and stimulate behavior (Leccese, 1991). Caffeine and nicotine are common mild stimulants. Amphetamines and cocaine have much stronger effects. These drugs speed up body functions (which is why amphetamines are known as "speed" or "uppers"), increase breathing and heart rates, heighten alertness, suppress appetite, and produce feelings of excitement, self-confidence, and even elation. For these reasons, stimulants have been used to stay awake, lose weight, and elevate mood. In large amounts, they can make a person anxious, jittery, and hyper-alert. As is often the case with psychoactive drugs, the user may come down from the high in a "crash" and feel tired, downbeat, and irritable. As with sedatives, there is also a risk of addiction.

Amphetamines are synthetic drugs, often taken in pill form, for the treatment of asthma, narcolepsy, depression, and obesity (Palfai & Jankiewicz, 1991). Chronic amphetamine use can trigger schizophrenia-like symptoms. Recently, amphetamine modifications have been synthesized in the pharmaceutical laboratory. One of these "designer drugs" is MDMA, or Ecstasy. In addition to its stimulant properties, MDMA is said to evoke a sense of well-being, particularly in relation to others (Shulgin, 1986).

Cocaine ("coke") is a natural drug derived from the leaves of the coca plant, a shrub native to South America. Its use as a stimulant was discovered hundreds of years ago by Peruvian Indians, who chewed coca leaves to overcome fatigue and increase stamina. Taken in this manner, small amounts of cocaine gradually enter the bloodstream. Today, cocaine in powder form is usually inhaled through the nose, resulting in a quick,

■ **stimulants** A class of drugs that excite the central nervous system and energize behavior (e.g., amphetamines, cocaine).

intense "rush." As seen in Figure 4.12, cocaine is one of the most abused illegal drugs in the United States. Its consciousness-altering effects, which last up to thirty minutes, are predictably followed by a "crash" caused by a temporary depletion in the supply of dopamine and norepinephrine. A highly potent form of cocaine known as "crack" is smoked in a pipe or injected directly into the bloodstream. Crack gives a higher "high" but is followed by a lower "low"—and a craving for another "hit." It is dangerous and highly addictive (Gawin, 1991).

Hallucinogens

Hallucinogens are the psychoactive drugs that cause the most dramatic alterations in consciousness. These drugs (which are also called psychedelics, from the Greek words meaning "mind expanding") distort perceptions of time and space and cause hallucinations—sensations without sensory input. The best-known hallucinogens are LSD and PCP. The latter (also called "angel dust") is a potent but dangerous pain killer. Marijuana, which has mixed sedative and stimulant effects, also acts as a mild hallucinogen.

LSD (lysergic acid diethylamide) is a synthetic drug that was first discovered in 1938 by Albert Hofman, a Swiss chemist. At one point, Hofman experimented on himself. He took what he thought to be a small dose of LSD and found himself in a world he would never forget: "Everything in my field of vision was distorted as if seen in a curved mirror. . . . Familiar objects and furniture assumed grotesque, threatening forms. . . . Fantastic images surged in on me, alternating, variegated, opening and closing themselves in circles and spirals, exploding in colored fountains" (Hofman, 1983). Drug companies, researchers, and intelligence agencies in search of a truth serum went on to experiment with LSD. Even when it is taken at low doses, acid "trippers" report that objects shimmer, colors become more vivid, the perception of time is slowed, old memories surface, and emotions range from euphoria to panic. Often, too, there is an eerie feeling of separation from one's own body. Researchers now believe that LSD and other hallucinogens produce these effects by blocking the activity of the neurotransmitter serotonin.

Marijuana is a milder and less potent hallucinogen. It is derived from the leaves and flowering tops of the hemp plant, *cannabis sativa,* and has been cultivated for 5,000 years in many parts of the world. Its major active ingredient is called THC (delta-9-tetrahydrocannabinol), but it contains other chemicals that also have psychoactive effects. Marijuana is usually smoked in hand-rolled "joints" or pipes, but it may also be mixed into foods such as brownies. At low doses, marijuana may act as a sedative, producing a relaxed state and possibly a mild euphoria. It may also heighten awareness of colors, sounds, tastes, smells, and other sensations. At higher doses, it may distort perceptions of time and space. In the United States, marijuana is the most commonly used illicit drug (see Figure 4.12).

There is widespread disagreement over the costs and benefits of marijuana use. Smoking marijuana, like tobacco, causes lung damage. It also slows reaction time and impairs coordination—hence the danger of driving while "stoned." Depending on the person and situation, it may also magnify feelings of anxiety, paranoia, or depression. Marijuana is not particularly addictive, however, and it does have important clinical uses. A signifi-

■ **hallucinogens** Psychedelic drugs that distort perceptions and cause hallucinations (e.g., LSD, marijuana).

cant body of research shows that marijuana combats nausea and weight loss in cancer and AIDS patients and helps to reduce pressure in the eyes of glaucoma patients. In a recent nationwide survey of cancer specialists, 48 percent said they would prescribe marijuana if it were legal, and 44 percent said they had already recommended marijuana to at least one patient—even though it's illegal (Doblin & Kleiman, 1991).

Opiates

Opiates are a class of drugs related to opium, and they include morphine, codeine, and heroin (McKim, 1991). Their most prominent effect is to produce euphoria and analgesia (they also cause constipation). Because they depress neural activity, opiates are widely prescribed for the alleviation of pain. The user becomes drowsy and lethargic, yet happy and euphoric. Changes in consciousness are not particularly striking. These drugs are highly addictive, as the user quickly develops an insatiable need for more and larger doses. Heroin can be injected, smoked, or inhaled. Those who are addicted risk death through overdose, contaminated drugs, and AIDS contracted by sharing drug-injection needles.

People all over the world have sought to alter their states of consciousness, often by the consumption of psychoactive drugs. Whatever the reasons for this desire, it is clear that drug use often turns to abuse, and that social factors—such as poverty, peer pressure, work stress, and a lack of personal fulfillment—play a role. In the United States, the number of people who use psychoactive drugs has declined over the past few years. Still, the problem is far from solved. And it is not clear, as a matter of public policy, how it can be solved. Thus, as policymakers debate the perennial question of whether to legalize the illicit drugs, psychologists concede that one cannot confidently predict the impact of such a policy (MacCoun, 1993).

CONSCIOUSNESS AND CONTROL

"A penny for your thoughts?" Over the years, psychologists have equated consciousness with attention and examined varying states of awareness ranging from sleep and dreams to hypnosis and the effects of mind-altering drugs. We have seen that people can often control the contents of consciousness. Research on selective attention shows that as we focus the spotlight of awareness on one stimulus, we can screen out irrelevant competing information. At times we can divide our attention, simultaneously engage in two or more activities, and process information without awareness.

Our ability to exert control over the contents of awareness is more impressive than most people realize. We saw earlier, for example, that lucid dreamers can sometimes control their dreams—and that almost anyone who is motivated can be trained to become a lucid dreamer. And we saw that while some of us can be hypnotized easily (a trait that requires the ability to focus attention and become absorbed), people cannot be hypnotized against their will—and those who are normally low in hypnotic susceptibility can learn to become more responsive to induction. Of course, when it comes to drug-induced altered states of consciousness, the choice is yours.

■ **opiates** A class of highly addictive drugs that depress neural activity and provide temporary relief from pain and anxiety (e.g., heroin, morphine).

Despite these impressive abilities, there are times when the control of consciousness seems out of reach. The mind may wander, you may slip into a daydream, you may become distracted despite your efforts at concentration. People who become dependent upon a psychoactive drug may lose the ability to control their states of consciousness. And those who suffer from various anxiety-related disorders may become literally obsessed with certain thoughts (see Chapter 16). Studying what he calls "ironic processes" in mental control, Daniel Wegner (1994) has found that, at times, the harder you try to control your thoughts, the less likely you are to succeed. Try *not* to think about a white bear for the next thirty seconds, and chances are, that very image will intrude upon your consciousness with remarkable frequency. Instruct a jury to disregard an item of inadmissible testimony, and that censored material is sure to pop to mind as they deliberate on a verdict. Try not to worry about how long it's taking to fall asleep, and you'll stay awake. Try not to think about an itch—well, you get the idea. According to Wegner, every conscious effort to control a thought is met by a concern about the failure to do so. For psychologists, and everyone else for that matter, the key is to learn how to minimize these ironic effects.

SUMMARY AND KEY TERMS

Attentional Processes

Psychologists generally define *consciousness* in terms of *attention*—an awareness of the sensations, thoughts, and feelings that one is attending to at a given moment. Three important processes governing consciousness are selective attention, divided attention, and influence without awareness.

Selective Attention

Studies of the *cocktail party effect* demonstrate that people can use *selective attention* to focus on one stimulus and virtually exclude other stimuli from consciousness.

Divided Attention

Other listening experiments show that *divided attention* is possible: some stimuli penetrate consciousness even when we are focusing on something else. Moreover, if we are so experienced at a particular process that it becomes automatic, we can do other things at the same time. The *Stroop test* demonstrates, for example, that experienced readers process word meanings automatically, without effort or awareness.

Influence Without Awareness

A number of studies show that people can be influenced by *subliminal messages*—information below the threshold of awareness. Two characteristic means of influencing a response, prior exposure to a stimulus and priming, both have an effect even when the stimulus is subliminal. People with *prosopagnosia*, who cannot recognize familiar faces, show glimmers of recognition without knowing they are doing so. And people with *blindsight* can react to certain visual cues without awareness.

There is no strong evidence, however, that subliminal persuasion can change our long-term behavior.

Sleep and Dreams

The Sleep-Wake Cycle

As biological organisms, humans experience regular fluctuations known as *biological rhythms*. Our day-long *circadian rhythm*, such as the sleep-wake cycle, is controlled by the suprachiasmatic nucleus of the hypothalamus, which seems to respond to light in the environment. Cut off from sunlight, humans tend to drift toward longer daily cycles. When our rhythms are disrupted, we may experience reactions such as jet lag.

The Stages of Sleep

Sleep follows its own cycle of distinct stages: presleep; stages 1–4 of deepening sleep, as the body relaxes and brain waves become larger and slower; and *REM sleep*, characterized by rapid eye movements, increased pulse rate and breathing, brain waves like those of presleep, and totally relaxed muscles. It is during REM sleep that vivid dreams occur. Each night, as we pass through several cycles, we gradually spend more time in REM sleep and less time in non-REM or *NREM sleep*.

Why Sleep?

Sleep is so necessary that when people try to stay awake for long periods, they fall into short microsleeps, a few seconds at a time. According to restoration theory, sleep helps us recover from the day's demands. Circadian theory offers an evolutionary explanation: sleep helps animals conserve energy and avoid predators when not searching for food or seeking a mate.

Dreams

Dreams, too, seem to serve an adaptive function. As shown by studies that measure the amount of REM sleep, people do their greatest amount of dreaming early in life when the brain is still developing. Common dream themes include falling and being chased or attacked. Both daily concerns and external stimuli influence dream content. Some people experience *lucid dreaming,* a semiconscious state in which they are aware of their own dreams and can even control them.

Freud accounted for the bizarre quality of dreams by theorizing that they are disguised expressions of unconscious wishes. To interpret dreams, Freud said, we have to go beyond the *manifest content* to uncover the unconscious meaning or *latent content.* A more recent hypothesis, the *activation-synthesis theory,* contends that dreams begin with random neural signals in the brainstem. When these signals spread up to the cortex, the brain tries to make sense of them by constructing images and stories.

Sleep Disturbances

Sleep disturbances are common. *Insomnia*—the inability to fall asleep, stay asleep, or get enough sleep—has many causes, including medical problems, depression, and drug abuse. Hypersomnia (sleeping too much) is less frequent but more dangerous. For instance, *narcolepsy*—characterized by sudden attacks of drowsiness and REM sleep—is a life-threatening disorder. Other sleep disturbances, known as parasomnias, include nightmares, night terrors, and sleepwalking.

Hypnosis

The Seeds of Controversy

Hypnosis, a heightened state of suggestibility induced by systematic attention-focusing procedures, has long been controversial.

The Hypnotic Induction

In the first stage of hypnosis, induction, the subject's attention is focused. In the second stage, suggestion, the subject responds to the hypnotist's cues.

Hypnotic Responsiveness

People differ in their degree of *hypnotic susceptibility.* Those who are most responsive to hypnosis tend to have vivid imaginations and long attention spans.

The Myths and Realities

Contrary to myth, people cannot be hypnotized against their will, nor can they be coerced into violating their consciences.

Evidence suggests, however, that hypnotized subjects may shed their inhibitions. Hypnosis can also reduce pain. Through *posthypnotic suggestion,* the hypnotist can influence a subject's behavior even after the session ends. *Posthypnotic amnesia* is also common, though not permanent. But *hypermnesia,* the supposed enhancement of memory by hypnosis, has not been confirmed by experiments; in fact, research indicates that hypnosis makes people more vulnerable to false memories.

Is Hypnosis an "Altered" State?

State theories maintain that hypnosis induces a unique, altered state of consciousness. *Nonstate theories* see hypnosis as an ordinary state characterized by phenomena that can be produced by other means. Many state theories contend that the subject experiences *dissociation,* a division of consciousness in which one part of the mind operates independent of another. Nonstate theories explain hypnotic phenomena as the result of social influence. Recent research suggests that both theories may be true: some subjects may reach a truly altered state, while others do not.

Psychoactive Drugs

Throughout history, people have sought altered states of consciousness, often by using *psychoactive drugs,* chemicals that change perceptions, moods, thoughts, or behavior. Such drugs can become addictive, creating either *physical dependence* or *psychological dependence.*

Sedatives

Among psychoactive drugs, *sedatives* such as alcohol, barbiturates, and benzodiazepines slow activity in the central nervous system.

Stimulants

Stimulants, including caffeine, nicotine, amphetamines, and cocaine, excite the central nervous system and energize behavior.

Hallucinogens

Hallucinogens or psychedelic drugs, such as LSD and marijuana, distort perceptions and cause hallucinations.

Opiates

The highly addictive *opiates,* such as heroin, morphine, and codeine, depress neural activity, relieve pain, and produce euphoria.

Consciousness and Control

As studies of attention and hypnosis illustrate, people have a great deal of command over their own consciousness. Yet there are times when our minds wander and we cannot control the distractions. Often we must contend with an irony: the harder we try to manage our thoughts, the less we succeed.

PART II

Are people rational or irrational? Competent or incompe-

tent? Among psychologists who study cognitive and affec-

tive processes, this question has sparked many debates. Part II opens

with Chapter 5 on *learning,* and includes the principles of classical

conditioning, operant conditioning, and modeling. Chapter 6 on

memory introduces information-processing models, the sensory reg-

ister, short-term memory, and long-term memory. The chapter also

reviews recent studies of autobiographical memory. Chapter 7 on

thought and language examines research on problem-solving, judg-

ment, and language in animals and humans. This part closes with

Chapter 8 on the physiological, expressive, and cognitive compo-

nents of *emotion.* Various types of emotions are distinguished, and

cultural and sex differences are discussed.

COGNITIVE AND AFFECTIVE PROCESSES

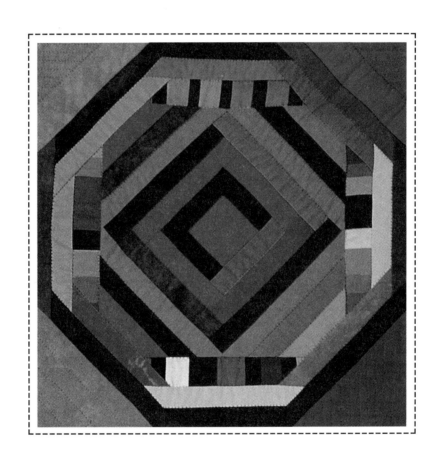

Chapter 5

Learning

Every spring, a tiny fresh-water fish called the stickleback performs an intriguing reproductive ritual. As the male's belly turns from dull gray to bright red, he builds a nest and performs a zigzag courtship "dance" to attract a female, occasionally brushing her belly with his stickles. He then escorts her to the nest, prods her tail to induce spawning, fertilizes her eggs, aerates the eggs by fanning the water, and vigorously attacks all red-bellied male intruders. Once the eggs hatch a week later, he guards the young and keeps them close by until they are ready to leave the nest.

Many land animals also exhibit adaptive, complex forms of behavior. When the herring gull mother returns to the nest with food, newly hatched chicks will peck at her bright yellow bill, causing her to regurgitate the food for their consumption. The honeybee uses a wax it secretes to build hives in which each comb consists of hexagonal cells that form a mathematically efficient, perfect design. The indigo bunting, a small bird, navigates south every winter, using as a guide the bright North Star, the only star in the Northern Hemisphere that maintains a fixed compass position through the night. Similarly prepared by instinct, the canary sings, the spider weaves its web, the beaver builds dams, and the newly hatched duckling follows the first moving object it sees, usually its mother. How do the stickleback and others know what to do? Simple. In many animal species, certain behaviors are programmed by *instinct*.

Programmed by instinct, bees build honeycombs and spiders weave webs.

 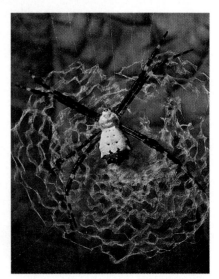

■ **ethology** The study of the behavior of animals in their natural habitat.

■ **fixed action pattern** A species-specific behavior that is built into an animal's nervous system and triggered by a specific stimulus.

Inspired by Darwin's theory of evolution, and led by Nobel Prize winners Konrad Lorenz and Nokilaas Tinbergen, **ethologists** study the behavior of animals in their natural habitat (Dewsbury, 1992; Eibl-Eibesfeldt, 1989). Based on their observations, these researchers refer to the instinctual behaviors as **fixed action patterns.** A fixed action pattern is a species-wide sequence of movements that is built into the nervous system and triggered or "released" by a specific stimulus. The response to the stimulus is automatic, like a reflex—no ifs, ands, or buts. Thus, the stickleback male attacks all red-bellied forms, even those that do not resemble a fish (see Figure 5.1). Similarly, the herring gull chick pecks at all moving red dots, even if they do not resemble another bird (see Figure 5.2).

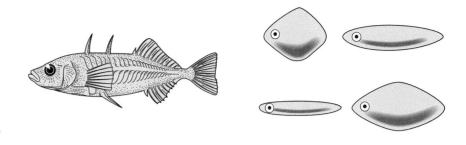

Figure 5.1

Stickleback Models

Research shows that various red-bellied objects trigger male attack, yet a replica of another male stickleback without a red belly does not. The red belly is the stimulus that releases this fixed action pattern (Tinbergen, 1951).

Do people exhibit fixed action patterns? Are we instinctual creatures? We'll see later that human newborns are equipped with adaptive, instinct-like behaviors in the form of reflexes. Upon birth, an infant will clutch anything that touches the palm of the hand, turn with an open mouth toward any object that grazes the cheek, start sucking when the lips are touched, and swallow when the back of the mouth is stimulated. These reflexes are not within the infant's control, and some disappear in a few months, never to return. Why are we less equipped with inborn, reflex-like rituals than the stickleback? Because we adapt to life's demands not by instinct but through learning, memory, thought, language, and emotion.

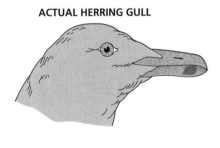

ACTUAL HERRING GULL　　**HERRING GULL MODELS**　　**SUPERNORMAL STIMULUS**

Figure 5.2

Herring Gull Models

Research shows that pecking is released by the movement of any red dot—even on objects, such as a pencil, that do not resemble the gull's beak (Hailman, 1969).

THE BIG PICTURE

When scientists compare human beings to other animals, they point to our superior intellect—to our ability to learn from experience, keep what we have learned in memory, think and reason in logical and abstract terms, and communicate to others through the use of language. Indeed, many cognitive psychologists have likened the information-processing capacities of the human mind to that of a computer. According to this view, people are capable of acquiring large amounts of information, converting it into a usable form, and storing it all in memory—to be retrieved as needed for solving problems, calculating probabilities, making decisions, and interacting with others. A good deal of research shows that people are competent, objective, and eminently rational.

And who would dispute it? In the first part of this book, we saw that the human brain is an extraordinarily complex organ. It weighs only three pounds yet contains more than 100 billion interconnected neurons and provides roughly 100 trillion synaptic connections that control our sensory systems, perceptions, consciousness, and other mental activities. Compared to all other animals, the cerebral cortex of the human brain is by far the most highly developed. Indeed, the triumphs of science, art, and civilization—our ability to split the atom, land on the moon, crack the genetic code, paint lifelike images on canvas, build pyramids and other architectural splendors, transplant organs to save lives, and invent the very computer to which we like to compare ourselves—are proof of what feats the human mind can achieve.

At the same time, researchers studying different aspects of human cognition have found that we are not machine-like in our processing of information. In Part I of this book, we saw that the human brain is in some ways like that of lower animals. The brain stem is similar to that found in other vertebrates, and the limbic system is similar to that of most other mammals. Indeed, whenever we fail to learn, repeat mistakes of the past, forget important names or dates, gamble away hard-earned money in games of chance, get fooled by con artists, make hasty decisions, or clench our teeth in fits of jealous rage, we reveal ourselves to be somewhat less competent, less objective, and less rational. To make matters worse, we are not always aware of our limitations, so we often feel overconfident about the accuracy of what we know. A great deal of research thus serves as a humbling reminder that each of us is an imperfect, sometimes lazy, and often emotional warm-blooded creature of habit—not a computer.

As we explore the psychology of learning, memory, thought, language, and emotion in Part II of this book, you'll find that there is an undercurrent of tension over the question of human competence and rationality. You'll also find, I think, that both views are correct. In some ways people are supremely competent, yet in other ways they are not. To illustrate the point, imagine that you are a subject in the following experiment.

What's Your Prediction?

THE SITUATION

As you enter the laboratory reception area, you are met by an experimenter, taken to a small room, and told that you will be taking part in a study of human memory. Next you're told that you will have seven minutes to examine the following strings of letters, and that you should try to "learn and remember as much as you can." The task is clear, so you have no questions. Ready, begin:

PVV	TSSSXXVV	TSXXTVPS	PVPXTVPS	TSSXXVV
TSXS	PTVPXVV	TXXTVPS	TXXTTTVV	PVPXVV
TSSXXVPS	TXXVPXVV	PTVPS	PTTTVPS	PTVPPXTVV
PVPXVPS	PTTVV	TXS	TSSSXS	TXXTVPS

You look at these meaningless items one by one, trying to memorize. P-V-V. T-S-X-S. You repeat them under your breath, over and over. After seven minutes, the experimenter stops you. Time's up. You can't wait to write down what you remember before you lose it—but the experimenter has other plans. He or she now reveals that the items were formed according to a set of rules, an "artificial grammar" if you will, and is interested in whether you know what the rules are. As the experimenter starts to explain the test you're about to take, you get a sinking feeling in the pit of your stomach. "Uh oh. There were rules? Did I miss something? I wasn't looking for rules!"

The test is straightforward. On slides, you will be shown 100 new items consisting of the same letters as before, one item per slide. Half of these will be grammatical (formed according to the rules), half will not. For each one, you are to press a button marked YES if you think the item is grammatical or one marked NO if you think it's not. You should also rate your level of confidence in each judgment on a scale marked from 1 to 5. Oh, one more thing: your responses will be timed.

The slide projector is turned on, the overhead lights are shut off, and you've got your fingers on the buttons ready to fire. First item: PTTTVPVS. It looks okay, as it contains the usual letters, and all. But are these letters ordered in a way that fits the grammar? "If I don't know," you ask, "should I just guess?" Instructed to respond to every item, you press a button and state your confidence. The next one is PVTVV. Same routine. Then PVPS. SVPXTVV. SXXVPS. PTTTVPS. TXXVV. TPVV. Sometimes you answer quickly; at other times you stare at the lit screen for a while before making a response. By the 100th slide, you're ready for a cool drink and a nap.

MAKE A PREDICTION

How well do you think subjects like yourself fare in this task? Having been in this experiment myself, I can tell you that many subjects shrug their shoulders in confusion. Based on what you've read, what do you think is the average test score? If all you did was guess, you would achieve roughly a 50 percent accuracy rate. Of course, if you came up with rules that were wrong, your score could be lower. If you knew the right rules, you would do better. So what is your estimate: 10 percent? 30? 50? 55? 59 or 60? Between 60 and 65? 90? Make a prediction:

0   5   10   15   20   25   30   35   40   45   50   55

60   65   70   75   80   85   90   95   100

THE RESULTS

For thirty years, cognitive psychologist Arthur Reber (1993) has used experiments like this one to study "implicit learning"—the tendency for people to acquire complex, abstract concepts without awareness or intention. Consistently, Reber finds that subjects cannot describe the grammar he uses to form the letter strings, nor can they explain the reasons for their YES-NO test responses. Yet in studies like the one just described, subjects did more than guess. They made the correct response 77 percent of the time, and usually did so quickly.

WHAT DOES IT ALL MEAN?

According to Reber, implicit learning, which occurs outside of conscious awareness, is a primitive but very powerful form of adaptation. Indeed, people learn his grammar—not by looking for it and not as a result of explicit instruction, but simply from exposure to properly formed letter strings. Without conscious effort, it just happens. It's the way we learn how to speak grammatically in our native tongue, or to behave appropriately in a new setting, or to "calculate" the trajectory of a ball in flight in order to make the catch. A good deal of research now confirms that these learning processes are not explicit and would be difficult to teach in step-by-step terms (Knowlton & Squire, 1994).

What if subjects are told that there's a grammar *before* seeing the items? Does active searching for rules improve learning? Would test scores rise to 80 percent, 90 percent, or higher? No. In fact, the opposite is true. Test performance declines when subjects try to discern the rules during exposure. As in real language, we may not be able to articulate the rules of grammar, but we know instantly when those rules have been violated. Call it intuition, if you want. The point is, people know far more than they can tell.

This distinction between implicit and explicit knowledge enables us to see both sides in the debate over human competence. Implicit learning is one instance. There are others. As we will see in Part II of this book, for example, cognitive psychologists find that people often seem to forget an experience, yet show the effects of that experience—indicating that there can be memory without awareness. We will also see that people have the ability to reason logically, yet often take mental shortcuts that steer them into making bad judgments. And we'll see that although our feelings are often based on the way we interpret events, emotions—like reflexes—are sometimes triggered without conscious awareness, leading us to feel before we think. Are human beings competent or incompetent? Rational or nonrational? These questions are important to the study of cognitive and affective processes—beginning with the topic of learning.

THE PSYCHOLOGY OF LEARNING

When psychologists talk about **learning,** they are referring to a relatively permanent change in knowledge or behavior that comes as a result of *experience.* Experience is necessary for us to speak, read, write, add and subtract, ride a bicycle, swim, play a saxophone or trumpet, or charm a romantic partner.

The topic of learning is near and dear to the heart of all psychologists—regardless of whether they specialize in the study of biological, cognitive, developmental, social, or clinical processes. Often what we learn makes us happier, healthier, and more successful; sometimes it does not. The beauty of adaptation by learning, however, is that it is flexible, not rigidly preset like a stickleback's dance-and-attack ritual. In principle, this means that each of us can learn to behave in ways that benefit rather than harm ourselves and others. The question is, How does this learning take place?

The simplest form of learning is **habituation**—the tendency to become familiar with a stimulus merely as a result of repeated exposure. The first time it happens, a sudden loud noise or a blast of cold air has a startling effect on us, and triggers an "orienting reflex." Among humans, the eyes widen, the eyebrows raise, muscles tighten, the heart beats faster, skin resis-

■ **learning** A relatively permanent change in knowledge or behavior that results from experience.

■ **habituation** The tendency of an organism to become familiar with a stimulus as a result of repeated exposure.

tance drops, and brain-wave patterns indicate a heightened level of physiological arousal (Sokolov, 1963). On the second and third exposures to the stimulus, the effect is weakened. As we become acclimated or "habituated" to the stimulus, the novelty wears off, the startle reaction disappears, and boredom sets in.

Habituation is a primitive form of learning and is found among mammals, birds, fish, insects, and all other organisms. For example, sea snails reflexively withdraw their gills at the slightest touch. Then after repeated tactile stimulation, the response disappears (Kandel, 1979). Habituation also occurs in human infants. If a picture or sound is presented over and over again, an infant will eventually get bored, lose interest, look away, and exhibit a lower heart rate (Bornstein, 1989). Think about everyday life, and numerous examples of habituation will come to mind. People who move from a large city to the country, or from a region of the world that is hot to one that is cold, often need time to adjust to the sudden change in stimulation. Once they do, the new environment seems less noisy, quiet, hot, or cold.

In habituation, an organism learns from mere exposure that a stimulus is familiar. Over the years, however, psychologists have focused more on the ways in which we learn relationships between events. In this chapter, three such processes are discussed: classical conditioning, operant conditioning, and observational learning.

CLASSICAL CONDITIONING

I will always remember the summer of 1969 on the beach—the body surfing, bikinis, Frisbees, rock 'n' roll, the feel of hot sand between the toes, low-flying sea gulls, and warm air blowing the scent of salt water and coconut-oil suntan lotion. To this day, these memories flood my mind whenever I hear a song that was a radio hit at the time.

In stark contrast, I will never forget a cold, dark night in January of 1976. I was in graduate school, and had eaten dinner with a friend. Driving back to campus, I hit a patch of ice and skidded. Before I knew it, the car had scraped the wall of a brick building, turned on its side, and stalled. My friend and I were shaken, but not hurt. Yet I vividly recall the lights flashing on the dashboard, the smell of burnt rubber, and the blast of cold air that hit my face when we climbed out through the door. I can also recall the song that played on the radio as we tried to escape. I still flinch whenever I hear it.

Following Aristotle, modern philosophers and psychologists have long believed that the key to learning is *association,* a tendency to connect events that occur together in space or time. Can learning by association be studied in a scientific manner? With the arrival of the twentieth century, psychology was poised and ready for one of its most important discoveries.

Pavlov's Discovery

Enter Ivan Pavlov, a Russian physiologist. After receiving his medical degree in 1882, he spent twenty years studying the digestive system and won a Nobel Prize for that research in 1904. Pavlov was the complete dedicated scientist. Rumor has it that he once reprimanded a lab assistant who was ten minutes late for an experiment because of street riots stemming from the Russian Revolution: "Next time there's a revolution," he said, "get up earlier!" (Hothersall, 1990).

Ironically, Pavlov's most important contribution was the result of an incidental discovery. In studying the digestive system, he strapped dogs in a harness, placed different types of food in their mouths, and measured the flow of saliva through a tube surgically inserted in the cheek (see Figure 5.3). But there was a "problem": after repeated sessions, the dogs began to salivate *before* the food was actually put in their mouths. In fact, they would drool at the mere sight of food, the dish it was placed in, the assistant who brought it, or even the sound of the assistant's approaching footsteps. Pavlov saw these "psychic secretions" as a nuisance, so he tried to eliminate the problem by sneaking up on the dogs without warning. He soon realized, however, that he had stumbled on a very basic form of learning. This phenomenon was **classical conditioning**, and Pavlov devoted the rest of his life to studying it.

Figure 5.3

Pavlov's Classical Conditioning Apparatus

Strapped into an apparatus like the one shown here, Pavlov's dogs were conditioned to salivate. Through a tube surgically inserted into each dog's cheek, saliva was recorded by a pen attached to a slowly rotating cylinder of paper.

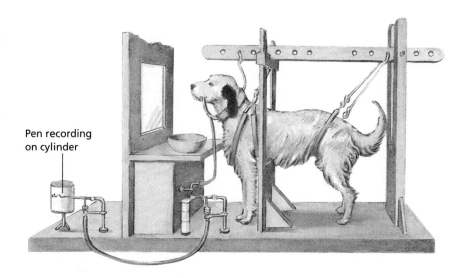

Pen recording on cylinder

■ **classical conditioning** A type of learning in which an organism comes to associate one stimulus with another (also called Pavlovian conditioning).

■ **unconditioned response (UR)** An unlearned response (salivation) to an unconditioned stimulus (food).

■ **unconditioned stimulus (US)** A stimulus (food) that triggers an unconditioned response (salivation).

To examine the classical conditioning systematically, Pavlov needed to control the delivery of food, a dry meat powder, as well as the events that preceded it. The animals did not have to be trained or "conditioned" to salivate. The salivary reflex is an innate **unconditioned response (UR)** that is naturally triggered by food in the mouth, an **unconditioned stimulus (US)**. There are numerous unconditioned stimulus-response connections. Tap your knee with a rubber mallet and your leg will jerk. Blow a puff of air into your eye and you'll blink. Turn the volume up on an alarm clock and, when it rings, your muscles will tighten. In each case, the stimulus automatically elicits the response—no ifs, ands, or buts. No experience is necessary.

Using the salivary reflex as a starting point, Pavlov (1927) sought to determine whether dogs could be trained by association to respond to a "neutral" stimulus—one that does not naturally elicit a response. To find out, he conducted an experiment in which he repeatedly rang a bell before plac-

Ivan Pavlov and some of the two hundred other scientists who worked with him during his illustrious career.

ing food in the dog's mouth. Bell, food. Bell, food. After a series of these paired events, the dog started to salivate to the sound alone. Because the bell, which was initially a neutral stimulus, came to elicit the response through its association with food, it became a **conditioned stimulus (CS)** and salivation, a **conditioned response (CR)**. With this experiment as a model, Pavlov and others trained dogs to salivate in response to buzzers, ticking metronomes, tuning forks, odors, lights, colored objects, and a touch on the leg. This classical conditioning procedure is diagrammed in Figure 5.4.

Figure 5.4   Classical Conditioning

Note the sequence of events before, during, and after Pavlov's study. At first, only the US (meat) elicits a UR (salivation). After a neutral stimulus (bell) repeatedly precedes the US, however, it becomes a CS and can elicit a CR (salivation) on its own.

■ **conditioned stimulus (CS)** A neutral stimulus (bell) that comes to evoke a classically conditioned response (salivation).

■ **conditioned response (CR)** A learned response (salivation) to a classically conditioned stimulus (bell).

BEFORE CONDITIONING

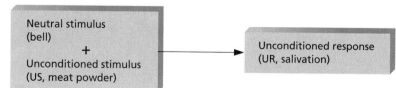

DURING CONDITIONING

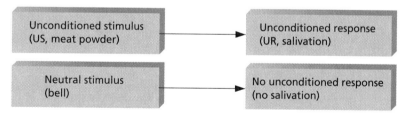

AFTER CONDITIONING

[Cartoon by John Chase]

As we'll see, classical conditioning affects us all in ways that we're often not aware of. We learn to salivate (CR) to lunch bells, menus, the smell of food cooking, and the sight of a refrigerator (CS) because these stimuli are often followed by eating (US). Similarly, we cringe at the sound of a dentist's drill because of past associations between that sound and pain. And we tremble at the sight of a flashing blue light on a highway because of its association with speeding tickets. For me, the beach—which was the site of so many good times of the past—is a conditioned stimulus that triggers peaceful, easy feelings.

Basic Principles

Inspired by his initial discovery, Pavlov spent more than thirty years examining the factors that influence classical conditioning. Other researchers throughout the world also became involved. As a result, we now know that various species can be conditioned to blink when they hear a click that is paired with a puff of air to the eye, to fear colored lights that signal the onset of painful electric shocks, and to develop a distaste for foods they ate before becoming sick to the stomach (Schwartz & Reisberg, 1991). We also know that there are four very basic principles of learning: acquisition, extinction, generalization, and discrimination.

Acquisition Classical conditioning seldom springs full blown after a single pairing of the CS and US. Rather, it takes some number of paired trials for the initial learning, or "acquisition," of a CR. In Pavlov's experiments, the dogs did not salivate the first time they heard the bell. As shown in the left panel of Figure 5.5, however, the CR increases rapidly over the next few pairings—until the "learning curve" peaks and levels off.

The acquisition of a classically conditioned response is influenced by various factors. The most critical are the order and timing of the presentation. In general, conditioning is quickest when the CS (the bell) precedes the onset of the US (food)—a procedure known as *forward* conditioning. Ideally, the CS should precede the US by about half a second and the two should

Figure 5.5

The Rise and Fall of a Conditioned Response

In classical conditioning, the CS does not evoke a CR on the first trial, but over time it increases rapidly until leveling off. During extinction, the CR gradually declines. After a brief delay, however, there is typically a spontaneous recovery, or "rebounding," of the CR—until it is completely extinguished.

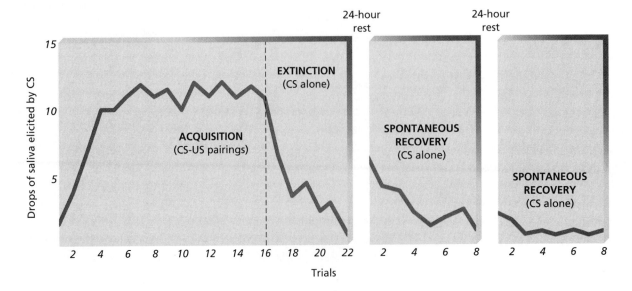

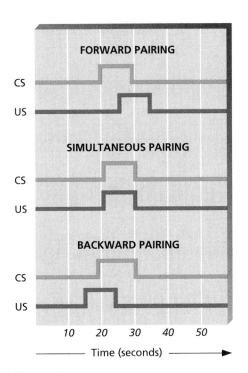

Figure 5.6

Temporal Relations in Classical Conditioning

A key factor in classical conditioning is the timing of the CS and US. Note that the three temporal patterns illustrated here are presented in order—from the most to least effective.

overlap somewhat in time. When the onset of the US is delayed, conditioning takes longer and the conditioned response is weaker. When the CS and US are *simultaneous,* it takes even longer. And when the US is presented before the CS (a procedure referred to as *backward* conditioning), learning often does not occur at all (see Figure 5.6).

Once a buzzer, light, or other neutral stimulus gains the power to elicit a conditioned response, it becomes a CS—and can serve as though it were US for yet another neutral stimulus. In one experiment, for example, Pavlov trained a dog to salivate to the sound of a bell, using meat powder as the US. After the CS-US link was established, he then presented a second neutral stimulus, a black square, followed by the bell—but no food. The result: after repeated pairings, the black square on its own elicited small amounts of salivation. Through a process of *higher-order conditioning,* as illustrated in Figure 5.7, one CS was used to create another CS. In effect, the black square came to signal the bell, which, in turn, signaled the appearance of food (Rescorla, 1980).

Extinction   In the acquisition phase of classical conditioning, a conditioned response is elicited by a neutral stimulus that is paired with a US. But what happens to the CR when the US is removed? Would a dog continue to salivate to a bell if the bell is no longer followed by food? Would the sound of a dentist's drill continue to send chills up the spine if it is no longer followed by pain? No. If the CS is presented often enough without the US, it eventually loses its response-eliciting power. This apparent reversal of learning is called **extinction** (see the middle panel of Figure 5.5).

Extinction is a gradual process. Indeed, Pavlov found that when the same dog was returned for testing a day or two after extinction, it once again salivated to the bell—a rebound effect known as **spontaneous recovery** (depicted in the right panel of Figure 5.5.) In fact, the dogs were easily reconditioned after just one repairing of the CS and US. Apparently, extinction does not erase what was previously learned—but only suppresses it.

Generalization   After an animal is conditioned to respond to a particular CS, other similar stimuli will often evoke the same response. In Pavlov's experiments, the dogs salivated not only to the original tone but also to other tones that were similar but not identical to the CS. Other researchers have

■ **extinction** The elimination of a learned response by removal of the unconditioned stimulus (in classical conditioning) or reinforcement (in operant conditioning).

■ **spontaneous recovery** The re-emergence of an extinguished conditioned response after a rest period.

Figure 5.7   Higher-Order Conditioning

After Pavlov trained a dog to salivate (CR) to a bell (CS), he preceded the bell with another neutral stimulus, a black square. After repeated pairings, the dog would salivate to the square itself. In effect, one CS was used to create another CS.

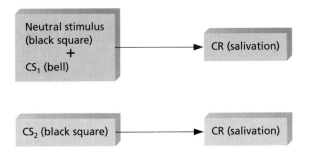

made the same observation. In one study, for example, rabbits were conditioned to blink to a tone of 1,200 Hz (a pitch that is roughly two octaves above middle C) that was followed by a puff of air to the eye. Later, they blinked to other tones ranging from 400 Hz to 2,000 Hz. The result: the more similar the tone was to the CS, the more likely it was to evoke a conditioned response. This tendency to respond to stimuli other than the original CS is called **stimulus generalization** (Pearce, 1987).

Discrimination   Stimulus generalization can be useful because it enables us to apply what we learn to new, similar situations. But there are drawbacks. As illustrated by the child who is terrified of all animals because of one bad encounter with a barking dog, or the adult who assumes that "they" are all alike, generalization is not always adaptive. Sometimes we need to distinguish between objects that are similar—a process of **discrimination.** Again, Pavlov was the first to demonstrate this process. He conditioned a dog to salivate in the presence of a black square (a CS) and then noticed that the response generalized to a gray-colored square. Next, he conducted a series of conditioning trials in which the black square was followed by food, while the gray one was not. The result: the dog continued to salivate only to the original CS. In a similar manner, it eventually learned to discriminate between the color black and darker shades of gray.

Pavlov's Legacy

Classical conditioning is so powerful and so basic that it occurs in animals as primitive as the flatworm (the body of the flatworm contracts in response to electric shock; if the shock is paired often enough with a light, the flatworm's body eventually contracts to the light alone) and as sophisticated as us humans (Turkkan, 1989). In recent years, psychologists have taken classical conditioning in two directions: some want to better *understand* the phenomenon—its extensions and its limitations—while others are eager to *apply* it to different aspects of the human experience.

Theoretical Advances   Inspired by their initial successes and by the Darwinian assumption that all animals share a common evolutionary past, Pavlov and other early behaviorists made a bold claim: that any organism can be conditioned to any stimulus. It does not matter if the subject is a dog, cat, rat, pigeon, or person. Nor does it matter if the conditioned stimulus is a bell, light, buzzer, or odor. Whenever an initially neutral stimulus is paired with an unconditioned stimulus, the result is classical conditioning.

The early behaviorists also insisted that a science of human behavior must focus only on external, objective, quantifiable events. A *stimulus* can be observed and measured. So can its effect on an overt *response*. Together, these form the basis for what is known as S-R psychology. As far as the organism itself is concerned—its instincts, drives, perceptions, thoughts, and feelings—the behaviorists refused to speculate. In fact, Pavlov was said to have fined lab assistants for using soft, "mentalistic" language. So where does the *organism* fit in? In recent years, researchers have come to appreciate some of the ways in which the "O" bridges the S and R—giving rise to

■ **stimulus generalization** The tendency to respond to a stimulus that is similar to the conditioned stimulus.

■ **discrimination** In classical and operant conditioning, the ability to distinguish between different stimuli.

a more flexible S-O-R brand of behaviorism. Two factors within the organism are particularly important: biological preparedness and cognitive representations.

Biological Preparedness   All animals are biologically programmed, for survival purposes, to learn some associations more easily than others. This limitation was first discovered by John Garcia and Robert Koelling (1966). While studying the effects of radiation exposure on laboratory rats, they noticed that the animals would not drink from the plastic water bottles inside the radiation chambers. Since the radiation (US) was causing nausea (UR), they reasoned, perhaps the rats had acquired an aversion (CR) to the "plastic" taste of the water (CS).

To test this hypothesis, the investigators rigged an apparatus that worked as follows: when a rat licked a plastic drinking tube, it tasted sweetened water, saw a flash of light, and heard a loud clicking noise—all at the same time. The rats were then exposed to a high dose of x-rays, which caused poisoning and nausea. The result: although the rats later avoided the sweetened water after radiation poisoning, they did not also learn to avoid the light or noise. The link between taste (CS) and poison (US) was so easily learned that it took only one experience—even though the rats did not get sick until hours later (a far cry from the split-second CS-US interval that is usually necessary). It is important to note that people acquire taste aversions, too. For example, cancer patients often react with disgust to distinctive foods they ate before receiving a chemotherapy treatment that causes vomiting (Bernstein & Borson, 1986).

Garcia and Koelling (1966) also found that when the US was a painful electric shock to the feet instead of x-ray poisoning, the rats continued to drink the water but avoided the audiovisual stimuli instead. Why was taste such a powerful CS when it was paired with poison but not with shock? And why were light and noise conditioned to the shock but not to the poison? Think about these associations for a moment, and one word will come to mind: adaptiveness. In nature, food is more likely to produce stomach poisoning than a pain in the foot. And external stimuli are more likely to cause a pain in the foot than stomach illness. If you get sick after eating dinner in a new restaurant, you are likely to blame your illness on something you ate, not on the decor or the music that played. Clearly, we are "prepared" by nature to learn some CS-US associations more easily than others.

Research on the classical conditioning of fear reactions also illustrates this point. As we'll see in Chapter 16, on psychological disorders, people all over the world develop some of the same fears. Particularly common are fears of darkness, height, snakes, and insects. One possible reason is that humans are predisposed to be wary of stimuli that were harmful to our prehistoric ancestors. Thus, when subjects are conditioned in the laboratory to fear an object (through the pairing of its exposure with electric shock), their reaction—as measured by physiological arousal—is acquired faster and lasts longer when the object is a snake, a spider, or an angry face than when it's a flower, a house, or a happy face (Ohman, 1986).

Cognitive Representations   According to Pavlov, classical conditioning occurs whenever a neutral stimulus is paired with an unconditioned stimulus. With dogs salivating to bells, it all seemed passive and automatic—a mechanical process in which the control of a reflex is passed from one stimulus to another. But is the process really that passive? Laboratory animals do not have to be geniuses to acquire a conditioned response, but they may be cognitively more active than Pavlov was willing to admit. Perhaps Pavlov's dogs salivated to his bells and tones because prior experience led them to *expect* food.

Based on years of research, Robert Rescorla (1988) concluded that classical conditioning is the process by which an organism learns that one event (CS) *predicts* another event (US). In other words, says Rescorla, a simple pairing of two stimuli is often not sufficient for conditioning. Rather, the organism must also learn that one event signals the coming onset of another. To demonstrate, Rescorla (1968) exposed rats to an electric shock (US) that was always paired with a tone (CS). In one condition, every shock was accompanied by the tone—so the CS reliably predicted the US. In a second condition, the rat experienced the same tone-shock pairs but was occasionally shocked without the tone as well. In other words, although the two events were paired, the CS did not reliably predict the US (see Figure 5.8). As Rescorla expected, the rats acquired a fear of the tone in the first condition but not in the second. Apparently, classical conditioning requires more than a simple pairing of a CS and US. It requires that there be a reliable predictive relationship.

Rescorla's redefinition is significant because it helps to explain various aspects of classical conditioning. It explains, for example, why a conditioned response is hard to produce by a backward conditioning procedure in which the CS *follows* the US. The two stimuli co-occur, but the CS cannot predict the US when it comes second in the sequence of events. Rescorla's model also explains why certain associations are learned more easily

CONDITION 1: CONTIGUITY PLUS PREDICTIVE RELATIONSHIP

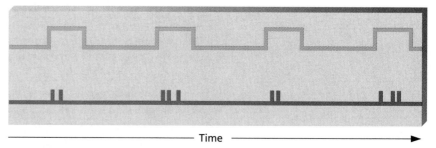

Time

Figure 5.8

Classical Conditioning: When the CS Predicts the US

Rescorla (1968) exposed rats to a shock (US) paired with a tone (CS). In one condition, every US was paired by the CS (top). In a second condition, shocks were sometimes administered without a tone—so the CS did not predict the US (bottom). Indicating that a predictive relationship is required, rats learned to fear the tone in the first condition but not in the second.

CONDITION 2: CONTIGUITY *WITHOUT* PREDICTIVE RELATIONSHIP

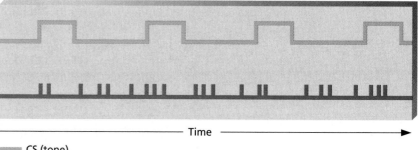

Time

CS (tone)
US (shock)

than others. In the taste-aversion study described earlier, rats quickly learned to avoid food that was paired with stomach poisoning, and lights and noise that were paired with electric shock. But they did not similarly link food to external pain, or lights and noise to stomach poisoning. Regardless of the CS-US links artificially created in the laboratory, food is more likely in nature to produce stomach illness than a pain in the foot, while lights and noise are more likely to predict the onset of electric shock than the onset of illness. As Rescorla (1988) put it, "Conditioning is not a stupid process by which an organism willy-nilly forms associations between any two stimuli that happen to co-occur. Rather the organism is better seen as an information seeker using logical and perceptual relations among events and its own preconceptions to form a sophisticated representation of its world."

Practical Applications   When Pavlov first found that he could train Russian dogs to drool at the sound of a dinner bell, nobody cared. In fact, E. B. Twitmyre, an American graduate student, had reported similar results at a psychology conference in 1904—the same year that Pavlov won the Nobel Prize. At the time, Twitmyre was studying the knee-jerk reflex in humans. Before each trial, he would ring a bell to warn subjects that a hammer was about to strike the knee. Like Pavlov, he found that the subject's leg would soon twitch in response to the bell—even before the knee was hit. Was this a profound development? Although one would think so, Twitmyre's presentation attracted little interest.

Conditioned Fears   Psychologists finally took notice of classical conditioning in 1914, when behaviorist John Watson described Pavlov's research to a group of American psychologists. To demonstrate the relevance of the phenomenon to humans, Watson and his assistant Rosalie Rayner (1920) conditioned an eleven-month-old boy named Albert to fear a white lab rat. "Little Albert" was a normal, healthy, well-developed infant. Like others his age, he was scared of loud noises but enjoyed playing with furry little animals. Enter John Watson. Modeled after Pavlov's research, Watson presented Albert with a harmless white rat. Then just as the boy reached for the animal, Watson made a loud, crashing sound by banging a steel bar with a hammer, which caused the startled boy to jump and fall forward, burying his head in the mattress he was lying on. After seven repetitions of this event, the boy was terrified of the animal. What's worse, his fear generalized, leading him to burst into tears at the sight of a rabbit, a dog, a Santa Claus mask, and even a white fur coat (see Figure 5.9).

From an ethical standpoint, Watson and Rayner's study was shameful. They infected an innocent baby with a fear that seemed to spread like a contagious disease from one white and furry stimulus to the next—and they never "de-conditioned" him (in case you're wondering, ethics committees would not approve this study today). Watson claimed that the boy was taken away before he had a chance to do so, but the historical record suggests that he knew well in advance that Albert's mother was going to remove her son from the research project (Harris, 1979). On the positive side, Little Albert's fear is a legend in the history of psychology because it established for the first time a link between Pavlov's dogs and an important aspect of the human experience. We now know that people can come to

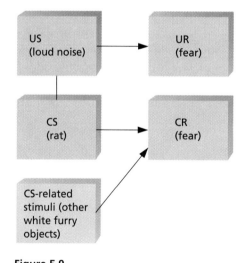

Figure 5.9

The Conditioning of Little Albert

By linking a harmless white rat to an aversive loud noise, Watson conditioned a baby boy to react with terror to the rat. In fact, the fear spread or "generalized" to other, superficially similar objects.

fear objects or places because they happened to be associated with aversive experiences. As we will see in Chapter 17, classical conditioning spawned a revolutionary method of treating these irrational fears and other anxiety-related disorders.

It is also important to note that babies can be conditioned to form positive *preferences* as well—for example, toward stimuli that are associated with maternal care. In one study, Regina Sullivan and her associates (1991) exposed newborns to a neutral odor. After each presentation, some were gently touched, an inherently pleasurable experience; others were not. The next day, all the infants were returned to the lab and tested. As predicted, those for whom the odor was paired with the tactile stimulation were more likely to turn their heads toward that odor rather than away from it. This effect occurs not only in human infants but also in young rats, mice, hamsters, deer, guinea pigs, squirrel monkeys, and other species (Leon, 1992).

Social Attitudes   Not everyone was happy about the possible uses of classical conditioning. In *Brave New World*, novelist Aldous Huxley (1932) warned us of a future in which diabolical leaders use Pavlov's methods to control their followers. These concerns are unfounded. However, classical conditioning does affect our lives in many ways. Think about the movie *Jaws*. Early in the film, pulsating bass music is followed by the sight of a shark's fin and the bloody underwater mutilation of a young swimmer. Then it happens again. And again. Before you know it, the music alone (CS)—even without the great white shark (US)—has the audience shaking and ducking for cover. Many other examples illustrate this point. Based on powerful associations, American politicians wrap themselves in stars and stripes, the swastika strikes terror in the hearts of Jewish people, and the burning cross arouses fear among African-Americans. In the words of Shelby Steele (1990), a black English professor, "there are objective correlatives everywhere that evoke a painful thicket of emotions . . . covering everything from Confederate flags and pickup trucks with gun racks to black lawn jockeys" (p. 154).

Through classical conditioning, people often react with strong emotions to once neutral objects such as red-white-and-blue flags, yellow ribbons, and other symbols.

These examples suggest that people form strong positive and negative attitudes toward neutral objects by virtue of their links to emotionally charged stimuli. Arthur and Carolyn Staats (1958) thus presented college students with a list of national names (German, Swedish, Dutch, Italian, French, and Greek), each repeatedly paired with words that had pleasant (*happy, gift, sacred*) or unpleasant (*bitter, ugly, failure*) connotations. When subjects later evaluated the nationalities by name, they were more positive in their ratings of those that had been paired with pleasant words rather than unpleasant words. Recognizing the power of this effect, advertisers link their products to positive emotional symbols, sexy models, happy tunes, and nostalgic images. This marketing strategy seems to work (Stuart et al., 1987), in part by heightening the consumer's attention to the product (Janiszewski & Warlop, 1993).

The Immune System   One of the most exciting new research developments is the finding that just as animal reflexes and human emotional reactions can be classically conditioned, so can the body's immune system (Ader & Cohen, 1993). Consisting of more than a trillion white blood cells, the immune system guards our health by warding off bacteria, viruses, and other foreign substances that invade the body. When this system fails, as it does when it is ravaged by the AIDS virus, disease and death are the certain outcome (see Chapter 18).

With that in mind, you can appreciate a striking discovery that was recently made. Psychologist Robert Ader had been using classical conditioning procedures with rats in which he paired sweetened water with cyclophosphamide, a drug that causes nausea. Water, drug. Water, drug. As expected, the rats developed a taste aversion to the sweetened water. Unexpectedly, however, many of them died because the drug Ader used had weakened the immune system by destroying certain types of white blood cells. To further explore this phenomenon, Ader joined with immunologist Nicholas Cohen (1985) in a series of experiments. They repeatedly fed the rats sweetened water, which is harmless, followed by the cyclophosphamide (US), which weakens the immune response (UR). The result: After several pairings, the sweetened water on its own (CS) caused a weakening of immunity, followed by sickness and sometimes death (CR). This breakthrough raises an exciting question: If the immune system can be weakened by conditioning, can it similarly be strengthened? Might it some day be possible to use classical conditioning to help people fight AIDS? Perhaps. This research is still in its preliminary stages, but promising results with animals have been reported (Ghanta et al., 1985; MacQueen et al., 1989).

OPERANT CONDITIONING

Several years ago, I took my children to Sea World. After watching a dazzling show that featured killer whales jumping through hoops, sea lions playing volleyball, and dolphins dancing on the water, my son, who was three years old at the time, asked, "How did the animals learn to do these tricks? . . . Did they go to college?"

Classical conditioning may explain why people salivate at the smell of food, cringe at the sound of a dentist's drill, run when someone yells "fire," or tremble at the sight of a flashing blue light in the rearview mirror. But it cannot explain how animals learn to perform complex acrobatics. Nor can it explain how we learn to solve equations, make people laugh, or behave in ways that earn love, praise, sympathy, or the respect of others. As we will see, the acquisition of voluntary, complex, and goal-directed behaviors such as these involves a second form of learning.

The Law of Effect

Before Pavlov had begun his research, an American psychology student named Edward L. Thorndike (1898) was blazing another trail. Interested in animal intelligence, Thorndike built a "puzzle box" from wooden shipping crates so he could observe how different animals learn to solve problems. In one study, for example, he put hungry cats into a cage, one at a time, with a door that could be lifted by stepping on a lever. He then placed a tantalizing chunk of raw fish outside the cage—and beyond reach. You can imagine what happened next. After sniffing around the box, the cat tried to escape by reaching with its paws, scratching the bars, and pushing at the ceiling. At some point, the cat accidentally banged on the lever. The door opened and the cat scampered out to devour the food. Thorndike repeated the procedure again. The cat went through its previous sequence of movements and eventually found the one that caused the latch to open. After a series of trials, Thorndike's cats became more efficient: they went straight to the latch, stepped on the lever, and ate the food (see Figure 5.10).

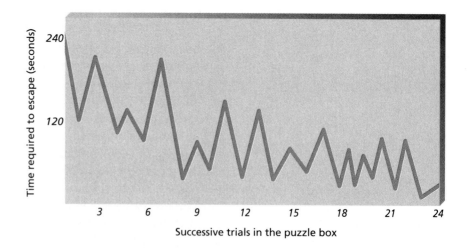

Figure 5.10

Thorndike's Law of Effect

Thorndike's hungry cats initially engaged in various behaviors—sniffing, pawing, scratching the bars, pushing the ceiling, and pressing the lever that opened the escape hatch. Over a series of trials, the cats took less and less time to press the lever (top). Accordingly, Thorndike proposed that behaviors followed by a reward are "stamped in," while others fade away (bottom).

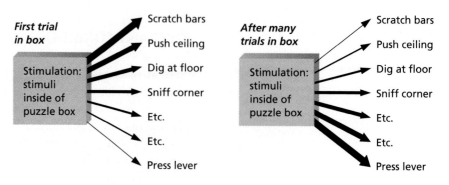

law of effect A law stating that responses followed by positive outcomes are repeated, while those followed by negative outcomes are not.

operant conditioning The process by which organisms learn to behave in ways that produce reinforcement.

"Behavioral psychology is the science of pulling habits out of rats."

DOUGLAS BUSCH

Based on studies like this one, Thorndike (1911) proposed the **law of effect**: behaviors that are followed closely in time by a satisfying outcome are "stamped in" or repeated, while those followed by a negative outcome or none at all are extinguished. In the puzzle box, cats spent progressively more time stepping on the latch, and less time poking at the bars and ceiling. In the case of humans, Thorndike's law of effect was used to describe the process of socialization. By using rewards and punishments, parents train their children to eat with a utensil, not to fling their mashed potatoes across the table. To the extent that we learn how to produce desirable outcomes, the process is adaptive.

Skinner's Principles of Reinforcement

Following in Thorndike's footsteps, B. F. Skinner transformed the landscape of modern psychology. But first things first. To study learning systematically, Skinner knew that he had to design an environment in which he controlled the organism's response-outcome contingencies. So as a graduate student in 1930, he used an old ice chest to build a soundproof chamber equipped with a stimulus light, a response bar (for rats) or pecking key (for pigeons), a device that dispenses dry food pellets or water, metal floor grids for the delivery of electric shock, and an instrument outside the chamber that automatically records and tabulates the responses. This apparatus came to be known as the *Skinner box* (see Figure 5.11).

Next, Skinner introduced a new vocabulary. To distinguish between the active type of learning that Thorndike had studied (whereby the organism operates on the environment) and Pavlov's classical conditioning (whereby the organism is a more passive respondent), Skinner coined the term *operant conditioning*. **Operant conditioning** is the process by which organisms learn to behave in ways that produce desirable outcomes. The behavior itself is called an "operant" because it is designed to operate on the environment. Thus, whereas classical conditioning involves the learning of associations between stimuli, resulting in a passive response, operant conditioning

Figure 5.11

The Skinner Box

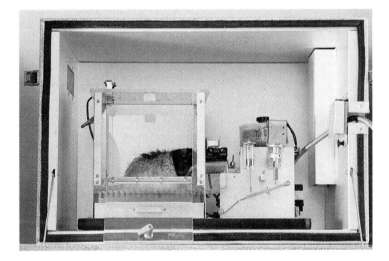
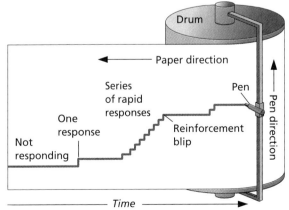

■ **reinforcement** In operant conditioning, any stimulus that increases the likelihood of a prior response.

■ **punishment** In operant conditioning, any stimulus that decreases the likelihood of a prior response.

involves the learning of an association between a spontaneously emitted action and its consequences (Rescorla, 1987).

To avoid speculating about an organism's inner state, Skinner also used the term **reinforcement** instead of "reward" or "satisfaction." Objectively defined, a reinforcer is any stimulus that increases the likelihood of a prior response. There are two types of reinforcers: positive and negative. A *positive reinforcer* strengthens a prior response through the presentation of a positive stimulus. In the Skinner box, the food that follows a bar press is a positive reinforcer. For humans, so are money, grades, hugs, kisses, and a pat on the back. Even mild electrical stimulation to certain parts of the brain, which releases the neurotransmitter dopamine, has a pleasurable effect and serves as a positive reinforcer (Olds & Milner, 1954; White & Milner, 1992; Wise & Rompre, 1989). In contrast, a *negative reinforcer* strengthens a response through the removal of an aversive stimulus. In a Skinner box, the termination of a painful electric shock is a negative reinforcer. Similarly, we learn to take aspirins to soften a headache, fasten our seatbelts to turn off the seatbelt buzzer, and rock babies to sleep to stop them from crying.

It is important to keep straight the fact that positive and negative reinforcers both have the same effect: to strengthen a prior response. Skinner was thus quick to point out that **punishment** is not negative reinforcement. Although the two are sometimes confused, punishment has the opposite effect: it decreases, not increases, the likelihood of a prior response. There are two types of punishment. A *positive punisher* weakens a response through the presentation of an aversive stimulus. Shocking a lab rat for pressing the response lever, scolding a child, locking a criminal behind bars, and boycotting a product are examples of this form of punishment designed to weaken specific behaviors. In contrast, a *negative punisher* weakens behavior through the removal of a stimulus typically characterized as positive. Taking food away from a hungry rat and grounding a teenager by suspending driving privileges are two examples. The different types of reinforcement and punishment are summarized in Table 5.1.

Shaping and Extinction   Modeled after the law of effect, Skinner's basic principle seemed straightforward. Responses that produce a reinforcement are repeated. But wait—if organisms learn by the consequences of their be-

Table 5.1

Types of Reinforcement and Punishment

Reinforcement strengthens a response through (1) the presentation of a positive stimulus or (2) the removal of a negative stimulus. Punishment weakens a response through (1) the presentation of a negative stimulus or (2) the removal of a positive stimulus.

Procedure	Effect on behavior	
	Increases	Decreases
Presentation of stimulus	Positive reinforcement (Feed the rat)	Positive punishment (Shock the rat)
Removal of stimulus	Negative reinforcement (Stop the shock)	Negative punishment (Withhold the food)

"Boy, do we have this guy conditioned. Every time I press the bar down he drops a pellet in."

[Jester of Columbia]

havior, where does the very first response come from? Before the first food pellet, how does the animal come to press the bar? As demonstrated by Thorndike, one possibility is that the response occurs naturally as the animal explores the cage. Skinner pointed to a second possibility: that the behavior is gradually *shaped*, or guided, by the reinforcement of responses that come closer and closer to the desired behavior.

Imagine that you are trying to get a hungry white rat to press the bar in a Skinner box. The rat has never been in this situation before, so it sniffs around, pokes its nose through the air holes, grooms itself, rears its hind legs, and so on. At this point, you can wait for the target behavior to appear on its own, or you can speed up the process. If the rat turns toward the bar, you drop a food pellet into the cage. Reinforcement. If it steps toward the bar, you deliver another pellet. Reinforcement. If the rat moves closer, or touches the bar, you deliver yet another one. Once the rat is hovering near the bar and pawing at it, you withhold the next pellet until it presses down, which triggers the feeder. Before long, your subject is pressing the bar at a rapid pace. By reinforcing "successive approximations" of the target response, you will have shaped a whole new behavior.

Shaping is the procedure that animal trainers use to get circus elephants to walk on their hind legs, bears to ride bicycles, chickens to play a piano, and dolphins to jump through hoops—which brings me back to Sea World. The dolphin trainer begins by throwing the dolphin a fish for turning toward a hoop, then for swimming toward it, swimming through it underwater, and finally jumping through a hoop that is many feet up in the air. The process applies to people as well. Young children are toilet trained, socialized to behave appropriately, and taught to read, through step-by-step reinforcement. Similarly, political candidates repeat statements that draw loud applause and abandon those that are met with silence—thereby creating messages that are shaped by what voters want to hear. Rumor has it that a group of college students once shaped the behavior of their psychology professor. Using eye contact as a reinforcer, the students trained this professor to lecture from a particular corner of the room. Whenever he moved in that

Using operant conditioning, Sea World animal trainers can get these orca whales to jump on cue.

B. F. Skinner was born in 1904 and received his psychology degree from Harvard in 1931. He published his first paper in 1930, his last in 1990. Skinner's behavioral approach was so influential that it spawned a separate division of the American Psychological Association, an independent professional organization with more than two thousand members, two private foundations, and an estimated twenty-three journals (Lattal, 1992). Skinner received thirty honorary degrees from colleges and universities around the world and is consistently ranked by his peers as one of the most important psychologists of all time (Korn et al., 1991).

On August 10, 1990, B. F. Skinner made his final public appearance in Boston (as shown in this photograph)—at the APA's annual convention. He was there to receive an award for Outstanding Lifetime Contribution to Psychology. I was there—and so, it seemed, was everyone else I knew. Upon his introduction, Skinner was greeted with a long and thunderous standing ovation. After all, everyone in the audience knew they were watching a living legend in action. The talk itself was vintage Skinner. He insisted, as always, that psychology could never be a science of the mind, only a science of behavior.

On the evening of August 17, 1990, one week after his Boston appearance, Skinner completed his last article, for the *American Psychologist*. He died the very next day.

direction, they looked up at him; otherwise, they looked down. Before long, he was lecturing from one corner of the classroom, not quite realizing that he had been "shaped."

In classical conditioning, repeated presentation of the CS without the US causes the CR to gradually weaken and disappear. *Extinction* also occurs in operant conditioning. If you return your newly shaped rat to the Skinner box and disconnect the feeder from the response bar, you'll find that after the rat presses the bar a few times without a reinforcement, its behavior will fade and become extinguished. By the same token, people stop smiling at those who don't smile back, stop helping those who never reciprocate, and stop working when their efforts are never successful.

Schedules of Reinforcement   Every now and then, scientists stumble into their greatest discoveries. Pavlov was a classic example. So was Skinner. Early in his research, Skinner would reinforce his animals on a continuous basis: every bar press produced a food pellet. Then something happened. At the time, Skinner had to make his own pellets by squeezing food paste through a pill machine and then waiting for them to dry. The process was time consuming. "One pleasant Saturday afternoon," Skinner recalled, "I surveyed my supply of dry pellets and, appealing to certain elemental theorems in arithmetic, deduced that unless I spent the rest of the afternoon and evening at the pill machine, the supply would be exhausted by 10:30 Monday morning" (1959, p. 368). Not wanting to spend the whole weekend in the lab, Skinner convinced himself that not *every* response had to be reinforced. He adjusted his apparatus so that the bar-pressing response would be reinforced on a partial basis—only once per minute. Upon his return the next week, however, he found response patterns that were far different from anything he had seen before. As a result, Skinner began to realize the powerful effects of "partial reinforcement." Indeed, he and others went on to identify four types of *schedules of reinforcement* (see Figure 5.12), each having different effects on behavior (Ferster & Skinner, 1957).

Fixed Interval (FI) Schedule   In the situation just described, reinforcement followed the first response made after a fixed interval of *time* had elapsed. In an FI-1 schedule, the response produces food after each new minute; or it may be made available only after every two (FI-2), ten (FI-10), or fifteen (FI-15) minutes. The schedule is fixed by time, and tends to produce a slow, "scalloped" response pattern. After the animal learns that a certain amount of time must elapse, it pauses after each reinforcer and then responds at an accelerating rate until the animal nears the end of the cycle—which signals the availability of the next reinforcement. The student whose rate of studying starts slow, increases before midterms, trails off, and picks up again before finals illustrates this reaction to an FI schedule.

Variable Interval (VI) Schedule   Once animals learn what the fixed pattern is, they press the bar only as they near the end of each interval. To counter this lazy response pattern, Skinner varied the interval around an average. In other words, an interval may average one minute in length (a VI-1 schedule), but the actual timing of a reinforcement is unpredictable from one interval to the next—say, after fifty seconds, then two minutes, ten seconds, and one minute. The result is a slow but steady, not scalloped, pattern of responses. Teachers who give pop quizzes are using a VI schedule to ensure

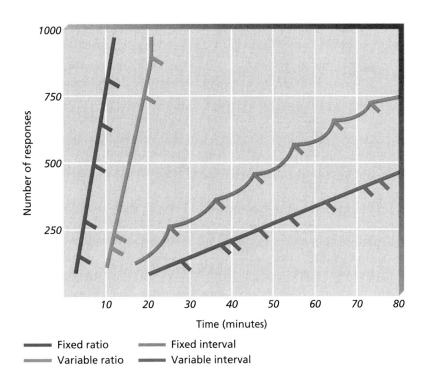

Figure 5.12

Schedules of Reinforcement

These curves show the response patterns typically produced by different schedules of reinforcement. The steeper the curve, the higher the response rate (the slash marks on each curve indicate the delivery of a reinforcement). As you can see, the rate of responding is higher under ratio than interval schedules.

In the gambling casino, slot machines are preset to pay off on a variable ratio schedule. This schedule leads gamblers to deposit their coins at a high rate.

that their students keep up with their reading rather than cram at the last minute.

Fixed Ratio (FR) Schedule In this situation, a reinforcer is administered after a fixed number of *responses*—say, every third response, or every fifth, tenth, or fiftieth. In an FR-10 schedule, it takes ten bar presses to get food. If thirty responses are needed, it is an FR-30 schedule. The response-to-reinforcement ratio thus remains constant. In a Skinner box, animals on an FR schedule exhibit a burst of bar presses until the food appears, pause briefly, then produce another burst. The result is a fast, step-like response pattern. Airlines that offer a free flight after 25,000 miles of travel, CD clubs that offer a free CD after every fifth purchase, and the employer who pays workers after they produce a certain number of products all operate on a fixed ratio schedule.

Variable Ratio (VR) Schedule In this situation, the reinforcement appears after some average number of responses is made—a number that varies randomly from one reinforcement to the next. On a VR-15 schedule a rat would have to press the bar an average of fifteen times, but the food may appear on the fifth response, then the twentieth, fourteenth, twenty-first response, and so on. Unable to predict which response will produce a food pellet, animals on a VR schedule respond at a constant high rate. In one case, Skinner trained pigeons to peck a disk ten thousand times for a single food pellet! Slot machines and lotteries are rigged to pay off on a VR schedule, leading gamblers to deposit coins and purchase tickets at a furious, addictive pace. Perhaps the next coin, or the next lottery ticket, or the one after that, will bring the jackpot. . . .

Reinforcement schedules affect extinction rates as well as learning. Specifically, the operant response is more enduring and, later, more resistant to extinction when the organism is reinforced on a partial basis than on a continuous, 100 percent schedule. This phenomenon is called the *partial-reinforcement effect.* The rat that is fed after every bar press is quick to realize once the feeder is disconnected that the contingency has changed. But the rat that is fed on only an occasional basis persists more before realizing that a reinforcement is no longer forthcoming. If you drop coins into a Coke machine and do not get the drink you ordered, you walk away. Since vending machines operate on a continuous-reinforcement basis, it would be apparent that this one is out of order. Deposit coins into a broken slot machine, however, and you may go on to lose hundreds more. After all, you expect slot machines to pay off on an irregular basis. The partial reinforcement effect has ironic implications. For example, parents who only sometimes give in to a child's temper tantrums create "little monsters" with more tenacious, hard-to-eliminate outbursts than do those who always give in.

Punishment   In 1948, Skinner wrote *Walden Two,* a novel about a fictional society in which socially adaptive behaviors were maintained by various schedules of reinforcement. The book was a blueprint for the use of "behavioral engineering" to design a healthy and productive community. Skinner never hesitated to preach the use of reinforcement. Yet he just as adamantly opposed the use of punishment, even though it is a common form of behavior control. Think about it. Parents scold their children, police officers fine motorists for speeding, referees penalize athletes for committing fouls, and employers fire workers who are lazy. So what's the problem? Aren't these forms of punishment effective?

Research shows that punishment has mixed effects (Axelrod & Apsche, 1983). When it is strong, immediate, consistent, and inescapable, punishment clearly does suppress unwanted behaviors. Shock a rat for pressing the response bar and it will quickly stop making the response. Yell "no!" at the top of your lungs to a child playing with matches, and it is unlikely to happen again. There is an episode of the TV show *Cheers* in which Clifford Claivin—an obnoxious, know-it-all postal worker—hires a behaviorist to shape his social skills so that he would be better liked. The two men enter the bar, and each time Claivin makes an offensive or boastful remark, the behaviorist jolts him with a hand-held, remote-controlled electric shock device. This scene is very funny, and it illustrates that punishment can be an effective deterrent.

It is important to know, however, that punishment can also have unwanted side effects. There are four specific problems. First, a behavior that is punished may be temporarily inhibited, or hidden from the punishing agent—but it is not necessarily extinguished. The child who lights matches and the teenager who smokes cigarettes may both continue to do so at school, at a friend's house, or at home when the parent is at work. Second, even when punishment does suppress an unwanted behavior, it does not replace that behavior with one that is more adaptive. It's okay to lock up the convicted criminal, but in order to change his or her future behavior, some form of rehabilitation program is necessary. Third, punishment can sometimes backfire because a stimulus thought to be aversive may, in fact, prove rewarding. The neglected child who acts up and is scolded by his or her busy parents may actually "enjoy" all the attention and make trouble again in the future. Fourth, punishment (especially if it is severe) can arouse fear, anger, frustration, and other negative emotions—leading the person to strike back, retaliate, tune out, or run away.

Properly administered, punishment can be used to suppress an unwanted behavior. As we have seen, however, it can also create more problems than it solves. It is better, advised Skinner, to use a combination of reinforcement (to increase alternative, desirable behaviors) and extinction (to decrease undesirable behaviors) in order to shape a new, more adaptive way of life.

Stimulus Control   In operant conditioning, organisms learn to respond in ways that are reinforced. But there is more to the story. A pigeon trained in a Skinner box learns to peck a key for food, but it may also learn that the response produces reinforcement only in the presence of certain cues. Since reinforcements are often available in one situation but not in another, it is adaptive to learn not only *what* response to make but *when* to make it. If pecking a key produces food only when a green disk is lit, a pigeon may learn to discriminate and to respond on a selective basis. The green light is a *discriminative stimulus* that "sets the occasion" for the behavior to be reinforced (Ross & LoLordo, 1987).

When people learn to respond in some situations and not others, their behavior is said to be under "stimulus control." In human terms, this is often important for treating behavioral disorders. Consider the problem of insomnia. Research shows that insomniacs too often use the bed for nonsleeping activities such as watching TV, listening to the radio, reading magazines, and worrying about personal problems. In other words, the bed is a discriminative stimulus for so many activities that it becomes a source of arousal, not relaxation. To counter this problem, insomniacs are advised, frequently with successful results, to lie in bed only for the purpose of sleeping (Morawetz, 1989).

An operant response may spread from one situation to another through the process of stimulus *generalization*. As in classical conditioning, the more similar a new stimulus is to the original discriminative stimulus, the more likely it is to trigger the response. In one study, for example, pigeons were reinforced for pecking a key that was illuminated with yellow light. They were then tested with lights of different colors. The more similar the test lights were to the yellow discriminative stimulus—for example, green and orange as opposed to red and blue—the more likely the pigeons were to peck at it (Guttman & Kalish, 1956). In another study, horses were trained to press a lever that was placed in their stalls, a response that released oats and hay into a feed tray. The animals were conditioned in the presence of an illuminated black circle 2.5 inches in diameter. They were then tested in the presence of circles that varied in size from this original. The closer the resemblance, the more likely the horses were to press the lever. The results for two horses, named Lady Bay and Bud Dark, are illustrated in Figure 5.13 (Dougherty & Lewis, 1991).

Discrimination and generalization are important aspects of human operant conditioning. From experience, a child might learn that temper tantrums bring results from busy parents but not from teachers, that studying increases grades in social studies but not math, that lewd remarks elicit laughter in the locker room but not in the classroom, and that aggression wins praise on the football field but not in other settings. As adults, of course, we routinely regulate our behavior according to situational cues.

Figure 5.13

Stimulus Generalization

The more similar a new stimulus is to a discriminative stimulus, the more likely it is to trigger the operant response. In this study, two horses trained to press a lever in the presence of a 2.5-inch circle later responded to new circles based on their level of similarity to the original (Dougherty & Lewis, 1991).

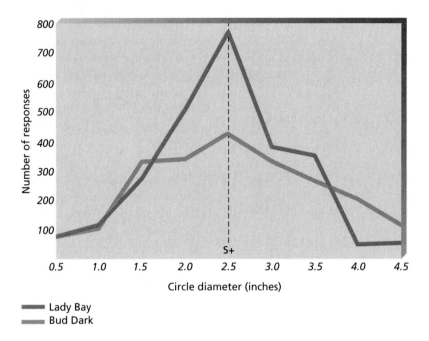

Lady Bay
Bud Dark

Practical Applications of Operant Conditioning

From the start, Skinner was interested in the practical applications of operant conditioning. In World War II, he worked for the United States government on a top-secret project in which he shaped pigeons to guide missiles toward enemy ships. Based on this work, the U.S. Navy recently trained dolphins and sea lions to locate explosive mines in the Persian Gulf and perform other dangerous underwater missions (Morrison, 1988). Similarly, the Coast Guard uses pigeons to search for people lost at sea. The birds are strapped under the belly of a rescue helicopter and trained to spot floating orange objects in the water (orange is the international color of life jackets). In response to this stimulus, the birds are conditioned to peck a key that buzzes the pilot (Simmons, 1981).

Skinner used operant conditioning in other ways as well. In 1945, he constructed an "air crib" for his infant daughter—a comfortable temperature-controlled box equipped with a roll of diapers, a window, and a shade. He also advised parents on how to raise children through the use of reinforcement, and he invented a "teaching machine" so that students could learn at their own individualized pace by solving a graded series of problems and receiving immediate feedback on their answers. Today, computer-assisted instruction in schools is based on this and other early work (Benjamin, 1988). Inspired by Skinner, other behaviorists apply the principles of operant conditioning to help people solve practical problems (Martin & Pear, 1992), and people even use them to help themselves (see box, pp. 198–199).

Operant conditioning is now used in the clinic, the workplace, the classroom, and other settings. For *clinical* purposes, it laid an important foundation for the techniques of behavior modification, in which reinforcement is used to change maladaptive thoughts, feelings, and behaviors (see Chapter 17, on treatment). It also forms the basis for "biofeedback"—a procedure by which people learn to control their own autonomic processes by receiving continuous information, or "feedback," in the form of visual or auditory displays. With the aid of electronic sensors to the body and an in-

Reinforcement schedules influence human behavior the way they do rats in a Skinner box. If you deposit a coin in a pay phone and do not get a dial tone you probably will not try that phone again. Trained on a continuous reinforcement basis, you would expect this particular phone to be out of order.

strument that amplifies the signals, people can monitor and regulate their heart rate, blood pressure, and muscular tension. Biofeedback is thus used in the treatment of hypertension, chronic back pain, migraine headaches, and other health problems (Hatch et al., 1987).

Operant conditioning has also been extensively used in the *workplace*. In a study conducted within a large department store, Fred Luthans and his colleagues (1981) observed sales clerks from sixteen departments for a period of four weeks. The employees in half of these departments were then reinforced for productive performance with cash, time off, or a chance to win a company-paid vacation. The other half were not offered added incentives. As shown in Figure 5.14, the two groups were equivalent in the first

Figure 5.14

Using Reinforcement to Boost Job Performance

As observed in many studies, department store sales clerks who were offered incentives improved their job performance, while those in the control group did not (Luthans et al., 1981).

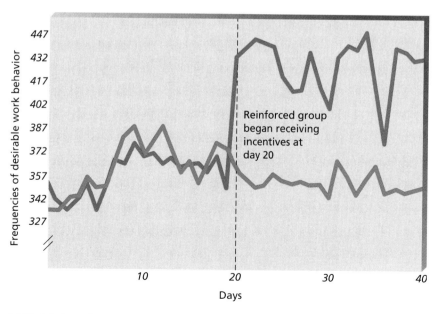

COGNITIVE PSYCHOLOGY   Health

Self-Help Through Operant Conditioning

Do you need to diet or exercise in order to lose weight? Would you like to stop smoking? Do you drink too much? Do you have trouble falling asleep at night? Are you painfully shy in large groups? Do you spend too much time bickering with your romantic partner, or too little time studying for classes? If you answered "yes" to any of these questions, then you can help yourself with an individualized program of operant conditioning, or "behavior modification." In a book on how to use self-modification for personal adjustment, David Watson and Roland Tharp (1989) outline the steps you must take to reach your behavioral goals:

1. Clearly identify the target behavior you want to change. For a program to work, your problem must be defined in precise, measurable terms ("I eat too much" or "I don't exercise enough"), not in terms that are more general and harder to pin down ("I am overweight").

2. Once you have defined the problem, you should begin by gathering three types of behavioral information about yourself: (a) First, record your existing response level, or *baseline*. If overeating is the problem, count the number of calories you consume in a seven-day period. If smoking is the problem, write down how many cigarettes you smoke each day. Whatever the goal, it is important to keep accurate written records in order to monitor your progress later on. In this regard, it may help to plot your data on a graph. (b) With each target response, you should note where you are, what you are doing, who you are with, and other aspects of the situation you're in. By monitoring *stimulus conditions* that precede the target response, you may notice that the problem is triggered by certain stimuli. For example, some people find that they tend to overeat when they are alone, are under job stress, or are studying for exams. (c) You should also monitor the *effects* of a target behavior to determine the ways in which it is maintained by reinforcement. If social gatherings make you

phase of the study. In the second phase, however, the reinforced group improved their performance dramatically, even after the reinforcement period, while the control group did not. Similar effects have been observed in different work settings (Pritchard et al., 1988; Petty et al., 1992). It is no wonder that so many business organizations now use reinforcement to increase worker satisfaction, motivation, and productivity. A survey of some 1,600 companies revealed that many of them use (1) individual or group incentive programs that offer an opportunity to earn time off or bonuses, (2)

There are many practical applications of operant conditioning. In the workplace, organizations recognize employees for their performance. In the classroom, computer games reward children for correct answers through colorful animated displays.

anxious, and if drinking or smoking calms you down, then your problem is being negatively reinforced by anxiety reduction.

3. Once you know the baseline of the target behavior, the stimulus conditions that precede it, and the consequences that tend to follow, you are ready to formulate a self-modification plan. (a) To *increase* the frequency of a *desirable* behavior, use positive reinforcement. To choose a reinforcer, think about objects or activities that you enjoy. The reinforcer can be anything: dinner at a favorite restaurant, a day at a shopping mall, the purchase of new CDs, or a long-distance call to an old friend. Whatever you choose, the key is to devise a plan, a schedule of reinforcement. The contingency should be challenging but realistic (for example, "If I run three miles a day for ten days, I earn a trip to the mall"). If you are not yet able to make the desired target response, shape your behavior using Skinner's method of successive approximations. If you cannot run a full three miles, for example, start by rewarding yourself for one mile a day for the first week, two miles a day for the next week, and so on. (b) To *decrease* the frequency of an *unwanted* behavior, you can take one of two approaches. First, try to avoid the stimulus conditions that seem to trigger the response. If you tend to overeat while talking on the kitchen telephone or watching TV, it would help to spend less time in these situations. An alternative is to extinguish the behavior by removing the existing reinforcers or by punishing yourself in some other way. To ensure that you follow through, the punishment should not be too severe.

4. Implement the plan that you have designed for yourself and continue to record the frequency of the target response. As before, it helps to mark progress by plotting your data on a graph. If you see little improvement, you should reexamine the program. The reinforcer may be too weak, or you may have set goals that are too difficult or too easy to reach. To further enhance your sense of commitment, it helps to sign a behavioral "contract" in front of friends or family members.

5. Once you have reached the final goal, it is important to realize that you are only half the way to success. The other half is to maintain the change into the future. In general, it is better to phase the program out gradually rather than all at once. This can be achieved by lowering the reinforcement-to-response ratio—until, eventually, the reinforcement is no longer necessary.

profit sharing plans, in which workers earn money from company profits, and (3) recognition programs, in which "employees of the month" are ceremoniously singled out for gifts, plaques, and trophies (Horn, 1987).

Finally, operant conditioning is commonly used in the *classroom*. Skinner's teaching machine is one application, but there are others as well. For example, many teachers establish large-scale reinforcement programs in which children earn gold stars, ribbons, or "tokens" for engaging in desired behaviors—tokens that can be exchanged for toys, extra recess time, and other privileges. Skinner (1988) himself described how a sixth-grade teacher gave her students a card every time they handed in an assignment. The students put their cards into a jar and, at the end of the week, one card was randomly drawn, with the winner receiving a prize—say, a portable radio. The result: a dramatic improvement in the number of assignments completed.

New Developments in Operant Conditioning

Believing that a science of behavior must restrict its focus to observable stimulus-response relationships, Pavlov overlooked aspects of the organism that influenced classical conditioning. In the realm of operant behavior, Skinner took the same narrow view, leaving others to study the impact of inborn biological predispositions and cognitive processes.

Biological Constraints   Behaviorists used to think that animals and humans alike could be trained to emit any response that they were physically capable of making. We now realize, however, that there are biological limits to what an animal can learn. In 1947, Keller and Marian Breland, former students of Skinner's, founded Animal Behavior Enterprises in Hot Springs, Arkansas. The Brelands were in the business of training animals to do tricks in county fairs, zoos, circuses, movies, and TV commercials. Indeed, they trained thousands of animals belonging to thirty-eight different species—including bears, whales, chickens, pigs, goats, and reindeer. Despite their professional success, however, the Brelands had to concede that biological predispositions often interfered with the shaping of a new behavior. At one point, for example, they tried to train a raccoon to pick up a wooden coin and deposit it into a piggy bank. But instead the raccoon would clutch the coin or rub two coins together, dip them into the container, pull them out, and rub them again—rather than make the deposit that was reinforced with food. The Brelands also sought to train a pig in the same routine, but after a while the pig would drop the coin, push it with its snout, toss it in the air, and drop it again. The problem? In an article entitled "The Misbehavior of Organisms," Breland and Breland (1961) concluded that animals revert to species-specific behavior patterns, a powerful tendency they called *instinctive drift*. In the wild, raccoons manipulate food objects and dunk or "wash" them, while pigs "root" for food in the ground—foraging instincts that inhibit the learning of new operant responses.

Biological predispositions may also constrain an animal's ability to learn how to escape from danger. For example, rats are easily conditioned to freeze, run from one place to another, or attack another rat—if these responses are reinforced by the termination of a painful electric shock. Yet they are slow to learn to escape by pressing a lever, a response they easily learn to make for food and water. Why? According to Robert Bolles (1970), an animal's innate defensive reactions compete with the learning of a new escape response. All this serves to remind us that behavior is guided by an organism's evolutionary past, not just by personal experience. As with classical conditioning, in which some associations are more easily learned than others, operant learning is limited by an organism's own adaptive ways (Gould & Marler, 1987).

Cognitive Perspectives   Up to the day he died, Skinner (1990) steadfastly refused to speculate about internal mental processes. Although this radical position still has its share of proponents (Poling et al., 1990), most psychologists now believe that it is important to understand internal cognitive processes—not only in humans but in animals as well (Ristau, 1991).

Latent Learning   The first prominent theorist to adopt a cognitive position was Edward Tolman. According to Tolman (1948), animals in their natural habitat learn more than just a series of stimulus-and-response connections. They also acquire a *cognitive map*—a mental spatial model of the layout—and do so regardless of whether their explorations are reinforced. Thus, when Tolman trained rats to run a maze, but then changed the starting place, or blocked the most direct routes, the animals behaved as if they were using a street map of their surroundings: they took the best available detours (see Figure 5.15).

Figure 5.15

Rats in a Maze: Evidence for a Cognitive Map

Tolman trained rats to run a maze like the one shown here, but he then blocked the most direct routes to the goal box. Operating as if they had a cognitive map, the animals took the best available detours.

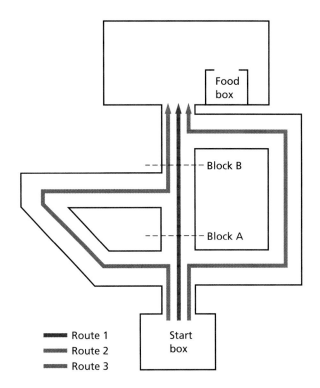

To examine whether spatial learning required that the rats be reinforced for their exploratory behavior, Tolman and Honzik (1930) conducted a classic experiment. Once a day for two weeks, they put three groups of rats into a complex maze and measured their speed in reaching the "goal box." One group was rewarded with food and improved considerably over time. A second group was not rewarded and did not improve much over time. From an operant standpoint, neither of these results is surprising. The third group, however, was the key to this experiment. In this group, the rats were not rewarded during the first ten days, but they received food beginning on the eleventh. The result: They showed immediate and dramatic improvement. On the eleventh day, before realizing that there was food in the goal box, they were just as slow as the no-reward group. But on the twelfth day, after one reinforcement, they were just as fast as the group that had been rewarded all along (see Figure 5.16). This result was significant because it demonstrated what Tolman called **latent learning**, learning that is not exhibited in overt performance until there is an incentive to do so. By making this distinction between "learning" and "performance," Tolman was able to demonstrate that animals learn from experience—with or without reinforcement. More recent research provides additional support for this phenomenon (Keith & McVety, 1988).

Locus of Control   Strict behaviorists claim that people are controlled by objective reinforcement contingencies. In contrast, a cognitive perspective holds that behavior is influenced more by our subjective interpretations of reinforcement. To illustrate the point, consider the following two incidents. The first was a demonstration by Skinner (1948) in which he dropped food pellets into a pigeon's cage on a random basis, leading the animal to repeat whatever it happened to be doing at the time. Soon this "superstitious" pigeon was busy turning, hopping on one leg, bowing, scraping, and raising

■ **latent learning** Learning that occurs but is not exhibited in performance until there is an incentive to do so.

Figure 5.16

Latent Learning

Tolman and Honzik (1930) put rats into a maze and measured how quickly they reached the goal box. Those rewarded with food improved; those without reward did not. A third group received no food until the eleventh day. Note that the rats in this last group showed a marked improvement from the eleventh day (before they knew there was food in the goal box) to the twelfth (after the first reward). These animals had exhibited latent learning, learning without reinforcement.

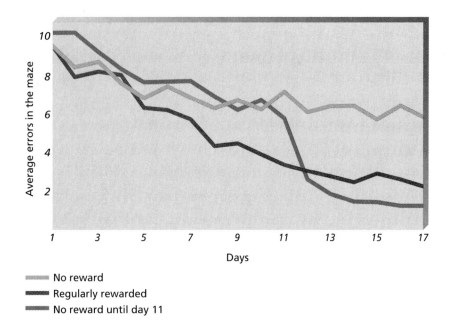

its head. This pigeon—like most humans, says Skinner—was under the illusion that it had control, even though it did not. The second story concerns a young male psychotherapy patient named Karl S. who was depressed because he felt incompetent to find a job, friends, or a woman. E. Jerry Phares (1976), Karl's therapist, tried to raise his expectancy for success through a series of small achievements—submitting a job application, striking up a conversation with a woman, and so on. Karl succeeded in these efforts but remained passive and pessimistic. The problem? He did not see the link between his actions and successful outcomes. In contrast to the superstitious pigeon, Karl had control but didn't realize it. So he didn't try.

According to Julian Rotter (1966), reinforcement can influence behavior only if we perceive the two as causally connected. For students who believe that studying increases their grades, for workers who think that hard work will be rewarded, and for citizens who believe that they can influence government policy, reinforcement strengthens behavior. But for students who believe that grades are arbitrarily determined, for workers who think that getting ahead requires more luck than effort, and for citizens who feel that they're at the mercy of powerful leaders, reinforcement does not strengthen behavior. Research shows that people differ in their "generalized expectancies" for personal control and in their responsiveness to reinforcement. Those who have a relatively *internal* locus of control tend to believe that they determine their own destiny. Those with an *external* locus of control believe that luck, fate, and powerful others determine their reinforcements. Compared to externals, internals achieve higher grades in school, persist longer at laboratory tasks, and play a more active role in political and social affairs (Strickland, 1989; Rotter, 1990).

Hidden Costs of Reward   By focusing on how people interpret reinforcement, the cognitive perspective raises a second issue. After someone is rewarded for an enjoyable task, what happens to his or her interest and motivation once that reward is no longer available? Does reinforcement

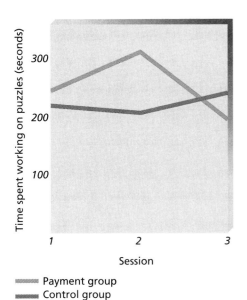

Figure 5.17

The Hidden Cost of Reward

Subjects worked three times on puzzles they found interesting. After each session the amount of free time spent on the puzzles indicated their level of motivation. During the second session, half the subjects were paid and half were not. Those who were paid were later less interested in the puzzles when the money was not available (Deci, 1971).

enhance motivation? To examine this question, Edward Deci (1971) recruited college students to work for three one-hour sessions on a set of fun block puzzles. During the first and third sessions, all subjects were similarly treated. In the second session, however, half the subjects were paid one dollar for each puzzle they completed. As a measure of their intrinsic motivation, or task interest, Deci left subjects alone during breaks and recorded the amount of free time they spent on the puzzles relative to other available activities. Compared to subjects in the nonrewarded group, those who were paid in the second session showed less interest in the puzzles in the third session—when the money was no longer available (see Figure 5.17).

Think for a moment about this paradoxical result. Why did payment undermine subjects' intrinsic motivation—that is, their desire to perform the activity for its own sake? There are two reasons. First, Mark Lepper and David Greene (1978) note that when we receive money, grades, or other rewards for an enjoyable task, our perceptions change, and we come to view the task as work ("I am doing this because I'm getting paid for it") rather than as play ("I am doing this because I enjoy it"). Offer people a large payment for engaging in a particular activity, and they will automatically assume that the activity must be tedious, risky, boring, or unpleasant (Freedman et al., 1992). Once that happens, the task no longer seems worth doing "for free." A second problem, say Edward Deci and Richard Ryan (1985), is that money and other reinforcers make us feel "controlled" rather than "in control"—an aversive feeling that further diminishes our intrinsic motivation. In a study of managers and workers in an office-machine company, Deci and his colleagues (1989) thus found that the less controlling managers were, the happier their workers were with the company as a whole.

This hidden cost of reward has serious implications. Take a child who loves to read and a teacher who awards gold stars for books completed. During the year, the child continues to read at a lively pace. But what will happen later on, when there are no gold stars? At that point, the child may begin to wonder for the first time if it is still worth the effort. Does this mean that reinforcement should never be used? No, not at all. If a person is not sufficiently motivated to start with, reward can help. For the child who doesn't normally read, gold stars provide a necessary incentive in much the same way food increases bar pressing in the Skinner box. Also, reward can be used to send different messages. When reward is presented as a "bonus" (for superior performance) rather than as a "bribe" (for mere task engagement), it actually enhances intrinsic motivation (Boggiano et al., 1985). To summarize, the lessons of the cognitive perspective are clear: People do not mindlessly repeat behaviors that are followed by reinforcement but, instead, are influenced by their perceptions, beliefs, and expectations.

OBSERVATIONAL LEARNING

Classical and operant conditioning are two ways in which organisms adapt and learn from experience. But something is missing. Forget the dogs, cats, rats, and pigeons that drool, press bars, peck keys, jump from shocks, and run in mazes. What about the human learning of complex behavior? Don't

■ **observational learning** Learning that takes place when one observes and models the behavior of others.

"Children have never been very good at listening to their elders, but they have never failed to imitate them."

JAMES BALDWIN

we sometimes learn without direct experience? Think about the first time you danced, drove a car, prepared dinner, or programmed a VCR. Now imagine how slow and inefficient you would have been if the skills had to be acquired from scratch—"shaped," as Skinner would say, through trial and error.

Complex new behaviors are often learned by watching and imitating others. The young zebra finch, a songbird, learns to reproduce precise song phrases by listening to adult "tutors" (Slater et al., 1988). Similarly, chimpanzees imitate others who are slapping their hands, stomping their feet, or using sticks to fish for insects (Goodall, 1986). Human infants also exhibit rudimentary forms of imitation. Research shows that they copy adults who stick out their tongues (Anisfeld, 1991), use a particular hand to reach, point, wave, and make other gestures (Harkins & Uzgiris, 1991), or utter sounds such as "meh," "dah," and "bee" (Poulson et al., 1991). Similarly, toddlers imitate others of their own age grasping, pulling, pushing, and poking at various toys (Hanna & Meltzoff, 1993). It is clear that imitation is adaptive: by observing their peers and elders, young members of a species learn to interact and develop the skills of past generations.

Studies of Modeling

According to Albert Bandura (1986), people learn by watching others. These others are called *models,* and the process is known as **observational learning.** In a classic experiment, nursery school children were exposed to a live adult model who behaved aggressively (Bandura et al., 1961). In a typical session, the child would be sitting quietly, drawing a picture. From another part of the room, an adult approached a Bobo doll, an inflatable clown-like toy that is weighted on the bottom so that it pops back up whenever it is knocked down. For the next ten minutes, the adult repeatedly abused the doll—sitting on it, pounding it with a hammer, kicking it, throwing balls at it, and yelling, "Sock him in the nose. . . . Kick him!"

After the outburst, the child was taken to a room filled with attractive toys but told that these toys were being saved "for the other children." Frustrated, the child was then taken to a third room containing additional toys, including—you guessed it—a Bobo doll. At that point, the child was left alone and observed through a one-way mirror. What happened? Compared to children exposed to a nonviolent model, or to no model at all, those who witnessed the aggressive display were far more likely to assault the doll. In fact, they often copied the model's attack, action for action, and repeated the same abusive remarks, word for word. The children had acquired a whole new repertoire of aggressive behavior. More recent research confirms the point: among children and adolescents, exposure to aggressive models on TV and in the movies triggers aggression—not just in the laboratory but in the classroom, the playground, and other settings as well (Wood et al., 1991).

Observational learning also has beneficial effects. In one study, snake phobics gained the courage to approach a live snake by first watching someone else do so—which is why models are often used in the treatment of phobias (Bandura et al., 1969). In a second study, bystanders were more likely to help a stranded motorist or donate money to the Salvation Army,

Based on studies showing that exposure to violent models increases aggression in children, a storm of controversy surrounds MTV's heavy-metal cartoon, *Beavis and Butt-head.*

two acts of generosity, if they had earlier observed someone else do the same (Bryan & Test, 1967). And in a third study, elementary school children learned by watching others how to sharpen their logical skills in the game of "twenty questions"—indicating that exposure to models can be used to facilitate the learning of new concepts and strategies (Johnson et al., 1991).

The Process of Modeling

According to Bandura (1977, 1986), observational learning is not a simple, automatic, reflex-like reaction to models. Rather, it consists of two-stages: acquisition and performance. You may recall that Edward Tolman had earlier made this distinction by noting that a newly acquired response often remains "latent" until the organism is motivated to perform it. Building on Tolman's work, Bandura described observational learning as a chain of events involving four steps: attention, retention, reproduction, and motivation.

Attention: To learn by observation, one must pay attention to the model's behavior and the consequences of that behavior. Due to their ability to command our attention, parents, teachers, political leaders, and TV celebrities are potentially effective models.

Retention: In order to model someone else's behavior minutes, days, weeks, months, or even years later, one must recall what was observed. Accordingly, modeling is likely to occur when the behavior is memorable, or when the observer thinks about or rehearses the behavior.

Reproduction: Attention and memory are necessary conditions, but observers must also have the motor ability to reproduce the modeled behavior. As closely as I watch, and as hard as I try, I will never be able to copy Michael Jordan's graceful flight to the basket.

Motivation: People may pay attention to a model, recall the behavior, and have the ability to reproduce it—all laying a necessary foundation for modeling. Whether an observer takes action, however, is then determined by his or her expectations for reinforcement—expectations that are based not only on personal experience but on the experiences of others. This last point is important because it illustrates the phenomenon of *vicarious reinforcement:* that people are more likely to imitate models who are rewarded for their behavior and less likely to imitate those who are punished. Apparently, learning can occur without direct, firsthand experience.

PERSPECTIVES ON LEARNING

For about a century now, psychologists have studied with remarkable intensity the basic laws of classical conditioning, operant conditioning, and observational learning. To a large extent, the knowledge gained from this research has had far-reaching implications for a wide range of animal and human behaviors. Inspired by Pavlov and Skinner, the psychology of learning is grounded in hard-nosed S-R behaviorism. Today, however, a vast majority of researchers recognize that biological dispositions, cognitive processes, and other factors residing within the person play a critical role. Thus, we now know that all organisms are genetically prepared to learn some associations more easily than others, that synaptic transmissions are modified as learning occurs, that beliefs about reinforcement can have a greater impact on behavior than the reinforcement itself, and that learning is also achieved by observing others.

In the remaining chapters of this section, we will see that cognitive psychologists are systematically exploring the inner workings of the human mind. Whether the focus is on neuronal changes that accompany learning, or on memory, thought, language, or emotion, there is tremendous interest in the "O" part of S-O-R psychology. Learning theorists are also studying the acquisition of complex human skills—such as how we learn to read, speak, understand stories, solve math problems, recognize music, play chess, use a computer, and drive a car (Holding, 1989). And they are interested in the way people learn complex material without really trying—through implicit, unconscious processes (Reber, 1993). Finally, there is a great deal of interest in the application of learning theory to instructional issues and the acquisition of knowledge (Glaser, 1990).

SUMMARY AND KEY TERMS

As in the case of the stickleback, *ethologists* have found that many aspects of animal behavior are programmed by inborn *fixed action patterns*. In contrast, human beings adapt primarily through learning, memory, thought, language, and emotion.

The Big Picture

In Part II of this book, there is an undercurrent of tension over the question of human competence and rationality. This point is illustrated in the implicit learning study described here.

The Psychology of Learning

Learning is a relatively permanent change in knowledge or behavior that comes from experience. The simplest form of learning, found even in lower organisms, is *habituation*.

Classical Conditioning

The key to learning is association, a tendency to connect events that occur together in space or time.

Pavlov's Discovery

Studying the digestive system in dogs, Pavlov stumbled upon *classical conditioning*. In his experiments, the salivary reflex was the *unconditioned response (UR)*, and it was elicited by food, an *unconditioned stimulus (US)*. Through pairing of a bell with the food, the bell became a *conditioned stimulus (CS)* that on its own could elicit salivation, a *conditioned response (CR)*. This experiment serves as a model of classical conditioning in humans.

Basic Principles

After Pavlov's initial experiment, he and others discovered four basic principles of learning: (1) the acquisition of a CR is influenced by the order and timing of the CS-US pairing; (2) in *extinction*, repeated presentation of the CS without the US causes the CR to lose its power, though there is an occasional rebound effect known as *spontaneous recovery;* (3) after an organism is conditioned to a CS, similar stimuli will often evoke the CR through *stimulus generalization;* and (4) *discrimination* is the opposite process, one of learning to distinguish between stimuli.

Pavlov's Legacy

As demonstrated by taste aversion studies, research shows that animals are biologically prepared to learn some associations more easily than others. The process seems to involve learning that one event (CS) predicts another event (US). There are many applications of classical conditioning. For example, people can be conditioned to develop fears or preferences, and positive or negative social attitudes. Recent studies show that the body's immune cells can be classically conditioned as well.

Operant Conditioning

The learning of voluntary, complex, goal-directed behaviors is achieved by a different form of learning, one that involves the link between an action and its consequences.

The Law of Effect

Using animals, Thorndike studied the *law of effect:* that actions followed by a positive outcome are repeated, while those followed by a negative outcome or no outcome are not.

Skinner's Principles of Reinforcement

Also using animals, Skinner systematically examined *operant conditioning,* the process by which we learn to behave in ways that produce reinforcement. As defined by Skinner, *reinforcement* is any stimulus that strengthens a prior response. There are two types of reinforcers: positive (the presentation of a desirable stimulus) and negative (the withdrawal of an aversive stimulus). In contrast to reinforcement, *punishment* has the opposite effect of weakening, not strengthening, a prior response. Punishers may be positive (presentation of an aversive stimulus) or negative (withdrawal of a desirable stimulus).

Skinner found that complex new behaviors can be "shaped" through reinforcement of successive responses that come closer and closer to the target behavior. He and others also identified four types of schedules of reinforcement (fixed interval, variable interval, fixed ratio, variable ratio), each having different effects on learning and extinction. Although punishment can often be used to suppress unwanted behavior, it has undesirable side effects and should be used cautiously. As in classical conditioning, generalization and discrimination are important aspects of operant learning.

Practical Applications of Operant Conditioning

Skinner was interested in practical applications. Following in his footsteps, many behaviorists use the principles of operant conditioning to solve practical problems in clinical settings, the workplace, and the classroom.

New Developments in Operant Conditioning

Although operant conditioning is broadly applicable, animal studies have revealed that species-specific biological predispositions often interfere with the shaping of a new behavior. And although Skinner refused to speculate about mental processes, others have not. Thus, researchers have found that animals exhibit *latent learning* (learning without reinforcement), that people are more influenced by the perception of control over reinforcement than by objective contingencies, and that rewards sometimes undermine our intrinsic motivation.

Observational Learning

Complex new behaviors are often learned not through direct experience but through the observation and imitation of others.

Studies of Modeling

According to Bandura, we learn by watching others. These others are called models, and the process is called *observational learning.* Studies indicate that both desirable (helping) and undesirable (aggressive) behaviors may be learned in this manner.

The Process of Modeling

Observational learning involves not simple, reflex-like imitation but a four-step process that requires attention, retention, reproduction, and motivation.

Perspectives on Learning

Inspired by Pavlov and Skinner, the psychology of learning is grounded in S-R behaviorism. Today, however, researchers are also interested in biological dispositions, cognitive processes, and other factors residing within the organism.

Chapter 6

Memory

On November 22, 1963, thousands of Dallas residents watched one of the most tragic events in modern American history: the assassination of John F. Kennedy. What happened? Some witnesses said they saw a lone gunman in the sixth-floor window of a nearby building; others recalled the presence of two or three men in the same window. Still others insisted that they saw shooting from a grassy knoll. To add to the confusion, some witnesses recalled that three shots were fired; others swore they heard five or six. Twenty-eight years later, in 1991, John Demjanjuk was identified by four survivors of a World War II concentration camp as "Ivan the Terrible," a Nazi guard who killed thousands of Jews. After forty-five years, these witnesses identified the elderly man as Ivan. Based on their testimony, Demjanjuk was convicted and sentenced to death in a Jerusalem courtroom—only to be released two years later when he was exonerated by evidence that had previously been withheld. It was also in 1991 that TV viewers watched in astonishment as law professor Anita Hill accused Supreme Court Justice Clarence Thomas of sexual harassment, and repeated—word for word—lewd remarks he allegedly made ten years earlier. Thomas adamantly denied all the charges.

These three cases have little in common, but they raise the same basic question: Can remembrances of the past be trusted? Human memory is often the subject of controversy. Sometimes we seem able to recall a face, a voice, the contents of a lecture, a foreign language, a news event, a first date, the birth of a child, or the death of a loved one, with precision and certainty. At other times, however, memory is limited, flawed, biased—as when you forget a phone number you just looked up, the items on the grocery list you left at home, coursework from last semester, or the name of someone you recently met. How are our experiences stored in the brain and later retrieved? What causes us to recall some events but not others? How accurate are our recollections of the past? To answer these questions, cognitive psychologists study *memory*, the process by which information is retained for later use.

After the 1963 assassination of John F. Kennedy, many eyewitnesses came forward. Some reported seeing one gunman in the sixth-floor window of a nearby building; others recalled two or three gunmen in the same building; still others thought the shots were fired from the ground. Such are the pitfalls of eyewitness memory.

AN INFORMATION-PROCESSING MODEL

■ **sensory memory** A memory storage system that records information from the senses for up to three seconds.

■ **short-term memory (STM)** A memory storage system that holds about seven items for up to twenty seconds before the material is transferred to long-term memory or forgotten.

■ **long-term memory (LTM)** A relatively permanent memory storage system that can hold vast amounts of information for many years.

According to Aristotle and Plato, memory was like stamping an impression into a block of wax. Over the years, others have likened memory to a switchboard, storage box, workbench, library, and tape recorder. Today, cognitive psychologists compare the human mind to a computer and memory to an information-processing system. If you've ever worked on a computer, you will appreciate the analogy. Your PC *receives* input from a keyboard, joystick, or mouse; *converts* the symbols into a special numeric code; *saves* the information on a hard or floppy disk; then *retrieves* the data from the disk by displaying it on the screen or sending it to a printer. If the computer crashes, if there's not enough space on the disk, if the file was deleted, or if you type in the wrong retrieval command, then the information becomes inaccessible, or "forgotten."

Using the computer as a model, memory researchers seek to trace the flow of "information" as it is "processed." In this model, a stimulus that registers on our senses is remembered only if it (1) draws *attention*, which brings it into consciousness, (2) is *encoded*, or transferred to *storage* sites in the brain, and (3) is *retrieved* for use at a later time (Atkinson & Shiffrin, 1968).

Within this information-processing approach, three types of memory have been distinguished: sensory, short-term, and long-term. **Sensory memory** stores all stimuli that register on the senses, holding literal copies for a brief moment ranging from a fraction of a second to three seconds. Sensations that do not draw attention tend to vanish, but those we "notice" are transferred to **short-term memory (STM)**, another temporary storage system that can hold seven or so items of information for about twenty seconds. Although STM fades quickly, information can be held for a longer period of time through repetition and rehearsal. When people talk about attention span, they are referring to short-term memory. Finally, **long-term memory (LTM)** is a somewhat permanent storage system that can hold vast quantities of information for many years. Science writer Isaac Asimov once estimated that LTM takes in a quadrillion separate bits of information in the course of a lifetime. And mathematician John Griffith estimated that, from birth to death, the average person stores five hundred times more information than the *Encyclopedia Britannica*. When people talk about memory, long-term memory is typically what they have in mind.

As depicted in the flow chart in Figure 6.1, this information-processing model is used to structure the present chapter. Note, however, that it is only a model and does *not* necessarily mean that there are three separate

Figure 6.1

An Information-Processing Model of Memory

Many stimuli register in sensory memory. Those that are noticed are briefly stored in short-term memory, and those that are encoded are then transferred to a more permanent facility. As you can see, forgetting may be caused by failures of attention, encoding, or retrieval.

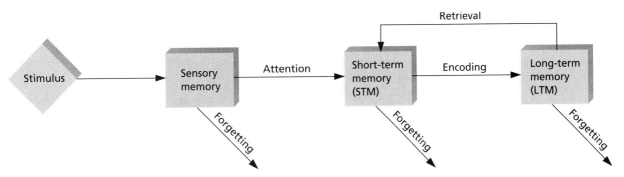

storage bins in the brain. It's also important to know that this is only one view of how memory works. We'll see later that many researchers believe there are multiple memory systems, each uniquely dedicated to a certain type of information. We'll also see that researchers have exposed some serious flaws and biases in human memory. As you read through this chapter, keep an eye on the recurring theme of cognitive psychology: that human beings are both competent and incompetent, rational and irrational.

THE SENSORY REGISTER

Take a flashlight into a dark room, turn it on, shine it on a wall, and wave it quickly in a circular motion. What do you see? If you're fast enough, the light will appear to leave a glowing trail, and you'll see a continuous circle. The reason: even though the light illuminates only one point in the circle at a time, your visual system stores a "snapshot" of each point as you watch the next point. The visual image is called an "icon," and the snapshot it stores is called *iconic memory* (Neisser, 1967).

Iconic Memory

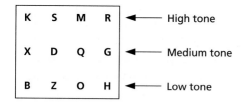

Figure 6.2

Testing for Iconic Memory

Here is an array of letters like that used by Sperling (1960). When subjects viewed this array for one-twentieth of a second and tried to name all the letters, they could recall only 4 or 5. But when they were signaled after the items to recall only one row, they were able to recall 3 or 4 per line—for an average of 10 letters.

People typically don't realize that a fleeting mental trace lingers after a stimulus is removed from view. Nor did cognitive psychologists realize it until George Sperling's (1960) ingenious series of experiments. Sperling instructed subjects to stare at the center of a blank screen. Then he flashed an array of letters for one-twentieth of a second and asked subjects to name as many of the letters as possible. Take a quick glance at Figure 6.2, and try it for yourself. You will probably recall about a handful of the letters. In fact, Sperling found that no matter how large the array, subjects could name only four or five items. Why? One possibility is that people can register just so much visual input in a single glance—that twelve letters is too much to see in so little time. A second possibility is that all the letters registered but the image faded before subjects could report them all. Indeed, many subjects insisted they were able to "see" the whole array but then forgot some of the letters before they could name them.

Did the information that was lost leave a momentary trace, as subjects had claimed, or did it never register in the first place? To test these alternative hypotheses, Sperling devised the "partial report technique." Instead of asking subjects to list all the letters, he asked them to name only one row in each array—a row that was not determined until *after* the array was shown. In this procedure, each presentation was immediately followed by a tone signaling which letters to name: a high-pitched tone indicated the top line; a medium pitch, the middle line; a low pitch, the bottom line. If the entire array was seen, subjects should have been able to report all the letters in a prompted row correctly—regardless of which row was prompted. Sperling was right: subjects correctly recalled 3.3 letters per row. In other words, 10 letters (9.9), not 4 or 5, were instantly registered in consciousness before fading, held briefly in iconic memory. To determine how long this type of memory lasts, Sperling next varied the time between the letters and the tone that signaled the row to be recalled. As depicted in Figure 6.3,

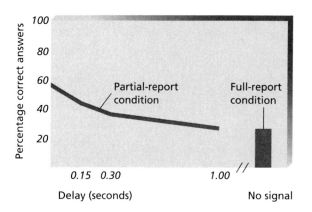

Figure 6.3

Duration of Iconic Memory

How long does an iconic memory last? Sperling (1960) varied the time between the letters and the tone signaling the row to be recalled. The iconic image started to fade after one-third of a second and vanished completely after one full second.

the visual image started to fade as the interval was increased to one-third of a second and had almost completely vanished two-thirds of a second later. Iconic memory lasts for just a fraction of a second (Coltheart, 1980; G. Loftus et al., 1992).

Echoic Memory

A similar phenomenon exists for auditory stimuli. The next time you listen to the radio, notice after you turn it off how an "echo" of the sound seems to reverberate in your head. This auditory sensory register is called *echoic memory*. How much auditory input is stored in echoic memory, and for how long? In a study modeled after Sperling's, Christopher Darwin and his colleagues (1972) put headphones on their subjects and simultaneously played three sets of spoken letters—in the right ear, in the left ear, and in both ears at once. Subjects then received a visual signal indicating which set to report. Based on this study and others, we now know that echoic memory holds only a few items but lasts for two or three seconds, and perhaps even longer, before fading (Cowan, 1988; Sams et al., 1993).

Whether a sensory memory system stores information for one third of a second or for three seconds, one wonders: What's the point of having a "memory" that is so quick to decay? To answer this question, try to imagine what your perceptions of the world would be like without sensory memories. Without the visual icon, for instance, we would lose track of what we see with every blink of the eye—as if we were viewing the world through a series of snapshots rather than on a continuous film. Similarly, it would be hard to understand spoken language without the persistent traces of echoic memory. Speech would sound like a series of staccato sounds rather than connected words and phrases. In fact, we have other sensory memories as well—for tactile (touch), olfactory (smell), and gustatory (taste) stimuli.

SHORT-TERM MEMORY

I recently traveled by Amtrak to New York City. As I climbed the stairs of Penn Station onto 34th Street, I was bombarded by sensations: the vibration under my feet from a train rumbling into the station; the sound of

The information-processing model of memory regards *attention* as a necessary first step. In a tennis match, as in other settings, people selectively tune in to stimuli that are adaptive, interesting, and important.

horns honking, a siren blaring, and a bus screeching to a stop; the faint aroma of freshly brewed coffee overwhelmed by the smell of exhaust fumes; and the sight of skyscrapers, traffic lights, street vendors, cars bouncing over bumps in the road, and white steam billowing through a hole in the ground.

I'm sure more stimuli reached my sensory registers than I can write about, but most never reached consciousness and were quickly "forgotten." The key is *attention*. As noted earlier, sensations that do not capture attention quickly tend to evaporate, while those we notice are transferred to *short-term memory,* a somewhat more lasting but limited storage facility. Attention is a selective process. Have you ever been engaged in conversation at a noisy gathering, yet managed to overhear someone say your name? If so, then you have experienced the *cocktail party effect,* the tendency to detect a single, often meaningful, stimulus in a complex environment (Moray, 1959). As we saw in Chapter 4 on consciousness, people are selective in their perceptions and can instantly direct their attention to stimuli that are interesting, adaptive, or important. During my visit to New York, I was so busy searching for a taxicab uptown that I focused on moving yellow objects to the exclusion of everything else.

From the sensory register, information is *encoded*—that is, converted into a form that can be stored in short-term memory. A stimulus may be encoded in different ways. After you read this sentence, for example, you might recall a picture of the letters and their placement on the page (visual encoding), the sound of the words themselves (acoustic encoding), or the meaning of the sentence as a whole (semantic encoding). Research shows that people usually encode information in acoustic terms. Thus, when subjects are presented with a string of letters and immediately asked to recall them, they make more "sound-alike" errors than "look-alike" errors. For example, subjects misrecall an *F* as an *S* or *X*, but not as an *E* or *B* (Conrad, 1964). Subjects are also more likely to confuse words that sound alike (*man, can*) than words that are similar in meaning (*big, huge*)—further indicating that information is more likely to be encoded in acoustic than in semantic terms (Baddeley, 1966).

Capacity

Attention limits what information comes under the spotlight of STM at any given time. To the extent that one stimulus captures our attention, others may be ignored—sometimes with startling effects on memory. For example, research on eyewitness testimony shows that when a criminal displays a weapon, witnesses are less able to identify that culprit than if no weapon is present (Steblay, 1992). Why? One reason is that the witness's eyes are fixed on the weapon like a magnet—drawing attention away from the face. To demonstrate, Elizabeth Loftus and her colleagues (1987) showed subjects slides of a customer who walked up to a bank teller and pulled out either a gun or a checkbook. By recording eye movements, these researchers found that subjects spent more time looking at the gun than at the checkbook. The result: an impairment in their ability to identify the criminal in a lineup.

Figure 6.4

Memory-Span Test

Try this memory-span task. Read the top row of digits, one per second, then look away and repeat them back in order. Next, try the second row, the third row, and so on, until you make a mistake. The average person's memory span can hold seven items of information.

5	7	3									
9	0	7	6								
8	5	4	0	2							
0	9	1	3	5	6						
8	6	0	4	8	7	2					
1	7	5	4	2	4	1	9				
9	6	5	8	3	0	8	0	1			
5	7	3	5	1	2	0	2	8	5		
3	1	7	9	2	1	5	0	6	4	2	
2	1	0	1	6	7	4	1	9	8	3	5

Limited by attentional resources, short-term memory can hold only a small number of items. How small a number? To appreciate the limited capacity of STM, try the *memory-span task* presented in Figure 6.4, or test a friend. By presenting increasingly long lists of items, researchers seek to identify the point at which subjects can no longer recall without error. In tasks like this one, the average person can store seven or so list items (usually between five and nine)—regardless of whether it consists of numbers, letters, words, or names. This limit is so consistent that George Miller (1956) described the capacity of STM by the phrase, "the magical number seven, plus or minus two."

Once short-term memory is filled to capacity, the storage of new information requires that existing contents be discarded or "displaced." Thus, if you're trying to memorize historical dates, chemical elements, or a list of vocabulary words, you may find that the eighth or ninth item pushes out those earlier on the list. It's like a computer screen. As you fill the screen with new information, old material scrolls out of view. This limited capacity seems awfully disabling. But is it absolutely fixed, or can we overcome the magical number seven?

According to Miller, STM can accommodate only seven items, but there's a hitch: although an item may consist of one letter or digit, these can be grouped into *chunks* of words, sentences, and large numbers—thus enabling us to use our storage capacity more efficiently. To see the effects of chunking on short-term memory, read the following letters, pausing at each space; then look up and name as many of the letters as you can in correct order: *CN NIB MMT VU SA.* Since this list contains twelve discrete letters, you probably found the task quite frustrating. Now try this next list, again pausing between spaces: *CNN IBM MTV USA.* Better, right? This list contains the same twelve letters. But because these letters are "repackaged" in familiar groups, you had to store only four chunks, not twelve—well within the "magical" capacity (Bower, 1970).

Chunking enables us to improve our short-term memory span by using our capacity in a more efficient manner. You may be limited to seven or so chunks, but you can learn to increase the size of those chunks. To demonstrate, a group of researchers trained two male college students, both long-distance runners of average intelligence, for several months. For an hour a day, three or four days a week, these students were asked to recall random

Figure 6.5

Increased Memory Span

Two students practiced memory-span tasks for an hour a day, three to four days a week, for six months. Remarkably, their short-term memory span increased from seven digits up to eighty (Ericsson & Chase, 1982). In fact, one subject now has a memory span that exceeds one hundred digits (Staszewski, 1988).

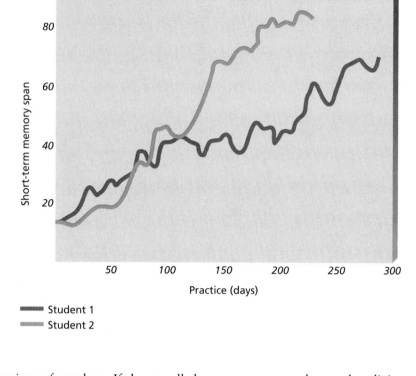

Practice (days)

Student 1
Student 2

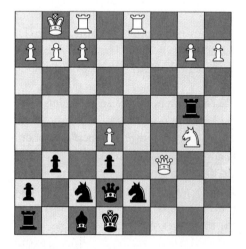

Figure 6.6

The Value of Chunking

Study this arrangement of chess pieces for five seconds. Then turn to the empty board on page 218 and try to reproduce the arrangement as best you can. Unless you are an experienced chess player, the number of pieces you place in the correct squares should approximate the magical number seven.

strings of numbers. If they recalled a sequence correctly, another digit was added to the next sequence and the task was repeated. If they made a mistake, the number of digits in the next sequence was reduced by one. As shown in Figure 6.5, the improvement was astonishing. Before practicing, their memory span was the usual seven digits. After six months, they were up to eighty items (Ericsson & Chase, 1982; Ericsson et al., 1980). In one session, for example, the experimenter read the following numbers in order: 8931944349250215784166850612094888856877273141 86105462 9748012949749659228. After two minutes of concentration, the subject repeated all seventy-three digits, in groups of three and four. How did he do it? Given no special instruction, the subject developed his own elaborate strategy: he converted the random numbers into ages ("89.3 years, a very old person"), dates (1944 was "near the end of World War II"), and cross-country racing times for various distances (3492 was "3 minutes and 49.2 seconds, nearly a world's record for the mile").

The value of chunking is evidenced by the way people retain information in their areas of expertise. Study the arrangement of pieces on the chessboard shown in Figure 6.6, and in five seconds memorize as much of it as you can. Chances are, you'll be able to reproduce approximately seven items. Yet after looking at the same arrangement for five seconds, chess masters can reproduce all the pieces and their row-and-column positions almost without error. It's not that chess masters are born with computer-like minds. When pieces are placed randomly on the board, they are no more proficient than the rest of us. But when the arrangement is taken from an actual game between good players, they chunk the configurations of individual pieces into familiar patterns such as the "Romanian Pawn Defense" and "Casablanca Bishop's Gambit" (De Groot, 1965; Chase & Simon, 1973). From their years of experience, experts in all domains—including computer programmers, sports fans, waitresses, and bartenders—chunk information to boost their short-term memory capacity (Cohen, 1989).

Have you ever had a waiter or waitress recall everyone's order at a table without the use of a notepad? Research shows that such "experts" learn to chunk information to boost their short-term memory capacity.

Duration

It has happened to me, and I'll bet it has happened to you too. You look up a telephone number, repeat it to yourself, put away the directory, and start dialing. Then it happens. You hit the first three numbers without a hitch, but then you go blank, get confused (was that a 5 or a 9?), and hang up in frustration. After just a few seconds, the phone number is gone, no longer in memory. Then there is the matter of names. I'll be at a party or social gathering and meet someone for the first time. We'll talk for a few moments, and then I will turn to introduce my wife—only to realize with embarrassment that I have already forgotten the name of my new acquaintance.

These types of experiences are common because short-term memory is limited not only in the *amount* of information it can store but also in the length of *time* it can hold that information. What is the duration of short-term memory? That is, how long does a memory trace last if a person does not actively rehearse or repeat it? To measure how rapidly information is forgotten, Lloyd and Margaret Peterson (1959) asked subjects to recall a set of unrelated consonants such as *MJK*. So that subjects could not rehearse the material, they were given a number and instructed to count backward from that number by threes: 564, 561, 558, 555, and so on. After varying lengths of time, subjects were cued to recall the consonants. After 18 seconds, performance plummeted to below 10 percent (see Figure 6.7).

Knowing the fleeting nature of short-term memory, one can prevent forgetting by repeating information silently or aloud. That's why, if I do not have a pen and paper handy, I will repeat a phone number over and over again until I have dialed it. And that's why I try to silently repeat the person's name while being introduced. Repetition extends the twenty-second

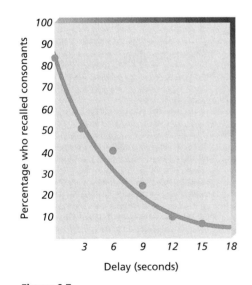

Figure 6.7

Duration of Short-Term Memory

What is the duration of short-term memory? When subjects are prevented from rehearsing material they are trying to recall, their short-term memory vanishes within 20 seconds (Peterson & Peterson, 1959).

■ **maintenance rehearsal** The use of sheer repetition to keep information in short-term memory.

duration of STM in the same way that chunking expands its seven-item capacity. (See box, p. 246, for ways to improve your memory.)

The retention benefits of sheer repetition, or **maintenance rehearsal**, were first demonstrated by Hermann Ebbinghaus (1885), a German philosopher who was a pioneer in memory research. Using himself as a subject, Ebbinghaus created a list of all possible nonsense syllables consisting of a vowel inserted between two consonants. Syllables that formed words were then eliminated—which left a list of unfamiliar items (*RUX, VOM, QEL, MIF*), each written on a separate card. To study the effects of rehearsal, Ebbinghaus would turn over the cards, one at a time, and say each syllable aloud to the ticking rhythm of a metronome. Then, after reading the items once, he would start again and go through the cards in the same order. This procedure was repeated until he could anticipate each syllable before turning over the card. Ebbinghaus found that he could recall a list of seven syllables after a single reading (there's that magical number again) but that he needed more practice for longer lists. The more often he repeated the items, the more he could recall. Numerous other studies confirm the point: "rehearsal" can be used to "maintain" an item in short-term memory for an indefinite period of time.

Functions of Short-Term Memory

Short-term memory's limitations may seem to be a handicap, but in fact they are necessary and adaptive. As with clearing outdated papers off a desk or purging old files from a computer, it is convenient to forget what is no longer useful. Otherwise, your mind would be cluttered with every sensation, every name, phone number, ZIP code, and morsel of trivia that ever entered the stream of your consciousness. If STM had unlimited capacity, you would constantly be distracted—possibly with devastating results. In Chapter 16, for example, we'll see that people who suffer from schizophrenia are often incoherent, jumping from one topic to the next as they speak, in part because they cannot filter out distractions.

In the computer we call the human mind, STM is like the screen. On a computer, material displayed on the monitor may be entered on a keyboard or retrieved from previously saved files. Similarly, STM contains both new sensory input and material that is pulled from long-term storage. All cognitive psychologists agree that people have fleeting memories that are limited in their capacity and duration (Shiffrin, 1993). It is important to note, however, that many researchers are now critical of the traditional view that STM is a passive storage depot where information is held until it either fades or is transferred to a more permanent warehouse. One problem with this account is that there's no physiological evidence for the existence of a special short-term facility in the brain (Crowder, 1993). The second problem is that short-term memory is not merely a passive storage site but an active workspace where information is processed. For that reason, Alan Baddeley (1992) and others prefer the term *working memory*. According to Baddeley, working memory consists of a "central executive" processor and two specialized storage-and-rehearsal systems—one for auditory input, the other for visual and spatial images. The adaptive significance of this active, short-term system is evident when researchers compare individuals who

If you have not already done so, turn to Figure 6.6 on p. 216 and follow the instructions.

■ serial position effect The tendency to recall items from the beginning and end of a list more effectively than those in the middle.

*"I remember opening the can,
and I remember washing the pot,
but I don't remember eating the chili."*

[Drawing by Frascino; © 1979 The New Yorker Magazine, Inc.]

differ in their working-memory capacity. For example, the more words or sentences people can hold for a brief period of time, the higher their scores will be on the verbal SAT test and other measures of language and reading comprehension (Engle et al., 1992; Just & Carpenter, 1992).

Research also suggests that it's important to distinguish between a short-term and a long-term memory. When people try to memorize any list of items, they typically exhibit the **serial position effect**: items from the beginning and end of the list are recalled more readily than those sandwiched in the middle. The enhanced recall of the early items on a list is the *primacy effect*; that for the later items is called the *recency effect*. These principles were first discovered in the 1890s by Mary Whiton Calkins, the first woman ever to serve as president of the American Psychological Association (Madigan & O'Hara, 1992). Since that time, numerous others have reported similar findings—not only in humans but in nonhuman primates as well (Castro & Larsen, 1992).

Two different factors seem to be responsible for the serial position effect: (1) the first few items receive more attention and are rehearsed more than later ones, so they are transferred into long-term memory, and (2) the last few items have not yet faded from short-term storage when the test begins. Unless an item is unique in some way, those caught in the middle of a serial list come too late to be adequately rehearsed but too early to be held in STM without rehearsal. So they are forgotten. Various studies support this explanation. For example, Murray Glanzer and Anita Cunitz (1966) presented two groups of subjects with fifteen words to memorize. One group was tested right after the presentation; the second was distracted for thirty seconds and then tested. As shown in Figure 6.8, the subjects who were tested immediately exhibited the usual effect: the first few items were recalled by rehearsal, and the last few had not yet faded. In the delayed-testing group, however, there was no recency effect, only primacy. After 30 seconds and no opportunity for rehearsal, the later items had vanished from short-term memory.

Figure 6.8

The Serial Position Effect

Subjects trying to memorize a list of words were tested either immediately or after 30 seconds of distraction. In the first group, subjects recalled the first and last few items the best, yielding the U-shaped serial position curve. In the delay group, however, there was no recency effect: after 30 seconds without rehearsal, subjects forgot the later items (Glanzer & Cunitz, 1966).

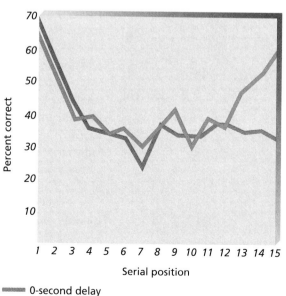

 0-second delay
30-second delay

■ **elaborative rehearsal** A technique for transferring information into long-term memory by thinking about it in a deeper way.

It's interesting that the serial position effect can also be found in long-term memory tasks—though presumably for other reasons. For example, how many U.S. presidents can you name in the correct order? Try it and see what happens. When Henry Roediger and Robert Crowder (1976) asked college students to complete this task, they found primacy, recency, and the usual decline in the middle. Let's see: Washington, Adams, Jefferson, . . . Lincoln, . . . Carter, Reagan, Bush, and Clinton. The one exception to the pattern is that Lincoln was recalled far more frequently than would be expected from his middle position—a performance "spike" that is common when a distinctive item is embedded in an otherwise homogenous list (Wallace, 1965; Schmidt, 1991).

LONG-TERM MEMORY

Do you remember your fourth birthday, the name of your first-grade teacher, or the smell of floor wax in the corridors of your elementary school? Can you describe a dream you had last night, or recite the words of the national anthem? To answer these questions, you would have to retrieve information from the mental warehouse of long-term memory. *Long-term memory* is a relatively enduring storage system that has the capacity to retain vast amounts of information for long periods of time. This section examines long-term memory of the recent and remote past—how it is encoded, stored, retrieved, forgotten, and even reconstructed in the course of a lifetime.

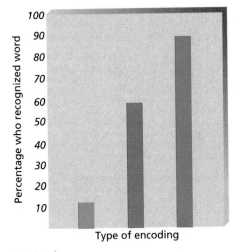

Figure 6.9

Elaborative Rehearsal

Subjects read a long list of words and for each one judged how it was printed (visual), how it sounded (acoustic), or what it meant (semantic). The more thought required to process the words, the easier they were to recognize later (Craik & Tulving, 1975).

Encoding

Information can be kept alive in STM by rote repetition, or maintenance rehearsal. But to transfer something into long-term memory, you would find it more effective to use **elaborative rehearsal**—to think about the material in a more meaningful way and associate it with other information stored in long-term memory. The more deeply you process information, the more likely you are to recall it at a later time.

To demonstrate, Fergus Craik and Endel Tulving (1975) showed subjects a list of words, one at a time, and for each asked them for (1) a simple visual judgment that required no thought about the words themselves ("Is _____ printed in capital letters?"), (2) an acoustic judgment that required subjects to at least pronounce the letters as words ("Does _____ rhyme with *small*?"), or (3) a more complex semantic judgment that compelled subjects to think about the meaning of the words ("Does the word fit the sentence 'I saw a _____ in the pond'?"). Subjects did not realize that their memory would be tested later. Yet words that were processed at a "deep" level, in terms of meaning, were more easily recognized than those processed at a "shallow" level (see Figure 6.9). Deep processing can also enhance our ability to recognize faces. Lance Bloom and Samuel Mudd (1991) displayed a series of faces and asked subjects to make judgments that were superficial

("Is the face male or female?") or more complex ("Is the face honest or dishonest?"). Those who had to process the pictures at a deep level spent more time looking, made more eye movements, and were more likely to recognize the faces later.

Perhaps the most effective form of elaborative rehearsal is the linking of new information to the self. In one study, subjects sat in front of a microcomputer and looked at forty trait adjectives (for example, *shy, friendly, ambitious*). In some cases, they were told to judge whether the words were self-descriptive; in others, they judged the words' length, sound, or meaning. When asked to list as many of the words as they could, subjects remembered more when they thought about the words in reference to themselves than for other purposes (Rogers et al., 1977). Apparently, the self is a memory aid: by viewing new information as relevant to our own experience, we consider that information more fully and organize it around common themes. The result is an improvement in memory (Greenwald & Banaji, 1989).

Memorizing—definitions, mathematical formulas, poems, or historical dates—usually requires conscious effort. When I teach a large class, I pass out index cards on the first day and ask students to write down their names and a unique personal detail that will help me remember who they are. Then I locate each student's photograph in the college "face book," match the face to the name, and run through the cards until I can identify each student. With tasks like this one, practice makes perfect. In 1885, Ebbinghaus read through a list of nonsense syllables 0, 8, 16, 24, 32, 42, 53, or 64 times, and checked his memory for the items twenty-four hours later. As predicted, the more learning time he spent the first day, the better his memory was on the second day.

But there's more. Ebbinghaus and others found that retention is increased through *overlearning*—that is, continued rehearsal even after the material appears to have been mastered (Driskell et al., 1992). For example, tutoring—a form of overlearning—enhances the long-term retention of material learned in college courses (Semb et al., 1993). Researchers also discovered that long-term memory is better when the practice is spread over time than when it is crammed in all at once, a phenomenon known as the *spacing effect* (Dempster, 1988). Harry Bahrick and Lynda Hall (1991) found that adults retained more of their high school math skills when they later practiced the math in college—and when that practice was extended over semesters rather than condensed into a single year.

Although the transfer of information to LTM often requires a good deal of effort, certain types of information are encoded automatically and without conscious control. When I meet someone for the first time, for example, I have to work on recalling that person's name but I can easily and without rehearsal remember the face. It just happens. Similarly, we encode information about time, spatial locations, and the frequency of events. In a study that provides evidence of this *automatic processing*, Lynn Hasher and Rose Zacks (1984) showed subjects a long list of words. Some subjects were warned in advance that they would be asked to recall how many times a certain word was presented. Yet others who were not similarly prepared were just as accurate in their later estimates. Apparently, numerical frequencies are encoded without conscious effort.

Storage

Whether the encoding process is effortful or automatic, cognitive psychologists have long been interested in the *format,* the *content,* and the *physiological bases* of long-term memory as it is represented in the brain.

Formats of Long-Term Memory   In long-term memory, information is stored in two forms or "codes": one semantic, the other visual. *Semantic coding* is easy to demonstrate. When we process verbal information—such as a spoken phrase, a speech, a written sentence, or a story—what we store is the meaning of the information, not specific words. In a demonstration of this phenomenon, Jacqueline Sachs (1967) had subjects listen to a tape-recorded passage. She then presented a series of sentences (for example, "He sent a letter about it to Galileo, the great Italian scientist") and asked if they were the same as or different from those of the original passage. Subjects correctly rejected sentences that changed the meaning ("Galileo, the great Italian scientist, sent him a letter about it"), but they did not reject sentences with the same meaning that were worded differently ("A letter about it was sent by him to Galileo, the great Italian scientist"). They apparently had stored the semantic content of the passage—not an exact, word-for-word representation. In fact, we often "read between the lines" and recall hearing not just what was said but what was *implied.* For example, people who heard that a paratrooper "leaped out of the door" often recalled that he "jumped out of the plane." And mock jurors who heard a witness testify that "I ran up to the burglar alarm" later assumed the witness had said, "I rang the burglar alarm" (Harris & Monaco, 1978).

Although verbal information is stored in a semantic form, visual inputs and many long-term memories (including some of our most cherished childhood recollections) are stored as visual images. In *visual coding,* a mental picture is generated of an object or scene—a process that has implications for how people retrieve the information. To demonstrate, Stephen Kosslyn (1980) showed subjects some drawings like the boat in Figure 6.10. Later, he asked the subjects to visualize each drawing, to focus on the right or left side of it, and then, as quickly as possible, to indicate whether or not a specific object was present by pressing a YES or NO button that stopped a clock. If the drawing is stored in a visual manner, reasoned Kosslyn, then it should take longer for subjects to "scan" their image for an answer when the object is located away from the subject's focus of attention. That is exactly what happened. When subjects were mentally focused on

Figure 6.10

Visual Coding

When subjects visualized the left rather than right side of this drawing, it took them longer to recall that a flag was present. This result suggests that subjects had "scanned" a mental image for the answer (Kosslyn, 1980).

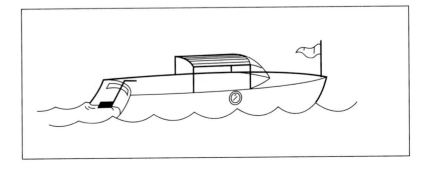

the left rather than the right side of the drawing, for example, it took them longer to determine that a flag was present on the boat.

Mental images play an important role in long-term memory. Popular books on how to improve your memory advise people to use imagery, and research shows that this advice is well founded. As an illustration, try to memorize the following list of word pairs so that the first word triggers your memory of the second: *lawyer-chair, snowflake-mountain, shoes-milk, dog-bicycle, chef-pickle, student-sandwich, boy-flag.* You might try to master the list by silently repeating the items over and over. But now take a different approach: for each item, form an image in your "mind's eye" that contains the two words of each pair interacting in some way. For example, imagine a brown *dog* chasing a *bicycle* or a *student* eating a foot-long *sandwich*. This method should improve performance (Bower & Winzenz, 1970; Paivio, 1969).

Consistent with the notion that imagery facilitates memory, concrete words that are easy to visualize (*fire, tent, statue, zebra*) are recalled better than abstract words that are difficult to represent in a picture (*infinite, freedom, process, future*). Also, certain types of mental images are better memory aids than others. For example, it is better to imagine the items-to-be-recalled as interactive, not as separate and static objects. And bizarre images are frequently more effective than common ones—perhaps because they are more carefully processed in the first place, or because they are distinctive and easy to retrieve from storage. Look again at the word pairs presented in the preceding paragraph and try to form images that are both interactive and bizarre. For example, you might imagine a scene in which a *dog* rides a *bicycle*, or in which a *student* stabs a *sandwich*. Using images like those in Table 6.1, researchers have found that the recall of word pairs improves more when subjects are provided with sentences that describe bizarre rather than common images (Einstein et al., 1989; Riefer & Rouder, 1992).

Table 6.1

Imagery and Recall

Consistent with the notion that imagery facilitates memory, recall of word pairs improves more when people are given sentences that describe bizarre rather than common images (Riefer & Rouder, 1992).

Common	Bizarre
1. The *chef* sliced the *pickle.*	1. The *chef* smoked the *pickle.*
2. The *lawyer* sat on the *chair.*	2. The *lawyer* argued with the *chair.*
3. The *snowflake* fell on the *mountain.*	3. The *snowflake* climbed the *mountain.*
4. The *shoes* were placed by the *milk.*	4. The *shoes* were filled with *milk.*
5. The *maid* spilled the *ammonia.*	5. The *maid* drank the *ammonia.*

Contents of Long-Term Memory Increasingly it appears that there is more than one type of long-term memory. Following Endel Tulving (1985), researchers now commonly distinguish two types. One is *procedural memory*, which consists of our stored knowledge of learned habits and skills—such as how to drive, swim, type, ride a bike, and tie shoelaces. The second type is *declarative memory*, which is memory for facts about ourselves and

There are two types of long-term memory. Procedural memory contains one's knowledge of various skills—such as how to swim. Declarative memory contains one's knowledge of facts—for example, what a pyramid is or where it can be found.

the world—such as where we went to school, who the U.S. president is, or what the word *gravity* means. This distinction is important, as we'll see later, because people with amnesia are often unable to recall facts and events (declarative memory), but they still retain many skills previously learned (procedural memory).

With all that's stored in long-term memory—learned skills, verbal information, and knowledge of words, names, dates, faces, pictures, personal experiences, and the like—it's amazing that anything can ever be retrieved from this vast warehouse. Surely our knowledge must be organized in memory, perhaps the way books are filed in a library. One popular view is that memories are stored in a complex web of associations, or **semantic networks.** According to proponents of this view, items in memory are linked together by a semantic relationship (see Figure 6.11). When an item is brought to mind, the pathways leading to meaningfully related items are *primed*—thus increasing the likelihood that they too will be retrieved (Collins & Loftus, 1975; Anderson, 1983).

A good deal of research supports the notion that memories are stored in semantic networks. When subjects are presented with a list of sixty words that fall into four categories (animals, professions, names, fruits)—even if the words are presented in a mixed order—the subjects later recall them in *clusters*. In other words, retrieving *tiger* is more likely to trigger one's memory for *baboon* than for *dentist, Jason,* or *banana* (Bousfield, 1953; Romney et al., 1993). Research on "lexical decision making" also illustrates the point. In these studies, people see a string of letters (*nart, wire, bent, tise*) and must decide as quickly as possible if they form a word. Consistently, people make these decisions more quickly when the letter string comes after a semantically related word than after an unrelated word. Thus, subjects are quicker to decide on *fire* when the preceding word was *red* than when it was *clouds.* By measuring response times in this way, researchers are able to map our underlying networks of associations (McNamara, 1992)—memory's filing system.

■ **semantic network** A complex web of semantic associations that link items in memory such that retrieving one item triggers the retrieval of others as well.

Physiological Bases of Long-Term Memory   Is it possible to pinpoint a site in the brain that houses these associations? Do memories leave a physi-

Figure 6.11

According to semantic network theories, memories are linked in a complex web of associations. The shorter the link between items, the more likely it is that the retrieval of one item will trigger that of the other (Collins & Loftus, 1975).

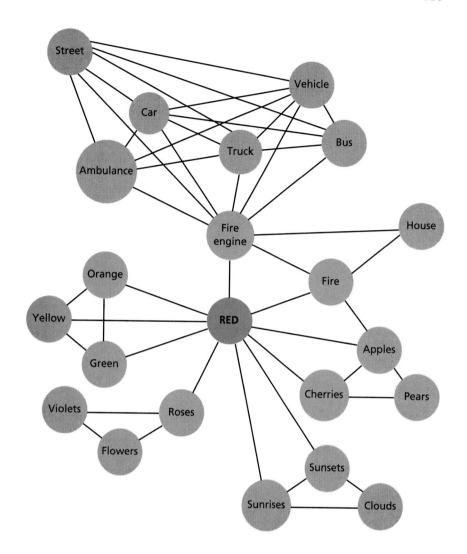

cal trace that can be "seen"? Are there drugs we can take to improve our memory? Neuroscientists have long been intrigued by such possibilities—but have also been led astray by various exciting developments.

In 1959, James McConnell and others reported that they had chemically transferred the memory of one flatworm to another. Specifically, they conditioned worms to contract to light, cut them in half, and found that the worms that regenerated from both the head and tail ends were quicker to condition than new worms—suggesting that they had inherited a "memory." This result captured the imagination (can you picture taking a pill that contains the information from this textbook?). But many researchers could not replicate the finding, and interest in memory transfer faded.

In another astonishing development, neurosurgeon Wilder Penfield reported that he had triggered long-forgotten memories through brain stimulation. In the 1940s, Penfield was treating epileptics by removing portions of their brains. To locate the damage, he stimulated different cortical areas with a painless electrical current. Sometimes, his patients—who were awake during the procedure—would "relive" long-lost events from the past. For example, one woman said she heard a mother calling her child when a certain spot was stimulated. From reports like this, Penfield concluded that experience leaves a permanent "imprint" that can be played

■ **anterograde amnesia** A memory disorder characterized by an inability to store new information in long-term memory.

■ **retrograde amnesia** A memory disorder characterized by an inability to retrieve long-term memories from the past.

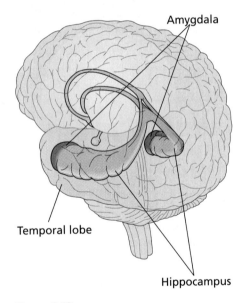

Amygdala

Temporal lobe

Hippocampus

Figure 6.12

The Hippocampal Region

As shown here, the hippocampus is located under the temporal lobe of the cerebral cortex. This structure is necessary for the encoding of new information into long-term memory.

back years later as though there was a tape recorder in the brain (Penfield & Perot, 1963). This observation sparked a good deal of excitement until cognitive psychologists scrutinized the data and made two sobering discoveries. First, the phenomenon itself was very rare, reported by only a handful of Penfield's 1,100 patients. Second, the "flashbacks" were more likely dream-like illusions, not real memories (Loftus & Loftus, 1980; Neisser, 1967).

Despite such "dead ends," today's researchers continue in hot pursuit of the *engram*—a term used to describe the physical trace of memory. There are two objectives in this endeavor: (1) to locate the anatomical structures in the brain where memories are stored, and (2) to understand the neural and biochemical changes that accompany these memories. Along these lines, let us examine some recent developments.

Anatomy: Where Is the Engram?   The search for memory traces in the brain was pioneered by Karl Lashley (1950). For thirty years, Lashley trained rats to run a maze, removed various structures from their brains, and then returned the rats to the maze to test their memory. No matter what structures he removed, however, the rats recalled at least some of what they had learned. Eventually, Lashley was forced to conclude that memories do not reside in any specific location.

Then along came H.M., a 27-year-old man who underwent brain surgery for severe epileptic seizures. The surgeon removed parts of both temporal lobes and the *hippocampus,* a curved structure in the limbic system (see Figure 6.12). The operation proceeded uneventfully and succeeded in controlling the patient's seizures. What made H.M. one of the most famous neurology cases of all time is that the surgery had an unexpected side effect: it produced **anterograde amnesia**, an inability to form new long-term memories. (This should not be confused with **retrograde amnesia**, which is an inability to retrieve long-term memories from the past.) H.M. still recalled the people, places, and events from before the surgery. He also performed as well as before on IQ tests and could still read, write, and solve problems so long as he stayed focused on the task. But he could not retain new information. He would meet someone new but then forget the person; or he would read an article without realizing that he had read it before; or he would not know what he ate during his last meal. At one point, H.M.'s family moved. Yet a year later, he still did not know the new address. It was as if new information "went in one ear, out the next" (Scoville & Milner, 1957; Milner et al., 1968).

H.M.'s case is important for two reasons. First, he exhibited a very specific information-processing deficit. H.M. could bring new information into short-term memory and he could retrieve long-term memories previously stored. But he could not form new long-term memories. Second, H.M.'s case was the first to prove what Lashley could not—that localized lesions in the brain can have disruptive effects on memory. In fact, it revealed that the hippocampus and perhaps other areas of the limbic system as well (notably, the amygdala and thalamus) play a key role.

Recent research involving animals and humans confirms this point: the hippocampus is essential for the explicit recollection of newly acquired information (Cohen & Eichenbaum, 1993; Squire, 1992). Hippocampal lesions that mimic H.M.'s surgery produce a similar impairment in rats, monkeys, and other animals. Thus, when the hippocampus is removed from black-capped chickadees—food-storing birds that are endowed with a larger hippocampus than that in nonstoring birds—they lose their natural ability to recover food they had stored in various scattered locations (Sherry, 1992). With respect to humans, brain scans reveal that the hippocampal region in amnesics is shrunken to 57 percent of the normal size, even though the surrounding areas of the temporal lobe are intact (Squire, 1992; see Figure 6.13).

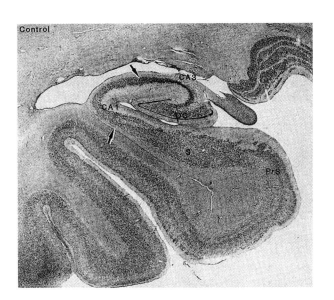 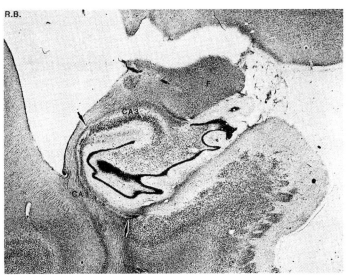

Figure 6.13

The Hippocampus and Memory

Brain scans often reveal damage to the hippocampus in amnesic patients (right), even though surrounding areas are intact. For comparison, the hippocampus of a normal control is also shown (left).

Is all of memory stored in the hippocampus? Probably not (Squire, 1992). This subcortical region of the brain seems to be necessary for the encoding of information into long-term memory, but it is not the storage facility. Also, not all aspects of memory require the hippocampus. As we'll see later, amnesics like H.M. often exhibit memory in indirect ways. They can be conditioned to blink to a tone previously paired with a puff of air to the eye, and they can remember how to work a maze they had practiced—but they cannot recall the training sessions. Similarly, they form preferences for new music they hear, yet do not recognize the melodies in a testing situation. For these types of memory tasks, different cortical structures may be involved. For example, David McCormick and Richard Thompson (1984) located a microscopic spot in the *cerebellum* that controls the classical conditioning of the eyeblink reflex. For something as complex as memory, many areas of the brain are needed (Desimone, 1992).

Biochemistry: What Is the Engram?   As some researchers try to locate where memories are stored, others seek to identify the accompanying biochemical changes that take place in the neural circuits. Most of these changes are likely to be found at the *synapses*—the tiny gaps between neurons that are linked by the release of *neurotransmitters* (Lynch & Baudry, 1984), as discussed in Chapter 2.

One neurotransmitter that seems to play an important role in memory is *acetylcholine*. Research shows that people who suffer from Alzheimer's disease—a degenerative brain disorder that is characterized by a striking loss of memory for new information (see Chapter 10)—have lowered levels of acetylcholine in the brain, a link supported by animal studies as well. In light of this finding, many are hopeful that Alzheimer's patients can be treated by boosting their levels of acetylcholine. Unfortunately, positive results have not been obtained yet—in part because Alzheimer's disease, and human memory in general, involves more than a single neurotransmitter (Thal, 1992).

Certain hormones are also involved in memory. For example, James McGaugh (1990) finds, in studies of rats, that increases in *epinephrine*—a hormone that is released in states of arousal—improves the retention of new information. Hormones do not enter the brain directly, but they appear to energize memory by causing the release of the sugar glucose (Gold, 1992). This discovery has exciting implications. One is that certain drugs may impair memory by blocking the activity of certain neurotransmitters. For example, alcohol disrupts the activity of serotonin, which could explain why eyewitnesses are less accurate in their reports of crime when slightly drunk than when sober (Yuille & Tollestrup, 1990). Another implication is that glucose treatments can be used to facilitate the formation of long-term memories, especially for people with memory disorders. Paul Gold (1993) had twenty-two healthy senior citizens listen to a taped passage and then drink lemonade sweetened with either glucose or saccharine, the sugar substitute. When tested the next day, those who had taken the glucose recalled 53 percent more information from the passage. The image of taking memory pills may seem like science fiction, but it has already been suggested that a glucose-based "cognitive enhancer" may not be far behind (Wenk, 1989).

Retrieval

Once information is stored, how do you know it exists? Since people can openly report on their recollections, this seems like a silly question. In fact, however, it is one of the thorniest questions confronting researchers. Hermann Ebbinghaus (1885) was not only the first person to study memory systematically but also the first to realize that memory may exist without awareness. In his words, "These experiences remain concealed from consciousness and yet produce an effect which is significant and which authenticates their previous experience" (p. 2).

Memory without awareness illustrates how human beings can be both competent and incompetent at the same time, and poses a profound challenge to the researcher: If people have memories they cannot report, how can we ever know if these memories exist? To his credit, Ebbinghaus devised a simple but clever technique. He tested memory by its effect on performance. Acting as his own subject, he would learn a set of nonsense syllables and then count the number of trials it later took him to relearn the same list. If it took fewer trials the second time around than the first, then he must have retained some of the material—even if he could not consciously recite it.

■ explicit memory The deliberate and conscious retrieval of recollections in response to direct questions.

■ implicit memory Nonconscious recollection of a prior experience that is measured indirectly, by its effects on performance.

In recent years, other techniques have also been devised. Basically, there are two types of tests, each of which assesses a different aspect of memory: one explicit, the other implicit. **Explicit memory** is a term used to describe the recollections of facts and events that people *consciously* retrieve in response to *direct* questions. **Implicit memory** is a term used to describe the *nonconscious* retention of information, as measured *indirectly* by its effects on performance (Jacoby et al., 1993; Rajaram & Roediger, 1993).

Why is this distinction made? The reason, as we'll see, is that people often exhibit *dissociations* between the two types of tasks. That is, people will consciously forget (have no explicit memory of) an experience but at the same time show the effects (have an implicit memory) of that experience. There are two ways to look at this pattern. Some theorists believe that explicit and implicit memory are two separate systems controlled by different parts of the brain (Squire, 1992; Schacter, 1992; Tulving & Schacter, 1990). In contrast, others believe that they signal differences in the encoding and retrieval of information (Jacoby et al., 1992; Roediger, 1990). Either way, it's important to consider these two aspects of memory separately (see Table 6.2).

Table 6.2

Differences Between Explicit and Implicit Memory

Explicit memory	Implicit memory
conscious retention	nonconscious retention
direct tests	indirect tests
disrupted by amnesia	intact with amnesia
encoded in the hippocampus	encoded elsewhere

Can you name the Seven Dwarfs? The answer appears at the bottom of p. 231.
[© The Walt Disney Company.]

Explicit Memory   Can you name all of Walt Disney's Seven Dwarfs? Try it. When I was put to the test, I could list only six. As hard as I tried, I could not come up with the seventh. This type of task, in which a person is asked to reproduce information without the benefit of external cues, is an example of a *recall* test of explicit memory. Other examples include taking an essay exam, describing a criminal's face to the police, and struggling to recall a childhood trauma.

Now try a different task. Consider the following names, and circle only those of the Seven Dwarfs: Grouchy, Gabby, Sleepy, Smiley, Happy, Jumpy, Droopy, Dopey, Sneezy, Goofy, Grumpy, Bashful, Cheerful, Wishful, Doc, and Pop. This task, in which a person must select a remembered item from a list of alternatives, is a form of *recognition* test. So are taking a multiple-choice exam and picking a criminal from a lineup or photograph.

Research shows that recall and recognition are both forms of explicit memory (Haist et al., 1992). There is, however, a key difference: people are usually better at recognition. The Seven Dwarfs task illustrates the point. When college students were asked to recall the characters on their own, they correctly produced an average of 69 percent of the names. When they made selections from a list, however, the accuracy rate was 86 percent (Meyer & Hilterbrand, 1984). Even I was able to recognize the name that I could not recall (it was Bashful). Harry Bahrick and his colleagues (1975)

ROW 1: John Milinovich, Mike Minelli, Bob Zimmerman, Frank Sherman. ROW 2: Pat Lamprecht, Carole Del Grande, Marsha Banen, Verlene Carpenter, Bonnie Schoenig, Sally Jolowsky, Carol Tappero, Mary Jane Svigel. ROW 3: Pierina Maracchini, Helen Taylor, Colleen Schulz, Barbara Rostvold, Barbara Satovich, Darlene Solinger, Jean Wright, Donna Urbia, Pat Baumgardner.

ROW 1: Stanley Nylund, Mike Jarmer, Dennis Hickman, Terry Mattson, Tom Pearson. ROW 2: Sharon Connors, Doreen Dom-

When shown old high school yearbook photos, people find it easier to *recognize* the names of their classmates from a list than to *recall* the names on their own. In this set of pictures was a student named Robert Zimmerman—better known as Bob Dylan.

reported the same difference in a study of long-term memory. They showed people pictures of classmates taken from their high school yearbooks. Seven years after they graduated, subjects could correctly *recall* only 60 percent of the names belonging to each face. But those who only had to *recognize* the right names from a list of possible alternatives were 90 percent accurate—even when tested fourteen years after graduation.

The fact that recognition is easier than recall suggests that forgetting sometimes occurs not because memory has faded but because the information is difficult to reclaim from storage. Retrieval failure is a common experience. Did you ever feel as though a word or a name was just out of reach—on the tip of your tongue? In a classic study of the *"tip of the tongue" phenomenon,* Roger Brown and David McNeill (1966) prompted this experience by giving students definitions of uncommon words and asking them to produce the words themselves. For example, what is "the green-colored matter found in plants" or "the art of speaking in such a way that the voice seems to come from another place"? Most often, subjects either knew the word immediately or were certain that they did not know it. But sometimes subjects were sure that they knew the word but could not recall it—a frustrating state that Brown and McNeill likened to being on the brink of a sneeze.

The experience is an interesting one. When something is on the tip of the tongue, subjects often come up with words that are similar in sound or meaning. Groping for "chlorophyll" subjects might say "chlorine" or "cholesterol." For "ventriloquism" they produce words such as "ventilate" and "vernacular." In fact, a surprising number of people will guess the correct first letter, last letter, and number of syllables contained in the missing word. These cases indicate that the information is in memory, but that subjects need additional retrieval cues to dislodge it (A. Brown, 1991).

Recognition is often easier than recall because recognition tasks contain retrieval cues, or reminders. A *retrieval cue* is a stimulus that helps us to ac-

With the names of American soldiers killed in action etched in black marble, the Vietnam Veterans Memorial in Washington, D.C., serves as a powerful retrieval cue for the veterans who survived and the loved ones of those who did not.

■ **encoding specificity** The principle that any stimulus encoded along with an experience can later jog one's memory of that experience.

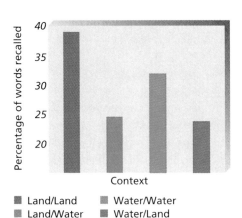

Figure 6.14

Context-Dependent Memory

Whether on land or at sea, deep-sea divers recalled more words when learning and retrieval took place in the same setting. This result illustrates the context dependence of memory (Godden & Baddeley, 1975).

From left to right, Snow White's Seven Dwarfs are Happy, Bashful, Grumpy, Doc, Sneezy (front row), and Dopey and Sleepy (back row).

cess information in long-term memory. According to Tulving's (1983) principle of **encoding specificity**, any stimulus that is encoded along with an experience can later trigger one's memory of that experience. The retrieval cue may be a picture, a location, a word, a song, another person, or even a fragrance.

When you stop to think about it, *smells* can be remarkably potent and nostalgic reminders of the past. A whiff of perfume, the top of a baby's head, freshly cut grass, a locker room, the musty odor of a basement, the floury aroma of a bakery, the smell of mothballs in the attic, and the leathery scent of a new car—each may trigger what Diane Ackerman (1990) has called "aromatic memories." Frank Schab (1990) tested this hypothesis in a series of experiments. In one, subjects were given a list of adjectives and instructed to write an antonym for each one. In half of the sessions, the sweet smell of chocolate was blown into the room. The next day, subjects were asked to list as many of the antonyms as they could—again, in the presence or absence of the chocolate aroma. As it turned out, the most words were recalled when the smell of chocolate was present at both the learning and recall sessions. The reason? The aroma was encoded along with the words, so it later served as a retrieval cue.

The retrieval of explicit memories is influenced by other *external* factors as well. In an unusual study, Duncan Godden and Alan Baddeley (1975) presented deep-sea divers with a list of words in one of two settings: fifteen feet underwater, or on the beach. Then they tested the divers in the same or another setting. Illustrating what is called *context-dependent memory*, the divers recalled 40 percent more words when the material was learned and retrieved in the same context (see Figure 6.14). The practical implications are intriguing. For example, recall may be improved if material is retrieved in the same room in which it was initially learned (Smith, 1979). Indeed, context seems to activate memory even in 3-month-old infants. In a series of studies, Carolyn Rovee-Collier and her colleagues (1992) trained infants to shake an overhead mobile equipped with colorful blocks and bells by kicking a leg that was attached to the mobile by a ribbon. The infants were later more likely to recall what they learned (in other words, to kick) when tested in the same crib and looking at the same visual cues than when there were differences. Apparently, it is possible to jog one's memory by reinstating the initial context of an experience. This explains why I will often march into my secretary's office for something, go blank, forget why I was there, return in defeat to my office, look around, and ZAP! suddenly recall what it was I needed.

Internal cues that become associated with an experience may also spark the retrieval of explicit memories. Illustrating the phenomenon of *state-dependent memory*, studies reveal that it is often easier to recall something when our state of mind is the same at testing as it was during encoding. If information is acquired when you are happy, sad, drunk, sober, calm, or aroused, that information is more likely to be retrieved under the same conditions (Bower, 1981; Eich, 1980; Eich et al., 1994). The one key complicating factor is that the mood we're in leads us to evoke memories that are congruent with that mood. When we are happy, the good times are most easy to recall; but when we feel depressed or anxious, our minds become flooded with negative events of the past (Blaney, 1986; Ucros, 1989).

Implicit Memory   In 1911, physician Edouard Claparede described an encounter he had with a young woman who suffered from *Korsakoff's syndrome*—a brain disorder, common among chronic alcoholics, that impairs the transfer of information into long-term memory. When Claparede was introduced to the woman, he hid in his right palm a pin that pricked her painfully as the two shook hands. The next day, he returned to the hospital. Due to her memory disorder, the patient did not recognize the doctor and could not answer questions about their prior interaction. Yet when he reached out to shake her hand, she pulled back abruptly at the last moment. Why did she refuse? After some confusion, all she could say was "Sometimes pins are hidden in people's hands" (Schwartz & Reisberg, 1991).

Implicit Memory in Amnesia Patients   Did Claparede's patient remember him or not? On the one hand, she knew enough to be afraid. On the other hand, she did not know why. It was as if she had a memory but didn't know it! As unusual as this story may seem, we now know that there are many others like it. As in the case of H.M., cognitive psychologists are keenly interested in people with amnesia. It used to be believed that amnesics lack the ability to encode or store information in long-term memory. They could still perform "skills"—but could not keep new "information" in memory.

Or could they? In 1970, Elizabeth Warrington and Lawrence Weiskrantz published an article in *Nature* that challenged the prevailing view. These researchers gave a list of words to four amnesics and sixteen normal control subjects. Four memory tests were then administered. Two were standard measures of explicit memory—one a recall task, the second involving recognition. The other tests were indirect measures of implicit memory in which the subjects were asked to complete word "fragments" (such as *k___ht, c_l__ge,* and *t___v_s_on*) and "stems" (for example, *kni___, col____,* and *tele_____*) with the first guess that came to mind. The results are shown in Figure 6.15. As was expected, the control subjects scored higher than the amnesics on the explicit-memory tests. But on the incomplete-word tasks, the amnesics were just as likely to form words that appeared on the original list. Like Claparede's Korsakoff's patient, they retained the information enough to use it. They just didn't realize it.

This dissociation—the tendency for amnesics to exhibit long-term retention of information without awareness—has since been replicated in studies involving different types of amnesia and different implicit-memory tests (Schacter, 1987; Shimamura, 1986; Squire & Butters, 1992). For example, a patient would not remember a story that was read, yet be able to read it faster a second time around. In one study, twenty-five *surgery patients* were read a list of word-pairs during their operations—after they were rendered "unconscious" by general anesthesia. Later on in the recovery room, and again two weeks after that, they could not recall or recognize the items. Yet these same patients often came up with the correct "guess" in response to the first word of each pair (Kihlstrom et al., 1990). In other studies, patients with *prosopagnosia* (a disorder that impairs one's ability to recognize faces) could not match names to famous faces in a multiple-choice test, but they reacted with greater increases in physiological arousal when the faces were named correctly than incorrectly (Bauer & Verfaellie, 1992; Bruyer,

Figure 6.15

Amnesic patients and normal controls were tested for their memory of words previously learned. As you can see, the amnesics performed more poorly on the measures of explicit memory (recall and recognition) but not on indirect measures of implicit memory (word-fragment and word-stem completion tasks). The amnesics had retained the information but didn't know it (Warrington & Weiskrantz, 1970).

EXPLICIT TESTS

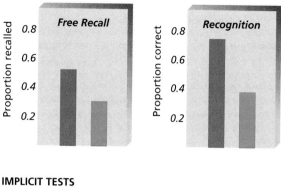

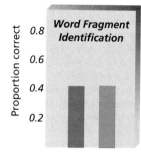

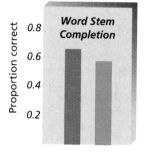

■ Control group
■ Amnesic patients

1991). Once again, there was an implicit memory—or, as Henry Roediger (1990) puts it, "retention without awareness."

Implicit Memory in Everyday Life You don't have to suffer from brain damage to exhibit a dissociation between memory and awareness. Have you ever had the eerie feeling that you've been in a situation before, even though you had not? This is called *déjà vu*, defined as the illusion that a new situation is familiar (the term is French for "already seen"). In a way, déjà vu is the opposite of amnesia. Whereas amnesics have memory without awareness or familiarity, the person with déjà vu has a sense of familiarity but no real memory. This experience is quite common. Charles Dickens (1849) described it in *David Copperfield;* so did Leo Tolstoy (1859) in *War and Peace* and Marcel Proust (1919) in *Remembrance of Things Past.* Estimates vary, but between 30 and 96 percent of people report having had such an episode (Sno & Linszen, 1990).

Déjà vu is not the only type of dissociation commonly experienced. It is now clear that retention without awareness occurs in us all—sometimes with interesting consequences. We now consider three of these consequences: false fame, eyewitness transference, and cryptomnesia.

1. *The false fame effect:* Is Sebastian Weisdorf famous? He is not. But Larry Jacoby and his colleagues (1989) found a way to make him and other no-names famous overnight. They had subjects read aloud a long list of made-up names, supposedly to test the speed and accuracy of their pronunciation. Some of the names appeared repeatedly, but others were read only once. The next day, subjects received a new list of

names—some famous, some nonfamous, and some from the first list that were nonfamous. Their task was to decide for each one whether it was the name of a famous person. This seems easy enough and, for the most part, it was. Subjects easily distinguished between names that were truly famous and those that were not, and they knew that the names repeatedly presented the day before were not famous. But they misjudged as famous many of the names previously presented only once. The reason? These names were familiar, but subjects did not know why. Not realizing that these names were from the first list, they made an assumption: if a name rings a bell, the person must be famous.

2. *Eyewitness transference:* False fame is amusing, but it can also have tragic consequences. Several years ago, I received a call from a San Francisco lawyer whose client was being tried for murder based on an eyewitness identification. In this case, a witness saw someone, late at night and from a distance, throw a road flare into a window of an apartment building. The building caught fire and a resident was killed. Due to the circumstances, the witness could give the police only a general description of the man (which did not match the defendant's appearance). One week later, the witness looked through a book of mugshots that included a picture of the defendant, but he could not make a selection. Weeks later, that same witness viewed a six-person lineup, recognized the defendant, and made an identification. Was the defendant familiar to the witness? Probably he was. But from the crime or the mugshots?

The problem illustrated by this case is that people often remember a face but forget the circumstances in which they saw it. In one study, for example, subjects witnessed a staged crime and looked through mugshots (Brown et al., 1977). A few days later, they were called in to view a lineup. The result was startling: subjects were just as likely to identify an innocent person whose photograph was in the mugshots as they were to pick the real criminal! This familiarity effect gives rise to the phenomenon of *eyewitness transference,* whereby a person seen in one situation is confused in memory with a person seen in a second situation (Loftus, 1979). Incidentally, the defendant I described was found guilty and sentenced to prison—based primarily on the eyewitness's identification.

3. *Cryptomnesia:* False fame and unconscious transference occur when one is aware that something is familiar but cannot pinpoint the correct source of that familiarity (Johnson et al., 1993; Mandler, 1980). In other words, the experience has an impact on behavior, but without one's conscious awareness. There is another possible consequence of implicit memory: *cryptomnesia,* or unintentional plagiarism. Several years ago, former Beatle George Harrison was sued for recording "My Sweet Lord"—a song that bore a striking resemblance to "He's So Fine," recorded in 1962 by the Chiffons. At trial, Harrison admitted that he'd heard the earlier song but denied that he copied it. The judge ruled against him, however, and concluded that he was unintentionally influenced by what was in his unconscious memory.

Have you ever had an insight you thought was original, only later to realize or be told that it was "borrowed" from another source? Are people who write, compose music, solve problems, or come up with creative ideas generally vulnerable to cryptomnesia? Alan Brown and Dana

Murphy (1989) had subjects in groups take turns generating items that fit a particular category (sports, four-legged animals, musical instruments, and clothing). After four rounds, they asked subjects individually to recall the items they personally had generated and to come up with new ones from the same categories. As it turned out, 75 percent of the subjects took credit for at least one item of someone else's, and 71 percent came up with a "new" item that was given earlier. Sometimes, subjects inadvertently plagiarized their own ideas, but most often they "stole" from others in the group. Additional research shows that the incidence of cryptomnesia increases with time and the difficulty of the task (Marsh & Bower, 1993). As in other research on implicit memory, these studies show that there is a bit of amnesia in us all.

Forgetting

Before we celebrate the virtues of memory and outline the techniques that we can use to improve it, let's stop for a moment and ponder the wisdom of William James (1890), who said, "If we remembered everything, we should on most occasions be as ill off as if we remembered nothing" (p. 680). James was right. Many years ago, Russian psychologist Alexander Luria (1968) described his studies of Solomon Shereshevskii, a man he called S., who had a truly exceptional memory. After one brief presentation, S. would remember lists containing dozens of items, recite them forward or backward, and still retain the information fifteen years later. But there was a drawback: no matter how hard S. tried, he could not forget. Images of letters, numbers, and other trivia were so distracting that he had to quit his job and support himself by entertaining audiences with his feats of memory. Sometimes it is better to forget.

"Memory is the thing you forget with."

ALEXANDER CHASE

The Forgetting Curve   Memory failure is a common experience in everyday life (see Table 6.3 on the next page). I wish I had a dollar for every time I left something I needed at home, neglected to bring up a point in conversation, or forgot the name of someone I met. To measure the rate at which information is forgotten, Ebbinghaus (1885) tested his own memory for nonsense syllables after intervals ranging from twenty minutes to thirty-one days. As shown in the *forgetting curve* plotted in Figure 6.16, Ebbinghaus

Figure 6.16

The Ebbinghaus Forgetting Curve

Ebbinghaus's forgetting curve indicates the rate at which nonsense syllables were forgotten. You can see that there was a quick decline in performance within the first hour, but also that the rate of forgetting leveled off over time.

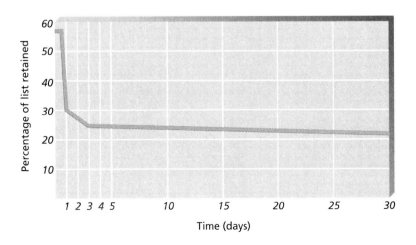

Table 6.3

Forgetting in Everyday Life

How's your memory? Read the statements and think about how often you've had the experiences described. The numbers in parentheses are the ratings given by the average person (Baddeley, 1990).

____ 1. Forgetting where you have put something; losing things around the house (5)

____ 2. Having to go back to check whether you have done something that you meant to do (4)

____ 3. Failing to recognize, by sight, close relatives or friends that you meet frequently (1)

____ 4. Telling friends a story or joke that you have told them once already (2)

____ 5. Forgetting where things are normally kept, or looking for them in the wrong place (2)

____ 6. Finding that a word is on the "tip of your tongue"; you know what it is but cannot quite find it (4)

____ 7. Forgetting important details of what you did or what happened to you the day before (1)

____ 8. Forgetting important details about yourself, such as your birthday or where you live (1)

____ 9. Completely forgetting to take things with you, or leaving things behind and having to go back and fetch them (3)

____ 10. Finding that the faces of famous people, seen on TV or in photographs, look unfamiliar (2)

Note: Subjects responded on the following scale: 1 = not at all in the last six months, 2 = about once in six months, 3 = more than once in the last six months, 4 = about once a month, 5 = more than once a month, . . . 9 = more than once a day.

found that there was a steep loss of retention within the first hour, that he forgot more than 60 percent of the items within nine hours, and that the rate of forgetting leveled off after that. How quickly we forget.

The Ebbinghaus forgetting curve shows a rapid loss of memory for meaningless nonsense syllables. Does it apply to real-life memories as well? Harry Bahrick (1984) tested nearly eight hundred English-speaking adults who took Spanish in high school. Depending on the subject, the interval between learning and being tested ranged from zero to fifty years. Compared to students who had just taken the course, those who were tested two to three years later had forgotten much of what they learned. After that, however, scores on vocabulary, grammar, and reading comprehension tests stabilized—even among people who had not used Spanish for forty or fifty years (see Figure 6.17). This impressive last result led Bahrick to argue that the knowledge had entered a *permastore*—a term he coined to describe permanent, very-long-term memory.

Why Do People Forget?   Knowing the rate at which information is lost is just the first step. The next important question is, Why? Do memory traces simply fade with time? Are they displaced by new memories? Or do memories get buried, perhaps blocked by unconscious forces? As we'll see, "forgetting" can result from one of four processes: a lack of encoding, decay, interference, or repression. In the first two, the information to be recalled is simply not in long-term memory storage. In the second two, the memory may exist but is difficult, if not impossible, to retrieve.

Encoding   Do you know what a penny looks like? Would you recognize one if you saw it? If you live in the United States, you have undoubtedly

Figure 6.17

A Longer-Term Forgetting Curve

This forgetting curve indicates the rate at which adults forgot the Spanish they took in high school. Compared to new graduates, those tested two to three years later had forgotten much of what they learned. After that, however, test scores stabilized (Bahrick, 1984).

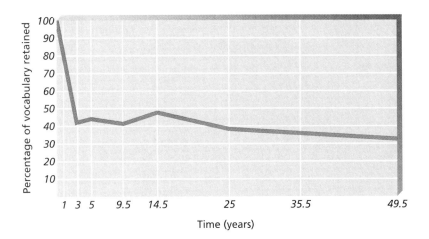

looked at, held, and counted thousands of copper pennies in your life. Yet many people cannot accurately draw one from memory, name its features, or distinguish between a real penny and a fake. Look at the coins in Figure 6.18. Do you know which is the real one? Raymond Nickerson and Marilyn Adams (1979) presented this task to college students and found that 58 percent did *not* identify the right coin. The reason for this result is not that the subjects forgot what a penny looks like—it's that the features were never encoded into long-term memory in the first place. And why should they be? So long as you can tell the difference between pennies and other objects, there is no need to focus on the fine details. Indeed, you may also have difficulty recalling the features of a dollar bill, a telephone dial, the front-page layout of your favorite newspaper, and other common objects.

Decay The oldest theory of forgetting is that memory traces erode with the passage of time. But there are two problems with this simple explana-

Figure 6.18

Can You Recognize a Penny?

Which of these pennies is the real thing? The answer appears on p. 238 (Nickerson & Adams, 1979).

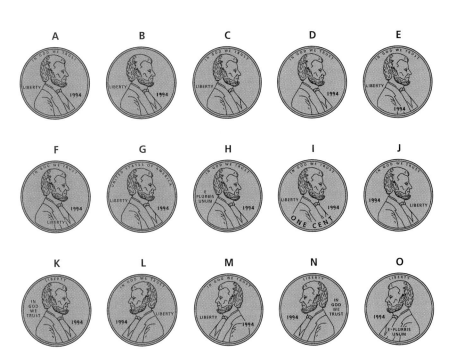

The correctly drawn penny is shown in (A).

tion. One is that there is no evidence of physiological decay that corresponds to the fading of memory. The second is that time alone is not the critical factor. As we saw earlier, memory for newly learned nonsense syllables fades in a matter of hours, but the foreign language learned in high school is retained for many years.

The key blow to the decay theory of forgetting was landed in 1924 by John Jenkins and Karl Dallenbach. Day after day, these researchers presented nonsense syllables to two subjects and then tested their memory after 1, 2, 4, or 8 hours. On some days, the subjects went to sleep between learning and testing; on other days, they stayed awake and kept busy. As shown in Figure 6.19, the subjects recalled more items after they had slept than when they were awake and involved in other activities. Jenkins and Dallenbach concluded that "forgetting is not so much a matter of the decay of old impressions and associations as it is a matter of interference, inhibition, or obliteration of the old by the new" (p. 612). To minimize forgetting, students may find it helpful to go to sleep shortly after studying, thus avoiding "new information" (Fowler et al., 1973).

Figure 6.19

Minimizing Forgetting

Subjects who studied nonsense syllables recalled more items after 1, 2, 4, or 8 hours when they slept than when they stayed awake between the learning and test sessions. This result suggests that forgetting may be caused by retroactive interference (Jenkins & Dallenbach, 1924).

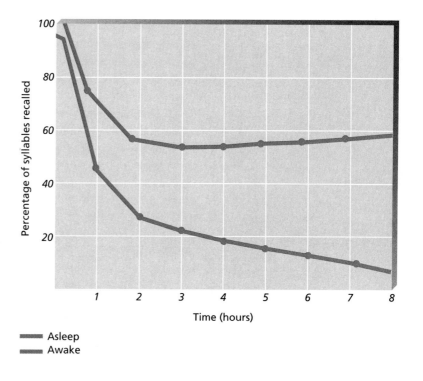

Asleep
Awake

Interference   By showing that memory loss may be caused by mental activity that takes place when we are awake, Jenkins and Dallenbach's study suggested a third explanation of forgetting—that something learned may be forgotten due to interference from other information. As summarized in Table 6.4, there are two kinds of interference.

In **proactive interference**, prior information inhibits one's ability to recall something new. If you try to learn a set of names, formulas, phone numbers, or vocabulary words, you will find it more difficult if you had earlier studied a similar set of items. Indeed, Benton Underwood (1957) found that the more nonsense-syllable experiments subjects had taken part in, the

■ **proactive interference** The tendency for previously learned material to disrupt the recall of new information.

Table 6.4

Interference and Forgetting

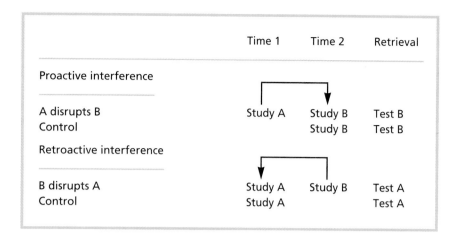

	Time 1	Time 2	Retrieval
Proactive interference			
A disrupts B	Study A	Study B	Test B
Control		Study B	Test B
Retroactive interference			
B disrupts A	Study A	Study B	Test A
Control	Study A		Test A

more forgetting they exhibited in a brand-new study. A related problem is **retroactive interference**, whereby new material disrupts memory for previously learned information. For example, Carla Chandler (1991) found that people were less likely to recognize pictures of nature scenes if they saw similar photographs before being tested. Clearly, one learning experience can displace or at least inhibit the retrieval of another.

Repression   In 1990, a young woman jogging in New York City's Central Park was raped, beaten unconscious, and left for dead by a gang of teenagers. After many months of recovery, the victim said she remembered running that day but could not recall anything about the attack itself. Her amnesia for the event may well have been caused by head injuries she had sustained—or it may have been due to motivated forgetting, or *repression*.

Many years ago, Sigmund Freud—the founder of psychoanalysis whom we will meet in Chapter 15—noted that his patients often could not recall unpleasant past events in their own lives. In fact, they would sometimes stop, pull back, and lose their train of thought just as they seemed on the brink of an insight. Freud called this repression, and said it was an unconscious defense mechanism that keeps painful personal memories under lock and key—and out of awareness. We'll see in Chapter 16 that people who suffer through childhood traumas such as war, abuse, and rape sometimes develop "dissociative disorders" characterized by huge gaps in their explicit memory. Although repression is not easily demonstrated in the laboratory, clinical case studies reveal that repressed memories are often recovered in psychotherapy (Erdelyi, 1985). In cases such as these, unfortunately, it's difficult to tell the difference between dormant memories of actual events and false memories, constructions of experiences that never occurred (Loftus, 1993a).

Reconstruction

■ **retroactive interference** The tendency for new information to disrupt the memory of previously learned material.

Up to now, we have likened human memory to a computer that faithfully encodes, stores, and retrieves information from the recent and distant past. Clearly, however, there is more to the story. As we'll see, remembering is an active process in which we *reconstruct* memories according to our beliefs, wishes, needs, and information received from outside sources.

■ **schemas** Preconceptions about persons, objects, or events that bias the way that new information is interpreted and recalled.

In 1932, Frederick Bartlett asked subjects to recall stories taken from the folklore of other cultures and found that although they correctly recalled the gist of these stories, they changed, exaggerated, added, and omitted certain details—resulting in passages that were more coherent to them. Without realizing it, subjects had reconstructed the material to fit their own **schemas**, a term that Bartlett used to describe the preconceptions that people have about persons and situations. Schemas distort memory, often by leading us to fill in missing pieces. After people look at close-ups of various scenes, for example, they mentally extend the borders by reporting details that are not in the picture but might plausibly exist outside the camera's field of view (Intraub et al., 1992).

There are numerous other examples as well. In one study, subjects were left waiting alone in a small cluttered room that the experimenter called an "office." (Before you read the next sentence, try the demonstration in Figure 6.20.) After thirty-five seconds, subjects were taken out and asked to

Figure 6.20

"Office" Schema

Look at this picture of an office for thirty seconds or so. Then list the objects you recall being in the room.

recall what was in the room. What happened? Nearly everyone remembered the desk, chair, and shelves—objects typically found in an office. But many of the subjects also mistakenly recalled seeing books—an item that fit the setting but was not actually present (Brewer & Treyens, 1981). Our schemas are sometimes so strong that an object that does not belong becomes particularly memorable. After spending time in an office, subjects were quick to remember the presence of a toy truck, blocks, and fingerpaints. But if that time was spent in a preschool classroom, they were more likely to recall the presence of textbooks, a typewriter, and an ashtray (Pezdek et al., 1989).

■ **misinformation effect** The tendency to incorporate post-event information into one's memory of the event itself.

"Do you swear to tell your version of the truth as you perceive it, clouded perhaps by the passage of time and preconceived notions?"

[Harris/Cartoonists & Writers Syndicate]

Clearly, memory is an active construction of the past—a construction that alters reality in ways that are consistent not only with prior expectations but also with *postevent information.* Consider the plight of those in Dallas who witnessed firsthand the assassination of President Kennedy. When it was over, they talked about the tragedy, read about it, heard other witnesses on TV, and knew what government officials were saying. By the time these witnesses were questioned, one wonders if their original memory was still "pure," uncontaminated by postevent information.

According to Elizabeth Loftus (1979), it probably was not. Based on her studies of eyewitness testimony, Loftus proposed a theory of *reconstructive memory.* After people observe an event, she says, later information about the event—whether it's true or not—becomes integrated into the fabric of their memory. A classic study by Loftus and John Palmer (1974) illustrates the point. Subjects watched a film of a traffic accident and answered the question, "About how fast were the cars going when they *hit* each other?" Other subjects heard the same question, except the verb *hit* was replaced by *smashed, collided with, bumped into,* or *contacted.* Even though all subjects saw the same film, the wording of the question biased their reports. Subjects asked the "smash" question estimated the fastest speed; those asked the "contact" question estimated the slowest. But there's more. A week later, subjects were called back for additional probing. Did the loaded question cause subjects to reconstruct their memories of the accident? Yes. When asked if there was broken glass at the accident, 32 percent of the "smash" subjects said there was; in fact, there was not. The reason, says Loftus, is that memory of the accident was reconstructed on the basis of two sources: the film itself and the postevent information (see Figure 6.21).

Additional studies have since confirmed what is called the **misinformation effect.** For example, Loftus and her colleagues (1978) presented a slide show in which a car hits a pedestrian after turning at an intersection. Subjects saw either a STOP sign or a YIELD sign in the slides, but were then

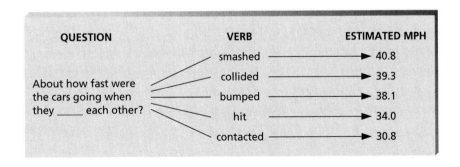

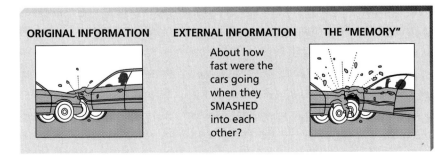

Figure 6.21

Reconstructive Memory

In a classic study of eyewitness testimony, subjects who heard a leading question about a car accident "reconstructed" their memory of the event (Loftus & Palmer, 1974).

COGNITIVE PSYCHOLOGY   Law

Eyewitness Identifications

"I'll never forget that face!" When these words are uttered, police officers, judges, and juries all take notice. Sometimes, however, eyewitnesses make mistakes. Consider the sad story of William Jackson, identified by two crime victims, convicted, and sent to prison. Five years later, Jackson was proven innocent so he was released. But the damage had been done. "They took away part of my life, part of my youth," he said.

An estimated 77,000 people a year are charged with crimes solely on the basis of eyewitness identifications (Goldstein et al., 1989). Many of these are accurate, but some are not. What factors influence the accuracy of a witness's testimony? Common sense tells us that brief exposure, long distance, poor lighting, and disguise limit our perceptions, and that a lineup has to be fair. Several years ago, a TV skit featured comedian Richard Pryor in a lineup alongside a nun, a refrigerator, and a duck. Sure enough, the witness picked Pryor. You don't have to be a cognitive psychologist to see what's wrong with this situation. But researchers have identified many less obvious problems as well (Wells & Loftus, 1984; Ross et al., 1994). Before reading this chapter, did you know that the presence of a weapon reduces one's ability to recognize a criminal? Or that your memory of a crime can be altered by your expectations, or by the way the questions are worded? The following factors are particularly important:

1. *Emotional arousal:* Often witnesses are asked to recall a bloody shooting, accident, or assault—emotional events that arouse high levels of stress. Arousal has a complex effect on memory. Realizing the importance of what they are seeing, highly aroused witnesses zoom in on the central features of an event—perhaps the culprit, the victim, or a weapon. As a direct result of this narrowed attention, arousal impairs a witness's memory for other details (Burke et al., 1992; Christianson, 1992).

2. *Race:* By varying the racial make-up of subjects and target persons, eyewitness researchers have discovered that people find it relatively difficult to recognize members of a race other than their own. This cross-race bias is found among subjects who are White, Black, Asian, and Hispanic. Although the reason for the bias is not clear, it appears that when people have little experience or contact with other racial and ethnic groups, "they all look alike" (Brigham & Malpass, 1985).

3. *Lineup composition:* In a live lineup, the police present their suspect to the witness along with five or six "foils" who are similar in their appearance. There are many structural and procedural aspects of the lineup that can lead witnesses to make false identifications (Buckhout, 1974; Wells, 1993). In this multiple-choice task, research shows, for example, that anything that makes one lineup member more distinctive than the others increases his or her chance of being selected. This may explain the case of Steve Titus, a man falsely accused of rape when a victim picked his photograph from a set of six. The other men generally resembled Titus, but his picture was smaller and was the only one without a border. He was also the only

asked a question that implied the presence of the other sign. The result was that most subjects later "recognized" a slide containing the wrong traffic sign. In a similar manner, researchers have misled subjects into recalling hammers as screwdrivers, Coke cans as cans of peanuts, *Vogue* magazine as *Mademoiselle,* breakfast cereal as eggs, a green object as yellow, and a clean-shaven man as having a mustache. What's worse, subjects are quick to respond and confident of the accuracy of these false memories (Loftus et al., 1989).

This provocative theory has aroused a lot of controversy. Does misinformation permanently impair a witness's real memory, never to be retrieved again (Belli, 1992; Belli et al., 1994)? Or do subjects merely follow the experimenter's leading "suggestion," leaving a true memory intact for retrieval under other conditions (Dodson & Reisberg, 1991; McCloskey &

man in the group with a smile on his face (Loftus & Ketcham, 1991).

4. *Lineup instructions:* The instructions that the police give to the witness are also critical. In a study by Roy Malpass and Patricia Devine (1981), students saw a staged act of vandalism and then attended a lineup. Half of the students were led to believe that the culprit was in the lineup; the others were informed that he may or may not be present. The result: subjects given the first, more suggestive instruction felt compelled to pick *someone*—so many identified an innocent person.

5. *Eyewitness confidence:* What makes the imperfections of an eyewitness so damaging is that his or her testimony is highly persuasive in court. In a series of experiments, Gary Wells, Rod Lindsay, and their colleagues staged a crime in front of unwary subjects who underwent cross-examination after trying to pick the culprit from mugshots. Other subjects, serving as jurors, watched the questioning and evaluated the witness. Time and again, jurors overestimated witness accuracy and could not tell the difference between those who made correct versus incorrect identifications (Lindsay et al., 1989; Wells et al., 1979). The problem is that jurors reasonably base their judgments on a witness's statement of self-confidence. Yet research indicates that confidence does not reliably predict accuracy. The witness who declares that "I am absolutely certain" is no more likely to be correct than the one who hems and haws (Wells & Murray, 1984).

Psychologists who study human memory are sometimes called to testify at trials involving eyewitness testimony. So what do they say to the judge and jury? A survey of sixty-three eyewitness experts reveals that in addition to testifying on the effects of emotional arousal, race, lineup composition, lineup instructions, and confidence, they describe other memory phenomena as well—many of which are discussed in this chapter (see the table below).

Memory Phenomena in Eyewitness Testimony

A survey of sixty-three eyewitness experts reveals that psychologists who testify in court inform judges and juries about the following factors (Kassin et al., 1989).

Wording of Questions	An eyewitness's testimony about an event can be affected by how questions put to that witness are worded.
Misinformation	Eyewitness testimony about an event often reflects not only what the witness actually saw but also information obtained later on.
Transference	Eyewitnesses sometimes identify as a culprit someone they saw in another situation or context.
Forgetting Curve	The rate of memory loss for an event is greatest right after the event and then levels off over time.
Weapon Focus	The presence of a weapon impairs an eyewitness's ability to accurately identify the perpetrator's face.
Schemas	An eyewitness's perception and memory for an event may be affected by his or her attitudes and expectations.

Zaragoza, 1985)? While the debate rages on, the important practical lesson remains: whether memory is truly altered or not, our *reports* are hopelessly biased by postevent information. This finding has serious implications for our legal system.

AUTOBIOGRAPHICAL MEMORY

Imagine sitting down to write your autobiography. What would you say? What experiences stand out in your mind? Would your reports of the past be accurate or distorted in some way? To answer such questions, psychologist Marigold Linton (1982) kept an extensive diary and later used it to test her memory for the events of her life. Every day for six years, she wrote the date on one side of an index card and a description of something that happened to her. In all, the diary contained 5,000 entries—some important, others trivial. Once a month, Linton pulled 150 cards at random from her file and tried to recall the events and date them correctly. Like Ebbinghaus, she found that as time passed, her personal memories took longer to recall, were harder to date, and were less detailed—but that this fading occurred at a slower, steadier rate than is typical for verbal material (she forgot only 1 percent of the items after one year, another 5 percent after two years, and 30 percent after six).

Many cognitive psychologists have traded in their nonsense syllables for the study of *autobiographical memory*—the recollections people have of the experiences that have touched their lives (Conway, 1990; Rubin, 1986). There are two key questions about this type of memory: (1) What aspects of our own past do we tend to preserve—and what are we likely to forget? (2) Are we generally accurate in our recollections, or does memory change as we get older?

What Events Do People Remember?

When people are prompted to recall their own experiences, they typically report more events that are recent than are from the distant past, and they often have difficulty dating these events. There are, however, two exceptions to these rules. One is that older adults retrieve a large number of personal memories from the age range of eleven to thirty years. This "reminiscence peak" may reflect the fact that late adolescence and early adulthood are formative and busy years in one's life (Fitzgerald, 1988). For example, William Mackavey and his colleagues (1991) analyzed the autobiographies of forty-nine eminent psychologists and found that their most important life experiences were concentrated between the ages of eighteen and thirty-five (see Figure 6.22). Second, although people cannot attach correct dates

Figure 6.22

Reminiscence Peak

Illustrating a reminiscence peak, an analysis of the autobiographies of forty-nine eminent psychologists revealed that most of their important experiences occurred between the ages of eighteen and thirty-five (Mackavey et al., 1991).

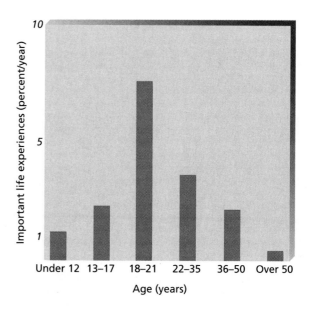

to past events, they make better estimates when they use personal or historical landmarks such as "my senior year," "after I broke up with my boyfriend," "the year the Giants won the Super Bowl," or "the night Clinton was elected President" (Friedman, 1993).

Obviously, not all experiences leave the same impression, and some dates are etched in memory for a lifetime. Marigold Linton (1982) found that unique events were easy to recall, but that routines were quickly forgotten. More specifically, David Rubin and Marc Kozin (1984) asked college students to describe their clearest memories and found that births, deaths, and weddings, accidents, injuries, sports events, romantic encounters, and vacations were among the highlights that topped the list. Some events are so vivid that they seem to occupy a particularly special status in memory. Ask people who are old enough to remember November 22, 1963, and the chances are they will tell you exactly what was happening, where they were, and with whom, the moment they heard the news that Kennedy had been shot. I, for one, will never forget that day—returning to my fifth-grade classroom after lunch, hearing the principal's voice crack over the loud speaker, watching my teacher gasp, the silence of the bus ride home, the TV blaring as I walked through the door, and the tears streaming down my mother's face.

Roger Brown and James Kulik (1977) questioned adults about that day and found that everyone had a memory that was as bold and vivid as a snapshot—not just of the assassination but of their own circumstances upon hearing the news. Brown and Kulik coined the term *flashbulb memory* to describe these surprisingly enduring and detailed recollections, and speculated that humans are biologically equipped for survival purposes to "print" highly dramatic events in memory (as you may recall, arousal triggers the release of hormones that enhance memory; see p. 228). Indeed,

Do you recall where you were and what you were doing on January 28, 1986, when you learned of the explosion of the space shuttle *Challenger*? Many people claim that this tragic event triggered a flashbulb memory.

COGNITIVE PSYCHOLOGY   Education

Ways to Improve Your Memory

Before taking office, President Clinton invited five hundred business leaders to an economic summit in Little Rock. When it was over, many of the guests marveled at Clinton's ability to address them all by name. I have always been impressed by stories like this one—by stories of stage actors who memorize hundreds of lines in only one week of rehearsal, of people who fluently speak five languages, and of waiters who take dinner orders without a note pad. How can these accomplishments be explained?

Over the years, psychologists have stumbled upon a few rare individuals who seemed equipped with extraordinary "hardware" for memory. But often the actors, waiters, multilinguists, and others we encounter use memory tricks called **mnemonics**—in other words, they vary their memory's "software." Can you boost your recall capacity through the use of mnemonics? Can you improve your study skills as a result? At this point, let's step back, consider the educational implications, and draw concrete advice from this chapter.

1. *Practice time:* To learn names, dates, vocabulary words, formulas, or the concepts in a textbook, you'll find that practice makes perfect. In general, the more time spent studying, the better. Skimming or speed-reading will not promote long-term retention. In fact, it pays to overlearn—that is, to review the material even after you think you have it mastered (see p. 221). It's also better to distribute your studying over time than to cram all at once. You will retain more information from four two-hour sessions than from one eight-hour marathon (see p. 221).

2. *Depth of processing:* The sheer amount of practice time is important, but only if it's "quality time." Mindless drills may help to maintain information in short-term memory, but, as noted in our discussion of elaborative rehearsal (see p. 220), long-term retention requires that you think actively and deeply about material—about what it means and how it is linked to what you already know. There are many ways to increase your depth of processing. Ask yourself critical questions about the material. Think about it in ways that relate to your own experiences. Talk about the material to a friend, thus forcing yourself to organize it in terms that can be understood.

3. *Hierarchical organization:* Once you have information to be learned, organize it hierarchically—as in an outline. Start with a few broad categories, then divide these into more specific subcategories and sub-subcategories. This is how many experts chunk new information, and it works. Thus, when Andrea Halpern (1986) presented subjects with 54 popular song titles, she found that recall was greater when the titles were organized hierarchically than when they were scrambled. The implication for studying is clear: organize the material in your notes, preferably in the form of an outline—and make sure to review these notes later (Kiewra et al., 1991).

4. *Verbal mnemonics:* Sometimes the easiest way to remember a list of items is to use verbal mnemonics, or "memory tricks." Chances are, you have already used popular methods such as *rhymes* ("*i* before *e*, except after *c*" is my favorite; "thirty days hath September, April, June, and November" is another) and *acronyms* that reduce the amount of information to be stored (for example, *ROY G BIV* can be used to recall the colors of the light spectrum: *r*ed, *o*range, *y*ellow, *g*reen, *b*lue, *i*ndigo, and *v*iolet). Relying on verbal mnemonics, advertisers create slogans to make their products memorable (see table).

5. *Imagery mnemonics:* Virtually all books on how to improve memory recommend that verbal information be represented as visual images, and research shows that this advice is well founded. One popular use of imagery is the *method of loci*, in which items to be recalled are mentally placed in familiar locations. This method is easy to use. First you memorize a series of objects along a familiar route. For example, you might imagine your morning walk from the bedroom, to the bathroom, to the kitchen,

■ **mnemonics** Memory aids designed to facilitate the recall of new information.

research shows that flashbulb memories are triggered by events that are important to a person and elicit an emotional response (Conway et al., 1994). Does this mean that information linked to emotional events is immune to forgetting? No, it now appears that such memories are not more accurate than normal (McCloskey et al., 1988). As time passes, however, people gain more and more confidence in these recollections (Weaver, 1993). Accurate or not, flashbulb memories "feel" special and serve as prominent landmarks in the biographies we write about ourselves.

Slogans and Products

Read the slogans and product names presented below. How many of the slogans can you match to the correct advertised products?

____ 1. Like a good neighbor
____ 2. Be all that you can be
____ 3. You deserve a break today
____ 4. Head for the mountains
____ 5. We bring good things to life
____ 6. You've got the right one, baby
____ 7. You're in good hands

(a) General Electric
(b) State Farm
(c) Busch Beer
(d) Allstate
(e) McDonald's
(f) Diet Pepsi
(g) U.S. Army

Answers: 1(b), 2(g), 3(e), 4(c), 5(a), 6(f), 7(d)

STEP 1 Memorize these pegwords in order	STEP 2 Hang new items on the pegwords	STEP 3 Form a bizarre, interactive image
one is a bun	bun—egg	
two is a shoe	shoe—apple	
three is a tree	tree—butter	
four is a door	door—cola	
five is a hive	hive—pasta	
six is sticks	sticks—tuna	
seven is heaven	heaven—steak	
eight is a gate	gate—sugar	
nine is wine	wine—chips	
ten is a hen	hen—lettuce	

The Peg-Word Mnemonic

Try it, and you'll see how easily it works. Most people are able to memorize ten new items in order with this mnemonic.

and out the door. As you follow this path, you visualize some of the objects you pass: your bed, then the bathroom door, shower, stairs, kitchen counter, and so on. These places become pigeonholes for items to be recalled. To memorize a shopping list, for example, you could picture a dozen eggs splattered on the bed, a bag of red apples hanging on the bathroom door, and butter in the soap dish of the shower. When you take a mental stroll through the house, the items on this list should pop to mind. The trick is to link new items to others already in memory.

Another powerful imagery mnemonic is the *peg-word method,* in which a list of words serves as memory "pegs" for the material to be recalled. The first step is to learn a list of pegwords that correspond to numbers. An example you may have heard of is this: "one is a bun, two is a shoe, three is a tree," and so on. Next you hang each item to be recalled on each of the pegs by forming a mental image of the two interacting. As illustrated in the figure, the images of an egg being laid on a hamburger bun, a shoe stuffed with apples, and trees made from sticks of butter are easier to recall than words on a page. The more bizarre and interactive the image, the better (see p. 223).

6. *Interference:* Because one learning experience can disrupt memory for another, it is wise to guard against the effects of interference. This problem is particularly common among college students, as material learned in one course can make it harder to retain that learned in another. To minimize the problem, follow two simple suggestions. First, study right before sleeping and review all the material right before the exam. Second, allocate an uninterrupted chunk of time to one course, and then do the same for your others as well. If you study psychology for a while, then move to biology, and then on to math and back to psychology, each course will disrupt your memory of the others— especially if the material is similar (see p. 238).

7. *Context reinstatement:* Information is easier to recall when people are in the setting in which it was acquired (see p. 231). That's why actors like to rehearse on the stage where they will later perform. So the next time you have an important exam to take, it may help to study in the room where the test will be administered.

In contrast, there is a period of life that seems entirely lost to us. Think back to your earliest memory. It probably was not the sight of the doctor's hands in the delivery room, or the first time you waved, or even the first real step you took as a toddler. An intriguing aspect of autobiographical memory is that most people cannot recall anything that happened before the age of three or four (Dudycha & Dudycha, 1941; Rubin, 1984). In one study, for example, David Pillener and his colleagues (1994) interviewed pre-adolescent children about a fire drill evacuation they had experienced in preschool. Those who were four and five years old when the incident occurred were able to recall it seven years later; those who were three years old at the time could not. This memory gap, which is quite common, is known as *childhood amnesia*.

Why should this be? One possibility is that the forgetting is caused simply by the passage of time and by interference from later experiences. The problem with this explanation is that a college student may be unable to recall events from eighteen years ago, but a thirty-five-year-old can easily recall his or her college days after the same amount of time. There are other explanations, too—that the hippocampus is not sufficiently developed in the first years of life, that young children lack the conceptual framework or self-concept for organizing the information to be stored, and the Freudian hypothesis that the early years are repressed because they are filled with trauma (Conway, 1990; Howe & Courage, 1993). Are early memories possible? It's hard to say. Some researchers have found that adults can recall certain critical events—moving, the birth of a sibling, being hospitalized, the death of a family member—from the age of two, suggesting that there are exceptions to the rule (Usher & Neisser, 1993). Others caution that these reports may not be memories at all but, rather, educated guesses or stories learned from parents and others (Loftus, 1993b). Still others argue that people have partial, implicit memories of the early years. For example, Nora Newcombe and Nathan Fox (1994) found that ten-year-old children sometimes reacted physiologically to slides of preschool classmates—even though they failed to "recognize" those classmates.

The Self as Personal Historian

"The nice thing about having memories is that you can choose."

WILLIAM TREVOR

By linking the present to the past and providing us with a sense of inner continuity, autobiographical memory is a vital part of a person's identity. Think about it. Who would you be if you could not remember your parents or childhood playmates, your successes and failures, the places you lived, the schools you attended, the books you read, and the experiences you had? Clearly, memories shape the self-concept. What's even more interesting is that the self-concept shapes our memory as well.

There are two ways in which memory is shaped by the self. First, people are motivated to distort the past in a manner that is self-inflated, or *egocentric*. According to Anthony Greenwald (1980), "The past is remembered as if it were a drama in which the self was the leading player." To illustrate, let's turn the clock back to a momentous event in American history: the Watergate hearings of 1973. The witness was John Dean, former counsel to President Nixon. Dean had submitted a 245-page statement in which he recounted word for word the details of conversations. Dean's memory seemed so flawless that he was dubbed "the human tape recorder." In an ironic twist of fate, it turned out that Nixon had actually taped the meetings Dean recalled. Was Dean accurate? A comparison of his testimony with the tapes revealed that he correctly remembered the gist of his White House conversations, but he exaggerated his own role in these events—leading Ulric Neisser (1981), the cognitive psychologist who analyzed Dean's testimony, to wonder, "Are we all like this? Is everyone's memory constructed, staged, self-centered?" Research shows that the answer is yes—there is a bit of John Dean in all of us.

A second important feature of autobiographical memory is the *hindsight bias,* the tendency to think after an event that we knew in advance what was going to happen. Historians are sometimes criticized for making the past seem inevitable in hindsight. We all do. After learning a new fact or an outcome—whether it's the result of a political election, an earthquake, the invasion of one country by another, or the winner of the last Super Bowl—people are quick to claim, "I knew it all along" (Fischhoff, 1975; Hawkins & Hastie, 1990).

When it comes to autobiographical memory, 20/20 hindsight leads people to revise their fading personal histories in ways that reflect favorably on the self. For example, George Goethals and Richard Reckman (1973) found that subjects whose attitudes about school busing were changed by a persuasive speaker later assumed that they had held their new attitude all along. Similarly, Michael Ross (1989) found that after subjects were persuaded by an expert that frequent tooth brushing was desirable, they reported in the context of a subsequent experiment having brushed more often in the previous two weeks. Illustrating that memory can be biased rather than objective, the subjects "updated" the past in light of their new attitude.

Contemplating the social implications, Ross suggested that our revisionist tendencies may account for the tendency of all generations of parents to complain that today's children are not equal to those who grew up in the good old days. According to Ross, adults wrongly assume that they used to be as they are in the present—which makes the next generation seem deficient by comparison. From studies of adult development, George Vaillant (1977) drew a similar conclusion: "It is common for caterpillars to become butterflies and then to maintain that in their youth they had been little butterflies. Maturation makes liars of us all" (p. 197).

"Needless to say, in the course of redefining myself I've taken certain liberties with the factual record."

[Drawing by Lorenz; © 1992 The New Yorker Magazine, Inc.]

SUMMARY AND KEY TERMS

An Information-Processing Model

Cognitive psychologists view memory as an information-processing system. *Sensory memory* stores sensations for a brief moment. Those that draw attention are transferred to *short-term memory (STM),* and those that are further encoded are stored in *long-term memory (LTM).*

The Sensory Register

The sensory register is the first step in the information-processing system.

Iconic Memory

The visual system stores images called "icons" in iconic memory. Using the "partial report technique," Sperling found that many items initially register in consciousness but that most last for only a fraction of a second before fading.

Echoic Memory

The auditory system stores sounds in echoic memory. Echoic memory holds only a few items but lasts two or three seconds, sometimes longer.

Short-Term Memory

Sensations that do not capture attention fade quickly, but those we notice are encoded (in visual, acoustic, or semantic terms) and transferred to short-term memory. People usually encode information in acoustic terms.

Capacity

Using a memory-span task, researchers found that short-term memory has a limited capacity. People can store seven items, plus or minus two. Our STM can be used more efficiently, however, if we group individual items into larger chunks.

Duration

STM is also limited in the length of time it can hold information. Experiments show that items are held in STM for up to twenty seconds. Through sheer repetition or *maintenance rehearsal*, however, items can be held for an indefinite period of time.

Functions of Short-Term Memory

STM contains new sensory input and material pulled from long-term memory. The limits of STM are adaptive, enabling us to discard information that is no longer useful. It is widely believed that STM is not just a passive storage depot but an active workspace. When people memorize a list of items, they exhibit the *serial position effect,* whereby those items from the beginning and end of a list are recalled better than those in the middle.

Long-Term Memory

LTM is a relatively enduring storage system that can hold vast amounts of information for long periods of time.

Encoding

To transfer input to LTM, we find it most effective to use *elaborative rehearsal*—specifically, by engaging in "deep" processing and associating the input with information already in LTM. Retention is increased through overlearning (continued rehearsal after the material is mastered) and through practice that is spaced over time rather than crammed in all at once.

Storage

In LTM, information may be stored in semantic or visual form. In semantic coding, people store the meaning of verbal information, not just specific words. In fact, memories are stored in complex webs of association called *semantic networks*. In visual coding, people store information as mental pictures. Use of imagery thus improves memory.

Is it possible to pinpoint a site in the brain that houses these associations? Neuroscientists have tried to identify the physical traces of memory. In the case of H.M., the hippocampus was removed, producing *anterograde amnesia*, the inability to form new long-term memories (not *retrograde amnesia,* the inability to pull memories from the past). Recent studies confirm that the hippocampus is involved in the encoding of information into long-term memory. Biochemically, the neurotransmitter acetylcholine plays a key role. So does the hormone epinephrine, which seems to facilitate memory by causing the release of glucose.

Retrieval

Basically, there are two techniques by which retrieval can be tested, and each assesses a different aspect of memory: explicit and implicit. *Explicit memories* are the recollections that people consciously retrieve in response to direct questions. *Implicit memories* refer to the nonconscious retention of information and are indirectly measured by their effects on performance. This distinction is important because people sometimes "forget" (have no explicit memory of) an experience and yet show the effects (have an implicit memory) of that experience.

In tests of explicit memory, people tend to perform better at recognition than recall. Apparently, forgetting sometimes occurs not because memory has faded but because the information is difficult to retrieve. Retrieval failure is indicated by the "tip of the tongue" phenomenon and by the fact that memory is aided by retrieval cues. Research on *encoding specificity* indicates that any stimulus that is encoded along with an experience—including smells, locations, and internal states—can later jog one's memory of that experience.

Implicit tests uncover memories of which people are not aware by measuring the effects of such memories on task performance. Studies show that many amnesia patients use previously obtained information that they cannot explicitly recall. As indicated by the false fame effect, unconscious transference in eyewitness testimony, and unconscious plagiarism, implicit memory is also common in everyday life.

Forgetting

Beginning with Ebbinghaus, researchers have found that there is an initial steep loss of retention, but that the forgetting rate levels off over time. Forgetting can result from one of four processes: a lack of encoding, physical decay, interference, or repression. There are two kinds of interference. In *proactive interference,* prior information inhibits one's ability to recall something new. In *retroactive interference,* new material disrupts memory for previously learned information.

Reconstruction

Remembering is an active process in which people construct memories based on *schemas,* or preconceptions, and information from outside sources. Experiments by Loftus and others reveal that memory is also "reconstructive"—that after one observes an event, postevent information becomes integrated into the fabric of memory. When that information is false, the result is known as the *misinformation effect.*

Autobiographical Memory

Autobiographical memory consists of the recollections people have of their own personal experiences. What aspects of our own past do we preserve? Are these memories accurate?

What Events Do People Remember?

People can best recall events from the recent rather than the distant past, though older adults report many personal memories from the age range of eleven to thirty years and tend to recall events that are particularly vivid, dramatic, and unique. So-called flashbulb memories "feel" accurate but may be no more so than ordinary memories. Most people cannot recall events from before the age or three or four, a memory gap called childhood amnesia.

The Self as Personal Historian

Autobiographical memory is vital to one's identity. Accordingly, our memories can be shaped by our need for self-esteem. People thus distort the past in a manner that is egocentric and think in hindsight that they knew all along what would happen.

Chapter 7

Thought and Language

Curare is a drug that is derived from tropical plants. It has been used by South American Indians to make poisoned arrows. The effect is devastating—a complete paralysis of the skeletal muscles. Imagine that you are placed on a table and injected with two and half times the amount of curare needed to paralyze the muscles that allow you to breathe. After one minute, you are dizzy and feeling weak in the jaw. At ten minutes, you cannot move your mouth to speak. At twenty minutes, you can't open your eyes. And within thirty minutes, you need artificial respiration because you are no longer capable of breathing on your own. Pretty scary. It makes you wonder, what would you be thinking?

Behaviorist John Watson (1925) would have predicted that you could *not* think at all if your muscles were paralyzed, that your mind would be blank. According to Watson, thought is nothing more than silent, subvocal speech—and, as such, requires the use of the vocal cords and related muscles. Consistent with this claim, Edmund Jacobson (1932) placed electrodes near the vocal cords and detected muscle movements whenever people engaged in mental activities.

There is more to the story, however. In 1947, a physician named Scott Smith actually allowed the curare experiment to be performed—using himself as the subject! The experiment was designed to evaluate the usefulness of curare in anesthesia, but it also served as a test of Watson's theory (Smith et al., 1947). The result: In contrast to what Watson would have predicted, Smith reported that even while completely paralyzed, kept alive by a respirator, he was conscious. He had lucid thoughts, was able to perform mental arithmetic, and heard all that was happening around him. Indeed, Smith's EEG readings were those of a normal alert subject. And when the drug wore off, he was able to recall the incidents and statements made during the experiment. Clearly, there was thinking without subvocal speech.

Today, psychologists view thought and language as separate but interconnected activities. Interest in these topics has been central to psychology from its beginning. Indeed, the capacity for abstract thought and language is what most clearly separates us from other animal species. Or does it? The question of whether these abilities are uniquely human is one of several controversies to be addressed in this chapter. In the coming pages, we will examine some of the basic processes of thought and language, and then return to the question of how they are related. But first, let's examine the building blocks of both thought and language: concepts.

THE BUILDING BLOCKS

Freedom. Sports. Plants. Animals. Education. Furniture. Sex. Peace. Music. Heroes. Happiness. Each one of these words represents a **concept**, a mental grouping of persons, ideas, events, or objects that share common properties.

In Chapter 6, we saw that long-term memory can be pictured as a complex, orderly network of semantic concepts. So, when one concept in the network is "activated"—as when you read a word or see an image—other semantically related concepts are *primed,* made more available for retrieval. Look at the semantic network depicted in Figure 7.1. The fact that

■ **concept** A mental grouping of persons, ideas, events, or objects that share common properties.

Figure 7.1

A Semantic Network

Long-term memory can be pictured as a complex web of concepts, some of which are cogitively closer than others. When one concept is "activated," others nearby in the network are primed.

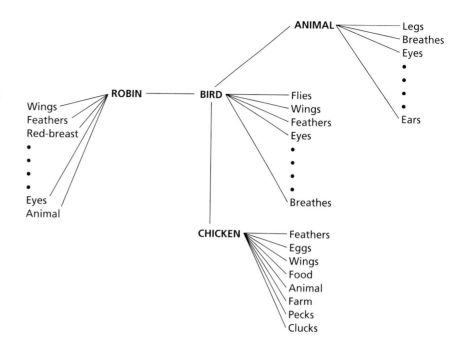

a robin is a type of bird is illustrated by their linkage, and this linkage in itself is a concept that is stored in your memory. What's interesting about semantic networks is that one concept can be used to bring others to mind. Once you hear the word *bird,* it becomes easier to pull *robin, chicken,* and *animal* from memory.

Is there any evidence that priming actually occurs? Yes. In one study, David Meyer and Roger Schvaneveldt (1971) presented subjects with pairs of letter strings and asked them to decide as quickly as possible if both letter strings formed words. On some trials, the two items in a pair were semantically related words (*nurse-doctor*). On other trials, the pairs included unrelated words (*bread-doctor*) or nonwords (*marb-doctor*). As it turned out, subjects were quickest to decide that the items were both words when they were related. Apparently, reading the first word of the pair primed semantically related words—thus giving the *nurse-doctor* subjects a "head start" on the second item and speeding up their decisions. Over the years, many more researchers have confirmed this point (McNamara, 1994).

There is another important feature of semantic networks: some concepts are more closely related than others. As shown in Figure 7.1, "chicken" is farther from the concept "bird" than "robin" is—even though both are members of the bird category. Assuming that it takes longer to reveal connections between concepts that are distant than between those that are closely related, reaction-time tasks are used to plot the psychological distances between concepts. If I were to time how long it takes you to verify the statement that "a chicken is a bird," and then compare that to the amount of time it takes you to verify that "a robin is a bird," you would respond more quickly to the second statement (Collins & Loftus, 1975).

Eleanor Rosch (1975) noted that some members of a category are perceived to be more "typical" than others, just as a robin seems more typical of birds than does a chicken, an ostrich, or a penguin—which have wings and feathers but do not fly. What makes a category member more or less typical? Look once again at Figure 7.1, and notice the partial list of characteristics that are linked to the concepts "bird," "robin," and "chicken."

When you hear the word *pet*, what image comes to mind? For this particular concept, some animals (golden retrievers) are more prototypical of the category than others (rabbits or iguanas).

When people are asked to list properties of different concepts, the typical members, which are called **prototypes**, have more properties that are true of the category as a whole (Medin & Ross 1992; Smith et al., 1974; Rosch & Mervis, 1975). Consider the categories listed in Table 7.1. The more prototypical an item is, the more easily we recognize that it is a member of a category and use that member to make judgments about the category as a whole (Whitney, 1986).

Table 7.1

Typicality of Members in Three Categories

Category	Typicality		
	High	Moderate	Low
Furniture	Chair	Lamp	Vase
Fruit	Apple	Lemon	Coconut
Vehicle	Car	Boat	Blimp

The use of prototypes is illustrated in many studies. For example, Lance Rips (1975) had subjects read a story about an island that was inhabited by sparrows, robins, eagles, hawks, ducks, geese, and ostriches. One group was then told that a disease had infected the robins, while a second group was told that the disease infected the ducks. Subjects were asked, How many of the other species would be infected? Based on what you've read about prototypes, can you anticipate the result? Subjects in the robin-infected group predicted that the disease would spread to all other bird species. In contrast, the duck group predicted that only geese, a "related" species, would be infected. Apparently, robins served as a prototype for the whole group, but ducks did not. Other research as well demonstrates the importance of prototypes. For example, Vicki Smith (1991) found that mock jurors were more likely to vote a defendant guilty of robbery when the crime was prototypical (money taken from the apartment of an elderly

■ **prototype** A "typical" member of a category, one that has most of the defining features of that category.

person, at night, by a man carrying a gun) than when it was not (money taken from the driver of a car, during the day, by an unarmed man on a street corner). Semantic networks affect not only what information is retrieved, and how quickly, but also the way we think and the judgments we make.

Let's step back for a moment and review. Stimuli from the external environment activate concepts in our semantic networks, and this activation primes related concepts. These related concepts are then easier to retrieve from memory and more likely to influence the judgments we make. For some problems, such as playing the TV game *Jeopardy!*, trying to recite the lyrics of a song you once knew, or trying to recall a recipe, the solution consists of retrieving the necessary information from memory. But what about the many problems we face that will not be solved by recitation, formula, or a mere regurgitation of facts? When you lock your keys in the car, or play chess against a formidable opponent, or choose between competing job offers, the solution you're looking for is not stored directly in memory. In these situations, you must combine and manipulate concepts in novel ways to solve the problem or make the necessary judgment. In the next section, we examine this more complex aspect of human thought.

SOLVING PROBLEMS

Problem solving consists of the mental processes we use to attain some goal when we cannot simply retrieve the answer from memory. In general, problem solving is a three-step process: (1) representing the problem, (2) generating possible solutions, and (3) evaluating these solutions (Glass & Holyoak, 1986; Ellis & Hunt, 1989). You should think of these steps not as a fixed series of stages but as a set of mental activities that are used in cycles. For example, you may be stuck on a problem, only to realize that you had not represented it correctly in the first place. At that point, you might start the process over with a new way to view the problem.

You don't have to be a scientist to engage in problem solving. To find a cure for cancer or even to repair a leak in the plumbing, one must (1) represent the problem, (2) generate possible solutions, and (3) evaluate these solutions.

Representing the Problem

Many problems we encounter come to us in the form of words, and representing these problems involves activating concepts from our semantic memory. There are other ways to depict a problem, however. One is through visual **images,** mental representations of visual information. To turn on the ignition of your car, do you turn the key to the right or to the left? What about the cold-water faucet in your kitchen sink? Which way do the hands of a clock move? (yes, it's clockwise, but describe what that means). And if you can picture a map of the world, identify which city is farther north—London or New York? To answer these questions, people generate visual images.

Margaret Intons-Peterson (1993) presented people with verbal descriptions of simple line drawings, like the one in Figure 7.2, and found that the more rotations that were involved, the longer time it took subjects to generate the image. These results suggest that people solve this problem by mentally rotating the visual image of one of the forms. Other evidence confirms this point. Martha Farah (1989) used brain imaging techniques to show that in tasks requiring imagery, the brain is active in the same areas that are involved in vision. These studies, and other research as well, suggest that some of our thought processes are visually based (Kosslyn, 1994).

Figure 7.2

Mental Rotation Tasks

Imagine a capital letter T. Rotate it 90° to the right. Put a triangle directly to the left of the figure so that it is pointing to the right. Now rotate the figure 90° to the right. Got it? Now look at the images below and pick the correct one. You can check your answer by drawing the figure on paper or looking on p. 260.

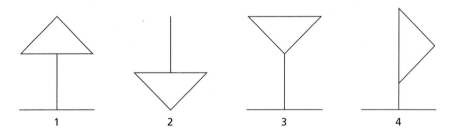

Consider another example using a verbally presented problem, devised by Karl Duncker (1945). After reading the problem, think about it and spend some time trying to solve it before reading on.

> One morning, exactly at sunrise, a Buddhist monk began to climb a tall mountain. A narrow path, no more than a foot or two wide, spiraled around the mountain to a glittering temple at the summit. The monk ascended at varying rates of speed, stopping many times along the way to rest and eat dried fruit he carried with him. He reached the temple shortly before sunset. After several days of fasting and meditation, he began his journey back along the same path, starting at sunrise and again walking at variable speeds with many pauses along the way. His average speed descending was, of course, greater than his average climbing speed. Prove that there must be a spot along the path that the monk will pass on both trips at precisely the same time of day.

■ **image** A mental representation of visual information.

So, how did you approach this task? Were you able to solve it? Many people think of this as an algebra problem, which starts them wondering about angles, speeds, and distances, or even writing down equations—only to become frustrated and fail. As revealed in Figure 7.3, however (on p. 260), the solution is simple if you construct a visual rather than mathematical representation of the problem. The way to do this is to construct a graph of the monk ascending and descending the mountain, or even imagine a second monk starting down from the top at the same time the first monk starts up from the bottom. You can vary their relative speeds, of course, which will alter the meeting spot. But that's irrelevant. This method shows that they will have to cross paths somewhere along the mountain. The point is, a single problem can be depicted in different ways—through words, graphs, diagrams, lists, tables, matrices, or pictures. Depending on the problem, some of these ways lead to solutions more readily than others.

At times, the problems that confront us are best represented in the form of **mental models,** which are intuitive theories of the way things work (Gentner & Stevens, 1983). When accurate, these theories can be powerful tools for reasoning. By having specific mental models of how computers, engines, bureaucracies, viruses, and other things work, people can diagnose malfunctions and adapt accordingly. The problem is that our mental models are sometimes wrong. Before reading on, look at the marble problem that is used to study what Michael McCloskey (1983) calls *intuitive physics—* mental models that people have about the laws of motion (see Figure 7.4). For tasks like this one, many people draw incorrect paths because they operate according to "impetus theory," which was abandoned in physics more than three hundred years ago. Interestingly, physics students do not always perform better on motion problems, suggesting that mental models can be difficult to change (Donley & Ashcraft, 1992).

Generating and Evaluating Solutions

Once a problem is represented, we try out possible solutions and test to see if they work. If the problem is solved, life goes on. If not, we go back to the proverbial drawing board in order to come up with new ideas. There are many different ways to find solutions, but there are four basic problem-solving processes: trial and error, algorithms, heuristics, and insight.

Trial and Error   **Trial and error** is the simplest problem-solving strategy there is, and it's often effective. You may recall from Chapter 5 that Edward Thorndike studied animal intelligence by putting cats in a "puzzle box," placing food outside a door, and timing how long it took for them to figure out how to escape. At first, the cats tried various ineffective behaviors. They tried reaching with their paws, but the food was too far away. They scratched at the bars, but that did not work. They pushed at the ceiling, but that did not work either. Then they would literally stumble upon the solution (which was to step on a lever, which opened the door) and repeat that solution whenever they were in the box. The cats solved the problem by trial and error.

As you can imagine, this rather aimless, hit-or-miss approach is not the most efficient way to proceed. Yet I must confess that when I tinker with a computer and run into problems, I often start pecking furiously at the keyboard, hoping that something I do will effect a change. Sometimes this strategy proves enlightening. For example, Thomas Edison—the most

Figure 7.4

Intuitive Physics

Subjects were asked to draw the path that a marble would take as it exited this curved tube. Most subjects incorrectly drew a curved path (dotted line) rather than the correct straight path (dashed line). Our mental models of motion are often wrong.

■ **mental models** Intuitive theories about the way things work.

■ **trial and error** A problem-solving strategy in which several solutions are attempted until one is found that works.

Figure 7.3

Solution to the Buddhist Monk Problem

By drawing a graph of the monk ascending and descending the mountain, you can see that the two paths will have to cross.*

Solution to Mental Rotation Tasks

The answer is (3).

*[From Cognition, Second Edition, by A. Glass and K. Holyoak. Copyright © 1985 by McGraw-Hill. Reprinted by permission of McGraw-Hill.]

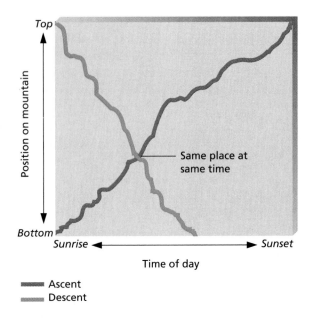

prolific inventor in American history—tested thousands of light bulb filaments before he found one that worked. The problem is, this strategy often takes too long or fails completely. If possible, it's better to take a more systematic, planned approach.

Algorithms and Heuristics   An **algorithm** is a step-by-step procedure that is guaranteed, eventually, to produce a solution. When you were taught in school how to solve two-digit addition problems, or long division, you learned an algorithm. An alternative is to use **heuristics,** mental shortcuts, or rules of thumb, that may or may not lead to the correct solution. The "i before e" heuristic for spelling *ie* words is a good example. To appreciate the difference between algorithms and heuristics, consider the following anagram problem: unscramble the letters *L K C C O* to make a word. One strategy is to use an algorithm, trying all possible letter combinations by systematically varying the letters in each position. Sooner or later, you will form the correct word. An alternative is to use a heuristic. For example, you could try the most familiar letter combinations. A common ending for English words is *ck,* so you might start with this combination and arrive quickly at the solution: *clock.*

If algorithms are guaranteed to produce solutions, why not use them all the time? The reason is that algorithms are not always available, and sometimes they take too much time to be practical. For example, chess experts do not consider all the possible moves on the board, because there are simply too many of them. This strategy is fine for high-speed computers such as "Deep Thought"—a computerized chess master that can analyze 750,000 different moves per second! But good players rely instead on heuristics, such as getting control of the center of the board.

Some heuristics are general, in that they can be used to solve a wide range of problems. One particularly important general heuristic is the **means-ends analysis** (Newell & Simon, 1972). This involves breaking a larger problem into a series of subgoals. For example, let's say you are starting a new job on Monday and have the problem of getting to work on

■ **algorithm** A systematic problem-solving strategy that is guaranteed to produce a solution.

■ **heuristic** A rule of thumb allowing one to make judgments that are quick but often in error.

■ **means-ends analysis** A problem-solving heuristic that involves breaking down a larger problem into a series of subgoals.

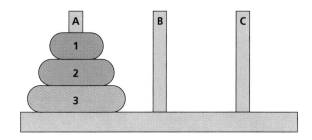

Figure 7.5

Tower of Hanoi Problem

Your mission is to move three rings from peg A to peg C. You may move only the top ring on a peg and may not place a larger ring above a smaller one. See solution on p. 262.

time. You could solve this problem by driving your car to work, but your car needs repair. Now you have a subgoal of getting your car repaired. But this might require other subgoals, such as finding out which mechanics in town are reliable. For some problems, the nested subgoals can get quite complex and involved. In fact, unless people carefully evaluate whether each step is bringing them closer to the final solution, it is possible to lose track of what part of the problem is actually being solved (Simon, 1975). The benefits of formulating subgoals can be seen in the *Tower of Hanoi problem,* depicted in Figure 7.5.

Another useful general heuristic is the use of **analogies** to solve problems. If you have previously solved some problem that is similar to a new dilemma, you can use the old solution as a model for the new one. The trick is to recognize that the second problem resembles the first. By way of illustration, take a few minutes to try and solve the following "radiation problem" (Gick & Holyoak, 1980):

> Suppose you are a doctor faced with a patient who has a malignant tumor in his stomach. It is impossible to operate on the patient, but unless the tumor is destroyed the patient will die. There is a kind of laser beam that can be used to destroy the tumor. If the rays reach the tumor all at once at a sufficiently high intensity, the tumor will be destroyed. Unfortunately, at this intensity the healthy tissue that the rays pass through on the way to the tumor will also be destroyed. At lower intensities the rays are harmless to healthy tissue, but they will not destroy the tumor either. What type of procedure might be used to destroy the tumor with the rays and, at the same time, avoid destroying the healthy tissue?

Do you have the answer? If not, read the following "parade-dispersion" story:

> A small country was controlled by a dictator. The dictator ruled the country from a strong fortress. The fortress was in the middle of the country, surrounded by farms and villages. Many roads radiated outward from the fortress like the spokes of a wheel. To celebrate the anniversary of his rise to power, the dictator ordered his general to conduct a full-scale military parade. On the morning of the anniversary, the general's troops were gathered at the head of one of the roads leading to the fortress, ready to march. However, a lieutenant brought the general a disturbing report. The dictator was demanding that this parade had to be more impressive than any previous parade. He wanted his army to be seen and heard at the same time in every region of the country. Furthermore, the dictator was threatening that if the parade was not sufficiently impressive he was going to strip the general of his medals and reduce him to the rank of private. But it seemed impossible to have a parade that could be seen throughout the whole country.

■ **analogy** A problem-solving heuristic that involves using an old solution as a model for a new, similar problem.

Solution to the Tower of Hanoi Problem
To complete this mission, it helps to break the task into subgoals. The first is to get ring 3 to the bottom of peg C (move ring 1 to peg C, ring 2 to peg B, and ring 1 from peg C to peg B; then put ring 3 at the bottom of peg C). Your second subgoal is to get ring 2 to peg C (move ring 1 to peg A and ring 2 to C). The third subgoal is now easy: just move ring 1 over to peg C—and you're done.

"Now I see your problem—linear thought."

[Drawing by Lorenz; © 1992 The New Yorker Magazine, Inc.]

■ **insight** A form of problem solving in which the solution seems to pop to mind all of a sudden.

The general, however, knew just what to do. He divided his army up into small groups and dispatched each group to the head of a different road. When all were ready he gave the signal, and each group marched down a different road. Each group continued down its road to the fortress, so that the entire army finally arrived together at the fortress at the same time. In this way, the general was able to have the parade seen and heard through the entire country at once, and thus please the dictator.

Okay, now go back to the radiation problem and try again. If you are still having trouble, here's a hint: think of the fortress in the parade-dispersion story as an analogy for the tumor in the radiation problem. Can you see the relevance of the general's strategy for the surgeon's dilemma? The radiation solution is similar to the general's: use a low-intensity ray that can be aimed at the tumor from several directions. When all the rays reach the tumor, their effects will add up to that of a single high-intensity beam at the site of the tumor, and no healthy tissue will be destroyed.

Demonstrating the usefulness of problem solving by analogy, Gick and Holyoak (1980) found that only 8 percent of "naive" subjects solved the radiation problem—but among those who first read the parade-dispersion story, the solution rate increased to 50 percent. In fact, some subjects were prepared with an even stronger analogy, one in which a general *attacked* a fortress from several different directions. As this story was easier to relate to the radiation problem, 76 percent of the subjects in this group found the solution. The more directly an old solution relates to a new problem, the more effective the analogy (Holyoak, 1990).

Insight   When people work on problems, they usually try to monitor their progress to evaluate whether they are closing in on a solution (Kotovsky et al., 1985). But have you ever puzzled over something, felt as if you were stumped, and then come up with the solution suddenly, out of the blue, as if a light bulb flashed inside your head? Aha! If so, then you have experienced problem solving by **insight**, a process in which the solution pops to mind all of a sudden—and the problem solver doesn't realize the solution is coming and cannot describe what he or she was thinking at the time (Metcalfe & Wiebe, 1987; Kaplan & Simon, 1990).

Insight is a common experience that arises when people switch from a poor strategy to a better one, represent the problem in a new way, or identify an analogy from prior experience (Simon, 1989). Some researchers believe that these apparent flashes of insight may actually be the result of a gradual, step-by-step process—and that people are often just not aware of the progress they're making (Weisberg, 1992). Is problem solving by insight gradual but nonconscious? It's hard to know for sure. But research shows that when people working on insight problems are asked to describe their thinking, which puts the process into consciousness, performance deteriorates (Schooler et al., 1993).

People often report that they tried unsuccessfully for hours to solve a problem and then, after taking a break, came back and it "clicked": an insight that quickly led to a solution. The improved ability to solve a problem after taking a break from it is called the *incubation effect*. One puzzle that psychologists have used to investigate incubation effects in the laboratory is the "cheap necklace problem" illustrated in Figure 7.6. Try it for at least five minutes before reading on.

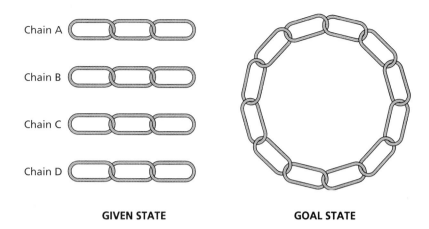

Figure 7.6

The Cheap Necklace Problem

Make a necklace out of the four separate chains. It costs 2 cents to open a link and three cents to close a link. You must make your necklace for 15 cents or less. The solution can be found on p. 265.

Using the cheap necklace problem, J. Silveira (1971) tested three groups of subjects. All groups worked on the same task for a total of thirty minutes. One group worked the whole time without a break. After fifteen minutes, however, the second group took a half-hour break and the third group took a four-hour break. During these rest periods, subjects were kept busy with other activities that kept them from continuing to work on the necklace problem. The results provided strong evidence for the incubation effect: subjects who took a break were more likely to solve the problem than those who did not. In fact, the longer the break was, the better the performance. The practical implication of this effect is clear. Sometimes it helps to take a break while trying to solve problems that require a single critical insight—as in the cheap necklace problem, where the key is to realize that you can't link all four chains (Anderson, 1990).

The history of science is filled with stories of discovery by insight. But is insight necessarily the product of great minds? No. In fact, many psychologists believe other animals are capable of insight as well, not just of trial-and-error problem solving. Many years ago, Wolfgang Kohler (1925) claimed that a chimpanzee named Sultan displayed insight in problem solving. Kohler put bananas and a long stick outside the chimp's cage, both out of reach, and put a short stick inside the cage. Sultan poked at the banana with the short stick, but it was too short. After repeatedly trying, he gave up, dropped the stick, and walked away. Then all of a sudden, Sultan jumped up, picked up the short stick, and used it to get the longer stick—which he then used to get the banana. Did this episode reveal insight? Many researchers are skeptical of such a claim and suggest that the apparent insight may be no more than an accumulation of learned behaviors (Epstein et al., 1984). Yet others agree with Kohler. Sociobiologist Edward O. Wilson tells a Sultan-like story of a chimp trying to reach some leaves: "He sat and looked at the tree for a long time, and went over to a log. He dragged it over to the tree, propped it against the trunk, then stood back and charged his ramp. It's extremely difficult to explain that, other than to say the chimp was consciously thinking" (Begley & Ramo, 1993).

This brings us to the question of whether problem solving is uniquely human. Do other animals have insight or use heuristics? Are they capable of conscious thought? These are difficult questions to resolve, and attempts to answer them have generated a lively area of debate in psychology (Timberlake, 1993). This research is controversial, but there is tantalizing evidence to suggest that chimpanzees and other apes can learn to solve problems that require the use of abstract symbols. We will take a closer look at this research later in the chapter when we discuss attempts to teach language to nonhuman primates.

"Blind Spots" in Problem Solving

Using trial and error, algorithms, heuristics, and insight, people often exhibit a remarkable capacity to solve problems. As we have seen time and again, however, our competencies are often compromised by certain "blind spots." To appreciate some of these shortcomings, try the problems in Figure 7.7 before reading on. The solutions are revealed in the upcoming paragraphs and then are illustrated on p. 266.

Figure 7.7(a)

The Nine-Dot Problem

Connect all nine dots with four straight lines without lifting your pencil from the paper.

Figure 7.7(b)

Duncker's Candle Problem

Using just the objects shown, how could you mount the candle on a wall?

Problems	Jar A capacity	Jar B capacity	Jar C capacity	Desired quantity
1	21	127	3	100
2	14	163	25	99
3	18	43	10	5
4	9	42	6	21
5	20	59	4	31
6	23	49	3	20
7	15	39	3	18
8	28	76	3	25
9	18	48	4	14
10	14	36	8	6

Figure 7.7(c)

Luchin's Water-Jar Problem

Try to solve the following ten problems. In each case, use Jars A, B, and C, with the capacities indicated, to pour out the desired quantities of water (far-right column). For example, if Jar A has a capacity of 27 cups, B has 20 cups, and C has 4 cups, you could measure out 50 cups of water by using the formula 2A – C, or 54 – 4.

Representation Failures   The difficulty of the "nine-dot problem" in Figure 7.7(a) illustrates that failure often results from an incorrect problem representation. Even though the instructions say nothing about staying inside an imaginary square formed from the dots, almost everyone behaves as though the outside dots form a boundary that cannot be crossed (to understand why, think back to the gestalt principles of perceptual grouping in Chapter 3). If you don't mentally handicap yourself in this way, the solution is simple. But people do, which is what makes the problem so difficult. Is this tendency to represent problems narrowly limited to laboratory puzzles and brainteasers? Sadly, no. As we'll see in Chapter 17, many clinical psychologists find that people suffer needlessly because they conceptualize problems in ways that make them seem insurmountable (Beck, 1985; Ellis, 1962).

■ **functional fixedness** The tendency to think of objects only in terms of their usual functions, a limitation that disrupts problem solving.

■ **mental set** The tendency to return to a problem-solving strategy that worked in the past.

■ **confirmation bias** The inclination to search only for evidence that will verify one's beliefs.

Functional Fixedness The "candle problem" in Figure 7.7(b) illustrates a more specific type of representation failure. The difficulty in this case is one of **functional fixedness**, a tendency to think of objects only in terms of their usual functions. In the candle problem, for example, you would struggle for as long as you see the matchbox as only a container, not as a possible shelf. A brick is a brick, but it can also be used as a paperweight. Finding new and creative solutions to practical problems often requires the kind of open-mindedness that enables us to see unusual uses for common objects (Sternberg & Lubart, 1991; Weisberg, 1986).

Mental Sets The "water-jar problem" in Figure 7.7(c) illustrates a related blind spot, the inability due to past experience to view the problem from a new perspective. If you haven't tried this one yet, please do; then come back. How was it? Were you able to solve the first water-jar problem? If so, you figured out the algorithm: B (127) − A (21) − 2C (6) = 100. Chances are, you also found problems 2 through 7 easy, and whizzed through them by using the same formula. But what about problems 8, 9, and 10, which required a new formula? If you're like most students, you probably struggled more on these—even though the solution (A − C) is simple. Why? The first few problems lead people to form a **mental set**, a tendency to use a strategy that has worked in the past. As with the use of analogy to solve problems, mental sets are not all bad. After all, carrying over the B − A − 2C formula helped you with items 2 through 7. The drawback is that we are often slow to shed our mental sets when we need to. As I said, students tend to slow down on problems 8, 9, and 10—unless they work on these first, so that no mental set is formed. (For an amusing look at mental sets in action, play hide-and-seek with young preschool children, and you'll find that they always go right back to the last place you hid.)

The Confirmation Bias The nine-dot, candle, and water-jar problems are tricky not because they are intellectually demanding but because people tend to be overly rigid in their thinking. But there's more. Once we think we have a solution, we fall prey to the **confirmation bias,** the tendency to look only for evidence that will verify our beliefs—which can prevent us from realizing that we are in error. To demonstrate, Peter Wason (1960) gave students a three-number sequence, 2-4-6, and challenged them to figure out the rule he had used to generate this set. How should they proceed? By making up their own sequences and asking the experimenter to indicate

Figure 7.8

Solution to the Cheap Necklace Problem
The key is to realize that you can't link all four chains. To solve the problem, open every link on one chain (this costs 6 cents), then use these open links to join the three remaining chains (which costs 9 cents).

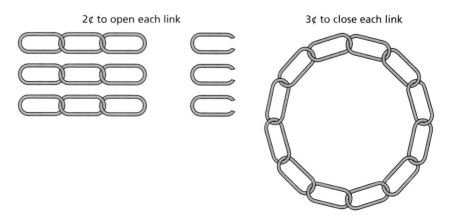

2¢ to open each link   3¢ to close each link

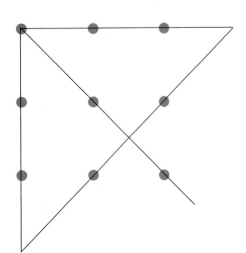

Figure 7.9

Solution to the Nine-Dot Problem

To solve this problem, you need to realize that all four lines must extend beyond the square of dots.

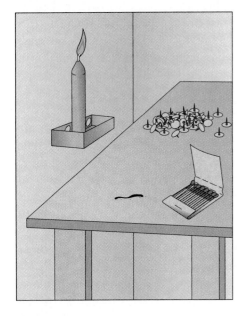

Figure 7.10

Solution to Duncker's Candle Problem

To solve this problem, you need to realize that the box can be used not only as a container but also as a shelf.

■ **belief perseverance** The tendency to cling to beliefs even after they have been discredited.

whether or not they fit the rule. Subjects were told they could test as many sequences as they wanted and to state the rule only if they felt certain that they knew it. The task was straightforward and the rule behind 2-4-6 was easy: any three increasing numbers. Yet out of twenty-nine subjects, only six discovered the correct rule without first seizing upon one that was incorrect. What happened was this: subjects would start with an initial hypothesis (adding by twos, even numbers, skipping numbers) and then search only for confirming evidence. Thinking that the rule was "adding by twos," a subject might test 6-8-10, 50-52-54, 21-23-25, and so on, yet never try disconfirming sets such as 6-8-4 or 3-2-1. When all the sequences fit, the subject would proudly and with confidence announce the wrong rule.

Belief Perseverance   As noted, people search for evidence that verifies their beliefs. But what happens when we confront information that plainly contradicts our beliefs? Do we revise our views, as logic would dictate? Not necessarily. In a series of studies, Craig Anderson and his colleagues (1980) found that our beliefs are often highly resistant to change. For example, subjects read case studies suggesting that the best firefighters are either risk takers or cautious types. Next, subjects were asked to come up with a theory for the suggested link. The possibilities are easy to imagine: "He who hesitates is lost" supports risk taking, and "You have to look before you leap" supports caution. Finally, when the experiment was supposedly over, subjects were told that the information they had received was totally false, manufactured for the sake of the experiment. Did this discrediting evidence erase subjects' newly formed beliefs? No, it was too late. Many subjects exhibited **belief perseverance:** they clung to their initial beliefs even after those beliefs had been discredited. Though hardly rational, it seems that our beliefs often outlive the evidence from which they sprung.

Many currently popular books on how to improve your problem-solving skills provide advice on how to eliminate blind spots (Bransford & Stein, 1984; Zechmeister & Johnson, 1992). We now know that people have to learn to be more flexible in the way they represent problems, the strategies they use, the way they evaluate their initial beliefs, and their responsiveness to discrediting information. At each stage, then, the key is to think flexibly and with an open mind.

MAKING JUDGMENTS

People have to make decisions every day. Occasionally we are faced with choices that have a major impact on the rest of our lives. Where should I go to school? Should I get married? Whom should I vote for? What career is right for me? Should I save my money or invest it in stocks? We all like to think of ourselves as thoughtful and logical decision makers who weigh the costs and benefits, calculate the probabilities, and act accordingly. But are we that logical, really? Researchers study human decision making in tasks ranging from formal logic to everyday reasoning. The results have given rise to some rather surprising discoveries about *Homo sapien,* the "rational animal."

Formal Logic

■ **syllogism** A logical problem in which the goal is to determine the validity of a conclusion given two or more premises.

Throughout history, philosophers, psychologists, economists, and others have assumed that our natural way of thinking followed the laws of formal logic. One way to test this assumption is to examine the ways in which people solve strictly logical problems.

Syllogistic Reasoning   One aspect of formal logic that is studied extensively in psychology is *syllogistic reasoning*. A **syllogism** is a logical problem in which you are given premises that you must assume are true, and then decide whether a certain conclusion can be drawn from these premises. For example, given the premises "all A are B" and "all B are C," is the conclusion "all A are C" a valid one? The answer is yes—given the premises, the conclusion must be true. Before reading further, try the syllogisms shown in Table 7.3, and try to figure out why some seem so much harder to solve than others.

Table 7.2

Syllogism Problems

For each set of premises, decide if the conclusion is valid. The answers appear below.

> 1. Some As are Bs.
>   All Bs are Cs.
>   Therefore, some As are Cs.
>
> 2. All As are Bs.
>   Some Bs are Cs.
>   Therefore, some As are Cs.
>
> 3. All robins are birds.
>   All birds are animals.
>   Therefore, all robins are animals.
>
> 4. All bananas are fruit.
>   Some fruits are yellow.
>   Therefore, some bananas are yellow.

Answers: (1) valid, (2) invalid, (3) valid, (4) invalid

In general, most people find syllogisms easier when they are stated concretely than in the abstract "all A are B" format. In fact, one strategy people use to solve abstract syllogisms is to rephrase them as more concrete problems. However, this method can lead us to make mistakes because we often fail to see that there can be more than one way to represent a given premise. Consider "some A are B." The diagram in Figure 7.11 can be used to make this syllogism more concrete. But note that although the left diagram seems more natural, the right one is also a valid way to show the premise, because whenever it is true that "all A are B," it is also true that "some A are B." In drawing a conclusion from this premise, people often don't double-check to see if the conclusion would be valid for *all* the different ways of representing it (Johnson-Laird, 1983).

A second disadvantage of making syllogisms more concrete is illustrated by the last item in Table 7.2. It's easy to make a mistake on this type of problem precisely because it is true based on general world knowledge. But

Figure 7.11

Different Representations of the Same Premise

"Some A are B."

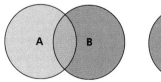

the actual truth of the matter has nothing to do with whether the conclusion follows logically from the premises. Sure, some bananas are yellow, as stated in the conclusion of the sample item, but that conclusion does not follow logically from the premises that are provided.

Conditional Reasoning   Another common type of problem derived from formal logic is that of *conditional reasoning*, which takes the form of "if-then" statements. To see what's involved in conditional reasoning, look at the problem shown in Figure 7.12. You are told that each of the four cards has a number on one side and a letter on the other. Your goal is to test the hypothesis that "*if* a card has a vowel on one side, *then* it has an even number on the other side." Using as few cards as necessary, which cards would you need to turn over in order to adequately test this hypothesis? Think

Figure 7.12

A Conditional-Reasoning Problem

Each of the four cards has a number on one side and a letter on the other. Using as few cards as necessary, test the hypothesis that if a card has a vowel on one side, then it has an even number on the other side (Wason, 1960).

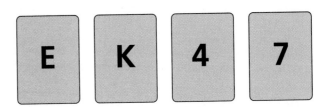

about it. What is your answer? Most people realize that the E has to be turned over. But another card is needed as well. Is it the one with the 4 showing? No, this card doesn't help. If there's a vowel on the other side, the rule could still be invalidated by another card. If there is a consonant, the rule is not invalidated (the rule does not state that a card with a consonant cannot have an even number on the other side). The correct choices are E and 7. A vowel on the other side of the 7 would invalidate the rule. Studies with college students show that only 4 percent of the subjects got the right answer. Most picked the E and the 4, probing only for evidence that was consistent with their hypothesis (Wason, 1960). So if you missed it, you are not alone.

This manifestation of the confirmation bias appears in a wide range of reasoning problems. For example, Deanna Kuhn (1991) interviewed people as to how they would evaluate their beliefs on important real issues (for example, the causes of criminal behavior and school failure) and found that very few subjects realized that to truly evaluate their beliefs, they would need to consider disconfirming evidence. Everyone is vulnerable, sometimes even motivated to confirm their initial beliefs. Case studies in "pathological science" reveal that scientists have been known to test their pet theories in ways that do not allow for disconfirmation (Rousseau, 1992).

Is the confirmation bias an inevitable, fatal flaw in the way human beings reason? Patricia Cheng and her colleagues (1986) found that, compared to people with no formal training in logic, those who had completed a full semester course in this discipline performed only 3 percent better. There is hope, however. Research shows that people perform well on conditional-reasoning tests using more familiar content. For instance, suppose you're trying to test this rule: "If a person is drinking beer, then he or she must be over twenty-one." In front of you are four cards, each with an age written

Figure 7.13

A Conditional-Reasoning Problem with Familiar Context

Each of the four cards has an age on one side and a drink on the other. Using as few cards as necessary, test the hypothesis that if a person is drinking beer, then he or she must be over 21.

on one side and what he or she is drinking written on the other. The four cards read "16," "25," "cola," and "beer." Look at the problem presented in Figure 7.13. Which cards would you turn over? In an actual experiment, 74 percent of the subjects chose "16" and "beer"—which is correct (Griggs & Cox, 1982). Why was there such an improvement, compared to the last experiment? It may be that, because subjects are accustomed to thinking about drinking-age violations, they were reminded in this case to search for disconfirming evidence.

What are the educational implications of this result? Can people be trained in the logic of conditional reasoning? To some extent, yes. But the key may be to teach this form of reasoning through the use of concrete problems, the way psychologists do—not through the presentation of abstract rules, as in philosophy. To test this hypothesis, Michael Morris and Richard Nisbett (1993) assessed the conditional-reasoning performance of first- and third-year graduate students enrolled in psychology or philosophy at Michigan, Chicago, and Brown universities. The results were quite striking. As shown in Figure 7.14, the philosophy students did not improve from the first year to the third. But the psychology students performed 33 percent better in their third year of study than in their first. After being trained to conduct experiments that test causal hypotheses, the psychology students had learned how to reason in "if-then" terms.

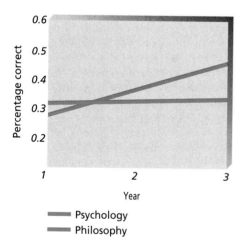

Figure 7.14

Can Conditional Reasoning Be Taught?

In this study, graduate students in psychology and philosophy were tested for conditional reasoning. As shown, psychology students improved from their first to their third year but those in philosophy did not (Morris & Nisbett, 1993).

Biases in Judgment

Should I buy the Toyota wagon or a Ford Taurus, a Macintosh or an IBM PC? Should my wife and I have more children? Should I coach little-league baseball again? Like everyone else, I could continue to list forever the kinds of decisions that are made every day—decisions that are based on intuitive judgments of probability, estimates we make of the likelihood of good and bad outcomes. How do we go about making these judgments? Do the decisions we make match those that we *should* have made, based on actual, objective probabilities? In a series of studies, Daniel Kahneman, Amos Tversky, and others (1982) have found that people consistently use two heuristics in making these kinds of judgments: availability and representativeness.

Availability   One mental shortcut people use is the **availability heuristic,** the tendency to estimate the likelihood of an event based on how easily instances of that event come to mind. To demonstrate, Tversky and Kahneman (1973) asked subjects to judge whether there are more words in English that begin with the letter *k* or the letter *t*. To answer this question, subjects tried to think of words that started with each letter. More words

■ **availability heuristic** A tendency to estimate the likelihood of an event in terms of how easily instances of it can be recalled.

■ **representativeness heuristic** A tendency to estimate the likelihood of an event in terms of how typical it seems.

came to mind that started with *t*, so most subjects correctly chose *t* as the answer. In this case, the availability heuristic was useful. It sure beat counting all the relevant words in the dictionary.

As demonstrated, the availability heuristic enables us to make judgments that are quick and easy—but often these judgments are in error. For example, Tversky and Kahneman asked some subjects the following question: Which is more common, words that start with the letter *k*, or words that contain *k* as the third letter? In actuality, the English language contains many more words with *k* as the third letter than the first; yet, out of 152 subjects, 105 guessed it to be the other way around. The reason for this disparity is that it's easier to bring to mind words that start with *k*, so these are judged more common.

The letter-estimation bias may seem cute and harmless, but the availability heuristic can lead us astray in important ways—as when uncommon events pop easily to mind because they are very recent or highly emotional. One possible consequence concerns the perception of risk. Which is a more likely cause of death in the United States, being killed by falling airplane parts or being attacked by a shark? Shark attacks get more publicity, and most people say it is a more likely cause of death. Yet the chances of dying from falling airplane parts are thirty times greater ("Death Odds," 1990). Similarly, people who are asked to guess the major causes of death tend to overestimate the number of those who die in shootings, fires, floods, terrorist bombings, accidents, and other dramatic events—and underestimate the number of deaths caused by strokes, heart attacks, diabetes, and other mundane and less memorable events (Slovic et al., 1982). With stories of drug dealing featured so prominently in the news, it is no wonder that Americans think that drug abuse is on the rise when, in fact, it is not (Eisenman, 1993).

A second consequence of the availability heuristic is that we are influenced more by one vivid life story than by hard statistical facts. Have you ever wondered why so many people buy lottery tickets despite the low odds, or why so many travelers are afraid to fly even though they're more likely to perish in a car accident? These behaviors are symptomatic of the fact that people are relatively insensitive to numerical probabilities and, instead, are overly influenced by graphic and memorable events like the sight of a multimillion-dollar lottery winner rejoicing on TV, or a photograph of bodies being pulled from the wreckage of a plane crash (Bar-Hillel, 1980). It may not be logical, but one memorable image is worth a thousand numbers.

Representativeness   A second rule of thumb that people use to make probability estimates is the **representativeness heuristic**—the tendency to judge the likelihood of an event by how typical it seems (Kahneman & Tversky, 1973). Like other heuristics, this one enables us to make quick judgments. With speed, however, comes bias and a possible loss of accuracy. For example, which sequence of boys (B) and girls (G) would you say is more likely to occur in a family with six children: (1) B,G,B,G,B,G, (2) B,B,B,G,G,G, or (3) G,B,B,G,G,B? In actuality, these sequences are all equally likely. Yet most people say that the third is more likely than the others because it looks typical of a random sequence. As we'll soon discuss (see box, pages 272–273), this use of the representativeness heuristic can give rise to a "gambler's fallacy" in games of chance.

The problem with this heuristic is that it often leads us to ignore numerical probabilities, or "base rates." Suppose I told you that there is a group of thirty engineers and seventy lawyers. In that group I randomly select a conservative man named Jack, who enjoys mathematical puzzles and has no interest in social or political issues. Question: Is Jack a lawyer or an engineer? When Kahneman and Tversky (1973) presented this item to subjects, most guessed that Jack was an engineer (because he seemed to fit the stereotyped image of an engineer)—even though he came from a group containing a 70 percent majority of lawyers. In this instance, representativeness overwhelmed the more predictive base rate.

Overconfidence Sometimes our judgments are correct, sometimes they are not. Nobody's perfect. But are we sufficiently aware of our own limitations? In a series of experiments, Baruch Fischhoff and his colleagues (1977) had people answer hundreds of general-knowledge questions and estimate the odds that each answer was correct. Consistently, the subjects were overly confident.

In more recent studies, David Dunning and others (1990) asked students to make judgments of a more social nature—to predict how a target person would react in different situations. Some of the subjects made predictions about a fellow student whom they had just met and interviewed, and others made predictions about their roommates. In both cases, the subjects reported their confidence in each prediction, and accuracy was determined by the responses of the target persons themselves. The results were clear: regardless of whether they judged a stranger or their own roommate, subjects consistently overestimated the accuracy of their predictions. These results are illustrated in Figure 7.15.

People even overestimate their ability to predict their own future behavior. When ninety-eight first-year students made 3,800 self-predictions about the upcoming academic year—predictions that were later verified ("Will you decide on a major?" "Will you have a steady boy/girlfriend?" "Will you call your parents more than twice a month?")—they estimated that they would be accurate 82 percent of the time but, in actuality, had an

Figure 7.15

The Overconfidence Effect

Students made 2,760 predictions about others that were later verified. Regardless of whether confidence was low, medium, high, or 100 percent, confidence levels consistently exceeded accuracy rates.

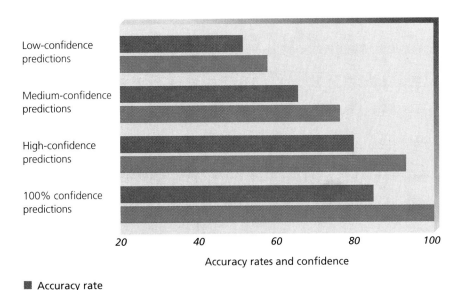

Accuracy rates and confidence

■ Accuracy rate
■ Confidence

Gambling: Irrational Thinking in the Casino

There are only two states that do *not* have some form of legal gambling: Utah and Hawaii.

"I hope to break even today," said one gambler to another. "Why is that?" "I really need the money." Anyone who has played poker for money, dropped coins into a slot machine, bet on a sports event, or bought lottery tickets knows how seductive gambling can be. Every year, people from all walks of life spend unimaginable amounts of money at casinos, racetracks, off-track betting parlors, state lotteries, bingo, and numbers games. Americans spend hundreds of billions of dollars a year in legal and illegal gambling activities, and predictably lose between 5 and 20 percent of that figure (Popkin, 1994).

Gambling is a truly puzzling phenomenon. Ordinarily, people do not like to take large financial risks. Offered a hypothetical choice between receiving a certain 1,000 dollars or a fifty-fifty shot at 2,500 dollars, most people choose the smaller but guaranteed alternative (Kahneman & Tversky, 1984). So why do so many people gamble, and persist in the face of defeat? There are different types of theories. From a cognitive perspective, there are three problems: (1) people seem to think that they have control over chance events, (2) they do not completely understand the laws of probability, and (3) they come up with biased explanations for their wins and losses.

In a series of experiments on the *illusion of control*, Ellen Langer (1975) found that people delude themselves into believing they can control the outcome in games of chance that mimic skill situations. When subjects cut cards against a competitor in a game of high-card, they bet more money when their opponent seemed nervous rather than confident. When subjects played the lottery, they were more reluctant to sell their tickets after choosing a number themselves than after getting an assigned number. This hardly seems rational. But don't many of us fall prey to these same illusions? Watch people playing slot machines and you'll see that they try to influence their luck by moving from one machine to another with coins in hand. Or watch players throwing dice in craps, backgammon, or Monopoly, and you'll notice that they often roll hard for high numbers and soft for low numbers (Henslin, 1967).

The effects on gambling are clear. To exploit our tendency to infuse games of chance with an illusion of control, states now provide an element of choice in their lotteries by having players pick number combinations themselves. Go to the racetrack, and you will find bettors sizing up the horses or studying the data contained in racing forms. In casinos, the dealers are instructed not to intimidate players by shuffling the cards in fancy ways. Why are we so easily fooled? According to Langer, people need to feel that they can control the important events in their lives. Additional research supports this hypothesis. Thankfully, people think more critically and are less vulnerable when the stakes are high (Dunn & Wilson, 1990).

Gambling can also be viewed as an unfortunate outgrowth of misguided notions of *probability* and the predictions that people make about chance events (Wagenaar, 1988). Suppose you flipped a coin six times. Which sequence of heads (H) and tails (T) would you be most likely to get—HHHTTT or HTTHTH? When asked this question, most subjects pick the second alternative. In fact, the two patterns are equally likely. Now suppose you could purchase a lottery ticket containing six numbers out of 40. Would you rather have the numbers 4 33 29 10 2 16, or 1 2 3 4 5 6? Most people would prefer the first ticket over the second. Yet out of the 3,838,380 possible combinations, both are equally likely. Consider another example. In the Pennsylvania Daily Number game, a number

accuracy rate of only 68 percent (Vallone et al., 1990). In later chapters, we'll see that self-confidence in general is a virtue that promotes happiness, health, and success. The key is to avoid becoming so overconfident that we take foolish risks and make hasty decisions.

Framing   Overall, research shows that human beings have some powerful reasoning tools, but that the process is flawed in serious ways. This theme repeats itself as we explore a topic that bridges thought and language. In a classic series of studies, Tversky and Kahneman (1981) found that deci-

Americans lose billions of dollars a year in gambling. Part of the problem is that people believe they can control the outcome of chance events.

machine addicts say that a machine is "hot" if it has not surrendered a jackpot for a long period of time.

Another problem with the way we judge probabilities stems from the *availability heuristic*, the tendency to overestimate the likelihood of dramatic, memorable events (Tversky & Kahneman, 1973). Think about it. One reason people buy lottery tickets despite the dreadfully low odds is that they are too influenced by the sight of multimillion-dollar winners rejoicing on TV. The same is true of casinos. The last time I visited one, I had to fight the sense that everyone was coming up a winner. All around me, people were shrieking with joy, bells, whistles, and sirens were blaring, lights were flashing, and coins were jingling loudly into metal coin trays. What about all those who were losing? They were invisible, a silent majority, nowhere to be seen or heard. If I didn't know any better, I would have thought that everyone was winning except me. Winning was "available" and easy to overestimate.

The fact that we often bet money on the basis of defective prediction strategies explains part of the gambler's dilemma. But it doesn't explain why people persist after losing over and over again. To understand this problem, it is important to know that gamblers generate *biased explanations* for their outcomes. Research shows that people are quick to take credit for success and to explain away failure. For example, Thomas Gilovich (1983) questioned subjects one week after they had bet on a series of pro football games. He found that although they accepted winning without scrutiny, they consistently cited fluke events to explain losses—a fumble on the goal line, an injury to a key player, or a close call by the referee—all to suggest that victory was otherwise close at hand. Can this bias inspire persistent gambling? In basketball, the shot that circles the rim and pops out may bolster the belief that a certain player is hot, but it may also be used to maintain the belief that another player is cold. Likewise, according to Gilovich, the gambler's ace in the hole is to recall a point in time when he or she was winning and should have quit. We have all heard those regretful last words: "I was close; I could have won if. . . ." Well, maybe next time.

between 000 and 999 is randomly drawn every day, and the payoff is always 500 to 1—regardless of how many winners there are. It is not possible to strategically influence one's chances. Yet a study of number selections showed that ticket purchasers shy away from numbers that have won in the recent past (Halpern & Deveraux, 1989). Why?

Kahneman and Tversky (1972) find that the *representativeness heuristic* leads people to falsely assume that any sequence of events, if the result of a truly random process, should "look" random. Since a large number of coin flips will produce roughly 50 percent heads and 50 percent tails, people think that this ratio would emerge even in a small sample of flips. This assumption gives rise to the *gambler's fallacy*— the belief that random processes are self-correcting, that temporary deviations in one direction will be matched by later deviations in the opposite direction. That's why, after a string of heads, people are likely to predict that the next coin will land on its tail; or why, after a long run of red numbers on the roulette wheel, people increase their betting on black numbers. The gambler's fallacy is also the reason many slot-

■ **framing effect** The biasing effects on decision making of the way in which a choice is worded, or "framed."

sions can be influenced by the language used to describe a dilemma. This tendency to be influenced by the way an issue is worded, or "framed," is called the **framing effect**. To demonstrate this phenomenon, researchers present two versions of a problem that are worded differently but are logically equivalent. Rationally speaking, our preferences should be the same in both versions. But that's not what happens.

In one study, a vast majority of subjects thought condoms were effective in stopping AIDS when condoms were said to have a "95 percent success rate," but not when they were said to have a "5 percent failure rate"

(Linville et al., 1992). In a second study, subjects were more likely to favor a new medical treatment when it was said to have a "50 percent success rate" than when it was said to have a "50 percent failure rate" (Levin et al., 1988). And in a third study, consumers preferred ground beef that was labeled "75 percent lean" rather than "25 percent fat" (Levin & Gaeth, 1988).

Framing effects seem to indicate that people's judgments are not always well reasoned. Still, it's important to note that we do tend to make satisfactory choices given time constraints and limitations in our ability to keep track of alternatives (Simon, 1991). Sure, we all make poor decisions that we later regret, but psychologists disagree on the extent of the problem (Payne et al., 1992). It's also helpful to know that people can be taught in college and other educational settings to reason in more logical ways (Lehman & Nisbett, 1990; Nisbett et al., 1987).

There is, finally, another lesson to be drawn from framing effects. At the beginning of this chapter, we briefly considered the relationship between thought and language. In that context, framing effects suggest that thinking may be shaped by language. We'll take up this issue again, after surveying what is known about the nature of language.

LANGUAGE

A colleague's friend, who happens to be an experimental psychologist, had a frightening experience a few years ago. While talking to a graduate student, he found himself suddenly unable to recall words that are basic to his work, like "data" and "experiment." These words were not on the tip of his tongue, waiting to be retrieved. Instead he was suffering from *anomia,* an inability to recall familiar words. While in this state, he knew what concepts he wanted to express but could not come up with the verbal labels. Fortunately, the experience lasted for only forty-five minutes. It was caused by a temporary reduction of blood flow to part of the left hemisphere of his brain. With surgery, doctors were able to prevent a relapse. If the anomia had resulted from brain damage—due to a stroke, for example—the effects would have been more lasting.

Two lessons relevant to the study of language can be drawn from this episode (Ashcraft, 1993). First, anomia suggests that there is an important distinction between concepts and the words used to represent them. Even when our semantic networks are functioning normally, we can lose the connections between concepts and their verbal representations. The implication is that thought and language are not identical. Second, anomia illustrates that in trying to understand the psychology of language, it often helps to study people with language disturbances, or **aphasias.** Anomia is one type of aphasia. Two other types are Broca's aphasia and Wernicke's aphasia. A person with *Broca's aphasia* can comprehend language but has difficulty producing fluent speech. A person with *Wernicke's aphasia* can speak fluently but suffers in comprehension.

People who lose part of their capacity for language find the experience to be terribly distressing. This is not surprising. Language is essential to social living and is one of the most important milestones in human evolution

■ **aphasias** Language disturbances, often caused by left-hemisphere damage, that disrupt speech production or comprehension.

(Pinker, 1990). One source of evidence for the evolutionary significance of language is that human beings acquired the capacity for speech despite some physical limitations that came with this capacity. For example, the human vocal tract is ideal for the production of many sounds, but the arrangement of the larynx and tongue make it unusually easy for humans, compared to other animals, to choke while swallowing food (Lieberman, 1984).

Communication in the Animal Kingdom

Among humans, language is a primary means of communication. Other animal species have complex forms of communication as well. *Ants* send chemical signals secreted from glands to share information about food and enemies with other members of the colony. When *honeybees* discover a source of nectar, they return to the hive and communicate its location to the other worker bees through an intricate dance that signals both direction and distance. Male *songbirds* of various species sing in the spring to attract a female mate and also to warn other males to stay away from his territory to avoid a fight. *Dolphins* talk to each other at great depths of the ocean by making a combination of clicking, whistling, and barking sounds. Vervet *monkeys* grunt quietly at each other in relaxed social situations but give off loud alarm calls that differ in sound according to whether the predator they see is a snake, eagle, or leopard.

There is no doubt that animals communicate with one another in ways that benefit their own survival. When the honeybee locates nectar and performs its dance, other bees leave the hive and buzz straight to the source—even if the one that discovered it is detained (von Frisch, 1974). And when a monkey produces an alarm call, other members of the group take action. Among East African vervets, for example, a snake alarm leads others in the group to stand tall and peer into the grass, an eagle call leads them to look

The spring song of the male bluebird and the howling of the desert coyote are two of the many adaptive forms of intraspecies communication found in the animal kingdom.

up and duck into bushes, and a leopard call leads them to run up into a tree (Cheney & Seyfarth, 1992). There are many other marvelous examples of adaptations that serve species well. So why do some scientists claim that "language" is a uniquely human capacity? To answer this question, we need to know more about what language is and the properties that are used to define it.

Characteristics of Human Language

According to *The Universal Almanac* of 1994, there are between four thousand and ten thousand languages worldwide, to say nothing of the different dialects within each language. When the dialects are taken into account, tens of thousands of variations can be distinguished. It's amazing how different the many languages seem. To appreciate this point, consider the principal languages, ranked in order of usage in the world's population: Chinese, English, Hindi, Arabic, Russian, Malay, Bengali, Spanish, French, Japanese, Portuguese, German, and Urdu. Despite the differences among them, however, all languages share three essential properties: semanticity, generativity, and displacement.

At a produce market in Beijing, this man and woman converse in Chinese—the most widely spoken language in the world.

■ **semanticity** The property of language that accounts for the communication of meaning.

■ **morphemes** In language, the smallest units that carry meaning (e.g., prefixes, root words, suffixes).

■ **phonemes** The basic, distinct sounds of a spoken language.

Semanticity   **Semanticity** refers to the fact that there are separate units in a language and that these units have *meaning*. The smallest unit that carries meaning is called a **morpheme**. Every word has one or more morphemes. Simple words like *dog, run,* and *think* contain one. The word *unthinkable* has three morphemes, the prefix *un-,* the root word *think,* and the suffix *able*—and each adds to the total meaning of the word.

In all spoken languages, morphemes are composed of **phonemes**, the basic *sounds* of a language. Each separate sound you hear when you pronounce the word *unthinkable* is one phoneme. English has twenty-six letters, but forty to forty-five phonemes. The word *tip* has three phonemes: *t, i,* and *p.* So do the words *ship* (*sh, i,* and *p*) and *chip* (*ch, i,* and *p*). Linguists estimate that human beings are physiologically capable of producing one hundred basic sounds. No one language uses all of these, however, as most languages contain between twenty and eighty phonemes. English speakers say *s* and *z* differently. In Spanish, they're one and the same. Due to such differences in experience, people sometimes have trouble pronouncing the phonemes of other languages. For example, many Americans struggle to roll the German *r* or to cough up the guttural *ch* sound of Arabic.

It is quite remarkable that human beings are able to master a full language vocabulary so well, and so quickly, given that most word sounds are unrelated to meaning. There is no reason why a cat is called a *C-A-T* as opposed to a *D-O-G*. It just happens to be that way. There are some exceptions to this rule, as some words resemble the sounds they signify (examples include the words *bang* and *crack*). Incidentally, some animal communication signals also seem arbitrary. For example, the East African vervet monkey makes a "chutter" sound to signify the presence of snakes, a two-syllable cough for eagles, and a loud barking call for leopards (Cheney & Seyfarth, 1992).

Generativity A second property of language is **generativity**, the capacity to use a finite number of words, and rules for combining words, to produce an infinite variety of novel expressions. Think about it. When I spoke to my mother last week, she said, "So what do you think, will you, Carol, and the kids be able to make it in this weekend for Lauren's birthday, I mean, can you take the time off?" It's a pretty mundane sentence. But I'll bet no one in history had ever uttered it before. Generativity gives language unlimited flexibility as a communication system.

There are two features of human language that enable this flexibility: iteration and recursion. *Iteration* means that a phrase can always be added to the end of a sentence in order to form an entirely new sentence. Through iteration, one can go from the sentence "I really like psychology" to "I really like psychology this semester" to "I really like psychology this semester, thanks to the professor," and so on. *Recursion* refers to a related fact of language, that one expression can always be inserted inside another. This makes possible the construction of long, embedded sentences.

People usually understand iterative and recursive sentences quite easily. But they can become mentally taxing. If you ever sat on a jury, you'd know exactly what I mean. At the end of every trial, the judge instructs the jury on the law that should guide their decision making. Jurors are ordinary folks, not law school graduates. Yet the instructions they receive are often so filled with iterations and recursions that it's practically impossible to understand them. The following instruction on the term *negligence,* commonly used by judges, illustrates the point:

> One test that is helpful in determining whether or not a person was negligent is to ask and answer whether or not, if a person of ordinary prudence had been in the same situation and possessed the same knowledge, he would have foreseen or anticipated that someone might have been injured by or as a result of his action or inaction (Kassin & Wrightsman, 1988, p. 150).

If language is so generative that we can produce limitless numbers of novel sentences, how are we able to comprehend each other as competently as we do? The key to managing generativity is **syntax**, rules of grammar

■ **generativity** The property of language that accounts for the capacity to use a limited number of words to produce an infinite variety of expressions.

■ **syntax** Rules of grammar that govern the arrangement of words in a sentence.

that govern how words can be arranged in a sentence. Expressions are not random strings of unrelated words but, rather, words that are combined in familiar and orderly ways. Every language has its own unique syntax. For example, adjectives usually come *before* the noun in English (*white wine*) but *after* the noun in Spanish (*vino blanca*). We'll see in Chapter 9 that children learn to speak correctly by the age of five, and do so without explicit instruction. Hardly anyone can explain the rules of grammar, yet most of us can instantly spot a statement that violates these rules. Which us brings another point to. . . .

This brings us to another point about the generativity of language: that any one thought can be expressed in different ways. Regardless of whether I say, "Briana won a medal," "A medal was won by Briana," or "What Briana won was a medal," you would grasp the underlying meaning. Linguist Noam Chomsky (1957) explained this phenomenon by distinguishing between the deep structure and surface structure of language. The *deep structure* refers to the underlying meaning of a statement, apart from the particular way that it is expressed. The *surface structure* consists of the words that are actually used to communicate that meaning. According to Chomsky, syntax provides us with a set of "transformational" rules for how to (1) put meaning into words when we speak, and (2) derive meaning from words when we are spoken to (see Figure 7.16).

Figure 7.16

Relationship Between Deep Structure And Surface Structure

According to Chomsky, syntax provides a set of rules for transforming meaning (deep structure) into words (surface structure), and vice versa. As shown, transformational rules enable us to express the same idea in different ways.

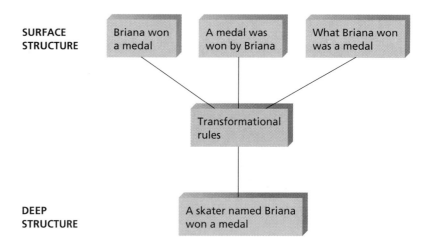

Some transformations are easier to process than others. For example, Daniel Slobin (1966) asked people to read active sentences ("The dog is chasing the cat") or passive sentences ("The cat is being chased by the dog") and to decide which of two pictures (a dog chasing a cat, or a cat chasing a dog) illustrated the sentence. He found that both children and adults were faster at choosing the correct picture when the sentence was active. Apparently, passively constructed sentences require extra transformations, and therefore more time, to get to the deep structure. The nature of the rules of transformation are not completely understood, and psychologists disagree over how such rules are implemented in the brain (Pinker, 1990; Rumelhart & McClelland, 1986). Still, the evidence suggests that we are on the right track in considering syntax to be separate from, but interacting with, meaning.

Displacement   A third property of language is displacement. **Displacement** refers to the fact that language can be used to communicate about things that are not in our immediate surroundings, matters that extend beyond the limits of the here-and-now. Thus, we reminisce about the good old days, talk about our hopes and dreams for the future, gossip about others behind their backs, and discuss abstract ideas concerning God, politics, social justice, and love.

As a means of communication, language is a social activity—and displacement enables us to tell others what we're thinking, how we're feeling, or what we plan to do next. These are complex messages, however, and social interaction is just that, a two-way interaction. To converse with others effectively, therefore, we need more tools than are provided by an extensive vocabulary and an arcane knowledge of grammar. We must also have a sense of the *pragmatics,* or social context, of language, along with an understanding of how to use it. In the words of Herbert Clark (1985), "Language is a social instrument. When we talk, we direct our words not to the air but to other people" (p. 179). Accordingly, says Clark, there are intricate rules that guide the way speakers and listeners position themselves physically from each other, take turns in conversation, and communicate through the face, voice, body, and other nonverbal channels. We also tailor our statements according to the person we're talking to and the situation we're in. People take language pragmatics for granted. Tension may thus result when these pragmatics break down—as when people from different cultures neglect to realize that the person they're trying to communicate with does not know their local expressions, jargon, and buzzwords (Axtell, 1993). In a book entitled *You Just Don't Understand,* sociolinguist Deborah Tannen (1990) claims that male-female conflicts often arise because of gender differences in communication style, or pragmatics.

To illustrate the importance of pragmatics, consider the story of an early attempt to use computers to translate text from one language to another. After programming a computer to translate material from English to Russian, researchers gave the computer the task of decoding "The spirit is willing, but the flesh is weak." As the story goes, the Russian translation came out, "The vodka is fine, but the meat is tasteless." So much for machines. In the absence of pragmatic knowledge, ironic or metaphoric expressions are likely to be interpreted in rather bizarre ways (Simpson, 1989).

Can Animals Learn Language?

Philosophers and scientists have long regarded the capacity for language and abstract thought as uniquely human, the dividing line between us and other animals. Is this still considered to be true, or has a new breed of "cognitive ethologists"—studying the once-taboo topic of animal thinking and awareness (Griffin, 1992; Ristau, 1991; Wasserman, 1993)—discovered something new?

The Talking Parrot   At center stage in this emerging area are research projects aimed at teaching rudimentary language to nonhuman animals. In one such project, Irene Pepperberg (1991) has spent more than fifteen years teaching English to Alex, a one-pound African gray parrot. Everyone

■ **displacement** The property of language that accounts for the capacity to communicate about matters that are not in the here-and-now.

Alex, the African gray parrot, prepares to answer the question, "What toy is blue and triangular?"

knows that these birds can "parrot" what people say, but do they understand the words they use? Pepperberg makes a compelling case. She'll pick up an object from a crowded tray and ask, "What toy?" In response, Alex will often name the object ("block") and respond at an 80 percent level of accuracy to questions about its color ("red"), shape ("square"), and substance ("wood"). Overall, Alex can use seventy-one words to name more than thirty objects, seven colors, five shapes, five numbers, actions, and materials. More often than not, he can also tell whether an object is the same as or different from, or bigger or smaller than, something else. He can even count how many items there are in a collection of items ranging from one to six (Pepperberg, 1994).

The Bottlenosed Dolphins   In Hawaii, Louis Herman and his colleagues (1993) have been studying the language capabilities of two bottlenosed dolphins, Phoenix and Akeakamai. In this project, the researchers communicate with one dolphin by using hand gestures and with the other dolphin through electronic whistle-like sounds transmitted through an underwater speaker system. In both cases, the distinct gestures or sounds refer to objects that are in the tank, the relationships between objects, actions to be taken, and location. The behavior of these sea mammals is astonishing in many ways. For example, when given commands consisting of two- to five-word sentences such as "right water left Frisbee fetch"—which means "take the Frisbee on your left to the stream of water on your right"—the dolphins perform to specification. Even more impressive is the fact that they are responsive to changes in syntax. The dolphins were trained in a system in which modifiers precede objects ("left Frisbee") and objects precede actions ("Frisbee fetch"). So, when a command violates these rules of grammar, they do not obey. Just how impressive are these dolphins? "If you accept that semantics and syntax are core attributes of human language," says Herman, "then we have shown that dolphins also account for these two features within the limits of this language" (Linden, 1993, p. 58).

What do these projects tell us about the capacity of animals for language? Cognitive ethologists believe they are shattering old assumptions and breaking new ground, while skeptics claim that these studies show little more than mimicry and rote learning. Before addressing this controversy, however, let's first examine the most impressive evidence for the claim—evidence derived from our closest animal relatives, the great apes.

"Although humans make sounds with their mouths and occasionally look at each other, there is no solid evidence that they actually comunicate with each other."

The Great Apes By today's standards, early attempts to teach language to apes were misguided. In 1933, psychologists Winthrop and Luella Kellogg raised a baby chimpanzee alongside their own son and tried to treat them in the same way. Their son learned to coo, babble, and speak on schedule; the chimp did not. A similar attempt was later made by Cathy Hayes (1951), who found that her chimpanzee could recognize pictures, categorize objects, and imitate complex behaviors, but could not speak more than a few rudimentary words. After six years of intensive training, all the chimp could say were "cup," "up," "mama," and "papa." Conclusion: apes do not have the cognitive capacity for language.

The problem with these studies is like the problem with Watson's definition of thought as subvocal speech. Chimps may not have the vocal musculature for uttering human phonemes, but is speech a necessary criterion for language? Of course not. What about the symbols on this page, the characters found in other alphabets, the printed characters in Braille that enable blind people to read, and the sign languages used by those who are deaf? To overcome the vocalization problem, psychologists had to take creative new approaches, and they did. David Premack (1971) taught a chimp named Sarah to communicate by placing colored plastic chips, symbolizing words, on a magnetic board. Duane Rumbaugh (1977) taught a chimp named Lana to communicate by pressing keys on a specially designed computer. Some of the most impressive projects involved the use of American Sign Language (ASL). Allen and Beatrice Gardner (1969) taught sign language to Washoe and four other chimps. Within four years, Washoe had a vocabulary of 132 words and the ability to combine signs in order to form simple sentences. Most astonishing is that Washoe and her friends communicated to each other in sign language, and she even taught her adopted young son 68 different signs (Fouts et al., 1989)—without the aid of human trainers! Also using sign language, Herbert Terrace (1986) trained a chimp he called Nim Chimpsky (after the famous linguist Noam Chomsky), and Francine Patterson and Eugene Linden (1981) trained a gorilla named Koko, whose 600-word vocabulary is the largest recorded so far.

Combining the various techniques, Sue Savage-Rumbaugh and her colleagues (1986) taught a young pygmy chimp named Kanzi to talk by making hand signals, pointing to geometric symbols on a laminated board, and punching these same symbols on a special keyboard. Kanzi also understands spoken English. What sets this project apart from the others was that Kanzi learned the language the way human children do: not by explicit instruction, but by mere exposure. The researchers had trained Kanzi's mother, and he learned by watching. As Savage-Rumbaugh put it, "If Kanzi could learn without instruction, I wondered, why teach?" (Linden, 1993, p. 57).

The Controversy The feats of Sarah, Lana, Washoe, Nim, Koko, Kanzi, and others are impressive, even to critics. Clearly, these animals are smart and quite capable of learning. But is what they learned "language"? Some say yes, others say no. What do *you* think? Let's stop for a moment and focus this debate on the question of whether these evolutionary relatives of ours show the properties of semanticity, generativity, and displacement in their "language" behavior.

Semanticity   Just about everyone agrees that the various language apes satisfy this criterion. With vocabularies ranging from 130 to 600, these apes can produce words for concrete objects (*me, chair*), action verbs (*tickle, eat*), and even adjectives (*big, happy*). And they know more than simple rote associations between signs or symbols and objects. Sherman, a chimp trained by Sue Savage-Rumbaugh, pointed to the symbol "food" when shown a real banana or the symbol for banana. Koko the gorilla signed "finger bracelet" to describe a ring and "eye hat" to describe a mask (Patterson & Linden, 1981). And Kanzi, the chimpanzee with the most advanced language skills, reacted appropriately to slightly different requests, such as "show me the light," "bring me the light," and "turn the light on" (Savage-Rumbaugh, 1990).

Kanzi, the chimpanzee with the most advanced language skills, can "talk" by making hand signals—and by pointing to symbols on a special board.

Generativity   Can the apes combine words in lawful ways to produce novel expressions? Some researchers find that their apes do not distinguish between two-word combinations based on how the words are ordered (Terrace, 1986). But others find that their apes do use syntax to combine words and form sentences they have never heard before. Syntax? Yes. When Washoe wanted to be tickled, she would sign, "You tickle Washoe." When she wanted to do the tickling, it was "Washoe tickle you" (Gardner & Gardner, 1978). When Lana wanted a caretaker's orange but had no word for this fruit, she improvised by punching in the symbols for "Tim give apple which-is orange" (Rumbaugh, 1977). Kanzi also understands sentences he never heard before. Once, with his back to the speaker, Kanzi heard "Jeanie hid the pine needles in her shirt." Immediately, he turned around, walked to Jeanie, and searched her shirt (Savage-Rumbaugh, 1990).

Displacement   The most demanding criterion for language is displacement, the use of words to talk about matters that are not in the immediate surroundings. People do it all the time, but what about the language apes? Florence Patterson claims that Koko the gorilla used signs to make statements about past events, and to express feelings—such as sadness over the death of her pet kitten (Patterson & Linden, 1981). Savage-Rumbaugh (1990) reports that Kanzi also refers to past events. When a trainer asked Kanzi about a wound on his body, he replied, "Matata hurt"—presumably referring to the fact that Matata, his mother, had bitten him over an hour earlier. These types of stories are not common, but they capture the imagination.

Conclusion   The evidence is tantalizing, but skeptics insist that it's open to interpretation. Herbert Terrace (1985) argues that many of the "spontaneous" signs may simply be imitations of or conditioned responses to subtle cues provided by the trainers. Further, he notes, researchers who work with the apes sometimes lose their objectivity and see what they're hoping to see. Maybe, maybe not.

In the most impressive study to date, Savage-Rumbaugh and her colleagues (1993) compared Kanzi's comprehension abilities to those of a two-year-old girl named Alia. Clearly, no ape can *produce* language the way a normal human child can, but how much do they *know*? Research with aphasia patients indicates that language *production* and *comprehension* are based in different parts of the brain, and research with toddlers indicates that they understand more than they're able to say, so there is reason to believe that this is an important distinction to make. In an extensive series of tests, which took nine months to complete, Kanzi and Alia were compared for their responses to 660 commands that were made in spoken English. The sentences were new to both subjects, they were structured in several different ways, and they often combined objects in ways that had never been encountered before ("Put the melon in the potty," "Go get the carrot in the microwave"). To ensure that the subjects could not pick up subtle clues from the experimenters' nonverbal behavior, the commands were given by one experimenter over an intercom, and the subjects' behavior was recorded by a second experimenter from behind a one-way mirror. As it turned out, Kanzi responded correctly to 74 percent of the sentences, Alia to 65 percent. Both exhibited comprehension of spoken language, semantics, and syntax. There's no doubt about it. Kanzi, and presumably other language apes as well, know far more than they can tell (see Table 7.3).

So what are we to conclude? It is clear that apes can be taught words and can understand sentences in which these words are combined according to rules of grammar. Anecdotes suggest that they can even "talk" about past events. It is equally clear, however, that the apes have a smaller vocabulary and a simpler syntax than is found in older children. There's also no evidence to suggest that they can talk about abstract matters, such as whether humans can master language. As far as many scientists are concerned, the bright line that separates "us" and "them" is not as bright as once thought. At this point, however, it's best to conclude that what these apes have learned is a "protolanguage"—a form of language that is cruder and more rudimentary than ours.

Table 7.3

Kanzi's Knowledge of English

This is a sample of the 660 requests made to Kanzi. Words and syntax were varied, and comprehension was measured by the correctness of his behavioral response, where C = correct, PC = partially correct, and N = incorrect (Savage-Rumbaugh et al., 1993).

Sentence	Kanzi's Response	Scoring
"Throw the orange to Rose."	Kanzi picks up the orange, turns, and hands it to Rose.	PC
"Make the snake bite the doggie."	He picks up the toy snake and puts it on top of the toy dog.	C
"Make the doggie bite the snake."	He picks up the toy dog and puts it on top of the snake.	C
"Can you pour the ice water in the potty?"	He picks up the bowl of ice water, heads toward the potty, and carefully pours it in.	C
"Take the telephone to the colony room."	He goes to the colony room, but takes nothing with him.	PC
"Put the raisins in the yogurt."	He pours the yogurt on the raisins.	N
"Put the monster mask on your head."	He drops the orange he is eating into the monster mask and puts it on his head.	C
"Give the lighter and the shoe to Rose."	He hands Rose the lighter, then points to some food in a bowl that he would like to eat.	PC
"Hide the toy gorilla, hide him."	He tries to push the toy gorilla under the fence.	C

THE RELATION BETWEEN THOUGHT AND LANGUAGE

This chapter opened with Watson's hypothesis that thinking is merely subvocal speech. We now know that Watson was wrong—and that thought and language are separate but interrelated cognitive activities. Having examined these two activities separately, we are faced with the question, What is the nature of their interrelationship?

The Linguistic Relativity Hypothesis

"The mystery of language was revealed to me . . . Everything had a name, and each name gave birth to a new thought."

HELEN KELLER

The traditional, intuitive position is that language is a tool for expressing thought, that thought → language. Consistent with this view, child development researchers often find that young children understand concepts before they have the words to explain them (Flavell et al., 1993). But what about the reverse sequence that language → thought? Does language have the power to shape thought? In the 5th century B.C., Herodotus, a Greek historian, argued that Greeks and Egyptians thought differently because the Greeks wrote from left to right and Egyptians from right to left. Inspired by anthropologist Edward Sapir, Benjamin Lee Whorf (1956), a self-educated

■ linguistic relativity hypothesis The hypothesis that language determines, or at least influences, the way we think.

linguist, theorized that the language we speak—the words, syntax, and so on—shapes the way we conceptualize the world. This notion, that our thoughts are "relative" to our linguistic heritage, is known as the **linguistic relativity hypothesis.**

Whorf's hypothesis gave rise to a profound prediction: that people of different cultures think in different ways (Lucy, 1992). To illustrate, Whorf pointed to cultural differences in the use of words to represent reality. He noted, for example, that although English has only one word for *snow*, Eskimos have several words—and that this enables them to make mental distinctions that others may miss between "falling snow, snow on the ground, snow packed hard like ice, slushy snow, wind-driven flying snow—whatever the situation may be" (p. 216). Even grammar shapes thought, claimed Whorf. For example, he compared English to the language of the Hopi Indians. In English you can use the same numerical modifier for units of time ("five days") as for concrete objects ("five pebbles"). In the Hopi language, by contrast, different numerical modifiers are used in each case. Whorf argued that this feature causes the speakers of each language to perceive time differently.

Evaluating the linguistic relativity hypothesis is not easy because people who speak different languages differ in other ways as well. Many bilingual people claim that Whorf is right, citing as personal evidence the odd sense that they think differently in each language—and get "lost in translation" (Hoffman, 1989; Wierzbicka, 1985). Critics, however, point to flaws in both the theory and the research. First, even if members of two cultures think differently, who's to say that the difference in language came first? Second, Eskimos may have more words for snow than do others of North America, but does that mean they think about snow differently? New Englanders, and presumably people from other regions as well, distinguish between slush, fresh powder, packed powder, wet snow, and the "loose granular" substance often found on ski slopes. We may not have an extensive vocabulary for snow, but we can still make the distinctions. The same is true of color. Eleanor Rosch (1973) studied the Dani, an aboriginal people living in Papua New Guinea. Compared to English, which has eleven basic color words, the Dani language has only two basic color words, one for light hues, one for dark. Can Dani speakers make fine color discriminations? Yes. They recognize differences among colors of the same name the way non-Eskimos distinguish between types of snow.

Today, nobody believes that language *determines* thought the way genes determine a person's height. But most psychologists do agree with a less radical claim, that language *influences* the way we think (Bloom, 1981; Hardin & Banaji, 1993; Hunt & Agnoli, 1991; Lucy, 1992). There are numerous examples to illustrate this point. In one study, researchers showed subjects line drawings and varied the label that accompanied each one (see Figure 7.17). Later, subjects redrew these figures from memory in ways that were distorted by the labels (Carmichael et al., 1932). In a second study, which was described in Chapter 6, subjects were shown a film of a collision and asked how fast the cars were going when they "hit," "smashed," "collided with," "bumped into," or "contacted" each other. Everyone saw the same film, yet subjects who received the "smash" question estimated the fastest speed whereas those who received the "contact" question estimated the slowest (Loftus & Palmer, 1974). In a third study,

Like Eskimos, skiers make distinctions between fresh powder, packed powder, loose granular, and other types of snow.

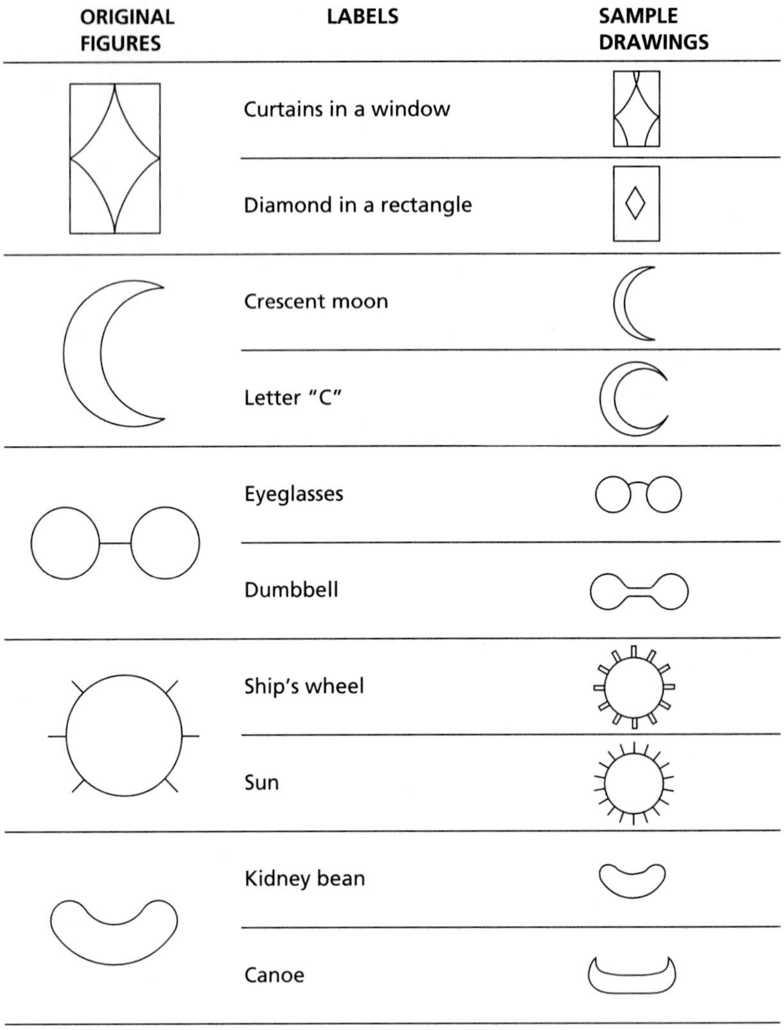

Figure 7.17

Words That Distort Memory for Images

Subjects who saw figures like those shown (left) later redrew these figures from memory in ways that fit the different labels they had been given (right).

ORIGINAL FIGURES	LABELS	SAMPLE DRAWINGS
	Curtains in a window	
	Diamond in a rectangle	
	Crescent moon	
	Letter "C"	
	Eyeglasses	
	Dumbbell	
	Ship's wheel	
	Sun	
	Kidney bean	
	Canoe	

subjects were presented with pictures of faces or color chips, and half were asked to describe them. Those who had put what they saw into words later had more difficulty recognizing the original faces and colors. Did language in this case disrupt thought? Yes, according to the investigators, "some things are better left unsaid" (Schooler & Engstler-Schooler, 1990).

Bringing linguistic relativity back to the cultural domain, Curt Hoffman and his colleagues (1986) studied bilingual Chinese-English speakers. These investigators presented descriptions of fictional characters whose personalities could be summarized easily by a single label in either Chinese or English, but not in both. For example, English has the stereotypic term *artistic* for someone who paints, lives an unconventional lifestyle, and is imaginative, moody, and intense (the Chinese language has a word for people who are talented in art, but this same word implies nothing about temperament or lifestyle). In contrast, Chinese has the term *shi gu* to describe someone who is worldly, experienced, socially skilled, devoted to family, and somewhat reserved (English does not have a single word for this particular collection of traits). Does having an economical term for a type of person make it easier to process information about others? By random assignment, some of the bilingual subjects took the experiment in English, others took it in Chinese. Consistent with the linguistic relativity hypothesis, subjects formed quicker, more stereotyped impressions of artistic types when they "thought" in English and of shi gu types when they "thought" in Chinese.

If language can influence thought, then words are tools that can be used to socialize our children, sell products, mold public opinion, and stir the masses. People in power are well aware of this connection, and go out of their way to choose their words carefully. As colorfully documented by author William Lutz (1989), the result is *doublespeak*—language that is designed to mislead, conceal, inflate, confuse, and distort meaning. Thus, we are told that the new tax is just a "user's fee," that acid rain is "poorly buffered precipitation," that a recession is "negative economic growth," that a bomb is a "vertically deployed anti-personnel device," that civilian war deaths are "collateral damage," and that plastic handbags are made of "genuine imitation leather."

Psychological Impact of Sexist Language

At the start of the 1993–1994 academic year, Williams College celebrated its bicentennial and rewrote its catalog. Despite two hundred years of tradition, the term *freshman* was replaced by *first-year student*. In that same year, controversy exploded at the University of Massachusetts over whether it should retain or change the name of its sports teams, now called the "Minutemen." In both cases, the existing terms were labeled sexist for using the generic masculine form.

Whatever the political arguments, the psychological question is, Does sexist language influence the way we think about men and women? What do you think? Is the term *mail carrier* rather than *mailman* silly and awkward, or does the change help break down gender stereotypes? Does it seem harmless or sexist to talk about "the evolution of *man*," our "fore*fathers*," "*brother*hood," and the "chair*man* of the board"? And what about the generic use of the masculine pronoun *he* to refer to all human beings? Is it okay to say that "a doctor must be well trained if *he* is to be competent?" Consistent with the linguistic relativity hypothesis, many people feel strongly about this issue.

For psychologists, the task is to determine whether the use of generic masculine nouns and pronouns triggers images of men to the exclusion of women. Consistently, the results of this research support the hypothesis: *man, he,* and other masculine words, even when used generically, lead people to think of men. In one study, for example, male and female college students were asked to make up stories based on a topic sentence: "In a large co-educational institution, the average student will feel isolated in _____ courses." Into the blank, the researchers inserted the pronoun *his, his or her,* or *their*. Did the pronoun in the topic sentence make a difference? Yes, when *his* rather than a neutral term was used, 65 percent of the stories written were about men (Moulton et al., 1978). Similar results have been found in studies of both adults and school-aged children (Hamilton, 1988; Hyde, 1984; Ng, 1990; Switzer, 1990).

In a study with particularly disturbing implications, John Briere and Cheryl Lanktree (1983) had one group of college students read a passage from a 1972 version of the American Psychological Association's statement of ethical standards (the statement has since been revised). For example, part of the passage read: "The psychologist believes in the dignity and worth of the individual human being. He is committed to increasing man's understanding of himself and others." Another group of students read the same passage, but rewritten in gender-neutral language. Subjects in both groups were asked to rate the attractiveness of a career in psychology for males and females. The result: Those given the original wording rated a career in psychology as less attractive for women than did subjects given the neutral wording. Clearly, the use of generic masculine terms is exclusive, not inclusive, of women. Some suggestions for how to avoid sexism in your own writing are presented in Table 7.4.

Table 7.4

Guidelines for Nonsexist Language

Common sexist terms	Nonsexist alternatives
man, mankind	people, humanity, human beings, the human species
manpower	work force, personnel, workers, human resources
freshman	first-year student
chairman	head, chair, chairperson
foreman	supervisor
policeman	police officer
he, his, him	he or she, his or her, him or her, *or* they, their, them
mothering	parenting, nurturing, caregiving
female doctor, male nurse	doctor, nurse

Whorf's original hypothesis, that we can think only in terms provided for in language, was undoubtedly overstated. But this should not blind us to the fact that language does make it easier to conceptualize the world in some ways rather than others. The use of sexist words is one practical implication of linguistic relativity, but there are other implications, too. In the global village, translating ideas from one language to another is tricky, and sometimes results in misunderstanding. We need to recognize that the people of the world do not just speak differently but also interpret events through different lenses. Certainly more research is needed to explore this link between language and thought and what it means for intercultural relations.

Learning to Think Critically

"Many people would sooner die than think. In fact, they do."

BERTRAND RUSSELL

Psychologists who study the processes of thought and language—like those who study learning and memory—have come to realize that people are complex, "two-headed" creatures, competent in some ways, flawed in others. Often we solve difficult problems through trial and error, algorithms,

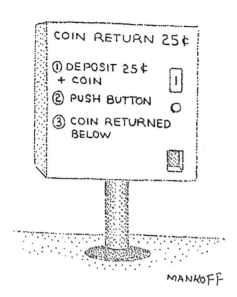

Con artists prosper from people who do not think critically.

© 1994 Robert Mankoff and The Cartoon Bank, Inc.

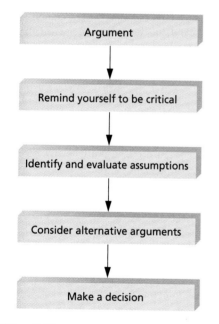

Figure 7.18

Steps in Critical Thinking

■ **critical thinking** The process of solving problems and making decisions through a careful evaluation of evidence.

heuristics, and a great capacity for creative insight. Yet often we get stuck, mentally, and fail to find obvious solutions because of functional fixedness, mental sets, and confirmation biases that keep us from fully testing out our ideas. The same dual portrait characterizes the way people make decisions. Sometimes, we're capable of performing feats of formal logic, as in problems involving syllogistic and conditional reasoning. Yet often we put our minds on "autopilot" and allow ourselves to be misled by availability, representativeness, framing effects, and other heuristics. Then there's language. Despite recent successes in teaching apes to communicate, it is clear that the human capacity for language—whether measured by semanticity, generativity, or displacement—is impressive and unmatched. Yet it is also clear that words can be used to shape, and sometimes distort, the way we think. People are complicated, multidimensional creatures, both competent and flawed at the same time.

The good news is, we have the capacity to improve upon the way we think and, therefore, upon our ability to adapt to changing circumstances. Earlier, we saw that even when we feel we're stumped on a problem, it is possible to find the insight we need by representing it in a different way, opening our minds to alternative approaches, or perhaps just taking a break. We also saw that people can be taught to reason in more logical ways. In short, there are many ways for us to maximize the use of our cognitive abilities.

The keys to success can be summarized by the term **critical thinking**. Critical thinking means solving problems and making decisions through a careful evaluation of evidence. When faced with important issues, forget old rules of thumb, scrutinize what others say, consider their motives and emotions, probe beneath the surface of words, and consider the logic of the arguments. And if you can—don't rush to judgment, take your time. Thinking critically about the arguments that others make, or that you make to yourself, can improve the quality of your decision making (Kuhn, 1991). See Figure 7.18 for a summary of the steps involved in critical thinking.

The first step is to adopt an attitude of healthy skepticism. Most of us are not in the habit of probing for logical flaws in arguments, especially in the claims we make to ourselves—as shown by the research on the confirmation bias. So, thinking critically requires conscious effort. The next step is to identify the assumptions that are quietly made in an argument and consider whether they should be challenged. At times, a speaker's assumptions are clear from his or her use of facts. The problem is, people often present as "facts" assumptions that need verification. It's also important to avoid being unduly influenced by smooth talking and jargon. A set of arguments may sound compelling, but are they, really? Next, open your mind, step out of your "mental set," and try to imagine and evaluate alternative arguments. Is it possible that these alternatives are better than the ones being proposed? This step is especially hard when you're trying to imagine alternatives to your own assertions (Kuhn, 1991; Zechmeister & Johnson, 1992). Still, with practice it can be done.

Critical thinking is as much an attitude as it is a skill. As you learn new material in psychology and in other courses, stop to think about the assumptions being made and evaluate the logic and plausibility of the material. Remember: You can't decide if you believe an argument until you understand it.

SUMMARY AND KEY TERMS

As the curare experiment demonstrated, thought can take place even when speech mechanisms are paralyzed. This finding disproved Watson's theory that thought was only subvocal speech. Psychologists today see thought and language as separate, interconnected activities.

The Building Blocks

Research shows that when a *concept* is activated in a person's mind, other related concepts in the semantic network are primed such that they emerge more readily from memory. *Prototypes,* concepts that seem "typical" of a particular category because they have most of its defining properties, come most readily to mind and have the strongest influence on our judgments.

Solving Problems

When we cannot find a solution by retrieving the answer from memory, we go through three steps: representing the problem, generating possible solutions, and evaluating those solutions.

Representing the Problem

Representing the problem often involves activating concepts from our semantic memory. It can also involve *images* of visual information and intuitive *mental models* of how things work. Our mental models, though very useful, are sometimes inaccurate.

Generating and Evaluating Solutions

Once we have represented a problem, we generally choose from four basic problem-solving strategies: trial and error, algorithms, heuristics, and insight.

Trial and error entails trying various solutions until one of them works. More systematically, we may use an *algorithm,* a step-by-step procedure guaranteed to produce a solution eventually. *Heuristics* are rules of thumb that lead to quicker but not always accurate solutions. One general heuristic is *means-end analysis,* the breaking down of a problem into subgoals. Another is the use of *analogies,* which involve taking an old solution as a model for a new problem. Sometimes, in a flash of *insight,* a solution pops to mind. In long problem-solving sessions, people often experience the incubation effect, whereby sudden insight occurs after they take a break.

"Blind Spots" in Problem Solving

Our mental "blind spots" in problem solving can result from a number of factors. For instance, the problem may be represented incorrectly. We may fall into *functional fixedness,* thinking of objects only in terms of their usual functions. A *mental set,* taking us back to a strategy that worked in the past, is a hindrance if that strategy proves useless. The *confirmation bias* disposes us to look only for evidence that supports our beliefs. And *belief perseverance* leads us to stick to our beliefs even when they have been discredited.

Making Judgments

Studies of decision making have brought further discoveries about the rationality of human beings.

Formal Logic

In solving logical *syllogisms,* people often restate the problem in concrete terms to make it easier, but doing so leads to many mistakes. Likewise, in conditional-reasoning problems, people err because of the confirmation bias.

Biases in Judgment

In making everyday judgments, we consistently rely on two heuristics. The *availability heuristic* estimates the likelihood of an event by how easily instances can be recalled. Although this approach is often helpful, we tend to remember vivid and dramatic events and weigh them more heavily than hard facts. The *representativeness heuristic* leads us to judge an event's likelihood by its apparent typicality, so that we ignore numerical probabilities. And studies of the *framing effect* demonstrate that decisions can be biased by the way an issue is worded. Despite these common types of biases, people are consistently overconfident about their judgment abilities.

Language

Studies of language disturbances known as *aphasias* have shed light on the distinction between thought and language. People with anomia, for instance, can remember concepts while forgetting the corresponding verbal labels.

Communication in the Animal Kingdom

Animals such as honeybees and dolphins communicate in ways that are crucial to their survival. Yet scientists have long maintained that "language" itself is uniquely human.

Characteristics of Human Language

All languages share the properties of semanticity, generativity, and displacement. *Semanticity* refers to the fact that language has separate units of meaning. The smallest meaningful units are *morphemes.* In all spoken languages, morphemes are made up of basics sounds called *phonemes.*

Through the property of *generativity,* language can turn a finite number of words into an infinite variety of expressions, using the processes of iteration and recursion. *Syntax,* the formal grammar, provides the rules for transforming the deep structure of a statement into various possible surface structures.

Finally, all languages are capable of *displacement,* or communication about things beyond the here-and-now. Such communication also involves pragmatics, our knowledge of the social context of language.

Can Animals Learn Language?

Animals as different as parrots, dolphins, and apes can apparently be taught some features of language. In experiments, apes have clearly met the semanticity criterion, and at times they seem to exhibit generativity and displacement. Still, there is controversy about whether the apes are producing language per se.

The Relation Between Thought and Language

If Watson's idea of language as subvocal speech is incorrect, what exactly is the relation between thought and speech?

The Linguistic Relativity Hypothesis

Going beyond the traditional view that thought shapes language, Whorf's *linguistic relativity hypothesis* predicts that language can shape the way we think. Some research indicates that people with different cultures do think differently, although investigators disagree about the interpretation. Today most psychologists believe, on the basis of experimental evidence, that language influences thought. People in power who use doublespeak are well aware of this influence.

Psychological Impact of Sexist Language

Consistent with the linguistic relativity hypothesis, research indicates that sexist language influences the way we conceptualize the roles of men and women.

Learning to Think Critically

Human thought and language are amazing and impressive, but they are also prone to illogic and distortion. Through careful evaluation of evidence, *critical thinking* can help us improve our problem solving and decision making. Thinking critically involves maintaining a skeptical attitude, probing underlying assumptions, and considering alternative arguments.

Chapter 8

Emotion

*S*ilence of the Lambs. *Ghost. Field of Dreams. Basic Instinct. Terms of Endearment. Dances with Wolves.* Go to the movies on a Saturday night, and you will witness firsthand the power of human emotion. In darkened theaters all over the world, audiences laugh at lines that tickle the funny bone, cry in sorrow, gasp in fear, scream in anger, and tingle with sexual delight. Cheers, tears, sweaty palms, tense muscles, and a pounding heart are a vital part of the entertainment experience.

When scientists compare human beings and other animals, they are quick to point to our superior intellect, to the cognitive processes of learning, memory, thought, and language. It is important to realize, however, that we humans are also intensely emotional, warm-blooded creatures. Love, hate, joy, sadness, pride, shame, hope, fear, jealousy, lust, boredom, surprise, embarrassment, guilt, and disgust are among the powerful feelings that color and animate our daily lives.

Emotion is a very difficult concept to define, in part because there are so many different emotions in the repertoire of human feelings. Some are universal, others are found only in certain cultures; some are intense, others are mild; some are positive, others negative; some motivate us to take action, others do not. Despite these vast differences, psychologists agree that emotions in general consist of three interacting components: (1) physiological arousal, (2) expressive behavior, and (3) a cognitive appraisal (see Figure 8.1). This chapter examines each of these components as well as various theories on how they combine to produce the conscious sensations we call emotions.

Figure 8.1

Three Components of Emotion

Based on many years of research, psychologists now agree that emotions are triggered by a combination of factors.

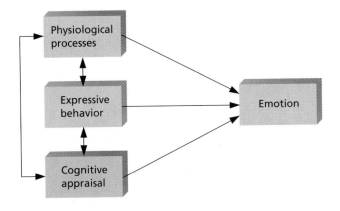

THE PHYSIOLOGICAL COMPONENT

The first time I gave a talk at a professional conference, I was very nervous. The symptoms were unmistakable. As I stepped to the podium and looked up at the audience, I had a knot in the pit of my stomach. My heart pounded, my hands shook, cold sweat dripped down my arms, and my mouth was bone dry. If that wasn't bad enough, my voice quivered the moment I started to speak. My body was sending me a message I did not want to hear and could not control. Was this a rare and unique experience? Not at all. Imagine what it feels like to fall head-over-heels in love, to be stranded on a dangerous street at night, to suffer the death of a loved one, or to get cheated out of something you desperately wanted and deserved. The physical sensations may vary, but the body is intimately involved in feelings of intense emotion.

A Historical Perspective

William James was the first psychologist to theorize about the role of bodily functions in emotion. Common sense tells us that we smile because we're happy, cry because we're sad, clench our fists because we're angry, and tremble because we're afraid. Thus, if you are crossing the street and see a car speeding at you, that stimulus will trigger fear, which, in turn, will cause your heart to pound as you try to escape. This seems reasonable, but in 1884, James turned common sense on its head by proposing what he thought to be a radical new idea (in fact, philosopher René Descartes had made a similar proposal in the seventeenth century): that people feel happy because they smile, sad because they cry, angry because they clench their fists, and afraid because they tremble. In other words, the perception of danger causes your heart to pound as you run for cover—and these physiological and behavioral reactions cause you to become afraid. This proposed chain of events, which was also suggested by a Danish physician named Carl Lange, is known as the **James-Lange theory** of emotion (see Figure 8.2).

Figure 8.2

The James-Lange Theory of Emotion

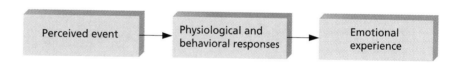

In 1927, physiologist Walter Cannon challenged the James-Lange theory on three grounds. First, said Cannon, bodily sensations alone cannot produce emotion. Indeed, when people are injected with epinephrine—a hormone that energizes the body—they report feeling "pumped up" and aroused but do not experience any specific emotion. Second, said Cannon, we sometimes feel fear, anger, and other emotions instantly, before all the systems of the body have had time to react. Third, the physical changes that do occur are often too general for us to distinguish between different emotions. Fear may make the heart beat faster, but so do anger, love, and other emotions.

As an alternative to the James-Lange theory, Cannon and a colleague named Philip Bard proposed that emotion originates in the thalamus, a part of the brain that simultaneously relays messages from the sensory organs to the autonomic nervous system (arousal), skeletal muscles (motor behavior), and cerebral cortex (conscious thought). According to the **Cannon-Bard theory,** the body and "mind" are activated independently in the experience of emotion. Thus, if you see a car swerving in your direction, your heart will start to pound, you'll run, and you'll become afraid—all at the same time (see Figure 8.3).

■ **James-Lange theory** The theory that emotion stems from the physiological arousal that is triggered by an emotion-eliciting stimulus.

■ **Cannon-Bard theory** The theory that an emotion-eliciting stimulus simultaneously triggers physiological arousal and the experience of emotion.

Figure 8.3

The Cannon-Bard Theory of Emotion

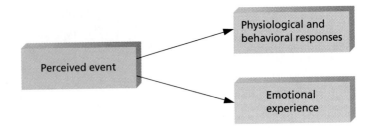

The debate between the James-Lange and Cannon-Bard theories was never resolved. Today, physiologically oriented emotion researchers are not quite as focused on the precise timing and sequence of internal events. Equipped with sophisticated new measurement devices, they seek instead to understand the role in emotion played by different brain structures, neural pathways, and autonomic arousal. We now consider each of these topics.

Brain Centers of Emotion

What role does the brain play in the experience of emotion? To begin with, research shows that many emotions are regulated by the *limbic system*—an evolutionarily primitive set of neural structures (including the thalamus, hypothalamus, hippocampus, and amygdala) that surrounds the brainstem and is found in lower mammals. Stimulate one part of the limbic system in a cat, and it withdraws in fear; stimulate an adjacent area, and the cat becomes enraged—snarling, hissing, and ready to attack. Electronic stimulation of limbic structures in humans, as is sometimes used in the treatment of epilepsy, has similar effects (Panskepp, 1986). In fact, recent research suggests that the *amygdala* triggers certain powerful emotions instantly—before information reaches the cortex and before we have had time to appraise the situation and formulate a response (LeDoux, 1989). This finding may help to explain our irrational fears, angry outbursts, and other emotional reactions that seem to defy logic.

Certain emotional reactions may be quick and automatic, but others involve the *cerebral cortex*—the seat of human intellect. One cannot pinpoint a single region of the cortex that regulates all feelings because different emotions involve distinct patterns of activity. There are hemispheric differences in the brain, however. In a series of experiments, Richard Davidson, Nathan Fox, and others have found that positive emotions evoke more electrical activity in the left cerebral hemisphere, while negative emotions elicit more activity in the right. In one study, Davidson and his colleagues (1990) had subjects watch films that evoked either pleasure (a puppy playing with flowers, a gorilla taking a bath in a zoo) or disgust (a third-degree burn victim, a gruesome leg amputation), videotaped their facial expressions with a hidden camera, and took EEG recordings in the brain. The result: Pleasure films increased activity in the left hemisphere, disgust films did so in the right. Very similar results have been found in infants. When newborn babies taste sugared water, or when ten-month-olds are approached by mom, the left hemisphere is primarily activated. When the taste is sour, however, or when the approaching adult is a stranger, there is greater activity in the right hemisphere (Fox, 1991).

■ **sympathetic nervous system** A branch of the autonomic nervous system that controls the involuntary activities of various organs and mobilizes the body for fight or flight.

■ **parasympathetic nervous system** A branch of the autonomic nervous system that calms the body and conserves energy.

Emotions evoke specific patterns of EEG activity. In the experiment depicted here, researcher Nathan Fox records brain waves in a four-month-old infant stimulated by toys.

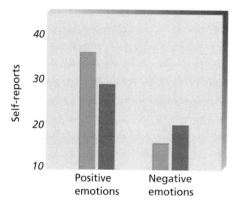

■ Left-hemisphere-active subjects
■ Right-hemisphere-active subjects

Figure 8.4

Brain Centers of Emotion

Compared to subjects who exhibited greater EEG activity in the right hemisphere, those with a more active left hemisphere experienced emotions that were more positive (left) and less negative (right) (Tomarken et al., 1992).

If approach and withdrawal *behaviors* are associated with the left and right hemispheres, respectively, could there be a link between brain activity and *personality?* Is it possible using EEG measures to distinguish between people who are characteristically outgoing and those who are shy and withdrawn? Yes, it appears so. Research shows that children and adults with a more active left hemisphere tend to be interested, joyful, and enthusiastic, while those with a more active right hemisphere are more fearful, nervous, avoidant, and depressed (Davidson, 1993; Finman et al., 1989; Tomarken et al., 1992). This asymmetry is illustrated in Figure 8.4.

Generalized Autonomic Arousal

When an event prompts an emotional response, the human body prepares for action (Thompson, 1988). To mobilize us for "fight" or "flight," the hypothalamus activates the **sympathetic nervous system**—the branch of the autonomic nervous system (ANS) that controls involuntary activities of the heart, lungs, and other organs. Specifically, the adrenal glands secrete more of the hormones epinephrine and norepinephrine (more commonly known as adrenaline and noradrenalin), which increase the heart rate and blood pressure, and heighten physiological arousal. Then all at once the liver pours extra sugar into the bloodstream for energy, the pupils dilate to let in more light, the breathing rate speeds up for more oxygen, perspiration increases to cool down the body, blood clots faster to heal wounds, saliva flow is inhibited, and digestion slows down to divert blood to the brain and skeletal muscles. Epinephrine and norepinephrine supply the physiological fuel for our many passions.

After an emotional event, the **parasympathetic nervous system** takes over and restores the body to its premobilized calm state. The heart stops racing,

Riding on a roller coaster activates the sympathetic nervous system. After the ride is over, the parasympathetic nervous system restores the body to its calm state.

blood pressure is lowered, the pupils contract, breathing slows down, saliva flows again, the digestive system resumes its normal functions, and energy is conserved. As the levels of epinephrine and norepinephrine in the bloodstream slowly diminish, there is a gradual lowering in the intensity of our feelings, enabling us to relax, cool down, and get on with our normal functions. This aspect of emotion is illustrated in Figure 8.5.

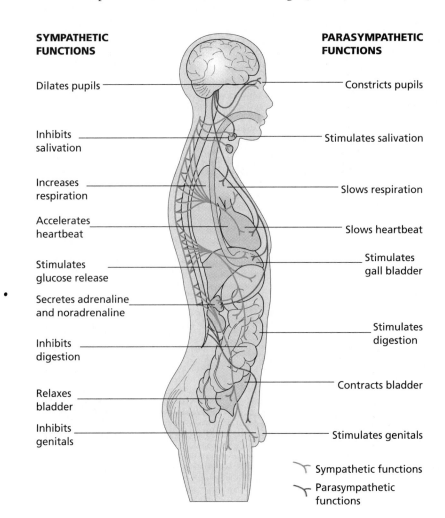

SYMPATHETIC FUNCTIONS

Dilates pupils

Inhibits salivation

Increases respiration

Accelerates heartbeat

Stimulates glucose release

Secretes adrenaline and noradrenaline

Inhibits digestion

Relaxes bladder

Inhibits genitals

PARASYMPATHETIC FUNCTIONS

Constricts pupils

Stimulates salivation

Slows respiration

Slows heartbeat

Stimulates gall bladder

Stimulates digestion

Contracts bladder

Stimulates genitals

⊤ Sympathetic functions

⊤ Parasympathetic functions

Figure 8.5

The Autonomic Nervous System

Note the differing functions of the sympathetic (arousing) and parasympathetic (calming) divisions of the autonomic nervous system.

Specific Patterns of Arousal

Clearly, physiological arousal intensifies an emotional experience. But are all emotions accompanied by the same state of arousal, or does each emotion have its own specific set of symptoms? Scholars have been debating this question for many years. William James (1884) and others have argued that each emotion feels different inside because each is associated with its own unique pattern of autonomic activity. Noting that love, rage, and fear all make the heart beat faster, however, Walter Cannon (1927) and, later, others have maintained that all emotions spark the same physiological arousal. Who is right? Does each emotion have its own autonomic "fingerprint," or do they all feel basically the same?

Recent research suggests there is a bit of truth to both positions. In one study, Paul Ekman and his colleagues (1983) trained subjects (many of whom were actors) to tense up the facial muscles that express happiness, anger, surprise, fear, sadness, or disgust. Aided by a mirror, subjects held each face for ten seconds and the researchers took various measures of autonomic arousal. As shown in Figure 8.6, the posed expressions produced physiological differences. For example, heart rate increased for both anger and fear, but anger increased skin temperature, while fear had the opposite effect. Other studies have since confirmed this point (Levenson, 1992): many emotions make the heart beat faster, but this similarity masks important differences, differences that are betrayed in the language we use to describe our feelings. Thus in anger, we say that we're "hot under the collar," that our "blood is boiling," and that we need to "cool off" and "simmer down." In contrast, we describe fear as a "bone chilling" emotion in which we "freeze" or get "cold feet" (Kovecses, 1990). Even more distinctive is the all-too-familiar pattern of arousal that accompanies embarrassment, a highly social emotion. When people are ashamed or embarrassed in front of others, they blush—an involuntary reflex characterized by redness in the cheeks and ears and a rise in body temperature (Shearn et al., 1990).

Clearly, autonomic nervous system activity is biologically programmed into the human organism—regardless of whether one lives in North America, South America, Europe, Asia, Africa, or the Pacific Islands. But are the

"Man is the only animal that blushes. Or needs to."

MARK TWAIN

Figure 8.6

Specific Patterns of Autonomic Arousal

In this study, subjects expressed various emotions in the face, while researchers recorded arousal. As shown, each emotion seems to have its own autonomic "fingerprint" (Ekman et al., 1983).

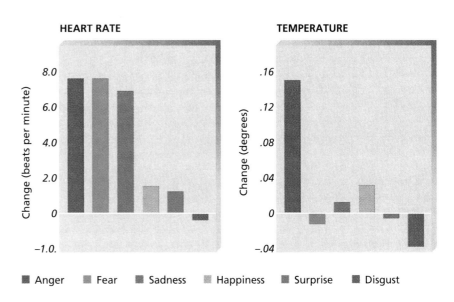

specific patterns of arousal similarly universal? Is anger associated with increased heart rate and skin temperature in all cultures? What about the link between fear and cooled skin temperature? To test the cross-cultural generality of Ekman's results, Robert Levenson and his colleagues (1992) studied the Minangkabau culture of Western Sumatra, an island of Indonesia. This culture is very different from ours in many ways: its members are Moslems and farmers, live in extended matrilineal families, and forbid the public display of negative emotions. Yet despite these differences, the Levenson team found that the Minangkabau exhibited patterns of autonomic arousal similar to those of American subjects.

In fact, people all over the world seem to know intuitively how the body reacts in different emotions. Klaus Scherer and Harald Walbott (1994) asked three thousand students from thirty-seven countries (including the United States, Brazil, France, Norway, Greece, Poland, Botswana, Malawi, Israel, India, Hong Kong, and New Zealand) to describe various emotional experiences and found that there was widespread agreement about the primary sensations. To be sure, there were some cultural differences as well. For example, Japanese subjects reported fewer symptoms than did American and European subjects—perhaps because they are less self-focused and less likely to attend to their own inner states. Still, the sensations that Japanese subjects did report were very similar to those described by other cultural groups (see Table 8.1).

The Lie-Detector Test

For centuries, people have known that lying is stressful and that the stress is revealed in involuntary physiological changes. The Bedouins of Arabia used to make crime suspects lick a hot iron; in India and China, suspects were forced to chew rice powder and then spit it out. Based on the assumption that lying produces a dryness in the mouth, those who burned their tongues or spit out dried powder were judged to be dishonest (Kleinmuntz & Szucko, 1984).

The modern lie-detector test is also based on the assumption that lying heightens autonomic arousal. Since this activity is not observable, law enforcement officials use the **polygraph**—an electronic instrument that can simultaneously record multiple channels of arousal. The physiological signals are picked up by sensors that are attached to different parts of the body. For example, rubber tubes are strapped around the subject's torso to measure breathing, or respiration; blood pressure cuffs are wrapped around the upper arm to measure pulse rate and other cardiovascular activity; and electrodes on the hand are used to monitor changes in sweat gland activity, or perspiration. These signals are then boosted by amplifiers and converted into a visual display.

It is important to keep in mind that the polygraph itself is merely a physiological recording device. It becomes a lie-detector test only when combined with an oral examination. Here's how it works. First, the examiner conducts a pretest interview to establish the subject's baseline level of arousal and convince the subject that the polygraph works. Next, the examiner compares the subject's reaction to arousing *crime-relevant* questions ("Did you steal the car last night?") and innocuous *control questions* that are arousing but not relevant to the crime ("Did you steal anything

■ **polygraph** An electronic device that records multiple channels of autonomic arousal and is often used as a lie-detector test.

Table 8.1

Shown here are some of the most frequently reported bodily symptoms of various emotions. These results are based on 2,235 respondents in 27 countries (Scherer & Walbott, 1994).

Emotions	Symptoms	% Reported
Joy	feeling warm	63
	fast heartbeat	40
	relaxed muscles	29
Fear	fast heartbeat	65
	tense muscles	52
	rapid breathing	47
	perspiration	37
	feeling cold	36
	lump in throat	29
	stomach trouble	22
Anger	fast heartbeat	50
	tense muscles	43
	rapid breathing	37
	feeling hot	32
	lump in throat	25
Sadness	lump in throat	56
	crying	55
	tense muscles	27
	fast heartbeat	27
	feeling cold	22
Shame	feeling hot	40
	fast heartbeat	35
	perspiration	26
Guilt	lump in throat	28
	fast heartbeat	27
Disgust	tense muscles	25
	fast heartbeat	23
	stomach trouble	21

when you were younger?"). In theory, crime-relevant questions should evoke more arousal than the control questions among subjects who are lying, but not among those who are telling the truth (see Figure 8.7).

Does the lie-detector test work? Many people think it is foolproof, but professional opinion is split. Some researchers report accuracy rates of about 90 percent (Horvath, 1984; Raskin, 1986). Others say that these claims are exaggerated and that the test is fraught with serious problems (Lykken, 1981). One well-documented problem is that truthful persons too often "fail" the test. A recent study of polygraph records obtained from police files revealed that although 98 percent of suspects later known to be guilty were correctly identified as such, 45 percent of those who were eventually found innocent were also judged as deceptive (Patrick & Iacono, 1991). A second problem is that the test can be faked. Studies show that you can beat the polygraph by tensing your muscles, biting your tongue, or squeezing your toes while answering the *control* questions. By artificially inflating your response to these "innocent" questions, you can mask the stress that is aroused by lying to the crime-relevant questions (Honts et al., 1994).

Figure 8.7

Lie-Detector Test

This polygraph recording depicts the physiological reactions of a crime suspect judged guilty. Note that heart rate and perspiration increased more in response to a crime-relevant question than to a control question (Raskin, 1982).

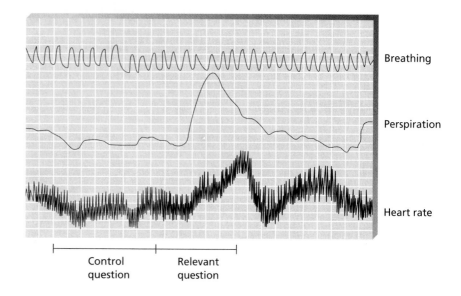

Breathing

Perspiration

Heart rate

Control
question

Relevant
question

What, then, are we to conclude? After carefully reviewing all of the polygraph research for the Congressional Office of Technology Assessment, Leonard Saxe and his colleagues (1985) concluded that there is no simple answer. Under certain conditions—for example, when the suspect is naive and the examiner is well trained—it is possible for polygraphers to make accurate judgments of truth and deception. The problems just described, however, remain hard to overcome—which is why many states refuse to allow polygraph test results into evidence. As an alternative, some researchers are now trying to develop a test that distinguishes between truth and deception through the measurement of involuntary electrical activity in the brain (Bashore & Rapp, 1993).

Until recently, many companies used the polygraph to screen employees and uncover theft in the workplace. Those who use it argue that it sharpens one's ability to hire employees who are honest. Opponents, however, argue that the test is an invasion of an individual's privacy, that it is often misused, and that the results are not sufficiently accurate. In light of these problems, the U.S. government in 1988 passed a law that limits the use of lie-detector tests to jobs involving matters of security and public safety. Accordingly, many companies now require job applicants to take "integrity tests"—questionnaires designed to assess a person's character by asking direct, pointed questions about drug use, drinking, shoplifting, petty theft, and other transgressions. At this point, research indicates that these tests can be used to predict counterproductive on-the-job behaviors such as theft, disciplinary problems, and absenteeism (Camara & Schneider, 1994; Ones et al., 1993).

THE EXPRESSIVE COMPONENT

Emotion may be an internal, purely subjective experience, but it also has an observable behavioral component. The links between our inner feelings and outward expressions are numerous: we smile when we're happy, cry when we're sad, blush when we're embarrassed, stand tall when we feel proud, drag our feet when we're down, press our lips in anger, grimace in pain, bow our heads in shame, and wrinkle our faces in disgust.

These behavioral expressions of emotion serve two functions. First, they provide us with a means of *nonverbal communication*. People often use words to tell others how they're feeling. But by smiling, frowning, crying, and turning red in the face, we also reveal our feelings nonverbally—which is what makes emotion an inherently social experience (Fridlund, 1992). A second function is *sensory feedback*. In 1872, Charles Darwin theorized that expression clarifies and intensifies an emotional experience by providing us with sensory feedback about how we feel. In short, the expressive component of emotion has two audiences: others and ourselves.

Nonverbal Communication

Knowing how another person is feeling can be tricky because people sometimes try to hide their true emotions. Think about it. Have you ever had to suppress your rage toward someone, mask your disappointment after failure, feign surprise, or pretend to like something just to be polite? Sometimes we come right out and tell people how we feel. Often, however, we actively try to conceal our feelings. In instances like these, observers tune into a silent language—the language of nonverbal behavior.

What kinds of nonverbal cues do people use to judge how someone is feeling? In *The Expression of the Emotions in Man and Animals,* Charles Darwin (1872) argued that the *face* communicates emotion in ways that are innate and understood by people all over the world. Contemporary research provides strong support for this notion. For example, Paul Ekman and his colleagues (1969) showed thirty photographs like those presented below to subjects from Argentina, Borneo, Brazil, Japan, New Guinea, and the United States, and asked them to guess the emotion that was portrayed in each photo. The results of this study, and of numerous others like it, indicate that people can reliably identify six emotions: joy, fear, anger, sadness, surprise, and disgust. In fact, subjects from ten different countries—Estonia, Germany, Greece, Hong Kong, Italy, Japan, Scotland, Sumatra, Turkey, and the United States—all exhibited high levels of agreement in their recognition of these same emotions (Ekman et al., 1987). Although questions have been raised about this research (Russell, 1994), it seems that from one end of the world to the other, a smile is a smile and a frown is a frown—and just about everyone knows what they mean.

Look at the photographs below and try to match each with one of the following emotions: (1) joy, (2) fear, (3) anger, (4) sadness, (5) surprise, and (6) disgust. Studies show that people from a diversity of cultures exhibit high levels of agreement on this task.

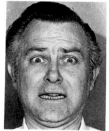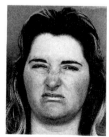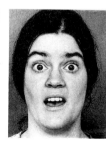

Further supporting the view that certain expressions are inborn is the fact that even infants—who are too young to speak and have yet to fully learn the lessons of their culture—make faces that are associated with basic emotions. Thus when Carroll Izard and his colleagues (1980) analyzed the facial expressions of very young infants, they were able to identify various emotions, each necessary for nonverbal infants to "communicate" from birth with their adult caretakers.

According to Izard (1991), certain emotional expressions are present at birth. These pictures depict young infants in moments of (1) joy, (2) fear, (3) anger, (4) sadness, (5) surprise, and (6) disgust.

According to Darwin, the ability to recognize emotion in others has survival value for all members of a species. This hypothesis suggests that some emotions are more important to identify than others. It is probably more adaptive, for example, to know when someone is angry (and prone to lash out in violence) than to know when someone else is happy, a nonthreatening emotion (see Figure 8.8). Are people more sensitive to signs of anger than to those of happiness? In a series of experiments, Christine and Ranald Hansen (1988) asked subjects to find discrepant facial expressions

Figure 8.8

The Face of Anger

Anger is universally recognized by geometric patterns on the face. In the examples shown, the left form in each pair seems angrier than the one on the right. In the threatening ceremonial masks of many cultures, anger is displayed by triangular eyes and hard, downward, angular lines (Aronoff et al., 1988, 1992).

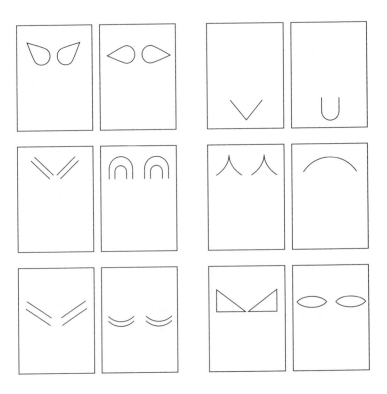

Featuring hard, downward, and angular lines, many of the masks worn by National Hockey League goalies have an intimidating, angry appearance.

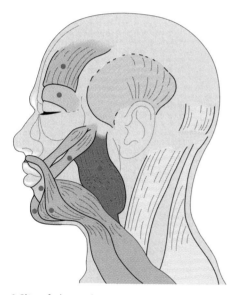

• Site of electrode

Figure 8.9

The Facial Electromyograph (EMG)

Electrodes placed on the face record activity in various muscles. These recordings reveal that positive emotions increase activity in the cheek muscles, while negative emotions increase activity in the forehead and brow areas (Cacioppo & Petty, 1981).

■ **facial electromyograph (EMG)** An electronic instrument used by emotion researchers to record activity in the facial muscles.

in pictures of large crowds, each crowd consisting of happy, neutral, or angry faces. In some pictures, everyone wore the same expression; in others, one was discrepant. As Darwin would have predicted, subjects exhibited the "face-in-the-crowd effect": they were quicker to spot discrepant angry faces than they were to locate discrepant faces that were happy or neutral. People are similarly sensitive to signs of fear, another emotion that signals danger (Lanzetta & Orr, 1986).

Emotion is accompanied by changes in facial expression—even when these changes are so subtle that they cannot be seen with the naked eye. It is estimated that the eighty muscles in the human face can create more than seven thousand different expressions. To measure the spontaneous activity of these muscles and their links to emotion, many researchers use a physiological device known as the **facial electromyograph (EMG).** In facial EMG studies, subjects are shown images that evoke positive or negative emotions, while electrodes attached to the face record the activity of various muscles (see Figure 8.9). The results of this research indicate that images that elicit positive emotions such as joy, interest, and attraction increase activity in the cheek muscles; those that arouse negative emotions such as anger, distress, and fear spark activity in the forehead and brow area. Apparently, the muscles in the human face reveal smiles, frowns, and other expressions that are otherwise hidden from view (Dimberg, 1990; Tassinary & Cacioppo, 1992).

Using the facial EMG, researchers have also discovered that there are two distinct types of smiles—one more genuine than the other. In a series of experiments, Ekman and his colleagues found that when people experience real joy, they beam smiles that raise the cheeks high enough to wrinkle up the skin surrounding the eyes and exhibit increased electrical activity in the left hemisphere of the brain. However, when people wear false "unfelt" smiles, perhaps to be polite or to pose for a photograph, the muscle activity in the lips and lower cheeks does not extend up to the eyes or trigger a predominance of left-hemisphere activity in the brain (Ekman & Davidson, 1993; Ekman et al., 1990; Frank et al., 1993).

Other nonverbal behaviors also communicate emotion, enabling us to make quick, sometimes accurate judgments of how others are feeling (Ambady & Rosenthal, 1992). One common form of expression is *body language*—the way people stand, sit, walk, and make gestures. For example, people who have a youthful walking style—who sway their hips, bend their knees, pick up their feet, and swing their arms in a bouncy rhythm—are seen as happier and more powerful than those who walk slowly, take shorter steps, and stiffly drag their feet (Montepare & McArthur, 1988). *Gaze,* or eye contact, is also a powerful form of communication. The eyes have been called "windows of the soul." In many cultures, people assume that someone who avoids looking them in the eye is evasive, cold, fearful, shy, or apathetic; that frequent gazing signals intimacy, sincerity, and confidence; and that the person who stares is tense, angry, and unfriendly. In fact, eye contact is often interpreted in light of pre-existing relationships. Among friends and lovers, frequent gaze means warmth and affection. Among enemies, it signals cold hostility (Kleinke, 1986; Patterson, 1983). Thus it has been said that if two people lock eyes for more than a few seconds, they are either going to make love or kill each other!

Emotion is sometimes communicated in a person's body language. Notice the slumped postures of the people in this scene. They are hurricane victims waiting in line for food.

Another nonverbal cue is *touch*—a congratulatory high-five, a sympathetic pat on the back, a joking elbow in the ribs, and a warm loving embrace are just a few examples. Physical touch is generally considered to be an expression of friendship, caring, and sexual interest. But it may also serve other functions. Nancy Henley (1977) observed that men, older persons, and those of high status are more likely to touch women, younger persons, and others of lower status, than the other way around. Her interpretation: Touching is an expression not only of intimacy but of dominance and control. Researchers are particularly intrigued by the sex differences reported by Henley. In one study, Brenda Major and her colleagues (1990) watched people in city streets, shopping malls, college campuses, beaches, bus stations, airports, and other public settings. Sure enough, men were more likely to touch women than women were to touch men—though this difference was not observed in places where friends ritually greet or say goodbye to each other. In another study, Judith Hall and Ellen Veccia (1990) observed 4,500 dyads and found in mixed-sex situations that although men were more likely to initiate contact with the hand, the difference was complicated when other kinds of touching were involved. For example, men are more likely to put their arms around women, while women are more likely to link arms with men.

Sensory Feedback

"Refuse to express a passion and it dies."
WILLIAM JAMES

Draw the corners of your mouth back and up and wrinkle your eye muscles. Relax. Now raise your eyebrows, open your eyes wide, and let your mouth drop open slightly. Relax. Now pull your brows down and together and clench your teeth. Relax. If you followed each of these directions, you would have appeared to others to be feeling first happy, then fearful, and finally angry. The question is, Do these expressions affect how you actually feel?

According to the **facial feedback hypothesis,** an expression does more than simply reflect one's emotion—it actually triggers an emotional experience. In an interesting first test of this hypothesis, James Laird (1974) told college students that they would take part in an experiment on the activity of the facial muscles. After attaching electrodes to the face, he showed the subjects a series of cartoons and asked them before each one to contract certain facial muscles in ways that made them smile or frown. The result: Subjects thought the material was funnier and reported feeling happier when they wore a smile than a frown. Similarly, other posed-expression studies show that people can also be induced to experience fear, anger, sadness, and disgust (Duclos et al., 1989).

According to Laird, facial expressions activate emotion through a process of self-perception: "If I'm smiling, I must be happy." But there is a second possible reason for this effect. Perhaps expressions trigger an emotional experience by eliciting physiological changes in the brain. According to Robert Zajonc (1993), for example, smiling causes facial muscles to increase the flow of air-cooled blood to the brain, which has a pleasant effect by lowering the brain's temperature. Conversely, frowning decreases blood flow, which produces an unpleasant state by raising brain temperature.

In an ingenious demonstration of this mechanism, Zajonc and his colleagues (1989) asked subjects to repeat certain vowels twenty times each, including the sounds "ah," "e," "u," and the German vowel "ü." As subjects uttered these sounds, temperature in the forehead was measured and subjects reported on how they felt. As shown in Figure 8.10, "ah" and "e" (vowel sounds that cause speakers to mimic smiling) lowered forehead temperature and elevated mood, while "u" and "ü" (vowels that cause speakers to mimic frowning) raised temperature and dampened mood. In other words, movement of the facial muscles influenced emotion even though subjects did not realize that they were wearing a particular expression. The lesson: If you want an emotional lift, just put on a happy face.

■ **facial feedback hypothesis** The hypothesis that changes in facial expression can produce corresponding changes in emotion.

Figure 8.10

Facial Feedback

In a study by Zajonc et al. (1989), subjects repeated certain vowel sounds. As shown, "ah" and "e"—sounds that cause speakers to smile—lowered brain temperature (left) and elevated mood (right). In contrast, "u" and "ü"—sounds that cause us to frown—raised brain temperature (left) and dampened mood (right).

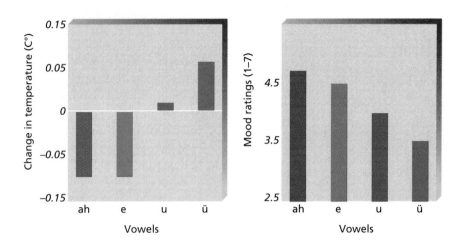

Other expressive behaviors such as body posture can also provide us with sensory feedback and influence how we feel. When people feel proud, they stand erect with their shoulders raised, chest expanded, and head held high (*expansion*). When people feel sad and dejected, however, they slump over with their shoulders drooping and head bowed (*contraction*). Clearly, your emotional state is revealed in the way you carry yourself. Is it also possible that the way you carry yourself affects your emotional state? Can people lift their spirits by expanding their posture, or lower their spirits through contraction? Yes. Sabine Stepper and Fritz Strack (1993) arranged for subjects to sit in a slumped or upright position by varying the height of the table they had to write on. Those who were forced to sit upright reported feeling more pride after succeeding at a task than did those who were put into a slumped position. In another study, subjects who were instructed to lean forward with their fists clenched during the experiment reported feeling anger, while those who sat slumped with their heads down said they felt sadness (Duclos et al., 1989). It appears that emotions can be triggered by sensory feedback from the body as well as from the face.

THE COGNITIVE COMPONENT

There is much more to emotion than physiological sensations and expressive behaviors. After all, the heart pounds in fear; but it also pounds in anger. We cry out in grief over the death of a loved one; but we also shed tears of joy at weddings and other happy occasions. We laugh when we're amused, but sometimes we laugh out of nervousness. Clearly, there is more to grief, joy, amusement, and nervousness than arousal and expression. The missing link is *cognitive appraisal*.

Psychologists have long been embroiled in a heated debate on the role of cognitive factors in emotion. Are your feelings, like inborn reflexes, triggered by certain stimuli without conscious thought or awareness, or does the way you feel depend on how you perceive, interpret, and evaluate the situation you're in? Do you think first and feel second, or is it the other way around? Theories of emotion provide different answers to these questions.

"Let's do it, let's fall in love."

Many researchers emphasize the role of cognitive factors in the experience of love and other emotions. [Drawing by Mankoff; © The New Yorker Magazine, Inc.]

Schachter's Two-Factor Theory of Emotion

When I was nineteen, my girlfriend and I were sitting upstairs in her home late at night. Her parents were away for the weekend and nobody else was in the house. The TV was on and we were on the verge of falling asleep. Then suddenly we heard scraping, clicking, the front door opening, and footsteps downstairs. There was an intruder in the house and we were terrified. My heart pounded so hard that I could feel my chest throb with every beat. Except for the trembling, I was frozen in place like a statue. The emotion we experienced that night was raw fear, plain and simple. How did I "know" that I was afraid and not sad, angry, disgusted, or ill?

According to Stanley Schachter (1964), two factors are necessary to have a specific emotion. First, the person must experience a heightened state of *physiological arousal,* such as a racing heart, sweaty palms, tightening of the stomach, rapid breathing, and so on—the kind of jitteriness you might feel after drinking too much coffee. Second, the person must find a *cognitive label* or attribution to explain the source of that arousal. The night that my girlfriend and I heard an intruder I had such an obvious explanation for my symptoms that labeling the emotion as fear was easy. In fact, I was shaky for quite some time afterward. (We called the police, and they arrived minutes later to find the front door wide open. Although they searched the house with flashlights, it was too late; the intruder had already left.) The same is true when people watch intensely emotional movies. When people saw *Silence of the Lambs,* they knew they were feeling disgusted rather than ashamed, angry, or sad, because the stimulus itself was unambiguous. At times, however, people become generally excited without knowing why—and must examine their surroundings in order to identify the emotion (see Figure 8.11).

To test this **two-factor theory of emotion,** Schachter and Jerome Singer (1962) injected male subjects with epinephrine, the hormone that produces physiological arousal. The subjects in one group were warned in advance about the side effects (they were drug-informed), but those in a second group were not (they were drug-uninformed). In a third group, the subjects were injected with a harmless placebo (this was the placebo control group). Before the drug—which was said to be a vitamin supplement—actually took effect, subjects were left alone with a male confederate introduced as another subject who had received the same injection. In some cases, the confederate's behavior was euphoric: he bounced around happily, doodled on paper, sank jump shots into the waste basket, flew paper airplanes across the room, and swung his hips in a hula hoop. In the presence of other subjects, the same confederate behaved angrily. At one point, for example, he ridiculed a questionnaire they were filling out and, in a fit of rage, ripped it up and hurled it into the waste basket.

Think for a moment about these various situations. In the *drug-informed* group, subjects began to feel their hearts pound, their hands shake, and their faces flush. Told to expect these side effects, however, they did not have to search very far for an explanation. In the *placebo* group, the subjects did not become aroused in the first place so they had no symptoms to explain. But now consider the predicament of the subjects in the *drug-uninformed* group, who suddenly became aroused without knowing why. Trying to identify the sensations, these subjects—according to the theory—

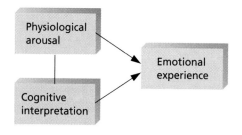

Figure 8.11

Two-Factor Theory of Emotion

■ **two-factor theory of emotion** The theory that emotion is based both on physiological arousal and on the cognitive interpretation of that arousal.

After dancing into a state of arousal, people are prone to react to new situations with more intense joy, fear, excitement, and other emotions. Autonomic arousal from one event can spill over to other events.

would take their cues from others in the situation, namely the confederate. The results generally supported this prediction. Drug-uninformed subjects reported that they felt more happy or angry depending on the confederate's actions. In some cases, they even exhibited similar kinds of behavior. For example, one subject "threw open the window and, laughing, hurled paper basketballs at passersby." Subjects in the drug-informed group, who attributed their arousal to the epinephrine, were not as influenced by these social cues. Neither were subjects in the no-drug placebo group—who, after all, were not physiologically aroused.

Schachter's (1964) two-factor theory has attracted a good deal of attention. Not all the research is supportive, but one general conclusion can be drawn: when people are aroused and do not know why, they try to identify their emotions by observing the situation they're in and making an attribution for their arousal (Reisenzein, 1983). This conclusion has interesting implications. One is that if people attribute their arousal to a nonemotional source they will experience less emotion (this is what happened in the drug-informed group, where subjects blamed their autonomic symptoms on the epinephrine). Another is that if people attribute their arousal to an emotional source they will experience more of that emotion (which was the experience of those in the drug-uninformed group). In short, once people are stimulated, they can cognitively intensify, diminish, and alter their own emotions.

One particularly intriguing implication of this theory is that the arousal produced by one source can be "misattributed" or "transferred" to another source. Suppose you just ran two miles, spent a full hour playing basketball, or danced hard at a party. Chances are, you would be sweating and gasping for breath. You would realize, of course, that these symptoms had been caused by physical exertion. But what if you went on to another activity? Since it takes time for one's pulse, body temperature, breathing, and other autonomic functions to return to normal, you might later attribute this residual arousal to a new source. Numerous studies of *excitation transfer* demonstrate this point. After strenuous physical exercise, subjects exhibit more anger when provoked by an insult and more sexual attraction for someone they meet of the opposite sex. Similarly, a heated argument or scary movie can spark sexual excitement, which, in turn, can intensify anger. In short, autonomic arousal from one event can sometimes spill over and fuel emotional reactions to another event (Zillman, 1983).

If it is possible to intensify an emotion by the transfer of arousal, it should also be possible to diminish emotion in the same way. Consider stage fright, or public-speaking anxiety—an unwanted emotion that claims many victims. As if the dry throat and quivering voice are not embarrassing enough, those who suffer from this common problem get even more anxious because they are anxious. But what if they had an alternative explanation for the symptoms? Is it possible to calm people with speech anxiety by providing face-saving attributions for their arousal? Using a technique of *misattribution*, James Olson (1988) led some subjects but not others to believe that a "subliminal noise" would make them feel anxious while speaking. The result: Those who thought that a noise made them more anxious gave smoother, more fluent speeches. By prompting these subjects to attribute their arousal to noise rather than to their own anxiety, Olson was able to calm them down and improve their performance. "What, me nervous? My heart may be racing, but thank goodness it's not me—it's just the noise."

Dimensions of Appraisal

According to cognitively oriented theorists, the emotions we experience are determined by the way we appraise the situation we're in—and certain appraisal dimensions are particularly important in this regard. To appreciate the cognitive approach, think about the last time you experienced a particular emotion—say, happiness. Picture the situation in your mind. Why were you happy? How pleasant was the experience? Did you feel as if you were in control? Were you responsible for what happened? How well did you understand the situation you were in? Did you know how things would turn out? Were you thinking about how you felt, or were you trying to shut your feelings out? Was the situation important to you? By asking people to answer questions like these about their own emotion experiences, researchers find that there are some clear links between our cognitive appraisals and emotional reactions (Frijda, 1986; Roseman et al., 1990; Smith & Ellsworth, 1985; Smith et al., 1993; Weiner, 1985).

The cognitive dimensions of appraisal that are most closely linked to emotion are the *pleasantness* of the situation (whether or not it's enjoyable), *attention* (whether or not one is focused on what's happening), *agency* (the belief that one is or is not in control), and *certainty* (the clarity of the situation and whether or not the outcome can be predicted). Research thus shows that pride, shame, boredom, interest, disgust, and other emotions can be distinguished by the cognitive appraisals people make along these dimensions (Smith & Ellsworth, 1985)—and that these dimensions are important not only in the United States but in many other countries as well (Mauro et al., 1992; Mesquita & Frijda, 1992). Consider the following examples:

- *Happiness* is a pleasant state that involves high levels of attention, control, and certainty (partying with friends, attending a graduation ceremony).
- *Surprise* is a pleasant, effortless state characterized by a high level of attention but low levels of certainty and control (getting an A in a course when a C was expected, receiving an unannounced visit from an old friend).
- *Shame* is an unpleasant state characterized by a desire to avoid thinking about the situation, by moderate levels of certainty, and by a high level of personal control in the form of self-blame (getting caught cheating, or gossiping about someone).
- *Anger* is an intensely unpleasant state that involves moderate levels of certainty and attention. The most prominent aspect of anger is the belief that one's misfortune is controlled by others (having one's car stolen, being insulted in public).
- *Sadness* is a highly unpleasant state in which there is uncertainty and a desire to minimize attention to the situation. Unlike situations that give

rise to anger, sadness events are blamed on circumstances rather than on other people (illness, divorce, the death of a loved one).

- *Fear* is also a highly aversive state. Like surprise, it is associated with high levels of uncertainty and low levels of personal control, particularly about one's ability to escape or avoid a dreaded outcome (being held at knife point, skidding on an icy winter road).

Is Cognition Necessary?

Schachter's two-factor theory as well as the theories of excitation transfer and cognitive appraisal are all based on the assumption that emotion requires thought. Cognitive emotion theorists would thus tell my intruder story as follows: I heard a noise (stimulus) and attributed that noise to someone in the house (cognition), thereby causing myself to feel scared (emotion) and to freeze (behavior). As we've seen, many psychologists believe that cognition plays a vital role in the experience of emotion. This claim is a source of controversy, however, and was the topic of a spirited exchange between Robert Zajonc (1984), who wrote an article on "the primacy of affect," and Richard Lazarus (1984), who countered with one on "the primacy of cognition."

According to Zajonc, people sometimes react with emotion instantly and without prior appraisal. In other words, sometimes we feel before we think. If you've ever banged your toe into a table, only to explode in anger and pound your fist, you would know that the link between pain and rage seems automatic—that you reacted with an angry outburst before realizing just how ridiculous it is to be mad at a piece of furniture. If you ever drank milk that was old and curdled, only to gag and spit it out, you would likewise know that the link between aversive tastes and disgust may also be automatic. This primacy of affect may help to explain why people develop intense, irrational, persistent fears of objects that are not inherently dangerous. It may also help to explain why infants make reflex-like facial expressions of pain, interest, joy, distress, anger, and disgust before they have the brain capacity to make the proposed cognitive appraisals (Izard, 1990).

According to Zajonc (1984), our emotions and thoughts are controlled by separate anatomical structures within the brain. In support of this argument, recent animal research indicates that certain emotions are triggered instantly—before it is even possible to appraise the situation and formulate a response. From studies aimed at tracing the neural pathways of emotion, Joseph LeDoux (1993) has found that there is a primitive, subcortical pathway in the limbic system (a pathway that connects the eyes and ears directly to the amygdala through the thalamus) that does not involve the cerebral cortex (and thus does not entail an initial processing of information). This pathway serves as an "early warning system," so that the amygdala can be activated quickly. When we are confronted with pain, noxious food substances, and other threats, this direct pipeline between sensation and emotion enables us to make a rapid-fire defensive motor response without having to stop for a cognitive appraisal.

Representing the cognitive approach, Richard Lazarus (1991) agrees that emotions can spring up quickly and without awareness, but he bluntly

"There is a road from the eye to the heart that does not go through the intellect."

G. K. CHESTERTON

maintains that it is not possible to have emotion without some kind of thought—even a thought that is quick, effortless, and unconscious. "Without cognitive activity to guide us," says Lazarus, "we could not grasp the significance of what's happening in our adaptational encounters with the environment, nor could we choose among alternative values and courses of action" (p. 353). According to Lazarus, an emotion is an individual's response to what he or she sees as the harms and benefits of a particular situation. Accordingly, Lazarus (1993) presents a list of fifteen emotions and the "core relational themes" (perceived harms and benefits) that set each of them off (see Table 8.2). Is cognition necessary to emotion? The debate rages on.

Table 8.2

Emotions and Their "Core Relational Themes"

According to Lazarus (1993), there are fifteen different emotions, each one triggered by a certain subjective predicament. ["From Psychological Stress to the Emotions: A History of Changing Outlooks" by R. S. Lazarus. Modified with permission from the author and the ANNUAL REVIEW OF PSYCHOLOGY, Volume 44, © 1993 by Annual Reviews Inc.]

Emotion	Core Relational Theme
Anger	A demeaning offense against me and mine
Anxiety	Facing an uncertain, existential threat
Fright	An immediate, concrete, overwhelming danger
Guilt	Having transgressed a moral imperative
Shame	Failing to live up to an ego-ideal
Sadness	Having experienced an irrevocable loss
Envy	Wanting what someone else has
Jealousy	Resenting a third party for the threat of losing another's affection or favor
Disgust	Taking in or being close to a repulsive object, person, or idea
Happiness	Making progress toward the realization of a goal
Pride	Ego-enhancement by taking credit for one's own achievement or that of someone identified with
Relief	A distressing condition that has changed for the better
Hope	Fearing the worst but wanting better
Love	Desiring affection that is often but not always reciprocated
Compassion	Being moved by another's suffering and wanting to help

HUMAN EMOTION: PUTTING THE PIECES TOGETHER

Knowing that emotions stem from physiological, expressive, and cognitive activities is only a first step. The next step is to determine how the different pieces of this puzzle fit together to produce an emotional experience.

Types of Emotions

The English language contains more than 2,000 words to describe categories of emotions. Are some of these universal, felt by people in all cultures? Over the years, psychologists have tried to classify emotions in various ways. Today, there is widespread agreement that fear, anger, joy, disgust, surprise, and sadness are "basic" human emotions: each is accompanied by a distinct facial expression, each is displayed by infants and very young children, and each is found in the words that people of diverse cultures use to describe their feelings. Other researchers believe that interest-excitement, acceptance, contempt, pride, shame, and guilt should be added to the list.

If there are only a few basic emotions, what accounts for the vast array of other feelings we so often experience? One possibility suggested by Robert Plutchik (1980) is that basic emotions provide the building blocks for more complex emotions in much the same way that the three primary colors combine to form the hues of the color wheel. According to Plutchik, the richness of human emotions is accounted for in three ways. First, there are eight basic types of emotions (he adds interest and acceptance to the original six). Second, each type comes in varying "shades," or levels of intensity (for example, intense disgust may be felt as hatred or loathing, and mild disgust as boredom). Third, new emotions are formed through mixtures of the eight basic ones (for example, love blends joy and acceptance, contempt blends disgust and anger, and nostalgia blends joy and sadness). Plutchik's three-dimensional model is illustrated in Figure 8.12.

It's easy to generate a list of emotions. The trick is to classify and compare the emotions along a small number of common dimensions. The most popular taxonomy is the *circumplex model,* in which all emotions are divided along two independent dimensions: pleasantness and intensity. Ac-

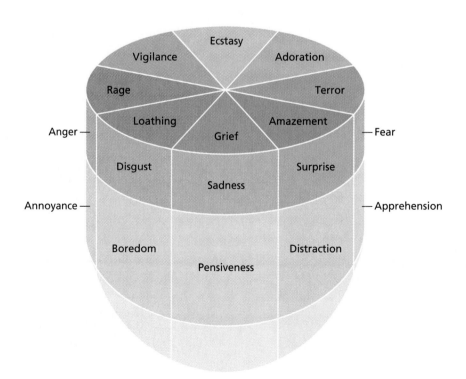

Figure 8.12

Plutchik's Three-Dimensional Model of Emotions

Figure 8.13

Russell's Circumplex Model

According to this circumplex model, there are four types of emotions: pleasant-intense, pleasant-mild, unpleasant-intense, and unpleasant-mild (Russell et al., 1980).

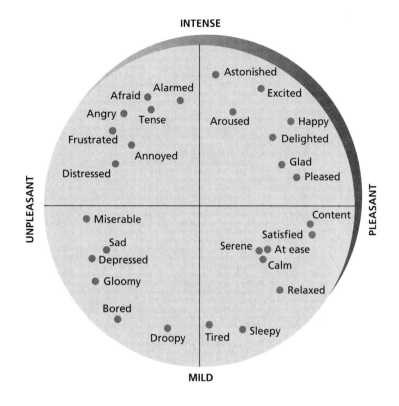

cording to James Russell (1980), emotions are either (1) pleasant or unpleasant, and (2) mild or intense. As illustrated in Figure 8.13, the result is a fourfold circle of emotions that are pleasant-and-intense ("delighted"), pleasant-and-mild ("relaxed"), unpleasant-and-mild ("bored"), and unpleasant-and-intense ("alarmed"). Research shows that when people are asked to sort emotion words into piles, this circular ordering consistently appears—not only in English but also in Chinese, Croatian, Estonian, Greek, Gujarati, Hebrew, Japanese, Polish, and Swedish (Larsen & Diener, 1992).

Certain emotions are "basic" to the human experience. Here, an Indian woman is stricken with grief after an earthquake killed most inhabitants of her hometown and a Texas woman expresses joy after a winning shot in the bowling alley.

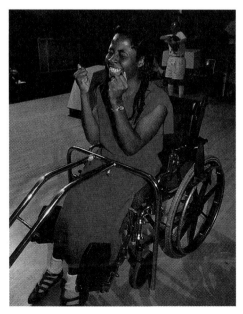

Weather and Emotion: Seasonal Affective Disorder

Anyone who lives in a four-season climate knows how easily emotional states can be influenced by the weather. Have you ever had a case of the "blues" after a succession of overcast days, only to be rejuvenated by a cheerful dose of sunshine? Have you ever caught "spring fever" after a dreary winter, the first time the sun and air were warm enough for you to shed your coat? If so, you have company. And lots of it.

Psychologists have recently discovered that although everyone is affected to a greater or lesser extent, some people suffer from *seasonal affective disorder*, or SAD—a form of depression that strikes during the dark days of autumn and winter. Every year, people with SAD who live in relatively cold regions of the world fall into a lethargic emotional state that resembles hibernation. They become listless, drowsy, and withdrawn. They also sleep more, eat more, crave carbohydrates, gain weight, lose interest in sex, and falter at work and in their social relationships. Consistent with the hypothesis that SAD is related to climate, as illustrated in the figure, surveys show that both SAD sufferers and people in general report feeling worse during the winter months (Kasper & Rosenthal, 1989)—and that the prevalence of SAD increases with a region's distance north of the equator. As shown in the table, SAD is more common in the states of Alaska and New Hamp-

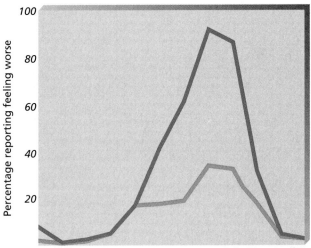

SAD sufferers
Normal subjects

Seasonal Differences in SAD
This graph depicts the percentage of sufferers and "normal" subjects who report feeling blue each month of the year. Most people feel worse in winter, a pattern that is exaggerated among those with SAD (Kasper & Rosenthal, 1989).

Dynamics of Emotion

"How strange would appear this thing that men call pleasure! And how curiously it is related to what is thought to be its opposite, pain! The two will never be found together in a man, and yet if you seek the one and obtain it, you are almost bound always to get the other as well, just as though they were both attached to one and the same head."

PLATO

I have always loved roller coasters. I find the speed and sharp turns frightening, the loops make me dizzy, and my neck muscles are often strained after tensing up for so long. But the feeling of relief that rushes through me when the terror-filled experience has ended is alone worth the price of admission. The scarier the ride, the greater the pleasure.

This common paradoxical experience illustrates an important point about emotion: it is dynamic, complex, and ever changing—not easily captured in a snapshot. To explain this type of paradox, Richard Solomon (1980) proposed the *opponent-process theory* of emotion. According to Solomon, an event triggers (1) a "primary state"—an unlearned, automatic response, which in turn triggers (2) an "opponent state"—a learned response that is the emotional opposite of the primary state. Thus, danger activates fear followed by relief, while happy events activate joy followed by sadness. The key difference between the two reactions is that the opponent state, compared to the primary state, starts later and lasts longer. It also gets stronger with repetition and experience. As illustrated in Figure 8.14, every positive emotional state is balanced in time by its negative counterpart—and vice versa.

Sampling Area	Latitude	SAD Cases (Estimated % of population)
Alaska	65°	28.3
New Hampshire	43°	20.7
New York City	41°	17.1
Maryland	39°	16.7
Florida	27°	4.0

Regional Differences in SAD
Combining severe and mild cases, the prevalence of SAD increases with latitude north of the equator.

gloom may begin to lift. Repeat this treatment until spring season brings in an abundance of natural sunshine; then put the lights away until the autumn leaves start to fall (Blehar & Rosenthal, 1989; Sack et al., 1990; Terman et al., 1989).

To combat SAD during the polar nights of winter, teenage girls in Tromsö, Norway, receive a daily dose of light therapy.

shire than in Maryland and Florida (Booker & Hellekson, 1992).

It's not yet clear why the winter months cause SAD, or why some people are affected more than others. One theory traces the problem to the pineal gland—a tiny structure in the brain that secretes melatonin, a hormone that causes drowsiness (light inhibits its secretion). Another theory is that the circadian rhythms of SAD sufferers, their internal biological clocks, are disrupted by the relative lack of sunshine. Whatever the specific cause, there is, happily, a simple, often effective solution: light therapy. Spend about two hours each day, preferably during the morning, in front of bright fluorescent lights with your eyes open. After a few days, the clouds of

Solomon cites various animal and human studies that support this point. One such study concerned the emotional reactions of skydivers. Right before their first jump, they were terrified: their bodies became stiff, their pupils dilated, their eyes bulged, and their breathing became irregular. Then, after their feet hit the ground, there was an initial stunned silence followed by relief, chatter, laughter, even a feeling of exhilaration. From their normal baseline state, fear had turned to elation. Research on the effects of mind-altering drugs also supports this point. At first, opiate drugs (if the dosage is right) produce a pleasurable "high" followed by a less intense state of euphoria. As the drug wears off, however, the user suffers through an agonizing state of withdrawal that is far less pleasant than his or her predrug state. Similarly, skydivers find that their fear subsides after several jumps, and drug users find that they must increase their dosage to get high.

The opponent-process theory offers some interesting insights into our changing emotional states. The hypothesis that every emotion triggers its opposite, perhaps to keep us emotionally balanced, may help to explain why women sometimes experience a "letdown" after the joy of childbirth, or why health enthusiasts enjoy hard physical exercise, hot and dry saunas, and other types of "good pain." Contemplating the implications, Solomon is quick to point out that the opponent-process theory is a puritan's theory: pleasure will enlarge the appetite for reward and make joy more elusive, while pain and suffering will enhance one's later sense of well-being. Pleasure has its costs, pain its benefits.

Figure 8.14

Opponent-Process Theory of Emotion

According to this theory, every primary state triggers its opposite. The result is a more balanced emotional experience in which a positive state is soon followed by a negative state, and vice versa.

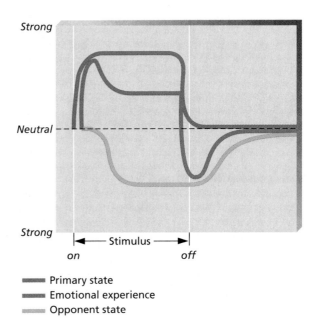

- ▬▬ Primary state
- ▬▬ Emotional experience
- ▬▬ Opponent state

The Cultural Context

Inspired by the writings of Charles Darwin, researchers have discovered several "universals" in human emotion. We saw earlier, for example, that people from diverse cultures react to emotion-filled events with similar arousal symptoms and widely recognized facial expressions. To some extent, people of different cultures and languages also categorize human emotions in similar ways. The following passage illustrates the point. "What are the feelings of men? They are joy, anger, sadness, fear, love, disliking, and liking. These seven feelings belong to men without their learning them." This statement may seem to have appeared earlier in this chapter. In fact, it is taken from *Li Chi*, a Chinese encyclopedia that was compiled in the first century B.C.

The physiological and expressive components of human emotion may be inborn and universal, and they may be related in important ways to environmental factors (see box). But there are also some cultural differences in the types of antecedent events that stir various emotions. According to Batja Mesquita and Nico Frijda (1992), certain events reliably trigger certain emotions. In all cultures, friendships and achievement elicit joy; insults and injustice elicit anger; novel experiences and risk-taking elicit fear; death, rejection, separation, and the breakup of relationships elicit sadness. The situations that awaken jealousy are also universal. In a cross-cultural study of the "green-eyed monster," college students from seven countries all said they would feel jealous if their boyfriend or girlfriend were to flirt with, kiss, or have sex with another person (Buunk & Hupka, 1987). Yet despite these similarities, the antecedents of emotion differ as a result of culturally specific living conditions. Among the Utku Eskimos, fear is triggered by thin ice, rough seas, and dangerous animals. However, among Israelis—for whom terrorism, the threat of war, and border clashes are constant—fear is most often awakened by interactions with strangers.

Culture also influences the way people categorize their experiences. Consider the words we use to describe our various emotions. Based on ethnographies and cross-cultural studies of language, James Russell (1991) finds that there are some striking differences between cultures. As noted earlier, the English language contains more than 2,000 words for categories of emotion. Yet there are only 1,501 emotion words in Dutch, 750 in Taiwanese, 230 in Malay, 58 among the Ifalukian of Micronesia, and 7 among the Chewong of Malaysia.

According to Russell, differences like these provide insight into a culture's folk theories of emotion. Among the Ilongot, a head-hunting tribe native to the Philippines, the word *liget* is used to describe both anger and grief—intense feelings for which head-hunting is an accepted form of release. Among the Gidjingali aborigines of Australia, the word *gurakadj* combines shame and fear; in Samoa, the word *alofa* is used to describe feelings of love, sympathy, and pity. Japanese lacks a word for "disappointed," Tahitian lacks a word for "sadness," and Gujarati, a language spoken in India, lacks a word for "excited."

In some cultures, emotion words are used that have no clear counterpart in the English language. For example, the German word *schadenfreude* specifically refers to pleasure derived from another person's suffering. In Indonesia, a distinction is made between *malu*, a feeling of shame brought on by one's own actions, and *dipermalukan*, a feeling of shame caused by someone else's deeds. Among the Baining of Papua New Guinea, *awumbuk* is an emotion that combines sadness, tiredness, and boredom that is brought on by the departure of visiting friends or relatives. Among the Utku Eskimos, *naklik* refers to the love of babies, sick people, and others in need of protection, while *niviuq* is a form of love felt toward those who are charming or admired. Similarly, the Utku distinguish among the fear of dangerous animals, evil spirits, thin ice, and an angry God.

The language of emotion provides clues about the emotional life of a culture. Consider, for example, comparisons often made between the United States and Japan. In America, parents teach their children to be independent, self-reliant, and assertive—a "cut above the rest." But in Japan, children are raised to fit into the community because "the nail that stands out gets pounded down." According to Hazel Markus and Shonobu Kitayama (1991), these cultures foster different conceptions of the individual in relation to others. In the United States—and in many other Western countries, too—people have an *independent* view of themselves as distinct, autonomous, and self-contained. In much of Asia, Africa, and Latin America, however, people hold a collective or *interdependent* view of themselves as part of a larger group in which social connections are more important than individual self-expression. These different outlooks are evident in the language of emotion (Matsumoto et al., 1988). So, while Americans are quick to express jealousy, anger, pride, and other "ego-focused" emotions, non-Westerners are more likely to feel sympathy, shame, respect, and embarrassment—"other-focused" emotions that promote interpersonal harmony

In Japan, it is more important that children learn to fit into the community than to stand out as individuals.

The Pursuit of Happiness

"In every adversity of fortune, to have been happy is the most unhappy kind of misfortune."   BOETHIUS

Long before psychology was born into science, philosophers regarded happiness to be the ultimate emotional state, one that all persons should strive for. In the Declaration of Independence, Thomas Jefferson thus cited life, liberty, and "the pursuit of happiness" as the most cherished of human rights. But what is happiness, and how is it achieved? Aristotle said it was the reward of an active life. Freud pointed to work and love. Others claim that happiness requires money, status, power, health and fitness, religion, beauty, the satisfaction of basic needs, and an ability to derive pleasure from the events of everyday life.

To study happiness (or as many psychologists now call it, "subjective well-being"), one must be able to measure it. How do researchers know if someone is happy? Simple: they just ask. Better yet, they use such questionnaires as the Satisfaction with Life Scale, in which subjects respond to statements such as, "If I could live my life over, I would change almost nothing." (Diener et al., 1984; Pavot & Diener, 1993). After all, said Marcus Aurelius, "no man is happy who does not think himself so."

Consistently, surveys show that 75 percent of those asked describe themselves as happy—and that happiness is associated with cheerful moods, self-esteem, physical and mental health, a sense of personal control, memory for positive rather than negative past events, and optimism about the future (Taylor, 1989; Seidlitz & Diener, 1993). It's no secret that your outlook on life becomes rosy right after you win a game, fall in love, land a great job, or make lots of money. Nor is it a secret that the world seems gloomy right after you lose, fall out of love, suffer a personal tragedy, or experience a financial setback. Predictably, the events of everyday life trigger fluctuations in our mood. For example, people are most happy on Fridays and Saturdays, and least happy on Mondays and Tuesdays (Larsen & Kasimatis, 1990). The

question is, what influences long-term satisfaction, and why are some people happier in general than others?

Seeking the roots of happiness, Ed Diener (1984) and others (Strack et al., 1991) reviewed many years of research and found that subjective well-being is not meaningfully related to such demographic factors as age, sex, race, ethnic background, IQ, or education level. However, there are three key predictors: (1) *social relationships* (people with an active social life, good friends, and a happy marriage are more satisfied than those who lack these intimate connections), (2) *employment status* (employed people are happier than those who are out of work—regardless of income), and (3) *health* (people who are physically fit and healthy are happier than those who are not).

Perhaps the most interesting relationship is between *income* and subjective well-being. Everyone knows the saying that "money can't buy happiness." But personally, I know very few people—particularly among those who are financially strapped—who truly believe it. Is wealth a key to happiness? Yes and no. Research reveals that there's a positive relationship: within a given country, the higher the income, the greater the satisfaction. For example, Ed Diener and his colleagues (1985) found that wealthy Americans reported being happy 77 percent of the time, while those of average means said they were happy 62 percent of the time. This 15-point difference is statistically significant, but it is also surprisingly small—especially considering that the wealthy respondents were selected from a list of the four hundred richest Americans! Also interesting is the finding that people who live in affluent countries such as the United States and Japan are not that much happier, and in some cases are less happy, than those who live in poorer countries such as Ireland, Argentina, and Hungary. Nor are increases in the standard of living within a single country accompanied by increases in reported happiness. Americans are twice as rich now as they were forty years ago—before we had personal computers, CD players, camcorders, big-screen color TVs, microwave ovens, digital

rather than conflict. Thus, the Japanese describe emotions such as *amae* (a pleasant feeling of trust and dependence), *oime* (feelings of indebtedness), *haji* (shame caused by immodest behavior), and *itoshii* (longing for an absent loved one). To a large extent, culture shapes our emotional lives (Kitayama and Markus, 1994).

Finally, there are some striking cultural differences in the *display rules* that determine when it is appropriate for people to express their feelings.

There is no formula for happiness, but enjoyment of one's work is undoubtedly an important ingredient.

watches, and fax machines. Yet during that same period of time, the percentage of Americans who describe themselves as "very happy" has not risen at all (Myers, 1993).

The reason money does not guarantee happiness is that our perceptions of wealth are relative to some standard. According to *social comparison theory,* people compare themselves to others, and feel content or deprived depending on how they fare in this comparison. To demonstrate, Ladd Wheeler and Kunitate Miyake (1992) asked ninety-two college students to keep for two weeks a written record of every time they mentally compared themselves—their grades, appearance, wealth, personality, or abilities—to someone else. Consistently, these diaries revealed that "upward comparisons" (to others who are better off) triggered negative feelings, while "downward comparisons" (to others who are worse off) triggered positive feelings. This result sheds light on why there is only a modest relationship between income and happiness. The middle-class worker whose friends and neighbors can't pay their bills feels successful. Yet the upper-class social

climber who moves into an affluent suburb and rubs elbows with the rich and famous feels relatively deprived. The trick is to avoid looking to the top of the ladder at others who are better off than you are.

It is also natural for people to use their own past lives as a standard of comparison. According to *adaptation level theory,* our satisfaction with the present depends on the level of success that we are accustomed to. Win a lottery, inherit a fortune, buy a new house, or make a killing in the stock market, and you will surely experience a wave of euphoria. Before long, however, the glitter will wear off, and you will adapt to your new wealth and raise your standard of comparison. In an intriguing test of this hypothesis, Philip Brickman and his colleagues (1978) interviewed twenty-two people who had won between $50,000 and $1 million in a state lottery, and found that they did not rate themselves as happier than in the past. In fact, in contrast to others from similar backgrounds, the winners said that they now derived less pleasure from routine activities such as shopping for clothes, reading a magazine, watching TV, eating breakfast, and talking to a friend. It seems that the more money you have, the more you need to stay happy. Adaptation level theory may explain why people who grew up during the Great Depression report higher-than-average levels of satisfaction with the present (Elder, 1974). It may also explain why, as Mihaly Csikszentmihalyi (1990) notes, "the waiting rooms of psychiatrists are filled with rich successful patients who, in their forties or fifties, suddenly wake up to the fact that a plush suburban home, expensive cars, and even an Ivy League education are not enough to bring peace of mind" (p. 44).

[© 1994 Charles Barsotti and The Cartoon Bank, Inc.]

The release of anger sparked by insult, jealousy, frustration, or a physical attack is a prime example. People all over the world exhibit similar patterns of autonomic arousal, but cultures teach us whether to manage that arousal by exploding or by suppressing our rage. Among the !Kung Bushmen of the Kalahari Desert, nomadic hunters and gatherers who forage as a group and share food, people must control their rage to survive. Japanese people also practice restraint, often masking their anger with a polite smile. In Japan, an angry outburst is seen as a shameful loss of control, so it is better to publicly "grin and bear it" (Matsumoto & Ekman, 1989). Yet among the Yanomamo Indians of the Amazon jungle, loud public displays of anger are common. Indeed, Yanomamo who are angry will often scream at the top of their lungs and launch into a barrage of personal insults: "You scaly ass, you bucktooth, you protruding fang, you caiman skin!" (Good & Chanoff, 1991).

Are There Sex Differences in Emotion?

When people are asked to describe the typical man and woman, they consistently say that women are more emotional than men are (or, to put it another way, that men are less emotional than women are). This belief is found in many different cultures and among young children as well as adults (Fabes & Martin, 1991; Williams & Best, 1982). In a study that illustrates just how deeply ingrained this stereotype is, adult subjects were shown a videotape of a nine-month-old baby. Half were told that they were watching a boy; the other half thought the baby was a girl. In fact, everyone saw the same tape. Yet when the baby burst into tears over a jack-in-the-box, subjects were gender-biased in their interpretations of the child's emotional state: *he* was *angry*, *she* was *frightened* (Condry & Condry, 1976).

Are there sex differences in emotion, or is this perception a mere illusion? The research is mixed, but certain differences do seem to emerge with regularity (Brody & Hall, 1993; Grossman & Wood, 1993; LaFrance & Banaji, 1992). On the one hand, women describe themselves as more emotional— or men describe themselves as less emotional—when asked direct questions about their emotionality. On the other hand, there is little support for the conclusion that the sexes differ in their actual feelings. Both men and women become happy when they achieve something that they have strived for. Similarly, both sexes experience sadness over the loss of a loved one, anger when frustrated, fearful when in danger, embarrassed when they slip up in front of others. Men and women also exhibit the same facial expressions and autonomic reactions to emotion-triggering events. People surely differ in their propensity for happiness, sadness, anger, embarrassment, fear, and other emotions, but these differences say more about us as individuals than as men or women.

So, in what ways are women more emotional than men? One clear finding is that regardless of how men and women actually feel, the sexes do often differ in their public expressions of emotion, or *self-disclosure*. Based on a review of 205 studies involving more than 23,000 subjects, Kathryn Dindia and Mike Allen (1992) concluded that women self-disclose to friends, parents, spouses, and others more than men do (in turn, people in general self-disclose more to women than to men). Women are also more likely to wear emotions on the face and show more muscle activity on the facial EMG (Dimberg, 1990). The result is that people in general can "read" women better than they can men. In one study, for example, male and female subjects saw slides that evoked feelings of joy, sadness, fear, surprise, anger, or disgust. As they watched, their facial reactions were recorded with a hidden camera, and the videotapes were later shown to observers. Observers were better at judging the emotions felt by the expressive female subjects (Wagner et al., 1986).

Why are women more open and expressive than men? One easy explanation is that girls more than boys are socialized at an early age to talk about their feelings. Researchers who analyze parent-child conversations in the home find that parents talk more about the emotional aspect of events with their daughters than with their sons ("That music was scary, wasn't it?" "You were happy, weren't you?")—even when the children are only two or three years old (Dunn et al., 1987; Kuebli & Fivush, 1992). Another reason, at least in our culture, is that although women are permitted if not encouraged to be expressive (except when it comes to rage and anger, emotions that men are allowed to express and women are supposed to contain), men are taught to be stoic—to fulfill the ideal of the strong, silent type. Masculinity norms demand that men publicly suppress their own fears, sorrows, and weaknesses. As the saying goes, "big boys don't cry" (Tavris, 1992).

Another possible basis for the perceived sex differences in emotion is that women outperform men at using nonverbal cues to make judgments about how *others* are feeling. In a series of studies, Robert Rosenthal and his colleagues (1979) showed subjects 220 two-second film clips of an actor revealing various emotions in her face, body, and/or voice. After each film, the subjects were asked to make a social judgment: Was she expressing love or trying to seduce someone? Was she saying a prayer or talking to a lost child? Research shows that women outscore men—not only in this test but in others like it (Hall, 1984). For example, Mark Costanzo and Dane Archer (1989) presented subjects with thirty videotaped scenes, each depicting a natural, spontaneous behavior and followed by a multiple-choice question. In one scene, for example, subjects saw two women interacting with an eleven-year-old boy and were asked to determine which woman was the boy's mother. In another scene, subjects watched a female student talking on the phone and were asked to determine whether she was talking to her mother, her boyfriend, or to a close female friend. Once again, sex differences were found, again suggesting that women are more attuned than men to the emotional state of others.

Now that we have explored the psychology of emotion, let us step back and reflect on what it says about human competence and rationality. You will recall that many cognitive psychologists liken people to computers, noting the ease with which we are able to learn, recall, reason, and communicate our knowledge. At the same time, however, research shows that performance often falls short of competence. Sometimes people fail to learn (or, instead, learn to behave in maladaptive ways), forget or distort their memories of past events, and use cognitive heuristics that steer them into making poor judgments. This two-headed portrait seems to characterize our emotional lives as well. In this chapter, for example, we saw that although emotion often follows from a rational interpretation of events, it also arises instantly and without conscious thought, perhaps leading us to feel before we think. In addition, we sometimes attribute our arousal sensations to the wrong source, causing us to mislabel our own emotions. In matters of the heart and mind, human beings are not entirely competent or incompetent but a complex and fascinating mixture of both.

SUMMARY AND KEY TERMS

Although emotion is a difficult concept to define, most psychologists agree that emotions consist of three interacting components: (1) physiological arousal, (2) expressive behavior, and (3) a cognitive appraisal.

The Physiological Component

The body is intimately involved in feelings of joy, fear, anger, and other emotions. The question is, in what capacity?

A Historical Perspective

According to the *James-Lange theory,* emotion follows from one's reactions to an emotion-eliciting stimulus (you're afraid because you are trembling). In contrast, the *Cannon-Bard theory* states that a stimulus elicits various reactions and emotion at the same time (perceiving a danger causes you to tremble and feel afraid). Today, physiologically-oriented emotion researchers seek to understand the role played by different brain structures, neural pathways, and autonomic arousal.

Brain Centers of Emotion

Many emotions are regulated by the limbic system—an evolutionarily primitive set of neural structures. Certain emotional reactions are automatic (triggered instantly by the amygdala); others involve the processing of information in the cerebral cortex. One cannot pinpoint a single region of the cortex that regulates all feelings, but research shows that positive emotions evoke higher levels of EEG activity in the left hemisphere, whereas negative emotions elicit more activity in the right.

Generalized Autonomic Arousal

When an event prompts an emotional response, the *sympathetic nervous system* mobilizes the body for an adaptive "fight or flight" response. Afterward, the *parasympathetic nervous system* restores the body to its premobilized calm state.

Specific Patterns of Arousal

Are all emotions associated with the same state of arousal, or does each emotion have unique symptoms? Research supports the latter alternative. For example, heart rate increases for both anger and fear, but anger increases skin temperature, while fear has the opposite effect.

The Lie-Detector Test

Based on the assumption that lying increases stress, law enforcement officials often use the *polygraph,* an instrument that records multiple channels of arousal. Subjects who exhibit more arousal to crime-relevant questions than to control questions are judged to be lying. Many professionals claim that lie-detector tests work, but researchers have uncovered some serious problems with such tests.

The Expressive Component

Behavioral expressions of emotion serve two functions. They provide us not only with a means of nonverbal communication to others but also with sensory feedback for the self.

Nonverbal Communication

The face communicates emotion in ways that are understood by people from different countries of the world. Further suggesting that these expressions are innate is the fact that even young infants make the faces that are associated with basic emotions. To measure the activity of facial muscles and their links to emotion, researchers use the *facial electromyograph (EMG).* This device has revealed that there are two distinct types of smiles, one more genuine than the other. Additional nonverbal behaviors that communicate emotion are body language, gaze, and touch.

Sensory Feedback

According to the *facial feedback hypothesis,* an expression not only reflects one's emotion but triggers an emotional state as well. Although psychologists disagree over the reason for this effect, research indicates that it does occur.

The Cognitive Component

Psychologists have long debated the role of cognitive factors in emotion. Different theories of emotion provide different points of view.

Schachter's Two-Factor Theory of Emotion

According to the *two-factor theory of emotion,* two factors are necessary to have a specific emotion: (1) a heightened state of arousal, and (2) a cognitive label. When people are aroused and do not know why, they determine their emotions by scanning the situation and making an attribution. Through a process of excitation transfer, arousal from one event can spill over and fuel our emotional reaction to another event.

Dimensions of Appraisal

According to cognitive theorists, the emotions we experience are determined by our appraisals of the situation we are in.

Is Cognition Necessary?

Some psychologists argue that people sometimes react with emotion instantly and without a cognitive appraisal, and that our emotions and thoughts are controlled by separate anatomical structures within the brain. Others maintain that it is not possible to have emotion without thought, even thought that is quick, effortless, and unconscious. This debate remains unresolved.

Human Emotion: Putting the Pieces Together

Knowing that emotions stem from physiological, expressive, and cognitive activities is only a first step. The next step is to determine how these elements combine to produce an emotional experience.

Types of Emotions

There is widespread agreement that fear, anger, disgust, joy, surprise, and sadness are basic human emotions. Some researchers speculate that other emotions are derived from mixtures of these, or that all emotions can be classified along two independent dimensions: pleasantness and intensity.

Dynamics of Emotion

According to the opponent-process theory of emotion, an event triggers a "primary state" (an unlearned response), which in turn activates an "opponent state" (a learned response that is the emotional opposite of the primary state). The opponent state starts later, lasts longer, and gets stronger with repetition. Every positive emotional state is thus balanced in time by its negative counterpart, and vice versa.

The Cultural Context

Certain physiological and expressive components of emotion may be inborn and universal, but culture influences the types of antecedent events that arouse various emotions, the way we think about and categorize emotions, and the display rules that determine when it is appropriate to express certain feelings.

Are There Sex Differences in Emotion?

People believe that women are more emotional than men, and certain differences do emerge. Women describe themselves as more emotional (or men as less emotional), are more self-disclosing to others, are more facially expressive, and are more accurate in their judgments about how others are feeling. Socialization practices may well account for these sex differences.

PART III

Are you programmed by nature, or is your fate molded by nurturing forces in the environment? As presented in Part III, the "nature-nurture" debate animates developmental psychology—the study of how people grow, mature, and change as they get older. Chapter 9 on *infancy and childhood* focuses on pre-natal development, the birth experience, and developmental processes in infants and young children. Chapter 10 then examines the biological, cognitive, and social changes that take place in *adolescence and adulthood,* and includes discussions of teenagers and mental health, old age, and the process of dying. Picking up on the nature-nurture debate, Chapter 11 on *intelligence* examines intelligence testing; theories on the nature of intelligence; racial, cultural, and gender-based differences; and the practical implications for schools and education.

HUMAN DEVELOPMENT

Chapter 9

Infancy and Childhood

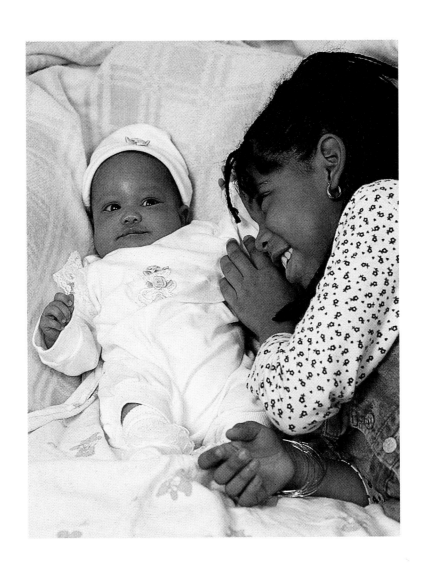

L ike most parents, my wife and I will never forget the birth of our daughter and then, three years later, our son. After nine long months of excitement and anticipation, the moment of truth had arrived. The "baby's room" was furnished and freshly painted, our work schedules were rearranged, anxious grandparents were called, the car was filled with gas, the hospital's birthing room was on reserve, and our obstetrician was ready for action. With these logistical pieces in place, every ounce of our attention turned to what was about to happen, and what it would mean for our lives. My head was spinning with questions. How long will the birthing process take? Will it go smoothly? Will the baby be okay? Will it be a boy or a girl? Who will the baby look like? Will he or she grow up to be happy, loving, smart, and successful? What will the future hold?

The study of **developmental psychology** examines the kinds of questions that parents often ask about their offspring, and that all of us ask about ourselves: How do individuals *change* as they get older? As we will see, developmental psychologists study how people grow, mature, and change across the entire life span, from conception through birth, infancy, and childhood; from adolescence through adulthood, old age, and death. Focusing on the first few years of human life, this chapter explores biological, cognitive, and social aspects of child development. But first let's step back and examine one of psychology's most enduring controversies: the nature-nurture debate.

THE BIG PICTURE

Joseph P. Kennedy is a young Massachusetts congressman, son of the late senator Robert Kennedy. Folk singer Arlo Guthrie is the son of Woody Guthrie, the folk singer who wrote "This Land Is Your Land," and entertainer Liza Minnelli is the daughter of Judy Garland, the singer who starred as a child in *The Wizard of Oz*. Ken Griffey, Jr., and Barry Bonds are outstanding major-league baseball players. Just a few years ago, so were their fathers. At first glance, these resemblances seem striking. But do they illustrate a rule, or exceptions to the rule? What do such similarities tell us about human development? One possible conclusion is that the similarities are built into nature, and that these famous sons and daughters are chips off the old block because of genetic similarity to their parents. But wait— these celebrities were also raised by their parents, were familiar with their careers, and learned from the experience.

The **nature-nurture debate** is a classic. The biological (nature) position states that just as you are programmed to grow to a certain height, you are predisposed to become shy, sociable, smart, athletic, cheerful, or depressed—according to a genetic blueprint. In contrast, the environmental (nurture) position says that your fate is molded more by life experiences, the way clay is molded by the hands of a sculptor. Psychologists who take this side of the debate trumpet the effects of learning, culture, family background, peer groups and critical life events.

Today, psychologists agree that the nature-nurture question should not be put in either-or terms. Asking whether behavior is caused by genes or the environment is like asking whether life is sustained by air or water. Both are essential. The real question is, How much does each factor con-

"We hold tomorrow in our hands when we hold our children in our arms."

BARBRA STREISAND, AT THE 1993 INAUGURATION OF PRESIDENT CLINTON

■ **developmental psychology** The study of how people grow, mature, and change over the life span.

■ **nature-nurture debate** The debate over the extent to which human behavior is determined by genetics and the environment.

■ **twin study method** A method of testing nature and nurture by comparing pairs of identical and fraternal twins of the same sex.

■ **adoption studies** A method of testing nature and nurture by comparing twins and other siblings reared together with those separated by adoption.

tribute, and how can we tease apart their combined influences? To answer the question, think about the logic of experiments, as described in Chapter 1. You may recall that in order to determine the effect of a factor on behavior, researchers try to vary that factor and keep all other variables constant. This principle suggests two possible ways to solve the nature-nurture dilemma: (1) vary the genetics but keep a constant environment, and (2) vary the environment but not the genetics.

Many years ago, Robert Tyron (1940) took the first approach in an animal study. Tyron identified white rats as "bright" or "dull" based on their performance in a maze. He then mated the bright males with bright females, and the dull males with dull females, and tested the maze performance of their offspring. Again, Tyron bred the "brightest of the bright" and the "dullest of the dull," and tested their offspring. After repeating this procedure for twenty-one generations, Tyron had two groups of rats so different from each other that even the lowest bright animals performed better than the highest dull animals. These results are no surprise to animal breeders. Whenever horses are bred for speed, or dogs for hunting, the genetic influences on behavior are evident.

Obviously, researchers cannot selectively breed humans. But sometimes life provides a natural laboratory in which conditions approximate the desired experiment. Two methods are particularly useful in the nature-nurture debate. The two strategies are summarized in Figure 9.1. The first is the **twin study method**: to estimate the role of genetics on individuals who share the same environment, researchers compare the similarity between pairs of *identical twins* (born of one sperm fertilizing one egg, and 100 percent genetic replicas of each other) and pairs of *fraternal twins* of the same sex (born of separate sperm fertilizing two eggs and, like other siblings, sharing only about 50 percent of the same genes). To the extent that heredity is an important factor in development, identical twins should grow up to be more similar to each other than fraternal twins.

Reversing the logic of using twins who live under the same roof, a second method capitalizes on natural variations in the environment but not in the genetics. To estimate the role of the environment on persons who are genetically related, researchers conduct **adoption studies**: they compare identical twins *raised together* in the same home to those who are separated after

Figure 9.1

Measuring the Effects of Nature and Nurture

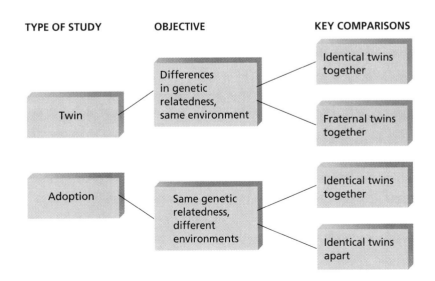

birth and *raised apart* by different parents. The contribution of the environment is thus measured by the extent to which the twins raised together are more similar to each other than those brought up in different homes. In a variation of this design, researchers may test the extent to which adopted children in general resemble their *biological* parents, siblings, and other blood relatives (evidence for the role of genetics) as opposed to their *adoptive* parents, siblings, and relatives (evidence for the role of environment). To fully appreciate these methods and their implications, imagine that you are part of a research team involved in the following project.

What's Your Prediction?

THE SITUATION

You know from past research that about 15 to 20 percent of all healthy babies are inhibited, shy, timid, and wary of strangers and unfamiliar situations. You also know that about 25 to 30 percent are uninhibited, outgoing, fearless, and eager to approach new people and situations. These basic differences are apparent at one or two years of age, and remain stable through childhood. So, where does this trait come from? Are some infants just born that way, as parents often assume, or does temperament arise from early experiences?

To tease apart the effects of nature and nurture, you decide to conduct a twin study. From monthly birth records, you contact all parents of recently born twins. Many agree to take part in your study, and you go on to recruit 178 pairs. About half are identical, or monozygotic (MZ); the others are fraternal, or dizygotic (DZ). Each set of twins is living together in the same home. You make appointments so that a mother and her children come to the laboratory when the twins are 14 months of age. Then they return for follow-up visits at 20 and 24 months old. Each session lasts for two and a half hours.

Along with two research assistants, you meet the mother and her twins in a reception room. You explain the procedure to the mother and place a bib with an identifying letter on each child. One child is randomly selected to join the mother and a second assistant in a playroom, while the other continues to play in the reception area. Once the testing is complete, the children switch places and the procedure is rerun. The playroom is simple but attractive. The floor is covered with toys. The mother sits on a sofa at one side of the room and is asked not to pay attention to the child unless needed. At this point, the child is free to play with the toys on the floor. Two events are then staged to provide additional opportunities to observe the child's behavior. The entire session is videotaped. First, a new assistant, a stranger to the child, enters the room holding a toy truck. After four minutes, she invites the child to play with her (if the child has not already done so). Next the assistant who brought the mother and child into the playroom opens up a cabinet and pulls out an unfamiliar object—either a blue stuffed toy monster, a robot made of tin cans and colored lights, or a gray remote-control plastic robot. After two minutes, the child is encouraged to approach the object (if he or she has not already done so).

To what extent is temperament genetically determined? First things first. To determine each child's level of inhibition, you review the session tapes and record how long it took the child to approach the toys, the stranger, and the unfamiliar object. You also record the percentage of time spent near the mother during these three phases. These standardized behavioral measures are then combined and the child is given an overall inhibition score.

Once all the sessions are scored, the data are ready to be analyzed. The question: What is the *correlation* between pairs of twins? If one twin is inhibited, is the other likely to be as well? If you paired unrelated children at random, the correlation would be 0 (remember, a correlation coefficient can range from 0 to plus or minus 1, and the higher the number, the stronger the link). At the other extreme, the behaviors of the MZ twin pairs—who share the same genes and the same environment—should be positively correlated. But what about the comparison group consisting of the DZ twins? If variations in child temperament are genetically determined, the correlation should be noticeably lower between DZ twins, even though raised in the same home. But if temperament stems from experience, the correlations should be about the same for the MZ and DZ twins. It would also be interesting to know whether the correlations remain stable from the first time the children are tested, at 14 months old, to the third time, after ten months of additional life experience.

MAKE A PREDICTION

You have two sets of twins, identical and fraternal, and for each set you have inhibition scores at 14, 20, and 24 months. To get you started, the correlation observed between 14-month-old MZ twins is presented below: .57. Using that number as a guideline, predict what you would expect for DZ twins at the same age. Remember, a number between 0 and .57 would indicate a greater role for genetic determination, while a number similar to .57 would indicate a greater role for experience. What do you think is at work in the case of inhibition? Is it nature or nurture? After making this initial prediction, fill in the correlations you would expect to see during the follow-up sessions:

Age	MZ Twins	DZ Twins
14 mo	.57	____
20 mo	____	____
24 mo	____	____

RESULTS

The research just described is based on a recent series of studies of infant and child temperament by Jerome Kagan and his colleagues (1988). In this particular twin study, JoAnn Robinson, along with Kagan and others (1992), sought to determine the extent to which individual differences in inhibition are the product of genetic heritage or environmental influences, nature or nurture. So, what did you predict? As shown below, the actual results provide two types of support for the contribution of genetic factors: (1) at 14 months, the correlation is higher between MZ twins than between DZ twins of the same sex, and (2) similar differences are found at 20 and 24 months, despite the additional exposure to environmental influences.

Age	MZ Twins	DZ Twins
14 mo	.56	.24
20 mo	.46	.17
24 mo	.58	.32

WHAT DOES IT ALL MEAN?

As researchers try to estimate the relative effects of heredity and environment, it is clear that both are important sources of influence on psychological characteristics. In this study of one- and two-year-olds, differences in temperament were attributable in part to genetic factors. But the correlations are far from perfect, even among MZ twins raised in the same home—thus suggesting that other influences are also at work. A second important point to note is that not all differences are rooted in genetics. In another study of the same twins, for example, the twin-pair correlations in performance on word comprehension and memory tasks were much lower (Plomin et al., 1993). Nature and nurture: The issues are complex, so let's briefly review some of the evidence for both factors.

Nature's Evidence

In 1979, Jim Springer and his identical twin brother Jim Lewis were reunited after thirty-nine years apart. Separated five weeks after birth, they were adopted by different families in Ohio. When University of Minnesota psychologist Thomas Bouchard, Jr., heard the story, he invited the Jim twins to take part in the ongoing research program dubbed the Minnesota twin study. What Bouchard and his colleagues (1990) found was astonishing: not only did both Jims have the same first name, but they both married women named Linda, divorced, and married women named Betty. Springer

Separated a few weeks after birth in 1940, the Jim twins were reunited in 1979.

named his oldest son James Allan, Lewis named his James Alan. In their childhood, both had dogs named Toy, and both liked math but hated spelling. As adults, both men were deputy sheriffs, and pumped gas and worked for McDonald's. Both drank Miller Lite beer, chain-smoked Salem cigarettes, chewed their fingernails, spent vacations on the same Florida beach, and enjoyed stock-car racing and woodworking. In fact, Springer and Lewis had even built similar white benches in their backyards! Additional similarities were revealed in their medical histories: both men gained and lost ten pounds at about the same age, both started to experience severe headaches at eighteen, and both suffered what seemed like a heart attack (Holden, 1980).

By administering various tests and collecting biographical data from pairs of identical twins reared apart, Bouchard and his colleagues (1990) found other odd similarities in mannerisms, abilities, tastes, habits, and the like (see also Holden, 1987; Lykken et al., 1992). These stories are fascinating, but what do they prove about the role of genetics in human development? In his book *Innumeracy,* mathematician John Allen Paulos (1988) pointed out that fluke similarities and coincidences like these are not as improbable as we might think. After all, there are so many ways to compare ourselves to others that at least some "striking" similarities are bound to be discovered. To take a more systematic approach, developmental psychologists search for statistical correlations used to calculate **heritability**—an estimate, for a given trait, of the extent to which the variation within a group is due to genetic factors rather than to the environment.

Is 5 percent, 50 percent, or 90 percent of the variability in personality traits attributable to genetics? What about intelligence, mental health, and other characteristics? In the temperament study described at the start of this chapter, the observed correlations enabled the investigators to estimate that roughly 57 percent of the variation in shyness among children was due to genetic influences (Robinson et al., 1992). In one of the Minnesota studies—which examined 217 MZ twins raised together, 114 DZ twins raised together, 44 MZ twins raised apart, and 27 DZ twins raised apart— heritability estimates averaged 48 percent (this is not to say that genes control 48 percent of your personality, but that genetic factors account for that much of the variation within a group.) On a wide range of personality measures, the evidence was clear: (1) when raised together, MZ twins were more similar than DZ twins, and (2) twins raised apart were almost as similar to each other as those raised together in the same home (Bouchard & McGue, 1990; Tellegen et al., 1988). Additional studies of twins and adoptees have extended nature's message even further: intelligence, verbal and spatial abilities, altruism, alcoholism, criminality, vocational interests, and various forms of mental illness all seem to have strong genetic roots (Bouchard et al., 1990; Loehlin et al., 1988; Lykken et al., 1993; Plomin & McClearn, 1993).

Nurture's Evidence

Does this wave of support for the forces of nature mean that one's environment is unimportant? Are the sons and daughters of shy parents doomed to become wallflowers? Are **young** children genetically programmed for high

Oskar Stohr and Jack Yufe are identical twins separated at birth. In an ironic twist of fate, one was raised by a Nazi family in Germany, and the other is Jewish.

■ **heritability** A term that refers to the statistic used to estimate the percentage of the variability of a trait caused by genetic factors.

Actor Macaulay Culkin has six brothers and sisters. So what makes him different? Researchers have come to realize that even if brothers and sisters grow up in the same home, they encounter somewhat different environments.

"It's a shame you missed the eighties."

[Drawing by W. Miller; © 1990 The New Yorker Magazine, Inc.]

or low math grades? Are violent criminals born, not made? No, not at all. Robert Plomin (1989) notes that twin studies and adoption research contain a second clear message that should not be drowned out: "that these same data provide the best available evidence for the importance of the environment" (p. 108).

This pro-nurture conclusion is based on two observations. The first is that, even among identical twins, heredity usually accounts for less than 50 percent of the variation in personality (heritability estimates are higher in intellectual domains)—which means that environmental factors are responsible for the rest. Second, children growing up in the same home are quite different from each other, regardless of whether they're related by blood or adoption. The reason is that no two siblings live in the same environment, even when they grow up together in the same house (Loehlin et al., 1987; Scarr & Weinberg, 1983). True, there is a *shared environment*. Siblings may have the same parents, attend the same school, take the same vacations, visit the same relatives, and celebrate the same holidays. But brothers and sisters also experience unique *nonshared environments*. Born at separate times, siblings are treated differently by their parents, have different friends and teachers, play on different sports teams, and so on. A particular sibling may even fall victim to illness, a serious accident, the death of a friend, or other traumas not endured by a brother or sister. The point is, the forces of nurture are vital to development, and they can steer us in different directions—not just between families but within a family as well (Dunn & Plomin, 1990; Hetherington et al., 1994).

As researchers struggle to tease apart the influences of nature and nurture, they must consider yet another complicating factor: the two factors are not independent. Research shows that identical twins receive more similar treatment from parents than fraternal twins do. In fact, the more genetically similar any two siblings are, the more similar their experience is in the home. To some extent, each of us selects and modifies our own environment—and our genetic makeup plays an important role in the kind of environment we create (Scarr & McCartney, 1983; Plomin et al., 1994).

THE UNBORN CHILD

Recognizing that the passage from the womb into the outside world is a profound one, westerners celebrate the birthday as the starting point in a person's development. In fact, birth is not so much a beginning as a transition. The real beginning occurs nine months earlier, at the moment of conception. That is why the Chinese calculate age from that moment and consider a baby to be a one-year-old at birth.

Genetic Building Blocks

Life begins when a tiny male *sperm* cell—one of hundreds of millions released into the Fallopian tube during intercourse—is united with the female's *ovum*, or egg cell. The fertilized ovum then forms a barrier that blocks the entry of other sperm. In the meantime, the nucleus of the male and female cells move toward each other, fusing within hours into a single, brand-new cell. This fusion marks the beginning of a new life, genetically endowed by a mother and father. Right from the start, this single cell has a full genetic heritage contained within 23 pairs of rod-like structures called **chromosomes**—half carried in the mother's ovum, and half in the father's sperm. Each of the 46 chromosomes contains strands of the molecule **deoxyribonucleic acid**, commonly known as **DNA.** In turn, each DNA molecule is made up of many thousands of segments called **genes**—the biochemical building blocks of an individual life (see Figure 9.2).

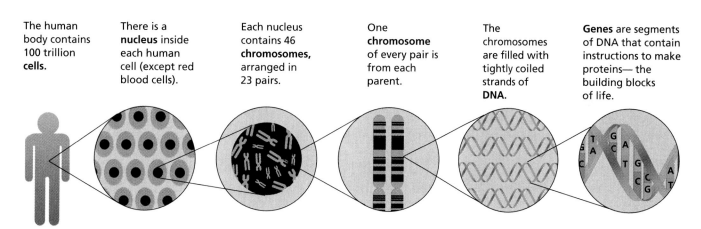

The human body contains 100 trillion **cells.**

There is a **nucleus** inside each human cell (except red blood cells).

Each nucleus contains 46 **chromosomes,** arranged in 23 pairs.

One **chromosome** of every pair is from each parent.

The chromosomes are filled with tightly coiled strands of **DNA.**

Genes are segments of DNA that contain instructions to make proteins— the building blocks of life.

Figure 9.2
Genetic Building Blocks

Like a photograph that has already been taken but not yet developed, genes determine your skin color, height, weight, blood type, and certain personality traits as well as medical and psychological disorders. All humans have certain genes in common, which is why you can walk and talk, but not fly, bark, or breathe underwater. At the same time, unless you are one of two identical twins, you have a distinct combination of genes that makes you unique among all past, present, and future humans. The 23rd pair of chromosomes controls your sex. Whereas everyone receives an X chromosome from the mother, there is an equal chance that the father will donate either an X or Y chromosome to the pair. If X, the offspring will be female (XX); if Y, it will be male (XY). The sex of a child thus depends on the father's contribution.

Prenatal Development

Prenatal development during the nine months of pregnancy is divided into three stages: *germinal* (the first two weeks after conception), *embryonic* (third to ninth weeks), and *fetal* (ninth week to birth). From one stage to the next, dramatic biological changes take place and environmental influences are plentiful. These developments are illustrated in Figure 9.3.

First, there is the germinal stage. Thanks to conception, life begins with one remarkable new cell called a **zygote**—about the size of the period at the end of this sentence, yet fully equipped with a rich genetic heritage. Very

■ **chromosomes** Rod-like structures, found in all biological cells, that contain DNA molecules in the form of genes.

■ **deoxyribonucleic acid (DNA)** The complex molecular structure of a chromosome that carries genetic information.

■ **genes** The biochemical units of heredity that govern the development of an individual life.

■ **zygote** A fertilized egg that undergoes a two-week period of rapid cell division and develops into an embryo.

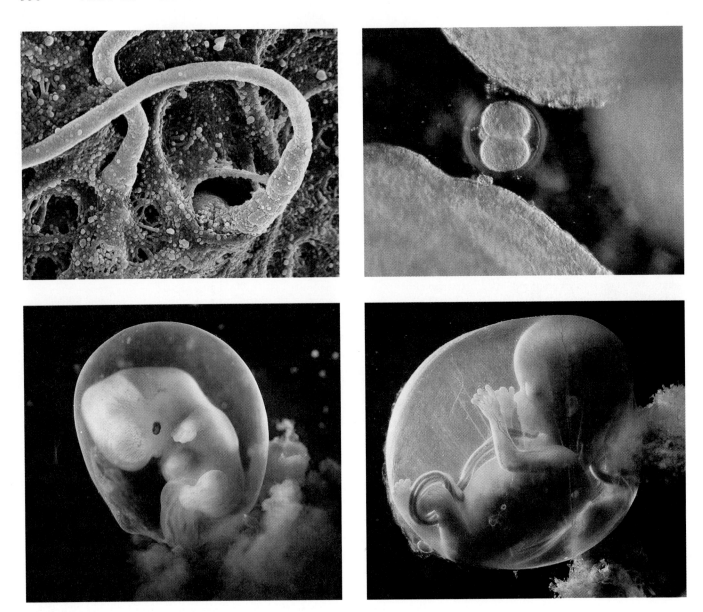

Figure 9.3

Prenatal Development

Just prior to conception, a sperm penetrates the ovum wall (top left). After thirty hours, the fertilized ovum divides for the first time and each cell contains genes from both the mother and the father (top right). After six weeks, the embryo's heart is beating and parts of its body have formed (bottom left). At four months, the fetus is 2 to 4 inches in length and takes on a conspicuously human appearance (bottom right).

■ **embryo** The developing human organism, from two weeks to two months after conception.

quickly, a process of cell division takes place: the first cell splits into two, four, eight, and so on. After two and a half days, there are twelve to sixteen cells. By the fourth day, there are more than a hundred cells clustered together in a ball, traveling from the Fallopian tube into the uterus, and increasing in both number and diversity. Some will form muscles and bone; others will form the stomach, liver, and so on. At two weeks, the ball of cells attaches to the uterine wall, braced and ready for eight and a half months in a new home. By the time this zygote is born, it will consist of hundreds of trillions of cells.

Once the zygote is firmly attached to the uterine wall, the germinal stage is over, and the zygote is called an **embryo**. It is at this point when all parts of the body begin to form—an oversized head with a primitive brain and central nervous system, eyes, ears, a nose, and a mouth with lips and teeth, a heart and circulatory system, arms, legs, fingers, toes, and a tail. During this stage, organs start to function, including a heart that pumps blood and beats for the first time. Also during this stage, the male hormone testosterone is secreted in embryos that are genetically male, but not in those des-

■ **fetus** The developing human organism, from nine weeks after conception to birth.

■ **teratogens** Toxic substances that can harm the embryo or fetus during prenatal development.

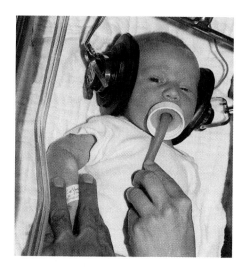

In this study, infants sucked on a nipple more vigorously to hear the sound of their mother's voice rather than that of an unfamiliar male (DeCasper & Fifer, 1980).

tined to become female. The embryo is an astonishing creature: all the pieces of an individual are in place, yet at eight weeks of age it is only an inch long and weighs a tenth of an ounce. You could hold one in the palm of your hand.

From the ninth week on, the embryo becomes a conspicuously human **fetus.** At first, the cartilage in the bones starts to harden and there is rapid growth of the brain, heart, lungs, genitals, and other internal organs and body parts. Depending on its age, the fetus can squirm, open its eyes, suck its thumb, kick its legs, curl its toes, and turn somersaults. By the seventh month, the key life-support systems are sufficiently developed so that the fetus can breathe, circulate blood, digest nutrients, and dispose of wastes. At this point, the two-pound fetus has a fighting chance to survive if delivered prematurely. If born on schedule, it will weigh an average of seven pounds.

Let's stop for a moment and ponder a fascinating prospect for parents. During the final three months of pregnancy, a fetus is developed enough to hear sounds from the outside world. Is it possible that the fetus can recognize mom's voice? Can expectant parents soothe, even teach, their unborn child by reading stories or playing music? Could I have pretrained my daughter and son to appreciate the thrills of baseball, suspense novels, and rock 'n' roll? In a fascinating series of experiments, Anthony DeCasper and his colleagues sought to answer these questions. In one study, 16 women—twice a day in the last six weeks of pregnancy—read passages either from Dr. Seuss's *The Cat in the Hat* or from *The King, the Mice, and the Cheese,* a child's story with a very different cadence. Three days after birth, the babies were brought to the laboratory where they wore headphones and sucked an electronic pacifier that activated a tape recording of one of these two stories, depending on the rate at which the nipple was sucked. As it turned out, 13 of the 16 babies "chose" by sucking faster or slower to hear the story the mother had read before birth (DeCasper & Spence, 1986). Along similar lines, newborns prefer to hear the familiar patterns and rhythms of the mother's voice or a heartbeat than the unfamiliar sound of a male voice (DeCasper & Fifer, 1980; DeCasper & Sigafoos, 1983).

Although fetal development follows a biological clock, it is heavily influenced by environmental factors as well. Depending on the biological stage of development, exposure to harmful substances called **teratogens** (from the Greek word *teras,* meaning "monster") can have devastating effects on the fetus. As obstetricians tell expectant mothers, malnutrition, stress, x-rays, AIDS, German measles and other viral infections, certain antibiotics, painkillers, large doses of aspirin, heavy exposure to paint fumes, and a long list of drugs can all prove dangerous (see Table 9.1). Some teratogens cannot be avoided—and some problems may arise without exposure to toxic substances. There are no guarantees. But expectant mothers can minimize the risks by controlling their intake of certain harmful substances (see box, p. 342).

THE BIRTH EXPERIENCE

Few transitions in life are as dramatic as one's emergence from the birth canal into the world. After spending nine months curled up inside a dimly

Table 9.1

Some of the Substances That Can Harm
the Developing Embryo and Fetus

Substance	Possible Danger
Alcohol	Excessive use can produce fetal alcohol syndrome. Even one or two drinks a day can cause damage—especially in the early stages of pregnancy.
Cigarettes	Smoking is linked to miscarriages, premature births, and low birth weight. Effects on behavior and cognitive functioning are harder to pinpoint.
Cocaine	Cocaine use results in lower birth weight and possibly permanent learning deficits.
Aspirin	Taken in large quantities, aspirin can cause prenatal bleeding, intestinal discomfort, respiratory problems, and low birth weight.
Marijuana	Heavy use can lead to premature birth and to babies with abnormal reactions to stimulation.
AIDS	AIDS can be transmitted to the fetus (or to the newborn during birth). AIDS-infected fetuses are often born with facial deformities and growth failure.
Rubella	Before the 11th week, rubella, or German measles, can cause heart problems, mental retardation, cataracts, and deafness.
X-rays	Heavy exposure can cause malformation of organs.

lit, warm sack of amniotic fluid, the baby is pulled out, poked, prodded, and exposed for the first time to cold dry air, bright lights, and high-pitched sounds. As an adult, you would probably feel rather dazed by this rude awakening. But what is it like for a newborn?

The Prenatal Environment

Research on the newborn's sensory experience right before and after birth has yielded some surprising findings. In the first place, the mother's womb is not a perfectly tranquil home free from stimulation. Amniotic fluid contains urine, sugars, cholesterol, and fatty acids, so the fetus can taste a mixture of sweet, sour, salty, and bitter flavors in the mouth. There is also a good deal of movement. Although cushioned from many of life's jolts, the early fetus tumbles around, and the more advanced fetus—which is too cramped for such gymnastics—fidgets and kicks. Finally, there is noise, and lots of it. Near the fetus, the mother's organs beat, rumble, and growl. And when the mother speaks, her voice travels like thunder down her lungs. The fetus is equipped to detect these sounds beginning in the seventh month. So, what is the prenatal experience like? Daphne and Charles Maurer (1988) put it this way: "To the adult, withdrawing into the womb would resemble flying cramped inside a light airplane, through turbulent weather, with the taste of air-sickness in your mouth" (p. 7).

The Postnatal Environment

Although the fetus is stimulated before being born, the first few moments after birth are different, to say the least. The typical delivery room is highly illuminated. Many parents don't realize that newborn babies can see as soon as they are born, and can follow moving objects with their eyes. The reason babies are born with their eyes shut is that the delivery room is too bright. By using invisible, infrared light to photograph eye movements, researchers found that in total darkness newborn babies open their eyes wide and scan back and forth, and that even dim light causes them to squint (Haith, 1980). Think about how it feels to catch a glimpse of the morning sun after a full night's sleep, and then imagine that you had slept for nine months. As we saw in Chapter 3, the eye that is adapted to the dark becomes hypersensitive to light.

Upon birth, sounds are not necessarily louder, but they are different. When the baby emerges at birth, the ears are plugged up with amniotic fluid, which muffles sound. It's just as well, too, because the delivery room is often filled with shrieks of pain, joy, and other noises. There is also a change in outside temperature. From constant warmth, the newborn emerges soaking wet and naked into a relatively cold room. Like anyone who steps out of a hot bath, the infant is chilled. Because newborns have a higher proportion of surface area from which to lose heat and less insulation in the form of fat, their body temperature drops sharply right after birth.

At birth, the newborn is thrust into a world that is brighter, louder, and colder than it is accustomed to.

THE REMARKABLE NEWBORN

In 1890, William James described the newborn's experience of the world as "one great booming, buzzing confusion." Some eighty years later, Lewis Lipsitt (1971) signaled the dawn of a new era in an article entitled "Babies: They're a Lot Smarter than They Look." Why is there such a discrepancy

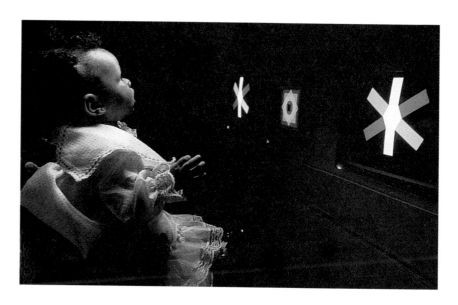

Infant researchers have developed sophisticated new techniques to measure what newborns cannot put into words.

DEVELOPMENTAL PSYCHOLOGY   Health

Drugs and the Fetus

Legally and illegally, people have used drugs throughout human history. The psychoactive effects of various substances on the user were described in Chapter 4. But are there health risks to a fetus when the user is an expectant mother? And if so, is the fetus more vulnerable during some stages of pregnancy than others? In recent years, researchers have studied the effects of various substances, including alcohol, tobacco, and cocaine.

Alcohol. In 1899, English doctor William Sullivan studied the babies born to women in prison. He compared the children of heavy-drinking mothers with those of nondrinkers and discovered that the rate of stillbirths and infant mortality was two and a half times higher among the children of drinking mothers. This discovery lay dormant for many years. Then in 1973, Kenneth Jones and his colleagues noticed that eleven babies of alcoholic mothers were born with a pattern of defects that included stunted growth, facial deformities (widely spaced eyes, a flattened nose, and a thin upper lip), and mental retardation. They called this pattern **fetal alchohol syndrome.**

The devastating impact of alcohol is not all that surprising in light of the immediate effects it has on the fetus. Soon after a mother takes a drink—whether it's beer, wine, or hard liquor—alcohol enters her bloodstream. It then passes through the placenta into the fetus's blood, flows to the brain, and impairs breathing. Using ultrasound to observe fetuses, researchers found that after the mothers drank a glass of orange juice, the fetuses breathed an average of 46 percent of the time. But after the mothers drank a "screwdriver"—a drink consisting of orange juice and vodka—breathing time decreased to 14 percent (Lewis & Boylan, 1979). It seems that when an expectant mother gets drunk, to some extent, so does her unborn child.

From more than a thousand animal experiments and recent studies with humans, the evidence is clear: alcoholic mothers are likely to have a "multihandicapped child"—one who suffers from brain damage, intellectual impairments, attentional disorders, speech problems, hyperactivity, and motor problems such as trembling, slow reflexes, lack of coordination, and a weak grip (Hill et al., 1989; West, 1986). But what about social drinking during pregnancy? Does an occasional glass of wine over dinner or a sip of bubbly champagne on New Year's Eve cause permanent damage to the unborn child? When it comes to social drinking, the evidence suggests that expectant mothers should exercise caution.

In one study, Sandra Jacobson and her colleagues (1993) tested infants born to women who drank varying degrees of alcohol during pregnancy. They found that infants whose

■ **fetal alcohol syndrome** A specific pattern of birth defects (stunted growth, facial deformity, and mental retardation) often found in the offspring of alcoholic mothers.

■ **habituation** The tendency for attention to a stimulus to wane over time (often used to determine whether an infant has "learned" a stimulus).

■ **recovery** Following habituation to one stimulus, the tendency for a second stimulus to arouse new interest (often used to test whether infants can discriminate between stimuli).

between James and Lipsitt? Babies are not more capable today than they used to be—they still sleep sixteen to twenty hours a day, shut their eyes under the bright sun, dirty their diapers, and cry a lot. The difference is that developmental psychologists now have high-tech equipment and sophisticated methods to measure what the newborn cannot tell us in words.

One particularly valuable research technique is based on the measurement of **habituation,** the tendency for attention to a novel stimulus to wane over time. If a picture or sound is presented over and over again, an infant will eventually get bored, lose interest, look away, and exhibit a change in heart rate—a sure sign that it has "learned" the stimulus and "remembered" the previous exposures (Bornstein, 1989). If the infant perks up, regains interest, and increases its looking time in response to a new stimulus, this **recovery** suggests that it has noticed a difference between the old and new. Using this technique, researchers can determine the age at which infants begin to distinguish different faces, voices, musical notes, speech sounds, colors, geometric shapes, and rudimentary concepts.

Other research techniques are also used. To determine what infants find interesting or surprising, researchers put different objects in front of

mothers had consumed at least two drinks a day processed information more slowly and were less likely to engage in playful imitation. In other research, Ann Streissguth, Helen Barr, and their colleagues interviewed more than 1,500 pregnant women in Seattle, most of whom were white, married, and middle class, and asked about their consumption of alcohol and other substances before and after they knew they were pregnant. Four and a half years later, 457 of these women's children were brought in for testing. Results revealed that the more alcohol consumed by the mother, the more serious the child's problems were later on. Two findings were especially alarming. First, even small doses of alcohol proved harmful. Children of mothers who consumed only about one drink a day while pregnant lacked balance, manual dexterity, and a steady hand. At three drinks a day, IQ scores dropped an average of five points. Second, damage was greatest when mothers drank during their third and fourth weeks of pregnancy, a time when the embryo's head was starting to take shape—but before many women realized they were pregnant (Barr et al., 1990; Streissguth et al., 1989). Unhappily, there seems to be no safe level of drinking, and the timing couldn't be worse.

Cigarettes. A second common teratogen is tobacco. When a woman smokes a cigarette, she inhales many chemicals—including nicotine, cyanide, and the same carbon monoxide that spews from the exhaust pipe of a car. How does all this affect the fetus? For starters, as soon as a pregnant woman lights up, oxygen is restricted and the fetus begins to breathe less. It's not surprising, then, that women who smoke are more likely to have miscarriages, premature babies, and full-term babies that are underweight (Neiberg et al., 1985). The long-term effects of smoking on the fetus are not as easy to pinpoint. A few years ago, several published studies showed a relationship between prenatal tobacco exposure and a host of behavioral problems, including deficits in aca-demic achievement, IQ, and social adjustment. It now appears, however, that women who smoke also tend to be younger, not well educated, less likely to eat a balanced diet, and more likely to drink large amounts of alcohol and coffee. Once these other factors are accounted for, it's no longer clear what kinds of long-term damage are caused by smoking per se (Streissguth et al., 1989).

Cocaine. Cocaine is a particularly harmful substance. In recent years, an estimated 5 percent of American women have used cocaine during pregnancy (Frank et al., 1988). The effects on the developing fetus are clear. Research shows that infants exposed in utero to cocaine are smaller at birth than comparable nonexposed infants. They also have difficulty learning. In one study, for example, cocaine-exposed infants learned less, showed less interest, and derived less pleasure from an enjoyable task at four to eight months old (Alessandri et al., 1993). This result is merely correlational, as cocaine-exposed and nonexposed infants may differ in other ways too. But animal researchers have found that when randomly assigned rats are injected with cocaine, they exhibit less nurturing parental behavior (Zimmerberg and Gray, 1992). Moreover, the pups of cocaine-exposed pregnant rats exhibit learning deficits that persist into their adulthood (Smith et al., 1989; Heyser et al., 1993).

them—dots, lines, balls, whatever—and use an eye-tracking device to record the amount of time spent looking at each object. Or, as in the Dr. Seuss study described earlier, an electronic pacifier can be used to allow infants to express their preferences by sucking on the nipple in a certain manner. As we'll see, there are numerous ways for a newborn to "communicate" to researchers. Body movements, facial expressions, and measured changes in brain waves, heart rate, and respiration are among the possibilities. When it comes to infants, says researcher Mark Strauss, "you can tell the wheels are turning. They're paying attention to the world in incredibly subtle ways" (cited in Grunwald & Goldberg, 1993).

The results of all the recent research are informative—and sometimes startling. For example, Karen Wynn (1992) showed five-month-old infants one or two Mickey Mouse dolls being put on a puppet stage and covered by a screen (see Figure 9.4). Next they saw her either add a doll to the one behind the screen (1 + 1) or take one away (2 − 1). The screen was then lowered, so the babies could see how many dolls were now on the stage. Sometimes the number was correct (2 in addition, 1 in subtraction); at other times it was incorrect (1 in addition, 2 in subtraction). Can infants

Figure 9.4

Can Infants Add and Subtract?

Five-month-olds saw a sequence of events that illustrated the addition (1 + 1 = 2) or subtraction (2 - 1 = 1) of Mickey Mouse dolls. In each case, a correct or incorrect outcome was revealed. The infants looked longer at outcomes that were incorrect and, apparently, unexpected (Wynn, 1992).

■ **grasping reflex** In infants, an automatic tendency to grasp an object that stimulates the palm.

■ **rooting reflex** In response to contact on the cheek, an infant's tendency to turn toward the stimulus and open its mouth.

add and subtract? If so, reasoned Wynn, then they would "expect" correct outcomes and be surprised by incorrect outcomes. That is what happened. By recording their looking time, Wynn found that the babies looked longer at the incorrect—and apparently unexpected—outcomes. This result suggests that five-month-olds have a rudimentary ability to add and subtract.

Reflexes

In light of research, developmental psychologists now have a profound respect for the newborn's capacities. To begin with, babies are prepared upon birth with many adaptive reflexes—automatic, unlearned reactions to certain types of stimulation. Press into a newborn's palm, and you will stimulate a **grasping reflex** that causes the baby to clutch your hand so hard that it can support its own weight. Touch the newborn's right or left cheek with a nipple, or even a finger, and you will stimulate a **rooting reflex**, causing the baby automatically to turn in that direction and open its mouth. Touch the newborn's lips, and it will try to squeeze your finger between its tongue and palate, breathe through the nose, and begin to *suck*. Move your finger to the back of the baby's mouth, and it will try to *swallow*. None of these reflexes are intentional or within the infant's control, and most disappear within three or four months, never to return. While they last, however, grasping, turning, opening the mouth, sucking, swallowing, and other reflexes are an important part of the newborn's adaptive machinery.

Sensory Capacities

Contrary to what maternity doctors and nurses used to tell new mothers, the newborn has the capacity to see, hear, taste, smell, and feel pain. The question is not whether newborns have these senses, but, rather, what are their limitations and what kinds of stimulation do they prefer?

Vision   At birth, portions of the eye and the visual cortex are not fully developed, and the newborn is nearsighted. In fact, to see an object as would an adult with 20/20 vision, the newborn needs to be twenty to thirty times closer—the best distance being about eight inches from the eyes (Banks & Salapatek, 1983). The problem is that the newborn's lens does not focus on objects at a distance. Newborns also cannot detect subtle differences in light, shading, or color. So, soft pastel colors in the crib or on wallpaper do not arouse as much interest as a newspaper with bold print or a checkerboard that has stark black-on-white contrast (Adams & Maurer, 1984). What would it be like to see through the eyes of a newborn baby? According to Daphne and Charles Maurer (1988), the world would look like "a badly focused snapshot that has been fading in the sun for so many years that you can barely identify the subject" (p. 127).

Newborns may be limited in their vision, but their sensory abilities develop quickly and they have marked preferences for certain kinds of stimulation. Just a few hours after birth, for example, infants distinguish between light and dark, stare at objects that show contrast, and track slow

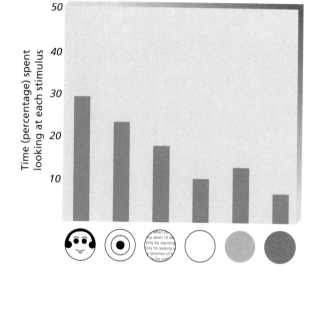

Figure 9.5

Fantz (1961) recorded the amount of time newborns spent gazing at various disks. As shown, they looked more at the patterns than at solids, and they looked most of all at the human face. [From "The Origin of Form Perception" by R. L. Fantz. Illustration by Alex Semenoick. Copyright © 1961 by Scientific American, Inc. All rights reserved.]

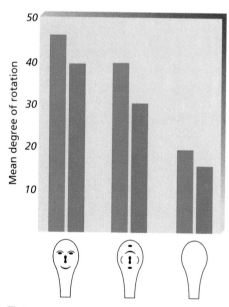

- ■ Eye movement
- ■ Head movement

Figure 9.6

In this study, a face, a scrambled pattern, or a blank form was moved past each infant's field of view. As you can see, the infants tracked the face more than they did the other patterns (Johnson et al., 1991).

movement with their eyes. Especially intriguing is a study in which Robert Fantz (1961) recorded the amount of time that two- to five-day-old infants spent gazing at each of the six disks illustrated in Figure 9.5—a human face, a bullseye, newsprint, and three solids colored red, white, and yellow. As shown, the infants preferred to look at the patterns over solids. Lo and behold, their favorite pattern was the human face. This finding raised an intriguing question: Do faces just happen to provide the right kind of visual stimulation, or is the human nervous system primed to pay special attention to social stimuli? Is the attraction a mere happy coincidence, or the clever design of evolution?

Research offers support for both interpretations. On the one hand, it now appears that newborns look at any object that has complexity, contrast, and a symmetrical pattern of eye-like dots in an outline—whether that object resembles a face or not (Kleiner, 1987). On the other hand, infants tested within an hour of birth exhibit a unique level of interest in face-like stimuli. To demonstrate, Mark Johnson and his colleagues (1991) presented newborns with white head-shaped forms that depicted a properly featured face, a scrambled face, or a featureless blank face. Each pattern was moved slowly across each infant's field of view, and the experimenter recorded the extent to which they rotated their head and eyes to follow the visual stimulus. As shown in Figure 9.6, the infants tracked the face-like pattern more than they did the scrambled and blank patterns. This study, and others like it, strongly suggests that humans are born with an orientation toward the face (Morton & Johnson, 1991).

Other lines of research also indicate that newborns are "tuned in" to the face as a social object. Andrew Meltzoff and Keith Moore (1983) found that within seventy-two hours of birth, babies not only look at faces but often mimic gestures such as moving the head or sticking out the tongue (see Figure 9.7). This form of imitation occurs even when the model is a stranger (Meltzoff & Moore, 1992). In another study, newborns were videotaped as they watched an adult wear a happy, sad, or surprised expression. Observers who later saw only the tape were able to guess the

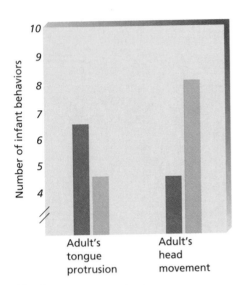

Figure 9.7

Newborn Imitation

An adult experimenter either stuck out his tongue or moved his head in front of newborn infants. Videotaped records showed that the infants were more likely to respond by imitating the same gesture (Meltzoff & Moore, 1989).

- ■ Infant's tongue protrusions
- ■ Infant's head movements

In talking to babies, people all over the world use "motherese"—a pattern of speech that is slow, clear, high-pitched, rhythmic, and song-like.

adult's expression from changes in the baby's face (Field et al., 1982). What do these findings mean? It is not clear that newborns are capable of deliberate and coordinated imitation. But they do seem to react automatically to certain facial cues, a reaction that has been observed among Asian Indian and American newborns (Reissland, 1988). It's almost as if babies were born with a "social reflex," to the delight of parents all over the world.

Hearing   Slam the nursery door while a newborn is asleep, and the baby will open its eyes wide and fling out its arms. Clearly, the newborn can hear. But what does it hear, and how well? As in vision, the human auditory system is not fully developed at birth. The baby's outer ear is small, its eardrum does not vibrate effectively, and the brain's auditory cortex is still immature. For the first week or so, the baby's ears are also clogged with amniotic fluid, which muffles sound. The result of all this is that the newborn baby is hard of hearing, compared to adults.

Though not in perfect form, the newborn reacts to life's sounds in consistent ways. If you stand on the baby's right or left side and shake a rattle, you'll notice that it slowly turns its head in your direction, as if trying to locate the source of the sound (see Chapter 3). Newborns have difficulty detecting low-pitched sounds, but they are particularly sensitive to high-pitched sounds, melodies, and the human voice (Aslin, 1989). They can tell the difference between tones that are one note apart on the musical scale, between the mother's voice and another woman's, and between speech sounds that are as similar as "pa" and "ba" (Maurer & Maurer, 1988). In light of these findings, it's interesting to consider the way adults talk to babies. In cultures all over the world, men, women, and children use babytalk, or "motherese"—a form of speech that is slow, clear, simple, high in pitch, rhythmic, and song-like, just the kinds of sounds that will seize a newborn's attention (Fernald et al., 1989). How marvelously adaptive for the development of language! It's no wonder that infants prefer to hear babytalk over ordinary adult conversation (Fernald, 1985).

Taste and Smell   Although nearsighted and somewhat hard of hearing, the newborn is well equipped for taste and smell. To illustrate, imagine the kind of face you'd make if a drop of sugar, lemon, or vinegar was put on your tongue. Regardless of age or culture, adults react to sweetness with a fleeting smile, to sour tastes with puckered lips, and to bitter tastes with a foul look of disgust. What about babies? To find out, researchers have tested newborns—many of whom were so young they had not yet been fed. As it turned out, these babies made the same kinds of facial expressions as adults do, but in a more exaggerated manner (Rosenstein & Oster, 1988; Steiner, 1979). The same is true of odors. When Steiner held sweet-smelling swabs under their noses, the babies smiled. Swabs of rotten egg made them grimace. The newborn's sense of smell is so well developed that at two weeks old, nursing infants are more attracted to the body odor of their own mother and other lactating females than to that of other women (Porter et al., 1992). No matter how tender the age, the nose knows.

The human newborn is not a miniature adult and is obviously too helpless to survive on its own. Thanks to recent research, however, we adults can now celebrate the newborn's impressive capacities. From the moment of birth, babies are equipped with many primitive but adaptive reflexes.

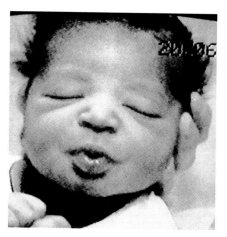
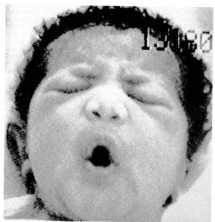
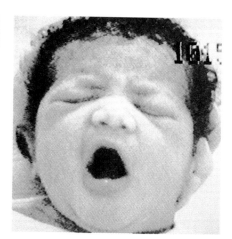

A newborn's sense of taste is evident from its behavior. As you can see, sweet, sour, and bitter tastes elicit different facial expressions (Rosenstein & Oster, 1988).

They are also prepared to experience many forms of sensory stimulation, especially those provided by human contact—faces, voices, and mother's scent. And they are capable of rudimentary forms of learning and memory. Carolyn Rovee-Collier (1988), for example, hung a mobile over the crib of six-week-olds, attaching the mobile by a ribbon to one of their legs so they could move it. When these infants were brought back two weeks later, they remembered which leg to kick. Newborn capacities like these have existed for generations, but only now are we beginning to appreciate them.

THE INFANT AND GROWING CHILD

The newborn has come a long way—both in our minds and in its own short history of development. But there is so much more to come. First, there is an *infant,* from the Latin word meaning "without language." The infant grows into a walking and talking toddler, who then graduates on the first day of school to the category of *child.* Puberty spurs the *adolescent,* though what it means to be an *adult* is anybody's guess. Throughout the rest of this chapter, and in the next chapter as well, we look at biological, cognitive, and social development, and consider the interplay among them.

Biological Development

During the first year or so, babies grow at a pace never to be equaled again. On average, babies double their birth weight in five months and triple it by their first birthday. They grow about ten inches in height during the first year, and another four to six inches the year after. To the distress of parents without hand-me-downs, a baby's clothing size changes almost every month. Though it is not always accurate, there's a general rule of thumb I find remarkable: by the second birthday, most babies have reached half of their adult height.

Matching the observable changes in body size, other aspects of growth also proceed at a fast pace. Cartilage turns to bone, muscle fibers thicken, and teeth break through the gums. Also impressive are the changes that

NEWBORN   **3 MONTHS**   **15 MONTHS**   **2 YEARS**

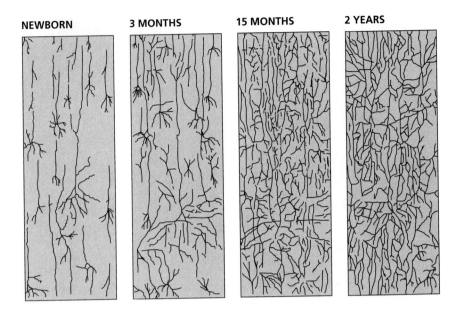

Figure 9.8

The Development of Neurons in the Cerebral Cortex

These drawings of brain tissue illustrate that, from birth to two years of age, neurons grow in size and increase in the number of synaptic connections.

occur in the brain and nervous system—and what these changes mean for cognitive and social development. At birth, an infant's brain weighs close to a pound and is fully equipped with all of its estimated billions of neurons. Yet the newborn brain and nervous system are immature. As children get older, the neural axons get longer and the dendrites increase in number—so there is a proliferation of new *synaptic connections* (see Figure 9.8). Also, the neurons become tightly wrapped with myelin sheath—a fatty substance that enhances the speed at which neural signals are transmitted through the nervous system. This process of *myelination* takes time and continues through infancy, childhood, and adolescence.

The maturation of the brain is linked in intimate ways to other aspects of psychological development. For example, natural increases in the number of synaptic connections or "pathways" in the brain are often accompanied by increases in cognitive ability (Fischer, 1987; Goldman-Rakic, 1987). Myelination shows similar patterns. At birth, the brainstem and spinal cord—which are responsible for simple reflexes—are well myelinated and in working order. The visual cortex is less well developed, as is the newborn's vision. Those parts of the cortex that control attention and information processing are not fully myelinated until the ages of four to seven years, just when children are considered ready for school (Parmelee & Sigman, 1983). In short, growth spurts in the brain correspond nicely to developments of the mind.

What's particularly exciting is that this correspondence is a two-way street: just as the brain influences how you experience the world, it can also be *affected* by that experience. As an example, consider a series of provocative experiments performed by Mark Rosenzweig (1984), who built an "amusement park" for rats to examine the effects of an enriched environment on neural development. Some rats lived together in a cage filled with ladders, platforms, boxes, and other toys, while others lived in solitary confinement. The enriched rats developed heavier, thicker brains than did the ones who were deprived. Those flooded with visual stimulation formed 20 percent more synaptic connections per neuron in the visual cortex than did those raised in darkness (Greenough et al., 1987). Trained to run between pylons on a series of elevated runways, "acrobatic" rats formed new synaptic connections in the cerebellum, a brain structure involved in balance and motor coordination (Greenough et al., 1990). In a very real sense, then, the developing brain is a dynamic structure—programmed in part by genetics, but also molded by the environment.

From infancy to childhood, physical growth—as measured by gains in height and weight—is the most predictable change that takes place. The second most predictable is the coordination of *motor skills*. As you can see in Figure 9.9, babies, on average, can lift their heads at 2 months, sit without support at 5.5 months, crawl at 10 months, and walk at 12 months. Children will differ somewhat in their *rate* of motor development, but the *sequence* of events is usually the same: lifting the head precedes sitting, which precedes crawling, and so on. More advanced activities such as running, jumping, climbing stairs, riding a bicycle, and throwing a ball develop later and are less predictable in their sequence. So are fine motor skills such as holding a pencil, tying a shoelace, and using a fork (Wade & Whiting, 1986).

It's important to realize that cultural factors may play an important role. For example, African infants sit at an earlier age than their American peers because their parents use rolled-up blankets to prop them up into sitting positions in a hole in the ground. Yet these same precocious sitters are

Figure 9.9

Milestones of Infant Motor Development

These bars show the average ages and variations for achievements ranging from lifting the head to walking without support (Frankenburg & Dodds, 1967).

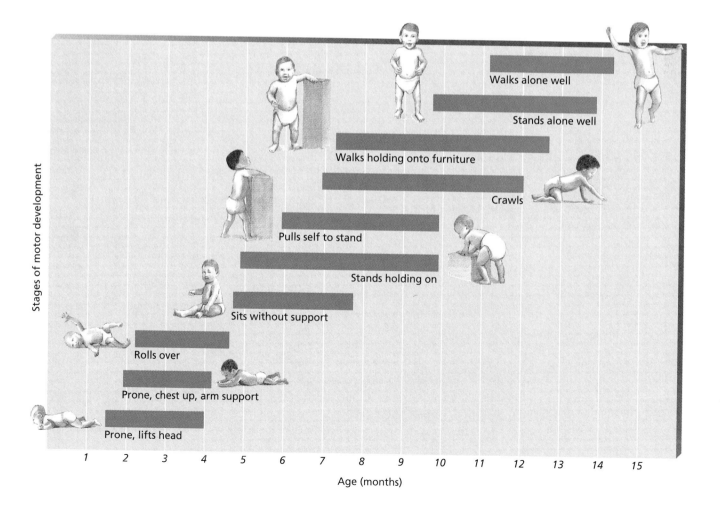

Walks alone well

Stands alone well

Walks holding onto furniture

Crawls

Pulls self to stand

Stands holding on

Sits without support

Rolls over

Prone, chest up, arm support

Prone, lifts head

Stages of motor development

1   2   3   4   5   6   7   8   9   10   11   12   13   14   15

Age (months)

slower to crawl because their parents discourage crawling (Rogoff & Morelli, 1989). Environmental factors are also important. A recent analysis of birthdates revealed that infants born in the summer and early fall began to crawl three weeks later than did those from the same area who were born in the winter and spring. By the time summer and fall babies are ready to move about, the day is shorter and the temperature is colder (Benson, 1993).

Cognitive Development

You don't have to be a psychologist to notice physical growth or the development of motor skills. The real challenge is to unravel the mystery of how children of different ages think—not just what they know but *how* they come to know it and the mistakes they make along the way. To understand this aspect of development, we turn to Jean Piaget (1896–1980), the most influential figure in the study of cognitive development.

Jean Piaget.

Piaget's Theory   Born in Switzerland, Piaget was a precocious boy interested in seashells, birds, and mechanics. He published his first article at the age of ten and was offered a curatorship at a natural history museum in Geneva while in high school. At twenty-one, Piaget earned a Ph.D. in biology, studied psychology in Paris, and took a job administering intelligence tests to schoolchildren. As luck would have it, this experience proved to be a turning point—for Piaget and for psychology.

While testing, Piaget became intrigued by the mistakes that children made. Far from being random or idiosyncratic, these errors signaled that young children use a logic that is foreign to adults. To understand it, Piaget had children explain their answers, a simple but informative method. From these interviews, Piaget published a series of articles, and in 1921 he was named director of a child development institute in Geneva. The seed was planted. In the years that followed, Piaget studied thousands of children, including his own. By the time he died in 1980, he had written more than forty books on how children come to think about people, nature, time, morality, and other aspects of the world (Piaget & Inhelder, 1969; Ginsburg & Opper, 1988). Today, anyone interested in cognitive development—whether parents, educators, or philosophers—begins with Piaget.

Piaget's theory rests on the assumption that as children get older, they advance through a series of chronological *cognitive stages*, each distinguished by a specific kind of thinking. For Piaget, the child's cognitive development is like climbing a staircase, one step at a time. This view of development has two implications. First, even though some children advance more quickly than others, the sequence is universally the same: the first stage must precede the second, the second must precede the third, and so on. In this way, each stage holds both the fruits of the past and the seeds of the future. Second, even though the cognitive stages build upon one another, these increments are qualitative and abrupt, not quantitative and gradual—in other words, like climbing stairs, not a ramp. As shown in Figure 9.10, Piaget described four stages in the development of the mind: (1) sensorimotor, (2) preoperational, (3) concrete operational, and (4) formal operational.

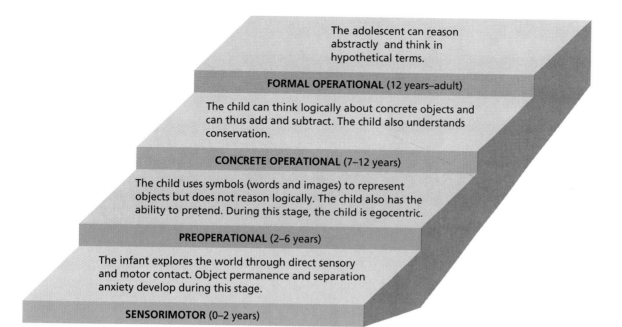

The adolescent can reason abstractly and think in hypothetical terms.

FORMAL OPERATIONAL (12 years–adult)

The child can think logically about concrete objects and can thus add and subtract. The child also understands conservation.

CONCRETE OPERATIONAL (7–12 years)

The child uses symbols (words and images) to represent objects but does not reason logically. The child also has the ability to pretend. During this stage, the child is egocentric.

PREOPERATIONAL (2–6 years)

The infant explores the world through direct sensory and motor contact. Object permanence and separation anxiety develop during this stage.

SENSORIMOTOR (0–2 years)

Figure 9.10

Piaget's Stages of Cognitive Development

■ **sensorimotor stage** Piaget's first stage of cognitive development, from birth to two years old, when infants come to know the world through their own actions.

■ **object permanence** Developing at six to eight months, an awareness that objects continue to exist after they disappear from view.

■ **separation anxiety** Among infants with object permanence, a fear reaction to the absence of their primary caretaker.

Sensorimotor Stage Beginning at birth and lasting about two years, infants come to know the world by touching, grasping, smelling, sucking, chewing, poking, prodding, banging, shaking, and manipulating objects. Piaget called this the **sensorimotor stage** of development. As far as infants are concerned, an object exists only for the moment and only insofar as it is in direct sensory contact. In fact, research shows that the way infants explore objects changes predictably with age. Beginning at one month old, they learn about the shape, texture, and substance of objects with the mouth (Gibson & Walker, 1984). At five months, they also acquire information with their hands (Streri & Pecheux, 1986), or by coordinating movement of the hands, eyes, and mouth together (Rochat, 1989). This sensorimotor mode can be seen in the way young babies try to stuff crayons, toys, and limbs into the mouth—and in the way they pull, push, shake, squeeze, and bang everything they can get their fingers on.

According to Piaget, the crowning cognitive achievement of the sensorimotor stage is the development of **object permanence,** an awareness that objects continue to exist after they disappear from view. This may not seem to be much of an accomplishment, but Piaget (1952) noticed that whenever he covered a toy with his beret or a handkerchief, babies younger than eight months old did not protest, made no effort to retrieve it, and were unaware of its absence—even when the toy made noise. Quite literally, out of sight means out of mind. Given this lack of object permanence, it is no wonder that until babies approach their first birthday, they never seem to tire of playing peek-a-boo, a game in which each round is met with a fresh look of surprise.

Object permanence may be linked to social development. It is probably not a coincidence that just as babies become aware of objects that are out of view, they also begin to experience **separation anxiety,** a fear reaction to the absence of their primary caretaker. The baby who is not aware of its mother when she isn't perceptible will not seem distressed by her absence. However, the baby who has achieved object permanence is capable of missing its mother and cries frantically the moment she slips out of sight. As

By uncovering the hidden toy, this baby demonstrates object permanence.

with other aspects of sensorimotor development, this pattern—object permanence accompanied by several months of separation anxiety—can be observed in cultures all over the world (Kagan, 1976; Werner, 1988; Whiting & Edwards, 1988). Figure 9.11 provides a clear illustration of this point.

Preoperational Stage   During the second year, developments in memory lend permanence to people no longer in view, and peek-a-boo games give way to hide-and-seek. At eight months old, a delay of 2 or 3 seconds is enough for babies to become distracted from the location of a hidden object. At ten months, they can wait eight seconds, and at sixteen months, 20 to 30 seconds (Kail, 1990). At twenty months old, babies who watched an adult hide a Big Bird doll in a desk drawer or behind a pillow were able to find the toy even on the next day (DeLoache & Brown, 1983). The second year is also a time when children become more verbal and more abstract in their thinking. For the first time, words and images are used to symbolize objects. And one object may be used as a symbol for another—as when children pretend that their spoon is an airplane and their mouth a runway (Harris & Kavanaugh, 1993).

Despite enormous cognitive gains, the two-year-old does not think like an adult, or even like a school-aged child. According to Piaget, preschoolers between two and six years of age are in a **preoperational stage** during which they reason in an intuitive, pre-logical manner, unable to perform mental operations. There are two important symptoms of preoperational thought. The first is that the child is **egocentric**, or self-centered—unable to adopt the perspective of another person. At this stage of development, children tend to assume that you can tell what they are thinking, or that you know all the people in their lives, or that you can see a picture in a book they are reading. Play a hiding game with three-year-olds, and they will

■ **preoperational stage** Piaget's second stage of cognitive development, when two- to six-year-olds become capable of reasoning in an intuitive, prelogical manner.

■ **egocentric** Self-centered, unable to adopt the perspective of another person.

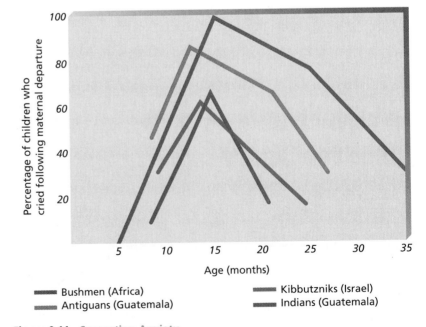

Figure 9.11   Separation Anxiety

Cross-cultural researchers have found that the rise and fall of separation anxiety follows a similar pattern among infants in different parts of the world (Kagan, 1976).

■ **conservation** The concept that physical properties of an object remain the same despite superficial changes in appearance.

stand in full view and cover their eyes—assuming that if they cannot see, then they cannot be seen. Or eavesdrop on a conversation between four-year-olds and you will hear each of them jabbering away and taking turns—oblivious to what the other is saying. These "collective monologues" are also evidence of egocentrism.

A second limitation at this stage is that the preoperational child does not understand **conservation**, the idea that physical properties of an object stay the same despite superficial changes in appearance. To illustrate, take a tall, thin 8-ounce glass of lemonade and pour it into an 8-ounce cup that is shorter and wider. You and I know that the quantity of liquid stays the same regardless of changes in shape, but to the preschooler the tall, thin glass holds more to drink. As illustrated in Figure 9.12, there are other examples as well. Flatten a ball of clay and the preoperational child will think there is less. Roll the clay into a long thin snake, and the child will think there is more. Or, take a handful of pennies and the child will think there are more if you spread them out than if you push them close together.

CONSERVATION OF LIQUID

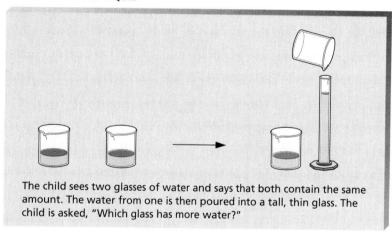

The child sees two glasses of water and says that both contain the same amount. The water from one is then poured into a tall, thin glass. The child is asked, "Which glass has more water?"

CONSERVATION OF SUBSTANCE

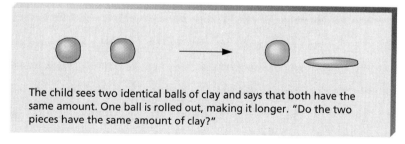

The child sees two identical balls of clay and says that both have the same amount. One ball is rolled out, making it longer. "Do the two pieces have the same amount of clay?"

CONSERVATION OF NUMBER

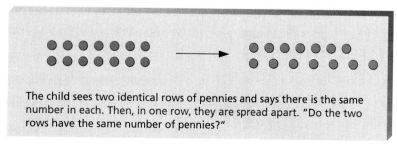

The child sees two identical rows of pennies and says there is the same number in each. Then, in one row, they are spread apart. "Do the two rows have the same number of pennies?"

Figure 9.12

Tasks Used to Test Conservation

According to Piaget, the ability to conserve marks the transition from the preoperational to the concrete operational stages of cognitive development.

DEVELOPMENTAL PSYCHOLOGY   Law

The Child Witness: Competent to Testify?

On August 12, 1983, Judy Johnson complained to the police in Manhattan Beach, California, that her two-and-a-half-year-old son had been molested at the McMartin Pre-School by Raymond Buckey, a teacher. Before long, the police had contacted other parents and children and charged that Ray and his mother, Peggy McMartin Buckey, had sexually abused hundreds of boys and girls. In interviews with a therapist, several three- to six-year-old children said they were forced to play "naked games" and then frightened into silence. Some of the children told bizarre stories of satanic rituals, which entailed digging up bodies at cemeteries, drinking blood, jumping out of an airplane, and sacrificing animals on a church altar.

Were the children's stories accurate? Were the children themselves competent to testify in a court of law? On the one hand, there were some striking consistencies in the reports of different children. On the other hand, the therapist who conducted the interviews often prompted the children with suggestive leading questions, urged them to describe acts they had initially denied, and pressured those who claimed ignorance. Based on the testimony of eleven children, the McMartin case went to trial. After thirty-three months—the longest criminal trial in American history—the jury found the defendants not guilty. As one juror explained, "I believe that the children believed what they were saying, but I couldn't tell if they were repeating what they had been told. . . . I had a hard time picking fact from fiction" (Mydans, 1990, p. A18).

Can leading questions cause children to confuse appearance and reality? Since the McMartin case, thousands of child sex-abuse cases involving preschool teachers, babysitters, family members, and strangers have inundated the courts. With each new complaint, judges struggle to decide: Are preschoolers competent to take the witness stand, or are they too suggestible, too prone to confuse reality and fantasy? In the McMartin trial, the jury did not trust the young children's recollections. Yet in the recent cases against the Little Rascals Day Care Center in North Carolina, the Wee Care Nursery School in New Jersey, and the Country Walk Babysitting Service in Florida, defendants were convicted and imprisoned solely on the basis of such testimony. To provide guidance to the courts, researchers have been studying children's eyewitness memory (Ceci & Bruck, 1993; Doris, 1991; Perry & Wrightsman, 1991).

Laboratory studies clearly show that preschoolers are more likely than older children and adults to incorporate misleading questions into the fabric of memory. For example, Stephen Ceci and his colleagues (1987) had subjects from three to twelve years old read a story with pictures about a girl who had an upset stomach after eating her breakfast eggs too fast. The next day, half the subjects were "reminded" of the girl who had a *headache* after eating her *cereal* too fast. Two days later, subjects tried to select the pictures—eggs or cereal, an upset stomach or headache—that fit the original story. The preschoolers who were not misled and the older children were accurate about 90 percent of the time. The preschoolers who had been misled, however, were fooled 63 percent of the time. Young children can be quite suggestible.

What all these demonstrations show is that, until roughly the age of seven, children can't seem to *center* on two object features at a time (height and width, for example) or mentally *reverse* such operations as pouring, rolling, flattening, or spreading. Very simply, "what you see is what you get."

Egocentrism and failures at conservation seem to have something in common: in both cases, the preoperational child cannot think about objects or events in more than one way. Unable to see from another person's point of view or to take another perspective on the same object, young children have trouble distinguishing reality (what they know) from appearance (what they see). John Flavell and his colleagues (1986), for example, let nursery school children feel a soft sponge that looked like a rock. When asked (1) what the object *really is,* and (2) what the object *looks like right now,* most children gave the same response to both questions. Those who knew it was a sponge said it *looked* like a sponge, and those who said it looked like a rock thought it *was* a rock. Several years ago, on Halloween

But are they too suggestible when it comes to stressful real-life experiences? On this question, the evidence is mixed. Gail Goodman and her colleagues (1991) questioned children who had received immunization shots at a health clinic and suggested events that did not occur (for example, "Did the doctor take you to another room?" "Did he kiss you?"). These researchers found that although preschoolers were easily misled about minor aspects of the experience, they seldom reported acts of abuse that were suggested but did not occur. Results like this have led some developmental psychologists to conclude that young children are not particularly vulnerable to suggestion (Melton, 1992).

At the same time, other researchers are finding that young children's reports are biased by expectations as well as by aspects of the questioning process. For example, Debra Poole and Lawrence White (1991) found that young children are more likely than others to change their answers when a memory question is asked repeatedly—a situation that implies that the answer given is not good enough. In another study, Ceci and his colleagues (in press) told nursery school children about a man named Sam Stone who was clumsy and always broke things. A month later, the man visited the school, spent some time in the classroom without incident, and left. The next day, the children were shown a ripped book and a soiled teddy bear and were asked what happened. Reasonably, no one said that they saw Stone cause the damage. Then, over the next ten weeks, they were asked suggestive questions ("I wonder if Sam Stone was wearing long pants or short pants when he ripped the book?"). The result: When a new, naive interviewer asked the children to describe what happened, 72 percent of the three- and four-year-olds blamed Stone for the damage, and 45 percent said they saw him do it. One child "recalled" that Stone took a paintbrush and painted melted chocolate on the bear. Others "saw" him spill coffee, throw toys in the air, rip a book in anger, and soak the book in warm water until it fell apart.

It's clear that young children are sometimes vulnerable to the biasing effects of leading questions. At this point, more research is needed to help the courts distinguish between true and false claims and prosecute only those who are guilty of crimes against young children. Ideally, this research will be used to establish a clear set of guidelines for interviewing child witnesses in an objective, nonbiasing manner.

Preschool teacher Kelly Michaels was found guilty of sexually molesting nineteen children. After she spent five years in jail, her conviction was overturned by an appeals court that questioned the accuracy of the children's testimony. "One day you're getting ready for work and making coffee, minding your business," said Michaels, "and the next minute you are an accused child molester."

I discovered this confusion the hard way. In front of my four-year-old daughter Briana, I put on a gorilla mask. She watched me put the mask on and knew it was me, but then burst into tears, making me feel awful. It was as if appearance had become reality.

Concrete Operational Stage   At about the age of seven, children advance to what Piaget called the **concrete operational stage,** during which they become capable of logical reasoning. As they enter school for the first time, children are able to take the perspective of another person and understand that various object properties stay the same despite surface changes in appearance. They can now group similar objects into categories, order the objects according to size or number, and appreciate the logic that if A is greater than B, and B is greater than C, then A is greater than C. Capable of performing concrete operations, the first grader can also be taught to add and subtract without counting (Resnick, 1989).

■ **concrete operational stage** Piaget's third stage of cognitive development, when six-year-olds become capable of logical reasoning.

Piaget believed that conservation marks the beginning of a major advance in cognitive development, one that lasts until the age of eleven or twelve. However, even though concrete operational children appear to reason like adults in response to a specific problem, they do not think on an abstract level. The child may know that 2 is an even number and that 2 + 1 is an odd number, and they may well realize the same for 4 + 1, 6 + 1, and 100 + 1 —but they will not necessarily put the pieces together to form the more general principle that any even number plus one yields an odd number. The ability to use methods of logic—inductive reasoning, deductive reasoning, and systematic hypothesis testing—is the hallmark of Piaget's next stage, the **formal operational stage** of cognitive development.

Formal Operational Stage   What distinguishes Piaget's third and fourth levels of development is the ability to think about solutions in advance and to reason on a logical, hypothetical level. To illustrate, imagine how you might approach the following test. You have four beakers, each containing a colorless chemical, and a dropper filled with potassium iodide. You are then told that when the potassium iodide is mixed with one or more of the four chemicals, it produces a bright yellow solution. Your task is to determine which chemicals to mix. Faced with this problem, the typical nine- or ten-year-old child will arbitrarily begin to mix chemicals, trying one combination after another until stumbling upon the solution. In contrast, the typical twelve- or thirteen-year-old will plan a systematic course of action, first adding potassium iodide to the individual beakers, then trying combinations of chemicals and keeping track of outcomes until the problem is solved (Inhelder & Piaget, 1958).

Unlike Piaget's first three stages, which appear on schedule in different cultures, formal operational thought is not used by many non-Western adults. In fact, as we saw in Chapter 7, even adults in Western cultures are not necessarily formal operational in their problem solving, often falling back on rules of thumb known as "heuristics." Piaget's point, however, is that adolescents and adults are cognitively *capable* of formal operations, whereas children are not.

Piaget's Legacy   Piaget was an astute observer of children, and his writings single-handedly brought the study of cognitive development to life (Beilin, 1992). Important practical lessons also stem from his theory—such as the idea that young children are often not developmentally ready for reading, writing, arithmetic, and other cognitive tasks. Today, many parents try to give their children a "jump start" on life by enrolling them in academically rigorous preschools. Thanks to Piaget, however, child development experts are now quick to warn that children should not be pushed "too early," before they have matured to the necessary next stage of development (Elkind, 1989; Zigler, 1987).

Two aspects of Piaget's theory have stirred controversy, and neo-Piagetian researchers are now revising and extending his work in important ways. One problem is that Piaget's interview method was crude by today's standards. As a result, he underestimated young children's cognitive abilities and taxed their capacity to process task-relevant information (Case, 1992). For example, Piaget thought that object permanence did not develop until eight months of age, when babies first try to retrieve toys that have been hidden from view. Using a more sensitive measure of what infants

■ **formal operational stage** Piaget's fourth stage of cognitive development, when adolescents become capable of logic and abstract thought.

know, however, Renée Baillargeon (1986) recorded eye movements and found that six-month-olds reacted with surprise when a hidden object seemed to disappear. This suggests that an out-of-sight object is not out of mind at this age—or even at four months old (Baillargeon & De Vos, 1991). Similarly, Piaget thought that three- and four-year-olds are egocentric, unable to take the perspective of another person. Yet other research shows that children at this age speak more simply to babies than to adults, and that they show toys and pictures to others with the front side facing the viewer (Gelman, 1979). Were Piaget's timetables wrong? Yes and no. Yes, it's clear that young children are often more precocious than Piaget had realized. But no, his developmental sequences—for example, the hypothesis that object permanence precedes conservation, which in turn precedes formal logic—have stood up well. Piaget may have underestimated the overall *rate* of development, but he was right about the *sequence* of achievements.

A second question is often raised that goes right to the heart of Piaget's theory: Does cognitive development progress through a series of distinct stages, like a staircase, or is it more gradual, like a ramp? Robert Thatcher and his colleagues (1986) measured electrical brain activity in 577 humans ranging from two months old to young adulthood, and spotted distinct growth spurts that corresponded roughly to the emergence of Piaget's stages. Yet Piaget's all-or-none view of development has been challenged inasmuch as children often master a concept in some tasks but not others. Four-year-olds can order colors from light to dark, but they can't order sticks by length. Similarly, six-year-olds understand conservation in the pennies problem before they can solve the liquid or clay problems. Inconsistencies like these tell us that cognitive concepts don't burst into mind all at once but, rather, are used one task at a time (Flavell, 1982). What, then, are we to conclude? Once again, Piaget was only partly accurate. The pace of development is more rapid at some ages than at others. But within these periods of rapid growth, it takes time for new skills to reach full maturity.

Information-Processing Perspectives   Today, many cognitive development researchers examine age-related changes in the way that information is processed. From this perspective, cognitive development is characterized not by the transition from one qualitative stage of logic to another, but by gradual increases both in the ability to attend to one stimulus and screen out distractions and in the ability to encode, store, and retrieve information from memory. These information-processing skills are acquired and refined throughout childhood. Again, from this perspective, young children may fail a Piagetian task not because of how they think or what logic they use—but because their attention wanders, they get distracted, and they forget elements of the problem (Kail & Bisanz, 1992; Klahr, 1989; Siegler, 1991).

One highly consistent change that takes place in childhood is in memory. On tests of short-term memory span, the average adult can recall about seven items of information (see Chapter 6). Among young children, this number increases steadily with age. Why? Some researchers have found that young children do not use the kinds of encoding, storage, and retrieval strategies that are common among adults. When you or I have to recall a phone number or grocery list, we try to repeat the items over and over. Not so among young children. In one experiment, children of varying ages were instructed to memorize objects presented in pictures, while a trained lip reader watched for signs of silent rehearsal. The result: The percentage of those who rehearsed increased from 10 percent among five-year-olds to 60 percent among seven-year-olds, to 85 percent among ten-year-olds (Flavell et al., 1966). Similar differences have been noted regarding the use of organizational strategies, note taking, and other memory aids (Kreutzer et al., 1975). The memory abilities of young children have also been the subject of controversy in the courtroom (see box p. 354).

The use of strategies may partly explain age differences in memory, but many researchers believe that the initial limitations and later increases are also related to maturation of the brain and the efficiency with which information is processed (Case, 1985; Pascual-Leone, 1970). Thus, there is a consistent age-related decline in performance *speed* at cognitive tasks. In a series of experiments, Robert Kail (1991) recorded the amount of time it took for seven- to twenty-one-year-old subjects to do various simple tasks. They were asked to name pictured objects, judge whether two letters flashed on a screen were the same, mentally rotate objects, move pegs from one side of a pegboard to the other, add two numbers, or press a button the moment they detected a target stimulus. The result: On all tasks, responses were quicker with age—and followed the same rate of change. As depicted in Figure 9.13, information processing speeded up between the ages of seven and twelve, then leveled off. According to Kail, this general increase in speed stems from the maturation of the brain (specifically, perhaps, from the increased myelination of axons, which facilitates the transmission of neural impulses). It may also account for some of the stage-like performance increments typically found in cognitive development research.

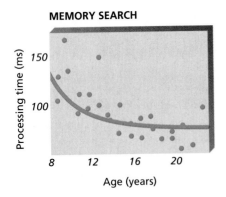

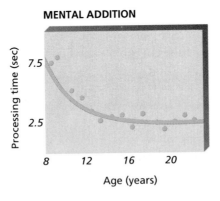

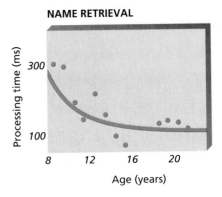

Figure 9.13

Speed of Information Processing

In general, response times decline between the ages of seven and twelve, then level off. This pattern appears in many tasks, including mental addition, memory search, and name retrieval (Kail, 1991).

Emergence of Language   Paralleling the changes that take place in the way children think is their development of language. Between the ages of one and six, children acquire a vocabulary consisting of an estimated 14,000 words, an average of 9 words per day. They also learn to combine words in ways that fit grammatical rules too complex for most of us to explain. What's amazing about these achievements is that boys and girls of all cultures, almost like sponges, absorb the words and grammar of language without formal instruction. It just happens. As in cognitive development, some children may speak sooner than others, but the sequence of achievements is the same for all (Brown, 1973; McNeil, 1970; Rice, 1989).

Developmental Sequence   Newborns communicate their needs by *crying*. In the second month, they also begin to use the tongue to make more articulated *cooing* sounds such as "oh" and "ah." In the sixth month or so, babies begin playful *babbling*, vocalizing for the first time in ways that sound like human speech—"ah boo," "da da," and "ah gee." Like crying and cooing, babbling is inborn. Whether the native language is English, French, Spanish, German, Hebrew, or Swahili, babies all over the world initially make the same sounds, including some they never hear at home (for example, the German *ch,* the clicks of certain African tribes, and rolled *r*'s). Even babies who are deaf and cannot *hear* speech babble right on schedule.

Some time near the first birthday, babies utter their first real *words*. The sounds are brief and not clearly pronounced, but they are used to communicate meaning in the native tongue—for example, "ba" for bottle. For the next few months, babies speak one-word utterances, and the number of words in their vocabulary increases from 4 or 5 at twelve months to 30 at eighteen months, to 250 at two years. These utterances are not random. Babies tend to name objects and actions they desire (a bottle, favorite toys, "more"), especially those that involve motion (cars, a pet dog)—just as Piaget would expect of a sensorimotor child (Nelson, 1973).

At about two years of age, there is a vocabulary explosion, as children learn and accumulate hundreds of new words a year. More important, they begin to form two- and three-word phrases. These early word combinations illustrate *telegraphic speech* because—as in telegrams, kept short for cost reasons—they include only nouns, verbs, and essential modifiers, and yet make sense to the listener ("More juice" for "I want more juice," or "no sit chair" for "I don't want to sit in the chair"). It's interesting that these primitive forms of sentence contain the seeds of grammar—"more juice" rather than "juice more," for example. It's also interesting that the statements are often *overextensions*. For example, until different animals can be distinguished, the two-year-old who uses the word "doggie" to call the family pet will use the same word to refer to a cat, horse, or circus elephant. Language can tell us a lot about a child's developing knowledge of the world.

By the age of three, four or five, the child's mind contains a small dictionary of words ready to be used correctly. Although new words are learned without explicit thought or instruction, an enriched linguistic environment can accelerate the process. For example, preschoolers who watch the educational TV show *Sesame Street* have larger vocabularies than those who do not (Rice et al., 1990). With increasing age, children construct longer and more complex sentences, learn to use plurals, pronouns, past tense, and other rules of grammar, and begin to appreciate puns and words with double meanings. At puberty, corresponding to the onset of Piaget's formal operational stage, children come to appreciate abstract metaphors—"like two ships passing in the night."

Developmental Theories   Nobody disputes the stages of language development in children or the sequence of those stages. But there are differences of opinion as to what it all means. Two issues in particular have been lively topics of controversy.

The first is our old friend, the nature-nurture debate. In 1957, behaviorist B. F. Skinner wrote a book entitled *Verbal Behavior* in which he argued that children learn to speak the way animals learn to run mazes. They associate objects and words, imitate adults, and repeat phrases that are met by social reinforcement. Through trial and error, for example, a baby of

English-speaking parents learns to repeat the babbling sounds that excite mom and dad, but not foreign sounds that leave them cold. In response to Skinner, linguist Noam Chomsky (1959, 1972) argued that the human brain is specially wired for the acquisition of language. The evidence in support of this biological position is impressive: language grows at a rate that exceeds all other kinds of learning, two-year-olds construct telegraphic statements they couldn't possibly hear from adults, and children learn to speak properly even though nobody stops to correct their grammar. Most psychologists now agree with Chomsky that humans are prepared for language the way computers are wired for programming. Environment may provide the software that determines *what* language you learn to speak, but biology provides the hardware that controls *how* you learn it.

The second debate concerns a chicken-and-egg problem: What comes first, thought or language? Piaget (1976) believed that children must understand a concept before they can use words to describe it. Thus, babies cannot say "all gone" or "bye-bye," or use other words that refer to the disappearance of objects, until they understand the concept of object permanence. However, other developmental psychologists believe that language shapes thought, and that children develop concepts in order to understand the words they hear from others. Thus, the child who hears "dog" tries to understand the word by searching for objects that might fit (Bruner, 1983). Which view is correct? Apparently both are. Words and concepts emerge at roughly the same time, and the causal arrow points in both directions. Sometimes children use words to communicate what they already know, and sometimes they form concepts to fit the words they hear (Rice, 1989).

Social Development

Born completely helpless, equipped with reflexes that orient toward people, responsive to human faces, voices, and odors, and prepared to cry and mimic facial expressions on cue, the newborn is an inherently social animal. For eager parents, the baby's first smile is the warmest sign of all. It's funny how nature finds ways to lubricate a parent-newborn relationship. If you gently stroke or blow on a newborn's face, it often reacts to this stimulation of the nervous system by contracting its muscles and pulling back its mouth into what looks like—you guessed it, a smile (Emde et al., 1976). In fact, babies don't crinkle up their eyes and flash "social smiles" at people until they are at least six weeks old (Bower, 1982).

The Parent-Child Relationship   Many developmental psychologists believe that a baby's first primary relationship to the mother or another caretaker sets the stage for social development. Clearly, it is critical in certain species of animals. Newly hatched ducks and geese, for example, will automatically follow their mother—an instinctive form of attachment called **imprinting**, which serves the purpose of keeping the young birds in proximity to their mother. Intrigued by how automatic the process is, Konrad Lorenz (1937) suspected that any moving, honking stimulus (whether it is the mother or not) will trigger this response. To demonstrate, he squatted, clucked, and moved about in front of birds hatched in an incubator. It worked like a charm. One of Lorenz's favorite pictures shows him strolling

■ **imprinting** Among newly hatched ducks and geese, an instinctive tendency to follow the mother.

Soon after hatching, ducklings will follow the first moving object they see. In this photograph, the imprinted object was ethologist Konrad Lorenz.

through high grass trailed by a line of geese imprinted by his actions. In fact, geese will follow a wide variety of first-seen moving objects—decoys, rubber balls, wooden blocks, and even a striped metal pipe (Hess, 1959).

If baby birds are to follow their mother, they must be exposed to her in the first day or so, a **critical period** for the development of imprinting. In humans, however, attachment is less automatic, the mother plays a more active role, and there is no "critical" period. But the infant does form a very deep and affectionate emotional bond called an **attachment**.

The First Attachment   Beginning in the second half of the first year, accompanying the development of object permanence, infants all over the world form an intense, exclusive attachment to their primary caretaker. This first relationship is highly charged with emotion and emerges with remarkable consistency from one culture to the next. Why? What motivates the infant? Years ago, psychologists assumed that infants become attached to anyone who feeds them and satisfies their basic physiological needs. That assumption was then put to rest by a classic series of dramatic experiments by Harry Harlow (1958, 1971).

In the 1950s, Harlow was breeding rhesus monkeys to study learning. Infant monkeys were separated from their mothers, fed regularly, and housed in cages equipped with a blanket. At one point, Harlow noticed that the infants had become passionately attached to their blankets—as they would be to their mothers. It is interesting that, like Linus of the comic strip *Peanuts*, many normal children in the United States, Sweden, New Zealand, and elsewhere clutch security blankets (Passman, 1987). At any rate, this observation sparked in Harlow an interest in the possible origins of attachment: Are infants in general drawn to mother for the comfort of her warm and cuddly body, or for the food and nourishment she provides?

To answer this question, Harlow placed newborn monkeys into a cage that contained two substitute mothers—one was a wire-mesh cylinder with a wooden head, the other was covered with soft terrycloth. Both provided a bottle of milk with a nipple. It was no contest. The infant monkeys spent almost all of their time with the terrycloth doll. In fact, they continued clinging to the cloth substitute even when it did not contain a bottle for feeding! Given the choice, the infant monkeys preferred "contact comfort" over food. In later variations of this study, Harlow found that warmth and rocking motions further intensified the contact comfort provided by a cloth mother. It is clear that infants need more from parents than milk and a clean diaper.

Sadly, Harlow found that the infant monkeys raised with inanimate cloth substitutes developed into unhealthy adults, terrified in new settings, socially awkward, and sexually unable to function. Fortunately, the discovery that contact comfort has therapeutic benefits for the isolated infant has proved useful. For example, consider the predicament of a typical premature baby—kept in an incubator without physical contact and at risk for a host of problems later in life. Working in the maternity ward of a hospital, Saul Schanberg and Tiffany Field (1987) treated a group of premature babies with a 45-minute body massage for ten days, and then compared their progress to others not receiving massage. The two groups drank the same amount of formula, yet the massaged infants gained 47 percent more weight, were more alert, active, and coordinated, and left the hospital an

■ **critical period** A period of time during which an organism must be exposed to a certain stimulus for proper development to occur.

■ **attachment** A deep emotional bond that an infant develops with its primary caretaker.

Premature babies will snuggle up to a "breathing" stuffed bear in their sleep. Shown here is the original Teddy Bear, created in 1902 and named after President Theodore Roosevelt, who had refused to shoot a trapped bear.

■ **strange-situation test** A parent-child "separation and reunion" procedure that is staged in a laboratory to test the security of a child's attachment.

■ **secure attachment** A parent-child relationship in which the baby is secure when the parent is present, distressed by separation, and delighted by reunion.

■ **insecure attachment** A parent-child relationship in which the baby clings to the parent, cries at separation, and reacts with anger or apathy to reunion.

average of six days earlier—for a savings of $3,000 per infant in expenses. This important finding has been replicated on numerous occasions (Scafidi et al., 1990). In another interesting intervention, Evelyn Thoman and her colleagues (1991) found that when the incubator was equipped with a soft blue teddy bear that gently "breathed" with the help of an air pump, premature babies snuggled up against the bear and slept more soundly in its presence. Additional research has shown that the breathing bear is a highly reinforcing source of stimulation (Thoman & Ingersoll, 1993).

Styles of Attachment   Watch different parents and infants, and you will notice that some attachments seem more intense than others. Is it possible to measure the intensity of this first relationship? How much of it depends on the parent? How much on the child? And can an infant's first attachments be used to predict the quality of its social relationships later in life?

To study the attachment process, Mary Ainsworth and her colleagues (1978) created the **strange-situation test** in which parents (usually the mother) bring their baby into an unfamiliar laboratory playroom, and proceed through a routine whereby the parent and a stranger come and go according to a fixed schedule. Based on how infants react to the separations and reunions, they are classified as having either a secure or insecure attachment. Infants with a **secure attachment** wander around and explore the environment when the mother is present, react with distress when she leaves, and beam with sheer delight when she returns. These babies shower the returning parent with waves, smiles, laughter, hugs, and kisses. Infants having an **insecure attachment** are less self-confident and more likely to cling to the mother; they cry when she leaves, and yet they react with anger or indifference when she returns. These babies often push the returning parent away, stiffen up, squirm, or even cry when picked up. The percentage of babies classified as securely attached varies somewhat from culture to culture. In the United States, about 70 percent of infants tested in the strange situation show secure attachments (Lamb et al., 1992; Van IJzendoorn & Kroonenberg, 1988).

It's hard to know for sure what causes a secure or insecure attachment. Clearly, parenting style is important, as mothers and fathers of securely attached babies are more affectionate, playful, and sensitive to the infant's moment-to-moment needs (Isabella et al., 1989). An infant's temperament also plays a role, however, as securely attached babies are by nature less fussy and more easygoing than those who are not securely attached (Goldsmith & Lansky, 1987; Kagan et al., 1992). After eight or nine months, the personalities of parent and child are so tangled up that trying to separate the effects of one on the other is like trying to untie a twisted knot.

How important is this first relationship? Does a secure, trusting attachment with a mother or father provide a foundation for close friendships later in life? And what is the fate of an insecurely attached infant? Developmental psychologists disagree about the long-term implications. On the one hand, research shows that infants classified as securely attached at twelve months old are more popular, independent, self-assured, and socially skilled as school-aged children years later (Ainsworth, 1989; Cassidy, 1988; Sroufe & Jacobvitz, 1989). On the other hand, it is important to realize that the infant-to-child correlation is far from perfect, and does not necessarily mean that early attachment *causes* the differences later in life.

Responsive parents and easygoing infants may well continue in their positive ways long after the initial attachment period has ended. These later interactions may be just as important (Lamb, 1987).

The Day-Care Controversy If you've seen black-and-white reruns of *Leave It to Beaver, Father Knows Best,* or other TV shows produced in the 1950s, you are no doubt familiar with the image of the traditional, all-American family: a working father and a mother who stays home to take care of the house and kids. Today, the typical American child grows up in a vastly different environment consisting of either a single parent or two parents who both work outside the home. As a result, many infants and preschoolers in the United States spend much of their "attachment time" with babysitters, in day-care centers, or at home with fathers and other relatives. This scenario is not true of all other societies. In China and Russia, mothers are encouraged to work full time while their children are cared for in state-supported institutions. And in Israel, mothers who live on rural collective settlements called *kibbutzim* work on the farm while child-care specialists raise the children in groups. The question is, does nonmaternal child care for infants disrupt the security of attachment?

To begin with, what is the modern father's role as a second attachment figure? As a result of social changes that have taken place over the years, researchers are just now starting to answer this question, and this is what we know: as a general rule, fathers spend less time with their infants than mothers do, and they are more likely to spend that time playing rather than feeding, bathing, dressing, or otherwise caring for the child. At home, infants seek contact with both parents equally and form attachments to both at about the same time. Yet in the strange-situation test, anxious infants prefer mothers to fathers (Cox et al., 1992; Parke, 1981; Lamb, 1986). This preference suggests that caring for the infant's needs is a key to attachment. Except for breastfeeding, fathers are as capable as mothers—and the more involved they are in the day-to-day routine, the stronger the attachment. Indeed, you can almost predict the closeness of the father-infant relationship just by counting how many diapers he changes in a week (Ross et al., 1975)!

As increasing numbers of wives join their husbands in the workplace, infants and preschoolers spend more and more of their time in day-care settings away from home. What is the impact of this experience? Should new parents—involved in careers, or struggling to make ends meet—worry about harmful long-term effects? As the research evidence mounts, professional opinion is sharply divided. Some developmental psychologists fear that full-time maternal employment may put infants at risk for minor adjustment problems (Barglow et al., 1987; Belsky, 1988). Others are far more optimistic about the impact of high-quality infant day care—as long as it is safe and stimulating, and has a low adult-to-child ratio (Scarr, 1986). So, what conclusions can be drawn from research that compares the children of working and nonworking mothers?

After reviewing the recent evidence, Alison Clarke-Stewart (1989) gave infant day care a cautious stamp of approval. Studies using the strange-situation test show that day-care infants whose mothers work full time are, on average, somewhat more likely than home-raised infants to appear insecurely attached; the proportions are 36 percent and 29 percent, respectively. As young children, they are also somewhat more aggressive with their peers and less willing to obey their parents. That's the bad news. The good news is that day-care infants are more outgoing and independent—and they get higher-than-average scores on tests of intelligence. In fact, recent studies indicate that preschoolers who are placed full time in high-quality day-care settings go on in grade school to become more sociable, more popular, and more affectionate toward classmates (Andersson, 1992; Field, 1991).

To summarize, there is no "bottom line." Day care and maternal care seem to foster somewhat different personal styles, though neither is necessarily better for healthy development. If an only parent has to work, or if both parents work outside the home, day care is a viable option. What matters is not the *quantity* of time spent in one setting or the other but the *quality* of that time (Hoffman, 1989).

Beyond Attachment   Attachment is just the first step in a long and complex relationship among mothers, fathers, sons, and daughters. Beginning at the age of two or three, children become more autonomous, independent, and even defiant. They stray from their parents, test the limits of authority, and spend increasing amounts of time playing with their brothers and sisters. Through TV and other cultural influences, boys and girls learn about sex roles and other stereotypes. The terrible two's, toilet training, sibling rivalry, the first day of school, outside friendships, homework, the facts of life, and puberty are among the challenges that confront the growing child. Through it all, the parents—their behavior, attitudes, and discipline styles, whether they are happily married or divorced, whether they value obedience to authority or independence, whether they are strict or permissive, and so on—exert a profound influence on the child's social development (Maccoby, 1980).

Peer Relationships   Developmental psychologists now realize that the mother-child attachment is only one factor in social development, and that children also form key relationships with grandparents, siblings, teachers, classmates, and neighbors. The older the child is, the more important are *horizontal relationships*—friendships among peers, or equals (Hartup, 1989).

The growth of friendships may not progress through discrete stages, as in cognitive development, but certain patterns are evident. At one year old, infants show little interest in each other, and come together only if drawn to the same person or toy. At first these interactions breed friction, but with experience infants learn to take turns and minimize conflict. By the age of two, children prefer playing near each other rather than alone. By the age of four or five, they show clear preferences for some playmates over others. Although these relationships are quickly formed, quickly broken, and based on convenience, they mark the beginning of what can be called friendship (Berndt & Ladd, 1989; Collins & Gunnar, 1990; Johnson, 1987).

It is interesting that almost all child relationships are between members of the same sex—not only in our culture but in others as well. Ask a three-year-old child to approach a peer, and he or she will stop farther away when that peer is of the opposite sex. Or, watch children on a school playground, and you will see that four-year-olds spend three times as much time with playmates of the same sex than of the opposite sex (see Figure 9.14). By the age of six, this ratio is even higher, at 11 to 1 (Maccoby &

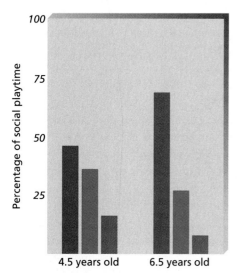

Figure 9.14

Gender Segregation at Playtime

Observations of young children reveal that they are most likely to play in same-sex groups—a tendency that increases between the ages of four and six years (Maccoby & Jacklin, 1987).

One reason for gender segregation in peer relationships is that boys and girls tend to play differently. Boys engage in rough-and-tumble group play, while girls prefer more intimate contact with one or two friends.

Jacklin, 1987)! From preschool to adolescence, only about 5 percent of all friendships are between boys and girls, and those that do exist often have sexual overtones (Thorne, 1986). Why is gender segregation so common? According to Eleanor Maccoby (1990), one reason is that boys and girls prefer different kinds of activities: boys like competitive, rough-and-tumble play that takes up lots of space and involves large groups, while girls prefer to congregate at home with one or two close friends.

Just as attachments inside the home are important to healthy social development, so is the formation of friendships outside the home. To study this aspect of development, researchers ask schoolchildren to rate themselves and to nominate the classmates they like the most and the least. They also get ratings from teachers and parents, observe behavior firsthand, and combine the results for each child. Using these methods, researchers have identified four types of school-aged children—compared to those in the "average" majority—based on their "sociometric" status among peers. As described by Andrew Newcomb and his colleagues (1993), children can be classified as *popular* (sociable, skilled, and well liked), *rejected* (aggressive or withdrawn, lacking in social skills, and disliked), *controversial* (sociable but aggressive, both liked and disliked), and *neglected* (less sociable and less aggressive than average, and seldom mentioned by peers). Of these four types, children who are rejected by classmates are the ones who are the most "at risk." Research shows that they suffer from loneliness (Cassidy & Asher, 1992) and are later more likely to drop out of school and have social adjustment problems as adults (Parker & Asher, 1987; Asher & Coie, 1990). At this point, it's hard to know from these correlations if peer rejection is just part of a deeper problem, or if it is the problem itself. And it's hard to know whether the emotional effects of peer rejection can be offset by family members, pets, or others. But it is clear that children's peer relations can be vital. Thus, Willard Hartup (1989) refers to friends as "developmental advantages" (p. 125).

THE MANY FACETS OF DEVELOPMENT

For the sake of convenience, developmental psychologists tend to separate the biological, cognitive, and social aspects of development. It's important to realize, however, that the way infants and children mature (the biological aspect), how they learn to think and speak (the cognitive aspect), and how they interact with others (the social aspect) are all intertwined. For example, only when the brain is sufficiently developed for infants to be capable of object permanence do they develop separation anxiety. The baby must have the capacity to be conscious of its mother and father when they are out of sight in order to be distressed by their absence (Kagan, 1984). Similarly, as suggested many years ago by Piaget, social relations inspire cognitive growth. By talking, sharing, playing, arguing, and watching one another, young children learn through peer interactions to shed their egocentric ways and acquire logical skills such as conservation (Kerwin & Day, 1985). In short, biological, cognitive, and social development are intimately linked.

Now that we have zoomed in on the fine details of child development, let's step back and take a wide-angle look at the "big picture." As the material in this chapter clearly shows, both biological and environmental factors contribute to growth-related changes. Each of us is born with genetic predispositions, yet unique aspects of our experience can steer us in different directions. Biology and environment: Both are vital parts of the big picture.

SUMMARY AND KEY TERMS

Developmental psychology studies how people grow, mature, and change through the stages of the human life span.

The Big Picture

Is behavior determined by a person's genetic blueprint or by environmental factors? This is the question posed by the *nature-nurture debate*. Recognizing that both factors are important, developmental psychologists try to measure their respective contributions. In the *twin study method*, researchers compare the degree of similarity between identical twins and fraternal twins. *Adoption studies* compare identical twins raised in the same household to those raised apart.

Nature's Evidence

Correlations from both twin and adoption studies can be used to calculate *heritability*, a statistic estimating the percentage of a trait's variability caused by genetic factors. Studies of heritability find strong genetic roots for many human characteristics, including personality and intelligence.

Nurture's Evidence

The research supporting genetic influence also shows the importance of environment. In studies of personality, heredity usually accounts for less than half the variation, meaning that environmental factors account for the rest. Moreover, children in a family are different from one another in part because they experience nonshared environments.

Complicating the nature-nurture debate is the fact that the two factors intertwine: people's genetic makeup can influence the environment they create.

The Unborn Child

Genetic Building Blocks

A sperm cell and ovum unite to produce a single cell with 46 rod-like *chromosomes*. The chromosomes are made up of *deoxyribonucleic acid* (DNA) molecules that contain many thousands of *genes*, the biochemical building blocks of an individual life.

Prenatal Development

In the germinal stage (the first two weeks after conception), the fertilized ovum, or *zygote*, divides into a cluster of cells that pass out of the Fallopian tube and attach to the uterine wall. At this point the zygote becomes an *embryo*. During the embryonic stage (third to ninth weeks), body parts begin to form and organs start to function. After the ninth week the embryo becomes a *fetus*, which develops movement, circulation, and even the ability to recognize its mother's voice.

Teratogens are toxic substances that can harm the embryo or fetus during development. Babies of alcoholic mothers often show a pattern of birth defects known as *fetal alcohol syndrome*; even small doses of alcohol seem to be harmful. Smoking, too, restricts the fetus's oxygen supply, and cocaine use by the mother correlates with learning difficulties for the infant.

The Birth Experience

Researchers have tried to discover how the newborn child experiences the rude awakening that we call birth.

The Prenatal Environment

Studies of the environment inside the womb suggest that, far from being tranquil, it is full of sensory stimulation.

The Postnatal Environment

Nevertheless, the world after birth is very different from the womb. Newborns can see the bright delivery-room lights, hear the noises, and feel the drop in temperature.

The Remarkable Newborn

To investigate how infants distinguish sights, sounds, and simple concepts, researchers often measure *habituation*, the tendency for attention to a novel stimulus to wane over time, and *recovery*, the tendency for a different stimulus to arouse new interest. Studies of this sort reveal that infants have remarkable abilites—even a rudimentary sense of arithmetic.

Reflexes

Babies are born with many adaptive reflexes, such as the *grasping reflex*, the *rooting reflex*, sucking, and swallowing.

Sensory Capacities

Though nearsighted, newborns can distinguish between light and dark, follow movements, notice face-like patterns, and mimic adult gestures. Though hard of hearing, they respond to the human voice, especially high pitches and melodic patterns. In taste and smell, newborns are very well developed.

The Infant and Growing Child

Biological Development

Babies grow most rapidly in the first year. As they grow, the brain and nervous system develop more synaptic connections and increased myelination. Motor skills also advance in a fairly predictable sequence. Yet these biological aspects of development are influenced by cultural and environmental factors.

Cognitive Development

Piaget described four stages in cognitive development. In the *sensorimotor stage* (birth to two years of age), infants learn about the world through direct sensory and motor contact. They develop *object permanence*, an awareness that objects continue to exist after they disappear from view, and *separation anxiety*, a fear reaction to the absence of the primary care-taker. In the *preoperational stage* (two to six years of age), children begin to reason in an intuitive, pre-logical way. They are *egocentric* (self-centered), and they do not understand *conservation*, the concept that an object's physical properties remain the same despite superficial changes in appearance. The *concrete operational stage* (six to twelve years of age) brings logical reasoning but not abstract thought. Finally, at the *formal operational stage* (roughly twelve years of age to adulthood), the individual learns to reason at an abstract, hypothetical level.

Recent research suggests that Piaget underestimated the rate of development, but he was right about the sequence. Likewise, he seems to have been only partly right about the sharp distinctions between stages. Many researchers now study age-related changes in information processing. This approach indicates that short-term memory and processing speed increase as children grow older.

Language development proceeds in a regular sequence: crying, cooing, babbling, words, telegraphic speech, full sentences. Evidence supports the view that humans are specially "wired" for language and that words and concepts develop jointly, each influencing the other.

Social Development

Some animals exhibit *imprinting*, an instinctive tendency to follow the mother during a *critical period* just after birth. In humans the process is less automatic, but infants do form an *attachment*, a deep, affectionate emotional bond with the primary caretaker. Studies with both humans and monkeys show that "contact comfort" is an important source of attachment. The *strange-situation test* helps researchers distinguish between *secure attachment* and *insecure attachment*, a difference that results from both parenting style and the infant's own temperament. Although securely attached infants tend to become more independent, popular, and socially skilled in later years, it isn't clear whether the early form of attachment causes these results.

Psychologists disagree about the effects of day care on attachment. Recent evidence suggests that high-quality day care has both benefits (greater independence and intelligence) and drawbacks (less secure attachment, less obedience, more aggression).

Horizontal (peer) relationships—mostly between children of the same sex—become more important as the child grows older. Children neglected by their peers are more at risk for later adjustment problems than those who are more popular.

The Many Facets of Development

Although psychologists tend to differentiate among biological, cognitive, and social development, all three areas are closely linked, and all are affected by both nature and nurture.

Chapter 10

ADOLESCENCE

Biological Development

Cognitive Development
Moral Reasoning / Alternative Conceptions

Social Development
Parent Relationships / Peer Influences / Sexuality

Adolescence and Mental Health

ADULTHOOD AND OLD AGE

Biological Development
The Adult Years / Old Age

Cognitive Development
Memory and Forgetting / Intelligence / Productivity

Social Development
Ages and Stages of Adulthood / Critical Events of Adulthood / Life Satisfaction

Dying and Death

PERSPECTIVES ON THE LIFE CYCLE

Adolescence and Adulthood

When it comes to understanding people, it often seems that poets, playwrights, philosophers, and artists are a step ahead of the rest of us. In the seventh century B.C., the Greek poet Solon described nine stages in human development, beginning in the cradle and ending in the grave. Then, in approximately the year 500 B.C., Chinese philosopher Confucius described six life phases spanning the ages of fifteen to seventy. At the end of the sixteenth century, William Shakespeare immortalized his vision of seven life stages. And in Sweden, an unnamed artist depicted the ages of man and woman in ten-decade pyramids that peak at the age of fifty. In some cultures, the life span is pictured as a straight line. In others, it is thought of as a circle, spiral, square, or as a change of seasons (Kotre & Hall, 1990).

In light of all the wisdom inherited from past generations, it is ironic that researchers only recently began to appreciate the theme of this chapter—that human development is a lifelong process. In Chapter 9, we examined the recurring controversy over the relative influences of nature and nurture. Over the years, developmental psychologists have also debated *stability* and *change*, a question concerning the extent to which humans change over the course of a lifetime. Will an infant with a precocious smile turn into a sociable adult? Is the early-walking toddler a future athlete? Is the preschooler who clings to mom fated to become a dependent spouse later in life? Is the overanxious college student doomed to a life of anxiety? As in the nature-nurture debate, there are two competing, though not mutually exclusive, points of view.

For many years, it was assumed that our individual life scripts were written in infancy and childhood, waiting only to be acted out during our adult years. Freud felt that personality is largely formed by the sixth birthday, while Piaget claimed that the ultimate stage of cognitive development typically blossoms with puberty. These narrow views of the early years of life as "critical" may well describe changes in height, whereby early growth spurts are followed by a leveling off in adulthood. But such views do not yield an accurate picture when it comes to the full range of biological, cognitive, and social development. In this chapter, we will see that even though infancy and childhood are in some ways "formative," each of us continues to change in important ways when we mature from adolescence to adulthood and old age. As our ancestors tried to tell us, development is a lifelong process.

Whether one's interest is in infants, children, adolescents, or adults, there are two approaches for studying developmental processes. In **cross-sectional studies**, people of different ages are examined at about the same time and their responses are compared. For example, intelligence researchers who test people in their twenties through seventies find that older adults consistently obtain lower scores than younger adults (Wechsler, 1972). This method of comparison is quick and easy to implement, but the results need to be interpreted with caution. Consider cross-sectional studies of intelligence. Is the pattern of decline a result of age, or could it reflect a "cohort effect"—that is, a difference between generations? Today's twenty-year-olds spend more years in school than did their grandparents, who grew up during World War II. Lower scores among the older adults may stem from a relative lack of educational opportunity—not from chronological age.

In longitudinal research, subjects are tested at different times in their lives. In a similar manner, Bobby Neel Adams creates "age maps" by photographing adults in poses that mimic earlier pictures. Shown here is a double portrait of Sally Woodbridge—in 1944, and again in 1992.

■ **cross-sectional studies** A method of developmental research in which people of different ages are tested and compared.

■ **longitudinal studies** A method of developmental research in which the same people are tested at different times to track age-related changes.

■ **adolescence** The period of life from puberty to adulthood, corresponding roughly to the ages of thirteen to twenty.

A second method is to conduct **longitudinal studies** in which the same subjects are retested at different times in their lives in order to measure truly age-related changes. Using this method, researchers interview people or administer questionnaires at one point in their lives, and then collect follow-up information days, weeks, months, or years later. In the research on age and intelligence, this strategy has revealed that there is somewhat less of a decline in performance as the same people grow older (Baltes et al., 1979; Schaie, 1983). Whereas cross-sectional studies reveal *differences*, longitudinal studies measure *change*. The main drawback is logistical. Longitudinal studies take a great deal of time—and require patience from researchers and cooperation from subjects.

ADOLESCENCE

Many cultures have initiation rites to celebrate the passage from childhood to adulthood. In the African Thonga tribe, the boy, upon reaching puberty, is beaten with clubs, shaved, stripped, exposed to cold, forced to eat unsavory foods, circumcised, and secluded for three months. Among the Cheyenne Indians of North America, the girl who menstruates for the first time is bathed, her body is painted red by older women, and she is then isolated for four days. The ritual may vary, but most cultures have ways of marking adolescence. Confirmation, bar mitzvah, the first communion, and the start of junior high school are some of the ways in which Westerners recognize this transitional time of life (Cohen, 1964).

Adolescence is to adulthood what infancy is to childhood—the start of a new era, a "second birth." Beginning with a biological event (puberty) and culminating in a social event (independence from parents), adolescence in

Many cultures celebrate the passage from childhood to adulthood. Dressed in buckskin and jewelry, an Apache girl is honored for her first menstrual period in an elaborate four-day ritual. At the age of thirteen, Jewish boys achieve their manhood in a religious ceremony known as a bar mitzvah.

■ **puberty** The onset of adolescence, as evidenced by rapid growth, rising levels of sex hormones, and sexual maturity.

the United States corresponds roughly to the teen years, thirteen to twenty. No longer a child but not yet an adult, the adolescent is in an important transitional phase of life—a time of biological, cognitive, and social change.

It is interesting to note that the way psychologists have viewed adolescence has changed over time. Robert Enright and his colleagues (1987) analyzed articles on the topic that were published over the past one hundred years and found that conceptions of adolescence have changed with changing social and economic conditions. During World Wars I and II, when young people were needed for factory work and military service, teenagers were described as competent and responsible, and adolescence was thought to end by about age sixteen. Yet during the economically depressed 1890s and 1930s, when work was hard to find, teenagers were portrayed as incompetent and immature, and adolescence itself was thought to end at a later age. Perhaps social and economic conditions bias the way psychologists view this phase of development—or perhaps these same conditions affect adolescent behavior. Either way, it is important to recognize that certain aspects of adolescence, and of other developmental periods as well, may differ somewhat from one generation and culture to the next.

Biological Development

The biological motor of adolescence is **puberty,** the onset of sexual maturation brought on by rising hormone levels—estrogen and progesterone in females, and testosterone in males. Plus or minus two years, girls reach puberty at the age of eleven, and boys at the age of thirteen. This sex difference is noticeable in the rapid growth that propels children to almost their full height. Look at Figure 10.1, and you will see that the growth

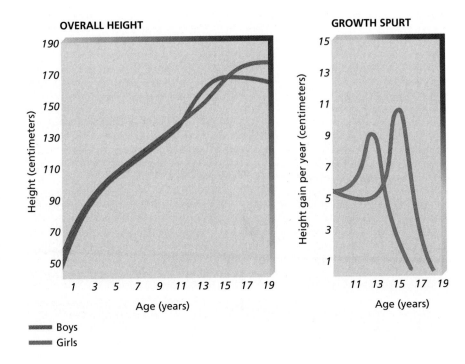

Figure 10.1

Adolescent Growth Spurts in Height

■ **menarche** A girl's first menstrual period.

spurt begins a bit earlier for girls but lasts longer for boys, eventually leaving adult men an average of five inches taller than women.

For girls, puberty is marked by the first menstrual period, called **menarche**. Menarche is often a memorable turning point in a girl's life, one that she recalls vividly and with a mixture of pride and embarrassment (Greif & Ulman, 1982). Two factors influence a girl's reaction both to her first period and to other physiological changes that signal her sexual maturity—budding breasts, pubic hair, and broadened hips. The first factor is *cultural practice*. For the Kurtatchi, who live on an island off the coast of New Guinea, menarche is a joyous village-wide event greeted by music, dance, food, and festivities. In many other cultures, however, menstruation—or "that time of the month"—is treated as too delicate a topic for conversation and the menstruating woman is viewed by men with a mixture of pity, fear, and disgust. It's no wonder that many girls are secretive about their first period, and tell only their mothers (Ruble & Brooks-Gunn, 1982).

The second factor that influences a girl's reaction to puberty is *timing*. Anne Petersen (1988) and her colleagues interviewed hundreds of adolescents and found that girls who mature earlier than most of their peers are less satisfied with their increased size, weight, and busty image. A well-developed seventh-grade girl towers over the boys in her class, gets teased about her appearance, and draws a watchful eye from parents worrying about their daughter's sexual activity. The result may be embarrassment in school and strained relations at home. Other researchers have found that early puberty presents additional adjustment problems. For example, girls who attain menarche early become more likely to spend time with older peers, date and have sex at an earlier age, get lower grades, and become involved in norm-breaking behaviors (Stattin & Magnusson, 1990). This timing effect is most true of those with a childhood history of behavior problems. In a longitudinal study conducted in New Zealand, Avshalom Caspi and Terrie Moffitt (1991) collected information from 348 girls, their parents, and their teachers—when the girls were nine, thirteen, and fifteen years old. They found that those who had problems before puberty *and* who reached puberty early were the most likely as adolescents to get into varying degrees of trouble (such as getting drunk, stealing items from classmates, getting into fights, sneaking into R-rated movies, breaking windows, cutting classes, and making prank telephone calls). In a follow-up study, Caspi and his colleagues (1993) found that early maturation is more of a problem for girls who attend mixed-sex schools than for those at all-girl schools. Although this correlation can be interpreted in different ways, these investigators speculated that the presence of boys in mixed-sex schools provides girls who are "at risk" with additional opportunities for participating in delinquent behavior.

It's interesting, by the way, that the timing of menarche is heavily influenced by environmental factors. In the 1800s, the average American girl didn't begin to menstruate until the age of seventeen. As a result of improved nutritional practices, the average girl now menstruates at a younger age, twelve or thirteen. Of course, there are vast individual differences—not only between cultures but within them as well. For example, many gymnasts, models, and ballet dancers who exercise and diet, and therefore lack body fat, reach menarche relatively late in their teens (Brooks-Gunn & Warren, 1985).

■ **spermarche** A boy's first ejaculation.

■ **moral reasoning** The way people think about and try to solve moral dilemmas.

For boys, puberty is marked by the growth of the penis and testes, accompanied by facial hair, pubic hair, increased muscle mass, lowered voice, and broadened shoulders. Akin to menarche, the high point of male puberty is **spermarche,** the boy's first ejaculation, which usually occurs at the age of thirteen or fourteen (although it is not until a year later that the semen holds live sperm cells ready for reproduction). As with girls, some boys reach puberty before others. For boys, however, spermarche is a generally positive experience (Gaddis & Brooks-Gunn, 1985; Stein & Reiser, 1994)—and early maturation is a social asset. Consistently, researchers have found that early-maturing males excel in sports, are popular among peers, take leadership roles, and are more poised and self-confident than those who mature later (Jones, 1957; Petersen, 1988). It's no wonder that the typical boy is on the lookout for whiskers, waiting for the chance to shave.

Cognitive Development

Paralleling the physical growth spurt brought on by puberty is what might be called a cognitive growth spurt. Adolescents who mature early get slightly higher scores on tests of intelligence than those who mature later (Newcombe & Baenninger, 1989). And you may recall Piaget's observation that adolescents are capable of logic, abstract thought, and hypothetical reasoning—hallmarks of the *formal operational* stage of cognitive development. This capacity for abstraction spurs teenagers to think critically, to challenge parents and society, and to contemplate possibilities. Eliot Turiel (1983) found that at the age of twelve or thirteen, adolescents begin to view social conventions—for example, appropriate clothing, or hairstyle, or the proper way to address a teacher—as arbitrary and unreasonable. It's important to keep in mind, however, that even as young adolescents start to flex their newly strengthened cognitive muscles, they are still somewhat *egocentric* in the way they think, and are highly self-conscious. Research shows that eighth- and ninth-graders always seem to think they are on "center stage"—the focus of everyone's attention and unique among their peers (Elkind, 1967; Elkind & Bowen, 1979).

As they enter the formal operational stage of development, adolescents begin to challenge parental and social conventions.

Moral Reasoning   According to Piaget (1932), the adolescent's capacity for abstraction gives rise to a more mature form of **moral reasoning.** Piaget noticed that young children take rules literally, without regard for a person's intentions, motives, or the circumstances. As far as the young child is concerned, the little leaguer who accidentally smacks a baseball into the windshield of a car is bad, and the parent who promises cookies only then to find the cupboard bare is a liar. Not until the age of ten or eleven do children think more flexibly about rules, and evaluate others not just by what they do but *why* they do it. In this more advanced stage of reasoning, the little leaguer is not considered a bad person or the parent a liar for actions that produced negative outcomes they did not intend (Lickona, 1976; Strichartz & Burton, 1990).

Building on the idea that moral reasoning requires cognitive sophistication, Lawrence Kohlberg argued that adolescence is a particularly rich time of life for moral development (Kohlberg, 1981, 1984; Colby & Kohlberg,

1987). Kohlberg presented stories containing moral dilemmas to children, adolescents, and adults, and asked them how these dilemmas should be resolved. To illustrate, consider the following classic story:

> In Europe, a woman was near death from cancer. One drug might save her, a form of radium that a druggist in the same town had recently discovered. The druggist was charging $2,000, 10 times what the drug cost him to make. The sick woman's husband, Heinz, went to everyone he knew to borrow the money, but he could only get together about half of what it cost. He told the druggist that his wife was dying and asked him to sell it cheaper or let him pay later. But the druggist said, "No." The husband got desperate and broke into the man's store to steal the drug for his wife. (Kohlberg, 1969, p. 379)

What do you think: Should Heinz have stolen the drug? Were his actions morally right or wrong, and why? Based on subjects' responses to stories like this one, Kohlberg proposed that people advance through three levels of moral thought, further divided into six stages. First, there is a *preconventional* level in which moral dilemmas are resolved in ways that satisfy self-serving motives—so an act is "moral" if it enables a person to avoid punishment or obtain reward. Second is a *conventional* level in which moral dilemmas are resolved in ways that reflect the laws of the land, or norms set by parents and other sources of authority. Thus, an act is moral if it meets with social approval or maintains the social order. Third, adolescents and adults who attain Piaget's formal operational stage of cognitive development may also reach a *postconventional* level of moral thought, one based on abstract principles such as equality, justice, and the value of life. At this level, an act is moral if it affirms one's conscience—even if it violates the law (see Table 10.1).

Is this theory of moral development valid? Over the years, Kohlberg has drawn an enormous amount of attention, support, and criticism. To his credit, Kohlberg and others have found that as children and adolescents mature, they climb his moral ladder in the predicted order, without skipping steps (Colby et al., 1983; Walker, 1989). Figure 10.2 shows that although most seven- to ten-year-olds are preconventional in their moral thinking, many thirteen- to sixteen-year-olds think in conventional terms.

Figure 10.2

Levels of Moral Reasoning

In response to standard moral dilemmas, most seven- to ten-year-olds exhibited preconventional reasoning, while most thirteen- to sixteen-year-olds thought in conventional terms. Very few of the subjects resolved these dilemmas on a postconventional level (Colby et al., 1983).

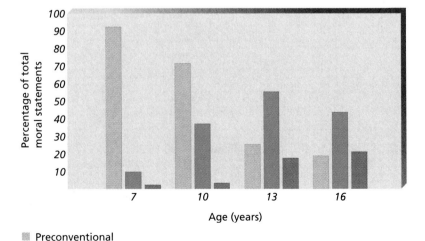

Levels	Stages	Moral reasoning in response to the Heinz dilemma	
		In favor of Heinz's stealing the drug	Against Heinz's stealing the drug
I. Preconventional	Stage 1 *Punishment and obedience orientation:* Motivation to avoid punishment	"If you let your wife die, you will get in trouble."	"You shouldn't steal the drug because you'll be caught and sent to jail if you do."
	Stage 2 *Instrumental relativist orientation:* Motivation to obtain rewards	"It wouldn't bother you much to serve a little jail term, if you have your wife when you get out."	"He may not get much of a jail term if he steals the drug, but his wife will probably die before he gets out, so it won't do him much good."
II. Conventional	Stage 3 *Good boy–nice girl orientation:* Motivation to gain approval and to avoid disapproval	"No one will think you're bad if you steal the drug, but your family will think you're an inhuman husband if you don't."	"It isn't just the druggist who will think you're a criminal, everyone else will too."
	Stage 4 *Society-maintaining orientation:* Motivation to fulfill one's duty and to avoid feelings of guilt	"If you have any sense of honor, you won't let your wife die because you're afraid to do the only thing that will save her."	"You'll always feel guilty for your dishonesty and law-breaking."
III. Postconventional	Stage 5 *Social-contract orientation:* Motivation to follow rational, mutually agreed-upon principles and maintain the respect of others	"If you let your wife die, it would be out of fear, not out of reasoning it out."	"You would lose your standing and respect in the community and break the law."
	Stage 6 *Universal ethical principle orientation:* Motivation to uphold one's own ethical principles and avoid self-condemnation	"If you don't steal the drug, . . . you would have lived up to the outside rule of the law but you wouldn't have lived up to your own standards of conscience."	"If you stole the drug, . . . you'd condemn yourself because you wouldn't have lived up to your own conscience and standards of honesty."

Table 10.1

Kohlberg's Theory of Moral Development

Interestingly, researchers find that very few adolescents—or adults, for that matter—resolve moral issues on a postconventional level.

Alternative Conceptions There are three major criticisms of Kohlberg's theory. The first is that his model is culturally biased. Research confirms that most children and adolescents—from Canada, Taiwan, Israel, Mexico, Turkey, and other countries—advance at the same rate through the first two levels, but that only educated, middle-class adults exhibit postconven-

■ **empathy** A feeling of joy for others who are happy and distress for those who are in pain.

tional forms of morality based on abstract principles (Edwards, 1981; Snarey, 1985). When presented with Kohlberg's written dilemmas, many nonwesterners—including Tibetan Buddhist monks, and respected village leaders in Kenya and Papua New Guinea—fail to reason at this third level. In cultures that value friendship and social responsibility more than rugged individualism, "conventional" moral reasoning is not only common but desirable. In a study that compared American and Indian children and adults, Joan Miller and David Bersoff (1992) found that in India, people possess an alternative postconventional moral code in which obligation to a friend is more principled than an obligation to justice.

A second criticism is that the model is gender biased. When Kohlberg first constructed his dilemmas, he tested only males and then used their responses as a moral yardstick. Yet according to Carol Gilligan (1982), women address moral issues "in a different voice." More concerned about compassion for others than about abstract rules, the female voice may be different, but it is not morally inferior. Gilligan's point has obvious intuitive appeal, but it lacks clear empirical support. On the one hand, public-opinion pollsters find that women care more deeply than men about social issues and interpersonal relations. On the other hand, moral development researchers do not find consistent sex differences in moral reasoning. On average, women and men obtain similar scores on Kohlberg's dilemmas (Rest, 1986; Walker, 1984).

Finally, many developmental psychologists have argued that Kohlberg's model is limited because morality is more than just an ability to think about hypothetical dilemmas in a manner that is cognitively sophisticated. Actions speak louder than words, say Kohlberg's critics. The real question is, Does moral *reasoning* breed moral *behavior*? Are postconventional thinkers kinder, or more caring, or more virtuous in their daily affairs than those lower on the cognitive ladder? Do society's model citizens use higher levels of moral reasoning than drug pushers, racists, mobsters, and corrupt business executives? Available research offers two answers to these questions.

First, moral reasoning and behavior are very often related. Juvenile delinquents tend to score lower on Kohlberg's dilemmas than normal adolescents, and those with higher scores tend to behave in ways that are considered more moral (Blasi, 1980; Kurtines & Gewirtz, 1984). The second answer, however, is that it's entirely possible to live a moral life without "elitist" levels of cognitive reasoning. Think about Kohlberg's theory, and then ask yourself: Are young children *a*moral, or less moral than their cognitively superior parents? Children may lack the cognitive equipment, but do they lack the emotional equipment underlying morality? According to Martin Hoffman (1984), morality in children is rooted in **empathy**—a capacity to experience joy for others who are happy and distress for those who are in pain. By this account, morality is present early in life. In the crib, infants will often cry when they hear the sound of another baby crying. They feel no pain of their own, yet they are distressed, a possible sign of empathy. At less than two years old, babies have been observed giving food, toys, hugs, and kisses to others who show signs of distress—again, a possible sign of empathy (Zahn-Waxler et al., 1992). At the sight of a homeless person curled up on the floor of a train station, even the young, preconventional child reacts with sorrow and a desire to offer help (Damon, 1988; Eisenberg & Mussen, 1989).

DEVELOPMENTAL PSYCHOLOGY   Law

Moral Dilemmas in Law: Euthanasia

Juries have long been confronted with moral dilemmas like those constructed by Kohlberg. Before the Civil War, northern juries regularly failed to convict people charged with aiding escaped slaves. During the turbulent Vietnam era, many juries refused to convict antiwar activists on political conspiracy charges. Today, cases involving battered women who retaliate against their abusive husbands and crime victims who kill their assailants in self-defense also present moral dilemmas to the jury. In cases of this nature, the jury has the power to vote its conscience, even if it means overruling or "nullifying" the law (Horowitz & Willging, 1991).

Two poignant stories illustrate different kinds of moral reasoning in action. The first involved the death of Emily Gilbert, a seventy-three-year-old woman who was suffering from Alzheimer's disease and a crippling case of osteoporosis. After years of agony, she pleaded with her husband Roswell to terminate her life. She was in such a state, Gilbert told his attorney, that "hospitals wouldn't take her, private nursing homes wouldn't take her. . . . In a state hospital, they'd have to strap her down. She'd be dehumanized." So one day, as

Emily sat on a sofa looking out a window in their tenth-floor condominium, he shot her twice in the back of her head. Tried for murder, Gilbert pleaded not guilty. Several witnesses, including many friends of the elderly couple, corroborated the claim that Emily had begged for her own death. Nevertheless, ten women and two men in Fort Lauderdale, Florida, convicted Gilbert of first-degree murder punishable by life imprisonment. One of the jurors said later, "We had no choice. The law does not allow for sympathy" (Associated Press, 1985).

The second case involved George Zygmanik, who was the tormented victim of a car accident that left him paralyzed from the neck down. From his hospital bed, Zygmanik cried to his younger brother Lester, "I want you to promise to kill me. I want you to swear to God." So one night, Lester complied with the request. He entered his brother's hospital room, shot him in the head with a 20-gauge sawed-off shotgun, dropped the gun by the bed, and turned himself in. He confessed to the killing immediately, and described it as an act of love for his brother. Zygmanik was charged with first-degree murder, which, in his home state of New Jersey, car-

Social Development

To many people, the word *teenager* is synonymous with torn jeans, loud music, wild hair, and long phone conversations. The teen years are a curious time of life. Absorbed in closer-than-ever friendships, newly aroused by sexual urges, needing to "fit in" and yet wanting to "stand out," feeling caught between parents and peers, and anxious about the future, teens are fraught with mixed emotions. The highs are high, the lows low, and the changes frequent.

According to Erik Erikson (1963), all people pass through a series of life stages, each marked by a "crisis" that has to be resolved in order for healthy development to occur. During the transitional period of adolescence, the central task is to form an *identity,* or self-concept—hence the term **identity crisis.** Some teenagers pass through this stage easily, clear about who they are, what values they hold, and what they want out of life. Others drift somewhat in confusion as they struggle to break from parents, find the right friends, establish their sexual orientation, and set career goals for the future. For Erikson, this identity crisis is best described by a sign he once saw hanging in a cowboy bar: "I ain't what I ought to be, I ain't what I'm going to be, but I ain't what I was" (1959, p. 93).

In the United States and other countries with an ethnically diverse population, minority adolescents—caught between two cultures—must also es-

■ **identity crisis** An adolescent's struggle to establish a personal identity, or self-concept.

ries a mandatory life prison sentence. During the trial, he testified that on the night of the killing, "I asked him if he was in pain. At this time, he couldn't speak at all. He just nodded that he was. He nodded yes. So I says, 'I am here to end your pain—is that all right with you?' And he nodded yes. And the next thing I knew, I shot him" (Mitchell, 1976, p. 195). The jury acquitted him.

The conflict in these events is profound: the law strictly prohibits *euthanasia,* or mercy killing, yet both Emily Gilbert and George Zygmanik desperately wanted to die. What should their loved ones have done, and how should society react? For killing his wife of fifty-one years, Roswell Gilbert was found guilty of murder and sent to prison until he was released in 1990, five years later. The reason for the jury's verdict? As we saw earlier, one juror—expressing a conventional level of morality—explained that "the law does not allow for sympathy." Yet Lester Zygmanik was found *not* guilty for very similar actions. Again, the reason? Exhibiting a postconventional level of morality, his jury felt that compassion for a loved one takes precedence over the letter of the law. Is it morally superior to condone rather than punish mercy killing? No, Kohlberg is quick to point out that moral development is measured not by *what* the decision is but by *how* it is reasoned. A postconventional jury could have convicted Gilbert, had it based its verdict not on the law but on the ethic that "human life should never be sacrificed."

The prosecution of Dr. Jack Kevorkian embodies a classic moral dilemma. Sometimes referred to as "Dr. Death," Kevorkian has assisted in the suicides of many terminally ill patients.

tablish an *ethnic identity.* Thus, the African-, Hispanic-, and Asian-American may identify with the language and customs of the "parent" culture, their new national culture, or both. Jean Phinney (1990) notes that the process of ethnic identity formation typically begins in adolescence with a passive acceptance of the dominant culture, is then followed in early adulthood by an awakening of interest in one's cultural roots, and culminates later in an ethnic identification. As you might expect, ethnic-group identity is stronger among immigrants who enter the host country as adults than it is among those who arrive at a younger, more formative age. This process is described further in Chapter 14.

Research shows that adolescents experiment with different possible selves—rebel, free spirit, workaholic, political activist, and so on—in search of their identity, and that the process takes time (Waterman, 1982). Indeed, first-year college students are less likely than seniors to say that "I know who I am and what I want out of life" (Constantinople, 1969). However long it takes, however, there are three aspects of social development that all adolescents must come to grips with: parent relationships, peer influences, and sexuality.

Parent Relationships   To the mother or father of a cuddly newborn baby, it's hard to imagine that the intense emotional bond could ever be broken. To the parent of a teenager, it's no longer so hard to imagine. Whether the

"When I was a boy of 14, my father was so ignorant I could hardly stand to have the man around. But when I got to be 21, I was astonished at how much he had learnt in 7 years."

MARK TWAIN

topic is a blaring stereo, school grades, money, or dirty laundry, it seems that parents and adolescents are often in a power struggle, involved in one squabble after another. As described by the mother of an eleven-year-old daughter, "It's like being bitten to death by ducks" (Steinberg, 1987, p. 36).

As children mature, what happens to their relationship with parents? Is conflict normal, or is it easily avoided? Can the bond that once seemed so secure be shattered? And what effect does it all have on the family? By administering questionnaires, interviewing family members, and observing interactions in the laboratory and in the home, researchers are now trying to answer these questions. What emerges from these studies is the following portrait of parents and teenagers: At the time of puberty and physical maturation, there is a sharp rise in tension between ten- to thirteen-year-olds trying to assert their independence—and parents, especially the mother. As shown in Figure 10.3, young adolescents and parents fight about twice a week, mostly over routine household matters like taking out the garbage—not explosive issues such as sex, religion, or politics (Hill, 1988; Steinberg, 1989). The conflict does not usually leave a permanent scar on the parent-child relationship, but it is hard on parents while it lasts, increasing personal stress and straining marital relations (Small et al., 1988; Silverberg & Steinberg, 1990).

Figure 10.3

What Do Parents and Teenagers Fight About?

Interviews with parents and adolescents of varying ages revealed that most arguments concern routine matters, not differences in deeply held values (Smetana, 1988).

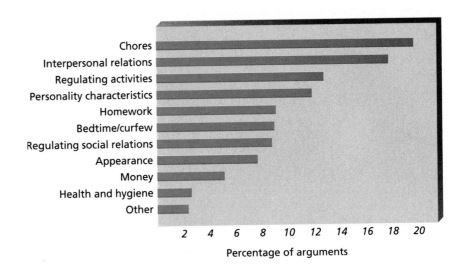

It may seem as if parents and teenagers are at war, like government and rebel forces, but research indicates that the so-called generation gap has been blown out of proportion. To be sure, there are frequent minor skirmishes. Some bickering between parents and teenagers is probably inevitable. Typically, however, there is peace. In questionnaires and interviews, a majority of adolescents say that they admire their parents and accept their parents' political and religious values (Adelson, 1986; Offer & Schonert-Reichl, 1992).

It's clear that the onset of puberty coincides with changes in the parent-child relationship. It's not clear, however, what to make of this correlation—so researchers, at least for now, can only speculate about the possible interpretations (Paikoff & Brooks-Gunn, 1991). Taking an evolutionary perspective, Laurence Steinberg (1989) argues that tensions within the family are triggered not by the adolescent's chronological age but by puberty. If it comes early, so does conflict. If puberty is late, the conflict is delayed. To clarify the complex link between the biology of adolescence and social relations at home, Steinberg notes that in many primate species living in the wild—gibbons and chimpanzees, for example—it's common for males and females at puberty to depart their group in order to search elsewhere for a mate and reproduce with others outside the family. Even among humans, there is historical precedence for separating parents and their teenagers. Before many countries became industrialized, adolescents lived in a state of "semiautonomy" (residing with parents, but working to earn money), and in some cultures they were subject to "extrusion" (sent to live in other households).

According to Steinberg, the problem that exists today may stem from the fact that sexually mature offspring spend more time in the company of parents than ever before. A hundred years ago, adolescents left home at sixteen or seventeen, roughly the age at which they became mature. Now adolescents reach puberty at twelve or thirteen but live at home until the age of eighteen or older. So what does all this tell us about parent-child relations? According to Steinberg (1987), everyone should feel reassured: "Telling parents that fighting over taking out the garbage is related to the reproductive fitness of the species provides little solace—and doesn't help get the garbage out of the house, either. But parents need to recognize that quarreling with a teenager over mundane matters may be a normal part of family life during adolescence" (p. 39).

Peer Influences   Another important aspect of adolescent social development is the heightened significance of peer groups and relations outside the home—long, gossipy phone conversations, flirtation, and dating. For the first time, the child becomes primarily oriented to the world outside the home and may not even want to be seen with parents. Compared to early childhood friendships, adolescent relationships can be highly intimate. It's not unusual for best friends to talk freely about their thoughts and feelings and to reveal some of their deepest, darkest secrets (Berndt & Ladd, 1989).

Although most adolescents tend to retain the fundamental values of their parents, they look to peers for guidance on how to dress or wear their hair, what music to listen to, how to speak, and how to behave in ways that are acceptable. As social beings, we all exhibit a tendency to conform, at least to some extent. Is this tendency more pronounced in adolescence? Are junior and senior high school students more vulnerable to peer pressure than adults? The answer is yes, especially during the early stages of adolescence. Thomas Berndt (1979) asked students in grades three, six, nine, and twelve how they would react if their friends tried to influence them to see a certain movie, go bowling, help a new kid on the block, or cheat on a test. The result: Conformity rose steadily with age, peaked in the ninth grade, then declined. The tendency to conform is weaker for actions that are immoral or illegal, but younger adolescents are consistently the most likely followers, wanting desperately to "fit in" (Brown et al., 1986; Gavin & Furman, 1989).

Whether conforming to a new generation means eating live goldfish, dressing punk, shaving the head, or piercing an ear, conformity satisfies important needs in a teenager's life. At the same time, there is the tragic possibility that adolescents can be pressured into using harmful drugs in order to attract peer approval. According to national surveys, an estimated 55 percent of American *junior* high school students try smoking cigarettes, 83 percent try alcohol, and 30 percent try illicit drugs such as marijuana (Newcomb & Bentler, 1989; Oetting & Beauvais, 1990). These numbers are higher among high school students and vary somewhat from one cultural group to the next. For example, substance-abuse rates for tobacco, alcohol, and marijuana are particularly high among certain groups of Native American youths (Moncher et al., 1990; Oetting & Beauvais, 1990).

What leads the young and impressionable teenager to use drugs? Is peer pressure partly to blame? Would the heavy demand for drugs subside if youngsters could "just say no"? There are no simple answers. Drug use is a complex problem that is influenced by personality traits, family background, education, culture, and socioeconomic factors. In this context, the pressure to conform seems to play an important but limited role. Teenagers may be seduced by peers into *experimenting* with drugs, but whether they become drug *abusers* also depends on their prior history of emotional adjustment. For those who are chronically anxious, alienated, or impulsive, experimentation may well turn to abuse (Shedler & Block, 1990).

Sexuality   Triggered by rising hormone levels and physical maturation, adolescent boys and girls are sexual beings, curious and easily aroused. Human sexuality is a very natural part of development. Adolescence is also a time when teenagers, in search of an identity, discover their sexual orientation. For most, it is clear. But for an estimated 10 percent of adolescents, there is a good deal of uncertainty and confusion (Gordun & Gillun, 1987). Whether teenagers *act* on their impulses, is influenced by changing times and cultural norms. Several decades ago, Alfred Kinsey and his associates (1948, 1953) conducted the first large-scale survey of sexual practices in America. A comparison of these data to more recent surveys suggests that although there has been a constant 50 to 70 percent rate of sexual activity among boys, the number of sexually active teenage girls climbed from a low of 10 percent in the 1940s to a high of 50 percent in the 1970s (Brooks-Gunn & Furstenberg, 1989).

Although American teenagers are sexually more active today than at the time of Kinsey's survey, they are surprisingly not better informed about the risks or more careful about the use of contraceptives. Thus the teenage pregnancy rate has reached epidemic proportions despite the availability of effective birth-control methods. In 1981, the Alan Guttmacher Institute estimated that 24 percent of all American girls become pregnant before the age of eighteen—and most of these pregnancies are unplanned and unwanted. All too often, the consequences are tragic—abortion, a hasty and unhappy marriage, or an out-of-wedlock birth that forces the mother out of school and plunges her into poverty (Hayes, 1987). Unprotected sex can also prove fatal. It is estimated that 20 million people, including 1.5 million Americans, are infected with HIV—the human immunodeficiency virus that causes AIDS (Mann, 1992). It is also estimated that one-fifth of these cases start in adolescence, a revelation that has alarming implications for the future (Gardner et al., 1991).

One reason for these difficulties is that many teenagers in the United States do *not* use contraceptives the first time they have sex—and this pattern of neglect persists, particularly among those who are young, poor, and uneducated. The percentages vary from one sample to another, but they all reveal the same problem. In a questionnaire anonymously taken by three hundred college students, a shocking 63 percent of the women and 57 percent of the men admitted that neither they nor their partners used a contraceptive the first time they had intercourse (Darling et al., 1992). Why not? One reason is that they were often caught off guard, especially the first time. As one sixteen-year-old girl put it, "The first time, it was like totally out of the blue. . . . I mean, you don't know it's coming, so how are you to be prepared?" (Stark, 1986, p. 28). A second reason is that many teenagers feel guilty about having sex, so they do not carry condoms or in any other way plan for contraception. If one is ambivalent, it's easier to justify getting "swept off your feet" and "carried away" than it is to have premeditated sex (Byrne & Fisher, 1983; Gerrard, 1987). A third reason is ignorance—and perhaps even the illusion of invulnerability ("it won't happen to me"). Many teenagers say they rely on withdrawal or the rhythm method as a means of birth control. Yet surveys consistently show that teenagers know surprisingly little about reproductive physiology or the safest time in the menstrual cycle (Morrison, 1985).

Clearly, improvements are needed in sex education. At home, too many parents communicate uneasily about birds and bees, urge girls not to have sex, and advise boys that "if worst comes to worst, be sure to use a rubber." In school, most sex education programs are brief, not comprehensive, and do not focus on matters pertaining to contraception (Brooks-Gunn & Furstenberg, 1989). Adolescent sexual behavior is complex inasmuch as it is influenced by hormones, pubertal status, risk taking, identity seeking, and other personality factors, parents, peers, the media, cultural institutions, and, of course, the influence of the prospective partner (Rodgers & Rowe, 1983). In short, there are no easy solutions to the kinds of problems that can arise. For the male and female adolescent, however, knowledge and protection are a necessary first step toward minimizing negative consequences.

To educate teenagers about the effects of unplanned pregnancies, instructors in this high school health class encourage students to wear a realistically shaped and weighted "empathy belly."

Adolescence and Mental Health

In 1904, G. Stanley Hall described adolescence as a time of "storm and stress," reflecting a widespread belief that teenagers suffer inner conflict and turmoil. Mood swings, identity crises, a rejection of moral values, depression, drugs, unsafe sex, and suicide are among the stereotypic images of the adolescent overcome by "raging hormones." Is there any truth to this image? Are teenagers really the hapless mental health victims of one hormone attack after another?

No. Research shows that despite some of the transitional "growing pains" and mood swings characteristic of adolescence, severe emotional distress is neither inevitable nor widespread (Buchanan et al., 1992; Powers et al., 1989; Whitaker et al., 1990). Many years ago, cultural anthropologists Margaret Mead (1928) and Ruth Benedict (1959) described several nonindustrialized societies in which puberty passes uneventfully, without hoopla or turmoil. More recently, Daniel Offer and his colleagues (1981) distributed questionnaires to more than 20,000 junior and senior high school students in different countries and found that most were happy and reasonably well adjusted. That's the good news. Unfortunately, some 20 percent do have serious emotional problems—a high percentage compared to younger children, and roughly the same percentage as in adults. It's important to realize that unhappy adolescents often grow up to be maladjusted, often with tragic consequences. Precisely for that reason, Offer (1987) urges parents and mental health professionals to abandon the storm-and-stress view of youth and to understand that the teenager who cries for help may be in real trouble, not just "passing through a stage." (See Table 10.2.) In some cases, the tragic result is an attempted suicide (Lewinsohn et al., 1994).

ADULTHOOD AND OLD AGE

It's not altogether clear what separates adolescence from early adulthood. In most states, a person is legally old enough to drive a car at sixteen, to vote at eighteen, and to drink at twenty-one. The average woman gets married at the age of twenty-three, the average man at twenty-five, and both are likely to become parents shortly thereafter. In educational terms, the average student in the United States graduates from high school at eighteen and from college at twenty-two. Those who go on to professional or graduate school typically remain students until age twenty-six or twenty-seven.

The starting point for adulthood may be debatable, but the endpoint is not. In all species of animals, there is a maximum **life span** that sets an upper limit on the oldest possible age of an organism under ideal conditions. Scientists have long held that just as a time clock has twenty-four hours in a day, our biological clocks contain a finite number of years in a life. Although that assumption still prevails, it is fast becoming a subject of controversy. In recent years, some biologists have extended the life span of certain fruit flies, roundworms, and rodents through selective breeding, genetic manipulation, and alterations in diet (Langreth, 1993).

In most species, the **life expectancy**—the actual number of years lived by an average member—is shorter than the maximum life span. On average,

"Some people mark off their life in years, others in events. I am one of the latter. . . . I did not become a young man at a particular year, like 13, but when a kid strolled into the store where I worked and called me 'mister.'"

RICHARD COHEN

■ **life span** The maximum possible age for members of a species.

■ **life expectancy** The number of years that an average member of a species is expected to live.

The universal teenager: common concerns	Australia	Bangladesh	Hungary	Israel	Italy	Japan	Taiwan	Turkey	United States	West Germany	International average
					Percent who agree						
A job well done gives me pleasure.	95	95	96	98	96	98	97	96	97	94	96
My parents are ashamed of me.	11	7	4	3	4	15	10	8	7	2	7
I like to help a friend whenever I can.	94	92	92	93	91	90	94	93	94	91	92
Very often I feel that my mother is no good.	11	10	9	9	9	17	15	6	13	6	9
At times I think about what kinds of work I will do in the future.	91	93	87	85	87	91	91	90	94	91	90
My parents will be disappointed in me in the future.	14	10	9	6	7	23	22	13	7	6	11
Being together with other people gives me a good feeling.	93	84	93	88	87	78	76	91	95	94	88
Very often I feel that my father is no good.	19	12	13	6	15	14	18	8	15	9	13
I feel empty emotionally most of the time.	27	39	12	20	29	29	47	42	18	8	27
I often feel that I would rather die than go on living.	30	38	17	19	15	20	14	25	19	19	22
I feel so lonely.	22	43	14	17	20	39	33	32	18	11	25
I find life an endless series of problems, with no solution in sight.	27	39	11	23	13	39	31	37	15	18	25
I frequently feel sad.	27	36	24	28	25	55	26	34	25	17	29

Table 10.2

Common Concerns Among Teenagers Around the World

Teenagers agreed or disagreed with each statement from the Offer Self-Image Questionnaire. The teens were surveyed in two age groups, thirteen to fifteen and sixteen to nineteen (Atkinson, 1988). ["Respectful, Dutiful Teenagers" by R. Atkinson from PSYCHOLOGY TODAY, October 1988, pp. 22, 28. Reprinted with permission from PSYCHOLOGY TODAY magazine, Copyright © 1988 (Sussex Publishers, Inc.)]

guinea pigs live to the tender age of three; dogs, ten to fifteen; chimpanzees, fifteen to twenty; elephants, thirty to forty; and eagles, one hundred and five (Lansing, 1959)! Among humans, the life expectancy is influenced not only by genetics but also by personality, nutrition, health practices, the environment, the quality of health care, and other factors. The average Roman in the year 1 A.D. lived to the age of twenty-two. In the United States, the life expectancy rose from thirty-six in the nineteenth century to forty-seven in the year 1900, and to seventy-five in 1990. Women outlive men by an average of seven years.

Based on these trends, the U.S. Census Bureau projects that the average

According to the Guinness Book of World Records *(1994), the oldest human being ever documented was Shigechiyo Izumi, a Japanese man who lived for 120 years and 237 days. In 1986, Izumi died of pneumonia.*

life expectancy will increase to seventy-six in 1995, seventy-seven in the year 2000, and seventy-eight in the year 2010 (*American Almanac,* 1993–1994). These numbers are somewhat deceptive, however, because most of the increase is due to a lowering of infancy and childhood mortality rates—not to the fact that people are living longer than their ancestors. Cultural variation is also common. Currently, the average life expectancy is forty-one in Ethiopia, fifty-three in Bolivia, fifty-eight in India, sixty-nine in Mexico, and seventy-eight in Japan (UNICEF, 1990). In the United States, there is also a racial gap, as white Americans live longer than blacks—on average, seventy-six years compared to seventy (U.S. National Center for Health Statistics, 1990).

Biological Development

At birth, a human infant has billions of brain cells. From that point on, however, there is a steady process of attrition: neurons die without replacement, and those that survive thin out. It's important to note that this process does not appear to have negative consequences—and that not all parts of the brain age at the same rate. In the brainstem, which controls many simple reflexes, there is little or no cell loss over time. Yet in the motor cortex and frontal lobes, which control motor and cognitive activity, thousands of neurons a day are lost, particularly after the age of fifty. By the time men and women are eighty, the brain weighs about 8 percent less than it did at the peak of adulthood. What's fascinating about this aspect of development is that the aging brain is simultaneously in a process of growth and decline. A newborn has an overabundance of brain cells, so maturation involves the death of cells that are not needed, coupled with the birth of new synaptic connections among those cells that remain. In the brain of a mature adult, more can be accomplished with less (Creasey & Rapoport, 1985).

The Adult Years   In addition to changes within the brain and nervous system, many other physical changes accompany adult development. Muscle strength, heart and lung capacity, speed of reflexes, and vision increase throughout the twenties, peak at about the age of thirty, and then gradually start to decline. Also at that time, metabolism slows down, leading both men and women to lose their youthful physique and to gain weight. Does this mean that young adults who rely on physical skills are "over the hill" by the age of thirty? Absolutely not. It depends on one's diet, health, and exercise habits, and on the physical demands of a particular activity. Baseball statistician Bill James (1982) as well as Richard Schulz and his colleagues (1994) analyzed the full career records of major-league ball players and found that batters and pitchers peaked at the age of twenty-six. Football, basketball, and tennis players follow a similar age pattern. Yet world-class sprinters and swimmers peak in their teens and early twenties, while professional bowlers and golfers reach the top of their game in their thirties. Age sets limits on what the body can do, but adults who keep in shape can minimize the effects of aging and stretch performance beyond the average. As we will see in Chapter 18, regular exercise benefits both physical

In sports, as in other walks of life, career paths vary. World-class sprinters like Gail Devers peak in their teens and early twenties. Major league baseball players peak at twenty-six, although Nolan Ryan peaked in his thirties and pitched to the age of forty-four.

and mental health—and may even be associated on a short-term basis with improved functioning of the immune system (Simon, 1991).

One inevitable biological event for women is **menopause,** the end of menstruation, which signals the end of fertility. At about the age of fifty, a woman's ovaries stop producing estrogen. The most common symptoms of this change are "hot flashes" (sudden feelings of warmth usually in the upper part of the body) and sometimes profuse sweating, dizziness, nausea, and headaches (Bates, 1981). Some women get moody, depressed, or anxious, but most are not terribly bothered by menopause, and most remain sexually active (Morokoff, 1988). In a survey of more than 8,000 middle-aged women, 70 percent said they felt relieved, liberated, or unaffected by the change (McKinlay et al., 1987). Among those who do suffer, it's not clear whether the negative experience is linked to lowered estrogen levels or to social factors. In youth-oriented cultures, as in the United States, menopause coincides with other life changes. Thus, when Bernice Neugarten (1967) asked 100 women what changes in middle age troubled them the most, very few cited menopause. Instead, most worried about cancer, the death of their husband, and their children leaving home.

For men, there is no biological equivalent to menopause. Testosterone levels (which peak during adolescence) diminish only gradually, and even

■ **menopause** Among middle-aged women, the end of menstruation and fertility.

FOR BETTER OR FOR WORSE copyright 1994 Lynn Johnston Prod., Inc. Reprinted with permission of UNIVERSAL PRESS SYNDICATE. All rights reserved.

though the sperm count may drop, there is only a gradual loss of fertility. Still, some men pass through a difficult midlife period, like the one that strikes adolescents, in which they question their marriage and career, worry about their health and sexual vigor, and feel frustrated about goals they did not achieve. For men and women alike, aging is not just a biological process but a psychological one as well.

Old Age As people enter their sixties and seventies, the cumulative effects of age begin to show and the process seems to accelerate. Inside the body, brain cells die at a faster rate, reflexes continue to slow down, muscles continue to lose strength, the immune system begins to fail, bones become brittle, joints stiffen, and there is a reduced sense of taste and smell. Resulting from a steady loss of visual acuity during adulthood, many older people are farsighted—and some have difficulty adapting to brightness or darkness (Fozard, 1990). There is also a noticeable loss of hearing, as many older people say they have difficulty hearing high-pitched sounds, normal speech, and background noises (Slawinski et al., 1993). Perhaps most obvious are the effects of chronological age on appearance—including wrinkles, stooped posture, thinned white hair, and height shrinkage (the average man will lose about an inch, the average woman two inches).

When Ponce de Léon left Spain in 1513 and discovered what is now the state of Florida, he was looking for the legendary fountain of youth. Biologists now know that it is impossible to reverse the body's aging process, but can it be slowed down? Can one's longevity be increased? According to current estimates, only one in a thousand readers of this textbook will live to celebrate a one hundredth birthday. Unfortunately, there is no secret formula. When Osborn Segerberg (1982) interviewed 1,200 centenarians, many of them cited peculiar reasons for their longevity ("because I sleep with my head to the north," "because I don't believe in germs"). In fact, what you need is a mixture of healthy genes, a hearty lifestyle, and luck (Palmore, 1982; Palmore & Jeffers, 1971).

It's often said that old age is a state of mind. But can a youthful mind produce a young body? Interested in this question, Ellen Langer (1989) and her associates designed a provocative experiment in which they tried to turn the clock back for men in their late seventies. Two groups of men were taken on a five-day country retreat. One group was encouraged to step back to the year 1959. These participants brought old photos and wrote autobiographical sketches in the present tense, but from the perspective of 1959. During their stay, these men listened to fifties-style music, saw old movies, talked about *The Honeymooners* and other classic TV shows, played *The Price Is Right* using 1950s prices, discussed old sports legends, read old issues of *Life* magazine, and listened over an old radio to a speech by President Eisenhower. The second group of men enjoyed a similar retreat, except that they spent their time reminiscing about the year 1959 from the perspective of the present. For these men, current photos were displayed, recent magazines were made available, and conversations referred to 1959 in the past tense.

After five short days, astonishing changes took place. When independent judges looked at photographs taken before and after the week, both groups of men looked younger. Even more striking, however, was the fact that the men who had mentally stepped back in time were in far better physical condition than those who had spent the same time reminiscing: they showed

Joining a small group of centenarians, comedian George Burns celebrates his 100th birthday.

measurable increases in sitting height and joint flexibility, improved vision in one eye, and higher scores on a test of manual dexterity. These results led Langer (1989) to speculate that "the regular and irreversible cycles of aging. . . may be a *product* of certain assumptions about how one is supposed to grow old" (pp. 112–113). To some extent, this concept makes sense. The biological process may be inevitable, but maybe the rate at which we exhibit the symptoms of old age is not. For Ponce de Léon, the fountain of youth may have resided within the human mind.

Cognitive Development

The human body peaks at thirty, then gradually declines. But what about the trajectory of *cognitive* development through later adulthood and old age? Does a weakened body signal a feeble mind, or are the two paths separate? At what age does "growth" turn to "aging" when it comes to memory, intelligence, and the ability to be productive at one's work?

Memory and Forgetting   The derogatory expression that "you can't teach an old dog new tricks" reflects a widespread stereotype that aging brings intellectual deterioration and a loss of memory. The image is clear: as we get older, we begin to forget names, faces, phone numbers, the car keys, messages, appointments, and whatever else is personally important. According to this stereotype, by the time men and women are ready to retire, they may be totally absent-minded, if not "senile."

A deterioration of cognitive abilities is *not* a necessary part of the aging process. Listen to the nostalgic remembrances of a parent or grandparent, and you will marvel at the ease with which he or she can vividly describe the details of an experience that took place a half-century ago. Research shows that certain experiences seem to leave an imprint on a person's memory, never to be erased. Sports, politics, disasters, crime, and entertainment are topics that leave clear traces of newsprint on the mind (Howes & Katz, 1988). Familiar smells may also leave a lasting impression, even in an older person. For example, a musty odor may trigger memories of playing in the basement as a child, and the smell of floor wax may bring back fleeting images of the first day of school (Schab, 1990). As Diane Ackerman (1990) put it, "Smells detonate softly in our memory like poignant land minds, hidden under the weedy mass of many years and experiences. Hit a tripwire of smell, and memories explode all at once" (p. 5).

Experiences that were once a daily part of life also seem to survive the adult years without too much forgetting. For example, Harry Bahrick and his colleagues (1975) tested 392 adults ranging in age from seventeen to seventy-four to see if they could remember the names and faces of their high school classmates. Some had just finished school; others had graduated as many as forty-seven years earlier. The result: Subjects became less able to retrieve names as they got older—even with the benefit of pictures. But their ability to *recognize* names and faces or to match them to each other was just as impressive after thirty-four years as it was after graduation. Similarly, Bahrick (1984) found that adults who took Spanish in high school or college exhibited very little loss of vocabulary or reading comprehension after thirty years, even though they had not used the language. As with riding a bicycle or playing a musical instrument, there is much about our past that we tend not to forget.

Although many autobiographical memories do not easily fade, there is an age-related decline in the ability to recall nonsense syllables, word lists, strings of numbers, written prose, the name of someone just introduced, and other newly learned material (Light, 1991; Craik, 1992). There are three possible contributing factors in this decline. The first is strictly cognitive. With advancing age, people lose some of the "brain power" needed to process information with speed and efficiency. This slowing down of neural processes can impair performance in memory-related tasks (Salthouse, 1991). A second possible factor is a lack of motivation. Older adults who have seen the world, established careers, and raised families may have no interest in memorizing useless material in a lab experiment (Perlmutter, 1978). Thus, there is less age-related decline in memory for "prospective" memory tasks in which a person is motivated to remember to do something that is planned—such as take a cake out of the oven (Einstein & McDaniel, 1990; Maylor, 1993). A third contributing factor is that as people get older, they lose confidence in their memory. When Jane Berry and her colleagues (1989) administered a "memory self-efficacy" scale (a test that measures people's beliefs about their own retention skills), they found that sixty- to eighty-year-old adults were less confident than eighteen- to thirty-year-olds (see Figure 10.4). Memory may in fact slip a bit with age, but negative stereotypes and a lack of confidence can worsen the problem (Levy & Langer, 1994). The person who fears that he or she cannot remember directions, an appointment, or an old friend may not even try.

Figure 10.4

How Good Is Your Memory?

Subjects were asked how confident they were (0–100) in their ability to perform various memory tasks. Consistently, elderly subjects were less confident than the younger subjects.

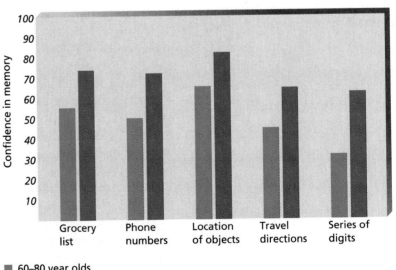

■ 60–80 year olds
■ 18–30 year olds

■ **dementia** An age-related brain disorder that results in severe cognitive impairments.

Although cognitive capacities do not decay as a natural part of aging, there are, sadly, many bright and sharp-witted adults who suffer from brain damage that causes **dementia**—an age-related mental disorder characterized by severe cognitive impairments. Dementia can occur at any time during adulthood, but it is most likely to happen after age sixty-five and to strike about 10 percent of the elderly population. It is not part of the nor-

■ **Alzheimer's disease (AD)** A progressive brain disorder that strikes older people, causing memory loss and other symptoms.

mal aging process but, rather, stems from damage to the brain caused by a stroke, a tumor, the long-term cumulative effects of alcohol, or certain kinds of diseases (Parks et al., 1993).

By far the most common cause of dementia is **Alzheimer's disease (AD)**, a progressive and irreversible brain disorder that afflicts mostly the elderly and kills brain cells at a terrifying pace. The statistics on AD are staggering. It is estimated that this disease claims as victims about 3 percent of adults aged sixty-five to seventy-four, 19 percent of those seventy-five to eighty-four, and 47 percent of those over eighty-five (Evans et al., 1989). At present, between 2 and 3 million people in the United States alone suffer from AD, which accounts for 40 to 50 percent of all nursing-home admissions. The estimated annual cost of AD in the United States is $80 billion (Zec, 1993).

Although the causes of cell death in AD are not fully known, researchers are in hot pursuit of clues (Parks et al., 1993). Many believe that AD results from a slow virus that invades the nervous system, or from an accumulation of environmental toxins in the brain. Others find that AD destroys brain cells that produce acetylcholine, a neurotransmitter that plays an important role in memory. Still others find that one form of the disease is linked to a genetic defect on the twenty-first chromosome, and another to the nineteenth chromosome. Whatever the cause, the effects of AD are devastating. It begins with lapses in memory and is soon followed by attention problems and an overall loss of cognitive functions. As the disease worsens over time, there are periods of disorientation, bursts of anger, depression, personality and mood changes, and a steady deterioration of physical functions. Alzheimer's victims may lose track of a conversation, neglect to turn off a faucet or the stove, forget where they parked the car, or forget the name of a loved one. Compared to others of the same age, Alzheimer's patients exhibit impairments in the simple classical conditioning of an eye-blink response (Solomon et al., 1991). To make matters worse, the victims often do not even realize the extent of their own problem (McGlynn & Kasczniak, 1991), and some lose the ability to recognize themselves in a mirror (Biringer et al., 1989). Typically, the onset of symptoms signals death within ten years.

There is no means of prevention and no cure for Alzheimer's disease. But there are adult day-care centers designed to help victims and provide relief and social support for the beleaguered families. For patients still in the early stages of AD, there are also memory-retraining programs that teach them how to use mnemonic devices and external memory aids. For more advanced AD patients, there are reality orientation programs to help them stay aware of who and where they are (Heston & White, 1991).

Intelligence   Psychologists used to think that native intelligence—a concept, as we'll see in Chapter 11, that is not easily defined or agreed upon—peaks during the early twenties, declines gradually up to the age of fifty, and then takes a dramatic downward turn from that point on. This view of development did not simply arise out of thin air, nor was it proposed by researchers extolling the power of youth. David Wechsler (1972), the psychologist who devised the most widely used adult intelligence test, was seventy-six years old when he wrote that "the decline of mental ability with age is part of the general process of the organism as a whole."

■ **fluid intelligence** A form of intelligence that involves the ability to reason logically and abstractly.

■ **crystallized intelligence** A form of intelligence that reflects the accumulation of verbal skills and factual knowledge.

In light of numerous studies, we now know that old age does not necessarily mean diminished intelligence. The reason today's researchers are more optimistic about intellectual development later in life is that most do not view intelligence as a single general trait. As we'll see in Chapter 11, theorists distinguish among different forms of intelligence—and although some forms decline with age, others do not. For example, Raymond Cattell (1963) and, later, John Horn (1982) distinguished between fluid and crystallized intelligence. **Fluid intelligence** is the ability to reason abstractly, solve problems of logic, detect letter or number sequences, or orient objects in two-dimensional space. In contrast, **crystallized intelligence** reflects an accumulation of factual knowledge, skill, or expertise—as measured, for example, by the size of one's vocabulary or the ability to add and subtract.

The distinction between fluid and crystallized intelligence is important because, when both are tested separately, two very different developmental patterns are found. In one large-scale study, for example, K. Warner Schaie and Sherry Willis (1993) tested hundreds of adults in age groups ranging from an average of twenty-nine to eighty-eight years old. As predicted, the fluid intelligence test scores started to decline steadily in middle and late adulthood, while measures of crystallized intelligence remained relatively stable—at least until subjects were in their seventies and eighties (see Figure 10.5).

Figure 10.5

Age Trends in Intelligence

In this cross-sectional study, 1,628 adults took a battery of tests. Shown on the right are the results of four measures: two involving fluid intelligence (spatial ability and inductive reasoning) and two involving crystallized intelligence (verbal ability and numeric ability).

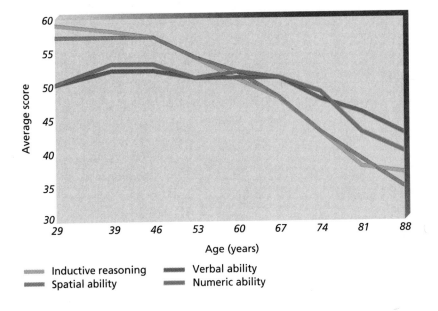

The fluid/crystallized distinction is related to two other developmental changes. First, people lose mental *speed* as they get older. Whether a task involves recognizing pictures, folding paper, solving arithmetic problems or verbal analogies, dialing a telephone, proofreading, or assembling cubes, we get slower and slower over the life span (Cerella, 1985; Bashore et al., 1989). This helps to explain why age-related declines are greater on tests that are timed rather than untimed (Hertzog, 1989; Schaie, 1989) and on mental problems that are complex rather than simple (Salthouse, 1992). To illustrate the point, let's reconsider the Schaie and Willis (1993) study of adults twenty-nine to eighty-eight years old. In that study, three multiple-

Despite age-related declines in fluid intelligence, many skills persist through old age. Now in her eighties, master chef Julia Child continues to cook at home and on TV. Here she sautés lobster for a lunch guest.

choice vocabulary tests were given to measure verbal ability, a form of crystallized intelligence: a standard untimed test, an untimed test consisting of difficult items, and a standard test that was timed. As shown in Figure 10.6, scores declined with age only in the speeded test. In the absence of time pressure, older subjects matched the performance of those literally half their age. It's worth noting, by the way, that older people can regain some of their diminished skills—even on measures of fluid intelligence—through cognitive training and practice (Willis, 1990; Schaie, 1994).

The second related change is that life experience, and hence age, is needed to cultivate *wisdom*—a form of intelligence that enables us to solve practical everyday problems (Baltes & Smith, 1990). Steven Cornelius and

Figure 10.6

Timed vs. Untimed Vocabulary Tests

To measure verbal ability, Schaie and Willis (1993) administered (1) a standard untimed test, (2) a difficult untimed test, and (3) a standard timed test. As you can see, scores declined with age only in the timed test. In fact, performance on the two untimed tests peaked at the age of sixty-seven.

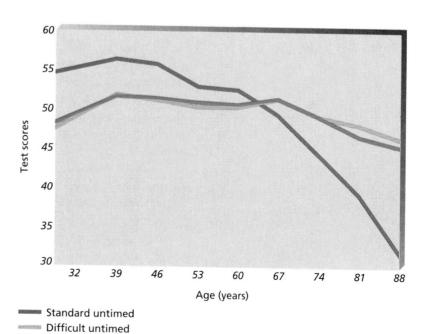

Avshalom Caspi (1987) asked adults ranging in age from twenty to seventy-eight to generate solutions to dilemmas that arise at home, at work, and with friends, family, and so on (for example, "Your landlord refuses to make some expensive repairs you want done. What should you do?"). The researchers measured problem-solving ability by having independent judges rate the quality of the solutions, and found that these ratings increased steadily and consistently with the age of the subject. As Plato once said, "The spiritual eyesight improves as the physical eyesight declines."

Productivity   Benjamin Franklin was eighty-one years old when he helped draft the U.S. Constitution. Italian composer Giuseppe Verdi was seventy-nine when he wrote the comic opera *Falstaff*. Marian Hart was eighty-four when she flew solo in a single-engine plane across the Atlantic. Architect Frank Lloyd Wright was eighty-nine when he designed New York's Guggenheim Museum. Anna Mary "Grandma" Moses first took up painting at the age of seventy-eight, continuing to the age of one hundred.

These men and women were extraordinary—an inspiration to everyone approaching the later years of life. But what typically happens to productivity in adulthood? Sure, athletes peak when the body is in its prime. But what about people whose careers demand high levels of cognitive activity? Does productivity in these domains diminish with memory and mental speed, or does it increase with knowledge and wisdom? Over the years, researchers have plotted the publication rates of academic psychologists, historians, philosophers, mathematicians, artists, and other scholars of different ages. Across all disciplines, the pattern found is one of rising achievement through the twenties and thirties, peaking around the age of forty, and declining from that point on (Lehman, 1953; Horner et al., 1986). Obviously not everyone follows the same path. For example, the average mathematician (whose work requires fluid intelligence) peaks in the early thirties, while the average historian (whose scholarly work benefits from crystallized intelligence) stays productive well into the fifties and sixties (Simonton, 1988).

In studies of government employees, military recruits, bank tellers, nurses, teachers, blue-collar workers, insurance agents, and others, there is little evidence to suggest that performance on the job dwindles with age (Rhodes, 1983). One reason is that workers learn how to compensate for their diminished physical abilities (Bäckman and Dixon, 1992; Morrow et al., 1994). To demonstrate this point, Timothy Salthouse (1984) tested the reaction time and skills of female typists ranging in age from nineteen to seventy-two years old. He found that the older, more experienced women were slower in their reaction times, yet able to type just as many words per minute. How? By scanning the text farther ahead. Indeed, when Salthouse limited the number of characters that could be viewed in advance, these veteran typists slowed down considerably. The same is true in complex games such as chess. Older players take longer to move and struggle more to remember board positions—but the moves they make are perfectly sound (Charness, 1985). As illustrated by the aging pitcher who learns to compensate for his lost fastball by outsmarting the batter, experience can be used to overcome the loss of youth.

In light of this research, it is vitally important that we debunk the myths about workers who are approaching retirement age. The problem is this:

ageism The combined effect of negative stereotypes, prejudice, and discrimination against older people.

objective measures of job performance do not decline with age, yet supervisors have a tendency to rate workers less favorably as they get older, perhaps in anticipation of phasing them out (Waldman & Avolio, 1986). In fact, many people are occasionally guilty of **ageism**—a prejudice against the elderly that is fueled by negative stereotypes. Think about it. If a young man locks his keys in the car, we say he's forgetful; if the same thing happens to grandpa, we wonder if his mind is fading. When people expect cognitive ability to diminish, they use a double standard in evaluating the performances of young and old (Erber et al., 1990; Parr & Siegert, 1993).

Social Development

Psychologists who study infants and young children can't help but be impressed by how accurately chronological age can be used to mark the milestones of social development. The first social smile is seen at six weeks, and is predictably followed by attachment behaviors, separation anxiety, crawling, walking, first words, and so on. Do adults similarly pass through an orderly succession of stages? Can chronological age be used to predict changes in self-concept, social relationships, or feelings of satisfaction? Some say yes, others no.

Ages and Stages of Adulthood In contrast to the once-prevailing view that life patterns are set in early childhood, Erik Erikson (1963) proposed a life-span theory of development. According to Erikson, people mature through eight psychosocial stages, each marked by a "crisis" that has to be resolved. Stages 1–4 unfold in infancy and childhood; stage 5, in adolescence (the "identity crisis"); and stages 6–8, in the years of adulthood. In Erikson's view, those who manage to emerge from adolescence with a sense of identity enter young adulthood, a time in which it's critical to fuse with someone else, to find *intimacy* through meaningful close friendships or marriage. The next stage is middle adulthood, a time when people feel the need to achieve *generativity,* by contributing to the welfare of a new generation—at work, at home, or in the community. The final stage is late adulthood, a time in which it's important to gain *integrity,* a feeling that one's life has been worthwhile. Those who were fortunate enough to resolve their earlier crises enjoy a feeling of serenity and fulfillment. Those who are not so fortunate live their final years in regret and despair (see Table 10.3).

Building on Erikson's model, other theorists have tried to describe the stages of adulthood in finer detail, with a special emphasis on the middle years, the so-called prime of life (Gould, 1978; Sheehy, 1976; Vaillant, 1977). The best known of these theories was proposed by Daniel Levinson and his colleagues (1978). Based on interviews with forty middle-aged males, biographies of famous men, and follow-up research on the lives of thirty-nine women, Levinson (1986) proposed that just as there are four seasons in a year, there are four eras in an individual's adult life: pre-adulthood, followed by early, middle, and late adulthood. According to Levinson, one's life runs in cycles, alternating from stressful periods of transition *between* eras to periods of relative calm *within* eras. An important part of this model is the prediction that each of us will encounter rough times when we cross the transitional bridges to early adulthood (ages seventeen

Table 10.3

Erikson's Eight Stages of Development

Stages and Ages	The primary "crisis"
Infancy (0–1 year)	*Trust vs. mistrust*
Toddler (1–2 years)	*Autonomy vs. shame and doubt*
Preschooler (3–5 years)	*Initiative vs. guilt*
Elementary school (6–12 years)	*Competence vs. inferiority*
Adolescence (13–19 years)	*Identity vs. role confusion* The adolescent struggles to break from parents and form an identity, or self-concept.
Young Adulthood (20–40 years)	*Intimacy vs. isolation* Having resolved the identity crisis, the young adult seeks intimacy in meaningful close relationships and marriage.
Middle Adulthood (40–65 years)	*Generativity vs. stagnation* Having achieved intimacy, the middle-aged adult seeks to contribute to a new generation at work, at home, and in the community.
Late Adulthood (65 and over)	*Integrity vs. despair* Reflecting on life, the older adult seeks integrity, a sense that his or her life was worthwhile.

to twenty-two), middle adulthood (ages forty to forty-five), and late adulthood (ages sixty to sixty-five). The stages are shown in Figure 10.7.

During the transition to early adulthood, young adults shed their adolescence, build dreams, and set goals for the future. Men and women have somewhat different dreams, said Levinson: men tend to focus on work, and women combine motherhood and career concerns. Either way, the early twenties is a time when everyone makes choices that seem permanent—a job, a spouse, a place to live. These choices are often reevaluated and modified around the age of thirty. At that point, however, people enter a busy but stable period in which they try to settle down, start a career, and raise a family.

As men and women approach the age of forty, they reach a second turning point at which they question the paths they have taken in careers and marriage, worry about their remaining years, and realize that the dreams of youth are slipping away (it has dawned on me, for example, that I never will play centerfield for the New York Yankees!). Levinson described the early forties as a time when "internal voices that have been muted for years now clamor to be heard" (p. 200), and found that most of the men he interviewed experienced a "midlife crisis."

Figure 10.7

Levinson's "Seasons" of the Life Cycle

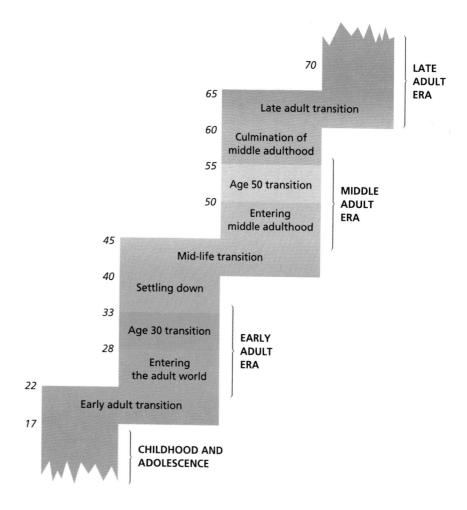

The final transition to late adulthood begins between the ages of sixty and sixty-five. Levinson could only speculate about this era, but others have found that it can prove gratifying to those who remain healthy and active. Edwin Shneidman (1989) interviewed a group of male professionals in their seventies and found that they talked often about their careers and families, and maintained a positive, healthy outlook on life until about the age of eighty. The same has been found among older women (Holahan, 1988). In the seasons of life, says Shneidman, the seventies are like "an Indian Summer, a last stretch of rather pleasant weather before the onset of an irreversible winter's frosting" (p. 692).

Critical Events of Adulthood Erikson, Levinson, and other age-and-stage theorists believe that adults change in predictable ways, and that these changes are linked to chronological age. However, in light of the diversity of lifestyles, which often lead people to take different developmental paths, other theorists believe that the course of adult development is influenced by critical events—regardless of the age at which they occur. So, what are these events? Ask people about turning points in their lives, and they inevitably mention their education, their first job, getting married, having children, moving from one home to another, the death of a loved one, health changes, and world events (Ryff, 1989). As counselor Nancy

"When 1,200 Americans were asked when middle age begins, 41 percent said it's when you worry about health care, 42 percent said it was when the last child moves out, and 46 percent said it was when you no longer recognize the names of music groups on the radio."

NEWSWEEK (1992)

■ **social clock** A set of cultural expectations concerning the most appropriate ages for men and women to leave home, marry, start a career, have children, and retire.

"We're pushing forty. Shouldn't we have a house, or something?"

[Drawing by Cline; © 1993 The New Yorker Magazine, Inc.]

THE TERRIBLE FORTY-TWOS

[Drawing by M. Twohy; © 1990 The New Yorker Magazine, Inc.]

Schlossberg put it, "Give me a roomful of 40-year-old women and you have told me nothing. What matters is what transitions she has experienced. Has she been 'dumped' by a husband, fired from her job, just had a breast removed, gone back to school, remarried, had her first book published? It is what has happened or not happened to her, and not how old she is that counts" (quoted in Rosenfeld & Stark, 1986, p. 69).

For life's major milestones, timing can also be critical. According to Bernice Neugarten (1979), people are very sensitive to the ticking of a **social clock**—the set of culturally shared expectations, known to us all, concerning the best age for men and women to leave home, marry, start a career, have children, retire, and complete other life tasks. Social clocks differ from one culture to the next, and from one generation to the next. In the 1950s, for example, most Americans believed that men and women should marry between the ages of nineteen and twenty-four, and start a career between twenty-four and twenty-six. Yet today we feel that it's more appropriate to marry and settle down at a later age. In Neugarten's view, social clocks provide us with a developmental guideline, and people who are "out of sync" (for example, those who leave home when they are too old or marry when they are too young) experience more stress than those who are "on time."

Not only are expected transitions important, but the fickle finger of fate can alter the course of development in profound and unpredictable ways. In a paper on the psychology of *chance encounters*, Albert Bandura (1982) noted that life paths are often twisted and turned by fortuitous events—as when a student is inspired to choose a career by a professor whose class happened to meet at a convenient hour, or when a talented young athlete is permanently injured and sidelined by a hit-and-run driver. My own children delight in pointing out how they owe their lives to my graduate-school roommate: had he not invited a crowd of his friends over one night, I would not have left the house, stumbled into a dance, and met their mother. These kinds of events cannot be anticipated, but they are important. Indeed, autobiographers reflecting on the direction of their own lives are often struck by the powerful influence of chance encounters (Handel, 1987).

Life Satisfaction How happy are you today, compared to when you were fifteen? How satisfied with life do you expect to be in twenty-five years? And what about others: Do you think men and women in general are happier at the age of twenty, forty-five, seventy, or eighty-five? As we saw earlier, researchers have debunked the myth that adolescence is a time inevitably filled with storm and stress. But consider other common assumptions: Are the twenties and thirties carefree and exciting? Do men and women in their forties suffer through a wrenching midlife crisis? Are the fifties calm and leisurely? Do the autumn years of retirement ring in sadness and depression? Recent studies cast new light on many of our beliefs.

Pollster Louis Harris (1987) asked thousands of American men and women how satisfied they were with their lives, and found that the percentage reporting high levels of satisfaction rose between the ages of eighteen and sixty-five. This steady upward slope is found not only among white

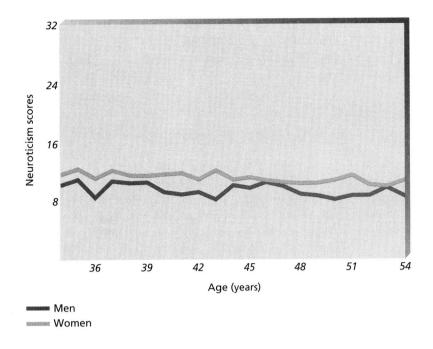

Figure 10.8

The Myth of a "Midlife Crisis"

Ten thousand adults filled out a questionnaire that measured emotional instability. As shown, neither males nor females peaked during the supposedly turbulent forties (McCrae & Costa, 1990).

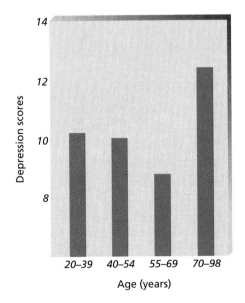

Figure 10.9

Are Older People More Depressed?

People from twenty to ninety-eight years old indicated how often they had depressive symptoms. The scores decreased from young adulthood to the middle and later years, and did not climb again until people approached eighty years old.

Americans but among black Americans as well (Chatters, 1988)—and is surprising for two reasons. First, there is no evidence for the turbulent midlife crisis popularized by Levinson, no dip in satisfaction during middle age. In fact, the rates of divorce, marital discord, job change, admission to psychiatric hospitals, and suicide do *not* increase among adults who are in their forties (Hunter & Sundel, 1989). To probe the matter, Robert Mc-Crae and Paul Costa (1990) administered to 350 men, thirty to sixty years old, a "Midlife Crisis Scale" that measured feelings of worthlessness and mortality, inner turmoil, confusion, and unhappiness with job and family. Scores did not peak, or even show a blip, in the midlife forties. Next they administered a questionnaire that measured emotional instability (anxious, guilt-prone, irritable, thin-skinned) to nearly 10,000 men and women, half of whom were between thirty-four and fifty-four. As illustrated by the flat curve shown in Figure 10.8, there was no one age at which men or women peaked in their emotional instability—no sign of a so-called midlife crisis. Let's be clear about what these results mean. Clearly, we have ups and downs as we move through life. But the downs are not more likely to occur in our forties than in our twenties, thirties, fifties, or sixties.

The second surprise is that life satisfaction does not decline later in life, which is a blow to the stereotypic image of the elderly as sad, demoralized, and chronically worried. Although it is true that people experience more medical problems as they get older, they are not more prone to complain about their health, say they are distressed, or fall into a state of depression (Aldwin et al., 1989; Kessler et al., 1992; Newmann, 1989). In one cross-sectional study, for example, people ranging from **twenty** to ninety-eight years old were asked how often they experienced depressive symptoms such as crying spells, loneliness, loss of appetite, a lack of energy, and interpersonal problems. As shown in Figure 10.9, depression scores decreased from young adulthood to the middle and later years, and did not rise again until the late seventies (Gatz & Hurwicz, 1990).

DEVELOPMENTAL PSYCHOLOGY   Business

Career Development and Retirement

Whenever I meet someone for the first time, the opening line of our conversation is predictable. Question: "So, what do you do?" Answer: "I'm a psychology professor. And you?" For many people, work is an integral part of their personal identity. To be sure, many of us would rather spend our Monday mornings lying on a warm and breezy beach, reading a novel, and sipping tropical fruit juice, but most people spend a lot more time working than playing. In 1973, the average American worked outside the home 40.6 hours a week. By 1985, that figure was up to 48.8 hours, an increase of 20 percent (Schor, 1991). In part, we work to make money. But our jobs also provide us with activity, a sense of purpose, and a social community. Thus, people who lose their jobs are psychologically devastated, even when they are not to blame for their predicament (as when a plant shuts down), and regardless of whether they have the money to carry them through a period of unemployment (Price, 1992). Think about it. If you suddenly won a multimillion-dollar lottery or inherited a large fortune, would you still work? Most people say yes.

Psychologists who study organizational behavior have found that the career paths people take are an important part of adult development. According to some theorists, the development of a career passes through a series of predictable stages (Hall, 1976; Super, 1985). The first is one of *exploration,* during which time a person, usually in his or her twenties, considers the alternatives, makes a tentative choice, seeks training, and enters the job market. Once this entry is achieved, there begins a period of *establishment,* as the person focuses on a specific occupation, learns the routine, and "settles in." If performance on the job improves, the person, now usually in his or her thirties and early forties, may advance through promotions, transfers, or movement from one organization to another. Eventually, the person encounters a stage of *maintenance,* during which he or she may continue to grow on the job, and then peak and level off. Usually in the middle to late forties, concern shifts from career advancement to maintenance. The final stage is often *decline,* or withdrawal, as the person—in his or her sixties or seventies—works fewer hours, or retires completely.

Research indicates that careers often but not always follow a path of upward movement, followed by maintenance and decline. Due to changing economic conditions, the desire to balance career and family concerns, and a recent emphasis on

You might wonder why life satisfaction increases as we get older, at least up to a point. Most psychologists agree that the recipe for "subjective well-being" contains two main ingredients: *love* and *work*. What's interesting is that these aspects of life are like bottles of wine—they seem to get better with age. To be sure, every individual's life path is unique. Some people get married, others do not; some are promoted at work, others get laid off. But there are some general tendencies. At home, for example, marital satisfaction tends to decline when a young couple first has children (Belsky & Pensky, 1988) and continues to drop until the kids leave home, at which point husbands and wives report *increasing* levels of happiness (White & Edwards, 1990). Having children is an enriching experience, and parents may be initially saddened by the departure of their last child—the so-called "empty nest syndrome." But raising a family is also a stressful experience that drains time, energy, and money from a relationship. So, marriages are often strained when the nest is full and rejuvenated when it is empty. Job satisfaction also follows an upward pattern later in life—as people consistently report their highest levels of job satisfaction in late adulthood, before retirement (Rhodes, 1983; Warr, 1992). As people get older they often advance to higher positions, get paid more money, and feel more committed to their work. In short, life satisfaction has more to do with the state of one's life at home and on the job than with chronological age.

job retraining, some people fail to become established in a particular line of work. Still others don't seem to decline much as they get older. However, large-scale studies consistently show that most workers report increases in job satisfaction through much of adulthood, to the age of sixty (Rhodes, 1983; Warr, 1992). With age and experience, people become more skilled at what they do, climb to higher or more desirable positions, feel more committed to their work—and make more money (see figure). As they get older, many workers become less concerned with advancement and derive greater enjoyment from the work itself and from day-to-day interactions.

One particularly significant developmental milestone is *retirement*. People retire at different ages and for different reasons. Job stress, physical limitations, financial incentives, failing health, interpersonal conflicts at work, a desire for more free time, and mandatory retirement age are a few of the reasons. For most people, retirement is generally satisfying, as it enables them to travel, relax, spend more time with the family, and pursue new activities and interests. For others—particularly those who are pressured into retirement, or who have financial or health problems—the transition is stressful and requires a period of adjustment (Floyd et al., 1992).

As in the building of a career, retirement is not a single discrete event but a developmental process. Once people know they are going to retire, they tend to distance themselves from the job and fantasize about the future. Afterward, many re-

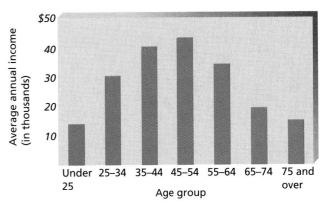

Age and Income
In the United States, average annual incomes (before taxes) climb through the early and middle adult years, peak between the ages of 45 and 54, and decline during and after retirement (*American Almanac,* 1992–1993).

tirees experience a "honeymoon" period during which time they pursue various recreational activities. This honeymoon may last for years, but longitudinal research suggests that it usually fades after six months, and is followed by a period of disenchantment until another, more stable pattern is established (Ekerdt et al., 1985). It is interesting that even after retirement, people continue to see themselves as teachers, accountants, doctors, police officers, plumbers, and so on (Atchley, 1976). As noted earlier, a person's work can indeed be an integral part of his or her identity.

Dying and Death

Humans are the only animals who know they are going to die or think about what it means. Many westerners view death as a transition point in which the body ceases to exist but a soul lives on. Hindus and Buddhists believe in reincarnation. Still others view death as a final parting, period. The ways in which death is viewed, the intense emotions it elicits, how it is talked about, how the dying are treated, and how the dead are mourned all vary from one person, time, and culture to the next (Kearl, 1989).

Whatever their beliefs, people try to find ways to cope with the experience of dying and the terrifying prospect of their own demise. After interviewing hundreds of terminally ill patients, psychiatrist Elisabeth Kübler-Ross (1969, 1974) proposed that when people know they're dying, they pass through five stages in the coping process: (1) *denial* of their terminal condition ("It's not possible, it must be a mistake"), (2) *anger* and resentment, often directed at physicians and family members ("Why me? It isn't fair!"), (3) *bargaining* for more time ("God, let me live longer, and I'll be virtuous"), (4) *depression* accompanied by crying and refusal to see visitors ("Now I've lost everything I ever cared for"), and finally (5) *acceptance* of one's fate, often marked by a sense of peace and calm ("Oh well, what has to be, has to be").

Kübler-Ross's observations offer us a glimpse at some of the ways in which people cope with dying. Not everyone passes in sequence through all the stages, however, and the experience can be quite different from one person to the next. Some patients struggle to the bitter end, while others accept their fate with quiet resignation (Kalish, 1981; Shneidman, 1984). For that reason, Kübler-Ross's stages should not be taken too literally. It may be reassuring for friends and relatives to know that irrational denial and the venting of anger are common reactions, but it is also important to respect the uniqueness of the process. When a patient lashes out in anger, or bursts into tears of depression, those close to the patient should treat these feelings with sensitivity, not dismiss them as mere signs of a person "just going through a stage."

The psychology of dying and death is fascinating but not well understood. We know that psychological factors such as a "will to live" can influence the timing of a person's death. For example, older people are more likely to die in the weeks that follow their birthday, or some other meaningful symbolic event, than in the weeks that precede it (Phillips & Feldman, 1973; Phillips et al., 1992). But we don't understand how the desire to live affects biological functions. We also know that many Americans support a terminal patient's "right to die" (Harris, 1987), and that a small but growing number of people are preparing a living will, a legal document that asserts the right "to be allowed to die and not be kept alive by medications, artificial means, or heroic measures." But we don't understand the factors that influence decision making in these matters. Finally, we know that at least some people who are pulled from the jaws of death, revived at the last moment, report having extraordinary "near-death experiences"—soft music, visions of spirits separating from their body, traveling through a dark tunnel with a light at the end, meeting deceased friends and relatives, and so on. But we don't know if these reports are sheer fabrications, or if they result from hallucinations induced by drugs, high fever, or other bodily changes (Siegel, 1980). For each of us, the psychological mystery of death will be solved only by experience. Still, many psychologists feel that it is important to understand the dying process in order to know "how death can serve life" (Feifel, 1990).

PERSPECTIVES ON THE LIFE CYCLE

"We do not count a man's years until he has nothing else to count."

RALPH WALDO EMERSON

In this chapter, we have seen that biological, cognitive, and social development continues across the entire life span. Adolescence is not a mere extension of childhood, but a time of rapid change—puberty, the capacity for sophisticated moral reasoning, identity formation, new relationships with parents, peer influences, and the onset of sexuality. Then come the various stages of adulthood and old age. Far from being one long and flat developmental plateau, these years are like a landscape filled with rolling hills, winding roads, peaks, and valleys. Physically, humans are in their prime at the age of thirty, and then lose speed, power, sensory acuity, and endurance. Cognitively, there are two courses of development. A small but steady decline occurs in mental speed, in the ability to recall new information, and in fluid intelligence. Yet autobiographical memories do not fade,

This medieval painting by Hieronymous Bosch depicts a bright light-filled tunnel, a common vision in near-death experiences.

and both crystallized intelligence and "wisdom" remain relatively stable with age. On the social front, the trajectories of development are more difficult to plot, as they are influenced more by critical life events, social expectations, and chance encounters than by chronological age. The one pattern that remains clear is that life satisfaction peaks in late adulthood and doesn't diminish until we are very old, nearing death.

Buried underneath all the documented changes is an important detail—support for the expression that "the more things change, the more they stay the same." There is a recurring controversy in developmental psychology over the extent to which personal characteristics are either stable or mutable over the course of life. It turns out that both conclusions are accurate. As you get older, certain biological, cognitive, and social changes will occur. You'll get slower, for example, and possibly wiser. Yet in other respects you are the same person today as you were ten years ago, and you will remain that person another ten years from now. Children who are well adjusted as adolescents are more likely than those who have problems to be cheerful in adulthood (Block, 1981). Likewise, longitudinal studies have revealed that among those who are smart, shy, outgoing, anxious, calm, hostile, impulsive, conscientious, or open-minded, their relative standing on these attributes will also stay basically the same. In other words, individuals who are more withdrawn or outgoing than most of their peers at one point in their adulthood are likely to remain so when they are older (McCrae & Costa, 1990).

There's one final point worth making about continuity and its relationship to how old we feel. I know someone who is thirty-nine going on seventy, and someone else who is forty going on eighteen. It's often said that

Figure 10.10

Subjective Age: How Old Do You Feel?

When people varying in age are asked this question, the results show that teenagers feel older than they really are, while maturing adults (particularly women) feel younger than they really are.

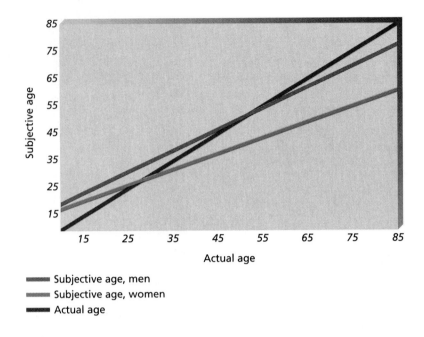

Subjective age (y-axis): 15, 25, 35, 45, 55, 65, 75, 85
Actual age (x-axis): 15, 25, 35, 45, 55, 65, 75, 85

— Subjective age, men
— Subjective age, women
— Actual age

age is a state of mind. Indeed, there is some truth to this statement. Chronology may provide us with a rough measure of adult development, but *subjective age*—that is, how old we feel—is as important psychologically as how old we really are. Do we accurately feel our age, or was financier and statesman Bernard Baruch right when he said that "old age is always fifteen years older than I am"? When people are asked their subjective age, the results form an interesting pattern: teenagers feel older than they really are, while maturing adults feel younger, a tendency that is more pronounced for women than for men (Montepare & Lachman, 1989). As you can see in Figure 10.10, we seem to age less in our minds than on the clock—a symptom, perhaps, of our inner continuity.

SUMMARY AND KEY TERMS

For years developmental psychologists have debated the question of stability versus change—whether characteristics evident early in life remain essentially the same as a person ages. It's true that early years are "formative" in some ways, but development is a lifelong process. The two main approaches for studying this process are *cross-sectional studies,* which compare people of different ages, and *longitudinal studies,* which involve testing the same people at different times in their lives.

Adolescence

Adolescence, the transition from childhood to adulthood, corresponds roughly to ages thirteen to twenty in our society.

Biological Development

Adolescence begins with *puberty,* the onset of sexual maturation marked by rising levels of sex hormones and rapid growth. For girls, puberty brings *menarche,* the first menstrual period.

Cultural practice, such as whether the culture considers menarche a joyous or a shameful event, influences a girl's reaction. So does the timing of menarche; those who reach puberty early tend to face embarrassment and adjustment problems.

For boys, puberty brings *spermarche,* the first ejaculation, as well as growth of the sexual organs, facial and pubic hair, increased muscle mass, and a lower voice. For boys, unlike girls, maturing earlier than their peers is a positive experience.

Cognitive Development

Along with physical growth, adolescence is a time of rapid cognitive growth. Entering what Piaget called the formal operational stage, teenagers begin to think critically and abstractly. In their *moral reasoning,* adolescents show a greater flexibility in interpreting rules than they did as children.

According to Kohlberg, moral reasoning develops in three stages, from the preconventional level to the conventional level and (sometimes) the postconventional level. But critics see both cultural and gender bias in this theory. Critics also question how moral reasoning relates to behavior. Although higher scores on Kohlberg's reasoning standards correlate with behavior that society considers moral, young children can act morally without such sophisticated reasoning. Children's morality is based on *empathy,* a feeling of joy for others who are happy and distress for those who are in pain.

Social Development

An adolescent's struggle to establish a personal identity, or self-concept, is often called an *identity crisis.* In an ethnically diverse society like the United States, finding one's personal identity can involve establishing an ethnic identity as well.

Young adolescents typically experience a rise in tension with their parents. At the same time, peer relationships become more important. In early adolescence, peer pressure creates a tendency toward conformity, which can play a role in drug abuse and other harmful behaviors. The expression of sexuality is a natural part of adolescent development, but it can sometimes bring confusion and harmful consequences. American adolescents are sexually more active today than two generations ago; yet the increased activity has not brought greater knowledge of risks or more care in using contraceptives.

Adolescence and Mental Health

Severe emotional distress is no more common among adolescents than among adults. Nevertheless, unhappy teenagers often become maladjusted adults, so parents should not dismiss mental health struggles as just a passing stage.

Adulthood and Old Age

Scientists generally agree that each species has a maximum possible *life span,* which is typically greater than the average *life expectancy.*

Biological Development

The number of brain cells drops steadily after birth. Muscle strength and reflexes peak at about age thirty, and then decline; also around age thirty, metabolism begins to slow, so that people tend to gain weight. For women, middle age brings *menopause,* the end of menstruation and fertility. For men, there is a gradual decline in fertility after adolescence, but no abrupt end. For both men and women, the psychological effects of the midlife period may be more problematic than the physical ones.

When people enter their sixties and seventies, the aging process accelerates. The senses may decline sharply, and the bones, joints, and immune system begin to deteriorate. Yet, as Langer's experiment demonstrated, a youthful state of mind can slow the rate at which people exhibit the symptoms of old age.

Cognitive Development

Aging does not necessarily mean cognitive decline. Autobiographical memories, for instance, survive into old age. Al-though lab experiments show an age-related decline in ability to remember new material, a slowing of neural processes is only one possible reason. Older people also seem to tend to lack the motivation and confidence needed for short-term memory tasks.

Dementia, a disorder resulting in severe cognitive impairments, strikes about 10 percent of the elderly population. The most common cause is *Alzheimer's disease (AD),* which progressively destroys brain cells, causing memory loss and other symptoms.

Studies show that *fluid intelligence,* the ability to reason logically and abstractly, declines steadily in middle and late adulthood. However, *crystallized intelligence,* reflecting the accumulation of skills and factual knowledge, remains relatively stable until people reach their seventies and eighties. Similarly, mental speed decreases with age, but wisdom—the ability to solve practical everyday problems—increases.

Objective measures of job performance do not decline with age. Still, work supervisors, like many others in our society, are sometimes guilty of *ageism,* a prejudice against older people based on negative stereotypes.

Social Development

Theorists such as Erikson and Levinson have described adulthood in terms of distinct stages. In this view, the stages are linked to chronological age, and the transitions produce stress or crisis. Other theorists believe that social development has less to do with age than with critical events such as marriage and having children. The *social clock* sets the expected times when major life events should occur. Another profound influence on social development is fate itself, in the form of chance encounters that change a person's life.

Despite prevailing stereotypes, recent research has found no evidence for a turbulent midlife crisis or demoralization of the elderly. In fact, life satisfaction increases with age and depression decreases, at least until the very late years. The critical ingredients—love and work—both seem to improve with age.

Dying and Death

Kübler-Ross proposed five stages that people go through in coping with the knowledge of impending death: denial, anger, bargaining, depression, and acceptance. Not everyone experiences these stages, though, and factors such as the "will to live" remain a mystery.

Perspectives on the Life Cycle

Overall, the evidence on human development suggests both stability and change. Biological, cognitive, and social changes do occur as people age. But on measures of many personal characteristics, such as intelligence and anxiety, people keep the same standing relative to their peers.

Chapter 11

Intelligence

Brace yourself, take a deep breath, and try to answer the following questions: How many miles apart are New York and California? If two apples cost 15 cents, what would be the cost of a dozen apples? In what ways are a lion and tiger alike? What does the word *disparate* mean? Why is copper used in electrical wires? Now read the following series of numbers and, without taking a second look, try to repeat it backwards: 4 7 5 2 8 6. If these questions ring a familiar bell, it's because they are taken from tests widely used to measure *intelligence*. The faster and more accurate you are, the higher your "IQ" will be. But what is an IQ, and what does the score mean? This chapter examines the controversial concept of human intelligence: (1) how it's defined, (2) how it's measured, (3) the debates it has sparked, and (4) the implications it has for education. As we'll see, this facet of human development raises many profound challenging questions.

Let's start with a definition: What is **intelligence**? In 1921, fourteen prominent psychologists and educators were invited to answer this question, and they came up with fourteen different definitions—such as "the ability to carry on abstract thinking," "the capacity to learn or profit by experience," and "the capacity to acquire capacity" (Thorndike et al., 1921). How do these sound to you? When railroad commuters, supermarket shoppers, and college students were handed a blank sheet of paper and asked to write down the characteristics of intelligence, they produced a long list of behaviors, including: reasons logically, makes sound decisions, sizes up situations well, speaks fluently, reads widely, is an expert on a particular subject, has many good ideas, accepts others for what they are, has an interest in world events, and thinks before speaking (Sternberg et al., 1981).

It appears that intelligence means different things to different people. In fact, it's important to realize that your definition is influenced by the culture in which you live. Many students I talk to are impressed by the combination of speed and general knowledge that enables contestants on TV game shows like *Jeopardy!* to win large sums of money. For the Puluwat Islanders of the South Pacific, however, intelligence is defined by one's ability to navigate the ocean from one island to the next. For the Kalahari Bushmen in Africa, it means having all the skills needed for hunting and gathering. For gang members of an inner city, "street smarts" is what matters most. To accommodate the many ways in which people all over the world exhibit their intelligence, many psychologists prefer to define the concept in general terms, as *a capacity to learn from experience and adapt successfully to one's environment*.

"Intelligence consists in recognizing opportunity."

CHINESE PROVERB

There are many different conceptions of intelligence. Some people associate it with the kind of general knowledge that is needed to play *Jeopardy!*

■ **intelligence** The capacity to learn from experience and adapt successfully to one's environment.

INTELLIGENCE TESTS

The study of intelligence begins with the instruments used to measure it. Like much of psychology, intelligence testing is long on tradition but short on history. About four thousand years ago, the Chinese used civil-service exams to measure aptitude. But it was not until the end of the nineteenth century that modern forms of assessment were born. The first psychologist to devise such "mental tests" was Sir Francis Galton (1883), Charles Darwin's cousin. Noticing that great human achievements run in families like his own, Galton believed that intelligence was inherited. Like it or not, he said, all men and women are *not* created equal. Taking a page from Darwin's book on evolution, Galton went on to suggest that if intelligence could be objectively measured, then the normally slow processes of "natural selection" and "survival of the fittest" could be hastened through selective-breeding policies in which only the brightest of adults are encouraged to reproduce.

How did Galton measure intelligence? If you had visited the Chicago World's Fair in 1883, or London's International Health Exhibition in 1884, you could have been one of thousands to find out. For a small fee, a technician using Galton's state-of-the-art equipment would measure your muscular strength, the size of your head, your speed at reacting to signals, your ability to detect slight differences between two weights, lights, and tones, and other biologically rooted abilities. Afterward, you would receive your intelligence score printed on a card (Johnson et al., 1985). These measures may seem intriguing, but by today's standards they are crude and without validity. Even Galton saw that bright, accomplished adults did *not* get higher-than-average test scores. What's worse, Galton's elitist proposal for raising the native intelligence of the human species through selective breeding laid the groundwork for what would become a bumpy road for the intelligence testing movement that followed (Weinberg, 1989).

The Stanford-Binet

Across the English Channel, French psychologist Alfred Binet sought to measure intelligence for humane reasons: to enhance the education of children needing special assistance. In 1904, a few years after a law was passed requiring all French children to attend school, the Minister of Public Instruction hired Binet to develop an objective means of identifying children who would have difficulty with normal classwork. With the help of Théophile Simon, Binet (1905) developed a test that contained questions on problem solving, numbers, vocabulary, logical reasoning, general knowledge, and memory—the kinds of skills necessary in an academic setting. Binet and Simon wrote hundreds of questions, tried them out on Paris students, and kept track of the average performance of children at different ages. Questions were retained if answered correctly by an increasing number of children from one grade level to the next.

Once the test was complete, questions were arranged in order of increasing difficulty and administered by someone trained to score and interpret the results. Assuming that children develop in similar ways but at different rates, Binet and Simon used their test to determine a student's **mental age,** the average age of children who pass the same number of items. In other words, the average ten-year-old would have a mental age of ten. Those who are exceptionally bright would have a mental age that is higher (like an average older child), while those who are slow to develop would have one that is lower (like an average younger child). Practically speaking, mental age was a convenient way to score a child's intelligence because it suggested an appropriate grade placement in school.

■ **mental age** In an intelligence test, the average age of the children who achieve a certain level of performance.

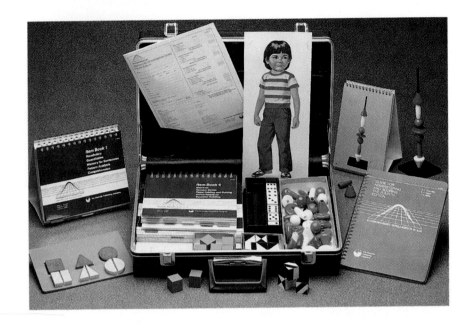

Materials used in the Stanford-Binet.

■ **Stanford-Binet** An American version of Binet's intelligence test that yields an IQ score with an average of 100.

■ **intelligence quotient (IQ)** Originally defined as the ratio of mental age to chronological age, an IQ score now represents a person's performance relative to same-aged peers.

After Binet died in 1911, the scale was translated into English and imported to the United States by Stanford University psychologist Lewis Terman (1916). The age norms in California were different from those in Paris, so Terman revised many of the questions, added items suitable for adults, published a set of American norms, and gave the test a new name, the **Stanford-Binet**. This test was revised four more times (in 1937, 1960, 1972, and 1986), takes about an hour to administer, and is still used today. Ironically, Binet's work was barely known in France until the Stanford-Binet caught on in America. Then in 1971, sixty years after Binet's death, he and Simon were honored by a commemorative plaque installed at the school in Paris where it all began.

Back at Stanford, Terman was busy developing tests that could be administered in groups (including the popular *Stanford Achievement Test*), theorizing about the roots of intelligence (he favored nature over nurture as an explanation), and conducting a massive longitudinal study of gifted children (to be discussed later). Yet his most notable contribution was the concept of **IQ**, which stands for **intelligence quotient**. Based on an idea offered by German psychologist William Stern, Terman proposed that performance on the Stanford-Binet be converted to a single score—a ratio derived by dividing mental age (MA) by the person's chronological age (CA), and then multiplying the result by 100 to eliminate the decimal point. The concept is elegantly simple, yet powerful: $IQ = (MA \div CA) \times 100$. Using this formula, you can see that people who are average (that is, those whose MA and CA are exactly the same) have an IQ of 100. A ten-year-old child with an MA of twelve has an IQ of 120, while a twelve-year-old with an MA of 10 has an IQ of 83.

Although IQ is a convenient way to represent a child's intelligence, it makes little sense for adults. The problem is that mental age does not continue to increase with chronological age, but levels off as we get older. An average ten-year-old may be two MA years ahead of the average eight-year-old, but you can't really say the same for someone who is twenty rather than eighteen, or thirty rather than twenty-eight. When you consider specific examples, you can see that the results are ludicrous: if at eighteen you get the same score as the average thirty-six-year-old, your IQ would be 200, yet if at thirty-six you had the same score as an average eighteen-year-old, your IQ would be 50. The solution was to drop Terman's quotient and assign IQ-like scores based instead on a person's performance *relative to the average of their same-aged peers*.

The Wechsler Scales

In schools and other settings, the WISC is the most widely used individually administered IQ test for children.

Galton, Binet, and Terman all developed tests that reduced intelligence to a single score. But is that the most informative approach? David Wechsler (1939) didn't think so, so he constructed a test for adults that distinguishes among different aspects of intelligence. Wechsler's test has eleven subscales grouped within two major scales—one yielding a *verbal* score, and the other a nonverbal *performance* score useful for people with language problems. He improved the test in 1955 and called it the **Wechsler Adult Intelligence Scale**, or **WAIS** (the test was revised again in 1981 and abbreviated WAIS-R). He also created similar tests for different age groups. For children six to sixteen years old, there is the *Wechsler Intelligence Scale for Children* (WISC III), and for preschoolers there is the *Wechsler Preschool and Primary Scale of Intelligence–Revised* (WPPSI-R).

Since the IQ scale was so deeply ingrained in public consciousness, Wechsler kept the same scoring system, setting the average at 100. Keep in mind, however, that if you took the WAIS, you would get three separate scores—verbal, performance, and total (even the most recent version of the Stanford-Binet also yields more than one score). To appreciate the kinds of skills measured on the test, try answering the questions in Figure 11.1. You'll see that the verbal items call for comprehension, arithmetic, vocabulary, general information, analogies, and the ability to recall strings of digits. In contrast, the items in the nonverbal performance scale ask you to find missing picture parts, reproduce block designs, arrange cartoons in a logical sequence, assemble pieces of a jigsaw-like puzzle, and copy symbols on paper. Today, Wechsler's scales are used more often in schools, research laboratories, and clinics than any other individually administered test (Lubin et al., 1984). Sometimes short forms are used in which only certain subtests or certain items are sampled (Silverstein, 1990).

■ **Wechsler Adult Intelligence Scale (WAIS)** The most widely used IQ test for adults, it yields separate scores for verbal and performance subtests.

Group Aptitude Tests

The Stanford-Binet and the Wechsler scales are used to test one person at a time and take about an hour. This procedure enables the examiner to interact with the test taker and observe whether he or she has trouble with instructions, loses attention, gets frustrated, or gives up too quickly. The disadvantage is that individualized tests are not practical for quick, large-scale assessment. During World War I, for example, the United States military needed an efficient way to screen recruits for service. With help from psychologists, two group tests were developed and administered to 1.7 million men—the Army Alpha Test, given in writing to those who could read

---

VERBAL SCALE

General Information
How many hours apart are Eastern Standard and Pacific time?

Similarities
In what way are boats and trains alike?

Arithmetic Reasoning
If eggs cost 96 cents a dozen, what does 1 egg cost?

Vocabulary
What does the word "procrastinate" mean?

Comprehension
Why do people buy automobile insurance?

Digit Span
Listen carefully to the following numbers. When I am through, I want you to repeat the numbers backwards: 4 8 7 5 2.

PERFORMANCE SCALE

Picture Completion
I'm going to show you a picture with an important part missing. Tell me what's missing:

Block Design
Using the sixteen blocks on the left, make the pattern shown on the right:

Object Assembly
If these pieces are put together correctly, they make something. Put them together as quickly as you can:

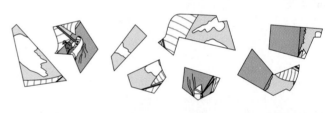

Picture Arrangement
The pictures tell a story. Put them in the right order to tell the story:

Coding
As quickly as you can, put the appropriate code symbols in the blank spaces:

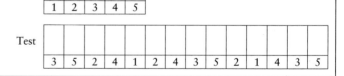

Figure 11.1

Sample Items from the WAIS

English, and the Army Beta Test, given orally to those who could not (Lennon, 1985).

Today, group testing is a regular part of our lives. You are no doubt familiar with the Scholastic Aptitude Test (SAT), a national rite of passage that many have learned to fear. The SAT is a grueling two-and-a-half-hour college entrance exam taken by 1.5 million high school seniors every year. The test, which was introduced in 1926, measures verbal and mathematical aptitude in a multiple-choice format. In 1994, the SAT was revised to include math questions that call for write-in answers (students can now use calculators), sentence-completion vocabulary items, and an increased emphasis on reading comprehension (see Figure 11.2). The SAT is designed to supplement grades as an objective predictor of academic performance. Many colleges and universities instead use the American College Test (ACT), a rival exam developed in 1939 that tests specific abilities in math, English, social studies, and natural sciences. Comparable tests are also used to screen applicants for advanced education. If you choose to go on to graduate school, you will have to take the Graduate Record Exam, or GRE. Similarly, you would take the Medical College Admission Test (MCAT), the Law School Aptitude Test (LSAT), or the Graduate Management Admission Test (GMAT).

Underlying all these exams is the assumption that what they measure is academic *aptitude* (a raw potential for a certain kind of learning), not just your past *achievements* (what you have already learned in school). In fact,

Figure 11.2

Sample Items from the Scholastic Aptitude Test (SAT)

VERBAL

Choose the word or phrase that is most nearly *opposite* in meaning to the word in capital letters.

WILT: (A) prevent (B) drain (C) expose (D) revive (E) stick

(93 percent correctly answered D)

GARNER: (A) disfigure (B) hedge (C) connect (D) forget (E) disperse

(26 percent correctly answered E)

Each question below consists of a related pair of words or phrases, followed by five lettered pairs of words or phrases. Select the lettered pair that *best* expresses a relationship similar to that expressed in the original pair.

PAINTING: CANVAS (A) drawing : lottery (B) fishing : pond (C) writing : paper (D) shading : crayon (E) sculpting : design

(92 percent correctly answered C)

SCOFF: DERISION (A) soothe : mollification (B) slander : repression (C) swear : precision (D) stimulate : appearance (E) startle : speediness

(21 percent correctly answered A)

MATHEMATICAL

If $x^3 + y = x^3 + 5$, then $y =$
(A) -5 (B) $-\sqrt[3]{5}$ (C) $\sqrt[3]{5}$ (D) 5 (E) 5^3

(93 percent correctly answered D)

In a race, if Bob's running speed was 4/5 Alice's and Chris's speed was 3/4 Bob's, then Alice's speed was how many times the average (arithmetic mean) of the other two runners' speeds?
(A) 3/5 (B) 7/10 (C) 40/31 (D) 10/7 (E) 5/3

(10 percent correctly answered D)

In the figure below, one side of the square is a diameter of the circle. If the area of the circle is p and the area of the square is s, which of the following must be true?

I. $s > p$ II. $s \gtreqless p$ III. $s < p$
(A) None (B) I only (C) II only (D) III only (E) I and II

(45 percent correctly answered B)

VERBAL

Ravens appear to behave ____ , actively helping one another to find food.

(A) mysteriously   (D) cooperatively
(B) warily   (E) defensively
(C) aggressively

An accurate assessment of this shore community's ____ is complicated by the ____ migrations of part-time residents.

(A) age..historical   (D) population..seasonal
(B) revenue..negligible   (E) environment..predictable
(C) geography..regional

ANSWERS: D; D

MATHEMATICAL

If the average of four numbers is 37 and the average of two of these numbers is 33, what is the average of the two other numbers?

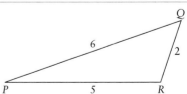

In Δ *PQR* above, point *S* (not shown) is on *QR* between *Q* and *R*. Grid in one possible value for the length of *PS*.

ANSWERS: 41; 5.1

"You're kidding! You count S.A.T.s?"

[Drawing by M. Twohy; © 1991 The New Yorker Magazine, Inc.]

■ **standardization** The procedure by which existing norms are used to interpret an individual's test score.

■ **reliability** The extent to which a test yields consistent results over time or using alternate forms.

■ **test-retest reliability** The degree to which a test yields consistent results when re-administered at a later time.

however, it's difficult to separate the contributions of aptitude and achievement. Your SAT score, for example, is influenced by whether you took high school calculus and advanced literature. Does this also mean that you can boost your "aptitude" to new heights by taking a six-week SAT-preparation course? According to the College Board, the SAT measures "developed abilities" acquired from an accumulation of life experiences both inside and outside the classroom (Donlon, 1984). Supporting this position is research showing that cramming for the SAT by taking a crash course increases scores by an average of only 15 points on the 200 to 800 scale (Kulik et al., 1984; Powers, 1986). Others claim that these courses can raise a student's total score by 100 points (DePalma, 1991). Whatever the number, high school students who review their class notes, practice their math, and take sample exams to learn the test format can prepare themselves too—without spending hundreds of dollars on a special course.

Are Intelligence Tests Accurate?

Every year, millions of dollars are spent on intelligence testing. But what's the bottom line? Are the tests "accurate"? To answer this question, it's important to know that all psychological tests—including those designed to measure intelligence—must contain three ingredients: standardization, reliability, and validity (Anastasi, 1988).

Standardization means that a test provides a standard of existing norms that can be used to interpret an individual's score. Suppose that, after taking a 150-item SAT, you received a letter indicating you had correctly answered 115 of the questions. How would you feel? Would you celebrate your success or lament your failure? As you can see, a raw score does not provide you with enough information. To interpret the score, you would need to compare it to the performance of others. Standardization is achieved by administering a test in advance to thousands of people similar to those for whom the test is designed. In the case of the Wechsler scales, the average was arbitrarily set at 100, with test scores distributed in a normal, bell-shaped curve in which roughly 68 percent of all scores fall between 85 and 115, 95 percent fall between 70 and 130, and 99 percent fall between 55 and 145. The SATs were first standardized in 1941 using a sample of more than 10,000 college-bound students. Scores were put on a scale ranging from 200 to 800, with the average for both verbal and math tests set at 500. In any case, regardless of whether a test's average is set at 100, 500, or 12 million, your *raw score*—that is, the number of questions answered correctly—must be converted into a standardized *test score* that reflects the distance between your performance and the norm (see Figure 11.3).

The second ingredient is **reliability**, the consistency of a test's results. Two types of consistency are sought. One is **test-retest reliability**, the extent to which a test yields similar results on different occasions. Just as you would not trust a bathroom scale that shows moment-to-moment fluctuations in your weight, psychologists would not trust an IQ test that shows radical changes from one session to the next. Intelligence is thought to be a relatively stable trait, not one that varies over a short period of time. To ensure that a scale has test-retest reliability, researchers test the same subjects

Figure 11.3

Distribution of Scores on the WAIS and SAT

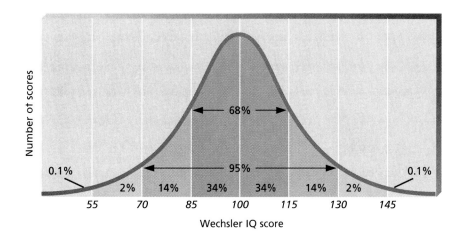

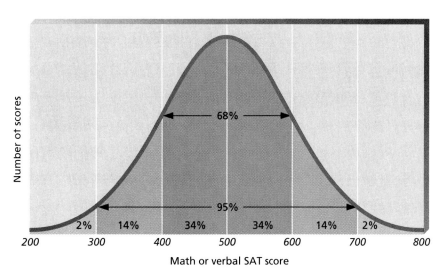

■ **split-half reliability** The degree to which alternate forms of a test yield consistent results.

■ **validity** The extent to which a test measures or predicts what it is designed to.

■ **content validity** The extent to which a test measures what it's supposed to measure.

on two occasions—say, a month or two apart—and calculate the correlation between their test and retest scores. The higher the correlation, the more reliable the scale (as you may recall, correlations range from −1.0 to +1.0).

The second kind of consistency is **split-half reliability**, the extent to which different forms of a test produce similar results. If you had two bathroom scales of the same brand and model, you would expect them to provide identical estimates of your weight. Likewise, alternate forms of an IQ test (often created by dividing it into odd and even items) should produce similar results. Using the test-retest and split-half methods, it's clear that the Stanford-Binet, WAIS, and SAT are reliable measures, all yielding correlations of about +.90. In fact, a study of 23,000 college seniors bound for graduate school showed a high correlation (+.86) between their scores on the GRE (an exam much like the SAT) and their SAT performances four years earlier (Angoff, 1988).

The third essential ingredient is **validity,** a test's ability to measure or predict what it's supposed to. IQ tests may yield consistent scores, but do they indicate intelligence? Do college entrance exams measure aptitude? Better yet, are these tests able to predict academic success? Two kinds of validity are necessary. The first is **content validity,** which means that test items

"You can't build a hut, you don't know how to find edible roots and you know nothing about predicting the weather. In other words, you do terribly on our IQ test."

[Harris/Cartoonists & Writers Syndicate]

should adequately measure what they are designed to measure. Just as a science exam has science questions and a history exam has history questions, an IQ test should contain items that correspond to our definitions of intelligence. The second kind of validity is **criterion validity**, a test's ability to predict a concurrent or future outcome. For intelligence tests, the bottom line is the prediction of academic achievement.

Are IQ tests valid? It depends on what it is you're trying to predict. If the goal is to assess *academic potential*, then the tests pass with flying colors, particularly in the earlier school years. In elementary school, there is a high correlation among IQ, class grades, and achievement test scores. There is a somewhat lower correlation between SAT scores and performance in college, but the combination of high school grades and SAT scores is highly predictive of a student's grade-point average (Jensen, 1980; Linn, 1982). However, if the goal is to predict achievement in nonacademic walks of life, then IQ tests are more limited in their validity. In fact, many psychologists are now convinced that although these tests measure academic performance, they do not measure our ability to adapt to life outside the classroom. The complex decisions made by successful business executives, the mental arithmetic used by hurried supermarket shoppers, and the handicapping strategies of gamblers at a racetrack are all instances of practical, real-world intelligence unrelated to IQ (Sternberg & Wagner, 1986).

Are Intelligence Tests Biased?

When Binet and Simon (1905) constructed their scale, they were trying to identify slow learners for placement in special classes. It soon became clear, however, that IQ tests can too easily be used as an instrument of prejudice and discrimination. One of the darkest episodes in psychology's history occurred just prior to World War I when immigrants from overseas arrived at Ellis Island, in the shadow of the Statue of Liberty. Just off the boat and exhausted from their long journey, the new arrivals were immediately tested—and in English, a language many of them could barely understand. Lo and behold, psychologist Henry Goddard (1917) concluded from the results that European Jews, Italians, Russians, and Hungarians were far less intelligent than the average American. Sadly, claims like this one may have fueled prejudice and contributed, at the time, to the passage of laws designed to restrict immigration.

Critics charge that intelligence tests are *culturally biased,* in that they favor some social groups over others. To the extent that a test calls for specific cultural knowledge, it *is* biased. That's why Terman had to "Americanize" Binet's French test. But what about IQ testing in the United States, where Americans don't all share a common cultural heritage? Consider an issue that has deeply troubled many psychologists. Ever since intelligence tests were first administered, African-Americans as a group have averaged 15 points lower than whites on IQ tests, and 100 points lower on the SAT verbal and math tests (Jensen, 1985; Loehlin et al., 1975). Everyone agrees that the difference exists. But disagreements arise as to what the difference means, and what the social implications are.

Later we'll see that there are many possible reasons for racial differences. But for now we'll examine one criticism in particular: that the question

■ **criterion validity** The extent to which a test can predict a concurrent or future outcome.

content within the tests favors the cultural and educational experiences of the white middle class (Garcia, 1981; Miller-Jones, 1989). If you take the Stanford-Binet or Wechsler test, for example, you may be asked, What is the color of rubies? What does C.O.D. mean? Who was Thomas Jefferson? To answer these questions, one needs to be familiar with the dominant culture. To illustrate the point, sociologist created a test in which blacks outscored whites on items that were derived from African-American culture (for example, Who is Bo Diddley? What are chitlings?). From a cultural perspective, a person's racial or ethnic background can also guide his or her perception of the testing situation, interpretation of the language in task instructions, motivation to succeed, trust in the examiner, and other aspects of the experience (Helms, 1992). There are many subtle ways in which test scores can be influenced by a person's background—independent of his or her intelligence.

Advocates of IQ testing have two replies to this criticism. The first is that racial differences exist even on test items that seem "culture-fair" (see Figure 11.4)—namely, nonverbal items that do not require extensive knowledge of a particular culture, tasks such as reciting a series of letters or digits, classifying objects, forming a pattern with blocks, or putting together the pieces of a picture puzzle (Cattell, 1949; Raven et al., 1985). Second, intelligence and aptitude tests are statistically valid predictors of academic performance, the purpose for which they were designed—regardless of whether students are black, white, Hispanic, or Asian (Kaplan, 1985).

Test bias has been debated not just in the laboratory but in the courtroom as well (Elliott, 1987). In the 1979 case of *Larry P.* v. *Wilson Riles,* the parents of six black students in San Francisco claimed that the school had harmed their children by placing them in "dead-end" classes for the educable mentally retarded (EMR), placements influenced by the results of IQ tests culturally biased against blacks. To bolster their case, these parents pointed out that 25 percent of all EMR children in the state of California were black, even though blacks constituted only 10 percent of the school population. On the opposing side, the school board maintained that IQ tests were administered only to students who had already fallen behind, and that the tests were valid—that is, predictive of the academic performance of black children as well as whites. The trial lasted six months, generated ten thousand transcript pages, and included testimony from more than fifty witnesses, most of them psychologists. In the meantime, a nearly identical dispute reached center stage in the Chicago case of *P.A.S.E.* v. *Hannon* (1980). Once again, black parents argued that the IQ tests administered to their children were biased, local school officials defended the measures, and experts testified on both sides.

Mirroring the disagreements within psychology (Snyderman & Rothman, 1987), the judges in these two cases reached opposite decisions. In San Francisco, the judge concluded that IQ tests were culturally biased and banned their use in the California schools for placement purposes—ironically the very reason they were designed. Yet the Chicago judge concluded from the same evidence that intelligence tests are not discriminatory, and that they offer a valid way to place children in appropriate classes. So, are IQ tests culturally biased, or not? Although the issue is far from settled, it seems that both sides are right. Minority groups are handicapped on standardized measures, but they're also handicapped in the classroom. If IQ

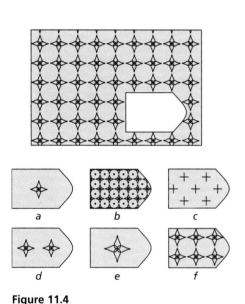

Figure 11.4

Sample Item from Raven's "Culture-Fair" Intelligence Test

In this test, the person is presented with a series of matrices and must complete each one by selecting the appropriate symbol from the accompanying choices.

Cultural Literacy: A Key to Success?

There's an old saying that "one man's garbage is another man's treasure." This expression may have some truth when it comes to the question of how important it is to learn the lessons of one's culture. Some say it's wrong for intelligence tests to include items that are "biased"—specific to the culture in which they are used. Yet in a controversial best seller entitled *Cultural Literacy: What Every American Needs to Know*, E. D. Hirsch, Jr. (1987), argues that "cultural literacy"—knowing basic facts in such topics as science, politics, literature, art, history, entertainment, history, sports, and geography—is a key to success.

According to Hirsch, every culture has a vocabulary of shared information. All Americans, for example, should know something about Shakespeare, Cinderella, the three branches of government, DNA, Superman, Martin Luther King Jr.'s "I have a dream" speech, evolution, the location of the Rocky Mountains, the Bible, the founder of communism, the New York Yankees, and so on. It's important to know these facts not just to play board games like Trivial Pursuit, but to thrive on a day-to-day basis. Cultural literacy is something we take for granted. But Americans who lack this vocabulary will have difficulty understanding what appears in daily newspapers, magazines, and popular books, all of which assume that readers know certain facts common within the culture.

Citing experiments showing that people read passages faster and with greater comprehension when they are familiar with the names, places, and contexts referred to in those passages, Hirsch argues that cultural literacy is "the oxygen of social intercourse" and that society's disadvantaged are doomed to failure without it. The solution, says Hirsch, is simple: schools must impart cultural information to all students. Indeed, the U.S. Department of Education concluded in a recent report entitled *America's Challenge* (1990) that because American students are poorly informed about basic subjects, they are not adequately prepared for life in the twenty-first century. At the heart of this issue, however, are some controversial questions: Who's to say what core knowledge is essential? In a pluralistic nation such as ours, what people, places, and events belong in culture's dictionary? What are the "basics" that *you* would include? For ideas, consider some items presented in a paperback book entitled *Test Your Cultural Literacy* (Zahler & Zahler, 1993).

1. If you "bury the hatchet," you
   a. ignore an insult.
   b. spend too much money.
   c. hide the evidence of a crime.
   d. make peace.

2. The area that became Israel in 1948 was formerly known as
   a. Palestine.   c. Syria.
   b. Jordan.   d. Arabia.

3. How is AIDS transmitted?
   a. by contact between skin and skin
   b. by exchange of body fluids
   c. by bacterial infection
   d. by an airborne virus

4. An economic recession is a period of
   a. high spending.
   b. low business activity.
   c. high prices.
   d. increased production.

tests are culturally biased, it is precisely because they are meant to predict success in schools that are themselves part of the dominant culture. As one expert said, blaming IQ tests for reflecting society's problems is like killing the messenger who delivers the bad news.

THE NATURE OF INTELLIGENCE

From the beginning, intelligence tests were constructed for strictly practical purposes—to identify fast and slow learners in school, assign new military

5. A silicon chip is part of a
   a. floppy disk.
   b. microcomputer.
   c. cassette.
   d. teleprinter.

6. What is the Koran?
   a. the ark in which the Jewish Holy Book is kept
   b. the church built over Christ's tomb in Jerusalem
   c. the name for Moses' Ten Commandments
   d. the holy book of Islam

7. In the case of *Brown* v. *Board of Education of Topeka,* the U.S. Supreme Court ruled that
   a. public schools must be desegregated.
   b. official school prayers were illegal.
   c. children could not work in factories.
   d. teenage girls could not get abortions.

8. Look at the map of Europe presented below. Which labeled section is Great Britain?
   a. I   b. II   c. III   d. IV

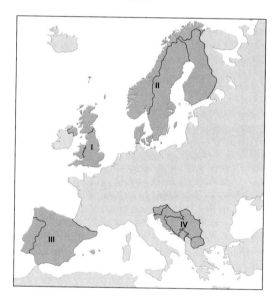

9. Who painted the portrait shown below?
   a. Rembrandt
   b. Picasso
   c. Leonardo da Vinci
   d. Michelangelo

10. What building is shown in the picture below?
   a. Mount Vernon
   b. the White House
   c. the Capitol
   d. Monticello

The correct answers are 1(d), 2(a), 3(b), 4(b), 5 (b), 6(d), 7(a), 8(a), 9(c), and 10(c).

recruits, and select college applicants. Unfortunately, the initial emphasis on tests and measurements may have stunted the growth of theories concerning the nature of intelligence—what it is, where it comes from, and how it develops. As one psychologist put it, "Intelligence is whatever an intelligence test measures" (Boring, 1923).

One of the most unsatisfying aspects of IQ tests is that they reduce intelligence to a single uncomplicated number. But does that number tell a rich enough story about a person's intellect? For me, it certainly doesn't. I can write a decent sentence, I have more inventive research ideas than I can manage, I can hold my own in a game of Trivial Pursuit, and I can cut to the heart of a logical argument in a matter of seconds. But I can't for the life of me solve a Rubik's Cube, I have a lousy sense of direction, and it takes an embarrassing amount of time for me to assemble the pieces of a child's toy. It's amazing how a person can feel so smart and yet so dense all at once. The point is, you have to wonder whether a person's intelligence can really be summarized by a single IQ score, or even by two scores as in the WAIS and SAT.

General Intelligence

Psychologists disagree about whether there is one intelligence, or many. Some theorists are "lumpers" who view different aspects of intelligence as part of a general underlying capacity. Others are "splitters" who divide intelligence into two or more specific abilities (Weinberg, 1989). Following in Binet's footsteps, all test developers make it a point to include many tasks and derive an IQ score by averaging a subject's performance on the different items. But is it meaningful to calculate an average level of intelligence? Yes, according to the "lumpers," some people are generally smarter and more capable than others—regardless of whether they are trying to program a computer, memorize a poem, learn a foreign language, solve a complex equation, or compose a story.

Charles Spearman (1904) was the first psychologist to propose that **general intelligence** (abbreviated as *g*) underlies all mental abilities. Spearman noticed that people who excel at one task—say, verbal analogies—also perform well on mazes, block designs, and other seemingly unrelated skills. To demonstrate the point, Spearman developed **factor analysis**, a statistical technique used to identify clusters of test items that correlate with one another. He administered different kinds of tests to subjects, calculated the between-item correlations, and found that although individuals may be more skilled in some areas than in others, all intellectual abilities are highly correlated. This pattern suggests that there is a general intelligence factor, *g*, that underlies our specific abilities. As far as Spearman was concerned, and others as well, an individual's intelligence could well be summarized by a single IQ score (Eysenck, 1982).

Shortly after Spearman uncovered *g*, Louis Thurstone (1938) administered fifty-six different tests to college students, used factor analysis to analyze the results, and concluded that intelligence consists of 7 factors, or "primary mental abilities." As far as he was concerned, a person's intellectual profile cannot be captured by a single number. Other researchers agree with Thurstone's emphasis on specific abilities, but they disagree on how many. John Horn and Raymond Cattell (1966) and Paul Kline (1991) say there are two types of intelligence. J. P. Guilford (1967) believed that intelligence consists of 120 different factors—a number he later increased to 150 (Guilford, 1985).

Research provides evidence for both a general intelligence and specific abilities. Scores on the eleven WAIS subscales are correlated (those who do well on one subscale also tend to do well on others)—evidence for a general intelligence. At the same time, it's not unusual for someone to score high on some subscales and low on others, as the correlations between subscales are far from perfect (usually in the .30 to .70 range)—evidence of separate

■ **general intelligence (*g*)** A broad intellectual-ability factor used to explain why performances on different intelligence test items are often correlated.

■ **factor analysis** A statistical technique used to identify clusters of test items that correlate with one another.

mental abilities. So what does an IQ score tell us about the nature of intelligence? Were Albert Einstein, Jane Austen, and King Solomon similarly able individuals, or is that like comparing apples, oranges, and cherries? Psychologists believe that there is much more to intelligence than IQ scores derived from paper-and-pencil tests. Two new and exciting theories are now shaping a much broader view of this controversial concept.

Gardner's "Frames of Mind"

"It is all very well to be able to write books, but can you waggle your ears?"

J. M. BARRIE

In his 1983 book *Frames of Mind*, Howard Gardner presents provocative evidence for the existence of **multiple intelligences**, each linked to a separate and independent system within the human brain. Gardner's main point is simple but revolutionary: the word *intelligence* is too narrowly used to describe cognitive abilities, and does not adequately encompass the kinds of genius found in great musicians, poets, orators, dancers, athletes, and inspirational leaders all over the world. When former basketball star Michael Jordan soared gracefully toward a hoop, evading blockers, and shooting with remarkable precision, wasn't he exhibiting a form of intelligence? Can't the same be said about Stephen King, the horror novelist who makes readers tremble with his masterful use of language? And what about Martin Luther King Jr., the black civil rights leader who stirred millions of Americans with his speeches and inspired massive social change?

Like a detective searching for fingerprints, witnesses, a smoking gun, and other clues, Gardner uses converging lines of evidence to marshal support for his theory that humans have multiple intelligences. He studies brain structures, diverse cultures, evolution, child development, and individuals with exceptional abilities—in other words, not just IQ tests. For example, the existence of *prodigies* (people who are generally normal, but precocious in a specific domain) and *idiot savants* (people who are mentally retarded, yet extraordinarily talented in some way) tells us that it's possible to have one kind of intelligence and to lack another. Similarly, brain-damaged patients, who lose certain abilities while retaining others, tell us that different intelligences can be traced to specific parts of the brain. Based on these kinds of evidence, Gardner has identified six types of intelligence: linguistic, logical-mathematical, spatial, musical, bodily-kinesthetic, and personal. The first three fit comfortably within existing conceptions of intelligence. The last three represent a radical departure from tradition.

1. *Linguistic intelligence* is a verbal aptitude that is rooted in the auditory and speech centers of the brain and consists of the skills involved in speaking, listening, reading, and writing. As far as Gardner is concerned, storytellers and poets who are sensitive to shades of meaning, syntax, sounds, inflections, and rhythm are linguistic geniuses. So are politicians, evangelists, and trial lawyers who know how to use language for persuasive purposes.

2. *Logical-mathematical intelligence* is the abstract reasoning ability necessary for solving a logical puzzle, programming a computer, breaking a complex code, and working out an equation. This specific form of intelligence blossoms early in childhood and is displayed with remarkable clarity by "human calculators"—prodigies and idiot savants who are

■ **multiple intelligences** Gardner's theory that there are six types of intelligence (linguistic, mathematical, spatial, musical, bodily-kinesthetic, and personal).

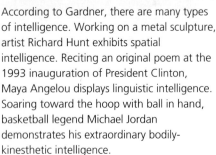

According to Gardner, there are many types of intelligence. Working on a metal sculpture, artist Richard Hunt exhibits spatial intelligence. Reciting an original poem at the 1993 inauguration of President Clinton, Maya Angelou displays linguistic intelligence. Soaring toward the hoop with ball in hand, basketball legend Michael Jordan demonstrates his extraordinary bodily-kinesthetic intelligence.

capable of rapid-fire mental arithmetic. In 1987, for example, a young Indian woman named Shakuntala Devi astonished mathematicians by multiplying in her head two 13-digit numbers randomly generated by a computer. It took her only twenty-eight seconds to calculate the right answer: 18,947,668,177,995,426,462,773,730 (*Guinness Book of World Records*, 1994).

3. *Spatial intelligence* is rooted in the right hemisphere of the brain, and consists of the ability to visualize objects, find one's orientation in space, and navigate from one location to another (if you ever tried to find your way through a fun-house maze, you'll know the skill it takes). A Vietnamese refugee named Minh Thai was a spatial genius. He was able to solve the Rubik's Cube, a highly complex three-dimensional puzzle, in under twenty-three seconds—a world record. Great pilots, architects, mechanics, chess masters, and visual artists also exhibit spatial intelligence. As described by Vincent van Gogh, "there are laws of proportion, of light and shadow, of perspective which one must know in order to be able to draw well" (Stone & Stone, 1960).

4. *Musical intelligence* can be found in all cultures, has existed throughout human history, flowers early in childhood, and involves basic skills that control our reactions to pitch and rhythm. Musical intelligence is an ability to appreciate the tonal qualities of sound, to sing, compose, and play an instrument. Gardner's argument for the existence of a "musical IQ" is supported by numerous case studies. Perhaps the most prolific musical prodigy of all was Mozart, who learned how to play the harpsichord at the age of three, composed music at the age of four, and made his first public appearance one year later. Then there is the lesser known but extraordinary case of Noel Patterson, an autistic young man living in an institution. Patterson has a WAIS IQ score of 61, is unable to read, and has almost no memory for verbal material. Yet he is fascinated with

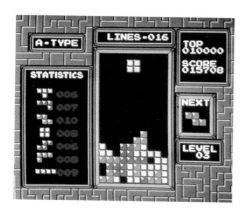

In the computer game "Tetris," players use spatial skills to rotate and orient different squared shapes to create a solid block.

music, can memorize melodies at the drop of a hat, and plays complicated classical pieces by ear on the piano (Radford, 1990).

5. *Bodily-kinesthetic intelligence* is the ability to control the gross and fine movements of the body. This kind of ability is rooted in the motor cortex and probably evolved in humans for running, climbing, swimming, hunting, combat, and self-defense. This form of intelligence can be seen in the figure skater who varies the timing and speed of her jumps, flips, and spins with clock-like precision, and lands softly on the blade of her skate. It can also be seen in skilled dancers, actors, athletes, and surgeons.

6. *Personal intelligence* has two facets that can be regarded as separate. One is *inter*personal intelligence—the ability to recognize faces and voices, predict and understand other people's actions, read facial expressions and nonverbal gestures, notice changes in their mood, and so on. Interpersonal intelligence can be found among successful leaders, salespersons, politicians, and others who need social skills to thrive. The second facet of personal intelligence is *intra*personal—the ability to achieve insight into your own inner thoughts and feelings, to understand the causes and consequences of your own behavior, and to regulate your actions accordingly. For Gardner, self-insight is a form of intelligence.

As you might expect, Gardner's theory is controversial. Some psychologists agree that intelligence should be defined broadly enough to encompass musical genius, exquisite use of the body, and personal insight. Others feel that the theory stretches the meaning of the concept too far. To his critics, Gardner says there is nothing magical about the word *intelligence*—that to define it narrowly is to place cognitive and academic endeavors on a pedestal. The point is, all kinds of intelligence should be valued—on tests, in school, and in life generally. Whether you agree or not, Gardner has raised consciousness and challenged the mainstream about what it means to have intelligence. Working in school systems, he is also exploring the implications of his theory for alternative, less standardized forms of education (Gardner, 1993). At this point, further research is needed to evaluate his provocative ideas.

Sternberg's Triarchic Theory

"I knew exactly what our school psychologist looked like. Whenever she entered the classroom, I would panic: her grand entry meant that we were about to take an IQ test, and the mere thought of it left me petrified. She was cold, impersonal, and as scary to me as the Wicked Witch of the West must have been to Dorothy. I really stunk on IQ tests" (quoted in Trotter, 1986, p. 56). Remarkably, this personal story is told by Robert J. Sternberg, now a psychology professor at Yale University and a leading expert on—you guessed it, intelligence.

Sternberg's initial poor performance piqued his curiosity about IQ tests. He overcame his test anxiety in the sixth grade, performed exceedingly well, and designed his own test of mental abilities as part of a science project. He then found a copy of the Stanford-Binet in a library book and administered the test to some of his classmates. The chief school psychologist

■ **triarchic theory of intelligence** Sternberg's theory that there are three kinds of intelligence—information processing, creative, and practical.

found out and threatened to burn the book if Sternberg brought it back to class, so he didn't. After graduating high school, however, Sternberg worked summers as a research assistant at Educational Testing Service in New Jersey, home of the SAT. "Thus began my lifelong interest in intelligence. Call it the lure of the forbidden; or perhaps it was the experience of flunking those earlier tests. Whatever the impetus, my interest had been sparked, and it would continue throughout my life" (Sternberg, 1988).

In a book entitled *The Triarchic Mind*, Sternberg (1988) proposed that there are three kinds of human intelligence: (1) information processing, (2) creative, and (3) practical. To bring this theory to life, Sternberg described three graduate students—Alice, Barbara, and Celia. *Alice* was smart according to conventional criteria and was admitted to Yale as a top pick. She had an undergraduate grade-point average of 4.0, high scores on the Graduate Record Exam (GRE), and solid letters of recommendation. As it turned out, however, Alice was *not* a strong graduate student. She did well on tests and was a sharp analytical thinker, but she lacked insight and could not generate creative research ideas. *Barbara* was different. Her GRE scores and grades were nothing to write home about, low by Yale's standards. But her college professors raved about her insight and creativity. Barbara was not accepted into Yale, but Sternberg hired her as a research associate and found her to be exceptional: "some of the most important work I've done was in collaboration with her," he said. *Celia* was the third student. Her grades, GRE scores, and letters were not great, but they were good enough for admission into Yale. Celia lacked Alice's analytical ability and Barbara's creativity. Four years later, however, she was the most successful student on the job market. The reason: Celia had practical intelligence, or "street smarts." She did the kind of research that was in demand, submitted her papers to the right journals, made the necessary contacts, and learned how to satisfy the requirements of her new profession. Like Barbara's creativity, hers was a form of intelligence that does not show up on IQ tests.

To summarize, Sternberg (1986, p. 62) argues that there are different ways to be smart. "What you want to do is take the components (Alice intelligence), apply them to your experience (Barbara), and use them to adapt to, select, and shape your environment (Celia)." His **triarchic theory of intelligence** is illustrated in Figure 11.5.

Figure 11.5

Sternberg's Triarchic Theory of Intelligence

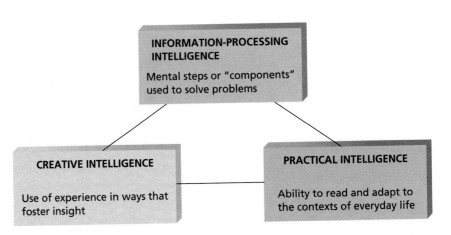

Information-Processing Intelligence   Alice's intelligence is what you might call "school smarts" and is characteristic of someone who tests well. Taking an *information-processing* approach to intelligence, Sternberg and others have tried to understand *how* people like Alice answer the kinds of questions that appear on traditional IQ tests—specifically, in terms of the mental steps or "components" they use to analyze math problems, syllogisms, analogies, and so on.

What does it mean to process information intelligently? In our culture, it is common to equate intelligence with computer-like mental speed. Thus, smart people are often described as "quick-witted" and as "fast learners." Is it true? Do students who get perfect SAT scores have quick minds? Studies show that people with high IQs are indeed quicker than average (in milliseconds) at reacting to flashing lights, at matching letters, at solving certain types of problems, and at retrieving general information from memory (Hunt, 1983; Vernon, 1987; Kranzler & Jensen, 1989). These initial findings led some information-processing theorists to propose that people with high IQs are equipped with a nervous system that relays signals rapidly—enabling them to learn more efficiently and accumulate a greater store of knowledge. In fact, recent experiments have shown that neural transmission in certain pathways in the brain are faster in people with high IQ scores (Reed & Jensen, 1992; Vernon & Mori, 1992). As this evidence accumulates, there is speculation that it may be possible in the future to devise a physiological intelligence test (Matarazzo, 1992).

Sternberg (1980) believes it's not that simple. In a series of studies, he asked subjects to solve multiple-choice analogies such as "*spouse* is to *husband* as *sibling* is to _____ (father, brother, uncle, son)." To answer these kinds of questions, a problem solver must first *identify* the meaning of each term and then *compare* the terms to each other. In the above sample problem, you have to recognize that *spouse* is a generic term for married person, that *husband* refers to a male spouse, that *sibling* is a general term for persons born of the same parents, and so on. Next, you have to match what you know about these terms to each other. To separate the two components of this task, Sternberg put subjects through a timed two-step procedure. First, they read the question part of the analogy and pressed a button to signal when they were ready to move on. Next, they saw the multiple choices and pressed another button to select a response option. It turned out that subjects with higher IQ scores spent *more* time than others on the initial identification part of the task, but were then quicker at making the necessary comparisons to find the answer. This study suggests that skilled performance on complex thought tasks cannot be equated with sheer mental speed. People who excel on IQ tests seem to know that the trick is to invest more time up front to comprehend the problem, and then pick up the pace (Galotti, 1989).

Creative Intelligence   Barbara did not have the type of school smarts that excites information-processing psychologists, but she was gifted with a creative mind—the second facet of Sternberg's (1988) theory. According to the dictionary, **creativity** refers to "the mental processes that lead to solutions, conceptualizations, ideas, artistic forms, theories or products that are unique and novel" (Reber, 1985). To Sternberg, the key is *insight*—an ability to know what information is relevant, find connections between the old

■ **creativity** Intellectual and motivational processes that lead to novel solutions, ideas, artistic forms, or products.

Displaying her creative intelligence, dancer-choreographer Martha Graham created the new and distinctive style of American modern dance.

and the new, combine facts that seem unrelated, and see the "big picture." It is certainly easy to come up with a list of creative geniuses who have used these skills in ways that have transformed our lives. Thomas Edison, inventor of the lightbulb, phonograph, and another 1,300 patented inventions, is an obvious choice. So are Rachel Carson, who pioneered the environmental movement in America, and Steve Jobs, the founder of Apple Computers who first came up with the idea of making PCs for the home.

Over the years, psychologists have tried to develop tests to measure our capacity for creative insight (Sternberg & Lubart, 1991). J. P. Guilford (1967) suggested that the critical factor is **divergent thinking,** the ability to think flexibly and open the mind to a wide range of possible solutions. Several tests have been devised to measure divergent thinking. Guilford asked people to name as many uses as they can for common objects such as a brick. If you are a skilled divergent thinker, you'd come up with many unconventional answers—use it to prop a door open, use it as a paper weight, break a window with it if you're locked out of the house, and so on. A second measure is the Symbolic Equivalents Test, in which people are asked to produce "symbolic equivalents" for various images. In response to the image of a candle burning low, for example, the divergent thinker is likely to imagine such analogous events as dying, a sunset, and water trickling down a drain (Barron, 1988). A third measure is the Remote Associates Test, in which people are shown three words and asked to come up with a fourth that is associated with all the others. For example, the words *piano, record,* and *baseball,* are all linked to "player." For *stool, powder,* and *ball,* the answer is "foot" (Mednick, 1962).

Creativity requires not only the mental processes that promote insight and divergent thinking, but also **intrinsic motivation**—an inner drive, passion, and enthusiasm for a task. In the words of Beth Hennessey and Teresa Amabile (1988), "People will be most creative when they feel motivated primarily by interest, enjoyment, satisfaction, and challenge of the work itself, not by external pressures" (p. 11). In fact, they say, the creative process unravels when people become more motivated by such *extrinsic* factors as the need to earn grades, make money, fulfill obligations, meet deadlines, win competitions, and impress others. Thus, Amabile and her colleagues (1985, 1986) find that when research subjects are *paid* or *evaluated* to draw pictures, write poems, or make paper collages, they produce lower-quality work than those who are not extrinsically motivated for these same activities. Once "play" begins to feel like "work," people lose some of their creative energy.

Psychologists are a long way from understanding creativity. It's clear that to compose music, write poetry, solve a difficult crime, or discover a chemical process, one needs the ability to process information and think in ways that spark flashes of insight. But it's also clear that creative achievements do not flow from great minds without lots of motivation, commitment, and hard work. Reflecting on his own prolific career, Thomas Edison concluded that "genius is one percent inspiration and ninety-nine percent perspiration."

■ **divergent thinking** The ability to think flexibly and entertain a wide range of possible solutions.

■ **intrinsic motivation** An inner drive for a task that motivates people in the absence of external reward and punishment.

Practical Intelligence According to Sternberg (1988), Celia epitomized the reason IQ tests often do not predict success outside the classroom.

■ **practical intelligence** The ability to size up new situations, and adapt to real-life demands.

The U.S. Department of Education (1993) estimates that 90 million Americans lack the competence at practical life tasks such as reading a bus schedule, computing the cost to carpet a room, writing a business letter, and balancing a checkbook.

Celia, you may recall, was the student who was the weakest on paper, but then the most successful on the job market. The reason is, she had street smarts, or **practical intelligence**—the ability to size up new situations, figure out the unspoken "rules of the game," and do what is necessary to adapt to life's demands. Whether you are trying to start a career, buy a house, or make friends, what you need is practical intelligence, not IQ points.

More and more, psychologists are coming to appreciate how important practical intelligence is in nonacademic settings. What skills are involved? Nancy Cantor and John Kihlstrom (1987) argue that what's critical is *social competence*—like Gardner's interpersonal intelligence, an ability to know the feelings, thoughts, and actions of other people. In a related vein, Paul Baltes and Jacqui Smith (1990) believe that what's important is *wisdom*—the knowledge that grows with age and experience, and enables us to make sound judgments in family matters, work, and other practical issues.

In a book entitled *The Cloak of Competence*, Robert Edgarton (1967) relates the story of a mentally retarded man who could not tell time and wore a broken watch. Then when he needed to know what time it was, he would approach a stranger and say, "Excuse me, but I notice my watch isn't working. Could you tell me the correct time?" Using this ingenious strategy, the man was able to overcome his handicap without embarrassment—a nice case of practical intelligence. In sharp contrast, I know a brilliant college professor with an intimidating intellect who eats the *New York Times* crossword puzzle for breakfast every morning. Yet he has no social skills whatsoever, lacks what you might call common sense, and can't seem to teach, get papers published, run a committee meeting, or balance his checkbook. In short, this man lacks practical, down-to-earth street smarts. The moral of the story: Intelligence is not something you *have*, but something you *use*.

New York City entrepreneur J.R. has practical intelligence, or street smarts. Each week he pays "scavengers" to collect bottles and cans. Then he carts thousands of them to a recycling center. For his efforts, J.R. averages $3,750 a week in profit.

THE GREAT DEBATES

Intelligence testing has become a "numbers game" with profound consequences for real people. IQ and aptitude scores help to determine which young children in need of parents are adopted quickly, and which students are accepted into a prestigious school. They determine whether a child is labeled as retarded or gifted, and placed in the "bluebirds" or "cardinals" group at school. Later, these scores help to determine which students are admitted into elite colleges, offered scholarships, and then job prospects. As Richard Weinberg (1989) put it, "IQ tests play a pivotal role in allocating society's resources and opportunities" (p. 100). With the stakes so high, it's easy to see why psychologists who study and measure intelligence find themselves in one emotional debate after another. In this section, we consider three heated issues: nature and nurture, racial and cultural differences, and sex differences.

Nature and Nurture

Is intelligence determined by *nature* (genetics) or by *nurture* (the environment)? More specifically, how much does each factor contribute? This question looms over all others, and is the most explosive. To see why this issue generates so much heat, let's step back in time and consider some of its social and political implications.

The Politics   Writing in the nineteenth century, Sir Francis Galton argued that since intelligence was inherited, only bright adults should be encouraged or even allowed to reproduce. Many years later, Henry Goddard (1917) tested new immigrants to America, determined that many were genetically inferior, and recommended that they be deported. Then in 1969, Arthur Jensen reviewed past research and concluded that IQ differences between black and white Americans were genetically rooted. Jensen was accused of racism and jeered on college campuses across the country. However, his views influenced physicist William Shockley (the winner of a Nobel Prize for inventing the transistor), who urged the U.S. government to establish a voluntary sterilization program: pay citizens with low IQ scores, many of whom are black, to undergo sterilization at a rate of $1,000 for each IQ point below 100. Along with several other Nobel Prize winners, Shockley deposited his sperm in a "sperm bank" for use by women of superior intelligence.

Over the years, nurture advocates have blamed intelligence deficits on poverty, nutritional deficiencies, bad schools, and feelings of despair. Focusing on the environment, they promote social policies designed to enrich the educational experiences of disadvantaged children. As early as 1905, Binet wanted to identify slow learners so they could receive special services (Binet & Simon, 1905). Sixty years later, in the United States, psychologists studying the effects of experience on intelligence helped to inspire **Project Head Start,** a nationwide preschool program for children born of poor families. Similar intellectual enrichment projects can now be found in other countries as well. In Venezuela, for example, an ambitious program provides prenatal care, infant nutrition, parent training, and classes that teach

■ **Project Head Start** A preschool intellectual-enrichment program for children born of poor families.

"thinking skills" to very young children (Walsh, 1981; Herrnstein et al., 1986).

In light of the political implications, it is perhaps not surprising that the nature-nurture debate has been mired in scandal. Jensen (1969) believed that racial differences were inherited and that educational enrichment programs were doomed to failure. He based these conclusions heavily on the research of Sir Cyril Burt, an eminent British psychologist who died in 1971. In a series of three studies published in 1943, 1955, and 1966, Burt had reported that the correlation in IQ scores was higher between identical twins reared apart than between fraternal twins reared together—convincing evidence for the role of genetics. When these data were closely inspected, however, they revealed a remarkable story. In *The Science and Politics of IQ*, Leon Kamin (1974) found that even though Burt kept adding new twins to his sample, the IQ correlations he reported never changed—a statistical outcome that is nearly impossible. Two years later, an article appeared in the *London Times* under the headline "Crucial data was faked by eminent psychologist" (Gillie, 1976), followed by a rash of letters-to-the-editor by other well-known researchers. Some say Burt not only fudged his statistics but made up the names of research assistants and subjects who did not exist (Hearnshaw, 1979). Others discredit Burt's results but conclude merely that he was careless (Fletcher, 1991; Joynson, 1989). Whatever the truth may be, the Burt affair stands as a tall reminder that on politically tender topics, psychological research findings should be handled with care and treated with caution.

The Science After many years of debate, most experts now agree that intelligence is influenced but not entirely determined by genetic factors. In support of this conclusion, Figure 11.6 summarizes the results of 111 studies of more than 100,000 twins and other relatives (Bouchard & McGue,

Figure 11.6

Nature's Influence on IQ Scores

Studies reveal that the greater the genetic similarity between individuals, the more similar are their IQ scores (evidence for the influence of nature). These same studies reveal that individuals reared together are more similar in their IQ scores than those reared apart (evidence for the influence of nurture).

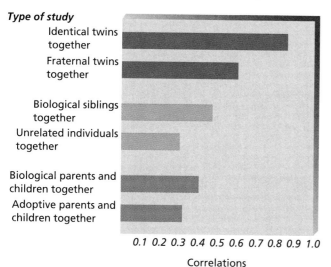

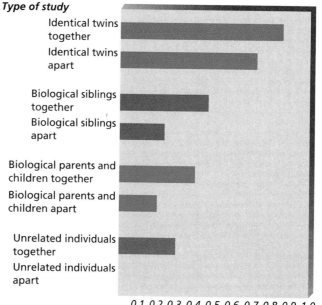

1981). You can see that genetically identical twins who grow up in the same home get highly similar scores on IQ tests—as if the same person had taken the test twice. But how much of this similarity is rooted in nature? To estimate the role of genetic factors, let's compare people who share a similar environment but differ in their genetic relatedness. Three such comparisons are worth noting: (1) identical twins who are reared together (in fact, even those reared apart) are more similar than fraternal twins also reared together, (2) siblings who grow up together are more similar than unrelated individuals who grow up in the same home (even biological siblings reared apart show some degree of similarity), and (3) children are more similar to their biological parents than to adoptive parents. New research ties the genetic knot around IQ even tighter. Studies that follow people over time show that the similarities do not diminish as blood relatives grow older—and that these similarities exist in verbal, mathematical, and spatial abilities, school grades, and vocational interests (McCartney et al., 1990; Plomin, 1988).

Nobody disputes the effect of genetics on IQ, but it's also important to realize that the same research provides evidence for environmental influences. This pro-nurture conclusion is based on comparisons of people who have the same genetic relationship but live in different environments. As you can see in Figure 11.6, there's more similarity between (1) identical twins, (2) siblings, (3) biological parents and children, and (4) unrelated individuals, whenever they live together than when they live apart. In all cases, different environments reduce the impact of genetic relatedness. Based on these results, it is estimated that heredity accounts for about 50 percent of the population variation in intelligence, meaning that environmental factors are responsible for the rest (Weinberg, 1989).

What environmental factors can influence intelligence? The possibilities are numerous: prenatal exposure to alcohol and other drugs, birth complications, malnutrition in the first few months of life, intellectual stimulation at home, high-quality education in school, and so on (Bouchard & Segal, 1985). One particularly interesting factor is *family configuration*—the number and birth order of children in the home. Many years ago, Robert Zajonc (1976) made a bold prediction: that the steady decline in SAT scores that began in 1963 would stop in 1980, at which point the scores would start to climb. As you can see in Figure 11.7, his prediction was right on target.

How was Zajonc able to forecast this trend? He based the prediction on his theory that a family's intellectual environment consists of the average absolute intelligence levels of all its members. Let's say, for example, that a family consisting of two adults with average IQs has an intellectual environment of 100. If the couple has a newborn baby whose mental age is zero, the family average drops to 67 (200/3). If a second baby is born the same year, the average drops even lower, to 50. As children get older, their mental ages increase and raise the family's average. Consistent with this model, IQ scores are slightly higher among first-borns and children from small families (who spend much of their time in the company of adults) than among later-borns and those in large families (who are surrounded by other children, unless their siblings are much older). As far as the SAT trends are concerned, Zajonc knew that high school students tested between 1963 and 1980 were born into increasingly large families during the post–World War II baby boom. He also knew that the birth rate had since

Figure 11.7

Zajonc's Bold Prediction: The Decline and Rise of the SAT

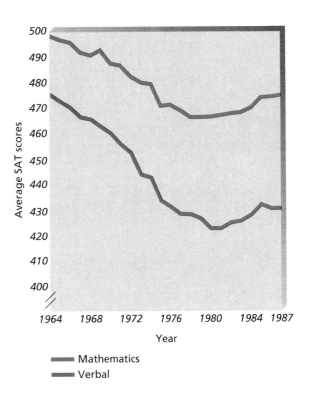

dropped and that students scheduled to take the test in 1980 would be from smaller families. Using this same logic, Zajonc predicts that the slow upward trend will continue to the year 2002 (Zajonc, 1986).

Head Start Programs   Parents who provide an enriched and stimulating home—by hanging mobiles in the crib, reading bedtime stories, playing games, traveling, and so on—foster their child's intellectual growth. Children deprived of these learning experiences thus begin life at a tremendous disadvantage. It's like the old chicken-and-egg problem: poverty lowers intelligence, and low intelligence leads people into poverty. Somehow, the vicious cycle must be broken.

In 1965, Project Head Start was launched as part of President Johnson's War on Poverty. Head Start is a group of preschool programs for children born into low-income families. In some programs, teachers make house calls to train parents and engage the children in playing with building blocks, naming colors, reading books, drawing, using pegboards, and other cognitive activities. In other programs, children attend special preschools outside the home. Dedicated to enhancing the development of those born into disadvantaged environments—many of whom are minorities—Head Start serves hundreds of thousands of families across the country each year at an estimated cost of $2,600 per child.

Skeptics wonder if it's worth the money. After many years of research, however, the program appears to be reasonably successful. It cannot boost IQ scores into the gifted range, but in some important ways, Head Start alumni surpass comparable others who don't participate. Entering school, they score about 10 points higher on IQ tests, are more confident, and are quicker to adjust to the demands of sitting in a classroom. Although the initial gain in IQ wears off over time (Woodhead, 1988), Head Start children are later found to be healthier, less likely to repeat grades or get placed in

Project Head Start is designed to enhance the intellectual development of children born into poverty.

remedial classes, and more likely to graduate high school and hold after-school jobs (Lee et al., 1990; McKey et al., 1985; Zigler & Berman, 1983). And perhaps the earlier children gain access to Head Start, the better. In programs that target infants who are "at risk" due to low birth weight, low income, or low parental IQ, intelligence test scores increase by as much as 9 points by the age of three (Brooks-Gunn et al., 1992; Ramey et al., 1992). When it comes to academic success and failure, getting off on the right foot can make a world of difference.

Racial and Cultural Differences

One reason the nature-nurture debate is so emotional is that certain racial and cultural groups get higher average IQ scores than others, differences that ignite blunt questions concerning genetic superiority and inferiority. Let's start with an often-cited empirical fact: African-Americans as a group average 15 points lower than whites on IQ tests, and 100 points lower on the SAT verbal and math tests (Jensen, 1985; Loehlin et al., 1975). Why? If heredity contributes to differences between individuals, can't it also be responsible for the differences between groups? No, not necessarily. Since the average white American grows up in a more affluent home with more educational opportunities than the average African-American, environmental differences alone are sufficient to account for the IQ gap.

Two key research findings support this point. The first is from a study that asked, What would happen to the IQ scores of black children adopted into white middle-class homes? Sandra Scarr and Richard Weinberg (1976) studied 99 cases of this sort in Minneapolis and found that the average IQ score was 110—well above the black average, and comparable to that of white children from similar families. When these adoptees were retested ten years later, the same results were found (Weinberg et al., 1992). The second finding involves recent historical trends. As a result of school desegregation and social programs like Head Start, African-Americans have had more educational doors opened in recent years than in the past. Paralleling these new opportunities, the racial gap in reading achievement, math achievement, and SAT scores has narrowed somewhat (Jones, 1984).

The recent achievements of Asian-American immigrants are raising the same questions once again. Compared to other groups, Asian-American students get higher grades and SAT math scores, are more likely to attend and graduate from college, and are more likely to win National Merit Scholarships, Westinghouse Science Talent Searches, and Presidential Scholarships. It's no wonder the news media refer to Japanese, Chinese, Korean, Vietnamese, Filipino, and Asian-Indian students collectively as "The New Whiz Kids" (Sue & Okazaki, 1990). Are Asians in general smarter than other groups? To find out, Harold Stevenson and his colleagues (1986) administered tests to elementary-age schoolchildren from Japan, Taiwan, and the United States. They found no differences in IQ, but the Japanese and Taiwanese students outscored the Americans in a math achievement test.

Researchers are struggling to understand this phenomenon. Some suggest that the achievements of the Asian-American community are influenced by genetic factors (Anderson, 1982). Others attribute the success to cultural

Lenny Ng is a son of Chinese immigrants. At ten, he scored a perfect 800 on the math SAT. At sixteen, he entered Harvard University. Julian Stanley, who founded the Study of Mathematically Precocious Youth at Johns Hopkins University, calls him "the most brilliant math prodigy I've ever met."

values that emphasize hard work, discipline, and a respect for education. Comparing Chinese and American children, Stevenson and his colleagues (1990) found that although Chinese children were superior in number concepts, computation, word problems, estimation, tables, graphs, and other aspects of math, the children themselves said they found it more difficult, were less confident of their own skills, and were evaluated less favorably by their parents and teachers. Indeed, American parents are more satisfied than Asian parents with their children's progress in math (Crystal & Stevenson, 1991). When you put these pieces together, the pattern suggests that Americans set lower standards and place a lower value on math-related achievements. Also consistent with this cultural explanation, Philip Ritter and Sanford Dornbusch (1989) surveyed thousands of high school students in California and found that (1) those of Asian descent were more likely than all others to believe that success in life is linked to what is learned in school, and (2) the longer an Asian family has lived in the United States, the lower is its level of achievement. Ironically, the cultural values that promote success for new Asian immigrants seem to erode as they become settled in their new homeland.

Sex Differences

When intelligence tests are constructed, a concerted effort is made to eliminate questions that prove more difficult for one sex than for the other, or at least to balance items favoring one sex with items favoring the other. As a result, general IQ scores are comparable for males and females. But what about specific mental abilities? Traditional gender stereotypes depict women as verbal creatures who are blessed with the gift of gab, but who should not "worry their pretty little heads" about numerical facts and figures. Is there any truth to this image? Are math and spatial relations masculine enterprises, and is language the art of woman? Eleanor Maccoby and Carol Jacklin reviewed the available research in 1974, and their conclusions supported the stereotype. However, since the issue can have staggering implications for how parents treat their sons and daughters, and for how teachers treat male and female students, psychologists are eager to know the extent of these differences. At this point, here is what we know:

1. On *verbal* aptitude tests (spelling, vocabulary, reading comprehension, writing, and so on), Janet Hyde and Marcia Linn (1988) analyzed studies involving millions of students tested between 1947 and 1980. They found that girls used to outscore boys, but that the gender gap has narrowed.

2. In *mathematics,* the gender gap has also narrowed but it has not completely disappeared. Boys and girls start counting at the age of two and are equally proficient at arithmetic in elementary school. Then males begin to surpass females in junior high school, a difference that continues through college and beyond, and is found in other countries as well. On the math part of the SAT, males outscore females by about 46 points. This sex difference is mostly evident among the most precocious of math students (Benbow, 1988; Hyde et al., 1990).

3. On *visual-spatial* tasks that involve mentally rotating objects in space to

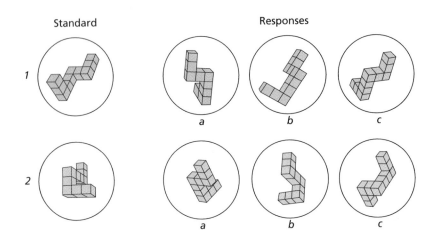

Figure 11.8

The Mental Rotation Test of Spatial Ability

For each standard shown on the left, which of the three responses on the right shows a different view of the same object? The answer appears on p. 436.

determine what they look like in another position (see Figure 11.8), males perform better than females. This skill is helpful for architectural design, carpentry, auto mechanics, navigation, and so on. It may also partly account for the gender gap in math—especially geometry, an area in which small sex differences still exist (Burnett, 1986; Linn & Petersen, 1985).

Why are there disparities in math and spatial relations? As you might expect, this question awakens the usual debate on the relative importance of biological and social factors. On the *biological* side, Camilla Benbow (1988) and others have speculated that sex differences in math and spatial abilities may stem from the prenatal effects of sex hormones on the brain—that the male hormone testosterone slows the fetal development of the left hemisphere, thereby enhancing the growth of the right hemisphere, the side of the brain associated with spatial intelligence. It turns out, for example, that highly talented math students are also more likely to be left-handed, nearsighted, and allergy sufferers—all traits thought to be linked prenatally to high levels of testosterone exposure.

One possible basis for observed sex differences in spatial skills is that boys are more likely to engage in video arcade games and other spatial activities.

On the *social* side, Jacquelynne Eccles (1985) and others attribute the gender gap to stereotypes of math as a masculine subject, less encouragement of girls by parents and teachers, and different experiences in childhood. Boys, for example, are often exposed to math through baseball cards and sports statistics, and to spatial skills through action-packed video games, construction sets, and "transformers" (plastic toys that can be "transformed" from one object to another). Indeed, recent studies show that playing action video games improves spatial performance—in boys and girls (Okagaki & Frensch, 1994; Subrahmanyan & Greenfield, 1994). Biology or socialization: At this point, it's too early to tell how much each factor contributes to the differences that now exist. Either way, however, it's important to realize that the average differences are between groups, not individuals. There are many, many women who are mathematically and spatially more talented than the average man.

EDUCATION

Now that we have examined the major IQ tests, theories of intelligence, and debates that have arisen, let's return to where it all started: the classroom. Ever since Binet's work in the schools of Paris, many psychologists have had uneasy feelings about the linkage between our conceptions of intelligence and education.

There are two key questions. First, by focusing on the prediction of academic performance, have we accepted too narrow a conception of intelligence? There are many influential theorists who think so. Gardner (1983) complains that IQ tests totally ignore musical, bodily-kinesthetic, and personal intelligences. Likewise, Sternberg (1988) says that these tests, like the school systems they service, don't sufficiently recognize the potential for achievement hidden within people who have creative insight or street smarts. The second question concerns the impact of IQ testing on the quality of education. Once schoolchildren are identified as fast, slow, or average learners, what next? Do those with unusually high or low IQ scores benefit from being identified as "special"? What are the educational implications? Since schools rely heavily on intelligence tests to sort children into academic categories, it's important to raise these kinds of critical questions.

Gifted Children

Popular stereotypes of gifted children include unflattering images of eccentric nerds and social misfits, doomed to a life of failure—hence the expression "Early ripe, early rot." The story of William James Sidis, considered the world's greatest child prodigy, is a case in point. Sidis was born in 1898 in New York City, to Russian immigrant parents. He was reading fluently by the age of two, using a typewriter at three, and speaking Russian, French, German, and English at five. Sidis started school at the age of six, and whizzed through seven grades in less than twelve months. That year, he devised a new table of logarithms and knew enough about human anatomy

According to the Guinness Book of World Records, *the highest IQ ever recorded was a test-shattering 210—obtained by Kim Ung-Yong, a South Korean boy born in 1963. At age four, Kim spoke four languages, wrote poetry, and could perform integral calculus.*

Answer to Mental Rotation Test
The correct answers are 1(a) and 2(b).

to pass a medical-school exam. At the age of eleven, Sidis was admitted into Harvard, where he astonished the Harvard Mathematical Club with a lecture on the fourth dimension. Despite this prodigious start, however, Sidis soon fizzled into obscurity. He dropped out of graduate school, failed as a teacher, and spent the rest of his life in low-paying clerical jobs. When Sidis died at the age of forty-six, he was living in a rooming house alone, unemployed, and penniless (Wallace, 1986).

Contrary to popular belief, this biographical pattern is atypical. In 1921, Lewis Terman (the Stanford psychologist who imported Binet's IQ scale) launched what was to become the most extensive longitudinal study of "genius" ever conducted. Terman studied 1,528 California schoolchildren, all with IQs over 135. He and subsequent researchers then followed the progress of their lives for years to come, and found that as a group these men and women were healthy, well adjusted, happily married, and successful in school and in their careers. Many went on to become eminent doctors, lawyers, book authors, scientists, and professors.

It's impossible to know why William Sidis floundered, while so many of Terman's subjects were successful. From an educational standpoint, however, it's important to know what it means to be "gifted" and how we can educate our bright and talented children. When Terman conducted his study, he selected subjects according to IQ tests. Today giftedness is viewed in broader terms. For example, Joseph Renzulli (1986) proposed a three-ring conception of giftedness as a combination of above-average intelligence, task commitment, and creativity. Following in the footsteps of Gardner and Steinberg, others maintain that giftedness is not a general trait but, rather, one that is specific to a particular domain. That's why many high school students who get perfect scores on one academic subtest of the ACT (math, English, social studies, natural sciences) do not fall within the gifted range on other subtests (Colangelo & Kerr, 1990). You can be a brilliant musician, physicist, writer, computer programmer, or painter without being an intellectual jack-of-all-trades.

As a matter of policy, society has mixed feelings about how gifted children should be treated (Reis, 1989). On the one hand, we are troubled by a feeling that it's unfair to provide special opportunities for an elite, chosen group of children, to the exclusion of all others. On the other hand, we recognize that it's important to challenge bright minds and harvest their full potential in order to build a better future for everyone. An accelerated curriculum, special resource rooms, and after-school programs are some of the ways to enhance the educational experience. In 1971, for example, Julian Stanley of Johns Hopkins University pioneered what is now a nationwide talent search for gifted math students. By administering the math portion of the SAT to bright seventh graders, Stanley and his colleagues identify as "mathematically precocious" those boys and girls with scores over 500 (a higher-than-average score for twelfth graders, and the top percentage of seventh graders). These students are offered advanced summer programs in math and science, accelerated college courses, and counseling for parents. Although more research is needed, it appears that participants enjoy the program and benefit from the experience, without showing signs of social or emotional stress (Stanley et al., 1974; Stanley & Benbow, 1986; Richardson & Benbow, 1990).

Mental Retardation

■ **mental retardation** A diagnostic category used for people with IQ scores below 70 who have difficulty adapting to the routine demands of life.

At the opposite end of the continuum, children whose IQ scores are below 70 are evaluated to see if they are mentally retarded. **Mental retardation** is a term used to describe people with limited intellectual ability. It used to be the case that anyone who scored in the lowest 3 to 5 percent was identified as mentally retarded. Since test performance has little to do with the ability to function in nonacademic settings, however, the American Psychiatric Association (1994) raised its criteria. To be diagnosed as mentally retarded, a person must now have (1) an IQ score below 70, and (2) difficulty adapting to routine needs of life such as self-care, social interactions, and so on. Other causes of poor test performance—for example, physical illness, or impaired vision or hearing—also have to be ruled out. Only about 1 percent of the population meets these criteria, with males outnumbering females (Landesman & Ramey, 1989).

There are four categories of mental retardation, varying in severity. As shown in Table 11.1, the vast majority are only mildly retarded. They have IQ scores in the 50 to 70 range, and are sometimes referred to as "educable" because they are capable of achieving a sixth-grade level in reading and math. Usually, mildly retarded children live at home and attend public schools. Once diagnosed, they are given individualized education programs designed to meet their academic, social, physical, and emotional needs, while keeping them as much as possible within the regular classroom (Schroeder et al., 1987). As Alfred Binet had hoped, these students can be

Table 11.1

Mental Retardation: Degrees of Severity

Level	Percentage of retarded persons	Typical IQ scores	Adaptation to demands of life
Mild	85%	50–70	May learn academic skills up to sixth-grade level. Adults may, with assistance, achieve self-supporting social and vocational skills.
Moderate	10%	35–49	May progress to second-grade level. Adults may contribute to their own support by labor in sheltered workshops.
Severe	4%	20–34	May learn to talk and to perform simple work tasks under close supervision, but are generally unable to profit from vocational training.
Profound	1%	Below 20	Require constant aid and supervision.

■ **self-fulfilling prophecy** The idea that a person's expectation can lead to its own fulfillment (as in the effect of teacher expectations on student performance).

taught at their own pace, enabling them to learn better and live more fulfilling lives. Unfortunately, the use of IQ tests for placement purposes can be risky, maybe even backfire. The problem is this: since the tests are not the perfect crystal ball, what happens to a child whose ability is underestimated? What happens if expectations are set too low?

The Self-Fulfilling Prophecy

In 1948, sociologist Robert Merton told a story about Cartwright Millingville, president of the Last National Bank during the Depression. Although the bank was solvent, a rumor began to spread that it was floundering. Within hours, hundreds of depositors lined up to withdraw their savings, until there was no money left to withdraw. The rumor was false, but the bank eventually failed. Using stories such as this, Merton proposed that a person's expectation can actually lead to its own fulfillment—a phenomenon known as the **self-fulfilling prophecy**.

Based on Merton's hypothesis, Robert Rosenthal and Lenore Jacobson (1968) wondered about the possible harmful effects of IQ testing. What happens to the educational experience of the child who receives a low score? Would it leave a permanent mark on his or her record, arouse negative expectations on the part of the teacher, and impair future performance? To examine the possible outcomes, Rosenthal and Jacobson told teachers in a San Francisco elementary school that certain pupils were on the verge of an intellectual growth spurt. The results of an IQ test were cited, but in fact the pupils were randomly selected. Rosenthal and Jacobson administered real tests eight months later, and found that the so-called late bloomers (but not children assigned to a control group) had actually improved their scores by as much as 30 points and were evaluated more favorably by their classroom teachers.

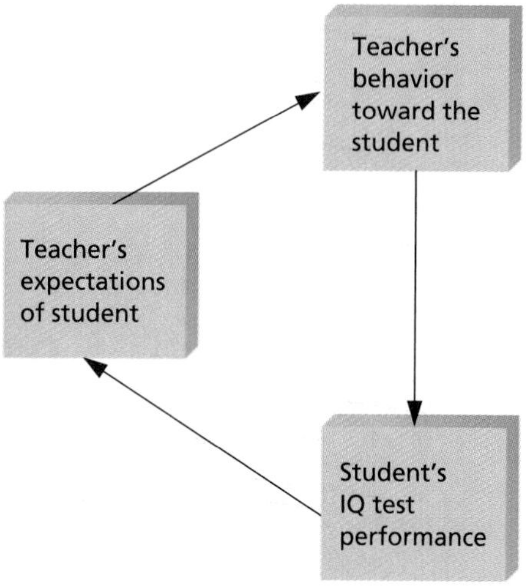

When this study was published, it was greeted with chagrin. If high teacher expectations can increase student performance, can low expectations have the opposite effect? Could it be that children who get high scores are destined for success, while those who get low scores are doomed to failure, in part because educators hold different expectations of them? Many researchers were critical of the study and skeptical about the generality of the results. Unfortunately, the phenomenon cannot be swept under the proverbial rug. In more than four hundred experiments that tested the hypothesis, teacher expectations significantly influenced student performance 36 percent of the time (Rosenthal, 1985). In fact, student expectations of a teacher can have similar effects. When high school classes were led to believe that their new English teacher was highly regarded, her impact was enhanced. Students became noticeably more attentive in class and achieved higher final grades as a result (Jamieson et al., 1987).

How does the self-fulfilling prophecy work? How are teacher expectations transformed into reality? As illustrated in Figure 11.9, the self-fulfilling prophecy can be viewed as a three-step process. First, the teacher forms an impression of the student early in the school year. This impression may be based on IQ test scores, or on the student's sex, background, reputation, or physical appearance. Second, the teacher behaves in a manner that is

Figure 11.9

Self-Fulfilling Prophecy

The self-fulfilling prophecy is a three-step process: (1) the teacher forms an impression of the student based on test scores and other information, (2) the teacher behaves in a way that is consistent with that impression, and (3) the student adjusts his or her behavior according to the teacher's actions.

consistent with that first impression. If expectations are high rather than low, the student receives more attention, praise, emotional support, and challenging homework. Third, the student unwittingly adjusts his or her own behavior according to the teacher's actions. If the signals are positive, the student may become energized. If not, there may be a loss of interest and self-confidence. Before you know it, the cycle is complete and the expectations confirmed. The self-fulfilling prophecy is a powerful psychological phenomenon (Cooper & Good, 1983; Harris & Rosenthal, 1985; Jussim, 1989).

A second way in which IQ tests can actually influence (not just reflect) academic performance is by steering students onto a fast or slow track in the school curriculum. If you've read Aldous Huxley's *Brave New World*, you may recall the opening scene in the "Hatchery and Conditioning Centre," where human embryos only a few hours old are transformed into Alphas, Betas, Gammas, Deltas, or Epsilons, and programmed accordingly for a high-class or low-class future. In the foreword to this novel, Huxley (1932) expressed his personal fear that a "science of human differences" could be used to sort people early in life into fixed, immutable social ranks. This may sound like fanciful science fiction, but critics charge that intelligence tests are being used in the same manner to separate children according to their IQ (Tobias, 1989).

To cope with the tremendous diversity of children who attend public schools, educators try to group students who have similar academic abilities. Indeed, teaching is easier and more effective when all students are on the same "wavelength." There are two ways to reduce student heterogeneity. One is *between-classroom grouping*, in which all the students in a grade are assigned to separate high-, average-, or low-level classes. A second way is *within-classroom grouping*, in which students mixed in the same classroom are put in separate instructional groups, usually for reading and math. What happens to students who are tracked at so young an age, often based on an IQ test? What difference does it make to a child's education and self-esteem to belong to the fast "sharks" rather than the slow "goldfish"?

The main argument for between-classroom grouping is that by separating whole groups of children by ability, a teacher can prepare one curriculum to meet the needs of all students. The level and pace of instruction can be raised for those in the high class and lowered for those in the low class. Yet, as reasonable as this policy seems, this practice can have harmful effects on students who are dumped into slow classes because they don't test well. In elementary school, teachers in low-ability classes spend much of their time managing disruptive students, to the detriment of all the others (Eder, 1981). In junior and senior high schools, high-track students read great literature, use computers, and learn critical thinking, expository writing, and other skills valuable for college. But in low-track classes, instructors are content to teach "functional literacy" (how to read signs, fill out forms, and so on), basic arithmetic, and rote memorization (Oakes, 1985). In short, a school's curriculum can be either enriched or watered down, depending on a student's placement—a placement that may constrain future performance. Ultimately, the rich get richer and the poor get poorer.

The alternative is within-classroom ability grouping, in which, as noted,

DEVELOPMENTAL PSYCHOLOGY Environment

The Physical Setting of a Classroom

From kindergarten through twelfth grade, the average person spends about 14,000 hours in school. When I think about those hours, the images that come to mind are of teachers, classmates, the work, the assemblies, lunches, recesses, school trips, and the bus ride home. An aspect of the experience that I never really thought about at the time, but one that can play a role in the learning process, is the physical environment of the classroom.

As educators tried to find the best way to group students of different abilities, they also experimented with factors such as lighting, carpeting, room size, class size, windows, furnishings, and the arrangement of tables and chairs. Paralleling the debate over the merits of between- versus within-classroom grouping is the debate over traditional versus open classrooms. The *traditional classroom* consists of rows and columns of student desks that face the teacher and a chalkboard at the front of the room. Beginning in the 1960s, however, many educators abandoned this old-fashioned "egg-carton" design in favor of an *open classroom* consisting of large areas of undivided flexible space that enables students to work in small groups (see figure).

Compared to the type of teaching that is effective within a traditional design, the less formal open classroom encourages students to move around from one area to the next and engage in "hands on" activities. Does this aspect of the physical setting play a role in learning? Some researchers have found that open-classroom students spend more time "on task" (Rosenfield et al., 1985). But most observe that students waste more time moving around and getting ready for new tasks—and spend less time actually working (Gump, 1987; Neill, 1982). Apparently, the open classroom is more stimulating, but it is also noisier and more distracting (Ahrentzen et al., 1982).

Classroom seating arrangements can also influence the nature of student participation. When seats are arranged in straight rows and columns, as in a lecture hall, students who sit in the front and middle participate more than those who sit in the back or on the sides (Sommer, 1967). In contrast, a U-shaped or horseshoe seating arrangement facilitates a more open and active discussion among students in a seminar, while a modular arrangement (with individual chairs around tables) is best for small work groups placed together to carry out specific tasks (Hurt et al., 1978). In schools, as in other settings, people are influenced by their physical environment.

mixed students from the same class are separated into groups assembled for math and reading instruction. Most schools favor this approach, though the issue is complicated. After reviewing fourteen studies, Robert Slavin (1987) concluded that students who are in heterogeneous classes achieve more when they are grouped for instruction than when the class is taught as a whole, and that between-class grouping is not similarly effective. So far, so good. But it's also important to consider the effects of such grouping on self-esteem. For many years, researchers were baffled by the fact that children in disadvantaged schools have higher academic self-esteem than those who attend more affluent schools. Apparently, children compare themselves to one another and feel smarter when they are surrounded by classmates who are relatively weak, academically. In this respect, it's better to be a large fish in a small pond than a small fish in a large pond (Marsh & Parker, 1984). In terms of classroom composition, however, heterogeneity is like a two-edged sword: high-ability students gain confidence through exposure to weaker peers, but low-ability students lose confidence through their exposure to stronger peers. This result led David Reuman (1989) to conclude that "choosing within-classroom versus between-classroom grouping policies involves complicated tradeoffs" (p. 187).

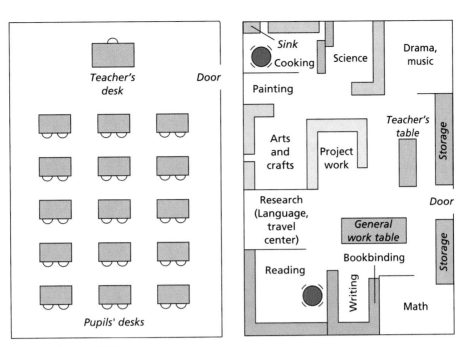

Classroom Environment
Furniture arrangements for (1) a traditional classroom, and (2) a sample open classroom.

PERSPECTIVES ON INTELLIGENCE

For about a century now, psychologists have been trying to define, measure, understand, and enhance intelligence, an elusive concept. You can tell by the common use of the Stanford-Binet, Wechsler scales, SAT, and other instruments that intelligence testing is a booming enterprise. It is also one that should be viewed with a critical eye to safeguard against possible abuses. Intelligence is a many-splendored concept—more than just IQ, a magical number used to predict school performance. Intelligence shows up in one person's flair for writing, art, or music, a second person's ability to wheel-and-deal in business, and a third person's fluent mastery of five languages. It's the ability to process information with efficiency, generate creative ideas, and use one's skills to get ahead in life.

Underlying much of the tension that surrounds the study of intelligence is the nature-nurture debate. It is clear that both genetic and environmental factors contribute to an individual's intelligence. It's also clear that because racial and cultural groups have distinct life experiences, intellectual differences at the group level are hard to interpret. The same is true of the small differences that exist between men and women. Finally, it's important to consider the educational implications of using IQ tests for identification and placement purposes. On the one hand, objective measures of intelligence help us predict academic potential and develop programs suitable for individual students. On the other hand, IQ tests can set in motion a self-fulfilling prophecy by arousing teacher expectations and steering students onto a fast or slow track in school. Either way, it's important to keep in mind that intelligence is not a tangible object, but a word that describes the skills that enable you to make a better life for yourself and others.

SUMMARY AND KEY TERMS

Many psychologists define *intelligence* as a capacity to learn from experience and adapt successfully to one's environment.

Intelligence Tests

The Stanford-Binet

In the early 1900s, Binet and Simon developed a test to determine a student's *mental age*—that is, the average age of children who achieve the same level of performance. Terman revised the test and renamed it the *Stanford-Binet*. Terman also proposed scoring the test by means of an *intelligence quotient (IQ)*: mental age divided by chronological age and multiplied by 100. Today, an IQ represents a person's performance relative to the average of same-aged peers.

The Wechsler Scales

To distinguish between different aspects of intelligence, the *Wechsler Adult Intelligence Scale (WAIS)* yields separate verbal and performance scores. There are also Wechsler scales for children.

Group Aptitude Tests

In contrast to the Stanford-Binet and Wechsler measures, which are individually administered, aptitude tests like the SAT and ACT are given to a number of people at a time. Although these tests attempt to distinguish aptitude from achievement, the two factors are difficult to separate.

Are Intelligence Tests Accurate?

To be accurate, intelligence tests must be standardized, reliable, and valid. *Standardization* means that the test provides a standard of existing norms that can be used to interpret an individual's score. *Reliability* means that the results are consistent. *Test-retest reliability* ensures that a test will yield similar results at different times; *split-half reliability* ensures that different forms of the test will produce similar results. *Validity* is the extent to which the test measures or predicts what it is supposed to. *Content validity* refers to whether test questions adequately measure the quality they were designed to measure (in this case, intelligence). *Criterion validity* concerns the test's ability to pre-

dict a concurrent or future outcome (such as academic achievement). IQ and aptitude tests do correlate with performance in school, but not necessarily with adaptation to life outside.

Are Intelligence Tests Biased?

According to critics, intelligence tests are culturally biased because scores are influenced by background factors such as the test taker's racial or ethnic group. Advocates of testing argue that racial differences occur even on "culture-fair" items and that intelligence tests do predict academic performance.

The Nature of Intelligence

General Intelligence

Some psychologists believe in *general intelligence (g),* a broad factor underlying all mental abilities. By developing *factor analysis,* a statistical technique used to identify clusters of test items that correlate with one another, Spearman found that all intellectual abilities are highly correlated. Other researchers, however, have divided intelligence into various components.

Gardner's "Frames of Mind"

Pursuing a theory of *multiple intelligences,* Gardner argued that different systems within the brain produce six different types of intelligence: linguistic, logical-mathematical, spatial, musical, bodily-kinesthetic, and personal. The last three types stretch the concept of intelligence beyond traditional notions.

Sternberg's Triarchic Theory

According to Sternberg's *triarchic theory of intelligence,* there are three basic types of intelligence. Information-processing intelligence, the kind needed for traditional IQ tests, may relate to the sheer speed of neural transmission in the brain.

Creativity, the second type, refers to the mental processes that lead to unique and novel solutions, ideas, artistic forms, or products. One key to creative insight may be *divergent thinking,* the ability to think flexibly and entertain a wide range of possible solutions. Another key is *intrinsic motivation,* an inner drive, passion, and enthusiasm for a task.

Practical intelligence, the last of Sternberg's three types, is the ability to size up new situations, figure out unspoken rules, and adapt to real-life demands. Other psychologists describe this sort of intelligence as social competence or wisdom.

The Great Debates

Since test scores affect so many aspects of our lives, debates about intelligence testing have been heated.

Nature and Nurture

People have long disputed whether intelligence is determined more by nature (genetics) or nurture (environment). Most experts now take a middle position. Studies of twins and other family members show that heredity and environment each account for about half the population's variation in intelligence.

The relation between intelligence and poverty is a vicious cycle. Research indicates that programs such as Head Start, which intervenes early in a child's life to break the cycle, have a measurable impact on IQ and school success.

Racial and Cultural Differences

Are group differences in average IQ and SAT scores brought about by nature or by nurture? Although the issue is clouded by emotion, research suggests that environmental factors explain both the relatively low scores by African-Americans and the relatively high scores by Asian-Americans.

Sex Differences

Boys on the average develop better mathematical and visual-spatial abilities than girls. Some studies suggest a biological sex difference, perhaps traceable to the prenatal effects of sex hormones. But others point to social explanations, such as a difference between boys' and girls' experiences in childhood

Education

Gifted Children

Contrary to stereotypes, gifted children as a group do well in later life. Today, many children identified by testing as gifted are offered special programs. Limited studies suggest that students can generally benefit from these programs without feeling undue social or emotional stress.

Mental Retardation

For students with *mental retardation*—who have low IQ scores and exhibit difficulty adapting to routine demands of life—individualized education programs can help meet special needs. On the other hand, test results may lead educators to underestimate a child's ability.

Self-Fulfilling Prophecy

According to studies of the *self-fulfilling prophecy*, teachers' expectations influence students' performance. If teachers expect little of a child because of a low IQ score, that child will likely perform accordingly. Moreover, grouping or tracking, often based on intelligence tests, can harm students assigned to the slower groups. Within-classroom grouping appears to be less harmful in this respect than between-classroom grouping.

Perspectives on Intelligence

Intelligence is a complex and elusive concept. It is expressed in many ways besides IQ. Because intelligence is influenced by both heredity and environment, group differences are hard to interpret. In education, intelligence testing can help identify students for special programs, but it can also limit the opportunities of those who don't score well.

PART IV

Do you ever behave in ways that are profoundly "out of character" to suit the situation you're in? Drawn together by the theme that situations have the power to overwhelm us, the chapters in Part IV focus on the influence of others on the individual. Chapter 12 on *social perception* examines the way that we form impressions of other people, how attraction develops at various stages of a relationship, and how cognitive and motivational factors form the roots of prejudice. Chapter 13 on *social influence* examines the link between attitudes and behavior and the processes of conformity, obedience, persuasion, and group influences. Also considered are two important social behaviors, aggression and altruism. Finally, Chapter 14 on *human diversity* summarizes recent research on the influences of culture, racial and ethnic background, gender, and sexual orientation.

SOCIAL PSYCHOLOGY

Chapter 12

Social Perception

E very now and then, an event comes along that seems to defy explanation. One such event took place in Los Angeles, in the spring of 1991. Police cars chased motorist Rodney King through the night, stopped his car, and cornered the unarmed black man on the street. A sergeant fired a 50,000-volt stun gun at King's chest, knocking him to the ground. Three other officers then clubbed him with their nightsticks, while eleven others looked on. The result: King suffered a fractured skull, a crushed cheekbone, burn marks on the chest, a broken ankle, and internal injuries. To many concerned citizens, this horrifying incident was an act of racism, like an old-fashioned lynching. But then on April 29, 1992, in the trial of four police officers charged with King's assault, a California jury returned verdicts of not guilty.

News of the jury's acquittals sparked a storm of anger in Los Angeles. At first, crowds gathered to protest the decision. But before long, mobs were rushing the streets, blocking traffic, setting buildings on fire, smashing windows, and looting stores. In a chilling incident that paralleled the King beating, members of a local gang pulled driver Reginald Denny from his

The videotaped beating of Rodney King (top left), the riots that erupted after the police officers were acquitted (top right), and a group of residents working together on the post-riot cleanup (bottom).

■ **social psychology** The study of how individuals think, feel, and behave in social situations.

truck, beat him senseless, and shot him in the leg. Thanks to four strangers who rushed Denny to the emergency room of a nearby hospital, he was able to survive the attack. Still, others were killed and parts of the city were destroyed. One year later, the federal government retried the four officers for violating King's civil rights. Two of the officers were convicted by a second jury. The tension subsided.

This entire episode—the beating, the verdict, the riots, and the retrial—raises many questions. Was the King incident racially motivated, influenced by the color of his skin? Why didn't the officers who watched the beating try to stop it? How did the jurors interpret the situation? What persuaded the first jury to vote for acquittal, and the second for conviction? What caused the mob violence that followed the first trial? And amidst the chaos, what inspired four courageous citizens to rescue the fallen trucker? These questions—about prejudice, conformity, the perceptions of others, persuasion, aggression, and altruism—are all questions of **social psychology**, the study of how individuals think, feel, and behave in social situations.

THE BIG PICTURE

Do you ever behave in ways that are "out of character" just to suit the situation you're in? Were you ever coaxed into doing something distasteful, even harmful to yourself or others? Why do good people sometimes behave badly? Why do reasonable people often do unreasonable things when in a large group? Driven by the belief that situations have the power to overwhelm even the best of us, social psychologists study the ways in which people influence—and are influenced by—one another. To illustrate the point, imagine that you are a subject in the following classic research.

What's Your Prediction?

THE SITUATION

You see a newspaper ad for a psychology experiment that pays well, so you sign up. As you arrive at the laboratory, located at Yale University, you meet two men. One is the experimenter, a young man dressed in a lab coat. The other is a pleasant forty-seven-year-old man named Mr. Wallace. You exchange introductions, and then the experimenter explains that you will be taking part in a study on the effects of punishment on learning. By a drawing of lots, it is determined that you will serve as the "teacher" and Mr. Wallace as the "learner." So far, so good.

Before you know it, however, the situation takes on a more ominous tone. You find out that your job is to test the learner's memory and administer electric shocks of increasing intensity whenever he makes a mistake. You are taken to another room where the experimenter straps Mr. Wallace in a chair, rolls up his sleeve, puts electrodes on his arm, and applies "electrode paste" to prevent blisters and burns. You overhear Mr. Wallace saying that he has a heart problem and the experimenter responding that although the shocks are painful, they will not cause permanent damage. You then go back to the main room, where you're seated in front of a shock generator—a machine with thirty switches that range from 15 volts (labeled "slight shock") to 450 volts (labeled "XXX").

Your task is easy. First you read a list of word pairs to Mr. Wallace through a microphone. Blue-phone. Girl-hat. Fish-spoon. Then you test his memory with a series of multiple-choice questions. The learner answers each question by pressing one of four switches that light up on the shock generator. If his answer is correct, you go to the next question. If it's incorrect, you announce the correct answer and shock him. As you press the shock switch, you hear a buzzer go off in the learner's room. After each wrong answer, you are told, the shock intensity should be increased by 15 volts.

You don't realize it, but the experiment is rigged, and Mr. Wallace—who works for the experimenter—is not feeling any shocks. As the session proceeds, the learner makes more and more errors, leading you to work your way up the shock scale. As you reach 75 volts, you hear the learner grunt in pain. At 120 volts, he shouts. If you're still in it at 150 volts, he cries out, "Experimenter! That's all. Get me out of here. I refuse to go on!" Screams of agony and protest follow. If you reach 300 volts, he absolutely refuses to go on. By the time you surpass 330 volts, the learner falls silent and is not heard from again. 360 volts. Zap. Not a peep. 420, 435, 450. Zap. Still no response. At some point, you turn to the experimenter for guidance. What should I do? Shouldn't I stop? Shouldn't we check on him? But in answer to your inquiries, the experimenter firmly repeats his commands: "Please continue." "The experiment requires that you continue." "It is absolutely essential that you continue." "You have no other choice, you *must* go on."

MAKE A PREDICTION

What do you do? Feeling caught between a rock and a hard place, do you follow your conscience or obey? Do you stop at 75 volts? 150? 300? How would other subjects react? Would *anyone* in their right mind keep shocking the hapless Mr. Wallace—all the way to 450 volts? Let's see how good a social psychologist you are. Based on what you know about people, try to predict the point at which most subjects stopped and defied the experimenter:

15 45 75 105 135 165 195 225 255 285 315
345 375 405 435 450 (circle one)

THE RESULTS

Over thirty years ago, social psychologist Stanley Milgram (1963) staged this situation to examine obedience to authority. When Milgram described the study to college students, adults, and a group of psychiatrists, they predicted that, on average, they would stop at 135 volts—and that almost *nobody* would go all the way. Look at Table 12.1, and you'll see that they were wrong. In Milgram's initial study, twenty-six out of forty men—that's 65 percent—delivered the ultimate punishment of 450 volts!

Table 12.1

Milgram's Obedience Results

Shock level	Subjects who stopped at this level	
	Number	Percentage
15–285	0	0.0
300	5	12.5
315	4	10.0
330	2	5.0
345	1	2.5
360	1	2.5
375–435	1	2.5
450	26	65.0

WHAT DOES IT ALL MEAN?

Why did so many subjects obey the experimenter, even while thinking they were hurting a fellow human being? One possible explanation for these scary results is that Milgram's men were unusually cruel and sadistic. Who were these guys? Or maybe the result says something about men in general. What if the subjects were women instead? How far up the shock scale would they go? In a later study, Milgram examined this question by putting forty women in the same situation. What do you suppose happened? Did most of the women stop at 75 volts? 150? 300? How many went all the way to 450 volts? Stop. Make a prediction and let's see how accurate you are. Ready? The result: 65 percent of the women tested administered 450 volts, identical to the number of men.

Hmm. Males and females, perhaps people in general, are willing if not eager to harm a fellow human being—even without commands to do so. As a sad commentary on human nature, perhaps Milgram's study says more about aggression than obedience. So how far would subjects go if *not* ordered to do so by a figure of authority? What if the experimenter did not constantly prod the subjects to increase the voltage level? On their own, would they stop at 75 volts? 150? 300? How many would go up to 450 volts? Think about this situation and make another prediction. The result: Only one subject out of forty (2.5 percent) pressed the last switch. Most stopped at 75 volts.

Milgram's subjects had acted out of obedience, not cruelty. In fact, they were visibly tormented by the experience. Many of those who administered 450 volts perspired, stuttered, trembled, bit their lips, and even burst into fits of nervous laughter. It was as if they wanted to stop but felt powerless to do so. What does it all mean? When Nazis were tried for war crimes after World War II, they used the defense, "I just followed orders." Intrigued by the power of authority implied by this statement, Milgram developed a laboratory situation to mimic the forces that operate in real-life crimes of obedience. In Chapter 13, we will revisit this study and discuss some of the ways Milgram found to reduce the level of obedience. As we'll see, this classic research cries out the message of social psychology loud and clear: other people can have a profound impact on our behavior.

FORMING IMPRESSIONS

■ **social perception** The processes by which we come to know and evaluate other persons.

To explain social behavior, we must begin by understanding the processes of **social perception,** the ways in which we come to know and evaluate other persons. This chapter addresses three major questions: (1) How do people form impressions of each other? (2) What attracts us to others, both in our opening encounters and at more advanced stages of a relationship? (3) How are social perceptions biased by stereotypes and prejudice, often giving rise to sexism, racism, and other forms of discrimination? As you read this chapter, you'll notice that these questions are considered from the perceiver's vantage point. Keep in mind, however, that in social interactions you are both a *perceiver* and a *target* of other people's perceptions.

Snap Judgments

"You're not at all like your answering machine."

[Drawing by M. Stevens; © 1991 The New Yorker Magazine, Inc.]

Did you ever meet someone for the first time and form a quick impression based on just a "snapshot" of information? As children, we were told that you cannot judge a book by its cover. As adults, however, we can't seem to help ourselves. There are two types of cues that guide our first impressions: physical appearance and nonverbal behavior.

Physical Appearances In 500 B.C., Hippocrates—the founder of modern medicine—looked into a patient's face to make a diagnosis. In the nineteenth century, physician Franz Gall introduced "phrenology" and said he could measure a person's character by bumps on the head. And in 1954, Harvard psychologist William Sheldon claimed that there was a link between an individual's physique and personality.

Research generally does not support the various claims made over the years about the significance of physical appearance. Yet first impressions are influenced in subtle ways by a person's height, weight, skin color, hair color, and so on. Among Americans, for example, blondes are considered fun-loving and sociable, while brunettes are thought to be dependable and smart; overweight people are considered weak, lazy, and dependent, while those who are thin are perceived as tense, stubborn, and suspicious. In the perception of men, even height is thought to be significant—a possibility suggested by the astonishing fact that between the years 1900 and 1992, the taller candidate for U.S. president won 21 out of 23 elections. Clearly, people believe that there is a connection between the body and personality (Alley, 1988; Bull & Rumsey, 1988; Herman et al., 1986).

The human face in particular attracts more than its share of attention. Diane Berry and Leslie Zebrowitz-McArthur (1986) find that adults who have baby-faced features—high eyebrows, large eyes, round cheeks, a large forehead, smooth skin, and a rounded chin—are seen as warm, kind, naive, honest, and submissive. In contrast, adults with mature features—small eyes, low brows, a small forehead, wrinkled skin, and an angular chin—are seen as stronger, more dominant, and less naive. These perceptions can have real consequences. At home, parents hold their baby-faced sons and daughters less responsible for misbehavior and punish them less severely (Zebrowitz et al., 1991a). In the workplace, baby-faced applicants are more likely to be recommended for jobs as day-care teachers, while mature-

■ **nonverbal behavior** Behavior that reveals a person's feelings without words—through facial expressions, body language, and vocal cues.

"We're going to get along just fine: we speak the same body language, you and I."

[© 1994 Liza Donnelly and The Cartoon Bank, Inc.]

Sometimes people inadvertently betray their feelings in their nonverbal behavior. When a peace agreement was reached between PLO leader Yasir Arafat and Israeli Prime Minister Itzhak Rabin, their bitter rivalry and ambivalence were quite evident. *Time* magazine used the term "grip-and-grimace" to describe the historical handshake.

faced adults are considered to be better suited for work as bankers (Zebrowitz et al., 1991b).

Nonverbal Behavior An easy first step in social perception is to know what a person is doing at a particular moment. The more difficult task is to determine how a person is feeling. Sometimes, people tell us how they feel. At other times, however, they do not tell us, or they're uncertain, or they try to conceal their true emotions. Thus, we often tune into a "silent" language, the language of **nonverbal behavior.** In 1872, Charles Darwin proposed that the human *face* expresses emotion in ways that are innate, understood by people all over the world. It now seems that Darwin was right. When people from all over the world view photographs similar to those on page 303, they reliably identify six emotions: happiness, fear, sadness, anger, surprise, and disgust (Ekman et al., 1987).

Sometimes, we draw conclusions about a person's emotional state from the situation he or she is in. In one study, for example, subjects looked at pictures of faces with a neutral expression. When subjects were told that the man or woman in the picture was being threatened by a vicious dog, they perceived the facial expression as fearful; when subjects were told the person had just won money in a TV game show, they interpreted the *same* expression as a sign of happiness (Trope, 1986).

Other nonverbal behaviors also influence our impressions. For example, we are fluent readers of *body language*—the ways that people stand, sit, walk, and express themselves through gestures. Thus men and women who have a youthful walking style—who sway their hips, bend their knees, pick up their feet, and swing their arms in a bouncy rhythm—are seen as happier and more powerful than those who walk slowly, take short steps, and drag their feet (Montepare & McArthur, 1988).

We are also quick to notice *gaze*, or eye contact. Eyes have been called "windows of the soul." For example, people tend to assume that someone who avoids eye contact is evasive, cold, shy, fearful, or indifferent; that frequent gazing signals intimacy, sincerity, and self-confidence; and that the person who stares is tense, angry, or unfriendly. As with facial expressions, however, we sometimes interpret gaze according to the situation. If a relationship is friendly, frequent gaze elicits a positive impression. If not, it is seen in negative terms. Thus it is said that if two people lock eyes for more than a few seconds, they are either going to make love or kill each other (Kleinke, 1986; Patterson, 1983)!

Another powerful nonverbal cue is *touch*—a congratulatory high-five, a sympathetic pat on the back, a joking elbow in the ribs, a loving embrace. Touching has long been regarded as an expression of friendship, nurturance, and sexual interest. But it may also serve other functions. Nancy Henley (1977) observed that men, older persons, and persons of high status were more likely to touch women, young persons, and those lower in status, than the other way around. According to Henley, touch can be an expression not only of intimacy but of dominance and control as well. In this regard, the sex differences are particularly intriguing. Brenda Major and her colleagues (1990) observed people in city streets, shopping malls, college campuses, airports, train stations, beaches, and other public settings. Sure enough, men were more likely to touch women than women were to touch men—a difference that did not exist among children, or in places where friends ritually greet each other.

Detecting Truth and Deception   Social perception can be tricky because people sometimes try to hide or stretch the truth about themselves. Poker players bluff to win, witnesses lie to protect themselves, and political candidates make campaign promises they don't intend to keep. On occasion, everyone engages in deception. We make excuses, try to present ourselves in a particular light, or pretend for the sake of being polite. Can social perceivers tell the difference? Can *you* tell when someone is lying?

Sigmund Freud once said that "no mortal can keep a secret. If his lips are silent, he chatters with his fingertips; betrayal oozes out of him at every pore" (1905, p. 94). Paul Ekman and Wallace Friesen (1974) revised Freud's observation by pointing out that some pores "ooze" more than others. Ekman and Friesen proposed that some channels of communication are difficult for deceivers to control, while others are relatively easy. To test this hypothesis, researchers recruit one group of subjects to make statements that are true or false, and then present other groups of subjects with transcripts, audiotapes, or videotapes of these statements. In general, this research shows that people are not particularly proficient as judges of truth and deception, often accepting what is said at face value and giving speakers the benefit of the doubt. As shown in Table 12.2, individuals who make these judgments for a living—police detectives, psychiatrists, trial judges, and government agents who administer lie-detector tests for the CIA, FBI, and the military—are also prone to error in these experimental situations (Ekman & O'Sullivan, 1991).

Table 12.2

Can the "Experts" Catch a Liar?

In this study, lie-detection experts with experience at judging truth and deception were shown brief videotapes of ten women—half of them telling the truth, the other half lying about their feelings. Considering that there was a 50-50 chance of guessing correctly, the accuracy rates were remarkably low. Only a sample of U.S. Secret Service agents posted a better-than-chance performance (Ekman & O'Sullivan, 1991).

Observer groups	Accuracy rates
College students	52.82
CIA, FBI, and military	55.67
Police investigators	55.79
Trial judges	56.73
Psychiatrists	57.61
U.S. Secret Service	64.12

What seems to be the problem? There are four channels of communication that provide relevant information: words, the face, the body, and the voice. When people have a reason to lie, *words* alone cannot be trusted. The *face* is also controllable, as deceivers sometimes mask their real feelings with "false smiles." The *body* is somewhat more revealing than the face, as deception is often accompanied by fidgety movements of the hands and feet, and by restless shifts in posture. But the *voice* is the leakiest, most revealing cue. When people lie, especially when they are desperate to do so, their voice rises in pitch and the number of speech hesitations increases. In light of these findings, it seems that there is a *mismatch*—between the behaviors actually associated with deception (body movements and vocal cues) and those to which the perceivers are attending (words and facial cues). Too easily seduced by the silver tongue and the smiling face, we often fail to notice the restless body and the quivering voice (Zuckerman et al., 1981).

Attributions

To interact effectively with others, we generally find it useful to know how they feel and if they can be trusted. To understand people well enough to predict their future behavior, however, we must also identify and form impressions of their "dispositions"—that is, relatively stable characteristics such as personality traits, attitudes, and abilities. These dispositions cannot actually be seen; rather they must be inferred from a person's behavior—and the perceived causes of that behavior.

Attribution Theory To make sense of our social world, we try to understand the causes of our own and other people's behavior. What kinds of explanations do we come up with, and how do we go about making them? In *The Psychology of Interpersonal Relations*, Fritz Heider (1958) took a first step in answering these questions. According to Heider, we are all scientists of a sort. To understand others, we observe, analyze, and try to explain their behavior. The explanations we come up with are called attributions, and the theory that describes the process is called **attribution theory.**

Although there are numerous possible explanations for the events of human behavior, Heider found it useful to group our attributions into two major categories: personal and situational. The juries that tried the four police officers in the Rodney King case, for example, had to decide: Was the beating caused by characteristics of the officers (a *personal attribution*), or had King somehow provoked their actions (a *situational attribution*)? For the attribution theorist, the task is not to determine the true causes of this event but, rather, to understand our *perceptions* of the causes.

Following Heider, Harold Kelley (1967) theorized that people make attributions according to the **covariation principle,** which states that for something to be the cause of behavior it must be present when the behavior occurs and absent when it does not. According to Kelley, three types of covariation information are particularly useful: consensus, distinctiveness, and consistency. To illustrate these concepts, imagine that you're standing on a street corner one hot, steamy evening, when all of a sudden a stranger bursts out of a cool, air-conditioned movie theater and blurts out, "Great movie!" Looking up, you don't recognize the film title, so you wonder what to make of this candid appraisal. Was the behavior (the rave review) caused by something about the person (the stranger), stimulus (the film), or circumstances (say, the comfortable theater)? Possibly interested in spending a night at the movies, how do you explain this incident?

Thinking like a scientist, you would probably seek *consensus information* to see how different persons react to the same stimulus. In other words, how do other moviegoers feel about this film? If others also rave about the film, the stranger's behavior is high in consensus and is thus attributed to the stimulus. If others are critical of the same film, the behavior is low in consensus and attributed to the person. Still thinking like a scientist, you might also seek *distinctiveness information* to see how the same person reacts to different stimuli. In other words, how does this moviegoer react to other films? If the stranger is critical of other films, the target behavior is high in distinctiveness and attributed to the stimulus. If the stranger raves about everything, however, the behavior is low in distinctiveness and attributed to the person.

■ **attribution theory** A set of theories that describe how people explain the causes of behavior.

■ **covariation principle** An attribution rule stating that for something to be the cause of a behavior it must be present when the behavior occurs and absent when it does not.

Finally, you might seek *consistency information* to see what happens to the behavior at another time when the person and the stimulus both remain the same. How does this moviegoer feel about this film on other occasions? If the stranger raves about the film on video as well as in the theater, the behavior is high in consistency. If the stranger does not always enjoy the film, however, the behavior is low in consistency. According to Kelley, behavior that is consistent is attributed to the stimulus when consensus and distinctiveness are also high, and to the person when they are low. Behaviors that are low in consistency are attributed to fleeting circumstances, such as the temperature of the movie theater.

Kelley's attribution theory is logical, but does it describe the way that you and I analyze the behavior of others? To some extent, yes. Research shows that when subjects are asked to make an attribution for someone's behavior, they often follow the logic of the covariation principle and make attributions from consensus, distinctiveness, and consistency information (Cheng & Novick, 1990; Fosterling, 1989; Hewstone & Jaspars, 1987). The theory and the predictions it makes are represented in Figure 12.1.

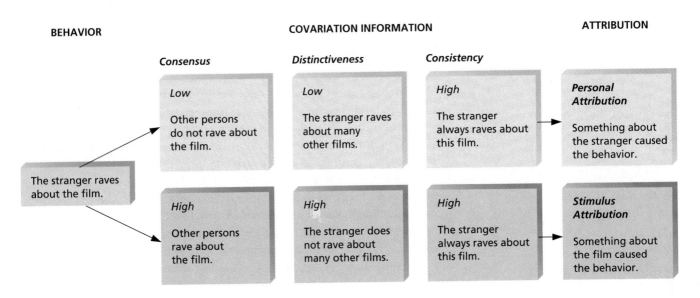

Figure 12.1

Kelley's Covariation Theory of Attribution

For behaviors that are consistent over time, attribution theory predicts that people make personal attributions under conditions of low consensus and distinctiveness (top row), and situational attributions under high consensus and distinctiveness (bottom row). Behaviors that are low in consistency (not shown) are attributed to passing circumstances.

Attribution Biases   When attribution theory was first proposed, many social psychologists wondered: Do people really analyze behavior as one might expect of a computer? Do social perceivers have the time, the desire, or the cognitive capacity for such mindful processes? Not always. With so much to explain and not enough time in the day, we often take mental shortcuts, cross our fingers, and get on with life (Fiske & Taylor, 1991). The problem is that with speed comes bias, and perhaps even a loss of accuracy. We now examine two types of biases in attribution.

The Fundamental Attribution Error   By the time you complete this section of this textbook, you will have learned the cardinal lesson of social psychology: people are influenced in profound ways by situations. This point

■ **fundamental attribution error** A tendency to overestimate the impact of personal causes of behavior and to overlook the role of situations.

TV viewers often think that an actor's behavior stems from a personal disposition rather than the role he or she plays. The fundamental attribution error may lead people to assume that actress Candice Bergen is like the character she plays, Murphy Brown.

seems obvious, right? So, why are parents often astonished to hear that their mischievous child, the family monster, is a perfect angel in school? And why are students often surprised to see that their favorite professor, an eloquent lecturer, can be awkward in informal conversation? These reactions are symptoms of a well-documented feature of social perception. When people explain the behavior of others, they typically underestimate the role of situational factors and overestimate the role of personal factors. This bias is so pervasive, and often so misleading, that it has been called the **fundamental attribution error** (Ross, 1977).

The fundamental attribution error was first discovered in a study by Edward Jones and Victor Harris (1967). In that study, subjects read a speech presumably written by a college student that was either for or against Fidel Castro, the communist leader of Cuba. Some subjects were told that the student had freely chosen his or her position; others were told that the student was assigned to that position by a professor. What was the student's true attitude? In response to this question, subjects were more likely to infer the student's attitude from the speech when the position was freely chosen than when it was assigned. So far, so good. But even when subjects knew that the student had no choice, they still inferred his or her attitude from the speech. This finding has been repeated many times. Unless people suspect the speaker of having an ulterior motive for the position taken (Fein et al., 1990), or unless the essay is perceived to have been half-heartedly written (Miller et al., 1990), the result is essentially the same (Jones, 1990).

A fascinating study by Lee Ross and his colleagues (1977) demonstrates the fundamental attribution error in a more familiar setting, the TV quiz show. By a flip of a coin, subjects were randomly assigned to play the role of either the questioner or the contestant in a quiz game, while spectators looked on. In front of the contestant and spectators, the experimenter told the questioner to write ten challenging questions from his or her own store of general knowledge. If you're a trivia buff, you can imagine how esoteric these questions might have been: Who was the first governor of Idaho? What team won the NHL Stanley Cup in 1968? It's no wonder that contestants correctly answered only about 40 percent of the questions asked. When the game was over, all participants rated the questioner's and contestant's general knowledge on a scale of 0 to 100.

Picture the events that transpired. The questioners appeared more knowledgeable than the contestants—after all, they knew all the answers. But a moment's reflection should remind us that the situation put the questioner at a distinct advantage. Did subjects take the situation into account, or did they assume that the questioners actually had greater knowledge? The results were startling. Spectators rated the questioners as above average in their general knowledge and the contestants as below average. The contestants even rated themselves as inferior to their partners. Like the spectators, they too were fooled by the loaded situation (see Figure 12.2).

What's going on here? Why do social perceivers consistently draw conclusions about persons, and fail to appreciate the impact of situations? According to Daniel Gilbert (1989), the problem stems from *how* attributions are made. Attribution theorists used to assume that people survey all the evidence and then decide on a personal or situational attribution. Instead, claims Gilbert, there is a two-step process: first we identify the behavior

Figure 12.2

Fundamental Attribution Error in a TV Quiz Show

The simulated quiz show placed questioners in position of advantage over contestants, yet observers rated the questioners as more knowledgeable (right). Questioners did not overrate their own general knowledge (left), but contestants, like the observers, rated themselves as inferior (middle). These results illustrate the fundamental attribution error.

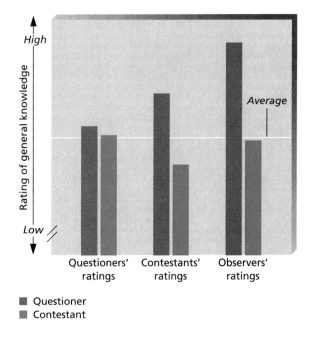

and make a quick personal attribution; then we correct or adjust that inference to account for situational influences. The first step is simple and automatic, like a reflex; the second one requires attention, thought, and effort. This model is depicted in Figure 12.3.

Figure 12.3

A Two-Step Model of the Attribution Process

Traditional attribution theories assumed that people analyze behavior by searching for personal and situational causes. A more recent, two-step model suggests that people make personal attributions automatically, and then make conscious adjustments to that inference to account for situational factors.

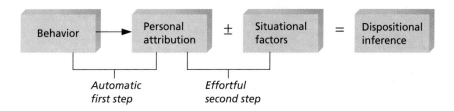

Why is it so natural for people to assume a link between another person's acts and personal dispositions? There are two explanations. One is that people infer dispositions from behavior because of a perceptual bias, something like an optical illusion. Think about it. When you listen to a speech or watch a quiz show, the actor is the conspicuous *figure* of your attention, while the situation fades into the *background* ("out of sight, out of mind," as they say). Indeed research shows that people attribute events to factors that are perceptually conspicuous, or *salient* (Taylor & Fiske, 1978).

The second explanation is cultural. Westerners are taught that individuals are autonomous and responsible for their own actions. In contrast, many non-Western cultures take a holistic view that focuses on the relationship between persons and their social roles. To see if these differing world views are related to attributions, Joan Miller (1984) asked Americans and Asian-Indians of varying ages to describe what caused certain positive and negative behaviors they had observed in their lives. Among the youngest children, there were no cultural differences. With increasing age, however, the American subjects made more personal attributions, while the

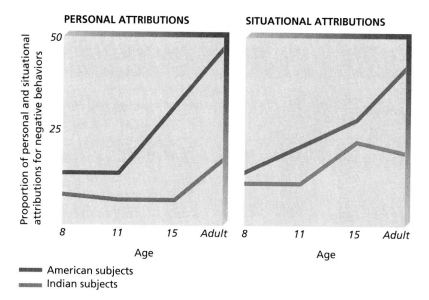

Figure 12.4

Fundamental Attribution Error: A Western Bias?

American and Asian-Indian subjects of varying ages described the causes of various behaviors. Among young children, there were no cultural differences. With age, however, Americans made more personal attributions, while Indian subjects made more situational attributions. This result raises a provocative question: Is the fundamental attribution error a strictly Western phenomenon?

Indian subjects became more situational. These findings suggest that the fundamental attribution error may be unique to Western cultures (see Figure 12.4).

Motivational Distortions   As logical as we try to be, our attributions are also sometimes biased by underlying motivations. When students receive their exam grades, those who do well take credit for the success; those who do poorly complain about the instructor and the questions. When researchers have articles accepted for publication, they assume it reflects on the high quality of their work; when articles are rejected, these same professors blame the editor and reviewers. When professional athletes win, they fill the sports pages with self-congratulatory quotes; when they lose, they complain about the officials, weather conditions, and opposing players. Clearly, people are biased in the attributions they make for their own behavior—taking credit for success but distancing themselves from failure (Schlenker et al., 1990).

When social perceivers observe others, different motives come into play. According to Melvin Lerner (1980), people have a deep-seated need to believe that the world is a just place where we "get what we deserve" and "deserve what we get"—where hard work and a virtuous lifestyle are rewarded, and where laziness and a sinful lifestyle are punished. To believe otherwise, after all, is to concede that we are vulnerable to the cruel twists and turns of fate. This **belief in a just world** gets jolted, however, when one is confronted by the innocent victims of crime, illness, accidents, and natural disasters. Terrified by the implication that these tragedies could happen to *us*, we psychologically defend ourselves by blaming the victims for their misfortune. Thus, we might assume that the homeless are lazy, that rape victims are promiscuous, that battered wives provoke their abusive husbands, and that AIDS sufferers lack moral integrity.

The tendency to disparage victims may seem like just another symptom of the fundamental attribution error: too much focus on the person, not enough on the situation. But there's more to it than that. Research shows that victims are held most responsible for their fate when the resulting

■ **belief in a just world** The assumption that the world is a just place where people get what they deserve.

■ **primacy effect** The tendency for impressions of others to be heavily influenced by information appearing early in an interaction.

harm is severe rather than mild (Walster, 1966), when the victim is in a situation similar to the perceiver's (Burger, 1981), and when a perceiver is emotionally aroused by the event (Thornton et al., 1986). In other words, the more personally shaken we are by an apparent injustice, the more we feel the need to blame the victim.

Confirmation Biases

Sometimes, we form impressions of people quickly, without much conscious thought or effort, based on superficial cues such as physical appearance and nonverbal behavior. At other times, our opinions of others are based on a causal analysis of their behavior. Either way, research shows that once we make up our minds about a person, we become less and less likely to revise our opinions in light of new evidence. First impressions can be powerful. The reason, as we'll see, is that people tend to *interpret* and *create* new information in ways that confirm their pre-existing beliefs.

The Power of First Impressions   It is often said that first impressions stick, and social psychologists are inclined to agree. In a classic demonstration of this phenomenon, Solomon Asch (1946) told a group of subjects that a person was "intelligent, industrious, impulsive, critical, stubborn, and envious." He then presented a second group with exactly the same list, but in reverse order. Logically, the two groups should have formed the same impression. Instead, however, subjects who heard the first list—in which the positive traits came first—were more favorable in their evaluations than those who heard the second list. Clearly, people are influenced more by information that appears early in an interaction than by information that appears later—a finding known as the **primacy effect.**

The primacy effect occurs for two reasons. The first is that perceivers become less attentive to subsequent behavioral evidence once they have formed an impression of a person. Thus, when subjects in one study read a series of statements about someone, the amount of time they spent reading each statement declined steadily as they proceeded through the list (Belmore, 1987). The second reason is more unsettling. Once people have formed an initial impression, they interpret new evidence in a biased manner. When people are told that a nice person is *calm,* they assume that he or she is gentle and serene. When a cruel person is said to be *calm,* however, that word is taken to mean shrewd and calculating. Similarly, the word *proud* can mean self-respecting or conceited, while *critical* can mean astute or picky (Hamilton & Zanna, 1974; Watkins & Peynircioglu, 1984).

A study by John Darley and Paget Gross (1983) illustrates the power of first impressions in an important setting. In their study, subjects were asked to evaluate the academic potential of a girl named Hannah. Half of the subjects were led to believe that she was from an upper-middle-class home with well-educated, professional parents (high expectations). The other half was told that she lived in a run-down neighborhood and had poorly educated working parents (low expectations). As illustrated in Figure 12.5, subjects in the first group were somewhat more positive in their ratings of Hannah's ability than were those in the second group. In each of these groups, however, half the subjects watched a videotape of Hannah taking a

"It is a capital mistake to theorize before you have all the evidence. It biases the judgment."

SIR ARTHUR CONAN DOYLE

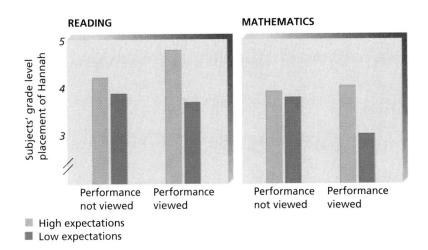

Figure 12.5

Mixed Evidence: Does It Extinguish or Fuel First Impressions?

Subjects evaluated the potential of a school-girl. Without seeing her test performance, those with high expectations rated her slightly higher than did those with low expectations. Among subjects who watched a tape of the girl taking a test, the expectations effect was even greater.

short achievement test. Her performance on the tape was not particularly high or low, but average—she correctly answered some hard questions but missed others that were easy. Since all of these subjects saw the same test performance, their initial expectations should carry less weight, right? Wrong. Among subjects who saw the tape, Hannah received even lower ability ratings from those with low expectations and even higher ratings from those with high expectations. Presenting the same body of mixed evidence did not extinguish the first impression bias, it *fueled* it.

In events that are ambiguous enough to support contrasting interpretations, perceivers see what they expect to see. Also biasing is the way we interpret evidence that plainly disconfirms our opinions. What happens, for example, when advocates and opponents of nuclear technology are confronted with evidence of a near-fatal accident? If a nuclear power plant breaks down, but the system's safeguards prevent a disaster, how do people react? Assuming that advocates will feel humbled by the breakdown, and that opponents will feel comforted by the effectiveness of the safeguards, the two sides should converge in their opinions. That's not what happens. After subjects with strongly pro- or anti-nuclear points of view read a story about a power plant accident that was not catastrophic, most became more certain, not less certain, of their initial positions. Advocates focused on the safeguards, and opponents focused on the breakdown—thus magnifying the initial differences of opinion (Plous, 1991). Additional studies show that we are quick to discredit evidence that contradicts the conclusions we want to reach (Ditto & Lopez, 1992; Kunda, 1990).

The Self-Fulfilling Prophecy   As social perceivers, we interpret new information in light of our existing beliefs and preferences. To make matters worse, we also at times *create* support for our beliefs and preferences. In Chapter 11, we saw that teachers who have positive or negative expectations of a student, perhaps based on an IQ score, alter their behavior toward that student, thus setting into motion a self-fulfilling prophecy (Rosenthal & Jacobson, 1968). The same process is at work in other settings as well. In a study of 34 corporate managers and 164 job applicants, Amanda Phillips and Robert Dipboye (1989) found that when the managers had positive expectations, they spent more interview time trying to

Social Perception Biases and the Jury

Every day, ordinary people are brought together, seated in a courtroom, and empowered to make important decisions. Jury trials are the heart and soul of the American judicial system. The jury trial consists of three stages. First, members of the community are summoned to court, sworn in, questioned, and selected. Next comes the presentation of testimony, arguments, and the judge's instructions. Third, jurors go off to deliberate as a group and strive to reach a common verdict.

By law, juries are instructed to base their decisions only on the evidence presented in court—not on extraneous factors. But is that ideal always achieved? What happens in cases that attract widespread media attention? Can jurors ignore pretrial publicity? Can they disregard testimony that the judge rules to be inadmissible? Can they set aside impressions of a defendant based on his or her physical appearance? Over the years, social psychologists have examined these possible sources of bias.

Pretrial Publicity

Think about some of the defendants whose trials have made the news in recent years—O.J. Simpson, Oliver North, Mike Tyson, William Kennedy Smith, "Hotel Queen" Leona Helmsley, Lorena Bobbitt, Jeffrey Dahmer, the four police officers who beat Rodney King, the Los Angeles rioters who beat trucker Reginald Denny, and the Menendez brothers who killed their parents. All of these cases were featured in the newspapers and on TV, as are many thousands of local trials held every year. Does exposure to pretrial publicity corrupt the jury?

Public opinion surveys consistently indicate that the more people know about a case, the more likely they are to presume the defendant guilty (Moran & Cutler, 1991). This result is not hard to explain. The information appearing in the news typically emanates from the police or district attorney's office, so it typically reveals facts unfavorable to the defense. The real question, of course, is whether this information overwhelms the evidence—and the jury. To examine the effects of pretrial publicity, Norbert Kerr and his colleagues (1991) played a videotaped reenactment of an armed robbery trial to hundreds of subjects participating in 108 mock juries. Before watching the tape, groups of subjects were exposed to TV reports and newspaper clippings on the case. Some received material that was neutral, while others received information that was incriminating—for example, revealing that the defendant had a prior record or was implicated in a hit-and-run accident. As in court, all subjects were instructed to base their decisions solely on the evidence. But the pretrial publicity had a marked effect. In groups exposed to the neutral story, 33 percent of the subjects voted guilty after the trial and deliberations. In groups exposed to prejudicial material, that figure increased to 48 percent.

Pretrial publicity is dangerous in part because jurors are exposed to it *before* they enter the courtroom. From what is known about primacy and the power of first impressions, the implication is clear. So, is there a solution? Since the biasing effect persists despite cautionary instructions, justice may demand that prospective jurors with prior knowledge of a case be excluded, or that highly publicized cases be postponed or moved to other, less informed communities.

impress rather than evaluate the applicant, and were more likely to make a favorable hiring decision. And in a study of 29 platoons that consisted of a thousand men in the Israeli Defense Forces, Dov Eden (1990) led some but not all platoon leaders to expect that the trainees they were about to receive had great potential—when, in fact, they were of average ability. After ten weeks, the trainees who were assigned to the high-expectation platoons obtained higher-than-average scores on written exams and exhibited a greater ability to operate a weapon.

How does this self-fulfilling prophecy work? How do social perceivers transform beliefs into reality? As shown by research on teacher expectations, the process involves a three-step chain of events (see Figure 12.6). First, a perceiver forms an impression of a target person—based on the target's physical appearance, reputation, gender, race, or initial interactions.

Inadmissible Evidence

Just as jurors are biased by news stories, they sometimes receive extralegal information during the trial itself. According to the law, a judge may exclude from evidence information that is inflammatory, unreliable, confusing, or illegally obtained. If such information is leaked during the trial, the judge will instruct jurors to disregard it. But can people really strike information from the mind the way court reporters can strike it from the written record? Can jurors resist the forbidden fruit of inadmissible testimony? Common sense would suggest that they cannot. So does the research.

In one study, a group of mock jurors read about a murder case based on evidence so weak that not a single subject voted guilty. A second group read the same case but was told that the prosecution introduced an illegally obtained tape recording of a phone call made by the defendant: "I finally got the money to pay you off. . . . When you read the papers tomorrow, you'll know what I mean." The defense argued that the illegal tape should not be admitted, but the judge allowed it into evidence and the conviction rate rose to 26 percent. In a third group, as in the second, the tape was introduced and the defense objected. But this time, the judge sustained the objection and told jurors to disregard the information. The result? Thirty-five percent voted for conviction (Sue et al., 1973).

Similar results were found in a study of "dirty tricks." Mock jurors read a trial transcript in which a lawyer implied in the context of a cross-examination question that the opponent's expert witness had a bad reputation: "Isn't it true, doctor, that your work is poorly regarded by your colleagues?" No proof of this allegation was offered, yet subjects who heard the question lowered their estimates of this witness's credibility. In fact, they devalued that witness regardless of whether the question was met with an admission, a denial, or an objection sustained by the judge (Kassin et al., 1990).

Physical Appearances

There is a third possible source of bias that is perhaps the most basic of all. Studies show that when people meet others whom they do not know, their initial impressions are influenced by physical appearances. Does this bias extend into the courtroom, or is justice truly blind? Do judges and juries evaluate defendants by the way they look? Sometimes, yes. One study revealed that Pennsylvania state judges were less likely to sentence convicted defendants to prison if they were physically attractive than if they were not (Stewart, 1980). Another study revealed that Texas judges set lower bails and imposed smaller fines on suspects who were attractive than on those who were not (Downs & Lyons, 1991).

Physical attractiveness is not the only aspect of appearance that can influence decisions. As we've seen, people with babyish faces are perceived to be youthful, naive, and honest, whereas those with mature faces are perceived as strong, mature, and dominant. To examine the possible legal consequences of these perceptions, Diane Berry and Leslie McArthur (1988) wrote two versions of a trial. In one, the defendant was charged with negligence because he forgot to warn a customer about the hazards of a product he was selling. In the other version, the defendant was said to have deliberately misled a customer in order to make a sale. As predicted, subjects found the baby-faced defendant negligent, a crime that "matched" his appearance. Yet they judged the mature-faced defendant as guilty of the crime of deception. A similar bias was uncovered in the decisions made by small-claims court judges (Zebrowitz & McDonald, 1991).

To summarize, the law states that verdicts should be based only on the evidence presented in court. But jurors are ordinary people—and that means they are subject to the biases of social perception. Having identified the problems, researchers are seeking ways to minimize these prejudicial effects.

Second, the perceiver behaves in a manner that is consistent with that first impression. Third, the target unwittingly adjusts his or her behavior to the perceiver's actions (Darley & Fazio, 1980; Harris & Rosenthal, 1985).

Figure 12.6

The Self-Fulfilling Prophecy

How do people transform beliefs into reality? (1) A perceiver forms an impression of a target person; (2) the perceiver then behaves in a manner consistent with those expectations; and (3) the target unwittingly adjusts his or her behavior according to the perceiver's actions.

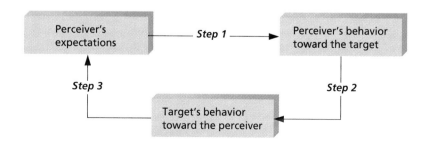

By steering interactions with others along a path narrowed by our initial beliefs, we set into motion the self-fulfilling prophecy—which keeps us from judging others in an objective manner. Fortunately, this bias is not an inevitable aspect of social perception. If we conceptualize the problem as a three-step process, it is possible to identify two links in the chain that can be broken to prevent a vicious cycle (Hilton & Darley, 1991; Snyder, 1993).

First there's the link between one's expectations and one's behavior toward the target. When perceivers are motivated to seek the truth (as when they evaluate the target as a possible teammate or opponent), or when they want the target to like them, they become more objective—and often do not confirm negative expectations (Neuberg, 1989; Neuberg et al., 1993). Next is the link between a perceiver's actions and a target's response. In most of the research, the target subjects are not aware of the perceiver's expectations. But what if they were? How would you react if *you* knew that you were being cast in a particular light? When it happens to research subjects—especially when they think they're being misjudged—they often behave in ways that contradict the perceiver's initial beliefs (Hilton & Darley, 1985; Swann & Ely, 1984). Indeed, the persons we perceive have their own prophecies to fulfill.

Thus far, we have discussed the way that people form and maintain their impressions of each other. It's important to recognize, however, that the process begins with a warm-blooded, passionate, motivated, and emotional human being whose impressions are often positive or negative. We now examine this evaluative aspect of social perception. First we look at some factors that promote positive evaluations, or *attraction.* Then we turn to the problem of *prejudice,* the dark side of social perception.

ATTRACTION

If you have ever had a crush on someone, or felt the excitement of "love at first sight," or enjoyed the warmth of an intimate friendship, then you know the meaning of the term *attraction.* The following section explores two aspects of this positive experience: (1) the desire to approach others upon initial encounters, and (2) the later development of close relationships (Berscheid, 1994).

Initial Encounters

When you meet someone for the first time, what personal characteristics do you look for? Common sense is filled with contradiction: Does familiarity breed fondness or contempt? Is beauty the object of our desire, or do we assume that appearances are deceiving? Do birds of a feather flock together, or do opposites attract? Over the years, researchers have identified various determinants of attraction. Among the most important of these are familiarity, physical attractiveness, and similarity.

Familiarity   The first rule of attraction is that for a relationship to develop, there must be contact. Indeed, people tend to like, befriend, and

■ **mere-exposure effect** The attraction to a stimulus that results from increased exposure to it.

marry others who live in the same neighborhood, attend the same school, belong to the same club, or work in the same office. In a classic study, for example, Theodore Newcomb (1961) found that close friendships in an experimental dormitory were far more likely to develop between roommates than between those who did not share a room.

To some extent, proximity promotes liking by providing opportunities for interaction. But there is another, very basic reason as well: the more exposure people have to a stimulus—say, a foreign word, an object, a melody, or a person—the more they like it (Zajonc, 1968; Bornstein, 1989). This phenomenon, known as the **mere-exposure effect,** can also influence our self-evaluations. Imagine, for example, that you had a photograph of yourself developed into two pictures—one that depicted your actual appearance, and the other a mirror-image copy. Which picture would you prefer? Which would a friend prefer? Theodore Mita and his colleagues (1977) tried this experiment with female college students and found that most preferred their own mirror images, while their friends liked the actual photos. In both cases, the preference was for the view of the face that was most familiar.

As a consequence of the mere-exposure effect, people (perhaps including Madonna) prefer their own familiar mirror images to actual-image photos.

The mere-exposure effect is powerful, but there are two limitations. The first is that if you initially dislike someone, increased familiarity may make the situation even worse, breeding contempt instead of attraction (Grush, 1976). The second limitation is based on the sheer frequency of exposure. Have you ever listened over and over again to a new song you liked, only to become sick of it after a while? This reaction is not uncommon. A stimulus that is frequently presented loses impact if it is "overexposed"—especially if it is repeatedly presented to people who are easily bored (Bornstein et al., 1990).

Physical Attractiveness   What do you look for most in a friend or romantic partner? Intelligence? Kindness? A sense of humor? How important is a person's looks? As children, we were told that "beauty is only skin deep." Yet as adults, we react more favorably to others who are physically attractive rather than unattractive. Studies show that physical attractiveness influences parents' expectations for their newborn babies, teachers' evaluations of schoolchildren, the hiring of job applicants, jury verdicts, and the sentencing of convicted felons (Hatfield & Sprecher, 1986). Thus it is not surprising that tall and slender "supermodels" are paid millions of dollars a year to sell products in magazine advertisements.

The Nature of Beauty   Is physical attractiveness an objective and measurable quality like height, weight, or hair color? Or is beauty more subjective, existing in the eye of the beholder?

Some researchers believe that some faces are inherently more attractive than others. There are two sources of evidence for this proposition. First, when subjects are asked to rate faces on a 10-point scale, there is typically a high level of agreement over which are more or less attractive. In fact, it appears that people like faces with eyes, noses, lips, and other features that are not too different from the average. Judith Langlois and Lori Roggman (1990) showed college students actual yearbook photos as well as computerized facial composites that "averaged" the features in these photos. The result was that subjects preferred the averaged composites to the actual faces. A second source of evidence is that babies—even though they are too young to have learned the cultural standards of beauty—exhibit a preference for faces considered attractive by adults. Indeed, judging from their eye movements, two-month-old infants spend more time gazing at attractive faces than at unattractive ones (Langlois et al., 1987).

Other researchers argue that beauty is subjective, and point to the influences of culture, time, and the circumstances of our perception. To enhance their appearance, people from different cultures use face painting, makeup, plastic surgery, scarring, hairstyling, the molding of bone structures, the filing of teeth, braces, and the piercing of ears, noses, and other body parts. What people find attractive in one part of the world may be repulsive in other parts of the world (Landau, 1989). Even within a culture, standards of beauty may change from one generation to the next. Brett Silverstein and others (1986) examined the measurements of female models appearing in women's magazines between 1901 and 1981, and found that "curvaceousness" (as measured by the bust-to-waist ratio) varied over time, with a boyish slender look becoming particularly desirable in recent years. Finally, judgments of beauty can be inflated or deflated by various circumstances. For example, we evaluate others as more physically attractive after we have grown to like them (Gross & Crofton, 1977). On the other hand, subjects who view nude models in *Playboy* and *Penthouse* magazines subsequently lower their attractiveness ratings of average-looking women—the unfortunate result of a contrast effect (Kenrick et al., 1989).

Social Stereotypes   The bias for beauty is pervasive. In one study, fifthgrade teachers were given background information about a boy or girl accompanied by a photograph of an attractive or unattractive child. All teachers received identical information, yet those who saw an attractive

Showing that beauty is in the eye of the beholder, people in different cultures enhance their appearance in different ways. Pictured here are a Mejecodoteri woman from Amazon, Venezuela (top left), a "punk" couple from the United States (top right), two Maasai men from Kenya (bottom left), and a woman from the state of Gujarat in India (bottom right).

child judged that child as smarter and more likely to do well in school (Clifford & Walster, 1973). In a second study, male and female experimenters approached students on a college campus and tried to get them to sign a petition. The more attractive the experimenter was, the more signatures he or she was able to get (Chaiken, 1979). And in a third study, mothers of facially deformed infants reported that they were more satisfied with parenthood, but, in fact, they were less responsive in their maternal behavior and less nurturant than the mothers of normal infants (Barden et al., 1989).

It seems so shallow, so superficial. Why are we drawn like magnets to people who are physically attractive? One possibility is that it is rewarding to be in the company of others who are aesthetically appealing, or "easy on the eyes." In other words, we derive pleasure from beautiful men and women the same way we enjoy breathtaking scenery. Second, people associate physical attractiveness with other desirable qualities. In children's fairy tales, Snow White and Cinderella are portrayed as beautiful *and* kind, while the witch and stepsisters are said to be ugly *and* cruel. Similarly, studies indicate that good-looking people are generally perceived to be smart, successful, well adjusted, happy, confident, assertive, socially skilled, and

As in the story of Cinderella, the perceived link between beauty and goodness is evident even in classic children's fairy tales. [© The Walt Disney Company.]

Actress Marilyn Monroe was beautiful but very insecure.

popular (Dion et al., 1972; Eagly et al., 1991). Is this stereotype accurate? Only to a limited extent. Good-looking people do have more friends, better social skills, and a more active sex life. But beauty is *not* related to objective measures of intelligence, personality, adjustment, or self-esteem. It appears that popular perceptions exaggerate the reality (Feingold, 1992).

So why does the physical attractiveness stereotype endure? One possibility is that social perceivers may create support for their biased impressions. Think about the three-step model of the self-fulfilling prophecy described earlier. Mark Snyder and his colleagues (1977) demonstrated this phenomenon in a classic study of interpersonal attraction. The subjects were unacquainted pairs of male and female college students. All subjects were given a biographical sketch of their partner, with men also receiving a photograph of a physically attractive or unattractive woman, supposedly their partner. At that point, the men rated their partners and then had a telephone-like conversation over headphones. The results were provocative. Men who thought that their partner was physically attractive rather than unattractive (1) formed more positive impressions of her personality and (2) were friendlier in their conversational behavior. And now for the clincher: (3) the female subjects whose partners had seen the attractive photograph were rated by listeners to the conversation as warmer, more confident, and more animated. Fulfilling their own prophecies, men who expected an attractive partner actually created one. This finding calls to mind the Greek myth of Pygmalion, who fell in love with the statue he had carved—and brought it to life.

It is interesting that despite the many social advantages associated with physical attractiveness, it is not a sure ticket to happiness and self-esteem. The life and death of Marilyn Monroe is a case in point. Monroe was considered one of the most ravishing women of her time and was one of the hottest talents in Hollywood. Yet she was terribly vulnerable and insecure. Why? One problem is that highly attractive people often can't tell whether all the attention and praise they receive from others is due to their talent or just to their good looks. In a study by Brenda Major and her colleagues (1984), male and female subjects wrote essays that were later positively evaluated by an unknown member of the opposite sex. Half the subjects were told that their evaluator could see them through a one-way mirror;

"I like walks in the rain, old barns, and
Edna St. Vincent Millay. Does that
ring any bells?"

[Drawing by Weber; © 1991 The New Yorker Magazine, Inc.]

the other half thought they could not be seen. The result: Physically attractive subjects who thought they could be seen attributed the positive evaluation to their appearance, not to the quality of their work.

Similarity   Imagine that you meet someone for the first time and strike up a conversation about politics, sports, restaurants, and your favorite rock band—only to realize that the two of you have a lot in common. Now imagine the opposite experience, of meeting someone who is very different in his or her interests, values, and outlook on life. Which of these two strangers would you want to see again, the one who is similar or the one who is different?

As a general rule, people prefer to associate with others who are similar to themselves. According to Donn Byrne and his colleagues (1986), this effect on attraction consists of a two-step process: (1) we avoid others who are very different, then (2) among those who are left, we seek out those people who are the most similar to us. As a result, friends and couples are more likely than are randomly paired persons to share common attitudes and interests. They are also more likely to be similar in age, religion, race, level of education, height, intelligence, and economic status. The more similar two individuals are, the better are the chances that their relationship will last (Byrne, 1971).

People also gravitate toward others with a similar level of physical attractiveness. Have you ever seen a couple in which one partner is beautiful and the other plain? If so, how did you react? Surprise, confusion, and shock are common reactions—and for good reason. Research shows that most people wish to date beautiful men and women, a preference that is often seen in laboratory choice studies (Walster et al., 1966). In real life, however, people tend to shy away from romantic encounters with others who are "out of their league." Among couples who are dating, living together, engaged, or married, the results instead support the **matching hypothesis**—the tendency to form close relationships with others who are equivalent in their level of attractiveness (Murstein, 1986).

The Social Marketplace   In the social marketplace, where physical attractiveness is a highly valued commodity, matching is an equitable arrangement. However, beauty may also be "exchanged" for economic resources. Trading looks for money sounds terribly old-fashioned and not very romantic, but it seems to accurately describe the partner-selection process. Various analyses of personal ads appearing in newspapers and magazines reveal that women tend to offer beauty and seek wealth, while men seek beauty and offer wealth (Harrison & Saeed, 1977; Rajecki et al., 1991). These preferences appear to be universal. In a large-scale cross-cultural study, David Buss (1989) asked men and women in thirty-three countries within North and South America, Asia, Africa, Europe, and the Pacific to rate how important various characteristics were in choosing a mate. In all countries, "good looks" were rated more highly by men, while "good financial prospect" was more important to women.

Why is this difference so prevalent, and what does it mean? Buss argues that the answer can be derived from *sociobiology*, the discipline that uses the principles of evolution to understand human social behavior. Since reproductive success is necessary for the survival of a species, sociobiologists

■ **matching hypothesis** The tendency to form close relationships with others of equivalent attractiveness.

When "Pretty Woman" Julia Roberts married Lyle Lovett, people were surprised. Why? The fact that she is considered much more attractive violates the matching hypothesis.

claim that people exhibit mating patterns that favor the conception, birth, and survival of their offspring. From this perspective, men lust for beautiful women because the features of physical attractiveness—such as smooth skin, lustrous hair, and full lips—also happen to be associated with youth and fertility. In turn, women need men with earning power in order to protect and provide for the welfare of their offspring. Interestingly, sociobiology is also used to explain a consistent sex difference in age preference. Research shows that men in their twenties are equally interested in younger women and slightly older women who are still of fertile age. But older men consistently seek women who are younger than they are, while women want men who are older (Kenrick & Keefe, 1992). For the sociobiologist, the personal ads that people write reveal the forces of evolution at work (Kenrick, 1994).

Nobody doubts the existence of these sex differences. Many social psychologists are quick to point out, however, that the differences may be more "socio" than "biological." Two specific points can be made in this regard. First, women may trade sex appeal for money, not for reproductive purposes, but because they are denied *direct* access to economic power. Second, the sex differences that exist are minor compared to the similarities. When Buss (1988) asked college students to rate various behaviors for their capacity to attract members of the opposite sex, the lists produced by male and female students were almost identical. A good sense of humor, a well-groomed appearance, sympathy, and helpfulness were all highly desirable—for everyone.

Close Relationships

Sometimes, initial interactions give rise to a deeper, more intimate relationship. There are different ways to define and measure the closeness of a relationship. Ellen Berscheid and her colleagues (1989) developed a questionnaire that asks partners to report on the amount of time they spend together, the range of activities they engage in together, and the degree of influence each has over the other's plans and decisions. This measure of closeness has some predictive value. A follow-up study of dating college students showed that closeness scores at the time of testing helped to predict whether or not the couple would still be together after nine months. Another measure of closeness is based on the idea that an intimate relationship is one in which the "line" between self and other becomes so blurred that *mine* and *yours* are one and the same. Indeed, Arthur Aron and his colleagues (1992) have found that the longevity of a romantic relationship can be predicted simply on the basis of which diagram in Figure 12.7 was chosen by subjects to describe their relationship. The more one incorporates a partner into the self, the more lasting the relationship is likely to be.

What specific form might a close relationship take? And when can the term *love* be used to describe the experience? Over the years, philosophers, poets, and songwriters have sought to define love. Elizabeth Barrett Browning thus asked, "How do I love thee? Let me count the ways." We now know that the number of ways is substantial. When a group of college students was asked to list the kinds of love that came to mind, they produced 216 different types—including friendship, parental, brotherly, sisterly, ro-

Please circle the picture below that best describes your relationship.

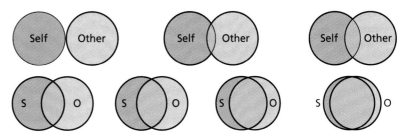

Figure 12.7

A Single-Item Measure of Relationship Closeness

mantic, sexual, spiritual, obsessive, possessive, and puppy love (Fehr & Russell, 1991). Social psychologists have also tried to distinguish among the different types of loving relationships. The most basic is Elaine Hatfield's (1988) two-pronged distinction between passionate and companionate love.

Passionate Love   **Passionate love** is an intense emotional state of positive absorption in another person. From the ecstatic highs to the agonizing lows, passionate love is the stuff of romance novels, popular music, and soap operas. What is it, and where does it come from? According to Ellen Berscheid and Elaine (Hatfield) Walster (1974), the key to understanding passionate love is to recognize that it is an emotion and can be analyzed like other emotions. Influenced by the two-factor theory of emotion presented in Chapter 8, Berscheid and Walster theorized that passionate love requires two essential ingredients: (1) a heightened state of physiological *arousal,* and (2) the *belief* that this arousal was triggered by the beloved person. Sometimes, the connection between arousal and love is obvious—as when a person feels a surge of sexual excitement while daydreaming about a romantic partner. At other times, however, the arousal—including such symptoms as a pounding heart, sweaty palms, and weak knees—is difficult to interpret. It may be joy, fear, or anxiety. In the company of an attractive person, the arousal may be attributed or even "misattributed" to passionate love.

Several researchers have tested the hypothesis that arousal from any source intensifies passionate feelings. In a series of experiments, male subjects rated women whom they had just met as more attractive when they were artificially aroused—by running in place, watching a comedy routine, or listening to a stressful event—than when they were not (Allen et al., 1989; White et al., 1981). Donald Dutton and Arthur Aron (1974) were the first to demonstrate this provocative phenomenon in a field study that took place on two bridges above British Columbia's Capilano River. One was a narrow, wobbly suspension bridge with a low handrail that sways 230 feet above rocky rapids. The other was wide, sturdy, and only ten feet from the ground. As young men walked over these bridges, they were met by an attractive woman who introduced herself as a research assistant, asked them to fill out a questionnaire, and gave her phone number in case they wanted more information about the project. As predicted, subjects who walked over the scary bridge—a highly stressful experience that could be misattributed to the research assistant—were more likely than those who crossed the stable bridge to call the woman later. Perhaps terror can fan the hot flames of romance.

■ **passionate love** An intense, emotional state of positive absorption in another person.

■ **companionate love** A deep and lasting affection between close friends or lovers.

Companionate Love   Arousal may animate our passions, but other kinds of love are different. According to Hatfield (1988), **companionate love** is a form of affection between close friends or lovers that is less emotionally intense, but deeper and more enduring. Resting on a foundation of mutual trust and respect, companionate love enables partners to exhibit high levels of *self-disclosure*—in other words, to bare their souls and reveal intimate details about themselves.

Self-disclosure is to companionate love what arousal is to passionate love. Self-disclosure follows three predictable patterns. One is that partners reveal more and more to each other as the relationship grows over time. Indeed, the more dating and married partners self-disclose, the happier they are with the relationship and the more likely they are to stay together (Hendrick, 1981). Second, we typically reciprocate another person's self-disclosure with one of our own—at a comparable level of intimacy (Berg, 1987). Third, women are more open than men are—which, perhaps, is why people in general prefer to confide in women more than in men (Derlega et al., 1985) and why women in general have more intimate same-sex friendships than men do (Sherrod, 1989).

Sexuality

Romantic relationships between partners of the same or opposite sex are multidimensional. Typically beginning in late adolescence, sexuality is a part of a relationship that is the most intimate, the most private, and, in some ways, the most difficult to study. During the 1940s, Alfred Kinsey and his colleagues (1948, 1953) conducted the first large-scale survey of sexual practices in America. Based on interviews of more than 17,000 men and women, these researchers sought to describe what nobody would talk about: patterns of sexual activity. Kinsey's goal was to uncover the hidden norms for such aspects of sexual behavior as masturbation, premarital sex, extramarital affairs, homosexuality, orgasms, and sexual disorders. Some of Kinsey's results were shocking, as he revealed that sexual activity was more frequent and varied than expected. His books quickly became best sellers. Although his sampling methods were flawed (most subjects were young, white, urban, and middle class), the findings are still used as a basis for comparison.

Since Kinsey's groundbreaking study, numerous sex surveys have been conducted. Although one can never know for sure how accurate these self-report results are, it is clear that cultural norms and practices have changed over the years. For example, sexual-activity levels peaked during the "sexual revolution" of the 1960s and 1970s, but the numbers have declined somewhat in recent years (Robinson et al., 1991). Thus when Meg Gerrard (1987) surveyed female college sophomores in the 1973–74 academic year, she found that 35 percent were sexually active. In 1978–79, that number was up to 51 percent. In 1983–84, it was down to 37 percent.

These survey-based population statistics provided only a glimpse into the sexual component of relationships, so more intensive research was needed. Enter sex researchers William Masters and Virginia Johnson. As reported in their 1966 book, *Human Sexual Response,* Masters and Johnson filmed and measured physiological activity in hundreds of male and female volunteers while they masturbated or had sexual intercourse in the laboratory.

■ **sexual response cycle** The four physiological stages of sexual responding—excitement, plateau, orgasm, and resolution.

Their observations revealed that despite male-female differences in anatomy, upbringing, norms, and attitudes, there are striking physiological similarities in the sexual response.

There are four stages in the **sexual response cycle**—and these are the same for men and women (see Figure 12.8). In the *excitement* stage, a stimulus sparks sexual arousal marked by increased blood flow to the pelvic region, which then causes the genitals to become engorged with blood. During this phase, the man's penis becomes partially erect, while the woman's vagina secretes a lubricant and her breasts become enlarged. This phase lasts from a few minutes to well over an hour. The excitement then builds to a *plateau* stage, when breathing and heart rates increase. The man's penis fills with a fluid that may contain live sperm, some of which may appear at the tip of the penis; his erection becomes firmer, the woman's vagina becomes wetter, and a "climax" feels moments away. During the *orgasm* stage, rhythmic genital contractions give rise to an intensely pleasurable feeling of sexual release, accompanied in men by the ejaculation of semen. For both men and women, the contractions are spaced at about eight-tenths of a second apart, with the first five or six contractions being the most intense. The feeling seems to be the same for both sexes. Afterward, the body slowly returns to its normal pre-aroused state and enters the *resolution* stage. In men, resolution is accompanied by a refractory period during which another orgasm is impossible. This "downtime" can last from just a few minutes to more than a day. Women, however, do not experience a lengthy refractory period, so they are capable of a rapid succession of orgasms if restimulated.

Figure 12.8

The Sexual Response Cycle

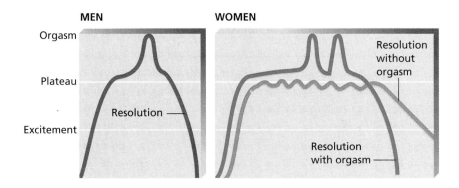

How important is sex in a romantic relationship? It's hard to tell. On the one hand, research suggests that dating relationships with sex last longer than those without sex. In one study, for example, college student couples who were sexually active rather than inactive were more likely to still be together when recontacted three months later (Simpson, 1987). On the other hand, married couples who live together before marriage—a situation that provides greater access to sexual activity—are more likely to have less satisfying relationships that end in divorce (Glenn, 1990). These correlations should be interpreted with caution, as there is no way of knowing the extent to which sex is a cause or an effect of relationship quality. What is clear, however, is that for both heterosexual and homosexual couples, sexual satisfaction is correlated with overall satisfaction in a relationship (Kurdek, 1991).

PREJUDICE

When people evaluate others positively and seek out their company, with or without sex, we speak of attraction, friendship, and love. At times, however, people evaluate others negatively—sometimes because of their affiliation with a particular group. When that happens, we speak of **prejudice**, the dark, hurtful side of social perception. Examples are not hard to find. In South Africa, a white ruling class discriminates against the black majority. In Germany, Neo-Nazi skinheads terrorize immigrants. In the Middle East, Israelis and Arabs fight what seems an eternal war. And in what used to be the Soviet Union, raging ethnic conflicts are almost too numerous to mention. The streets of the United States are also filled with bigotry—and the ivory tower is no exception. At one university, fraternity members painted their faces black and held a mock slave auction. At another, the Jewish Student Union was spray-painted with a swastika. On a third campus, rocks and bottles were thrown at gay men and women during a parade.

Stories like these make the news on a regular basis, bringing to life an important point: our impressions of others are sometimes biased by their membership in a social group. Prejudice is one of the most tenacious social problems of modern times. Regardless of whether its victims are women, minorities, homosexuals, senior citizens, the handicapped, or newly arrived immigrants, there are often two roots to the problem: one cognitive, the other motivational.

Cognitive Roots

To some extent, prejudice is a by-product of the beliefs we hold and the way we think. The beliefs are called stereotypes, and the cognitive process that promotes stereotyping is called social categorization (Stangor & Lange, 1994).

A **stereotype** is a belief that associates a group of people with certain traits. When you stop to think about it, the list of well-known stereotypes seems endless. Consider some examples: the Japanese are sneaky, athletes are brainless, Italians are emotional, Jewish people are materialistic, Californians are laid back, accountants are dull, college professors are absent-minded, blacks are athletic, and used-car salesmen cannot be trusted as far as you can throw them. Now, how many of these images ring a bell? More important, how do they influence our perceptions and evaluations of each other? There are many theories on how stereotypes like these are born within the history of a culture. Social psychologists, however, ask a different question: How do stereotypes operate in the minds of individuals, and how do they affect our perceptions of others?

From a cognitive perspective, the problem begins with the fact that people naturally divide others into groups based on sex, race, age, nationality, religion, and other attributes. The process is called **social categorization**. In some ways, social categorization is natural and adaptive. By grouping people the way we do foods, animals, furniture, and other objects, we form impressions quickly and easily and use past experience to guide new interactions (Macrae et al., 1994). The problem is that categorizing people leads us to magnify the differences *between* groups and overlook the differences

■ **prejudice** Negative evaluation of others based solely on their membership in a certain group.

■ **stereotype** A belief that associates a group of people with certain traits.

■ **social categorization** The classification of persons into groups based on common attributes.

In sports and other rivalries, the process of social categorization leads us to assume that although "we" are diverse, "they" are all alike.

among individuals *within* groups (Wilder, 1986). Also a problem is that social perceivers are themselves members or nonmembers of social categories. Groups you identify with—your country, religion, political party, even your hometown sports team—are called *ingroups,* while groups other than your own are called *outgroups.*

Research shows that the distinction between ingroups and outgroups has important psychological and social consequences. Part of the problem is that once we carve the world up into "us" and "them," there is a pervasive tendency to assume that "they" are all alike—a phenomenon known as the **outgroup homogeneity bias** (Ostrom & Sedikides, 1992). Examples abound. People who arrive in America from Korea, China, Vietnam, and Taiwan see themselves as different from one another, but to the Western eye they are all Asian. Likewise, the people of Mexico, Puerto Rico, Central America, and Cuba distinguish among themselves, but others refer to them all as Hispanic. Business majors talk about "engineering types," engineers lump together "business types," conservatives see liberals as all the same, and while the natives of New York City proclaim their cultural and ethnic diversity, outsiders talk of the typical New Yorker.

As a result of the outgroup homogeneity bias, people are quick to generalize from a single individual to a whole group. In one experiment, for example, students from Rutgers and Princeton—rival universities in the state of New Jersey—watched a videotape of a subject in a decision-making study. After being led to believe that the study was held at either Rutgers or Princeton, subjects watched the target person make a series of choices (for example, classical or rock music, verbal or math problems). When later asked to predict the percentage of other subjects who made the same choices, students assumed that there was more similarity between the target person and other subjects at the rival university than at their own (Quattrone & Jones, 1980). It appears that for groups other than our own, "If you've seen one, you've seen them all."

There are two reasons for the tendency to perceive outgroups as homogeneous. First, we do not notice subtle differences among outgroup members as we do among ingroup members because we have less personal contact with them. Indeed, the more familiar people are with an outgroup, the less likely they are to perceive that group as homogeneous (Linville et al., 1989). The second reason is that people often do not encounter a representative sample of outgroup members. The Princetonian who sees only those Rutgers students who cruise into town for a football game, screaming at the top of their lungs, is seeing only those rivals who are the most avid fans, hardly a diverse lot (Quattrone, 1986).

Motivational Roots

From a cognitive perspective, stereotypes spring from the process of social categorization and the distinctions that are made between ingroups and outgroups. In other words, stereotypes are a by-product of the way people think. But is that all there is to it? If people could somehow be prevented from categorizing one another, would all of the prejudice in the world be eliminated? Doubtful. The way we *think* about social groups is important, but there's another factor to consider: our *motivations* to perceive the groups we encounter in a particular light.

■ **outgroup homogeneity bias** The tendency to assume that "they" (members of groups other than our own) are all alike.

Sexism in the Workplace: Taking the Case to Court

Brenda Taylor, a Florida attorney, was fired because she dressed for work in designer blouses, tight-fitting skirts, and ornate jewelry. The problem? According to Taylor's supervisor, her appearance in court "created the impression that she was a bimbo interested only in meeting men" (Associated Press, 1988). Did Taylor's clothing undermine her credibility? Studies show that women's clothing can have this effect. When banking and marketing administrators saw videotaped interviews of female applicants for a management position, the women received higher recommendations when they were dressed in a "masculine" navy suit with a blazer jacket than when they wore a softer, "feminine" light-colored dress (Forsythe, 1990). The question confronting Brenda Taylor and other working women is whether the "dress for success" rules are fair. According to Taylor, a professional woman should not have to dress like a man.

In contrast was the case of Ann Hopkins—an accountant who was said to be too "masculine." Hopkins was hoping to become a partner in a major accounting firm. On paper, her record was impeccable. In just a few years, Hopkins had single-handedly brought in over $25 million in contracts, the tops among her peers. Yet she was denied partnership, while several less productive male candidates were promoted. Why? According to Hopkins, it was because she was a woman. As in most disputes, however, there are two sides to the story. The firm claimed that Hopkins was overbearing, abrasive, and difficult to work with. One member of the firm was said to have quit and sought employment elsewhere, presumably because he could not tolerate working with her.

Was Ann Hopkins rejected because of her personality, her gender, or a combination of the two? Hopkins took the case to court, where she testified that she was described by one

There are two major motivational theories of prejudice. The first is **realistic conflict theory**, which begins with a simple observation: that many intergroup conflicts in the world today stem from direct competition for valuable but limited resources (Levine & Campbell, 1972). As a matter of economics, one group may fare better than a neighboring group in a struggle for land, jobs, or power. The losers become frustrated, the winners feel threatened, and before long the conflict heats to a rapid boil. It has been suggested, for example, that the recent surge in racial tensions in the United States is linked to increased resentment among white Americans who are bitter about affirmative action policies that give preference to minorities (D'Souza, 1991).

Realistic conflict accounts for part of the problem, as frustration evokes hostility, aggression, and the search for a "scapegoat." Between the years 1882 and 1930, for example, the number of black Americans lynched in the Deep South increased as cotton prices fell—a sign of economic frustration (Hovland & Sears, 1940; Beck & Tolnay, 1990). The argument seems compelling, but wait—individuals are often prejudiced even when their own quality of life is *not* directly threatened by an outgroup. Surveys of white residents in Los Angeles and Louisville (Kentucky), for example, showed that their opposition to affirmative action and other liberal racial policies was the same whether or not they were personally affected (Sears & Kinder, 1985).

A series of laboratory studies poses additional challenges to realistic conflict theory. In the first of these, Henri Tajfel and his colleagues (1971) showed subjects a sequence of dotted slides and asked them to estimate the number of dots on each. The slides were flashed in rapid-fire succession so

■ **realistic conflict theory** The theory that prejudice stems from intergroup competition for limited resources.

partner as a "macho" lady who should attend "charm school." She was even advised to "wear makeup, have my hair styled, and wear jewelry." To make the case that these comments reveal sex discrimination, Hopkins called on social psychologist Susan Fiske to testify as an expert on stereotypes. Citing research on social perception, Fiske testified that Hopkins's aggressive manner was offensive only because it clashed with traditional conceptions of women, and that her token status in a predominantly male environment put her in the limelight where everything she did was noticed, scrutinized, and blown out of proportion. Fiske concluded that Hopkins was a victim of sex discrimination, and the trial judge agreed. By a 6 to 3 vote, so did the U.S. Supreme Court (Fiske et al., 1991).

Despite her exceptional record, Ann Hopkins was denied partnership at the accounting firm for which she worked. Was it because she is a woman perceived to be too much like a man?

■ **ingroup favoritism** The tendency to discriminate in favor of ingroups over outgroups.

■ **social identity theory** The theory that people discriminate against outgroups to enhance their own self-esteem.

the dots could not be counted. The experimenter then told subjects that some people are chronic "overestimators," others "underestimators." As part of a second task, subjects were then divided, supposedly for the sake of convenience, into groups of overestimators and underestimators (in fact, the assignments were random). Knowing who was in their group, subjects allocated points to each other for various tasks, points that reflected favorable judgments and could be cashed in for money. This procedure created "minimal groups"—persons categorized by trivial similarities. The overestimators and underestimators were not bitter rivals, had no history of antagonism, and were not competing for a limited resource. Yet subjects allocated more points to members of their own group than to those of the outgroup. This pattern of discrimination, known as **ingroup favoritism,** is consistently observed—even when groups are assembled by a mere flip of a coin (Messick & Mackie, 1989).

Why do people favor ingroups over outgroups in the absence of realistic conflict, when personal interests are not at stake? According to the **social identity theory** of Tajfel (1982) and John Turner (1987), the answer is simple: personal interests *are* at stake because prejudice is nourished by a concern for oneself. Social identity theory states that each of us strives to enhance our self-esteem, which has two components: a *personal* identity and various *social* identities that are rooted in the groups to which we belong. In other words, people can boost self-esteem not only through their own achievements but by perceiving their ingroups as better and more deserving than outgroups. What's nice about the need for social identity is that it leads us to derive a sense of pride from our connections with others. What's sad, however, is that we sometimes need to belittle "them" in order to feel

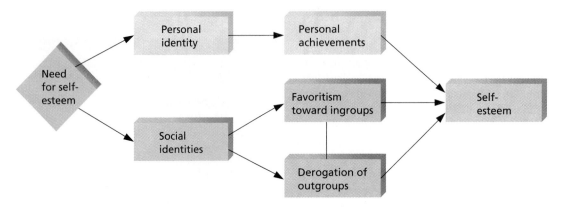

Figure 12.9

Tajfel (1982) and Turner (1987) claim that people strive to enhance self-esteem, which has two components: a personal identity and various social identities based on the groups to which they belong. People can thus boost their self-image by viewing ingroups more favorably than outgroups.

secure about "us." Religious fervor, racial and ethnic pride, and patriotism may all serve to fulfill this aspect of our social identity. The theory is summarized in Figure 12.9.

Social identity theory makes two predictions: (1) threats to self-esteem heighten the need for prejudice, and (2) expressions of prejudice should, in turn, enhance one's self-esteem. Research generally supports these predictions (Hogg & Abrams, 1990)—though one important factor to consider is the relative size of the ingroup. Noting that people want to belong in groups that are small enough for them to feel unique, Marilyn Brewer (1991) has found that ingroup loyalty—and the prejudice that follows from it—is more intense for minority groups than for members of a large, overly inclusive majority.

So far, we have seen that stereotypes lead us to overlook the diversity within outgroups and rush to judgment about others. We have also seen that prejudice stems both from competition and from the need to favor ingroups to boost one's self-esteem. In Chapter 14, we'll see that these principles can help us to understand sexism and racism, two common forms of social discrimination.

SUMMARY AND KEY TERMS

Social psychology is the study of how individuals think, feel, and behave in social situations.

The Big Picture

Milgram's classic experiments showed that a high percentage of subjects would follow orders, even if they thought they were harming a fellow human. This finding illustrates a basic message of social psychology: that people can influence each other's behavior in profound ways.

Forming Impressions

To understand social behavior, we need to study *social perception,* the processes of coming to know and evaluate other people.

Snap Judgments

We often make snap judgments of other people. One major cue we use is physical appearance. People with baby-faced features, for instance, are seen as warmer and kinder than those with more mature looks. Another cue is *nonverbal behavior;* as people draw conclusions about others on the basis of facial expressions, body language, gaze, and touch.

Despite these cues, most people are not very good at detecting deception by others. Voice is the cue most likely to reveal deception, but perceivers often pay more attention to a person's words and face.

Attributions

In addition to making snap judgments, we make attributions for the causes of other people's behavior. Heider, who first developed *attribution theory*, distinguished between personal and situational attributions. Kelley theorized that our attributions follow the *covariation principle*: for something to be the cause of a behavior, it must be present when the behavior occurs and absent when it does not. According to Kelley, we use three types of covariation information: consensus (do other people react in the same way?), distinctiveness (how does the person react to different stimuli?), and consistency (does the person react the same way at different times?).

Other studies point to our frequent errors in attribution. In explaining the behavior of others, we typically underestimate the role of the situation and overestimate the role of personal factors; this is the *fundamental attribution error*. Some research suggests that the fundamental attribution error may be unique to Western cultures, which tend to emphasize individual responsibility.

Our attributions can be biased by our motivations as well. We often take personal credit for our successes but blame the situation for our failures. Since our *belief in a just world* convinces us that people generally get what they deserve, we tend to blame victims for their misfortune, especially when we are personally shaken by it.

Confirmation Biases

Whether our opinions of others are based on snap judgments or on attributions, we tend to be biased in interpreting further information. Because of the *primacy effect*, our impressions are more heavily influenced by early information than by what we learn later. In fact, we often use later information to confirm our initial bias, and we discredit evidence that contradicts it. Further, we often create a self-fulfilling prophecy: by behaving according to our biases, we can influence the other person's behavior, which then confirms what we thought in the first place.

Attraction

Initial Encounters

Researchers have identified several factors that influence the attraction of people who are getting to know each other. The first is familiarity. Because of the *mere-exposure effect*, increased exposure to any stimulus (including another person) tends to produce greater attraction.

Physical attractiveness is also important. Not only do we value good looks in themselves, but we associate other desirable qualities with physical beauty, and our behavior toward attractive people can help fulfill our own prophecies.

A third key to attraction is similarity. People usually prefer to associate with others who are similar to themselves in interests, values, and even attractiveness. Studies support the *matching hypothesis*, which holds that we tend to form close relationships with others of equivalent attractiveness.

In the social marketplace, matching sometimes involves an exchange of beauty for wealth. An extensive cross-cultural study has found that men tend to seek beauty in a partner, while women look for good financial prospects. According to sociobiology, this difference makes evolutionary sense. But many social psychologists stress social explanations rather than biological ones.

Close Relationships

Although there are different ways to measure closeness and define love, Hatfield makes a basic distinction between passionate and companionate love. *Passionate love*, an intense emotional state of positive absorption in another person, requires both a heightened state of physiological arousal and a belief that the other person has triggered this arousal. *Companionate love*, though less intense, is a deep and lasting affection between close friends or lovers that generally involves high degrees of self-disclosure.

Sexuality

Overall levels of sexual activity in our society have varied over the years. But the *sexual response cycle* is predictable, and men and women both experience the same four stages: excitement, plateau, orgasm, and resolution. Sexual satisfaction correlates with overall satisfaction in a relationship.

Prejudice

Prejudice refers to negative evaluation of others based solely on their membership in a certain group. Its roots can be both cognitive and motivational.

Cognitive Roots

The cognitive roots of prejudice involve *stereotypes*—beliefs that associate a group of people with certain traits. Through the process of *social categorization*, we divide people into groups based on common attributes, such as race or religion. We also distinguish ingroups (those we identify with) from outgroups (groups not our own). Although this process is natural and adaptive, the *outgroup homogeneity bias* leads us to assume that members of outgroups are all alike. As a consequence, we miss the distinctions among individuals.

Motivational Roots

Our motivations also play a role in prejudice. The *realistic conflict theory* holds that prejudice stems from intergroup competition for limited resources. But this explanation does not account for the pattern of *ingroup favoritism* that appears even when resources aren't limited. *Social identity theory* points to a social as well as a personal component in our identities. Because of the social component, we can bolster our self-esteem by discriminating against outgroups. Research generally confirms that threats to self-esteem raise the need for prejudice, and that expressions of prejudice in turn enhance self-esteem.

Chapter 13

Social Influence

Advertisers hire celebrities and supermodels to sell soft drinks, sneakers, and other products. Politicians try to win votes by making speeches, shaking hands, and passing out bumper stickers. Sports fans spread the "wave" and chant "de-fense" in a spectacular show of unison. Protestors, lost in a massive sea of anonymous faces, shed their inhibitions and become transformed into a violent mob. Performers with stage fright tremble, turn pale, and freeze before appearing in front of an audience. And bystanders on a city street see a victim cry for help but fail to react.

As the above examples illustrate, people affect one another in profound and varied ways. These "social influences" come in different shapes and sizes. The source may be a person or a group, the effect may be a change in attitudes or behavior, and the change may be constructive (helping others) or destructive (hurting others). These various aspects of social influence are examined in this chapter.

ATTITUDES AND BEHAVIOR

Do you favor or oppose gun control? What about abortion? Should smoking be banned in public places? Would you rather listen to rock music or jazz, work on an IBM computer or a Mac? As these questions suggest, people have positive and negative reactions to all sorts of persons, objects, and ideas. These evaluative reactions are called **attitudes** (Eagly & Chaiken, 1993).

It is common to assume that *attitudes influence behavior*—that voter opinions of opposing candidates predict the winner on election day, that consumer preferences for competing products influence the purchases they make, or that feelings of prejudice trigger acts of discrimination. Interestingly, however, the link between attitudes and behavior is far from automatic.

Sociologist Richard LaPiere (1934) made this observation many years ago. At a time when anti-Asian prejudice was widespread, LaPiere took a young Chinese couple on a three-month car trip and visited 250 restaurants, campgrounds, and hotels in the United States. The couple was welcomed in all but one location. When LaPiere wrote back to the places they had visited, however, and asked if they would serve Chinese patrons, more than 90 percent of the respondents said they would not. In short, self-reported attitudes did not correspond with behavior.

LaPiere's study was flawed in many ways (for example, attitudes were recovered several months after the trip, and during that time the attitudes may have changed). But it was the first of many studies to reveal that attitudes are only weakly correlated with behavior, if at all (Wicker, 1969). Sobered by this finding, social psychologists—who, after all, conduct opinion polls and surveys in order to predict behavior—went on to find that there is a link between attitudes and behavior, but only under certain conditions. Indeed, behavior is influenced not only by attitudes but also by social pressures and other external factors (Fishbein, 1980; Ajzen, 1991).

Social influence is not one process but many. A change in someone's attitude may precipitate a change in his or her behavior; sometimes it is the other way around. This chapter separately explores the ways in which be-

■ **attitude** A positive or negative reaction to any person, object, or idea.

havior and attitudes are changed. Then it explores the factors that influence two important types of interpersonal behavior: aggression and altruism.

SOCIAL INFLUENCES ON BEHAVIOR

As social animals, we are all vulnerable to subtle, reflex-like influences. We yawn when we see others yawning, and laugh when we hear others laughing. In one study, research confederates stopped on a busy street in New York City, looked up, and gawked at a window of a nearby building. A camera stationed behind the window showed that roughly 80 percent of passersby stopped and gazed up when they saw these confederates (Milgram et al., 1969). Knowing that people are quick to imitate others, TV producers infuse sitcoms with canned laughter to make viewers think the shows are funny, political candidates trumpet inflated results from their own public opinion polls as a way of attracting new voters, and bartenders stuff dollar bills into empty tip jars to draw more money from their customers. As they say, "monkey see, monkey do."

People are often influenced in strange ways by the behavior of others. Look at this baby yawning, for example, and you too may start to yawn.

Street musicians will often put dollar bills into their instrument cases as a way of prompting others to do the same.

Conformity

Conformity, the tendency for people to bring their behavior in line with group norms, is a powerful fact of social life. Cast in a positive light, it promotes harmony, group solidarity, and peaceful coexistence—as when people assume their places in a waiting line. Cast in a negative light, conformity also has harmful effects—as when people drink too heavily at parties or tell offensive ethnic jokes because others are doing the same. For the social psychologist, the goal is not to make moral judgments but, rather, to determine the factors that promote conformity and the reasons for it.

The Early Classics   In 1936, Muzafer Sherif published a classic laboratory experiment on how norms develop in small groups. The subjects in his study, thinking they were in a visual perception experiment, sat in a dark room, saw a beam of light, and then estimated the distance the light had

■ **conformity** A tendency to alter one's opinion or behavior in ways that are consistent with group norms.

Religion is a powerful force in producing conformity. Here, thousands of Muslims converge on Mecca, the holiest city of the Islamic faith.

moved. This procedure was repeated several times. Subjects didn't realize it, but the light never moved. The movement they thought they saw was merely an optical illusion. At first, subjects sat alone and reported their perceptions only to the experimenter (most estimates stabilized in the range of one to ten inches). Then, during the next few days, subjects returned to participate in three-person groups. Each time a beam of light was flashed, subjects stated their estimates one by one. As shown in Figure 13.1, initial esti-

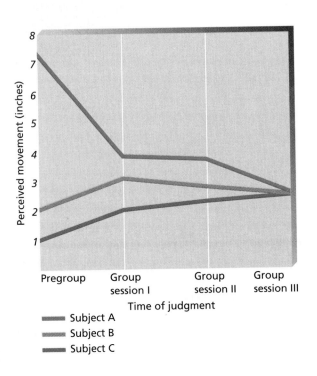

Figure 13.1

A Classic Case of Suggestibility

These findings from one group in Sherif's study illustrate how subjects' estimates of the apparent movement of light converged over time. Gradually, the group established its own set of norms.

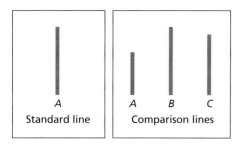

Figure 13.2

Line-Judgment Task in Asch's Study

Which comparison line—A, B, or C—is the same length as the standard line?

mates varied considerably, but subjects eventually converged on a common perception, each group establishing its own set of norms.

Fifteen years after Sherif's experiment, Solomon Asch (1951) constructed a different situation. Imagine yourself as a subject in his study. You sign up for a psychology experiment, and when you arrive you find six other students waiting around a table. You take an empty seat, and the experimenter explains that he is measuring people's ability to make visual discriminations. As a warm-up, he asks you and the others to indicate which of three comparison lines is identical in length to a standard line (see Figure 13.2).

That seems easy enough. The experimenter then asks you all to take turns in order of your seating position. Starting on his left, the experimenter asks the first person for a judgment. Seeing that you are in the next-to-last position, you patiently await your turn. The opening moments pass uneventfully. The task is clear and everyone agrees on the answers. On the third set of lines, however, the first subject selects the wrong line. Huh? What happened? Did he suddenly lose his mind, his eyesight, or both? Before you know it, the next four subjects choose the same wrong line. Now it's your turn. Faced with what seems like an easy choice, you rub your eyes and take another look. What do you think? Better yet, what do you do? As you may have guessed by now, the other "subjects" were confederates trained to make incorrect judgments on certain trials. The right answers were clear. In a control group, where subjects made their judgments alone, performance was virtually errorless. Yet subjects in the experimental group went along with the incorrect majority 37 percent of the time—a surprising level of conformity that was replicated just a few years ago (Larsen, 1990).

After two uneventful rounds in Asch's line-judgment study, the subject (number 6) faces a dilemma. Confederates 1 through 5 all gave the same wrong answer. Should he give his own, or conform to theirs?

Both Sherif and Asch found that people are influenced by the behavior of others. But there is an important difference in the types of conformity exhibited in these studies. Sherif's subjects were literally "in the dark"—uncertain of their own perceptions. Wanting to be correct, they looked to others for guidance and adopted the average of their estimates. In Asch's situation, however, the task was simple enough for subjects to see the lines with their own eyes. These subjects knew that the majority was wrong but went along to avoid becoming social outcasts. In short, there are two different types of social influence: informational and normative (Deutsch & Gerard, 1955; Campbell & Fairey, 1989). **Informational influence** leads people to conform because they assume that the majority is correct. In the case of **normative influence**, people conform because they fear the social rejection

■ **informational influence** Conformity motivated by the belief that others are correct.

■ **normative influence** Conformity motivated by a fear of social rejection.

that accompanies deviance. For good reason. Research shows that people who stray from the norm are disliked, and often ridiculed and laughed at (Levine, 1989)—especially in groups that need to reach a consensus (Kruglanski & Webster, 1991).

The distinction between the two types of social influence is important because they produce different types of conformity—private and public. Like beauty, conformity may be skin-deep, or it may penetrate beneath the surface. In *private conformity*, people change not only their behavior but their minds as well. To conform at this level is to be genuinely persuaded that the majority is right. In contrast, *public conformity* refers to a temporary and superficial change in which people outwardly comply with the majority in their behavior but privately maintain their own beliefs.

Majority Influence   Realizing that people can be pressured by others is only the first step in understanding the process of social influence. The next step is to identify the situational factors that make us more or less likely to conform. One obvious factor is the size of a group. Common sense suggests that as a majority increases in size, so does its impact. Actually, it is not that simple. Asch (1956) varied the size of his groups, by using one, two, three, four, eight, or fifteen confederates, and found that conformity increased only up to a point. After four confederates, the amount of *additional* influence was negligible, subject to the law of diminishing returns (see Figure 13.3). Bibb Latané (1981) likens this impact on an individual to the way light bulbs illuminate a surface. Add a second bulb in a room, and the effect is dramatic. Add a tenth bulb, and its impact is barely noticed.

Figure 13.3

Group Size and Conformity

By varying the number of confederates, Asch found that conformity increased with the size of the majority, but only up to a point. As you can see, fifteen had no more impact than did four.

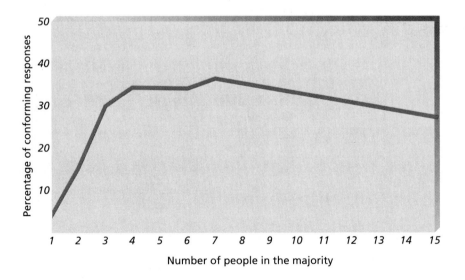

In Asch's initial study, subjects were pitted against a unanimous majority. But what if they had an ally, a partner in dissent? Put yourself in this situation: How do you think having an ally would affect *you?* Varying this aspect of his experiment, Asch found that the presence of just one confederate who gave the correct answer reduced conformity by almost 80 percent. In fact, any dissenter—even one whose competence is called into question—can break the spell cast by a unanimous majority and reduce the pressure to conform (Allen & Levine, 1971).

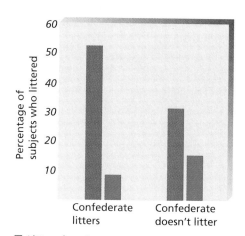

Figure 13.4

Conformity to a Social Norm

In a parking garage that was either clean or littered with trash, subjects saw a confederate either throw paper on the ground (left) or not (right). As shown, there was greater conformity—that is, more littering when the garage was messy than clean—after the confederate had littered, an act that drew attention to the existing social norm.

It may not be easy, but individuals sometimes resist the social pressure to conform.

[Drawing by C. Barsotti; © 1992 The New Yorker Magazine, Inc.]

Although the size of a majority and the presence of an ally influence the amount of pressure that is felt, people are most likely to conform when their attention is drawn to social norms. To demonstrate this point, Robert Cialdini and his colleagues (1991) observed patrons in an indoor parking garage that was kept either *clean* or *cluttered* with candy wrappers, cigarette butts, and other trash. On some occasions, a research confederate brought this clean or cluttered norm to the subject's attention by crumpling up a piece of paper and throwing it to the ground. At other times, the confederate passed without incident. Upon reaching their cars, subjects found a PLEASE DRIVE SAFELY handbill tucked under the windshield wiper. Did they toss the paper to the ground or take it with them? As shown in Figure 13.4, subjects conformed to the situation—in other words, they littered more when the garage was cluttered than when it was clean—only when they had seen the confederate litter, which drew their attention to the existing norm. For social norms to influence our behavior, they must be "activated" or brought to mind.

Finally, cultural factors play an important role. In many Western cultures—most notably, the United States, Australia, Great Britain, Canada, and the Netherlands—autonomy and fierce independence are highly valued. In contrast, many cultures of Asia, Africa, and Latin America place a value on social harmony and "fitting in" for the sake of the community. Among the Bantu of Zimbabwe, for example, an African tribe in which deviance is scorned, 51 percent of the subjects placed in an Asch-like study conformed to the majority's wrong answer—more than the number typically obtained in the West (Triandis, 1994).

Minority Influence   It is not easy for individuals who express unpopular views to enlist support from others. Philosopher Bertrand Russell once said that "conventional people are roused to frenzy by departure from convention, largely because they regard such departure as criticism of themselves." Russell may have been right. People who challenge the status quo are perceived as competent, but they are intensely disliked (Bassili & Provencal, 1988).

Maintaining independence in the face of social pressure to conform is difficult, but it is not impossible. In *The Dissenters*, anthropologist Langston Gwaltney (1986) interviewed "ordinary" nonconformists—an Irish man who befriended blacks in a racist community, a New England grandmother who risked arrest to protest nuclear weapons, and a group of nuns who sued their church. Laboratory research also provides relevant evidence. Think about it. Asch's subjects conformed on 37 percent of the trials, but the flip side of the coin is that they openly refused to acquiesce in the other 63 percent—a result that bears witness to the human spirit of independence (Friend et al., 1990).

How do nonconformists tolerate the pressure to change? Better yet, how do they sometimes manage to sway the majority? According to Serge Moscovici (1985), majorities exert power by their sheer numbers, but those in a minority derive their power by sticking to their positions in a persistent, unwavering, and self-confident manner. By holding firm, dissenters get others to sit up, take notice, and rethink their own positions. Moscovici and his colleagues (1969) first observed this phenomenon by confronting real subjects with a *minority* of confederates who made incorrect judgments. In groups of six, subjects took part in what was believed to be a study of color perception. They viewed a series of blue slides and, for each, took turns naming the color. The task was simple—until two confederates described the slides as green. When these confederates were *consistent*— that is, when both made incorrect green judgments for all slides—one-third of all subjects incorrectly reported seeing at least one green slide.

People are sometimes influenced in important but subtle ways by minority opinion. Because of social pressures, we may be too intimidated to admit or even recognize the influence. But it is there, and is especially likely to materialize when subjects give their answers anonymously or in an indirect way (Clark & Maass, 1990; Moscovici & Personnaz, 1991).

Obedience

Allen Funt, creator of the TV program *Candid Camera,* used to spend as much time observing people as most psychologists do. His conclusion: "The worst thing is how easily people can be led by any kind of authority figure, or even the most minimal signs of authority." Funt went on to describe the time he put up a road sign that read DELAWARE CLOSED TODAY. The reaction? "Motorists didn't question it. Instead they asked, 'Is Jersey open?'" (Zimbardo, 1985, p. 47).

Blind obedience may seem funny, but as the pages of history attest, the implications are sobering. In World War II, Nazi officials participated in the deaths of millions of Jewish men, women, and children. When they came to trial for these crimes, their defense was always the same: "I was just following orders." Was this a fluke? An historical aberration? No, crimes of obedience are still being committed all over the world, even today (Kelman & Hamilton, 1989). On one extraordinary occasion, such obedience was carried to its limit: in 1978, nine hundred men and women of the People's Temple cult obeyed an order from the Reverend Jim Jones to kill themselves.

To study the power of authority, Stanley Milgram conducted the dramatic experiments described at the start of Chapter 12. These experiments culminated in his 1974 book, *Obedience to Authority.* In total, Milgram

One nonconformist "hero" who calls himself Darkmoon strapped himself into a California redwood. To keep loggers from felling the tree, he spent thirty-three days on a tiny platform, eating food sent up on a line. The tree survived.

Taken to the extreme, blind obedience can have devastating results. In World War II, Nazi officials killed millions, many said, "because I was just following orders." In 1978, nine hundred followers of Reverend Jim Jones committed mass suicide at his command.

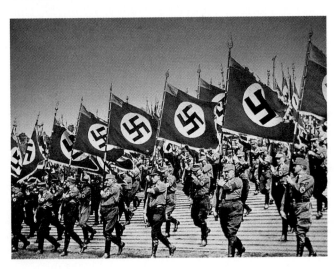

put one thousand subjects into a situation in which they were ordered by an experimenter to administer painful electric shocks to a confederate. Recall that subjects thought they were "teachers" in a study of the effects of punishment on learning, and that each time the "learner" made a mistake, they were to deliver a shock of increasing intensity. The subjects could not actually see the learner, but they could hear grunts of pain, complaints, objections, loud screams, and eventual silence. Yet at each step, they were ordered to continue up the shock scale. Despite the pain that subjects thought they were inflicting, and despite the guilt and anguish they themselves were experiencing, 65 percent of the subjects in Milgram's initial study delivered the ultimate punishment of 450 volts.

Milgram's subjects used the shock generator shown here to seemingly deliver up to 450 volts to the confederate who was strapped into his chair.

At first, these grim results led people to conclude that Milgram's subjects were sick, heartless, and cruel, not "normal" like you and me. On the contrary. All of the subjects were tormented by the experience—and comparable levels of obedience were later found among men, women, and college students all over the world (Miller, 1986). The results were so powerful that one author felt compelled to ask, *Are we all Nazis?* (Askenasy, 1978).

The lesson of Milgram's research is clear: although some people are more obedient than others (Blass, 1991), even decent human beings can be pushed to behave in ways that violate the conscience. Think about it. To me, the most striking aspect of Milgram's findings is that a psychology experimenter, unlike one's boss or military superior, cannot ultimately enforce his or her commands. Can you imagine the power that is wielded by real-life figures of authority? Not content merely to demonstrate obedience, Milgram altered aspects of his experimental situation in order to identify the factors that affect levels of obedience. Three factors in particular were systematically varied:

The authority: When Milgram moved his experiment from the prestigious campus of Yale University to a rundown city office building, arranged for the experimenter to issue his commands by telephone, or replaced the experimenter with an ordinary person, obedience levels dropped.

The victim: In Milgram's main experiment, subjects were physically separated from the learner, so they could distance themselves emotionally from his pain and suffering. When the subject and learner were seated in the same room, however, especially when subjects had to touch the learner, levels of obedience declined.

The commands: Two aspects of the experimenter's command contributed to the high level of obedience: (1) he explicitly assumed responsibility for the victim's welfare, and (2) full obedience was reached gradually, each step requiring only 15 volts more than the previous level. As Milgram (1965) put it, people become "integrated in a situation that carries its own momentum. The subject's problem . . . is to become disengaged from a situation which is moving in an altogether ugly direction" (p. 73).

SOCIAL INFLUENCES ON ATTITUDES

People often change their behavior in response to social pressure from a group or figure of authority. These changes, however, are typically limited to one act in one situation at a fleeting moment in time. For the effects to endure, it is important to change attitudes, not just behavior. Whether the goal is to win votes on election day, get consumers to buy a product, raise funds for a worthy cause, or combat discrimination in the workplace, attitude change is the key to a deeper, more lasting form of social influence.

Persuasive Communications

Persuasion, the process of changing attitudes, is a part of everyday life. The most common approach is to make a persuasive communication. Appeals made in person and through the mass media rely on the spoken word, the written word, and the picture that is worth a thousand words. What determines whether an appeal succeeds or fails? To understand why some approaches work and others do not, we need a road map of the persuasion process.

Two Routes to Persuasion   It's a familiar scene in American politics: every four years, presidential candidates launch extensive campaigns for office. In a way, if you've seen one election, you've seen them all. The names and dates may change, but over and over again opposing candidates accuse each other of ducking the issues and turning the election into a popularity contest. Whether or not the accusations are true, they illustrate that politicians are keenly aware that votes can be won through two very different methods. They can stick to the issues, or they can base their appeal on other grounds.

To account for these varying approaches, Richard Petty and John Cacioppo (1986) proposed a two-track model of persuasion. When people have the ability and motivation to think critically about the contents of a message, they take the **central route to persuasion**. In these instances, people are influenced by the strength and quality of the arguments. When people do not have the ability or motivation to pay close attention to the issues, however, they take mental shortcuts along the **peripheral route to persuasion**. In this case, people may be influenced by a speaker's appearance, slogans, one-liners, emotions, audience reactions, and other superficial cues. This two-track model of persuasion, and others like it (Chaiken et al., 1989), helps to explain how voters, consumers, juries, and other targets

■ **central route to persuasion** A process in which people think carefully about a message and are influenced by its arguments.

■ **peripheral route to persuasion** A process in which people do not think carefully about a message and are influenced by superficial cues.

of persuasion can seem so logical on some occasions, yet so illogical on others.

To understand the conditions that produce change on one route or the other, it's helpful to view persuasion as the outcome of three factors: a *source* (who), a *message* (says what, and how), and an *audience* (to whom). If a speaker is clear, if the message is important, if there is a bright and captive audience that cares deeply about the issues, then that audience will take the effortful central route. But if the source speaks too fast to comprehend, if the message is trivial, or if the audience is distracted, pressed for time, or uninterested, then the less strenuous peripheral route is taken. A major determinant of the target listener's approach is his or her personal involvement and concern about the message. High involvement leads us to take the central route; low involvement, the peripheral route (Johnson & Eagly, 1989; Petty & Cacioppo, 1990). This model of persuasive communication is illustrated in Figure 13.5.

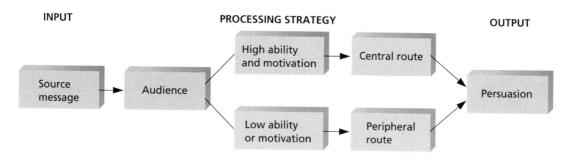

INPUT   **PROCESSING STRATEGY**   **OUTPUT**

Figure 13.5

Two Routes to Persuasion

Based on aspects of the source, message, and audience, people take either a "central" or "peripheral" route to persuasion. On the central route, we are influenced by strong arguments and evidence. On the peripheral route, we are influenced more by superficial cues.

The Source   Once he announced that he had the virus that causes AIDS, basketball star Magic Johnson became a powerful spokesman for health organizations seeking to educate the public. Johnson was not a medical expert or a professional speaker, but he was very effective. Why? What makes some communicators more persuasive than others?

Holding a press conference outside the White House, former basketball star Magic Johnson became a highly visible spokesman for AIDS awareness the moment he announced that he was infected with the HIV virus.

To begin with, *credibility* is an important characteristic. To have credibility, a communicator must be perceived as an expert who can be trusted to tell the truth. Experts—for example, dentists recommending a brand of toothpaste—have a remarkably disarming effect on us. We assume they are knowledgeable, so when they speak, we listen. To engender trust, a source must also be willing to state a position honestly and without compromise. If a communicator has been bought and paid for, has an ax to grind, or has something else to gain, then he or she will not be persuasive.

More than anything else, Magic Johnson's impact as an AIDS spokesman is based not on his credibility but on his *likability*—his personal charm, his winning smile. As Dale Carnegie (1936) implied in the title of his classic, *How to Win Friends and Influence People*, being liked and being persuasive go hand in hand. Hence the speaker who is similar to us or physically attractive has a unique advantage. In one study, Diane Mackie and her colleagues (1990) found that college students were more influenced by a speech on the use of the SATs when the speaker was said to be from their own university than from another school. In another study, Shelly Chaiken (1979) had male and female experimenters try to get students to sign a petition, and found that the more attractive the experimenters were, the more signatures they collected. It is no wonder that advertisers spend millions of dollars a year on celebrity endorsements from Nancy Kerrigan, Michael Jordan, Jamie Lee Curtis, Shaquille O'Neal, and other popular stars.

Does the source hold the key to success? Are we so impressed by experts and so drawn to beautiful models that we uncritically embrace whatever they have to say? In light of what we know about the central and peripheral routes to persuasion, the answer is, it depends. When a target's involvement is low, superficial source characteristics make a difference. Under high involvement, however, a lack of substance cannot be masked by style (Chaiken, 1980; Petty et al., 1981).

The Message   How can a message be constructed for maximum impact? Should it be crammed with facts or short and to the point? Does it help to ask rhetorical questions? What about the length of a message, one-sided versus two-sided arguments, and visual versus auditory media? After many years of research, it is now clear that there are no simple answers, no specific formulas. To illustrate, let us consider two strategic questions that confront all communicators.

First, how extreme a position should be taken? Before making an appeal, the astute communicator recognizes that members of the audience are not blank slates but human beings endowed with pre-existing attitudes and values. Knowing this, how discrepant a position should one advocate from that of an audience? Is it better to stake out an extreme position in the hope of stimulating the most change, or to preach moderation in order to avoid being rejected outright? There are two answers to this question: (1) It is important to ensure that one's arguments are based on premises that are acceptable to an audience (Holtgraves & Bailey, 1991), and (2) communicators should take a position that is moderately discrepant from that of the audience. The more discrepant the message, the greater the change. But there is a breaking point, beyond which too much discrepancy produces less change (Bochner & Insko, 1966).

A second common question concerns the arousal of emotion. Is it better to recite only facts and rational arguments, or to stir up primitive emotions? This issue is often raised in discussions of the persuasive effects of fear, a common device. Research shows that fear can motivate change (see box p. 494).

Interestingly, so do positive emotions. Food, drinks, soft lights, tender memories, funny movies, and a scenic landscape can lull us into a positive emotional state—ripe for persuasion. There are two reasons for this phenomenon. First, when people are in a good mood, they want to savor the moment and prolong the rosy glow, not ruin it by concentrating on new information (Isen, 1987). Second, a good mood can be distracting, causing the mind to wander and making it more difficult to think critically about a persuasive message (Mackie & Worth, 1989). Lacking both the motivation and the ability to scrutinize a communication, people who are in a positive emotional state are often easy to persuade through the use of superficial cues (Schwarz et al., 1991).

The Audience   Source and message factors are important, but no persuasion strategy is complete without a consideration of the audience. Presentations that work on some people may fail with others. Are some individuals easier to persuade than others? No, not as a general rule. It used to be assumed, for example, that the more intelligent the target, the more difficult it is to change his or her attitude. But William McGuire (1968) found that intelligence is unrelated to persuasion. The reason, according to McGuire, is that persuasion requires that a message first be learned, and then accepted. Smart people are quick to grasp the message, but they are also likely to be critical of it; less intelligent people are prone to accept the message, but they do not always understand it. The net result: Neither group is necessarily more vulnerable to persuasion than the other, a prediction supported by a good deal of research (Rhodes & Wood, 1992).

Conceding that individuals are not consistently easy or hard to persuade, researchers now try to "match" the type of message to its intended audience. For example, some people are more likely than others to take the central route to persuasion—and, therefore, to be focused on content. According to Cacioppo and Petty (1982), individuals differ in terms of how much they enjoy effortful cognitive activities or, as they call it, the *need for cognition*. Those with a high need for cognition are influenced by strong, information-oriented messages; people who are low in the need for cognition are swayed by a speaker's reputation, the applause of an audience, and other peripheral cues (Axsom et al., 1987; Cacioppo & Petty, 1982).

According to Mark Snyder (1987), people who are highly concerned about their public image exhibit *self-monitoring:* a tendency to modify their behavior from one social situation to the next. As measured by the Self-Monitoring Scale (Snyder & Gangestad, 1986), high self-monitors tend to say that "I would probably make a good actor," and that "in different situations and with different people, I often act like different persons." As targets of influence, high self-monitors are thus drawn to messages that promise a desirable social image. In one study, subjects read information-oriented or image-oriented magazine advertisements. In an ad for Irish Mocha Mint Coffee, for example, a man and woman were shown relaxing

SOCIAL PSYCHOLOGY   Health

Promoting Health Through the Arousal of Fear

Before the twentieth century, the principal causes of death were infectious diseases such as polio, smallpox, tuberculosis, and pneumonia. In the United States, none of these illnesses is now a leading killer. Instead, Americans are most likely to die from heart disease, cancer, strokes, and accidents (AIDS is eleventh on the list)—problems that can often be prevented by changes in attitudes and behavior. For social psychologists, then, the challenge is to find ways to promote public health through mass persuasive communication.

Turn on the TV or open a magazine, and you're sure to find a public service announcement designed to convince people to drive safely, fasten seat belts, exercise, use condoms when having sex, or stop smoking, drinking, taking drugs, and eating fatty foods. Are such messages effective? How should public health campaigns be designed so as to modify unhealthy behaviors?

According to Ronald Rogers (1983), a persuasive message must achieve two goals to be effective. First, it has to convince people that a genuine threat exists—and that they, personally, are at risk. This may seem like a simple objective, but in fact people tend to harbor *illusions of invulnerability,* which lead them to underestimate the risks to their own health and safety. Surveys consistently reveal that people see themselves as less likely than peers to experience a heart attack, cancer, tooth decay, obesity, alcohol dependence, a migraine headache, a sexually transmitted disease, an unwanted pregnancy, an automobile accident, and other negative events (Weinstein, 1982; Quadrel et al., 1993). As Magic Johnson (1991) admitted shortly after his AIDS disclosure, "To me, AIDS was someone else's disease" (p. 19). A second goal is to convince people that certain healthful behaviors can be used to overcome the threat—and that they have the ability to carry out these behaviors. Regardless of whether they are trying to quit smoking, curb drinking, lose weight, or lower their cholesterol level, self-confidence is a key for success.

Over the years, persuasion researchers have found that fear motivates change. Many religious cults use scare tactics to indoctrinate new members. So do public heath organizations that vividly portray the victims of cigarette smoking, drugs, reckless driving, and unsafe sex. Magazine ads for condoms often use fear appeals—the most extreme being "I enjoy sex

in a candlelit room over a cup of coffee. The image-oriented ad promised to "Make a chilly night become a cozy evening;" the informational ad read, "A delicious blend of three great flavors." As predicted, high self-monitors said they would pay more for products that were presented through image-oriented than informational ads (Snyder & DeBono, 1985). To be most persuasive, a message should meet the psychological needs of its audience.

Self-Persuasion

Anyone who has ever acted on stage knows how easy it is to become so absorbed in a role that the experience seems real. Forced laughter can make an actor feel happy, and fake tears can turn to sadness. Even in real life, the effect can be dramatic. In 1974, Patty Hearst—a sheltered young college student from a wealthy family—was kidnapped by a revolutionary group. By the time she was arrested months later, she carried a gun and called herself Tania. How could someone be so totally converted? In Hearst's own words, "I had thought I was humoring [my captors] by parroting their cliches and buzzwords without believing in them. . . . In trying to convince them I convinced myself."

The Patty Hearst case illustrates the powerful effects of role playing. Of

but I don't want to die for it" (Struckman-Johnson et al., 1990). Similarly, ads tell us that smoking "is a matter of life and breath" and that "this [a fried egg] is your brain on drugs." Even commercial advertisers try to scare us into buying their products. After all, who wants to get caught with bad breath, dandruff, body odor, or a ring around the collar?

Does fear persuade, and, if so, is it better to arouse just a little nervousness or a full-blown anxiety attack? To answer this question, researchers have measured the amount of attitude change produced by messages varying in fearfulness. Their results suggest that high-fear messages produce more change than low-fear messages—but only when they also provide reassurance and instructions on how to avoid the threatened danger (Gleicher & Petty, 1992; Leventhal, 1970). Without guidance on how to cope, people panic and tune out. In one study, for example, subjects who had a chronic fear of cancer were less likely than others to detect logical errors in a message that advocated regular checkups (Jepson & Chaiken, 1990). But when clear instructions are included, fear arousal is effective. Antismoking films elicit more negative attitudes about cigarettes when they show gory scenes of lung-cancer patients rather than charts filled with dry statistics (Leventhal et al., 1967). Similarly, driving-safety films are more effective when they show bloody accident victims instead of controlled collisions using dummies as passengers (Rogers & Mewborn, 1976).

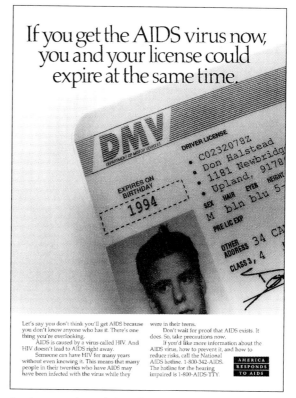

Fear is a persuasion technique that is frequently used.

course, you don't have to be terrorized to be coaxed into behavior that contradicts your inner convictions. People often engage in attitude-discrepant behavior—as part of a job, for example, or to please others. This raises a profound question: What happens when people behave in ways that do not follow from their attitudes? We know that attitudes influence behavior. Can the causal arrow be reversed? That is, can a forced change in behavior spark a change in attitude?

Cognitive Dissonance Theory   The answer to this question was provided by Leon Festinger's (1957) provocative theory of **cognitive dissonance**. According to Festinger, we hold many cognitions about ourselves and the world around us—and sometimes these cognitions clash. For example, you say you're on a diet, and yet you just dove head first into a chocolate mousse. Or you waited on line for hours to get into a concert, but then the band was disappointing. Or you baked your body under the hot summer sun, even though you knew of the health risks. In each case, there is inconsistency and conflict. You already committed yourself to a course of action, but you realize that your behavior contradicts your attitude.

According to Festinger, these kinds of discrepancies often produce an unpleasant state of tension that he called cognitive dissonance. Attitude-discrepant behavior doesn't **always** arouse dissonance. If you broke a diet

■ **cognitive dissonance** An unpleasant psychological state often aroused when people behave in ways that are discrepant with their attitudes.

for a holiday dinner, or if you thought that the mousse you ate was low in calories, you would be relatively free of tension. Attitude-discrepant behavior that is performed *freely* and with *knowledge* of the consequences, however, does arouse dissonance—and the motivation to reduce it. There are different ways to cope with this unpleasant state. Often the easiest is to change your attitude so that it becomes consistent with your behavior.

To understand dissonance theory, imagine for a moment that you are a subject in the classic study by Leon Festinger and J. Merrill Carlsmith (1959). Upon arrival, you are greeted by an experimenter who says that he is interested in various measures of performance. He hands you a wooden board containing forty-eight pegs in square holes and asks you to turn each peg to the left, then to the right, then back to the left, and again to the right. The routine seems endless. After thirty minutes, the experimenter comes to your rescue. Or does he? Just when you think things are looking up, he hands you another board, another assignment. For the next half-hour, you are to take twelve spools of thread off the board, put them back on, take them off, and put them back on again. By now, you're just about ready to tear your hair out. As you think back over better times, even the first task begins to look good.

Finally, you're done. After one of the longest hours of your life, the experimenter lets you in on a secret: there's more to this experiment than meets the eye. You were in the control group. To test the effects of motivation on performance, the experimenter will tell other subjects that the experiment is fun. You don't realize it, but you're being set up for a critical part of the study. Would you tell the next subject that the experiment is enjoyable? As you hem and haw, the experimenter offers to pay for your service. Some subjects, like you, are offered one dollar; others, twenty dollars. Before you know it, you're in the waiting room trying to dupe an unsuspecting fellow student.

By means of this staged presentation, subjects were goaded into an attitude-discrepant behavior, an act that contradicted their private attitudes. They knew the experiment was dull, but they raved anyway. Was cognitive dissonance aroused? It depended on how much subjects were paid. Suppose you were one of the lucky ones offered twenty dollars. By today's standards, that amount would be worth over eighty dollars—certainly a sufficient justification for telling a little white lie. Being well compensated, these subjects did not experience dissonance. But wait. Suppose you were offered only one dollar. Surely your integrity is worth more than that, don't you think? In this case, you do not have sufficient justification for going along. Thus, you cope by changing your view of the task. If you can convince yourself that the experiment was interesting, then there is no conflict.

When the experiment was presumably over, subjects were asked to rate the peg-board tasks. Control group subjects, who did not mislead a confederate, admitted the tasks were boring. So did those in the twenty dollar condition who had ample justification for what they did. Those paid only one dollar, however, rated the tasks as more enjoyable. After engaging in an attitude-discrepant behavior without sufficient justification, these subjects felt internally pressured to change their attitudes in order to reduce cognitive dissonance (see Figure 13.6).

Cognitive dissonance theory makes another interesting prediction: that people will change their attitudes to justify their effort, money spent, time,

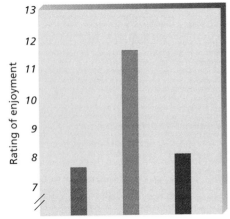

■ Control group
■ Group paid $1
■ Group paid $20

Figure 13.6

Festinger and Carlsmith's Classic Dissonance Study

How interesting is a boring task? Compared to subjects who did not have to lie and those paid $20 to do so, subjects paid only $1 later rated the task as more enjoyable. Having engaged in an attitude-discrepant behavior, the latter subjects reduced dissonance by changing their attitude.

According to cognitive dissonance theory, we are motivated to justify our efforts. This could help to explain why sororities, fraternities, and other groups that are hard to join often foster such lifelong loyalties.

or suffering. In the first test of this hypothesis, Eliot Aronson and Judson Mills (1959) invited female students to join a discussion group about sex. To get admitted into the group, subjects were told they would have to pass an "embarrassment test." One set of subjects underwent a severe test (they had to recite obscene words and lurid passages), a second set took a mild test (they read a list of mildly sexual words), and a third set was admitted without an initiation. Subjects then listened in on a dreadfully boring discussion. How attractive was this discussion group? As predicted, those who had to endure a severe initiation liked the group more than the others did. There are some interesting implications. Research shows, for example, that the harder psychotherapy patients work at their own treatment, the better they say they feel later (Axsom, 1989). Cognitive dissonance theory may also explain why college fraternities and sororities foster such lifelong loyalties, or why 58 percent of Vietnam veterans, compared to 29 percent of others, say that "the U.S. was right to get involved in the Vietnam war" (Witteman, 1990). Perhaps even today, those who had risked their lives feel a need to justify the nightmare they had experienced in that war.

"New Looks" at Cognitive Dissonance Following in Festinger's footsteps, a generation of social psychologists have refined the basic theory. Nobody disputes the fact that when people are coaxed into performing an attitude-discrepant behavior, they often go on to change their attitudes. But under what conditions, and why? According to Joel Cooper and Russell Fazio (1984), four conditions are necessary for this change to occur: (1) the behavior has *negative consequences*; (2) the person feels *responsible* for these consequences; (3) the person becomes *physiologically aroused*, experiencing a tension that needs to be reduced; and (4) the person *attributes* that arousal to his or her behavior.

The "why" question is still a matter of controversy. Some theorists argue that the change in attitude is not fueled by the need to justify our actions, but instead occurs as a rational process through which people draw conclusions about their attitudes by observing their own behavior. In other words, subjects in the Festinger and Carlsmith study who lied about the boring task for a dollar reflected upon their actions and concluded that the task "must have been" interesting—or else why would they have said so (Bem, 1967)? Other theorists claim that the predominant motive is not to be consistent but to *appear* consistent, or favorable, to others. According to this view, Festinger and Carlsmith's subjects simply did not want the experimenter to think they had sold out for a paltry sum of money (Tedeschi et al., 1971). Still others claim that the change in attitude is necessary for one's self-concept. According to this view, Festinger and Carlsmith's subjects had to view the task as enjoyable in order to repair the damage done to their self-esteem (Steele, 1988; Thibodeau & Aronson, 1992).

GROUP PROCESSES

When individuals assemble in groups, profound changes take place. The beating of Rodney King by four police officers is one example. So are the Los Angeles riots that broke out when the officers were initially acquitted, the random violence and vandalism of street gangs, avid sports fans who

SOCIAL PSYCHOLOGY   Environment

Population Density, Architecture, and Social Behavior

While social psychologists focus on the influences of other people on our behavior, environmental psychologists study the impact of physical settings. One of the most consistent findings in this area is that crowding often triggers antisocial behavior. From overpopulated cities to tightly packed neighborhoods, office buildings, subway cars, dormitories, classrooms, playgrounds, and prisons, this aspect of the physical environment influences our social interactions.

Researchers have found it useful to distinguish between density and crowding (Stokols, 1972). *Density* is an objective and quantifiable measure of the number of persons per unit space—and can be defined by square footage, number of housing units per acre, number of rooms per building, and so on. In contrast, *crowding* is a psychological state that arises when one feels that there are too many people in a given space. This distinction helps to explain why high density can be experienced either as enjoyable (as in a basketball arena packed with thousands of hometown fans) or as aversive (as in a jam-packed shopping mall during the week before Christmas). Apparently, feeling crowded is based not only on physi-cal characteristics of the environment, but on various personal, cultural, and architectural factors as well.

Many years ago, animal researchers found that high-density laboratory environments increased aggression among monkeys, rats, cats, hermit crabs, hogs, chickens, gerbils, fruit flies, and other species. For example, John Calhoun (1962) built different "rat universes," varied the population, and found that, despite an ample supply of food and water, the high-density conditions increased hyperactivity, aggression, cannibalism, withdrawal, and illness. Research with humans also shows the effects of high-density living. In dormitories, college students who were assigned three to a room rather than the usual two felt more crowded, disliked their roommates more, were less satisfied with the living conditions, felt a lack of control, and had lower grades (Baron et al., 1976; Gormley & Aiello, 1982). In off-campus housing, students who live in crowded apartments are less likely to seek or offer social support to housemates, or even to a stranger in need of support in an unrelated setting—a symptom of social withdrawal (Evans & Lepore, 1993). In prisons, studies reveal that as the number of inmates in a given facility increases, so

scream at the top of their lungs to celebrate victory, high-powered business groups that make unusually risky decisions, and bloodthirsty lynch mobs seeking revenge. It's as if the group casts a spell over the individual.

Social Facilitation

First things first. How does the mere presence of others affect our behavior? Appropriately, this most basic question in social psychology was also the first to be tested. In 1898, Norman Triplett studied bicycle racing records, and discovered that cyclists were faster when they competed alongside others than when they biked alone against the clock. Intrigued by this finding, Triplett asked forty children to wind a fishing reel—sometimes alone, other times in pairs. Again, performance was faster among those who worked together than alone. Triplett's conclusion: The presence of others triggers "nervous energy," thereby enhancing performance.

■ **social facilitation** The tendency for the presence of others to enhance performance on simple tasks and impair performance on complex tasks.

Subsequently, many researchers confirmed that the presence of others speeds up performance on various cognitive and motor tasks (even ants excavate more, and chickens eat more, in the company of other members of their species). At the same time, however, other researchers were observing performance declines. Why did the presence of others have such different

Overcrowding can cause residents to lash out or withdraw. At the University of Cincinnati, Sander Hall—a twenty-six-story dorm that housed 1,300 students—was so beset by violence and vandalism that in 1991, the university literally blew the building up.

do levels of stress, violence, discipline problems, and deaths (Paulus, 1988).

High-density living may be overstimulating, arousing, and invasive of one's privacy and control, but the aversiveness of the experience can also be influenced by architectural design. In an illustrative study (further discussed in Chapter 18), Andrew Baum and Stewart Valins (1979) found that first-year college students living in corridor-style dormitories—compared to those residing in dorms that were divided into suites—complained more about crowding and a lack of privacy, sought to avoid others inside and outside the dorm, and had fewer friends among floormates. The two types of residences had the same amount of space per person, the same number of residents per floor, and comparable furnishings. Yet due to the spatial layout, the students living in the corridor-style dorms had to share more space (including bathrooms), found it harder to control their social contacts, and were under more stress. Various aspects of architectural design and décor can be used to offset the adverse effects of density. For example, roommates feel less crowded in rooms where the floor space has been opened up with bunk beds. Rooms also feel larger when they are rectangular in shape rather than square, when walls are straight-edged rather than curved, and when there are windows, sunlight, light-colored walls, and high ceilings (McAndrew, 1993).

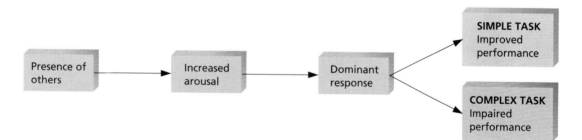

Figure 13.7

Social Facilitation

As proposed by Zajonc, the presence of others increases arousal, which strengthens the "dominant" response. The result: The presence of others improves performance on simple tasks but impairs performance on tasks that are complex.

effects on task performance? In 1965, Robert Zajonc solved the problem. The key, he noted, is to realize that (1) the presence of others increases arousal, and (2) arousal enhances the "dominant" response—that is, whatever response is most likely to occur. When a task is easy, the dominant response is a correct one; when a task is difficult, it is incorrect. The presence of other people thus improves performance on simple tasks but has a negative effect on tasks that are complex. To demonstrate, Zajonc found that subjects who tried to memorize simple word associations (*mother-father*) performed better in the presence of others than alone, but that those who tried to learn difficult associations (*mother-algebra*) did worse. This phenomenon is known as **social facilitation** (see Figure 13.7).

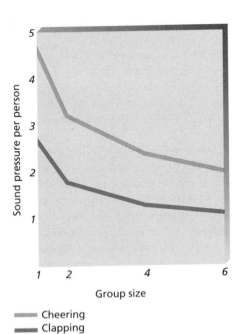

Group size

- ▬▬▬ Cheering
- ▬▬▬ Clapping

Figure 13.8

Social Loafing

Subjects were told to clap or cheer "as loud as you can"—either alone or in groups of two, four, or six. The more others there were, the less effort was exerted by each individual subject (Latané et al., 1979).

When contributions to a joint task are pooled, as on a rowing team, individual members may "loaf," exerting less effort than they would if performing alone.

Is the mere presence of other actors or observers sufficient to produce social facilitation, as Zajonc suggested? Some social psychologists argue that we are aroused by others only when they are in a position to *evaluate* our performance. Others claim that we are aroused only when others drive us to *distraction*. Whatever the cause of the arousal, one fact is clear: in the company of other people, we perform better on tasks we're good at but worse on those we find difficult (Guerin, 1986).

Social Loafing

Social facilitation effects are found for *individual* tasks such as running a race, solving a problem, or memorizing a list of words. In these types of activities, one's own performance is easy to identify. But what about cooperative *joint* activities for which individual contributions are pooled? In a tug-of-war, say, does each person exert more effort when they compete as part of a team or alone?

To find out, Alan Ingham and his colleagues (1974) asked blindfolded subjects to pull on a rope "as hard as you can," and found that subjects pulled 18 percent harder when they knew they were alone than when they thought that three other subjects were pulling with them. In another study, Bibb Latané and his associates (1979) asked subjects to clap or cheer "as loud as you can"—either alone or in groups of two, four, or six. The result: As individuals, subjects produced less noise when they thought they were part of a group than when they thought they were alone.

The Latané team (1979) coined the term **social loafing** to describe this group-produced reduction in individual effort. As illustrated in Figure 13.8, social loafing increases with group size: the more others there are, the less effort each subject exerts. In the clapping and cheering study, for example, two-person groups performed at only 71 percent of their individual capacity, four-person groups at 51 percent, and six-person groups at 40 percent.

Why do people slack off when others are there to pick up the slack? There are several reasons. One is that people see their own contribution as unessential to the group's success. A second is that people are less concerned about being personally evaluated—in part because individual performance standards within a group are unclear. A third possibility is that people slack off in order to guard against looking like the "sucker" who works harder than everyone else. Putting the pieces together, researchers have concluded that social loafing occurs because individuals often do not perceive the link between their own effort and the desired outcome (Karau & Williams, 1993; Sheppard, 1993).

Social loafing threatens work groups throughout Western society and, to a lesser extent, in Eastern cultures as well (Gabrenya et al., 1983). But it is not inevitable. For example, research shows that people are less likely to take a "free ride" when they are led to believe that their individual performance can be separated from the group's, when their own effort is needed for the group to succeed, when success will be amply rewarded, when the task is personally meaningful, or when the group consists of friends rather than strangers (Brickner et al., 1986; Karau & Williams, 1993; Williams et al., 1981).

Group Polarization

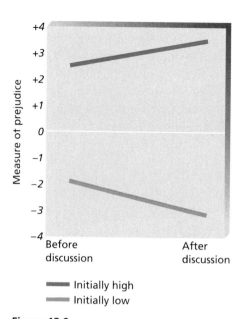

Figure 13.9

Group Polarization

Following discussions among like-minded subjects, prejudice increased among those who were initially high in prejudice, and decreased for those who were low. This finding shows that discussion intensifies prevailing attitudes in the group.

If you've ever watched political conventions on TV, you may have noticed that the Democrats often sound more liberal and the Republicans more conservative when they meet in their own groups than on an individual basis. Why? What happens to the members of each party who hold moderate views? Common sense suggests that when you put people together, their differences of opinion will result in a compromise, as everyone moves toward the group center. But that isn't what happens. Instead, individuals who start with roughly similar views become more extreme after group discussion. Put a group of moderate liberals together and they become more liberal; put a group of moderate conservatives together and they become ultra-conservative.

The tendency for social interaction to intensify initial opinions is called **group polarization** (Moscovici & Zavalloni, 1969; Myers & Lamm, 1976). For example, David Myers and George Bishop (1970) created like-minded groups of high school students—based on whether they scored high or low on a pre-measure of racial prejudice—for a discussion of racially charged issues. Afterward, in a post-discussion measure of prejudice, those in the low-prejudice groups scored even *lower*, while those in the high-prejudice groups scored even *higher*, (see Figure 13.9).

There are two reasons why opinions are polarized by group discussion (Isenberg, 1986). First, when group members lean in a particular direction—conservative or liberal, prejudiced or nonprejudiced—most arguments that are aired reinforce this initial view. Second, as group members reveal their positions, perhaps by taking a straw poll, a social norm is established. Motivated to cast themselves in a favorable light, group members make it a point to show extra-strong support for this norm. If believing X is considered good, then arguing for Triple X is even better.

Groupthink

In 1961, President Kennedy and his top advisers set into motion a half-baked plan to attack the Bay of Pigs in Cuba with 1,400 CIA-trained Cuban exiles. The invasion resulted in a quick and humiliating defeat, leaving Kennedy to wonder how such poor judgement could have come about. Curious to know the answer, Irving Janis (1972, 1989) studied the decision-making procedures leading up to the Bay of Pigs fiasco, along with other miscalculations (such as the escalation of the Vietnam war, the Watergate coverup, and NASA's tragic decision to launch the Challenger space shuttle). What happened in the groups that made these blundering decisions? Was the process rational or irrational?

According to Janis, decision-making groups in politics, business, education, and other settings often fall prey to **groupthink**—a concurrence-seeking process in which the members convince themselves that their policies are correct. Insulated, tightly knit groups that value harmony and have a strong leader are most vulnerable to this conspiracy of silence. Groupthink seems to operate at two levels. In some cases, members suppress personal doubts on their own, often without realizing they are doing so; in other cases, they are openly and actively pressured into submission by a

■ **social loafing** The tendency for people to exert less effort in group tasks for which individual contributions are pooled.

■ **group polarization** The tendency for discussion to enhance or "polarize" a group's initial position.

■ **groupthink** A group decision-making style by which group members convince themselves that they are correct.

"This might not be ethical. Is that a problem for anybody?"

In insulated decision-making groups, members often fail to challenge existing policies.
[Drawing by Vietor; © 1987 The New Yorker Magazine, Inc.]

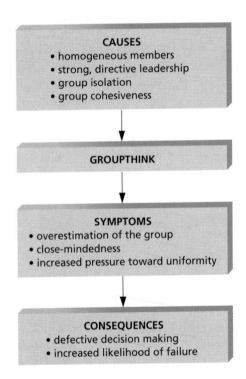

CAUSES
- homogeneous members
- strong, directive leadership
- group isolation
- group cohesiveness

GROUPTHINK

SYMPTOMS
- overestimation of the group
- close-mindedness
- increased pressure toward uniformity

CONSEQUENCES
- defective decision making
- increased likelihood of failure

Figure 13.10

Groupthink

majority intolerant of dissent (McCauley, 1989). Some researchers disagree with Janis about the specific conditions that put decision-making groups "at risk" (Aldag & Fuller, 1993; Tetlock et al., 1992). In a recent laboratory experiment, however, Marlene Turner and her colleagues (1992) assembled small problem-solving groups and found that when the groups were cohesive (the members wore name tags and thought about their similarities) and when they were under pressure (they feared the consequences of faulty decision making), they came up with lower-quality solutions.

The behavioral symptoms of groupthink are manifested in three ways. First, the group tends to overestimate its own capacity. Group members harbor an illusion of invulnerability, an illusion of unanimity, and an exaggerated belief in the morality of their views. Second, group members become close-minded. They rationalize their own actions, often by stereotyping the targets of these actions. And third, there is tremendous pressure toward uniformity. In the interests of group unity, members censor their own thoughts and act as "mindguards" to prevent all expressions of dissent. By inviting the pathological decision making outlined in Figure 13.10, groupthink raises the odds of miscalculation and failure.

Can groups inoculate themselves against this problem? After the Bay of Pigs fiasco, President Kennedy took active steps to make his decision-making process more constructive. Based on the safeguards Kennedy later adopted, Janis (1989) offered the following advice: (1) to avoid isolation, experts should be brought in and members should consult with impartial outsiders; (2) to reduce conformity pressures, the leader should not take a strong public stand early in the group discussion; and (3) to establish a norm of critical review, subgroups should be formed to separately discuss the same issue, a member should be assigned to play devil's advocate, and a "second-chance" meeting should be held to reconsider the preliminary decision.

AGGRESSION

In August 1989, six teenagers roamed through New York City's Central Park looking for trouble. Like a pack of wolves hunting for prey, they beat two men senseless. Then they attacked a twenty-eight-year-old female jogger with a metal pipe, gang-raped her, cracked her skull with a brick, and left her for dead. Three years later, in February 1992, a Milwaukee jury heard graphic evidence of fifteen grisly murders. Jeffrey Dahmer had lured young men into his home, drugged them, drilled holes in their heads, had sex with the corpses, and ate parts of the bodies. After the trial, traumatized jurors were given psychological counseling. In the fall of 1993, Lorena Bobbitt cut off her sleeping husband's penis. Then, just weeks before the 1994 Olympics, figure skater Nancy Kerrigan was clubbed in the knee. The list of violent stories seems endless.

In some ways, these acts of violence were so deviant and so grotesque that they shed little light on "normal" human nature. In other ways, however, these events serve to remind us that aggression—behavior that is intended to inflict harm—is a common and contagious social disease. Every

In June of 1994, football hall-of-famer O.J. Simpson was charged with the murders of his ex-wife, Nicole Brown Simpson, and her friend Ronald Goldman. Soon after the news broke, it was revealed that Simpson had assaulted Nicole before and that she had feared for her life. Even among the rich and famous, domestic violence and other forms of aggression are a persistent problem.

day, people all over the world are victims of wars between nations, conflicts between ethnic and religious groups, terrorist bombings, racism, street gangs, drug dealers, organized crime, sexual assaults, domestic violence, police brutality, and suicide. Aggression is so prevalent that psychologists have desperately tried to pinpoint the origins of this troubling behavior. Some argue that aggression is programmed into human nature by instincts, genes, hormones, and other biological factors. Others emphasize the role of culture, social learning, and environmental stressors. As always, human behavior is not the product of either nature or nurture, but the interaction of both (Berkowitz, 1993).

Biological Roots

On November 11, 1918, World War I ended. Shell-shocked, covered in mud, and lungs blasted by gas, millions of soldiers had died on the battlefields of Europe. What sinister forces of human nature could possibly explain the bloodshed? For Sigmund Freud (1920), who had earlier proposed that people were motivated by powerful life instincts, the war suggested that human beings are also driven by a self-destructive "death instinct." In the conflict between these opposing forces, said Freud, the death instinct is redirected—from oneself to others.

Based on his observations of animal behavior, Konrad Lorenz (1966) also viewed aggression as an inborn and adaptive instinct. According to Lorenz, successful aggressors gain access to food, water, and desirable mates. Hence natural selection favors the evolution of an aggressive instinct. Are wars, crimes, and other acts of violence inevitable, then? Not necessarily. Both Freud and Lorenz argued that instinctual aggressive impulses can be channeled into hunting, contact sports, intellectual debates, and other socially acceptable outlets.

Instinct theories—which are based on the assumption that aggression is unlearned and characteristic of the whole species—have little influence today. One problem is that there are vast differences in aggression between cultures that cannot be explained by instinct alone. The Arapesh of New Guinea live peacefully, for example, while the Yanomamo of the Amazon jungle are ferocious tribal warriors. A second problem is that instinct-based explanations are logically circular: people are aggressive because of an instinct—which we know exists because people are aggressive.

Whether or not human aggression is fixed by instincts, it is subject to biological influences. Twin and adoption studies suggest that there is a genetic component (DiLalla & Gottesman, 1991). In one study, for example, identical twins were more likely than fraternal twins to give the same response when asked if they have a violent temper (Rushton et al., 1986). There are also consistent sex differences: compared to women, men report engaging in more physical aggression (Buss & Perry, 1992), behave more aggressively in the laboratory (Eagly & Steffen, 1986), and commit more violent crimes (Federal Bureau of Investigation, 1987). Why? One possibility is that aggression is linked to the male sex hormone testosterone. In rats and other animals, testosterone injections increase levels of aggression, while castration—which lowers testosterone—has the opposite effect

(Svare, 1983). In humans, correlational research shows that violent criminals have naturally higher levels of testosterone than those convicted of nonviolent crimes (Dabbs et al., 1987).

Finally, there is strong evidence to implicate alcohol in the commission of homicides, stabbings, child abuse, and other criminal acts of violence. In laboratory experiments as well, alcohol has this effect (Bushman & Cooper, 1990). In one study, for example, subjects delivered more painful shocks, supposedly to another person, after drinking beverages spiked with 100-proof vodka or bourbon than after consuming nonalcoholic beverages (Taylor & Leonard, 1983). Why does alcohol unleash aggression? According to Claude Steele and Robert Josephs (1990), people self-disclose more, gamble more, take more risks, and behave more aggressively when they're drunk than sober. The reason, they say, is that alcohol leads us to become short-sighted about the consequences of our actions—thus evoking a state of "drunken excess."

Social Influences

Aggression has biological roots, but it is also learned from experience and then triggered by factors within the environment. What kinds of events unleash our aggressive impulses? And how can social influences be used to promote peace and nonviolence?

Aversive Stimulation   Put two rats in a cage together, subject them to painful shocks, loud noise, or intense heat, and a fight is likely to break out. Put people in unpleasant conditions—perhaps an overcrowded ghetto, a noisy construction site, a room full of cigarette smoke, or the company of an obnoxious co-worker—and they too may lash out (see box, p. 498). As a general rule, aversive stimulation sparks aggression (Berkowitz, 1983).

One type of aversive event that we all experience at times is frustration. In 1939, John Dollard and his associates proposed the hypothesis that frustration leads to aggression—either against the source of frustration or against an innocent but vulnerable substitute, or "scapegoat." Testing the implications of this **frustration-aggression hypothesis**, Carl Hovland and Robert Sears (1940) examined the link between economic hard times and racial violence. As noted in Chapter 12, they analyzed the records from fourteen southern states during the years 1882 to 1930 and discovered a strong negative correlation between the value of cotton and lynchings: as the price of cotton fell, the number of lynchings increased. The same relationship has been verified in more recent analyses (Beck & Tolnay, 1990; Hepworth & West, 1988). Although this correlation cannot be interpreted in causal terms, experiments have confirmed that frustration sparks aggression in many contexts, by arousing anger, fear, and other negative emotions (Berkowitz, 1989).

The high temperatures of a "long, hot summer" also spark acts of violence. Based on worldwide weather records and crime statistics, correlational analyses reveal a strong link between heat and aggression. More violent crimes occur in the summer than in the winter, during hot years than in cooler years, and in hot cities than in cooler cities. As you can see in Figure 13.11, the numbers of political uprisings, riots, homicides, assaults, rapes,

■ **frustration-aggression hypothesis** The theory that frustration causes aggression.

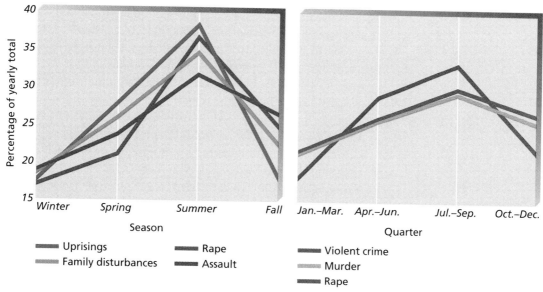

Figure 13.11

The Link Between Heat and Violence

Worldwide weather records and crime statistics reveal that more violent crimes are committed during the summer than in the other seasons (Anderson, 1989).

Research suggests that the sight of a weapon can trigger aggression in people who are predisposed.

and reports of family violence all peak in the months of June, July, and August (Anderson, 1989). Indirect acts of aggression also increase in excessive heat. As temperatures rise above 90° F, laboratory subjects become more likely to interpret ambiguous events in a hostile manner (Rule et al., 1987), drivers in cars without air-conditioning are more likely to honk their horns at another motorist (Kenrick & MacFarlane, 1984), and major-league baseball pitchers are more likely to hit a batter with a pitch (Reifman et al., 1991). When people are "hot under the collar," tempers flare.

Situational Cues   Frustration, heat, and other aversive events predispose us to aggression by arousing negative affect. Once we are in this state of readiness, the presence of stimuli associated with aggression may then prompt us to act on this predisposition. Aversive events "load the gun," but situational cues get us to "pull the trigger." What situational cues have this effect?

Weapons   The sights and sounds of violence are everywhere. In the United States, millions of adults own handguns. Daily TV news reports flood us with images of war, terrorism, and weapons of mass destruction. Does any of this matter? Yes. According to Leonard Berkowitz, the mere sight of an aggressive stimulus influences behavior. In a classic demonstration of this point, Berkowitz and Anthony LePage (1967) had male subjects administer electric shocks to a confederate—who had insulted half the subjects right before the session. In one condition, only the shock-generating apparatus was present in the lab. In a second condition, a .38-caliber pistol and a 12-gauge shotgun were on the table near the shock button—supposedly left over from a previous experiment. As measured by the number of shocks given, aggression was increased by the sight of the weapons. Specifically, subjects who were angered, and primed for aggression, retaliated more in the presence of the weapons than in their absence.

This provocative "weapons effect" has been replicated in some experiments but not in others. By statistically combining all the research, Michael Carlson and his colleagues (1990) concluded that the presence of weapons does increase aggression—except among subjects who figure out the true purpose of the experiment (when subjects figure out that the guns are intended to heighten their aggression, they bend over backward to present themselves in the opposite manner). Do guns kill, or are people the problem? As Berkowitz himself put it, "The finger pulls the trigger, but the trigger may also be pulling the finger."

Media Violence   As if reality did not provide enough of a stimulus, the entertainment industry adds fuel to the fire. In an eighteen-hour sampling of television shows, *TV Guide* researchers taped the programs on ten major channels and counted a total of 1,846 acts of violence—including 175 killings, 389 assaults, 588 scenes depicting gunplay or menacing threats with a weapon, and 673 physical acts such as punching, pushing, and dragging. Among the culprits were news shows, movies, TV dramas, rock music videos, and toy commercials. The most violent programs of all are children's cartoons, in which heroes, villains, and Ninja Turtles fight an average of 26 battles an hour (Hickey, 1992).

Does exposure to TV violence promote aggression? Literally hundreds of studies have addressed this important question, often with alarming results. Correlational studies reveal that there is a link between the amount of TV violence watched by young boys and their subsequent level of aggression—a link commonly observed in the United States and Europe (Huesmann & Eron, 1986). In a longitudinal development study, for example, Leonard Eron (1987) found that a boy's exposure to TV violence at eight years old predicted criminal activity twenty-two years later. Critics are quick to point out that these correlations cannot be used to draw conclusions about cause and effect. After all, does exposure to TV violence cause aggression, or does being aggressive cause children to seek out violence on TV? Is it possible that poverty and other external conditions cause the tendency both to watch and to commit acts of aggression? (Freedman, 1988).

Playing violent video games, like watching violence on TV, may increase aggression in children.

■ **deindividuation** A loss of individuality, often experienced in a group, that results in a breakdown of internal restraints against deviant behavior.

To pin down cause and effect, researchers observe subjects who are randomly assigned to watch violent or nonviolent events. Controlled laboratory studies of this sort show that exposure to aggressive models, either live or on film, have negative effects. In the first of these experiments, for example, Albert Bandura and his colleagues (1961) found that preschool children were more likely to attack an inflated doll after watching an aggressive adult model than after watching a nonaggressive model. In a more recent study, Nicola Schutte and her associates (1988) found that children were more likely to hit another child after playing "Karetka," a violent video game, than after playing "Jungle Hunt," an exciting nonviolent game. Among children and adolescents, exposure to aggressive models clearly increases aggression—not just in the laboratory but in the classroom, the playground, and other settings (Wood et al., 1991).

Deindividuation   Earlier, we saw that the presence of others can arouse us (social facilitation) or relax us (social loafing), depending on the situation. At times, the influence of a group is even more profound and more troubling. Hidden in a faceless crowd, people tend to shed their normal inhibitions—sometimes resulting in violent acts of racism, looting, vandalism, sexual assaults, and riots. How can normal, law-abiding citizens turn into frenzied mobs that take the law into their own hands? The problem is that in large groups, people lose their sense of individuality, resulting in a breakdown of their internal controls against deviant behavior. This depersonalized state of mind is called **deindividuation**.

Large groups promote deindividuation in two ways. First, people feel anonymous, if not "invisible," and less accountable for their actions. *Anonymity* has powerful effects. In one study, subjects who were dressed in white coats and Ku Klux Klan–style hoods, thus masking their bodies and faces, punished a confederate with longer electric shocks than did subjects who wore their regular clothing and name tags (Zimbardo, 1970). In a second study, Halloween trick-or-treaters who were invited to take one piece of candy from a bowl were more likely to grab extras when they were nameless and in groups than when they appeared alone and were asked for their names (Diener et al., 1976).

A second aspect of deindividuation is a *loss of self-consciousness*. Have you ever been at a rock concert or a party with music blaring so loud that you could feel the room vibrate and your identity slipping away? When attention is diverted from the self by intense environmental stimulation, people momentarily lose track of their own values, morals, and internal standards of conduct—resulting in behavior that is impulsive, uninhibited, and often aggressive (Prentice-Dunn & Rogers, 1989). This effect may even grow with the size of the group. Indeed, when Brian Mullen (1986) analyzed newspaper accounts of sixty lynchings that occurred between 1899 and 1946, he discovered that the more people there were in the lynch mob, the more vicious were their actions.

The anonymity that comes with wearing masks and costumes promotes deindividuation—and a lowering of inhibitions.

ALTRUISM

Bob Dylan, Bruce Springsteen, Paul McCartney, Sting, Elton John, Bette Midler, and Ziggy Marley recorded children's songs for an album designed

Trapped in fire, Peter Lewis crawled out onto a ledge twelve stories above Times Square. As onlookers below shouted "Don't jump!" firefighter Kevin Shea dropped down from the roof and risked his own life to make a heroic rescue. Was this an act of altruism?

■ **altruism** Helping behavior that is motivated primarily by a desire to benefit others, not oneself.

■ **empathy-altruism hypothesis** The proposition that an empathic response to a person in need produces altruistic helping.

to raise money for pediatric AIDS. These stars were not paid for their services, so why did they perform? Why do people give blood, donate money to charity, and volunteer their time for worthy causes? And why, during World War II, did hundreds of German citizens risk their lives to hide their Jewish neighbors from the Nazis?

Focusing on the brighter side of human nature, many social psychologists study **altruism**, helping behavior that is motivated primarily by a desire to benefit a person other than oneself. When people are asked to list instances of helping in their own lives, they mention helping a classmate with homework, listening to a friend's problems, giving moral support, lending books or CDs, giving directions to someone who is lost, giving rides, holding doors, helping with groceries, helping to find lost keys, and so on (McGuire, 1994). Everyday examples are not hard to find. Yet psychologists ask, Does altruism really exist, or is helping always selfishly motivated? And why do we sometimes fail to come to the rescue of someone who is in danger or in need of assistance? These are just some of the puzzling questions often asked about helping and the factors that influence this important social behavior.

The Altruism Debate

On the surface, altruism—as an act of self-sacrifice—seems personally maladaptive. The hero who risks life and limb to save a crime victim and the philanthropist who donates large sums of money both come out losers in the exchange. Or do they? Sociobiologists claim that in the fight for survival, helpfulness can perpetuate our own "selfish" genes (Dawkins, 1976). One way this may operate is that people of all cultures follow the norm of reciprocity—a moral code that directs us to help, not hurt, those who have helped us. Helping can thus be considered a long-term investment in the future. Sociobiologists also point out that people are quick to help their own offspring, followed by other family members in proportion to their genetic relatedness, and strangers who are similar to themselves. The result: self-sacrificing behavior that, paradoxically, promotes one's own genetic immortality (Rushton, 1989).

It is often said that helpfulness serves short-term personal interests as well. According to some theorists, people decide whether to intervene on behalf of another person by weighing the costs (time, money, discomfort, the risk of injury) against the benefits (financial reward, praise, social approval, a feeling of satisfaction). This decision making may not be conscious, but if the anticipated benefits exceed the anticipated costs, we help; if not, we stay put. In other words, helping is motivated by self-serving goals (such as a desire to experience a "helper's high" or to avoid feeling guilty for not helping), not by altruism (Cialdini et al., 1973; Piliavin et al., 1981).

Are humans ever truly altruistic, or is our behavior always selfishly motivated? C. Daniel Batson (1991) argues that an act of assistance should be considered altruistic when the helper's main goal is to benefit the person in need—independent of the consequences for the helper. According to Batson's **empathy-altruism hypothesis**, diagrammed in Figure 13.12, people have two emotional reactions to someone in need: *personal distress* (guilt,

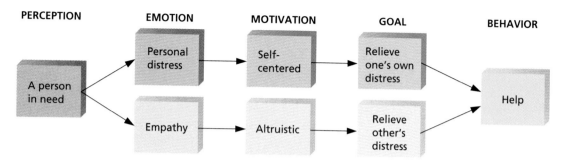

Figure 13.12

Two Pathways to Helping

In response to someone in need of assistance, people experience a combination of personal distress and empathy. Accordingly, there are two paths to helping: one is self-centered (aimed at the relief of one's own discomfort), and the other is altruistic (designed to alleviate the other's suffering).

"This guy's organ-donor card specifies 'For any deserving conservative.'"

Although many psychologists challenge the sociobiological view of altruism, research shows that people are more likely to help strangers who are similar in some way to themselves. [Drawing by D. Reilly; © 1992 The New Yorker Magazine, Inc.]

anxiety, and discomfort) and *empathy* (sympathy and compassion for the other person). When the first reaction predominates, we help primarily to relieve our own discomfort—a self-centered, "egoistic" motivation. When the second reaction predominates, however, we help in order to alleviate the other's suffering—an altruistic motivation. In other words, says Batson, helping can satisfy both selfish and noble motives.

If Batson is correct, then empathy—a genuine, gut-level compassion for another person—is the engine that drives pure altruism. Parents who feel their child's joy and anguish as if it were their own have it; child abusers do not (Miller & Eisenberg, 1988). Can empathy alone inspire helping? How can the two helping motives be distinguished? According to Batson, people who come face-to-face with a needy person—say, a beggar on the street or an accident victim—can relieve their *own* distress by offering help or by escaping the situation (out of sight, out of mind). For people with empathy for the victim, however, there is no mental escape. The *victim's* distress can be reduced only by helping.

To demonstrate, Batson and his colleagues (1981) devised a situation in which subjects observed a female accomplice, posing as another subject, take electric shocks as part of an experiment. Over closed-circuit TV, subjects saw that she was upset and heard her say that she had suffered an electrical accident as a child. What next? Given a choice, would subjects leave the experiment, having already completed their part in it (escape), or would they volunteer to trade places with this other subject (help)? As predicted by Batson, the choice that subjects made depended on their empathy for the woman. Among those low in empathy (because her values were different from their own), only 18 percent agreed to trade places. However, among subjects who were high in empathy (because she shared similar values), 91 percent agreed to the trade. These latter subjects could have made themselves feel better by leaving, but instead they stayed to help the other person. Does this mean that pure altruism exists? Some say yes (Batson et al., 1989; Dovidio et al., 1990), others say no (Cialdini et al., 1987; Schaller & Cialdini, 1988). The debate continues.

Bystander Intervention

This debate about human nature is fascinating, but what initially inspired social psychologists to study helping were hair-raising news stories about bystanders who fail to take action even when someone else's life is in danger. The problem first made headlines in March 1964. Kitty Genovese was walking home from work in Queens, New York, at 3:20 in the morning. As she crossed the street from her car to her apartment, a man with a knife appeared. She ran, but he caught up and stabbed her. Genovese cried frantically for help and screamed, "Oh my God, he stabbed me! . . . I'm dying, I'm dying!"—but to no avail. The man fled, but then returned, raped her, and stabbed her eight more times, until she was dead. In the still of the night, the attack lasted for over half an hour. Thirty-eight neighbors heard the screams, turned lights on, and came to their windows. One couple even pulled chairs up to their window and turned out the light to see better. Yet nobody came down to help. Until it was over, nobody even called the police.

What happened? How could people have been so heartless and apathetic? How could they have remained passive while a neighbor was being murdered? Rather than blame the bystanders, Bibb Latané and John Darley (1970) focused on the social factors at work in this situation. In a series of experiments, they staged emergencies, varied conditions, and observed the behavior of their subjects. The question: Is it possible to transform ordinary people into unhelpful bystanders in the controlled setting of a psychology experiment?

In one study, Darley and Latané (1968) took subjects to a cubicle and asked them to discuss the kinds of personal problems that college students face. For confidentiality purposes, they were told, subjects would communicate over an intercom system and the experimenter would not be listening. The subjects were also told to speak one at a time and to take turns. Some were assigned to two-person discussions, others to larger groups. The opening moments were uneventful, though one subject (an accomplice) mentioned in passing that he had a seizure disorder that was sometimes triggered by study pressures. Sure enough, when it came his turn to speak again, this subject struggled and pleaded for help:

> "I could really-er-use some help so if somebody would-er-give me a little h-help-uh-er-er-er c-could somebody-er-er-help-er-uh-uh-uh (choking sounds). . . . I'm gonna die-er-er-I'm . . . gonna die-er-help-er-er-seizure-er."

If you were in this situation, how would you react? Would you interrupt the experiment, dash out of your cubicle, and try to find the experimenter? As it turned out, subjects' responses were strongly influenced by the size of their group. Actually, all subjects participated alone, but they were led to believe that others were present and that there was a real crisis. Almost all the subjects who thought they were involved in a two-person discussion left the room immediately to try to get help. In the larger discussion groups, however, subjects were less likely to intervene, and slower to do so when they did. In fact, the larger the group was supposed to be, the less helping occurred (see Figure 13.13). This result led to a chilling conclusion known as the **bystander effect**: the more bystanders there are, the less likely a victim is to get help. In an emergency, the presence of others inhibits helping.

At first, this pioneering research seemed to defy all common sense. Isn't there safety in numbers? Don't we feel more secure rushing in to help when others are there for support? To fully understand what went wrong, Latané and Darley (1970) provided a careful, step-by-step analysis of the decision-making process in emergency situations. According to their scheme, bystanders help only when they *notice* the incident, *interpret* it as

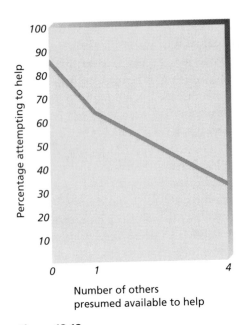

Figure 13.13

The Bystander Effect

When subjects thought that they alone heard a seizure victim in need, the vast majority sought help. As the number of bystanders increased, however, subjects became less likely to intervene (Darley & Latané, 1968).

■ **bystander effect** The finding that the presence of others inhibits helping in an emergency.

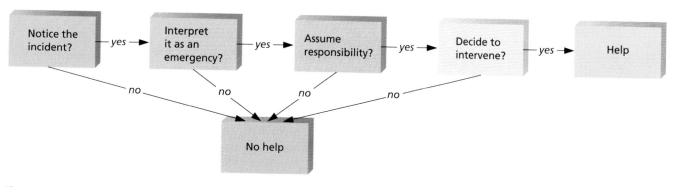

Figure 13.14

A Model of Bystander Intervention

This step-by-step analysis suggests several reasons for the fact that bystanders often do not help in emergencies.

an emergency, *take responsibility* for helping, *decide* to intervene, and then *act* on that decision (see Figure 13.14).

This analysis of the intervention process sheds light on the bystander effect, as the presence of others can inhibit helping at each of the five steps. Consider, for example, the second requirement that bystanders interpret an event as an emergency. Have you ever heard screaming from a nearby house, and the sound of crashing objects, only to wonder if you were overhearing an assault or just a family quarrel? Cries of pain may sound like shrieks of laughter, and heart attack victims may be mistaken for drunk. How do other bystanders influence our interpretation? Faced with a sudden, possibly dangerous event, everyone pretends to stay calm. As each person sees that others seem indifferent, they shrug it off. As a result, the event no longer feels like an emergency.

This process was observed in a study in which Latané and Darley (1970) had subjects fill out questionnaires alone or in groups of three. Shortly after the experimenter left, white smoke was pumped into the room through a vent. Alone, most subjects worried that there was a fire and quickly reported the smoke to the experimenter. Yet in the company of others, most subjects did not seek help. In some groups, the smoke was so thick that subjects coughed, rubbed their eyes, and waved the fumes away from their face as they worked on the questionnaires, but they did not call for help. Why not? In post-experiment interviews, these subjects said they assumed the smoke was harmless steam, air-conditioning vapors, or even "truth gas"—but not a fire.

The presence of others also inhibits helping by causing a **diffusion of responsibility**, a belief that others will intervene. Thirty-eight people watched from their separate apartments and did nothing while Kitty Genovese was attacked. Subjects in the group conditions of the seizure study also did not intervene. When subjects thought that they alone could hear the victim, making them solely responsible for his welfare, they took action. Many of those who thought that others were also present, however, behaved like the neighbors of Kitty Genovese: they did not help because they assumed someone else had or would.

The bystander effect is powerful and scary. Over the years, researchers have observed behavior in different kinds of staged crises. Would subjects report a theft or a possible fire? Would they stop for a stranded motorist, help a woman who faints or sprains an ankle, or try to break up a fight? Would they rush to the aid of a seizure victim, a subway passenger who staggers and falls to the ground, or an experimenter who has an asthma

■ **diffusion of responsibility** In groups, a tendency for bystanders to assume that someone else will help.

Table 13.1

Some Facts About Helping

As a general rule, helping is most likely to occur under the following conditions:

1. When the bystander is in a good mood
2. When the bystander feels guilty or is low in self-esteem
3. When the bystander observes someone else helping
4. When the bystander is not pressed for time
5. When the bystander is male and the victim female
6. When the victim makes a direct request for help
7. When the victim is physically attractive
8. When the victim appears to deserve help
9. When the victim is similar in some way to the bystander
10. In a small town or rural area, not a large city

attack? What are the odds that a person in need will actually receive help? Clearly, helping depends in complex ways on characteristics of the victim, the bystanders, and the situation (see Table 13.1). The fact remains, however, that a person is less likely to intervene in a group than when alone. Perhaps even more remarkable is that victims are more likely to get help from some*one* when their welfare rests on the shoulders of a single potential helper than when many others are present (Latané & Nida, 1981).

Driven by the belief that social situations influence each of us in profound ways, social psychologists have studied a wide range of important behaviors—and in a wide range of important settings. From studies of conformity, obedience, persuasion, the group processes of social facilitation, social loafing, group polarization, groupthink, aggression, and altruism, the research message is clear: we are influenced by the words and actions of other people.

SUMMARY AND KEY TERMS

Attitudes and Behavior

We commonly assume that our *attitudes*—evaluative reactions to persons, objects, or ideas—guide our behavior. But the connection is not automatic. Social influence works on both attitudes and behavior through a variety of processes.

Social Influences on Behavior

Conformity

Classic studies of *conformity,* our tendency to alter our opinions or behavior to match group norms, show two types of social influence at work. People demonstrating *informational influence* go along with the group because they believe the others are correct. *Normative influence* leads people to conform because they fear social rejection. These two kinds of influence produce different types of conformity: private (marked by actual change in beliefs) and public (compliance without changing one's beliefs).

Conformity increases with group size (up to a point) and with the salience of social norms. Conformity decreases when

an ally is present. Cultural factors are also important. Some cultures value independence, while others stress social harmony.

Although nonconformists are often unpopular, studies show that minorities can influence majority opinion by sticking to their positions with consistency and confidence. This influence can occur even when majority members do not recognize or admit its presence.

Obedience

History offers many examples of terrible crimes committed in the name of obedience. Milgram's research showed that even decent human beings can violate the conscience at the command of an authority figure.

Social Influences on Attitudes

To have the most lasting effects, social influence must change not just immediate behavior but also people's attitudes.

Persuasive Communications

Persuasion, the process of changing attitudes, can occur in two ways. On the *central route to persuasion,* people think carefully about a message and are influenced by its arguments. On the *peripheral route to persuasion,* they rely instead on superficial cues. The central route requires the ability and motivation to process the communication carefully.

Persuasive communication is the outcome of three factors: source, message, and audience. Source credibility and likability increase persuasiveness, at least when the audience's involvement is low. With regard to the message, persuasion works best if the position taken is moderately discrepant from the audience's. Messages that arouse fear often work well, as long as they provide reassurance and ways to avoid the threat; but messages that play on positive emotions are also influential. Finally, the persuasiveness of different kinds of messages depends on audience characteristics such as the need for cognition and the degree of self-monitoring.

Self-Persuasion

Just as attitudes influence behavior, behavior can influence attitudes. Festinger argued that behaving in ways discrepant with our attitudes often produces an unpleasant state of *cognitive dissonance.* This in turn leads us to change our attitudes to match or justify our behavior. There is evidence to support this basic effect, and researchers have identified conditions under which it occurs. Theorists continue to debate the reasons for it.

Group Processes

Social Facilitation

Through *social facilitation,* the presence of others tends to enhance performance on simple tasks but impair performance on complex tasks. According to Zajonc's explanation, the mere presence of others increases arousal and triggers our dominant response. Other researchers maintain that this arousal occurs only when others can evaluate our performance or drive us to distraction.

Social Loafing

In joint activities, people often exert less effort than they would alone. This *social loafing* increases with group size because individuals do not see the link between their own effort and the desired group outcome.

Group Polarization

Discussions among people of similar views tend to produce *group polarization,* an intensification of initial opinions. This phenomenon occurs because the arguments expressed reinforce the original view and because a social norm is established.

Groupthink

Groupthink, a process in which members convince themselves they are correct, is especially likely in groups that are isolated, cohesive, and homogeneous and that have strong leadership. By producing overestimation of the group's capacity, close-mindedness, and great pressure toward uniformity, groupthink raises the odds of miscalculation and failure.

Aggression

Aggression, like other aspects of human behavior, is rooted in both human biology and social factors.

Biological Roots

Although instinct theories of aggression do not account for differences among cultures, there are biological influences. Men, for example, seem to be more aggressive than women, perhaps because of testosterone levels.

Social Influences

In general, aversive stimulation tends to spark aggression. For example, studies of the *frustration-aggression hypothesis* show that frustration correlates with aggressive behavior. Higher summer temperatures are also linked to aggressive responses. Once aversive stimulation arouses negative emotion, situational cues, such as the sight of weapons and exposure to mass-media violence, prompt us to turn the feeling into aggressive action.

Another form of social influence is *deindividuation,* a loss of individuality that people sometimes experience in a large group. Prompted by feelings of anonymity and a loss of self-consciousness, deindividuation results in a breakdown of internal controls against deviant behavior.

Altruism

Does *altruism*—that is, helping behavior primarily motivated by a desire to benefit others—really exist? And why do we sometimes fail to help others?

The Altruism Debate

Sociobiologists argue that by helping others we selfishly promote the long-term success of our own genes. Others say that helping is motivated by short-term benefits, such as receiving praise or avoiding guilt. According to Batson's *empathy-altruism hypothesis,* however, we react to someone else's need with both personal distress and empathy. When the latter reaction predominates, we have a truly altruistic motivation.

Bystander Intervention

Studies of helping behavior demonstrate a *bystander effect:* in an emergency, the presence of others inhibits helping. Bystanders reduce our tendency to interpret the event as an emergency, and they also create a *diffusion of responsibility,* a belief that others will provide the necessary help.

Chapter 14

Human Diversity

The first time I heard the song was at the 1964 World's Fair in Queens, New York. I was eleven years old at the time, and the exhibit was called "It's a Small World." After waiting in line, my family and I were seated in a boat that transported us from one room of the exhibit to another and treated us to a fantasy-like display that left a lasting imprint in my memory. There were hundreds of animated dolls colorfully dressed as children from all the continents of the world. As the dolls circled and moved about on mechanical platforms, you could hear children's voices all singing in their native languages. The message of this exhibit was that despite differences in language, customs, and geography, the peoples of the world share a common bond.

It's now thirty years later, and millions of people continue to tour this exhibit in the Disney parks of Florida, California, Paris, and Tokyo. And the message—that it's a small world—rings truer today than ever before. As many as a billion people have watched the Olympics on TV. Via satellite, the outbreak of war, floods, earthquakes, volcanic eruptions, and royal weddings are broadcast live to all corners of the globe. In Moscow, you can wear Levi jeans, watch MTV, drink Coke, and eat burgers and fries at McDonald's. And in the United States, you can drive a Japanese car, wear clothes made in Taiwan, and eat in restaurants that serve enchiladas, lasagna, wonton soup, pita bread, sushi, sausages, curried lamb, and other international delights.

It's a sign of the times that Coca-Cola is being sold at Red Square in Moscow.

Computers, high-speed jumbo jets, satellite communications, international trade agreements, educational exchanges, and the like invite an important question: What challenges lie ahead as we approach the twenty-first century, when East meets West and North meets South in the global village? Does the smallness of our world homogenize different cultures and other groups, or does it sharpen our awareness of human diversity? And what about migration patterns within countries? Consider the rapid changes in the American landscape caused by recent influxes of immigrants. Over the next few years, ethnic minority groups will constitute a majority of the population in a number of U.S. cities. Will this increased heterogeneity breed tolerance of others who are different, or will it fuel prejudice? What about recent changes in the social roles played by men and women? As more and more women enter professional schools, join the work force, and seek positions of leadership, new questions are raised about the nature of men and women and the extent to which sex differences are rooted in biological or social factors. Finally, what do psychologists know about sexual orientation? How prevalent is homosexuality, and to what extent is it rooted in biological or social factors?

Over the years, social psychologists have found that people are profoundly affected by the situations they are in (Milgram's obedience experiments illustrate this point in a dramatic way). In this regard, we'll see that cultural factors—such as childrearing practices, social norms, and stereotypes—play a particularly prominent role. The various issues addressed in this chapter converge on another important point: for people to get along with their neighbors, co-workers, fellow citizens, members of the opposite sex, and others with whom we share this planet, there needs to be mutual tolerance, understanding, and an appreciation for the diversity of human life. If I had to sum up all of psychology—and the theme of this chapter—in just one sentence, it would be this: everyone is basically the same, yet no two people are alike.

The similarities among us are so self-evident that they are invisible, taken for granted. Regardless of whether you are male or female, regardless of whether the color of your skin is black, white, brown, red, yellow, or olive-toned, regardless of whether you are gay or straight, and regardless of where in the world you live—you squint your eyes in bright sunlight, prefer sweet foods to bitter, get light-headed when you drink too much, smile when you're happy, speak in "baby talk" to infants, have the capacity to

Despite cultural diversity, there are many similarities among the peoples of the world. Children crave the sweet taste of candy in Texas—and everywhere else. Teenagers flirt and think about sex in Honduras—and everywhere else.

hold seven or so items in short-term memory, forget events that took place when you were two years old, repeat behaviors that produce reinforcement, seek the company of others who are similar, respond to social pressure from peers, and react to trauma with anxiety or depression. Similarly, babies all over the world babble before uttering a word, fear strangers in the first year of life, think concretely before using abstract logic, and start thinking about sex during adolescence.

Despite the "universals" of human behavior, there are some differences—(1) between cultures, (2) between racial and ethnic groups within a culture, (3) between men and women, and (4) between gays and straights. We'll see that some of these differences are rooted in biology, while others result from the various physical, economic, and social environments in which people live. Either way, it is clear that there's a good deal of diversity among us.

CROSS-CULTURAL PERSPECTIVES

For every two ticks of the second hand on your watch, nine new babies are born and three people die. The net increase of three human lives per second means that the world's population grows by 10,600 per hour, 254,000 per day, 1.8 million per week, 7.7 million per month, and 93 million per year. According to the United Nations, there are now 5.5 billion people in the world's population, a number that is projected to reach 6 billion by 1998 and 10 billion before the year 2050.

Immersed in our own ways of life, it is all too easy to overlook an important fact: there is no dominant world culture. Look at Table 14.1, for example, and you'll see that of every 100 people in the two hundred or so nations of the world, only 5 live in the United States. We humans are a heterogeneous lot. As a matter of *geography*, some of us live in large, heavily populated cities, while others live in small towns, affluent suburbs, rural farming communities, hot and humid jungles, expansive deserts, high-altitude mountains, tropical islands, and icy arctic plains. Excluding the dialects, more than 6,000 different *languages* are spoken—the most common being Chinese, English, Hindi, Arabic, Russian, Malay, Bengali, Spanish, French, Japanese, Portuguese, and German, in that order. There are also hundreds of *religions* that people identify with—the most popular being Christianity (32 percent), Islam (17 percent), Hinduism (14 percent), Buddhism (6 percent), Chinese folk religions (4 percent), New Asian religions (2 percent), various African tribal religions (2 percent), and Judaism (.4 percent). The remaining 20 percent of the world's population are atheists or simply unaffiliated with a religion.

21	China
16	India
5	United States
5	former Soviet Union
4	Indonesia
3	Brazil
2	Bangladesh
2	Japan
2	Mexico
2	Nigeria
2	Pakistan
1	Egypt
1	Ethiopia
1	France
1	Germany
1	Iran
1	Italy
1	Philippines
1	Thailand
1	Turkey
1	United Kingdom
1	Vietnam
25	all remaining countries

Table 14.1

Where in the World People Live

In 1991, the U.S. Census Bureau estimated that of every 100 people in the world, 21 live in China, 16 live in India, 5 live in the United States, and so on.

Cultural Diversity: A Fact of Life

Linked together by space, language, religion, and historical bonds, each cultural group has its own ideology, folklore, music, forms of artistic expression, political system, family structure, sexual mores, fashions, and foods. In China, food is flavored primarily with soy sauce, rice wine, and

After China, India is the second most populous country in the world. This scene shows a Hindu woman at the holy river Ganges.

"Very nice, but now can you take us to McDonald's?"

Immersed in our own way of life, we sometimes fail to appreciate the richness and diversity of other cultures. [Published in *Hemisphere*; © Bob Schocket.]

■ **social norms** Implicit rules of conduct according to which each culture operates.

ginger root; in Greece, olive oil, lemon, and oregano are often used; in Morocco, the food is seasoned with coriander, cumin, cinnamon, onion, and fruit; and in Mexico, tomatoes and hot chile pepper are used (Rozin, 1983).

As world travelers well know, the variations in food are matched by variations in local customs. Visit an outdoor market in Iraq, and you should expect to barter or negotiate the price of everything you purchase. Dine in an Indian home, and you should leave some food on the plate to show the host that the portions were generous and you had enough to eat. Plan a meeting with a native of Brazil, and don't be surprised if he or she is late. Nothing personal. In North America, it is common to sit casually opposite someone with your legs outstretched. Yet in Nepal, it is considered an insult to point the bottom of your feet at a person. In Turkey, it is okay for heterosexual men to embrace, kiss on the cheek, and walk together hand in hand. Yet in North America, such public displays between men are considered unmanly. In Iran, Islamic women wear veils over the face; in many other countries, women paint their lips, shadow their eyes, and powder their faces with makeup. People in some parts of the world eat with forks and knives; others use chopsticks, bread, or their bare hands. Some people exchange greetings by shaking hands or waving; others lower the head and bow. Even the way we space ourselves from each other is culturally determined. Americans, Germans, the British, and Northern Europeans maintain a polite distance between themselves and others—and feel "crowded" by the more intimate, touchier, nose-to-nose style of the French, Greeks, Arabs, Mexicans, and people of South America. In the affairs of day-to-day living, each culture operates according to its own implicit rules of conduct, or **social norms** (see Table 14.2).

Just as cultures differ in their social norms, so too they differ in the extent to which people adhere to those norms. As an example, compare the United States and Japan. In the United States, it is said that "the squeaky wheel gets the grease"—so parents teach their children to be independent, self-reliant, and unique. In Japan, however, it is said that "the nail that

- *Greetings.* Waving and shaking hands may seem universal, but there are different rules for greeting. In Finland you should give a firm handshake, in France you should loosen the grip, in Zambia you should use your left hand to support the right, and in Bolivia you should extend your arm if your hand is dirty. In Japan people bow, in Thailand they put both hands together in a praying position on the chest, and in Fiji they smile and raise their eyebrows. In Venezuela, Paraguay, and certain other parts of Latin America, it is common for people to hug, embrace, and kiss upon meeting. In most Arab countries, men greet one another by saying *salaam alaykum,* then shaking hands, saying *kaif halak,* and kissing each other on the cheek.

- *Nonverbal Communication.* When you don't speak the native language, it's natural to use gestures. Watch out. In Bulgaria, nodding your head means "no" and shaking your head sideways means "yes." In Germany and Brazil, the American "okay" sign (forming a circle with your thumb and forefinger) is an obscene gesture. Personal space habits also vary across cultures. Japanese people prefer to keep a comfortable distance while interacting. But in Puerto Rico and much of Latin America, people stand very close—and backing off is considered an insult. Also beware of what you do with your eyes. In Latin America locking eyes is a must, yet in Japan too much eye contact shows a lack of respect. If you're in the habit of stroking your cheek, you should know that in Italy, Greece, and Spain it means you find the person you're talking to attractive. And whatever you do, don't ever touch someone's head while in Buddhist countries, especially Thailand. The head is sacred.

- *Table Manners.* So much human social activity revolves around eating that acceptance of local foods and table manners is important. First, be prepared for foods you may consider "exotic." For example, you may be served sheep's eyes in Saudi Arabia, raw fish in Japan, bear's paw soup in China . . . and lobster in the United States. Be mindful of strict religious prohibitions, and don't ask for beef in India or pork in Islamic countries. Table etiquette is also tricky. In Zambia, the guest should ask to be served because it's impolite for the host to offer food first. In Saudi Arabia, you show your appreciation of a meal by stuffing yourself. As a dinner guest in Bolivia, you should clean your plate to prove you enjoyed the meal, but in India you should leave some food to signal to the host that you've had enough to eat. In parts of Pakistan, India, Malaysia, and Indonesia, you should never pass, accept, or touch food with your left hand.

- *Gifts.* Giving and accepting gifts is a customary part of social interaction. It also presents an opportunity for misunderstanding. In Japan, gift giving is used to express friendship, gratitude, and respect. But beware: If you receive a gift, you should reciprocate—so don't get caught empty-handed. When you give a gift in Japan, however, make sure that it is not wrapped in white paper (white is associated with death). In China, avoid using red ink (messages written in red imply the severing of a relationship). Of course, what you give is as important as how you present it. Never present a bottle of wine to a Muslim because the Islamic faith prohibits alcohol. In Hong Kong, avoid clocks (which symbolize death) and sharp objects (which signify the breakup of a relationship). Flowers are nice, but in Guatemala white flowers are reserved for funerals, and in Chile yellow flowers signify contempt. If you visit someone in Greece, Morocco, and many Arab countries, be careful not to admire or praise any possession too much or your host will feel obligated to give it to you.

Table 14.2

Helpful Tips for the World Traveler

Social norms from one country to the next are so different that people who travel on business or for pleasure should know the local customs. Here are a few tips from the 1993 edition of Roger Axtell's best-seller, *Do's and Taboos Around the World.*

stands out gets pounded down"—so children are taught the values of conformity, loyalty, and harmony within the community. As we'll see, this comparison indicates that there are two very different cultural orientations toward persons and the groups to which they belong. One orientation centers on the individual, the other on the group.

Individualism and Collectivism: A Tale of Two Cultures

In the movie *Mr. Baseball,* actor Tom Selleck plays an aging American baseball star who signs a contract with a team in Japan. Selleck plays a brash and colorful character who always swings for the home run, loafs at practice, defies his manager, argues with umpires, and throws his bat when

■ **individualism** A cultural orientation in which independence, autonomy, and self-reliance take priority over group allegiances.

■ **collectivism** A cultural orientation in which interdependence, cooperation, and group harmony take priority over purely personal goals.

he is frustrated—a personal style that offends the Japanese sense of decorum. Eventually, Selleck's antics become so publicly humiliating to the team that he is suspended. American and Japanese values were caricatured in this film for the sake of art. But there is an underlying truth to the distinction. Baseball is popular in both countries and is played by the same set of rules. But while American players seek personal glory as all-stars and national heroes, Japanese coaches caution their players that "lone wolves are the cancer of the team."

This comparison reveals just the tip of an iceberg. Over the years, social scientists have observed that cultures differ in the extent to which they value **individualism** and the virtues of independence, autonomy, and self-reliance, or **collectivism** and the virtues of interdependence, cooperation, and social harmony. Under the banner of individualism, personal goals take priority over group allegiances. In collectivist cultures, however, the person is, first and foremost, a loyal member of a family, team, company, church, state, and other groups (see Table 14.3). In what countries are these differing orientations most extreme? In a worldwide study of 116,000 employees of IBM, Geert Hofstede (1980) found that the most fiercely individualistic people are from the United States, Australia, Great Britain, Canada, and the Netherlands, in that order. The most collectivistic people are from Venezuela, Colombia, Pakistan, Peru, Taiwan, and China.

Table 14.3

Individualistic and Collectivist Orientations

Read these statements and note whether you agree or disagree with each one. People from collectivist cultures tend to agree with the *C* statements, while those from individualistic cultures tend to agree with the *I* staements. Where do you stand in your cultural orientation? (Hui, 1988; Triandis et al., 1988)

1. If the group is slowing me down, it is better to leave it and work alone. (*I*)

2. To be superior, a person must stand alone. (*I*)

3. I can count on my relatives for help if I find myself in any kind of trouble. (*C*)

4. If you want something done right, you've got to do it yourself. (*I*)

5. It is reasonable for a son to continue his father's business. (*C*)

6. In the long run, the only person you can count on is yourself. (*I*)

7. I enjoy meeting and talking to my neighbors every day. (*C*)

8. I like to live close to my good friends. (*C*)

9. The bigger the family, the more family problems there are. (*I*)

10. There is everything to gain and nothing to lose for classmates to group themselves for study and discussion. (*C*)

What determines whether a culture becomes individualistic or collectivist? Speculating on the origins of the two orientations, Harry Triandis (1989) suggests that there are three key factors. The first is the *complexity* of a society. As people live in increasingly complex industrialized societies—compared, for example, to a life of food gathering among desert nomads—there are more groups to identify with (family, hometown, alma mater, place of employment, church, political party, sports teams, social clubs, and so on), which means less loyalty to any one group and more of a

Exhibiting a collectivist orientation, two hundred Amish men and women come together for a barn-raising. After an arsonist set fire to several barns in this Pennsylvania Amish community, the men built a new structure, while the women prepared lunch. The barn was completed in ten hours.

focus on personal rather than collective goals. Second is the *affluence* of a society. As people prosper, they gain financial independence from one another, a condition that promotes social independence, mobility, and, again, a focus on personal rather than collective goals. The third factor is *heterogeneity*. Societies that are homogeneous or "tight" (where members share the same language, religion, and social customs) tend to be rigid and intolerant of those who veer from the norm. In contrast, societies that are culturally diverse or "loose" (where two or more cultures coexist) are more permissive of dissent—thus allowing for greater individual expression.

It is interesting that individualistic values in the United States are even greater today than in the past. Consider this question: If you were a parent, what traits would you like your child to develop? When this question was asked of American mothers in 1924, many chose "strict obedience," "loyalty," and "good manners"—key characteristics of collectivism. But when American mothers were asked the same question fifty-four years later, in 1978, they cited "independence" and "tolerance of others"—important aspects of individualism. Due perhaps to the greater complexity, affluence, and diversity of Western life in general, similar trends were also found in surveys conducted in Germany, Italy, and England (Remley, 1988).

Conceptions of the Self   Individualism and collectivism are so deeply ingrained in a culture that they mold our very self-conceptions and identities. According to Hazel Markus and Shinobu Kitayama (1991), people who grow up in individualistic countries see themselves as entities that are *independent*—distinct, autonomous, self-contained, and endowed with unique dispositions. By contrast, people from collectivist countries hold an *interdependent* view of the self as part of a larger social network that includes family, co-workers, friends, and others with whom they are socially connected. In one study, David Trafimow and his colleagues (1991) had American and Chinese college students complete twenty sentences beginning with "I am . . ." The Americans were more likely to fill in the blank with trait descriptions ("I am shy"), while the Chinese were more likely to identify themselves by their group affiliations ("I am a college student"). It's no

Figure 14.1

Markus and Kitayama (1991) find that people from individualistic cultures see themselves as independent and distinct from others. In contrast, people in collectivist cultures see themselves as interdependent, as part of a larger social network.

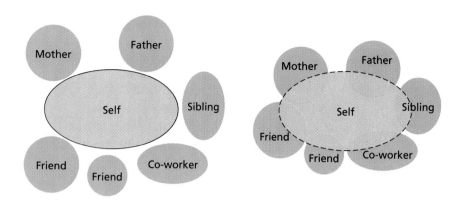

wonder that in China, the family name comes *before* one's personal name. These conceptions are illustrated in Figure 14.1.

Do these conceptions of the self influence the way people perceive themselves in relation to others? Markus and Kitayama (1991) found three interesting differences between East and West. First, American college students see themselves as less similar to others than do Asian-Indian students. This finding reinforces the idea that people with independent conceptions of the self believe they are unique. Second, while North Americans are quick to express envy, anger, pride, and other "ego-focused" emotions that affirm the self as distinct, many nonwesterners feel "other-focused" emotions that promote interpersonal harmony rather than conflict. As described in Chapter 8, for example, people in Japan describe the emotions of *oime* (indebtedness), *fureai* (connection with others), and *sitasimi* (familiarity to others). Third, people in individualistic cultures strive for personal achievement, but those in collectivist cultures derive more self-esteem through the status and accomplishments of a valued group. Thus, whereas North Americans tend to overestimate their own contribution to a team effort, take credit for success, and blame others for failure, Japanese people tend to underestimate their own role and present themselves in more modest, humble terms.

Developmental Influences The culturally prescribed socialization practices that breed independence or interdependence begin soon after a baby is born. In the United States, a vast majority of middle-class parents who can afford it put their babies to bed in a separate room. Indeed, pediatrician Benjamin Spock (1945), author of the best-selling child-care book, advised that it is better "not to take the child into the parents' bed for any reason" (p. 101). When my children were younger, my wife and I never even thought twice about it. Separate sleeping arrangements were just a part of independence training. Yet in most other countries of the world, it is common for young children to sleep in the same room, even in the same bed, with their parents (Whiting & Edwards, 1988). Perhaps that is all part of *inter*dependence training. To many non-Americans, it is merciless to force helpless babies to lie alone in a dark room. Thus, when Mayan mothers from Guatemala were told of this practice, they reacted with shock, disapproval, and pity. As one disbelieving mother asked, "But there's someone else with them there, isn't there?" (Morelli et al., 1992).

Socialization fosters different cultural orientations in other ways, too. In individualistic cultures, parents are quick to wean infants from the breast and toilet-train their toddlers out of diapers. Teenagers fight to separate from parents, and adults struggle to resolve the "identity crisis" that seems to plague us all. With all the focus on "me," the individual, it's no wonder that bookstore shelves are lined with paperbacks on how to "get in touch with your feelings," "speak your mind," "fulfill your potential," and become "self-actualized." In many ways, we take our cultural orientations for granted. In cultures that value freedom and individual rights, for example, we assume that people should marry for love and romance. Not so in all corners of the world. In parts of India, even today, families make arrangements at birth for the future marriage of their children.

Social Consequences   Try as they do to be objective, cross-cultural researchers cannot help but make value judgments about the individualist and collectivist orientations. Is one orientation better, or more adaptive, or more productive, or more humane? There is no quick and simple answer. Predictably, individualists are less likely than collectivists to follow social norms. In Chapter 13, we saw that when American subjects were confronted with confederates who made incorrect perceptual judgments, they conformed to this incorrect majority 37 percent of the time. When similar tasks were given to subjects from collectivist cultures, conformity rates were even higher. Among the Bantu of Zimbabwe, an African tribe in which deviance is punished, 51 percent conformed. In fact, John Berry (1979) compared subjects from seventeen cultures and found that conformity rates ranged from a low of 18 percent among Eskimo hunters of Baffin Island to a high of 60 percent among village-living Temne farmers of West Africa. Is conformity a desirable or undesirable characteristic? Cast in a positive light, it promotes harmony and group solidarity—qualities that keep societies from being torn apart by dissension. Cast in a negative light, however, a lack of independence may lend itself to narrow-mindedness, cowardice, and blind obedience.

There is a drawback to individualism. If everyone focuses on personal goals, then the group as a whole may suffer. The baseball player who worries more about his batting average than the team's winning percentage is a case in point (there's a scene in *Mr. Baseball* in which Tom Selleck defies his manager's call for a sacrifice bunt and strikes out swinging for a home run). We saw in Chapter 13 that people often exert less effort, or "loaf" on the job, when they work as part of a group than when they work alone (Latané et al., 1979). To many of us, it seems natural to slack off somewhat when others are there to pick up the slack. But social loafing is not equally strong all over the world. In fact, research shows that Chinese subjects in Taiwan work harder in a group than they do for themselves alone (Gabrenya et al., 1983). In collectivist cultures, what's good for the group is good for the self.

Ironically, the benefit of collectivism may also be its main flaw. Intimately connected to groups, collectivists are loyal and team-spirited, willing to sacrifice personal gain for their group's long-term well-being, and sometimes even willing to fight and die for their group. But how do collectivists behave toward members of other groups? Because they identify so strongly with their own, collectivists may be more likely to see their own norms as universal and exploit outsiders for competitive gain. In a study of interpersonal conflict, Kwok Leung (1988) found that Chinese subjects were less likely than Americans to pursue a conflict with a friend, but they were more likely to confront a stranger. As Harry Triandis put it, "While collectivists are very nice to those who are members of their own groups, they can be very nasty, competitive, and uncooperative toward those who belong to other groups" (quoted in Goleman, 1990, p. 41). The result: The collective "we" may fuel intergroup tensions and promote ethnic, regional, national, and religious fighting against the collective "them."

MULTICULTURAL PERSPECTIVES

In June 1993, three hundred Chinese men, women, and children left their families, crowded into a creaky, rusted freighter called the *Golden Venture*, traveled for four months over 17,000 miles, endured a ferocious Atlantic storm, and landed at 2 A.M. in Rockaway Beach, New York. Two hundred yards from the shore, the passengers clambered down the side of the vessel and swam to the beach, where they were met by authorities. Most appeared dazed, disoriented, shivering cold, hungry, and in poor health. Why did these people pay thousands of dollars to illegal alien smugglers and risk their lives on this dangerous and uncertain journey? Upset by the political and economic climate back home, they desperately wanted to start a new life.

Seeking a new life, would-be immigrants from China wait off the coast of Mexico for entrance into the United States.

Ethnic Diversity: A Fact of Life

The names, dates, and places may change, but this script is replayed over and over again. In 1991, thousands of Albanians seeking political freedom stole into the night and sailed across the Adriatic Sea to Italy. Most but not all were sent back. In just the past few years, thousands of Haitian refugees received political asylum in neighboring countries, Mexicans crossed the

Portrait of an American Family. In 1912, Joseph Ashear left his home in Aleppo, Syria, traveled by sea to the United States, and married Rae Shweky, whose parents were also from the Middle East. This Jewish immigrant couple raised and educated four children whose sons and daughters married others with ancestors from Poland, Rumania, Russia, Austria, and elsewhere in Europe. This modern American family, like so many others, is rooted in a diversity of cultures.

Americans use 68 percent more spices today than a decade ago. The use of red pepper rose by 105 percent, basil by 190 percent (American Spice Trade Association).

In 1976 there were 67 Spanish-speaking radio stations in the United States. Now there are 311 (Market Segment Research, Inc.).

■ **multiculturalism** The study of diverse racial and ethnic groups within a culture.

border into the United States, Afghans escaped war to Pakistan, Pakistanis moved into Great Britain, Turks sought employment in Germany, and Russian Jews moved from the defunct Soviet Union to Israel. Immigration is not the only source of ethnic diversity within a culture. In some cases, ethnic groups inhabit a country because they do not have their own homeland. Thus, many Sikhs live in India and Pakistan, Kurds inhabit Turkey and Iraq, the Basques live in Spain, the Tamils live in Sri Lanka, Palestinians are scattered throughout the Middle East, and the Navajo, Sioux, and other Native Americans are all citizens of the United States (Demko, 1992). In short, many countries are ethnically diverse.

Like most countries, the United States has a culturally mixed population—which is becoming even more so with time. According to the 1990 census, there are 248 million U.S. citizens, 22 million of whom were born in another country. As categorized by the Census Bureau, 80 percent of the population are white; 12 percent are black; 3 percent are Asians or Pacific Islanders; one percent are Native Americans, Eskimos, and Aleuts; 4 percent are of "other races." Overall, 9 percent of the people in these racial groups are of Hispanic origin and trace their roots to Mexico, Puerto Rico, Central America, Cuba, and other Spanish-speaking countries.

Growing racial and ethnic diversity within many countries around the world presents us all with new challenges and an uncertain future. How do the different groups within a culture coexist? Why so often is there animosity and conflict? More specifically, what are the causes and effects of prejudice, and how can this chronic social disease be treated? These and other questions have triggered an examination of **multiculturalism,** the study of racial and ethnic groups within a culture.

Acculturation and Ethnic Identity

When people migrate from one country to another, they bring with them a cultural heritage and lifestyle that reaches deep into the past. The result is that each racial or ethnic group is unique—similar to the dominant culture

■ **acculturation** The process by which persons are changed by their immersion in a new culture.

in some ways, different in others. For example, black psychologist James Jones (1991) argues that compared to white American culture, black Americans tend to be more present-oriented, improvisational, expressive, spiritual, and emotional. Originating in Africa or among slaves of the American South, many blacks have adopted a colorful and conspicuous behavior style—as seen in a certain slow, casual, rhythmic walk; in handshakes such as the "high five" and "thumb grasp"; and in sports, where athletes "spike" footballs into the endzone and "slam dunk" basketballs through the hoop (Majors, 1991).

Regardless of where racial or ethnic groups come from, how they get there, or why they leave their land of origin, all face the same core dilemma: whether to blend in and "assimilate" into the new culture or retain a separate identity, language and all. There are two radically different historical perspectives on how this conflict between old and new should be managed. One is the romantic American ideal that all immigrant groups discard their heritage culture and blend into the American way of life. This assimilationist view is captured by the image of a *melting pot* in which different ethnic groups are mixed together to produce one harmonious mainstream culture. In the United States, this ideal is formalized in laws that require immigrants to renounce other citizenships, pass a test of American history, and take an oath of loyalty. The second approach encourages immigrants to retain their ancestral heritage, producing a culture that is ethnically diverse. In 1971, Canada adopted a policy of multiculturalism, in which the melting pot image was replaced by one of a colorful *mosaic* whereby each cultural group takes pride in its own unique identity and tolerates the differences between groups. Research shows, for example, that many recent Greek, Arab, and Italian immigrants to North America want their children to retain their own cultural identity (Moghaddam et al., 1993).

Torn between the need to fit in and a desire to retain their own heritage, ethnic-group members differ in the way they manage **acculturation**—the process by which persons are changed by their immersion in a new culture. According to John Berry and his colleagues (1989), there are four types of

Ethnic diversity is a fact of American life. In Dorchester, Massachusetts, these children represent twenty-four different nationalities.

coping strategies. At one extreme is *assimilation,* in which the person abandons the old for the new and completely embraces his or her host culture—its language, customs, identity, and ways of life. At the opposite extreme is *separation,* a pattern characterized by a desire to maintain one's ethnic traditions and not become part of the host culture. Native Americans who live on Indian reservations and the Amish who live in Lancaster, Pennsylvania, are good examples. A third strategy is *integration*, a bicultural pattern in which the person tries to make the best of both worlds by retaining old traditions while, at the same time, adapting to the new way of life. The fourth strategy is *marginalization,* in which the person has no desire to maintain traditional ties or adopt the new culture, perhaps due to discrimination. These four types of acculturation strategies are summarized in Figure 14.2.

Figure 14.2

Acculturation Strategies

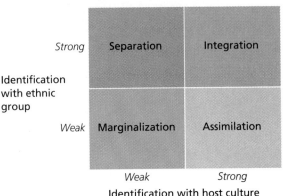

As a result of acculturation pressures, people who are caught between cultures come to identify with one or both of these cultures in the formation of an **ethnic identity**. Thus, French-speaking residents of Quebec may think of themselves as French, Canadian, French-Canadian, or neither; Irish-Americans may identify themselves as Irish, American, or Irish-American. Jean Phinney (1990) notes that our ethnic identities are revealed in the way we label ourselves, our sense of belonging to a group, our pride in that group, and the extent to which we speak the language, study the history, follow the customs, and enjoy the food, music, dance, literature, holidays, and traditions. Phinney also notes that ethnic-identity formation typically begins in adolescence with a passive acceptance of the dominant culture, is followed in early adulthood by an awakening of interest in one's roots, and culminates later on in an ethnic identification. As you might expect, ethnic-group identification is stronger among immigrants who enter the host country as adults than it is among those who arrive at a younger, more formative age.

Regardless of *how* immigrants, refugees, displaced natives, and other ethnic minorities adapt to their cultural environment, some individuals have a more difficult time than others in making the adjustment. The problem used to be called "culture shock." Now the term **acculturative stress** is used. Either way, studies show that entering a new culture may be accompanied by anxiety, depression, and other mental health problems—and that these problems are linked to language barriers, a lack of familiarity with

■ **ethnic identity** The part of a person's identity that is defined by an ethnic heritage, language, history, customs, and so on.

■ **acculturative stress** The stress and mental health problems often found in immigrants trying to adjust to a new culture.

Many cultural and ethnic groups in the United States like to retain the traditions of their homeland. Chinese-Americans across the country honor the Chinese New Year, and Mexican-Americans celebrate Cinco de Mayo.

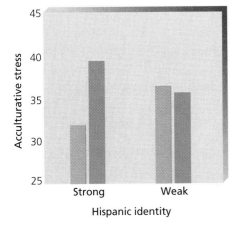

Figure 14.3

The Link Between Cultural Identity and Acculturative Stress

In Miami, Hispanic-American students answered questions about their Hispanic and American identities and acculturative stress. As shown, students who were "integrated" (leftmost bar) reported less stress than those who did not identify with one or both cultures.

the host culture, a lack of education, rejection of one's group, prejudice, the absence of social support services, and other factors (Berry et al., 1992). For example, Hispanic newcomers to the United States who were interviewed said they felt pressured to learn English, found it difficult to find suitable work, felt guilty about leaving their family and friends behind, did not make use of social services for fear of being deported, and felt that they were rejected because they were Latinos. Needless to say, these immigrants were under more stress at home and in the workplace than were Hispanics born in the United States (Cervantes et al., 1991).

Is there a healthy, optimum way for Hispanic-Americans and others to cope with being strangers in a strange land, fish swimming outside of the mainstream? Consider the acculturation strategies described earlier. Is it better to become "integrated" and bicultural, or should immigrants shed their native past in an effort to become fully "assimilated" into the host culture?

At this point, there is no clear answer. However, a study by Juan Sanchez and Diana Fernandez (1993) provides an important starting point. In Miami, these investigators administered questionnaires to 164 Hispanic college students who were born in Cuba, Puerto Rico, South America, Central America, or the United States. One questionnaire measured the extent to which subjects identified with their ethnic group ("I have a sense of belonging to Hispanic heritage"), a second measured the extent to which they identified with American culture ("I consider myself an American"), and the third assessed feelings of acculturative stress ("People look down on me if I practice customs of my culture," "It is difficult to show off my family"). As shown in Figure 14.3, students who were integrated—that is, those who had a strong ethnic identification *and* embraced American culture—reported less acculturative stress than students who did not identify with one or both cultures. This correlation should be interpreted with caution, however. It may mean that identification with one's host culture reduces stress, or that a lack of acculturative stress promotes identification. Either way, it is consistent with the increasingly popular notion that bicultural competence is psychologically adaptive, as it enables a person to alternate, without tension, between the two cultures (LaFromboise et al., 1993). As multiculturalist trends continue throughout the world, additional research should help provide some answers.

Discrimination

■ **discrimination** Behavior directed against persons because of their affiliation with a social group.

■ **racism** A deep-seated form of prejudice that is based on the color of a person's skin.

Of the many obstacles that confront ethnic minorities in any culture, the most vicious is **discrimination**—behavior directed against persons because of their affiliation with a social group. It is tempting to think of discrimination as a sin of the past. Unfortunately, recent incidents suggest that it still exists, and that its victims are avoided, excluded, rejected, belittled, and attacked, often because of their skin color or ethnic background. Discrimination has both cognitive and emotional roots. From a cognitive standpoint, it can often be traced to *stereotypes*—simplistic beliefs that associate whole groups of people with certain, sometimes unflattering, traits.

Stereotypes have a depersonalizing effect on the way people perceive ethnic minorities. In addition, discrimination is often motivated by deep-seated *prejudice*—feelings of hatred toward others based on their membership in a particular group. Whether the targets are blacks, whites, men, women, immigrants, or older people, prejudice is pervasive—and always has been.

Racism in America

Slave trading. The Deep South. Abolitionists. The Civil War. Lynch mobs. Separate but equal. The Ku Klux Klan. Jackie Robinson. The NAACP. Sitting in the back of the bus. Martin Luther King, Jr. Civil rights. Malcolm X. School busing. *Roots.* Affirmative action. Rodney King. Race relations in the United States have had a checkered, troubled, and emotional history—a history marked by both hatred and guilt, violent riots and peaceful marches, tolerance and intolerance, advances and setbacks. At the heart of it all, **racism:** a deep-seated form of prejudice that is based on the color of a person's skin. In the United States, this conflict is multidirectional, as all groups exhibit prejudice in one form or another.

The Ku Klux Klan's burning cross is a powerful, spine-chilling symbol of racism.

The Problem I have been told, and I believe it, that because I am white I'll never really understand what it feels like to be black and living in the United States. In a poignant, very personal book titled *Race,* Studs Terkel (1992) interviewed ordinary Americans, black and white, about what he calls "the American obsession." Terkel tells penetrating real-life stories that reveal the depth and scope of the problem.

In some cases, he observes overt, old-fashioned prejudice—for example, the new construction worker who complained bitterly about affirmative action because, as he said of all blacks, "they live like low lifes. Don't like to work. Let their homes run down." In other cases, the prejudice is more subtle—as when Terkel's friend's wife, who is white and who thinks of herself as colorblind, drove through a black neighborhood in Chicago: "The people at the corners were all gesticulating at her. She was very frightened, turned up the windows, and drove determinedly. She discovered after several blocks, she was going the wrong way on a one-way street and they were trying to help her. Her assumption was they were blacks and were out to get her."

Another instance involved Terkel himself. He boarded a bus one morning and deposited his fare, only to have the driver, a young black man, say he was a dime short. Terkel was sure he had paid the right amount and was upset. But he fished into his pocket and dropped another dime into the box. "Oh, I understood the man," he thought. "I know the history of his people's bondage. It was his turn—a show of power, if only in a small way. If that's how it is, that's how it is. Oh, well." Then it happened. "As I was about to disembark, I saw a dime on the floor. My dime. I held it up to him. 'You were right.' He was too busy driving to respond. I waved: 'Take it easy.' 'You, too,' he replied. I've a hunch he'd been through something like this before" (p. 6).

This very subtle form of racism may seem invisible, but it is painful and humiliating to its victims. Terkel interviewed a young black woman who said, "It infuriates me to think that some little white woman would get on the elevator with my father and assume, just by the color of his skin, that he's going to harm her, and clutch her purse tighter. To think that my father, who's worked hard all his life, put us through school, loves us, took care of us—to think that she would clutch her purse because he's there. The thought of it makes me so angry." Similarly, a professor talked about the time a black professional he knows, a college graduate who lived in the suburbs, visited a nearby country club. "Someone handed him a bag of golf clubs," he said. "They thought he was a caddy" (p. 96).

The Symptoms Racism in the 1990s is a two-way problem that poisons social relations between blacks and whites. Detecting racism is not as easy as it may seem. In 1933, Daniel Katz and Kenneth Braly found that many white college students believed that black Americans were lazy, happy-go-lucky, aggressive, and ignorant. Thankfully, follow-up surveys taken in 1951, 1967, and 1982 showed that these bigoted images had faded (Dovidio & Gaertner, 1986). Or had they? These days, very few white Americans openly express racist sentiments. But can public opinion polls be trusted, or has racism simply gone underground (see box, p. 532). And what about the distrust of whites that many black Americans harbor? If

SOCIAL PSYCHOLOGY   Business

Minorities in the Workplace

Today, a majority of white Americans believe that racial discrimination in the workplace is on the decline (Sigelman & Welch, 1991). African-Americans disagree. Interviews with black MBA graduates from prestigious business schools revealed that 84 percent believe that their race has a negative impact on their salaries, evaluations, and promotions (Jones, 1986). Similarly, *Sports Illustrated* surveyed three hundred highly paid professional athletes who play in the NFL, the NBA, and Major League Baseball (Johnson, 1991). As shown in the figure, the disparity in perceptions was striking: 63 percent of black respondents, compared to only 2 percent of their white teammates, thought that blacks in their sport were the victims of discrimination—in wages, fan support, treatment by coaches, opportunities for management, and commercial endorsements. One black football player said, "Black players who make too much, or talk too much, or don't play three times better than whites get cut" (p. 45). Yet a white player from the same league insisted that "there are more instances of discrimination against white athletes" (p. 45). Who is right? The difference of opinion does not prove that there is discrimination in sports. But is there,

in fact, a lingering scent of discrimination in the workplace of the 1990s?

It's not that clear. Granted, there are fewer instances of overt discrimination now than in the past. When Jackie Robinson broke the color barrier in baseball in 1947, it was news. Today, there are no such explicit barriers. In fact, research does *not* support the claim that on-the-job evaluations are biased by race (Waldman & Avolio, 1991; Sackett & DuBois, 1991). But does the same "glass ceiling" that blocks career women also block minorities? If so, what are these transparent barriers?

One may be the face-to-face job interview. In the context of such an interview, Carl Word and his colleagues (1974) found that when white subjects questioned an applicant who was black rather than white, they sat farther away, made more speech errors, and held shorter interviews—factors that add up to a distant social style that causes people to behave in a more nervous and awkward manner. It would be interesting to see if a similar result were to be found today, some twenty years later. For minority men and women on the job market, such a result would prove sobering.

Figure 14.4   How Racist Beliefs Distort Perception

After looking at this drawing, one subject described it to a second, who described it to a third, and so on. After six rounds of communication, the final report often placed the razor blade held by the white man into the black man's hand (Allport & Postman, 1947).

Once in the workplace, minority employees may face additional institutional barriers. Thomas Pettigrew and Joanne Martin (1987) cite three biases. First, negative racial stereotypes may lead supervisors and co-workers to hold low expectations for performance that may be difficult to overcome. Second, in organizations that hire few minorities, those who are hired draw more than their fair share of attention, leading others to exaggerate both the positive and the negative. Third, it is often believed that minorities are hired as "tokens," or to fill affirmative action quotas, thus raising even more doubts about their competence. Together, these biases subject minorities to what Pettigrew and Martin call "triple jeopardy." In fact, there may be a fourth problem: minorities often feel excluded, socially, from informal work groups; are not well "networked"; and lack the kinds of sponsors, role models, and "mentors" that are necessary for moving up in an organization (Irons & Moore, 1985).

At this point, it is hard to separate perceptions of bias and discrimination from actual practices in the workplace. More research is thus needed to document the problem, the reasons for it, and, where needed, the solutions.

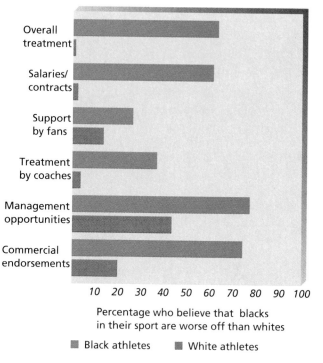

Is There Racial Discrimination in Sports?
In a recent survey, *Sports Illustrated* found that more black athletes, compared to their white teammates, believe that blacks in their sport are victims of discrimination.

people who are prejudiced will not admit it to pollsters, or even to themselves, how can we know that this chronic social disease still exists? What are the symptoms? Better yet, what is the cure?

People may not openly express their prejudices, but racism can be subtle, coloring our perceptions and our behavior. In an old and classic demonstration of this point, Gordon Allport and Leo Postman (1947) showed subjects a picture of a subway train filled with passengers. In the picture were a black man dressed in a suit and a white man holding a razor (see Figure 14.4). One subject viewed the scene briefly and described it to a second subject who had not seen it. The second subject communicated the description to a third subject and so on, through six rounds of communication. The result: The final subject's report often indicated that the black man, not the white man, was holding the razor. Some subjects even reported that he was waving the weapon in a threatening manner.

The way people *interpret* an event may also be influenced by race, even today. In one study, white subjects watched on a TV monitor an interaction involving two men. A discussion developed into a heated argument and one man seemed to shove the other. When the antagonist was white and the victim was black, only 17 percent of the subjects saw the shove as an act of violence. Most said it was just "horseplay." Yet when the antagonist was black and the victim white, the number of "violence" interpretations rose to 75 percent (Duncan, 1976). Similar results were found among children (Lawrence, 1991; Sagar & Schofield, 1980).

Using Schools to Combat Racism

Forty years ago, the United States Supreme Court launched a bold and historic experiment in race relations. In the case of *Brown* v. *Board of Education of Topeka*, the Court ruled that racially separate schools were unequal, in violation of the Constitution. This opinion was informed by research suggesting that segregation had an adverse effect on the self-esteem and academic performance of black students, and on prejudice itself (Allport et al., 1953).

At the time, the Court's decision was controversial. Many Americans opposed school desegregation and argued that forcing interracial contact would only worsen matters. Others pinned their hopes on the *contact hypothesis*—which states that under certain conditions, direct contact between members of different groups will improve relations. For contact to have this effect, it was proposed, four conditions have to be met: (1) the two groups should be of *equal status* within the contact situation, (2) there should be *personal interactions* between individual members, (3) the groups should have a common goal that requires their *cooperation*—so that "them" can become part of "us," and (4) the contact should be supported by *social norms*, as set in part by people in authority.

Despite the Court's ruling, desegregation proceeded slowly. Indeed, many schools remained untouched until the early 1970s. Then as the dust began to settle, research brought the sad news that little had changed, that race relations were not improving (Stephan, 1986). Was the contact hypothesis wrong? Maybe not. School desegregation had not produced the desired changes, but the conditions necessary for effective intergroup contact had not been met. Nobody ever said that deeply rooted racism would be erased overnight just by throwing blacks and whites together. In fact, the four conditions necessary for contact to succeed did not exist in the public schools.

First, the two groups did not come together on equal status terms. When the public schools were desegregated, the white children were from more affluent families, were better prepared, and thus were favored more in class than their black peers (Cohen, 1984). Second, personal interactions among black and white children were uncommon. Studies show that schools are not a melting pot. After the bus arrives, students gravitate toward members of their own race in the cafeteria, the playground, and the classroom. What's more, the prob-

■ **contact hypothesis** The proposition that in certain conditions, direct contact between members of rival groups will improve relations.

Racist beliefs can also be detected without asking direct questions. Researchers have found that *reaction time*—the speed it takes to answer a question—can be used to uncover hidden prejudices. In one study, for example, white subjects read word pairs and pressed a button whenever they thought the words fit together. In each case, the word *blacks* or *whites* was paired with either a positive trait (*clean, smart,* etc.) or a negative trait (*stupid, lazy,* etc.). The results were revealing. Subjects did not openly associate blacks with negative terms or whites with positive terms. And they were equally quick to reject the negative terms in both cases. However, subjects were quicker to respond to the positive words when they were paired with *whites* than with *blacks*. Since it takes less time to react to information that fits existing attitudes, this finding suggests that subjects were unconsciously predisposed to associate positive traits with whites more than with blacks (Gaertner & McLaughlin, 1983).

This result may seem subtle, but it suggests that racial prejudice may be so deeply ingrained in our culture that the negative images are as difficult to break as a bad habit (Devine, 1989). That's why the wife of Studs Terkel's friend was quick to assume that the black pedestrians who were gesturing at her posed a threat when, in fact, they were trying to let her know she was driving the wrong way on a one-way street. And that is why Terkel himself jumped to the conclusion that the black bus driver who said he was a dime short was being difficult when, in fact, the dime had fallen

lem is compounded when students are "tracked" based on grades, a policy that further separates the advantaged white students from disadvantaged blacks. In other words, desegregation does not ensure integration (Epstein, 1985; Schofield, 1982). Third, the typical classroom is filled with competition for a teacher's attention, grades, and so on—not with the kinds of cooperative activities that bring people together to achieve a common goal. Fourth, school desegregation, at least initially, was not supported by social norms. Many principals, teachers, and politicians objected, and many parents boycotted busing—hardly an ingredient for success.

Although problems have plagued school desegregation efforts, research shows that prejudice *can* be reduced in situations that satisfy the chief requirements of the contact hypothesis (Cook, 1985). In the classroom, Elliot Aronson and his colleagues (1978) developed a cooperative learning method they called the "jigsaw classroom." In newly desegregated elementary schools in Texas and California, they assigned fifth-graders to small, racially and academically mixed groups. The material to be learned within each group was divided into subtopics, much the way a jigsaw puzzle is broken into pieces. Each student was responsible for learning one piece of the puzzle, after which all members took turns teaching their material to one another. Under this system, everyone—regardless of race, ability, or self-confidence—needs everyone else if the group as a whole is to succeed. The

In cooperative learning, racially mixed groups of children work together on a common problem.

method produced impressive results. Compared to children in traditional classes, those in jigsaw classrooms grew to like one another more, were less prejudiced, liked school more, and had higher self-esteem. In addition, academic test scores improved for minority students and remained the same for white students. Like an interracial sports team, the jigsaw classroom offers a promising way to create a truly integrated educational setting. It also provides a model of how to use contact to promote greater tolerance of diversity among children of all colors.

on the floor. The problem may be more common than we realize. Indeed, many nonprejudiced white Americans admit that they are not always fair to blacks—an insight that causes them to feel embarrassed, guilty, and ashamed of themselves (Devine et al., 1991).

The Treatment   Racism is a social disease that gets transmitted from one generation to the next and afflicts millions. Can it be treated? Can stereotypes and prejudice be wiped out by a mass-media blitz designed to inform people that their expectations and fears are unfounded? Social psychologists used to think that such efforts at persuasive communication would prove effective, but they do not. Indeed, when you consider the many sources of stereotypes and prejudice, the prospects seem dim. There is, however, reason for hope. The key is to expose children to diversity, and the ideal setting is the school (see box).

GENDER: THE GREAT DIVIDE?

Do you sleep in the nude? Nineteen percent of men say yes, compared to only 6 percent of women. How much TV-watching time do you spend working the remote control? Men estimate 55 percent, women 34 percent.

How many articles of clothing do you buy in a year? Women estimate 52, men only 33. Are you afraid to walk at night within a mile of your home? Sixty-two percent of women say yes, compared to 26 percent of men. Are you more likely to refuse sex than your partner is? Forty-three percent of women say yes, compared to only 22 percent of men (see Table 14.4).

Table 14.4

Self-Reported Differences Between Men and Women

In search of the so-called gender gap, pollsters have uncovered differences along every imaginable dimension—and then some (Weiss, 1991).

Items	Males	Females
% who consider themselves handsome or pretty	42	28
% who say they cry when they're blue	4	23
% married who think private time is important	32	46
% who look forward to hearing the telephone ring	20	37
% who consider themselves happy	90	90
% who believe in life elsewhere in the universe	41	32
% who frequently pray	26	39
% who feel guilty after eating candy	17	48
% who speak to their parents at least once a week	64	72
% who like to watch daytime soaps	7	33
% who think the U.S. president is underpaid	28	17
% who say they can be trusted	41	41
% who saw an X-rated movie last year	31	17

As these examples illustrate, it is common for pollsters to find a "gender gap" in the ways that men and women describe their beliefs, attitudes, preferences, and behavior (Weiss, 1991). What exactly do these results mean? Why are people so fascinated by even the silliest and most trivial of sex differences? And why, as Carol Jacklin (1989) put it, has the study of sex differences become a "national preoccupation"? Browse the shelves of any bookstore and you'll see one paperback title after another that addresses this intriguing topic. There are books for men and books for women, books that preach the masculine ideal and books that tell us how to be more feminine, books that portray men and women as similar and books that focus on the differences. In *You Just Don't Understand*, sociolinguist Deborah Tannen (1990) argues that women and men have different conversational styles, a situation that often leads to misunderstanding. In *Brain Sex*, Ann Moir and David Jessel (1989) conclude from scientific evidence that men and women are different psychologically "because their brains are different" (p. 5). In *The Mismeasure of Woman*, psychologist Carol Tavris (1992) claims there are no "essential" differences between the sexes—but that scientists perpetuate stereotypes to devalue women. As shown on p. 537, even cartoonists have gotten into the act.

On the topic of sex differences, two sets of questions need to be addressed. First, in what ways are men and women *truly* different, and in what ways are they similar? Second, what are the biological and environmental bases for sex differences? In the following section, we try to distinguish between the facts and the fiction.

Differences Between Men and Women

To children, the notion that there are innate differences between the sexes is immortalized in a poem: "What are little boys made of? Frogs and snails and puppy dogs' tails. . . . What are little girls made of? Sugar and spice and all that's nice." Ingredients aside, are males and females really that different?

Certain biological sex differences are a fact of life that cannot be denied. At puberty, the onset of sexual maturation is brought on by rising hormone levels—estrogen and progesterone in females, and testosterone in males. Girls reach puberty at about the age of eleven, boys at the age of thirteen. On average, adult men are 5 inches taller than women and 20 to 30 pounds heavier, have 40 percent more muscle and 12 percent less fat, and sweat more. The average woman can arm-curl 52 percent as much weight as the average male and bench-press 37 percent as much. The average man has a million more red blood cells in each drop of blood, absorbs 30 percent less alcohol into his bloodstream (controlling for differences in body weight, this explains why men hold their liquor better than women), and has 10 percent more lung volume than women of the same size. Men are also more likely to be left-handed, snore in their sleep, become bald as they age, have a deficiency in color vision, and die of a heart attack. At birth, the average American female is expected to live for 78 years, the average American male for 71 years (Weiss, 1991).

Statistics such as these seem innocent enough—and are not the subject of debate. The biological approach becomes politically charged, however, when psychological differences between men and women are found *and* when these differences are attributed to sex hormones, brain anatomy, and other biological factors. The reason for the political heat is clear: our views of the nature of men and women will inform important policy questions such as whether military women should be allowed into combat, or whether men should be given equal consideration in child custody suits. Are there reliable sex differences in behavior? If so, are the differences innately determined? Some scientists claim men and women are so innately different that to suggest otherwise is "to build a society based on a biological and scientific lie" (Moir & Jessel, 1989, p. 5). Yet others argue just as forcefully that "there is nothing *essential*—that is, universal and unvarying—in the natures of women and men" (Tavris, 1992, p. 21). Let's look at some of the evidence and consider the arguments on both sides.

Sexuality   One way in which men and women differ is in their sexual attitudes and behavior. Surveys conducted worldwide consistently show that men are more sexually promiscuous than women are. Among adolescents, boys report higher levels of sexual activity than girls do. Later in life, men are more likely to enjoy pure sex without emotional involvement or commitment, more likely to be excited by pornographic material, and more

"Do you have any of those books that understand men?"

"Talk to me, Alice. I speak woman."

Cartoonists often play up the popular notion that men and women have little in common.
[Top: Drawing by Weber; © 1993 The New Yorker Magazine, Inc. Bottom: Drawing by M. Stevens; © 1992 The New Yorker Magazine, Inc.]

Aware of political sensitivities, Diane Halpern (1992) precedes her presentation of the biological perspective with these words: "WARNING: Some of the research and theories described in this chapter may be disturbing to your basic belief systems."

Research shows that men are more likely than women to interpret mixed-sex social interactions in sexualized terms.

likely to make the first move to initiate sexual encounters (Brehm, 1992). Men are also more permissive than women in their attitudes toward casual premarital sex and extramarital affairs (Oliver & Hyde, 1993). A recent national survey of 2,765 Americans also revealed that men masturbate more than women, have more premarital sex, prefer a variety of sexual techniques, sleep with more partners, and have less negative attitudes about one-night stands. Women, on the other hand, are more likely to have been sexually molested as children and sexually harassed as adults (Janus & Janus, 1993).

Compared to women, men also seem to view the world in more "sexualized" terms. In one study, Antonia Abbey (1982) arranged for pairs of male and female college students to talk for five minutes, while other students observed these interactions. When she later questioned the actors and observers, Abbey found that the males were more sexually attracted to the females than vice versa—and that they rated the female actors as more promiscuous and seductive than the women had rated themselves. In another study, male subjects who read stories of various heterosexual dating scenarios were more likely than female subjects to assume that the women in these scenarios wanted to have sex (Muehlenhard, 1988). Other research confirms this point: among men more than women, eye contact, a friendly remark, a brush against the arm, a compliment, and an innocent smile are often seen as sexual come-ons (Kowalski, 1993). These misperceptions occur not only in the laboratory but also between strangers, acquaintances, and casual friends who meet at parties, school, work, and other settings (Abbey, 1987; Saal et al., 1989).

Aggression   Hunting, combat, rough-and-tumble play, barroom brawls, contact sports, and murder. No matter when, where, or how you measure it, males exhibit more physical aggression than females. In most species of the animal kingdom, males are more likely than females to attack and fight (Archer, 1988). On the playground, boys are more likely than girls to engage in rambunctious and competitive group games (Maccoby, 1990). And in all countries in which criminal records are kept, more men than women commit violent crimes (Kenrick, 1987). According to FBI statistics, for example, 82 percent of all those arrested are male—a figure that rises to 89 percent for violent offenses such as murder, rape, and aggravated assault. In U.S. prisons, men outnumber women by a ratio of 18 to 1. In laboratory experiments in which subjects believe they are administering painful electric shocks to another person, men select higher voltage shocks than women (Eagly & Steffen, 1986). Finally in public opinion polls, more men than women favor military solutions to world problems, the use of physical punishment to discipline children, and the death penalty (Weiss, 1991).

Cognitive Skills   When intelligence tests are constructed, problems that prove more difficult for one sex or the other are taken out or balanced by questions that have the opposite effect. Accordingly, there are no discernible sex differences in IQ. But are there differences in specific skills? Consider mathematics—and related fields such as physics, engineering, and computers. Despite increasing numbers of women in the work force, men continue to outnumber women in these occupations. Is it possible that the disparity is based on sex differences in math ability?

In Chapter 11, we saw that both boys and girls start to count at the age of two and are equally skilled at arithmetic in elementary school (Kimball, 1989). Then in junior high school, males surpass females in mathematical problem solving—and this difference is carried into college and adulthood. On the math part of the SAT, male high school seniors outscore their female classmates by an average of 50 points (Hyde et al., 1990). This difference is particularly evident among the most precocious of math students. Among seventh-graders who score over 700 on the math SATS, boys outnumber girls by a ratio of 100 to 1 (Benbow, 1988). And in the U.S.A. Mathematical Olympiad Contest for high school students, 142 of its 144 winners from 1972 to 1989 were male (Stanley, 1990).

Males also perform better on certain visual-spatial tasks—for example, imagining how three-dimensional objects will appear when rotated, how flat objects appear when folded, or how solid objects appear when unfolded; visually locating the vertical or horizontal plane in space; or finding a simple figure embedded in a complex pattern (see Figure 14.5). These skills are used for playing chess, assembling objects, reading maps and blueprints, and navigating from one location to another. The sex difference in spatial performance may also account for part of the gender gap in math, especially geometry (Burnett, 1986; Linn & Petersen, 1985).

SPATIAL PERCEPTION
Align the rod within these frames so that it is vertical.

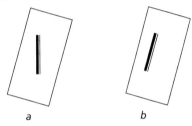

a   b

MENTAL ROTATION
Are these pairs of figures the same except for their orientation?

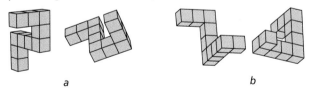

a   b

SPATIAL VISUALIZATION
Is Figure (a) part of Figure (b)?

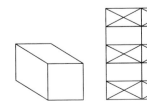
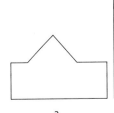
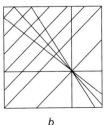

a   b   a   b

Figure 14.5

Sample Tests of Visual-Spatial Ability

In general, men outscore women on these tests (Halpern, 1992).

Paralleling the apparent male advantage in math and spatial relations, women typically perform better at spelling, grammar, reading comprehension, and verbal fluency tasks that require people to quickly come up with appropriate words, phrases, or sentences (see Figure 14.6). Further suggesting that there is a female advantage in verbal fluency are education statistics which show that boys are four times more likely than girls to stutter and five to ten times more likely to have dyslexia, a reading disorder (Halpern, 1992). Women are also more socially sensitive than men are. Whether or not you call it "female intuition," research shows that women are better at using facial expressions, tone of voice, and other nonverbal cues to determine how other people are feeling (Hall, 1984).

Are male-female differences like the ones just described rooted in innate biological differences between the sexes? Or do these same disparities stem from the unequal social experiences that affect men and women? Let's examine these two different perspectives.

Figure 14.6

Sample Tests of Verbal Abilities

These tests tap different types of verbal ability. In general, women tend to outscore men on such tests (Halpern, 1992).

1. Name as many words as you can that start with the letter "k."

2. Select the word that is most nearly the same in meaning:

   vivacious
          (A) honest
          (B) mediocre
          (C) lively
          (D) brat

3. igloo: Indian:: tepee:

   (A) ice (B) canvas (C) Eskimo (D) home

4. Answer the questions based on the information provided in this passage.

   The literature with regard to sex differences in verbal abilities has been mixed with some researchers reporting large differences and others reporting no statistically significant differences. It seems that the controversy can be resolved by looking at the types of verbal tasks in which differences are found and determining how they differ from tasks in which differences are not found. It may be that tasks like solving verbal analogies are more similar to mathematical problem solving than to some of the other verbal tasks.

   (A) What is the "controversy" that is referred to in the second sentence?

   (B) Why does the author suggest that verbal analogies are similar to mathematical problems?

5. Which is correct?

   (A) Give the money to Bob and I.

   (B) Give the money to Bob and me.

The Biological Perspective

Even before a baby is born, it has a full genetic heritage contained within its 23 pairs of chromosomes. The twenty-third pair controls one's sex. Everyone receives an X chromosome from the mother, but there's an equal chance that the father will donate an X or a short, stumpy Y chromosome to the pair. If the chromosome is an X, the offspring will be female (XX); if Y, it will be male (XY).

Six or so weeks after conception, the male and female embryos look the same and are similarly equipped. In those that are genetically female, ovaries are formed. In those that are genetically male, however, undescended testes form and secrete the male hormone *testosterone*. The presence of testosterone sparks the growth of the male sex organs; its absence results in the development of female sex organs. In other words, having an XY or XX genetic endowment does not itself guarantee male or female development. If for some reason testosterone is not secreted in an XY embryo, the genetically male baby will be born with a girl's genitals. If testosterone is injected into an XX embryo, the genetic female will have the genitals of a normal male (Kelly, 1991). Prenatal exposure to sex hormones also affects sexual behavior. In studies with rats, mice, and certain other mammals, female embryos given testosterone later mount other females upon sexual maturity, while male embryos deprived of testosterone do not (Hines, 1982).

Many researchers have recently become interested in male-female differences in the brain. The most obvious place to start this search is in the *hypothalamus*—the small limbic structure perched over the brainstem that controls sexual behavior. In rats, Roger Gorski and his colleagues (1978) found that an area of the hypothalamus called the "sexually dimorphic nucleus" is larger in males than in females—and is increased by prenatal injections of testosterone. In humans, this area is more than twice the size in males than in females (Allen et al., 1989).

Another brain structure that has attracted attention is the *corpus callosum*, the bundle of nerve fibers that connects the right and left hemispheres. Using post-autopsy measurements and MRI images of live healthy adults, some researchers have found that certain regions of the corpus callosum are thicker and more bulbous in women's brains than in men's (de Lacoste-Utamsing & Holloway, 1982; Clarke et al., 1989). At this point, however, it is not clear to researchers how reliable this difference is or even if the width of the corpus callosum—and presumably the number of fibers separating the two hemispheres—has any psychological significance (Byne et al., 1988).

Many researchers who believe there are innate psychological differences between men and women also believe that the sex hormones, testosterone and estrogen, are the key distinguishing ingredients (Gerall et al., 1992). In the prenatal life of an organism, these hormones have long-term "organizational" effects on the developing nervous system. Later in life, beginning at puberty, fluctuating hormone levels can also have short-term "activational" effects on behavior.

It is widely believed that testosterone fuels male sexual behavior. For that reason, castration (the surgical removal of the testes, which lowers testosterone production) has been used over the years to prepare harem guards, ensure celibacy, cure masturbation, and rehabilitate sex offenders. Research shows that castration may have the intended effect: testosterone is not essential for sexual performance, but men with lowered levels often have less sexual interest and desire. There appears to be a similar link between ovarian hormones and the sexual behavior of women. Estrogen is not necessary for performance, but sexual motivation may fluctuate across the menstrual cycle (Carter, 1991).

There's also a strong connection between testosterone and aggression. If testosterone is injected into immature male mice, they attack other males; if they're castrated, aggression levels subside. Similarly, castration transforms a wild stallion into a gentle horse and a snarling dog into a domesticated pet. In rats, monkeys, deer, and many other animal species, the males become increasingly aggressive at the onset of sexual maturation, at a time when testosterone levels surge, and less so as testosterone levels decline in adulthood (this may explain why the crime rate is always high among teenagers). James Dabbs and his co-workers (1987) measured testosterone in saliva samples taken from male prisoners and found that those who had committed unprovoked violent crimes had the highest concentration levels. Dabbs and his associates (1990) then compared men of different occupational groups and found that football players had higher levels of testosterone than ministers did. These correlations cannot be used to prove that testosterone *causes* human aggression (competition triggers the release of testosterone, so the link may be the other way around!). However, a good deal of animal research suggests that it does play a role (Archer, 1991; Monaghan & Glickman, 1992).

Testosterone may also have an effect on cognitive skills. According to Norman Geschwind and Peter Behan (1982), prenatal testosterone washes over the fetal brain, slowing the development of the left hemisphere, where language skills are housed, and permitting enhanced growth of the right hemisphere, which is associated with spatial skills. Supporting the hypothesis that the male brain is right-dominated is the fact that more males than females are left-handed (you may recall from Chapter 2 that the right hemisphere controls the left half of the body and vice versa). This male right-dominance, say Geschwind and Behan, can explain why most talented math students are male, why men perform better on visual-spatial tasks, and why women excel instead in various language-related tests.

Is there really a link between sex hormones and intellectual performance? There are some tantalizing results consistent with this controversial hypothesis. In one study, males who reached puberty late due to abnormally low testosterone levels performed worse on spatial ability tasks than other males. In a second study, normal men were better at the same tasks than those with very high levels (in fact, most males score higher on spatial tests in the spring, when their testosterone levels are low, than in the fall, when testosterone levels are higher). In a third study, women with high testosterone levels did better on these spatial tasks than other women. Put these puzzle pieces together and what do you see? Elizabeth Hampson and Doreen Kimura (1992) reviewed this research and concluded that testosterone is correlated with sharpened spatial skills, at least up to a point. As depicted in Figure 14.7, too little or too much is associated with a decline in performance (Gouchie & Kimura, 1991).

According to Kimura (1989), cognitive performance may also be affected by estrogen and progesterone. Hampson and Kimura (1988) tested women at different phases of the menstrual cycle and found that they performed somewhat better at spatial tasks when their estrogen and progesterone levels were low rather than high. Also interesting is that performance on tests of verbal fluency, in which women typically excel, was better when these levels were high rather than low. Do sex hormones provide a continuing basis for existing differences in cognitive performance? Although the theoretical implications are exciting for biologically oriented researchers, some of whom have replicated these results (Heister et al., 1989), Kimura is quick to caution that the differences are small—too small to make predictions about individual men and women.

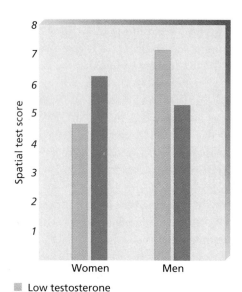

Low testosterone
High testosterone

Figure 14.7

The Link Between Testosterone and Spatial Skills

Gouchie and Kimura (1991) measured testosterone (T) in saliva samples and found that spatial test scores were higher for high-T women and low-T men than for low-T women (whose T levels were the lowest) and high-T men (whose T levels were highest). Too little or too much testosterone appears to be associated with a decline in spatial performance.

The Environmental Perspective

When a baby is born, the first question everyone asks is the same: "Is it a boy or a girl?" The newborn is then given a male or female name, dressed in blue or pink clothing, and showered with masculine or feminine gifts. Over the next few years, the typical boy receives toy trucks, baseball bats, building blocks, tools, guns, and chemistry sets, while his sister plays with dolls, stuffed animals, kitchen toys, sewing kits, and tea sets. In school, boys are guided into math and science, and girls are expected to seek out art, music, and social activities. These distinctions persist in college, as male students are more likely to major in math, economics, and hard sciences, while females predominate in education, arts, and humanities. At work, men become doctors, builders, airline pilots, engineers, and bankers; women become secretaries, nurses, teachers, flight attendants, and bank tellers. The moral of the story: The human male and female may love, work, play, and have families together, but to some extent, they live in different worlds.

Gender Roles   The fact that males and females have different life experiences may explain the sex differences often observed. If you grew up in the United States, for example, you were probably taught to believe that it's more important for boys than for girls to learn to compete, fight, and defend themselves. Chances are, you also think it's more appropriate for the man to ask the woman out for a date as well as to pay, drive, and initiate the good-night kiss.

Experience promotes sex differences through a process of *social learning*. Parents, teachers, and other socializing agents communicate **gender roles** to children at an early age, serve as same-sex role models, and use reward and punishment to shape up behaviors that are gender-appropriate. The models that surround children are a powerful source of influence. For example, Gary Levy (1989) found that girls with mothers who worked outside the home were more flexible in their perceptions of male and female sex roles than were those whose mothers worked in the home.

What transpires in the home is only part of what influences gender roles. Hugh Lytton and David Romney (1991) summarized the results of 172 studies and found that although parents tend to direct children to engage in sex-typed activities, in other ways they treat their sons and daughters in a similar manner. The problem is, the social learning of gender roles is supported by a host of cultural institutions. Studies show that "Dick and Jane" readers, cartoons, TV shows, and magazines overportray their male and female characters in traditional roles. Gone are the days when women were depicted merely as housewives who frantically shopped, cooked, polished, and fretted over the husband's "ring around the collar." Still, some sex stereotyping remains—for example, in TV commercials (Lovdal, 1989) and in children's books (Purcell & Stewart, 1990). Even current MTV rock music videos overportray men and women in sex-stereotyped ways (Hansen, 1989). The result of all this is that boys are taught to be masculine, while girls are taught to be feminine.

Experience shapes not only our behavior but our beliefs as well. According to Sandra Bem (1981), experience leads people to form **gender schemas**—beliefs about men and women that influence the way we perceive

■ **gender roles** Sex-typed behaviors promoted by social learning.

■ **gender schemas** Beliefs about men and women that influence the way we perceive ourselves and others.

ourselves and others. Research shows that nine-month-old infants can distinguish between male and female faces (Leinbach & Fagot, 1993), and that children identify themselves as boys or girls by the age of three—and divide the world into masculine and feminine categories soon after that (Biernat, 1991; Martin et al., 1990). People who have rigid gender schemas are more likely to pay attention to a person's sex and form negative impressions of others who break the norms for acceptable male and female conduct (Frable, 1989).

In some cultures of the world, "sexist" traditions are quite strong. In Sudan, currently ruled by Islamic fundamentalists, women must wear veils over the face and may not leave the country without permission from their fathers, husbands, or brothers. In Israel, where Jewish religious law prevails, a wife cannot get divorced without the consent of her husband—leaving thousands of women known as the Agunot ("the anchored") married against their will. In India, a Hindu system of dowries requires that the bride's family pay the groom cash and gifts equal to his social standing. The result is that girls are considered a burden on their parents. And in China, where males are economically more valuable than females, and where the government controls population growth by limiting each couple to one or two children, many female infants are aborted, abandoned, given to relatives for adoption, or killed at birth. In the Guangdong province, men between thirty and forty-five years of age cannot find wives because they outnumber women due to such past practices (*Time*, 1990). And the problem is getting worse. Aided by ultrasound tests that reveal the sex of a fetus, parents are aborting increasing numbers of girls. Worldwide, 105 males are born for every 100 females. In China, however, the sex ratio is now 118 to 100 (see Figure 14.8).

Needless to say, prescribed sex roles vary widely from one culture to the next. Consider your reaction to statements such as, "The first duty of a woman with young children is to home and family" and "When a man and woman live together, she should do the housework and he should do the heavier chores." People living in Nigeria, Pakistan, India, and Japan agree more with these statements than people from Germany, the Netherlands, Finland, or England—with Americans and Canadians falling between the two extremes (Williams & Best, 1990).

Even in places where gender barriers of the past have eroded, these barriers have not disappeared. In the United States, 57 million women were employed in 1990—nearly double that of the 1960s. The number of women who now go on to become doctors, lawyers, accountants, and other professionals has increased significantly in recent years. And at home, more men today than in the past are cooking, cleaning, shopping, changing diapers, and doing household chores. Despite these impressive changes, however, men and women continue to play different roles in the home. From interviews with working parents, sociologist Arlie Hochschild (1989) argues that wives more than husbands come home after work to a "second shift" of domestic and child-care duties. When the number of hours spent working outside and inside the home are combined, what emerges is a "leisure gap" that favors men.

Gender Stereotypes   Cultures vary in their sex-role traditions, but stereotypes about men and women are universal. If you had to describe the typical man and woman, what would you say? In a large-scale study, 2,800

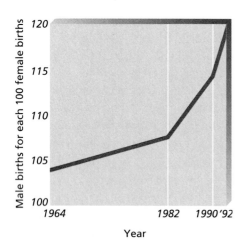

Figure 14.8

Sex Ratios in China

Birth statistics reveal that 118 boys are born for every 100 females in China (by nature, this ratio is 105 to 100). Considered less valuable, female fetuses are being aborted in increasing numbers (Kristof, 1993).

college students from thirty countries across the world were asked to check off adjectives from a list that are believed to describe men or women. Consistently, men were said to be adventurous, strong, dominant, assertive, task-oriented, aggressive, enterprising, and independent. Just as consistently, women were said to be sensitive, gentle, dependent, emotional, sentimental, weak, submissive, and people-oriented (Williams & Best, 1982). These stereotypes are also evident in children's descriptions of others (Best & Williams, 1993).

Male and female stereotypes are so deeply ingrained that they influence our behavior literally from the moment a baby is born. In a fascinating study, first-time parents of fifteen girls and fifteen boys were interviewed within twenty-four hours of the birth. There were no differences between the male and female newborns in height, weight, or superficial physical appearance. Yet the parents of girls rated their babies as softer, smaller, and more finely featured, while the fathers of boys described their sons as stronger, larger, better coordinated, and more alert (Rubin et al., 1974). Could there have been differences that only the parents were able to discern? Doubtful. In a second study, men and women were shown a videotape of a nine-month-old baby. Half were told they were watching a boy; the other half, a girl. Although all subjects saw the same tape, their perceptions were influenced by the gender manipulation. At one point, for example, the baby burst into tears over a jack-in-the-box. The reaction? *He* was *angry*, and *she* was *frightened* (Condry & Condry, 1976).

Gender stereotypes are so widespread that you may wonder if they are accurate and, if not, why they persist. Enlightened by years of research on sex differences, psychologists can now draw the following conclusion: conventional wisdom contains a small kernel of truth, but it oversimplifies and exaggerates that truth (Maccoby & Jacklin, 1974; Eagly & Wood, 1991). Yes, most men are somewhat more competitive and aggressive than most women. And yes, most women are more socially sensitive and cooperative than most men. But our stereotypes about male-female differences are greater than the differences themselves.

A study by Carol Lynn Martin (1987) illustrates the point. She presented male and female adults with a list of thirty traits that were "masculine," "feminine," or neutral, and asked them to circle those that were self-descriptive. A separate group of subjects received the same list and estimated for each trait the percentage of men and women in general for whom it was an accurate description. By comparing the percentage of male and female subjects who *actually* found the traits self-descriptive with the *estimated* percentages, Martin found that expectations outstripped reality. In actuality, the masculine traits were just slightly more self-descriptive of men and the feminine traits of women, but the estimated differences were substantial. Like the cartoonist who draws caricatures, we mentally stretch, expand, and enlarge the ways in which men and women differ.

If men and women are more similar than we think, why do exaggerated perceptions of difference endure? Alice Eagly's (1987) **social roles theory** provides a possible explanation. According to Eagly, perceived sex differences, although based in part on actual differences, are magnified by the unequal social roles occupied by men and women. The process involves three steps. First, through a combination of biological and social factors, a division of labor between the sexes has emerged over time—at home and in the work setting. Men are more likely to work in construction or business;

■ **social roles theory** The theory that perceived sex differences are magnified by the unequal social roles occupied by men and women.

Women in the Workplace

In recent years, women in the United States and many other countries have made great strides in moving from the homefront to the workplace. Despite their progress, however, gender equality is a seldom-achieved ideal. Specifically, gender gaps exist in three important areas: (1) occupational choice, (2) income, and (3) leadership opportunities.

Occupational Choice

How many female airline pilots have you met recently? What about male secretaries? Look at the table, and you'll see that even today, in the 1990s, there are some striking sex differences in the workplace.

Part of the problem is that sex discrimination in childhood—for example, greater encouragement of boys in math, science, computers, and mechanical pursuits—paves the way for diverging career paths later in life (Eccles et al., 1990). Another problem is that employers discriminate against men and women who try to cross gender lines in their occupation. A study by Peter Glick and his colleagues (1988) illustrates the point. These investigators sent a fictitious résumé to 212 business professionals. In all cases, the applicant was a recent college graduate named either Ken or Kate Norris. In one version of the résumé, Ken or Kate was said to have worked in a sporting goods store and on a grounds crew and had led the varsity basketball team (a masculine profile). In a second version, Ken or Kate had worked in a jewelry store, taught aerobics, and was captain of a cheerleading squad (a feminine profile). After reading the résumés, subjects indicated whether they would interview the applicant for three jobs—sales manager for a machinery company (masculine job), dental receptionist (feminine job), and administrative bank assistant (gender-neutral job). The result? Regardless of the applicant's own background, men were favored for the so-called masculine job, and women for the so-called feminine job. It seems that once an occupation is typecast as male or female, it is difficult to write a new gender-free script.

Occupation	% Men Employed	% Women Employed
Airline pilot	97	03
Auto mechanic	99	01
Bartender	46	54
Child-care worker	04	96
Computer programmer	66	34
Dentist	90	10
Dental assistant	02	98
Elementary school teacher	14	86
College-level instructor	59	41
Lawyer, judge	81	19
Librarian	17	83
Physician	80	20
Registered nurse	05	95
Telephone repairer	93	07
Telephone operator	11	89

Sex Differences in Occupation
U.S. Department of Labor statistics for 1991 reveal that men and women occupy very different positions in the work force.

■ **sexism** Discrimination that is based on a person's gender.

women, to care for children and to take the lower-status jobs (see box). Second, since people behave in ways that fit the roles they play, men are more likely than women to wield physical, social, and economic power. Third, these behavioral differences provide a continuing basis for sex stereotypes, leading us to perceive men as dominant "by nature" and women as domestic "by nature," when, in fact, the differences reflect the roles they play. In other words, says Eagly, our stereotypes are shaped by (and also confused with) the unequal distribution of men and women into different social roles (see Figure 14.9).

Social Roots of Sex Differences   Clearly, the behavior of men and women all over the world is scripted by the gender roles they're expected to play.

Income

There always has been and still is a gender gap in wages. It has been narrowing, but at a snail's pace. In 1980, women earned 60 cents for every dollar that males were paid. By 1990, that figure was up only slightly, to 68 cents. It is no wonder that in a recent survey of college seniors, women expected to earn $1,238 less upon entering the job market and $18,659 less at the peak of their careers (Jackson et al., 1992).

There are several reasons for this difference. First, women expect less pay than men do, even when they're just as qualified—resulting, perhaps, from a history of discrimination (Major & Konar, 1984). Second, women seem to care less than men about money and more about interpersonal relationships (Crosby, 1982). Third, women tend to evaluate themselves less favorably than do men—so even when they work harder and perform better, they feel less entitled (Major et al., 1984). Will working women of the future be content to remain underpaid? Is the gender wage gap here to stay? Not necessarily. If the difference in reward expectations is rooted in experience, it should diminish as new generations of women become established in high-paying careers.

Sex differences in occupations are sometimes so striking that we're quick to notice female construction workers and others who break the mold.

Leadership Opportunities

Look at the top of the list of America's Fortune 500 companies, and you will find that only 3.6 percent of board-of-directors members are women. Even today, despite the recent progress that has been made in entry- and middle-level positions, working women who seek positions of leadership are said to be blocked by a "glass ceiling"—a barrier so subtle that it's transparent, yet so strong that it keeps them from climbing to the top of the corporate ladder (Morrison & Von Glinow, 1990).

Clearly, women are as qualified as men for positions of power. Research shows that male and female managers have similar aspirations, values, and skills (Dobbins & Platz, 1986; Howard & Bray, 1988). The only difference is that women are more open and democratic in their style, more likely to invite subordinates to participate in decision making (Eagly & Johnson, 1990). This result is consistent with Judy Rosener's (1990) conclusion that today's leading women draw effectively on feminine qualities. It is also consistent with Sally Helgesen's (1990) observation that female managers interact more with subordinates, share power and information, and spin extensive networks, or "webs of inclusion"—a leadership style she calls the "feminine advantage."

So what's wrong? If women are competent for leadership, why have so few managed to reach the top? For women, the path to power is like an "obstacle course" (Ragins & Sundstrom, 1989). One reason is that many women are deeply conflicted about having to juggle a career and family (Crosby, 1991). Another reason is societal. Lingering stereotypes portray women as followers, not leaders, so people are uneasy about women who assume leadership roles. Combining the results of sixty-one studies, Alice Eagly and her colleagues (1992) found that female leaders are often devalued compared to equivalent males—particularly when they adopt a "masculine" task-focused leadership style or occupy "masculine" positions such as business manager or athletic coach.

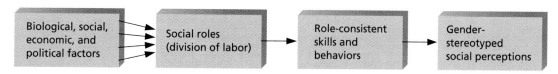

Figure 14.9

A Theory of Gender Stereotypes

According to social roles theory, stereotypes of men as dominant and women as nurturant or subordinate persist because of the different roles they play.

To what extent are the sex differences described earlier the product of socially constructed gender roles? Is it possible, for example, that men's strengths in mathematical problem solving and spatial skills are socially constructed? What about the interpersonal sensitivity of women?

Biologically oriented researchers argue that sex differences in math and spatial tests are so consistent over time and across cultures that they must be innate. Socially oriented researchers, however, warn that these comparisons are misleading because boys and girls are not raised on a level playing field. Boys receive more support in math from parents and teachers (Chipman et al., 1985; Jacobs, 1991). Studying the development of quantitative skills in children from hundreds of families, Jacquelynne Eccles and her colleagues (1990) found that parents who believe that girls are generally weak at math see their daughters as less competent, set lower expectations for them, and guide them in other directions. As a result, these girls lose interest and confidence and avoid future math-related pursuits. This may be why elementary school girls—even though they do as well in math as boys do—see themselves as less competent (Eccles et al., 1993). The single best predictor of math achievement test scores is the number of math courses one has taken. But girls take fewer math courses than boys do (Yee & Eccles, 1988).

A similar argument can be made about the extent to which boys and girls are exposed to computers. As we approach the twenty-first century and confront the challenges of high technology, computer literacy has become an essential skill and a top-dollar commodity. Yet it's clear that the computer—from the bells, whistles, and space wars of the video arcade to more serious programming applications—is becoming a male enterprise. Why? A survey of twenty-three summer computer camps that enroll a total of five thousand students revealed that boys outnumber girls by a 3-to-1 ratio—and that this disparity increases with the cost, grade level, and difficulty level of the camp (Hess & Miura, 1985). Why are boys so much more interested in computers? One possible reason is that educational software is designed primarily with them in mind. Thus when forty-three educators were asked to invent a new grammar game for students in general, their programs resembled those they had otherwise designed specifically for boys (Huff & Cooper, 1987). Expecting the users to be male, software developers flood the market with male-oriented products—a situation that can set self-fulfilling prophecies in motion and help to *create* differences between the sexes.

The strongest evidence for a cognitive gender gap is performance on visual-spatial tasks. Is it possible that the male advantage at these skills stems from differences in experience? Perhaps. Research shows that boys are permitted to stray farther from home than girls and engage in more "scouting" activities. Boys are more likely to own building blocks, erector sets, and other toys that involve spatial manipulation. They're also more likely to play billiards, basketball, and other sports that involve making judgments of moving objects. To some extent, the more spatial experience one has, the better is one's performance on visual-spatial tests (Baenninger & Newcombe, 1991). Spatial skills can be improved with training. In one study, four-year-old boys *and girls* who were trained with wooden blocks, dominoes, tinker toys, and geometric shapes later scored higher on a spatial test than children who were not similarly trained.

Turning from the cognitive to the social domain, studies reveal that women are more sensitive than men to how others are feeling—a skill often referred to as "female intuition." Some researchers speculate that this advantage is rooted in the left-dominant female brain (Moir & Jessel, 1989). Others argue that women acquire interpersonal sensitivity out of social necessity. According to Sara Snodgrass (1985), women are better than men at reading others for self-protective reasons—because they occupy subordinate roles in society. Think about it. Isn't it more important for workers to know how the boss is feeling, and for students to know how their professor is feeling, than vice versa? To test this hypothesis, Snodgrass paired a man and a woman in each of several work teams and assigned one or the other to be the leader. In general, she found that the subordinate was more sensitive to the leader's nonverbal cues than the leader was to the subordinate's—regardless of gender. Snodgrass thus suggested that "women's intuition" be called "subordinate's intuition" to reflect the fact that low status, not sex, is what motivates our insight into others.

Putting Sex Differences in Perspective   Every year, the psychology department I work in offers a senior seminar in which students debate current controversies. One of the staples of this seminar is the question, "Should we be more impressed by the similarities or by the differences between the sexes?" The last time my students and I prepared for a debate on the subject, we talked about sexual behavior, aggression, and cognitive skills. The more I thought about the well-established principles of psychology, however, the more I realized that men and women are similar in so many ways that we take for granted. Differences make news, similarities do not.

Ponder the material presented elsewhere in this book and you'll see the point. Boys and girls alike crawl, walk, and smile at about the same age, and both become curious about sex in adolescence. Similarly, both men and women see better in daylight than in the dark, fall prey to optical illusions, and behave in ways that bring reward. Both men and women can hold about seven items in short-term memory, retrieve more information in recognition tests than through free recall, and use shorthand cognitive heuristics in making judgments. In their social behavior, both men and women are biased by their first impressions, are attracted to others who are similar, and are more likely to help others when they're alone than in a group of bystanders. The list of similarities that escape our daily notice is long and impressive. As fellow human beings, men and women are more alike than they are different.

Sexual Orientation

As national leaders, policy makers, and the general public debate such issues as gay rights and the ban on gays and lesbians in the military, political and emotional rhetoric too often substitute for hard scientific information. How common is homosexuality? Where does it come from? Why are openly gay men and lesbians the frequent targets of prejudice and discrimination? Today, no discussion of human diversity is complete without a consideration of differences in **sexual orientation**, as defined by one's sexual preference for members of the same sex (homosexuality), opposite sex (heterosexuality), or both sexes (bisexuality).

■ **sexual orientation** An enduring sexual preference for members of the same sex (homosexuality), the opposite sex (heterosexuality), or both sexes (bisexuality).

The Numbers Game   Throughout history, and in all cultures, a vast majority of people have been heterosexual in their orientation. But just how vast a majority is this? For years, researchers have tried to estimate the number of gays and lesbians in the population, and for years these surveys have produced a range of results—and a great deal of controversy. A debate over numbers may not seem an emotionally charged issue, but gay

Although some men and women are openly gay, as shown in this wedding announcement for a lesbian couple, researchers can only estimate the prevalence of homosexuality in the population.

rights leaders and opponents believe that the more gay men and lesbians there are perceived to be, the greater is their political clout (Rogers, 1993).

Seizing upon certain combinations of numbers in Alfred Kinsey's sex surveys of the 1940s and 1950s, the popular media have often held that approximately 10 percent of the population is homosexual. Consistently, however, recent studies have yielded much smaller estimates. A 1970 survey funded by the Kinsey Institute revealed that 3.3 percent of American men sampled said that they had frequent or occasional homosexual sex (Fay et al., 1989). Then between 1989 and 1992, the National Opinion Research Center reported that 2.8 percent of men and 2.5 percent of women reported having exclusive homosexual activity. Although the number of adults who say they've had at least one homosexual experience is much higher (in the 20 percent range for men, 15 percent for women), large-scale surveys conducted in the United States and in countries throughout Europe, Asia, and the Pacific together suggest that the size of the homosexual population is roughly 5 percent among men, and about half that number among women (Diamond, 1993).

Social Reactions   Several years ago, a group of gay students at a large state university picked a date and announced, "If you are gay, wear blue jeans today." Nobody sought to quantify the result, but can you guess what may have happened? (Fewer students than usual wore blue jeans.) Studies show that although most Americans support equal rights, attitudes toward gay men and lesbians are generally negative (Herek, 1988). Based on a recent poll, *Time* magazine found that 53 percent of American adults believe that homosexual relationships between consenting adults are morally wrong, and 64 percent believe that marriage between homosexuals should not be recognized by law (Henry, 1994).

Not everyone harbors anti-gay prejudice, of course, and there is a wide range of individual differences of opinion. The problem is that people with negative attitudes toward homosexuals may also discriminate in important matters. In one study, Geoffrey Haddock and his colleagues (1993) told student subjects that their university's student government had to cut funding to campus-wide organizations by 20 percent—and that they wanted to hear student opinions on where to make these cuts (two weeks earlier, each subject's attitude toward homosexuals had been assessed). Subjects were then given a list of ten campus organizations, including one for gays and lesbians. As you might expect, negative attitudes were linked to discriminatory decisions. Those with the most anti-gay sentiment proposed an average budget cut of 45 percent, compared to 26 percent among subjects with the least negative attitudes. Discrimination can take on many forms. In a recent survey of 800 American adults, 75 percent said they would shop at a store owned by a homosexual, but only 48 percent said they would vote for a homosexual political candidate and only 39 percent said they would see a homosexual doctor (Henry, 1994).

Origins of Homosexuality   What are the origins of homosexuality? As in discussions of gender differences, both biological and psychological theories have been proposed. Aristotle believed that homosexuality was inborn but strengthened by habit, psychoanalysts argue that it stems from a disturbed family environment and the child's overattachment to a parent of the same or opposite sex, and learning theorists point to reinforcing homosexual experiences in childhood. There is very little evidence, however, to support any of these claims. In the most comprehensive study, Alan Bell and his colleagues (1981) intensively interviewed hundreds of homosexual and heterosexual men and women about their lives, and compared the responses. No differences were found in their family backgrounds, numbers of brothers and sisters, the absence of a male or female parent, their relationships with parents, sexual abuse by someone of the same or opposite sex, age of puberty, or high school dating. Except for the fact that homosexual adults were somewhat less conforming as children, the two groups could not be distinguished by their past experiences. In fact, both groups felt that their sexual orientation was determined long before it became "official."

More and more, researchers are now searching for and finding biological clues. In one highly publicized study, neurobiologist Simon LeVay (1991) autopsied the brains of nineteen homosexual men who had died of AIDS; sixteen heterosexual men, some of whom had died of AIDS; and six heterosexual women. Influenced by existing research on gender differences, LeVay analyzed a tiny structure in the hypothalamus—the "sexually dimorphic nucleus"—that helps regulate sexual behavior and is larger in heterosexual men than in women. All the specimens were numerically coded, so LeVay did not know whether the donor he was examining was male, female, straight, or gay. The result: In the homosexual brains he studied, the nucleus was on average less than half as large as in the heterosexual brains—comparable in size to those in the female brains. The difference was probably not due to AIDS because in the male heterosexual brains the nucleus was the same size regardless of whether these men had died of AIDS. This research is fully described in LeVay's (1993) book, *The Sexual Brain.*

Stop for a moment and ponder the implications. What is your reaction? When LeVay's report appeared in *Science,* there erupted a storm of controversy. Emerging from the laboratory, LeVay soon found himself in the spotlight on TV news shows, on talk shows, and in magazines. Within the

When asked about LeVay's study, playwright Jonathan Tolins (1993) said, "The truth is, I knew, as just about any gay person did, that it was only a matter of time. I knew in my bones that my own sexuality was not a decision but a natural part of who I am."

Some people disparage gay men with AIDS and blame them for their fate. But is one's sexual orientation selected as a matter of choice, or is it biologically determined?

gay community, reactions were polarized. Worried that the findings could somehow be used to discriminate against gay people, some called LeVay "homophobic" and referred to his work as anti-homosexual. But wait. LeVay himself has been openly gay since he was a teenager. Still, "one critic said that I wanted to prove that it's not my fault I'm gay" (quoted in Nimmons, 1994, p. 68). A more common reaction, however, was to enthusiastically embrace the whole idea that sexual orientation is a natural biological condition so that people would tolerate it rather than make discriminatory moral judgments. Thus, LeVay reported that "many gay men sent my study to their parents . . . and parents, in turn, wrote to say the study helped them understand their kids."

It's important to recognize that this study reveals only a correlation between sexual orientation and the size of this one hypothalamic nucleus—and cannot be used to draw conclusions about cause and effect. LeVay himself is quick to caution that "I didn't show that gay men are born that way" and that "since I looked at adult brains, we don't know if the differences I found were there at birth or if they appeared later" (Nimmons, 1994, p. 66). Even before this study, other researchers were focused on the role of prenatal hormones. Studies showed, for example, that men whose mothers were under extreme stress during pregnancy (which lowers prenatal testosterone levels) are somewhat more likely to be homosexual (Ellis & Ames, 1987).

Currently, the strongest support for a biological model of sexual orientation comes from twin studies that reveal a genetic predisposition. Michael Bailey and Richard Pillard (1991) interviewed 167 gay men and surveyed their twins and/or adopted brothers. Overall, 52 percent of the identical twins were also gay, compared to only 22 percent of the fraternal twins and 11 percent of the adoptive brothers. Two years later, in a study of both male and female homosexuals, Frederick Whitam and his colleagues (1993) found that 66 percent of the identical twins were also homosexual, compared to only 30 percent of the fraternal twins. As in other recent research (Bailey & Benishay, 1993), the results were similar for gay men and lesbians.

The origins of homosexuality are complex and may never be fully understood. Although the biological approach has its critics (Byne & Parsons, 1993), the evidence is mounting that there may be a genetic link, a natural source of diversity (LeVay & Hamer, 1994).

SUMMARY AND KEY TERMS

As the world becomes a global village, it's important to understand both the diversity among human groups and the fact that people around the world are remarkably similar.

Cross-Cultural Perspectives

Cultural Diversity: A Fact of Life

People vary not only in their language, religion, and the geography of their surroundings but also in their *social norms*—a cul-

ture's implicit rules of conduct—and in the degree to which they follow these norms.

Individualism and Collectivism: A Tale of Two Cultures

Cultures differ in their orientation toward *individualism* and *collectivism*. Individualistic cultures value independence, autonomy, and self-reliance, while collectivist cultures stress interdependence, cooperation, and group harmony. The United States, traditionally individualistic, is even more so today than in the past. According to Triandis, societies that are complex, affluent, and heterogeneous are the most likely to be individualistic.

Individualism and collectivism mold our self-conceptions. Cultural orientation also influences socialization practices throughout a person's life. The age of weaning, the choice of where a baby sleeps, decisions about whether to marry for love and other considerations relate to society's individualism or collectivism.

Each cultural orientation has advantages and disadvantages. In collectivist societies, people are more likely to follow social norms, which promotes harmony and loyalty and discourages social loafing. But collectivism can also produce narrow-mindedness and a confrontational attitude toward outsiders.

Multicultural Perspectives

Ethnic Diversity: A Fact of Life

As ethnic diversity increases in the United States and elsewhere, more attention is being paid to *multiculturalism,* the study of diverse racial and ethnic groups within a culture.

Acculturation and Ethnic Identity

All ethnic groups face the dilemma of how to adapt to the larger society. Should they blend into a single "melting pot" or retain their heritage as part of a cultural "mosaic"? *Acculturation,* the process of change that occurs when people are immersed in a new culture, entails one of four basic coping strategies: assimilation (abandoning the old culture for the new), separation (maintaining one's heritage and keeping apart from the host culture), integration (retaining the old *and* adapting to the new), or marginalization (identifying with neither culture).

Through acculturation, each person establishes an *ethnic identity,* which is revealed in language, customs, and the individual's sense of belonging. But immigrants may also experience *acculturative stress,* resulting in anxiety, depression, and other mental health problems. The strategy of integration seems to correlate with less acculturative stress than the other three strategies.

Discrimination

The most vicious obstacle for ethnic minorities is *discrimination,* behavior directed against people because of their affiliation with a social group. It stems from stereotypes and feelings of prejudice.

Racism in America

Racism, a deep-seated form of prejudice based on the color of a person's skin, is not as overt in the United States as it used to be, but studies still find evidence of it in the workplace and in other settings. It influences both our perceptions and our interpretations of events.

Gender: The Great Divide?

Pollsters commonly find a "gender gap" between men and women, but is it real, and is its origin biological or environmental?

Differences Between Men and Women

Some biological sex differences are indisputable. Research has also established differences in the areas of sexuality, aggression, and cognitive skills. Around the world, men are more sexually promiscuous and permissive than women, and they see life in more "sexualized" terms. Males are also more physically aggressive than females. On average, males perform slightly better in mathematical problem solving and on some visual-spatial tasks. Females typically exhibit greater verbal fluency and social sensitivity.

The Biological Perspective

Some studies have identified sex differences in the hypothalamus and the corpus callosum, and much research has focused on the role of the sex hormones. Testosterone, the male sex hormone, has been linked to aggression. A high level of testosterone—but not too high—also seems to enhance spatial skills. Conversely, high levels of the female sex hormones estrogen and progesterone are linked to lower spatial skills and higher verbal fluency.

The Environmental Perspective

Despite the biological evidence, sex differences may result from the different life experiences of males and females. Through a process of social learning, children come to understand *gender roles* they are expected to play. Experience also leads us to form *gender schemas,* beliefs about men and women that influence the way we perceive ourselves and others.

In some cultures, sexist traditions are especially strong. Even in the United States, where many gender barriers have fallen, men and women continue to play different roles in the home and in the workplace. Research shows that our gender stereotypes hold a small kernel of truth, but they are greatly exaggerated. According to *social roles theory,* the sex differences we perceive are magnified by the unequal social roles occupied by men and women.

Some researchers argue that environmental influences account for various sex differences. Boys may be better at visual-spatial tasks because they roam farther from home and use more spatial manipulation in their play. Girls may learn interpersonal sensitivity because their subordinate social roles demand it. Either way, it's important to recognize that men and women are more similar than different.

Sexual Orientation

Sexual orientation refers to an enduring sexual preference for members of the same sex (homosexuality), opposite sex (heterosexuality), or both sexes (bisexuality). Cross-cultural surveys suggest that about 5 percent of men and 2.5 percent of women are homosexual. Socially, gays and lesbians in the United States face discrimination because of generally negative attitudes toward them.

The origins of homosexuality have long been disputed. Evidence is growing that there may be a biological basis, but the debate is far from resolved.

PART V

I s personality set in stone, or do people have a capacity for change? Part V presents clinical psychology, the subfield that is concerned with the diagnosis, understanding, and treatment of psychological disorders. The section opens with Chapter 15 on *personality.* This chapter examines psychoanalysis, cognitive social-learning theory, the humanistic approach, and the trait approach to personality. Chapter 16 on *psychological disorders* then examines the different models of abnormality and diagnosis, and describes what is known about anxiety disorders, somatoform disorders, dissociative disorders, depression, schizophrenia, and personality disorders. Finally, Chapter 17 on *treatment* describes psychoanalysis, behavior modification, and other psychological methods of therapy as well as the effects of psychoactive drugs and other forms of medical intervention.

CLINICAL PSYCHOLOGY

Chapter 15

Personality

Browse through any bookstore, and you will notice that the shelves are lined with pop-psych books that promise to reveal your true, hidden personality. All you have to do, they say, is analyze your diet (you are what you eat), your color preferences (if you like red, for example, you're said to be emotional and hot-tempered), handwriting (short, clipped strokes mean that you are stingy), astrology (I've been told that I have a typical Taurus-like stubborn streak), facial characteristics (people with eyes set close together cannot be trusted), and the shape of your body (round people are outgoing party animals).

Self-insight is not the only reason for all the interest in personality. Marketing experts try to categorize consumers so they can develop advertisements that appeal to certain segments of the market. Trial lawyers hire consultants to select jurors personally disposed to favor their client's case. Insurance companies try to develop profiles of high-risk clients prone to accidents. The government hires psychologists to analyze the minds of terrorists and serial killers. Guidance counselors administer tests to tell whether someone is suited to working alone or with people. Even novelists use vivid personality sketches to develop the characters of their heroes.

So what is **personality?** Although the word comes from the Latin *persona*, which means "mask," personality is more than just a face we wear in public. It's also what lies behind the mask—an enduring "inner core" that embodies an individual's distinct pattern of thoughts, feelings, motives, and behaviors. The study of personality seeks to describe individuals, the ways in which they are similar to one another, and the ways in which each of us is unique. The study of personality is also central to **clinical psychology**, an area that is concerned with the classification, understanding, and treatment of psychological disorders.

THE BIG PICTURE

Psychology has always led a dual existence. As a science, the field was born in 1879, in Leipzig, where Wilhelm Wundt established the first formal laboratory for the study of consciousness. From then on, human and animal research labs sprung up in universities all over the world. Quite independently, Sigmund Freud and other physicians were working in hospitals treating patients who were suffering from nonmedical illnesses. Freud gradually formulated a theory of personality and a method of conducting psychotherapy. Others, many of whom were also trained in medicine, went on to develop alternative approaches.

There are three basic subject areas of clinical psychology, and each is represented in a chapter of this book: (1) the healthy human personality, (2) psychological disorders, and (3) the treatment of disorders. Among those seeking to understand what precipitates a decline in mental health, and how that process can be reversed, there is an underlying tension between the forces of continuity and change. Thus they ask, To what extent is personality set in stone, and to what extent do people have a capacity for change (Heatherton & Weinberger, 1994)? To address this empirical question, imagine that you are a researcher in the following study.

■ **personality** An individual's distinct and relatively enduring pattern of thoughts, feelings, motives, and behaviors.

■ **clinical psychology** The branch of psychology that deals with the diagnosis and treatment of mental disorders.

What's Your Prediction?

THE SITUATION

Based on recent research, you know that one way to describe personality is by comparing where individuals stand on five broad traits: (1) *neuroticism* (a proneness to anxiety and distress), (2) *extraversion* (a desire for social interaction, stimulation, and activity), (3) *openness* (a receptiveness to new experiences and ideas), (4) *agreeableness* (a selfless concern for others), and (5) *conscientiousness* (a tendency to be reliable, disciplined, and ambitious). Does one's relative standing on these traits stay basically the same over time, or does personality change with age, experience, and other factors? If you're generally calm, outgoing, and open-minded now, will that be your profile later in life?

To determine the stability of personality, you decide to contact a large group of adults who had completed a personality test six years earlier as part of another study. The test they had filled out was designed to measure the top three major traits (neuroticism, extraversion, openness). Overall, 635 people had initially taken the test—365 men and 270 women, ranging in age from twenty-five to ninety-one years old. Your goal now is to retest these same people on a newer version of the same scale. Most agree to take part in your study. But others, you come to learn, have died, moved, become disabled, or lost interest. In the end, you are able to recruit 398 of the original subjects. To each one, you mail the test, the instructions, and a stamped self-addressed envelope.

The questionnaire that you use is called the Neuroticism-Extraversion-Openness Personality Inventory, or NEO-PI, a test that is often used in research (Costa & McCrae, 1992). The NEO-PI contains 181 statements ("I am usually cheerful," "I really like most people I meet," "I have a very active imagination"). Next to each one, subjects rate on a 5-point scale how much they agree or disagree. The items measuring neuroticism, extraversion, and openness are dispersed throughout the test, but afterward you total the scores separately for each "subscale"—a procedure that yields three scores per subject. Once all tests are scored, the data are ready to be analyzed.

So, what next? To determine the stability of the traits you measured, you need to take a *longitudinal* approach by comparing each subject's scores in the first and second test. What is the *correlation* between the two sets of scores? If personality, like mood, were to fluctuate from one moment to the next, or if you were to pair the scores of one subject with those of a randomly selected other subject, the correlation would be 0 (remember, a correlation coefficient ranges from 0 to plus or minus 1). At the other extreme, if personality were completely fixed or if the same subjects were retested only 6 days, weeks, or months apart, the two sets of scores should be strongly and positively correlated, in the .90 range. The question is, How strongly correlated would the two sets of scores be after 6 full years?

MAKE A PREDICTION

Your 398 subjects take the test twice, and each yields three trait scores: one for neuroticism, another for extraversion, and a third for openness to experience. How high do you think the correlations are between the two sets of scores? To give you a basis of comparison, the correlation co-efficients that are found when the test is re-administered after six months appear in the left-hand column. On a scale ranging from 0 (no correlation, no stability) to +1 (a perfect correlation, total stability), and using the 6-month numbers as a guideline, predict the correlations that are found after 6 years:

Trait	6 Months	6 Years
Neuroticism	.87	_____
Extraversion	.91	_____
Openness	.86	_____

RESULTS

The research just described is based on recent studies of adult personality that were conducted by Robert McCrae and Paul Costa (1990). So, what did you predict? Does one's personality stay basically the same or does it change over time? As shown below, the results revealed an extraordinary degree of stability—comparable, in fact, to that found after only 6 months!

Trait	6 Months	6 Years
Neuroticism	.87	.83
Extraversion	.91	.82
Openness	.86	.83

WHAT DOES IT ALL MEAN?

Think for a moment about your own personality—your basic feelings, attitudes, and ways of relating to others. Have you changed at all, or stayed pretty much the same? When McCrae and Costa (1990) asked their subjects this question, 51 percent said they stayed the same, 35 percent said they changed a little, and 14 percent said they changed a good deal. Were these self-perceptions accurate? Not necessarily. Costa and McCrae recalculated the test-retest correlations for only those subjects who said they had changed a lot—and the numbers were just as high.

As a general rule, personality is stable over time. Indeed, if it were not, you could not predict the kind of person you would be tomorrow, set a future career goal, or commit yourself to a marriage partner. Of course, this is not to say that we all stay the same as we get older. As we saw in Chapter 10, the aging process itself is accompanied by physical, sensory, and cognitive changes. As a result of life experiences, we may also change our habits, attitudes, and behaviors. Even subtle shifts in personality are possible. When adults of different age groups are tested, those who are older tend to score slightly lower on neuroticism, extraversion, and openness.

For clinical psychologists who work at helping people in distress, this research raises a critical question: Can people who are suffering from chronic anxiety, depression, or other types of mental disorders be helped? In Chapter 17, we'll see that the answer is yes—and that both psychological and drug treatments have proved successful. But to the question of how much change is possible, and how difficult it is to facilitate that change, the answer that you get to this question depends in part on who you ask. Specifically, this chapter presents four major approaches to the study of personality: (1) psychoanalysis, (2) the cognitive social-learning approach, (3) the humanistic approach, and (4) the trait approach. Each perspective contains a set of theories that share certain assumptions about human nature—how personality forms and then develops; whether people are inherently good, bad, or neutral; the relative importance of biological and environmental factors; the role of unconscious determinants of behavior; and, of course, the question of stability and change. As we'll see, the study of personality integrates theory, methods of assessment, research on specific topics, and an interest in the clinical implications.

PSYCHOANALYSIS

On the evening of May 6, 1856, at 6:30 P.M., a baby boy was born in what is now the Czech Republic to Jakob and Amalie Freud. The boy arrived in a caul, a membrane that envelops a fetus and sometimes covers the infant's head at birth. Superstition has it that to be born in a caul is a good-luck omen—a sign that the baby will one day achieve fame and fortune. After one year of marriage, Jakob and Amalie had little money, but they were thrilled. They named the first of their six children Sigmund.

The boy grew up to be strong, healthy, and bright, at the top of his class in school. He enrolled at the University of Vienna at the age of seventeen, received a medical degree eight years later, and became a practicing neurologist. By his own admission, Freud was a driven young man, one who sorely wanted to make his mark on the world. In 1884, however, his quest for fame took a curious turn. He had heard about a "magic drug" with anesthetic possibilities, tried it, and enjoyed its uplifting effects on his mood and work. Thinking he was on the verge of a medical breakthrough, Freud prescribed the drug to a friend, who became hopelessly addicted and died of an overdose. The drug was cocaine. Having lost a friend, a patient, and a measure of respect in the medical community, Freud abandoned the drug and pursued other interests.

The Birth of Psychoanalysis

In 1885, Freud moved to Paris to study under Jean Charcot, an eminent French neurologist. Charcot was studying *hysteria,* a "conversion disorder" in which the patient experiences symptoms such as paralysis of the limbs, blindness, deafness, convulsions, and the like—without an organic basis (see Chapter 16). What's fascinating about hysteria is that the patient is not faking, yet there's nothing physically wrong. Charcot found that hysterical disorders often started with a traumatic event in the patient's childhood, and that he could make the symptoms vanish by putting the patient under

Sigmund Freud and his daughter Anna—who went on to become a psychoanalyst in her own right.

hypnosis. You can imagine how dazzled Freud was by the sight of "paralyzed" patients suddenly able to walk, and those who were "blind" suddenly able to see. Demonstrations like these filled Freud with a profound regard for the power of unconscious forces.

Back in Vienna, Freud became intrigued by the case of Anna O., a patient who suffered from hysterical paralysis of three limbs, impaired vision and speech, and a nervous cough. With the help of her physician Josef Breuer, Anna was able to recall the events that precipitated her symptoms. As if a large block had been removed from her mind, Anna's symptoms slowly disappeared. Breuer had invented a *talking cure.* But something else happened that would also prove significant. After many sessions, Anna had become emotionally attached to Breuer. Freud was puzzled by the intensity of Anna's feelings, until the day came when he had the same experience. Without provocation, a female patient lovingly threw her arms around Freud's neck. Freud had not sought the patient's affection, and assumed he was not the real target of her passion. Without realizing it, he thought, this patient must have been transferring her feelings for someone else (maybe her father) onto him, a phenomenon Freud called *transference.*

Freud went into private practice, but he did not have much luck using hypnosis. Apparently, not everyone could be hypnotized and the so-called cures produced in hypnosis often did not last. To help patients recall and talk freely about their past, Freud came up with his first technique of psychotherapy, *free association.* The rules are simple: the patient lies on a couch, relaxes, and says whatever comes to mind, no matter how trivial, embarrassing, or illogical it may seem. After many sessions, Freud noticed something curious. Although patients could produce streams of ideas leading to the unconscious, many seemed unable to talk or even think about painful and unpleasant memories. In fact, once on the brink of an important insight, they would often stop, go blank, lose their train of thought, or change the subject. Freud called this phenomenon *resistance,* and concluded that it was part of an unconscious defensive process designed to keep unwanted thoughts under lock and key—and out of awareness.

Freud's Theory of Personality

Freud's clinical experiences laid a foundation for the theory he later developed. He was convinced that the traumas and conflicts of early childhood can have lasting effects, that we are ruled by unconscious forces, that what's unconscious can be brought out through free association, that we try to resist painful self-insights, and that we often transfer our feelings for one object onto another. Slowly but surely, the pieces were falling into place. In 1896, Freud used the term **psychoanalysis** for the first time. Then in 1900 he published *The Interpretation of Dreams,* the first of twenty-four books and the one that marked the birth of what would become one of the most influential theories in modern history. The theory is summarized in Freud's (1940) last book, *An Outline of Psychoanalysis,* published one year after his death.

■ **psychoanalysis** Freud's theory of personality and method of psychotherapy, both of which assume that our motives are largely unconscious.

The Unconscious   Underlying psychoanalysis is the assumption that personality is shaped largely by *unconscious forces.* To illustrate, Freud com-

"Every man has reminiscences which he would not tell to everyone but only to his friends. He has other matters in mind which he would not reveal even to his friends, but only to himself, and that in secret. But there are other things which a man is afraid to tell even to himself, and every decent man has a number of such things stored away in his mind."

FEODOR DOSTOEVSKY

pared the human mind to an iceberg. Like the small tip of the iceberg that floats on the water, the *conscious* part consists of all that a person is aware of at a particular moment. Below the surface is the vast region of the *unconscious*, which contains thoughts, feelings, and memories that are hidden from view. Part of this region lies just beneath the surface, in an area called the *preconscious*. Preconscious material is not threatening, just temporarily out of awareness and easy to bring to mind. The rest of the unconscious, however, is a deep, dark sea of secret urges, wishes, and drives. According to Freud, the mind keeps these unacceptable impulses out of awareness. Still, they rumble, make waves, and surface for air—in our dreams, slips of the tongue, the jokes we tell, the people we're attracted to, the anxieties we feel, and so on. In other words, only through psychoanalysis can we achieve meaningful insight into our personality.

What's in the unconscious? According to Freud, two major instincts motivate all of human behavior. The first is collectively referred to as the *life instincts*, which include the need for food, water, air, and sex. As you can imagine, the sex part raised eyebrows. Yet Freud felt it was critical: many of the childhood traumas that his patients told about were sexual in nature. Later on, after living through the stark horrors of World War I, Freud also proposed that there is a second, darker side of human nature—that buried within the unconscious is a *death instinct*, a need to reduce all tensions by returning to a calm lifeless state. Since these self-destructive impulses conflict with the more powerful life forces, reasoned Freud, they are turned away from the self and directed instead toward others. The fated result is aggression, a problem that has plagued humans throughout history.

The Structure of Personality   Have you ever had a burning urge to kiss or embrace someone you're attracted to, or to hit someone who has angered you, only to hear the haunting voice of your conscience? How do you resolve these dilemmas? Based on his clinical experiences, Freud believed that people are driven by inner conflicts (conscious vs. unconscious, free association vs. resistance, life vs. death)—and that compromise is a necessary solution. Freud thus divided the human personality into three interacting parts: the id, ego, and superego.

The **id** is the most primitive part of personality. Present at birth, it is a reservoir of instincts and biological drives that energize us. According to Freud, the id operates according to the **pleasure principle**, motivating us to seek immediate and total gratification of all desires. When a person is deprived of food, water, air, or sex, a state of tension builds until the need is satisfied. The id is thus a blind, pleasure-seeking part of us that aims for the reduction of all tension. If the impulsive, id-dominated infant could speak, it would scream: "I want it, and I want it *now!*"

The **superego** is a socially developed aspect of personality that motivates us to behave in ways that are moral, ideal, even perfect. Whereas the id pushes us to seek immediate gratification, the superego is a prude, a moralist, a part of us that shuns sex, aggression, and other innate sources of pleasure. Where does the superego come from? According to Freud, children learn society's values from their parents. Through repeated experiences with reward for good behavior and punishment for bad, children eventually develop internal standards of what's right and wrong. There are two components to the superego. One is the *ego-ideal*, an image of the ideals we should strive for. The other is the *conscience*, a set of prohibitions that

■ **id** In psychoanalysis, a primitive and unconscious part of personality that contains basic drives and operates according to the pleasure principle.

■ **pleasure principle** In psychoanalysis, the id's boundless drive for immediate gratification.

■ **superego** In psychoanalysis, the part of personality that consists of one's moral ideals and conscience.

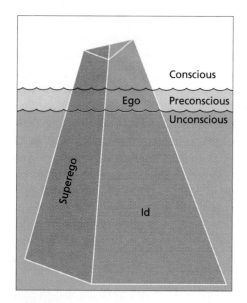

Figure 15.1

The Structure of Personality According to Freud

define how we should not behave. Once the superego is developed, people reward themselves internally for moral acts by feeling pride, and they punish themselves for immoral acts by suffering pangs of guilt.

The third aspect of personality is the **ego,** which mediates the conflict between the "wants" of the id and the "shoulds" of the superego. According to Freud, the ego is a pragmatic offshoot of the id, the part of personality that helps us achieve realistic forms of gratification. In contrast to the id (which strives for immediate gratification) and the superego (which seeks to inhibit the same impulses), the ego operates according to the **reality principle**—the goal being to reduce one's tensions, but only at the right time, in the right place, and in a socially appropriate manner. The ego is thus a master of compromise, the part of us that tries to satisfy our needs without offending our morals. The ego, said Freud, is the executive officer of the personality, the part that controls our behavior. Freud's model is illustrated in Figure 15.1.

Psychosexual Development   Over and over again, Freud the physician listened to patients tell wild tales about childhood traumas—tales involving sexual and aggressive encounters with mothers, fathers, neighbors, and dirty old uncles. Eventually, Freud came to believe that although some of the stories he heard were true, many of them were sheer fantasies, a product of overactive imaginations. From this experience, Freud drew two developmental conclusions: (1) that personality is shaped during the first few years of life, and (2) that the resolution of "psychosexual" conflicts is the key contributor. He went on to propose that children pass through an odyssey of **psychosexual stages** of development, with each stage defined by a different "erogenous zone," a part of the body that's most sensitive to erotic stimulation.

First comes the *oral stage,* which occurs in the first year of life, a time when the baby's mouth is the pleasure-seeking center of attention. Oral activity begins with the sucking of nipples, thumbs, and pacifiers, then moves on to biting, chewing, cooing, and other oral activities. In this stage, the infant is totally dependent on caretakers, feeding is a key activity, and weaning (the transition away from the breast or bottle) is a major source of conflict. Next comes the *anal stage,* which occurs during the second and third years of life, when the baby derives pleasure in the sensation of holding in and letting go of feces. There is a regular and enjoyable cycle of tension buildup and release. In this stage, however, toilet training brings the parent ("wait!") and child ("I don't want to!") into sharp conflict. Between the ages of four and six, the child then enters the *phallic stage,* a time when pleasure is felt in the genital area. In this stage, children become fascinated with the body and can often be seen playing with their own sex organs in public, a habit that once again brings them into conflict with parents. To Freud, the single most dramatic event in psychosexual development takes place at this point.

There's a famous Greek tragedy in which the hero, a once abandoned infant who goes on to become King Oedipus, returns as a young man to kill his father and marry his mother, both without realizing who they were. According to Freud, this legend exposes an unconscious human wish he called the **Oedipus complex**—a tendency for children to become sexually attracted to the parent of the opposite sex, and to develop feelings of jealousy

■ **ego** In psychoanalysis, the part of personality that operates according to the reality principle and mediates the conflict between the id and superego.

■ **reality principle** In psychoanalysis, the ego's capacity to delay gratification.

■ **psychosexual stages** Freud's stages of personality development during which pleasure is derived from different parts of the body (oral, anal, phallic, and genital).

■ **Oedipus complex** In psychoanalysis, a tendency for young children to become sexually attracted to the parent of the opposite sex, and hostile toward the parent of the same sex.

According to Freud, psychosexual development progresses through stages, each defined by a part of the body that is most sensitive to stimulation. In the oral stage (top left), everything is put into the mouth. During the anal stage (top center), toilet training brings the child and parents into conflict. For both boys and girls, the phallic stage (top right) centers around the Oedipus complex. Middle childhood is characterized by a relatively calm latency period (bottom left) when sexual urges lie dormant. Beginning at puberty, the genital stage (bottom right) is marked by the emergence of adult-like sexual desires.

■ **identification** In psychoanalysis, the process by which children internalize their parents' values and form a superego.

and rage toward the rival parent of the same sex. Freud's theory of male development is clear: the young boy wants his mother and hates his father for standing in the way. Since the father is bigger and more powerful, however, the boy develops *castration anxiety*, a fear that the father will retaliate by cutting off his son's prized genitals. For defensive reasons, the boy represses his sexual urge for the mother and tries to emulate the father, a process known as **identification**. As a result, the boy becomes less anxious, derives partial satisfaction of his repressed wish for mom, and adopts his father's

■ **fixation** In psychoanalysis, a tendency to get "locked in" at early, immature stages of psychosexual development.

moral values. Freud was quick to admit that his theory of female development is less clear. At some point, he says, the girl notices that her father has a penis, but that she and her mother do not. Unconsciously, the girl blames and resents her mother for the predicament, develops *penis envy,* and seeks to become daddy's little girl. Eventually, she realizes the futility of these feelings, represses her envy, and identifies with her mother. For both boys and girls, then, the identification part of the process is important: It means that the superego springs full blown from the Oedipus complex.

Once Oedipal conflicts are resolved, the child enters a long *latency period,* which lasts roughly between the ages of seven and twelve. In these middle years of childhood, sexual impulses lie dormant, as boys and girls concentrate on friends of the same sex and schoolwork. As parents come to appreciate, this is a time of calm between storms. Indeed, it precedes the fourth and final stage of psychosexual development—the *genital stage.* Starting at puberty, boys and girls emerge from their latency shells and feel the stirring of adult-like sexual urges for the first time. Once again, the ego must cope with an undeclared state of war between biological drives and social prohibitions.

According to Freud, one must pass successfully through all psychosexual stages in order to form a healthy personality and enjoy mature adult relationships. If children receive *too much* or *too little* gratification at an earlier stage, they will become stuck or "fixated" at that stage. **Fixation** is thus responsible for the development of the following personality types:

Oral: If you were weaned too early or too late as an infant, you would become fixated at the oral stage and feel the need to smoke, drink, bite your nails, chew on pencils, or spend hours talking on the phone. You might also seek symbolic forms of oral gratification by becoming passive, dependent, and demanding—like a nursing infant.

Anal: If, as a toddler, you were toilet trained in a harsh and rigid manner, you would become anally fixated and react in one of two ways—by becoming tight, stubborn, punctual, and overcontrolled (the holding-on, "anal-retentive" type), or by being rebellious, messy, and disorganized (the letting-go, "anal-expulsive" type).

Phallic: If you masturbated freely during the preschool years, or if all genital contact was prohibited, resulting in frustration, you would develop a phallic personality—one that is entirely self-centered, vain, arrogant, and in constant need of attention. The macho man who seems obsessed with building his muscles, wearing expensive clothing, and conquering women is a classic example.

"Every impulse we strive to strangle broods in the mind, and poisons us."

OSCAR WILDE

The Dynamics of Personality   Influenced by the science of physics, Freud believed that the human mind has a constant, finite amount of "psychic energy," energy that cannot be created or destroyed, only transformed from one state to another. What this means for personality is that even though the id's instinctual impulses can be temporarily suppressed, that energy must find an outlet, a way to leak out. According to Freud, the ego searches for safe and normal outlets for these needs.

You may recall from Chapter 4 that in Freud's theory the dreams you remember in the morning are a disguised, nonthreatening expression of your unconscious wishes. Pent-up energy is released while you're asleep, but in ways that are confusing, and therefore harmless. The same is true of the so-called *Freudian slips* of the tongue and, as we'll see later, a defense mechanism known as *sublimation*. Even humor can serve as an outlet, as when people tell ethnic jokes to relieve hostile impulses and dirty jokes to ease sexual tension. Disguised wish fulfillment—it's the compromise we strike with ourselves (see Figure 15.2).

Figure 15.2

The Dynamics of Personality According to Freud

In psychoanalysis, unconscious sexual and aggressive impulses find acceptable forms of expression.

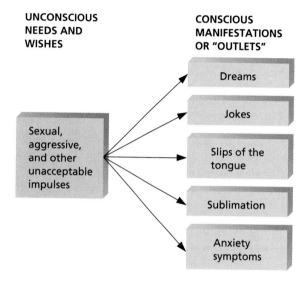

To help minimize the anxiety that results from the clash between our wishes, morals, and reality, the ego uses powerful weapons—unconscious **defense mechanisms** that deny and distort our self-perceptions. Here are some common defense mechanisms described by Freud. See if you recognize any of them:

- **Repression** occurs when anxiety-provoking thoughts and memories are "forgotten" and pushed out of awareness. Freud believed that people repress unacceptable sexual and aggressive urges, traumas, and guilt feelings. In the 1990 case of the Central Park jogger who was stripped, raped, beaten, and left for dead by a gang of teenagers, the victim testified that she could barely remember the attack—a possible sign of repression. According to Freud, this mechanism of defense is a necessary prerequisite for all the others, but is seldom a final solution.

- **Denial** is a primitive form of repression in which anxiety-filled external events are not only forgotten but barred from awareness in the first place (see no evil, hear no evil). Denial is common among terminally ill patients and in families who sometimes refuse to admit that a loved one is dying. It is also characteristic of smokers who refuse to recognize the health risks of their habit, husbands and wives who ignore signs of marital conflict, and politicians who manage to overlook corruption that takes place right under their noses.

- **Projection** occurs when people attribute or "project" their own unacceptable impulses onto others. In Freud's view, a person who is sexually attracted to a friend's spouse, or to anyone else who is "off limits,"

■ **defense mechanisms** Unconscious methods of minimizing anxiety by denying and distorting reality.

■ **repression** A defense mechanism in which personally threatening thoughts, memories, and impulses are banned from awareness.

■ **denial** A primitive form of repression in which anxiety-filled external events are barred from awareness.

■ **projection** A defense mechanism in which people attribute or "project" their own unacceptable impulses onto others.

"And then I say to myself, 'If I really wanted to talk to her, why do I keep forgetting to dial 1 first?'"

Freud often interpreted forgetting as an unconscious but disguised form of wish fulfillment. [Drawing by Modell; © 1981 The New Yorker Magazine, Inc.]

Sam: Why is it what you just said strikes me as a mass of rationalizations?
Michael: Don't knock rationalization. Where would we be without it? I don't know anyone who could get through the day without two or three juicy rationalizations. They're more important than sex.
Sam: Ah, come on. Nothing's more important than sex.
Michael: Oh yeah? You ever gone a week without a rationalization?

THE BIG CHILL (1982)

■ **reaction formation** A defense mechanism in which one converts an unacceptable feeling into its opposite.

■ **rationalization** A defense mechanism that involves making excuses for one's failures and shortcomings.

■ **sublimation** In psychoanalysis, the channeling of repressed sexual and aggressive urges into socially acceptable substitute outlets.

might repress those feelings and consciously come to believe that the friend's spouse is attracted to him or her. In this way, "I lust for this person" is transformed into "this person lusts after me." Similarly, people who are prejudiced against certain racial or ethnic groups are quick to attribute their own hostile impulses to "them."

■ **Reaction formation** involves converting an unacceptable feeling into its opposite. Someone who brags may be masking feelings of inadequacy. Similarly, hatred can be transformed into love, and sadness into joy. Compared to "true" feelings, reaction formations often appear exaggerated. Examples include the mother who smothers with affection an unwanted child she secretly resents, the schoolboy who goes out of his way to taunt a girl he really likes, the anti-pornography crusader who deep down inside is aroused by sexually explicit material, and the vocal anti-gay activist who fights to cover up his own homosexual impulses.

■ **Rationalization** involves making excuses for one's failures and shortcomings. The fox in Aesop's fable who refused the grapes he could not reach "because they were sour" used rationalization. So do failing students who say they don't really care about grades, gamblers who justify their massive losses as entertainment costs, and scorned lovers who find fault with those who reject them.

■ **Sublimation** is the channeling of the id's repressed urges into socially acceptable substitute outlets. Freud saw this as the healthiest defense mechanism because it represents a genuine compromise among the id, ego, and superego. Thus, a person with pent-up hostile impulses may derive satisfaction by becoming a surgeon, football player, or critic. Similarly, a person may sublimate sexual needs by listening to others talk about sex, or through music, art, dance, and other activities. Freud believed that civilization's greatest achievements spring from the wells of sexual and aggressive energy. He suggested, for example, that Leonardo da Vinci painted the famous *Mona Lisa* as a sublimation of his need for intimacy with a mother from whom he was separated at an early age. As for other men, the lyrics of an old song hint at how substitute gratification for repressed Oedipal urges can be achieved: "I want a girl just like the girl that married dear old dad!"

Freud's Legacy

Freud was born and raised in the prudish Victorian era, so you can imagine how people reacted to his theory (Gay, 1988). Unconscious conflicts, dreams, jokes, and slips of the tongue that hold hidden meaning, erotic impulses churning in the innocent newborn, repression and other defense mechanisms that keep us from falling apart at the seams—it all seemed pretty wild. Still, Freud's legacy is remarkable. As we'll see, his ideas gave rise to other psychoanalytic theories and a whole class of personality tests. He also provided a target for psychologists of other theoretical persuasions to shoot at.

Neo-Freudian Theorists   Despite the controversy, Freud's emerging theory immediately attracted a group of followers, many of whom went on to propose competing theories. Make no mistake about it—these dissenters were psychoanalytically oriented. Following Freud, they assumed that unconscious factors play a critical role, that people need to resolve inner conflicts, and that personality is formed early in childhood. The main sticking point was and still is Freud's emphasis on s-e-x as a driving force.

Carl Jung was a favorite within Freud's inner circle, heir apparent to the throne of psychoanalysis. Jung (1928), however, complained that Freud viewed the brain "as an appendage to the genital glands," and sought to change the theory in two ways. First, he maintained that the unconscious consists not only of repressed material from one's personal life but also of universal symbols and memories from our ancestral past—an inherited **collective unconscious.** That's why, said Jung, so many humans are born with an irrational fear of snakes, why we're drawn like magnets to fire, water, wind, and other natural elements, and why certain common themes appear in cultural myths around the world. Jung's second shift in emphasis concerned the subject of personality development. He agreed that people strive for the satisfaction of biological drives. But he also felt that at the age of forty or so, we undergo a midlife transition, a time during which the youthful, vigorous pursuit of biological needs is replaced by deeper, more cerebral, even spiritual concerns. As far as Jung was concerned, personality development continues into adulthood.

Alfred Adler was another major theorist within Freud's inner circle. Like the others, Adler was trained in medicine. He soon broke with Freud, however, because he felt that personality was formed more from social conflicts than from sexual tension. According to Adler (1927), all humans feel small, weak, and helpless in the first few years of life, symptoms of an "inferiority complex." As a result, we grow up trying unconsciously to compensate for these feelings and "strive for superiority," while at the same time taking an interest in the welfare of others. Adler felt that Freud was so preoccupied with the triangle of relationships among mother, father, and child that he neglected other family influences. Adler wrote, for example, about the impact of being a first-, middle-, or later-born within the family, and he coined the term *sibling rivalry*.

Later generations of psychoanalytic theorists either viewed themselves as classical Freudians (Brenner, 1982) or extended the theory in two directions. One group followed in Adler's path by emphasizing that humans are *social* animals. Erich Fromm (1941) argued that as Western civilization abandoned the caste system, people felt freer and more independent, but also more isolated. Fromm thus argued that we unconsciously seek to "escape from freedom" by falling in love, getting married and having children, joining religious groups, and rallying behind powerful leaders. What distinguishes individuals from one another are the ways in which they resolve the conflict between freedom and unity. Karen Horney (1945) similarly claimed that all humans need love and security, and become highly anxious when they feel isolated and alone. According to Horney, people have different ways of coping with this anxiety: some are unconsciously driven to be loved, others to be feared, and still others to be admired. Again, the goal is to satisfy needs that are social, not biological.

A second group of psychoanalysts known as *ego psychologists* enlarged the role of the ego in personality. For Freud, the ego existed in order to accommodate the id and yet also to operate within the boundaries of reality, appease the superego, and ward off anxiety through the use of defense

■ **collective unconscious** As proposed by Jung, a kind of memory bank that stores images and ideas that humans have accumulated over the course of evolution.

mechanisms. But according to daughter Anna Freud, Heinz Hartmann, David Rapaport, Erik Erikson, and others, the ego is more than simply the id's brainy assistant. In their view, the ego is present at birth, is every bit as basic as the id, and is the reason why people are often thoughtful as well as passionate. This ego helps to organize our thoughts, feelings, and memories, and leads us to grow and pursue creative activities for the sake of enjoyment, not simply the reduction of tension (Westen, 1990). As ego psychologist Robert White (1975) put it, "Human beings have intrinsic urges which make them want to grow up."

Projective Personality Tests   Psychoanalysis is founded on the assumption that the most meaningful parts of personality are locked away in an unconscious part of the mind. What this means is that one cannot truly get to know someone by asking direct questions. Searching for the key to this warehouse of personal secrets, Freud tried hypnosis, free association, and the interpretation of dreams—the "royal road to the unconscious." Is it possible to explore the mind without psychotherapy? Seeking a shortcut to the unconscious, psychoanalytic researchers and practitioners devised what's known as **projective tests.** A projective test asks people to respond to an ambiguous stimulus—a word out of context, an incomplete sentence, an inkblot, a fuzzy picture. The assumption is that if a stimulus has no inherent meaning and can accommodate a multitude of interpretations, then whatever people "see" must be a *projection* of their own needs, wishes, hopes, fears, and conflicts.

The most popular of the projective tests is the **Rorschach,** introduced in 1921 by Swiss psychiatrist Hermann Rorschach, and consisting of a set of ten symmetrical inkblots—some in color, others in black and white. Look, for example, at the inkblot in Figure 15.3. What do you see? Is it a man with a beer belly, wearing a bow tie? Two bats hanging from a wall? Two women bending over a pot? An upside-down frog? A bearskin rug? A butterfly? As you can imagine, stimuli like this can be interpreted in different ways. You may see crawling insects, animals, humans, sexual organs, weapons, or other inanimate objects. You may see a single large image, or you might dissect the inkblot into many smaller images. In fact, the examiner is interested not only in what you see but also in how you approach the task—whether you take two seconds per card, or five minutes; whether you're sensitive to form, or to color; and whether the images you report are common or uncommon. I'll never forget the time a graduate-school friend of mine was learning to work with the Rorschach as part of her clinical training, and used me as a guinea pig. Following a series of black-and-white inkblots, she turned over a bright, multicolored design. "Wow, nice!" was my immediate reaction, at which point my friend raised an eyebrow and quickly jotted down some notes. Later I was told that not everyone reacts as I did to the color, that my animated reaction means I'm an emotional person.

Over the years, many elaborate systems have been developed for scoring the Rorschach, which is still widely used in clinical settings. Critics say there are two problems. The first is that it lacks reliability, which means that two examiners often reach different conclusions from the same set of responses. The second problem is that the test lacks validity, which means that it does not discriminate among groups known to have different per-

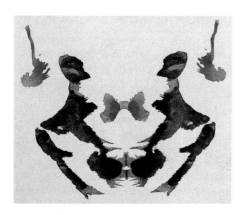

Figure 15.3

Sample Rorschach Card

According to psychoanalytically oriented psychologists, what you see in this inkblot—and how you see it—can be used to assess your personality.

■ **projective tests** Psychoanalytic personality tests that allow people to "project" unconscious needs, wishes, and conflicts onto ambiguous stimuli.

■ **Rorschach** A projective personality test in which people are asked to report what they see in a set of inkblots.

sonalities (Hertz, 1986). Despite these criticisms, Rorschach users are now becoming more sophisticated. Based on past research John Exner, Jr. (1986) developed a new, comprehensive, computerized scoring system. Recent research in general shows that there are higher levels of reliability and validity now than in the past (Parker et al., 1988)—but these levels are still lower than is found in the kinds of "objective" tests to be described later (Acklin et al., 1992). Nevertheless, as far as avid Rorschach proponents are concerned, skillful examiners can use the test to understand how people think and to explore depths of personality that do not otherwise surface in questionnaires, interviews, or behavioral observations (Blatt, 1990).

A second popular projective instrument is the **Thematic Apperception Test,** or **TAT,** introduced by Henry Murray. Murray (1938) had formulated a personality theory that distinguishes people by the kinds of psychological needs that motivate their behavior (examples include the needs for power, achievement, nurturance, and affiliation). To measure these needs, Murray (1943) developed a set of nineteen drawings of characters in ambiguous situations (plus one blank card, the ultimate projective test!), and asked subjects to tell a story about the "hero." Look, for example, at the picture presented in Figure 15.4. What do you think is going on? Who are the characters, and what is their relationship? What led up to this situation, and how will it all turn out? You can see that the possibilities are limitless—like a blank page awaiting your personal signature. The last time I showed this particular card to my students, I received a remarkable range of stories. Some said the woman in the shawl is the girl's mother, disappointed in her daughter's choice of a husband or career, or the fact that she's a lesbian. Others said the girl is looking into the mirror, seeing herself as an old lady, alone and without a family. Still others say the young woman is angry at her mother for driving her father out of the house.

The TAT is based on the assumption that people identify with the heroes and project their own needs into their responses. If someone tells one story after another about the loss of a loved one, resistance to authority, the struggle to achieve success, or a fear of rejection, chances are that particular theme is an important one for the person. As with the Rorschach, the TAT has been criticized for lacking reliability and validity (Anastasi, 1988). At the same time, certain TAT pictures can be used to identify specific motives and predict behavior. Research shows, for example, that people whose TAT stories reveal a high rather than low *need for intimacy* think more about social relationships, and spend more time talking, self-disclosing, smiling, and making eye contact when they're engaged in conversation (McAdams et al., 1984). In contrast, people whose stories reveal a high rather than low *need for achievement* set more realistic goals, persist more in the face of failure, are more likely to succeed at work, and derive more pride from their accomplishments (Atkinson, 1957; McClelland, 1985; Spangler, 1992).

Current Perspectives on Psychoanalysis   On November 29, 1993, *Time* magazine had a picture of Sigmund Freud on the cover, accompanied by three words: "Is Freud Dead?" It has now been over a hundred years since Freud started putting together the pieces of psychoanalysis, a bold theory that would alter the course of psychology as a discipline. Needless to say, Freud and other psychoanalysts have always attracted their share of critics,

Figure 15.4

Sample TAT Picture

This ambiguous picture is used in the Thematic Apperception Test.

■ **Thematic Apperception Test (TAT)** A projective personality test in which people are asked to make up stories from a set of ambiguous pictures.

as new research developments within psychology lead us to modify or reject some propositions, while accepting others.

There are three major criticisms. One is that psychoanalysis as a theory of personality paints too bleak a portrait of human nature. It was bad enough when Copernicus exposed the myth that Earth is at the center of the universe, and when Darwin noted that humans were descended from apes. But when Freud claimed that we are driven even as infants by lustful, incestuous desires and antisocial aggressive impulses, and that we are all at the mercy of unconscious forces beyond our control, he went too far. The theory was simply too pessimistic for many people to accept. Before World War II, for example, Albert Einstein wrote Freud and asked if he thought that war could be avoided. Freud wrote back a fourteen-page letter. The essence of his answer was no, war is inevitable.

The second criticism of psychoanalysis is that it does not meet acceptable standards of science. From the start, Freud based his whole theory on observations of his Vienna patients, hardly a representative group. He then proceeded to use the theory to explain family dynamics, mental illness, love and attraction, homosexuality, smoking, alcoholism, war, religion, suicide, crime and punishment, and the course of human history. Of course, after-the-fact explanations are easy, very much like betting on a horse after the race has been run. But can Freud's theory predict these kinds of events in advance?

The critics say no, leading to the third major criticism of psychoanalysis: that carefully controlled research fails to support many of its propositions. One important example concerns the assumption that personality is completely formed in the first few years of life. In light of recent research, we now know that although early childhood experiences are formative, and can have a lasting impact on us, development is a lifelong process (see Chapter 10). Freud's theory that childhood conflicts cause people to become fixated at certain psychosexual stages has also not stood the test of time. Research shows that although oral, anal, and phallic personality types can be identified, they don't necessarily arise from difficulties in weaning, toilet training, masturbation, or other psychosexual experiences. Even the Oedipus complex, the centerpiece of Freud's development theory, receives little support. Young boys and girls often do favor the opposite-sexed parent and identify with the same-sexed parent, but there's no evidence for castration anxiety, penis envy, or other sex-related motives (Fisher & Greenberg, 1977; Daly & Wilson, 1990).

So, is Freud dead? The man is, but his influence is not. In its classic form, psychoanalysis has some shortcomings and relatively few adherents. But many of its concepts have become so absorbed into mainstream psychology, not to mention popular culture, that it is very much alive—and continues to inspire new theories and research. As a physician, Freud almost single-handedly managed to convince the world that mental disorders are often psychological, not medical, in origin. As a personality theorist, he drew attention to the profound importance of the attachment bond between parents and the young child, the powerful unconscious filled with inner turmoil, and our arsenal of nonrational coping mechanisms. The theory may paint an unflattering portrait, psychoanalysts admit, but one must recognize the dark shadows of human nature in order to deal with them. Freud had the courage to expose this side of us, and to penetrate beneath the surface of our behavior.

Perhaps the most enduring of Freud's ideas is his view of the mind as an iceberg. Today, virtually everyone agrees that the unconscious is vast and important—and that people have a limited awareness of why they think, feel, and behave as they do (Singer, 1990). Psychologists disagree, however, about the nature of the unconscious. Some are influenced by the view that it consists of repressed traumas and wishes actively blocked from awareness for self-protective reasons (Erdelyi, 1992). Others maintain that the unconscious consists of innocent material that is not attended to, or else is forgotten, for strictly cognitive reasons (Greenwald, 1992; Kihlstrom et al., 1992). In a series of studies, Lloyd Silverman and his colleagues found that subjects are influenced by psychoanalytically charged messages flashed on a screen for 4 milliseconds—too quick to register in awareness. For example, after the Oedipal message "Mommy and I are one" is flashed, male subjects often report feeling happier and less anxious, even though they don't seem to know that a message was presented (Silverman & Weinberger, 1985). Researchers are now trying to determine just how reliable this provocative result is, and why it occurs (Balay & Shevrin, 1988; Hardaway, 1990).

A second enduring legacy of Freud's theory was his analysis of defense mechanisms. Based on the resistance shown by so many of his patients, Freud argued that people distort reality to ward off anxiety. Research shows he was absolutely right. Some of us may be more defensive than others, but everyone harbors illusions about the self—illusions that foster mental health. Thus, we take credit for success, make excuses for failure, exaggerate our power over uncontrollable events, compare ourselves to others who are less fortunate, and think more optimistically than we should about our own future (Taylor, 1989). Even young children exhibit the use of defense mechanisms (Cramer, 1990). Indeed, this part of Freud's theory can shed light on some of the most irrational, atrocious acts of humankind. After interviewing twenty-eight Nazi doctors who aided in the murder of millions of concentration-camp victims in World War II, for example, Robert Jay Lifton (1986) found that these men psychologically covered their tracks through denial, rationalization, "psychic numbing," and other unconscious forms of self-deception.

If he were alive, Freud would have liked Lifton's analysis of the Nazi doctors. Freud himself had to escape Vienna when the Nazis stormed his hometown. He died in 1939 in London, at the age of eighty-three, and sixteen years later a statue was unveiled in the courtyard of the University of Vienna, where he used to walk as a student. On the statue the inscription read, "Sigmund Freud: who divined the famed riddle and was a man most mighty."

THE COGNITIVE SOCIAL-LEARNING APPROACH

■ **cognitive social-learning theory** An approach to personality that focuses on social learning (modeling) and cognitive factors (expectancies, values), and emphasizes the person-situation interaction.

In contrast to psychoanalysis, **cognitive social-learning theory** is an approach that views personality as the product of a continuous interaction between persons and environments. This theory has its roots in the behavioral principles of classical and operant conditioning, social-learning theory, and cognitive psychology. Let's trace the evolution of this important second approach.

Principles of Learning and Behavior

As psychoanalysis was emerging in Europe, a second movement was being conceived in animal laboratories in the United States and Russia. At the time, animal researchers were discovering some very powerful principles of learning, and spreading the new word of *behaviorism*—a scientific approach to psychology that focuses on environmental determinants of observable behavior. To the hardcore behaviorist, personality was a nonscientific figment of the Freudian imagination. After all, behaviorists had refused to muddy the scientific study of behavior by speculating about inner states of "mind." As we saw earlier in this book, the first spokesman for this countermovement was John Watson, whose message was loud and clear:

> Give me a dozen healthy infants, well-formed, and my own specified world to bring them up in, and I'll guarantee to take any one at random and train him to become any type of specialist I might select—doctor, lawyer, artist, merchant-chief and, yes, even beggar-man and thief, regardless of his talents, penchants, tendencies, abilities, vocations, and race of his ancestors. (1924, p. 104)

At the same time that Freud was writing his classic book on dreams, animal researchers were discovering five simple but very powerful principles of learning (these are more fully described in Chapter 5). The first was *classical conditioning,* based on Pavlov's finding that the dogs in his laboratory would start to salivate before they were fed, in anticipation of the meal they were about to eat. By repeatedly sounding a buzzer before the presentation of food, Pavlov found that eventually the dogs would salivate as soon as the buzzer was sounded. Thus, the animals were trained to react to a neutral stimulus if it was associated with food, an unconditioned stimulus that naturally elicits the reaction. The second major principle was *operant conditioning,* first shown by Edward Thorndike's discovery that organisms repeat behaviors that are rewarded. Working with cats and, later, with humans, Thorndike found that whatever solution succeeded for a subject on one puzzle was later tried on other puzzles as well. A few years later, B. F. Skinner trained rats to press bars and pigeons to peck at keys for food in order to test the effects of reinforcement schedules on their behavior.

Both classical and operant conditioning researchers were making parallel discoveries not yet relevant to the study of personality. The first is *stimulus generalization,* the principle that once a response is learned in one situation, it may also be evoked in other, similar situations—as when Pavlov's dogs learned to salivate to tones that were similar but not identical to the conditioned stimulus. The second, opposite principle is *discrimination,* the learned tendency to distinguish between a conditioned stimulus and other stimuli—as when a child learns that having tantrums works on parents, but not on teachers and friends. The third principle is *extinction,* the tendency for a conditioned response to diminish if not reinforced. Pavlov's dogs eventually stopped salivating to the buzzer if it was no longer followed by meat, and Skinner's animals stopped pressing bars when food pellets were no longer forthcoming.

These principles of learning and behavior were momentous discoveries in psychology, the new science of behavior. But what did drooling dogs, puzzled cats, and key-pecking pigeons have to do with personality? In a crude attempt to answer this question, John Watson and his assistant Rosalie

Rayner (1920) conducted a well-known but ethically questionable demonstration. As you may recall from Chapter 5, Watson and Rayner brought an eleven-month-old boy named Albert into contact with a harmless white rat, then repeatedly made a loud sound every time the boy reached for the animal. Soon poor Albert was terrified not only of the rat but also of rabbits, dogs, and a white furry coat. What was the point? Poking fun at Freud and his followers, Watson declared that some day a psychoanalyst will meet a man named Albert with a fur coat phobia, analyze his dreams, and conclude that his fear is related to a scolding he received from his white-haired mother. Such are the pitfalls of a nonscientific approach to personality, said Watson.

Picking up where Watson left off, B. F. Skinner emerged as behaviorism's most forceful and dedicated proponent. He coined the term *operant conditioning*, studied different schedules of reinforcement, and wrote about how these principles could be used to socialize and educate children, increase worker productivity, extinguish behavioral disorders, and build a better society. As far as Skinner was concerned, personality is nothing more than a collection of behavior patterns developed, maintained, and—if necessary—modified by one's unique history of reinforcement.

Social-Learning Theory

Although Skinner offered a welcome change of pace from psychoanalysis, many psychologists found his focus on behavior too narrow and rejected his unwillingness to study thoughts, feelings, motivations, and the richness and texture of the human personality. At the very least, it seemed that behaviorism had to be extended in two ways. Enter *social-learning theory*, an approach that examines the social and cognitive factors involved in learning and the development of personality. Leading the way were Albert Bandura, Julian Rotter, and Walter Mischel.

The first problem was to account for the fact that people often acquire new behavior patterns without having had personal experience with reward and punishment. According to Bandura (1977), people learn by observing and imitating others, a process called **modeling.** Children, for example, absorb what their parents say and how they act, pay close attention to TV characters and sports heroes, and emulate peers whom they admire. Research shows that modeling is a multistep process: we look, we learn, we store in memory (learning). And then, if we are capable and motivated, and if the time is right, we imitate (performance). Bandura thus reminds us that learning often takes place in a social context, and that people learn to become aggressive, helpful, fearful, moral, and so on, by observing others (see Chapter 5).

The second important extension of behaviorism was to examine how our thoughts can influence the link between reinforcement and behavior. Skinner had insisted that behavior is determined by actual reinforcement contingencies, but Julian Rotter (1954) argued that what really matters is how we perceive and interpret and value the rewards in our lives. According to Rotter, human behavior in any given situation is determined by two factors: (1) our subjective *expectancy* that a specific act will be reinforced, and (2) the *value* of that reinforcement to us. If you expect that reading the rest

■ **modeling** The social-learning process by which behavior is observed and imitated.

■ **locus of control** A term referring to the expectancy that one's reinforcements are generally controlled by internal or external factors.

On one natural leg, this man competes in the long jump at the Paralympic Games. Such determination and persistence are hallmarks of an internal locus of control.

of this textbook will help you learn psychology and earn a high grade for the course, and if these strike you as desirable outcomes, you'll probably read on. If you don't expect to learn from this book, or if you don't really care, this may be the last paragraph you read. As far as personality is concerned, research shows that individuals differ in the amount of control they expect to have over outcomes in their lives and in the kinds of outcomes they value (Rotter et al., 1972).

Expanding on Rotter's model, Walter Mischel (1973, 1990) proposed a "cognitive" social-learning theory. According to Mischel, it is important to consider five "person variables" to understand how individuals interact with their environment. These person variables are (1) *competencies*—your mental and physical abilities, social skills, and creative talents, all of which influence what you strive for and what you can do; (2) *encoding strategies*—how you process information about other people and situations (for example, whether you tend to evaluate others in terms of their intelligence, friendliness, power, or physical appearance); (3) *expectancies*—your beliefs about the causes of success and failure, and about other possible consequences of your actions (there are two types of expectancies: whether you can perform a particular behavior, and whether that action will be reinforced); (4) *subjective values*—the kinds of outcomes you find more or less reinforcing (for example, whether you strive for love, security, excitement, respect, or dominance); and (5) *self-regulatory systems*—your ability to set goals, monitor and evaluate your progress, delay your short-term needs for gratification, and plan for the future. Self-regulation is an important and adaptive person variable. For example, Mischel and his colleagues (1989) have found that preschoolers who show they can defer their gratification in the laboratory by waiting for a larger but delayed reward grow up to become more competent, attentive, deliberate, and able to cope with real frustrations later in life.

Locus of Control   According to cognitive social-learning theory, behavior is influenced not by actual reinforcements, as Skinner had maintained (see Chapter 5), but by our perceptions of control. Think about it. Is there a connection between how hard you study and the grades you receive, or does grading sometimes seem arbitrary? Does getting ahead require hard work and persistence, or is it simply a matter of being in the right place at the right time? Can individuals influence government policies, or are we at the mercy of powerful leaders? And what about the quality of your health, relationships, and financial well-being—are you in control?

According to Rotter (1966), individuals differ in their **locus of control**, defined as a "generalized expectancy" for the control of reinforcement. People who have an *internal* locus of control believe they are masters of their own destiny. Those who have an *external* locus of control feel they are at the mercy of luck, fate, and powerful others. To assess these contrasting orientations, Rotter constructed a questionnaire known as the I-E Scale (see Table 15.1). Using this instrument, researchers have found that, compared to externals, internals are more inquisitive, active, optimistic, hardworking and persistent. They are also more likely to take preventive health measures, play an active role in political and social affairs, achieve high grades in school, and cope actively with stressful life events (Findley & Cooper, 1983; Lefcourt, 1982; Strickland, 1989; Rotter, 1990).

Table 15.1

Here are six items from the I-E Scale. For each item, circle the letter (a or b) of the statement you agree with more. Give yourself one point for each of the following answers: 1(a), 2(b), 3(a), 4(b), 5(b), 6(a). Next add your total number of points (from zero to six). The higher your score, the more *external* is your generalized expectancy for control (Rotter, 1966).

1. a. No matter how hard you try, some people just don't like you.
    b. People who can't get others to like them don't understand how to get along with others.
2. a. One of the major reasons we have wars is because people don't take enough interest in politics.
    b. There will always be wars, no matter how hard people try to prevent them.
3. a. Sometimes I can't understand how teachers arrive at the grades they give.
    b. There is a direct connection between how hard I study and the grades I get.
4. a. The average citizen can have an influence in government decisions.
    b. This world is run by a few people in power, and there is not much the little guy can do about it.
5. a. Becoming a success is a matter of hard work; luck has little or nothing to do with it.
    b. Getting a good job depends mainly on being in the right place at the right time.
6. a. Most people don't realize the extent to which their lives are controlled by accidental happenings.
    b. There really is no such thing as "luck."

An internal orientation is adaptive—except in situations that are not truly controllable.

Although people differ in their locus of control, there are two important qualifications to note. The first is that it is entirely possible to have an internal orientation in some life situations but not in others. Look again at Table 15.1, and you'll see that the I-E Scale asks about control expectancies for a wide range of domains—including health, academics, friendships, career pursuits, and remote political and social events. Second is that individuals also differ in the extent to which they *want* control. Some of us care more deeply than others about making our own decisions, or having an influence over others. People with a strong desire for control—regardless of whether they are internal or external in their expectancies—are more likely to become stressed in situations that make them feel helpless (Burger, 1991).

Is an expectation for control adaptive? At first glance, it seems that an internal orientation is a key to health, success, and happiness. In one study, nursing-home patients who by random assignment were given more control over minor daily affairs were happier, more active, and more alert when tested eighteen months later (Rodin, 1986). "No doubt about it," I tell my kids, "you need to believe in yourselves, take charge of your lives, open doors, and make things happen. As they say, the buck stops here (point to yourself)." But wait. Is an internal orientation *always* adaptive, or are there times when it's better to see life's reinforcements as beyond our command?

This is a tough question because there are two exceptions to the rule that it's better to be internal than external. First, an internal orientation can cause problems if we don't carefully distinguish between truly controllable and uncontrollable events. For example, the person with an inflated sense of control may be at risk to lose money gambling on games of pure chance (Langer, 1975). Second, an internal orientation can cause problems if it

Type A and B Cities: The Pace of Life and Death

In the 1950s, cardiologists Meyer Friedman and Ray Rosenman were studying the relationship between cholesterol and coronary heart disease when they stumbled upon the idea that psychological stress may also play a role. In a study of more than 3,500 healthy middle-aged men, they found that those who were the most hard-driving, competitive, time-conscious, restless, and quick to anger were more likely than those who were more relaxed to suffer heart attacks during the next few years. The hard-driving men they referred to as Type A's; and the more relaxed ones, as Type B's (Rosenman et al., 1975).

As we'll see in Chapter 18, the Type A behavior pattern of the so-called workaholic consists of many traits, including a sense of time urgency, high levels of competitive achievement, a strong need for control, and hostility (Booth-Kewley & Friedman, 1987; Matthews, 1988; Wright, 1988). In general, researchers have focused on *individuals* who differ in their Type A and B patterns of behavior. But is it also possible that these orientations are triggered by factors within the environment?

Anyone who has been to Wall Street and stood on the crowded floor of the New York City Stock Exchange will vividly recall the frantic pace, the running, the noise, and the flashing stream of stock prices changing from one moment to the next. In contrast, anyone who has enjoyed an early morning stroll along the main street of a small, sleepy town in the rural Midwest will recall an experience of calm and relaxation. It's hard to believe that these two settings coexist on the same planet. This comparison does suggest, however, that just as we may be predisposed by our personalities to exhibit Type A or Type B behavior, environments can also lead us to behave in ways that pose more or less of a health risk.

Do cities around the world, or even inside the borders of the United States, have different tempos? Do New Yorkers really live life in the fast lane? Are Californians as laid back as

Frantic, time-urgent Type A behavior is a daily routine on the floor of the New York Stock Exchange.

the popular image suggests? Indeed, can the pace of city life be measured, and, if so, how does it relate to the incidence of heart disease among inhabitants? Interested in these questions, Robert Levine (1990) examined thirty-six American cities of various sizes, nine from each of four regions (Northeast, Midwest, South, and West). In each city, Levine determined the "pace of life" by combining four measures: (1) the walking speed of downtown pedestrians on a clear summer weekday, (2) the amount of time it took bank tellers to fulfill a simple request for change, (3) the talking speed of postal clerks in response to a standardized question, and (4) the percentage of adults on the street wearing wristwatches. Levine also looked at health statistics on the local death rates from heart disease (adjusted in each city for the average age of the population).

As you can see in the figure, the Northeastern cities that were sampled had the fastest pace of life, and the Western cities had the slowest (the fastest city was Boston and the

leads us to develop an "overcontrolling," stress-inducing style of behavior—whether that means having the last word in a conversation, driving from the back seat of a car, or planning every detail of a leisurely vacation (see box). Sometimes it is better to just let go (Wright et al., 1990).

Self-Efficacy   As noted, locus of control refers to the expectation that our behaviors can produce satisfying outcomes. But people also differ in the extent to which they think they can perform these reinforced behaviors in the first place. According to Bandura (1989), these latter expectations are

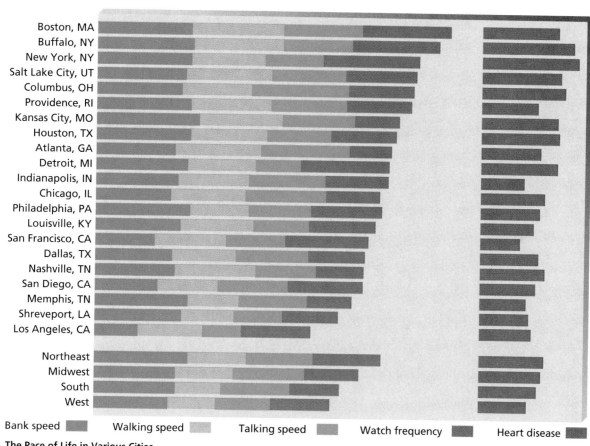

Boston, MA
Buffalo, NY
New York, NY
Salt Lake City, UT
Columbus, OH
Providence, RI
Kansas City, MO
Houston, TX
Atlanta, GA
Detroit, MI
Indianapolis, IN
Chicago, IL
Philadelphia, PA
Louisville, KY
San Francisco, CA
Dallas, TX
Nashville, TN
San Diego, CA
Memphis, TN
Shreveport, LA
Los Angeles, CA

Northeast
Midwest
South
West

Bank speed ■   Walking speed ■   Talking speed ■   Watch frequency ■   Heart disease ■

The Pace of Life in Various Cities

slowest was Los Angeles). More important, the correlations showed that the quicker the pace, the higher was the incidence of death from heart disease. Why are residents of fast-paced environments more prone to heart disease? From the correlations alone, it is hard to tell. One possible interpretation is that a city's pace causes its inhabitants to develop the kinds of personality traits that are necessary for survival (in other words, maybe one has to acquire the classic Type A behavior pattern in order to cope with life in the Northeast).

Another alternative is that people who are by nature Type A's seek out fast cities, while those who are Type B's tend to migrate to slower-paced lifestyles. Still other interpretations are that fast-paced cities are found in colder climates, or may lead people to smoke cigarettes and engage in other stress-reducing but harmful habits. Whatever the explanation, the link between the pace of city life and heart disease prompted Levine to suggest that the environment in which we live can be used to predict our health.

■ **self-efficacy** The belief that one is capable of performing the behaviors required to produce a desired outcome.

based on feelings of competence, or **self-efficacy.** Although some people are generally more confident than others, Bandura believes that self-efficacy is a state of mind that varies from one specific task and situation to another. In other words, you may have a high self-efficacy about meeting new people, but not about raising your grades. Or you may have a high self-efficacy about solving a calculus problem, but not about writing a paper.

There are now volumes of research on self-efficacy, and this research indicates that the more of it you have at a particular task, the more likely you are to engage in an activity, exert yourself, persist in the face of failure, and

It's common for people to have feelings of self-efficacy in some life domains but not others. [Drawing by Mankoff; © 1993 The New Yorker Magazine, Inc.]

MANKOFF

"Amazing, three failed marriages, scores of disastrous relationships, many financial reversals, and countless physical ailments, but through it all I've always had good luck parking."

succeed. The implications for health are particularly striking. For example, people with a high self-efficacy on health-related matters are more likely, if they want, to stop smoking, abstain from alcohol, stay physically fit, and tolerate the pain of arthritis, migraine headaches, and childbirth (Maddux, 1991). Evidence also suggests that among people who have a high self-efficacy about their ability to cope with stress, there is an enhanced functioning of the immune system (Wiedenfeld et al., 1990).

Perspectives on Cognitive Social-Learning Theory

Cognitive social-learning theorists believe that personality is rooted in the basic principles of learning. In contrast to psychoanalysis, this approach rests on the assumption that human behavior is caused more by external factors than by instincts, and that personality is shaped by reinforcement, observation, and the development of abilities, expectancies, values, and information-processing strategies.

Although all learning-based theories of personality share this assumption, the more recent approach has come a long way from that taken by the hardcore behaviorists. In his facetious call for a dozen healthy infants, Watson claimed that he could mold people like clay through the use of reward and punishment. Years later, Skinner similarly argued that human behavior is shaped by external forces, by reinforcement contingencies beyond our awareness and control. Yet cognitive social-learning theorists say that personality emerges from an ongoing mutual interaction among persons, their actions, and their environments, a concept Bandura (1986) calls **reciprocal determinism.** The point is, environmental forces may help shape our personalities, but we can also choose and alter the situations we encounter, and interpret these situations in light of our own points of view. In Bandura's words, "Your behavior, internal personal factors, and environmen-

■ **reciprocal determinism** The view that personality emerges from a mutual interaction of individuals, their actions, and their environments.

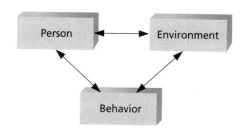

Figure 15.5

Reciprocal Determinism

tal influences all operate interactively as determinants of each other" (p. 23). This concept is illustrated in Figure 15.5.

To measure personality, cognitive social-learning theorists use fairly direct forms of assessment. One method is behavioral observation, in which subjects are observed either in real-life settings or in the laboratory. Another involves asking subjects to report their own expectancies, values, and past behaviors using standardized interviews, or questionnaires like the I-E Scale. Whatever the specific technique may be, information about an individual is measured in ways that are direct and to the point. No inkblots, no fuzzy pictures. To those in hot pursuit of the unconscious, the cognitive social-learning approach is doomed to shed light on only the tip of the iceberg. To others, this approach permits the study of personality in an objective and scientific manner.

THE HUMANISTIC APPROACH

Faced with a choice between psychoanalysis and behaviorism, many personality psychologists in the 1940s and 1950s had an uneasy feeling that something was missing, something vital about human nature. Freud had drawn attention to the dark forces of the unconscious, and Skinner was interested only in the effects of reinforcement on observable behavior. But what about the conscious mind, free will, subjective experiences, and the capacity for self-reflection? If we want to know about someone, can't we just ask? Are people really that mechanical? And isn't there a brighter side to human nature? In short, where's the *person* as we know it in personality? To fill the void, a "third force" was born—the **humanistic theory** of personality. Inspired by theorists Carl Rogers and Abraham Maslow, a group of psychologists founded the Association of Humanistic Psychology, and adopted four basic principles: (1) the experiencing person is of primary interest; (2) human choice, creativity, and self-actualization are the preferred topics of investigation; (3) meaningfulness must precede objectivity in the selection of research problems; and (4) ultimate value is placed on the dignity of the person.

Carl Rogers

Enter Carl Rogers, the first self-proclaimed humanistic theorist. Born into a religious family in a Midwest farming community, Rogers attended a theological seminary for two years before deciding to become a clinical psychologist. He then received his degree in 1931, the same year in which B. F. Skinner got his. Like Freud, Rogers spent his early years as a therapist treating emotionally troubled "clients." Yet unlike Freud, who was impressed by his patients' efforts to resist their own cures, Rogers was struck by how often his clients reflected on who they are ("I'd like to be more independent, but that just isn't me," "I just haven't been myself lately"), and by their natural will to get better and reach their full potential. Sure, Rogers saw signs of temporary resistance and other ego defense mechanisms. But he was much more impressed by the self-concept and the will to improve. If

■ **humanistic theory** An approach to personality that focuses on the self, subjective experience, and the capacity for growth and fulfillment.

■ **unconditional positive regard** An attitude of unqualified acceptance of another person.

therapists provide warmth, a gentle, guiding hand, and a climate of uncritical acceptance, he said, clients will ultimately solve their own problems and find the road to health, happiness, and fulfillment. As far as Rogers was concerned, there is in each of us an inner wisdom.

Rogers' Theory   The seeds of a new and different approach to personality were thus planted in fertile ground. From a humanist's standpoint, Rogers went on to develop client-centered therapy (1951) and a theory of personality, as described in his book *On Becoming a Person* (1961). According to Rogers, all living organisms are innately endowed with an *actualizing tendency*, a forward drive not only to survive but to grow and reach their full genetic capacity (see Table 15.2). For thinking and feeling humans, there is also a natural *need for self-actualization*, a drive to behave in ways that are consistent with one's conscious identity, or self-concept. So far, so good. The problem is that we are social animals, born helpless, and dependent on others for approval, support, and love. In other words, there also develops within us a competing need, a *need for positive regard*. And therein lies the potential for conflict in the development of personality.

Driven as humans are by the needs for self-actualization and positive regard, one of two general outcomes is possible. If you are fortunate enough to receive **unconditional positive regard** from parents and significant oth-

Table 15.2

The Actualizing Tendency, as Described by Rogers

Carl Rogers was born and raised on a farm. Before he died in 1987, he spent many hours working in his garden. Influenced by his experiences, Rogers saw parallels among humans, plants, and other forms of life. He summarized his portrayal of human nature in the following poetic passage:

During a vacation weekend some months ago I was standing on a headland overlooking one of the rugged coves which dot the coastline of Northern California. Several large rock outcroppings were at the mouth of the cove, and these received the full force of the great Pacific combers which, beating upon them, broke into mountains of spray before surging into the cliff-lined shore. As I watched the waves breaking over these large rocks in the distance, I noticed with surprise what appeared to be tiny palm trees on the rocks, no more than two or three feet high, taking the pounding of the breakers. Through my binoculars, I saw that these were some type of seaweed, with a slender "trunk" topped off with a head of leaves. As one examined a specimen in the interval between the waves it seemed clear that this fragile, erect, top-heavy plant would be utterly crushed and broken by the next breaker. When the wave crunched down upon it, the trunk bent almost flat, the leaves were whipped into a straight line by the torrent of the water, yet the moment the wave had passed, here was the plant again, erect, tough, resilient. It seemed incredible that it was able to take this incessant pounding hour after hour, day after night, week after week, perhaps for all I know, year after year, and all the time nourishing itself, extending its domain, reproducing itself; in short, maintaining and enhancing itself in this process which, in our shorthand, we call growth. Here in this palmlike seaweed was the tenacity of life, the forward thrust of life, the ability to push into an incredibly hostile environment and not only hold its own, but to adapt, develop, become itself. (1974, pp. 1–2)

ers—that is, if the important people in your life are loving and respectful despite your failures and setbacks, no ifs, ands, or buts—then life is rosy. Your need for positive regard is met, and you've got the green light to freely and openly pursue the all-important need for self-actualization. However, if you are subject to *conditional positive regard*—that is, if your parents, spouse, and close friends withdraw their love when your actions and life choices don't meet with their approval—then you get hung up trying to strike a balance between your true self and the kind of person others want you to become. The result is frustration, anxiety, emptiness, and feelings of incongruence or "discrepancy" within the self.

The Self-Concept   From the start, Rogers sought empirical verification for his newly formulated theory. To evaluate the importance of the *self-concept*, he taped, transcribed, and analyzed many of his therapy sessions and found that, as treatment progressed, clients made more and more positive statements about themselves. Whatever self-discrepancies there were tended to diminish. More recent research confirms that people have clear, often complex ideas about the self. According to Hazel Markus (1977), the self-concept is multifaceted, made up of a collection of *self-schemas*—specific beliefs about the self that influence how we process self-relevant information and interpret our life experiences. In fact, it appears that we also think about our "possible selves"—images of what we might become, would like to become, and are afraid of becoming in the future (Markus & Nurius, 1986).

Picking up where Rogers left off, E. Tory Higgins (1989) confirmed the hypothesis that *self-discrepancy*—defined as a mismatch between your self-concept and other desired self-images—breed emotional turmoil. In a series of studies, Higgins and his colleagues had subjects describe their own "ideal" self (what they want to be), "ought" self (what they think they should be), and "self-concept" (what they actually are). He then assessed their emotional well-being. The result was interesting. Subjects whose self-concepts fell short of their ideals were most likely to feel sad, dejected, unfulfilled, even depressed. Those whose self-concepts were at odds with their "ought" selves were more likely to feel guilty, shameful, fearful and anxious. Based on a large body of supportive research, these emotional and mental health effects are summarized in Figure 15.6 (Scott & O'Hara, 1993; Strauman, 1989; Strauman & Higgins, 1987).

Figure 15.6

The Personality Theory of Carl Rogers

According to Rogers, the needs for self-actualization and positive regard present a potential for conflict. Unconditional positive regard permits self-actualization, but conditional positive regard can result in self-discrepancies. Higgins's more recent theory details the mental health consequences of these self-discrepancies.

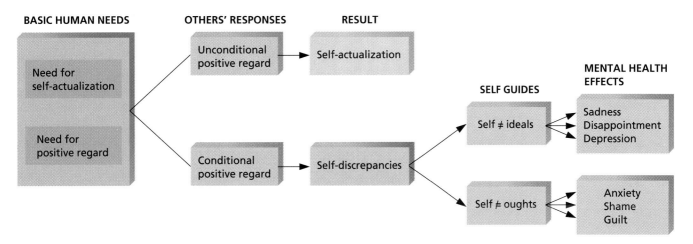

Abraham Maslow

Abraham Maslow was the second influential spokesman for the humanistic approach to personality. Oddly enough, Maslow started out as a behaviorist conducting learning experiments with monkeys. Then came the birth of his first child. As most parents would agree, this was an eye-opening experience. Said Maslow, "I was stunned by the mystery and by the sense of not really being in control. I felt small and weak and feeble before all this. I'd say anyone who had a baby couldn't be a behaviorist." Over the years, Maslow (1954, 1968) went on to formulate a motivational theory of personality, focusing on how people strive to fulfill their utmost potential.

Maslow's Theory   Have you ever met someone who seems to have it all—great looks, money, successful career, nice home, loving spouse, and wonderful children—and yet seems unsatisfied, searching for more? If so, then you'll appreciate the essence of Maslow's theory. According to Maslow (1954), all people are motivated to fulfill a **hierarchy of needs,** from those most basic for survival up to those that promote self-enhancement (see Figure 15.7).

Figure 15.7

Maslow's Pyramid of Needs

Maslow theorized that everyone is motivated to fulfill a hierarchy of needs ranging from those most basic for survival up to those that promote self-enhancement.

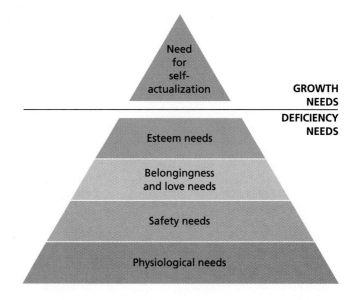

■ **hierarchy of needs** Maslow's list of basic needs that have to be satisfied before one can become self-actualized.

■ **self-actualization** In humanistic personality theories, the need to fulfill one's unique potential.

At the base of the hierarchy are the physiological needs for food, water, oxygen, sleep, sex, and shelter. Once these needs are met, people seek safety, financial security, stability at home, and a predictable environment. Next on the ladder is the need for belongingness and love, a craving for affection, close relationships, family ties, and group membership (if these needs are not satisfied, we feel lonely and alienated). Next is the need for esteem, which includes our desires for achievement, status, recognition, and respect from others (failing to satisfy this need, we feel inferior and unimportant). In short, each of us strives in our own way to be biologically content, safe, loved, and respected. Only once these needs are met are we ready, willing, and able to strive for **self-actualization**—the distinctly human need to become everything one is capable of becoming. In Maslow's

(1968) words, "A musician must make music, an artist must paint, a poet must write, if he is ultimately to be at peace with himself. What a man *can* be, he *must* be" (p. 46).

Research shows that not everyone climbs Maslow's pyramid in the prescribed order. For example, some people seek love before esteem, while others try to establish a career before a family (Goebel & Brown, 1981). Either way, Maslow's interest was in self-actualizing, the ultimate state. Indeed, he went out of his way to study happy, healthy, and productive individuals who embody the best that human nature has to offer. He interviewed a select group of acquaintances, and he used biographies to examine the lives of great historical figures such as Ludwig van Beethoven, Abraham Lincoln, Albert Einstein, and Eleanor Roosevelt. What did these self-actualized people have in common? Maslow (1968) saw self-actualization as a rare state of being in which a person is open to new experiences, spontaneous, playful, loving, realistic, accepting of others, creative, energetic, independent rather than conforming, and problem-focused rather than self-centered. If this set of traits sounds almost too good to be true, you're right. Maslow estimated that fewer than 1 percent of the world's adults are self-actualized. The rest of us are too busy trying to overcome obstacles in order to satisfy lower, more basic needs.

The State of Self-Actualization Are you self-actualized? Based on Maslow's theory, Everett Shostrom (1965) developed the Personal Orientation Inventory, a lengthy questionnaire designed to assess various aspects of self-actualization—for example, the capacity for intimate contact, spontaneity, and self-acceptance (see Table 15.3). This scale was endorsed by Maslow and is used in clinical settings. Research shows that people with high scores are psychologically healthier than those who receive low scores (Campbell et al., 1989; Knapp, 1976).

Table 15.3

Are You Self-Actualized?

Here is a sample of ten statements from the Personal Orientation Inventory. How many of the values thought to be associated with self-actualization do you possess?

1. I live in terms of my wants, likes, dislikes, and values.
2. I believe that man is essentially good and can be trusted.
3. I don't feel guilty when I'm selfish.
4. I believe it is important to accept others as they are.
5. I am not afraid of making mistakes.
6. I believe in saying what I feel in dealing with others.
7. I often make decisions spontaneously.
8. I welcome criticism as an opportunity for growth.
9. I enjoy detachment and privacy.
10. For me, work and play are the same.

If you're wondering what it must feel like to experience self-actualization at least temporarily, try this: "Think about the most wonderful experiences of your life; happiest moments, ecstatic moments, moments of rapture, perhaps from being in love, or from listening to music or suddenly 'being hit' by a book or a painting, or from some great creative moment" (Maslow, 1968, p. 71). According to Maslow, self-actualized individuals have more

Self-actualization is a state of mind that we achieve on a temporary basis during peak experiences.

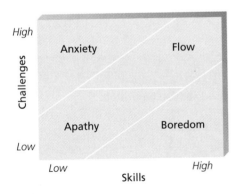

Figure 15.8

Flow, the Optimal Experience

Csikszentmihalyi claims that a state of "flow" arises when we engage in activities that we are skilled at and at levels that are challenging but not too difficult.

moments like these than everyone else. Still, many of us enjoy an occasional *peak experience*, a fleeting but intense moment of self-actualization in which we feel happy, absorbed, and capable of extraordinary performance. Music, sexual love, religion, nature, running, sports, creative pursuits, childbirth, and reminiscing are the most common triggers of a peak experience (Privette, 1983).

Inspired by Maslow's ideas, Mihaly Csikszentmihalyi (1975, 1990) has conducted extensive research on a state of mind he calls "flow," the "optimal experience." Under what conditions, Csikszentmihalyi asks, do we tend to become so fully immersed in an activity that we lose all track of time and all awareness of the self, forget our worries, and concentrate our energy on what we're doing, much to our benefit and enjoyment? I sometimes have this exquisite experience when I write, play baseball, or listen to my favorite music. Csikszentmihalyi interviewed athletes, dancers, artists, rock climbers, factory workers, chess masters, surgeons, sailors, elderly Korean women, Japanese motorcyclists, Navajo shepherds, and farmers in the Italian Alps, and found that people from all parts of the world and from all walks of life describe a similar kind of experience—when what they're doing seems effortless and perfect, when they're so completely tuned in that nothing else seems to matter.

What precipitates flow? From his research, Csikszentmihalyi finds that the state arises when people engage in activities at which they are skilled, and at levels that are challenging in relation to their ability (tasks that are too easy result in boredom, those that are too difficult cause anxiety). Also important is the capacity of these activities to present clear goals and immediate feedback. In one series of studies, for example, subjects carried portable beepers for a week and stopped to record what they were doing, thinking, and feeling whenever the beeper went off. Supporting the theory, subjects reported feeling happy, excited, strong, motivated, open, and in control at those times when they were involved in high-skill, high-challenge activities (Csikszentmihalyi & Csikszentmihalyi, 1988). This model is illustrated in Figure 15.8.

Perspectives on the Humanistic Approach

When Carl Rogers (1974) looked back on his career and his impact on psychology, counseling, education, and parenting, he concluded that "I expressed an idea whose time had come." The "idea," of course, was that people are inherently good, that conscious mental experience is important, and that the self-concept lies at the heart of personality.

Humanistic psychologists have received praise for drawing our attention to this idea, for providing an alternative view of personality, and for stimulating interest among serious researchers in previously neglected topics related to the self. At the same time, they have been severely criticized for taking a nonscientific approach based on personal impressions, for naively taking people's self-report statements at face value, and for painting too rosy a picture of human nature while ignoring our demonstrated capacity for evil. Focused on the all-important quest for self-actualization, humanistic psychologists have also been accused of inadvertently promoting the self-indulgent, "be true to yourself" approach to life that's associated with the so-called me generation. Sure the self is important, say critics, but where does the rest of the world fit in?

THE TRAIT APPROACH

In 1919, a twenty-two-year-old psychology student from Indiana wrote a letter to Sigmund Freud to say he'd be traveling in Europe and would like to meet. Freud was the master, known worldwide, and the student wanted to feel his presence, maybe get an autograph. A meeting was arranged, so the student took a train to Vienna, arrived on schedule, and entered the master's inner office. But Freud just sat there in silence, staring, waiting for his young, wide-eyed admirer to state his mission. Desperate to break the awkward stalemate, the student told about an incident he witnessed on the train that day involving a young boy who appeared to have a "dirt pho-bia." The boy complained that the seats were soiled, and pleaded with his mother to keep dirty passengers from sitting nearby. The mother, it turned out, was a dominant, "well-starched" woman. Isn't that an interesting case? When the student finished telling his story, Freud paused, then leaned over and said in a soft voice, "And was that little boy you?"

Freud's young admirer was terribly embarrassed. Wishing he could dis-appear, he nervously changed the subject, babbled a bit, excused himself, and left. How could Freud have been so wrong? Was he so accustomed to analyzing the hidden motives of anxious patients that he couldn't appreci-ate a man's simple curiosity? It turns out that the student was Gordon All-port, who went on to become one of the most important personality psy-chologists of all time. In an autobiography published the year he died, Allport (1967) said this experience convinced him that before personality theorists search for deep, analytical explanations, they should start by try-ing to *describe* and *measure* the basic units of personality. In other words, first things first. This rule now guides what is known as the trait approach.

The Building Blocks of Personality

Working from the ground up, Allport and his colleague Henry Odbert (1936) combed through an unabridged English dictionary, and came up with a list of 18,000 words that could be used to describe people. By elimi-nating synonyms, obscure words, and words referring to temporary states, they brought the list down to 4,500, then grouped words that were similar into about 200 clusters of related traits. For Allport, these **traits** were the building blocks of personality (though he was quick to point out that not all traits are relevant to all people, nor do they all have an influence on be-havior).

To reduce Allport's list to a more manageable size, and to construct a sci-ence of personality, Raymond Cattell (1965) used *factor analysis*, a statisti-cal technique designed to identify clusters of items that correlate with one another. You may recall from Chapter 11 that this technique was first used

■ **trait** A relatively stable predisposition to behave in a certain way.

to distinguish among different types of intelligence. Cattell—who was a chemistry major in college—wanted to uncover the basic units of personality, much like chemistry's periodic table of elements. Are individuals who are passive also thoughtful, calm, and even-tempered? And do those who describe themselves as sociable also say they're easygoing, lively, and talkative? How many trait clusters are needed to fully describe personality? To answer these questions, Cattell collected people's ratings of themselves and others on various traits, crunched the numbers through factor analysis, and found that personality consists of 16 distinct units, or *source traits*. What

Figure 15.9

Cattell's Sixteen Personality Factors

Cattell's sixteen "source traits" are described below. Through testing, Cattell plotted the average profiles of different groups—including criminals, airline pilots, and college professors (Cattell, 1965).

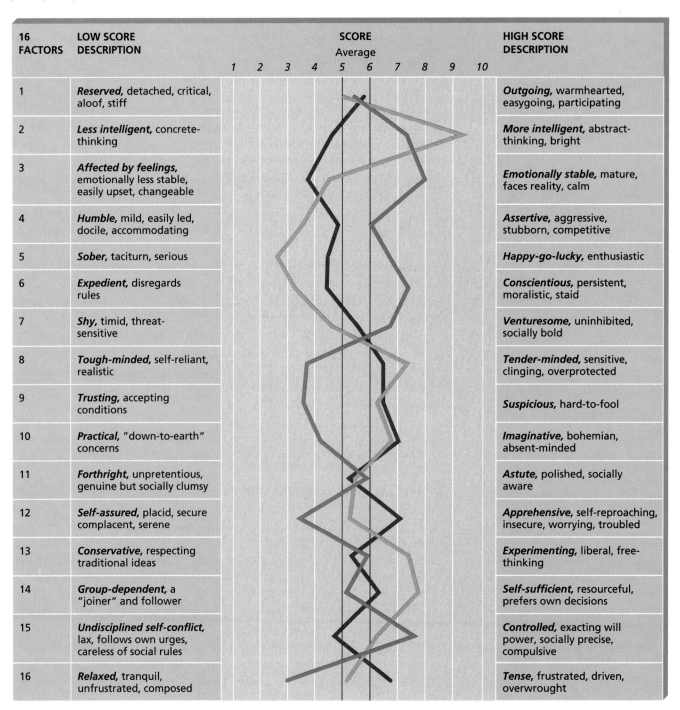

■ **five-factor model** A model of personality that consists of five basic traits: neuroticism, extraversion, openness, agreeableness, and conscientiousness.

distinguishes one individual from another, said Cattell, is that each of us has a unique combination of traits—a high level of some, a low level of others—a pattern that is summarized by a personality "profile." To derive this profile, Cattell devised the Sixteen Personality Factors Questionnaire, a 187-item scale that yields 16 separate scores, one for each factor. Figure 15.9 presents these factors as well as the average profiles of certain groups.

As factor analysis became more sophisticated, researchers began to notice that Cattell's model could be simplified even further—and that five major factors always seemed to emerge from self-ratings, ratings of others, and an assortment of personality questionnaires. Indeed, this **five-factor model** emerges consistently in studies of children, college students, and older adults, in men and women, in different languages, and in testing conducted in the United States, Canada, Finland, Germany, Japan, Poland, and other countries. As a result, these factors are called the *Big Five* (Goldberg, 1990, 1993; Digman, 1990; McCrae & John, 1992; Paunonen et al., 1992).

As shown in Table 15.4, many researchers are now convinced that the best way to describe personality and individual differences is to find where people stand on the following dimensions: (1) neuroticism, (2) extraversion, (3) openness to experience, (4) agreeableness, and (5) conscientiousness. New tests have thus been developed to specifically measure these broad traits (Costa & McCrae, 1992). It has also been suggested that people with highly extreme scores on one or more of these dimensions are likely to be diagnosed as having a personality disorder, which is described in Chapter 16 (Costa & Widiger, 1994).

Table 15.4

The "Big Five" Personality Factors

Factor	Description of Traits
Neuroticism	anxious vs. relaxed insecure vs. secure emotional vs. calm self-pitying vs. content
Extraversion	sociable vs. withdrawn fun-loving vs. sober friendly vs. aloof seeks excitement vs. calm
Openness	original vs. conventional imaginative vs. down-to-earth broad interests vs. narrow interests receptive vs. closed to new ideas
Agreeableness	good-natured vs. irritable soft-hearted vs. ruthless courteous vs. rude sympathetic vs. tough-minded
Conscientiousness	well-organized vs. disorganized dependable vs. undependable hardworking vs. lazy ambitious vs. easy-going

Using Personality Tests in Personnel Selection

Anyone who has applied for a full-time job knows that you sometimes have to climb hurdles and jump through hoops to get hired. It's a familiar routine. You submit a résumé and a list of references, fill out an application, and maybe take the "hot seat" in a face-to-face interview. You may even be asked to bring in samples of your work, or to take a standardized test of your intelligence, physical, perceptual, and cognitive abilities, vocational interests, or personality. When it comes to personnel selection in business and industry, there are numerous methods—all designed to predict performance in the workplace (Landy et al., 1994).

The use of personality tests for employment purposes has been a source of controversy. Can scores on trait inventories be used to predict worker productivity, motivation, satisfaction, loyalty, or other aspects of job performance? For many years, the MMPI was used to assess a candidate's personality—even though it had been developed for the purpose of diagnosing mental disorders, and even though there was no clear link between MMPI test scores and performance at work (Guion, 1965). Questions were also raised about whether it was ethical, or a violation of privacy, to require the testing of all prospective employees. People are free to refuse to take a test administered as part of the application process, but 52 percent of personnel managers surveyed said they automatically reject applicants who refuse to take a test (Blocklyn, 1988).

Construction of Multitrait Inventories

As Allport noted, the study of personality must begin not only with description but with measurement. And so it did. One of the most important contributions of trait psychology is the construction of *personality inventories,* questionnaires designed to assess a whole multitude of traits (Wiggins & Pincus, 1992). Cattell's Sixteen Personality Factors Questionnaire is one such instrument. There are many others. The most widely used is the **Minnesota Multiphasic Personality Inventory,** or **MMPI,** a 550-item questionnaire originally developed in the 1940s to help in the diagnosis of psychological disorders (Hathaway & McKinley, 1983).

The MMPI is to personality measurement what the Stanford-Binet was to intelligence testing. Taking an empirical approach, Alfred Binet developed his test by generating a large number of problems, testing schoolchildren, and retaining those problems that successfully discriminated between fast and slow learners. The MMPI developers used a similar strategy. They wrote hundreds of true-false statements, gave them to both "normal" adults and "clinical" patients with a variety of psychiatric diagnoses (depressed, paranoid, and so on), and then included in the final test only those items that were answered differently by the two groups—even if the content made little sense. The MMPI is filled with discriminating but odd items (for example, hysterical patients are more likely than others to answer "yes" to "My fingers sometimes feel numb"). Indeed, satirist Art Buchwald once wrote a spoof of MMPI-like personality tests by creating his own items. Among them: "I think beavers work too hard," "Frantic screams make me nervous," and "My mother's uncle was a good man."

Many of the original items were dated, and the norms had been based on a predominantly white, rural, middle-class group of subjects. To bring the test up to date, new items were written and a more ethnically diverse cross-

■ **Minnesota Multiphasic Personality Inventory (MMPI)** A large-scale test designed to measure a multitude of psychological disorders and personality traits.

For predictive purposes, many organizations have sought more "scientific" methods of evaluation. It has been estimated, for example, that 3,000 firms in the United States and many more in Europe use "graphology," or handwriting analysis, to predict job-relevant traits such as honesty, sales ability, and leadership potential (Rafaeli & Klimoski, 1983). Yet controlled research does not support the claim that handwriting can be used in this way. In one study, professional graphologists were asked to predict various aspects of job performance by analyzing the handwriting contained in the autobiographical sketches of bank employees. From the information contained in the same materials, the researchers themselves also made predictions. A comparison of predicted and actual employee performance revealed that the graphologists were no more effective than were the researchers. In fact, they were no more accurate than they would have been by flipping a coin (Ben-Shakhar et al., 1986).

Despite the initial problems and occasional misdirections, it now appears that certain personality tests can be used to predict a whole range of worker outcomes, including leadership potential, helpfulness toward co-workers, absenteeism, and theft (Gough, 1984; Hogan & Hogan, 1989). In particular, researchers have found that performance across different occupations can be significantly predicted by questionnaires that measure the "Big Five" personality factors. For example, extraverts are more likely than introverts to succeed as managers and salespersons, while workers in general benefit more from job training if they are high rather than low in their openness to new experiences. Indeed, recent reviews of this research have revealed that the personality factors of agreeableness and conscientiousness are highly predictive of performance in a variety of professional, skilled, and unskilled jobs (Barrick & Mount, 1991; Tett et al., 1991). Quite clearly, personality traits—not just physical, perceptual, and cognitive abilities—are useful for predicting success and failure in the workplace (Goldberg, 1993).

section of the United States was sampled. The result is a newer 567-item version known as MMPI-2 (Butcher et al., 1989; Butcher & Williams, 1992; Graham, 1990). As in the original test, MMPI-2 contains the ten *clinical scales* presented in Table 15.5. Eight of these are designed to distinguish between "normals" and diagnostic groups. The others measure normal variations on the traits of masculinity-femininity and social introversion. In addition, the MMPI and MMPI-2 contain a set of *validity scales* designed to expose test takers who are evasive, confused, lying to make a good impression, or defensive. Someone who says yes to many socially desirable but implausible statements like "I never get angry" is assumed to be trying too hard to project a healthy image. In contrast to the Rorschach and TAT, in which two examiners may reach different conclusions, the MMPI scoring is so objective that a test taker's responses can be converted into a personality profile by computer. That's one reason why the test has been translated into more than a hundred languages and is popular in both clinical and research settings.

The MMPI-2 is so easy to administer and score that test administrators must be cautious about how to use it and how to interpret the results. The test has good reliability and validity, but it is far from perfect (Helmes & Reddon, 1993). One needs to be particularly careful in interpreting the responses of test takers from subcultural groups that share different beliefs, values, ideals, and experiences. A pattern of responses may be normal in one culture and deviant in another.

Biological Roots of Personality

Many trait theories, even those that predate psychology's birth as a discipline, assume that there is a linkage between biological and personal

Clinical scales	Descriptions	Sample items
1. Hypochondriasis	Excessive concern about self and physical health, fatigue, a pattern of complaining	"I have a great deal of stomach trouble."
2. Depression	Low morale, pessimistic about the future, passive, hopeless, unhappy, and sluggish	"I wish I could be as happy as others seem to be."
3. Hysteria	Use of physical symptoms to gain attention from others or avoid social responsibility	"I have had fainting spells."
4. Psychopathic Deviation	Disregard for social rules and authority, impulsive, unreliable, self-centered, has shallow relationships	"In school I was sometimes sent to the principal for cutting up."
5. Masculinity-Femininity	Identification with masculine and/or feminine sex roles	"I enjoy reading love stories."
6. Paranoia	Feelings of persecution and/or grandeur, suspiciousness, hypersensitivity, use of blame and projection	"I am sure I get a raw deal from life."
7. Psychasthenia	Anxiousness as exhibited in fears, self-doubt, worries, guilt, obsessions and compulsions	"I feel anxiety about something or someone almost all the time."
8. Schizophrenia	Feelings of social alienation, aloofness, confusion and disorientation, bizarre thoughts and sensations	"I often feel as if things were not real."
9. Mania	Hyperactivity, excitement, flakiness, elation, euphoria, and excessive optimism	"At times my thoughts raced ahead faster than I could speak them."
10. Social Introversion	Withdrawal from social contact, isolation, shyness, a reserved, inhibited, self-effacing style	"Whenever possible I avoid being in a crowd."

Validity scales	Descriptions	Sample items
Cannot Say	Evasiveness, as indicated by a high number of noncomittal, "cannot say" responses	(None; this score consists of the number of "cannot say" responses)
Lie Scale	Tendency to present oneself favorably, not honestly, to fake a good impression	"I always tell the truth."
Infrequency Scale	Tendency to "fake bad" by reporting unusual weaknesses and problems	"Everything tastes the same."
Correction	Subtle test-taking defensiveness, or lack of self-insight	"I have never felt better in my life than I do now."

Table 15.5

Clinical and Validity Scales of the MMPI

These MMPI Scales have been used for more than fifty years. In recent revisions, supplementary clinical scales were added. These new scales include items that measure Anxiety, Repression, Dominance, Ego Strength, Dependency, Social Status, Overcontrolled-Hostility, Alcoholism, and Prejudice.

dispositions. In 400 B.C., the Greek physician Hippocrates said that people could be classified into four temperament types, depending on which of their "humors," or body fluids, predominated: an excess of blood was associated with cheerfulness, black bile with sadness, yellow bile with anger, and phlegm with sluggishness. In the nineteenth century, German physician Franz Gall introduced "phrenology," a theory that tried to link personality to brain structures that could be seen in the bumps on our head. There were also those who used "physiognomy," the idea that a person's character is revealed in the features of the face (for example, people with thin lips were said to be conscientious; those with thick lips, emotional).

Although these early theories were rejected, there is now a great deal of interest in the connections between biology and personality. In 1954, William Sheldon studied thousands of adult men, and concluded that there are three kinds of physique, each linked to a distinct type of personality. The *ectomorph*, said Sheldon, has a thin, frail body and a restrained, anxious, shy disposition. The *endomorph* has a soft, plump body and is relaxed, sociable, and easygoing. The *mesomorph* has a strong, muscular build and is bold, assertive, and energetic. Sheldon reported high correlations between body types and personality, but his methods were flawed and later research produced less impressive results.

Are there *any* biological underpinnings to personality? Yes, absolutely. Recall the nature-nurture debate and the twins study presented in Chapter 9. For a wide range of traits—including the Big Five—studies show that (1) raised together, identical twins are more similar than fraternal twins, and (2) twins raised apart are just as similar as those raised in the same home. As seen in Figure 15.10, it's estimated that personality differences in the population are about 50 percent genetically determined (Bouchard & McGue, 1990; Loehlin, 1992; Tellegen et al., 1988).

Much to the surprise of many researchers, recent twin studies have revealed that there are genetic links to characteristics that would seem to be

Figure 15.10

Genetic Influences on Personality

Based on twin studies, these percentages represent the estimated degrees to which various personality characteristics are inherited. Note that some traits have stronger genetic roots than others.

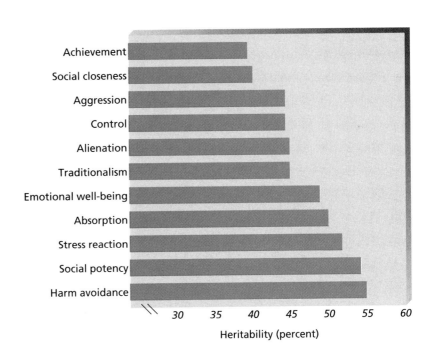

■ **extravert** A kind of person who seeks stimulation, and is sociable and impulsive.

■ **introvert** A kind of person who avoids stimulation, and is low-key and cautious.

determined entirely by personal experience. Specifically, identical twins are more similar than fraternal twins of the same sex in the risk of getting divorced (McGue & Lykken, 1992), in their attitudes toward sexuality, religion, and the death penalty (Tesser, 1993), and in their vocational and recreational interests (Lykken et al., 1993). Perhaps there are certain basic personality traits that predispose us to seek out certain types of people, situations, and experiences.

Introversion and Extraversion

Psychologists may disagree over whether personality consists of two, five, sixteen, or two hundred traits, but they all agree that the single most powerful dimension—one that can be seen in infants as well as adults, in cultures all over the world, and in questionnaires as well as behavior—is introversion-extraversion, one of the Big Five traits. The ancient Greeks and Romans noticed it, as have philosophers, physicians, and creative writers through the ages. Carl Jung wrote about individual differences on this dimension. So did Allport and Cattell. Even Pavlov noticed that some of the dogs in his laboratory were more outgoing than others! But it was British psychologist Hans Eysenck who most clearly defined the trait, constructed a test to measure it, and proposed a provocative theory to explain its origin.

As described by Eysenck (1967) the typical **extravert** is someone who has many friends, likes parties, craves excitement, seeks adventure, takes chances, acts on the spur of the moment, and is uninhibited. In contrast, the typical **introvert** is low-keyed, has just a few close friends, shies away from stimulation, acts cautiously, and distrusts the impulse of the moment. Based on past writings, personal observations, and factor analyses of trait questionnaires, Eysenck developed a test that includes a measure of introversion and extraversion (see Table 15.6). Using this instrument, researchers find that extraverts are generally more talkative, prefer occupations that involve social contact, and take greater risks. They are also more "sensation seeking"—a trait that leads people to seek out loud music, drink, smoke, fight, play contact sports, have sex, ride roller coasters, and gamble (Eysenck & Eysenck, 1985; Zuckerman, 1979). The question is, What accounts for this broad, pervasive aspect of personality?

At the 1993 Superbowl, this avid fan demonstrates what it means to be extraverted.

Table 15.6

Are You an Introvert or an Extravert?

If you said "yes" on most odd-numbered questions and "no" on the even-numbered ones, you are relatively extraverted. If it's the other way around, then you're more of an introvert. Many people fall somewhere in the middle of the continuum (Eysenck & Eysenck, 1964).

1. Are you usually carefree?
2. Do you generally prefer reading to meeting people?
3. Do you often long for excitement?
4. Are you mostly quiet when you're with others?
5. Do you often do things on the spur of the moment?
6. Are you slow and unhurried in the way you move?
7. Would you do almost anything for a dare?
8. Do you hate being in a crowd who plays jokes on one another?
9. Do you enjoy wild parties?
10. Do you like the kind of work you need to pay close attention to?

"So you're bored. You knew when you married me that I can't stand media or any other stimulus."

[Farris/Cartoonists & Writers Syndicate]

Eysenck argues that individual differences are biologically rooted and that introverts have central nervous systems that are more sensitive to stimulation. According to Eysenck, people seek a moderate, comfortable level of central nervous system arousal. Introverts are internally overaroused, so they avoid additional sources of excitement, while extraverts are internally underaroused, which leads them to approach high levels of excitement. Research provides reasonably good support for this hypothesis (Bullock & Gilliland, 1993; Eysenck, 1990; Zuckerman, 1990). For example, studies show that when drops of natural lemon juice are placed on the tongue, most introverts salivate more than most extraverts (Deary et al., 1988). Other studies show that introverts are more easily aroused by caffeine and other "uppers"—and are less easily relaxed by alcohol and other depressants (Stelmack, 1990). In short, says Eysenck, each of us is born with a nervous system that predisposes us to either love or hate large crowds, bright lights, blaring music, fast cars, spicy foods, and other, more social stimulants. In fact, as we saw in Chapter 9, these temperament differences can be seen in infants and young children—some of whom are naturally shy, inhibited, and easily aroused by even mildly stressful situations (Kagan et al., 1990; Kagan, 1994).

Perspectives: Do Traits Exist?

Intuitively, we are all trait psychologists. We use trait terms to describe ourselves and others, and we have preconceptions about how various characteristics relate to one another and to behavior. We assume that people who are unpredictable are also dangerous, and that people who talk slowly are also slow-witted. We're surprised when a polite and unassuming co-worker erupts in violence, or when the sweet girl from next door turns out to be the "other woman." Each of us tends to notice some traits more than others: one person may measure everyone by an intellectual yardstick, while others look for physical beauty, friendliness, a sense of humor, or a firm handshake. When I was younger, I used to think I could instantly tell all about people—whether they were relaxed or intense, competitive or cooperative, cautious or adventurous, and so on, by the way they played board games like Scrabble, Risk, and Monopoly.

Although it seems natural to think about people and their behavior in terms of traits, critics complain that the approach is limited. Psychoanalysts say it is superficial, cognitive social-learning theorists say it neglects situational factors, and humanists say it is cold and impersonal. By far the most serious attack, however, was Walter Mischel's (1968) startling claim that traits simply do not exist. After reviewing forty years of research, Mischel concluded that (1) personality test scores are not predictive of behavior, and (2) individuals do not act with trait-like consistency from one situation to the next. To illustrate, he cited a classic study by Hugh Hartshorne and Mark May (1928) in which they observed the moral conduct of thousands of children in school, at home, on the playground, at parties, and so on. Expecting to find evidence for a trait of honesty, Hartshorne and May found that the children exhibited remarkably little cross-situational consistency in behavior. A child might pass up a chance to cheat in class or steal money from a dropped wallet, but then be quick to cheat in an athletic event or lie to parents. Thus, said Mischel (1968), traits—as measured by personality tests—cannot reliably predict behavior.

Mischel's critique whipped up a tremendous controversy among personality psychologists wondering if traits were a mere figment of the imagination. Now, after many years of debate and new research, two main conclusions can be drawn. First, as noted by Seymour Epstein (1979), traits are highly informative—but only when they're used to predict an *aggregation* of behaviors. To measure personality, psychologists derive test scores by combining answers to several related questions. Similarly, says Epstein, behavior should be measured by combining several trait-related acts. Just as an IQ score is not expected to predict a grade in a particular class, your score on an introversion-extraversion scale cannot be expected to predict whether you will tell jokes at a particular party. By the same token, just as an IQ score can predict grade point *averages,* a personality test can predict general behavior tendencies (Epstein & O'Brien, 1985; Moskowitz, 1982; Rushton et al., 1983).

The second important conclusion is that behavior springs from an *interaction* between traits and situations (Magnusson & Endler, 1977; Snyder & Ickes, 1985; Kenrick & Funder, 1991). This interaction can take many forms. First, personality traits are expressed only in relevant situations. If you're the anxious type, you may break out in a cold sweat before a first date or a public presentation, but not when you're lying around at home watching TV. Second, traits are expressed only in situations that do not constrain our behavior. Nearly everyone is quiet and reserved in churches, libraries, and elevators, but our unique personalities are free to emerge at home, in a bar, or in the street. Third, individuals influence the situations they are in. The way we treat our friends, family, and others influences the treatment we receive in turn. Child development researchers who used to focus on how parents shape their children now realize that children, even infants, shape their parents as well. Fourth, people choose settings that are compatible with their personalities. Extraverts craving excitement are likely to visit amusement parks, casinos, and keg parties, while introverts seek out quiet restaurants, hiking trails, and other out-of-the-way places. Fifth, your personality influences how you interpret and react to situations. Optimists see the proverbial glass as half-full, while pessimists see the same glass as half-empty. As Allport (1961) said, "The same fire that melts the butter hardens the egg" (p. 102).

PERSONALITY IN PERSPECTIVE

Now that you are familiar with the four major approaches to personality, you are in a position to evaluate each perspective for yourself. If you were to stop and think about your own life, say, to write your autobiography, which of the four approaches would best describe your personality and explain how you got that way?

To summarize, psychoanalysis emphasizes deep, unconscious conflicts, sex and aggression, defensive behavior, anxiety, and early childhood influences. Cognitive social-learning theory views personality as a socially acquired pattern of behavior, a learned response to how people perceive, interpret, and value the external reinforcements in their lives. Humanists believe that people are inherently good, that we have self-insight, and that personality springs from the desire and struggle to reach our full potential. The trait approach makes few value judgments about human nature, but it assumes that everyone can be compared on a standard set of dispositions that are consistent over time and, at least to some extent, genetically determined.

The four approaches also differ in their perspectives on change and in their approaches to the treatment of psychological disorders. Beginning with Freud, most psychoanalysts see the early years of childhood as formative, if not critical, to the development of personality—with relatively little room for change in adulthood. In fact, psychoanalytic therapists say that patients unconsciously resist the recovery process. The trait approach, with its emphasis on genetic determinants and the stability of core dispositions, also takes a relatively dim view of change. According to this view, people are biologically introverted or extraverted, and calm or anxious—thus leaving little room for variation. In contrast, the behavioral and cognitive social-learning theorists see people as flexible, and influenced by environmental factors. According to this view, psychological disorders are learned—and can be unlearned just as well. The humanistic approach is equally clear in its view that people have not only the capacity but the will to change, and specifically, to strive toward self-actualization.

It is important to realize that although we have discussed the four approaches as distinct, you don't necessarily have to choose a favorite, or accept any one approach completely. Many personality psychologists are *eclectic*, which means that they accept bits and pieces of the different theories. Mix in some of Freud's unconscious, hold the sex, add a dash of reinforcement and a pinch of self-actualization, then administer a multitrait personality inventory, and you will have formed a new perspective from a blending of existing ingredients. It is also instructive to consider the possibility that each approach may better account for some aspects of personality than for others. Psychoanalysis may shed light on why we inexplicably feel troubled and anxious, cognitive social-learning theory may explain why having control is often so important to us, humanism may capture the experience of pursuing and catching lifelong dreams, and the trait approach may offer the best way to measure our unique predispositions. The human personality is so complex and multifaceted that all perspectives may be necessary.

SUMMARY AND KEY TERMS

The study of *personality*—an individual's distinct and relatively enduring pattern of thoughts, feelings, motives and behaviors—is central to *clinical psychology*, the branch of the discipline concerned with diagnosis and treatment of psychological disorders.

The Big Picture

Research shows that personality characteristics are remarkably stable over time. There are four major approaches to the study of personality. Each has its own theories, assessment procedures, and research methods, as well as its own answer to the question of how much personality can change.

Psychoanalysis

The Birth of Psychoanalysis

Just before the turn of the twentieth century, Freud used his clinical experience with hysteria to formulate *psychoanalysis*.

Freud's Theory of Personality

Psychoanalysis assumes that *unconscious forces* and inner conflicts play a large part in shaping personality. Freud divided the personality into three parts. The *id,* a primitive, unconscious reservoir of basic instincts and drives, operates according to the *pleasure principle,* a drive for immediate, total gratification. The personality's moral part, the *superego,* consists of the ego-ideal and the conscience. The *ego* mediates between the id's "wants" and the superego's "shoulds" and follows a *reality principle* that allows for gratification of needs in a socially appropriate manner.

Freud believed that personality is shaped by conflicts that arise during the *psychosexual stages* of development. Young children pass through the oral stage, the anal stage, and then the phallic stage. During the phallic stage (roughly ages four to six), children experience the *Oedipus complex,* a tendency to become sexually attracted to the parent of the opposite sex and hostile to the parent of the same sex. By resolving this complex, children form an *identification* with the same-sex parent, internalizing the parent's values. When boys and girls enter puberty, the genital stage begins. Too much or too little gratification in any of the first three stages can result in *fixation* at that stage and a distinct type of personality.

According to Freud, we feel anxiety when our impulses clash with morals, so the ego uses unconscious *defense mechanisms* that deny and distort reality. *Repression* helps us "forget" threatening thoughts, memories, and impulses by pushing them out of awareness. In *denial* we not only forget anxiety-filled events but bar them from awareness in the first place. Through *projection,* we attribute our own unacceptable impulses to others. Through *reaction formation,* we convert an unacceptable feeling into its opposite. *Rationalization* involves making excuses for our failures and shortcomings. And through *sublimation,* the healthiest defense mechanism, we channel repressed urges into socially acceptable substitute outlets.

Freud's Legacy

Freud's followers continued to focus on unconscious factors, inner conflicts, and early childhood influences. Jung proposed that people are influenced by a *collective unconscious* consisting of memories from our ancestral past, and argued that personality development continues into adulthood. Adler stressed social conflicts, developing the notions of sibling rivalry and the inferiority complex. More recent theorists have emphasized social needs or the role of the ego.

Psychoanalytic researchers also developed *projective tests* to reveal the unconscious through responses to ambiguous stimuli. The *Rorschach* uses inkblots. The *Thematic Apperception Test (TAT)* asks people to make up stories from a set of pictures.

Critics of psychoanalysis say that it takes too bleak a view of human nature, that it doesn't meet scientific standards, and that it is not supported by controlled research. Yet Freud's ideas, particularly those about the unconscious and defense mechanisms, have become an integral part of psychology.

The Cognitive Social-Learning Approach

Unlike psychoanalysis, *cognitive social-learning theory* sees personality as the result of a continuous interaction between the person and the environment.

Principles of Learning and Behavior

Early behaviorists investigated classical conditioning, operant conditioning, and other key principles of learning. Watson and Skinner applied these principles to the study of personality.

Social-Learning Theory

Social-learning theory extended behaviorism to include social and cognitive factors. Through *modeling,* people can learn behavior by observing and imitating. Rotter and Mischel further showed that thoughts influence the link between reinforcement and behavior.

According to cognitive social-learning theory, people differ in *locus of control*—expectations about the control of reinforcement. Internal (individuals who believe that they control their own fate) are generally happier, healthier, and more successful. People also differ in *self-efficacy,* the belief that they can perform the behaviors needed for a desired outcome. The more self-efficacy people have for a task, the more likely they are to succeed.

Perspectives on Cognitive Social-Learning Theory

Cognitive social-learning theory emphasizes *reciprocal determinism,* the notion that personality emerges from an ongoing interaction among individuals, their actions, and their environments. Environmental forces shape up our personalities, but we can choose, alter, and interpret the situations we encounter. To assess personality, cognitive social-learning theorists use direct methods such as behavioral observations and self-reports.

The Humanistic Approach

By the 1940s, some psychologists began to develop a *humanistic theory* of personality.

Carl Rogers

Impressed by his patients' self-insight and will to improve, Rogers theorized that we all have a natural need for self-actualization—that is, a drive to behave in ways consistent with our self-concepts. As social beings, however, we also have a competing need for positive regard. *Unconditional positive regard* from significant others frees us to pursue self-actualization. But if we receive only conditional positive regard, we experience frustration, anxiety, and self-discrepancies.

Abraham Maslow

Maslow believed that all people are motivated to fulfill a *hierarchy of needs,* from basic physiological needs to more complex social and psychological ones. At the top of the pyramid is *self-actualization,* the distinctly human need to become everything one is capable of becoming. Few people reach this state, though it is common to have momentary peak experiences.

Perspectives on the Humanistic Approach

Humanistic psychologists have been praised for focusing on the good in human beings, on the self-concept, and on conscious mental experiences. They have been criticized for ignoring the darker side of human nature and relying too heavily on people's self-reports.

The Trait Approach

The Building Blocks of Personality

To study the basic units of personality, Allport compiled a list of about 200 personality *traits*. With factor analysis Cattell reduced these to 16 source traits. More recently, researchers condensed the list to a *five-factor model* consisting of five major traits: neuroticism, extraversion, openness, agreeableness, and conscientiousness.

Construction of Multitrait Inventories

The trait approach gave rise to the construction of personality inventories such as the *Minnesota Multiphasic Personality Inventory (MMPI).*

Biological Roots of Personality

Different traits show different degrees of genetic linkage. According to recent estimates, many personality factors are about 50 percent genetically determined.

Introversion and Extraversion

One of the most powerful trait dimensions is introversion-extraversion. An *extravert* is sociable and impulsive and seeks stimulation. An *introvert* is low-keyed and cautious and avoids stimulation. Research suggests that introverts have more easily aroused nervous systems.

Perspectives: Do Traits Exist?

Debates about trait theory lead to two major conclusions. First, traits can predict an aggregation of behaviors but not specific acts. Second, behavior springs from an interaction between traits and situations.

Personality in Perspective

Each of the major approaches to personality has a different emphasis. To account for the full range of human experience, we may need to draw eclectically on all four theories.

Chapter 16

Psychological Disorders

Have you ever lost a loved one to death, only to be stricken by grief, despair, and the numb feeling that life is not worth living? Have you ever been so nervous before making a speech or going on a date that your heart raced, your voice trembled, and your stomach tightened up? Have you ever been the victim of a car accident, and then blocked out the whole experience? Have you ever jumped out of bed in the middle of the night, startled by a terrifying nightmare you couldn't seem to shake, or by creaking noises you imagined to be the sound of an intruder? Have you ever been haunted by a tune you kept humming and couldn't get out of your mind, no matter how hard you tried? And have you ever heard the sound of laughter as you entered a room, only to wonder for a moment if everyone was looking and laughing at *you?*

Chances are, one or more of these experiences will ring a familiar bell and provide you with a personal glimpse into the unhappy, disturbing, and sometimes scary world of psychological disorders. You don't have to be "crazy" to have these kinds of episodes. For some of us, they are rare and last for only brief periods of time. For others however, they are frequent, prolonged, and intense. Based on survey results, it is estimated that in any given one-year period, 28 or 29 percent of the adult population in the United States suffers from some form of psychological disorder. In the course of a lifetime, one third to one half of all Americans will suffer from a problem that is serious enough to be diagnosed as a psychological disorder (Kessler et al., 1994; Regier et al., 1988, 1993).

These surveys, supplemented by clinical case studies, tell us that psychological disorders are often a temporary condition. No one is invulnerable in times of great stress, but most people are resilient in their capacity for recovery. For the clinical psychologist, the key point is that people experience changes in the status of their mental health, sometimes for the better, at other times for the worse. In this chapter, we examine the negative form of change—the causes and effects of psychological disorders.

PSYCHOLOGICAL DISORDERS: A GENERAL OUTLOOK

Before we discuss the unusual array of mental health problems that plague people all over the world, three general questions must be asked. First, when are thoughts, feelings, and behaviors defined as disordered? That is, when does a person cross that invisible line between health and illness, psychology and psycho*pathology,* normal and *abnormal?* Second, what biological and environmental factors put our psychological well-being at risk? Third, how can different problems be distinguished for the sake of understanding and treating those in need of assistance?

Defining Normal and Abnormal

In a recent journey through a subway station in New York City, I passed by a middle-aged gentleman in a neatly pressed blue suit who stood on a bench, waved his arms, and urged commuters to repent for their sins because the planet was about to explode. On the same bench, an older

"Button King" Dalton Stevens covers all sorts of objects, including himself, with buttons. Is this behavior normal or abnormal? A hobby or an obsession?

bearded man in a heavy wool coat lay all curled up, with his arms folded together, his eyes cast down to the ground, and a brown liquor bottle peaking out of his coat pocket. Once on the train, I sat next to a woman who seemed to be having an animated conversation with herself, and watched a man who kept moving from one seat to the next, switching about twenty times during the ride. Crazy? For all I know, the other passengers—who slept, hid behind walls of newspapers, tuned into headphones, read books and minded their own business—were wondering about me, the nosy guy who couldn't stop spying on everyone else.

People-watching experiences like this demonstrate how tricky it can be to determine whether someone has a psychological disorder. Various criteria have been proposed over the years, and all have sparked controversy. A frequently cited definition is provided by the American Psychiatric Association (APA). According to the APA (1994), a pattern of behavior can be considered a **mental disorder** if, and only if, it satisfies three conditions:

1. The person experiences significant pain or distress, an inability to work or play, an increased risk of death, or a loss of freedom in important areas of life.
2. The source of the problem resides within the person, due to biological factors, learned habits, or mental processes, and is not simply a normal response to specific life events such as the death of a loved one.
3. The problem is not a deliberate reaction to conditions such as poverty, prejudice, government policy, or other conflicts with society.

These criteria suggest some key points about a definition. One is that the term *abnormal* means more than just different from the norm, in a statistical sense. Geniuses and Olympic gold medalists are also atypical, but they're not clinically troubled. Also, normative behavior in one cultural or ethnic group may be deviant in another. A second point is that normal and abnormal are merely locations along a continuum, not distinct conditions separated by a bright line. Think about it. At what point should

■ **mental disorder** A condition in which a person's pattern of behavior is judged to be dysfunctional.

■ **medical model** The perspective that mental disorders are caused by biological conditions and can be treated through medical intervention.

nervousness be called "anxiety," or sadness "depression"? How much pain, distress, or impairment is too much? When is a person who is deeply but reasonably upset by a tragic life event in need of psychological assistance? And when it comes to people who are poverty-stricken, homeless, and victimized by crime, how can we tell that their actions are not a normal response to a hostile environment? These are difficult questions that can be addressed only on a case-by-case basis. A third point is that certain behavior patterns are considered abnormal not because they are disabling to the individual but because they threaten the safety and welfare of others. The model citizen who holds a prestigious, well-paying job but then abuses his wife or children is an all-too-familiar example.

Finally, it's important to note that the criteria used to identify mental disorders do not in themselves explain the source of those disorders or imply a particular form of treatment. As we will see, the unhealthy mind is sometimes the product of an unhealthy body and, hence, treatable with drugs. Yet often the problem stems from deep-seated personal conflicts, bad habits, negative life experiences, stress, faulty processing of information, and sociocultural factors. Before describing the kinds of disorders from which so many of us suffer, let's examine these theoretical models.

Models of Abnormality

When archaeologists unearth human bone fragments from thousands of years ago, they sometimes find a small hole that was drilled into the skull. The reason, some experts speculate, is that our prehistoric ancestors believed that mental disorders were caused by the intrusion of evil spirits into the body, and that these spirits needed an opening to escape. In more recent times, these disorders were variously attributed to witchcraft, demonic possession, full moons, and other supernatural forces. Evil spirits were thus "driven out" through exorcism, torture, primitive forms of surgery, noise making, bloodletting, bitter potions, and starvation.

The Medical Perspective   Today, there are more enlightened, naturalistic models of abnormality—medical, psychological, and sociocultural. According to the **medical model,** disordered thoughts, feelings, and behaviors are caused by physical disease. In 400 B.C., Greek physician Hippocrates, the father of medicine, proposed that psychological disorders are caused by body-fluid imbalances. This perspective is an important one today, as researchers try to identify genetic links, damage to parts of the brain and nervous system, hormone imbalances, and neurotransmitter activity that is associated with various problems. The medical model is powerfully evoked by the language used to describe abnormality. Thus we speak of "diagnosing" mental "illness" in "patients" so that "treatment," "hospitalization," and "therapy" will relieve the "symptoms" and produce a "cure." In short, a strictly medical model holds that although mental disorders take on a psychological appearance, the underlying problems are physical in nature.

Medicine is more humane than demonology, but this approach is not without its critics. Psychiatrist Thomas Szasz (1961), for example, wrote a book entitled *The Myth of Mental Illness,* in which he argued that mental illness is a socially defined, relative concept used to cast aside people who are deviant ("If you talk to God, you are praying; if God talks to you, you

■ **psychological model** The perspective that mental disorders are caused and maintained by one's life experiences.

have schizophrenia"). Szasz (1987) charges that psychologists, psychiatrists, and other mental health experts are too quick to guard society's norms and values. What's worse, he claims, the label "sick" invites those with real problems to become passive—dependent upon doctors and drugs rather than relying upon their own inner strengths. On the one hand, these criticisms raise important and provocative questions. On the other hand, mental illness is *not* a myth and it would be cruel to deny that many psychological disorders have biological origins, consequences, and treatment possibilities.

The Psychological Perspective   A second major approach to abnormal behavior is based on the **psychological model,** which holds that mental disorders are caused and maintained by a person's past and present life experiences. The list of negatively impactful events is a long one. Examples include prolonged illness, natural disasters, sex abuse, domestic violence, war, divorce, poverty, punitive parents, the death of a loved one, a lack of friendships, and persistent failure. This perspective was born of Freud's interest in hysteria, a disorder in which the patient experiences bodily symptoms in the absence of physical damage. Freud and others believed that this disorder usually began with a traumatic event in childhood, and that it could be treated successfully with *psycho*therapy, a form of "talking cure."

Today, there is not one psychological model of abnormality but many. Paralleling the major approaches to personality that were described in Chapter 15, three broad perspectives are worth keeping in mind. The first is psychoanalysis, which emphasizes the role of parental influences, unconscious conflicts, guilt, frustration, and an array of defense mechanisms used to ward off anxiety. According to this view, psychological disorders spring from inner conflicts so intense that they overwhelm our normal defenses. The second perspective is rooted in behaviorism and cognitive social-learning theories. In this view, abnormal behavior is a learned response to reward and punishment, further influenced by our perceptions, expectations, values, and role models. The third perspective is humanistic, which holds that mental disorders arise when we are blocked in our efforts to grow and achieve self-actualization. In this view, the self-concept is all-important.

Psychological disorders often stem from stressful and traumatic experiences—as when recent flooding in the Midwest left many people homeless.

The Sociocultural Perspective   Whether one prefers to think in medical or psychological terms, it is important to realize that the sociocultural context in which we live affects the kinds of stresses we're exposed to, the kinds of disorders we're likely to experience, and the treatment we're likely to receive. Particularly impressive evidence for this perspective comes from the fact that different types of disorders appear in different cultures. One example is provided by John Weisz and his colleagues (1993), who, in the process of studying behavioral and emotional problems in adolescents, compared teenagers from the United States and Thailand. Problems are evident in both countries, but they take very different forms. In the United States, troubled teenagers tend to "act out" by bullying others, getting into fights, or disobeying teachers in school. But in the Buddhist country of Thailand, where people are taught to inhibit expressions of emotion, troubled teenagers are more likely to sulk, refuse to talk, sleep too much, or become constipated.

Additional evidence of sociocultural influence comes from the fact that some disorders are almost completely limited to specific groups. One such example is *anorexia nervosa,* an eating disorder in which the person, usually an adolescent girl, becomes so fearful of gaining weight that she limits her eating, becomes emaciated, and sometimes even starves to death. Closely related is *bulimia nervosa,* another eating disorder found among young women that is marked by cycles of extreme binge eating followed by self-induced vomiting and the overuse of laxatives. A most telling fact about these eating disorders is that they did not begin to appear with frequency until the 1970s, and even then they seemed to strike only middle- and upper-class women of westernized cultures. Why? As a matter of speculation, the problem may be that our culture—its diet centers, health spas, exercise videos, and shapely fashion models—places too much pressure on women to maintain their slender appearance (Brumberg, 1988; Ruderman & Besbeas, 1992). Although estimates vary, recent studies suggest that although only half of 1 percent of American women have anorexia, between 2 and 4 percent have bulimia—and these numbers are higher among female college students (Kendler et al., 1991). As you read this chapter, then, keep in mind that the kinds of experiences that trigger psychological disorders sometimes occur in specific sociocultural contexts.

Jane Fonda poses in her exercise video "Lean Routine." Fonda recently admitted that she used to suffer from bulimia nervosa.

■ **diagnosis** The process of identifying and grouping mental disorders with similar symptoms.

■ **DSM-IV** Nickname for the American Psychiatric Association's *Diagnostic and Statistical Manual of Mental Disorders (4th Edition).*

Diagnosis: A Necessary Evil

In science, as in other life pursuits, it helps to group people, objects, and situations that share similar properties. Biologists classify animals into species, archaeologists divide time into eras, and geographers split the earth into regions. Likewise, mental health professionals find it enormously useful, for the sake of prediction, understanding, and treatment, to categorize mental disorders that involve similar patterns of behavior, or *syndromes*. This process of grouping and naming mental disorders is referred to as **diagnosis**.

The most widely used classification scheme in the United States is the American Psychiatric Association's *Diagnostic and Statistical Manual of Mental Disorders (4th Edition),* mercifully nicknamed **DSM-IV**. This manual provides a comprehensive list of more than two hundred mental disor-

Table 16.1

DSM-IV Mental Disorders Described in This Chapter

1. *Anxiety disorders*
   Disorders in which intense anxiety is the main symptom. Includes generalized anxiety and panic disorders, phobias, obsessive-compulsive disorder, and post-traumatic stress disorder.

2. *Somatoform disorders*
   Disorders involving physical symptoms, such as paralysis or sensory loss, that are psychological in origin. Includes hypochondriasis and conversion disorder (formerly known as "hysteria").

3. *Dissociative disorders*
   Disorders in which part of one's experience is separated or "dissociated" from consciousness. Includes amnesia, fugue states, and multiple personality disorder.

4. *Mood disorders*
   Disorders marked by severe mood disturbances, such as major depression, mania (elation), or an alternating pattern of both.

5. *Schizophrenic disorders*
   A group of psychotic disorders characterized by a loss of contact with reality, hallucinations, delusions, disturbed thought and affect, and bizarre behavior.

6. *Personality disorders*
   Long-term, inflexible, maladaptive patterns of behavior. Includes borderline, antisocial, paranoid, obsessive-compulsive, narcissistic, dependent, and histrionic personality disorders.

Note: In addition to those described in this chapter, DSM-IV includes *disorders diagnosed in infancy and childhood* (such as mental retardation, learning disabilities, separation anxiety, bed wetting, hyperactivity, and stuttering), *cognitive disorders* (such as Alzheimer's disease and other dementias), *substance use disorders* (a dependence on alcohol and other drugs), *sexual disorders* (abnormal sex practices and disruptions in sexual fuctioning), *sleep disorders* (such as sleepwalking, insomnia, and nightmares), *factitious disorders* (in which symptoms are deliberately produced or faked), *impulse control disorders* (such as pathological gambling and kleptomania), *eating disorders* (anorexia and bulimia nervosa), *adjustment disorders* (inability to recover from divorce, financial setback, and other stressors), and other conditions that may be a focus of clinical attention.

ders grouped into seventeen broad categories. (Those discussed in this chapter are summarized in Table 16.1.) For each disorder, prominent symptoms are described in concrete behavioral terms. Also presented are the prevalence rates for men and women, predisposing factors, the normal age of onset, and the expected outcome. Accompanying the manual are books with illustrative case studies and standardized interviews to assist in diagnosis (Spitzer et al., 1994; Widiger et al., 1994). It is important to realize that DSM-IV, which was published in 1994, is only one link in an evolving chain of diagnostic schemes. Indeed, this version was preceded by four earlier ones. DSM was first published in 1952, was substantially revised in 1968 (DSM-II), substantially revised again in 1980 (DSM-III), and then updated in 1987 (DSM-III-R).

Over the years, critics of psychiatric diagnosis have voiced three concerns. The first was that the system lacked *reliability*. If two mental health

CLINICAL PSYCHOLOGY   Education

Attention Deficit Hyperactivity Disorder

This chapter is primarily focused on adult psychological disorders. Among the diagnostic categories appearing in DSM-IV, however, is one that pertains to problems that arise in infancy, childhood, or adolescence—often with adverse effects on academic achievement (Gaddes & Edgell, 1994).

Almost every elementary school classroom has one: a child, usually a boy, who is always on the go, lacks patience, and cannot sit still or sustain attention for an extended period of time. Among parents and teachers, children who fit this description are labeled "hyperactive." Because these children are also highly distractable and find it difficult to stay focused on a single task, they are diagnosed in DSM-IV as having Attention Deficit Hyperactivity Disorder, or *ADHD*.

Research shows that the average two-year-old can attend to a constant stimulus for about seven minutes, that three-year-olds can do so for nine minutes, four-year-olds for thirteen minutes, and five-year-olds for fifteen minutes. The average first-grader can be expected to sit and work for up to an hour. Yet children with ADHD are highly distractable, impulsive, easily stimulated, quick to move from one task to another, and constantly on the lookout for new activities. In school, these children often have difficulty remaining in their seats, listening to the teacher, following instructions, standing in line, awaiting their turn to speak, and working quietly at tasks that involve reading, writing, and problem solving (Barkley, 1990).

ADHD affects an estimated 3 to 6 percent of all elementary

experts interview the same person, what are the chances that they will independently come up with the same diagnosis? Research on the earliest versions of DSM revealed low levels of reliability. However, more recent versions, including DSM-IV, base classifications on observable behavior and provide a checklist of specific, objective items to guide the diagnosis. As in medicine, the system is still not perfect, but reliability estimates are much higher now than in the past (Matarazzo, 1983).

A second concern is that clinical judgments, like all other judgments, may be biased by stereotypes about gender, race, age, socioeconomic status, ethnic background, and other social factors (Lopez, 1989). Gender provides a common example. In general, men and women suffer equally from mental disorders, but certain specific problems are more common among men, others among women. Could these well-known differences influence a mental health expert's judgment? We saw in Chapter 12 that people tend to see what they expect to see. Could the same be said of clinical diagnosis?

To examine this possibility, Maureen Ford and Thomas Widiger (1989) mailed a case history of a fictitious male or female adult to 354 clinical psychologists and asked them for a diagnosis. For some, the case depicted a classic "antisocial personality," a predominantly male disorder characterized by a pattern of self-centered behavior and a reckless disregard for rules. For others, it portrayed a "histrionic personality," a mostly female disorder characterized by excessive attention-seeking, emotionality, and flirtatiousness. As shown in Figure 16.1, the diagnostic judgments were quite clearly biased by gender. Regardless of which case history was read, the male patient was more likely to be labeled antisocial, and the female histrionic. Similar research suggests the possibility that black Americans are more often misdiagnosed as schizophrenic than are white patients with the same symptoms (Mukherjee et al., 1983).

school–age children in North America, and is far more prevalent among boys than girls (Barkley, 1990; Shaywitz & Shaywitz, 1991). Many children with ADHD experience rather serious behavioral and learning disabilities—and have trouble adjusting to the structured setting of a classroom. They tend to do poorly in school and have difficulty at reading, complex problem solving, and tasks that require fine motor coordination. These problems often continue into adolescence. A sad but common result: poor grades, failure, and expulsion or early withdrawal from school (Klein & Mannuzza, 1991).

There are many theories about the causes of ADHD. According to one theory, children with ADHD exhibit extremely low levels of arousal in the central nervous system—and seek stimulation in order to raise that arousal level (Zentall & Zentall, 1983). In contrast, other researchers have examined differences in brain activity, dietary factors, neurotransmitters, parenting styles, and social learning. Whatever its origins, ADHD can often be treated (though not cured) with Ritalin, a stimulant drug that increases arousal and the production of the neurotransmitters norepinephrine and dopamine. Ritalin is prescribed for roughly 600,000 children a year in the United States—the equivalent of 1 to 2 percent of the school-age population. In many cases, this form of treatment is effective. A majority of ADHD children who are on Ritalin exhibit short-term increases in attention span, reductions in motor activity, and improvements in classroom behavior and academic performance (Carlson & Bunner, 1993; Pelham et al., 1993; Douglass et al., 1986).

It is important to be cautious in diagnosing ADHD (and thus to avoid identifying as "hyperactive" those children who are merely active and rambunctious). It's also important, if Ritalin is prescribed, to combine its use with psychologically oriented therapies and classroom teaching strategies aimed at modifying the child's behavior and problem-solving skills. In this intersection of clinical psychology and education, it is best for elementary school teachers, psychologists, and primary-care physicians to collaborate in their efforts (Pelham, 1993).

Figure 16.1

Gender Bias in Psychiatric Diagnosis

Clinical psychologists diagnosed a fictitious patient as "antisocial" when he was male, and as "histrionic" when she was female—regardless of which disorder was described by the case history. Apparently, a diagnosis can be biased by gender stereotypes.

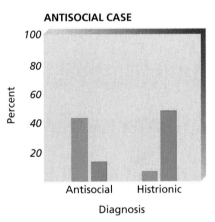

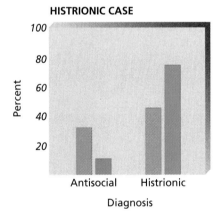

■ Male patients
■ Female patients

A third concern is that diagnostic labels can adversely affect the way we perceive and treat those who suffer from mental disorders. In a provocative demonstration of how a label can take on a life of its own, psychologist David Rosenhan (1973) and seven colleagues visited twelve mental hospitals in five states, gave false names and occupations, and complained of hearing an unfamiliar disembodied voice say the words "thud," "empty," and "hollow." On the basis of these reports, all the pseudopatients were diagnosed as schizophrenic and admitted for treatment. From that point on, however, they answered all questions truthfully, behaved normally, followed instructions, and reported hearing no voices. Yet it took an average of nineteen days for Rosenhan and the others to get released (one was kept for fifty-two days), and not one psychiatrist, psychologist, social worker, or nurse uncovered the fraud (ironically, many of the real patients suspected that the researchers were journalists or investigators). Written case reports revealed that staff members sometimes interpreted normal behaviors in abnormal ways. When one pseudopatient paced the halls out of boredom, for example, he was said to be "anxious." Another who was seen taking notes was said to be "paranoid." Once a label is in place, it can be hard to remove.

Thanks to the objective criteria provided in DSM-IV, and through the use of structured interviews and careful assessments of the patient's social and occupational functioning, diagnostic reliability has never been better. To some extent, however, the critics of diagnosis are correct in stating that it is an imperfect human enterprise. As in medicine, mental health professionals sometimes disagree on a patient, their judgments may subtly be influenced by stereotypes, and there is the ever-present danger that the labels themselves will color the way those with disorders are perceived. Still, diagnosis is necessary. Just as physicians have to distinguish among heart disease, cancer, and pneumonia in order to prescribe the right treatment, psychologists and psychiatrists must distinguish among the different mental disorders. To ease the stigma of diagnostic labels, the American Psychiatric Association (1994) recommends that we apply the labels to behaviors, not individuals. It's better to say that a person has schizophrenia or an alcohol dependence than to call that person a schizophrenic or alcoholic—terms that imply permanence.

In the remainder of this chapter, we consider some of the most common as well as some of the most bewildering disorders identified in DSM-IV. But first a word of caution: Watch out for "medical student's disease," the tendency to see in yourself the disorders described in this chapter. If you are troubled or if you find it hard to function on a day-to-day basis, see someone about your problems. Otherwise, don't be alarmed. Bear in mind that normal and abnormal are points along a continuum, and that everyone experiences some of the symptoms some of the time.

ANXIETY DISORDERS

Anyone who has faced military combat, the interview of a lifetime, a championship game, major surgery, or the menacing sound of a prowler in one's home knows what anxiety feels like. On occasion, we all do. It's a nervous, jittery feeling of apprehension accompanied by a pounding heart, trembling hands, cold and sweaty palms, quivering voice, a dry mouth, dizziness, light-headedness, a shortness of breath, an upset stomach, or diarrhea.

Generalized Anxiety Disorder

■ **generalized anxiety disorder** A psychological disorder that is characterized by a constant state of anxiety not linked to an identifiable source.

Anxiety is a normal response to threatening and stressful situations. It is estimated, however, that about 15 percent of all Americans will at some time in life experience anxiety that is so intense, persistent, and disabling that it is considered a disorder (Regier et al., 1988). Over the course of a lifetime, an estimated 5 percent of adults suffer what is known as **generalized anxiety disorder**—a persistent, gnawing undercurrent of "free-floating" (not linked to an identifiable source) anxiety (Wittchen et al., 1994). Feeling aroused and not knowing why, the person with a generalized anxiety disorder is highly sensitive to criticism, has difficulty making decisions, dwells on past mistakes, and worries constantly about money, work, family matters, and illness (Barlow, 1988). It is not clear, however, whether these are effects rather than causes of the disorder. Research suggests that people with generalized anxiety disorder are hypersensitive before they seek treatment—and remain so after the disorder is in remission (Eysenck, 1992).

Many people have anxiety attacks that are more focused. In particular, three such disorders are described in this section: panic, phobias, and obsessive-compulsive disorders. Before you read on, however, two points are worth noting. First, although the different anxiety disorders are in some ways distinct, most people who have one type are likely to exhibit the symptoms of at least one other type as well (Brown & Barlow, 1992; Sanderson et al., 1990). Second, although people all over the world suffer from intense anxiety, the specific symptoms are influenced by the forces of culture (Good & Kleinman, 1985).

Consider the case of a twenty-five-year-old Chinese American patient. Shortly after having sexual intercourse with a prostitute, the man complained of a sudden burning pain in his penis, accompanied by a fear that his genitals were shrinking. He became terrified that his penis would retract into his abdomen, causing him to suffer and die. In a state of panic, he tried to masturbate in order to assure himself that all was well, but he could not achieve an erection. The young man became so desperate that he contemplated suicide. This patient's case may sound unique, but in fact what he suffered from was *Koro* (also called "suo-yang" in Chinese medical books), an anxiety disorder that has existed for hundreds of years in Southeast Asia. Typically found in young males, Koro is characterized by an acute panic attack lasting for days or weeks and by a fear that one's sexual organs will disappear into the body, causing death. A Koro epidemic swept through Singapore in 1967. Shortly after the Vietnam war, a thousand cases were reported in Thailand. Then in the 1980s, two waves of Koro spread through China. Many Koro patients link the onset of their disorder to a sexual escapade, and treatment often consists of wearing a clamp that prevents retraction of the penis (Bernstein & Gaw, 1990).

Koro is only one example of an anxiety disorder that is restricted to a cultural group. There are other examples. In Mexico and certain South American cultures, people may experience *susto*—an intense fear reaction, insomnia, and irritability, believed to be brought on by the "evil eye" of voodoo or black magic. In Japan, there is *shinkeishitsu*—an emotional disorder in which people become so self-conscious and perfectionistic that they feel too inadequate to interact with others. And in China, there is *paleng*—a disorder in which sufferers wear several layers of clothing, even in the summer, because of a morbid fear that they will die from a loss of body heat.

What do these cross-cultural comparisons tell us? At this point, two conclusions can be drawn. First, anxiety is universal and the *physiological* symptoms are the same from one culture to the next. Regardless of where one is born and raised, anxiety is a bodily reaction characterized by a shortness of breath, racing heart, trembling, sweating, dizziness, nausea, diarrhea, chills, chest pains, insomnia, dryness in the mouth, and a "lump" in

■ **panic disorder** A disorder characterized by sudden and intense rushes of anxiety, in the absence of any apparent reason.

the throat. Second, culture influences the *cognitive* component of anxiety. What symptoms people worry about, how they interpret those symptoms, and their beliefs about the causes of anxiety all depend on the values and ideologies to which they are exposed (Barlow, 1988; Good & Kleinman, 1985).

Panic Disorder

Norwegian artist Edvard Munch (1863–1944) was a troubled man who knew all too well the meaning of the word *panic*. In 1893, Munch painted *The Scream,* a nightmarish portrait of a terrified person standing on a bridge under a blood-streaked sky, covering his or her ears and screaming in anguish as two ominous, shadowy people approach from behind. Said Munch, this image was inspired one day when "I was walking . . . and I felt a loud, unending scream piercing nature." Sometimes a picture really is worth a thousand words.

People who suffer from **panic disorder** experience frequent, sudden, intense rushes of anxiety, usually lasting for several minutes. The symptoms of a panic attack include chest pains and heart palpitations, a shortness of breath, choking and smothering sensations, and fainting. These are often accompanied by feelings of unreality and detachment from one's body, and by a fear of going crazy, losing control, or dying (see Table 16.2). Interestingly, research shows that panic strikes most frequently between the hours of 1:30 and 3:30 A.M., while people are asleep; that heart rates increase an average of thirty-nine beats per minute; and that the episodes last for approximately sixteen minutes, followed by exhaustion (Taylor et al., 1986).

The Scream (Edvard Munch, 1893).

Table 16.2

The Panic Button: Symptoms

Presented here are the percentages of panic-disordered patients who experience various symptoms. An attack is considered "panic" if it includes four or more of these symptoms (Barlow, 1988).

Symptoms	Percentages
Shortness of breath	75
Heart palpitations	87
Chest pains	38
Choking sensation	50
Dizziness or faintness	87
Depersonalization	57
Numbness or tingling sensations	58
Hot flashes or chills	74
Excessive sweating	70
Trembling or shaking	86
Nausea or abdominal distress	56
Fear of dying	52
Fear of going crazy or losing control	76

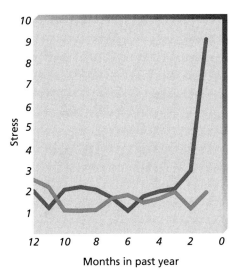

Figure 16.2

Stress and Panic Disorder

Faravelli and Pallanti (1989) assessed the amount of stress experienced by 64 panic disorder patients and a group of "normal" controls. As shown, the patients had experienced a sharp increase in stress during the month just prior to the onset of their symptoms.

"A man who fears suffering is already suffering from what he fears."

MICHEL DE MONTAIGNE

■ **agoraphobia** An anxiety disorder in which the main symptom is an intense fear of public places.

■ **phobic disorder** An anxiety disorder characterized by an intense and irrational fear.

■ **simple phobia** An intense, irrational fear of a specific object or situation.

What's worse, those who get panic attacks worry so much about embarrassing themselves in front of others (by falling, fainting, vomiting, gasping loudly for air, or losing bladder control) that they very often develop **agoraphobia,** a fear of being in public places that are hard to escape. People with agoraphobia are frequently prisoners in their own homes—afraid to stray into shopping malls, restaurants, sports events, theaters, airports, or train stations. The word itself comes from a Greek term meaning "fear of the marketplace."

Approximately one-third of all adults report that they have experienced a panic attack during the past year (Norton et al., 1992). However, only one or two out of every hundred suffer from a chronic panic disorder, the majority of them women (Eaton et al., 1994; Telch et al., 1989). What causes panic disorder? There are two perspectives—one biological, the other psychological. Supporting a biological point of view, research shows that panic attacks tend to strike without warning or provocation (patients say it just comes "out of the blue") and that the experience can be induced as well as treated with drugs (Barlow, 1988; Gorman et al., 1989). The psychological approach is supported by three kinds of evidence. First, many patients report that their first attack occurred shortly after an illness, miscarriage, or some other traumatic event (see Figure 16.2). Second, people who panic are also prone to "catastrophic thinking" about their bodily sensations. Feeling aroused, they are quick to conclude that they are experiencing a heart attack, or a stroke, or some other life-threatening ordeal—and this belief fuels the fire (Ehlers & Breuer, 1992). Third, psychological forms of therapy—such as relaxation training, breathing exercises, and various behavioral and cognitive techniques—can help alleviate panic attacks without the use of drugs (McNally, 1990; Michelson & Marchione, 1991; Rachman & Maser, 1988). To sum up: The human panic button can be activated by biological or psychological means.

Phobic Disorder

Every Sunday afternoon during football season, John Madden broadcasts a National Football League game on television. From one week to the next, regardless of whether the game is played in Philadelphia, Houston, Green Bay, or San Diego, Madden drives hundreds of miles in his own private bus. As inconvenient as this may seem, it is the only way Madden will travel. The reason? Despite his 260-pound, 6'4" frame and rough exterior, Madden is terrified of flying on airplanes.

Whereas panic strikes suddenly and without warning, phobias are focused and predictable. A **phobic disorder** is one in which a person reacts to an object or event with high levels of anxiety, knows that the reaction is irrational, and copes by avoidance. The word *phobia* comes from the name of the Greek God Phobos, who instilled fear in his enemies. The disorder itself is experienced by one out of eight Americans. There are two types of phobias. A **simple phobia** is an intense, irrational fear of a specific object or situation. The most common are a fear of heights, airplanes, closed spaces, blood, snakes, and spiders. But there are other, more idiosyncratic phobias as well. TV entertainer Johnny Carson used to joke about having a fear of backing into doorknobs. And I once had a friend who would grip his car

Table 16.3

Over the years, hundreds of phobias have been identified and named—some common, others unusual. How many on this list sound familiar? How many can you figure out from the prefix?

Phobia	Feared object or situation
Claustrophobia	closed spaces
Agoraphobia	public places
Acrophobia	heights
Aerophobia	flying
Zoophobia	animals
Ophidiophobia	snakes
Arachnaphobia	spiders
Entomophobia	insects
Hematophobia	blood
Aquaphobia	water
Nycytophobia	darkness
Mysophobia	dirt and germs
Xenophobia	strangers
Taphephobia	being buried alive
Homilophobia	sermons
Brontophobia	thunderstoms
Astraphobia	lightning
Monophobia	being alone
Ocholophobia	crowds
Aichmophobia	sharp pointed objects
Triskaidekaphobia	the number thirteen
Porphyrophobia	the color purple
Gephyrophobia	bridges
Genophobia	sex
Parthenophobia	virgins

seat, stiffen up, and break into a cold sweat whenever we drove over a drawbridge with a metal-grating surface. Table 16.3 presents a partial list of simple phobias that have been identified and named over the years (Maser, 1985).

A second type of phobic disorder is the **social phobia,** an exaggerated fear of situations that invite public scrutiny and the risk of embarrassment. Probably the most familiar example is public-speaking anxiety, or stage fright—a performer's worst nightmare. If you've ever had to make a public presentation, only to feel weak in the knees and hear your voice quiver, you will have endured at least a hint of this disorder. For the social phobic, unbearable levels of self-consciousness are evoked by many other situations as well. Examples include eating at a public lunch counter, signing a check in front of a store clerk, and, for males, urinating in a crowded men's room. In private, these behaviors pose no problem. In the presence of others, however, they arouse so much fear that the situations are avoided at all costs. In extreme cases, the reaction is so debilitating that the person just stays at home (Turner & Beidel, 1989).

■ **social phobia** An intense fear of situations that invite public scrutiny.

Certain phobic disorders occur with greater frequency than others. Some of the most common are ophidiophobia (a fear of snakes), acrophobia (a fear of heights), and claustrophobia (a fear of closed spaces).

What causes phobic disorders? Many years ago, Freud argued that people with phobias are anxious about hidden impulses, and cope by displacing their anxiety onto substitute objects that are less threatening and easier to avoid. To illustrate, he wrote about the classic case of "Little Hans," a five-year-old boy who would not leave home because he was terrified that he would be bitten by a horse. According to Freud (1909), Hans was in the midst of an Oedipal conflict, and had converted an unconscious fear that his father would castrate him into a conscious fear of getting bitten by a horse. From a psychoanalytic perspective, then, the phobic object is merely a symbol for a deeper, more troubling problem.

In reaction to Freud's case study, behaviorist John Watson demonstrated with a baby named Little Albert that phobias can develop through conditioning (see Chapter 5). Since that time, researchers have found that phobias are learned by classical conditioning (Ost, 1992) and by the observation of someone else's fear reaction to an object. For example, Susan Mineka and Michael Cook (1993) found that when laboratory-raised rhesus monkeys saw wild monkeys of the same species react fearfully to the presence of a snake, they too became distressed and acquired an intense fear of snakes. To the behaviorist, then, phobias are derived from an experience or observation, and then may spread through a process of stimulus generalization (thus, if a child is locked in a closet at a tender young age, he or she may acquire a specific fear of closets, or a more general case of claustrophobia). In this view, the reason phobias last long after the precipitating experience is forgotten is that we avoid phobic objects, denying ourselves an opportunity to unlearn the fear.

A third view is that humans are genetically programmed or "prepared" to develop certain kinds of phobias. Think about it. All over the world, large numbers of men and women fear darkness, heights, snakes, insects, and other harmless objects, some of which are never encountered. Yet few of us are terrified of automobiles, electrical outlets, appliances, or other objects that are potentially dangerous. According to Martin Seligman (1971), the reason is that humans are prepared by evolution to fear things that were harmful to our prehistoric ancestors. Thus, when college students were trained to react with anxiety to certain objects (through the pairing of pictures with electric shock), their newly conditioned fears persisted longer when the pictured object was a snake than when it was a house, a flower,

■ **obsessive-compulsive disorder (OCD)**
An anxiety disorder characterized by persistent thoughts (obsessions) and the need to perform repetitive acts (compulsions).

or some other "neutral" object (McNally, 1987). When, in the rhesus monkey studies just described, observer monkeys saw the model react with fear to a snake in a bed of flowers, they developed an intense fear of the snake, a potentially dangerous object, but not of the flowers (Cook & Mineka, 1990).

Obsessive-Compulsive Disorder

Howard Hughes had it all. He was a billionaire, famous pilot, entrepreneur, and Hollywood producer. There was just one hitch—Hughes was tormented by an uncontrollable preoccupation with germs, eventually causing him to live the life of a hermit. He sealed all windows and doors with tape and spent many hours a day washing himself. His aides had to open doors with their feet to avoid contaminating doorknobs, wear white cotton gloves before serving his food, and deliver newspapers in stacks of three so he could slide the middle one out with a tissue. Toward the end of his life, Hughes became so overwhelmed by his routines that he was incapable of self-care. When he died at the age of sixty-nine, his body was filthy and emaciated, his beard was scraggly, his teeth were rotted, and his fingernails were so long that they curled in on themselves—a sad and ironic ending for a man who had once said, "I want to live longer than my parents, so I avoid germs" (Fowler, 1986, p. 33).

Along with an estimated 4 million other Americans, Howard Hughes suffered from **obsessive-compulsive disorder (OCD)**—a crippling anxiety ailment characterized by constant *obsessions* (the intrusion into consciousness of persistent, often disturbing thoughts) and *compulsions* (behavior rituals performed in response to obsessions). OCD usually begins in late adolescence and early adulthood, affects men and women equally, and is found in India, England, Norway, Egypt, Nigeria, Japan, Hong Kong, and other countries around the world (Insel, 1984). People with OCD know that their habits are crazy, but they just can't stop themselves. Fearing shame and humiliation, many of them try to keep their actions a secret, and wait years before seeking treatment.

What kinds of thoughts and behaviors haunt OCD patients? In a book entitled *The Boy Who Couldn't Stop Washing*, psychiatrist Judith Rapoport (1989) described one boy who washed his hands so much they became raw and bloodied from all the scrubbing; another boy who ran up and down a flight of stairs exactly sixty-three times in forty-five minutes every day; a woman who checked and rechecked her stove repeatedly to make sure it was turned off; and a woman who was so determined to keep her eyebrows symmetrical that she plucked out each and every hair. As bizarre as these stories sound, research shows that they accurately reflect the kinds of behaviors that plague OCD sufferers (Jenicke et al., 1986). The most common themes of this disorder are presented in Table 16.4.

Everyone has a few mild obsessions and compulsions. You may double- and triple-check your alarm clock at night, try to avoid stepping on sidewalk cracks, or feel a burning need to straighten out crooked wall hangings. Professional athletes are especially well known for their compulsive rituals. Many baseball players, for example, adjust their cap, tug at their shirt, bang their shoes, and run through a complicated sequence of supersti-

[© 1994 Frank Cotham and The Cartoon Bank, Inc.]

What Do OCD Sufferers Obsess About?		What Rituals Do OCD Sufferers Perform?	
Obsessive themes	Percentage	Ritualistic behaviors	Percentage
Dirt, germs, contamination	55	Checking	79
Aggressive impulses	50	Washing	58
Forbidden sexual impulses	32	Counting	21
Bodily concerns	35		
Need for symmetry	37		

Table 16.4

Obsessive-Compulsive Disorder

As reported in interviews with 100 OCD patients, these were the most common themes of their disorder. Most patients had multiple obsessions and compulsions (Jenicke et al., 1986).

tious gestures before every pitch. If these examples don't apply to you, try this: Do *not* imagine a white bear. Seriously, put this book down, and try not to think about white bears. See the problem? Daniel Wegner (1989) finds that when people actively try to suppress a particular thought, that thought intrudes into consciousness with remarkable frequency—like a newly developed obsession. What distinguishes these mild quirks from OCD is the intensity of the accompanying anxiety and the extent to which it interferes with one's life.

There are many different theories about the causes of OCD. Psychoanalysts maintain that obsessive thoughts leak forbidden sexual and aggressive urges into consciousness, compelling the person to devise elaborate rituals as a countermeasure. In this view, compulsive washing symbolizes a person's need to "cleanse" the soul of "dirty" impulses. Behaviorally oriented theorists note that compulsions last for long periods of time because they are reinforced by a reduction of the anxiety aroused by obsessive thoughts. Indeed, many compulsions can be extinguished within a few weeks by forcibly preventing the patient from responding to his or her obsession—for example, no washing allowed despite the buildup of anxiety (Foa et al., 1985). Biological factors also play a role. PET scans on the brains of OCD patients reveal abnormalities in the basal ganglia, a portion of the brain that acts as a relay station between thought and motor processes and is involved in the activation and inhibition of learned habitual reactions. In addition, the use of antidepressant drugs enables some sufferers of OCD to terminate their rituals (Rapoport, 1989).

SOMATOFORM DISORDERS

■ **somatoform disorder** A type of mental disorder in which a person experiences bodily symptoms that are psychological rather than medical in nature.

Long before psychology became a discipline, physicians struggled with the problem of treating patients who complain of muscular aches and pains, upset stomachs, and other ailments for which an organic basis cannot be found. According to DSM-IV, many of these patients have a **somatoform disorder** (the word *somatoform* means "bodylike"), in which they experience bodily symptoms that are psychological rather than medical in origin.

Somatoform disorders are not easy to diagnose. People who complain of an illness are not necessarily faking (a condition known as "malingering"), nor do their psychological problems trigger physical damage (the way stress causes ulcers and migraine headaches, conditions that are "psychosomatic"). Illustrating that mind and body are hopelessly interlocked are two types of somatoform disorder: hypochondriasis and conversion disorder.

Hypochondriasis

While on his famed *Beagle* voyage around the world, Charles Darwin was constantly seasick. Then, beginning when his wife Emma became pregnant with their first of ten children, and lasting for the rest of his life, he complained of numbness in the fingertips, nausea, indigestion, dizzy spells, inability to sleep, chest pains, and other assorted ailments. The result: Darwin was so pampered by his family that "the whole day was planned out to suit him, to be ready for reading aloud to him, to go on his walks with him, and to be constantly at hand to alleviate his daily discomforts" (Colp, 1977, p. 92).

If Darwin were alive today, he would be diagnosed as having **hypochondriasis,** a disorder characterized by a chronic, unwarranted preoccupation with one's own physical health. Hypochondriacs are highly sensitive to normal bodily sensations. Equipped with do-it-yourself medical books, thermometers, blood pressure kits, and shelves lined with vitamins, they become alarmed the moment they sneeze, cough, feel warm, feel cool, get an itch, pull a muscle, or skip a heartbeat. Not wanting to hear words of reassurance, they also tend to jump from one doctor to the next until they find one who takes their complaints seriously (Baur, 1988; Kellner, 1987).

Some psychologists have speculated that hypochondriasis is a reaction to separation anxiety and the desire to stay helpless, or that it is symptomatic of society's preoccupation with health. Others believe that it is caused by an overly sensitive nervous system. Research shows, for example, that hypochondriacs are not only quicker to notice symptoms of illness but also more distressed than others in general by loud noises, high and low temperatures, and hunger pains (Barsky et al., 1988). And the more attention one pays to a body sensation, the more intense it gets. In a study by James Pennebaker (1982), male subjects walked on an exercise treadmill and listened either to a tape of city sounds or to their own breathing. Afterward, those who had heard their own breathing reported more headaches, racing hearts, and other symptoms of overexertion—even though there were no physiological differences between the two groups.

Whatever the causes of hypochondriasis, three points are clear. First, the disorder can easily become a lifelong pattern nourished by sympathy, attention, relief from work, excuse for failure, and other social rewards. Even Darwin realized before he died that "my head would have failed years ago had not my stomach saved me from a minute's over-work" (Colp, 1977, p. 70). Second, there is no truth to the stereotype that people become hypochondriacal as they get old. Research shows that although the elderly are more likely than younger adults to seek medical help, their health complaints are as genuine (Costa & McCrae, 1985). Third, our sensitivity to

"Nothing is more fatal to Health, *than the* Over Care *of it."*

BENJAMIN FRANKLIN

■ **hypochondriasis** A disorder characterized by an unwarranted preoccupation with one's physical health.

bodily sensations falls on a continuum on which both extremes are maladaptive. Just as the hypochondriac is too health-conscious, others are not sensitive enough to the symptoms of illness, choosing instead to deny the body's warning signals, often to their own detriment (Strauss et al., 1990).

Conversion Disorder

A second somatoform disorder is **conversion disorder,** in which the person temporarily loses a bodily function without a physical cause. This problem is primarily found in young women, which is why Hippocrates in 400 B.C. called it *hysteria* (from the Greek word for uterus)—and prescribed marriage as a cure. In the nineteenth century, Freud theorized that hysteria was precipitated by a traumatic event, and that anxiety over unconscious conflicts was "converted" into physical ailments. The classic symptoms mimic neurological disorders such as paralysis, blindness, deafness, epilepsy, and anesthesia (a loss of feeling in a limb). This disorder was illustrated in a wave of recent cases. In the 1970s, there was a reign of terror in what used to be Cambodia. Shortly afterward, many women—who had been tortured or, even worse, had seen their own children being tortured and murdered—became psychologically blind. One woman, a refugee whose family had been killed, and who managed to escape to the United States, said, "I cried for four years. When I stopped crying, I was blind" (Rozee & Van Boemel, 1989).

How can you tell the difference between conversion disorder and actual nerve damage? It's not always easy. One clue is that the reported symptoms are sometimes not anatomically possible, as in the case of "glove anesthesia" described in Figure 16.3. Another is that the symptoms may all of a sudden disappear—as when a "blind" patient manages to walk right through the doctor's office without bumping into furniture, or a "paralyzed" patient walks in his or her sleep. How can a conversion disorder be distinguished from conscious faking? No diagnosis is foolproof, but there is one clue: whereas people who fake ailments are evasive and defensive about examination, true conversion patients tend to display *la belle indifférence,* a nondefensive attitude and a curious lack of concern about their condition (Ford & Folks, 1985).

Sociocultural context seems to play an important role in the outbreak of somatoform disorders. Cases of hysterical paralysis that Freud and his contemporaries had reported on no longer seem to exist. Perhaps it's because we are too sophisticated now to believe that a person could truly be paralyzed for no apparent reason. But there is a new and puzzling ailment known as *chronic fatigue syndrome (CFS)* that may serve the same purpose. Cases of CFS first started appearing a few years ago among young, aspiring professionals who complained of a lack of energy, weakness, and an assortment of aches and pains (the media referred to it as "yuppie flu"). The condition can last for months, sometimes even years. Yet despite efforts to discover a medical basis for the disorder, none has been found. At present, many psychologists and psychiatrists speculate that CFS may be a type of somatoform disorder found in people who are unhappy with their careers or other aspects of their lives (Abbey & Garfinkel, 1991).

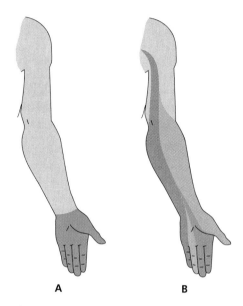

A   **B**

Figure 16.3

Glove Anesthesia: A Conversion Disorder

A person with "glove anesthesia" reports numbness in the hand from the wrist to the fingertips, but continued sensation in other parts of the arm (a). This complaint can be diagnosed as a conversion disorder because it is anatomically impossible. If there is actual nerve damage, the sensory loss would extend to upper parts of the arm as well (b).

■ **conversion disorder** A disorder in which a person temporarily loses a bodily function in the absence of a physical cause.

DISSOCIATIVE DISORDERS

■ **dissociative disorder** A condition marked by a temporary disruption in one's memory, consciousness, or self-identity.

Have you ever found yourself listening to someone talk, only to realize that you missed most of what was said? Were you ever in a place that was familiar, but could not remember having been there before? And did you ever have trouble figuring out whether an experience you had was real, or just a dream? These phenomena are possible signs of *dissociation,* a process by which a portion of one's life becomes separated, or "dissociated," from one's identity or conscious memory. Look at the experiences listed in Table 16.5. Some of these should ring a familiar bell. In a survey of a thousand adults, for example, 83 percent said they had occasionally "spaced out" on chunks of a conversation (Ross et al., 1990).

Table 16.5

Types of Dissociative Experiences

The following items are taken from the Dissociative Experiences Scale (Bernstein & Putnam, 1986). How many of these have you had, and how often? Some are quite common.

1. Suddenly realizing, when you are listening to someone talk, that you did not hear part or all of what the person said.
2. Finding yourself in a place and having no idea how you got there.
3. Finding yourself dressed in clothes that you don't remember putting on.
4. Suddenly realizing, when you are driving a car, that you don't remember what has happened during all or part of the trip.
5. Losing the memories of important events in your life, such as your wedding or graduation.
6. Looking in a mirror and not recognizing yourself.
7. Feeling sometimes that other people, objects, and the world around you are not real.
8. Becoming so absorbed in a fantasy or daydream that it feels as though it was really happening to you.
9. Feeling sometimes as if you were looking at the world through a fog such that people and objects appear far away or unclear.
10. Feeling sometimes that your body does not seem to belong to you.

In contrast to these normal episodes that we all experience, people diagnosed with a **dissociative disorder** have serious long-term memory gaps. In essence, these people have learned to cope with intense trauma and stress by mentally erasing unwanted parts of life from their memory. There are three types of dissociative disorders: amnesia, fugue state, and multiple personality.

Amnesia and Fugue States

The most common dissociative disorder is **amnesia,** a partial or complete loss of memory. Amnesia can last for varying periods of time, and can be caused by physical trauma such as head injury or alcohol intoxication. In a 1991 basketball game, for example, former Los Angeles Lakers star Magic Johnson fell on his back, hit his head on the hardwood floor, and was momentarily unable to recall the city he was in or the team he was playing

amnesia A dissociative disorder involving a partial or complete loss of memory.

fugue state A form of amnesia in which a person "forgets" his or her identity, wanders from home, and starts a new life.

multiple personality disorder (MPD) A dissociative disorder in which a person develops two or more distinct personalities.

against—a case of organic amnesia. Alternatively, the problem can sometimes be traced to a stressful event such as a car accident, a rape, or a physical beating. In these cases of "psychogenic" amnesia, only self-relevant memories are blocked. Amnesia victims may forget who they are and where they live, but they remember clearly how to speak, read, drive a car, and recite information from general knowledge (Weingartner et al., 1983).

Psychogenic **fugue states** (*fugue*, as in the word *fugitive*, means "flight") are more extensive than simple amnesia. In extreme cases, someone who slips into a fugue state not only forgets his or her name but wanders from home, takes on a new identity, remarries, gets a new job, and starts a new life. Then, just as suddenly, the person will "wake up"—disoriented, confused, oblivious to what had transpired, and eager to return home as if no time had passed. Fugue states may last for hours, or for years. Sometimes, the victim's new life is more exciting and uninhibited than the old routine. At other times it provides an escape from responsibility and danger. Fugue states are quite common, for example, among soldiers bound for combat. Either way, it is difficult—if not impossible—to tell whether a fugue victim has a genuine dissociative disorder or is faking (Schacter, 1986).

Multiple Personality

Chris Sizemore was the subject of *The Three Faces of Eve,* the 1957 film about a woman with multiple personality disorder. Sizemore claims that she had formed 22 different personalities to cope with "traumatic death experiences" she had at two years old.

The most dramatic instance of dissociation is **multiple personality disorder (MPD)**, an extremely rare condition in which a person displays two or more distinct personalities. Sometimes, two opposing identities battle for control, as in the classic tale of Dr. Jekyll and Mr. Hyde. In other instances, there are three personalities, as in *The Three Faces of Eve,* a book about a woman who alternated among Eve White, a timid housewife; Eve Black, a sexually promiscuous woman; and Jane, a balanced blend of the other two. In some cases, one dominant or "core" identity is accompanied by a host of subordinate personalities, as in the case of Sybil Dorsett, whose sixteen personalities were portrayed by actress Sally Field in the film *Sybil*.

Multiple personality disorder is such a strange phenomenon that you might think it springs from the imaginative minds of playwrights and novelists. What are the facts and fictions about MPD? According to DSM-IV, it is nine times more prevalent among women than men, and is ordinarily preceded by a childhood history of repeated abuse. Summarizing five major studies of 843 MPD patients, for example, Colin Ross and his colleagues (1990) found that more than 88 percent had been the victims of sexual, physical, or emotional child abuse—a striking statistic that was confirmed in a later study conducted within the Netherlands (Boon & Draijer, 1993). This finding makes a great deal of sense. Children who are brutally traumatized and utterly defenseless learn early in life to cope with their victimization by tuning out, divorcing a part of themselves from the pain and suffering, and constructing alternative persons within which to live (Ross, 1994).

In almost all MPD cases, at least one personality is unable to recall what happens to the others (Putnam et al., 1986). In fact, the differences between personalities are at times extraordinary. Each may have its own voice, speech pattern, habits, memories, sexual orientation, clothing, and handwriting. Physical changes may also occur, as when two personalities within

Table 16.6

Interviews with 102 people with MPD yielded the following percentages associated with each of these symptoms (Ross et al., 1990, p. 599).

Symptoms	Percentages
Another person existing inside	90
Voices talking	87
Amnesia for childhood	83
Referring to self as "we" or "us"	74
Blank spells	68
Being told by others of unremembered events	63
Feelings of unreality	57
Strangers know the patient	44
Noticing that objects are missing	42
Coming out of a blank spell into a strange place	36
Objects are present that cannot be accounted for	31
Different handwriting styles	28

the same patient exhibit different brain-wave patterns, blood pressure readings, eyeglass prescriptions, or reactions to medicine. One man, for example, had a severe allergic skin reaction to orange juice when one personality was in control, but not another (Braun, 1988). The most common symptoms of MPD are presented in Table 16.6.

If you find MPD hard to believe, you are not alone. Since the first case was reported in 1817, fewer than two hundred appeared in psychiatric journals up to the year 1970. Since that time, however, thousands of new cases have been reported (Boor, 1982; Kluft & Fine, 1993). Indeed, MPD can be found in most societies, but the frequency of the disorder and the form it takes vary from one generation and culture to the next (Spanos, 1994). All this has skeptics wondering: Is the disorder really on the rise? There are two alternative explanations. One is that patients often try to fake MPD for personal gain, and clinicians are unable to distinguish between true and false cases. A second explanation is that clinicians are overdiagnosing MPD or, worse, are suggesting and reinforcing the possibility of its presence in patients, thus producing a "psychiatric growth industry" (Weissberg, 1993).

To see the opposing points of view in action, consider the case of Kenneth Bianchi, otherwise known as the "Hillside Strangler." Based on convincing evidence, Bianchi was charged with brutally murdering ten California women. At first, he denied the charges. But then a psychologist hired to determine whether Bianchi was legally sane used hypnosis to uncover hidden parts of his personality. During the hypnosis session, the psychologist said to Bianchi, "I've talked a bit to Ken, but I think perhaps there might be another part of Ken that I haven't talked to. . . .Would you please come, Part, so I can talk to you?" Lo and behold, a completely new personality named Steve Walker came out. Ranting and raving, using foul language, and smoking no-filter cigarettes, Steve confessed to the crimes and said he hated Ken because he was a "goodie two-shoes." According to Steve, Ken was innocent.

Was Steve a real personality, or was he born of convenience to help Ken escape punishment for his crimes? MPD is a genuine problem, one that inflicts profound suffering on those who have it. In this case, however, the local police were suspicious, so they hired psychiatrist Martin Orne to conduct further tests. At one point, Orne mentioned to Bianchi that real multiples usually have three or more personalities, not just two. The trap was set, and Ken fell in: the next time he was under hypnosis, Ken produced a third personality. Orne's trick, along with the discovery that Bianchi owned a huge stack of books on psychology, hypnosis, and multiple personality, was convincing evidence. The jury that tried Bianchi found him guilty of murder (Orne et al., 1984; Schwarz, 1981).

MOOD DISORDERS

Personal experience tells us that mood can powerfully shade our view of ourselves, the world, and the future. On the roller coaster of life, the range of feelings is familiar to all of us: the exhilarating highs are on one end of the continuum, and the depths of despair are on the other. Land the job of your dreams, fall head over heels in love, or win a lottery, and you fly elatedly "on cloud nine." Lose a job or money, break up with a lover, struggle in school, or watch a tear-jerker of a movie, and you become sad, even depressed. These kinds of fluctuations are normal. Problems arise, however, when someone's mood state is so intense and so prolonged that it profoundly impairs the ability to function. There are two main types of **mood disorders:** major depression and bipolar disorder.

Major Depression

A chronic sufferer of depression, Winston Churchill referred to his condition as the "black dog" that followed him around. He was certainly not alone. Roughly 5 to 10 percent of American males and 10 to 20 percent of females will become depressed at some point in life, a rate that has increased dramatically in recent years (Klerman & Weissman, 1989). The problem is so widespread that Churchill's black dog has been called the "common cold" of mental disorders.

Depression is a mood disorder characterized by deep sadness and despair. Since these feelings are sometimes an appropriate and normal reaction to tragedy, someone is considered clinically depressed only if the episode arises without a discernible cause and lasts for two or more weeks. In addition to the effects on mood, symptoms include: (1) diminished pleasure or interest in food, sex, social banter, and other joys; (2) intense feelings of worthlessness, guilt, and self-blame; (3) restlessness and agitation, marked by difficulty sleeping, concentrating on work, and making decisions; (4) fatigue, slowness, and a lack of energy (in extreme cases, there is such a paralysis of the will that the person has to be pushed out of bed, washed, dressed, and fed by others); and (5) recurring thoughts of suicide

Kenneth Bianchi, otherwise known as the "Hillside Strangler," was found guilty of brutally murdering ten women. Bianchi said he suffered from a multiple personality disorder and was legally insane.

"When you're depressed, you feel like you've got a thousand pounds on every limb of your body."

ROD STEIGER

■ **mood disorder** A condition characterized by prolonged emotional extremes ranging from mania to depression.

■ **depression** A mood disorder characterized by sadness, despair, feelings of worthlessness, and low self-esteem.

Van Gogh's *Crows over the Wheatfield* is an intense and haunting portrayal of the French countryside under "troubled skies." This may have been Van Gogh's last painting before he committed suicide in 1890.

and death. Indeed, an alarming 15 percent of people who are clinically depressed go on to kill themselves (Charney & Weissman, 1988).

Consider some quick facts about depression. One consistent finding is that twice as many women than men seek treatment for depression—in part, perhaps, because women tend to confront their feelings, while men resort to alcohol, physical activity, and other means of distraction (Nolen-Hoeksema, 1990, 1993). Age is also a key factor (see Figure 16.4). Depression is seldom identified for the first time until adolescence, but then the age of first onset increases sharply, rises through adulthood, peaks at middle age, and then declines (Lewinsohn et al., 1986). Regardless of one's sex or age, it's reassuring to know that depressive episodes usually last only a few weeks or months. On the other hand, about half of those who recover from one major depression subsequently fall into another (Belsher & Costello, 1988).

As we saw in Chapter 8, some people exhibit the symptoms of depression on a seasonal basis, after a succession of overcast days. This condition is known as *seasonal affective disorder (SAD)*, and it strikes during the short, dark days of autumn and winter (Rosenthal et al., 1984). Every year, people with SAD who live in cold winter regions of the world become listless, drowsy, and withdrawn. They sleep more, eat more, crave carbohydrates, gain weight, lose interest in sex, and falter at work and in social relation-

Figure 16.4

Depression: Ages of First Onset

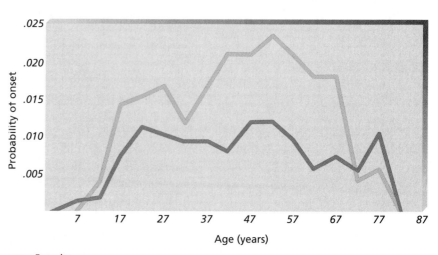

ships. As described in Chapter 8, however, there is a possible solution: light therapy. For many SAD sufferers, two hours each morning in front of bright fluorescent lights seem to help lift the clouds of depression (Blehar & Rosenthal, 1989; Terman et al., 1989).

Theories of Depression

As you might expect, psychologists have tried for many years to find a cure for this "common cold" of mental disorders. In order to treat and prevent depression, however, one must understand where it comes from and what factors serve to maintain it.

Biological Factors Ernest Hemingway killed himself with a shotgun. So did his father, and so did his brother. Clearly, say researchers, the depression that gives rise to suicide runs in families. But does this mean that depression is genetically determined, or that it is the product of shared environments? Research shows that if one fraternal twin suffers a major depression, there is a 10 to 20 percent chance that the other will too, at some point. Yet the rate for identical twins is closer to 50 percent—a comparison that reveals a genetic linkage (Allen, 1976; Tsuang & Faraone, 1990). This finding suggests two compatible conclusions: (1) there is a genetic basis of depression, but (2) environmental factors also play a prominent role.

In all likelihood, genes influence mood disorders by acting on neurotransmitters, the biochemicals that relay impulses from one neuron to another. In the 1950s, doctors noticed that drugs used to treat blood pressure and tuberculosis often had dramatic side effects on a patient's mood—sometimes causing depression, at other times euphoria. Researchers then found that the same drugs also increase the supply of norepinephrine and serotonin, neurotransmitters that regulate moods and emotions. So what does it all mean? When the two strands of evidence were brought together, they gave rise to the hypothesis that depression is caused by lower-than-normal levels of these neurotransmitters, and that mania is caused by an overabundance. As we'll see in Chapter 17, the practical result was the development of drugs popularly known as "antidepressants."

It is now clear that the link between biological states and mood is more complicated than was once believed. Antidepressants are effective for many people but not for everyone, and some drugs work without altering norepinephrine or serotonin levels (Depue & Iacono, 1989; McNeal & Cimbolic, 1986). Other biological factors may play a role as well. For example, certain infectious diseases, neurological disorders, thyroid problems, and vitamin deficiencies have mood-altering effects (Hollandsworth, 1990); many depressed people have higher-than-normal levels of cortisol, a stress hormone (Nemeroff, 1989); and people who suffer from the chronic pain of rheumatoid arthritis are also prone to become depressed (Brown, 1990). Researchers are currently trying to understand how and why these biological states are linked to depression, and whether they are causes or effects in the chain of events.

Psychological Factors In a 1917 paper entitled "Mourning and Melancholia," Sigmund Freud noted similarities between depression and the kind of grief that accompanies the death of a loved one. According to Freud, "melancholia," like "mourning," is a reaction to *loss*. The loss may involve the breakup of a relationship, financial decline, or failure to reach an important goal. Not everyone overreacts to these kinds of events. Among those who were abandoned or neglected as children, however, even a minor setback may cause them to retreat into a passive, dependent, child-like state. It can also awaken intense anger that is turned inward, or "internalized"—which is why people who are depressed often punish themselves with self-blame, feelings of worthlessness, and suicide.

Behaviorally oriented psychologists trace depression to our history of reinforcement and perception of control. According to Peter Lewinsohn (1974), people get depressed when they are unable to produce for themselves a high rate of positive reinforcement. Similarly, Martin Seligman (1975) has argued that depression is a form of **learned helplessness,** an expectation that one cannot control important life outcomes. In a series of experiments during the 1960s, Seligman found that dogs strapped into a harness and exposed to painful electric shocks soon became passive and gave up trying to escape—even in new situations where escape was possible. As applied to humans, this finding suggests that prolonged exposure to uncontrollable outcomes may similarly cause apathy, inactivity, a loss of motivation, and pessimism.

Realizing that perception is more important than reality, many psychologists now focus on the social-cognitive aspects of depression. Several years ago, psychiatrist Aaron Beck (1967) noticed that his depressed patients viewed themselves, their world, and the future through dark glasses. According to Beck, these patients distorted reality by focusing more attention on negative events than on positive ones—a pattern consistently found in research (Haaga et al., 1991). This bleak outlook is pervasive. Research shows that depressed people are not only down on themselves but also down on their parents and romantic partners (Gara et al., 1993).

Lynn Abramson and her colleagues (1989) further proposed that depression is a state of *hopelessness* brought on by negative thinking—in this case, by the attributions people make for failure. Specifically, some people have a *depressive explanatory style,* a tendency to attribute bad events to factors that are internal rather than external ("It's my fault"), stable rather than unstable ("It will not change"), and global rather than specific ("It affects other parts of my life"). Many studies now provide support for this proposition. Whether people are trying to explain social rejection, a sports defeat, low grades, or their inability to solve an experimenter's puzzle, those who are depressed are more likely than others to blame factors that are within the self, unlikely to change, and broad enough to impair other aspects of life. The result is a feeling of hopelessness and despair (Metalsky et al., 1993; Metalsky & Joiner, 1992; Seligman, 1990).

Finally, humanistic theorists believe that people become depressed if they fail to achieve self-actualization. Consistent with this hypothesis, studies show that people feel unfulfilled and depressed when they perceive that there is a discrepancy between their actual and ideal selves (Higgins, 1989)—particularly when the discrepancy is large and when attention is focused on the self (Strauman, 1989; Pyszczynski & Greenberg, 1987; Morrow & Nolen-Hoeksema, 1990). Within this framework, suicide is viewed as the last desperate attempt of an unfulfilled person to escape from his or her self (Baumeister, 1990).

■ **learned helplessness** A learned expectation that one cannot control important life outcomes, resulting in apathy and depression.

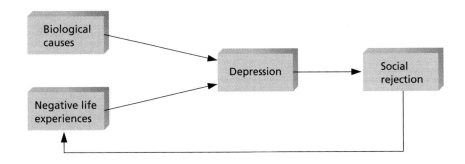

Figure 16.5

The Vicious Cycle of Depression

The Vicious Cycle of Depression

It is one of the saddest ironies for men and women with depression: they desperately need social support and a shoulder to cry on, yet they behave in ways that drive away the most important people in their lives. The result is a vicious, self-perpetuating cycle: depression elicits social rejection, which in turn worsens the depression (see Figure 16.5).

Do depressed people really elicit negative reactions and rejection? Are we all so cold-hearted that we turn our backs on those in need of emotional support? Sometimes, yes. When people are severely depressed, friends do try to cheer them up and offer a sympathetic ear, a shoulder to lean on, and advice. However, as psychotherapists are the first to admit, these efforts usually fail and the depression persists. Then, as if that were not bad enough, the suffering person is filled with complaints, regrets, and self-pity, all of which makes social interaction unpleasant if not painful to endure. The result: We react to others who are depressed with mixed emotions—sorrow laced with irritation, anger, and a desire to avoid future contact (Coyne, 1976; Strack & Coyne, 1983; Sacco & Dunn, 1990). This vicious cycle may help to explain why strained friendships, marital conflict, and even divorce are commonly associated with depression (Coyne et al., 1987).

Suicide: The Ultimate "Solution"

"The thought of suicide is a great source of comfort; with it a calm passage is to be made across many a bad night."

FRIEDRICH WILHELM NIETZSCHE

"I don't believe it. I just saw him last week, and he looked fine." "I knew she was depressed, but I had no idea it was this bad. Why didn't she call me?" These statements are typical of how people react when someone they know commits suicide. Every year, an estimated 31,000 Americans kill themselves (that's an average of one suicide every half-hour). And for every one person who actually commits suicide, there are ten to twenty others who try. To the average person, nothing about human behavior seems more senseless. To those who are depressed, however, it often seems like the quickest solution to a painful problem (Shneidman, 1987).

Who tries to commit suicide, and why? Statistics show that women are three times more likely to attempt suicide, but men are three times more likely to succeed. This difference reflects the fact that men often shoot themselves, while women usually take an overdose of sleeping pills—a slower and less certain method. Either way, 75 percent of suicides are committed by people who are depressed. In the vast majority of these cases, the single best predictor of suicide potential is hopelessness. In one study, for example, more than 2,000 psychiatric outpatients were tested and followed for up to seven years. Of the 17 who went on to commit suicide, 16 had initially gotten high scores on a "hopelessness scale" (Beck et al., 1990). In a survey of college students who had actually attempted suicide, the other factors most frequently cited were loneliness, depression, problems with boyfriends, girlfriends, or parents, feelings of helplessness, grades, and money (Westefeld & Furr, 1987).

When do people who feel hopeless resort to suicide? Roy Baumeister (1990) proposed the provocative theory that suicide is an "escape from self." According to this theory, people think about suicide when they (1) fail to achieve an important life goal, (2) blame themselves for the failure, (3) focus too much attention on the self, (4) become sad and depressed, (5) think in short-sighted terms as a way to escape mentally from the anguish, and, as a result, (6) shed the inhibitions that normally prevent people from contemplating such drastic measures. In other words, suicide is a last resort whose main purpose is "oblivion"—a complete loss of self-consciousness. Although it is impossible to test this theory directly, Baumeister presented an array of suicide research statistics compatible with his propositions. These are summarized in Table 16.7.

Shocked friends and relatives always wonder: Should I have known? Could I have done something to prevent it? These are tough personal questions. Suicide is difficult to predict, and nobody should feel guilty about getting caught by surprise. But there are patterns to watch for (Shneidman, 1987). First, people who are depressed and who use drugs are particularly vulnerable—not while they are in the depths of despair, as you may think, but afterward, as they start to regain their energy and spirit. Second, about 80 percent of all suicides are preceded by remarks about one's death ("I may as well be dead," "Sometimes I wonder if life is worth living"). Third, people who attempt suicide once are at a higher-than-average risk to do so again, even much later in life (Clark et al., 1989). Is there a way to prevent suicide? If you are concerned about someone you know, certain actions are recommended. Stay close, communicate openly, offer sympathy, suggest options, and most important of all—make sure the person gets professional help. In case of a crisis, call for help yourself. The national suicide hotline number is 1-800-621-4000.

These teenagers have all attempted suicide. Among the reasons most often cited in such cases are loneliness, depression, problems with boyfriends and girlfriends, grades, money, and feelings of helplessness.

Table 16.7

Suicide: An Escape from Self?

This table summarizes Baumeister's (1990) provocative theory of suicide and some of the evidence used to support it.

1. *Falling short of standards and expectations*

   Suicide is most likely when high hopes are followed by failure. Consistent with a high-expectations hypothesis, the suicide rate is higher in prosperous nations, in states with high standards of living, in geographical areas with mild weather, and during the pleasant months of late spring and summer.

   Consistent with the failure hypothesis, suicide rates are highest during the first month of imprisonment or hospitalization, among people newly separated or divorced, right after weekends and holidays, and when an economy begins to take a downward turn.

2. *Self-blame for failure*

   People who commit suicide are low in self-esteem, often have undergone recent drops in self-esteem, feel powerless and guilty, and view themselves unfavorably relative to others.

3. *Self-focus of attention*

   Compared to notes written by people who face death from illness, suicide notes contain more first-person pronouns ("I" and "me").

   The suicide rate is higher in cultures that emphasize pride and shame, two self-focusing emotions.

   Research shows that other self-destructive behaviors, such as excessive use of alcohol, are caused by high levels of self-awareness after failure.

4. *Feelings of negative affect*

   People with suicidal tendencies often feel guilty for past deeds. Most who attempt suicide report feeling sad, depressed, lonely, worried, and, in some cases, angry.

5. *Rigid, narrow-minded thinking*

   To escape mentally from the negative affect and unfavorable implications for the self, suicidal people focus on the present moment. They use fewer future-tense verbs, and seem unable to imagine improvement.

   Compared to the abstract, meaningful notes written by people who face involuntary death ("Teach my son to be a good man"), suicide notes are often concrete and focused on trivial, short-term details ("Don't forget to pay the electric bill").

   Research shows that suicidal people have "tunnel vision": they think in black-or-white terms and are unable to generate creative solutions to problems.

6. *Disinhibition*

   As a result of rigid thinking, normal inhibitions may cease to operate. Consistent with this hypothesis, research shows that people with suicidal tendencies become more impulsive and less emotional, and think of themselves as passive "victims."

■ **bipolar disorder** A rare mood disorder characterized by wild fluctuations ranging from mania (a euphoric, overactive state) to depression (a state of hopelessness and apathy).

Bipolar Disorder

In contrast to major depression, a *unipolar* disorder in which moods range from neutral to depressed, **bipolar disorder** is characterized by wild fluctuations that range from *manic* (a euphoric, overactive state) to *depressed* (a

Figure 16.6

The PET scans shown on the right were taken from the brain of a bipolar disorder patient who alternated every 24–48 hours from depression (top) to mania (middle), and back to depression (bottom). (Dark blues and greens mark low levels of activity; red, orange, and yellow mark higher levels of activity.)

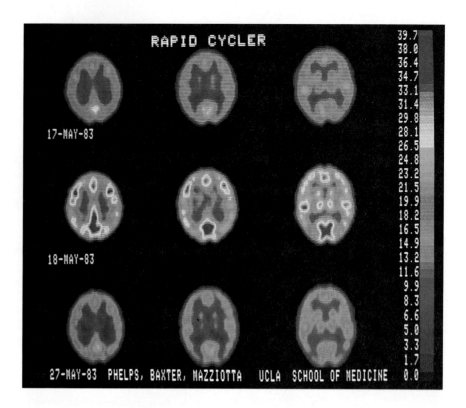

state of hopelessness and apathy). In what used to be called "manic depression," bipolar disorder patients alternate uncontrollably between the two extremes, in cycles that last from a few days to several months. One week, they are flying as high as a kite, bursting with energy and optimism. The next week, they have sunk to the depths of despair (see Figure 16.6).

What does the manic phase of this disorder feel like? What are the symptoms? In its early stages, mania is an exhilarating state of mind that many of us have enjoyed from time to time. The mildly manic person is boundless in energy, filled with self-esteem, and confident that no challenge is too daunting. With the mind racing at full speed, the manic person is sociable, entertaining, witty, quick to see connections between ideas, and filled with ambitious and creative schemes.

More than one hundred years ago, the German psychiatrist Emil Kraeplin (1883) observed that manic excitement "sets free powers that otherwise would be constrained by inhibition." History suggests he was right. In a book entitled *Touched with Fire*, Kay Redfield Jamison (1993) notes that among the many creative geniuses who had bipolar disorder were composers Robert Schumann and George Frideric Handel, artist Vincent van Gogh, and writers Edgar Allan Poe, Ernest Hemingway, Eugene O'Neill, Sylvia Plath, F. Scott Fitzgerald, and Virginia Woolf. The contagious optimism of the manic state may also be a key trait for leaders in times of adversity. Of the world's charismatic leaders, Oliver Cromwell, Martin Luther, Napoleon Bonaparte, Abraham Lincoln, Robert E. Lee, Winston Churchill, and Benito Mussolini are all believed to have suffered from bipolar disorder (Goodwin & Jamison, 1990). As the philosopher Nietzsche once said, "One must harbor chaos within oneself to give birth to a dancing star."

Before jumping to the conclusion that this disorder is worth having, you should know that there is a much darker side. As the disorder progresses,

"Oh, yeah? Well, I think you're the one with the biochemical imbalance."

[Drawing by Mankoff; © 1992 The New Yorker Magazine, Inc.]

mania accelerates out of control, and "high" becomes "too high." The person becomes easily distracted, moves from one project to another, stays awake at night, and is extremely sensitive to stimulation. It has been said that to the manic person, a gentle breeze feels like a slap on the face, and the dropping of a pin sounds like a clanging noise. People in an advanced state of mania also harbor delusions (false beliefs) of grandeur. They make promises they cannot keep, buy things they cannot afford, start new sexual relationships, and drag others into risky money-making schemes that are bound to fail. Socially, the charm and wit give way to behavior that embarrasses others. Fitting the stereotype of the "raving maniac," the person becomes loud, fast-talking, frenzied, and explosive. Even mild criticism may trigger anger and hostility. Finally, the manic phase is sometimes followed by major depression. Illustrating that what goes up must come down, bipolar disorder sufferers either return to normal or hit the ground in a crash landing. Many creative geniuses who reaped the benefits of their manic energy later killed themselves while depressed (Goodwin & Jamison, 1990).

Although bipolar disorder is a close relative of depression, they are quite different. To begin with, bipolar disorder has a stronger genetic component. Thus, if one twin has it, the odds are roughly 72 percent that an identical twin will have it too, compared to only 14 percent for a fraternal twin of the same sex (Allen, 1976; Blehar et al., 1988; Tsuang & Faraone, 1990). As we'll see in Chapter 17, bipolar disorder can be treated with the drug *lithium*.

SCHIZOPHRENIC DISORDERS

When you stop to think about "madness" or "insanity," what comes to mind? For many of us, the words alone evoke stereotyped images of people who stare blankly into space, talk gibberish to themselves, see imaginary pink animals, walk around in circles, and erupt in fits of rage and violence. These images are not that accurate, as we'll see, but they do come close to describing schizophrenia—the most dreaded of psychological disorders.

Schizophrenic disorders are marked by gross distortions of thought and perception, and by a loss of contact with reality. In some cases, the disorder strikes suddenly between the ages of seventeen and twenty-five and is followed by a full recovery. In other cases, it develops slowly, deteriorates over a period of years, and casts a life sentence on its victim—no parole, no time off for good behavior. Schizophrenia is found in all cultures of the world and affects men and women equally. It is estimated that slightly more than 1 percent of all Americans will suffer a schizophrenic disorder within the course of a lifetime (Regier et al., 1988). The most likely age of first onset is eighteen to twenty-five for men, twenty-six to forty-five for women. This sex difference in age of onset shows up all over the world, and researchers are puzzled by it (Gottesman, 1991; Straube & Oades, 1992).

schizophrenic disorders Disorders involving gross distortions of thought and perception, and loss of contact with reality.

Psychological Symptoms

Translated from Greek, the word *schizophrenia* means "split brain." The so-called split is not between two or more inner selves, as in multiple

■ delusions False beliefs that often accompany schizophrenia and other psychotic disorders.

■ hallucinations Sensory experiences that occur in the absence of actual stimulation.

"A monkey winked at me this morning."

Common in schizophrenia are delusions of reference, false beliefs that one is the recipient of others' actions. [Drawing by Booth; © 1992 The New Yorker Magazine, Inc.]

"What is madness? To have erroneous perceptions and to reason correctly from them."

VOLTAIRE

personality disorder, but rather between thoughts, beliefs, perceptions, emotions, motor behavior, and other brain functions. People with schizophrenia often say it's like being stuck in the "Twilight Zone" (Torrey, 1988).

There are five major symptoms of schizophrenia. First and foremost, it is a disorder characterized by *incoherent thinking*. The person is mentally disorganized and confused, on a different wavelength than the rest of us. This problem is most evident in speech. Listen to people with schizophrenia talk, and you may well hear them make up new words and drift illogically from one topic to another, making their statements sound like something of a "word salad." Often, for example, they will string together utterances that are only loosely associated. Eugen Bleuler (1911), the Swiss psychiatrist who gave schizophrenia its name, cited an example from one of his patients: "I wish you a happy, joyful, healthy, and fruitful year, and many good wine years to come as well as a healthy and good apple-year, and sauerkraut and cabbage and squash and seed year." In this sample of speech, the word *fruitful* set off a chain of food-related associations. The reason is that people with schizophrenia have difficulty focusing attention on one stimulus and filtering out distractions (McGhie & Chapman, 1961; Freedman et al, 1987). In the autobiographies of 50 former patients, concentration problems were the most frequent thought-related complaint (Freedman, 1974).

A second symptom is the presence of **delusions,** or false beliefs. In schizophrenic minds all over the world, certain delusional themes appear with remarkable frequency. Among the most common are delusions of influence—the belief that one's thoughts are being broadcast to the world, "stolen" from one's mind, or controlled by evil forces. Thus one patient believed that his thoughts were publicized to others on a "mental ticker-tape," another spoke of having her thoughts "sucked out of my mind by a phrenological vacuum extractor," and a third believed "a radio was implanted in my skull." Also common are delusions of grandeur (that one is a famous or powerful person, capable of controlling weather, the movement of planets, and other people), delusions of reference (that one is the recipient of others' actions), and delusions of persecution (that one is a target of secret plots by others).

A third symptom is the presence of **hallucinations,** which are sensory experiences that occur without actual stimulation. To hallucinate is to see, hear, smell, taste, or feel something that does not exist. The most common hallucinations are auditory. Schizophrenics report that they "hear" the swishing or thumping sound of a heartbeat, musical choirs, or disembodied voices that comment on their lives, make accusations, and issue commands. "Son of Sam" David Berkowitz, who terrorized New York City in the 1970s by killing innocent young women, claimed that he was ordered to stalk and shoot his victims by the demonic voice of a barking dog. Sometimes, though less often, hallucinations occur in other sensory systems as well. People may "see" heavenly creatures, "smell" foul body odors, "taste" poison in their food, or "feel" a tingling, burning, or pricking sensation on their skin. Other perceptual distortions are also evident. According to numerous reports, lights seem brighter, colors more vibrant, and sounds more intense. And people's bodies often appear longer, shorter, smaller, rounder, or otherwise deformed—like viewing the world through a funhouse mirror.

The thoughts and emotions of people with schizophrenia can often be seen in their creative expressions. In the words of artist Sandra Milne, "This painting was done in response to my doctor's suggestion that I paint who I really was. Each person represents a side of me" (left). Artist Herman Greenblatt says, "This painting represents the inner emotion of love of a human being and his animal" (right).

The fourth symptom is a *disturbance of affect*, or emotional experience. Some schizophrenics have a "flattened affect." They sit still for hours, wear a blank expression on the face, speak in a low and monotonic voice, avoid eye contact, and show little interest or concern in anything. As one psychiatrist described, "It is uncannily like interacting with a robot" (Torrey, 1988). Others express feelings that are exaggerated or inappropriate to the situation—crying after happy news, breaking into laughter during tragedy, or screaming in fear or anger without external provocation.

The fifth symptom is *bizarre behavior*. Absorbed in an inner world of stimulation, and confused by their distorted perceptions of the outer world, people with schizophrenia often withdraw, go into social "exile," and cease to function effectively at work. They may talk to themselves, repeat what others say like parrots, spend hours in statue-like poses, walk backward or in circles, take their clothes off in public, and so on. Remarkably, they also lack self-insight. Indeed, people with schizophrenia think that their speech is coherent, their delusions and hallucinations real, and their emotions appropriate. As one former patient said, "I felt I was the only sane person in the world gone crazy" (see Table 16.8). Approximately 12 percent of people with schizophrenia commit suicide (Caldwell & Gottesman, 1990).

Types of Schizophrenia

Even before Bleuler named the disorder, it was obvious that there are different kinds of schizophrenia. In DSM-IV, five major types are distinguished (McGlashan & Fenton, 1991): (1) *disorganized*, a category used to describe those who exhibit illogical thinking, incoherent speech, a neglect of personal hygiene, exaggerated displays of emotion, and mannerisms that

Table 16.8

Schizophrenia: A View from the Inside

The following excerpts are taken from a personal account written by a woman who was once diagnosed with schizophrenia. Which symptoms described in the text did she experience?

A little knowledge, people say, is a dangerous thing. My problems first started when I decided to go back to college at the age of 27. After taking a psychology course, I recognized signs of stress in myself and went for help. I was taking 16 credits, working full time in my business which was a day-care center, and taking care of my children in the absence of their father. He was working out of town and came home on weekends. During that school term, certain remarks made by my professors led me to the conclusion that they were working to rescue me from what they thought was an abusive marriage. And I, contrarily, was convinced that I wanted to stay married.

I felt particularly influenced by a foreign language instructor. I was convinced that this professor and I had a private means of communication and, because of this, interpreted what he said in class as personally relating to me. Sometimes the things I heard in class had no relation to the class purpose. One time, the professor asked the room at large, 'So your husband used to be a minister?' I had not divulged that information to him, but because I had recently told my babysitter that, I felt the incident was more than coincidence. I felt that there was a large network of people finding out about me, watching me on the street for some unknown reason. This feeling of lack of privacy soon grew into thinking my house was bugged, a fear I would have off and on for the next eight years. The bizarre and illogical things I heard people say were later dismissed as auditory hallucinations. They seemed very real to me, however.

On one occasion, I saw a personal experience of mine written on the blackboard in French and English. I did not recognize it as a hallucination at that time. This caused me considerable anguish, but I continued to act as normal as I could for fear that any bizarre behavior would cause me to lose my job. I did not talk about these things, so the only noticeable signs of my illness were that I became silent and withdrawn, not my usual ebullient and smiling self. I did not think I was sick, but that these things were being done to me. I was still able to function though I remember getting lunch ready very slowly as if working in molasses, each move an effort.

By Christmas, I heard an actor call me a liar over the TV, and I felt sure the media also knew about me. When I went to the store, I bought things that symbolically meant something else to me; each fruit, flavor, or color had a meaning that tied in with my delusion. For example, I would not buy Trix cereal, because it was associated with prostitution in my mind, but I bought a lot of Cheerios to make my day happier. The world of delusion soon became a world of imagined depravities that were a torment to my moralistic mind. I felt I was the only sane person in the world gone crazy (Anonymous, 1990, pp. 547-548).

---

are silly and childish; (2) *catatonic,* a rare form of the disorder that features extremes in motor behavior ranging from motionless "stupors" to bursts of hyperactivity; (3) *paranoid,* in which the main symptom is a preoccupation with one or more delusions or hallucinations, often accompanied by extreme suspiciousness and hostility; (4) *undifferentiated,* a catch-all category

A catatonic stupor is an extreme form of withdrawal. While in this state, the person does not move or speak. In fact, an uncomfortable statue-like pose may be held for so long that the limbs become stiff and swollen.

for cases that exhibit a mixture of the major symptoms and do no clearly fit into one of the other types; and (5) *residual*, a diagnostic category that is used for people who had prior episodes of schizophrenia but are currently not experiencing the major symptoms.

Many clinical researchers prefer to divide schizophrenia into two basic types (Crow, 1980; Andreasen et al., 1990; Kay, 1990). *Type I schizophrenia* is defined by behavioral excesses, or "positive symptoms" such as incoherent speech, delusions, hallucinations, exaggerated displays of emotion, and bizarre behavior. In contrast, *Type II schizophrenia* is characterized by behavioral deficits, or "negative symptoms" such as apathy, blank looks, blunted affect, slowed movement and speech, and social withdrawal. Based on a study of 111 schizophrenic outpatients in an Iowa hospital, the estimated prevalence of both positive and negative symptoms is presented in Table 16.9.

Can people with schizophrenia be neatly classified into the two general types? On the one hand, research suggests that people with positive symptoms have a better pre-disorder state and a greater chance of recovery than those suffering from the negative symptoms. On the other hand, many people exhibit both kinds of symptoms, so the two disorders often coexist (McGlashan & Fenton, 1992). In an assessment of over a hundred schizophrenic patients, for example, the vast majority had a "mixed" form of the disorder (Andreasen et al., 1990).

Theories of Schizophrenia

Can anyone stressed by adverse life circumstances "catch" a schizophrenic disorder, or are some of us more prone than others? Can the outbreak of schizophrenia in an adult be predicted in childhood? Indeed, are the causes biological, psychological, or a combination of both?

Biological Factors   Family, twin, and adoption studies reveal a strong genetic basis for schizophrenic disorders (Holzman & Matthysse, 1990). You

Table 16.9   Positive and Negative Symptoms of Schizophrenia

In a study of 111 individuals with schizophrenia, the following symptoms were exhibited by varying percentages of subjects. Note that delusions were the most common positive symptom and apathy the most common negative symptom (Andreason, 1987, pp. 16–17).

Positive Symptoms	Percentage	Negative Symptoms	Percentage
Hallucinations	69	Flattened Affect	88
Delusions	84	Slowed or No Speech	53
Bizarre Behavior	26	Apathy	90
Thought Disorders	43	Social Withdrawal	88
		Inattention	66

Table 16.10

Genetic Relationships and Schizophrenia

As shown, the lifetime risk of schizophrenia increases as a function of how genetically related a person is to someone else who is known to have schizophrenia (Gottesman, 1991, p. 96).

Relationship	Genetic relatedness	Risk
Identical twin	100%	48%
Offspring of two schizophrenic parents	100%	46%
Fraternal twin	50%	17%
Offspring of one schizophrenic parent	50%	17%
Sibling	50%	9%
Nephew or niece	25%	4%
Spouse	0%	2%
Unrelated person	0%	1%

may recall that slightly more than 1 percent of the American population is diagnosed with schizophrenia at some point in life. However, the more closely related you are to someone with schizophrenia, the greater the risk (see Table 16.10). When one fraternal twin has it, the odds are 17 percent for the other. With an identical twin, however, the odds increase even further to 48 percent—a number that remains high regardless of whether the twins are raised together or apart (Gottesman & Shields, 1982; Gottesman, 1991).

Searching for the biological origins of schizophrenia, many researchers find that the positive symptoms are associated either with overactivity in synapses where dopamine is the neurotransmitter or with an oversensitivity to dopamine. Three kinds of evidence support this linkage. The first is that "antipsychotic" drugs that block the activity of dopamine in the brain also lessen hallucinations, delusions, and other positive symptoms. Second, amphetamines both increase dopamine activity and intensify positive symptoms (long-term usage or overdoses can even trigger schizophrenic-like episodes in normal people). Third, autopsies on the brains of schizophrenic patients often reveal an overabundance of dopamine receptors (Davis et al., 1991; Meltzer & Stahl, 1976; Wong et al., 1986).

Interestingly, the negative symptoms of schizophrenia are typically not affected by antipsychotic drugs or amphetamines. Instead, these symptoms—flat affect, apathy, lack of speech, attention problems, immobility, and withdrawal—may be linked to structural defects in the brain. CAT scans of people with this type of schizophrenia thus reveal a shrinkage or "atrophy" of the cerebral cortex and an enlargement of fluid-filled spaces called "cerebral ventricles" (Shelton & Weinberger, 1986; Raz & Raz, 1990).

■ **diathesis-stress model** A theory stating that certain mental disorders (such as schizophrenia) develop when people with a genetic or acquired vulnerability are exposed to high levels of stress.

Psychological Factors   Although there is a genetic basis for schizophrenia, 54 percent of those people born to two schizophrenic parents do *not* themselves develop the disorder. In other words, heredity may increase the risk, but it does not by itself predetermine one's fate. This notion has given rise to the **diathesis-stress model**, which states that people with a genetic or acquired vulnerability, or "diathesis," develop schizophrenia when exposed to high levels of stress (Meehl, 1962; Zubin & Spring, 1977; Fowles, 1992). The question is, What experiences act as triggering mechanisms?

To identify the factors that predict the development of schizophrenia, researchers in the United States, Canada, Israel, Finland, Denmark, and Sweden are now conducting longitudinal studies in which high-risk children (those who have at least one schizophrenic parent) are followed closely as they grow older. The life experiences of the children who go on to develop schizophrenia are then compared to those who do not. So far, the results show that high-risk subjects who become schizophrenic were more likely to have had complications at birth, to have been separated from their mothers at an early age, to have fathers hospitalized for a mental disorder, to grow up in homes filled with conflict, to have trouble concentrating, and to have social problems in school (Asarnow, 1988). Can the future of a high-risk child be predicted? Perhaps. When psychology graduate students were shown old home movies of future schizophrenic patients and their healthy siblings—all of whom were normal while growing up—78 percent guessed correctly which of the children in the films went on to develop the disorder (Walker & Lewine, 1990).

As always, it is easier to identify factors that *predict* the onset of a disorder than to pinpoint its psychological *causes*. To see why, consider two classic findings that are interesting but hard to interpret. First, schizophrenia is most prevalent in the lowest socioeconomic classes of society. This pattern appears in studies all over the world, and is sometimes taken to mean that poverty causes schizophrenia. Or is it the other way around? Perhaps schizophrenia—precisely because it is characterized by massive cognitive and social impairment—leads its sufferers to drop out of school, lose jobs, and drift downward into poverty. A second example is the well-publicized observation that parents of schizophrenics communicate to their offspring in ways that are inconsistent and confusing. This finding is often taken to suggest that faulty communication patterns at home can cause schizophrenia. Again, however, it is equally possible that the behavior of parents is not a cause but a *response* to the problem of communicating with pre-schizophrenic children. Which comes first, the chicken or the egg? Either way, it seems that biological and environmental forces combine to produce this very devastating disorder.

PERSONALITY DISORDERS

You have your own unique personality. So do I. We all do. You may be sloppy or meticulous, calm or emotional, self-centered or altruistic, cautious or impulsive, a loner or a social butterfly. However, if someone has a personality that is highly inflexible and maladaptive, and causes distress, that person is diagnosed as having a **personality disorder** (Millon, 1990).

Among the disorders classified in DSM-IV, these are among the most controversial. People with personality disorders—an estimated 5 to 10 percent of the population—are not swamped with anxiety, depression, or confusion, nor have they lost touch with reality. In fact, they are not particularly motivated to change. The problem is, they are trapped by their own rigid ways in self-defeating patterns of behavior, patterns that begin to form in adolescence and then harden like plaster for the rest of life.

■ **personality disorders** A group of disorders characterized by a personality that is highly inflexible and maladaptive.

There are eleven personality disorders listed in DSM-IV; many of them quite colorful. Examples include the isolated and emotionally detached "schizoid personality," the perfectionistic "obsessive-compulsive personality," the highly sensitive and suspicious "paranoid personality," the melodramatic, attention-seeking "histrionic personality," the self-centered, ego-inflated "narcissistic personality," and the "avoidant personality" who so fears rejection that he or she does not start new relationships or make social commitments. Two in particular have attracted widespread attention: (1) the borderline personality, which is quite common, and (2) the antisocial personality, which is socially destructive.

Borderline Personality

Marilyn Monroe was famous for her beauty and her tremendous success in Hollywood. She was also known for being unpredictable, impulsive, insecure, impossible to live with, and yet desperately afraid to be alone. At the age of thirty-six, she shocked the world by killing herself with an overdose of sleeping pills. From what is known about her life, Marilyn Monroe did not have a serious anxiety, somatoform, conversion, or dissociative disorder, nor was she schizophrenic. At times, she was depressed. If she were alive today, however, she might well be diagnosed, along with 20 percent of all psychiatric patients and 3 to 5 percent of everyone else, as having a *borderline personality disorder* (Frances & Widiger, 1986).

Borderline personality disorder features a lack of identity and a pattern of instability in self-image, mood, and social relationships. People with this disorder (approximately two-thirds are women) are uncertain of who they are—in terms of their career goals, friends, values, and sometimes their sexual orientation. They complain of feeling empty and bored, can't stand to be left alone, and are desperate for the company of others. Unhappily, people with a borderline personality cling to others with such fierce dependence that their relationships are stormy and do not last. They are also impulsive—in the habit of running away, getting into fights, and jumping into bed with strangers. As a way to get attention, they are also notorious for committing acts of self-destruction. In a study of the lives of fifty-seven borderline patients, there were 42 suicide threats, 40 overdoses, 38 cases of drug abuse, 36 acts of self-mutilation (slashing wrists, banging heads, burning skin with cigarettes, pulling out hair), 36 instances of sexual promiscuity, and 14 car accidents caused by reckless driving (Gunderson, 1984).

Antisocial Personality

Every now and then, a crime story appears on the news that is so horrible it sends chills up my spine. Three high school students pour gasoline on their teacher and set her on fire. A man slashes the face of a model with a razor blade in exchange for two hundred dollars. What kind of person is capable of such atrocities? Who are these cold-blooded monsters? In the nineteenth century, they were described as morally insane. Subsequently, they were called psychopaths, or sociopaths. Today, the term **antisocial personality disorder** is used to describe people with "ice in their veins"—those who

"Tell me, do you respond to treatment?"

People with a narcissistic personality disorder are chronically vain, boastful, and pretentious. [Drawing by Rini; © 1992 The New Yorker Magazine, Inc.]

■ **antisocial personality disorder** A personality disorder characterized by a chronic pattern of self-centered, manipulative, and destructive behavior toward others.

behave in ways that are completely self-centered, irresponsible, and destructive, without regard for the welfare of others.

According to DSM-IV, antisocial personality (ASP) is a disorder that applies to those who (1) before the age of fifteen, were always cutting school, running away from home, vandalizing property, setting fires, harming animals, stealing, cheating, and fighting; and who (2) as adults, exhibit abusive behavior, wasteful spending, gambling, failure to honor commitments or pay debts, reckless driving, assault, and other unlawful activities. As you might expect, a person with ASP is unable to hold a job or maintain a close relationship. But the most striking feature is that he (80 percent are men) *lacks a conscience*—and feels no guilt, remorse, or empathy for his victims. He uses others for pleasure or profit, then discards them. When endowed with intelligence, the person with ASP is a cool, manipulative, superficially charming, clever con artist—one who can seduce romantic companions with empty words of love, lie to business partners with a straight face, and sweet-talk his way out of trouble (Cleckley, 1976; Hare et al., 1991). Among ex-prisoners, those with an antisocial personality are more likely than others to violate the terms of their parole (Hart et al., 1988).

For many years, researchers have speculated about the causes of ASP (Reid et al., 1986). Some have tried to trace the problem to broken homes, neglectful parents, and faulty role models that impede the formation of a superego and moral development. Others measure brain-wave patterns and heart rates—and find that the antisocial personality is not as excitable as the average person, is not as easily startled, and remains relatively calm in the face of electric shock and other tense situations (Patrick et al., 1993). Still others find that people diagnosed with ASP lack the ability to control their impulses or alter their behavior in response to punishment—problems that are further worsened by their tendency to abuse alcohol and other disinhibiting drugs. Whatever the causes, society can take some comfort in the fact that criminals with antisocial personalities tend to "burn out" and commit fewer crimes after age forty (Hare et al., 1988).

WHAT NEXT?

Psychological disorders keep people from adapting in the most effective way to their environment. In this chapter, six types of disorders were described, each featuring different primary symptoms: intense anxiety, physical ailments and complaints, dissociation of the self from memory, extreme moods ranging from depression to euphoria, schizophrenic devastation of mental functions, and self-defeating patterns of behavior. Yet there are many, many more—such as disorders involving sex, sleep, impulse control, drug abuse, and development. Clearly, no aspect of our existence is immune to breakdown.

Now that you've seen the list of psychological disorders, you should note two ways in which the picture is more complicated than it appears. First, although each disorder is presented separately in its own neat and tidy package, people diagnosed with one disorder often have symptoms of others as well—a phenomenon known as **comorbidity** (Kendall & Clarkin, 1992; Kessler et al., 1994). People with phobias often suffer from obsessive-compulsive disorder, many of those with general anxiety disorder

■ **comorbidity** The tendency for people diagnosed with one mental disorder to exhibit symptoms of other disorders as well.

CLINICAL PSYCHOLOGY   Law

The Insanity Defense

On July 22, 1991, Milwaukee police officers entered a one-bedroom apartment and encountered one of the most monstrous and disgusting crime scenes in American history. The stench was unbearable. There were photographs of dismembered bodies tacked on the walls, severed human heads, organs, and genitals in the refrigerator, and other body parts immersed in a vat of acid. The police soon arrested Jeffrey Dahmer, a thirty-one-year-old chocolate factory worker, who went on to confess to a total of seventeen murders. In each case, he said, he would lure a young man to his apartment, drug, rape, and kill him, dismember the body, and store or eat the remains. Dahmer went to trial and entered a plea of insanity. After hearing two weeks of testimony, however, a Milwaukee jury voted by a 10-to-2 margin that he was sane. Dahmer was sentenced to life in prison.

Was Jeffrey Dahmer really sane? How could a jury draw this conclusion about someone so calculating and so brutal? What does it mean to be sane, and when can a person be considered insane? To begin with, it's important to realize that *insanity* is a legal concept, not a psychological one. Insanity is not a diagnostic category and does not appear in DSM-IV. But it is an important concept in criminal law. Individuals who are charged with a crime can plead guilty or not guilty, or argue that they should not be held responsible in light of extraordinary circumstances. The law provides a variety of excusing conditions for this purpose. If a person commits a crime by accident, or was coerced, or acted in self-defense, then he or she may argue for a verdict of not guilty. In a similar manner, the law permits an insanity defense to protect from punishment those who cannot morally be faulted for their actions because they were mentally impaired while committing the crime (Hermann, 1983; Golding, 1992).

What does it mean to be mentally impaired, or insane? Over time, the courts have defined insanity in several different ways. In the nineteenth century, Great Britain and the United States adopted the rule that defendants were legally insane if, as a result of mental illness, they did not know what they were doing or that it was wrong. Critics argued that this definition too narrowly focused on a defendant's cognitive state and excluded those who knew what they were doing but could not control themselves. Some states thus added the "irresistible impulse" test by which defendants are considered insane if they lack the capacity to control their actions. Throughout the years, other definitions have been proposed. Today, the most common is one that combines three key elements. As defined by the Model Penal Code, defendants are not responsible for criminal conduct if (1) as a result of mental disorder, they cannot (2) appreciate the wrongfulness of their conduct, or (3) conform to the law.

The insanity plea is a constant source of controversy. In

are also depressed, and people with schizophrenia often abuse drugs (Vincent van Gogh had bipolar disorder, but he also experienced schizophrenic hallucinations, paranoid delusions, and alcohol abuse). In a similar manner, psychological disorders do not exist in caricature-like terms. Depression is considered a mood disorder, but it has cognitive symptoms; schizophrenia is considered a thought disorder, but it has a marked impact on emotion.

The second complication is that normal and abnormal are not distinct, well-defined categories but, rather, points on a continuum. Hence, people who are otherwise happy, healthy, and well adjusted may experience some of the symptoms of psychological disorders. On occasion, most of us have felt panic, phobic anxiety, mania, and depression. Most of us know what it's like to lose sleep when we're nervous or worry excessively about our health when a contagious disease begins to spread. Most of us know what it's like to "tune out" for short periods of time and dissociate mentally from our surroundings. Sometimes we even catch brief, mild glimpses of schizophrenic symptoms. For example, the new parent who "hears" his or

1843, a Scotsman named Daniel M'Naghten tried to assassinate British Prime Minister Robert Peel and mistakenly killed Peel's secretary. M'Naughten suffered from delusions of persecution and believed that Peel had plotted against him. He went to trial—but was found not guilty by reason of insanity. The public was outraged. In 1981, John Hinckley, Jr., shot and wounded President Reagan and was quickly apprehended. The shooting was witnessed by millions of TV viewers. Hinckley was tried in the District of Columbia, but this jury, too, returned a verdict of not guilty by reason of insanity. Again, the public was outraged (Low et al., 1986).

Understandably, many people fear that the insanity defense opens up a loophole through which massive numbers of criminals can escape punishment for their crimes. Is that fear justified? Consider the following three questions: (1) What percentage of criminal defendants enter a plea of insanity? (2) Of those who do, what percentage succeed? (3) Of those who succeed, how many are set free?

Eric Silver and his colleagues (1994) compared public opinions on these questions to the actual figures gathered from forty-nine counties in eight different states. The results showed that respondents clearly overestimated the overall impact of the insanity defense in criminal justice. Specifically, the public estimated that 37 percent of all criminal defendants raise the insanity defense, that 44 percent are acquitted, and that 26 percent of those acquitted are set free. In actuality, fewer than 1 percent of all defendants plead insanity, 26 percent are acquitted, and 15 percent of those acquitted are set free (the others are committed to a mental hospital). Put these numbers together, and you'll see that public opinion is highly distorted. For every 1,000 cases, people estimate that 163 defendants are acquitted by reason of insanity, and that 47 are set free. In actuality, 2 defendants in 1,000 are acquitted by reason of insanity, and only 3 in 10,000 are set free. In most cases, the person found to be insane spends as much time confined to a hospital as he or she would have spent in prison.

Despite the moral underpinnings of the insanity defense and the reassuring odds concerning the frequency of its usage, there are problems in its implementation. One is that many defendants who are evaluated for insanity engage in some degree of malingering, or faking (Rogers, 1988). To overcome this problem, psychologists are now developing tests and interview methods to detect such faking (Rogers et al., 1991; Schretlen et al., 1992). A second problem is that judges often turn for expert opinion to clinical psychologists and psychiatrists—who are trained to diagnose mental disorders, not to resolve questions of criminal responsibility. Predictably, many insanity trials feature a battle of opposing experts who disagree in their assessments of the defendant (Dawes et al., 1989).

Is there a solution to the insanity dilemma? On the one hand, it seems inhumane to punish people who are not responsible for their own actions. On the other hand, it seems repugnant to provide a loophole for murderers and other violent criminals. In recent years, many courts have reformed their laws to discourage acquittals by reason of insanity. Although it remains to be seen what effect these changes will have on judges and juries, controversy will clearly continue to surround this awkward relationship between clinical psychology and the law.

her newborn cry, only to see that the baby is fast asleep, is having an auditory hallucination. And the person who dines all alone in a restaurant and self-consciously thinks everyone is watching is under some kind of delusion. In short, psychological order and disorder are not always black-and-white categories, but shades of gray. At times, diagnosis is a judgment call based on how intense, frequent, prolonged, and disabling the symptoms are.

Once psychological disorders are identified and diagnosed, and once we understand their causes, what next? At this point, we must return our attention to the key underlying challenge of clinical psychology: the potential for positive *change*. As we saw in Chapter 15, personality tends to remain relatively stable throughout adulthood. But what about the psychological disorders that afflict so many people? What about episodes of anxiety or depression? For those in need of professional help, the answer is treatment—through drugs, counseling and psychotherapy, and other forms of intervention. Reflecting the hope and the reality that people can help other people change, these are the topics of our next chapter.

SUMMARY AND KEY TERMS

Psychological Disorders: A General Outlook

Since psychological disorders are widespread, though often temporary, it's important to ask how they are defined, what factors put us at risk, and how different problems can be distinguished.

Defining Normal and Abnormal

The term *mental disorder* has been defined in various ways. The APA definition stresses significant pain or dysfunctional behavior and an internal, involuntary source. Whatever definition is used, there is no strict line between normal and abnormal.

Models of Abnormality

The *medical model* attributes mental disorders to biological conditions. The *psychological model* locates the cause of disorder in past and present experiences. The sociocultural perspective stresses the importance of the social and cultural context.

Diagnosis: A Necessary Evil

Today the process of *diagnosis,* the grouping and naming of mental disorders, is based on the list of disorders and categories in the *DSM-IV.* Although diagnosis is more reliable than in the past, stereotypes can bias the process, and the diagnostic label can then affect the way people are received and treated.

Anxiety Disorders

Anxiety is a nervous feeling of apprehension accompanied by physical symptoms, such as a pounding heart and trembling hands.

Generalized Anxiety Disorder

A constant state of anxiety, not linked to an identifiable source, is the mark of *generalized anxiety disorder.* Cross-cultural studies show that anxiety and its physiological symptoms are universal, but the cognitive component (the particular set of worries and interpretations) depends on the culture.

Panic Disorder

Panic disorder—characterized by frequent, sudden, intense rushes of anxiety for no apparent reason—is often accompanied by *agoraphobia,* a fear of public places. There is evidence for both biological and psychological causes.

Phobic Disorder

A *phobic disorder*—an intense, irrational fear—can be a *simple phobia* (involving a specific object or situation) or a *social phobia* (involving a situation that invites public scrutiny). Freud attributed phobias to anxiety about hidden impulses; behaviorists

stress experience and learning; others have linked common phobias to evolutionary programming or "preparation."

Obsessive-Compulsive Disorder

In *obsessive-compulsive disorder (OCD),* the person is plagued by obsessions (persistent thoughts) and compulsions (the need to perform repetitive acts or rituals). Psychoanalysts, behaviorists, and biological researchers have all offered explanations.

Somatoform Disorders

People with a *somatoform disorder* have bodily symptoms that are psychological rather than medical in origin.

Hypochondriasis

A disorder involving unwarranted preoccupation with one's physical health, *hypochondriasis* can become a lifelong pattern.

Conversion Disorder

Conversion disorder—a temporary loss of a bodily function without a physical cause—mainly affects young women. Sociocultural context plays a role, as is suggested by the recent emergence of chronic fatigue syndrome.

Dissociative Disorders

Many people have experiences in which a portion of their lives becomes dissociated from their identity or memory. A severe condition of this sort is known as a *dissociative disorder.*

Amnesia and Fugue States

Amnesia is a partial or complete loss of memory. Causes include physical trauma, alcohol, and stressful events. In the rarer forms known as *fugue states,* people forget their identity, wander away, and start a new life.

Multiple Personality

In *multiple personality disorder (MPD),* the person develops two or more distinct personalities. Women exhibit this disorder much more often than men and usually have a history of abuse as children. Reported cases of MPD are on the rise.

Mood Disorders

People normally have many fluctuations of mood. But prolonged emotional extremes that impair the ability to function are diagnosed as *mood disorders.*

Major Depression

Depression, a widespread mood disorder, brings feelings of deep sadness and despair that occur without a discernible cause and last two weeks or more. Other symptoms include feelings of worthlessness and a lack of energy.

Theories of Depression

Twin studies show a genetic foundation for depression. Early research stressed the role of neurotransmitters, but now it appears that the connection between biology and mood is more complicated.

Psychological factors have also been noted. Freud considered depression a reaction to loss. Behaviorists link it to *learned helplessness,* an expectation that we cannot control important life outcomes. Social-cognitive theorists say that depressed people tend to focus on negative events, blame themselves, and assume that things will not change. Humanistic theories associate depression with a failure to reach self-actualization.

The Vicious Cycle of Depression

Depressed people often behave in ways that alienate others. Social rejection then intensifies the depression—a vicious cycle.

Suicide: The Ultimate "Solution"

Three-quarters of suicides are committed by depressed people. Baumeister sees suicide as an "escape from self" into oblivion. Clinically, scales of hopelessness are the best predictor. Among friends or relatives, signs of potential suicide include depression and drug use, remarks about death, and previous attempts.

Bipolar Disorder

People with *bipolar disorder* experience wild mood swings from depression at one extreme to mania (a euphoric, overactive state) at the other. Many famous artists and political leaders evidently had bipolar disorder, and their manic phases contributed to their brilliance. But mania may also spiral out of control, producing delusions and embarrassing behavior. Though related to depression, bipolar disorder has a stronger genetic component.

Schizophrenic Disorders

Marked by gross distortions of thought and perception and a loss of contact with reality, *schizophrenic disorders* are equally common in women and men, though they tend to strike women at a later age.

Psychological Symptoms

Schizophrenia's major symptoms are incoherent thinking, *delu-* *sions* (false beliefs), *hallucinations* (sensory experiences without actual stimulation), disturbance of affect (flattened, exaggerated, or inappropriate emotion), and bizarre behavior.

Types of Schizophrenia

DSM-IV lists five major types of schizophrenia: disorganized, catatonic, paranoid, undifferentiated, and residual. Some researchers make a two-fold distinction instead between Type I schizophrenia, marked by behavioral excesses or "positive symptoms," and Type II schizophrenia, defined by behavioral deficits or "negative symptoms." Many patients exhibit symptoms of both kinds.

Theories of Schizophrenia

Twin, family, and adoption studies reveal a genetic basis for schizophrenia, linked to the neurotransmitter dopamine or to structural brain defects. But psychological factors are also involved. Some evidence supports the *diathesis-stress model,* which holds that people with genetic or acquired vulnerability develop schizophrenia when exposed to a high level of stress.

Personality Disorders

A person with a highly inflexible and maladaptive personality is said to have a *personality disorder.*

Borderline Personality

People with *borderline personality disorder* lack identity, cling to others, act impulsively, and are prone to self-destruction.

Antisocial Personality

Of those who have *antisocial personality disorder,* 80 percent are men. The condition produces a chronic pattern of self-centered, manipulative, and destructive behavior toward others. Its most notable feature is lack of conscience.

What Next?

Two facts make the picture of mental disorders more complicated than the categories suggest. First, people diagnosed with one disorder often show symptoms of other disorders as well—a phenomenon called *comorbidity.* Second, normality and abnormality are points on a continuum, with many points in between.

After a mental disorder is diagnosed, what comes next? Chapter 17 turns to the underlying concern of clinical psychology: the potential for positive change.

Chapter 17

Treatment

I n a book entitled *Love's Executioner and Other Tales of Psychotherapy,* Irvin Yalom (1989) tells the story of Betty, a twenty-seven-year-old female patient who was 5'2" tall and weighed 250 pounds. A few moments into their first meeting, Yalom asked his standard opening question, "So what ails?" Betty's reply: "Everything." She worked sixty hours a week, had no friends, cried every night, had frequent headaches, and spent weekends at home eating in front of the TV. According to Betty, she was too heavy for people to accept, yet too depressed to lose weight. Had she sought professional help before? Yes, but without much success.

Throughout the first few weeks of therapy, Betty did not really open up. According to Yalom, she droned on about trivial work problems, giggled constantly, and put on silly accents—but she revealed nothing truly intimate about herself. To break the ice, Yalom confronted Betty with her avoidant tactics. Soon she began to open up (a frightening prospect, she said, "like jumping out of a plane without a parachute"), becoming more engaged in the sessions and more interesting to talk to, but also more anxious. To speed up the process and provide a supportive social network, Yalom then put Betty into a therapy group, which worked wonders. She enrolled in an eating disorder program, joined a bowling league, devoured her last honey-glazed doughnut, and went on a diet. As the months passed, Betty lost a great deal of weight, down to 160 pounds. With each new low, she would have flashbacks of emotionally charged events that had occurred when she was at that particular weight. At 150, for example, she recalled the death of her father. Swarms of painful memories poured out—her father's affectionate manner, his fight with cancer, how alone she felt when he died, and how afraid she was of dying the same way. There was one insight after another, until Betty became a happier, healthier, more confident woman. Then, after fifteen months, the therapist and his patient had their final session together. They reminisced about the past, looked forward to the future, embraced, and said goodbye.

As this story illustrates, the treatment of mental distress is not only a science but an art. Whereas some psychologists study the human mind and behavior in experiments and other types of research, practicing clinical psychologists help people cope with their problems. Sometimes the goal is to treat the symptoms of a specific disorder; at other times it is to foster growth in those of us who are "normal" but not happy or content with the state of our lives. Either way, this chapter addresses three questions: (1) What treatments are available to people in need of psychological help? (2) Are the treatments effective? and (3) If so, why?

PERSPECTIVES ON TREATMENT

The subject matter of this chapter cuts to the heart of clinical psychology and the study of personality, disorders, and treatment. The fundamental issue concerns the possibilities and limits of change. In a book entitled *Human Change Processes,* Michael Mahoney (1991) raised three core questions, each simple to ask but more difficult to answer: Can humans change? Can humans help humans change? And are some forms of helping better than others?

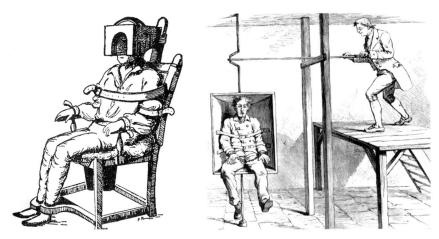

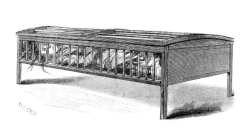

Figure 17.1

Old-Fashioned "Cures" for Mental Illness

In the nineteenth century, many crude devices were used to treat mental illness. Among the more popular were the crib, used to restrain people who were violent; the tranquilizing chair, used to calm those who were manic; and the circulating swing, used to treat depression through high-speed rotation. Twentieth-century gadgets included cold packs, hot steam showers, vibrating helmets, infrared lightbulb cabinets, and electric "mummy bags."

The treatment of mental disorders is far from perfect, but we've come a long way in a few short years (see Figure 17.1). Our prehistoric ancestors believed that people with psychological disorders were inhabited by evil spirits, so they drilled holes in the skull large enough for these spirits to escape. In the seventeenth century, mental disorders were attributed to witchcraft and demonic possession, and "treated" with exorcism, noise making, bloodletting, beating, bitter potions, starvation, and torture. By the eighteenth century, people with mental disorders were considered ill, but were hidden from view—chained to the walls of dark, dungeon-like hospitals called "asylums." Then in the nineteenth century, a spirit of humanitarian reform swept through the United States and Europe. The inmates were unchained, housed in clean rooms with windows, and permitted to walk outside on hospital grounds.

At the turn of the twentieth century, major advances were made on two fronts. One was the finding that hysterical symptoms such as paralysis and blindness could be treated with hypnosis. The other was the discovery that a schizophrenic-like disorder known as general paresis—marked by hallucinations, delusions, personality changes, and death—was caused by syphilis, a sexually transmitted genital infection. These developments now stand as symbols for the two predominant models of treatment: one psychological, the other medical. Today, as we'll see, these two models complement rather than compete with each other.

PSYCHOLOGICAL THERAPIES

The term **psychotherapy** is used to describe all forms of treatment in which a trained professional employs psychological techniques to help persons in need of assistance. Psychotherapy comes in many different forms. The "trained professional" may be a *clinical psychologist* (who attends graduate school, earns a Ph.D. in psychology, and conducts testing, diagnosis, treatment, and research), *psychiatrist* (who attends medical school, receives an M.D., does a residency in psychiatry, and is the only mental health professional who can prescribe drugs), *counseling psychologist* (who receives a Ph.D. in counseling to help people with minor adjustment problems), or

■ **psychotherapy** A term used to describe all forms of treatment in which a trained professional uses psychological techniques to help persons in need of assistance.

psychiatric social worker (who earns a two-year master's degree in social work and special training in counseling). The "person in need of assistance" also varies from one case to another. He or she may suffer from one of the many mental disorders listed in DSM-IV or may simply feel inadequate, lonely, unimportant, or unloved, and want more from life.

There is now a vast array of "psychological techniques" used in the practice of psychotherapy. Indeed, it has been estimated that there are more than 250 brands of psychotherapy to choose from (Herenk, 1980). A small number of therapists, who get too much attention in the media, use "faddish" techniques—for example, insulting patients to shake them up, or encouraging them to scream at the top of their lungs, listen to subliminal taped messages, or "regress" to infancy and the womb. However, the vast majority of therapists are serious professionals who work with individuals, families, and groups, and who are trained in one of the four major approaches: psychoanalytic, behavioral, cognitive, and humanistic. These approaches are described in the following pages.

Psychoanalysis

Imagine you are lying outstretched on a couch, with a soft pillow tucked underneath your head. You stare at the walls and ceiling, noticing subtle streaks of white paint, shadows, razor-thin cracks in the plaster, and dust on the drapes. You fixate on a small, neatly drilled hole in the wall from which a picture must have been hung. As your eyes examine every nook and cranny, however, your mind is elsewhere—in another time and place. You recall the tantrum you had on your first day of school, or the fight your parents had after putting you to bed one night, or the moment you heard that your favorite grandfather died, or the peculiar dream you had the night before, or the way the family used to get together on Thanksgiving to eat, drink, and watch the parade on TV. As an image comes to mind, you talk about it and relive the emotions you had felt. You laugh, you cry, you clench your teeth in anger as you become reabsorbed in the events of your own life. But you're not alone. Sitting behind you, listening to every word you say, commenting from time to time, and passing the Kleenex, is your "analyst."

Orthodox Psychoanalysis   Ever since Josef Breuer and Sigmund Freud (1895) found that people often feel better after purging their minds of material buried in the unconscious, *psychoanalysis* has had a pervasive influence on the treatment of mental disorders. You may recall from Chapter 15 that Breuer treated a young female patient named Anna O. who suffered from hysterical blindness, paralysis of an arm, a nervous cough, and other symptoms of conversion disorder. This case was important in three ways. First, Breuer found that when Anna talked about herself, she sometimes stumbled upon memories that had been repressed for many years. Second, these insights often brought about a relief of her symptoms. Third, Anna became intensely attached to Breuer, eventually causing him, a married man, to terminate their sessions.

From this experience, and others like it, Freud went on to develop psychoanalysis, the first systematic "talking cure." Psychoanalysis is designed to achieve two goals: *catharsis,* a release of bottled-up psychic tension, and

■ **free association** A key technique of psychoanalysis in which patients say whatever comes to mind—freely and without censorship.

insight, or self-understanding. As we will see, these goals are achieved through the therapist's interpretation of three types of behavior: free association, resistance, and transference.

Free Association   For Freud, the principal technique of psychoanalysis was born in 1892 with a patient named Elisabeth. At first Freud had her lie down, close her eyes, think hard about a symptom, and try to recall the moment it started. Meanwhile, he asked pointed questions and pressed his hand against her forehead to help her concentrate. Then at one point, after many futile attempts, Elisabeth had an insight—but concerning a part of her life that was unrelated to the symptom she was trying to recall. Freud was taken by surprise. Why did you wait so long to reveal something so important? "I could have told you that the first time, but I didn't think that it was what you wanted," she said (quoted in Jones, 1953, p. 243). Humbled by this turn of events, Freud came up with a new set of rules. From now on, he said, follow your own train of thought. Elisabeth was agreeable but, in turn, asked Freud to stop asking irrelevant questions and pressing on her forehead. This humorous episode marked the first use of **free association,** the backbone of psychoanalysis. In free association, the patient sits back, relaxes, and talks about thoughts, wishes, memories, fantasies, physical sensations, dreams, and whatever else comes to mind—no matter how trivial, embarrassing, or crazy it may seem. No censorship, no interruption. In the meantime, the analyst listens attentively, trying to put together the pieces of an emerging puzzle.

Beginning with Freud's (1900) classic, *The Interpretation of Dreams,* psychoanalysts have encouraged patients to free associate about their dreams—the "royal road to the unconscious." This emphasis is based on the theory that pent-up psychic energy from repressed sexual and aggressive impulses is released when we're asleep, though in ways that are confusing and hard to interpret. In other words, the dreams you remember in the morning are well-disguised expressions of deep, hidden impulses. Thus, as patients describe the conscious *manifest* content of dreams, their analysts are busy trying to unmask the underlying *latent* content—what the dreams "really" mean (see Chapter 4).

To encourage patients to relax, Freud had them recline on the couch in his study while he sat out of view. You can see this couch by visiting Freud's historic home in Vienna.

"Do you think your failure to bloom could be caused not just by improper location but also by a fear of having your blooms compared with those of other African violets?"

[Drawing by H. Martin; © 1992 The New Yorker Magazine, Inc.]

"In a sonata all the themes that are going to appear are stated at the beginning. . . . One might think of one's first relationships as the themes of one's interpersonal life and all subsequent relationships as the development and recapitulation of those themes."

MICHAEL KAHN

■ **resistance** In psychoanalysis, the tendency for patients to actively block or "resist" psychologically painful insights.

■ **transference** In psychoanalysis, the tendency of patients to displace intense feelings for others onto the therapist.

Resistance Free association was only the beginning. Right from the start, Freud noticed something curious. His patients could talk for long periods of time and produce endless streams of ideas, but they often would not face unpleasant memories. On the brink of an important but painful insight, patients would stop, go blank, lose their train of thought, change the subject, criticize the therapist, "forget" the next appointment, make jokes, call it quits, or seek another therapist. Freud called this pattern of avoidance **resistance**, and concluded that it was part of an unconscious defensive process designed to keep threatening personal insights under lock and key—and out of awareness.

In psychoanalysis, resistance is a double-edged sword. On the one hand, it slows down the course of therapy, and may even bring it to a grinding halt. On the other hand, it signals that the patient is on the verge of exposing a psychic raw nerve, and that therapy is moving in the right direction. Where there's smoke, there's fire; where there's resistance, there's emotional turmoil. The analyst's goal is to make the patient aware of the resistance by carefully interpreting what it means. "I notice you never want to talk about your mother" and "Why do you always make jokes when you discuss your illness?" are the kinds of interpretive statements analysts make in order to work through problems and nudge patients toward difficult self-insights.

Transference Also critical in psychoanalysis is the therapist-patient relationship. Just as Anna O. became attached to Breuer, many of Freud's patients developed intense, unsolicited feelings toward him. Freud assumed he was not the real target of these passions, and concluded that people have an unconscious tendency to transfer feelings for parents, siblings, lovers, and other significant persons onto the therapist—a phenomenon he called **transference**. Sometimes the patient reacts with passionate love and affection (positive transference), at other times with hatred, anger, and hostility (negative transference). In both instances, the therapist is merely a convenient substitute for the person for whom these feelings are really meant. In fact, said Freud, therapists need to beware of their own tendency to "countertransfer" feelings they have for others onto patients. In *Love's Executioner,* for example, Yalom (1989) freely admitted that when he started to treat Betty, the woman who weighed 250 pounds, he had to fight a lifelong aversion to people who are overweight—an aversion he traced to his own childhood.

As with resistance, transference is a welcome disruption in psychoanalysis. It may slow down and complicate matters, but it also provides a window to the unconscious. When deeply rooted feelings are awakened in therapy, patients can more easily slip into the past and recall events from childhood. Again, the goal is for people to gain insight into their current relationships—to understand why they are attracted to certain kinds of people, or why they shy away from commitments, need constant reassurance, or become fiercely possessive and jealous. To foster these kinds of transference-related insights, the psychoanalyst sits behind the patient, maintains a shadowy presence, and then interprets the transference reaction. Examples include: "You always seem to want my approval, the way you must have needed your mother's approval" and "You're angry because I won't tell you how to run your life, and you think I don't care. Is that why you're always upset with your boyfriend? He isn't bossy, so you think he doesn't care?"

Based on material provided by free association, resistance, and transference, psychoanalysts seek insight through a process of interpretation (see Table 17.1). The key factor in this endeavor is timing. Someone who is emotionally prepared to face painful memories and conflicts will feel relieved and enlightened by an interpretation. But for someone who is not, the technique will backfire, heightening anxiety and resistance. Psychoanalysis is thus a long, hard, and expensive process—typically requiring four or five 50-minute sessions a week, costing about a hundred dollars a

Table 17.1

Psychoanalysis in Action

Taken from an actual therapy session, this dialogue illustrates one psychoanalyst's use of interpretation (Baker, 1985, pp. 41–42).

Patient:	You know, I really didn't want to come today. I just don't seem to have very much to talk about. (long silence) I'm just not really sure what to say; maybe you can suggest a topic.
Therapist:	You'd like for me to tell you what to talk about, to give you some structure?
Patient:	Sure, after all, that's what I'm paying you for. (pause) It seems that you just sit there all the time not saying anything. I'm not really sure this is helping very much.
Therapist:	Perhaps we should talk about your feeling that I'm not giving you what you want.
Patient:	It's not so much want, it's what I *need*. You always just sit there; you never give me advice; you never tell me what to do. I thought therapy would be different from this.
Therapist:	You expected more?
Patient:	I expected *something*. You know, it's a little irritating to pay out good money and feel like you're not getting your money's worth.
Therapist:	So it feels as if I'm cheating or depriving you in some way. Perhaps that is why you're feeling so angry today.
Patient:	I'm not feeling angry. (pause) Well . . . I guess I am a little. In fact, I really didn't even want to come.
Therapist:	Perhaps there's a relationship between those feelings . . . feeling angry and then wanting to withdraw.
Patient:	You know, I think I do that a lot. I feel uncomfortable being angry at you. It doesn't seem justified somehow and yet I do feel angry and feel like I just want to not come and not talk; or not pay my bill or do something to get even. I guess I do that a lot. I mean, when I get angry, I get quiet and I just don't talk.
Therapist:	Perhaps that is why you were so quiet at the beginning of the hour. It was a way of indirectly letting me know that you were angry, while at the same time protecting yourself and me from that anger and your fears of what it might do.
Patient:	I guess you are right. I *am* afraid of anger and I have a lot of difficulty letting people know directly when I feel they have done something bad or hurt me in some way. So I just . . . withdraw.

session, and lasting for many years. It's interesting that Freud's patients seldom stayed in psychoanalysis for more than a year. Since then, however, the process has become very long and drawn out (it's been said that analysis used to last a year and marriage a lifetime, but that now it's the opposite). If you ever saw the movie *Sleeper,* you'll recall that after spending two hundred years in a frozen state, Woody Allen wakes up and says, in a semi-serious tone, "If I had kept seeing my analyst, I'd almost be cured by now!"

Brief Psychoanalytic Therapies   Inspired by neo-Freudian theorists such as Jung, Adler, Fromm, Horney, and Erikson (see Chapter 15), and by a practical need for a shorter-term, less costly form of treatment, most contemporary psychoanalytic therapists use modified, nonorthodox techniques. They still share key aspects of Freud's approach—such as an appreciation for the importance of past experiences and unconscious processes. In general, however, these newer therapies are briefer, less intense, and more flexible. Sessions are usually scheduled once a week and last for a limited period of time—usually just a few months, rather than years. To cut to the heart of matters and accelerate the therapy process, many analysts now sit face-to-face with their patients and take a more active conversational role, often asking direct questions and prompting certain lines of inquiry. Unconscious resistance is still interpreted, and transference is still considered a useful vehicle for insight, but today's analyst tries to minimize these reactions, or else facilitate the process through role-playing exercises. There is also less time spent plunging into the past, and more time spent addressing current life problems (Alexander & French, 1946; Crits-Christoph & Barber, 1991; Davanloo, 1980; Luborsky, 1984).

Controversies in Psychoanalysis   Ever since Freud claimed that we are driven from birth by lustful desires and aggressive impulses, and are at the mercy of unconscious forces beyond our control, psychoanalysis as a theory has been steeped in controversy. It is also controversial as a form of treatment. There are three main criticisms. The first, aimed at orthodox psychoanalysis, is that it takes too long and is too expensive, available to only the most affluent among us. The second is that psychoanalytic interpretations can never be disproved. If a therapist interprets a patient's late arrival as a sign of resistance and the patient accepts this interpretation, it stands confirmed. Yet if the patient emphatically denies the interpretation, the denial itself becomes proof of resistance, also "confirming" the initial interpretation ("heads I win, tails you lose"). A third criticism is that psychoanalysis is not truly therapeutic, that people are no better off after they come out than before they went in. As we will see later, this claim is unfair. Studies show that psychoanalytic therapy, like other types of psychotherapy, is generally effective. But must people dive head first into the past and open old wounds in order to solve current life problems? Many psychologists and psychiatrists do not think so. Psychoanalysis is thus on the decline, leaving many of its adherents in the United States wondering, "Is there a future for American psychoanalysis?" (Kirsner, 1990).

Despite the criticisms, psychoanalysis has left a permanent imprint on clinical practice. Therapists from all theoretical orientations agree that resistance is a typical behavior among psychotherapy patients (Mahoney, 1991). Indeed, research shows that defensiveness and self-deception in general are normal, often adaptive parts of human nature (Lockard & Paulhus,

1988; Taylor, 1989). Many practitioners also agree that transference, and other aspects of the therapist-patient relationship, are key to success (Horvath & Luborsky, 1993; Kahn, 1991). In addition, studies support Freud's claim that patients bring into therapy unique, consistent, and largely unconscious interaction styles from past relationships (Luborsky & Crits-Christoph, 1990). Finally, many of us now take for granted the psychoanalytic assumptions that mental disorders are often rooted in childhood, that deep-seated conflicts are often repressed, and that insight has therapeutic value.

Behavior Therapy

Psychoanalysis is an intensive form of therapy in which people are opened up, taken apart, and reassembled before they can be cured. In this approach, you have to get to the root of the "problem" in order to eliminate the "symptoms." Then along came Pavlov, Watson, Skinner, and other behaviorists. Armed with the principles of classical and operant conditioning, they argued that psychological disorders are learned by reinforcement, and can be unlearned in the same manner. Afraid to fly? Depressed? Think everyone is out to get you? Well, said the behaviorists, forget the past, ignore your dreams, keep unconscious urges in the closet, and stop waiting for pearls of wisdom to fall from the lips of your all-knowing analyst. Instead, tell me what it is you want to change about yourself. Then we'll make a list of concrete behavioral goals and try to achieve these goals as quickly as we can. Eliminate the symptom, and you have solved the problem.

Whether one has a phobia, test anxiety, a sexual disorder, or an inability to stop smoking, it can very often be treated by classical and operant conditioning, and other well-established principles of learning. In a book on behavioral techniques, 158 specific procedures were described, including "anger control therapy," "verbal satiation therapy," "implosion therapy," and "dry pants training" (Bellack & Hersen, 1985). Taken together, these numerous techniques are known as **behavior therapy** (Bandura, 1969; Wolpe, 1982; O'Leary & Wilson, 1987; Emmelkamp, 1994).

Classical Conditioning Therapies As we saw in Chapter 5, *classical conditioning* is the Pavlovian process by which a once-neutral stimulus (a bell) comes to elicit an emotional or behavioral response (salivation) after being paired repeatedly with an unconditioned stimulus (food) that already has the power to elicit that reaction. In 1920, Watson and Rayner used this model to train a baby to react with fear to a white rat by pairing the rat with a loud, aversive noise. If phobias and other disorders develop through classical conditioning, suggested Watson, then perhaps they can be erased in the same manner.

Flooding If Watson was right, it should be possible to treat psychological disorders through *extinction*. After repeated presentations of a bell without food, Pavlov's dogs eventually stopped salivating in response to the sound. Similarly, people who confront a fearful situation without a negative consequence should come to realize that the fear is unfounded. This idea gave rise to **flooding**—a behavioral technique in which a person is exposed to or

■ **behavior therapy** A set of techniques used to modify disordered thoughts, feelings, and behaviors through the principles of learning.

■ **flooding** A behavior therapy technique in which the patient is continually exposed to a fear-provoking stimulus until the anxiety becomes extinct.

CLINICAL PSYCHOLOGY   Law

Putting Repressed Memories on Trial

It is sometimes ironic how history repeats itself. It was the year 1900. While formulating his theory of psychoanalysis, Freud was listening to patients recount horrifying stories of early childhood abuse. One after another, they told of rape, incest, beatings, and other traumas, often sexual in nature. But Freud soon came to believe that at least some of the stories he was being told were false, figments of overactive imaginations. This development was a terrible blow, and Freud felt betrayed—until he realized that patients were not really lying to him. They truly believed that the incidents they talked about had happened.

Turning the clock forward, we find ourselves in the year 1990. In Redwood City, California, fifty-one year-old George Franklin stood trial for the murder of an eight-year-old girl that had taken place more than twenty years earlier. For years, the crime was left unsolved. Then Eileen Franklin, the victim's friend who was also eight years old at the time, came forward to implicate the defendant, her father. According to Eileen, she had totally forgotten the incident and just recently started to have flashbacks. She now remembered playing with her friend in the family van when the attack took place. She remembered seeing her father sexually assault the girl and raise his hands up, holding a rock. And she remembered screams, a struggle, and the sight of her friend covered with blood, with a smashed silver ring on her finger. Based solely on her testimony, Franklin was convicted of first-degree murder and sentenced to prison. It was the first time that someone had been tried and convicted of murder on the basis of a newly recovered repressed memory.

The Franklin conviction was followed by a barrage of new allegations. Actress Roseanne Barr Arnold recalled in therapy that her mother had abused her for six years from the time she was an infant. Other victims soon appeared in courtrooms and on daytime TV talk shows to tell horrifying tales of abuse, often at home, sometimes in the context of satanic cult rituals. In many states, the laws that kept people from bringing cases forward after long periods of time were modified for those who recovered long-lost memories. As a result, thousands of men and women filed criminal charges and multimillion-dollar lawsuits against family members and others in their distant past. The response was an emotional backlash against the use of repressed memories. The mothers, fathers, and grandparents accused in many cases sought help and formed the False Memory Syndrome Foundation, a nationwide support group with thousands of members. These people, too, had stories to tell—about having their lives, families, and reputations torn apart by false accusations. Many repressed-memory accusers withdrew their claims, and some even joined their families in suing the therapists who brought these so-called memories out in the first place (Jaroff, 1993).

Childhood sex abuse is a crime that can have devastating and lasting consequences for mental health—and it may be far more common than was previously realized. To be sure, people sometimes repress traumatic events, and these memories sometimes surface years later, to be corroborated by independent evidence (Daro, 1988). But what should be done when there is no independent evidence? On one side of the debate are Ellen Bass and Laura Davis (1988), authors of *The*

"flooded" with an anxiety-provoking stimulus until the anxiety is extinguished. Sometimes the person is told to imagine the dreaded stimulus; at other times the experience is firsthand. Someone with agoraphobia (a fear of being in public places), for example, might be taken by a reassuring therapist into a shopping mall and kept there for hours until the fear subsides. This procedure is repeated for several weeks, until the anxiety is completely diminished. Flooding is generally effective, but success is not guaranteed. Some people refuse to confront their feared situation; others agree to, but then panic, escape, and become even more anxious; still others complete the program but later experience a relapse (Barlow, 1988).

Systematic Desensitization   Another powerful antidote for anxiety is *counterconditioning*—a procedure in which a person is trained to react to a feared stimulus with a positive response that is incompatible with anxiety.

In November 1993, Steven Cook (left) filed a lawsuit against Cardinal Joseph Bernardin (right) in which he claimed that Bernardin had sexually molested him many years ago. In March 1994, however, Cook dropped the charges when he realized that his "memories" (which had been "recovered" under hypnosis) were false. "My life will never be the same because of this," said Bernardin afterward.

Courage to Heal, a book that is often described as the "bible" for the survivors of incest and childhood sex abuse. Though not trained in psychology, Bass and Davis provide their readers with a list of symptoms to watch for, such as anxiety, depression, loss of appetite, intimacy problems, and dependence. And when a reader is in doubt? "If you are unable to remember any specific instances. . . but still have a feeling that something abusive happened to you, it probably did" (p. 21). On the other side, Elizabeth Loftus (1993) warns that often a person's memories for remote past events are not memories at all, but images and ideas suggested by therapists eager to find the source of a patient's distress. In some cases, pa-

tients who were led to believe they were abused later concluded that their newly found memories were false (Jaroff, 1993).

Is it really possible for one person to plant a false trauma memory into the mind of another? In a compelling demonstration, Loftus and Coan (in press) recruited subjects, contacted a close family member for each, and arranged for that person to "remind" the subject of a time he or she was lost in a shopping mall. For example, a fourteen-year-old subject named Chris was told by his older brother Jim that he got lost in a mall when he was five years old and was found crying by a tall older man wearing a flannel shirt. A few days later, Chris "recalled" being scared, being asked by an older man if he was lost, and being scolded afterward by his mother. Then two weeks later, he described more fully what had happened: "I was with you guys for a second and I think I went over to look at the toy store. . . I thought I was never going to see my family again. I was really scared, you know. And then this old man, I think he was wearing blue flannel, came up to me . . . he was kind of old. He was kind of bald on top . . . he had like a ring of gray hair . . . and he had glasses."

As judges and juries struggle to sort the facts from the fictions, it is important to balance our concerns for both the victims of child abuse and the victims of false accusations. On the one hand, Freud was right in alerting psychologists to the powerful forces of repression. On the other hand, researchers have found that people can seldom, if ever, recall the first three years of life—and that old memories are often reconstructed in light of new information (see Chapter 6). Are repressed memories authentic and accurate? If *you* were on the Franklin jury, or on one in a similar trial, how would you vote? As the debate rages on, it is becoming clearer and clearer that these questions can be answered only on a case-by-case basis and with the help of independent evidence.

■ **systematic desensitization** A behavior therapy technique used to treat phobias and other anxiety disorders by pairing gradual exposure to an anxiety-provoking situation with relaxation.

Mary Cover Jones (1924), a student of Watson's, sought to demonstrate that anxiety could be erased by associating a feared stimulus with a pleasurable experience. Specifically, Jones treated a three-year-old boy named Peter who had developed an intense fear of rabbits and other furry animals. One afternoon, Jones took Peter into a room with a caged rabbit, sat him at a table, and fed him milk and crackers. This routine was duplicated several times, and each time the rabbit was moved closer as the boy devoured his snack. After a few weeks, Peter was holding the rabbit on his lap, stroking it with one hand and eating with the other. Through the process of stimulus *generalization*, he shed his fear of other animals as well.

Thirty-four years after Jones reported on this case, Joseph Wolpe (1958) devised **systematic desensitization**, a technique that is widely used in the treatment of phobias and other anxiety disorders. Based on the fact that a person cannot simultaneously feel anxious and relaxed, systematic desensitization is designed to condition people to respond to a feared stimulus with calm, not anxiety. There are three steps in this procedure: (1) relaxation training, (2) the construction of an anxiety hierarchy, and (3) gradual exposure. To see how systematic desensitization works, imagine that you are afraid to fly, and that whenever you see an airplane on a runway, hear the thunderous noise of its engines, smell the fuel, or feel the vibrations, your heart races and you break into a cold sweat. You make an appointment with a behavior therapist, and before you know it you're ready to begin.

The first step is to learn how to relax in response to a cue from the therapist. This is accomplished through *relaxation training*—a procedure in which you are taught to concentrate on what it feels like to tighten and then relax various muscle groups throughout the body. Try it. Sit back comfortably, loosen your clothing, take your shoes off, take a deep breath, and let your muscles get loose and heavy. Now wrinkle up your forehead, wrinkle it tighter, tighter again. Hold it for a few seconds. Now stop tensing, relax, and smooth it out. Picture your entire forehead and scalp becoming smoother. . . . Now frown and crease your brows. Close your eyes, tighter and tighter. Feel the tension. Now relax, and let go. Keep your eyes closed gently, and notice the relaxation. . . . Now clench your jaw and purse your lips, tighter and tighter. Press your tongue hard against the roof of your mouth, and feel the tension. All right, now relax. Relax your jaw, loosen your lips, let your mouth hang open, and let your tongue return to a comfortable position. Notice how relaxed you are all over. Let all your muscles go limp and feel the smoothness and relaxation in your scalp, forehead, eyes, mouth, and lips. See how it feels to be relaxed.

The next step is to come up with an *anxiety hierarchy,* a graduated sequence of fear-provoking situations that you rate on a 100-point scale, ranging from mild to terrifying. In your case, the hierarchy might begin with "You see a newspaper ad for discount airfares," and progress to "You look out the window as the plane leaves the ground" (see Table 17.2).

Prepared with the ability to relax on command and with a hierarchy of fear-provoking situations, you brace yourself for the third and final step. At this point, the therapist talks you into a state of relaxation and guides you through a gradual series of *exposures.* You're instructed to close your eyes and imagine the mildest fear-provoking situation in the hierarchy. If you keep your cool while visualizing this scene, you move on to the next item on the list. If you begin to get anxious, however, the therapist will instruct you to tune out and relax. The scene is then revisited, until it ceases to arouse anxiety. Lasting several sessions, this routine is repeated for all items in the hierarchy, until you are "cured" of the fear. This technique, in which the person mentally confronts the anxiety-provoking stimulus, is known as *imaginal exposure.* To ensure long-term success, however, many therapists conclude with "in vivo" desensitization, by having the person confront the feared situations in real life. The ultimate test of whether you have conquered the fear of flying is in your ability to board an airplane, stay calm during the flight, and make the return trip later on.

Systematic desensitization is a common and effective form of therapy, and has been used to treat the fear of dogs, mice, snakes, blood, heights, open spaces, crowds, balloons, feathers, violins, dentists, tunnels, needles, and eating in public (Marks, 1987)—sometimes in a single session (Ost, 1989; Zinbarg et al., 1992). According to Wolpe (1982), systematic desensitization works through counterconditioning, by associating a new re-

Table 17.2

A Sample Anxiety Hierarchy

The scenes in this hierarchy are typical of those used in the systematic desensitization of a fear of flying. The numbers to the left of each item represent one patient's subjective rating of how anxiety-provoking a situation is, on a scale from 0 to 100.

5	You see a newspaper ad for discount airfares.
10	You see a TV commercial for an airline.
20	A group of friends talks about arranging a trip that requires flying.
30	You visit a travel agent to make plane reservations.
35	The week before the trip, you get your plane tickets in the mail.
40	The night before the trip, you pull out your suitcase to pack.
55	You park your car near the departure terminal.
60	You check in, and the agent asks if you want a window or aisle seat.
65	The announcement is made that your flight is ready for passenger boarding.
70	You're on line, with ticket in hand, ready to board.
80	You are in your seat, and the flight attendant says, "Fasten your seatbelts for takeoff."
90	You feel the plane begin to roll down the runway.
95	You look out the window as the plane leaves the ground.

sponse (relaxation) to the feared stimulus. However, others find that exposure per se is all that's needed—with or without the relaxation (Rachman, 1990). Many home-bound agoraphobics, for example, benefit from an *in vivo exposure* treatment in which they are taken by their therapist, spouse, or a companion into crowded streets, shopping malls, and other progressively difficult situations (Foa & Kozak, 1986). Similarly, behavior therapists can sometimes treat people with an obsessive-compulsive disorder by putting them into situations that evoke obsessive thoughts, but then preventing them from carrying out their compulsive rituals (Emmelkamp, 1982). This technique has also been used to help women with bulimia, an eating disorder that is characterized by cycles of binge eating and purging. That is, the women are fed but prevented from vomiting (Wilson et al., 1986). In all cases, "exposure and response prevention" causes an initial build-up of anxiety that eventually subsides, often with lasting success (see Figure 17.2).

Sometimes it helps to watch the harmless exposure of others to an anxiety-provoking situation. In a study on the therapeutic effects of *modeling,* Albert Bandura and his colleagues (1969) had persons with snake phobias observe a filmed or live model handling snakes, and found that these exposures—especially to the live model—increased the extent to which subjects were able to approach a live snake without anxiety. In another study, medical patients who needed "hyperbaric oxygen therapy" (a stressful form of treatment in which they are locked for an hour in a narrow chamber containing pressurized oxygen) were more relaxed, completed more prescribed treatments, and required fewer days in the hospital when they first watched a filmed model coping with the same situation than when they did not (Allen et al., 1989). Even more effective is *participant modeling,* which combines passive exposure to a model with gradual practice (Ost et al., 1991).

Figure 17.2

Therapeutic Effects of Exposure and Response Prevention

A woman with a compulsive handwashing ritual was hospitalized and permitted for a week to wash as desired (baseline). During the next week she was told to try to break the habit (instruction). This was followed by three days of denied access to running water (response prevention), another instruction, and another round of response prevention. This treatment was highly effective. After just a few weeks, the woman was washing less often and getting fewer urges (Mills et al., 1973).

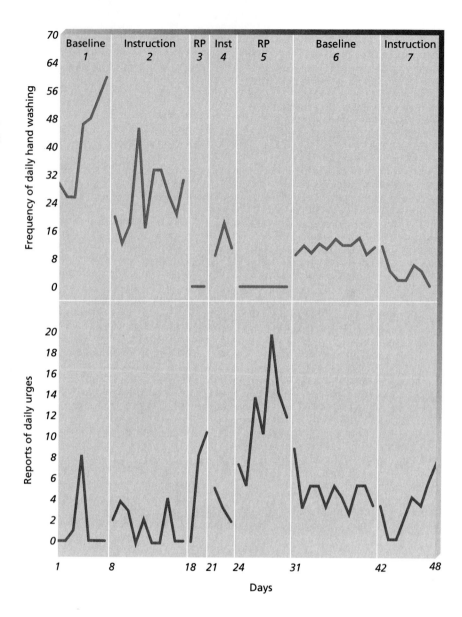

■ **aversion therapy** A behavior therapy technique for classically conditioning people to react with aversion to alcohol, tobacco, and other harmful substances.

Aversive Conditioning The purpose of systematic desensitization is to get people to stay calm in safe situations. When people are attracted to activities that are harmful—smoking, drinking, overeating, and other bad habits—just the opposite effect is sought. In these cases, behavior therapists use **aversion therapy,** a technique designed to elicit an aversive, rather than pleasurable, reaction to a harmful stimulus.

In the treatment of alcoholism, the goal of aversion therapy is to cause heavy drinkers to feel sick to the stomach at the sight, smell, and taste of liquor. The alcoholic is taken to a darkened room (one designed to look much like a bar), injected with antebuse (a drug that causes nausea), and served beer, wine, gin, whiskey, and other favorites. After a few minutes, the person vomits uncontrollably. This treatment generally results in total abstinence after five or six visits, followed by an occasional booster session (Cannon et al., 1981). In a study of 685 hospitalized alcoholics treated with aversion therapy, 63 percent were "dry" after one year, and 33 percent were still dry after three full years (Wiens & Menustik, 1983). Aversion

Using the "rapid smoking technique," behavior therapists force smokers to puff every few seconds for a prolonged period of time until they feel sick and disgusted with cigarettes.

therapy is similarly used to help cigarette smokers who can't seem to break the habit. In what is known as the "rapid-smoking technique," the person is forced to smoke continuously, taking a puff every few seconds. Eventually, the smoker feels so sick that "I don't ever want to see another cigarette for the rest of my life!" This procedure is repeated several times, often with lasting success (Lichtenstein, 1982; Glasgow & Lichtenstein, 1987).

Operant Conditioning Therapies   While some behaviorists were discovering the principles of reinforcement by training lab animals to peck keys, press bars, and jump over barriers for food pellets, water droplets, or the termination of electric shock, others began using the methods of *operant conditioning* for clinical purposes. On the assumption that all the world's a Skinner box, *reinforcement* can be used to promote behaviors that are desirable and to extinguish those that are not.

Reward and Punishment   It is sometimes necessary to establish clear reinforcement programs to treat people who are severely disordered. In one case, for example, a female patient with schizophrenia wore 25 pounds of clothing, including several dresses, sweaters, shawls, turbans, stockings, and coats. To control this bizarre behavior, the therapist in charge required this woman to weigh in at the door of the dining room before meals. Whether she was then allowed to enter and eat was contingent on a steadily decreasing clothing weight. After thirteen weeks, the problem was solved (Ayllon, 1963). Sometimes, in institutional settings, the staff establishes large-scale reinforcement programs called *token economies*. In a token economy, patients earn plastic chips or "tokens" for engaging in desirable behaviors (such as prompt attendance at group therapy meetings). Like money, these tokens can then be used to purchase candy, TV privileges, weekend passes, books, fluffy pillows, and other commodities (Ayllon & Azrin, 1968). In general, this is an effective way to shape behavior—not only in psychiatric wards but also in classrooms, homes for juvenile delinquents, and other settings (Kazdin, 1982).

Reward usually produces impressive changes, but punishment is sometimes necessary to eliminate dangerous, self-destructive behavior. In one study, for example, punishment was used on nineteen autistic preschoolers who were uncommunicative, and who injured themselves by pulling out hair, biting chunks of skin, and banging their heads against the wall. With help from their parents, these children were put in a two-year home treatment program in which they were ignored, interrupted, or slapped on the thigh whenever they engaged in violent, self-abusive acts. By the first grade, nine of them were functioning normally in school, a remarkable accomplishment compared to those not treated with punishment, and in light of previous failures with similar children (Lovaas, 1987).

Biofeedback   Yoga specialist Swami Rama once astonished psychologists by proving in controlled laboratory tests that he could voluntarily slow down or speed up his pulse rate, stop his heart from pumping blood for 17 seconds, raise or lower the temperature in his hand, and alter his brain-wave patterns. Is it possible? Can people control their physiological behavior? Absolutely. In 1969, Neil Miller found that heart rates in animals could be conditioned to increase or decrease in response to rewarding,

The Behavioral Treatment of Headaches

Have you ever had a headache so excruciating that you had to just lie down and close your eyes? If so, you're not alone. Surveys reveal that more than 90 percent of all adolescents and young adults have at least one headache per year (Linet et al., 1989). In fact, between 10 and 20 percent of respondents said "yes" to the question, "Do you have a headache today?" (Rasmussen et al., 1991). For most people, these are infrequent, mild, and easily treated with aspirins and rest in a dark, quiet room. But an estimated 11 million Americans suffer from headaches that are frequent, severe, and disabling (Stewart et al., 1992).

There are more than a hundred different kinds of headaches. The two most common are migraines and tension types. *Migraine* headaches tend to strike several times a month, usually on one side of the head, and often around the eye. They are accompanied by throbbing pain, nausea and vomiting, and a heightened sensitivity to noise, light, and physical exertion. In contrast, *tension-type* headaches are characterized by feelings of muscle tightness on both sides, of-

ten in the back of the neck or forehead. Studies show that headaches are more common among women than men (Stewart et al., 1992). They may be caused by such factors as high blood pressure, stress, too much or too little sleep, heat or cold, eyestrain, food allergies, alcohol, high altitude, and menstruation. Mild tension headaches can usually be treated with analgesics. For people who suffer from a chronic barrage of headaches, however, overuse of aspirin and other pain killers can trigger even more headaches and lose some of their impact over time (Hatch, 1993).

As an alternative, behaviorally oriented psychologists have successfully trained headache sufferers in the use of progressive muscle relaxation training and biofeedback. In one series of studies, for example, Edward Blanchard and his colleagues showed that biofeedback can help people with tension-type headaches. In some cases, patients are provided with electromyographic (EMG) recordings of muscle tension in the face and scalp. For example, they may watch a light on an instrument panel that brightens as the muscles in the forehead,

■ **biofeedback** An operant procedure in which people learn to control heart rate and other physiological processes by receiving "feedback" about their internal states.

■ **social skills training** A form of behavior therapy designed to teach interpersonal skills through modeling, rehearsal, and reinforcement (e.g., assertiveness training).

pleasurable brain stimulation. As an outgrowth of this research, psychologists developed **biofeedback,** a procedure by which people learn how to control their own autonomic processes by receiving continuous information or "feedback" in the form of visual or auditory displays. With the aid of electronic sensors attached to parts of the body and an instrument that records and amplifies the various signals, people can monitor and eventually regulate not only their heart rate but also blood pressure, skin temperature, gastric acidity, hormonal secretions, and muscular tension.

Today, behavior therapists use biofeedback in the treatment of hypertension, chronic back pain, ulcers, bedwetting, and other health problems (Hatch et al., 1987). In one series of studies, Edward Blanchard and his colleagues showed that biofeedback can help people with tension-related migraine headaches. In some cases, the headache sufferers are provided with electromyographic (EMG) recordings of muscle tension in the forehead (for example, they might watch a light that brightens as these muscles tighten and dims as they relax), enabling them over time to control the EMG displays by relaxing the right muscles (see box). In other cases, sensors are attached to a finger, and a beeping signal slows in rhythm as temperature rises. With experience, people can learn to raise finger temperature, which means greater blood flow in the limb—away from the head. Overall, these forms of biofeedback training seem to benefit more than 50 percent of tension headache sufferers on a long-term basis (Blanchard, 1992; Blanchard et al., 1982).

neck, or upper back tighten and dims as these muscles relax. Over time, this feedback enables the patient to control the EMG displays by learning to relax the right muscles (see figure). Another approach, typically used in the treatment of migraine headaches, is to provide patients with thermal biofeedback. In this procedure, sensors are attached to a finger and a beeping signal slows in rhythm as temperature rises. With experience, people learn to warm the finger, or even a hand or foot, thus bringing greater blood flow to that limb—and away from the head. Overall, biofeedback benefits more than 50 percent of tension headache sufferers on a permanent, long-term basis (Blanchard, 1992, 1994). These results compare favorably with those produced by drug treatments—yet without any adverse side effects.

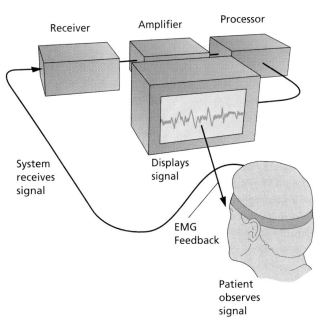

Biofeedback and the Tension Headache
Using biofeedback, a headache sufferer learns to relax the forehead muscles by monitoring EMG recordings of muscle tension in this region. Although biofeedback is effective, psychologists have found that relaxation can often be learned without this expensive equipment.

Social Skills Training   For people who are painfully shy, unresponsive, or socially awkward, there is **social skills training**—lessons on how to speak clearly, make eye contact, maintain a comfortable amount of social distance, and respond appropriately to questions (Curran & Monti, 1982). In social skills training, the therapist models the desired behaviors, the patient imitates and rehearses these behaviors in role-playing exercises, and the therapist responds with a combination of praise and constructive criticism. This reinforcement-based therapy produces impressive results. Studies show, for example, that it helps people with schizophrenia to interact with others more easily and to feel more comfortable in public situations (Benton & Schroeder, 1990).

One type of social skills training that is currently popular is *assertiveness training* (Alberti & Emmons, 1986). Imagine you are waiting in a long line for concert tickets, and someone cuts in front of you. Or you are in a movie theater, and the people behind you talk so loud you can't concentrate. Or a friend asks you for a lift to the airport, but you're too busy at the time. Or you take your car in for repairs, but when you pick it up you get a bill that is twice the estimated cost. How would you react in these situations? Would you speak up and assert yourself, or hold your tongue and say nothing? For people who are passive and easily manipulated, assertiveness training—through the use of modeling and reinforcement—teaches people how to protect their own self-interests, resulting in treatment gains that may be enduring (Baggs & Spence, 1990).

Cognitive Therapy

■ **cognitive therapy** A form of psychotherapy in which people are taught to think in more adaptive ways.

■ **rational-emotive therapy (RET)** A form of cognitive therapy in which people are confronted with their irrational, maladaptive beliefs.

"If you keep saying things are going to be bad, you have a good chance of being a prophet."

ISAAC BASHEVIS SINGER

Figure 17.3

Ellis's A-B-C Theory of Emotional Distress
According to Ellis, emotional distress is caused by irrational thoughts and the assumptions people make. This distress, in turn, helps to sustain the irrational beliefs.

Hardcore behaviorists seek to modify maladaptive behavior through the use of classical and operant conditioning. But what matters most, stimulus-response connections and reinforcement per se, or the way we perceive these events? Reflecting psychology's increased interest in information processing, many therapists have turned to a more cognitive, or "rational" approach. The result is **cognitive therapy,** a form of treatment designed to alter the maladaptive ways in which people interpret significant events in their lives (Hollon & Beck, 1994). To the cognitive therapist, "As you think, so shall you feel."

There are different brands of cognitive therapy, but all have certain features in common. Based on the assumption that anxiety, depression, and other emotional disorders spring from the way we think, the goal is for people to open their minds, challenge their assumptions, and think about old problems in new ways. Cognitive therapy is short term, often limited to twenty sessions, and the therapist acts as a partner, friend, and teacher all rolled into one. Sessions are centered on concrete problems, and the therapist maintains a brisk, business-like pace. Among the most prominent pioneers of this approach are Albert Ellis and Aaron Beck.

Rational-Emotive Therapy Though initially trained in psychoanalysis, Albert Ellis (1962, 1993) went on to develop **rational-emotive therapy,** or **RET.** According to Ellis, anxiety, depression, and other forms of mental distress are caused not by upsetting events per se but by the rigid and maladaptive ways in which people construe these events. In other words, A (activating events) gives rise to B (beliefs), which in turn triggers C (emotional consequences). This A-B-C model is illustrated in Figure 17.3. The problem, said Ellis, is that too many of us hold beliefs that set us up for emotional turmoil. "I have to be liked by everyone," "I have to be perfect at whatever I do," and "Everyone gets what they deserve" are common beliefs that Ellis sees as irrational. The solution? "My approach to psychotherapy," said Ellis, "is to zero in as quickly as possible on the client's basic philosophy of life; to get him to see exactly what this is and how it is inevitably self-defeating; and to persuade him to work his ass off, cognitively, emotively and behaviorally, to profoundly change it" (quoted in Warga, 1988, p. 57).

It's not easy to rid people of their lifelong assumptions or to get them to open their minds to new ways of thinking. To meet the task, RET therapists use blunt, confrontational techniques. "Why do you always have to make mountains out of tiny molehills?" "Where is it written that life is supposed to be fair?" "Who says you'll die if your marriage breaks up?" "What makes you think you'll be happier with more money?" are some of the argumentative questions typically asked. RET therapists also encourage

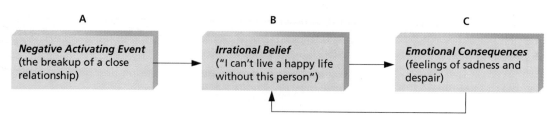

A	**B**	**C**
Negative Activating Event (the breakup of a close relationship)	**Irrational Belief** ("I can't live a happy life without this person")	**Emotional Consequences** (feelings of sadness and despair)

their clients to step out of character, try new behaviors, and engage in "shame exercises." In one case, for example, Ellis instructed a shy young woman to sing at the top of her lungs in the subway, strike up conversations in the supermarket, flirt with men she liked, and even ask them for dates—so she could see that these actions did not bring life to a crashing end. Another part of RET is "psychoeducation," in which clients are lectured on the ABC's of emotional distress and given tapes of their own therapy sessions to review at home, along with booklets and audiotapes that teach the cognitive approach. Ellis himself made a series of self-help tapes, with straight-shooting titles such as "How to Stubbornly Refuse to Be Ashamed of Anything" (Bernard & DiGiuseppe, 1989).

Ellis's approach to psychotherapy may seem unconventional, but as a pioneer of the cognitive approach, he has made a substantial impact on the practice of psychotherapy. Although it is difficult to know precisely the extent to which patients benefit from RET (Haaga & Davison, 1993), studies designed to measure its effects on a patient's later adjustment and well-being have revealed positive results (Engels et al., 1993; Lyons & Woods, 1991).

Beck's Cognitive Therapy Like Ellis, Aaron Beck was trained in psychoanalysis, but he went on to devise a cognitive therapy when he noticed that his patients were filled with self-defeating beliefs (Beck, 1991). People who are depressed, for example, view themselves, their world, and the future through dark-colored glasses. To someone who is depressed, "It's my fault," "I can't do anything right," "It's the story of my life," "I'm a hopeless case" (Beck et al., 1979). People with anxiety disorders also think in ways that are maladaptive. They exaggerate the likelihood that they will fall victim to fatal accidents or diseases, and they engage in "catastrophic thinking" about their own bodies. When panic disorder sufferers become aroused, for example, they often assume they're having a heart attack or a stroke—beliefs that further heighten their anxiety (Beck et al., 1985). Whether the problem is an eating disorder, a sexual disorder, an obsessive-compulsive disorder, hypochondriasis, drug abuse, or a fear of speaking in public, the problem contains an element of irrational thinking that can and should be changed (Beck, 1993).

All cognitive therapists share the same objectives, but they differ in style. Following Ellis, RET therapists hound clients, and forcefully confront them with their irrational beliefs. In contrast, Beck—who has a soft, folksy manner, like an old-fashioned country doctor—uses a gentler, more collaborative approach, helping people by means of a Socratic style of questioning. For a Beckian cognitive therapist, questions commonly asked include, "What's the evidence for this idea?" "Are these facts, or your interpretation of the facts?" "Is there another way to look at the situation?" and "What's the worst that could happen?" (see Table 17.3).

Two additional techniques play an important role in Beck's cognitive therapy. One is to get clients to experience their emotional distress in therapy. In one case, for example, an eighteen-year-old woman who had frequent panic attacks was instructed to hyperventilate, which heightened her physiological arousal and triggered a state of panic. The therapist then helped her to interpret her bodily sensations in noncatastrophic terms. After only four sessions, the woman's panic attacks subsided: "Every time my

Table 17.3

Beck's Cognitive Therapy in Action

The following dialogue between Beck and a client epitomizes Beck's approach to therapy. When the client came in, he was upset over the poor job he did wallpapering a kitchen. Note how Beck gets the client to realize that he was exaggerating his negative appraisal (Beck et al., 1979, pp. 130–131).

Therapist:	Why didn't you rate wallpapering the kitchen as a mastery experience?
Patient:	Because the flowers didn't line up.
Therapist:	You did in fact complete the job?
Patient:	Yes.
Therapist:	Your kitchen?
Patient:	No, I helped a neighbor do his kitchen.
Therapist:	Did he do most of the work?
Patient:	No, I really did almost all of it. He hadn't wallpapered before.
Therapist:	Did anything else go wrong? Did you spill paste all over? Ruin the wallpaper? Leave a big mess?
Patient:	No, the only problem was that the flowers didn't line up.
Therapist:	Just how far off was this alignment of the flowers?
Patient:	(holding his fingers about an eighth of an inch apart) About this much.
Therapist:	On each strip of paper?
Patient:	No . . . on two or three pieces.
Therapist:	Out of how many?
Patient:	About twenty or twenty-five.
Therapist:	Did anyone else notice it?
Patient:	No, in fact my neighbor thought it was great.
Therapist:	Could you see the defect when you stood back and looked at the whole wall?
Patient:	Well, not really.

heart rate increased, I'd say, it's okay, it's no big deal" (Alford et al., 1990, p. 232). Homework assignments are a second important part of Beck's approach. Clients are given books that explain the cognitive basis of their psychological distress. Indeed, research shows that people benefit from reading cognitive-therapy self-help books that communicate the message, "You feel the way you think" (Scogin et al., 1989). Clients are also encouraged to keep a daily log in which they describe the situation they were in, how they felt, what they were thinking, and how rational these thoughts were, when they are upset. These assignments provide a basis for discussion and learning from one session to the next (a sample form is presented in Figure 17.4).

Cognitive therapy is popular among clinical psychologists. As noted, Ellis and Beck are the pioneers of the approach, but there are others as well (Freeman et al., 1989). For example, Donald Meichenbaum (1985) uses "stress-inoculation training" in which people are taught to make optimistic, positive self-statements—to insulate them from stress the way vaccines inoculate us against medical disease. Others in the cognitive tradition focus on problem-solving skills (Turk & Salovey, 1988), feelings of self-efficacy (Goldfried & Robbins, 1982), and behavioral self-control (Mahoney, 1993). Whatever the specific technique may be, cognitive therapy is

DATE	EMOTION(S) What do you feel? How bad is it (0–100)?		SITUATION What were you doing or thinking about?	AUTOMATIC THOUGHTS What exactly were your thoughts? How far do you believe each of them (0–100%)?	
8th December	Tense Angry Despair	90 90 75	Dog next door barked for half an hour	I can't stand this. Why can't they shut up? We've saddled ourselves with a house that will always be spoiled by that dog barking and we'll never get away from it.	80%
9th December	Panic Anxiety	80 80	Car engine overheating; icy road, getting dark	I don't know what to do. It's too dangerous to go on—I'll do something to the car. But I can't stop here or I'll cause an accident.	100% 80% 80%
14th December	Lonely Helpless Unhappy	70 60 90	At work people grumbling, not wanting or trying to make things work	I don't want to be here. I can't leave because I need the money. They don't care, so I have to do everything. I have nothing in common with anyone here.	100% 100% 90% 90%

Figure 17.4

Daily Record of Dysfunctional Thoughts

In Beck's cognitive therapy, people are asked to keep a daily log in which the describe the situation they're in, how they feel, what they're thinking, and how rational these thoughts are when they are upset. These assignments provide a basis for discussion and learning (Fennell, 1989, p. 221).

now the most frequently taught orientation in American clinical psychology graduate programs (Nevid et al., 1987) and is an effective form of treatment for a wide range of problems (Robins & Hayes, 1993)—two sure signs that it's here to stay.

Humanistic Therapy

When Carl Rogers was a young therapist, he noticed that his clients had a strong sense of "self" and an inner drive to grow, improve, and fulfill their potential. All the therapist has to do, he said, is provide warmth, a gentle, guiding hand, and a climate of uncritical acceptance, and clients will find the way to happiness and personal fulfillment. With this simple advice, the humanistic approach to psychotherapy was born. This approach (1) trusts a client's growth instincts, (2) focuses on feelings, not cognitions or behavior, (3) is oriented in the here-and-now, not in the distant past, and (4) makes the client responsible for change. Over the years, two types of humanistic therapy have had a marked impact on clinical practice: person-centered therapy and Gestalt therapy.

Person-Centered Therapy When 415 psychotherapists were asked to name the person who most influenced their work, Carl Rogers was cited more often than anyone else (Smith, 1982). The reason? In a profound way, Rogers redefined the role that a therapist should play—not detective, teacher, or adviser, but a *facilitator* for the client. As Rogers put it, "Therapy is not a matter of doing something *to* the individual or inducing him to do something about himself. It is instead a matter of freeing him for normal growth and development" (1940, p. 7). Believing that people know what's right for themselves, Rogers let his clients call the shots. At various times

■ **person-centered therapy** A humanistic psychotherapy in which a warm and accepting environment is created to foster self-insight and acceptance.

■ **Gestalt therapy** A humanistic form of psychotherapy in which clients are aggressively prompted to express their feelings.

he referred to this approach as "nondirective," "client-centered," and "person-centered."

Person-centered therapy is designed to provide a safe haven for people to clarify their feelings, their sense of who they are, and their hopes for what they would like to become, without fear of punishment or disapproval. To foster this process of self-exploration and discovery, person-centered therapists create a warm and caring relationship with the client. Specifically, they need to exhibit *empathy* (an ability to take the client's perspective in order to understand how he or she feels) and to offer *unconditional positive regard* (an unwavering acceptance of the client as a person)—and these qualities have to be *genuine* (honest and sincere, not put on) for people to open up and reveal themselves. Believing that counselors should not preach right or wrong, interpret problems, or give Dear Abby–like advice, person-centered therapists also use *reflection,* a nondirective, minimum-intervention technique in which the therapist "actively" listens to a client's statements, and responds by paraphrasing what was said, and seeking clarification. No interruption, no analysis, no evaluation. In this way, the therapist serves as a human mirror into which clients can see their feelings reflected clearly and without distortion. If psychotherapy were a dance, the person-centered client would lead, and the therapist would follow (see Table 17.4).

Gestalt Therapy   Have faith in human nature, encourage people to introspect, listen with a sympathetic ear, and guide with a gentle hand, and you are a humanistic psychologist in the mold of Carl Rogers. Focus on feelings that are unconscious, show an interest in dreams, and use techniques that are dramatic and confrontational, and you have **Gestalt therapy,** devised by humanistic psychologist Frederick (Fritz) Perls. Like Rogers, Gestalt therapists try to make people responsible for their own growth and development. In other ways, however, there is little resemblance. Forget about nondirective beating around the bush, Perls used to say. Instead, put clients on the "hot seat." When they speak in ways that are not brutally honest—by slipping into the past to avoid the present, or by talking in general, abstract terms rather than in first-person—they should be challenged. "Do you really *need* to stay in this abusive relationship, or do you *want* to?" "Do you *have* to work for seven days a week, or do you *choose* to?" "Is it that you *can't* say no, or that you *won't*?" "Why do you squirm in your seat, fold your arms, and cross your legs every time you say your sex life is fine?" "When you say it's hard for *people* to express anger, what you really mean is that *you* find it hard to show *your* anger. If that's what you mean, say so!" (Perls et al., 1951; Perls, 1969).

Group Therapy Approaches

In the case study described at the start of this chapter, Yalom (1989) put Betty, his patient, into a therapy group. She felt isolated, craved companionship, and needed a new perspective. Betty resisted the idea at first, but went along. It worked like a charm. At one point, a young man named Carlos revealed to the group that he was dying of cancer, the disease that had

Table 17.4

Person-Centered Therapy in Action

The following dialogue between Carl Rogers and a young man, who is upset over his relationship with his mother, illustrates the technique of reflection. Note how skillfully Rogers helped his client clarify his feelings toward his stepfather. Without prompting, he moved from a blunt statement of mutual hatred, to one of unilateral hatred, to an expression of respect and the reasons for that respect (Raskin, 1985, pp. 167–168).

Client:	You see I have a stepfather.
Therapist:	I see.
Client:	Let's put it this way. My stepfather and I are not on the happiest terms in the world. And so, when he states something and, of course, she goes along, and I stand up and let her know that I don't like what he is telling me, well, she usually gives in to me.
Therapist:	I see.
Client:	Sometimes, and sometimes it's just the opposite.
Therapist:	But part of what really makes for difficulty is the fact that you and your stepfather, as you say, are not . . . the relationship isn't completely rosy.
Client:	Let's just put it this way, I hate him and he hates me. It's that way.
Therapist:	But you really hate him and you feel he really hates you.
Client:	Well, I don't know if he hates me or not, but I know one thing, I don't like him whatsoever.
Therapist:	You can't speak for sure about his feelings because only he knows exactly what those are, but as far as you are concerned . . .
Client:	. . . he knows how I feel about it.
Therapist:	You don't have any use for him.
Client:	None whatsoever. And that's been for about eight years now.
Therapist:	So for about eight years you've lived with a person whom you have no respect for and really hate.
Client:	Oh, I respect him.
Therapist:	Ah. Excuse me. I got that wrong.
Client:	I have to respect him. I don't have to, but I do. But I don't love him, I hate him. I can't stand him.
Therapist:	There are certain things you respect him for, but that doesn't alter the fact that you definitely hate him and don't love him.
Client:	That's the truth. I respect anybody who has bravery and courage, and he does. . . .
Therapist:	. . . You do give him credit for the fact that he is brave, he has guts or something.
Client:	Yeah. He shows that he can do a lot of things that, well, a lot of men can't.
Therapist:	M-hm, m-hm.
Client:	And also he has asthma, and the doctor hasn't given him very long to live. And he, even though he knows he is going to die, he keeps working and he works at a killing pace, so I respect him for that, too.
Therapist:	M-hm. So I guess you're saying he really has . . .
Client:	. . . what it takes.

terrified Betty ever since it took the life of her father. At first, these encounters with Carlos made Betty acutely anxious. She became physically ill, and was obsessed with the fear that she too would get cancer, lose weight, and shrivel away. No wonder Betty was obese, they all thought—she was fighting the skin-and-bones image of her father before he died. Whether true or not, this insight was a key to Betty's problems. Soon she began to diet, with her therapy group acting as a supportive community, rooting her on with every pound she shed. One male member half-jokingly said he would take her to Hawaii for the weekend when she lost a hundred pounds. It was the first time a man had ever shown an interest in her.

As this story illustrates, **group therapy** provides a valuable alternative to individual psychotherapy. Typically, one or two therapists work with four to ten clients at a time, and often the clients have similar problems. The benefits are numerous, as groups furnish social support and encouragement, new outlooks on old problems, and interpersonal experience for those who are shy or socially awkward. The format and goals of a therapy group differ according to theoretical orientation.

In psychoanalytic groups, therapists interpret each member's interactions with the others in the same way that resistance and transference are interpreted in individual sessions. One psychoanalytic form of group therapy is "transactional analysis" (TA), in which the therapist analyzes the interactions between group members for clues concerning the individuals. In contrast, behavioral and cognitive groups seek to modify thoughts and behaviors, using members who have the same problem as both models and reinforcers. For example, social skills training is often conducted in groups, as is systematic desensitization for people who have the same anxiety disorder (as when a group of people with agoraphobia are taken on a trip away from home). Among humanistic psychologists, groups are brought together to enhance personal development. One outgrowth of this approach is the *sensitivity training* group in which business executives, teachers, and others, in groups ranging in size from twelve to twenty persons, are taught to interact openly and with sensitivity. A close cousin of this is the *encounter group* developed by Carl Rogers. In an encounter group, members express themselves with complete and brutal honesty—crying, yelling, laughing, and so on.

Encounter groups are not as popular now as they were in the 1960s and 1970s, but they gave rise to more specialized *self-help* groups in which people who share a common problem come together for mutual help and social support. The best known is Alcoholics Anonymous, or AA. Many others are available—for AIDS victims, battered women, parents without partners, compulsive gamblers, teenage mothers, drug addicts, rape victims, weight watchers, smokers, newly arrived immigrants, families of cancer victims, and so on. The American Psychiatric Association (1989) estimates that in the United States alone, thousands of self-help groups now service up to 15 million Americans. People helping one another is a promising concept no one wants to oppose. But are self-help groups effective? At present, these programs have not been adequately evaluated, so firm conclusions cannot be drawn (Christensen & Jacobson, 1994).

Since people often enter therapy because of problems that arise at home, many psychologists prefer to treat families, not individuals. There is no single approach, but *family therapies* in general treat the family as an interde-

Rooted in the humanistic approach, Outward Bound and other groups bring participants together for sensitivity training and personal enhancement.

■ **group therapy** The simultaneous treatment of several clients in a group setting.

Alcoholics Anonymous is a successful self-help group that ensures anonymity—which is why these members show only their backs to the camera.

pendent social "system" in which the whole is greater than the sum of its parts. The therapist observes the family members together, how they relate, what roles they play, and what alliances they form. Indeed, researchers have tried to analyze these therapy interactions systematically (Friedlander & Heatherington, 1989). Problems within the system vary—a boy acts out to get attention from two busy working parents; a husband and wife don't get along and use their daughter as a scapegoat; a child reaches adolescence, but the parents don't recognize her need for independence; a father drinks too much, but everyone denies it and says "he's just under the weather." Whatever the problem, whole families are gathered in an effort to heal old wounds and prevent further conflict (Gurman et al., 1986; Hazelrigg et al., 1987; Wynne, 1988).

Perspectives on Psychotherapy

At the heart of all psychotherapy is the assumption that people have a capacity for change. Hence two questions loom over the entire enterprise: (1) Can humans help humans change? and (2) Are some forms of helping better than others? (Mahoney, 1991). To those interested in the answers to these questions, Allen Bergin and Sol Garfield's (1994) *Handbook of Psychotherapy and Behavior Change*, provides a comprehensive up-to-date review of all the research.

The Bottom Line: Does Psychotherapy Work? Read case studies written by psychotherapists, and you'll have the impression that success is guaranteed. Ask people who have undergone psychotherapy, and three out of four will say they were "satisfied" or "very satisfied" with the outcome (Lebow, 1982). With such glowing reports, is there any reason to question the value of psychotherapy?

Personal endorsements like these are important, but they do not provide hard evidence—for two reasons. First, both therapists and clients are motivated to believe that the experience was successful. Therapists want to affirm their professional value and integrity, and clients need to justify their

"Two strangers meet by prearrangement; their purpose, to wrestle with life itself; their goal, to win from deadness more life for one of them; their risk, that one or both of them will find life filled with pain and anxiety for some period of time; their certainty, that if they persist in good faith with their struggle both will be changed in some measure."

JAMES F. T. BUGENTAL

investment of time and money. Thus, independent measures of improvement are necessary—for example, pre- to post-treatment changes in test scores, behavior, or third-party evaluations. The second problem is that many people improve without treatment, by "spontaneous remission." This improvement may occur as a result of support received from friends, teachers, and family members, or simply because "time heals all wounds." (You know what they say about the common cold: take medicine and your stuffy nose will disappear in seven days, do nothing and it will last a whole week.) If psychotherapy is to be judged as effective, then, those who receive treatment should improve more than comparable others who do not. The question is, do they?

In 1952, Hans Eysenck reviewed twenty-four psychotherapy studies and found that roughly two-thirds of all patients showed improvement. So far, so good. But there was a hitch: 72 percent of the people who were on waiting lists for therapy but were not actually treated also improved in the same period of time, thanks to spontaneous remission. Eysenck's blunt, provocative, pessimistic conclusion: psychotherapy is worthless. Eysenck's article caused a major controversy. Psychologists were quick to attack the methods used in the original studies as well as Eysenck's analysis of the results. It turns out, for example, that many of the control group subjects were healthier initially than those who received treatment, that some of the controls were taking drugs prescribed by physicians, and that the rate of spontaneous remission was actually only 43 percent (Bergin & Lambert, 1978).

Despite its shortcomings, Eysenck's article inspired an active, more sophisticated generation of clinical researchers determined to evaluate psychotherapy outcomes. By 1980, the year in which Mary Lee Smith and her colleagues reviewed all the available research, there were 475 published studies involving literally thousands of patients! Using a meta-analysis to statistically combine the results of these different studies, they found that psychotherapy was effective for a whole range of problems, including anxiety disorders, low self-esteem, interpersonal difficulties, and addiction. As shown in Figure 17.5, the average psychotherapy patient showed more improvement than 80 percent of no-treatment controls, a finding that holds up on closer scrutiny (Lambert & Bergin, 1994). From this analysis, Smith and her colleagues (1980) concluded that "psychotherapy benefits people

Figure 17.5

Benefits of Psychotherapy

Summarizing the results of 475 studies, Smith et al. (1980) found that the average psychotherapy client shows more improvement than 80 percent of the no-treatment controls.

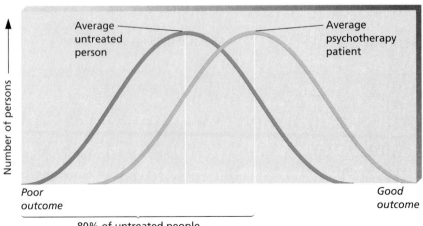

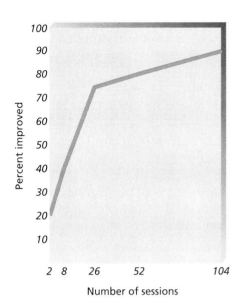

Figure 17.6

Improvement in Psychotherapy: The More the Better?

A summary of fifteen studies indicates that there is continued improvement over 26 sessions, but that the rate of improvement then levels off. At one session per week, six months seems to be an ideal amount of time to spend in psychotherapy.

of all ages as reliably as schooling educates them, medicine cures them, or business turns a profit" (p. 183).

Although some psychologists continue to question the benefits of psychotherapy (Dawes, 1994), clinical researchers are busy exploring the links between processes and outcomes. If a person started psychotherapy today, for example, how long would it take to feel better? Is there a timetable? Based on fifteen studies of more than 2,400 clients, Kenneth Howard and his colleagues (1986) found that the percentage of people who improve increases with the number of therapy sessions *up to a point*. After six months, or twenty-six sessions, 70 percent of the outcomes are successful. From that point on, however, the improvement rate levels off and additional sessions contribute little more to the final outcome (see Figure 17.6). In a follow-up study, Howard and his colleagues (1993) found that the pattern of self-reported improvement depends on the desired outcome. The patients reported "feeling better" early on, but it took longer before they saw actual changes in their ability to function at work, at home, and in relationships.

Are Some Therapies Better than Others? Eighty percent of all therapy patients improve more than no-treatment controls. Seventy percent of those who improve do so within six months. These figures are interesting, you may think, but they are just averages, generalities. Don't some people derive more or less benefit than the average? Aren't some problems more amenable to change than others? And what about the differences among the psychoanalytic, behavioral, cognitive, and humanistic approaches? Interestingly, Smith and her colleagues (1980) did compare the different types of therapies, and found a surprising result: all approaches were effective, and all were *equivalent*—that is, despite radical differences in techniques, no single approach was consistently superior to another. This conclusion, supported by others as well (Stiles et al., 1986), is called the "Dodo bird verdict" after the *Alice in Wonderland* character who declared, after a race, that "everyone has won, and all must have prizes."

The "Dodo bird verdict" poses a puzzling question: How can such different forms of treatment—from a probing analysis of unconscious childhood conflicts, to a hard-nosed modification of behaviors or cognitions, to warm and nondirective reflection—produce the same results? There are three good answers to this question. First, specific techniques are less critical to the final outcome than are personal characteristics of the client and therapist (Lambert, 1989; Lambert & Bergin, 1994). Second, the different approaches may well be equivalent on average, but the effectiveness of any one technique depends on the problem to be solved. Behavior therapy is perfect for extinguishing phobias, compulsions, shyness, and other specific anxiety-related ailments (Bowers & Clum, 1988). But cognitive therapy is more potent in the battle against depression (Dobson, 1989), and person-centered therapy is ideally suited to raising self-esteem (Smith et al., 1980). With so many disorders listed in DSM-IV, maybe therapists should act as "matchmakers" and use different techniques with different clients. A third explanation is that all psychological therapies are more similar in important ways than one might think. In other words, despite their surface differences, all psychotherapies have a lot in common at a deeper level—and these common factors, not the specific techniques, are the active ingredients necessary for change (Stiles et al., 1986).

Regardless of the specific techniques that are used, all forms of psychotherapy provide a supportive relationship.

What Are the Active Ingredients?   Regardless of theoretical orientation, there are three key ingredients in psychotherapy. First, all therapists provide a *supportive relationship* characterized by warmth, trust, concern, encouragement, reassurance, acceptance, and a shoulder to cry on. Indeed, the better the "working alliance" is between a therapist and client, the more favorable the outcome—especially from the client's standpoint (Horvath & Symonds, 1991; Horvath & Luborsky, 1993). In one study, for example, schizophrenic patients who had a good rapport with their therapists were more likely than those who did not to remain in therapy, take their prescribed drugs, and improve in the end (Frank & Gunderson, 1991). Why is this human relationship so important? In the words of psychoanalyst Hans Strupp (1989), "For many people it is a novel and deeply gratifying experience to be accepted and listened to respectfully."

Second, all therapies offer a ray of *hope* to people who are typically unhappy, anxious, depressed, demoralized, and down on themselves. In all aspects of life, people are motivated by faith, positive expectations, and optimism (Seligman, 1991). The same is true in psychotherapy. In fact, it's been suggested that high expectations alone are sufficient, even when they are not justified (Prioleau et al., 1983). This suggestion is based on the **placebo effect,** the well-established medical phenomenon whereby patients show more improvement when they are given an inactive drug or "placebo" than when they are not. Somehow, believing can help make it so—which is how faith healers and witch doctors have been known to perform "miracle cures" with empty rituals. So is that *all* there is to psychotherapy, just one big placebo effect? No, carefully controlled studies show that although people who are randomly assigned to receive a placebo therapy (bogus exercises, group discussions, self-help tapes, and sugar pills) improve more than those who do not, they typically do not improve as much as those who undergo actual psychotherapy (Barker et al., 1988). Hope may be necessary, but it's not sufficient.

A third common ingredient is that all psychotherapies offer an ideal setting for *opening up,* a chance for people to confide in someone, spill their guts and talk freely about their troubles—maybe for the first time ever. In a series of controlled studies on the healing power of opening up, James Pen-

■ **placebo effect** The curative effect of an inactive treatment that results simply from the patient's belief in its therapeutic value.

nebaker (1990) brought college students into a laboratory and asked them to write for twenty minutes about either past traumas or trivial events. He found that when people wrote about having been abused, the divorce of their parents, the death of a family pet, and other traumas, their systolic blood pressure levels rose during disclosure, but then dipped below pre-experiment levels. Afterward, they felt better, had a more positive outlook, and exhibited a decline in number of visits to the campus health center over the next six months.

Why does it help to open up? Why do *you* sometimes feel the need to talk out your problems? One possibility, recognized many years ago by Freud, is that the experience itself provides a much-needed catharsis, a discharge of psychic tension—like taking the lid off a boiling pot of water to slow the boiling. Another interpretation, favored by most psychotherapists, is that talking about a problem helps you to sort out your thoughts, understand it better, and gain insight, in cognitive terms. Whatever the explanation, it is clear that psychotherapy provides an ideal setting for self-disclosure: the listener is patient, caring, and nonjudgmental—and what's said is kept confidential.

The Eclectic Alternative   Psychoanalysis emerged from the medical model, behaviorists and humanists came forward in response to psychoanalysis, and cognitive therapies evolved from a desire to soften up hardcore behaviorism. Clearly, each approach staked out a position that seemed radically different from others. All that is changing now. Psychoanalytic therapists are playing a more active role than in the past to speed up the healing process. Behavioral and cognitive approaches have formed a hybrid known as "cognitive-behavior therapy"—and some of them now talk about unconscious processes and self-concepts. Person-centered therapists are more directive than they used to be, while many behaviorists are less directive.

As illustrated in Figure 17.7, national surveys show that more psychotherapists describe themselves as *eclectic*—which means that they borrow ideas and techniques from different approaches, as needed—than identify themselves with any single orientation (Smith, 1982; Beitman et al., 1989). More recent surveys suggest that this percentage has risen even higher over the past few years. Why is the trend toward an eclectic approach? And why are many psychotherapy researchers predicting more of the same as we approach the twenty-first century? The reasons are pragmatic. As health costs skyrocket and as people turn for insurance to managed health care programs, there is an increasing need for effective

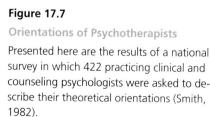

Figure 17.7

Orientations of Psychotherapists

Presented here are the results of a national survey in which 422 practicing clinical and counseling psychologists were asked to describe their theoretical orientations (Smith, 1982).

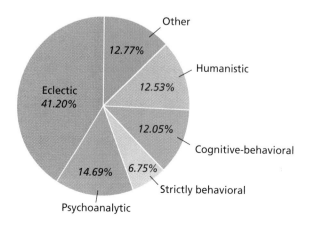

short-term therapies (Lazarus et al., 1992). Accordingly, specific treatment techniques should be chosen on a case-by-case basis, depending on the client, his or her problem, and the desired outcome (Norcross, 1991).

MEDICAL INTERVENTIONS

For people who suffer from severe anxiety, mood disorders, and schizophrenia, medical interventions provide an alternative to psychotherapy. Based on established links among the brain, mind, and behavior, three major types of medical treatment are available: psychoactive drugs, shock therapy, and psychosurgery.

Psychoactive Drug Therapies

In 1952, French psychiatrists Jean Delay and Pierre Deniker eliminated the symptoms of a schizophrenic patient with a wonder drug called *chlorpromazine*. From then on, the use of drugs in the treatment of psychological disorders has risen in popularity. There are now dozens of different drugs for different disorders (Meltzer, 1987). Most work by acting on neurotransmitters, the biochemicals that relay impulses between neurons. For thousands of people who used to languish in psychiatric hospitals, these drugs opened the door to life in the community. Michael Gitlin's (1990) *The Psychotherapist's Guide to Psychopharmacology* describes these drugs in clear, nontechnical language—their trade names, purposes, dosage levels, effects on the brain and behavior, benefits, potential side effects, and dangers. The main types are summarized in Table 17.5.

Antianxiety Drugs   Whether the cause is internal or external, and whether the condition is chronic or acute, there are many possible sources of anxiety, and many people who at times suffer through it. Thus, it is no wonder there has always been a great demand for—and abuse of—**antianxiety drugs,** or tranquilizers. During the 1950s, many doctors prescribed *barbiturates* such as Phenobarbital for anxious patients. Barbiturates combat anxiety by depressing central nervous system activity. They are effective, but highly addictive; they help us to relax, but also cause us to become clumsy and drowsy.

In the 1960s, a new class of tranquilizers was developed. Called *benzodiazepines*, they include chlordiazepoxide (Librium), diazepam (Valium), and alprazolam (Xanax). These drugs have the same desired calming effect and are less likely than barbiturates to cause drowsiness or addiction. Their impact is almost immediate, and they are most effective in treating generalized anxiety disorder, if taken regularly. Benzodiazepines are often prescribed by family doctors, not psychiatrists, for people who are in the midst of a stressful time of life. These drugs are not as safe as once thought, however. They are dangerous when combined with alcohol, and they may produce temporary side effects such as slurred speech, dry mouth, lightheadedness, and diminished psychomotor control. When a regular user stops taking them, the result may be a two-week "rebound anxiety" more intense than ever (Julien, 1992). A drug called *buspirone*, which was first released in

■ **antianxiety drugs** Tranquilizers used in the treatment of anxiety.

Table 17.5

Types of Psychoactive Drug Treatments

Drug type	Trade name	Potential effects
Antianxiety drugs chlordiazepoxide diazepam alprazolam buspirone	Librium Valium Xanax BuSpar	Act as a tranquilizer and, if taken regularly, can be used in the treatment of generalized anxiety disorder. Except for buspirone, which is slower-acting, these may cause physical dependence.
Antidepressants imipramine amitriptyline fluoxetine	Tofranil Elavil Prozac	Have mood-elevating effects and can relieve depression. They are not addictive, but may have minor side effects such as dry mouth, blurred vision, fatigue, and constipation.
Mood stabilizers lithium	Lithium Carbonate	Calms mania, and if taken continuously, may reduce the mood swings of bipolar disorder. Overdoses can prove fatal, and side effects include dry mouth, weight gain, fatigue, and tremors.
Antipsychotic drugs chlorpromazine clozapine	Thorazine Clozaril	Reduce hallucinations, delusions, jumbled speech, and other positive symptoms of schizophrenia. May cause stiffness, weight gain, sluggishness, and blunted affect. Except for clozapine, they may also cause shaking and a loss of control over voluntary movements.

1986, provides an alternative. It acts more slowly, usually taking a few days or weeks to have an effect, but it is also less likely to promote dependence or have unpleasant side effects (Lickey & Gordon, 1991).

Antidepressants   In the 1950s, doctors noticed that drugs being used to treat high blood pressure and tuberculosis had dramatic side effects on mood—sometimes causing depression, other times euphoria. At about the same time, researchers found that these drugs also increased levels of the neurotransmitter norepinephrine, a chemical cousin of adrenaline found in a part of the brain that regulates mood and emotion. Together, these strands of evidence suggested that depression is associated with lower-than-

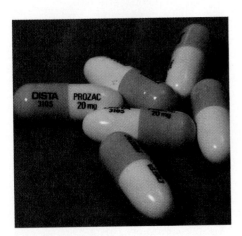

Encased in a small green-and-white capsule, Prozac is the most widely used antidepressant in the world. It is also mired in controversy because it is being prescribed for nondepressed people who find that it makes them more cheerful and self-confident.

■ **antidepressants** Drugs that relieve depression by increasing the supply of norepinephrine, serotonin, or dopamine.

■ **lithium** A drug used to control mood swings in people with bipolar disorder.

■ **antipsychotic drugs** Drugs that are used to control the positive symptoms of schizophrenia and other psychotic disorders.

needed norepinephrine levels. Later research also linked depression to serotonin. The practical result was the development of **antidepressants** such as *imipramine* (Tofranil) and *amitriptyline* (Elavil)—drugs that increase the supply of these chemicals and elevate mood. Studies have shown that the antidepressants are effective. They are not addictive, and cause only minor side effects such as dry mouth, constipation, blurred vision, and fatigue.

Today, a new drug called *fluoxetine*—better known by its trade name, Prozac—is the most widely used antidepressant in the world (Cowley, 1994). By zeroing in on serotonin, without affecting other neurotransmitters, Prozac is effective with relatively mild side effects (one researcher claimed that Prozac increased the risk of suicide, but others have failed to confirm this danger). It is also now the subject of controversy. Many psychiatrists have observed that in some patients, Prozac does more than relieve depression. It also seems to "transform" their personality, making them happier, more self-confident and productive at work, and more engaged and relaxed in social situations. As a result, it appears that this "wonder drug" in a little green-and-white capsule is sometimes being prescribed for people who are not clinically depressed. This last development is unsettling, and raises hard ethical questions concerning the proper use of psychoactive drugs (Kramer, 1993).

For bipolar disorder—which is characterized by manic-depressive mood swings—different, mood-stabilizing drugs are used. The best known of these is **lithium**—a mineral found in rocks, water, plants, and animals. Taken on a continuous basis, lithium can usually prevent moods from reeling out of control. Common side effects include dry mouth, thirst, weight gain, excessive urination, fatigue, and tremors. Taken in dosages that are too high, lithium can prove dangerous, even life-threatening. For bipolar patients who do not respond to lithium, or who cannot tolerate the side effects, other mood stablilizing drugs can be used instead (Pope et al., 1991).

Antipsychotic Drugs   Not that long ago, people with schizophrenia who exhibited hallucinations, delusions, confused speech, exaggerated displays of emotion, paranoia, and bizarre behavior used to be dismissed as a lost cause. All that changed in the 1950s, however, with the discovery of **antipsychotic drugs,** which reduced the intensity of these positive "uncontrollable" symptoms. As noted earlier, the first in this class of drugs was *chlorpromazine,* better known as Thorazine. By blocking the activity of dopamine, the neurotransmitter that has been linked to schizophrenia, antipsychotic drugs enable many people previously confined to hospital wards to live relatively normal lives.

Chlorpromazine has two drawbacks. The first is that it often does not relieve the negative symptoms of schizophrenia—symptoms such as flat affect, apathy, immobility, and social withdrawal, which may be linked to structural defects in the brain, not to dopamine (see Chapter 16). The second drawback is that very unpleasant side effects are common. In the worst of cases, these include Parkinson disease–like symptoms such as shaking and a loss of control over voluntary movements, stiff muscles, sluggishness, blunted affect, weight gain, and sexual impotence in men. These symptoms can sometimes be treated with other drugs. Still, psychiatrists and patients must weigh the benefits of relief from the symptoms of schizophrenia against the costs of drug-induced side effects (Gitlin, 1990).

"*Before Prozac, she* loathed *company.*"

[Drawing by Lorenz; © 1993 The New Yorker Magazine, Inc.]

Recent research suggests that *clozapine* (Clozaril), an antipsychotic medication first released in 1990, may be more effective than its predecessors. Clozapine operates through a different mechanism. Although it is effective at controlling hallucinations and other psychotic symptoms (even in some patients who do not respond to Thorazine), it does not have the undesirable side effects on motor functions. Unfortunately, for about 2 percent of those who take it, clozapine increases the risk of developing a fatal blood disorder (Lickey & Gordon, 1991).

Perspectives on Drug Therapies   "There's a place for drugs for some people, but they are overrated and overprescribed. In comparisons of psychotherapy and drugs, by and large drugs do not appear to be the superior treatment." "To say that psychiatric drugs are overrated is a stupid statement. . . . For a wide range of psychiatric disorders, it's well documented that these drugs are the most effective treatments." The first of these remarks was made by psychologist Roger Greenberg, the second by psychiatrist Paul Wender (quoted in Goleman, 1989). Which of these statements is more true? Is psychotherapy preferable to drug therapy, or is it the other way around?

The psychotherapy vs. drugs debate is as old as the split between psychology and medicine. In fact, there is no winner, no right or wrong answer, no contest. In the spirit of taking an eclectic approach to the treatment of disorders, mental health professionals should make their judgments on an individual case basis and not exclude either approach as a matter of principle. Clearly, psychoactive drugs have helped hundreds of thousands of men and women once hidden away in psychiatric institutions, and they will continue to do so in years to come. And clearly, there are people with disorders who do not respond as well to psychological forms of treatment. There are reasons for caution, however. One is that some psychoactive drugs produce side effects that are unpleasant and, at times, dangerous under high dosage levels. A second is that some drugs can produce a physical or psychological dependence, leading patients to play a passive role in their own healing process. The person who gets into the habit of taking Valium at the first sign of tension learns how to control the aversive symptoms of anxiety but not how to cope with the source of the problem.

In an effort to match treatments to specific disorders, many researchers are currently evaluating the relative effectiveness of psychological and drug therapies. So far neither approach has emerged as uniformly more effective. For example, the National Institutes of Mental Health recently compared cognitive therapy, an "interpersonal" form of psychotherapy, an antidepressant, and a placebo control treatment in which the patients were given an inactive pill, attention, and encouragement. A total of 239 patients in three cities were randomly assigned to receive one form of treatment for four months. Among those in the placebo group, 29 percent were no longer depressed when the "treatment" was ended. In the other groups, that number was near 50 percent—and both the psychological and drug therapies were found to be equally effective (Elkin et al., 1989). Other research shows that the outcome changes over time—that for those who are depressed, cognitive therapy is somewhat slower than antidepressants to take effect, but is then more likely to prevent a relapse (Dobson, 1989; Hollon et al., 1991).

Electroconvulsive Therapy

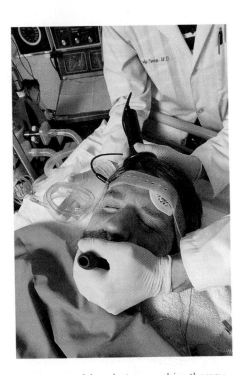

A person receiving electroconvulsive therapy. As shown, the shock is delivered to the right side of the head.

It used to be a terrifying experience, a Frankenstein-like nightmare come to life. The patient would be dragged kicking and screaming to a hospital table, and strapped down by the arms and legs, only to watch as a white-coated physician leaned over to administer the pain. The patient would then be jolted by 100 volts of electricity to both sides of the skull, triggering seizures, unconsciousness, and muscle spasms so violent that they sometimes resulted in broken bones. The shock also had a mind-scrambling effect, causing confusion and amnesia for chunks of time before and after the treatment.

Electroconvulsive therapy (ECT) has a curious history. Based on the notion that mental illness could be cured by quite literally shocking the system, ECT was introduced in 1938 by an Italian physician named Ugo Cerletti. From the start, it was clear that ECT provided relief from depression. It was widely used in the 1950s and 1960s, but fell out of favor as antidepressant drugs became available; then it made a quiet comeback when procedures were made safer and more humane. Today, consenting ECT patients are given a general anesthetic and a muscle relaxant to prevent injury from convulsions. They then receive briefer, milder shock to the right side of the head, which sets off a brain seizure that lasts for a minute or so. As in surgery, patients regain consciousness within minutes, unable to remember what happened. The entire process consists of ten or so sessions administered over a two-week period.

ECT is now a viable alternative for people who are deeply depressed, suicidal, and not responsive to psychological or drug therapies. It has also been used with some success in the treatment of the manic episodes exhibited by people with bipolar disorder (Mukherjee et al., 1994). The convulsions triggered by electrical current to the brain provide quick, sometimes permanent relief. ECT is also safe, resulting in only 2 deaths per 100,000 treatments, a mortality rate lower than that for childbirth (Abrams, 1988; Endler & Persad, 1988). The reason ECT is effective, however—whether it works by stimulating inactive parts of the brain, inhibiting overactive parts, or triggering the release of scarce neurotransmitters—remains a mystery (Janicak et al., 1985; Sackheim, 1988; Weiner & Coffey, 1988). Before-and-after brain scans of ECT patients show no signs of structural brain damage (Coffey et al., 1991). And as far as side effects are concerned, the only problem is that ECT patients experience a temporary state of confusion. When they regain consciousness, they cannot recall events of the recent past, and are disoriented about where they are and how they got there—a small price to pay for the benefits received.

Psychosurgery

■ **electroconvulsive therapy (ECT)** Electric shock treatments that often relieve severe depression by triggering seizures in the brain.

■ **psychosurgery** The surgical removal of portions of the brain for the purpose of treating psychological disorders.

The most controversial of interventions is **psychosurgery**, the removal of portions of the brain for the purpose of treating psychological disorders. In 1935, Portuguese neurologist Egas Moniz performed the first "lobotomy," a surgical procedure in which he cut the nerves that connect the frontal lobes to the rest of the brain, in order to "tame" patients who were agitated, manic, and violent. The operation was so highly regarded that in 1949, Moniz was awarded a Nobel Prize in Medicine. As reported in the

New York Times, "Hypochondriacs no longer thought they were going to die, would-be suicides found life acceptable, sufferers from persecution complex forgot the machinations of imaginary conspirators. . . . Surgeons now think no more of operations on the brain than they do of removing an appendix" (1949).

Was the lobotomy all that it was cracked up to be? In a book entitled *Great and Desperate Cures,* Elliot Valenstein (1986) describes how thousands of mentally ill adults around the world were mutilated on the operating table: "After drilling two or more holes in a patient's skull, a surgeon inserted into the brain any of various instruments—some resembling an apple corer, a butter spreader, or an ice pick—and, often without being able to see what he was cutting, destroyed parts of the brain" (p. 3). The results were often tragic. The lobotomy was supposed to relieve patients of crippling emotions, but it also profoundly altered their personalities, creating people who were like robots: lethargic, emotionless, unmotivated, and unable to make or keep plans of action.

Today, psychosurgery is "high tech" and more sophisticated, enabling neurosurgeons to "damage the brain to save the mind" (Rodgers, 1992). Specific regions of the brain can be destroyed with precision through ultrasonic irradiation, or by sending electrical currents through fine wire electrodes. For people who are stricken with uncontrollable seizures, for example, the nerve fibers involved can be deactivated. Psychosurgery is also used sparingly, but with some success, on people incapacitated by chronic anxiety and depression who are not responsive to other forms of treatment. Still, there is debate over the science and ethics of psychosurgery, a treatment of last resort. After all, whether the outcome is positive or negative, the effect is irreversible.

CONSUMER'S GUIDE TO MENTAL HEALTH SERVICES

Over the years, the number of Americans seeking professional help for psychological problems has climbed dramatically. The helpers are psychiatrists and clinical psychologists, psychiatric nurses and social workers, and pastoral, marital, and family counselors. The kinds of help provided range from intensive one-on-one psychoanalysis to behavioral, cognitive, humanistic, and group therapies. In a small number of cases, obscure therapies are practiced, such as Mandala Therapy, Electric Sleep Therapy, Body-Image Therapy, Deprivation Therapy, Alpha Wave Therapy, and the Zaraleya Psychoenergetic Technique. And in a growing number of cases, people are turning to nonprofessionals, such as the many self-help and support groups that are widely available (Christensen & Jacobson, 1994).

Faced with an overwhelming array of treatment alternatives, people in the market for professional help are in a bind. One problem is that although someone must have a professional degree and supervised training to get licensed as a psychologist, anyone can legally hang up a shingle, offer a service, and call it "therapy." From among those who are qualified, how do you select a therapist, and what kind of experience can you expect to have? Should you seek psychotherapy, or medical treatment? If you need help and don't know where to turn, it's probably best to start with personal recommendations from a close friend, relative, family doctor, or teacher. Or you might check with the college counseling service, which is free, or a community mental health center. If you have health insurance that covers psychological services, find out if the policy covers what you want. If not, the hourly rates vary. Shop around and talk to two or three therapists until you're satisfied that you have found one you like, respect, and can work with. Talk openly about your goals and inquire about fees, credentials, orientations, and values, to determine whether the two of you are on the same wavelength. Remember: The working relationship between therapist and client is a necessary first step on the road to successful treatment.

All this brings us back to our major theme in the study of personality, disorders, and treatment: the possibility of change. Under normal conditions, personality remains relatively stable throughout adulthood. Individuals who are highly introverted or extraverted at one point in time are likely to remain that way later in life. But changes in behavior can be made—as when someone seeks to overcome shyness. When people suffer through a mental disorder, the need for change takes on an added dimension of importance. Some problems are relatively easy to overcome, others quite difficult. Through psychological and medical forms of therapy, however, the possibilities for recovery are real. Whether the specific goal is to overcome a fear, lower anxiety, lift depression, or clear the mind of illogical thoughts and perceptions, there is reason for hope, which is necessary for change.

SUMMARY AND KEY TERMS

Perspectives on Treatment

Treatment raises the basic question of the possibilities and limits of human change. There are two primary models of treatment, psychological and medical.

Psychological Therapies

The term *psychotherapy* refers to all forms of treatment in which a trained professional uses psychological techniques to help people in need of assistance. The four major approaches are psychoanalytic, behavioral, cognitive, and humanistic.

Psychoanalysis

Orthodox psychoanalysis aims for both catharsis and insight. Its key technique, pioneered by Freud, is *free association*, in which patients say whatever comes to mind without censoring it. Often the patient free associates about dreams, while the therapist tries to get behind the manifest content to the latent content. *Resistance*—a patient's tendency to block painful memories or insights—can be an obstacle but can also signal that the therapy is heading in the right direction. The same is true of *transference*, whereby the patient displaces intense feelings for others onto the therapist. On the basis of these behaviors, the therapist offers interpretations to help the patient gain insight.

Since orthodox psychoanalysis is usually long and expensive, recent therapists have developed briefer, less intense, more flexible kinds of therapy. The analyst takes a greater part in the conversation, focuses less on the patient's past, and puts more emphasis on current life problems.

Psychoanalysis has faced three major criticisms. First, it is time-consuming and expensive. Second, psychoanalytic interpretation can't be proved. Third, some people claim that psychoanalysis is not therapeutic. Despite the criticisms, psychoanalysis has left a strong mark on therapeutic practice.

Behavior Therapy

Rather than search for deep problems, *behavior therapy* uses learning principles to modify the symptoms. Classical conditioning therapies often rely on *flooding* the patient with an anxiety-provoking stimulus until the anxiety is extinguished. *Systematic desensitization*, a form of counterconditioning, pairs gradual exposure to an anxiety-provoking stimulus with relaxation training. *Aversion therapy* produces an aversive reaction to a harmful stimulus.

Other behavioral therapies use the reinforcement principles of operant conditioning. Token economies reward patients for desirable behaviors; for dangerous behavior, punishment may be necessary. *Biofeedback*—learning to control physiological processes with the aid of feedback from instruments—is useful for health problems such as tension-related headaches. Assertiveness training and other types of *social skills training* use modeling, rehearsal, and reinforcement to teach interpersonal skills.

Cognitive Therapy

Cognitive therapy focuses on maladaptive perceptions and thoughts. Developed by Ellis, *rational-emotive therapy (RET)* bluntly confronts people with their irrational beliefs and provides "psychoeducation" on ways to change. Beck's cognitive therapy takes a gentler, more collaborative approach, giving clients homework assignments and leading them to experience their emotional distress during therapy. These and other cognitive approaches are now the most frequently taught forms of therapy in clinical psychology graduate programs.

Humanistic Therapy

Acting as a facilitator, Rogers developed *person-centered therapy,* which creates a warm, caring environment to promote self-insight and acceptance. Person-centered therapists offer genuine empathy and unconditional positive regard. Through reflection, the therapist becomes an emotional mirror for the client. *Gestalt therapy,* developed by Perls, similarly makes clients responsible for their own change, but it takes a greater interest in unconscious feelings and dreams, and it aggressively challenges clients to express their feelings.

Group Therapy Approaches

An alternative to individual therapies, group therapy involves working with several clients simultaneously in a group setting. In transactional analysis, a psychoanalytic therapist analyzes the interactions among group members. Behavioral and cognitive therapies can also take place in groups. Humanistic psychology has spawned sensitivity training groups, encounter groups, and various self-help groups. In family therapies, the members of a family are treated as an interdependent social system.

Perspectives on Psychotherapy

People have long argued about psychotherapy's effectiveness. Meta-analysis has shown that psychotherapy patients experience more improvement, on average, than people who are not treated. After about six months of therapy, however, improvement appears to level off. Overall, the different forms of psychotherapy are equally effective. Some may work better on particular problems than others, but all offer the same key ingredients: (1) a supportive relationship; (2) hope, which, as the *placebo effect* demonstrates, can itself produce improvement; and (3) an ideal setting in which the patient is able to open up. Today, most therapists use an eclectic strategy, borrowing ideas and techniques from various approaches.

Medical Interventions

Medical interventions take three major forms: psychoactive drugs, electroconvulsive or shock therapy, and psychosurgery.

Psychoactive Drug Therapies

Antianxiety drugs, or tranquilizers, include buspirone and the widely used class of benzodiazephines. Research linking depression to neurotransmitters led to the development of *antidepressants,* such as the controversial new drug fluoxetine (Prozac). The mood stabilizer *lithium,* a mineral found in nature, can control mood swings in bipolar disorder. For schizophrenia and other psychotic disorders, *antipsychotic drugs* often reduce the positive symptoms, although they may not relieve the negative symptoms.

In the debate about the relative merits of psychoactive drugs and psychotherapy, there is no one answer. On the one hand, drugs have helped hundreds of thousands of patients; on the other, drugs can have unpleasant or dangerous side effects, and some produce physical or psychological dependence.

Electroconvulsive Therapy

Though once a nightmare-like experience, *electroconvulsive therapy (ECT)* now provides milder electric shock that can relieve severe depression by triggering seizures in the brain.

Psychosurgery

Psychosurgery, the most controversial medical intervention, involves removing portions of the brain to treat a psychological disorder. The technique of lobotomy, once popular, has fallen into disrepute. Today's psychosurgery is more sophisticated, targeting specific regions of the brain with ultrasonic irradiation or electrical currents.

Consumer's Guide to Mental Health Services

As more Americans look for help with psychological problems, a bewildering array of services have become available. Consumers should seek personal recommendations and talk frankly with prospective therapists. Although basic personality traits tend to remain stable, psychological and medical therapies do offer hope for change and recovery from mental disorder.

PART VI

As we've seen, psychology can be divided into biological, cognitive, developmental, social, and clinical subfields. Part VI brings together these different areas in a final "capstone" chapter on *health and well-being.* Following a brief discussion of mind over matter, this chapter examines current research on the self, the processes of stress and coping, and the exciting new work being done in the area of psychoneuroimmunology.

PUTTING THE PIECES TOGETHER

Chapter 18

Health and Well-Being

We've seen throughout this textbook that psychology is a remarkably diverse and eclectic discipline. Some psychologists define what they do as the study of the mind; others prefer to focus on behavior. Some are interested in the biological roots of human nature; others are interested in cognitive and affective processes, growth and development, social factors, personality, or clinical disorders. Some of us build theories and conduct research to understand basic processes; others want to apply what is known to improve health, education, law, the workplace, our interactions with the environment, and other aspects of the human condition. It has all become so diverse that Sigmund Koch (1993)—a prominent psychology historian—believes the discipline should be renamed "The Psychological Studies."

Koch may have a point. A more important point, however, is that although psychology appears fragmented on the surface, many researchers in different areas of specialization unite in sharing a common objective: *to help improve upon our health and well-being, and to enhance the quality of our lives.* In this chapter, we'll try to put psychology's puzzle pieces together. Beginning with the concept of the self, and moving to the link between the mind and body, we'll examine some of the new and exciting health-related questions that are captivating researchers of the 1990s.

MIND OVER MATTER

Australian Aborigines believe that sorcerers have the power to cause death by pointing a bone at someone. The !Kung of Africa believe that malaria can be caused by the death of a loved one. Many Western religious leaders maintain that faith heals all wounds. Shortly after the death of their wives, men die at a rate three times greater than others of the same age. In Fiji and other Pacific Islands, natives walk barefoot across a bed of glowing hot coals without pain, burns, or blisters. Many doctors say they can prolong the lives of terminally ill patients through visualization (close your eyes, concentrate on the cancer in your body, and imagine that your disease-fighting white blood cells are gobbling up the cancer cells like Pac-Man). Still others advocate the power of positive thinking, laughter, confession, psychotherapy, prayer, meditation, yoga, jogging, subliminal self-help tapes, hypnosis, biofeedback, massage, social support, family pets, and screaming at the top of your lungs. Some of this advice is frivolous and without merit. As we'll see, however, a good deal of research does support the general point that people can improve their health by learning to control their minds and behavior.

In *The Healing Brain,* Robert Ornstein and David Sobel (1987) contend that "the brain minds the body," for the brain's primary function is not sensation, perception, consciousness, learning, thought, language, memory, or emotion—but health maintenance. According to Ornstein and Sobel, "The brain is the largest organ of secretion in the body, and the neuron, far from being like a chip within a computer, is a flesh-and-blood little gland, one that produces hundreds of chemicals. These chemicals do not, for the most part, serve thought or reason. They serve keeping the body out of

Walking barefoot on red-hot coals is an annual event at Mount Takao, Japan. This ritual may seem to demonstrate the power of mind over matter, but actually the wood coals are poor conductors of heat—and fire walkers often wet their feet before walking.

trouble" (p. 11). Taking the argument one step further, Howard Friedman (1991), author of *The Self-Healing Personality*, notes that although he never saw a death certificate marked "death due to unhealthy personality," there is a link to chronic conditions such as headaches, ulcers, asthma, arthritis, and even cancer. It all rings familiar the expression "mind over matter."

"Mind over matter" is a recurring theme in psychology. Elsewhere in this book, we saw that perceptions of an object's size are determined not just by the size of its retinal image but also by the perceiver's knowledge of what the object is and its distance from the eye. We saw that accident victims who have an arm or leg amputated often feel pain in the missing limb even though no pain receptors are stimulated. And we saw that people often develop intense fears of harmless objects, exaggerate in memory the role they played in past events, cure headaches with biofeedback, elevate their mood by smiling, and create self-fulfilling prophecies by behaving in ways that confirm their own beliefs.

One of the most profound illustrations of this theme is the widely documented *placebo effect*—a psychological form of treatment routinely observed in medical circles. A placebo is any medical intervention (including inactive drugs, counseling, or surgery) designed to improve one's condition through the power of suggestion. In past years, sick people were forced to consume potions made of frog sperm, lizard tongues, crocodile dung, fly specks, unicorn horns, and ground snake. They were also subjected to shock treatments, bloodletting, forced vomiting, freezing, and blistering. It seems a miracle anyone survived. Yet accounts of early medical practices indicate that many people were "cured" by these peculiar remedies. Clearly, the patient's faith and hope are important parts of the healing process (White et al., 1985; Shapiro, 1960).

In a powerful demonstration of the placebo effect, Robert Sternbach (1964) gave to volunteer subjects a white sugar pill that contained no active ingredients. At first, subjects were told that the pill contained a drug that would stimulate a strong churning sensation in the stomach. The next time, they were told that it would reduce their stomach activity and make them feel full. On a third occasion, they were informed that the pill was only a placebo. The result: Subjects always swallowed the same tablet, yet they exhibited measurable changes in stomach activity consistent with expectations.

In another striking demonstration reported by Henry Beecher (1961), participating coronary heart disease patients were randomly assigned to receive either a prescribed surgical procedure or a sham operation. In both groups, the patient was wheeled into the operating room and given a general anesthetic. And in both groups an incision was made in the chest and sewn up. But while half the patients had their arteries tied, which was the prescribed remedy, the other half received no treatment. Amazingly, the second group improved as much as the first did. Placebos have similarly been used to treat allergies, headaches, insomnia, skin rashes, constipation, upset stomachs, chronic pain, and a host of other ailments. Somehow, beliefs transform reality.

The placebo effect is not a magical occurrence, a miracle, a wonder drug, or even a purely mental phenomenon. Nor would psychologists accept the claims made in the medical community solely on the basis of stories, anecdotes, and case studies. So how do placebos work? Although the process is not well understood, research shows that positive treatment expectations—as communicated by an expert who projects enthusiasm and confidence—trigger in the brain the release of endorphins, morphine-like substances that provide a temporary relief from pain (Levine et al., 1978). By raising expectations, placebos also relieve people of their anxiety about being sick, thereby dampening the release of adrenaline and other stress hormones that break down the body's resistance (Taylor, 1986). As we'll see later in this chapter, the mind can help the body make the most of its own resources. This is the theme of many books, including *Head First: The Biology of Hope* by Norman Cousins (1989).

This chapter will describe recent developments in psychology on two fronts. First, we explore the topic of the self—the ways in which people think and feel about themselves and the consequences of this self-awareness for mental health. Next, we examine the topic of stress—what causes it, what effects it has on the body, and what coping mechanisms are most adaptive. As we'll see, people can often use their minds to improve the quality of their lives.

THE SELF AND WELL-BEING

Have you ever been at a noisy gathering and yet managed to hear someone at the other end of the room mention your name? As noted in Chapter 4, this phenomenon is known as the *cocktail party effect*—the ability to pick a personally relevant stimulus out of a complex environment. This phenomenon shows that people are selective in their perceptions of the world. It also shows that the self is not just another stimulus—but an important object of our attention.

The Need for Self-Esteem

You and I and just about everyone else are motivated by a need for **self-esteem,** and satisfying that need is critical to our entire outlook on life. People with high self-esteem tend to be happy, healthy, productive, and successful. They tend to persist longer at difficult tasks, sleep better at night, have fewer ulcers. They are also more accepting of others and less likely to conform to peer pressure. In contrast, people with low self-esteem are more anxious, depressed, pessimistic about the future, and prone to failure (Brown, 1991).

Part of the problem is that people lacking in self-esteem also lack confidence, so they bring to new tasks a defeatist attitude that traps them in a vicious cycle (see Figure 18.1). Expecting to fail, they become anxious, exert less effort, and "tune out" on life's important challenges. Then, when they do fail, people who are low in self-esteem blame themselves—which makes them feel even more incompetent (Brockner, 1983). If that's not bad enough, people with low self-esteem are also prone to illness. Recent research suggests that making people aware of their negative self-evaluations has adverse effects on the immune system, the body's capacity to ward off disease (Strauman et al., 1993).

Figure 18.1

Vicious Cycle of Low Self-Esteem

Low self-esteem is accompanied by negative expectations, which impair performance and, in turn, reinforce low self-esteem.

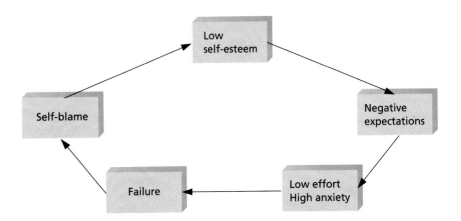

■ **self-esteem** A positive or negative evaluation of the self.

■ **self-discrepancy theory** The theory that your emotional well-being is defined by the match between how you see yourself and how you want to see yourself.

What determines how people feel about themselves? According to the **self-discrepancy theory** of E. Tory Higgins (1989), your self-esteem is defined by the match between how you see yourself and how you want to see yourself. To demonstrate, try the following exercise, which briefly appeared in Chapter 15. On a blank sheet of paper, write down ten traits that describe the kind of person you think that you *actually* are. Next write down the traits that describe the kind of person you think you *ought* to be—characteristics that would enable you to meet your sense of obligation, duty, and responsibility. Then list the traits that describe an *ideal* of what you'd like to be, an ideal that embodies all your hopes, wishes and dreams. If you follow these instructions, you should have three lists—your actual self, ought self, and ideal self.

Research shows that these trait lists can be used to predict your self-esteem and emotional well-being. The first list is your *self-concept.* The

■ **self-awareness theory** The theory that self-focused attention leads people to notice their shortcomings, thus motivating a change in behavior or an escape from self-awareness.

other two represent your personal standards or *self-guides*. To the extent that you fall short of meeting these standards, you will have a lowered self-esteem, unpleasant emotions, and, in extreme cases, an emotional disorder. As also noted in Chapter 15, the specific consequence depends on which of the self-guides you fail to achieve. If there's a discrepancy between your actual and ought selves, you'll feel guilty, ashamed, and resentful. You might even suffer from excessive fears and anxiety disorders. If there's a discrepancy between your actual and ideal selves, you'll feel disappointed, frustrated, unfulfilled, and possibly even depressed (Scott & O'Hara, 1993; Strauman, 1989).

Everyone must cope with some degree of self-discrepancy. After all, nobody is perfect. Yet we are not all anxious and depressed. Why not? According to Higgins (1989), the emotional consequences of self-discrepancy depend on two factors. First is the *amount* of discrepancy: the more of it there is, the more intense is our discomfort. The second factor is *accessibility:* the more aware of the discrepancies we are, then, again, the greater is the emotional discomfort. This second factor raises an important question. Assuming that everyone has self-discrepancies to cope with, what influences their accessibility? What is it that makes you self-conscious about *your* personal shortcomings?

The Self-Awareness "Trap"

If you carefully review your daily routine—classes, work, leisure activities, social interactions, meals, and so on—you would probably be surprised at how little time you actually spend thinking about yourself. In a study that illustrates this point, more than a hundred people, ranging in age from nineteen to sixty-three, were equipped for a week with electronic beepers that sounded on average every two hours between 7:30 A.M. and 10:30 P.M. Each time the beepers went off, subjects interrupted whatever they were doing, wrote down what they were thinking at that moment, and filled out a questionnaire. Out of 4,700 observations, only 8 percent of all recorded thoughts were about the self. Even more interesting is that when subjects did think about themselves, they reported feeling relatively unhappy, and wished they were doing something else (Csikszentmihalyi & Figurski, 1982).

This is an interesting correlation. Is it really unpleasant to think about ourselves? Is self-awareness a mental trap from which we need to escape? Perhaps. Many psychologists find that self-focus brings out our personal shortcomings the way staring into a mirror draws our attention to every blemish on the face. According to **self-awareness theory**, certain situations predictably force us to turn inward and become the object of our own attention. When we talk about ourselves, glance in a mirror, stand before an audience or camera, watch ourselves on videotape, or behave in a conspicuous manner, we enter a state of heightened self-awareness that leads us to compare our behavior to some standard. This comparison often results in a negative discrepancy and a drop in self-esteem as we discover that we fall short of our ideal and ought selves (Wicklund, 1975).

Just as certain situations can trigger self-awareness, some people are generally more self-focused than others. As measured by the Self-Conscious-

Looking into a mirror increases self-awareness—and often draws attention to our personal shortcomings.

ness Scale, research shows that individuals differ in the tendency to introspect on their inner thoughts and feelings, their concern for how they appear to others, and social anxiety—an emotion that includes feelings of public shame and embarrassment (Fenigstein et al., 1975; Buss, 1980). A sample of items used to measure these traits is presented in Table 18.1.

Table 18.1

Self-Consciousness

The following sample items are among those used to measure the trait of self-consciousness. How many of these statements do you agree with?

I'm always trying to figure myself out.

I usually worry about making a good impression.

One of the last things I do before leaving the house is look in the mirror.

I'm alert to changes in my mood.

I get embarrassed very easily.

I have trouble working when someone is watching me.

Large groups make me nervous.

I'm constantly examining my motives.

Self-consciousness is a characteristic not just of people but of situations as well. In a provocative book entitled *Escaping the Self,* Roy Baumeister (1991) argues that contemporary Western culture places so much emphasis on selfhood and identity—as embodied in the so-called me generation—that it is a constant burden to keep up. Just to maintain a positive self-image for ourselves and others, we strive for prestigious credentials, read books on how to make a good impression, replace clothes that are not worn out if they are no longer fashionable, starve ourselves to be thin, spend thousands of dollars on cosmetic surgery, buy cars that project a desired image, rehearse conversations in advance, rationalize failure and rejection, and blush when we say something foolish in front of others. The more energy we invest in the self, the more we have to lose. Society is so enamored of, obsessed with, and addicted to the self, writes Baumeister, that "maintaining self-esteem can start to seem like a full-time job!" (p. 12).

If focusing on the self is a problem, can it be solved? Self-awareness theory suggests that there are two ways to cope with the discomfort: (1) behave in ways that reduce one's self-discrepancies, or (2) withdraw from self-awareness. According to Charles Carver and Michael Scheier (1981), the solution chosen depends on whether you expect that you can successfully reduce the self-discrepancy—and whether you're satisfied with the progress you make once you try (Duval et al., 1992). If you are, you'll match your behavior to the standard; if not, you'll tune out, seek distractions, and turn attention away from the self. This process is depicted in Figure 18.2 (p. 692).

In general, research supports these predictions of self-awareness theory (Gibbons, 1990). When people are self-focused, they are more likely to behave in ways that are consistent with their values and socially accepted ideals. When the prospects for discrepancy reduction seem grim, however, they take the second route: escape from self-awareness. In one experiment,

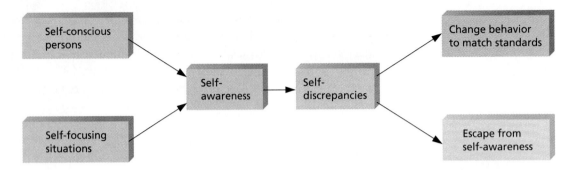

Figure 18.2

Self-Awareness Theory

Focusing attention on the self makes us aware of self-discrepancies. This awareness pressures us to match our behavior to ideal standards or else to tune out.

"More wine! Less truth!"

People often drown their troubles in a bottle to escape the negative implications of self-awareness. [Drawing by Cline; © 1991 The New Yorker Magazine, Inc.]

for example, subjects worked on a task in a room that did or did not have a full-length mirror facing them. Subjects who received negative feedback about their task performance were quicker to leave the room when it had a mirror than when it did not (Duval & Wicklund, 1972).

There are some disturbing health-related implications of escape as a coping strategy. One concerns the use of alcohol. According to Jay Hull, people will often drown their sorrows in a bottle as a way to flee mentally from the negative effects of self-awareness. To test this hypothesis, Hull and Richard Young (1983) administered what was supposed to be an IQ test to male subjects, and gave them false feedback suggesting they had either succeeded or failed. Supposedly as part of a separate study, subjects were then asked to taste and evaluate different wines. They did not realize it, but the experimenters kept track of how much they drank during the fifteen-minute tasting period. As predicted, subjects who had high scores on the Self-Consciousness Scale drank more wine after failure than after success, presumably to escape the implications for their self-esteem. Among the subjects low in self-consciousness, there was no difference in alcohol consumption. Similar results were obtained in a study of men who had been hospitalized for alcoholism and then released. After three months, those who were both self-conscious and under stress were the most likely to relapse into heavy drinking (Hull et al., 1986). Indeed, many people expect alcohol to provide mental relief from their problems (Leigh & Stacy, 1993).

According to Claude Steele and Robert Josephs (1990), alcoholic intoxication provides more than just a means of tuning out on the self. By causing people to lose touch with reality and shed their inhibitions, it also evokes a state of "drunken self-inflation." In one study, for example, subjects rated their actual and ideal selves on thirty-five traits—some important to their self-esteem, others not important. After drinking either an 80-proof vodka cocktail or a harmless placebo, subjects re-rated themselves on the same traits. As measured by the discrepancy between actual and ideal selves, subjects who had been drinking expressed inflated views of themselves on traits they considered important (Banaji & Steele, 1989). As discussed in Chapter 16, attempted suicide is the ultimate form of oblivion, or escape from self-awareness (Baumeister, 1990).

Mechanisms of Self-Deception

Self-awareness can cause discomfort and lower self-esteem by focusing attention on discrepancies, so we tune out. How else do people cope with their own inadequacies, faults, and an uncertain future? Simple. Using cog-

■ **self-deception** The processes by which people distort and hide unpleasant truths from themselves.

nitive strategies like the unconscious defense mechanisms described by Freud (see Chapter 15), we guard ourselves through **self-deception**—the processes by which we distort and hide unpleasant truths from ourselves.

Let's begin with a stark fact about human behavior: most people think and speak highly of themselves. Time and again, researchers find that subjects see positive traits as more self-descriptive than negative ones, rate themselves more highly than they rate others, overestimate their own contribution to a joint effort, exaggerate their control over life events, predict a bright future rather than a bleak one, and seek more information about their strengths than weaknesses (Taylor & Brown, 1988). In what is known as the "mere ownership effect," people even rate the letters contained in their own name as more attractive than the other letters of the alphabet (Hoorens & Nuttin, 1993). It's not that we deliberately flatter ourselves, either. The response is more like a reflex action. Thus, when subjects are busy or distracted as they make self-ratings, the judgments they come up with are quicker and even more favorable (Paulhus et al., 1989). Everyone can't be perfect, nor can we *all* be better than average. So what supports these positive illusions?

One support mechanism is that people often make self-promoting *biased attributions* for important life outcomes. When students receive their exam grades, those who get A's take credit for the success; those who do poorly whine about the instructor and test questions. When college professors have their articles accepted for publication, they assume this decision reflects on the quality of their work; when articles are rejected, these same professors blame the editor, the reviewers, and the shortage of journal space. When gamblers win bets, they see themselves as skillful; when they lose, they complain about random, fluke events that transformed near victory into defeat. When professional athletes win, they fill the sports pages with self-congratulatory quotes; when they lose, they blame the officials, weather, and opposing players. Whether people explain their behavior to others or in private, and whether they are trying to be honest or to make a good impression, there is bias: we are prone to take credit for success and distance ourselves from failure (Schlenker et al., 1990).

On the soccer field, as in other settings, people are more likely to take credit for success than blame for failure.

People also exhibit *unrealistic optimism*. As presented in Figure 18.3, college students asked to predict their own future compared to that of their classmates believed they were more likely to graduate higher in the class, get a better job, earn a higher salary, have a happier marriage, and bear a gifted child. They also believed they were less likely to get fired, get divorced, have a drinking problem, become depressed, or suffer from a heart attack (Weinstein, 1980). Numerous other examples illustrate this point. In polls taken between 1952 and 1980, American voters—regardless of whether they favored the ultimate winner or the loser—expected their favorite candidate to prevail by a 4-to-1 ratio (Granberg & Brent, 1983). Similarly, sports fans let their team preferences interfere with the bets they place, even when they're trying to be "objective" (Babad & Katz, 1991). In one study, college students gave themselves only a 20 percent chance of getting divorced—even though they knew that the divorce rate for new marriages is 50 percent (Kunda, 1987).

Figure 18.3

Unrealistic Optimism

When students were asked to predict their own future compared to that of their classmates of the same sex, they rated their own chances as above average for positive events and as below average for negative events.

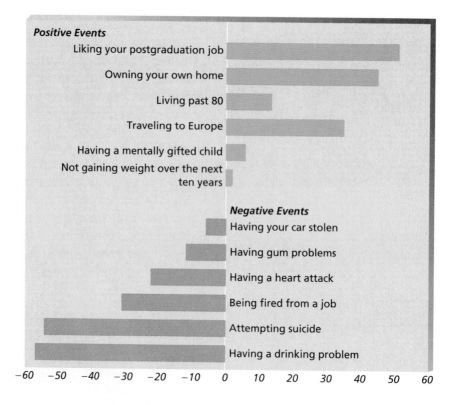

A third strategy that people use to preserve their self-esteem is perhaps the most interesting of all. When people fail or anticipate defeat, they make excuses (Snyder et al., 1983). "I had a headache," "I don't test well," "I was out partying all last night," and other creative admissions shield us from what could be the most shattering implication of failure—a lack of ability. It seems paradoxical, but at times we may even sabotage our own performance as a way to preserve our self-esteem (Higgins et al., 1990).

First described by Stephen Berglas and Edward Jones (1978), **self-handicapping** refers to actions people take to hinder their own performance

■ **self-handicapping** Behaviors designed to sabotage one's own performance and provide a subsequent excuse for failure.

This college student sits drunk on a Texas beach during spring break. People may drink heavily to escape from a past failure—and to set up a face-saving excuse for future failure.

in order to build an excuse for possible failure. To demonstrate, Berglas and Jones recruited college students for an experiment supposedly on the effects of drugs on intellectual performance. All subjects worked on a twenty-item test of analogies and were told that they had done well, after which they expected to work on a second, similar test. For one group, the problems were relatively easy, leading subjects to expect more success; for a second group, the problems were insoluble, leaving subjects confused about their initial performance and worried that they would fail. Before taking the second test, subjects were given a choice of two drugs: "actavil," which was supposed to improve performance, or "pandocrin," which was supposed to impair it. Although no drugs were actually administered, most subjects who were confident about the upcoming test selected the actavil; in contrast, male subjects (but not the females) who feared the outcome of the second test chose the pandocrin. By handicapping themselves, these men set up a convenient excuse for failure.

Some people more than others use self-handicapping as a defense—and there are different ways to do so. For example, men often handicap themselves by taking drugs or neglecting to practice, while women tend to cite stress and physical symptoms instead (Hirt et al., 1991). People also differ in the reasons they have for self-handicapping. Dianne Tice (1991) found that for people who are low in self-esteem, self-handicapping provides a defensive, face-saving excuse in case they fail (it's not your fault), while for those who are high in self-esteem, it offers an opportunity to claim bonus credit if they succeed (you must be amazing). Whatever the goal, self-handicapping seems an ingenious strategy: with the odds stacked against you, the self is insulated from failure and enhanced by success. Unfortunately, this strategy is not without considerable cost. Sure, it may ease the pressure to succeed, but sabotaging yourself—by not studying or practicing, or by drinking too much, using drugs, or faking illness—also increases the risk of failure. Sometimes you just have to take chances in order to get ahead in life.

A fourth way that people psychologically boost their spirits is by making "downward" *social comparisons*. When victimized by tragic life events (perhaps a crime, accident, disease, or the death of a loved one), people like to *affiliate* with others in the same situation who are adjusting well, role models who offer hope and guidance—but they prefer to *compare* themselves with others who are less successful, less happy, or less fortunate (Taylor & Lobel, 1989). It helps to know that life could be worse. That's why many cancer patients contrast themselves to other patients who are *not* coping well (Wood et al., 1985), and why most believe that they're better off than their peers (Taylor et al., 1986). Interviews with breast-cancer patients tell the story. One woman who had only a lump removed wondered "how awful it must be for women who have had a full mastectomy." An older woman who had a mastectomy said: "The people I really feel sorry for are these young gals. To lose a breast when you're so young must be awful." Yet a young mastectomy patient derived comfort from the fact that "if I hadn't been married, this thing would have really gotten to me" (Taylor, 1989, p. 171). As these quotes poignantly demonstrate, there's always someone else with whom we can favorably compare. In the words of a dying patient who appeared on the CBS documentary *A Time to Die,* "It's not the worst thing that could happen."

Reality, Illusions, and Mental Health

Psychologists used to think that an accurate perception of reality is vital to mental health. More and more, however, this view is being challenged by research on the mechanisms of self-deception. Consistently, people delude themselves with biased attributions, unrealistic optimism, self-handicapping, excuses, and downward social comparison. The question is, are these illusions a sign of well-being or symptoms of disorder?

When Shelley Taylor and Jonathon Brown (1988) reviewed the relevant research, they found that people who are depressed or low in self-esteem have less inflated and more realistic views of themselves than do others who are better adjusted. Their self-appraisals are more likely to match appraisals of them made by neutral others; they make fewer self-serving attributions for success and failure; they are less likely to exaggerate their control over uncontrollable events; and they make more balanced predictions about the future. Taylor and Brown thus drew the provocative conclusion that when it comes to the self, positive illusions—not accurate perceptions of reality—promote happiness, the desire to care for others, and the ability to work. In short, "these illusions help make each individual's world a warmer and more active and beneficent place in which to live" (1988, p. 205).

Taylor and Brown are not alone in their conclusion. Many psychologists believe that self-deception is adaptive (Lockard & Paulhus, 1988). Again, correlations indicate that the higher a person's self-esteem, the more likely he or she is to employ the mechanisms of self-deception. But these correlations do not prove that self-deception raises self-esteem. Besides, would you expect an illusional pattern always to be adaptive? Are *you* better off overestimating your abilities or the control you can exert over the events in your life? Are you better off the eternal optimist, or the hard realist? Baumeister and Steven Scher (1988) are not so sure. Looking at a wide range of self-defeating behaviors, these investigators conclude that illusions can give rise to chronic patterns of self-destruction. Think about it. People may escape from self-awareness through alcohol and drugs, self-handicap themselves into failure and underachievement, and deny health-related problems until it's too late for treatment. Research also shows that people who blame others for their own misfortune—having a miscarriage, giving birth to a deformed child, getting hurt in an automobile accident, or suffering from cancer, heart disease, or arthritis—are later more emotionally scarred than those who do not externalize the blame (Tennen & Affleck, 1990). Reality or illusion, which is more adaptive? As researchers debate the short-term and long-term consequences of positive illusions, it is clear that there is no simple answer (Colvin & Block, 1994; Taylor & Brown, 1994).

Shyness and Social Anxiety

■ **social anxiety** Feelings of discomfort in the presence of others, typically accompanied by shyness.

Have you ever felt so conspicuous upon entering a roomful of people that you thought all eyes were staring at you? Do you get nervous about asking someone for a date? Is it difficult for you to make oral presentations or to speak up in class? Do you look down and blush whenever someone compliments you? Do you hate being at the center of attention? When people are overly self-conscious, they often experience **social anxiety**—feelings of discomfort in the presence of others.

Social anxiety is often found in people who are low in self-esteem. It is also frequently accompanied by *shyness,* a form of inhibition and social awkwardness. Shyness is a pervasive problem. Roughly 40 percent of all Americans describe themselves as shy. So do 31 percent of people in Israel, 40 percent in Germany, 55 percent in Taiwan, and 60 percent in Japan (Zimbardo, 1977). People who are shy find it very hard to approach strangers (particularly members of the opposite sex), introduce themselves, phone someone for a date, speak up in class, participate in groups, and mingle at parties (see Table 18.2). Social situations like these may even produce bodily symptoms of anxiety such as sweating, an upset stomach, a racing heart, and trembling. Some people become so fearful of being scrutinized and embarrassed—a potentially shattering blow to the self—that they avoid all interpersonal contact and are clinically diagnosed as having a social phobia (see Chapter 16).

Table 18.2

How Shy a Person Are You?

To assess your own level of shyness, respond to the ten statements at right on a 1–5 point scale (1 = very untrue, 5 = very true), then calculate the average of your responses. The average item mean is 2.55 (Cheek & Briggs, 1990).

1. I feel tense when I'm with people I don't know well.
2. I am socially somewhat awkward.
3. I am often uncomfortable at parties and other social functions.
4. When in a group of people, I have trouble thinking of the right things to talk about.
5. It is hard for me to act natural when I am meeting new people.
6. I feel nervous when speaking to someone in authority.
7. I have trouble looking someone right in the eye.
8. I feel inhibited in social situations.
9. I am more shy with members of the opposite sex.
10. During conversations with new acquaintances, I worry about saying something dumb.

Shyness can arise from different sources. In some cases, it may be an inborn personality characteristic. As we saw in Chapter 9, Jerome Kagan and his colleagues (1990) have found that some infants are highly sensitive to stimulation, inhibited, and cautious even at birth. In other cases, shyness develops as a learned reaction to failed interactions with others. Clearly, social problems of the past ignite social anxieties about the future (Leary, 1983). Whatever the source, the problem is real—and it has painful consequences for a person's self-esteem. Studies show that shy people evaluate themselves negatively, expect to fail in their social encounters, blame themselves when they do, and conform out of a fear of rejection. Worst of all, many shy people go into self-imposed isolation, which makes them feel lonely, only to sink deeper and deeper into distress (Cheek & Melchior, 1990).

Loneliness is indeed a sad and heart-wrenching emotion (see Table 18.3). In general, surveys show that people who are romantically unattached are lonelier than those who have romantic partners, and people who are unemployed are lonelier than those who go to work every day. And contrary to

Table 18.3

Statements That Describe Loneliness

(Russell et al., 1980, p. 475)

There is no one I can turn to.

No one really knows me well.

People are around me but not with me.

I feel left out.

I feel isolated from others.

My interests and ideas are not shared by those around me.

I lack companionship.

I am unhappy being so withdrawn.

Surveys show that adolescents and young adults are the loneliest age group in American society.

■ **health psychology** The study of the links between psychological factors and physical health and illness.

the stereotypic image of the lonely old retired man passing time on a park bench and feeding pigeons, the loneliest groups in American society are adolescents and young adults, eighteen to thirty years old. In fact, loneliness declines over the course of adulthood—at least until health problems in the seventies limit social activities (Peplau & Perlman, 1982).

At one time or another, we have all felt lonely. It's not fun. So how do people cope with this distressing state of mind? When college students were asked about the behavioral strategies they use to combat loneliness, 96 percent said they sometimes or often tried harder to be friendly to other people; 94 percent took their minds off the problem by reading or watching TV; 93 percent tried extra hard to succeed at another aspect of life; 88 percent distracted themselves by running, shopping, washing the car, or engaging in other busy activities; 82 percent looked for new ways of meeting people; 80 percent tried to improve their physical appearance; 60 percent talked to a friend or relative about the problem; 36 percent used alcohol or drugs to wash away feelings of loneliness; and 9 percent sought help from a counselor or therapist (Rook & Peplau, 1982). In some ways, these students actively tried to improve their situation. In other ways, they coped with being alone by redirecting attention away from the self through various forms of distraction.

STRESS AND HEALTH

The reason for psychology's interest in mental health and well-being is obvious. But the field has also had a long-standing interest in physical health, a domain normally associated with medicine. Influenced by psychoanalysis, many clinical psychologists used to study "psychosomatic" ailments such as asthma, ulcers, headaches, and constipation, which were thought to result from unconscious conflicts. Working from a behavioral perspective, others studied "psychophysiological" disorders. Either way, the subject matter was basically the same (Gatchel & Blanchard, 1993).

Over the past few years, increasing numbers of researchers have become interested in **health psychology**, the application of psychology to the pro-

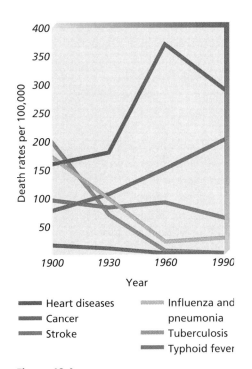

Figure 18.4

Leading Causes of Death, 1900–1990

As shown, heart disease, cancer, and strokes have replaced infectious diseases as the major causes of death in the United States.

motion of physical health and the prevention and treatment of illness (Adler & Matthews, 1994). You may wonder, what does psychology have to do with catching a cold, having a heart attack, or being afflicted by cancer? If you could turn the clock back a few years and ask your family doctor, his or her answer would be "very little." In the past, illness was considered a purely biological event. But this strict medical perspective is now giving way to a *biosocial model,* which holds that health is a joint product of biological, social, cognitive, developmental, and clinical factors.

Part of the reason for this broadened view is that illness patterns over the years have changed in significant ways. Before the twentieth century, the principal causes of death were contagious diseases such as polio, smallpox, typhoid fever, tuberculosis, malaria, influenza, and pneumonia. In the United States, none of these infectious illnesses is currently a leading killer. Instead, Americans are most likely to die, in order of risk, from heart disease, cancer, strokes, and accidents (AIDS is eleventh on the list)—problems that are sometimes preventable through changes in mind and behavior (see Figure 18.4).

Although it's not possible to quantify the extent of the problem, psychological stress is known to be a particularly potent killer. Regardless of who you are, when you were born, or where you live, you have no doubt experienced stress. Sitting in a rush-hour traffic jam, interviewing for the job of your dreams, rushing to make an appointment, packing your belongings to move, getting married or divorced, losing hours of work to a computer crash, cramming for the next morning's exam, getting into an argument with a close friend, rooting for your favorite sports team in a championship game, worrying about an unwanted pregnancy or the health of your child, getting mugged on the street, living in a noisy and overcrowded building, visiting the dentist, struggling to make financial ends meet, and caring for a loved one who is sick—these are the kinds of stresses and strains we all must learn to live with. Whether they are short-term or long-term, serious or mild, no one is immune and there is no escape. But there are ways to cope.

In this section, we examine three interrelated questions of relevance to your health and well-being: (1) What are some of the primary sources of stress? (2) What are the effects of stress on the body? and (3) What are the most adaptive ways of coping with stress? Together, the answers to these questions provide a useful model of the stress-and-coping process (see Figure 18.5).

Figure 18.5 Stress and Coping

Advances in health psychology show that although stressful events have effects on the body, the way we cope with stress can promote health or illness.

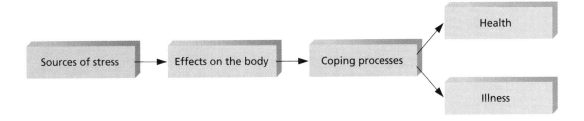

The Sources of Stress

■ **stress** An aversive state of arousal triggered by the perception that an event threatens our ability to cope effectively.

■ **posttraumatic stress disorder** An anxiety disorder triggered by an extremely stressful event, such as combat.

Stress is an unpleasant state of arousal that arises when we perceive that an event threatens our ability to cope effectively. There are many different sources of stress, or *stressors*. Try writing down the stressors in your own life, and you'll probably find that the items in your list can be divided into three major categories: catastrophes, major life events, and daily hassles.

Catastrophes   As the water level rose, Nick and Crystal Goedereis and their four children removed whatever valuables they could from their farm in Quincy, Illinois. To the bitter end, they spent nights in sleeping bags on their bare living room floor. After many weeks of heavy rain, however, the Mississippi River engulfed their five-bedroom home and ripped it apart. And they were not alone. Throughout the Midwest, major rivers reached record-high levels, causing levees to burst, causing billions of dollars of property and crop damage, and displacing thousands of families from their homes. In parts of Illinois, Missouri, Wisconsin, Kansas, South Dakota, Nebraska, Iowa, and Minnesota, the great flood of 1993 was an unprecedented disaster (Sidey, 1993).

The flood dealt a devastating blow to many people. Other events that have traumatic effects include rape, homelessness, automobile accidents, nuclear accidents, hurricanes, and earthquakes. The harmful impact of catastrophic stressors on health is well documented. For example, Paul and Gerald Adams (1984) examined the public records in Othello, Washington, both before and after the 1980 eruption of the Mount Saint Helens volcano, which spewed thick layers of ash all over the community. They discovered that there were dramatic post-eruption increases in calls made to a mental health crisis line, police reports of domestic violence, referrals to the alcohol treatment center, and visits to the local hospital emergency room. Based on a review of fifty-two additional studies, Anthony Rubonis and Leonard Bickman (1991) concluded that high rates of psychopathology are common in the wake of large-scale environmental disasters.

It has long been known that war in particular leaves deep and permanent psychological scars. Soldiers who experience combat see horrifying injuries, death, and destruction on a routine basis, and are left with images and emotions that do not fade. In World War I, the problem was called "shell shock." In World War II, it was known as "combat fatigue." Now called **posttraumatic stress disorder**, it is identified by such symptoms as sleeplessness, anxiety, depression, alcoholism, and social withdrawal. To evaluate the extent of the problem, researchers at the Centers for Disease Control (1988) compared 7,000 Vietnam combat veterans with 7,000 noncombat veterans who served in the military at the same time, more than twenty years ago. They found that although the Vietnam war is only a distant memory to most Americans, 15 percent of those who saw combat—twice as many as in the comparison group—reported lingering symptoms of posttraumatic stress disorder. Those who had particularly traumatic experiences (crossing enemy lines, being ambushed or shot at, handling dead bodies) were five times more likely to have nightmares, vivid flashbacks, startle reactions, and concentration problems (Goldberg et al., 1990). Similar results are found among older veterans of World War II and the Korean War (Fontana & Rosenheck, 1994; Spiro et al., 1994).

Tornadoes have such devastating power that those who survive often exhibit posttraumatic stress disorder.

Major Life Events   Some people are lucky enough to avoid major catastrophes. But nobody can avoid stress. The reason, say some psychologists, is that change, any kind of change—because it forces us to adapt to new circumstances—causes stress. This hypothesis was first proposed by Thomas Holmes and Richard Rahe (1967), who interviewed hospital patients and found that their illnesses were often preceded by major changes in some aspect of their lives. Some of the changes were negative (getting hurt, divorced, or fired), but others were quite positive (getting married or promoted, or having a baby). To measure life stress, Holmes and Rahe thus devised the Social Readjustment Rating Scale (SRRS)—a checklist of forty-three major life changes, each assigned a numerical value based on the amount of readjustment it requires (see Table 18.4).

Table 18.4

Sample Items from the Social Readjustment Rating Scale

For the events listed, circle those that happened to you in the past year. Your total number of points can be used to estimate the amount of stress in your life. Notice that this scale omits many events that are common for college students—changes in grades, summer job status, graduation, divorce of parents, and relationships with friends and lovers.

Life event	Value
1. Death of spouse	100
2. Divorce	73
3. Jail term or imprisonment	63
4. Death of a close family member	63
5. Major personal injury or illness	53
6. Marriage	50
7. Losing one's job	47
8. Pregnancy	40
9. Sexual difficulties	39
10. Addition of a new family member	39
11. Change in financial state	37
12. Death of a close friend	36
13. Change to a different line of work	36
14. Taking out a large mortgage (e.g., for a house)	31
15. Change in status at work	29
16. Son or daughter leaving home	29
17. Outstanding personal achievement	28
18. Major change in work hours or conditions	20
19. Move to a new residence	20
20. Transfer to a new school	20
21. Taking out a small loan (e.g., for a new car)	17
22. Change in sleeping habits (time of day, amount)	16
23. Change in eating habits (time, amount, etc.)	15
24. Vacation	13
25. Minor law violations (traffic tickets, etc.)	11

You may have seen the SRRS, or other questionnaires like it, in a book or magazine. The claim made is that the number of stress points or "life-change units" you accumulate in a recent period of time predicts your susceptibility to stress-related illnesses. I recall filling out such a questionnaire the year I finished graduate school. I had just received my Ph.D. Right away, my wife and I got married, moved to a new state, rented a new apartment, and started new jobs. For the first and only time in her life, my wife developed an ulcer. Her doctor's first question: "Has anything changed in your life?"

The simple notion that change is inherently stressful has an intuitive ring about it. Indeed, research shows that people with high scores on the SRRS are more likely to come down with various physical illnesses (Dohrenwend & Dohrenwend, 1978; Maddi et al., 1987). But is change per se necessarily harmful? There are two problems with this interpretation. First, although there is a statistical link between negative events and health, research does not similarly support the claim that positive stressors—taking a vacation, graduating, winning a lottery, starting a new career, or getting married— are also harmful (Stewart et al., 1986). Look again at the SRRS items in Table 18.4, and you'll see that most events on the list are negative. The second complicating factor is that the impact of any change depends on who the person is and how that change is interpreted. For example, moving to a new country is less stressful to immigrants who know their new language and culture (Berry et al., 1992), and having an abortion is less stressful to women who have the support of their family, partners, and friends (Major et al., 1990). To summarize, the amount of change in a person's life may provide crude estimates of stress and future health, but the predictive equation is far more complex.

Microstressors   Think for a moment about the sources of stress in your life, and catastrophes or exceptional events spring quickly to mind. Researchers are now finding, however, that the most significant source of stress arises from the hassles that irritate us on a daily basis. Environmental factors such as population density, loud noise, extreme heat or cold, and cigarette smoke are all possible sources of stress. Car problems, waiting in line at the supermarket, losing our keys, getting into an argument with a friend, nosy neighbors, final exams, a bad day at work, worrying about money, and other "microstressors" also place a constant strain on us (see Table 18.5). Unfortunately, there is nothing "micro" about the impact of these stressors on our health and well-being. Studies show that the accumulation of daily hassles is more predictive of illness than are major life events (DeLongis et al., 1982; Eckenrode, 1984; Weinberger et al., 1987).

There is one source of stress that plagues many people on a routine basis. At work, relentless job pressures can grind away at a person and, over time, cause *burnout*—a state of emotional exhaustion characterized by a cynical attitude toward others and a diminished sense of accomplishment. People

Waiting helplessly in traffic is one of the most common microstressors in daily life.

Table 18.5

The following are among the daily events that stress children, college students, and adults (Kanner et al., 1981, pp. 24–29; Kanner et al., 1991, pp. 168–169; Kohn et al., 1990, pp. 628–629).

Children and early adolescents

Having to clean up your room
Being bored and having nothing to do
Seeing that another kid can do something better
Getting punished for doing something wrong
Having to go to bed when you didn't want to
Being teased at school

College students

Conflicts with a boyfriend or girlfriend
Dissatisfaction with your athletic skills
Having your trust betrayed by a friend
Struggling to meet your own academic standards
Not having enough leisure time
Gossip concerning someone you care about
Dissatisfaction with your physical appearance

Middle-aged adults

Concerns about weight
Health of a family member
Social obligations
Inconsiderate smokers
Concerns about money
Misplacing or losing things
Home maintenance
Job security

---

who are "burned out" thus describe themselves as used up, drained, frustrated, callous, hardened, apathetic, lacking in energy, and without motivation (Maslach, 1982). Researchers used to think that only teachers, doctors, nurses, police officers, and others in the human-service professions were at risk. It now appears, however, that anyone who experiences prolonged stress in the workplace is vulnerable (Pines & Aronson, 1988).

The Physiological Effects of Stress

The term *stress* was popularized by Hans Selye (1936, 1976), an endocrinologist. As a young medical student, Selye noticed that patients who were hospitalized for different illnesses often had similar symptoms, such as muscle weakness, a loss of weight and appetite, and a lack of ambition. Maybe these symptoms were part of a generalized response to an attack on the body, he thought. In the 1930s, Selye tested this hypothesis by exposing laboratory rats to various stressors, including heat, cold, heavy exercise, toxic substances, food deprivation, and electric shock. As anticipated, these different stressors all produced a similar physiological response: enlarged adrenal glands, shrunken lymph nodes, and bleeding stomach ulcers. Selye called the reaction *stress*, a word that quickly became part of everyday language.

According to Selye, the body naturally responds to stress in a three-staged process he called the **general adaptation syndrome** (see Figure 18.6). Sparked by the recognition of a threat, any threat—predator, enemy soldier, speeding automobile, or virus—the body has an initial *alarm* reaction. To meet the challenge, adrenaline and other hormones are poured into the bloodstream, thus heightening physiological arousal. At this stage, the body is ready to mobilize all its resources to ward off the threat. Next comes a *resistance* stage, during which the body remains aroused and on the alert. There is a continued release of stress hormones, and local defenses are activated (if there is a virus, for example, immune-system antibodies are called into action). However, if the stress persists for a prolonged period of time (as in a bad marriage, high-pressure job, or poverty), the body will fall into an *exhaustion* stage. According to Selye, our antistress resources are limited. Eventually, resistance breaks down, putting us at risk for illness and even death.

Figure 18.6

The General Adaptation Syndrome

According to Selye, the human body responds to threat in three phases: alarm, resistance, and exhaustion.

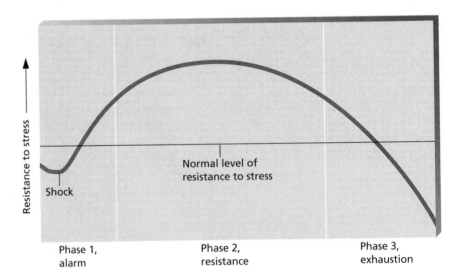

Research reveals that different types of stressors elicit somewhat different bodily responses. Still, Selye's basic model makes an important point: stress may be an adaptive, short-term reaction to threat, but over time it compromises our health and well-being. As we'll see in the coming pages, stress is linked to coronary heart disease and the functioning of the immune system.

Coronary Heart Disease   Coronary heart disease (CHD) is a narrowing of the blood vessels that carry oxygen and nutrients to the heart muscle. It is currently the leading cause of death in the United States. An estimated 69 million Americans suffer from CHD. For many, the result is a heart attack, which occurs when the blood supply to the heart is blocked. This causes an uncomfortable feeling of pressure, fullness, squeezing, or pain in the center of the chest—and sometimes also sweating, dizziness, nausea, fainting, and a shortness of breath. Every year, 1.5 million Americans have heart attacks. One-third do not survive.

■ **general adaptation syndrome** A three-staged process (alarm, resistance, and exhaustion) by which the body responds to stress.

■ **Type A personality** A personality characterized by an impatient, hard-driving, competitive, and anger-prone pattern of behavior.

■ **Type B personality** A personality characterized by an easygoing, relaxed pattern of behavior.

"It's for you!"

Talking on the phone while driving is symptomatic of a hurried Type A lifestyle. [© 1994 Jack Ziegler and The Cartoon Bank, Inc.]

Several factors are known to increase the risk of CHD. The three most important are hypertension, or high blood pressure; cigarette smoking; and high cholesterol (others include a family history of CHD, obesity, and lack of exercise). People who experience one of these three major risk factors are twice as likely to develop CHD, those with two risk factors are 3.5 times as likely, and those with all three are six times as likely. These statistics are compelling and should not be taken lightly. But combined, these factors account for fewer than half the known cases of CHD. What's missing from the equation is a fourth major risk factor: stress.

In 1956, cardiologists Meyer Friedman and Ray Rosenman were studying the relationship between cholesterol and coronary heart disease. After noticing that husbands were more likely than their wives to have CHD, they speculated that work-related stress might be the reason (at the time, most women did not work outside the home). To test this hypothesis, Friedman and Rosenman interviewed 3,000 healthy middle-aged men. Those who seemed to be the most hard-driving, restless, competitive, impatient, time-conscious, and quick to anger were classified as having a **Type A personality.** Roughly an equal number of those who were easygoing, relaxed, and laid back were classified as **Type B's.** Did this classification scheme predict health outcomes? Yes. Out of 258 men who had heart attacks over the following nine years, 69 percent were Type A's and only 31 percent were Type B's (Rosenman et al., 1975).

As described in Chapter 15, the Type A personality of the so-called workaholic comprises not one trait but many—and includes a sense of time urgency, competitive drive, and a dangerous mix of anger, cynicism, and hostility (Friedman & Booth-Kewley, 1988; Matthews, 1988; Smith, 1992; Wright, 1988). Type A people walk fast, talk fast, speed up at yellow traffic lights, interrupt speakers in mid-sentence, get angry with people who are late, eat on the run, work late into the night, get impatient about waiting in line, lash out at others in frustration, strive to win at all costs, and save time by doing several things all at once (see Table 18.6).

Table 18.6

The Type A Personality

These questions are among those used to uncover the Type A personality. Note, however, that *how* a person answers these questions in an interview can be more revealing than the answers themselves (Friedman and Rosenman, 1974).

——— 1. Do you find it difficult to restrain yourself from hurrying others' speech (finishing their sentences for them)?

——— 2. Do you often try to do more than one thing at a time (such as eat and read simultaneously)?

——— 3. Do you often feel guilty if you use extra time to relax?

——— 4. Do you tend to get involved in a great number of projects at once?

——— 5. Do you find yourself racing through the yellow lights when you drive?

——— 6. Do you need to win in order to derive enjoyment from games and sports?

——— 7. Do you generally move, walk, and eat rapidly?

——— 8. Do you agree to take on too many responsibilities?

——— 9. Do you detest waiting in lines?

———10. Do you have an intense desire to better your position in life and impress others?

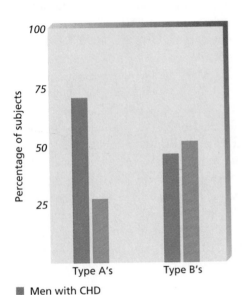

Figure 18.7

Personality and Coronary Heart Disease

Studies of middle-aged men reveal that Type A's are more likely than Type B's to have CHD (Miller et al., 1991).

The link between Type A behavior and coronary heart disease is not as strong as was initially believed, but the numbers are still impressive. In their haste to pursue this provocative line of health research, many psychologists tried to identify Type A people using quick, easy-to-administer questionnaires instead of the kinds of time-consuming interviews that Friedman and Rosenman conducted. These questionnaires, however, were not predictive. Indeed, the Type A personality is more evident from the subject's interview *behavior* (whether he or she constantly checks the time, interrupts the interviewer, speaks quickly and forcefully, makes restless fidgety movements) than from his or her *self-reports*. Recent research thus shows that when interviews are used to make the diagnosis, 70 percent of men who have CHD are classified as Type A—compared to only 46 percent of those who are healthy (Miller et al., 1991). These results are illustrated in Figure 18.7.

There are at least two possible reasons for the connection between Type A behavior and coronary heart disease (see Figure 18.8). First, Type A's may be less health-conscious than Type B's. People who feel stressed smoke more, consume more caffeine and alcohol, exercise and sleep less, and eat less healthy foods (Conway et al., 1981; Ketterer & Maercklein, 1991; Krietler et al., 1991). Second, Type A's are physiologically more reactive. Particularly in uncontrollable and frustrating situations, Type A's react with greater increases in pulse rate, blood pressure, and adrenaline—a hormone that accelerates the build-up of fatty plaques on the artery walls, causing a hardening of the arteries (Krantz & Manuck, 1984; Harbin, 1989).

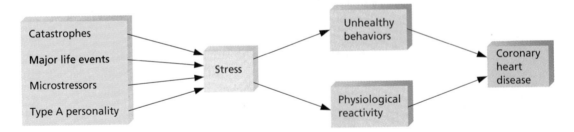

Figure 18.8 **Pathways from Stress to CHD**

Under stress, people (1) engage in less healthy behaviors (they smoke more, sleep less, and consume more caffeine and alcohol), and (2) are more physiologically reactive (they exhibit larger increases in pulse rate, blood pressure, and adrenaline level).

■ **immune system** A biological surveillance system that detects and destroys "nonself" substances that invade the body.

The Immune System   When it comes to the interaction between mind and body, the link between stress and the heart is just the tip of the iceberg. It now appears that stress may also increase the risk of chronic back pain, diabetes, arthritis, appendicitis, upper respiratory infections, herpes, gum disease, the common cold, and even some forms of cancer. How can stress have such a wide range of disabling effects? Answer: By compromising the body's immune system—the first line of defense against illness (Coe, 1993; Herbert & Cohen, 1993b).

The **immune system** is a complex surveillance system that fights bacteria, viruses, parasites, fungi, and other "nonself" substances that invade the body. The system consists of more than a trillion specialized white blood

■ **lymphocytes** Specialized white blood cells that secrete chemical antibodies and facilitate the immune response.

cells called **lymphocytes** that originate in the bone marrow (*B cells*) and thymus (*T cells*), migrate to various organs, circulate through the bloodstream, and secrete chemical antibodies. These sharklike search-and-destroy cells protect us by patrolling the body twenty-four hours a day and then attacking trespassers. Sometimes, however, they overreact and strike at benign material. This can result in "autoimmune" diseases such as multiple sclerosis, trigger allergic reactions to harmless pollen and ragweed, and cause the body to reject surgically transplanted organs. The immune system is also equipped with large scavenger cells known as *macrophages* ("big eaters") and *natural killer cells* (NK cells) that specifically attack viruses and cancerous tumors. Serving as a "sixth sense" for foreign invaders, the immune system continually renews itself. During the few seconds it takes to read this sentence, your body will have produced 10 million new lymphocytes (see Figure 18.9).

Figure 18.9

The Immune System

Originating in the bone marrow, lymphocytes move into certain organs and circulate continuously through the bloodstream (right). As pictured below left, a B cell migrates from the bone marrow to a blood vessel. Below right, two T cells use surface receptors to detect an infected cell.

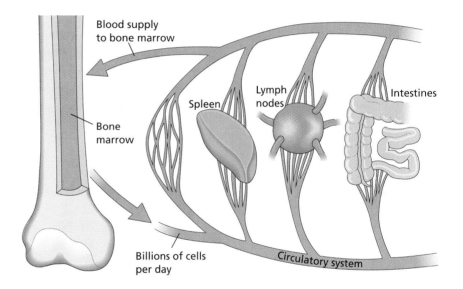

Blood supply to bone marrow

Bone marrow

Spleen

Lymph nodes

Intestines

Billions of cells per day

Circulatory system

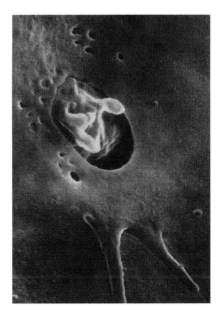

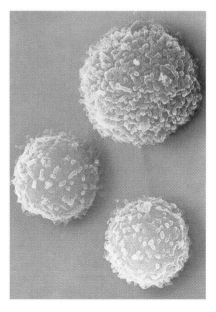

■ **psychoneuroimmunology (PNI)** A new subfield of psychology that examines the interactions among psychological factors, the nervous system, and the immune system.

Following their nine days in orbit, these NASA astronauts pose soon after touching ground. Given what is known about the link between stress and immunity, their immune responses may have been in a weakened state when this picture was taken.

Today, health psychologists are interested in the connections among the mind, the brain, and the immune system. Accordingly, many researchers take blood samples from animal and human subjects exposed to varying stressors in order to evaluate the effects of stress on the number and activity of the lymphocytes. This new field—which focuses on the complex interplay between psychology and the immune system—is called **psychoneuroimmunology, or PNI** (Ader et al., 1991; Goleman & Gurin, 1993).

There is now mounting evidence that stress has a harmful effect on immunity. The medical community used to reject the idea, but no longer. What changed? Animal experiments showed that rats exposed to noise, overcrowding, or inescapable shocks, and primates separated from their social companions, exhibit a drop in immune cell activity (Coe, 1993; Dunn, 1989). Then a link was observed among humans. Intrigued by the fact that people often get sick and die shortly after they are widowed, R. W. Barthrop and his colleagues (1977) took blood samples from twenty-six men and women whose spouses had just died. Compared to nonwidowed controls, these grief-stricken spouses exhibited a weakened immune response, as measured by T cell activity. This was the first demonstration of its kind. Additional studies soon revealed weakened immune responses in other stressed-out groups as well: NASA astronauts after reentry into the atmosphere and splashdown, subjects deprived of sleep for more than forty-eight hours, students in the midst of final exams, men and women recently divorced or separated, people who are caring for a family member with Alzheimer's disease, people with snake phobia exposed to a live snake, and workers who have recently lost their jobs (O'Leary, 1990).

How do grief, stress, or other psychological states "get into" the immune system? It is known that organs that play a central role in the immune system (the thymus, bone marrow, and lymph nodes) are richly endowed with nerve fibers, providing a direct pipeline to the brain. But what explains the link between stress and the activity of the lymphocytes? There are two possible mechanisms (see Figure 18.10). First, as was described earlier, people who are under stress tend to smoke more, use more alcohol and drugs, sleep less, exercise less, and have poorer diets. These unhealthy behaviors can weaken key aspects of the immune system. For example, research shows that there is a correlation between the amount of sleep one gets and natural-killer-cell activity (Irwin et al., 1992). Second, stress triggers the release of adrenaline and certain other hormones into the bloodstream—and these hormones suppress lymphocyte activity. The result is a lowering of the body's resistance and increased susceptibility to illness (Cohen & Williamson, 1991).

Figure 18.10

Pathways from Stress to Illness

Negative emotional states may cause illness in two ways: (1) by promoting unhealthy behaviors (more alcohol, less sleep, and so on), and (2) by triggering the release of hormones that weaken the immune system by suppressing activity of the lymphocytes.

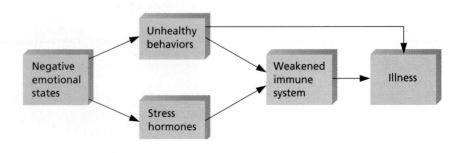

In Chapter 2, we saw that a link between stress and illness was established in a study of stress and the common cold. In that study, Sheldon Cohen and his colleagues (1993) recruited healthy women and men, administered blood tests and a medical examination, and had them complete a battery of questionnaires concerning negative life events and stress. Using nasal drops, the experimenters then exposed subjects to one of five respiratory viruses or to a harmless saline solution. The subjects were then quarantined and held for a seven-day observation period. Medical tests revealed that not all subjects who were exposed became infected with the virus—and not all those who were infected actually caught a cold. Stress was a factor in this outcome: 53 percent of the infected subjects who were under high levels of stress developed cold symptoms, compared to only 40 percent of those who were under lower levels of stress.

Stress and other negative emotions may even hasten the spread of cancer. In an early effort to test this hypothesis, Madeline Visintainer and her colleagues (1982) implanted tumorous cancer cells into a group of rats, and then exposed the rats to shocks they could escape by pressing a bar (a situation that promoted a feeling of mastery), inescapable shocks (a situation that promoted helplessness and despair), or no shocks at all. Within a month, 50 percent of the rats in the no-shock control group died; the others rejected the tumor. In the helplessness group, the death rate climbed to 73 percent. In the mastery group, it was only 30 percent. This study was among the first to demonstrate that psychological states can influence the spread of cancer. How does this happen? Research shows that inescapable shock and other traumas suppress activities of the immune system (Laudenslager et al., 1983).

The growth of tumors in helpless white laboratory rats is interesting, but does the same principle apply to people? For obvious ethical reasons, researchers cannot fill human subjects with despair or inject lethal tumors into their bodies to test the cause-and-effect chain directly. But they can examine the medical records of people whose lives are struck by tragedy. Investigations of this sort reveal that cancer appears more often than normal among people who are in a negative emotional state (Sklar & Anisman, 1981). In one large-scale study, researchers followed up on two thousand male workers of the Western Electric Company in Chicago whose personalities had been assessed in 1958. At the time, test scores indicated that some of the men were low in self-esteem, oversensitive, unhappy, and depressed. The result? Twenty years later, these men were more likely than their co-workers to have died of cancer (Persky et al., 1987). In fact, numerous studies show that people who are clinically depressed have weakened immune systems and a higher death rate from cancer and other killer diseases (Herbert & Cohen, 1993a; Weisse, 1992).

Toward the end of his life, Albert Schweitzer was asked for his opinion of traditional African medicine and the witch doctors who practice it. His reply: "The witch doctor succeeds for the same reason all the rest of us succeed. Each patient carries his own doctor inside him." More recently, Robert Ornstein and David Sobel (1987) referred to the human brain as an "internal pharmacy dispensing a stream of powerful drugs" (p. 89). Whether it involves pharmacists or doctors, recent work in psychoneuroimmunology suggests that the key is to find ways for each of us to tap our own inner resources.

COPING WITH STRESS

Stress is inevitable. No one can prevent it. But we can try to minimize its harmful *effects* on our health. To understand how some people keep their composure while others crumble under the pressure, it is useful to examine the *coping* process and ask the question, what are some adaptive ways to cope with stress?

Coping Strategies

Leaving home. Taking exams. Breaking up with my college sweetheart. Working long nights on my thesis. Seeking employment in a competitive job market. Having children. Raising children. Facing academic pressures to publish or perish. Struggling to meet the deadline to complete this text. I could have coped with these sources of stress in any number of ways. In each case, I might have focused on solving the problem, talked to friends, invited distractions to pass the time, drunk myself silly, smiled and pretended that all was well—or I could have just freaked out.

Richard Lazarus and Susan Folkman (1984) distinguished two general types of coping strategies. The first is *problem-focused coping,* designed to reduce stress by overcoming the source of the problem. Difficulties in school? Study harder, hire a tutor, or reduce your workload. Marriage on the rocks? Talk it out or see a counselor. Problems at work? Consult with your boss or look for another job. The goal is to attack the source of your stress. A second approach is *emotion-focused coping,* in which one tries to manage the emotional turmoil, perhaps by learning to live with the problem rather than changing it. If you're struggling at school, at work, or in a relationship, you can keep a stiff upper lip, and ignore the situation or make the best of it. According to Lazarus and Folkman, we take an active problem-focused approach when we think we can overcome the stressor, but fall back on an emotion-focused approach when we perceive the problem to be out of our control.

Many researchers prefer to make finer distinctions among the various strategies that people use. Based on the self-reports of many people, Charles Carver and his colleagues (1989) constructed a multidimensional questionnaire called COPE that measures twelve distinct methods of coping (see Table 18.7). Some of the methods are more problem-focused (figuring out how to remove a stressor, waiting until the time is right, setting aside distractions, seeking advice from others, taking specific steps to get rid of the problem); others are primarily emotion-focused (accepting the problem, or denying it, taking on a new perspective, letting go of pent-up feelings, giving up, trying not to think about the stress).

Thought Suppression   One emotion-focused strategy people often use is to block unwanted stressful thoughts from awareness. I have used this strategy myself. As I recline in the dentist's chair with my mouth wide open and a bright light blinding my eyes, the sound of the drill and the grinding on my teeth send chills up my spine. To endure the pain, I try to lock eyes

Table 18.7

Ways of Coping with Stress

These sample statements describe different coping strategies that people say they use. They are listed in order from those that are relatively common to those that are less common (Carver et al., 1989).

Planning/Active Coping

- I try to come up with a strategy about what to do
- I take additional action to try to get rid of the problem

Positive Reinterpretation

- I look for something good in what is happening
- I try to make it seem more positive

Acceptance

- I learn to live with it
- I accept that this has happened and can't be changed

Seeking Social Support

- I talk to someone about how I feel
- I ask people who had similar experiences what they did

Restraint Coping

- I force myself to wait for the right time to do something
- I make sure not to make matters worse by acting too soon

Focusing on/Venting Emotions

- I get upset and let my emotions out
- I let my feelings out

Suppression of Competing Activities

- I put aside other activities to concentrate on this
- . . . if necessary let other things slide a little

Mental Disengagement

- I turn to work . . . to take my mind off things
- I go to the movies or watch TV, to think about it less

Turning to Religion

- I seek God's help
- I try to find comfort in my religion

Behavioral Disengagement

- I give up the attempt to get what I want
- I admit to myself that I can't deal with it

Denial

- I refuse to believe that it has happened
- I pretend that it hasn't really happened

Alcohol and Drugs

- I drink alcohol or take drugs to think about it less

---

with a gigantic toothbrush hanging on the wall or imagine that I'm lying on a warm, sunny beach. Ignore the noise and the pain, I say to myself. Think about something else.

This strategy, which is called *thought suppression,* has a peculiar, paradoxical effect. To demonstrate, Daniel Wegner (1989) conducted a series of experiments in which he had subjects say whatever came to mind into a

Try not to think of a white bear, and this image is likely to intrude into consciousness with remarkable frequency.

microphone—and instructed half of them *not* to think about a white bear. Try it, and you'll see the dilemma. As we saw in Chapter 16, Wegner found that subjects could not keep the image from popping to mind. It's like trying not to think about food when you're on a diet or the itchy insect bite you're not supposed to scratch. What's more, when subjects were permitted later to think about a white bear, those who had earlier tried to suppress the image were unusually preoccupied with it, providing evidence of a "rebound" effect. It is difficult to follow the command "Don't think about it"—and the harder you try, the less likely you are to succeed. There is, however, a solution: focused self-distraction. Wegner told subjects to imagine a little red Volkswagen whenever the forbidden white bear intruded into consciousness, and the rebound effect vanished.

What do white bears and red cars have to do with coping? Lots. When people try to force stressful thoughts or painful sensations out of awareness, they are doomed to fail. In fact, the problem may worsen. That's where focused self-distraction comes in. In a study of pain tolerance, Delia Cioffi and James Holloway (1993) had subjects put a hand into a bucket of ice-cold water and keep it there until they could no longer bear the pain. One group was instructed to avoid thinking about the sensation in their hand. A second group was instructed to form a vivid mental picture of their room at home. Regardless of the strategy used, subjects kept their hand in the water for just over two minutes. Afterward, however, subjects who had coped through suppression were slower to recover from the pain than were those who had used focused self-distraction. To manage stress—whether it's caused by physical pain, a strained romance, final exams, or problems at the office—distraction (which specifies what to *do;* for example, "think about lying on the beach") is a better coping strategy than mere suppression (which specifies what *not* to do; for example, "don't think about the dentist's drill").

Relaxation   There are also ways of managing the physical symptoms of stress. One very popular technique is *relaxation.* Cardiologist Herbert Benson (1975), an expert on meditation, finds that people can lower their blood pressure, heart rate, and oxygen consumption by learning to relax in times of stress. According to Benson, anyone can be taught this "relaxation response." Sit quietly and comfortably, close your eyes, and relax all the muscles from your feet to your face. Then breathe deeply through the nose, and each time you exhale, silently utter some word (such as "one . . . one . . . one . . ."). As you proceed, let your mind drift freely. If anxiety-provoking thoughts intrude, however, refocus your attention on the word you are chanting and stay calm. Repeat this exercise once or twice a day, each time for about twenty minutes.

Is relaxation effective? Yes. In one study, Meyer Friedman and his colleagues randomly assigned hundreds of heart attack patients to one of two treatment groups (see Figure 18.11). In one group, they received standard medical advice on drugs, exercise, work, and diet. In the second group, they were also counseled on how to slow down their pace and relax. After three years, the relaxation patients had suffered only half as many repeat heart attacks as those in the control group (Friedman & Ulmer, 1984). In another study, Janice Kiecolt-Glaser and her colleagues (1985) found that relaxation also fortifies the immune system. Among a group of elderly resi-

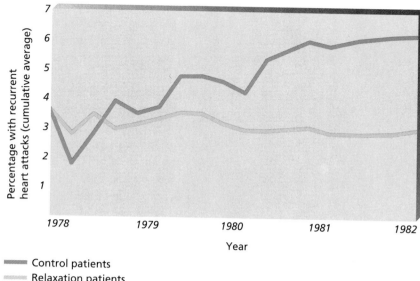

Figure 18.11

Relaxation and the Heart

After three years, heart attack victims who were taught to relax their pace suffered fewer recurrences than did those who received only standard medical advice (Friedman & Ulmer, 1984).

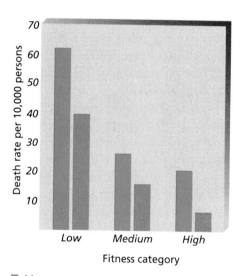

Figure 18.12

Exercise and Longevity

In a study of death rates, men and women varying in their physical fitness were compared. As shown, moderate and high levels of fitness were associated with increased longevity (Blair et al., 1989).

dents in an independent living facility, those who were trained in relaxation three times a week for one month felt better and exhibited an increase in natural-killer-cell activity compared to others in a no-treatment control group.

Aerobic Exercise   A second way to manage stress is through *aerobic exercise*—sustained, vigorous physical activity designed to build heart and lung capacity and to enhance the body's use of oxygen. Walking, running, swimming, bicycling, cross-country skiing, and dancing are ideal forms of aerobic exercise. The health benefits seem clear. One large-scale study showed that men who burned at least 2,000 calories a week through exercise lived longer than those who were less active (Paffenbarger et al., 1986). As illustrated in Figure 18.12, another study of both men and women showed that even a moderate amount of exercise is associated with increased longevity (Blair et al., 1989).

For both mother and daughter, running is a form of aerobic exercise that benefits health in many ways.

"Those who think they have not time for bodily exercise will sooner or later have to find time for illness."

EDWARD STANLEY

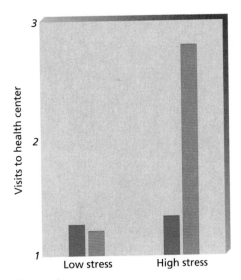

Figure 18.13

Fitness, Stress, and Health

In a recent study of college students, life stress was associated with increased visits to the health center among students low in aerobic fitness. Those who were high in fitness absorbed the stress without illness (Brown, 1991).

■ **hardiness** A personality style—characterized by commitment, challenge, and control—that acts as a buffer against stress.

Don't jump from these correlations to the causal conclusion that if you start running you'll live longer. It is possible, for example, that people who exercise regularly are also more health-conscious about eating, smoking, wearing seat belts, and other factors that contribute to longevity. Still, the effects of exercise on physical health are extensive. Research shows that exercise strengthens the heart, lowers blood pressure, aids in the metabolism of fats and carbohydrates, boosts self-esteem, elevates mood, improves cognitive functioning, and relieves depression (Simon, 1991). Physical fitness may also soften the harmful impact of stress on health. To demonstrate, Jonathon Brown (1991) brought college students into the lab, measured their aerobic fitness on an exercise bicycle, inquired about recent stressful events, and counted the number of illness visits they made to the university health center that year. The result: Life stress was linked to illness only among students who were out of shape. Those who were more physically fit absorbed more stress without an increase in illness (see Figure 18.13).

The "Self-Healing Personality"

For years, psychologists have speculated about very specific correlations between personality traits and illness. People who are anxious are doomed to get ulcers, we're told, just as angry types are prone to headaches, depressives are prone to cancer, weak and dependent types suffer from asthma, and workaholics die of heart attacks. In light of recent work on psychology and the immune system, others have considered the alternative possibility that there's a generic "disease-prone personality" consisting of a cluster of negative emotional states. According to this view, anger, anxiety, hostility, and depression all lead us to complain of bodily ailments (Watson & Pennebaker, 1989) and perhaps put us at risk for a whole range of illnesses (Friedman & Booth-Kewley, 1987). Whether the links are specific or general is a matter of dispute. However, most health researchers believe that certain traits are healthier and more adaptive than others (Adler & Matthews, 1994)—that there is, in essence, a "self-healing personality" (Friedman, 1991).

Hardiness   Stress affects people differently, an observation that led Suzanne Kobosa (1979) to wonder why some of us are more resilient than others. Kobosa studied two hundred business executives who were under a good deal of stress. Many said they were frequently sick, affirming the link between stress and illness; but others had managed to stay healthy. The two groups were similar in terms of age, education, job status, income, and ethnic and religious background. But psychological tests revealed that they differed in their attitudes about themselves, their jobs, and the people in their lives. Based on these differences, Kobosa identified a personality style she called **hardiness** and concluded that hardy people have three characteristics: (1) *commitment*, a sense of purpose and involvement in work, family, and other domains; (2) *challenge*, an openness to new experiences and a desire to embrace change; and (3) *control*, the belief that one has the power to influence important future outcomes.

In general, research supports the point that hardiness acts as a buffer against stress (Funk, 1992)—and that control is a key ingredient. Studies show that the harmful effects of noise, crowding, and other stressors are reduced when people think they can exert control over these aspects of their environment. Thus, rats exposed to electric shock are less likely to develop ulcers if they are trained to know they can avoid it, children awaiting a doctor's injection cope better when they're prepared with a pain-reducing cognitive strategy, elderly nursing-home residents become healthier and more active when they're given more control over daily events, and cancer patients are much better adjusted, emotionally, when they think that they can influence the course of their illness (Rodin, 1986; Thompson, 1981).

[© 1994 Robert Mankoff and The Cartoon Bank, Inc.]

Optimism and Hope A second important trait in the self-healing personality is *optimism,* defined as a generalized tendency to expect positive outcomes. Are *you* an optimist or a pessimist? Do you look on the bright side and expect good things to happen, or do you tend to believe that if something can go wrong, it will? By asking questions like these, Michael Scheier and Charles Carver (1985) categorized college students along this dimension and found that dispositional optimists reported fewer illness symptoms during the semester than did pessimists. Correlations between optimism and health are common. Other studies have shown that optimists are more likely to take a problem-focused approach to coping with stress; complete a rehabilitation program for alcoholics; make a quicker, fuller recovery from coronary artery bypass surgery; and, among gay men concerned about AIDS, take a more active, less avoidant approach to the threat (Scheier & Carver, 1992).

In a book entitled *Learned Optimism,* Martin Seligman (1991) argues that optimism and pessimism are rooted in our "explanatory styles"—in the ways we explain good and bad past events. Based on a large number of studies (Sweeney et al., 1986; Abramson et al., 1989), Seligman describes the typical *pessimist* as someone who attributes failure to factors that are internal ("It was my fault"), permanent ("I'm all washed up"), and global ("I'm bad at everything") and success to factors that are external ("I lucked out"), temporary ("The task was easy"), and specific ("It was my strength"). This explanatory style breeds despair and low self-esteem. In contrast, the typical *optimist* is someone who makes the opposite attributions. According to Seligman, he or she blames failure on factors that are external, temporary, and specific, while crediting success to factors that are internal, permanent, and global—an explanatory style that fosters hope, effort, and a high regard for oneself (see Figure 18.14 and Table 18.8).

Figure 18.14

Optimistic and Pessimistic Explanatory Styles

Many studies show that optimists and pessimists differ in the way they explain positive and negative events.

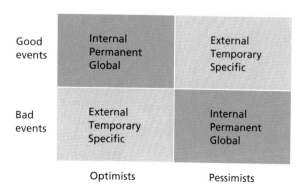

Table 18.8

Explanatory Styles Test

Do you interpret events as an optimist or pessimist? Imagine the following situations and circle cause A or B, whichever you think is most likely. When you're done, count the number of points earned (in parentheses). A score of 0 indicates a high degree of pessimism; a score of 8 indicates a high degree of optimism (Seligman, 1991).

1. You forget your boyfriend's (girlfriend's) birthday
   A. I'm not good at remembering birthdays (0)
   B. I was preoccupied with other things (1)

2. You stop a crime by calling the police
   A. A strange noise caught my attention (0)
   B. I was alert that day (1)

3. You were extremely healthy all year
   A. Few people around me were sick, so I wasn't exposed (0)
   B. I made sure I ate well and got enough rest (1)

4. You fail an important examination
   A. I wasn't as smart as the others taking the exam (0)
   B. I didn't prepare for it well (1)

5. You ask someone to dance, and he (she) says no
   A. I am not a good enough dancer (0)
   B. He (she) doesn't like to dance (1)

6. You gain weight over the holidays and you can't lose it
   A. Diets don't work in the long run (0)
   B. The diet I tried didn't work (1)

7. You win the lottery
   A. It was pure chance (0)
   B. I picked the right numbers (1)

8. You do extremely well in a job interview
   A. I felt extremely confident during the interview (0)
   B. I interview well (1)

"Cheerfulness is the very flower of health."

JAPANESE PROVERB

In the course of a lifetime, everyone experiences failure, defeat, tragedy, and other setbacks. Do optimists weather the storms better? Are they happier, healthier, and more successful? Do they have, in the words of Alan McGinnis (1987, p. 16), "the gift for turning stumbling blocks into stepping stones"? To find out, Christopher Peterson and his colleagues (1988) collected personal essays that were written in the 1940s by ninety-nine men who had just graduated from Harvard, and analyzed these materials to determine what each subject's explanatory style was in his youth. Were these men optimists or pessimists? What eventually happened to them? Remarkably, health at age sixty was predictable from explanatory styles thirty-five years earlier. Young optimists were healthier than young pessimists later in life. Why? A recent study by Leslie Kamen-Siegel and colleagues (1991) provides a clue. These researchers measured explanatory style, took blood samples, and found that pessimists had a weaker immune response than optimists.

As usual, we should be cautious in interpreting correlations—in this case, between explanatory styles and life outcomes. It's certainly possible that optimism causes happiness, health, and success. But it's also possible that the causal arrow points in the opposite direction, that being happy, healthy, and successful provides a realistic basis for optimism. Assuming that optimism is adaptive, Seligman (1991) says that pessimists can be retrained—not through "mindless devices like whistling a happy tune," "the pink Sunday school world of happy events," or simply "saying positive things to yourself," but by learning a new set of cognitive skills. According to Seligman, people can train themselves to make optimistic explanations by following three steps: (1) think about situations of adversity (losing in a sports competition, having a friend not return your calls); (2) consider the way you normally explain these events, and if it is pessimistic (I always choke under pressure, my friend does not really care about me); then (3) dispute these explanations by looking closely at the facts (my opponent played a great game, my friend has been very busy). Practice this exercise over and over again. You may find that changing a pessimistic explanatory style is like breaking a bad habit.

Social Support

We hear it all the time: no man (or woman) is an island, human beings are social animals, people need people, and to get by you need a little help from your friends. Is all this true? Do close family ties, lovers, buddies, community support groups, and relationships at work serve as a buffer against stress? Yes. An overwhelming amount of evidence shows that **social support** has therapeutic effects on our psychological and physical health (Cohen, 1988; House et al., 1988; Wills, 1990).

A study by Lisa Berkman and Leonard Syme (1979) illustrates the point. These investigators surveyed seven thousand residents of Alameda County, California, conducted a nine-year follow-up of mortality rates, and found that the more social contacts people had, the longer they lived. In fact, those who lived alone, had very few close friends or relatives, and did not participate in community groups died at a rate two to five times greater than those with more extensive social networks. This was true of both men and women, young and old, rich and poor, and people from all racial and ethnic backgrounds.

Research findings like these are common. Married people are more likely than unmarried people to survive cancer for five years (Taylor, 1990), gay men infected with HIV are less likely to contemplate suicide if they have close ties than if they are socially isolated (Schneider et al., 1991), and people who suffer from one heart attack are less likely to have a second if they are living with someone than if they live alone (Case et al., 1992). Among students who are stressed by schoolwork and among spouses of cancer patients, more social support is also associated with a stronger immune response (Baron et al., 1990; Jemmott & Magloire, 1988). Clearly, isolation can be hazardous to your health.

Why is social support so important? Our connections with other people are therapeutic for many reasons. Friends help by encouraging us to get out and exercise, eat regularly, stop smoking or drinking, or seek professional help. Emotionally, friends shower us with sympathy and reassurance in times of stress—and are there to listen when we feel the need to cry, scream, and release bottled-up tensions. Perhaps having a good friend around boosts our confidence, self-esteem, and sense of security. On an intellectual level, having someone to talk to helps by providing a sounding board, new perspectives, and advice and information, as we try to find the solutions to our problems. Communicating helps us sort things out in our own minds (Clark, 1993).

■ **social support** The healthful coping resources provided by friends and other people.

Pets provide us with companionship and "social" support.

According to James Pennebaker (1990), it's important to talk about upsetting and painful experiences. In a series of studies, Pennebaker had college students talk to a hidden experimenter or into a tape recorder, or else simply write about a trauma they had experienced. While speaking, subjects were physiologically aroused and upset. Many tearfully recounted accidents, failures, instances of sex abuse, loneliness, rape, the divorce of their parents, embarrassing moments, shattered relationships, death, and their fears about the future. Soon, however, these subjects were feeling better than ever. Blood samples taken after the experiment revealed a heightened immune response relative to the level measured beforehand, and in the ensuing months subjects who had "opened up" made 50 percent fewer visits to the campus health center. A comparison group of students who talked only about trivial matters did not similarly benefit from the experience.

The value of social support may be so basic that *any* bond formed with another living being—even the companionship of a pet—promotes health and survival (Beck & Katcher, 1983). In one study, heart attack victims who owned dogs, cats, birds, and other pets were found to be more likely to survive the year than those without pets (Friedmann et al., 1980). In a second study, elderly men and women made fewer visits to the doctor in times of stress if they had pet dogs than if they did not (Siegel, 1990). It may be that animals have a calming influence on us, and are a source of comfort. Indeed, Karen Allen and her colleagues (1991) found that when female subjects (all of whom owned pet dogs) were put to work on a stressful experimental task, those who had their pets with them became less physiologically aroused (as measured by changes in their blood pressure, perspiration, and pulse rate) than those who were alone or had a human friend present. As companions, pets are wonderfully nonjudgmental.

PROSPECTS FOR THE FUTURE

Psychologists from all areas of the discipline are seeking to better understand the factors that promote human health and well-being. With this goal in mind, we have made tremendous strides in recent years. We now know that self-awareness may lower rather than raise our self-esteem, that it's sometimes healthier to harbor positive illusions than to demand an accurate perception of reality, that stress can kill people by weakening the immune system, and that certain coping strategies, personality styles, and social support can be used to restore the body's natural defenses. The mind is a powerful tool. The more we know about how to use it, the better off we'll be.

Psychology's latest discoveries are exciting, but it is also important to recognize their limitations. Recently established links among mind, behavior, and the immune system, for example, raise the hope that perhaps each of us has the power to slow the spread of cancer and other diseases. This is not an invitation to believe in miracles, however, nor does it mean that we should reject standard medical treatments and try instead to wish away our illnesses. If we smoke, if we're exposed to radiation, if we breathe polluted air or spend too much time baking in the hot sun, we will increase the risk of cancer—regardless of how relaxed, fit, determined, or upbeat we are, and regardless of how many friends we have to support us. While appreciating the powers of the mind to influence the body, it's also important that we guard against blaming the victims of terminal illness for their condition and making them feel guilty—as if dying were their ultimate failure. As Howard Friedman (1991) put it, "We must walk a fine line between blaming patients on the one hand and absolving them of any role in their health on the other" (p. 96).

Nowhere is this more true than with people who suffer from acquired immune deficiency syndrome, or AIDS. Earlier, we noted that heart attacks, cancer, strokes, and accidents are now more common causes of death than infectious diseases. Among American men between the ages of twenty-five and forty-four, however, AIDS may soon top the list. As shown in Figure 18.15, it is already the second leading cause of death in this group. AIDS is a microbiological time bomb that just recently exploded. In 1981, 5 homosexual men in America were diagnosed as having AIDS, and were among 189 cases reported that year. By the end of 1992, the number of AIDS cases in the United States had skyrocketed to 233,907—and included heterosexual men, women, and children. And these figures were just the beginning: currently, an estimated 20 million people, including 1.5 million Americans, are infected with HIV—the human immunodeficiency virus that causes AIDS. The World Health Organization projects that by the year 2000, the number of people infected worldwide will reach between 40 and 110 million. From Africa to North America, South America, Asia, and Europe, AIDS is the first truly global epidemic (Mann, 1992).

Figure 18.15

AIDS Deaths

New figures indicate that the AIDS virus may soon be the top killer of American men aged 25–44. As shown, the threat to young women is growing as well (Centers for Disease Control and Prevention, 1993).
[NEWSWEEK, July 19, 1993, Centers for Disease Control and Prevention, p. 8.]

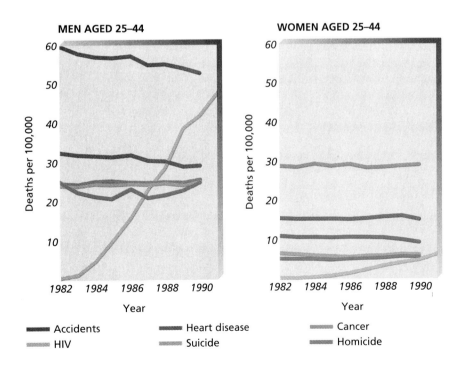

The AIDS virus is transmitted from one person to another in infected blood, semen, and vaginal secretions. People who are HIV-positive may have no symptoms for a few years, and may not even realize they are infected. Eventually, however, the virus will ravage their immune systems by destroying lymphocytes that help them ward off disease. What's so scary about AIDS is that it is fatal, that it is increasing at a rate of one new case every fifteen seconds, and that there is no vaccine or satisfactory treatment for it (Greene, 1993).

At present, the only way to control the spread of AIDS is to alter people's beliefs, motivations, and risk-taking behavior (Fisher & Fisher, 1992)—and that's where psychology comes in. As president of the Health Psychology Division of the American Psychological Association, Margaret Chesney (1993) notes that with the approach of the twenty-first century, psychologists need to design programs to encourage voluntary AIDS testing, provide counseling to assist those who are positively identified, identify the nonbiological factors that influence the progression of AIDS in those who are infected, educate the public about the disease, and convince everyone—particularly adolescents—to limit their sexual activity and use condoms as a means of protection. As always, we can use our minds to help protect our lives.

SUMMARY AND KEY TERMS

Although psychology is a diverse field, all its branches share the objective of improving our health and well-being.

Mind over Matter

The mind's influence on the body, a frequent theme in psychology, can be seen in the placebo effect. Research suggests that positive expectations increase the release of pain-relieving endorphins and suppress adrenaline and other stress hormones that reduce the body's resistance.

The Self and Well-Being

As the "cocktail party effect" demonstrates, the self is an important object of our attention.

The Need for Self-Esteem

Satisfying our need for *self-esteem* is vital in our lives. People with high self-esteem tend to be happy, healthy, and successful. Those with low self-esteem are more anxious, pessimistic, and prone to failure. Their lack of confidence traps them in a vicious cycle: they fail because they expect to fail, thereby lowering their self-esteem even further.

According to *self-discrepancy theory,* self-esteem stems from a match between the way we see ourselves and the way we want to see ourselves. If our self-concepts fall short of our self-guides, our self-esteem declines. The more discrepancy there is, and the more accessible it is to awareness, the more discomfort we feel.

The Self-Awareness "Trap"

According to *self-awareness theory,* certain situations raise our self-awareness and prompt us to compare our behavior to our standards, often resulting in a sense of discrepancy and a loss of self-esteem. Individuals differ, however, in their tendencies toward self-consciousness.

We can cope with self-awareness either by reducing self-discrepancies (trying to make our behavior match our standards) or by withdrawing from self-awareness and seeking an escape. The escape strategy sometimes involves harmful actions such as getting intoxicated.

Mechanisms of Self-Deception

We also cope with our inadequacies through *self-deception,* distorting and hiding unpleasant truths from ourselves. We tend to see ourselves in favorable terms, using biased attributions to take credit for success and shun responsibility for failure. Unrealistic optimism leads us to expect better outcomes for ourselves than for others. Sometimes we set up advance excuses by *self-handicapping,* and we boost our spirits by making "downward" social comparisons with people who do not fare as well as we do.

Reality, Illusions, and Mental Health

Does self-deception produce well-being or disorder? Some research indicates that self-deception may be adaptive: it correlates with self-esteem, happiness, and health. On the other hand, certain kinds of self-deception can cause self-destructive behaviors.

Shyness and Social Anxiety

Many people who are low in self-esteem experience *social anxiety,* or feelings of discomfort around others. These feelings are often accompanied by shyness. Shy people evaluate themselves negatively, expect to fail in social encounters, and blame themselves when they do. Worse, many shy people become lonely and isolated.

Stress and Health

In line with the movement from a medical to a biosocial model of health, researchers have taken a growing interest in *health psychology*, which applies psychology to the promotion of physical health and the prevention and treatment of illness. Among psychological influences on health, stress is especially important.

The Sources of Stress

Stress is an unpleasant state of arousal that occurs when we perceive that an event threatens our ability to cope effectively. Catastrophes are one major type of stressor. *Posttraumatic stress disorder* among combat veterans produces symptoms ranging from sleeplessness to social withdrawal.

According to some psychologists, any major life event—such as marriage, divorce, or promotion—causes stress. Research does show a link between negative life events and health problems, but no such connection for positive events. It's also important to recognize that people interpret events differently.

Daily hassles—microstressors—can have even more impact than major life events. Job pressures may cause stress and burnout. Environmental factors such as crowding also play a role.

The Physiological Effects of Stress

Selye saw the body's response to stress as a *general adaptation syndrome* marked by the stages of alarm, resistance, and exhaustion. This model suggests that stress may be adaptive in the short term but a threat to health in the long term.

Other researchers have linked stress to coronary heart disease (CHD). People with a workaholic, competitive, time-conscious *Type A personality* make up a greater percentage of those with CHD than people with an easygoing, relaxed *Type B personality*. Stress also compromises the *immune system*, which relies on *lymphocytes* (specialized white blood cells) to fight bacteria, viruses, and other invaders. Stress reduces the activity of the lymphocytes known as T cells and increases susceptibility to various diseases. The new field of *psychoneuroimmunology* studies this interplay between the mind and the immune system.

Coping with Stress

Although we cannot prevent stress, we can minimize its effects on our health by means of coping strategies.

Coping Strategies

Coping strategies can be divided broadly into problem-focused coping (overcoming the source of the problem) and emotion-focused coping (managing the emotional turmoil). Thought suppression, an emotion-focused strategy, doesn't usually work unless accompanied by focused self-distraction—deliberately thinking about something else. Relaxation techniques have been shown to boost the immune system. Aerobic exercise, which correlates with longevity and physical health, may also reduce the impact of stress.

The "Self-Healing Personality"

The personality style known as *hardiness*, which includes a strong sense of control, seems to be a buffer against stress. Another important trait is optimism, which has been linked with health and a strong immune response. Optimism and pessimism are often related to explanatory style, and some researchers believe that people can train themselves to use optimistic explanations.

Social Support

Social support from friends and family members—or even pets—can reduce stress and promote health. People with more social contacts survive illness better and live longer.

Prospects for the Future

Although psychology reveals strong connections between the mind and physical health, we should not assume that the mind can work miracles, nor should we blame people for their illnesses. Instead, we can use psychology to help us design public health programs—an especially important endeavor during the current global epidemic of AIDS.

Appendix

Statistics in Psychological Research

Understanding and interpreting the results of psychological research depends on *statistical analyses,* which are methods for describing and drawing conclusions from data. Chapter 1 introduced some terms and concepts associated with *descriptive statistics*—the numbers that psychologists use to describe and present their data—and with *inferential statistics*—the mathematical procedures used to draw conclusions from data and to make inferences about what they mean. Here, we present more details about these statistical analyses that will help you to evaluate research results.

DESCRIBING DATA

To illustrate our discussion, consider a hypothetical experiment on the effects of incentives on performance. The experimenter presents a simple list of mathematics problems to two groups of subjects. Each group must solve the problems within a fixed time, but for each correct answer, the low-incentive group is paid ten cents, while the high-incentive group gets one dollar. The hypothesis to be tested is the **null hypothesis,** the assertion that the independent variable manipulated by the experimenter will have no effect on the dependent variable measured by the experimenter. In this case, the null hypothesis holds that the size of the incentive (the independent variable) will not affect performance on the mathematics task (the dependent variable).

Assume that the experimenter has obtained a random sample of subjects, assigned them randomly to the two groups, and done everything possible to avoid the confounds and other research problems discussed in Chapter 1. The experiment has been run, and the psychologist now has the data: a list of the number of correct answers given by each subject in each group. Now comes the first task of statistical analysis: describing the data in a way that makes them easy to understand.

The Frequency Histogram

The simplest way to describe the data is to draw up something like Table A.1, in which all the numbers are simply listed. After examining the table, you might discern that the high-incentive group seems to have done better

■ **null hypothesis** The assertion that the independent variable manipulated by the experimenter will have no effect on the dependent variable measured by the experimenter.

Table A.1

A Simple Data Set

Here are the test scores obtained by thirteen subjects performing under low-incentive conditions and thirteen subjects performing under high-incentive conditions.

Low Incentive	High Incentive
4	6
6	4
2	10
7	10
6	7
8	10
3	6
5	7
2	5
3	9
5	9
9	3
5	8

than the low-incentive group, but the difference is not immediately obvious. It might be even harder to see if more subjects had been involved and if the scores included three-digit numbers. A picture is worth a thousand words, so a more satisfactory way of presenting the same data is in a picturelike graphic known as a **frequency histogram** (see Figure A.1).

Construction of a histogram is simple. First, divide the scale for measuring the dependent variable (in this case, the number of correct solutions) into a number of categories, or "bins." The bins in our example are 1–2, 3–4, 5–6, 7–8, and 9–10. Next, sort the raw data into the appropriate bin. (For example, the score of a subject who had 5 correct answers would go into the 5–6 bin, a score of 8 would go into the 7–8 bin, and so on.) Finally, for each bin, count the number of scores in that bin and draw a bar up to the height of that number on the vertical axis of a graph. The set of bars makes up the frequency histogram.

Because we are interested in comparing the scores of two groups, there are separate histograms in Figure A.1: one for the high-incentive group and one for the low-incentive group. Now the difference between groups that was difficult to see in Table A.1 becomes clearly visible: more people in the high-incentive group obtained high scores than in the low-incentive group.

Histograms and other pictures of data are useful for visualizing and better understanding the "shape" of research data, but in order to analyze data statistically, the data making up these graphic presentations must be handled in other ways. For example, before we can tell whether two histograms are different statistically or just visually, the data they represent must be summarized using descriptive statistics.

■ **frequency histogram** A graphic presentation of data that consists of a set of bars, each of which represents how frequently different values of variables occur in a data set.

Descriptive Statistics

The four basic categories of descriptive statistics (1) measure the number of observations made; (2) summarize the typical value of a set of data; (3) summarize the spread, or variability, in a set of data; and (4) express the correlation between two sets of data.

Figure A.1

Frequency Histograms

The height of each bar of a histogram represents the number of scores falling within each range of score values. The pattern formed by these bars gives a visual image of how research results are distributed.

(A) LOW INCENTIVE

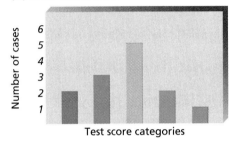

(B) HIGH INCENTIVE

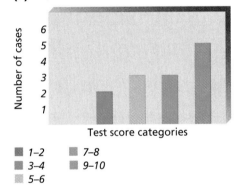

■ 1–2   ■ 7–8
■ 3–4   ■ 9–10
■ 5–6

N The easiest statistic to compute, abbreviated as *N*, simply describes the number of observations that make up the data set. In Table A.1, for example, *N* = 13 for each group, or 26 for the entire data set. Simple as it is, *N* plays a very important role in more sophisticated statistical analyses.

Measures of Central Tendency It is apparent in the histograms in Figure A.1 that there is a difference in the pattern of scores between the two groups. But how much of a difference? What is the typical value, the *central tendency*, that represents each group's performance? As described in Chapter 1, there are three measures that capture this typical value: the mode, the median, and the mean. Recall that the *mode* is the value or score that occurs most frequently in the data set. The *median* is the halfway point in a set of data: half the scores fall above the median, half fall below it. The *mean* is the arithmetic average. To find the mean, add the values of all the scores and divide by the number of scores.

Measures of Variability The variability, or spread, or dispersion of a set of data is often just as important as its central tendency. This variability can be quantified by measures known as the *range* and the *standard deviation*.

As described in Chapter 1, the range is simply the difference between the highest and the lowest value in a data set. For the data in Table A.1, the range for the low-incentive group is 9 – 2 = 7; for the high-incentive group, the range is 10 – 3 = 7.

The standard deviation, or SD, measures the average difference between each score and the mean of the data set. To see how the standard deviation is calculated, consider the data in Table A.2. The first step is to compute the mean of the set—in this case, 20/5 = 4. Second, calculate the difference, or *deviation* (*D*), of each score from the mean by subtracting the mean from each score, as in column 2 of Table A.2. Third, find the average of these deviations. However, if you calculated the average by finding the arithmetic mean, you would sum the deviations and find that the negative deviations exactly balance the positive ones, resulting in a mean difference of 0. Obviously there is more than zero variation around the mean in the data set. So, instead of employing the arithmetic mean, we compute the

Table A.2

Calculating the Standard Deviation

The standard deviation of a set of scores reflects the average degree to which those scores differ from the mean of the set.

Raw Data	Difference from Mean = D		D^2
2	2 – 4	= – 2	4
2	2 – 4	= – 2	4
3	3 – 4	= –1	1
4	4 – 4	= 0	0
9	9 – 4	= 5	25
Mean = 20/5 = 4			$\Sigma D^2 = 34$

$$\text{Standard deviation} = \sqrt{\frac{\Sigma D^2}{N}} = \sqrt{\frac{34}{5}} = \sqrt{6.8} = 2.6$$

■ **normal distribution** A dispersion of scores such that the mean, median, and mode all have the same value. When a distribution has this property, the standard deviation can be used to describe how any particular score stands in relation to the rest of the distribution.

standard deviation by first squaring the deviations (which removes any negative values), summing these squared deviations, dividing by N, and then taking the square root of the result. These simple steps are outlined in more detail in Table A.2.

The Normal Distribution   Now that we have described histograms and reviewed some descriptive statistics, we will re-examine how these methods of representing research data relate to some of the concepts discussed elsewhere in the book.

In most subareas in psychology, when researchers collect many measurements and plot their data in histograms, the pattern that results often resembles that shown for the low-incentive group in Figure A.1. That is, the majority of scores tend to fall in the middle of the distribution, with fewer and fewer occurring as one moves toward the extremes. As more and more data are collected, and as smaller and smaller bins are used (perhaps containing only one value each), the histograms tend to smooth out, until they resemble the bell-shaped curve known as the **normal distribution,** or *normal curve,* which is shown in Figure A.2a. When a distribution of scores

(A) Normal distribution, showing the smoothed approximation to the frequency histogram

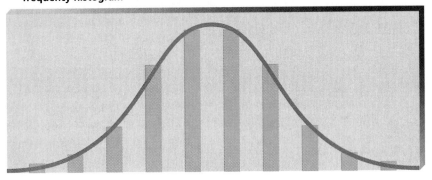

(B) The normal distribution of IQ

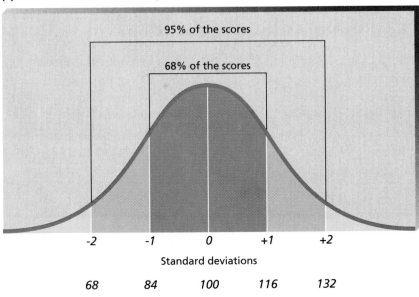

Figure A.2

The Normal Distribution

Many kinds of research data approximate the symmetrical shape of the normal curve, in which most scores fall toward the center of the range.

follows a truly normal curve, its mean, median, and mode all have the same value. Furthermore, if the curve is normal, we can use its standard deviation to describe how any particular score stands in relation to the rest of the distribution.

IQ scores provide an example. They are distributed in a normal curve, with a mean, median, and mode of 100 and an SD of 16 (see Figure A.2b). In such a distribution, half of the population will have an IQ above 100, and half will be below 100. The shape of the true normal curve is such that 68 percent of the area under it lies within one standard deviation above and below the mean. In terms of IQ, this means that 68 percent of the population has an IQ somewhere between 84 (100 minus 16) and 116 (100 plus 16). Of the remaining 32 percent of the population, half falls more than 1 SD above the mean, and half falls more than 1 SD below the mean. Thus, 16 percent of the population has an IQ above 116, and 16 percent scores below 84.

The normal curve is also the basis for percentiles. A **percentile score** indicates the percentage of people or observations that fall below a given score in a normal distribution. In Figure A.2b, for example, the mean score (which is also the median) lies at a point below which 50 percent of the scores fall. Thus, the mean of a normal distribution is at the 50th percentile. What does this mean for IQ? If you score 1 SD above the mean, your score is at a point above which only 16 percent of the population falls. This means that 84 percent of the population (100 percent minus 16 percent) must be below that score; so this IQ score is at the 84th percentile. A score at 2 SDs above the mean is at the 97.5 percentile, because only 2.5 percent of the scores are above it in a normal distribution.

Scores may also be expressed in terms of their distance in standard deviations from the mean, producing what are called **standard scores**. A standard score of 1.5, for example, is 1.5 standard deviations from the mean.

Correlation   Histograms and measures of central tendency and variability describe certain characteristics of one dependent variable at a time. However, psychologists are often concerned with describing the *relationship* between two variables. Measures of correlation are often used for this purpose. We discussed the interpretation of the *correlation coefficient* in Chapter 1; here we describe how to calculate it.

Recall that correlations are based on the relationship between two numbers associated with each subject or observation. The numbers may represent, say, a person's height and weight or the IQ of a parent and child. Table A.3 contains this kind of data for four subjects from our incentives study who took the test twice. (As you may recall from Chapter 11, the correlation between their scores would be a measure of *test-retest reliability*.) The formula for computing the Pearson product-moment correlation, or *r*, is as follows:

$$r = \frac{\Sigma(x - M_x)(y - M_y)}{\sqrt{\Sigma(x - M_x)^2 \Sigma(y - M_y)^2}}$$

where:

x = each score on variable 1 (in this case, test 1)
y = each score on variable 2 (in this case, test 2)
M_x = the mean of the scores on variable 1
M_y = the mean of the scores on variable 2

The main function of the denominator in this formula is to ensure that the coefficient ranges from +1.00 to –1.00, no matter how large or small the values of the variables being correlated. The "action element" of this formula is the numerator. It is the result of multiplying the amounts by which each of two observations (x and y) differ from the means of their respective distributions (M_x and M_y). Notice that, if the two variables "go together" (so that, if one is large, the other is also large, and if one is small, the other is also small), then either both will tend to be above the mean of their distribution or both will tend to be below the mean of their distribution. When this is the case, $x - M_x$ and $y - M_y$ will both be positive, or they will both be negative. In either case, their product will always be positive, and the correlation coefficient will also be positive. If, on the other hand, the two variables go opposite to one another, such that, when one is large, the other is small, one of them is likely to be smaller than the mean of its distribution, so that either $x - M_x$ or $y - M_y$ will have a negative sign, and the other will have a positive sign. Multiplying these differences together will always result in a product with a negative sign, and r will be negative as well.

Now compute the correlation coefficient for the data presented in Table A.3. The first step (step a in the table) is to compute the mean (M) for each variable. M_x turns out to be 3 and M_y is 4. Next, calculate the numerator by finding the differences between each x and y value and its respective mean and by multiplying them (as in step b of Table A.3). Notice that, in this example, the differences in each pair have like signs, so the correlation coefficient will be positive. The next step is to calculate the terms in the denominator; in this case, as shown in steps c and d in Table A.3, they have values of 18 and 4. Finally, place all the terms in the formula and carry out the arithmetic (step e). The result in this case is an r of +.94, a high and positive correlation suggesting that performances on repeated tests are very closely related. A subject doing well the first time is very likely to do well again; a person doing poorly at first will probably do no better the second time.

Table A.3

Calculating the Correlation Coefficient

Though it appears complex, calculation of the correlation coefficient is quite simple. The resulting r reflects the degree to which two sets of scores tend to be related, or to co-vary.

Subject	Test 1	Test 2	$(x - M_x)(y - M_y)$ (b)	
A	1	3	$(1 - 3)(3 - 4) = (-2)(-1)$	= + 2
B	1	3	$(1 - 3)(3 - 4) = (-2)(-1)$	= + 2
C	4	5	$(4 - 3)(5 - 4) = (1)(1)$	= + 1
D	6	5	$(6 - 3)(5 - 4) = (3)(1)$	= + 3
	(a)$M_x = 3$	$M_y = 4$	$\Sigma (x - M_x)(y - M_y)$	= + 8

(c) $\Sigma(x - M_x)^2 = 4 + 4 + 1 + 9 = 18$

(d) $\Sigma(y - M_y)^2 = 1 + 1 + 1 + 1 = 4$

(e) $r = \dfrac{\Sigma(x - M_x)(y - M_y)}{\sqrt{\Sigma(x - M_x)^2 \Sigma(y - M_y)^2}} = \dfrac{8}{\sqrt{18 \times 4}} = \dfrac{8}{\sqrt{72}} = \dfrac{8}{8.48} = +.94$

INFERENTIAL STATISTICS

The descriptive statistics from the incentives experiment tell the experimenter that the performances of the high- and low-incentive groups differ. But there is some uncertainty. Is the difference large enough to be important? Does it represent a stable effect or a fluke? The researcher would like to have some *measure of confidence* that the difference between groups is genuine and reflects the effect of incentive on mental tasks in the real world, rather than the effect of the particular subjects used, the phase of the moon, or other random or uncontrolled factors. One way of determining confidence would be to run the experiment again with a new group of subjects. Confidence that incentives produced differences in performance would grow stronger if the same or a larger between-group difference occurs again. In reality, psychologists rarely have the opportunity to repeat, or *replicate,* their experiments in exactly the same way three or four times. But *inferential statistics* provide a measure of how likely it was that results came about by chance. They put a precise mathematical value on the confidence or probability that rerunning the same experiment would yield similar (or even stronger) results.

Differences Between Means: The t Test   One of the most important tools of inferential statistics is the **t test**. It allows the researcher to ask how likely it is that the difference between two means occurred by chance rather than as a function of the effect of the independent variable. When the t test or other inferential statistic says that the probability of chance effects is small enough (usually less than 5 percent), the results are said to be *statistically significant*. Conducting a t test of statistical significance requires the use of three descriptive statistics.

The first component of the t test is the size of the observed effect, the difference between the means. Recall that the mean is calculated by summing a group's scores and dividing by the number of scores. In the example shown in Table A.1, the mean of the high-incentive group is 94/13, or 7.23, and the mean of the low-incentive group is 65/13, or 5. Thus, the difference between the means for the high- and low-incentive groups is 7.23 −5 = 2.23.

Second, the standard deviation of scores in each group must be known. If the scores in a group are quite variable, the standard deviation will be large, indicating that chance may have played a large role in producing the results. The next replication of the study might generate a very different set of group scores. If the scores in a group are all very similar, however, the standard deviation will be small, which suggests that the same result would probably occur for that group if the study were repeated. Thus, the *difference* between groups is more likely to be significant when each group's standard deviation is small. If variability is high enough that the scores of two groups overlap (in Table A.1, for example, some people in the low-incentive group actually did better on the math test than some in the high-incentive group), the mean difference, though large, may not be statistically significant.

Third, we need to take the sample size, N, into account. The larger the number of subjects or observations, the more likely it is that a given difference between means is significant. This is so because, with larger samples, random factors within a group—the unusual performance of a few people who were sleepy or anxious or hostile, for example—are more likely to be canceled out by the majority, who better represent people in general. The same effect of sample size can be seen in coin tossing. If you toss a quarter five times, you might not be too surprised if heads comes up 80 percent of the time. If you get 80 percent heads after one hundred tosses, however, you might begin to suspect that this is probably not due to chance alone and that some other effect, perhaps some bias in the coin, is significant in producing the results. (For the same reason, a relatively small correlation coefficient—between diet and grades, say—might be statistically significant if it was based on 50,000 students. As the number of subjects increases, it becomes less likely that the correlation reflects the influence of a few odd-ball cases.)

To summarize, as the differences between the means get larger, as N increases, and as standard deviations get smaller, t increases. This increase in t raises the researcher's confidence in the significance of the difference between means.

Analysis of Variance   Many experiments in psychology are considerably more complex than simple comparisons between two groups. They often involve three or more experimental and control groups. Some experiments also include more than one independent variable. For example, suppose we had been interested not only in the effect of incentive size on performance but also in the effect of problem difficulty. We might then create six groups whose subjects would perform easy, moderate, or difficult problems with low or high incentives.

In an experiment like this, the results might be due to the incentive, the problem difficulty, or the combined effects (known as the *interaction*) of the two. Analyzing the size and source of these effects is typically accomplished through procedures known as *analysis of variance*. The details of analysis of variance are beyond the scope of this book; for now, note that the statistical significance of each effect is influenced by differences between means, standard deviation, and sample size in much the same way as described for the t test.

For more detailed information about how analysis of variance and other inferential statistics are used to understand and interpret the results of psychological research, consider taking courses in research methods and statistical or quantitative methods.

SUMMARY AND KEY TERMS

Psychological research generates large quantities of data. Statistics are methods for describing and drawing conclusions from data.

Describing Data

Researchers often test the *null hypothesis,* which is the assertion that the independent variable will have no effect on the dependent variable.

The Frequency Histogram

Graphic representations such as *frequency histograms* provide visual descriptions of data, making the data easier to understand.

Descriptive Statistics

Numbers that summarize a set of data are called descriptive statistics. The easiest statistic to compute is N, which gives the number of observations made. A set of scores can be described by giving two other types of descriptive statistic: a measure of central tendency, which describes the typical value of a set of data, and a measure of variability. Measures of central tendency include the mean, median, and mode; variability is typically measured by the range and by the standard deviation. Sets of data often follow a *normal distribution,* which means that most scores fall in the middle of the range, with fewer and fewer scores occurring as one moves toward the extremes. In a truly normal distribution the mean, median, and mode are identical. When a set of data shows a normal distribution, a data point can be cited in terms of a *percentile score,* which indicates the percentage of people or observations falling below a certain score, and in terms of *standard scores,* which indicate the distance, in standard deviations, that a score is located from the mean. Another type of descriptive statistic, a correlation coefficient, is used to measure the correlation between sets of scores.

Inferential Statistics

Researchers use inferential statistics to quantify the probability that conducting the same experiment again would yield similar results.

Differences Between Means: The t Test

One inferential statistic, the *t test,* assesses the likelihood that differences between two means occurred by chance or reflect the effect of an independent variable. Performing a *t* test requires using the difference between the means of two sets of data, the standard deviation of scores in each set, and the number of observations or subjects.

Analysis of Variance

When more than two groups must be compared, researchers typically rely on analysis of variance in order to interpret the results of an experiment.

Credits (continued from copyright page)

Chapter 1: **p. 4:** The Bettmann Archive. **p. 5:** (top) Brown Brothers; (bottom) Historical Pictures/Stock Montage. **p. 11:** (left) © Dan McCoy/Rainbow; (right) © Bob Daemmrich/Stock Boston. **p. 16:** (left) © Jeff Greenberg/PhotoEdit; (right) © T. Clark/The Image Works. **p. 18:** © Joe McNally/Sygma. **p. 20:** UPI/Bettmann Newsphotos. **p. 21:** P. Breese/Gamma-Liaison. **p. 29:** (left) © Srulik Haramaty/Phototake; (right) © Paul Conklin. **Chapter 2:** **p. 38:** The Warren Anatomical Museum, Harvard Medical School. **p. 41:** © A. Glauberman/Photo Researchers. **p. 45:** © Custom Medical Stock Photo. **p. 46:** © Howard Sochurek. **p. 47:** © CNRI/ Science Photo Library/Photo Researchers. **p. 50:** © Dan Cabe/Photo Researchers. **p. 51:** © Myron Taplin/Tony Stone Images. **p. 53:** © Catherine Pouedras/Science Photo Library/Photo Researchers. **p. 54:** (top) John Mazziota, UCLA Medical School; (bottom) © Dan McCoy/Rainbow. **p. 55:** © Dan McCoy/Rainbow. **p. 57:** "Partial Complex," 28 × 35" watercolor, 1991 by Craig Smith. **p. 68:** *Figure 2.20* "Hemisphere Deconnection and Unity in Conscious Awareness," by Sperry from *American Psychologist*, 23, 723–733. Copyright © 1968 by the American Psychological Association. Reprinted by permission. **p. 69:** *Figure 2.22* "Perception of Bilateral Chimeric Figures following `Hemispheric Disconnection'" by J. Levy, C. Trevarthen and R. W. Sperry from Brain, 95, 61–78. Copyright © 1972 by Oxford University Press. Used by permission of Oxford University Press. **p. 72:** Courtesy of S. Petersen & M. Riachle at Washington University School of Medicine. *Figure 2.24* From *Brain, Mind and Behavior 2/e* by Bloom and Lazerson. Copyright © 1988 by Educational Broadcasting Corporation. Used with permission of W.H. Freeman and Company. **Chapter 3:** **p. 83:** *Table 3.1:* Some Absolute Thresholds from "Contemporary Psychophysics" by E. Galanter in New Directions in Psychology edited by R. Brown, E. Galanter. **p. 84:** © Bob Krist/Tony Stone Images. **p. 88:** © Lennart Nilsson, *Behold Man*, Little, Brown and Company. **p. 92:** Fritz Goro, *Life Magazine* © Time Warner. **p. 94:** These plates have been reproduced from Ishihara's Tests for Color Blindness published by Kanehara & Co., Ltd., Tokyo, Japan, but tests for color blindness cannot be conducted with this material. For accurate testing, the original plates should be used. **p. 96:** © Lennart Nilsson, *Behold Man*, Little, Brown and Company. **p. 98:** (top) © James M. Kubus; (bottom) © Gary Campbell; **p. 99:** © Lennart Nilsson, *Behold Man*, Little, Brown and Company. **p. 103:** © Omikron/Photo Researchers. **p. 104:** © Terry Vine/Tony Stone Images. **p. 106:** Intersport Television. **p. 108:** © Bob Daemmrich. **p. 110:** *Figure 3.22* From *Mind Sights* by Shepard. Copyright © 1990 by Roger N. Shepard. Used with permission of W.H. Freeman and Company. **p. 112:** © David Austen/Tony Stone Images. **p.113:** *Figure 3.23* from *Sensation & Perception*, Third Edition by Stanley Coren and Lawrence M. Ward, copyright © 1989 by Harcourt Brace & Company, reproduced by permission of the publisher. **p. 114:** Susan Schwartzenberg/The Exploratorium. **p. 116:** (top left) © J. Sohm/The Image Works; (top right) © L. Fleming/The Image Works; (bottom left) © Wernher Krutein/Gamma-Liaison. **p. 117:** (left) © Granitsas/The Image Works; (right) © Everton/The Image Works. **p. 119:** *Figure 3.28* "Pictorial Depth Perception in Sub-Cultural Groups in Africa" by W. Hudson from *Journal of Social Psychology*, 52, 183–208. Reprinted with permission of the Helen Dwight Reid Educational Foundation. Published by Heldref Publications, 1319 Eighteenth St., N.W., Washington, D.C. 20036–1802. Copyright © 1960. **p. 121:** *Figure 3.31* "Ambiguity of Form: Old and New" by G.H. Fisher from *Perception and Psychophysics*, vol. 4, pp. 189–192. Reprinted by permission of Psyconomic Society, Inc. **p. 122:** © Peter Pearson/Tony Stone Images. **p. 123:** © Michael Dwyer/Stock Boston. **p. 124:** (left) © Michael J. Howell/Stock Boston; (right) © Rod Planck/Tony Stone Images. **Chapter 4:** **p. 133:** *Figure 4.1* From *Human Information Processing: An Introduction to Psychology*, Second Edition by Peter H. Lindsay and Donald A. Norman, copyright © 1977 by Harcourt Brace & Company, reproduced by permission of the publisher. *Figure 4.2* "Selective Looking: Attending to Visually Specified Events" by U. Neisser & R. Becklen from *Cognitive Psychology*, 7, 480–494. Copyright © 1975 by Academic Press, Inc. Reprinted by permis-

494. Copyright © 1975 by Academic Press, Inc. Reprinted by permission. **p. 134:** *Figure 4.3* Source: Stroop, J.R. (1935), "Studies of Interference in Serial Verbal Reactions." *Journal of Experimental Psychology*, 18, 643–662. **p. 135:** © Paul Conklin. **p. 138:** © Thomas Ives. **p. 141:** © Yoav Levy/Phototake. *Figure 4.6* Reproduced from *Some Must Watch While Some Must Sleep* by William C. Dement. Copyright © 1972, 1974, 1976 by William C. Dement and the Stanford Alumni Association, Stanford, CA. **p. 143:** © Hank Morgan/Rainbow. **p. 145:** © Arnulf Husmo/Tony Stone Images. **p. 149:** © J.A. Hobson/Harvard Medical School/Photo Researchers. **p. 154:** © Bob Daemmrich/Stock Boston. **p. 160:** The Bettmann Archive. **p. 161:** (top left) © Dan McCoy/Rainbow; (top right) © Clark/The Image Works; (bottom left) © Cary Wolinsky/Tony Stone Images. **p. 163:** © Tony Stone Images. **Chapter 5:** **p. 172:** (left) © Treat Davidson/National Audubon Society/ Photo Researchers; (right) © Norbert Wu/Tony Stone Worldwide. **p. 179:** The Bettmann Archive. **p. 180:** *Figure 5.5* From *Conditioned Reflexes* by I. Pavlov. **p. 186:** J.-L. Atlan/Sygma. **p. 189:** © Yoav Levy/Phototake; **p. 191:** Jan Kopec/Tony Stone Images. **p. 192:** © Ellen Shub 1990. **p. 193:** © Fabricius-Taylor/Gamma-Liaison. **p. 196:** *Figure 5.13* "Stimulus Generalization, Discrimination, and Peak Shift in Horses" by D.M. Dougherty & P. Lewis from *Journal of the Experimental Analysis of Behavior*, 56, 97–104. Copyright © 1991 by the Society for the Experimental Analysis of Behavior, Inc. Reprinted by permission. **p. 197:** © Guido A. Rossi/The Image Bank. *Figure 5.14* "An Experimental Analysis of the Impact of Contingent Reinforcement on Salespersons' Performance Behavior" by F. Luthans, R. Paul & D. Baker from *Journal of Applied Psychology*, 66, 314–323. Copyright © 1981 by the American Psychological Association. Reprinted by permission. **p. 198:** (left) © Jon Riley/Tony Stone Images; (right) © Rob Nelson/Black Star. **pp. 198–199:** *Steps for Self-help from Self-Directed Behavior: Self-Modification for Personal Adjustment* by D. L. Watson & R. G. Tharp. **p. 201:** *Figure 5.15* "Cognitive Maps in Rats and Men" by E. C. Tolman from *Psychological Review*, Vol. 55, pp. 189–208, 1948. **p. 202:** *Figure 5.16* Source: Tolman, E.C., and Honzik, C.H. (1930), "Introduction and Removal of Reward and Maze Performance in Rats." *University of California Publications in Psychology*, 4, 257–275. **p. 203:** *Figure 5.17* Effects of Externally Mediated Awards on Intrinsic Motivation" by E.L. Deci from *Journal of Personality and Social Psychology*, 18, 105–115. Copyright © 1971 by the American Psychological Association. Reprinted by permission. **p. 204:** Wide World Photos. **Chapter 6:** **p. 210:** Zapruder Film: Copyright 1967 LMH Co., c/o James Lorin Silverberg, Esq., Washington, D.C. 202-332-7978. All Rights Reserved. **p. 213:** *Figure 6.3* "The Information Available in Brief Visual Presentations," by G. Sperling from *Psychological Monographs*, Vol. 74, pp. 1–29, 1960. **p. 214:** © Dave Cannon/Tony Stone Images; **p. 216:** *Figure 6.5* "Skilled Memory and Expert Mental Calculation" by J.J. Staszewski in M.T.H. Chi, R. Blaser, and M.J. Farr (Eds.), *The Nature of Expertise*. Copyright © 1988 by Lawrence Erlbaum Associates, Inc. Reprinted by permission. **p. 217:** © Donna Bise/Gamma-Liaison. *Figure 6.7* "Short-term Retention of Individual Verbal Items" by L.R. Peterson & M.J. Peterson from *Journal of Experimental Psychology*, 58, 193–98. **p. 219:** *Figure 6.8* "Two Storage Mechanisms in Free Recall" by M. Glanzer and A. Cunitz from *Journal of Verbal Learning and Verbal Behavior*, vol. 5, pp. 351–360. Copyright © 1966 by Academic Press. Reprinted by permission. **p. 220:** *Figure 6.9* "Depth of Processing and the Retention of Words in Episodic Memory" by F.I.M. Craik & E.Tuving from *Journal of Experimental Psychology: General*, 104, 268–294. Copyright © 1975 by the American Psychological Association. Reprinted by permission. **p. 224:** (left) © Lori Adamski Peek/Tony Stone Images; (right) © Kathleen Campbell/Gamma-Liaison. **p. 225:** *Figure 6.11* "A Spreading Activation Theory of Semantic Processing" by A.M. Collins & E.F. Loftus from *Psychological Review*, 82, 407–428. Copyright © 1975 by the American Psychological Association. Reprinted by permission. **p. 227:** Courtesy of Larry R. Squire, Ph.D. **p. 230:** (top) © R. Maiman/Sygma; (bottom) © Christopher Morris/Black Star. **p. 233:** *Figure 6.15* "Amnethe

(Credits continue following index)

Glossary

absolute threshold   The smallest amount of stimulation that can be detected.

accommodation   The visual process by which lenses become rounded for viewing nearby objects and flatter for viewing remote objects.

acculturation   The process by which persons are changed by their immersion in a new culture.

acculturative stress   The stress and mental health problems often found in immigrants trying to adjust to a new culture.

acetylcholine (ACh)   A neurotransmitter found throughout the nervous system that links the motor neurons and muscles.

action potential   An electrical impulse that surges through an axon, caused by an influx of positive ions in the neuron.

activation-synthesis theory   The theory that dreams result from the brain's attempt to make sense of random neural signals that fire during sleep.

adolescence   The period of life from puberty to adulthood, corresponding roughly to the ages of thirteen to twenty.

adoption studies   A method of testing nature and nurture by comparing twins and other siblings reared together with those separated by adoption.

afterimage   A visual sensation that persists after prolonged exposure and removal of a stimulus.

ageism   The combined effect of negative stereotypes, prejudice, and discrimination against older people.

agoraphobia   An anxiety disorder in which the main symptom is an intense fear of public places.

algorithm   A systematic problem-solving strategy that is guaranteed to produce a solution.

altruism   Helping behavior that is motivated primarily by a desire to benefit others, not oneself.

Alzheimer's disease (AD)   A progressive brain disorder that strikes older people, causing memory loss and other symptoms.

amnesia   A dissociative disorder involving a partial or complete loss of memory.

amygdala   A limbic structure that controls fear, anger, and aggression.

analogy   A problem-solving heuristic that involves using an old solution as a model for a new, similar problem.

anterograde amnesia   A memory disorder characterized by an inability to store new information in long-term memory.

antianxiety drugs   Tranquilizers such as Librium, Valium, and Xanax sometimes used in the treatment of anxiety.

antidepressants   Drugs that relieve depression by increasing the supply of norepinephrine, serotonin, or dopamine.

antipsychotic drugs   Drugs that are used to control the positive symptoms of schizophrenia and other psychotic disorders.

antisocial personality disorder   A personality disorder characterized by a chronic pattern of self-centered, manipulative, and destructive behavior toward others.

aphasias   Language disturbances, often caused by left-hemisphere damage, that disrupt speech production or comprehension.

applied research   Research that aims to solve practical human problems.

association cortex   Areas of the cortex that communicate with the sensory and motor areas and house the brain's higher mental processes.

attachment   A deep emotional bond that an infant develops with its primary caretaker.

attention   A state of awareness consisting of the sensations, thoughts, and feelings that one is attending to at a given moment.

attitude   A positive or negative reaction to any person, object, or idea.

attribution theory   A set of theories that describe how people explain the causes of behavior.

audition   The sense of hearing.

auditory localization   The ability to judge the direction a sound is coming from.

autonomic nervous system   The branch of the peripheral nervous system that connects the CNS to the involuntary muscles, organs, and glands.

availability heuristic   A tendency to estimate the likelihood of an event in terms of how easily instances of it can be recalled.

aversion therapy   A behavior therapy technique for classically conditioning people to react with aversion to alcohol, tobacco, and other harmful substances.

axon   Extension of the cell body of a neuron that sends impulses to other neurons.

basic research   "Pure science" research that tests theories and builds a foundation of knowledge.

behavioral neuroscience   The subfield of psychology that studies the links among the brain, nervous system, mind, and behavior.

behaviorism   A school of thought that defines psychology as the scientific study of observable behavior.

behavior therapy   A set of techniques used to modify disordered thoughts, feelings, and behaviors through the principles of learning.

belief in a just world   The assumption that the world is a just place where people get what they deserve.

belief perseverance The tendency to cling to beliefs even after they have been discredited.

binocular disparity A binocular cue for depth perception whereby the closer an object is to a perceiver, the more different the image is in each retina.

biofeedback An operant procedure in which people learn to control heart rate and other physiological processes by receiving "feedback" about their internal states.

biological rhythm A periodic, more or less regular fluctuation in a biological organism.

bipolar disorder A rare mood disorder characterized by wild fluctuations ranging from mania (a euphoric, overactive state) to depression (a state of hopelessness and apathy).

blind spot A part of the retina through which the optic nerve passes. Lacking rods and cones, this spot is not responsive to light.

blindsight A condition caused by damage to the visual cortex of the brain in which a person encodes visual information without awareness.

brainstem The inner core of the brain that connects to the spinal cord and contains the medulla, pons, and reticular formation.

Broca's area A region in the left hemisphere of the brain that directs the muscle movements in the production of speech.

bystander effect The finding that the presence of others inhibits helping in an emergency.

Cannon-Bard theory The theory that an emotion-eliciting stimulus simultaneously triggers physiological arousal and the experience of emotion.

case studies A type of research that involves making in-depth observations of individual persons.

CAT (computerized axial tomograph) scan A series of x-rays taken from different angles and converted by computer into an image that depicts a horizontal slice of brain.

central nervous system (CNS) The network of nerves contained within the brain and spinal cord.

central route to persuasion A process in which people think carefully about a message and are influenced by its arguments.

cerebellum A primitive brainstem structure that controls balance and coordinates complex voluntary movements.

cerebral cortex The outermost covering of the brain, largely responsible for higher-order mental processes.

cerebral lateralization The tendency for each hemisphere of the brain to specialize in different functions.

chromosomes Rod-like structures, found in all biological cells, that contain DNA molecules in the form of genes.

circadian rhythm A biological cycle, such as sleeping and waking, that occurs approximately every twenty-four hours.

classical conditioning A type of learning in which an organism comes to associate one stimulus with another (also called Pavlovian conditioning).

clinical psychology The branch of psychology that deals with the diagnosis and treatment of mental disorders.

cocktail party effect The ability to attend selectively to one person's speech in the midst of competing conversations.

cognition A general term that refers to mental processes such as thinking, knowing, and remembering.

cognitive dissonance An unpleasant psychological state often aroused when people behave in ways that are discrepant with their attitudes.

cognitive social-learning theory An approach to personality that focuses on social learning (modeling) and cognitive factors (expectancies, values), and emphasizes the person-situation interaction.

cognitive therapy A form of psychotherapy in which people are taught to think in more adaptive ways.

collective unconscious As proposed by Jung, a kind of memory bank that stores images and ideas that humans have accumulated over the course of evolution.

collectivism A cultural orientation in which interdependence, cooperation, and group harmony take priority over purely personal goals.

comorbidity The tendency for people diagnosed with one mental disorder to exhibit the symptoms of other disorders as well.

companionate love A deep and lasting affection between close friends or lovers.

concept A mental grouping of persons, ideas, events, or objects that share common properties.

concrete operational stage Piaget's third stage of cognitive development, when six-year-olds become capable of logical reasoning.

conditioned response (CR) A learned response (salivation) to a classically conditioned stimulus (bell).

conditioned stimulus (CS) A neutral stimulus (bell) that comes to evoke a classically conditioned response (salivation).

conduction deafness Hearing loss caused by damage to the eardrum or bones in the middle ear.

cones Cone-shaped photoreceptor cells in the retina that are sensitive to color.

confirmation bias The inclination to search only for evidence that will verify one's beliefs.

conformity A tendency to alter one's opinion or behavior in ways that are consistent with group norms.

consciousness An awareness of the sensations, thoughts, and feelings that one is attending to at a given moment.

conservation The concept that physical properties of an object remain the same despite superficial changes in appearance.

contact hypothesis The proposition that in certain conditions, direct contact between members of rival groups will improve relations.

content validity The extent to which a test measures what it's supposed to measure.

control group The condition of an experiment in which subjects are not exposed to the independent variable.

convergence A binocular cue for depth perception involving the turning inward of the eyes as an object gets closer.

conversion disorder A disorder in which a person temporarily loses a bodily function, in the absence of any physical cause.

cornea The clear outer membrane that bends light so that it is sharply focused in the eye.

corpus callosum A bundle of nerve fibers that connects the left and right hemispheres.

correlation A statistical measure of the extent to which two variables are associated.

covariation principle An attribution rule that states that for something to be the cause of a behavior it must be present when the behavior occurs and absent when it does not.

creativity Intellectual and motivational processes that lead to novel solutions, ideas, artistic forms, or products.

criterion validity The extent to which a test can predict a concurrent or future outcome.

critical period A period of time during which an organism must be exposed to a certain stimulus for proper development to occur.

critical thinking The process of solving problems and making decisions through a careful evaluation of evidence.

cross-cultural research A body of studies designed to compare and contrast people of different cultures.

cross-sectional studies A method of developmental research in which people of different ages are tested and compared.

crystallized intelligence A form of intelligence that reflects the accumulation of verbal skills and factual knowledge.

dark adaptation A process of adjustment by which the eyes become more sensitive to light in a dark environment.

deception A research procedure used to mislead subjects about the true purposes of a study.

defense mechanisms Unconscious methods of minimizing anxiety by denying and distorting reality.

deindividuation A loss of individuality, often experienced in a group, that results in a breakdown of internal restraints against deviant behavior.

delusions False beliefs that often accompany schizophrenia and other psychotic disorders.

dementia An age-related brain disorder that results in severe cognitive impairments.

dendrites Extensions from the cell body of a neuron that receive incoming impulses.

denial A primitive form of repression in which anxiety-filled external events are barred from awareness.

Deoxyribonucleic acid (DNA) The complex molecular structure of a chromosome that carries genetic information.

dependent variable A variable that is being measured in an experiment. (The dependent variable is the proposed effect.)

depression A mood disorder characterized by sadness, despair, feelings of worthlessness, and low self-esteem.

depth perception The use of visual cues to estimate the depth and distance of objects.

developmental psychology The study of how people grow, mature, and change over the life span.

diagnosis The process of identifying and grouping mental disorders with similar symptoms.

diathesis-stress model A theory stating that certain mental disorders (such as schizophrenia) develop when people with a genetic or acquired vulnerability are exposed to high levels of stress.

diffusion of responsibility In groups, a tendency for bystanders to assume that someone else will help.

discrimination Behavior directed against persons because of their affiliation with a social group.

discrimination In classical and operant conditioning, the ability to distinguish between different stimuli.

displacement The property of language that accounts for the capacity to communicate about matters that are not in the here-and-now.

dissociation A division of consciousness that permits one part of the mind to operate independent of another part.

dissociative disorder A condition marked by a temporary disruption in one's memory, consciousness, or self-identity.

divergent thinking The ability to think flexibly and entertain a wide range of possible solutions.

divided attention The ability to distribute one's attention and simultaneously engage in two or more activities.

dopamine A neurotransmitter that functions as an inhibitor and is involved in the control of voluntary movements.

DSM-IV Nickname for the American Psychiatric Association's *Diagnostic and Statistical Manual of Mental Disorders (4th Edition)*.

dualism The assumption that the body and mind are separate, though perhaps interacting, entities.

ego In psychoanalysis, the part of personality that operates according to the reality principle and mediates the conflict between the id and superego.

egocentric Self-centered, unable to adopt the perspective of another person.

elaborative rehearsal A technique for transferring information into long-term memory by thinking about it in a deeper way.

electroconvulsive therapy (ECT) Electric shock treatments that often relieve severe depression by triggering seizures in the brain.

electroencephalograph (EEG) An instrument used to measure electrical activity in the brain through electrodes placed on the scalp.

embryo The developing human organism, from two weeks to two months after conception.

empathy A feeling of joy for others who are happy and distress for those who are in pain.

empathy-altruism hypothesis The proposition that an empathic response to a person in need produces altruistic helping.

encoding specificity The principle that any stimulus encoded along with an experience can later jog one's memory of that experience.

endocrine system A collection of ductless glands that regulate aspects of growth, reproduction, metabolism, and behavior by secreting hormones.

endorphins A morphine-like neurotransmitter that is produced in the brain and linked to pain control and pleasure.

ethnic identity The part of a person's identity that is defined by an ethnic heritage, language, history, customs, and so on.

ethology The study of the behavior of animals in their natural habitat.

experiment A type of research in which the investigator varies some factors, keeps others constant, and measures the effects on randomly assigned subjects.

experimental group Any condition of an experiment in which subjects are exposed to the independent variable.

explicit memory The deliberate and conscious retrieval of recollections in response to direct questions.

extinction   The elimination of a learned response by removal of the unconditioned stimulus (in classical conditioning) or reinforcement (in operant conditioning).

extravert   A kind of person who seeks stimulation, and is sociable and impulsive.

facial electromyograph (EMG)   An electronic instrument used by emotion researchers to record activity in the facial muscles.

facial feedback hypothesis   The hypothesis that changes in facial expression can produce corresponding changes in emotion.

factor analysis   A statistical technique used to identify clusters of test items that correlate with one another.

fetal alcohol syndrome   A specific pattern of birth defects (stunted growth, facial deformity, and mental retardation) often found in the offspring of alcoholic mothers.

fetus   The developing human organism, from nine weeks after conception to birth.

five-factor model   A model of personality that consists of 5 basic traits: neuroticism, extraversion, openness, agreeableness, and conscientiousness.

fixation   In psychoanalysis, a tendency to get "locked in" at early, immature stages of psychosexual development.

fixed action pattern   A species-specific behavior that is built into an animal's nervous system and triggered by a specific stimulus.

flooding   A behavior therapy technique in which the patient is continually exposed to a fear-provoking stimulus until the anxiety becomes extinct.

fluid intelligence   A form of intelligence that involves the ability to reason logically and abstractly.

formal operational stage   Piaget's fourth stage of cognitive development, when adolescents become capable of logic and abstract thought.

fovea   The center of the retina, where cones are clustered.

framing effect   The biasing effects on decision making of the way in which a choice is worded, or "framed."

free association   A key technique of psychoanalysis in which patients say whatever comes to mind--freely and without censorship.

frustration-aggression hypothesis   The theory that frustration causes aggression.

fugue state   A form of amnesia in which a person "forgets" his or her identity, wanders from home, and starts a new life.

functional fixedness   The tendency to think of objects only in terms of their usual functions, a limitation that disrupts problem solving.

fundamental attribution error   A tendency to overestimate the impact of personal causes of behavior and to overlook the role of situations.

gate-control theory   The theory that the spinal cord contains a neurological "gate" that blocks pain signals from the brain when flooded by competing signals.

gender roles   Sex-typed behaviors promoted by social learning.

gender schemas   Beliefs about men and women that influence the way we perceive ourselves and others.

general adaptation syndrome   A three-staged process (alarm, resistance, exhaustion) by which the body responds to stress.

general intelligence (g)   A broad intellectual ability factor used to explain why performances on different intelligence test items are often correlated.

generalizability   The extent to which a finding applies to a broad range of subject populations and circumstances.

generalized anxiety disorder   A psychological disorder that is characterized by a constant state of anxiety not linked to an identifiable source.

generativity   The property of language that accounts for the capacity to use a limited number of words to produce an infinite variety of expressions.

genes   The biochemical units of heredity that govern the development of an individual life.

Gestalt psychology   A school of thought rooted in the idea that the whole (perception) is greater than the sum of its parts (sensation).

Gestalt therapy   A humanistic psychotherapy in which clients are aggressively prompted to express their feelings.

glial cells   Nervous system cells that provide structural support, insulation, and nutrients to the neurons.

grasping reflex   In infants, an automatic tendency to grasp an object that stimulates the palm.

group polarization   The tendency for discussion to enhance or "polarize" a group's initial position.

group therapy   The simultaneous treatment of several clients in a group setting.

groupthink   A group decision-making style by which group members convince themselves that they are correct.

gustatory system   The structures responsible for the sense of taste.

habituation   The tendency for attention to a stimulus to wane over time (often used to determine whether an infant has "learned" a stimulus).

habituation   The tendency of an organism to become familiar with a stimulus as a result of repeated exposure.

hallucinations   Sensory experiences that occur in the absence of actual stimulation.

hallucinogens   Psychedelic drugs that distort perceptions and cause hallucinations (e.g., LSD, marijuana).

hardiness   A personality style—characterized by commitment, challenge, and control—that acts as a buffer against stress.

health psychology   The study of the links between psychological factors and physical health and illness.

heritability   A term that refers to the statistic used to estimate the percentage of the variability of a trait caused by genetic factors.

heuristic   A rule of thumb allowing one to make judgments that are quick but often in error.

hierarchy of needs   Maslow's list of basic needs that have to be satisfied before one can become self-actualized.

hippocampus   A limbic structure that plays a key role in the formation of new memories.

hormones   Chemical messengers secreted from endocrine glands, into the bloodstream, to various organs throughout the body.

humanistic theory   An approach to personality that focuses on the self, subjective experience, and the capacity for growth and fulfillment.

hypermnesia A term referring to the unsubstantiated claim that hypnosis that can be used to facilitate the retrieval of past memories.

hypnosis A heightened state of suggestibility induced by systematic attention-focusing procedures.

hypnotic susceptibility The characteristic extent to which an individual is responsive to hypnosis.

hypochondriasis A disorder characterized by an unwarranted preoccupation with one's physical health.

hypothalamus A tiny limbic structure in the brain that helps regulate the autonomic nervous system, endocrine glands, emotions, and basic drives.

hypothesis A specific testable prediction, often derived from a theory.

id In psychoanalysis, a primitive and unconscious part of personality that contains basic drives and operates according to the pleasure principle.

identification In psychoanalysis, the process by which children internalize their parent's values and form a superego.

identity crisis An adolescent's struggle to establish a personal identity, or self-concept.

image A mental representation of visual information.

immune system A biological surveillance system that detects and destroys "nonself" substances that invade the body.

implicit memory Nonconscious recollection of prior experience that is measured indirectly by its effects on performance.

imprinting Among newly hatched ducks and geese, an instinctive tendency to follow the mother.

independent variable Any variable that the researcher manipulates in an experiment (the proposed cause).

individualism A cultural orientation in which independence, autonomy, and self-reliance take priority over group allegiances.

informational influence Conformity motivated by the belief that others are correct.

informed consent The ethical requirement that prospective subjects be given enough information to permit them to decide freely whether or not to participate in a study.

ingroup favoritism The tendency to discriminate in favor of ingroups over outgroups.

insecure attachment A parent-child relationship in which the baby clings to the parent, cries at separation, and reacts with anger or apathy to reunion.

insight A form of problem solving in which the solution seems to pop to mind all of a sudden.

insomnia An inability to fall asleep, stay asleep, or get the amount of sleep needed to function during the day.

intelligence The capacity to learn from experience and adapt successfully to one's environment.

intelligence quotient (IQ) Originally defined as the ratio of mental age to chronological age, an IQ score now represents a person's performance relative to same-aged peers.

interneuron Central nervous system neurons that connect sensory inputs and motor outputs.

intrinsic motivation An inner drive for a task that motivates people in the absence of external reward and punishment.

introspection Wundt's method of having trained observers report on their conscious, moment-to-moment reactions.

introvert A kind of person who avoids stimulation, and is low-key and cautious.

iris The ring of muscle tissue that gives eyes their color and controls the size of the pupil.

James-Lange theory The theory that emotion stems from the physiological arousal that is triggered by an emotion-eliciting stimulus.

just-noticeable difference (JND) The smallest amount of change in a stimulus that can be detected.

kinesthetic system The set of structures distributed throughout the body that give us a sense of position and movement of body parts.

latent content According to Freud, the unconscious, censored meaning of a dream.

latent learning Learning that occurs but is not exhibited in performance until there is an incentive to do so.

law of effect A law stating that responses followed by positive outcomes are repeated, while those followed by negative outcomes are not.

learned helplessness A learned expectation that one cannot control important life outcomes, resulting in apathy and depression.

learning A relatively permanent change in knowledge or behavior that results from experience.

lens A transparent structure in the eye that focuses light on the retina.

life expectancy The number of years that an average member of a species is expected to live.

life span The maximum possible age for members of a species.

light adaptation The process of adjustment by which the eyes become less sensitive to light in a bright environment.

limbic system A set of loosely connected structures in the brain that help regulate motivation, emotion, and memory.

linguistic relativity hypothesis The hypothesis that language determines, or at least influences, the way we think.

lithium A drug used to control mood swings in people with bipolar disorder.

locus of control A term referring to the expectancy that one's reinforcements are generally controlled by internal or external factors.

longitudinal studies A method of developmental research in which the same people are tested at different times in order to track age-related changes.

long-term memory A relatively permanent memory storage system that can hold vast amounts of information for many years.

lucid dreaming A semiconscious dream state in which a sleeper is aware that he or she is dreaming.

lymphocytes Specialized white blood cells that secrete chemical antibodies and facilitate the immune response.

magnetic resonance imaging (MRI) A brain-scanning technique that uses magnetic fields and radio waves to produce clear, three-dimensional images.

maintenance rehearsal The use of sheer repetition to keep information in short-term memory.

manifest content According to Freud, the conscious dream content that is remembered in the morning.

matching hypothesis The tendency to form close relationships with others of equivalent attractiveness.

means-ends analysis A problem-solving heuristic that involves breaking down a larger problem into a series of subgoals.

medical model The perspective that mental disorders are caused by biological conditions and can be treated through medical intervention.

medulla A brainstem structure that controls vital involuntary functions.

menarche A girl's first menstrual period.

menopause Among middle-aged women, the end of menstruation and fertility.

mental age In an intelligence test, the average age of the children who achieve a certain level of performance.

mental disorder A condition in which a person's pattern of behavior is judged to be dysfunctional.

mental models Intuitive theories about the way things work.

mental retardation A diagnostic category used for people with IQ scores below 70 who have difficulty adapting to the routine demands of life.

mental set The tendency to return to a problem-solving strategy that worked in the past.

mere-exposure effect The attraction to a stimulus that results from increased exposure to it.

meta-analysis A set of statistical procedures used to review a body of evidence by combining the results of individual studies.

Minnesota Multiphasic Personality Inventory (MMPI) A large-scale test designed to measure a multitude of psychological disorders and personality traits.

misinformation effect The tendency to incorporate post-event information into one's memory of the event itself.

mnemonics Memory aids designed to facilitate the recall of new information.

modeling The social-learning process by which behavior is observed and imitated.

monocular depth cues Distance cues, such as linear perspective, that enable us to perceive depth with one eye.

mood disorder A condition characterized by prolonged emotional extremes ranging from mania to depression.

moon illusion The tendency for people to see the moon as larger when it's low on the horizon than when it's overhead.

moral reasoning The way people think about and try to solve moral dilemmas.

morphemes In language, the smallest units that carry meaning (e.g., prefixes, root words, suffixes).

motor cortex The area of the cortex that sends impulses to voluntary muscles.

motor neurons Motion-producing neurons that transmit commands from the central nervous system to the muscles, glands, and organs.

Müller-Lyer illusion An illusion in which the perceived length of a line is altered by the position of other lines that enclose it.

multiculturalism The study of diverse racial and ethnic groups within a culture.

multiple intelligences Gardner's theory that there are six types of intelligence (linguistic, mathematical, spatial, musical, bodily-kinesthetic, and personal).

multiple personality disorder (MPD) A dissociative disorder in which a person develops two or more distinct personalities.

myelin sheath A layer of fatty cells that is tightly wrapped around the axon to insulate it and speed the movement of electrical impulses.

narcolepsy A sleep disorder characterized by irresistible and sudden attacks of REM sleep during the day.

naturalistic observation The observation of behavior as it occurs naturally in real-world settings.

nature-nurture debate The debate over the extent to which human behavior is determined by genetics and the environment.

nerve deafness Hearing loss caused by damage to the structures of the inner ear.

neural graft A technique of transplanting healthy tissue from the nervous system of one animal into that of another.

neurons Nerve cells that serve as the building blocks of the nervous system.

neurotransmitters Chemical messengers in the nervous system that transmit information by crossing the synapse from one neuron to another.

nonstate theories Theories that view hypnosis as an ordinary state of consciousness.

nonverbal behavior Behavior that reveals a person's feelings without words--through facial expressions, body language, and vocal cues.

normative influence Conformity motivated by a fear of social rejection.

NREM sleep The stages of sleep not accompanied by rapid eye movements.

object permanence Developing at six to eight months, an awareness that objects continue to exist after they disappear from view.

observational learning Learning that takes place when one observes and models the behavior of others.

obsessive-compulsive disorder (OCD) An anxiety disorder characterized by persistent thoughts (obsessions) and the need to perform repetitive acts (compulsions).

Oedipus complex In psychoanalysis, a tendency for young children to become sexually attracted to the parent of the opposite sex, and hostile toward the parent of the same sex.

olfactory system The structures responsible for the sense of smell.

operant conditioning The process by which organisms learn to behave in ways that produce reinforcement.

opiates A class of highly addictive drugs that depress neural activity and provide temporary relief from pain and anxiety (e.g., heroin, morphine).

opponent-process theory The theory that color vision is derived from three pairs of opposing receptors. The opponent colors are blue and yellow, red and green, and black and white.

optic nerve The pathway that carries visual information from the eyeball to the brain.

outgroup homogeneity bias The tendency to assume that "they" (members of groups other than our own) are all alike.

panic disorder A disorder characterized by sudden and intense rushes of anxiety, in the absence of any apparent reason.

parapsychology The study of ESP and other claims that cannot be explained by existing principles of science.

parasympathetic nervous system A branch of the autonomic nervous system that calms the body and conserves energy.

parasympathetic nervous system The division of the autonomic nervous system that reduces arousal and restores the body to its pre-energzied state.

passionate love An intense, emotional state of positive absorption in another person.

perception The set of processes by which people select, organize, and interpret sensations.

perceptual illusions Patterns of sensory input that give rise to misperceptions.

perceptual set The effects of prior experience and expectations on interpretations of sensory input.

peripheral nervous system (PNS) The network of nerves that radiate from the central nervous system to the rest of the body. The PNS comprises the somatic and autonomic nervous systems.

peripheral route to persuasion A process in which people do not think carefully about a message and are influenced by superficial cues.

personality An individual's distinct and relatively enduring pattern of thoughts, feelings, motives, and behaviors.

personality disorders A group of disorders characterized by a personality that is highly inflexible and maladaptive.

person-centered therapy A humanistic psychotherapy in which a warm and accepting environment is created to foster self-insight and acceptance.

PET (positron emission tomograph) scan A visual display of brain activity, as measured by the amount of glucose being used.

pheromones Chemicals secreted by animals that transmit signals to others, usually of the same species.

phobic disorder An anxiety disorder characterized by an intense and irrational fear.

phonemes The basic, distinct sounds of a spoken language.

phrenology The pseudoscientific theory that psychological characteristics are revealed by bumps on the skull.

physical dependence A psychological addiction in which a drug is needed to prevent symptoms of withdrawal.

pituitary gland A tiny gland in the brain that regulates growth and stimulates hormones in other endocrine glands at the command of the hypothalamus.

placebo effect The curative effect of an inactive treatment that results simply from the patient's belief in its therapeutic value.

pleasure principle In psychoanalysis, the id's boundless drive for immediate gratification.

polygraph An electronic device that records multiple channels of autonomic arousal and is often used as a lie-detector test.

pons A portion of the brainstem that plays a role in sleep and arousal.

Ponzo illusion An illusion in which the perceived length of a line is affected by linear perspective cues.

posthypnotic amnesia A reported tendency for hypnosis subjects to forget events that occurred during the induction.

posthypnotic suggestion A suggestion made to a hypnosis subject to be carried out *after* the induction session is over.

posttraumatic stress disorder An anxiety disorder triggered by an extremely stressful event, such as combat.

practical intelligence The ability to size up new situations, and adapt to real-life demands.

prejudice Negative evaluation of others based solely on their membership in a certain group.

preoperational stage Piaget's second stage of cognitive development, when two- to six-year-olds become capable of reasoning in an intuitive, prelogical manner.

primacy effect The tendency for impressions of others to be heavily influenced by information appearing early rather than late in an interaction.

proactive interference The tendency for previously learned material to disrupt the recall of new information.

Project Head Start A preschool intellectual enrichment program for children born of poor families.

projection A defense mechanism in which people attribute or "project" their own unacceptable impulses onto others.

projective tests Psychoanalytic personality tests that allow people to "project" unconscious needs, wishes, and conflicts onto ambiguous stimuli.

prosopagnosia A condition stemming from damage to the temporal lobes of the brain that disrupts the ability to recognize familiar faces.

prototype A "typical" member of a category, one that has most of the defining features of that category.

psychoactive drug A chemical that alters perceptions, thoughts, moods, or behavior.

psychoanalysis Freud's theory of personality and method of psychotherapy, both of which assume that our motives are largely unconscious.

psychological dependence A condition in which drugs are needed to maintain a sense of well-being or relief from negative emotions.

psychological model The perspective that mental disorders are caused and maintained by one's life experiences.

psychology The scientific study of behavior and the mind.

psychoneuroimmunology (PNI) A subfield of psychology that examines the interactions among psychological factors, the nervous system, and the immune system.

psychophysics The study of the relationship between physical stimulation and subjective sensations.

psychosexual stages Freud's stages of personality development during which pleasure is derived from different parts of the body (oral, anal, phallic, and genital).

psychosurgery The surgical removal of portions of the brain for the purpose of treating psychological disorders.

psychotherapy A term used to describe all forms of treatment in which a trained professional uses psychological techniques to help persons in need of assistance.

puberty   The onset of adolescence, as evidenced by rapid growth, rising levels of sex hormones, and sexual maturity.

punishment   In operant conditioning, any stimulus that decreases the likelihood of a prior response.

pupil   The small round hole in the iris of the eye through which light passes.

racism   A deep-seated form of prejudice that is based on the color of a person's skin.

random assignment   The procedure whereby subjects are assigned to conditions of an experiment in an arbitrary manner.

random sample   A method of selection in which everyone in a population has an equal chance of being chosen.

rational-emotive therapy (RET)   A form of cognitive therapy in which people are confronted with their irrational, maladaptive beliefs.

rationalization   A defense mechanism that involves making excuses for one's failures and shortcomings.

reaction formation   A defense mechanism in which one converts an unacceptable feeling into its opposite.

realistic conflict theory   The theory that prejudice stems from intergroup competition for limited resources.

reality principle   In psychoanalysis, the ego's capacity to delay gratification.

reciprocal determinism   The view that personality emerges from a mutual interaction of individuals, their actions, and their environments.

recovery   Following habituation to one stimulus, the tendency for a second stimulus to arouse new interest (often used to test whether infants can discriminate between stimuli).

reflex   An inborn automatic response to a sensory stimulus.

reinforcement   In operant conditioning, any stimulus that increases the likelihood of a prior response.

reliability   The extent to which a test yields consistent results over time or using alternate forms.

REM sleep   The rapid-eye-movement stage of sleep associated with dreaming.

replication   The process of repeating a study to see if the findings are reliable enough to be duplicated.

representativeness heuristic   A tendency to estimate the likelihood of an event in terms of how typical it seems.

repression   A defense mechanism in which personally threatening thoughts, memories, and impulses are banned from awareness.

resistance   In psychoanalysis, the tendency for patients to actively block or "resist" psychologically painful insights.

reticular formation   A group of nerve cells in the brainstem that help to control sleep, arousal, and attention.

retina   The rear multilayered part of the eye where rods and cones convert light into neural impulses.

retroactive interference   The tendency for new information to disrupt the memory of previously learned material.

retrograde amnesia   A memory disorder characterized by an inability to retrieve long-term memories from the past.

reversible figure   A drawing that one can perceive in different ways by reversing figure and ground.

rods   Rod-shaped photoreceptor cells in the retina that are highly sensitive to light.

rooting reflex   In response to contact on the cheek, an infant's tendency to turn toward the stimulus and open its mouth.

Rorschach   A projective personality test in which people are asked to report what they see in a set of inkblots.

schemas   Preconceptions about persons, objects, or events that bias the way that new information is interpreted and recalled.

schizophrenic disorders   Disorders involving gross distortions of thought and perception, and loss of contact with reality.

secure attachment   A parent-child relationship in which the baby is secure when the parent is present, distressed by separation, and delighted by reunion.

sedatives   A class of depressant drugs that slow down activity in the central nervous system (e.g., alcohol, barbiturates).

selective attention   The ability to focus awareness on a single stimulus to the exclusion of other stimuli, as in the cocktail party effect.

self-actualization   In humanistic personality theories, the need to fulfill one's unique potential.

self-awareness theory   The theory that self-focused attention leads people to notice their shortcomings, thus motivating a change in behavior or an escape from self-awareness.

self-deception   The processes by which people distort and hide unpleasant truths from themselves.

self-discrepancy theory   The theory that your emotional well-being is defined by the match between how you see yourself and how you want to see yourself.

self-efficacy   The belief that one is capable of performing the behaviors required to produce a desired outcome.

self-esteem   A positive or negative evaluation of the self.

self-fulfilling prophecy   The idea that a person's expectation can lead to its own fulfillment (as in the effect of teacher expectations on student performance).

self-handicapping   Behaviors designed to sabotage one's own performance to provide a subsequent excuse for failure.

self-report   A method of observation that involves asking people to describe their own thoughts, feelings, or behavior.

semanticity   The property of language that accounts for the communication of meaning.

semantic network   A complex web of semantic associations that link items in memory such that retrieving one item triggers the retrieval of others as well.

sensation   The set of processes by which our sense organs receive information from the environment.

sensorimotor stage   Piaget's first stage of cognitive development, from birth to two years old, when infants come to know the world through their own actions.

sensory memory   A memory storage system that records information from the senses for up to three seconds.

sensory neurons   Neurons that send signals from the senses, skin, muscles, and internal organs to the central nervous system.

separation anxiety   Among infants with object permanence, a fear reaction to the absence of their primary caretaker.

serial position effect   The tendency to recall items from the beginning and end of a list more effectively than those in the middle.

sexism   Discrimination that is based on a person's gender.

sexual orientation   An enduring sexual preference for members of the same sex (homosexuality), the opposite sex (heterosexuality), or both sexes (bisexuality).

sexual response cycle   The four physiological stages of sexual responding--excitement, plateau, orgasm, and resolution.

shape constancy   The tendency to see an object as retaining its form despite changes in orientation.

short-term memory   A memory storage system that holds about seven items for up to twenty seconds before the material is transferred to long-term storage or forgotten.

signal-detection theory   The theory that detecting a stimulus is jointly determined by the signal and the subject's response criterion.

simple phobia   An intense, irrational fear of a specific object or situation.

size constancy   The tendency to view an object as constant in size despite changes in the size of the retinal image.

social anxiety   Feelings of discomfort in the presence of others, typically accompanied by shyness.

social categorization   The classification of persons into groups based on common attributes.

social clock   A set of cultural expectations concerning the most appropriate ages for men and women to leave home, marry, start a career, have children, and retire.

social facilitation   The tendency for the presence of others to enhance performance on simple tasks and to impair performance on complex tasks.

social identity theory   The theory that people discriminate against outgroups to enhance their own self-esteem.

social loafing   The tendency for people to exert less effort in group tasks for which individual contributions are pooled.

social norms   Implicit rules of conduct according to which each culture operates.

social perception   The processes by which we come to know and evaluate other persons.

social phobia   An intense fear of situations that invite public scrutiny.

social psychology   The study of how individuals think, feel, and behave in social situations.

social roles theory   The theory that perceived sex differences are magnified by the unequal social roles occupied by men and women.

social skills training   A form of behavior therapy designed to teach interpersonal skills through modeling, rehearsal, and reinforcement (e.g., assertiveness training).

social support   The healthful coping resources provided by friends and other people.

soma   The cell body of a neuron.

somatic nervous system   The branch of the peripheral nervous system that transmits signals from the sensory organs to the CNS, and from the CNS to the skeletal muscles.

somatoform disorder   A type of mental disorder in which a person experiences bodily symptoms that are psychological rather than medical in nature.

somatosensory cortex   The area of the cortex that receives sensory information from the touch receptors in the skin.

spermarche   A boy's first ejaculation.

split brain   A surgically produced condition in which the corpus callosum is severed, thus cutting the link between the left and right hemispheres of the brain.

split-half reliability   The degree to which alternate forms of a test yield consistent results.

spontaneous recovery   The re-emergence of an extinguished conditioned response after a rest period.

standardization   The procedure by which existing norms are used to interpret an individual's test score.

Stanford-Binet   An american version of Binet's intelligence test that yields an IQ score with an average of 100.

state theories   Theories that maintain that hypnosis induces a unique "altered" state of consciousness.

statistics   A branch of mathematics that is used for analyzing research data.

stereotype   A belief that associates a group of people with certain traits.

stimulants   A class of drugs that excite the central nervous system and energize behavior (e.g., amphetamines, cocaine).

stimulus generalization   The tendency to respond to a stimulus that is similar to the conditioned stimulus.

strange-situation test   A parent-child "separation and reunion" procedure that is staged in a laboratory to test the security of a child's attachment.

stress   An aversive state of arousal triggered by the perception that an event threatens our ability to cope effectively.

Stroop test   A color-naming task that demonstrates the automatic nature of highly practiced activities such a reading.

sublimation   In psychoanalysis, the channeling of repressed sexual and aggressive urges into socially acceptable substitute outlets.

subliminal message   A stimulus that is presented below the threshold for awareness.

superego   In psychoanalysis, the part of personality that consists of one's moral ideals and conscience.

survey   A research method that involves interviewing or giving questionnaires to a large number of people.

syllogism   A logical problem in which the goal is to determine the validity of a conclusion given two or more premises.

sympathetic nervous system   A branch of the autonomic nervous system that controls the involuntary activities of various organs and mobilizes the body for fight or flight.

sympathetic nervous system   The division of the autonomic nervous system that heightens arousal and energizes the body for action.

synapse   The junction between the axon terminal of one neuron and the dendrites of another neuron.

syntax   Rules of grammar that govern the arrangement of words in a sentence.

systematic desensitization   A behavior therapy technique used to treat phobias and other anxiety disorders by pairing gradual exposure to an anxiety-provoking situation with relaxation.

teratogens   Toxic substances that can harm the embryo or fetus during prenatal development.

test-retest reliability   The degree to which a test yields consistent results when re-administered at a later time.

thalamus   A limbic structure that relays neural messages between the senses and areas of the cerebral cortex.

Thematic Apperception Test (TAT)   A projective personality test in which people are asked to make up stories from a set of ambiguous pictures.

theory   An organized set of principles that describes, predicts, and explains some phenomenon.

trait   A relatively stable predisposition to behave in a certain way.

transduction   The process by which physical energy is converted into sensory neural impulses.

transference   In psychoanalysis, the tendency of patients to displace or "transfer" intense feelings for others onto the therapist.

trial and error   A simple problem-solving strategy in which several solutions are attempted until one is found that works.

triarchic theory of intelligence   Sternberg's theory that there are three kinds of intelligence—information processing, creative, and practical.

trichromatic theory   A theory of color vision stating that the retina contains three types of color receptors—for red, blue, and green—and that these combine to produce all other colors.

twin study method   A method of testing nature and nurture by comparing pairs of identical and fraternal twins of the same sex.

two-factor theory of emotion   The theory that emotion is based both on physiological arousal and on the cognitive interpretation of that arousal.

Type A personality   A personality characterized by an impatient, hard-driving, competitive, and anger-prone pattern of behavior.

Type B personality   A personality characterized by an easygoing, relaxed pattern of behavior.

unconditional positive regard   An attitude of unqualified acceptance of another person.

unconditioned response (UR)   An unlearned response (salivation) to an unconditioned stimulus (food).

unconditioned stimulus (US)   A stimulus (food) that triggers an unconditioned response (salivation).

validity   The extent to which a test measures or predicts what it is designed to.

vestibular system   The set of inner ear and brain structures that give us a sense of equilibrium.

visual cliff   An apparatus used to test depth perception in infants and animals.

Weber's law   The principle that the just-noticeable difference of a stimulus is a constant proportion, despite variations in intensity.

Wechsler adult intelligence scale (WAIS)   The most widely used IQ test for adults, it yields separate scores for verbal and performance subtests.

Wernicke's area   A region in the left hemisphere of the brain that is involved in the comprehension of language.

white noise   A hissing sound that results from a combination of all frequencies of the sound spectrum.

zygote   A fertilized egg that undergoes a two-week period of rapid cell division and develops into an embryo.

References

Abbey, A. (1982). Sex differences in attributions for friendly behavior: Do males misperceive females' friendliness? *Journal of Personality and Social Psychology, 42,* 830–838.

Abbey, A. (1987). Misperceptions of friendly behavior as sexual interest: A survey of naturally occurring incidents. *Psychology of Women Quarterly, 11,* 173–194.

Abbey, S. E., & Garfinkel, P. E. (1991). Neurasthenia and chronic fatigue syndrome: The role of culture in the making of a diagnosis. *American Journal of Psychiatry, 148,* 1638–1646.

Abrams, R. (1988). *Electroconvulsive therapy.* New York: Oxford University Press.

Abramson, L. Y., Metalsky, G., & Alloy, L. B. (1989). Hopelessness depression: A theory-based subtype. *Psychological Review, 96,* 358–372.

Ackerman, D. (1990). *A natural history of the senses.* New York: Random House.

Acklin, M., McDowell, C., II, & Orndoff, S. (1992). Statistical power and Rorschach: 1975–1991. *Journal of Personality Assessment, 59,* 366–379.

Adams, P. R., & Adams, G. R. (1984). Mount Saint Helens's ashfall: Evidence for a disaster stress reaction. *American Psychologist, 39,* 252–260.

Adams, R. J., & Maurer, D. (1984). Detection of contrast by the newborn and 2-month-old infant. *Infant Behavior and Development, 7,* 415–422.

Adelson, J. (1986). *Inventing adolescence: The political psychology of everyday schooling.* New Brunswick, NJ: Transaction.

Ader, R., & Cohen, N. (1985). CNS-immune system interactions: Conditioning phenomena. *Behavioral and Brain Sciences, 8,* 379–426.

Ader, R., & Cohen, N. (1993). Psychoneuroimmunology: Conditioning and stress. *Annual Review of Psychology, 44,* 53–85.

Ader, R., Felten, D. L., & Cohen, N. (Eds.). (1991). *Psychoneuroimmunology* (2nd ed.). San Diego: Academic Press.

Adler, A. (1927). *The practice and theory of individual psychology.* New York: Harcourt, Brace & World.

Adler, N., & Matthews, K. (1994). Health psychology: Why do some people get sick and some stay well? *Annual Review of Psychology, 45,* 229–259.

Ahrentzen, S., Jue, G. M., Skorpanich, M. A., & Evans, G. W. (1982). School environments and stress. In G. W. Evans (Ed.), *Environmental stress.* New York: Cambridge University Press.

Ainsworth, M.D.S. (1989). Attachments beyond infancy. *American Psychologist, 44,* 709–716.

Ainsworth, M.D.S., Blehar, M. C., Waters, E., & Wall, S. (1978). *Patterns of attachment: A psychological study of the Strange Situation.* Hillsdale, NJ: Erlbaum.

Ajzen, I. (1991). The theory of planned behavior. *Organizational Behavior and Human Decision Processes, 50,* 179–211.

Akil, L. (1982). On the role of endorphins in pain modulation. In A. L. Beckman (Ed.), *The neural bases of behavior* (pp. 311–333). New York: Spectrum.

Alan Guttmacher Institute (1981). *Teenage pregnancy: The problem that hasn't gone away.* New York: Alan Guttmacher Institute.

Alberti, R. E., & Emmons, M. L. (1986). *Your perfect right: A guide to assertive living* (5th ed.). San Luis Obispo, CA: Impact Publishers.

Aldag, R. J., & Fuller, S. R. (1993). Beyond fiasco: A reappraisal of the groupthink phenomenon and a new model of group decision processes. *Psychological Bulletin, 113,* 533–552.

Aldwin, C. M., Spiro, A., Bosse, R., & Levenson, M. R. (1989). Longitudinal findings from the normative aging study: 1. Does mental health change with age? *Psychology and Aging, 4,* 295–306.

Alessandri, D. M., Sullivan, R. W., Imaizumi, S., & Lewis, M. (1993). Learning and emotional responsivity in cocaine-exposed infants. *Developmental Psychology, 29,* 989–997.

Alexander, F., & French, T. M. (1946). *Psychoanalytic therapy: Principles and application.* New York: Ronald Press.

Alford, B. A., Freeman, A., Beck, A. T., & Wright, F. D. (1990). Brief focused cognitive therapy of panic disorder. *Psychotherapy, 27,* 230–234.

Allen, J. B., Kenrick, D. T., Linder, D. E., & McCall, M. A. (1989). Arousal and attraction: A response-facilitation alternative to misattribution and negative-reinforcement models. *Journal of Personality and Social Psychology, 57,* 261–270.

Allen, K. D., Danforth, J. S., & Drabman, R. S. (1989). Videotaped modeling and film distraction for fear reduction in adults undergoing hyperbaric oxygen therapy. *Journal of Consulting and Clinical Psychology, 57,* 554–558.

Allen, K. M., Blascovich, J., Tomaka, J., & Kelsey, R. M. (1991). Presence of human friends and pet dogs as moderators of autonomic responses to stress in women. *Journal of Personality and Social Psychology, 61,* 582–589.

Allen, L. S., Hines, M., Shryne, J. E., & Gorski, R. A. (1989). Two sexually dimorphic cell groups in the human brain. *Journal of Neuroscience, 9,* 497–506.

Allen, M. G. (1976). Twin studies of affective illness. *Archives of General Psychiatry, 33,* 1476–1478.

Allen, V. L., & Levine, J. M. (1971). Social support and conformity: The role of independent assessment of reality. *Journal of Experimental Social Psychology, 7,* 48–58.

Alley, T. R. (1988). *Social and applied aspects of perceiving faces.* Hillsdale, NJ: Erlbaum.

Allison, T., & Cicchetti, D. V. (1976). Sleep in mammals: Ecological and constitutional correlates. *Science, 194,* 732–734.

Allport, F. H., et al. (1953). The effects of segregation and the consequences of desegregation: A social science statement. *Minneapolis Law Review, 37,* 429–440.

Allport, G. W. (1937). *Personality: A psychological interpretation.* New York: Holt, Rinehart & Winston.

Allport, G. W. (1961). *Pattern and growth in personality.* New York: Holt, Rinehart & Winston.

Allport, G. W. (1967). Gordon W. Allport. In E. G. Boring and G. Lindzey (Eds.), *A history of psychology in autobiography* (Vol. V). New York: Appleton-Century-Crofts.

Allport, G. W., & Odbert, H. S. (1936). Trait-names: A psycholexical study. *Psychological Monographs, 47*(Whole No. 1).

Allport, G. W., & Postman, L. J. (1947). *The psychology of rumor.* New York: Holt.

Amabile, T. M. (1985). Motivation and creativity: Effects of motivational orientation on creative writers. *Journal of Personality and Social Psychology, 48,* 393–399.

Amabile, T. M., Hennessey, B. A., & Grossman, B. S. (1986). Social influences on creativity: The effects of contracted-for reward. *Journal of Personality and Social Psychology, 50,* 14–23.

Ambady, N., & Rosenthal, R. (1992). Thin slices of expressive behavior as predictors of interpersonal consequences: A meta-analysis. *Psychological Bulletin, 111,* 256–274.

American Almanac, 1992–1993 (113th ed.). Austin, TX: The Reference Press.

American Psychiatric Association (1987). *Diagnostic and statistical manual of mental disorders* (3rd ed., rev.). Washington, DC: American Psychiatric Association.

American Psychiatric Association (1989). *Treatments of psychiatric disorders.* Washington, DC: APA.

American Psychological Association (1992). Ethical principles of psychologists and code of conduct. *American Psychologist, 47,* 1597–1611.

Amoore, J. E., Johnston, J. W., & Rubin, M. (1964). The stereochemical theory of odor. *Scientific American, 210,* 42–49.

Anand, B. K., & Brobeck, J. R. (1951). Localization of a "feeding center" in the hypothalamus of the rat. *Proceedings of the Society for Experimental Biology and Medicine, 77,* 323–324.

Anastasi, A. (1988). *Psychological testing* (6th ed.). New York: Macmillan.

Anderson, A. (1982). The great Japanese IQ increase. *Nature, 297,* 180–181.

Anderson, C. A. (1989). Temperature and aggression: Ubiquitous effects of heat on occurrence of human violence. *Psychological Bulletin, 106,* 74–96.

Anderson, C. A., Lepper, M. R., & Ross, L. (1980). Perseverance of social theories: The role of explanation in the persistence of discredited information. *Journal of Personality and Social Psychology, 39,* 1037–1049.

Anderson, J. R. (1983). *The architecture of cognition.* Cambridge, MA: Harvard University Press.

Anderson, J. R. (1990). *Cognitive psychology and its implications.* (3rd ed.). New York: W. H. Freeman.

Andersson, B. (1992). Effects of day-care on cognitive and socioemotional competence of thirteen-year-old Swedish school children. *Child Development, 61,* 20–36.

Andreasen, N. C. (1987). The diagnosis of schizophrenia. *Schizophrenia Bulletin, 13,* 1–8.

Andreasen, N. C. (1988). Brain imaging: Applications in psychiatry. *Science, 239,* 1381–1388.

Andreasen, N. C., Flaum, M., Swayze, V. W., Tyrrell, G., & Arndt, S. (1990). Positive and negative symptoms in schizophrenia: A critical reappraisal. *Archives of General Psychiatry, 47,* 615–621.

Angoff, W. H. (1988). The nature-nurture debate, aptitudes, and group differences. *American Psychologist, 43,* 713–720.

Anisfeld, M. (1991). Neonatal imitation. *Developmental Review, 11,* 60–97.

Annett, J. (1985). *Left, right, hand and brain: The right shift theory.* London: Erlbaum.

Anonymous (1990). Behind the mask: A functional schizophrenic copes. *Schizophrenia Bulletin, 16,* 547–549.

Archer, J. (1988). *The behavioural biology of aggression.* Cambridge: Cambridge University Press.

Archer, J. (1991). The influence of testosterone on human aggression. *British Journal of Psychology, 82,* 1–28.

Aron, A., Aron, E. M., & Smollan, D. (1992). Inclusion of other in the self scale and the structure of interpersonal closeness. *Journal of Personality and Social Psychology, 63,* 596–612.

Aronoff, J., Barclay, A. M., & Stevenson, L. A. (1988). The recognition of threatening facial stimuli. *Journal of Personality and Social Psychology, 54,* 647–655.

Aronoff, J., Woike, B. A., & Hyman, L. M. (1992). Which are the stimuli in facial displays of anger and happiness? Configurational bases of emotion recognition. *Journal of Personality and Social Psychology, 62,* 1050–1066.

Aronson, E., Blaney, N., Stephan, C., Sikes, J., & Snapp, M. (1978). *The jigsaw classroom.* Beverly Hills, CA: Sage.

Aronson, E., & Mills, J. (1959). The effect of severity of initiation on liking for a group. *Journal of Abnormal and Social Psychology, 59,* 177–181.

Asarnow, J. R. (1988). Children at risk for schizophrenia: Converging lines of evidence. *Schizophrenia Bulletin, 14,* 613–631.

Asch, S. E. (1946). Forming impressions of personality. *Journal of Abnormal and Social Psychology, 41,* 258–290.

Asch, S. E. (1951). Effects of group pressure upon the modification and distortion of judgments. In H. Guetzkow (Ed.), *Groups, leadership, and men.* Pittsburgh, PA: Carnegie Press.

Asch, S. E. (1955). Opinions and social pressure. *Scientific American, 193,* 31–35.

Asch, S. E. (1956). Studies of independence and conformity: A minority of one against a unanimous majority. *Psychological Monographs, 70,* 416.

Aschoff, J. (1981). *Handbook of behavioral neurobiology: Vol. 4. Biological rhythms.* New York: Plenum.

Aserinsky, E., & Kleitman, N. (1953). Regularly occurring periods of eye motility and concomitant phenomena during sleep. *Science, 118,* 273.

Ashcraft, M. H. (1989). *Human memory and cognition.* Glenview, IL: Scott, Foresman.

Ashcraft, M. H. (1993). A personal case history of transient anomia. *Brain and Language, 44,* 47–57.

Asher, S. R., & Coie, J. D. (1990). *Peer rejection in childhood.* New York: Cambridge University Press.

Askenasy, H. (1978). *Are we all Nazis?* Secaucus, NJ: Lyle Stuart.

Aslin, R. N. (1989). Discrimination of frequency transitions by human infants. *Journal of the Acoustical Society of America, 86,* 582–590.

Associated Press (1985, May 10). Man, 75, gets life for wife's death. *Kansas City Times,* p. A4.

Associated Press (1988, October 10). Skirting the issue? *National Law Journal,* p. 43.

Atchley, R. C. (1976). *The sociology of retirement.* New York: Halstead Press.

Atkinson, J. W. (1957). Motivational determinants of risk-taking behavior. *Psychological Review, 64,* 359–372.

Atkinson, R. (1988, October). Respectful, dutiful teenagers. *Psychology Today,* pp. 22, 26.

Atkinson, R. C., & Shiffrin, R. M. (1968). Human memory: A proposed system and its control processes. In K. Spence & J. Spence (Eds.), *The psychology of learning and motivation: Advances in research and theory* (Vol. 2). New York: Academic Press.

Axelrod, S., & Apsche, J. (Eds.). (1983). *The effects of punishment on human behavior.* New York: Academic Press.

Axsom, D. (1989). Cognitive dissonance and behavior change in psychotherapy. *Journal of Experimental Social Psychology, 25,* 234–252.

Axsom, D., Yates, S., & Chaiken, S. (1987). Audience response as a heuristic cue in persuasion. *Journal of Personality and Social Psychology, 53,* 30–40.

Axtell, R. E. (1993). *Do's and taboos around the world* (3rd ed.). New York: Wiley.

Ayllon, T. (1963). Intensive treatment of psychotic behaviour by stimulus satiation and food reinforcement. *Behaviour Research and Therapy, 1,* 53–61.

Ayllon, T., & Azrin, N. H. (1968). *The token economy.* New York: Appleton-Century-Crofts.

Babad, E., & Katz, Y. (1991). Wishful thinking—against all odds. *Journal of Applied Social Psychology, 21,* 1921–1938.

Backlund, E. O., Grandburg, P. O., & Hamberger, B. (1985). Transplantation of adrenal medullary tissue to striatum in Parkinsonianism: First clinical trials. *Journal of Neurosurgery, 62,* 169–173.

Backman, L., and Dixon, R. A. (1992). Psychological compensation: A theoretical framework. *Psychological Bulletin, 112,* 259–283.

Baddeley, A. (1966). Short-term memory for word sequences as a function of acoustic, semantic, and formal similarity. *Quarterly Journal of Experimental Psychology, 18,* 362–365.

Baddeley, A. (1990). *Human memory: Theory and practice.* Boston: Allyn & Bacon.

Baddeley, A. (1992). Working memory. *Science, 255,* 556–559.

Baenninger, M., & Newcombe, N. (1989). The role of experience in spatial test performance: A meta-analysis. *Sex Roles, 20,* 327–344.

Baggs, K., & Spence, S. H. (1990). Effectiveness of booster sessions in the maintenance and enhancement of treatment gains following assertion training. *Journal of Consulting and Clinical Psychology, 58,* 845–854.

Bahill, A. T., & Karnavas, W. J. (1993). The perceptual illusion of baseball's rising fastball and breaking curveball. *Journal of Experimental Psychology: Human Perception and Performance, 19,* 3–14.

Bahrick, H. P. (1984). Semantic memory content in permastore: Fifty years of memory for Spanish learned in school. *Journal of Experimental Psychology: General, 113,* 1–35.

Bahrick, H. P., Bahrick, P. O., & Wittlinger, R. P. (1975). Fifty years of memory for names and faces: A cross-sectional approach. *Journal of Experimental Psychology: General, 104,* 54–75.

Bahrick, H. P., & Hall, L. K. (1991). Lifetime maintenance of high-school mathematics content. *Journal of Experimental Psychology: General, 120,* 20–33.

Bailey, J. M., & Benishay, D. S. (1993). Familial aggregation of female sexual orientation. *American Journal of Psychiatry, 150,* 272–277.

Bailey, J. M., & Pillard, R. C. (1991). A genetic study of male sexual orientation. *Archives of General Psychiatry, 48,* 1089–1096.

Baillargeon, R. (1986). Representing the existence and the location of hidden objects: Object permanence in 6- and 8-month-old infants. *Cognition, 23,* 21–41.

Baillargeon, R., & De Vos, J. (1991). Object permanence in young infants: Further evidence. *Child Development, 62,* 1227–1246.

Baker, E. L. (1985). Psychoanalysis and psychoanalytic therapy. In S. J. Lynn & J. P. Garske (Eds.), *Contemporary psychotherapies: Models and methods.* Columbus, OH: Merrill.

Balay, J., & Shevrin, H. (1988). The subliminal psychodynamic activation method: A critical review. *American Psychologist, 43,* 161–174.

Baltes, P. B., Cornelius, S. W., & Nesselroade, J. R. (1979). Cohort effects in developmental psychology. In J. R. Nesselroade & P. B. Baltes (Eds.), *Longitudinal research in the study of behavior and development* (pp. 61–87). New York: Academic Press.

Baltes, P. B., & Smith, J. (1990). Toward a psychology of wisdom and its ontogenesis. In R. J. Sternberg (Ed.), *Wisdom: Its nature, origins, and development* (pp. 87–120). New York: Cambridge University Press.

Banaji, M. R., & Steele, C. M. (1989). Alcohol and self-evaluation: Is a social cognition approach beneficial? *Social Cognition, 7,* 137–151.

Bandura, A. (1969). *Principles of behavior modification.* New York: Holt, Rinehart & Winston.

Bandura, A. (1977). *Social learning theory.* Englewood Cliffs, NJ: Prentice-Hall.

Bandura, A. (1982). The psychology of chance encounters and life paths. *American Psychologist, 37,* 747–755.

Bandura, A. (1986). *Social foundations of thought and action: A social-cognitive theory.* Englewood Cliffs, NJ: Prentice-Hall.

Bandura, A. (1989). Human agency in social cognitive theory. *American Psychologist, 44,* 1175–1184.

Bandura, A., Blanchard, E. B., & Ritter, B. (1969). Relative efficacy of desensitization and modeling approaches for inducing behavioral, affective, and attitudinal changes. *Journal of Personality and Social Psychology, 13,* 173–199.

Bandura, A., Ross, D., & Ross, S. A. (1961). Transmission of aggression through imitation of aggressive models. *Journal of Abnormal and Social Psychology, 63,* 575–582.

Banks, M. S., & Salapatek, P. (1983). Infant visual perception. In M. M. Haith & J. J. Campos (Eds.), *Handbook of Child Psychology: Vol. 2. Infancy and Developmental Psychobiology* (4th ed., pp. 435–571). New York: Wiley.

Barasch, M. (1993, August). The mind-body revolution. *Psychology Today,* pp. 58–63, 86, 90, 92.

Barbaro, N. M. (1988). Studies of PAG/PVG stimulation for pain relief in humans. *Progress in Brain Research, 77,* 165–173.

Barber, T. X. (1969). *Hypnosis: A scientific approach.* New York: Van Nostrand Reinhold.

Barden, R. C., Ford, M. E., Jensen, A. G., Rogers-Salyer, M., & Salyer, K. E. (1989). Effects of craniofacial deformity in infancy on the quality of mother-infant interactions. *Child Development, 60,* 819–824.

Barglow, P., Vaughn, B. E., & Molitor, N. (1987). Effects of maternal absence due to employment on the quality of infant-mother attachment in a low-risk sample. *Child Development, 58,* 945–954.

Bar-Hillel, M. (1980). The base-rate fallacy in probability judgments. *Acta Psychologica, 44,* 211–213.

Barker, S. L., Funk, S. C., & Houston, B. K. (1988). Psychological treatment versus nonspecific factors: A meta-analysis of conditions that engender comparable expectations for improvement. *Clinical Psychology Review, 8,* 579–594.

Barkley, R. A. (1990). *Attention-deficit hyperactivity disorder: A handbook for diagnosis and treatment.* New York: Guilford Press.

Barlow, D. H. (1988). *Anxiety and its disorders.* New York: Guilford Press.

Baron, R. M., Mandel, D. R., Adams, C. A., & Griffin, L. M. (1976). Effects of social density in university residential environments. *Journal of Personality and Social Psychology, 34,* 434–446.

Baron, R. S., Cutrona, C. E., Hicklin, D., Russell, D. W., & Lubaroff, D. M. (1990). Social support and immune function among spouses of cancer patients. *Journal of Personality and Social Psychology, 59,* 344–352.

Barr, H. M., Streissguth, A. P., Darby, B. L., & Sampson, P. D. (1990). Prenatal exposure to alcohol, caffeine, tobacco, and aspirin: Effects on fine and gross motor performance in 4-year-old children. *Developmental Psychology, 26,* 339–348.

Barrick, M. R., & Mount, M. K. (1991). The big five personality dimensions and job performance: A meta-analysis. *Personnel Psychology, 44,* 1–26.

Barron, F. (1988). Putting creativity to work. In R. Sternberg (Ed.), *The nature of creativity* (pp. 76–98). New York: Cambridge University Press.

Barsky, A. J., Goodson, J. D., Lane, R. S., & Cleary, P. D. (1988). The amplification of somatic symptoms. *Psychosomatic Medicine, 50,* 510–519.

Barthrop, R. W., Lazarus, L., Luckhurst, E., Kiloh, L. G., & Penny, R. (1977). Depressed lymphocyte function after bereavement. *Lancet, 1,* 834–839.

Bartlett, F. C. (1932). *Remembering: A study in experimental and social psychology.* Cambridge: Cambridge University Press.

Barton, J. (1994). Choosing to work at night: A moderating influence on individual tolerance to shift work. *Journal of Applied Psychology, 79,* 449–454.

Bartoushuk, L. M., & Beauchamp, G. K. (1994). Chemical senses. *Annual Review of Psychology, 45,* 419–449.

Baruss, I. (1987). Meta-analysis of definitions of consciousness. *Imagination, Cognition and Personality, 6,* 321–329.

Bashore, T. R., Osman, A., & Heffley, E. F. (1989). Mental slowing in elderly persons: A cognitive psychophysiological analysis. *Psychology and Aging, 4,* 235–244.

Bashore, T. R., & Rapp, P. E. (1993). Are there alternatives to traditional polygraph procedures? *Psychological Bulletin, 113,* 3–22.

Bass, E., & Davis, L. (1988). *The courage to heal.* New York: Harper & Row.

Bassili, J. N., & Provencal, A. (1988). Perceiving minorities: A factor-analytic approach. *Personality and Social Psychology Bulletin, 14,* 5–15.

Bates, G. W. (1981). On the nature of the hot flash. *Clinical Obstetrics and Gynecology, 24,* 231.

Batson, C. D. (1991). *The altruism question: Toward a social-psychological answer.* Hillsdale, NJ: Erlbaum.

Batson, C. D., Batson, J. G., Griffitt, C. A., Barrientos, S., Brandt, J. R., Sprengelmeyer, P., & Bayly, M. J. (1989). Negative-state relief and the empathy-altruism hypothesis. *Journal of Personality and Social Psychology, 56,* 922–933.

Batson, C. D., Duncan, B. D., Ackerman, P., Buckley, T., & Birch, K. (1981). Is empathic emotion a source of altruistic motivation? *Journal of Personality and Social Psychology, 40,* 290–302.

Bauer, R. M., & Verfaellie, M. (1992). Memory dissociations: A cognitive psychophysiology perspective. In L. R. Squire & N. Butters (Eds.), *Neuropsychology of memory* (2nd ed., pp. 58–71). New York: The Guilford Press.

Baum, A., & Valins, S. (1979). Architectural mediation of residential density and control: Crowding and the regulation of social contact. *Advances in Experimental Social Psychology, 12,* 131–175.

Baumeister, R. F. (1990). Suicide as escape from the self. *Psychological Review, 97,* 90–113.

Baumeister, R. F. (1991). *Escaping the self.* New York: Basic Books.

Baumeister, R. F., & Scher, S. J. (1988). Self-defeating behavior patterns among normal individuals: Review and analysis of common self-destructive tendencies. *Psychological Bulletin, 104,* 3–22.

Baur, S. (1988). *Hypochondria: Woeful imaginings.* Berkeley: University of California Press.

Bayliss, G. C., Rolls, E. T., & Leonard, C. M. (1985). Selectivity between faces in the responses of a population of neurons in the cortex in the superior temporal sulcus of the monkey. *Brain Research, 342,* 91–102.

Beck, A. T. (1967). *Cognitive therapy and the emotional disorders.* New York: International Universities Press.

Beck, A. T. (1985). Cognitive therapy. In H. I. Kaplan & J. Sadock (Eds.), Comprehensive textbook of psychiatry (4th ed.). Baltimore: Williams & Wilkins.

Beck, A. T. (1991). Cognitive therapy: A 30-year retrospective. *American Psychologist, 46,* 368–375.

Beck, A. T. (1993). Cognitive therapy: Past, present, and future. *Journal of Consulting and Clinical Psychology, 61,* 194–198.

Beck, A. T., Brown, G., Berchick, R. J., Stewart, B. L., & Steer, R. A. (1990). Relationship between hopelessness and ultimate suicide: A replication with psychiatric outpatients. *American Journal of Psychiatry, 147,* 190–195.

Beck, A. T., Emery, G., & Greenberg, R. L. (1985). *Anxiety disorders and phobias: A cognitive perspective.* New York: Basic Books.

Beck, A. T., & Katcher, A. (1983). *Between pets and people: The importance of animal companionship.* New York: Putnam.

Beck, A. T., Rush, A. J., Shaw, B. F., & Emery, G. (1979). *Cognitive therapy of depression.* New York: Guilford Press.

Beck, E. M., & Tolnay, S. E. (1990). The killing fields of the Deep South: The market for cotton and the lynching of blacks, 1882–1930. *American Sociological Review, 55,* 526–539.

Beecher, H. K. (1961). Surgery as placebo: A quantitative study of bias. *Journal of the American Medical Association, 176,* 1102–1107.

Begley, S., & Ramo, J. C. (1993, November 1). Not just a pretty face. *Newsweek,* pp. 63–67.

Beilin, H. (1992). Piaget's enduring contribution to developmental psychology. *Developmental Psychology, 28,* 191–204.

Beitman, B. D., Goldfried, M. R., & Norcross, J. C. (1989). The movement toward integrating the psychotherapies: An overview. *American Journal of Psychiatry, 146,* 138–147.

Bell, A. P., Weinberg, M. S., & Hammersmith, S. K. (1981). *Sexual preference: Its development in men and women.* Bloomington: Indiana University Press.

Bellack, A. S., & Hersen, M. (Eds.). (1985). *Dictionary of behavior therapy techniques.* New York: Pergamon.

Belli, R. F., Lindsay, D. S., Gales, M. S., & McCarthy, T. T. (1994). Memory impairment and source misattribution in postevent misinformation experiments with short retention intervals. *Memory and Cognition, 22,* 40–54.

Belli, R. F., Windschitl, P. D., McCarthy, T. T., & Winfrey, S. E. (1992). Detecting memory impairment with a modified test procedure: Manipulating retention interval with centrally presented event items. *Journal of Experimental Psychology: Learning, Memory, and Cognition, 18,* 356–367.

Belmore, S. M. (1987). Determinants of attention during impression formation. *Journal of Experimental Psychology: Learning, Memory, and Cognition, 13,* 480–489.

Belsher, G., & Costello, C. G. (1988). Relapse after recovery from unipolar depression: A critical review. *Psychological Bulletin, 104,* 84–96.

Belsky, J. (1988). The "effects" of infant daycare reconsidered. *Early Childhood Research Quarterly, 3,* 235–272.

Belsky, J., & Pensky, E. (1988). Marital changes across the transition to parenthood. *Marriage and Family Review, 12,* 133–156.

Bem, D. J. (1967). Self-perception: An alternative interpretation of cognitive dissonance phenomena. *Psychological Review, 74,* 183–200.

Bem, D. J., & Honorton, C. (1994). Does Psi exist? Replicable evidence for an anomalous process of information transfer. *Psychological Bulletin, 115,* 4–18.

Bem, S. L. (1981). Gender schema theory: A cognitive account of sex-typing. *Psychological Review, 88,* 354–364.

Benbow, C. P. (1988). Sex differences in mathematical reasoning ability in intellectually talented preadolescents: Their nature, effects, and possible causes. *Behavioral and Brain Sciences, 11,* 169–232.

Benca, R. M., Obermeyer, W. H., Thisted, R. A., & Gillin, J. C. (1992). Sleep and psychiatric disorders: A meta-analysis. *Archives of General Psychiatry, 49,* 651–658.

Benedict, R. (1959). *Patterns of culture.* Boston: Houghton Mifflin.

Benjamin, L. T., Jr. (1988). A history of teaching machines. *American Psychologist, 43,* 703–712.

Benjamin, L. T., Jr., Durkin, M., Link, M., Vestal, M., & Acord, J. (1992). Wundt's American doctoral students. *American Psychologist, 47,* 123–131.

Ben-Shakhar, G., Bar-Hillel, M., Bilu, Y., Ben-Abba, E., & Flug, A. (1986). Can graphology predict occupational success? Two empirical studies and some methodological ruminations. *Journal of Applied Psychology, 71,* 645–653.

Benson, H. (1975). *The relaxation response.* New York: Morrow.

Benson, J. B. (1993). Season of birth and onset of locomotion: Theoretical and methodological implications. *Infant Behavior and Development, 16,* 69–81.

Benton, M. K., & Schroeder, H. E. (1990). Social skills training with schizophrenics: A meta-analytic evaluation. *Journal of Consulting and Clinical Psychology, 58,* 741–747.

Berg, J. H. (1987). Responsiveness and self-disclosure. In V. J. Derlega & J. H. Berg (Eds.), *Self-disclosure* (pp. 101–130). New York: Plenum.

Bergin, A. E., & Garfield, S. L. (Eds.). (1994). *Handbook of psy-*

chotherapy and behavior change (4th ed.). New York: Wiley.

Bergin, A. E., & Lambert, M. J. (1978). The evaluation of therapeutic outcomes. In S. L. Garfield & A. E. Bergin (Eds.), *Handbook of psychotherapy and behavior change* (2nd ed., pp. 139–189). New York: Wiley.

Berglas, S., & Jones, E. E. (1978). Drug choice as a self-handicapping strategy in response to noncontingent success. *Journal of Personality and Social Psychology, 36,* 405–417.

Berkman, L., & Syme, S. L. (1979). Social networks, host resistance, and mortality: A nine-year follow-up study of Alameda County residents. *American Journal of Epidemiology, 109,* 186–204.

Berkowitz, L. (1983). Aversively stimulated aggression: Some parallels and differences in research with animals and humans. *American Psychologist, 38,* 1135–1144.

Berkowitz, L. (1989). Frustration-aggression hypothesis: Examination and reformulation. *Psychological Bulletin, 106,* 59–73.

Berkowitz, L. (1993). *Aggression: Its causes, consequences, and control.* New York: McGraw-Hill.

Berkowitz, L., & LePage, A. (1967). Weapons as aggression-eliciting stimuli. *Journal of Personality and Social Psychology, 7,* 202–207.

Bernard, M. E., & DiGiuseppe, R. (Eds.). (1989). *Inside rational-emotive therapy.* New York: Academic Press.

Berndt, T. J. (1979). Developmental changes in conformity to peers and parents. *Developmental Psychology, 15,* 606–616.

Berndt, T. J., & Ladd, G. W. (Eds.). (1989). *Peer relationships in child development.* New York: Wiley.

Bernstein, D. A., Clarke-Stewart, A., Roy, E. J., Srull, T. K., & Wickens, C. D. (1994). *Psychology* (3rd ed.). Boston: Houghton Mifflin.

Bernstein, E. M., & Putnam, F. W. (1986). Development, reliability, and validity of a dissociation scale. *Journal of Nervous and Mental Disease, 174,* 727–735.

Bernstein, I. L., & Borson, S. (1986). Learned food aversion: A component of anorexia syndromes. *Psychological Review, 93,* 462–472.

Bernstein, R., & Gaw, A. (1990). Koro: Proposed classification for DSM-IV. *American Journal of Psychiatry, 147,* 1670–1674.

Berridge, A. P., & Valenstein, E. S. (1991). What psychological process mediates feeding evoked by electrical stimulation of the lateral hypothalamus? *Behavioral Neuroscience, 105,* 3–14.

Berridge, K. C., Venier, I. L., & Robinson, T. E. (1989). Taste reactivity analysis of 6-hydroxydopamine-induced aphagia: Implications for arousal and anhedonia hypotheses of dopamine function. *Behavioral Neuroscience, 103,* 3645.

Berry, D. S., & McArthur, L. Z. (1986). Perceiving character in faces: The impact of age-related craniofacial changes in social perception. *Psychological Bulletin, 100,* 3–18.

Berry, D. S., & McArthur, L. Z. (1988). What's in a face? Facial maturity and the attribution of legal responsibility. *Personality and Social Psychology Bulletin, 14,* 23–33.

Berry, J. M., West, R. L., & Dennehey, D. M. (1989). Reliability and validity of the memory self-efficacy questionnaire. *Developmental Psychology, 25,* 701–713.

Berry, J. W. (1979). A cultural ecology of social behavior. *Advances in Experimental Social Psychology, 12,* 177–206.

Berry, J. W., Kim, U., Power, S., Young, M., & Bujaki, M. (1989). Acculturation attitudes in plural societies. *Applied Psychology, 38,* 185–206.

Berry, J. W., Poortinga, Y. H., Segall, M. H., & Dasen, P. R. (1992). *Cross-cultural psychology: Research and applications.* New York: Cambridge University Press.

Berscheid, E. (1994). Interpersonal relationships. *Annual Review of Psychology, 45,* 79–129.

Berscheid, E., Snyder, M., & Omoto, A. M. (1989). The Relationship Closeness Inventory: Assessing the closeness of interpersonal relationships. *Journal of Personality and Social Psychology, 57,* 792–807.

Berscheid, E., & Walster, E. (1974). A little bit about love. In T. Huston (Ed.), *Foundations of interpersonal attraction* (pp. 356–379).

New York: Academic Press.

Best, D. L., & Williams, J. E. (1993). A cross-cultural viewpoint. In A. E. Beall & R. J. Sternberg (Eds.), *The psychology of gender* (pp. 215–248). New York: Guilford Press.

Beyer, S. (1990). Gender differences in the accuracy of self-evaluations of performance. *Journal of Personality and Social Psychology, 59,* 960–970.

Biederman, I. (1987). Recognition-by-components: A theory of human image understanding. *Psychological Review, 94,* 115–147.

Biernat, M. (1991). Gender stereotypes and the relationship between masculinity and femininity: A developmental analysis. *Journal of Personality and Social Psychology, 61,* 351–365.

Binet, A., & Simon, T. (1905). Methodes nouvelles pour le diagnostic du niveau intellectuel des anormaux. *L'Annee Psychologique, 11,* 191–244.

Biringer, F., Anderson, J. R., & Strubel, D. (1989). Self-recognition in senile dementia. *Experimental Aging Research, 14,* 177–180.

Bjorklund, A. (1991). Neural transplantation—an experimental tool with clinical possibilities. *Trends in the Neurosciences, 14,* 319–322.

Blair, S. N., Kohl, H. W., Paffenbarger, R. S., Clark, D. G., Cooper, K. H., & Gibbons, L. W. (1989). Physical fitness and all-cause mortality: A prospective study of healthy men and women. *Journal of the American Medical Association, 262,* 2395–2401.

Blakeslee, S. (1993, June 1). Scanner pinpoints sites of thoughts as people see or speak. *New York Times,* pp. C1, C3.

Blanchard, E. B. (1992). Psychological treatment of benign headache disorders. *Journal of Consulting and Clinical Psychology, 60,* 537–551.

Blanchard, E. B. (1994). Behavioral medicine and health psychology. In A. E. Bergin & S. L. Garfield (Eds.), *Handbook of psychotherapy and behavior change* (4th ed. pp. 701–733.) New York: Wiley.

Blanchard, F. A., Lilly, T., & Vaughn, L. A. (1991). Reducing the expression of racial prejudice. *Psychological Science, 2,* 101–105.

Blaney, P. H. (1986). Affect and memory: A review. *Psychological Bulletin, 99,* 229–246.

Blasi, A. (1980). Bridging moral cognition and moral action: A critical review of the literature. *Psychological Bulletin, 88,* 1–45.

Blass, T. (1991). Understanding behavior in the Milgram obedience experiment: The role of personality, situations, and their interactions. *Journal of Personality and Social Psychology, 60,* 398–413.

Blatt, S. J. (1990). The Rorschach: A test of perception or an evaluation of representation. *Journal of Personality Assessment, 55,* 394–416.

Blehar, M. C., & Rosenthal, N. E. (1989). Seasonal affective disorders and phototherapy: Report of a National Institute of Mental Health-sponsored workshop. *Archives of General Psychiatry, 46,* 469–474.

Blehar, M. C., Weissman, M. M., Gershon, E. S., Hirschfeld, R. M. A. (1988). Family and genetic studies of affective disorders. *Archives of General Psychiatry, 45,* 289–292.

Bleuler, E. (1911). *Dementia praecox oder gruppe der schizophrenien.* Leipzig: F. Deuticke.

Block, J. (1981). Some enduring and consequential structures of personality. In A. I. Rabin (Ed.), *Further explorations in personality.* New York: Wiley.

Block, J. R., & Yuker, H. E. (1989). *Can you believe your eyes?* New York: Gardner Press.

Blocklyn, P. L. (1988) Preemployment testing. *Personnel, 65,* 63–65.

Bloom, A. (1981). *The linguistic shaping of thought.* Hillsdale, NJ: Erlbaum.

Bloom, L. C., & Mudd, S. A. (1991). Depth of processing approach to face recognition: A test of two theories. *Journal of Experimental Psychology: Learning, Memory, and Cognition, 17,* 556–565.

Bochner, S., & Insko, C. A. (1966). Communicator discrepancy, source credibility, and opinion change. *Journal of Personality and Social Psychology, 4,* 614–621.

Boer, F., & Dunn, J. (Eds.). (1992). *Children's sibling relationships.* Hillsdale, NJ: Erlbaum.

Bogen, J. E. (1978). The callosal syndrome. In K. M. Heilman & E. Valenstein (Eds.), *Clinical Neuropsychology* (2nd ed.), pp. 308–359. New York: Oxford University Press.

Boggiano, A. K., Harackiewicz, J. M., Bessette, M. M., & Main, D. S. (1985). Increasing children's interest through performance-contingent reward. *Social Cognition, 3,* 400–411.

Bolanowski, S. J. Jr., & Gescheider, G. A. (Eds.). (1991). *Ratio scaling of psychological magnitude: In honor of the memory of S. S. Stevens.* Hillsdale, NJ: Erlbaum.

Bolles, R. C. (1970). Species-specific defense reactions and avoidance learning. *Psychological Review, 77,* 32–48.

Boneau, C. A. (1990). Psychological literacy: A first approximation. *American Psychologist, 45,* 891–900.

Boneau, C. A. (1992). Observations on psychology's past and future. *American Psychologist, 47,* 1586–1596.

Booker, J. M., & Hellekson, C. J. (1992). Prevalence of seasonal affective disorder in Alaska. *American Journal of Psychiatry, 149,* 1176–1182.

Boon, S., & Draijer, N. (1993). Multiple personality disorder in the Netherlands: A clinical investigation of 71 patients. *American Journal of Psychiatry, 150,* 489–494.

Boor, M. (1982). The multiple personality epidemic. *Journal of Nervous and Mental Disease, 170,* 302–304.

Booth-Kewley, S., & Friedman, H. S. (1987). Psychological predictors of heart disease: A quantitative review. *Psychological Bulletin, 101,* 343–362.

Borbely, A. (1986). *The secrets of sleep.* New York: Basic Books.

Boring, E. G. (1923). Intelligence as the tests test it. *New Republic, 35,* 35–37.

Bornstein, M. H. (1989). Information processing (habituation) in infancy and stability in cognitive development. *Human Development, 32,* 129–136.

Bornstein, R. F. (1989). Exposure and affect: Overview and meta-analysis of research, 1968–1987. *Psychological Bulletin, 106,* 265–289.

Bornstein, R. F. (1992). Subliminal mere exposure effects. In R. F. Bornstein & T. S. Pittman (Eds.), *Perception without awareness: Cognitive, clinical, and social perspectives* (pp. 191–210). New York: Guilford Press.

Bornstein, R. F., Kale, A. R., & Cornell, K. R. (1990). Boredom as a limiting condition on the mere exposure effect. *Journal of Personality and Social Psychology, 58,* 791–800.

Bornstein, R. F., & Pittman, T. S. (Eds.). (1992). *Perception without awareness: Cognitive, clinical, and social perspectives.* New York: Guilford Press.

Bouchard, T. J., Jr., Lykken, D. T., McGue, M., Segal, N. L., & Tellegen, A. (1990). Sources of human psychological differences: The Minnesota study of twins reared apart. *Science, 250,* 223–228.

Bouchard, T. J., Jr., & McGue, M. (1981). Familial studies of intelligence. *Science, 212,* 1055–1059.

Bouchard, T. J., Jr., & McGue, M. (1990). Genetic and rearing environmental influences on adult personality: An analysis of adopted twins reared apart. *Journal of Personality, 58,* 263–292.

Bouchard, T. J., Jr., & Segal, N. L. (1985). Environment and IQ. In B. B. Wolman (Ed.), *Handbook of intelligence: Theories, measurements, and applications* (pp. 391–464). New York: Wiley.

Bousfield, W. A. (1953). The occurrence of clustering in the recall of randomly arranged associates. *Journal of General Psychology, 49,* 229–240.

Bower, G. H. (1970). Organizational factors in memory. *Cognitive Memory, 1,* 18–46.

Bower, G. H. (1981). Mood and memory. *American Psychologist, 36,* 129–148.

Bower, G. H., & Winzenz, D. (1970). Comparison of associative learn-

ing strategies. *Psychonomic Science, 20,* 119–120.

Bower, T.G.R. (1982). *Development in infancy* (2nd ed.). San Francisco: W. H. Freeman.

Bowers, K. S. (1976). *Hypnosis for the seriously curious.* Monterey, CA: Brooks/Cole.

Bowers, T. G., & Clum, G. A. (1988). Relative contribution of specific and nonspecific treatment effects: Meta-analysis of placebo-controlled behavior therapy research. *Psychological Bulletin, 103,* 315–323.

Boynton, R. M. (1988). Color vision. *Annual Review of Psychology, 39,* 69–100.

Bradshaw, J. L., & Nettleton, N. C. (1981). The nature of hemispheric specialization in man. *Behavioral and Brain Sciences, 4,* 51–91.

Bransford, J. D., & Stein, B. S. (1984). *The ideal problem solver.* New York: W. H. Freeman.

Braun, B. G. (1988). *Treatment of multiple personality disorder.* Washington, DC: American Psychiatric Press.

Brean, H. (1958, March 31). What hidden sell is all about. *Life,* pp. 104–114.

Bregman, A. S. (1990). *Auditory scene analysis.* Cambridge MA: MIT Press.

Brehm, S. S. (1992). *Intimate relationships.* New York: McGraw-Hill.

Breland, K., & Breland, M. (1961). The misbehavior of organisms. *American Psychologist, 16,* 681–684.

Brenner, C. (1982). *The mind in conflict.* New York: International Universities Press.

Breuer, J., & Freud, S. (1895). *Studies on hysteria.* In J. Strachey, *The standard edition of the complete psychological works of Sigmund Freud.* London: Hogarth Press. (Reprinted in 1955)

Brewer, M. B. (1991). The social self: On being the same and different at the same time. *Personality and Social Psychology Bulletin, 17,* 475–482.

Brewer, W. F., & Treyens, J. C. (1981). Role of schemata in memory for places. *Cognitive Psychology, 13,* 207–230.

Brickman, P., Coates, D., & Janoff-Bulman, R. J. (1978). Lottery winners and accident victims: Is happiness relative? *Journal of Personality and Social Psychology, 36,* 917–927.

Brickner, M. A., Harkins, S. G., & Ostrom, T. M. (1986). Effects of personal involvement: Thought-provoking implications for social loafing. *Journal of Personality and Social Psychology, 51,* 763–769.

Briere, J., & Lanktree, C. (1983). Sex role-related effects of sex bias in language. *Sex Roles, 9,* 625–632.

Brigham, J. C., & Malpass, R. S. (1985). The role of experience and contact in the recognition of faces of own- and other-race persons. *Journal of Social Issues, 41,* 139–155.

Broca, P. (1861). Paul Broca on the speech centers (M. D. Boring, Trans.). In R. J. Herrnstein & E. G. Boring (Eds.), *A source book in the history of psychology.* Cambridge, MA: Harvard University Press. (Reprinted in 1965.)

Brockner, J. (1983). Low self-esteem and behavioral plasticity: Some implications. In L. Wheeler & P. Shaver (Eds.), *Review of personality and social psychology* (Vol. 4, pp. 237–271). Beverly Hills, CA: Sage.

Brody, L. R., & Hall, J. A. (1993). Gender and emotion. In M. Lewis & J. M. Haviland (Eds.), *Handbook of emotions* (pp. 447–460). New York: Guilford Press.

Brooks-Gunn, J., & Furstenberg, F. F., Jr. (1989). Adolescent sexual behavior. *American Psychologist, 44,* 249–257.

Brooks-Gunn, J., Gross, R. T., Kraemer, H. C., Spiker, D., & Shapiro, S. (1992). Enhancing the cognitive outcomes of low birth weight, premature infants: For whom is the intervention most effective? *Pediatrics, 89,* 1209–1215.

Brooks-Gunn, J., & Warren, M. P. (1985). The effects of delayed menarche in different contexts: Dance and nondance students. *Journal of Youth and Adolescence, 14,* 163–189.

Broughton, R. S. (1991). *Parapsychology: The controversial science.* New York: Ballantine Books.

Brown, A. S. (1991). A review of the tip-of-the-tongue experience. *Psychological Bulletin, 109,* 204–223.

Brown, A. S., & Murphy, D. R. (1989). Cryptomnesia: Delineating inadvertent plagiarism. *Journal of Experimental Psychology: Learning, Memory, and Cognition, 15,* 432–442.

Brown, B. B., Clasen, D. R., & Eicher, S. A. (1986). Perceptions of peer pressure, peer conformity dispositions, and self-reported behavior among adolescents. *Developmental Psychology, 22,* 521–530.

Brown, E. L., Deffenbacher, K. A., & Sturgill, W. (1977). Memory for faces and the circumstances of encounter. *Journal of Applied Psychology, 62,* 311–318.

Brown, G. K. (1990). A causal analysis of chronic pain and depression. *Journal of Abnormal Psychology, 99,* 127–137.

Brown, J. D. (1990). Evaluating one's abilities: Shortcuts and stumbling blocks on the road to self-knowledge. *Journal of Experimental Social Psychology, 26,* 149–167.

Brown, J. D. (1991). Staying fit and staying well: Physical fitness as a moderator of life stress. *Journal of Personality and Social Psychology, 60,* 555–561.

Brown, R. (1973). *A first language: The early stages.* Cambridge, MA: Harvard University Press.

Brown, R., & Kulik, J. (1977). Flashbulb memories. *Cognition, 5,* 73–99.

Brown, R., & McNeill, D. (1966). The "tip of the tongue" phenomenon. *Journal of Verbal Learning and Verbal Behavior, 5,* 325–337.

Brown, T. A., & Barlow, D. H. (1992). Comorbidity among anxiety disorders: Implications for treatment and DSM-IV. *Journal of Consulting and Clinical Psychology, 60,* 835–844.

Brumberg, J. J. (1988). *Fasting girls: The emergence of anorexia nervosa as a modern disease.* Cambridge, MA: Harvard University Press.

Bruner, J. S. (1983). *Child's talk: Learning to use language.* New York: Norton.

Bruner, J. S., & Potter, M. C. (1964). Interference in visual recognition. *Science, 144,* 424–425.

Brunner, D. P., Kijk, D. J., Tobler, I., & Borbely, A. A. (1990). Effect of partial sleep stages and EEG power spectra: Evidence for non-REM and REM sleep homeostasis. *Electroencephalography and Clinical Neurophysiology, 75,* 492–499.

Bruyer, R. (1991). Covert face recognition in prosopagnosics: A review. *Brain and Cognition, 15,* 223–235.

Bryan, J. H., & Test, M. A. (1967). Models and helping: Naturalistic studies in aiding behavior. *Journal of Personality and Social Psychology, 6,* 400–407.

Buchanan, C. M., Eccles, J. S., & Becker, J. B. (1992). Are adolescents the victims of raging hormones? Evidence for activational effects of hormones on moods and behavior in adolescence. *Psychological Bulletin, 111,* 62–107.

Buck, L., & Axel, R. (1991). A novel multigene family may encode odorant receptors: A molecular basis for odor recognition. *Cell, 65,* 175–181.

Buckhout, R. (1974). Eyewitness testimony. *Scientific American, 231,* 23–31.

Bull, R., & Rumsey, N. (1988). *The social psychology of facial appearance.* New York: Springer-Verlag.

Bullock, W. A., & Gilliland, K. (1993). Eysenck's arousal theory of introversion-extraversion: A converging measures investigation. *Journal of Personality and Social Psychology, 64,* 113–123.

Burger, J. M. (1981). Motivational biases in the attribution of responsibility for an accident: A meta-analysis of the defensive-attribution hypothesis. *Psychological Bulletin, 90,* 496–512.

Burger, J. M. (1991). Control. In V. Derlega, B. Winstead, & W. Jones (Eds.), *Personality* (pp. 287–312). Chicago: Nelson-Hall.

Burke, A., Heuer, F., & Reisberg, D. (1992). Remembering emotional events. *Memory and Cognition, 20,* 277–290.

Burnett, S. A. (1986). Sex-related differences in spatial ability: Are they trivial? *American Psychologist, 41,* 1012–1014.

Bushman, B. J., & Cooper, H. M. (1990). Effects of alcohol on human aggression: An integrative research review. *Psychological Bulletin, 107,* 341–354.

Buss, A. H. (1980). *Self-consciousness and social anxiety.* San Francisco, CA: W. H. Freeman.

Buss, A. H., & Perry, M. (1992). The aggression questionnaire. *Journal of Personality and Social Psychology, 63,* 452–459.

Buss, D. M. (1988). The evolution of human intrasexual competition: Tactics of mate attraction. *Journal of Personality and Social Psychology, 54,* 616–628.

Buss, D. M. (1989). Sex differences in human mate preferences: Evolutionary hypotheses tested in 37 cultures. *Behavioral and Brain Sciences, 12,* 1–14.

Butcher, J. N., Dahlstrom, W. G., Graham, J. R., Tellegen, A., & Kaemmer, B. (1989). *MMPI-2: Minnesota Multiphasic Personality Inventory—2. Manual for administration and scoring.* Minneapolis: University of Minnesota Press.

Butcher, J. N., & Williams, C. L. (1992). *Essentials of MMPI-2 and MMPI-A interpretation.* Minneapolis: University of Minnesota Press.

Buunk, B., & Hupka, R. B. (1987). Cross-cultural differences in the elicitation of sexual jealousy. *Journal of Sex Research, 23,* 12–22.

Byne, W., Bleier, R., & Houston, L. (1988). Variations in human corpus callosum do not predict gender: A study using magnetic resonance imaging. *Behavioral Neuroscience, 102,* 222–227.

Byne, W., & Parsons, B. Human sexual orientation: The biological theories reappraised. *Archives of General Psychiatry, 50,* 228–239.

Byrne, D. (1971). *The attraction paradigm.* New York: Academic Press.

Byrne, D., Clore, G. L., & Smeaton, G. (1986). The attraction hypothesis: Do similar attitudes attract anything? *Journal of Personality and Social Psychology, 51,* 1167–1170.

Byrne, D., & Fisher, W. A. (1983). *Adolescents, sex, and contraception.* Hillsdale, NJ: Erlbaum.

Cacioppo, J. T., & Petty, R. E. (1982). The need for cognition. *Journal of Personality and Social Psychology, 42,* 116–131.

Cairns, R. B., Gariepy, J. L., & Hood, K. E. (1990). Development, microevolution, and social behavior. *Psychological Review, 97,* 49–65.

Caldwell, C. B., & Gottesman, I. I. (1990). Schizophrenics kill themselves too: A review of risk factors for suicide. *Schizophrenia Bulletin, 16,* 571–589.

Calhoun, J. B. (1962). Population density and social pathology. *Scientific American, 206,* 139–148.

Camara, W. J., & Schneider, D. L. (1994). Integrity tests: Facts and unresolved issues. *American Psychologist, 49,* 112–119.

Campbell, D. J., & Lee, C. (1988). Self-appraisal in performance evaluation: Development versus evaluation. *Academy Management Review, 13,* 302–313.

Campbell, J. D., & Fairey, P. J. (1989). Informational and normative routes to conformity. *Journal of Personality and Social Psychology, 57,* 457–468.

Campbell, J. M., Amerikaner, M., Swank, P., & Vincent, K. (1989). The relationship between the Hardiness Test and the Personal Orientation Inventory. *Journal of Research in Personality, 23,* 373–380.

Campos, J. J., Langer, A., & Krowtiz, A. (1970). Cardiac responses on the visual cliff in prelocomotor infants. *Science, 170,* 196–197.

Cannon, D. S., Baker, T. B., & Wehl, C. K. (1981). Emetic and electric shock alcohol aversion therapy: Six- and twelve-month follow-up. *Journal of Consulting and Clinical Psychology, 49,* 360–368.

Cannon, W. B. (1927). The James-Lange theory of emotion: A critical examination and an alternative theory. *American Journal of Psychology, 39,* 106–124.

Cannon, W. B., & Washburn, A. L. (1912). An explanation of hunger. *American Journal of Physiology, 29,* 441–454.

Cantor, N., & Kihlstrom, J. F. (1987). *Personality and social intelligence.* Englewood Cliffs, NJ: Prentice-Hall.

Caramazza, A., & Hillis, A. E. (1991). Lexical organization of nouns and verbs in the brain. *Nature, 349,* 788–790.

Carlson, C. L., & Bunner, M. R. (1993). Effects of methylphenidate on the academic performance of children with attention deficit hyperactivity disorder and learning disabilities. *School Psychology Review, 22,* 184–198.

Carlson, M., Marcus-Newhall, A., & Miller, N. (1990). Effects of situational aggressive cues: A quantitative review. *Journal of Personality and Social Psychology, 58,* 622–633.

Carmichael, L., Hogan, H. P., & Walter, A. (1932). An experimental study of the effect of language on the reproduction of visually perceived form. *Journal of Experimental Psychology, 15,* 73–86.

Carnegie, D. (1936). *How to win friends and influence people.* New York: Pocket Books. (Reprinted in 1972)

Carskadon, M. A. (1993). Microsleep. In M. Carskadon (Ed.), *Encyclopedia of sleep and dreaming* (pp. 373–374). New York: Macmillan.

Carter, C. S. (1991). Hormonal influences on human sexual behavior. In J. B. Becker, S. M. Breedlove, & D. Crews (Eds.), *Behavioral endocrinology* (pp. 131–142). Cambridge, MA: MIT Press.

Cartwright, R. (1978, December). Happy endings for our dreams. *Psychology Today,* pp. 66–77.

Carver, C. S., & Scheier, M. F. (1981b). *Attention and self-regulation: A control-theory approach to human behavior.* New York: Springer-Verlag.

Carver, C. S., Scheier, M. F., & Weintraub, J. K. (1989). Assessing coping strategies: A theoretically based approach. *Journal of Personality and Social Psychology, 56,* 267–283.

Case, R. (1985). *Intellectual development: Birth to adulthood.* New York: Academic Press.

Case, R. (1992). *The mind's staircase.* Hillsdale, NJ: Erlbaum.

Case, R. B., Moss, A. J., Case, N., McDermott, M., & Eberly, S. (1992). Living alone after myocardial infarction: Impact on prognosis. *Journal of the American Medical Association, 267,* 515–519.

Caspi, A., Lynam, D., Moffitt, T. E., & Silva, P. A. (1993). Unraveling girls' delinquency: Biological, dispositional, and contextual contributions to adolescent misbehavior. *Developmental Psychology, 29,* 19–30.

Caspi, A., & Moffitt, T. E. (1991). Individual differences are accentuated during periods of social change: The sample case of girls at puberty. *Journal of Personality and Social Psychology, 61,* 157–168.

Cassidy, J. (1988). Child-mother attachment and the self in six-year-olds. *Child Development, 59,* 121–134.

Cassidy, J., & Asher, S. R. (1992). Loneliness and peer relations in young children. *Child Development, 63,* 350–365.

Castro, C. A., & Larsen, T. (1992). Primacy and recency effects in nonhuman primates. *Journal of Experimental Psychology: Animal Behavior Processes, 18,* 335–340.

Cattell, R. B. (1949). *The culture-free intelligence test.* Champaign, IL: Institute for Personality and Ability Testing.

Cattell, R. B. (1963). Theory of crystallized and fluid intelligence: A critical experiment. *Journal of Educational Psychology, 54,* 1–22.

Cattell, R. B. (1965). *The scientific analysis of personality.* Baltimore, MD: Penguin Books.

Cece, S. J., & Bruck, M. (1993). Suggestibility of the child witness: A historical review and synthesis. *Psychological Bulletin, 113,* 403–439.

Ceci, S. J., Leichtman, M., & White, T. (in press). Interviewing preschoolers: Remembrances of things planted. In D. P. Peters (Ed.), *The child witness: Cognitive, social, and legal issues.* Netherlands: Kluwer.

Ceci, S. J., Ross, D. F., & Toglia, M. P. (1987). Suggestibility of children's memory: Psycholegal implications. *Journal of Experimental Psychology: General, 116,* 38–49.

Ceci, S. J., Ross, D. F., & Toglia, M. P. (Eds.). (1989). *New directions in child witness research.* New York: Springer-Verlag.

Centers for Disease Control and Prevention (1993, July 19). *Newsweek,* p. 8.

Centers for Disease Control Vietnam Experience Study (1988). Health status of Vietnam veterans: I. Psychosocial characteristics. *Journal of the American Medical Association, 259,* 2701–2707.

Cerella, J. (1985). Information processing rates in the elderly. *Psychological Bulletin, 98,* 67–83.

Cernoch, J. M., & Porter, R. H. (1985). Recognition of maternal axillary odors by infants. *Child Development, 56,* 1593–1598.

Cervantes, R. C., Padilla, A. M., & de Snyder, N. S. (1991). The Hispanic Stress Inventory: A culturally relevant approach to psychosocial adjustment. *Psychological Assessment: A Journal of Consulting and Clinical Psychology, 3,* 438–447.

Chaiken, S. (1979). Communicator physical attractiveness and persuasion. *Journal of Personality and Social Psychology, 37,* 1387–1397.

Chaiken, S. (1980). Heuristic versus systematic information processing and the use of source versus message cues in persuasion. *Journal of Personality and Social Psychology, 39,* 752–766.

Chaiken, S., Liberman, A., & Eagly, A. (1989). Heuristic and systematic information processing within and beyond the persuasion context. In J. Uleman and J. A. Bargh (Eds.), *Unintended thought* (pp. 212–252). New York: Guilford Press.

Chandler, C. C. (1991). How memory for an event is influenced by related events: Interference in modified recognition tests. *Journal of Experimental Psychology: Learning, Memory, and Cognition, 17,* 115–125.

Charness, N. (Ed.). (1985). *Aging and human performance.* Chicester, England: Wiley.

Charney, E. A., & Weissman, M. M. (1988). Epidemiology of depressive and manic syndromes. In A. Georgotas & R. Cancro (Eds.), *Depression and mania* (pp. 26–52). New York: Elsevier.

Chase, M. H., & Morales, F. R. (1983). Subthreshold excitatory activity and motorneuron discharge during REM periods of active sleep. *Science, 221,* 1195–1198.

Chase, W. G., & Simon, H. A. (1973). Perception in chess. *Cognitive Psychology, 4,* 55–81.

Chatters, L. M. (1988). Subjective well-being evaluations among older Black Americans. *Psychology and Aging, 3,* 184–190.

Cheek, J. M., & Briggs, S. R. (1990). Shyness as a personality trait. In W. R. Crozier (Ed.), *Shyness and embarrassment: Perspectives from social psychology* (pp. 315–337). New York: Cambridge University Press.

Cheek, J. M., & Melchior, L. A. (1990). Shyness, self-esteem, and self-consciousness. In H. Leitenberg (Ed.), *Handbook of social and evaluation anxiety.* New York: Plenum.

Cheney, D. L., & Seyfarth, R. M. (1990). *How monkeys see the world.* Chicago: University of Chicago Press.

Cheney, D. L., & Seyfarth, R. M. (1992). Precis of *How monkeys see the world. Behavioral and Brain Sciences, 15,* 135–182.

Cheng, P. W., Holyoak, K. J., Nisbett, R. E., & Oliver, L. M. (1986). Pragmatic versus syntactic approaches to training deductive reasoning. *Cognitive Psychology, 18,* 293–328.

Cheng, P. W., & Novick, L. R. (1990). A probabilistic contrast model of causal induction. *Journal of Personality and Social Psychology, 58,* 545–567.

Cherry, E. C. (1953). Some experiments on the recognition of speech, with one and with two ears. *Journal of the Acoustical Society of America, 25,* 975–979.

Chesney, M. A. (1993). Health psychology in the 21st century: Acquired Immunodeficiency Syndrome as a harbinger of things to come. *Health Psychology, 12,* 259–268.

Chipman, S. F., Brush, L. R., & Wilson, D. M. (Eds.). (1985). *Women and mathematics.* Hillsdale, NJ: Erlbaum.

Cholewiak, R., & Collins, A. (1991). Sensory and physiological bases of touch. In M. A. Heller & W. Schiff (Eds.), *The psychology of touch* (pp. 23–60). Hillsdale, NJ: Erlbaum.

Chollar, S. (1989, November). Body-wise: Safe solutions for night work. *Psychology Today,* p. 26.

Chomsky, N. (1957). *Syntactic structures.* The Hague: Morton Publishers.

Chomsky, N. (1959). A review of B. F. Skinner's "Verbal Behavior." *Language, 35,* 26–58.

Chomsky, (1972). *Language and mind.* New York: Harcourt Brace Jovanovich.

Christensen, A., & Jacobson, N. S. (1994). Who (or what) can do psychotherapy: The status and challenge of nonprofessional therapies. *Psychological Science, 5,* 8–14.

Christianson, S. (1992). Emotional stress and eyewitness memory: A critical review. *Psychological Bulletin, 112,* 284–309.

Chumlea, W. C. (1982). Physical growth in adolescence. In B. Wolman (Ed.), *Handbook of developmental psychology.* Englewood Cliffs, NJ: Prentice-Hall.

Cialdini, R. B. (1988). *Influence: Science and practice* (2nd ed.). Glenview, IL: Scott, Foresman.

Cialdini, R. B., Darby, B. L., & Vincent, J. E. (1973). Transgressional altruism: A case for hedonism. *Journal of Personality and Social Psychology, 9,* 502–516.

Cialdini, R. B., Kallgren, C. A., & Reno, R. R. (1991). A focus theory of normative conduct: A theoretical refinement and reevaluation of the role of norms in human behavior. *Advances in Experimental Social Psychology, 24,* 201–234.

Cialdini, R. B., Schaller, M., Houlihan, D., Arps, K., Fultz, J., & Beaman, A. L. (1987). Empathy-based helping: Is it selflessly or selfishly motivated? *Journal of Personality and Social Psychology, 52,* 749–758.

Cioffi, D., & Holloway, J. (1993). Delayed costs of suppressed pain. *Journal of Personality and Social Psychology, 64,* 274–282.

Clark, D. C., Gibbons, R. D., Fawcett, J., & Scheftner, W. (1989). What is the mechanism by which suicide attempts predispose to later suicide attempts? A mathematical model. *Journal of Abnormal Psychology, 98,* 42–49.

Clark, H. H. (1985). Language use and language users. In G. Lindzey & E. Aronson (Eds.), *Handbook of social psychology* (3rd ed., pp. 179–231). New York: Random House.

Clark, L. F. (1993). Stress and the cognitive-conversational benefits of social interaction. *Journal of Social and Clinical Psychology, 12,* 25–55.

Clark, R. D., & Maass, A. (1990). The effects of majority size on minority influence. *European Journal of Social Psychology, 20,* 99–117.

Clarke, S., Kraftsik, R., Van der Loos, H., & Innocenti, G. M. (1989). Forms and measures of adult and developing human corpus callosum: Is there sexual dimorphism? *Journal of Comparative Neurology, 280,* 213–230.

Clarke-Stewart, K. A. (1989). Infant day care: Maligned or malignant? *American Psychologist, 44,* 266–273.

Cleckley, H. (1976). *The mask of sanity* (5th ed.). St. Louis: Mosby.

Clifford, M. M., & Walster, E. H. (1973). The effect of physical attractiveness on teacher expectations. *Sociology of Education, 46,* 248–258.

Coe, C. L. (1993). Psychosocial factors and immunity in nonhuman primates: A review. *Psychosomatic Medicine, 55,* 298–308.

Coffey, C. E., et al. (1991). Brain anatomic effects of electroconvulsive therapy: A prospective magnetic resonance imaging study. *Archives of General Psychiatry, 48,* 1013–1021.

Cohen, E. G. (1984). The desegregated school: Problems in status power and interethnic climate. In N. Miller & M. B. Brewer (Eds.), *Groups in contact: The psychology of desegregation* (pp. 77–96). New York: Academic Press.

Cohen, G. (1989). *Memory in the real world.* Hillsdale, NJ: Erlbaum.

Cohen, N. J., & Eichenbaum, H. (1993). *Memory, amnesia, and the hippocampal system.* Cambridge, MA: MIT Press.

Cohen, S. (1988). Psychosocial models of the role of social support in the etiology of physical disease. *Health Psychology, 7,* 269–297.

Cohen, S., Tyrrell, D.A.J., & Smith, A. P. (1991). Psychological stress and susceptibility to the common cold. *New England Journal of Medicine, 325,* 606–612.

Cohen, S., Tyrrell, D.A.J., & Smith, A. P. (1993). Negative life events, perceived stress, negative affect and susceptibility to the common cold. *Journal of Personality and Social Psychology, 64,* 131–140.

Cohen, S., & Williamson, G. (1991). Stress and infectious disease in humans. *Psychological Bulletin, 109,* 5–24.

Cohen, Y. (1964). *The transition from childhood to adolescence: Cross-cultural studies of initiation ceremonies, legal systems, and incest taboos.* Chicago: Aldine.

Coile, D. C., & Miller, N. E. (1984). How radical animal activists try to mislead humane people. *American Psychologist, 39,* 700–701.

Colangelo, N., & Kerr, B. A. (1990). Extreme academic talent: Profiles of perfect scorers. *Journal of Educational Psychology, 82,* 404–409.

Colby, A., & Kohlberg, L. (1987). *The measurement of moral judgment* (Vols. 1–2). New York: Cambridge University Press.

Colby, A., Kohlberg, L., Gibbs, J., & Lieberman, M. (1983). A longitudinal study of moral judgment. *Monographs of the Society for Research in Child Development, 48*(1–2, Serial No. 200).

Coleman, R. M. (1986). *Wide awake at 3:00 a.m.: By choice or by chance?* New York: W. H. Freeman.

Collins, A. M., & Loftus, E. F. (1975). A spreading-activation theory of semantic processing. *Psychological Review, 82,* 407–428.

Collins, W. A., & Gunnar, M. R. (1990). Social and personality development. *Annual Review of Psychology, 41,* 387–416.

Colp, R., Jr. (1977). *To be an invalid: The illness of Charles Darwin.* Chicago: University of Chicago Press.

Coltheart, M. (1980). Iconic memory and visual persistence. *Perception and Psychophysics, 27,* 183–228.

Colvin, C. R., and Block, J. (1994). Do positive illusions foster mental health? An examination of the Taylor and Brown formulation. *Psychological Bulletin, 116,* 3–20.

Condry, J., & Condry, S. (1976). Sex differences: A study of the eye of the beholder. *Child Development, 47,* 812–819.

Conel, J. L. (1939–1963). *The postnatal development of the human cerebral cortex* (Vols. I–VI). Cambridge, MA: Harvard University Press.

Conrad, R. (1964). Acoustic confusions in immediate memory. *British Journal of Psychology, 55,* 75–84.

Constantinople, A. (1969). An Eriksonian measure of personality development in college students. *Developmental Psychology, 1,* 357–372.

Conway, M. A. (1990). *Autobiographical memory: An introduction.* Philadelphia: Open University Press.

Conway, M. A., Anderson, S. J., Larsen, S. F., Donnelly, C. M., McDaniel, M. A., McClelland, A.G.R., Rawles, R. E., & Logie, R. H. (1994). The formation of flashbulb memories. *Memory and Cognition, 22,* 326–343.

Conway, T. L., et al. (1981). Occupational stress and variation in cigarette, coffee, and alcohol consumption. *Journal of Health and Social Behavior, 22,* 155–165.

Cook, M., & Mineka, S. (1990). Selective association in the observational conditioning of fear in monkeys. *Behaviour Research and Therapy, 25,* 349–364.

Cook, S. W. (1985). Experimenting on social issues: The case of school desegregation. *American Psychologist, 40,* 452–460.

Cook, T. D., Cooper, H., Cordray, D. S., Hartmann, H., Hedges, L. V., Light, R. J., Louis, T. A., & Mosteller, F. (1992). *Meta-analysis for explanation: A casebook.* New York: Russell Sage Foundation.

Cooper, H., & Good, T. (1983). *Pygmalion grows up: Studies in the expectation communication process.* New York: Longman.

Cooper, J., & Fazio, R. H. (1984). A new look at dissonance theory. In L. Berkowitz (Ed.), *Advances in experimental social psychology* (Vol. 17, pp. 229–267). New York: Academic Press.

Corballis, M. C. (1989). Laterality and human evolution. *Psychological Review, 96,* 492–505.

Coren, S. (1993). *The left-hander syndrome.* New York: Vintage Books.

Coren, S., & Aks, D. J. (1990). Moon illusion in pictures: A multimechanism approach. *Journal of Experimental Psychology: Human Perception and Performance, 16,* 365–380.

Coren, S., & Halpern, D. F. (1991). Left-handedness: A marker for decreased survival fitness. *Psychological Bulletin, 109,* 90–106.

Coren, S., & Ward, L. M. (1989). *Sensation and perception* (3rd ed.). San Diego: Harcourt Brace Jovanovich.

Corina, D. P., Vaid, J., & Belugi, U. (1992). The linguistic basis of left-hemisphere specialization. *Science, 255,* 1258–1260.

Cornelius, S. W., & Caspi, A. (1987). Everyday problem solving in adulthood and old age. *Psychology and Aging, 2,* 144–153.

Corwin, J. T., & Cotanche, D. A. (1988). Regeneration of sensory hair cells after acoustic trauma. *Science, 240,* 1772–1774.

Costa, P. T., Jr., & McCrae, R. R. (1985). Hypochondriasis, neuroticism, and aging: When are somatic complaints unfounded? *American Psychologist, 40,* 19–28.

Costa, P. T., Jr., & McCrae, R. M. (1992). *Revised NEO personality inventory: NEO PI and NEO Five Factor Inventory (NEO FFI Professional Manual).* Odessa, FL: Psychological Assessment Resources, Inc.

Costa, P. T., Jr., & Widiger, T. A. (Eds.). (1994). *Personality disorders and the five factor model of personality.* Washington, DC: American Psychological Association.

Costanzo, M., & Archer, D. (1989). Interpreting the expressive behavior of others: The Interpersonal Perception Task. *Journal of Nonverbal Behavior, 13,* 225–245.

Cousins, N. (1989). *Head first: The biology of hope.* New York: Dutton.

Cowan, N. (1988). Evolving concepts of memory storage, selective attention, and their mutual constraints within the human information-processing system. *Psychological Bulletin, 104,* 163–191.

Cowey, A., & Stoerig, P. (1991). The neurobiology of blindsight. *Trends in Neuroscience. 14,* 140–145.

Cowey, A., & Stoerig, P. (1992). Reflections on blindsight. In A. D. Milner & M. D. Rugg (Eds.), *The Neuropsychology of Consciousness.* London: Academic Press.

Cowley, G. (1994, February 7). The culture of Prozac. *Newsweek,* pp. 41–42.

Cox, M. J., Owen, M. T., Henderson, V. K., & Margand, N. A. (1992). Prediction of infant-father and infant-mother attachment. *Developmental Psychology, 28,* 474–483.

Coyne, J. C. (1976). Depression and the responses of others. *Journal of Abnormal Psychology, 85,* 186–193.

Coyne, J. C., Kessler, R. C., Tal, M., Turnbull, J., Wortman, C., & Greden, J. (1987). Living with a depressed person: Burden and psychological distress. *Journal of Consulting and Clinical Psychology, 55,* 347–352.

Craik, F.I.M. (1992). In F. Craik & T. A. Salthouse (Eds.), *Handbook of aging and cognition.* Hillsdale, NJ: Erlbaum.

Craik, F.I.M., & Tulving, E. (1975). Depth of processing and the retention of words in episodic memory. *Journal of Experimental Psychology: General, 104,* 268–294.

Cramer, P. (1990). *The development of defense mechanisms: Theory, research, and assessment.* New York: Springer-Verlag.

Crawford, H. J., Brown, A. M., & Moon, C. E. (1993). Sustained attentional and disattentional abilities: Differences between low and highly hypnotizable persons. *Journal of Abnormal Psychology, 102,* 534–543.

Crawford, H. J., Kitner-Triolo, M., Clarke, S. W., & Olesko, B. (1992). Transient positive and negative experiences accompanying stage hypnosis. *Journal of Abnormal Psychology, 101,* 663–667.

Creasey, H., & Rapoport, S. I. (1985). The aging human brain. *Annals of Neurology, 17,* 2–11.

Crits-Christoph, P., & Barber, J. (Eds.). (1991). *Handbook of short-term dynamic psychotherapy.* New York: Basic Books.

Crocker, J., & Major, B. (1989). Social stigma and self-esteem: The self-protective properties of stigma. *Psychological Review, 96,* 608–630.

Crocker, J., Voelkl, K., Testa, M., & Major, B. (1991). Social stigma: The affective consequences of attributional ambiguity. *Journal of Personality and Social Psychology, 60,* 218–228.

Crosby, F. (1982). *Relative deprivation and working women.* New York: Oxford University Press.

Crosby, F., Bromley, S., & Saxe, L. (1980). Recent unobtrusive studies of black and white discrimination and prejudice: A literature review. *Psychological Bulletin, 87,* 546–563.

Crosby, F. J. (1991). *Juggling.* New York: Free Press.

Crow, T. J. (1980). Positive and negative schizophrenic symptoms and the role of dopamine. *British Journal of Psychiatry, 137,* 383–386.

Crowder, R. G. (1993). Short-term memory: Where do we stand? *Memory and Cognition, 21,* 142–145.

Crystal, D. S., & Stevenson, H. W. (1991). Mothers' perceptions of children's problems with mathematics: A cross-national comparison. *Journal of Educational Psychology, 83,* 372–376.

Csikszentmihalyi, M. (1975). *Beyond boredom and anxiety.* San Francisco: Jossey-Bass.

Csikszentmihalyi, M. (1990). *Flow: The psychology of optimal experience.* New York: Harper & Row.

Csikszentmihalyi, M., & Csikszentmihalyi, I. S. (Eds.). (1988). *Optimal experience: Psychological studies of flow in consciousness.* New York: Cambridge University Press.

Csikszentmihalyi, M., & Figurski, T. J. (1982). Self-awareness and aversive experience in everyday life. *Journal of Personality, 50,* 15–28.

Curran, J. P., & Monti, P. M. (1982). *Social skills training: A practical handbook for assessment and treatment.* New York: Guilford Press.

Cytowic, R. E. (1989). *Synesthesia: A union of the senses.* New York: Springer-Verlag.

Czeisler, C. A., Johnson, M. P., Duffy, J. F., Brown, E. N., Ronda, J. M., & Kronauer, R. E. (1990). Exposure to bright light and darkness to treat physiologic maladaptation to night work. *New England Journal of Medicine, 322,* 1253–1259.

Czeisler, C. A., Kronauer, R. E., Allan, J. S., & Duffy, J. F. (1989). Bright light induction of strong (Type O) resetting of the human circadian pacemaker. *Science, 244,* 1328–1333.

D'Souza, D. (1991). *Illiberal education: The politics of race and sex on campus.* New York: Free Press.

Dabbs, J. M., de La Rue, D., & Williams, P. M. (1990). Testosterone and occupational choice: Actors, ministers, and other men. *Journal of Personality and Social Psychology, 59,* 1261–1265.

Dabbs, J. M., Jr., Frady, R. L., Carr, T. S., & Besch, N. F. (1987). Saliva testosterone and criminal violence in young adult prison inmates. *Psychosomatic Medicine, 49,* 174–181.

Dallenbach, K. M. (1927). The temperature spots and end organs. *American Journal of Psychology, 54,* 431–433.

Daly, M., & Wilson, M. (1990). Is parent-offspring conflict sex-linked? Freudian and Darwinian models. *Journal of Personality, 58,* 163–189.

Damon, W. (1988). *The moral child.* New York: Free Press.

Damos, D. (1992). *Multiple task performance.* London: Taylor & Francis.

Darley, J. M., & Fazio, R. (1980). Expectancy confirmation processes arising in the social interaction sequence. *American Psychologist, 35,* 867–881.

Darley, J. M., & Gross, P. H. (1983). A hypothesis-confirming bias in labeling effects. *Journal of Personality and Social Psychology, 44,* 20–33.

Darley, J. M., & Latané, B. (1968). Bystander intervention in emergencies: Diffusion of responsibility. *Journal of Personality and Social Psychology, 8,* 377–383.

Darling, C. A., Davidson, J. K., & Passarello, L. C. (1992). The mystique of first intercourse among college youth: The role of partners, contraceptive practices, and psychological reactions. *Journal of Youth and Adolescence, 21,* 97–117.

Daro, D. (1988). *Confronting child abuse.* New York: Free Press.

Darwin, C. (1872). *The expression of the emotions in man and animals.* London: John Murray.

Darwin, C. (1963). *The origin of species.* New York: Washington Square Press. (Original work published 1859)

Darwin, C. J., Turvey, M. T., & Crowder, R. G. (1972). An auditory analogue of the Sperling partial report procedure: Evidence for brief auditory storage. *Cognitive Psychology, 3,* 255–267.

Davanloo, H. (1980). *Short-term dynamic psychotherapy.* New York: Jason Aronson.

Davidson, R. J. (1993). The neuropsychology of emotion and affective style. In M. Lewis & J. M. Haviland (Eds.), *Handbook of emotions* (pp. 143–154). New York: Guilford Press.

Davidson, R. J., Ekman, P., Saron, C. D., Senulis, J. A., & Friesen, W. V. (1990). Approach-withdrawal and cerebral asymmetry: Emotional expression and brain physiology I. *Journal of Personality and Social Psychology, 58,* 330–341.

Davis, K., Kahn, R., Ko, G., & Davidson, M. (1991). Dopamine in schizophrenia: A review and reconceptualization. *American Journal of Psychiatry, 148,* 1474–1486.

Davis, M. (1992). The role of the amygdala in fear and anxiety. *Annual Review of Neuroscience, 15,* 353–375.

Dawes, R. (1994). *House of cards: Psychology and psychotherapy built on myth.* New York: Free Press.

Dawes, R. M., Faust, D., & Meehl, P. E. (1989). Clinical versus actuarial judgment. *Science, 243,* 1668–1674.

Dawkins, R. (1976). *The selfish gene.* New York: Oxford University Press.

Dawson, M. D., & Schell, A. M. (1982). Electrodermal responses to attended and nonattended significant stimuli during dichotic listening. *Journal of Experimental Psychology: Human Perception and Performance, 8,* 315–324.

De Groot, A. D. (1965). *Thought and chance in chess.* The Hague: Moulton.

de Lacoste-Utamsing, C., & Holloway, R. L. (1982). Sexual dimorphism in the human corpus callosum. *Science, 216,* 1431–1432.

De Longis, A., Coyne, J. C., Dakof, G., Folkman, S., & Lazarus, R. S. (1982). Relations of daily hassles, uplifts, and major life events to health status. *Health Psychology, 1,* 119–136.

Deary, I. J., Ramsay, H., Wilson, J. A., & Riad, M. (1988). Stimulated salivation: Correlations with personality and time of day effects. *Personality and Individual Differences, 9,* 903–909.

"Death Odds" (1990, September 24). *Newsweek,* p. 10.

DeCasper, A. J., & Fifer, W. P. (1980). Of human bonding: Newborns prefer their mothers' voices. *Science, 208,* 1174–1176.

DeCasper, A. J., & Sigafoos, A. D. (1983). The intrauterine heartbeat: A potent reinforcer for newborns. *Infant Behavior and Development, 6,* 19–25.

DeCasper, A. J., & Spence, M. J. (1986). Prenatal maternal speech influences newborns' perception of speech sounds. *Infant Behavior and Development, 9,* 133–150.

Deci, E. L. (1971). Effects of externally mediated rewards on intrinsic motivation. *Journal of Personality and Social Psychology, 18,* 105–115.

Deci, E. L., Connell, J. P., & Ryan, R. M. (1989). Self-determination in a work organization. *Journal of Applied Psychology, 74,* 580–590.

Deci, E. L., & Ryan, R. M. (1985). *Intrinsic motivation and self-determination in human behavior.* New York: Plenum.

DeLoache, J. S., & Brown, A. L. (1983). Very young children's memory for the location of objects in a large-scale environment. *Child Development, 54,* 888–897.

Dement, W. C. (1978). *Some must watch while others must sleep.* New York: W. W. Norton.

Dement, W. C., & Kleitman, N. (1957). The relation of eye movements during sleep to dream activity: An objective method for the study of dreaming. *Journal of Experimental Psychology, 53,* 339–346.

Demko, G. J. (1992). *Why in the world: Adventures in geography.* New York: Anchor Books.

Dempster, F. N. (1981). Memory span: Sources of individual and developmental differences. *Psychological Bulletin, 89,* 63–100.

Dempster, F. N. (1988). The spacing effect: A case study in the failure to apply the results of psychological research. *American Psychologist, 43,* 627–634.

DePalma, A. (1991, December 18). S.A.T. coaching raises scores, report says. *New York Times,* p. C1.

Depue, R. A., & Iacono, W. G. (1989). Neurobehavioral aspects of affective disorders. *Annual Review of Psychology, 40,* 457–492.

Deregowski, J. B. (1989). Real space and represented space: Cross-cultural perspectives. *Brain and Behavioral Sciences, 12,* 51–119.

Derlega, V. J., Winstead, B. A., Wong, P.T.P., & Hunter, S. (1985). Gender effects in an initial encounter: A case where men exceed women in disclosure. *Journal of Social and Personal Relations, 2,* 25–44.

Desimone, R. (1992). The physiology of memory: Recordings of things past. *Science, 258,* 245–246.

Deutsch, M., & Gerard, H. B. (1955). A study of normative and informational social influences upon individual judgment. *Journal of Abnormal and Social Psychology, 51,* 629–636.

DeValois, R. L., & DeValois, K. K. (1975). Neural coding of color. In E. C. Carterette & M. P. Friedman (Eds.), *Handbook of perception: Vol. V. Seeing* (pp. 117–168). New York: Academic Press.

Devine, P. G. (1989). Stereotypes and prejudice: Their automatic and controlled components. *Journal of Personality and Social Psychology, 56,* 5–18.

Devine, P. G., Monteith, M. J., Zuwerink, J. R., & Elliot, A. J. (1991). Prejudice with and without compunction. *Journal of Personality and Social Psychology, 60,* 817–830.

Dewsbury, D. A. (1992). Comparative psychology and ethology: A reassessment. *American Psychologist, 47,* 208–215.

Diamond, M. (1993). Homosexuality and bisexuality in different populations. *Archives of Sexual Behavior, 22,* 291–310.

Diener, E. (1984). Subjective well-being. *Psychological Bulletin, 95,* 542–575.

Diener, E., Emmons, R. A., Larsen, R. J., & Griffin, S. (1984). The Satisfaction with Life Scale. *Journal of Personality Assessment, 49,* 71–75.

Diener, E., Fraser, S. C., Beaman, A. L., & Kelem, R. T. (1976). Effects of deindividuation variables on stealing among Halloween trick-or-treaters. *Journal of Personality and Social Psychology, 33,* 178–183.

Diener, E., Horwitz, J., & Emmons, R. A. (1985). Happiness of the very wealthy. *Social Indicators Research, 16,* 263–274.

Digman, J. M. (1990). Personality structure: Emergence of the five factor model. *Annual Review of Psychology, 41,* 417–440.

DiLalla, L. F., & Gottesman, I. I. (1991). Biological and genetic contributions to violence—Widom's untold tale. *Psychological Bulletin, 109,* 125–129.

Dimberg, U. (1990). Facial electromyography and emotional reactions. *Psychophysiology, 27,* 481–494.

Dindia, K., & Allen, M. (1992). Sex differences in self-disclosure: A meta-analysis. *Psychological Bulletin, 112,* 106–124.

Dinges, D. F., Whitehouse, W. G., Orne, E. C., Powell, J. W., Orne, M. T., & Erdelyi, M. H. (1992). Evaluating hypnotic memory enhancement (hypermnesia and reminiscence) using multitrial forced recall. *Journal of Experimental Psychology: Learning, Memory, and Cognition, 18,* 1139–1147.

Dion, K. K., Berscheid, E., & Walster, E. (1972). What is beautiful is good. *Journal of Personality and Social Psychology, 24,* 285–290.

Ditto, P. H., & Lopez, D. F. (1992). Motivated skepticism: Use of differential decision criteria for preferred and nonpreferred conclusions. *Journal of Personality and Social Psychology, 63,* 568–584.

Dobbins, G. H., & Platz, S. J. (1986). Sex differences in leadership: How real are they? *Academy of Management Review, 11,* 118–127.

Doblin, R., & Kleiman, M.A.R. (1991). Medical use of marijuana. *Annals of Internal Medicine, 114,* 809–810.

Dobson, K. S. (1989). A meta-analysis of the efficacy of cognitive therapy for depression. *Journal of Consulting and Clinical Psychology, 57,* 414–419.

Dodson, C., & Reisberg, D. (1991). Indirect testing of eyewitness memory: The (non)effect of misinformation. *Bulletin of the Psychonomic Society, 29,* 333–336.

Dohrenwend, B. S., & Dohrenwend, B. P. (1978). Some issues in research on stressful life events. *Journal of Nervous and Mental Diseases, 166,* 7–15.

Dollard, J., Doob, L. W., Miller, N. E., Mowrer, O. H., & Sears, R. R. (1939). *Frustration and aggression.* New Haven, CT: Yale University Press.

Donley, R. D., & Ashcraft, M. H. (1992). The methodology of testing naive beliefs in the physics classroom. *Memory and Cognition, 20,* 381–391.

Donlon, T. F. (Ed.). (1984). *The College Board technical handbook for the scholastic aptitude test and achievement tests.* New York: College Entrance Examination Board.

Donnerstein, E., & Berkowitz, L. (1981). Victim reactions in aggressive erotic films as a factor in violence against women. *Journal of Personality and Social Psychology, 41,* 710–724.

Donnerstein, E., Linz, D., & Penrod, S. (1987). *The question of pornography.* New York: Free Press.

Doris, J. (Ed.). (1991). *The suggestibility of children's recollections: Implications for eyewitness testimony.* Washington, DC: American Psychological Association.

Dostoevsky, F. (1960). *Notes from underground* (R. E. Matlaw, Trans.). New York: Dutton (Original work published 1864)

Doty, R. L., Applebaum, S., Zusho, H., & Settle, R. G. (1985). Sex differences in odor identification ability: A cross-cultural analysis. *Neuropsychologia, 23,* 667–672.

Dougherty, D. M., & Lewis, P. (1991). Stimulus generalization, discrimination, and peak shift in horses. *Journal of the Experimental Analysis of Behavior, 56,* 97–104.

Douglas, V. I., Barr, R. G., O'Neill, M. E., & Britton, B. G. (1986). Short-term effects of methylphenidate on the cognitive, learning and academic performance of children with attention deficit disor-

der in the laboratory and the classroom. *Journal of Child Psychiatry and Psychology, 27,* 191–211.

Dovidio, J. F., Allen J. L., & Schroeder, D. A. (1990). Specificity of empathy-induced helping: Evidence for altruistic motivation. *Journal of Personality and Social Psychology, 59,* 249–260.

Dovidio, J. F., & Gaertner, S. L. (Eds.). (1986). *Prejudice, discrimination, and racism: Theory and research.* Orlando, FL: Academic Press.

Downs, A. C., & Lyons, P. M. (1991). Natural observations of the links between attractiveness and initial legal judgments. *Personality and Social Psychology Bulletin, 17,* 541–547.

Driskell, J. E., Willis, R. P., & Copper, C. (1992). Effect of overlearning on retention. *Journal of Applied Psychology, 77,* 615–622.

Duclos, S. E., Laird, J. D., Schneider, E., Sexter, M., Stern, L., & Lighten, O. V. (1989). Emotion-specific effects of facial expressions and postures on emotional experience. *Journal of Personality and Social Psychology, 57,* 100–108.

Dudycha, G. J., & Dudycha, M. M. (1941). Childhood memories: A review of the literature. *Psychological Bulletin, 38,* 668–682.

Duncan, B. L. (1976). Differential social perception and attribution of intergroup violence: Testing the lower limits of stereotyping of blacks. *Journal of Personality and Social Psychology, 34,* 590–598.

Duncker, K. (1945). On problem-solving (L. S. Lees, Trans.). *Psychological Monographs, 58*(No. 270).

Dunn, A. J. (1989). Psychoneuroimmunology for the neuroendocrinologist: A review of animal studies of nervous system-immune system interactions. *Psychoneuroendocrinology, 14,* 251–274.

Dunn, D. S., & Wilson, T. D. (1990). When the stakes are high: A limit to the illusion-of-control effect. *Social Cognition, 8,* 305–323.

Dunn, J., Bretherton, I., & Munn, P. (1987). Conversations about feeling states between mothers and their young children. *Developmental Psychology, 23,* 132–139.

Dunn, J., & Plomin, R. (1990). *Separate lives: Why siblings are so different.* New York: Basic Books.

Dunning, D., Griffin, D. W., Milojkovic, J. D., & Ross, L. (1990). The overconfidence effect in social prediction. *Journal of Personality and Social Psychology, 58,* 568–581.

Dutton, D. G., & Aron, A. P. (1974). Some evidence for heightened sexual attraction under conditions of high anxiety. *Journal of Personality and Social Psychology, 23,* 510–517.

Duval, S., Duval, V. H., & Mulilis, J. P. (1992). Effects of self-focus, discrepancy between self and standard, and outcome expectancy favorability on the tendency to match self to standard or to withdraw. *Journal of Personality and Social Psychology, 62,* 340–348.

Duval, S., & Wicklund, R. A. (1972). *A theory of objective self-awareness.* New York: Academic Press.

Dywan, J., & Bowers, K. (1983). The use of hypnosis to enhance recall. *Science, 222,* 184–185.

Eagly, A. H. (1987). *Sex differences in social behavior: A social-role interpretation.* Hillsdale, NJ: Erlbaum.

Eagly, A. H., Ashmore, R. D., Makhijani, M. G., & Longo, L. C. (1991). What is beautiful is good, but. . . : A meta-analytic review of research on the physical attractiveness stereotype. *Psychology Bulletin, 110,* 107–128.

Eagly, A. H., & Chaiken, S. (1993). *The psychology of attitudes.* Fort Worth, TX: Harcourt Brace Jovanovich.

Eagly, A. H., & Johnson, B. T. (1990). Gender and leadership style: A meta-analysis. *Psychological Bulletin, 108,* 233–256.

Eagly, A. H., Makhijani, M. G., & Klonsky, B. G. (1992). Gender and evaluation of leaders: A meta-analysis. *Psychological Bulletin, 111,* 3–22.

Eagly, A. H., & Steffen, V. J. (1986). Gender and aggressive behavior:

A meta-analytic review of the social psychology literature. *Psychological Bulletin, 100,* 309–330.

Eagly, A. H., & Wood, W. (1991). Explaining sex differences in social behavior: A meta-analytic perspective. *Personality and Social Psychology Bulletin, 17,* 306–315.

Eagly, A. H., Wood, W., & Chaiken, S. (1981). An attribution analysis of persuasion. In J. Harvey, W. Ickes, & R. Kidd (Eds.), *New directions in attribution research* (Vol. 3, pp. 37–62). Hillsdale, NJ: Erlbaum.

Eaton, W. W., Kessler, R. C., Wittchen, H. U., & Magee, W. J. (1994). Panic and panic disorder in the United States. *American Journal of Psychiatry, 151,* 413–420.

Ebbinghaus, H. (1913). *Memory: A contribution to experimental psychology* (H. Ruger & C. Bussenius, Trans.). New York: Teachers College Press. (Original work published 1885)

Eccles, J. (1965). *The brain and unity of conscious experience: The 19th Arthur Stanley Eddington Memorial Lecture.* Cambridge: Cambridge University Press.

Eccles, J. P. (1985). Sex differences in achievement patterns. In T. B. Sonderegger (Ed.), *Nebraska symposium on motivation: Psychology and gender.* Lincoln: University of Nebraska Press.

Eccles, J. S., Jacobs, J. E., & Harold, R. D. (1990). Gender role stereotypes, expectancy effects, and parents' socialization of gender differences. *Journal of Social Issues, 46,* 183–201.

Eccles, J., Wigfield, A., Harold, R. D., & Blumenfeld, P. (1993). Age and gender differences in children's self- and task perceptions during elementary school. *Child Development, 64,* 830–847.

Eckenrode, J. (1984). Impact of chronic and acute stressors on daily reports of mood. *Journal of Personality and Social Psychology, 46,* 907–918.

Eden, D. (1990). Pygmalion without interpersonal contrast effects: Whole groups gain from raising manager expectations. *Journal of Applied Psychology, 75,* 394–398.

Eder, D. (1981). Ability grouping as a self-fulfilling prophecy: A microanalysis of teacher-student interaction. *Sociology of Education, 54,* 151–161.

Edgarton, R. (1967). *The cloak of competence.* Berkeley: University of California Press.

Edwards, B. (1979). *Drawing on the right side of the brain: A course in enhancing creativity and artistic confidence.* Los Angeles: Tarcher.

Edwards, C. P. (1981). The comparative study of the development of moral judgment and reasoning. In R. H. Munroe, R. L. Munroe, & B. B. Whiting (Eds.), *Handbook of cross-cultural human development.* New York: Garland Press.

Efron, R. (1990). *The decline and fall of hemispheric specialization.* Hillsdale, NJ: Erlbaum.

Ehlers, A., & Breuer, P. (1992). Increased cardia awareness in panic disorder. *Journal of Abnormal Psychology, 101,* 371–382.

Eibl-Eibesfeldt, I. (1989). *Human ethology.* New York: Aldine de Gruyter.

Eich, E., Macaulay, D., & Ryan, L. (1994). Mood dependent memory for events of the personal past. *Journal of Experimental Psychology: General, 123,* 201–215.

Eich, J. E. (1980). The cue-dependent nature of state-dependent retrieval. *Memory and Cognition, 8,* 157–173.

Einstein, G. O., & McDaniel, M. A. (1990). Normal aging and prospective memory. *Journal of Experimental Psychology: Human Learning and Memory, 16,* 717–726.

Einstein, G. O., McDaniel, M. A., & Lackey, S. (1989). Bizarre imagery, interference, and distinctiveness. *Journal of Experimental Psychology: Learning, Memory, and Cognition, 15,* 137–146.

Eisenberg, N., & Mussen, P. H. (1989). *The roots of prosocial behavior in children.* New York: Cambridge University Press.

Eisenberger, R. (1992). Learned industriousness. *Psychological Review, 99,* 248–267.

Eisenman, R. (1993). Belief that drug usage in the United States is increasing when it is really decreasing: An example of the availability heuristic. *Bulletin of the Psychonomic Society, 31,* 249–252.

Ekerdt, D. J., Bosse, R., & Levkoff, S. (1985). An empirical test for phases of retirement. *Journal of Gerontology, 40,* 95–101.

Ekman, P., & Davidson, R. J. (1993). Voluntary smiling changes regional brain activity. *Psychological Science, 4,* 342–345.

Ekman, P., Davidson, R. J., & Friesen, W. V. (1990). The Duchenne smile: Emotional expression and brain physiology II. *Journal of Personality and Social Psychology, 58,* 342–353.

Ekman, P., & Friesen, W. V. (1974). Detecting deception from the body or face. *Journal of Personality and Social Psychology, 29,* 288–298.

Ekman, P., Friesen, W. V., O'Sullivan, M., Chan, A., Diacoyanni-Tarlatzis, I., Heider, K., Krause, R., LeCompte, W. A., Pitcairn, T., Ricci-Bitti, P., Scherer, K., Tomita, M., & Tzavaras, A. (1987). Universals and cultural differences in the judgments of facial expressions of emotion. *Journal of Personality and Social Psychology, 53,* 712–717.

Ekman, P., Levenson, R. W., & Friesen, W. V. (1983). Autonomic nervous system activity distinguishes among emotions. *Science, 221,* 1208–1210.

Ekman, P., & O'Sullivan, M. (1991). Who can catch a liar? *American Psychologist, 46,* 913–920.

Elder, G. H. (1974). *Children of the Great Depression.* Chicago: University of Chicago Press.

Elkin, I., et al. (1989). National Institute of Mental Health treatment of depression collaborative research program. *Archives of General Psychiatry, 46,* 971–983.

Elkind, D. (1967). Egocentrism in adolescence. *Child Development, 38,* 1025–1034.

Elkind, D. (1989). *Miseducation: Preschoolers at risk.* New York: Knopf.

Elkind, D., & Bowen, R. (1979). Imaginary audience behavior in children and adolescents. *Developmental Psychology, 15,* 38–44.

Elliott, R. (1987). *Litigating intelligence: IQ tests, special education, and social science in the courtroom.* Dover, MA: Auburn House.

Ellis, A. (1962). *Reason and emotion in psychotherapy.* New York: Lyle Stuart.

Ellis, A. (1989). Rational-emotive therapy. In R. J. Corcini & D. Wedding (Eds.), *Current psychotherapies* (4th ed.). Itasca, IL: Peacock.

Ellis, A. (1993). Reflections on rational-emotive therapy. *Journal of Consulting and Clinical Psychology, 61,* 199–201.

Ellis, A., & Dryden, W. (1987). *The practice of rational emotional therapy.* New York: Springer-Verlag.

Ellis, A., & Hunt, R. R. (1989). *Fundamentals of human memory and cognition* (4th ed.). Dubuque, IA: W. C. Brown.

Ellis, L., & Ames, M. A. (1987). Neurohormonal functioning and sexual orientation: A theory of homosexuality-heterosexuality. *Psychological Bulletin, 101,* 233–258.

Emde, R. N., Gaensbauer, T. J., & Harmon, R. J. (1976). Emotional expression in infancy: A biobehavioral study. *Psychological Issues, 10*(Monograph 37).

Emmelkamp, P. M. G. (1994). Behavior therapy with adults. In A. E. Bergin & S. L. Garfield (Eds.), *Handbook of psychotherapy and behavior change,* (4th ed.). New York: Wiley.

Emmelkamp, P.M.G. (1982). *Phobic and obsessive-compulsive disorders: Theory, research, and practice.* New York: Plenum.

Endler, N. S., & Persad, E. (1988). *Electroconvulsive therapy: The myths and the realities.* Toronto: Hans Huber Publishers.

Engels, G. I., Garnefski, N., & Diekstra, R. (1993). Efficacy of rational-emotive therapy: A quantitative analysis. *Journal of Consulting and Clinical Psychology, 61,* 1083–1090.

Engen, T. (1982). *The perception of odors.* New York: Academic Press.

Engle, R. W., Cantor, J., & Carullo, J. J. (1992). Individual differences in working memory and comprehension: A test of four hypotheses. *Journal of Experimental Psychology: Learning, Memory, and Cognition, 18,* 972–992.

Enright, R. D., Levy, V. M., Harris, D., & Lapsley, D. K. (1987). *Journal of Youth and Adolescence, 16,* 541–559.

Epstein, J. L. (1985). After the bus arrives: Resegregated schools. *Journal of Social Issues, 41*, 23–43.

Epstein, R., Kirshnit, C. E., Lanza, R. P., & Rubin, L. C. (1984). "Insight" in the pigeon: Antecedents and determinants of an intelligent performance. *Nature, 308*, 61–62.

Epstein, S. (1979). The stability of behavior: I. On predicting most of the people much of the time. *Journal of Personality and Social Psychology, 37*, 1097–1126.

Epstein, S., & O'Brien, E. J. (1985). The person-situation debate in historical and current perspective. *Psychological Bulletin, 98*, 513–537.

Erber, J. T., Szuchman, L. T., & Rothberg, S. T. (1990). Everyday memory failure: Age differences in appraisal and attribution. *Psychology and Aging, 5*, 236–241.

Erdelyi, M. H. (1985). *Psychoanalysis: Freud's cognitive psychology.* New York: W. H. Freeman.

Erdelyi, M. H. (1985). Psychodynamics and the unconscious. *American Psychologist, 47*, 784–787.

Erdelyi, M. H. (1992). Psychodynamics and the unconscious. *American Psychologist, 47*, 784–787.

Ericsson, K. A., & Chase, W. G. (1982). Exceptional memory. *American Scientist, 70*, 607–615.

Ericsson, K. A., Chase, W. G., & Faloon, S. (1980). Acquisition of a memory skill. *Science, 208*, 1181–1182.

Ericsson, K. A., Krampe, R. T., & Tesch-Romer, C. (1993). The role of deliberate practice in the acquisition of expert performance. *Psychological Review, 100*, 363–406.

Erikson, E. H. (1959). Identity and the life cycle. *Psychological Issues* (Monograph 1). New York: International Universities Press.

Erikson, E. H. (1963). *Childhood and society.* New York: Norton.

Eron, L. D. (1987). The development of aggressive behavior from the perspective of a developing behaviorism. *American Psychologist, 42*, 435–442.

Evans, D. A., et al. (1989). Prevalence of Alzheimer's disease in a community population of older persons: Higher than previously reported. *Journal of the American Medical Association, 262*, 2551–2556.

Evans, G. W., & Lepore, S. J. (1993). Household crowding and social support: A quasiexperimental analysis. *Journal of Personality and Social Psychology, 65*, 308–316.

Exner, J. E., Jr. (1986). *The Rorschach—A comprehensive system: Vol. 1. Basic foundations* (2nd ed.). New York: Wiley.

Eysenck, H. J. (1952). The effects of psychotherapy: An evaluation. *Journal of Consulting Psychology, 16*, 319–324.

Eysenck, H. J. (1967). *The biological basis of personality.* Springfield, IL: Thomas.

Eysenck, H. J. (1982). *A model for intelligence.* Berlin: Springer-Verlag.

Eysenck, H. J. (1990). Biological dimensions of personality. In L. A. Pervin (Ed.), *Handbook of personality theory and research* (pp. 244–276). New York: Guilford Press.

Eysenck, H. J., & Eysenck, M. W. (1985). *Personality and individual diferences: A natural science approach.* New York: Plenum.

Eysenck, H. J., & Eysenck, S.G.B. (1964). *Manual of the Eysenck Personality Inventory.* London: University of London Press.

Eysenck, M. W. (1992). *Anxiety: The cognitive perspective.* Hillsdale, NJ: Erlbaum.

Fabes, R. A., & Martin, C. L. (1991). Gender and age stereotypes of emotionality. *Personality and Social Psychology Bulletin, 17*, 532–540.

Fantz, R. L. (1961). The origin of form perception. *Scientific American, 204*, 66–72.

Farah, M. J. (1989). The neural basis of mental imagery. *Trends in Neuroscience, 12*, 395–399.

Faravelli, C., & Pallanti, S. (1989). Recent life events and panic disorders. *American Journal of Psychiatry, 146*, 622–626.

Farrell, P. A., Gates, W. K., Maksud, M. G., & Morgan, W. P. (1982). Increases in plasma beta-endorphin/beta-lipotropin immunoreactivity after treadmill running in humans. *Journal of Applied Psychology, 52*, 1245–1249.

Fay, R. E., Turner, C. F., Klassen, A. D., & Gagnon, J. H. (1989). Prevalence and patterns of same-gender sexual contact among men. *Science, 243*, 343–348.

Fechner, G. T. (1860). *Elements of psychophysics* (H. E. Alder, Trans.). New York: Holt, Rinehart & Winston. (Translated edition 1966.)

Federal Bureau of Investigation. (1987). Uniform crime reports: Arrests, by sex. In *The world almanac and book of facts* (p. 820). New York: World Almanac.

Fehr, B., & Russell, J. A. (1991). The concept of love: Viewed from a prototype perspective. *Journal of Personality and Social Psychology, 60*, 425–438.

Feifel, H. (1990). Psychology and death: Meaningful rediscovery. *American Psychologist, 45*, 537–543.

Fein, S., Hilton, J. L., & Miller, D. T. (1990). Suspicion of ulterior motivation and the correspondence bias. *Journal of Personality and Social Psychology, 58*, 753–764.

Feingold, A. (1992). Good-looking people are not what we think. *Psychological Bulletin, 111*, 304–341.

Fenigstein, A., Scheier, M. F., & Buss, A. H. (1975). Public and private self-consciousness: Assessment and theory. *Journal of Consulting and Clinical Psychology, 43*, 522–527.

Fennell, M. J. (1989). Depression. In K. Hawton, P. Salkovskis, J. Kirk, & D. Clark (Eds.), *Cognitive behaviour therapy for psychiatric problems* (pp. 167–234). New York: Oxford Medical Publications.

Fernald, A. (1985). Four-month-old infants prefer to listen to motherese. *Infant Behavior and Development, 8*, 181–195.

Fernald, A., Taeschner, T., Dunn, J., Papousek, M., Boysson-Bardies, B. D., & Fukui, I. (1989). A cross-linguistic study of prosodic modifications in mothers' and fathers' speech to preverbal infants. *Journal of Child Langauge, 16*, 477–501.

Fernandez, E., & Turk, D. C. (1992). Sensory and affective components of pain: Separation and synthesis. *Psychological Bulletin, 112*, 205–217.

Ferster, C. B., & Skinner, B. F. (1957). *Schedules of reinforcement.* New York: Appleton-Century-Crofts.

Festinger, L. (1957). *A theory of cognitive dissonance.* Stanford, CA: Stanford University Press.

Festinger, L., & Carlsmith, J. M. (1959). Cognitive consequences of forced compliance. *Journal of Abnormal and Social Psychology, 58*, 203–210.

Field, T. (1991). Quality infant day-care and grade school behavior and performance. *Child Development, 62*, 863–870.

Field, T. M., Woodson, R., Greenberg, R., & Cohen, D. (1982). Discrimination and imitation of facial expressions by neonates. *Science, 218*, 179–181.

Findley, M. J., & Cooper, H. M. (1983). Locus of control and academic achievement: A literature review. *Journal of Personality and Social Psychology, 44*, 419–427.

Finman, R., Davidson, R. J., Colton, M. B., Straus, A. M., & Kagan, J. (1989). Psychophysiological correlates of inhibition to the unfamiliar in children (Abstract). *Psychophysiology, 26*(No. 4A), S24.

Firestein, S., & Werblin, F. (1989). Odor-induced membrane currents in vertebrate-olfactory receptor neurons. *Science, 244*, 79–82.

Fischer, K. W. (1987). Relations between brain and cognitive development. *Child Development, 58*, 623–632.

Fischhoff, B. (1975). Hindsight/foresight: The effect of outcome knowledge on judgment under uncertainty. *Journal of Experimental Psychology: Human Perception and Performance, 1*, 288–299.

Fischhoff, B., Slovic, P., & Lichtenstein, S. (1977). Knowing with certainty: The appropriateness of extreme confidence. *Journal of Experimental Psychology: Human Perception and Performance, 3*, 552–564.

Fishbein, M. (1980). A theory of reasoned action: Some applications and implications. In H. E. Howe & M. M. Page (Eds.), *Nebraska Symposium on Motivation* (Vol. 27, pp. 65–116). Lincoln: University of Nebraska Press.

Fisher, G. H. (1968). Ambiguity of form: Old and new. *Perception and Psychophysics, 4,* 189–192.

Fisher, J. D., & Fisher, W. A. (1992). Changing AIDS-risk behavior. *Psychological Bulletin, 111,* 455–474.

Fisher, S., & Greenberg, R. P. (1977). *The scientific credibility of Freud's theories and therapy.* New York: Columbia University Press.

Fiske, S. T., Bersoff, D. N., Borgida, E., Deaux, K., & Heilman, M. E. (1991). Social science research on trial: Use of sex stereotyping research in *Price Waterhouse* v. *Hopkins. American Psychologist, 46,* 1049–1060.

Fiske, S. T., & Taylor, S. E. (1991). *Social cognition.* New York: McGraw-Hill.

Fitzgerald, J. M. (1988). Vivid memories and the reminiscence phenomenon: The role of self-narrative. *Human Development, 31,* 261–273.

Flavell, J. H. (1982). Structures, stages, and sequences in cognitive development. In W. A. Collins (Ed.), *The concept of development: The Minnesota symposia on child psychology* (Vol. 15). Hillsdale, NJ: Erlbaum.

Flavell, J. H., Beach, D. R., & Chinsky, J. M. (1966). Spontaneous verbal rehearsal in a memory task as a function of age. *Child Development, 37,* 283–299.

Flavell, J. H., Green, F. L., & Flavell, E. R. (1986). Development of knowledge about the appearance-reality distinction. *Monographs of the Society for Research in Child Development, 51*(1, Serial No. 212).

Flavell, J. H., Miller, P. H., & Miller, S. A. (1993). *Cognitive development* (3rd ed.). Englewood Cliffs, NJ: Prentice-Hall.

Fleming, I. A., Baum, A., & Weiss, L. (1987). Social density and perceived control as mediators of crowding stress in high-density residential neighborhoods. *Journal of Personality and Social Psychology, 52,* 899–906.

Fletcher, R. (1991). *Science, ideology, and the media: The Cyril Burt scandal.* New Brunswick, NJ: Transaction Publishers.

Floyd, F. J., Haynes, S. N., Doll, E. R., Winemiller, D., Lemsky, C., Burgy, T. M., Werle, M., & Heilman, N. (1992). Assessing retirement satisfaction and perceptions of retirement experiences. *Psychology and Aging, 7,* 609–621.

Foa, E. B., & Kozak, M. J. (1986). Emotional processing of fear: Exposure to corrective information. *Psychological Bulletin, 99,* 20–35.

Foa, E. B., Steketee, G., & Grayson, J. B. (1985). Imaginal and in vivo exposure: A comparison with obsessive-compulsive checkers. *Behavior Therapy, 16,* 292–302.

Fontana, A., & Rosenheck, R. (1994). Traumatic war stressors and psychiatric symptoms among World War II, Korean, and Vietnam War veterans. *Psychology and Aging, 9,* 27–33.

Ford, C. V., & Folks, D. G. (1985). Conversion disorders: An overview. *Psychosomatics, 26,* 371–374, 380–383.

Ford, M. R., & Widiger, T. A. (1989). Sex bias in the diagnosis of histrionic and antisocial personality disorders. *Journal of Consulting and Clinical Psychology, 57,* 301–305.

Forsythe, S. M. (1990). Effects of applicant's clothing on interviewer's decision to hire. *Journal of Applied Social Psychology, 20,* 1579–1595.

Fosterling, F. (1989). Models of covariation and attribution: How do they relate to the analogy of analysis of variance? *Journal of Personality and Social Psychology, 57,* 615–625.

Foulke, E. (1991). Braille. In M. A. Heller & W. Schiff (Eds.), *The psychology of touch* (pp. 219–233). Hillsdale, NJ: Erlbaum.

Fouts, R. S., Fouts, D. H., & Van Cantfort, T. E. (1989). The infant Loulis learns signs from cross-fostered chimpanzees. In R. A. Gardner, B. T. Gardner, & T. E. Van Cantfort (Eds.), *Teaching sign language to chimpanzees* (pp. 280–292). Albany: State University of New York Press.

Fowler, M. J., Sullivan, M. J., & Ekstrand, B. R. (1973). Sleep and memory. *Science, 179,* 302–304.

Fowler, R. D. (1986, May). Howard Hughes: A psychological autopsy. *Psychology Today,* pp. 22–33.

Fowles, D. C. (1992). Schizophrenia: Diathesis-stress revisited. *Annual Review of Psychology, 43,* 303–336.

Fox, N. A. (1991). If it's not left, it's right: Electroencephalograph asymmetry and the development of emotion. *American Psychologist, 46,* 863–872.

Fozard, J. L. (1990). Vision and hearing in aging. In J. E. Birren & K. W. Schaie (Eds.), *Handbook of the psychology of aging* (3rd ed.). San Diego: Academic Press.

Frable, D. E. S. (1989). Sex typing and gender ideology: Two facets of the individual's gender psychology that go together. *Journal of Personality and Social Psychology, 56,* 95–108.

Frances, A. J., & Widiger, T. (1986). The classification of personality disorders: An overview of problems and solutions. *Annual Review of Psychiatry, 5,* 240–257.

Frank, A. F., & Gunderson, J. G. (1991). The role of the therapist alliance in the treatment of schizophrenia: Relationship to course and outcome. *Archives of General Psychiatry, 47,* 228–236.

Frank, D. A., et al. (1988). Cocaine use during pregnancy: Prevalence and correlates. *Pediatrics, 82,* 888–895.

Frank, M. G., Ekman, P., & Friesen, W. V. (1993). Behavioral markers and recognizability of the smile of enjoyment. *Journal of Personality and Social Psychology, 64,* 83–93.

Frankenburg, W. K., & Dodds, J. B. (1967). The Denver developmental screening test. *Journal of Pediatrics, 71,* 181–191.

Freedman, B. J. (1974). The perceptual experience of perceptual and cognitive disturbances in schizophrenia: A review of autobiographical accounts. *Archives of General Psychiatry, 30,* 333–340.

Freedman, J. L. (1988). Television violence and aggression: What the evidence shows. *Applied Social Psychology Annual, 8,* 144–162.

Freedman, J. L., Cunningham, J. A., & Krismer, K. (1992). Inferred values and the reverse-incentive effect in induced compliance. *Journal of Personality and Social Psychology, 62,* 357–368.

Freedman, R., et al. (1987). Neurobiological studies of sensory gating in schizophrenia. *Schizophrenia Bulletin, 13,* 669–678.

Freeman, A., Simon, K. M., Beutler, L. E., & Arkowitz, H. (1989). *Comprehensive handbook of cognitive therapy.* New York: Plenum.

Freud, S. (1900). *The interpretation of dreams.* In Vols. 4 and 5 of the *Standard edition.* London: Hogarth.

Freud, S. (1909). Analysis of a phobia in a five-year-old boy. In *Collected works of Sigmund Freud* (Vol. 10). London: Hogarth. (Reprinted in 1956)

Freud, S. (1920). *Beyond the pleasure principle: A study of the death instinct in human aggression* (J. Strachey, Trans.). New York: Bantam Books. (Reprinted in 1959)

Freud, S. (1924). Mourning and melancholia. In J. Riviere (Trans.), *Collected papers* (Vol. 4). London: Hogarth Press. (Original work published 1917)

Freud, S. (1940). *An outline of psychoanalysis.* In Vol. 23 of the *Standard edition.* London: Hogarth.

Freud, S. (1959). Fragments of an analysis of a case of hysteria. *Collected papers* (Vol. 3). New York: Basic Books. (Original work published 1905)

Fridlund, A. J. (1992). The behavioral ecology and sociality of human faces. *Review of Personality and Social Psychology, 13,* 90–121.

Friedlander, M. L., & Heatherington, L. (1989). Analyzing relational control in family therapy interviews. *Journal of Counseling Psychology, 36,* 139–148.

Friedman, H. S. (1991). *The self-healing personality.* New York: Henry Holt and Company.

Friedman, H. S., & Booth-Kewley, S. (1987). The "disease-prone personality": A meta-analytic view of the construct. *American Psy-*

chologist, 42, 539–555.

Friedman, M., & Rosenman, R. F. (1974). *Type A behavior and your heart.* New York: Alfred A. Knopf.

Friedman, M., & Ulmer, D. (1984). *Treating Type A behavior—and your heart.* New York: Alfred A. Knopf.

Friedman, W. J. (1993). Memory for the time of past events. *Psychological Bulletin, 113,* 44–66.

Friedmann, E., Katcher, A. H., Lynch, J. J., & Thomas, S. A. (1980). Animal companions and one-year survival of patients after discharge from a coronary care unit. *Public Health Reports, 95,* 307–312.

Friend, R., Rafferty, Y., & Bramel, D. (1990). A puzzling misinterpretation of the Asch "conformity" study. *European Journal of Social Psychology, 20,* 29–44.

Frijda, N. H. (1986). *The emotions.* New York: Cambridge University Press.

Fromm, E. (1941). *Escape from freedom.* New York: Farrar & Rinehart.

Funk, S. C. (1992). Hardiness: A review of theory and research. *Health Psychology, 11,* 335–345.

Fuster, J. M. (1989). *The prefrontal cortex: Anatomy, physiology, and neuropsychology of the frontal lobe.* New York: Raven Press.

Gabrenya, W. K., Jr., Latané, B., & Wang, Y. E. (1983). Social loafing in cross-cultural perspective: Chinese in Taiwan. *Journal of Cross-Cultural Psychology, 14,* 368–384.

Gaddes, W. H., & Edgell, D. (1994). *Learning disabilities and brain function: A neuropsychological approach* (3rd ed.). New York: Springer-Verlag.

Gaddis, A., & Brooks-Gunn, J. (1985). The male experience of pubertal change. *Journal of Youth and Adolescence, 14,* 61–69.

Gaertner, S. L., Mann, J. A., Dovidio, J. F., Murrell, A. J., & Pomare, M. (1990). How does cooperation reduce intergroup bias? *Journal of Personality and Social Psychology, 59,* 692–704.

Gaertner, S. L., & McLaughlin, J. P. (1983). Racial stereotypes: Associations and ascriptions of positive and negative characteristics. *Social Psychology Quarterly, 46,* 23–30.

Galanter, E. (1962). Contemporary psychophysics. In R. Brown, E. Galanter, H. Hess, & G. Mandler (Eds.), *New directions in psychology.* New York: Holt, Rinehart & Winston.

Galotti, K. M. (1989). Approaches to studying formal and everyday reasoning. *Psychological Bulletin, 105,* 331–351.

Galton, F. (1883). *Inquiries into human faculty and its development.* London: Dent.

Gara, M. A., Woolfolk, R. L., Cohen, B. D., Goldston, R. B., Allen, L. A., & Novalany, J. (1993). Perception of self and other in major depression. *Journal of Abnormal Psychology, 102,* 93–100

Garcia, J. (1981). The logic and limits of mental aptitude testing. *American Psychologist, 36,* 1172–1180.

Garcia, J., & Koelling, R. A. (1966). The relation of cue to consequence in avoidance learning. *Psychonomic Science, 4,* 123–124.

Gardner, H. (1983). *Frames of mind: The theory of multiple intelligences.* New York: Basic Books.

Gardner, H. (1993). *Multiple intelligences: The theory in practice.* New York: Basic Books.

Gardner, R. A., & Gardner, B. I. (1969). Teaching sign language to a chimpanzee. *Science, 165,* 664–672.

Gardner, R. A., & Gardner, B. T. (1978). Comparative psychology and language acquisition. *Annuals of the New York Academy of Science, 309,* 37–76.

Gardner, W., Millstein, S. G., & Wilcox, B. (1991). *Adolescents in the AIDS epidemic: New directions for child development.* San Francisco: Jossey-Bass.

Gatchel, R. J., & Blanchard, E. B. (Eds.). (1993). *Psychophysiological disorders.* Washington, DC: American Psychological Association.

Gatz, M., & Hurwicz, M. L. (1990). Are old people more depressed? Cross-sectional data on Center for Epidemiological Studies depression scale factors. *Psychology and Aging, 5,* 284–290.

Gavin, L., & Furman, W. (1989). Age differences in adolescents' perceptions of their peer groups. *Developmental Psychology, 25,* 827–834.

Gawin, F. H. (1991). Cocaine addiction: Psychology and neurophysiology. *Science, 251,* 1580–1586.

Gay, P. (1988). *Freud: A life for our time.* New York: Norton.

Gazzaniga, M. S. (1967). The split brain in man. *Scientific American,* 24–29.

Gazzaniga, M. S. (1970). *The bisected brain.* New York: Appleton-Century-Crofts.

Gazzaniga, M. S. (1985). *The social brain.* New York: Basic Books.

Gazzaniga, M. S., & LeDoux, J. E. (1978). *The integrated mind.* New York: Plenum.

Geldard, F. A. (1972). *The human senses* (2nd ed.). New York: Wiley.

Gelman, R. (1979). Preschool thought. *American Psychologist, 34,* 900–905.

Gentner, D., & Stevens, A. L. (Eds.). (1983). *Mental models.* Hillsdale, NJ: Erlbaum.

Gerall, A. A., Moltz, H., & Ward, I. L. (Eds.). (1992). *Handbook of behavioral neurobiology: Vol. 11. Sexual differentiation.* New York: Plenum.

Gerrard, M. (1987). Sex, sex guilt, and contraceptive use revisited: The 1980s. *Journal of Personality and Social Psychology, 52,* 975–980.

Gescheider, G. A. (1985). *Psychophysics: Method, theory, and application* (2nd ed.). Hillsdale, NJ: Erlbaum.

Geschwind, N. (1979). Specializations of the human brain. *Scientific American, 241,* 180–199.

Geschwind, N., & Behan, P. (1982). Left-handedness: Association with immune disease, migraine, and left-handed learning disorder. *Proceedings of the National Academy of Sciences, 79,* 5097–5100.

Gesell, A. L. (1940). *The first five years of life: A guide to the study of the preschool child.* New York: Harper.

Ghanta, V. K., Hiramoto, R. N., Salvason, H. B., & Spector, N. H. (1985). Neural and environmental influences on neoplasia and conditioning of NK activity. *Journal of Immunology, 135,* 848–852.

Gibbons, F. X. (1990). Self-attention and behavior: A review and theoretical update. In M. P. Zanna (Ed.), *Advances in experimental social psychology,* (Vol. 23, pp. 249–303). New York: Academic Press.

Gibson, E., & Walk, R. D. (1960). The visual cliff. *Scientific American, 202,* 80–92.

Gibson, E. J., & Walker, A. S. (1984). Development of knowledge of visual-tactual affordances of substance. *Child Development, 55,* 453–461.

Gibson, J. J. (1962). Observations on active touch. *Psychological Review, 69,* 477–491.

Gibson, J. J. (1979). *The ecological approach to visual perception.* Boston: Houghton Mifflin.

Gick, M. L., & Holyoak, K. J. (1980). Analogical problem solving. *Cognitive Psychology, 12,* 306–355.

Gilbert, A. N., & Wysocki, C. J. (1987, October). The smell survey results. *National Geographic,* 514–525.

Gilbert, D. T. (1989). Thinking lightly about others: Automatic components of the social inference process. In J. S. Uleman & J. A. Bargh (Eds.), *Unintended thought: Limits of awareness, intention, and control* (pp. 189–211). New York: Guilford Press.

Gillie, O. (1976, October 24). Crucial data was faked by eminent psychologist. *London Sunday Times.*

Gilligan, C. (1982). *In a different voice: Psychological theory and women's development.* Cambridge, MA: Harvard University Press.

Gilovich, T. (1983). Biased evaluation and persistence in gambling. *Journal of Personality and Social Psychology, 40,* 797–808.

Gilovich, T. (1991). *How we know what isn't so: The fallibility of human reason in everyday life.* New York: Free Press.

Ginsburg, H., & Opper, S. (1988). *Piaget's theory of intellectual development* (3rd ed.). Englewood Cliffs, NJ: Prentice-Hall.

Gitlin, M. J. (1990). *The psychotherapist's guide to psychopharmacology.* New York: Free Press.

Glanzer, M., & Cunitz, A. (1966). Two storage mechanisms in free recall. *Journal of Verbal Learning and Verbal Behavior, 5,* 351–360.

Glaser, R. (1990). The reemergence of learning theory within instructional research. *American Psychologist, 45,* 29–39.

Glasgow, R. E., & Lichtenstein, E. (1987). Long-term effects of behavioral smoking cessation interventions. *Behavior Therapy, 18,* 297–324.

Glass, A. L., & Holyoak, K. J. (1986). *Cognition* (2nd ed.). New York: Random House.

Glass, D. C. (1977). *Behavior patterns, stress, and coronary disease.* Hillsdale, NJ: Erlbaum.

Gleicher, F., & Petty, R. E. (1992). Expectations of reassurance influence the nature of fear-stimulated attitude change. *Journal of Experimental Social Psychology, 28,* 86–100.

Glenn, N. D. (1990). Quantitative research on marital quality in the 1980s: A critical review. *Journal of Marriage and the Family, 52,* 818–831.

Glick, P., Zion, C., & Nelson, C. (1988). What mediates sex discrimination in hiring decisions? *Journal of Personality and Social Psychology, 55,* 178–186.

Goddard, H. H. (1917). Mental tests and the immigrant. *The Journal of Delinquency, 2,* 243–277.

Godden, D. R., & Baddeley, A. D. (1975). Context-dependent memory in two natural environments: On land and underwater. *British Journal of Psychology, 66,* 325–332.

Goebel, B. L., & Brown, D. (1981). Age differences in motivation related to Maslow's need hierarchy. *Developmental Psychology, 17,* 809–815.

Goethals, G. R., & Reckman, R. F. (1973). The perception of consistency in attitudes. *Journal of Experimental Social Psychology, 9,* 491–501.

Gold, P. E. (1992). Modulation of memory processing: Enhancement of memory in rodents and humans. In L. Squire & N. Butters (Eds.), *Neuropsychology of memory* (2nd ed., pp. 402–414). New York: Guilford Press.

Gold, P. E. (1993). *Cognitive enhancers in animals and humans: From hormones to brains.* Paper presented at the annual meeting of the American Psychological Society. Chicago, IL.

Goldberg, J., True, W. R., Eisen, S. A., & Henderson, W. G. (1990). A twin study of the effects of the Vietnam war on posttraumatic stress disorder. *Journal of the American Medical Association, 263,* 1227–1232.

Goldberg, L. R. (1990). An alternative "description of personality": The big-five factor structure. *Journal of Personality and Social Psychology, 59,* 1216–1229.

Goldberg, L. R. (1993). The structure of phenotypic personality. *American Psychologist, 48,* 26–34.

Goldberg, L. R., Grenier, J. R., Guion, R., Sechrest, L. B., & Wing, H. (1991). *Questionnaires used in the prediction of trustworthiness in pre-employment selection decisions: An A.P.A. Task Force Report.* Washington, DC: American Psychological Association.

Goldfried, M. R., & Robbins, C. (1982). On the facilitation of self-efficacy. *Cognitive Therapy and Research, 6,* 361–380.

Golding, S. L. (1992). The adjudication of criminal responsibility: A review of theory and research. In D. Kagehiro & W. Laufer (Eds.), *Handbook of psychology and law.* New York: Springer-Verlag.

Goldman-Rakic, P. S. (1987). Development of cortical circuitry and cognitive function. *Child Development, 58,* 601–622.

Goldsmith, H. H., & Lansky, J. A. (1987). Maternal and infant temperamental predictors of attachment: A meta-analytic review. *Journal of Consulting and Clinical Psychology, 55,* 805–816.

Goldstein, A. G., Chance, J. E., & Schneller, G. R. (1989). Frequency of eyewitness identification in criminal cases: A survey of prosecutors. *Bulletin of the Psychonomic Society, 27,* 71–74.

Goleman, D. (1989, October 17). Critics challenge reliance on drugs in psychiatry. *New York Times,* p. C1.

Goleman, D. (1990, December 25). The group and the self: New focus on a cultural rift. *New York Times,* pp. 37, 41.

Goleman, D., & Gurin, J. (Eds.). (1993). *Mind body medicine.* Yonkers, NY: Consumer Reports Books.

Good, B. J., & Kleinman, A. M. (1985). Culture and anxiety: Cross-cultural evidence for the patterning of anxiety disorders. In A. H. Tuma & J. D. Maser (Eds.), *Anxiety and the anxiety disorders.* Hillsdale, NJ: Erlbaum.

Good, K., & Chanoff, D. (1991). *Into the heart.* New York: Simon & Schuster.

Goodall, J. (1986). *The chimpanzees of Gombe: Patterns of behavior.* Cambridge, MA: Harvard University Press.

Goodard, H. H. (1917). Mental tests and the immigrant. *Journal of Delinquency, 2,* 243–277.

Goodman, G. S., Aman, C., & Hirschman, J. (1987). Child sexual and physical abuse. In S. Ceci, M. Toglia, & D. Ross (Eds.), *Children's eyewitness testimony* (pp. 1–23). New York: Springer-Verlag.

Goodman, G. S., Hirschman, J., Hepps, D., & Rudy, L. (1991). Children's memory for stressful events. *Merrill Palmer Quarterly, 37,* 109–158.

Goodwin, F. K., & Jamison, K. R. (1990). *Manic depressive illness.* New York: Oxford University Press.

Gordon, S. (1986, October). What kids need to know. *Psychology Today,* pp. 22–26.

Gordun, S., & Gillun, J. F. (1987). Adolescent sexuality. In V. B. Van Hasselt & M. Hersen (Eds.), *Handbook of adolescent psychology.* New York: Pergamon Press.

Gorman, J. M., Liebowitz, M. R., Fyer, A. J., & Stein, J. (1989). A neuroanatomical hypothesis for panic disorder. *American Journal of Psychiatry, 146,* 148–161.

Gormley, F. F., & Aiello, J. R. (1982). Social density, interpersonal relationships, and residential crowding stress. *Journal of Applied Social Psychology, 12,* 22–36.

Gorski, R. A., Gordon, J. H., Shryne, J. E., & Southam, A. M. (1978). Evidence for a morphological sex difference within the medial preoptic area of the rat brain. *Brain Research, 143,* 333–346.

Gottesman, I. I. (1991). *Schizophrenia genesis: The origins of madness.* San Francisco: W. H. Freeman.

Gottesman, I. I., & Shields, J. (1982). *Schizophrenia: The epigenetic puzzle.* New York: Cambridge University Press.

Gouchie, C. T., & Kimura, D. (1991). The relationship between testosterone levels and cognitive ability patterns. *Psychoneuroendocrinology, 16,* 323–334.

Gough, H. G. (1984). A managerial potential scale for the California Psychological Inventory. *Journal of Applied Psychology, 69,* 233–240.

Gould, J. L., & Marler, P. (1987). Learning by instinct. *Scientific American, 256* (1), 74–75.

Gould, R. L. (1978). *Transformations: Growth and change in adult life.* New York: Simon & Schuster.

Graham, J. R. (1990). *MMPI-2: Assessing personality and psychopathology.* New York: Oxford University Press.

Granberg, D., & Brent, E. (1983). When prophecy bends: The preference-expectation link in U.S. presidential elections. *Journal of Personality and Social Psychology, 45,* 477–491.

Green, D. M., & Swets, J. A. (1966). *Signal detection theory and psychophysics.* New York: Wiley.

Greene, W. C. (1993, September). AIDS and the immune system. *Scientific American,* pp. 99–105.

Greenough, W. T., Black, J. E., Isaacs, K., Anderson, B., & Alcantara, A. (1990, July). *Neurobiology.*

Greenough, W. T., Black, J. E., & Wallace, C. S. (1987). Experience and brain development. *Child Development, 58,* 539–559.

Greenwald, A. G. (1980). The totalitarian ego: Fabrication and revision of personal history. *American Psychologist, 35,* 603–618.

Greenwald, A. G. (1992). New Look 3: Unconscious cognition reclaimed. *American Psychologist, 47,* 766–779.

Greenwald, A. G., & Banaji, M. R. (1989). The self as a memory system: Powerful but ordinary. *Journal of Personality and Social Psychology, 57,* 41–54.

Greenwald, A. G., Spangenberg, E. R., Pratkanis, A. R., & Eskenazi, J. (1991). Double-blind tests of subliminal self-help audiotapes. *Psychological Science, 2,* 119–122.

Gregory, R. L. (1990). *Eye and brain: The psychology of seeing* (4th ed.). Princeton, NJ: Princeton University Press.

Greif, E. B., & Ulman, K. J. (1982). The psychological impact of menarche on early adolescent females: A review of the literature. *Child Development, 53,* 1413–1430.

Griffin, D. R. (1992). *Animal minds.* Chicago: University of Chicago Press.

Griggs, R. A., & Cox, J. R. (1982). The elusive thematic-materials effect in Wason's selection task. *British Journal of Psychology, 73,* 407–420.

Gross, A. E., & Crofton, C. (1977). What is good is beautiful. *Sociometry, 40,* 85–90.

Gross, C. G., Rocha-Miranda, E. C., & Bender, D. B. (1972). Visual properties of neurons in the inferotemporal cortex of the macaque. *Journal of Neurophysiology, 35,* 96–111.

Grossman, M., & Wood, W. (1993). Sex differences in intensity of emotional experience: A social role interpretation. *Journal of Personality and Social Psychology, 65,* 1010–1022.

Grunwald, L., & Goldberg, J. (1993, July). The amazing minds of infants. *Life,* pp. 46–56.

Grush, J. E. (1976). Attitude formation and mere exposure phenomena: A nonartifactual explanation of empirical findings. *Journal of Personality and Social Psychology, 33,* 281–290.

Guerin, B. (1986). Mere presence effects in humans: A review. *Journal of Experimental Social Psychology, 22,* 38–77.

Guilford, J. P. (1967). *The nature of human intelligence.* New York: McGraw-Hill.

Guilford, J. P. (1985). The structure-of-intellect model. In B. B. Wolman (Ed.), *Handbook of intelligence: Theories, measurements, and applications* (pp. 225–266). New York: Wiley.

Guinness Book of World Records (1994). New York: Bantam Books.

Guion, R. M. (1965). *Personnel testing.* New York: McGraw-Hill.

Gump, P. V. (1987). School and classroom environments. In D. Stokols & I. Altman (Eds.), *Handbook of Environmental Psychology* (Vol. 1). New York: John Wiley & Sons.

Gunderson, J. G. (1984). *Borderline personality disorder.* Washington, DC: American Psychiatric Press.

Gurman, A. S., Kniskern, D. P., & Pinsof, W. M. (1986). Research on the process and outcome of marital and family therapy. In S. L. Garfield & A. E. Bergin (Eds.), *Handbook of psychotherapy and behavior change* (2nd ed.). New York: Wiley.

Guttman, N., & Kalish, H. (1956). Discriminability and stimulus generalization. *Journal of Experimental Psychology, 51,* 79–88.

Gwaltney, L. (1986). *The dissenters.* New York: Random House.

Haaga, D., & Davison, G. C. (1993). An appraisal of rational-emotive therapy. *Journal of Consulting and Clinical Psychology, 61,* 215–220.

Haaga, D. A., Dyck, M. J., & Ernst, D. (1991). Empirical status of cognitive theory of depression. *Psychological Bulletin, 110,* 215–236.

Haddock, G., Zanna, M. P., & Esses, V. M. (1993). Assessing the structure of prejudicial attitudes: The case of attitudes toward homosexuals. *Journal of Personality and Social Psychology, 65,* 1105–1118.

Hailman, J. P. (1969). How an instinct is learned. *Scientific American, 221,* 98–106.

Haist, F., Shimamura, A. P., & Squire, L. R. (1992). On the relationship between recall and recognition memory. *Journal of Experimental Psychology: Learning, Memory, and Cognition, 18,* 691–702.

Haith, M. (1980). *Rules that babies look by.* Hillsdale, NJ: Erlbaum.

Hall, C. S., & Van de Castle, R. (1966). *The content analysis of dreams.* New York: Appleton-Century-Crofts.

Hall, D. T. (1976). *Careers in organizations.* Glenview, IL: Scott, Foresman.

Hall, G. S. (1904). *Adolescence.* New York: Appleton-Century-Crofts.

Hall, J. A. (1984). *Nonverbal sex differences: Communication accuracy and expressive style.* Baltimore: Johns Hopkins University Press.

Hall, J. A., & Veccia, E. M. (1990). More "touching" observations: New insights on men, women, and interpersonal touch. *Journal of Personality and Social Psychology, 59,* 1155–1162.

Halpern, A. R. (1986). Memory for tune titles after organized or unorganized presentation. *American Journal of Psychology, 99,* 57–70.

Halpern, A. R., & Deveraux, S. D. (1989). Lucky numbers: Choice strategies in the Pennsylvania Number game. *Bulletin of the Psychonomic Society, 27,* 167–170.

Halpern, D. F. (1992). *Sex differences in cognitive abilities.* Hillsdale, NJ: Erlbaum.

Halpern, D. F., & Coren, S. (1993). Left-handedness and life span: A reply to Harris. *Psychological Bulletin, 114,* 235–241.

Hamilton, D. L., & Zanna, M. P. (1974). Context effects in impression formation: Changes in connotative meaning. *Journal of Personality and Social Psychology, 29,* 649–654.

Hamilton, M. C. (1988). Using masculine generics: Does generic "he" increase male bias in the user's imagery? *Sex Roles, 19,* 785–799.

Hampson, E., & Kimura, D. (1988). Reciprocal effects of hormonal fluctuations on human motor and perceptual-spatial skills. *Behavioral Neuroscience, 102,* 456–459.

Hampson, E., & Kimura, D. (1992). Sex differences and hormonal influences on cognitive function in humans. In J. B. Becker, S. M. Breedlove, & D. Crews (Eds.), *Behavioral endocrinology* (pp. 357–398). Cambridge, MA: MIT Press.

Handel, A. (1987). Personal theories about the life-span development of one's self in autobiographical self-presentations of adults. *Human Development, 30,* 83–98.

Hanna, E., & Meltzoff, A. N. (1993). Peer imitation by toddlers in laboratory, home, and day-care contexts: Implications for social learning and memory. *Developmental Psychology, 29,* 701–710.

Hansen, C. H. (1989). Priming sex-role stereotypic event schemas with rock music videos: Effects on impression favorability, trait inferences, and recall of a subsequent male-female interaction. *Basic and Applied Social Psychology, 10,* 371–391.

Hansen, C. H., & Hansen, R. D. (1988). Finding the face in the crowd: An anger superiority effect. *Journal of Personality and Social Psychology, 54,* 917–924.

Harbin, T. J. (1989). The relationship between the Type A behavior pattern and physiological responsivity: Quantitative review. *Psychophysiology, 26,* 110–119.

Hardaway, R. A. (1990). Subliminally activated symbolic fantasies: Facts and artifacts. *Psychological Bulletin, 107,* 177–195.

Hardin, C., & Banaji, M. R. (1993). The influence of language on thought. *Social Cognition, 11,* 277–308.

Hare, R. D., Hart, S. D., & Harpur, T. (1991). Psychopathy and the DSM-IV criteria for antisocial personality disorder. *Journal of Abnormal Psychology, 100,* 391–398.

Hare, R. D., McPherson, L. M., & Forth, A. E. (1988). Male psychopaths and their criminal careers. *Journal of Consulting and Clinical Psychology, 56,* 710–714.

Harkins, D. A., & Uzgiris, I. C. (1991). Hand-use matching between mothers and infants during the first year. *Infant Behavior and Development, 14,* 289–298.

Harlow, H. F. (1958). The nature of love. *American Psychologist, 13,* 673–685.

Harlow, H. F. (1971). *Learning to love.* San Francisco: Albion.

Harlow, J. M. (1868). Recovery from the passage of an iron bar through the head. *Massachusetts Medical Society Publication, 2,* 327–347.

Harris, B. (1979). Whatever happened to Little Albert? *American Psychologist, 34,* 151–160.

Harris, L. (1987). *Inside America.* New York: Vintage Books.

Harris, L. J. (1988). Right-brain training: Some reflections on the application of research on cerebral hemispheric specialization to education. In D. L. Molfese & S. J. Segalowitz (Eds.), *Brain lateralization in children,* pp. 207–235. New York: Guilford Press.

Harris, L. J. (1993). Do left-handers die sooner than right-handers? Commentary on Coren and Halpern's (1991) "Left-handedness: A marker for decreased survival fitness. *Psychological Bulletin, 114,* 203–234.

Harris, M. J., & Rosenthal, R. (1985). Mediation of interpersonal expectancy effects. *Psychological Bulletin, 97,* 363–386.

Harris, P. L., & Kavanaugh, R. D. (1993). Young children's understanding of pretense. *Monographs of the Society for Research in Child Development, 58*(1, Serial No. 231).

Harris, R. J., & Monaco, G. E. (1978). Psychology of pragmatic implication: Information processing between the lines. *Journal of Experimental Psychology: General, 107,* 1–22.

Harrison, A. A., & Saeed, L. (1977). Let's make a deal: An analysis of revelations and stipulations in lonely hearts advertisements. *Journal of Personality and Social Psychology, 35,* 257–264.

Hart, S. D., Knapp, P. R., & Hare, R. D. (1988). Performance of male psychopaths following conditional release from prison. *Journal of Consulting and Clinical Psychology, 56,* 227–232.

Hartshorne, H., & May, M. (1928). *Studies in deceit.* New York: Macmillan.

Hartup, W. W. (1989). Social relationships and their developmental significance. *American Psychologist, 44,* 120–126.

Hasher, L., & Zacks, R. T. (1984). Automatic processing of fundamental information: The case of frequency. *American Psychologist, 39,* 1372–1388.

Hassett, J. (1978). *A primer of psychophysiology.* San Francisco: W. H. Freeman.

Hatch, J. P. (1993). Headache. In R. J. Gatchel & E. B. Blanchard (Eds.), *Psychophysiological disorders* (pp. 111–150). Washington, DC: American Psychological Association.

Hatch, J. P., Fisher, J. G., & Rugh, J. D. (1987). *Biofeedback: Studies in clinical efficacy.* New York: Plenum.

Hatfield, E. (1988). Passionate and companionate love. In R. J. Sternberg & M. L. Barnes (Eds.), *The psychology of love.* New Haven, CT: Yale University Press.

Hatfield, E., & Sprecher, S. (1986). *Mirror, mirror . . . The importance of looks in everyday life.* Albany, New York: State University of New York Press.

Hathaway, S. R., & McKinley, J. C. (1983). *Minnesota Multiphasic Personality Inventory: Manual for administration and scoring.* New York: Psychological Corporation.

Hawkins, S. A., & Hastie, R. (1990). Hindsight: Biased judgments of past events after the outcomes are known. *Psychological Bulletin, 107,* 311–327.

Hayes, C. (1951). *The ape in our house.* New York: Harper.

Hayes, C. D. (Ed.). (1987). *Risking the future* (Vol. 1). Washington, DC: National Academy Press.

Hazelrigg, M. D., Cooper, H. M., & Borduin, C. (1987). Evaluating the effectiveness of family therapies: An integrative review and analysis. *Psychological Bulletin, 101,* 428–442.

He, L. F. (1987). Involvement of endogenous opioid peptides in acupuncture analgesia. *Pain, 31,* 99–121.

Hearnshaw, L. S. (1979). *Cyril Burt: Psychologist.* Ithaca, New York: Cornell University Press.

Heatherton, T. F., & Weinberger, J. L. (Eds.). (1994). *Can personality change?* Washington, DC: American Psychological Association.

Heider, F. (1958). *The psychology of interpersonal relations.* New York: Wiley.

Heister, G., Landis, T., Regard, M., & Schroeder-Heister, P. (1989). Shifts of functional cerebral asymmetry during the menstrual cycle. *Neuropsychologica, 27,* 871–880.

Helgesen, S. (1990). *The female advantage: Women's ways of leadership.* New York: Doubleday Currency.

Heller, M. A., & Schiff, W. (Eds.). (1991). *The psychology of touch: Theory and application.* Hillsdale, NJ: Erlbaum.

Hellige, J. B. (1990). Hemispheric asymmetry. *Annual Review of Psychology, 41,* 55–80.

Helmes, E., & Reddon, J. R. (1993). A perspective on developments in assessing psychopathology: A critical review of the MMPI-2. *Psychological Bulletin, 113,* 453–471.

Helmholtz, H. von. (1852). On the theory of compound colours. *Philosophical Magazine, 4,* 519–534.

Helms, J. E. (1992). Why is there no study of cultural equivalence in standardized cognitive ability testing? *American Psychologist, 47,* 1083–1101.

Hendrick, S. S. (1981). Self-disclosure and marital satisfaction. *Journal of Personality and Social Psychology, 40,* 1150–1159.

Henley, N. M. (1977). *Body politics: Power, sex, and nonverbal communication.* Englewood Cliffs, NJ: Prentice-Hall.

Hennessey, B. A., & Amabile, T. M. (1988). The conditions of creativity. In R. J. Sternberg (Ed.), *The nature of creativity* (pp. 11–38). New York: Cambridge University Press.

Henry, K. R. (1984). Cochlear damage resulting from exposure to four different octave bands of noise at three different ages. *Behavioral Neuroscience, 1,* 107–117.

Henry, W. A. (1994). Pride and prejudice. *Time,* June 27, pp. 54–59.

Hensel, H. (1981). *Thermoreception and temperature regulation.* London: Academic Press.

Henslin, J. M. (1967). Craps and magic. *American Journal of Sociology, 73,* 316–330.

Hepper, P. G., Shahidullah, S., & White, R. (1990). Origins of fetal handedness. *Nature, 347,* 431.

Hepworth, J. T., & West, S. G. (1988). Lynchings and the economy: A time-series reanalysis of Hovland and Sears (1940). *Journal of Personality and Social Psychology, 55,* 239–247.

Herbert, T. B., & Cohen, S. (1993a). Depression and immunity: A meta-analytic review. *Psychological Bulletin, 113,* 472–486.

Herbert, T. B., & Cohen, S. (1993b). Stress and immunity in humans: A meta-analytic review. *Psychosomatic Medicine, 55,* 364–379.

Herek, G. M. (1988). Heterosexuals' attitudes toward lesbians and gay men: Correlates and gender differences. *Journal of Sex Research, 25,* 451–477.

Herenk, R. (Ed.). (1980). *The psychotherapy handbook: The A to Z guide to more than 250 therapies in use today.* New York: New American Library.

Hering, E. (1878). *Outlines of a theory of the light sense* (L. Hurvich & D. Jameson, Trans.). Cambridge, MA: Harvard University Press.

Herman, C. P., Zanna, M. P., & Higgins, E. T. (1986). *Physical appearance, stigma, and social behavior: The Ontario Symposium* (Vol. 3). Hillsdale, NJ: Erlbaum.

Herman, L. M., Kuczaj, S. A., & Holder, M. D. (1993). Responses to anomalous gestural sequences by a language-trained dolphin: Evidence for processing of semantic relations and syntactic information. *Journal of Experimental Psychology: General, 122,* 184–194.

Hermann, D.H.J. (1983). *The insanity defense: Philosophical, historical, and legal perspectives.* Springfield, IL: C. C. Thomas.

Herrnstein, R. J., Nickerson, R. S., de Sanchez, M., & Swets, J. A. (1986). Teaching thinking skills. *American Psychologist, 41,* 1279–1289.

Hershenson, M. (Ed.). (1989). *The moon illusion*. Hillsdale, NJ: Erlbaum.

Hertz, M. R. (1986). Rorschach bound: A 50-year memoir. *Journal of Personality Assessment, 50*, 396–416.

Hertzog, C. (1989). Influences of cognitive slowing on age differences in intelligence. *Developmental Psychology, 25*, 636–651.

Hess, E. H. (1959). Imprinting. *Science, 130*, 133–144.

Hess, R. D., & Miura, I. T. (1985). Gender differences in enrollment in computer camps and classes. *Sex Roles, 13*, 193–203.

Heston, L. L., & White, J. A. (1991). *The vanishing mind: A practical guide to Alzheimer's disease and other dementias*. New York: W. H. Freeman.

Hetherington, A. W., & Ranson, S. W. (1942). The spontaneous activity and food intake of rats with hypothalamic lesions. *American Journal of Physiology, 136*, 609–617.

Hetherington, E. M., Reiss, D., & Plomin, R. (Eds.). (1994). *Separate social worlds of siblings: The impact of nonshared environment on development*. Hillsdale, NJ: Erlbaum.

Hewstone, M., & Jaspars, J. (1987). Covariation and causal attribution: A logical model of the intuitive analysis of variance. *Journal of Personality and Social Psychology, 53*, 663–672.

Heyser, C. J., Spear, N. E., & Spear, L. P. (1993). Effects of prenatal exposure to cocaine on conditional discrimination learning in adult rats. *Behavioral Neuroscience, 106*, 837–845.

Hickey, N. (1992, August 22). How much violence? *TV Guide*, pp. 10–11.

Higgins, E. T. (1989). Self-discrepancy theory: What patterns of self-beliefs cause people to suffer? In L. Berkowitz (Ed.), *Advances in experimental social psychology* (Vol. 22, pp. 93–136). New York: Academic Press.

Higgins, E. T., Bond, R. N., Klein, R., & Strauman, T. (1986). Self-discrepancies and emotional vulnerability: How magnitude, accessibility, and type of discrepancy influence affect. *Journal of Personality and Social Psychology, 51*, 5–15.

Higgins, R. L., Snyder, C. R., & Berglas, S. (1990). *Self-handicapping: The paradox that isn't*. New York: Plenum.

Hilgard, E. R. (1982). Hypnotic susceptibility and implications for measurement. *International Journal of Clinical and Experimental Hypnosis, 30*, 394–403.

Hilgard, E. R. (1986). *Divided consciousness: Multiple controls in human thought and action*. New York: Wiley-Interscience.

Hilgard, E. R. (1987). *Psychology in America: A historical survey*. San Diego: Harcourt Brace Jovanovich.

Hilgard, E. R. (1992). Divided consciousness and dissociation. *Consciousness and Cognition, 1*, 16–31.

Hilgard, E. R., Morgan, A. H., & MacDonald, H. (1975). Pain and dissociation in the cold pressor test: A study of "hidden reports" through automatic key-pressing and automatic talking. *Journal of Abnormal Psychology, 84*, 280–289.

Hilgard, J. R. (1979). *Personality and hypnosis: A study of imaginative involvement*. Chicago: University of Chicago Press.

Hill, J. P. (1988). Adapting to menarche: Familial control and conflict. In M. R. Gunnar & W. A. Collins (Eds.), *Development during the transition to adolescence: The Minnesota symposia on child psychology* (pp. 43–77). Hillsdale, NJ: Erlbaum.

Hill, R. M., Hegemeir, S., & Tennyson, L. M. (1989). The fetal alcohol syndrome: A multihandicapped child. *Neuro-Toxicology, 10*, 585–596.

Hilton, J. L., & Darley, J. M. (1991). The effects of interaction goals on person perception. *Advances in Experimental Social Psychology, 24*, 235–267.

Hines, M. (1982). Prenatal gonadal hormones and sex differences in human behavior. *Psychological Bulletin, 92*, 56–80.

Hirsch, E. D., Jr. (1987). *Cultural literacy: What every American needs to know*. Boston: Houghton Mifflin.

Hirt, E. R., Deppe, R. K., & Gordon, L. J. (1991). Self-reported versus behavioral self-handicapping: Empirical evidence for a theoretical distinction. *Journal of Personality and Social Psychology, 61*, 981–991.

Hobbes, T. (1919). *Leviathan*. London: J. M. Dent. (Original work published 1651)

Hobson, J. A. (1988). *The dreaming brain*. New York: Basic Books.

Hobson, J. A. (1989). *Sleep*. New York: Scientific American.

Hobson, J. A., & McCarley, R. W. (1977). The brain as a dream state generator: An activational-synthesis hypothesis of the dream process. *American Journal of Psychiatry, 134*, 1335–1348.

Hochberg, J. E. (1978). *Perception* (2nd ed). Englewood Cliffs, NJ: Prentice-Hall.

Hochschild, A. R. (1989). *The second shift: Working parents and the revolution at home*. New York: Viking.

Hoffer, B. J., & Olson, L. (1991). Ethical issues in brain cell transplantation. *Trends in the Neurosciences, 14*, 384–388.

Hoffman, C., Lau, I., & Johnson, D. R. (1986). The linguistic relativity of person cognition: An English-Chinese comparison. *Journal of Personality and Social Psychology, 51*, 1097–1105.

Hoffman, E. (1989). *Lost in translation: A life in a new language*. New York: Dutton.

Hoffman, L. W. (1989). Effects of maternal employment in the two-parent family. *American Psychologist, 44*, 283–292.

Hoffman, M. L. (1984). Empathy, its limitations, and its role in a comprehensive moral theory. In J. Gewirtz & W. Kurtines (Eds.), *Morality, moral development, and moral behavior* (pp. 283–302). New York: Wiley.

Hoffner, C., & Badzinski, D. M. (1989). Children's integration of facial and situational cues to emotion. *Child Development, 60*, 411–422.

Hofstede, G. (1980). *Culture's consequences*. Beverly Hills, CA: Sage.

Hogan, J., & Hogan, R. (1989). How to measure employee reliability. *Journal of Applied Psychology, 74*, 273–279.

Hogg, M. A., & Abrams, D. (1990). Social motivation, self-esteem and social identity. In D. Abrams & M. Hogg (Eds.), *Social identity theory: Constructive and critical advances* (pp. 28–47). New York: Springer-Verlag.

Holahan, C. K. (1988). Relation of life goals at age 70 to activity participation and health and psychological well-being among Terman's gifted men and women. *Psychology and Aging, 3*, 286–291.

Holden, C. (1980, November). Twins reunited. *Science, 80*, 55–59.

Holden, C. (1987, September). Genes and behavior: A twin legacy. *Psychology Today*, pp. 18–19.

Holding, D. H. (1989). *Human skills* (2nd ed.). New York: John Wiley.

Hollandsworth, J. G., Jr. (1990). *The physiology of psychological disorders*. New York: Plenum.

Hollins, M., Faldowski, R., Rao, S., & Young, F. (1993). Perceptual dimensions of tactile surface texture: A multidimensional scaling analysis. *Perception and Psychophysics, 54*, 697–705.

Hollon, S. D., Shelton, R. C., & Loosen, P. T. (1991). Cognitive therapy and pharmacotherapy for depression. *Journal of Consulting and Clinical Psychology, 59*, 88–99.

Holmes, T. H., & Rahe, R. H. (1967). The Social Readjustment Rating Scale. *Journal of Psychosomatic Research, 11*, 213–218.

Holtgraves, T., & Bailey, C. (1991). Premise acceptability and message effectiveness. *Basic and Applied Social Psychology, 12*, 157–176.

Holyoak, K. J. (1990). Problem solving. In D. M. Osherson & E. E. Smith (Eds.), *Thinking: An invitation to cognitive science* (Vol. 3). Cambridge, MA: MIT Press.

Holyoak, K. J., & Spellman, B. A. (1993). Thinking. *Annual Review of Psychology, 44*, 265–315.

Holzman, P. S., & Matthysse, S. (1990). The genetics of schizophrenia: A review. *Psychological Science, 1*, 279–286.

Honts, C. R., Raskin, D. C., and Kircher, J. C. (1994). Mental and physical countermeasures reduce the accuracy of polygraph tests. *Journal of Applied Psychology, 79,* 252–259.

Hooper, J., & Teresi, D. (1986). *The 3-pound universe—the brain.* New York: Laurel.

Hoorens, V., & Nuttin, J. M. (1993). Overvaluation of own attributes: Mere ownership or subjective frequency? *Social Cognition, 11,* 177–200.

Horn, J. C. (1987). Bigger pay for better work. *Psychology Today, 21*(1), 54–57.

Horn, J. L. (1982). The aging of human abilities. In B. B. Wolman (Ed.), *Handbook of developmental psychology* (pp. 847–870). Englewood Cliffs, NJ: Prentice-Hall.

Horn, J. L., & Cattell, R. C. (1966). Refinement and test of the theory of fluid and crystallized general intelligences. *Journal of Educational Psychology, 57,* 253–270.

Horne, J. (1988). *Why we sleep.* Oxford: Oxford University Press.

Horne, J., & Minard, A. (1985). Sleep and sleepiness following a behaviorally "active" day. *Ergonomics, 28,* 567–575.

Horner, K. L., Rushton, J. P., & Vernon, P. A. (1986). Relation between aging and research productivity of academic psychologists. *Psychology and Aging, 1,* 319–324.

Horney, K. (1945). *Our inner conflicts.* New York: Norton.

Horowitz, I. A., & Willging, T. E. (1991). Changing views of jury power: The nullification debate, 1787–1988. *Law and Human Behavior, 15,* 165–182.

Horvath, A. O., & Luborsky, L. (1993). The role of the therapeutic alliance in psychotherapy. *Journal of Consulting and Clinical Psychology, 61,* 561–573.

Horvath, A. O., & Symonds, B. D. (1991). Relation between working alliance and outcome in psychotherapy: A meta-analysis. *Journal of Counseling Psychology, 38,* 139–149.

Horvath, F. (1984). Detecting deception in eyewitness cases: Problems and prospects in use of the polygraph. In G. Wells & E. Loftus (Eds.), *Eyewitness testimony: Psychological perspectives* (pp. 214–255). New York: Cambridge University Press.

Hothersall, D. (1990). *History of psychology* (2nd ed.). New York: McGraw-Hill.

House, J. S., Landis, K. R., & Umberson, D. (1988). Social relationships and health. *Science, 241,* 540–545.

Hovland, C. I., & Sears, R. R. (1940). Minor studies in aggression: VI. Correlation of lynchings with economic indices. *Journal of Psychology, 9,* 301–310.

Howard, A., & Bray, D. W. (1988). *Managerial lives in transition.* New York: Guilford Press.

Howard, I. P. (1986). The perception of posture, self-motion, and the visual vertical. In K. R. Boff, L. Kaufman, & J. P. Thomas (Eds.), *Handbook of perception and human performance* (Vol. I). New York: Wiley.

Howard, K. I., Kopta, S. M., Krause, M. S., & Orlinsky, D. E. (1986). The dose-effect relationship in psychotherapy. *American Psychologist, 41,* 159–164.

Howard, K. I., Lueger, R. L., Maling, M. S., & Martinovich, Z. (1993). A phase model of psychotherapy outcome: Causal mediation of change. *Journal of Consulting and Clinical Psychology, 61,* 678–685.

Howe, M. L., & Courage, M. L. (1993). On resolving the enigma of infantile amnesia. *Psychological Bulletin, 113,* 305–326.

Howes, J. L., & Katz, A. N. (1988). Assessing remote memory with an improved public events questionnaire. *Psychology and Aging, 3,* 142–150.

Hubel, D. H. (1979). The brain. *Scientific American.*

Hubel, D. H. (1988). *Eye, brain, and vision.* New York: Scientific American Library.

Hubel, D. H., & Wiesel, T. N. (1962). Receptive fields, binocular interaction and functional architecture in the cat's visual cortex. *Journal of Physiology, 160,* 106–154.

Hubel, D. H., & Wiesel, T. N. (1979). Brain mechanisms of vision. *Scientific American, 241,* 150–162.

Hudson, W. (1960). Pictorial depth perception in sub-cultural groups in Africa. *Journal of Social Psychology, 52,* 183–208.

Hudspeth, A. J. (1985). The cellular basis of hearing: The biophysics of hair cells. *Science, 230,* 745–752.

Huesmann, L. R., & Eron, L. D. (Eds.). (1986). *Television and the aggressive child: A cross-national comparison.* Hillsdale, NJ: Erlbaum.

Huff, C., & Cooper, J. (1987). Sex bias in educational software: The effect of designers' stereotypes on the software they design. *Journal of Applied Social Psychology, 17,* 519–532.

Hugdahl, K., Satz, P., Mitrushina, M., & Miller, E. N. (1993). Left-handedness and old age: Do left-handers die earlier? *Neuropsychologia, 31,* 325–333.

Hughes, J., Smith, T. W., Kosterlitz, A. W., Fothergill, L. A., Morgan, B. A., & Morris, H. R. (1975). Identification of two related pentapeptides from the brain with potent opiate against activity. *Nature, 258,* 577–579.

Hui, C. H. (1988). Measurement of individualism-collectivism. *Journal of Research in Personality, 22,* 17–36.

Hull, J. G., & Young, R. D. (1983). Self-consciousness, self-esteem, and success-failure as determinants of alcohol consumption in male social drinkers. *Journal of Personality and Social Psychology, 44,* 1097–1109.

Hull, J. G., Young, R. D., & Jouriles, E. (1986). Applications of the self-awareness model of alcohol consumption: Predicting patterns of use and abuse. *Journal of Personality and Social Psychology, 51,* 790–796.

Hunt, E. (1983). On the nature of intelligence. *Science, 219,* 141–146.

Hunt, E., & Agnoli, F. (1991). The Whorfian hypothesis: A cognitive psychology perspective. *Psychological Review, 9,* 377–389.

Hunter, S., & Sundel, M. (Eds.). (1989). *Midlife myths: Issues, findings, and practice implications.* Newbury Park, CA: Sage.

Hurt, H. T., Scott, M. D., & McCroskey, J. C. (1978). *Communication in the classroom.* Reading, MA: Addison-Wesley.

Huxley, A. (1932). *Brave new world.* London: Chatto & Windus.

Hyde, J. S. (1994). Children's understanding of sexist language. *Developmental Psychology, 20,* 697–706.

Hyde, J. S., Fennema, E., & Lamon, S. (1990). Gender differences in mathematics performance: A meta-analysis. *Psychological Bulletin, 107,* 139–155.

Hyde, J. S., & Linn, M. C. (1988). Gender differences in verbal ability: A meta-analysis. *Psychological Bulletin, 104,* 53–69.

Hyman, R. (1989). *The elusive quarry: A scientific appraisal of psychical research.* Buffalo, New York: Prometheus Books.

Hyman, R. (1994). Anomaly or artifact? Comments on Bem and Honorton. *Psychological Bulletin, 115,* 19–24.

Iaccino, J. F. (1993). *Left brain-right brain differences: Inquiries, evidence, and new approaches.* Hillsdale, NJ: Erlbaum.

Ingham, A. G., Levinger, G., Graves, J., & Peckham, V. (1974). The Ringelmann effect: Studies of group size and group performance. *Journal of Experimental Social Psychology, 10,* 371–384.

Ingram, R. E. (1990). Self-focused attention in clinical disorders: Review and a conceptual model. *Psychological Bulletin, 107,* 156–176.

Inhelder, B., & Piaget, J. (1958). *The growth of logical thinking from childhood to adolescence.* New York: Basic Books.

Insel, T. R. (Ed.). (1984). *New findings in obsessive-compulsive disorder.* Washington, DC: American Psychiatric Press.

Intons-Peterson, M. (1993). Imaginal priming. *Journal of Experimental Psychology: Learning, Memory, and Cognition, 19,* 223–235.

Intraub, H., Bender, R. S., & Mangels, J. A. (1992). Looking at pictures but remembering scenes. *Journal of Experimental Psychology: Learning, Memory, and Cognition, 18,* 180–191.

Irons, E. D., & Moore, G. W. (1985). *Black managers: The case of the banking industry.* New York: Praeger.

Irwin, M., Smith, T. L., & Gillin, J. C. (1992). Electroencephalographic sleep and natural killer cell activity in depressed patients and control subjects. *Psychosomatic Medicine, 54,* 10–21.

Isabella, R. A., Belsky, J., & von Eye, A. (1989). *Developmental Psychology, 25,* 12–21.

Isen, A. M. (1987). Positive affect, cognitive processes, and social behavior. In L. Berkowitz (Ed.), *Advances in experimental social psychology* (Vol. 20, pp. 203–253). New York: Academic Press.

Isenberg, D. J. (1986). Group polarization: A critical review and meta-analysis. *Journal of Personality and Social Psychology, 50,* 1141–1151.

Izard, C. E. (1990). Facial expressions and the regulation of emotions. *Journal of Personality and Social Psychology, 58,* 487–498.

Izard, C. E. (1993). Four systems for emotion activation: Cognitive and noncognitive processes. *Psychological Review, 100,* 68–90.

Izard, C. E., Huebner, R., Risser, D., McGinnes, G., & Dougherty, L. (1980). The young infant's ability to produce discrete emotion expressions. *Developmental Psychology, 16,* 132–140.

Jacklin, C. N. (1989). Female and male: Issues of gender. *American Psychologist, 44,* 127–133.

Jackson, H. J. (1958). In J. Taylor (Ed.), *Selected writings of John Hughlings Jackson.* New York: Basic Books.

Jackson, L. A., Gardner, P. D., & Sullivan, L. A. (1992). Explaining gender differences in self-pay expectations: Social comparison standards and perceptions of fair pay. *Journal of Applied Psychology, 77,* 651–663.

Jacobs, J. E. (1991). Influence of gender stereotypes on parent and child mathematics attitudes. *Journal of Educational Psychology, 83,* 518–527.

Jacobson, E. (1932). Electrophysiology of mental activities. *American Journal of Psychology, 44,* 677–694.

Jacobson, S. W., Jacobson, J. L., Sokol, R. J., Martier, S. S., & Ager, J. W. (1993). Prenatal alcohol exposure and infant information processing ability. *Child Development, 64,* 1706–1721.

Jacoby, L. L., Kelley, C. M., Brown, J., & Jasechko, J. (1989). Becoming famous overnight: Limits on the ability to avoid unconscious influences of the past. *Journal of Personality and Social Psychology, 56,* 326–338.

Jacoby, L. L., Lindsay, D. S., & Toth, J. P. (1992). Unconscious influences revealed: Attention, awareness, and control. *American Psychologist, 47,* 802–809.

Jacoby, L. L., Toth, J. P., & Yonelinas, A. P. (1993). Separating conscious and unconscious influences on memory: Measuring recollection. *Journal of Experimental Psychology: General, 122,* 139–154.

James, B. (1982). *The Bill James Baseball Abstract.* New York: Ballantine.

James, W. (1884). What is an emotion? *Mind, 9,* 188–205.

James, W. (1890). *Principles of psychology* (Vols. 1–2). New York: Holt.

Jamieson, D. W., Lydon, J. E., Stewart, G., & Zanna, M. P. (1987). *Journal of Educational Psychology, 79,* 461–466.

Jamison, K. R. (1993). Touched with fire: Manic-depressive illness and the artistic temperament. New York: The Free Press.

Janicak, P. G., Davis, J. M., Gibbons, R. D., Ericksen, S., Chang, S., & Gallagher, P. (1985). Efficacy of ECT: A meta-analysis. *American Journal of Psychiatry, 142,* 297–302.

Janis, I. L. (1972). *Groupthink.* Boston: Houghton Mifflin.

Janis, I. L. (1982). *Groupthink* (2nd ed.). Boston: Houghton Mifflin.

Janis, I. L. (1989). *Crucial decisions: Leadership in policy-making and crisis management.* New York: Free Press.

Janiszewski, C., & Warlop, L. (1993). The influence of classical conditioning procedures on subsequent attention to the conditioned brand. *Journal of Consumer Research, 20,* 171–189.

Janus, S. S., & Janus, C. L. (1993). *The Janus Report on sexual behavior.* New York: Wiley.

Jaroff, L. (1993, November). Lies of the mind. *Time,* pp. 52–59.

Jemmott, J. B., III, & Magloire, K. (1988). Academic stress, social support, and secretory immunoglobin. *Journal of Personality and Social Psychology, 55,* 803–810.

Jenicke, M. A., Baer, L., & Minichiello, W. E. (1986). *Obsessive-compulsive disorders: Theory and management.* Littleton, MA: PSG.

Jenkins, J. G., & Dallenbach, K. M. (1924). Oblivescence during sleep and waking. *American Journal of Psychology, 35,* 605–612.

Jennings (Walstedt), J., Geis, F. L., & Brown, V. (1980). Influence of television commercials on women's self-confidence and independent judgment. *Journal of Personality and Social Psychology, 38,* 203–210.

Jensen, A. R. (1969). How much can we boost IQ and scholastic achievement? *Harvard Educational Review, 39,* 1–123.

Jensen, A. R. (1980). *Bias in mental testing.* New York: Free Press.

Jensen, A. R. (1985). The nature of the black-white differences on various psychometric tests: Spearman's hypothesis. *Behavioral and Brain Sciences, 8,* 193–263.

Jepson, C., & Chaiken, S. (1990). Chronic issue-specific fear inhibits systematic processing of persuasive communications. *Journal of Social Behavior and Personality, 5,* 61–84.

Jessell, T. M., & Kelly, D. D. (1991). Pain and analgesia. In E. R. Kandel, J. H. Schwartz, & T. M. Jessell (Eds.), *Principles of neural science* (3rd ed., pp. 385–399). New York: Elsevier.

John, E. R., Prichep, L. S., Fridman, J., & Easton, P. (1988). Neurometrics: Assisted differential diagnosis of brain dysfunction. *Science, 239,* 162–169.

John, O. P. (1990). The "Big Five" factor taxonomy: Dimensions of personality in the natural language and in questionnaires. In L. A. Pervin (Ed.), *Handbook of personality theory and research* (pp. 66–100). New York: Guilford Press.

Johnson, B. T., & Eagly, A. H. (1989). Effects of involvement on persuasion: A meta-analysis. *Psychological Bulletin, 106,* 290–314.

Johnson, D. (1990). Animal rights and human lives: Time for scientists to right the balance. *Psychological Science, 1,* 213–214.

Johnson, E. (1991, November 18). I'll deal with it (Interview with "Magic" Johnson). *Sports Illustrated, 75,* 16–45.

Johnson, J. E., Christie, J. F., & Yawkey, T. D. (1987). *Play and early childhood development.* Glenview, IL: Scott, Foresman.

Johnson, K. M., Gutkin, T. B., & Plake, B. S. (1991). Use of modeling to enhance children's interrogative strategies. *Journal of School Psychology, 29,* 81–88.

Johnson, M. H., Dziurawiec, S., Ellis, H. D., & Morton, J. (1991). Newborns' preferential tracking of faces and its subsequent decline. *Cognition, 40,* 1–19.

Johnson, M. K., Hashtroudi, S., & Lindsay, D. S. (1993). Source monitoring. *Psychological Bulletin, 114,* 3–28.

Johnson, R. C., McClearn, G. E., Yuen, S., Nagoshi, C. T., Ahern, F. M., & Cole, R. E. (1985). Galton's data a century later. *American Psychologist, 40,* 875–892.

Johnson, W. O. (1991). How far have we come? *Sports Illustrated, 75*(6), 39–47.

Johnson-Laird, P. N. (1983). *Mental models.* Cambridge, MA: Harvard University Press.

Jones, E. (1953). *The life and work of Sigmund Freud.* New York: Basic Books.

Jones, E. E. (1990). *Interpersonal perception.* New York: W. H. Freeman.

Jones, E. E., & Harris, V. A. (1967). The attribution of attitudes. *Journal of Experimental Social Psychology, 3,* 1–24.

Jones, E. E., & Pulos, S. M. (1993). Comparing the process in psychodynamic and cognitive-behavioral therapies. *Journal of Consulting and Clinical Psychology, 61,* 306–316.

Jones, E. W. (1986). Black managers: The dream deferred. *Harvard Business Review, 64,* 84–93.

Jones, J. L. (Ed.). (1991). *Black psychology* (3rd ed.). Berkeley, CA: Cobb & Henry.

Jones, K. L., Smith, D. W., Ulleland, C. N., & Streissguth, A. P. (1973). Patterns of malformation in the offspring of chronic alcoholic mothers. *Lancet, 1,* 1267–1271.

Jones, L. V. (1984). White-black achievement differences: The narrowing gap. *American Psychologist, 39,* 1207–1213.

Jones, M. C. (1924). A laboratory study of fear: The case of Peter. *Journal of Genetic Psychology, 31,* 308–315.

Jones, M. C. (1957). The late careers of boys who were early- or late-maturers. *Child Development, 28,* 115–128.

Joynson, R. B. (1989). *The Burt affair.* London: Routledge.

Judd, C. M., & Park, B. (1993). Definition and assessment of accuracy in social stereotypes. *Psychological Review, 100,* 109–128.

Julien, R. M. (1992). *A primer of drug action* (6th ed.). New York: W. H. Freeman.

Jung, C. G. (1928). *Contributions to analytical psychology.* New York: Harcourt Brace.

Jussim, L. (1989). Teacher expectations: Self-fulfilling prophecies, perceptual biases, and accuracy. *Journal of Personality and Social Psychology, 57,* 469–480.

Just, M. A., & Carpenter, P. A. (1992). A capacity theory of comprehension: Individual differences in working memory. *Psychological Review, 99,* 122–149.

Kagan, J. (1994). Galen's prophesy: Temperament in human nature. New York: Basic Books.

Kagan, J. (1976). Emergent themes in human development. *American Scientist, 64,* 186–196.

Kagan, J. (1984). *The nature of the child.* New York: Basic Books.

Kagan, J., Reznick, J. S., & Snideman, N. (1990). Biological bases of childhood shyness. *Science, 240,* 167–171.

Kagan, J., Snidman, N., & Arcus, D. M. (1992). Initial reactions to unfamiliarity. *Current Directions in Psychological Science, 1,* 171–174.

Kahn, M. (1991). *Between therapist and client: The new relationship.* New York: W. H. Freeman.

Kahneman, D., Slovic, P., & Tversky, A. (Eds.). (1982). *Judgement under uncertainty: Heuristics and biases.* New York: Cambridge University Press.

Kahneman, D., & Tversky, A. (1973). On the psychology of prediction. *Psychological Review, 80,* 237–251.

Kahneman, D., & Tversky, A. (1984). Choices, values, and frames. *American Psychologist, 39,* 341–350.

Kail, R. (1990). *The development of memory in children* (3rd ed.). New York: W. H. Freeman.

Kail, R. (1991). Developmental changes in speed of processing during childhood and adolescence. *Psychological Bulletin, 109,* 490–501.

Kail, R., & Bisanz, J. (1992). The information-processing perspective on cognitive development in childhood and adolescence. In R. J. Sternberg & C. A. Berg (Eds.), *Intellectual development.* New York: Cambridge University Press.

Kalish, R. A. (1981). *Death, grief, and caring relationships.* Monterey, CA: Wadsworth.

Kamen-Siegel, L., Rodin, J., Seligman, M.E.P., & Dwyer, J. (1991). Explanatory style and cell-mediated immunity in elderly men and women. *Health Psychology, 10,* 229–235.

Kamin, L. J. (1974). *The science and politics of IQ.* New York: Wiley.

Kandel, E. R. (1979). Small systems of neurons. *Scientific American, 241,* 66–87.

Kane, J. M., Honigfeld, G., Singer, J., Meltzer, H., & The Clozaril Collaborative Study Group (1988). Clozapine for the treatment-resis-

tant schizophrenic. *Archives of General Psychiatry, 45,* 789–796.

Kanner, A. D., Coyne, J. C., Schaefer, C., & Lazarus, R. S. (1981). Comparison of two modes of stress measurement: Daily hassles and uplifts versus major life events. *Journal of Behavioral Medicine, 4,* 1–39.

Kanner, A. D., Feldman, S. S., Weinberger, D. A., & Ford, M. F. (1991). Uplifts, hassles, and adaptational outcomes in early adolescents. In A. Monat & R. S. Lazarus (Eds.), *Stress and coping: An anthology* (pp. 158–181). New York: Columbia University Press.

Kaplan, C. A., & Simon, H. A. (1990). In search of insight. *Cognitive Psychology, 22,* 374–419.

Kaplan, R. M. (1985). The controversy related to the use of psychological tests. In B. B. Wolman (Ed.), *Handbook of intelligence: Theories, measurements, and applications* (pp. 465–504). New York: Wiley.

Karau, S. J., & Williams, K. D. (1993). Social loafing: A meta-analytic review and theoretical integration. *Journal of Personality and Social Psychology, 65,* 681–706.

Kasper, S., & Rosenthal, N. E. (1989). Anxiety and depression in seasonal affective disorders. In P. Kendall & D. Watson (Eds.), *Anxiety and depression: Distinct and overlapping features* (pp. 341–375). San Diego: Academic Press.

Kassin, S. M., Ellsworth, P. C., & Smith, V. L. (1989). The general acceptance of psychological research on eyewitness testimony. *American Psychologist, 44,* 1089–1098.

Kassin, S. M., Williams, L. N., & Saunders, C. L. (1990). Dirty tricks of cross-examination: The influence of conjectural evidence on the jury. *Law and Human Behavior, 14,* 373–384.

Kassin, S. M., & Wrightsman, L. S. (1988). *The American jury on trial: Psychological perspectives.* Washington, DC: Hemisphere.

Katz, D., & Braly, K. (1933). Racial stereotypes of 100 college students. *Journal of Abnormal and Social Psychology, 28,* 280–290.

Kaufman, L., & Rock, I. (1962). The moon illusion. (Vol I). *Science, 136,* 953–961.

Kay, S. R. (1990). Significance of the positive-negative distinction in schizophrenia. *Schizophrenia Bulletin, 16,* 635–652.

Kazdin, A. E. (1982). The token economy: A decade later. *Journal of Applied Behavior Analysis, 15,* 431–445.

Kearl, M. C. (1989). *A sociology of death and dying.* New York: Oxford University Press.

Keith, J. R., & McVety, K. M. (1988). Latent place learning in a novel environment and the influences of prior training in rats. *Psychobiology, 16,* 146–151.

Kelley, H. H. (1967). Attribution theory in social psychology. In D. Levine (Ed.), *Nebraska Symposium on Motivation* (Vol. 15, pp. 192–241). Lincoln, NE: University of Nebraska Press.

Kellman, P. J., & Spelke, E. S. (1983). Perception of partly occluded objects in infancy. *Cognitive psychology, 15,* 483–524.

Kellner, R. (1987). Hypochondriasis and somatization. *Journal of the American Medical Association, 258,* 2718–2722.

Kellogg, W. N., & Kellogg, L. A. (1933). *The ape and the child.* New York: McGraw-Hill.

Kelly, D. D. (1991). Disorders of sleep and consciousness. In E. R. Kandel, J. H. Schwartz & T. M. Jessell (Eds.), *Principles of neural science* (3rd. ed., pp. 805–819). New York: Elsevier.

Kelly, D. D. (1991). Sexual differentiation of the nervous system. In E. R. Kandel, J. H. Schwartz, & T. M. Jessel (Eds.), *Principles of neural science* (3rd ed., pp. 959–973). New York: Elsevier.

Kelman, H. C., & Hamilton, V. L. (1989). *Crimes of obedience: Toward a social psychology of authority and responsibility.* New Haven, CT: Yale University Press.

Kendall, P. C., & Clarkin, J. F. (1992). Introduction to special section: Comorbidity and treatment implications. *Journal of Consulting and Clinical Psychology, 60,* 833–834.

Kendler, H. H. (1993). Psychology and the ethics of social policy. *American Psychologist, 48,* 1046–1053.

Kendler, K. S., MacLean, C., Neale, M., Kessler, R., Heath, A., & Eaves, L. (1991). The genetic epidemiology of bulimia nervosa. *American Journal of Psychiatry, 148,* 1627–1637.

Kenrick, D. T. (1987). Gender, genes, and the social environment. *Review of Personality and Social Psychology, 8,* 14–43.

Kenrick, D. T. (1994). Evolutionary social psychology: From sexual selection to social cognition. *Advances in Experimental Social Psychology, 26,* 75–121.

Kenrick, D. T., & Funder, D. C. (1991). The person-situation debate: Do personality traits really exist? In V. Derlega, B. Winstead, & W. Jones (Eds.), *Personality* (pp. 149–174). Chicago: Nelson-Hall.

Kenrick, D. T., Gutierres, S. E., & Goldberg, L. L. (1989). Influence of popular erotica on judgments of strangers and mates. *Journal of Experimental Social Psychology, 25,* 159–167.

Kenrick, D. T., & Keefe, R. C. (1992). Age preferences in mates reflect sex differences in human reproductive strategies. *Behavioral and Brain Sciences, 15,* 75–91.

Kenrick, D. T., & MacFarlane, S. W. (1984). Ambient temperature and horn-honking: A field study of the heat/aggression relationship. *Environment and Behavior, 18,* 179–191.

Kerr, N. L., Kramer, G. P., Carroll, J. S., & Alfini, J. J. (1991). On the effectiveness of voir dire in criminal cases with prejudicial pretrial publicity: An empirical study. *The American University Law Review, 40,* 665–701.

Kerwin, M.L.E., & Day, J. D. (1985). Peer influences on cognitive development. In J. Pryor & J. Day (Eds.), *The development of social cognition* (pp. 211–228). New York: Springer-Verlag.

Kessler, R. C., Foster, C., Webster, P. S., & House, J. S. (1992). The relationship between age and depressive symptoms in two national surveys. *Psychology and Aging, 7,* 117–126.

Kessler, R. C., McGonagle, K. A., Zhao, S., Nelson, C. B., Hughes, M., Eshleman, S., Wittchen, H. U., & Kendler, K. S. (1994). Lifetime and 12-month prevalence of DSM-III-R psychiatric disorders in the United States. *Archives of General Psychiatry, 51,* 8–19.

Ketterer, M. W., & Maercklein, G. H. (1991). Caffeinated beverage use among Type A male patients suspected of CAD/CHD: A mechanism for increased risk? *Stress Medicine, 7,* 119–124.

Kiecolt-Glaser, J. K., Cacioppo, J. T., Malarkey, W. B., & Glaser, R. (1992). Acute psychological stressors and short-term immune changes: What, why, for whom, and to what extent? *Psychosomatic Medicine, 54,* 680–685.

Kiecolt-Glaser, J. K., Glaser, R., et al. (1985). Psychosocial enhancement of immunocompetence in a geriatric population. *Health Psychology, 4,* 25–41.

Kiecolt-Glaser, J. K., & Glaser, R. (1992). Psychoneuroimmunology: Can psychological interventions modulate immunity? *Journal of Consulting and Clinical Psychology, 60,* 569–575.

Kiecolt-Glaser, J. K., & Glaser, R. (1993). Mind and immunity. In D. Goleman & J. Gurin (Eds.), *Mind body medicine* (pp. 39–61). Yonkers, NY: Consumer Reports Books.

Kiewra, K. A., et al. (1991). Note-taking functions and techniques. *Journal of Educational Psychology, 83,* 240–245.

Kihlstrom, J. F. (1985). Hypnosis. *Annual Review of Psychology, 36,* 385–418.

Kihlstrom, J. F., Barnhardt, T. M., & Tataryn, D. J. (1987). The psychological unconscious: Found, lost, and regained. *American Psychologist, 47,* 788–791.

Kihlstrom, J. F., Schacter, D. L., Cork, R. C., Hurt, C. A., & Behr, S. E. (1990). Implicit and explicit memory following surgical anesthesia. *Psychological Science, 1,* 303–306.

Kimball, M. M. (1989). A new perspective on women's math achievement. *Psychological Bulletin, 105,* 198–214.

Kimble, D. P. (1990). Functional effects of neural grafting in the mammalian central nervous system. *Psychological Bulletin, 108,* 462–479.

Kimble, D. P. (1988). *Biological Psychology.* NY: Holt, Rinehart and Winston.

Kimmel, A. J. (1991). Predictable biases in the ethical decisionmaking of American psychologists. *American Psychologist, 46,* 786–788.

Kimura, D. (1989, November). How sex hormones boost—or cut—intellectual ability. *Psychology Today,* 62–66.

Kinnunen, T., Zamankski, H. S., and Block, M. L. (1994). Is the hypnotized subject lying? *Journal of Abnormal Psychology, 103,* 184–191.

Kinsey, A. C., Pomeroy, W. B., & Martin, C. E. (1948). *Sexual behavior in the human male.* Philadelphia: W. B. Saunders.

Kinsey, A. C., Pomeroy, W. B., Martin, C. E., & Gebhard, P. H. (1953). *Sexual behavior in the human female.* Philadelphia: W. B. Saunders.

Kirsch, I., Silva, C. E., Carone, J. E., Johnston, J. D., & Simon, B. (1989). The surreptitious observation design: An experimental paradigm for distinguishing artifact from essence in hypnosis. *Journal of Abnormal Psychology, 98,* 132–136.

Kirsner, D. (1990). Is there a future for American psychoanalysis? *Psychoanalytic Review, 77,* 175–200.

Kitayama, S., and Markus, H. R. (Eds.) (1994). *Emotion and culture: Empirical studies of mutual influence.* Washington, D. C.: American Psychological Association.

Klahr, D. (1989). Information-processing perspectives. In R. Vasta (Ed.), *Annals of child development* (Vol. 6, pp. 133–185). Greenwich, CT: JAI Press.

Klein, R., & Mannuzza, S. (1991). Long-term outcome of hyperactive children: A review. *Journal of the American Academy of Child and Adolescent Psychiatry, 30,* 383–387.

Kleiner, K. A. (1987). Amplitude and phase spectra as indices of infants' pattern preferences. *Infant Behavior and Development, 10,* 49–59.

Kleinke, C. L. (1986). Gaze and eye contact: A research review. *Psychological Bulletin, 100,* 78–100.

Kleinmuntz, B., & Szucko, J. J. (1984). Lie detection in ancient and modern times. *American Psychologist, 39,* 766–776.

Kleitman, N. (1963). *Sleep and wakefulness.* Chicago: University of Chicago Press.

Klerman, G. L., & Weissman, M. M. (1989). Increasing rates of depression. *Journal of the American Medical Association, 261,* 2229–2235.

Kline, P. (1991). *Intelligence: The psychometric view.* New York: Routledge, Chapman & Hall.

Klivington, K. A. (Ed.). (1989). *The science of mind.* Cambridge, MA; MIT Press.

Kluegel, J. R. (1990). Trends in whites' explanations of the black-white gap in socioeconomic status, 1977–1989. *American Sociological Review, 55,* 512–525.

Kluft, R. P., & Fine, C. G. (1993). *Clinical perspectives on multiple personality disorder.* Washington, DC: American Psychiatric Press.

Knapp, R. R. (1976). *Handbook for the Personal Orientation Inventory.* San Diego: Edits Publishers.

Knowlton, B. J., & Squire, L. R. (1994). The information acquired during artificial grammar learning. *Journal of Experimental Psychology: Human Learning and Memory, 20,* 79–91.

Kobosa, S. C. (1979). Stressful life events, personality, and health: An inquiry into hardiness. *Journal of Personality and Social Psychology, 37,* 1–11.

Koch, S. (1993). "Psychology" or "the psychological studies"? *American Psychologist, 48,* 902–904.

Koffka, K. (1935). *Principles of gestalt psychology.* New York: Harcourt, Brace & World.

Kohlberg, L. (1981). *Essays on moral development: Vol. 1. The philosophy of moral development.* New York: Harper & Row.

Kohlberg, L. (1984). *Essays on moral development: Vol. 2. The psychology of moral development.* New York: Harper & Row.

Kohler, W. (1925). *The mentality of apes.* New York: Harcourt Brace Jovanovich.

Kohler, W. (1947). *Gestalt psychology.* New York: Liveright.

Kohlstrom, J. F., Barnhardt, T. M., & Tataryn, D. J. (1992). The psychological unconscious: Found, lost, regained. *American Psychologist, 47,* 788–791.

Kohn, P. M., Lafreniere, K., & Gurevich, M. (1990). The inventory of college students' recent life experiences: A decontaminated hassles scale for a special population. *Journal of Behavioral Medicine, 13,* 619–630.

Kolb, B., & Whishaw, I. Q. (1990). *Fundamentals of human neuropsychology* (3rd ed.). New York: W. H. Freeman.

Korn, J. H., Davis, R., & Davis, S. F. (1991). Historians' and chairpersons' judgments of eminence among psychologists. *American Psychologist, 46,* 789–792.

Kosslyn, S. M. (1980). *Image and mind.* Cambridge, MA: Harvard University Press.

Kosslyn, S. M. (1994). *Image and brain: The resolution of the imagery debate.* Cambridge, MA: MIT Press.

Kotovsky, K., Hayes, J. R., & Simon, H. A. (1985). Why are some problems hard? Evidence from Tower of Hanoi. *Cognitive Psychology, 17,* 248–294.

Kotre, J., & Hall, E. (1990). *Seasons of life.* Boston: Little, Brown.

Kovecses, Z. (1990). *Emotion concepts.* New York: Springer-Verlag.

Kowalski, R. M. (1993). Inferring sexual interest from behavioral cues: Effects of gender and sexually relevant attitudes. *Sex Roles, 29,* 13–36.

Kraeplin, E. (1923). *Textbook of psychiatry.* New York: Macmillan. (Original work published 1883)

Kramer, P. D. (1993). *Listening to Prozac.* New York: Viking.

Krantz, D. S., & Manuck, S. B. (1984). Acute psychophysiologic reactivity and risk of cardiovascular disease: A review and methodological critique. *Psychological Bulletin, 96,* 435–464.

Kranzler, J. H., & Jensen, A. R. (1989). Inspection time and intelligence: A meta-analysis. *Intelligence, 13,* 329–347.

Kreitler, S., Weissler, K., Krietler, H., & Brunner, D. (1991). The relation of smoking to psychological and physiological risk factors for coronary heart disease. *Personality and Individual Differences, 12,* 487–495.

Kreutzer, M. A., Leonard, C., & Flavell, J. H. (1975). An interview study of children's knowledge about memory. *Monographs of the Society for Research in Child Development, 40*(1, Serial No. 159), 1–58.

Kristof, N. D. (1993, July 21). Peasants of China discover new way to weed out girls. *New York Times,* pp. A1, A6.

Kruglanski, A. W., & Webster, D. M. (1991). Group members' reactions to opinion deviates and conformists at varying degrees of proximity to decision deadline and of environmental noise. *Journal of Personality and Social Psychology, 61,* 212–225.

Krumhansl, C. L. (1991). Music psychology: Tonal structures in perception and memory. *Annual Review of Psychology, 42,* 277–303.

Kübler-Ross, E. (1969). *On death and dying.* New York: Macmillan.

Kübler-Ross, E. (1974). *Questions and answers on death and dying.* New York: Macmillan.

Kuebli, J., & Fivush, R. (1992). Gender differences in parent-child conversations about past emotions. *Sex Roles, 27,* 683–698.

Kuffler, S. W. (1953). Discharge patterns and functional organization of mammalian retina. *Journal of Neurophysiology, 16,* 37–68.

Kuhn, D. (1991). *The skills of argument.* Cambridge: Cambridge University Press.

Kulik, J. A., Bangert-Drowns, R. L., & Kulik, C. (1984). Effectiveness of coaching for aptitude tests. *Psychological Bulletin, 95,* 179–188.

Kunda, Z. (1987). Motivated inference: Self-serving generation and evaluation of causal theories. *Journal of Personality and Social Psychology, 53,* 636–647.

Kunda, Z. (1990). Motivated reasoning. *Psychological Bulletin, 108,* 480–498.

Kuntz-Wilson, W., & Zajonc, R. B. (1980). Affective discrimination of stimuli that cannot be recognized. *Science, 207,* 557–558.

Kurdek, L. A. (1991). Sexuality in homosexual and heterosexual couples. In K. McKinney & S. Sprecher (Eds.), *Sexuality in close relationships* (pp. 177–191). Hillsdale, NJ: Erlbaum.

Kurtines, W. M., & Gewirtz, J. L. (Eds.). (1984). *Morality, moral behavior, and moral development.* New York: Wiley.

LaBerge, S. P. (1992). *Physiological studies of lucid dreaming.* Hillsdale, NJ: Erlbaum.

LaFrance, M., & Banaji, M. (1992). Toward a reconsideration of the gender-emotion relationship. *Review of Personality and Social Psychology, 14,* 178–201.

LaFromboise, T., Coleman, H., & Gerton, J. (1993). Psychological impact of biculturalism: Evidence and theory. *Psychological Bulletin, 114,* 395–412.

Laird, J. D. (1974). Self-attribution of emotion: The effects of expressive behavior on the quality of emotional experience. *Journal of Personality and Social Psychology, 33,* 475–486.

Lamb, M. (1986). *The father's role: Applied perspectives.* New York: Wiley.

Lamb, M. (1987). Predictive implications of individual differences in attachment. *Journal of Consulting and Clinical Psychology, 55,* 817–824.

Lamb, M., Sternberg, K. J., & Prodromidis, M. (1992). Nonmaternal care and the security of the infant-mother attachment: A reanalysis of the data. *Infant Behavior and Development, 15,* 71–83.

Lambert, M. J. (1989). The individual therapist's contribution to psychotherapy process and outcome. *Clinical Psychology Review, 9,* 469–485.

Lambert, M. J., & Bergin, A. E. (1994). The effectiveness of psychotherapy. In A. Bergin & S. Garfield (Eds.), *Handbook of psychotherapy and behavior change* (4th ed., pp. 143–189). New York: Wiley.

Land, M. F., & Fernald, R. D. (1992). The evolution of eyes. *Annual Review of Neuroscience, 15,* 1–29.

Landau, T. (1989). *About faces: The evolution of the human face.* New York: Anchor Books.

Landesman, S., & Ramey, C. (1989). Developmental psychology and mental retardation: Integrating scientific principles with treatment practices. *American Psychologist, 44,* 409–415.

Landy, F. J., Shankster, L. J., & Kohler, S. S. (1994). Personnel selection and placement. *Annual Review of Psychology, 45,* 261–296.

Langer, E. J. (1975). The illusion of control. *Journal of Personality and Social Psychology, 32,* 311–328.

Langer, E. J. (1989). *Mindfulness.* Reading, MA: Addison-Wesley.

Langley, G. (Ed.). (1989). *Animal experimentation: The consensus changes.* New York: Chapman & Hall.

Langlois, J. H., & Roggman, L. A. (1990). Attractive faces are only average. *Psychological Science, 1,* 115–121.

Langlois, J. H., Roggman, L. A., Casey, R. J., Ritter, J. M., Rieser-Danner, L. A., & Jenkins, V. Y. (1987). Infant preferences for attractive faces: Rudiments of a stereotype? *Developmental Psychology, 23,* 363–369.

Langreth, R. (1993, November). Can we live to 150? *Popular Science,* pp. 77–82.

Lansing, A. K. (1959). General biology of senescence. In J. E. Birren (Ed.), *Handbook of aging and the individual.* Chicago: University of Chicago Press.

Lanzetta, J. T., & Orr, S. P. (1986). Excitatory strength of expressive faces: Effects of happy and fear expressions and context on the extinction of a conditioned fear response. *Journal of Personality and Social Psychology, 50,* 190–194.

LaPiere, R. T. (1934). Attitudes vs. action. *Social Forces, 13,* 230–237.

Larry P. v. *Wilson Riles,* 495 F. Supp. 926 (N. D. Cal. 1979).

Larsen, K. S. (1990). The Asch conformity experiment: Replication and transhistorical comparisons. *Journal of Social Behavior and Personality, 5,* 163–168.

Larsen, R. J., & Diener, E. (1992). Promises and problems with the circumplex model of emotion. *Review of Personality and Social Psychology, 13,* 25–59.

Larsen, R. J., & Kasimatis, M. (1990). Individual differences in entrainment of mood to the weekly calendar. *Journal of Personality and Social Psychology, 58,* 164–171.

Lashley, K. S. (1950). In search of the engram. In *Society for Experimental Biology, Symposium 4,* 454–482.

Latané, B. (1981). The psychology of social impact. *American Psychologist, 36,* 343–356.

Latané, B., & Darley, J. M. (1970). *The unresponsive bystander: Why doesn't he help?* New York: Appleton-Century-Crofts.

Latané, B., & Nida, S. (1981). Ten years of research on group size and helping. *Psychological Bulletin, 89,* 308–324.

Latané, B., Williams, K., & Harkins, S. (1979). Many hands make light the work: The causes and consequences of social loafing. *Journal of Personality and Social Psychology, 37,* 822–832.

Lattal, K. A. (1992). B. F. Skinner and psychology: Introduction to the special issue. *American Psychologist, 47,* 1269–1272.

Laudenslager, M. L., Ryan, S. M., Drugan, R. C., Hyson, R. L., & Maier, S. F. (1983). Coping and immunosuppression: Inescapable but not escapable shock suppresses lymphocyte proliferation. *Science, 231,* 568–570.

Lawrence, V. W. (1991). Effect of socially ambiguous information on white and black children's behavioral and trait perceptions. *Merrill-Palmer Quarterly, 37,* 619–630.

Lazarus, A. A., Beutler, L. E., & Norcross, J. C. (1992). The future of technical eclecticism. *Psychotherapy, 29,* 11–20.

Lazarus, R. S. (1984). On the primacy of cognition. *American Psychologist, 39,* 124–129.

Lazarus, R. S. (1991). Cognition and motivation in emotion. *American Psychologist, 46,* 352–367.

Lazarus, R. S. (1993). From psychological stress to the emotions: A history of changing outlooks. *Annual Review of Psychology, 44,* 1–21.

Lazarus, R. S., & Folkman, S. (1984). *Stress, appraisal, and coping.* New York: Springer.

Leahey, T. H. (1992). The mythical revolutions of American psychology. *American Psychologist, 47,* 308–318.

Leary, D. E. (1992). William James and the art of human understanding. *American Psychologist, 47,* 152–160.

Leary, M. R. (1983). *Understanding social anxiety: Social, personality, and clinical perspectives.* Beverly Hills, CA: Sage.

Lebow, J. (1982). Consumer satisfaction with mental health treatment. *Psychological Bulletin, 91,* 244–259.

Leccese, A. P. (1991). *Drugs and society.* Englewood Cliffs, NJ: Prentice-Hall.

LeDoux, J. E. (1989). Cognitive-emotional interactions in the brain. *Cognition and Emotion, 3,* 267–289.

LeDoux, J. E. (1993). Emotional networks in the brain. In M. Lewis & J. M. Haviland (Eds.), *Handbook of emotions* (pp. 109–118). New York: Guilford Press.

LeDoux, J. E., Wilson, D. H., & Gazzaniga, M. S. (1977). A divided mind: Observation on the conscious properties of the separated hemispheres. *Annals of Neurology, 2,* 417–421.

Lee, V. E., Brooks-Gunn, J., Schnur, E., & Liaw, F. R. (1990). Are Head Start effects sustained? A longitudinal follow-up of comparison of disadvantaged children attending Head Start, no preschool, and other preschool programs. *Child Development, 61,* 495–507.

Lefcourt, H. M. (1982). *Locus of control: Current trends in theory and research.* Hillsdale, NJ: Erlbaum.

Lehman, D. R., & Nisbett, R. E. (1990). A longitudinal study of the effects of undergraduate training on reasoning. *Developmental Psychology, 26,* 952–960.

Lehman, H. C. (1953). *Age and achievement.* Princeton, NJ: Princeton University Press.

Leibowitz, H. W., Brislin, R., Perlmutter, L., & Hennessy, R. (1969). Ponzo perspective illusion as a manifestation of space perception. *Science, 166,* 1174–1176.

Leigh, B. C., & Stacy, A. W. (1993). Alcohol outcome expectancies: Scale construction and predictive utility in higher-order confirmatory models. *Psychological Assessment, 5,* 216–229.

Leinbach, M. D., & Fagot, B. I. (1993). Categorical habituation to male and female faces: Gender schematic processes in infancy. *Infant Behavior and Development, 16,* 317–332.

Lennon, R. T. (1985). Group tests of intelligence. In B. Wolman (Ed.), *Handbook of intelligence: Theories, measurement, and applications* (pp. 825–845). New York: Wiley.

Leon, M. (1992). The neurobiology of filial learning. *Annual Review of Psychology, 43,* 377–398.

Lepper, M. R., & Greene, D. (Eds.). (1978). *The hidden costs of reward.* Hillsdale, NJ: Erlbaum.

Lerner, M. J. (1980). *The belief in a just world: A fundamental delusion.* New York: Plenum.

Leung, K. (1988). Some determinants of conflict avoidance. *Journal of Cross-Cultural Psychology, 19,* 125–136.

LeVay, S. (1991). A difference in hypothalamic structure between heterosexual and homosexual men. *Science, 253,* 1034–1037.

LeVay, S. (1993). *The sexual brain.* Cambridge, MA: MIT Press.

LeVay, S., & Mamer, D. H. (1994). Evidence for a biological influence in male homosexuality. *Scientific American, 270* (5), 44–49.

Levenson, R. W. (1992). Autonomic nervous system differences among emotions. *Psychological Science, 3,* 23–27.

Levenson, R. W., Ekman, P., Heider, K., & Friesen, W. V. (1992). Emotion and autonomic nervous system activity in the Minangkabau of West Sumatra. *Journal of Personality and Social Psychology, 62,* 972–988.

Leventhal, H. (1970). Findings and theory in the study of fear communications. In L. Berkowitz (Ed.), *Advances in experimental social psychology* (Vol. 5). New York: Academic Press.

Leventhal, H., Watts, J. C., & Pagano, F. (1967). Effects of fear and instructions on how to cope with danger. *Journal of Personality and Social Psychology, 6,* 313–321.

Levin, I. P., & Gaeth, J. (1988). How consumers are affected by the framing of attribute information before and after consuming the product. *Journal of Consumer Research, 15,* 374–378.

Levin, I. P., Schnittjer, S. K., & Thee, S. L. (1988). Information framing effects in social and personal decisions. *Journal of Experimental Social Psychology, 24,* 520–529.

Levine, J. D., Gordon, N. C., & Fields, H. L. (1978). The mechanism of placebo analgesia. *Lancet, 2,* 654–657.

Levine, J. M. (1989). Reaction to opinion deviance in small groups. In P. B. Paulus (Ed.), *Psychology of group influence* (2nd ed., pp. 187–231). Hillsdale, NJ: Erlbaum.

Levine, R. A., & Campbell, D. T. (1972). *Ethnocentrism: Theories of conflict, ethnic attitudes, and group behavior.* New York: Wiley.

Levine, R. V. (1990). The pace of life. *American Scientist, 78,* 450–459.

Levinson, D. J. (1986). A conception of adult development. *American Psychologist, 41,* 3–13.

Levinson, D. J., Darrow, C. N., Klein, E. B., Levinson, M. H., McKee, B. (1978). *The seasons of a man's life.* New York: Knopf.

Levy, B., & Langer, E. (1994). Aging free from negative stereotypes: Successful memory in China and among the American deaf. *Journal of Personality and Social Psychology, 66,* 989–997.

Levy, G. D. (1989). Relations among aspects of children's social environments, gender schematization, gender role knowledge, and flexibility. *Sex Roles, 21,* 803–823.

Levy, J., Trevarthen, C., & Sperry, R. W. (1972). Perception of bilateral chimeric figures following hemispheric disconnection. *Brain, 95,* 61–78.

Lewinsohn, P. M. (1974). A behavioral approach to depression. In R. Friedman & M. Katz (Eds.), *The psychology of depression: Con-*

temporary theory and research. Washington, DC: Winston-Wiley.

Lewinsohn, P. M., Duncan, E. M., Stanton, A. K., & Hautzinger, M. (1986). Age at first onset for nonbipolar depression. *Journal of Abnormal Psychology, 95,* 378–383.

Lewinsohn, P. M., Rohde, P., & Seeley, J. R. (1994). Psychosocial risk factors for future adolescent suicide attempts. *Journal of Consulting and Clinical Psychology, 62,* 297–305.

Lewis, P., & Boylan, P. (1979). Fetal breathing: A review. *American Journal of Obstetrics and Gynecology, 134,* 587–598.

Lichtenstein, E. (1982). The smoking problem: A behavioral perspective. *Journal of Consulting and Clinical Psychology, 50,* 804–819.

Lickey, M. E., & Gordon, B. (1991). *Medicine and mental illness.* New York: W. H. Freeman.

Lickona, T. (1976). Research on Piaget's theory of moral development. In T. Lickona (Ed.), *Moral development and behavior.* New York: Holt, Rinehart & Winston.

Lieberman, P. (1984). *The biology and evolution of language.* Cambridge, MA: Harvard University Press.

Lifton, R. J. (1986). *The Nazi doctors.* New York: Basic Books.

Light, L. L. (1991). Memory and aging: Four hypotheses in search of data. *Annual Review of Psychology, 42,* 333–376.

Linden, E. (1993, March 22). Can animals think? *Time,* pp. 52–61.

Lindsay, P. H., & Norman, D. A. (1977). *Human information processing.* New York: Academic Press.

Lindsay, R.C.L., Wells, G. L., & O'Conner, F. J. (1989). Mock-juror belief of accurate and inaccurate eyewitnesses: A replication and extension. *Law and Human Behavior, 13,* 333–339.

Lindvall, O., et al. (1990). Grafts of fetal dopamine neurons survive and improve motor function in Parkinson's disease. *Science, 247,* 574–577.

Linet, M. G., Stewart, W. F., Celentano, D. D., Ziegler, D., & Sprecher, M. (1989). An epidemiologic study of headache among adolescents and young adults. *Journal of the American Medical Association, 261,* 2211–2216.

Linn, M. C., & Petersen, A. (1985). Emergence and characterization of sex differences in spatial ability: A meta-analysis. *Child Development, 56,* 1479–1498.

Linn, R. L. (1982). Ability testing: Individual differences, prediction, and differential prediction. In A. K. Wigdor & W. R. Garner (Eds.), *Ability testing: Uses, consequences, and controversies* (Part II). Washington, DC: National Academy Press.

Linton, M. (1982). Transformations of memory in everyday life. In U. Neisser (Ed.), *Memory observed: Remembering in natural contexts* (pp. 77–91). San Francisco: W. H. Freeman.

Linville, P. W., Fischer, G. W., & Fischhoff, B. (1992). Perceived risk and decision-making involving AIDS. In J. B. Pryor & G. D. Reeder (Eds.), *The social psychology of HIV infection.* Hillsdale, NJ: Erlbaum.

Linville, P. W., Fischer, G. W., & Salovey, P. (1989). Perceived distributions of the characteristics of in-group and out-group members: Empirical evidence and a computer simulation. *Journal of Personality and Social Psychology, 57,* 165–188.

Linz, D., Donnerstein, E., & Penrod, S. (1988). Effects of long-term exposure to violent and sexually degrading depictions of women. *Journal of Personality and Social Psychology, 55,* 758–768.

Lipsitt, L. (1971, December). Babies: They're a lot smarter than they look. *Psychology Today,* p. 23.

Liu, S. S. (1971). Differential conditioning and stimulus generalization of the rabbit's nictitating membrane response. *Journal of Comparative and Physiological Psychology, 77,* 136–142.

Livingstone, M., & Hubel, D. (1988). Segregation of form, color, movement, and depth: Anatomy, physiology, and perception. *Science, 240,* 740–749.

Lockard, J. S., & Paulhus, D. L. (1988). *Self-deception: An adaptive mechanism?* Englewood Cliffs, NJ: Prentice-Hall.

Loehlin, J. C. (1992). *Genes and environment in personality development.* Newbury Park, CA: Sage Publications.

Loehlin, J. C., Lindzey, G., & Spuhler, J. N. (1975). *Race differences in intelligence.* San Francisco: W. H. Freeman.

Loehlin, J. C., Willerman, L., & Horn, J. M. (1987). Personality resemblance in adoptive families: A 10-year follow-up. *Journal of Personality and Social Psychology, 53,* 961–969.

Loehlin, J. C., Willerman, L., & Horn, J. M. (1988). Human behavior genetics. *Annual Review of Psychology, 38,* 101–133.

Loftus, E. F. (1979). *Eyewitness testimony.* Cambridge, MA: Harvard University Press.

Loftus, E. F. (1979). The malleability of human memory. *American Scientist, 67,* 313–320.

Loftus, E. F. (1993a). The reality of repressed memories. *American Psychologist, 48,* 518–537.

Loftus, E. F. (1993b). Desperately seeking memories of the first few years of childhood: The reality of early memories. *Journal of Experimental Psychology: General, 122,* 274–277.

Loftus, E. F., & Coan, D. (in press). The construction of childhood memories. In D. Peters (Ed.), *The child witness in context: Cognitive, social and legal perspectives.* New York: Kluwer.

Loftus, E. F., Donders, K., Hoffman, H. G., & Schooler, J. W. (1989). Creating new memories that are quickly accessed and confidently held. *Memory and Cognition, 17,* 607–616.

Loftus, E. F., & Ketcham, K. (1991). *Witness for the defense: The accused, the eyewitness, and the expert who puts memory on trial.* New York: St. Martin's Press.

Loftus, E. F., & Klinger, M. R. (1992). Is the unconscious smart or dumb? *American Psychologist, 47,* 761–765.

Loftus, E. F., & Loftus, G. R. (1980). On the permanence of stored information in the human brain. *American Psychologist, 35,* 409–420.

Loftus, E. F., Loftus, G. R., & Messo, J. (1987). Some facts about "weapon focus." *Law and Human Behavior, 11,* 55–62.

Loftus, E. F., Miller, D. G., & Burns, H. J. (1978). Semantic integration of verbal information into visual memory. *Journal of Experimental Psychology: Human Learning and Memory, 4,* 19–31.

Loftus, E. F., & Palmer, J. C. (1974). Reconstruction of automobile destruction: An example of the interaction between language and memory. *Journal of Verbal Learning and Verbal Behavior, 13,* 585–589.

Loftus, G. R., Duncan, J., & Gehrig, P. (1992). On the time course of perceptual information that results from a brief visual presentation. *Journal of Experimental Psychology: Human Perception and Performance, 18,* 530–549.

Logan, G. (1992). Attention and preattention in theories of automaticity. *American Journal of Psychology, 105,* 317–340.

Logothetis, N. K., & Schall, J. D. (1989). Neuronal correlates of subjective visual perception. *Science, 245,* 761–763.

Logue, A. W. (1991). *The psychology of eating and drinking: An introduction.* New York: W. H. Freeman.

Lopez, S. R. (1989). Patient variable biases in clinical judgment: Conceptual overview and methodological considerations. *Psychological Bulletin, 106,* 184–203.

Lorenz, K. (1937). Imprinting. *The Auk, 54,* 245–273.

Lorenz, K. (1966). *On aggression.* New York: Harcourt, Brace & World.

Lovaas, O. I. (1987). Behavioral treatment and normal educational and intellectual functioning in young autistic children. *Journal of Consulting and Clinical Psychology, 55,* 3–9.

Lovdal, L. T. (1989). Sex role messages in television commercials: An update. *Sex Roles, 21,* 715–724.

Low, P. W., Jeffries, J. C., & Bonnie, R. J. (1986). *The trial of John Hinckley, Jr.: A case study in the insanity defense.* Mineola, NY: Foundation Press.

Lubin, B., Larson, R. M., & Matarazzo, J. D. (1984). Patterns of psychological test usage in the United States: 1935–1982. *American Psychologist, 39,* 451–454.

Luborsky, L. (1984). *Principles of psychoanalytic psychotherapy*. New York: Basic Books.

Luborsky, L., & Crits-Christoph, P. (1990). *Understanding transference: The CCRT method*. New York: Basic Books.

Lucy, J. A. (1992). *Language diversity and thought: A reformulation of the linguistic relativity hypothesis*. New York: Cambridge University Press.

Luria, A. R. (1968). *The mind of a mnemonist*. New York: Basic Books.

Luthans, F., Paul, R., & Baker, D. (1981). An experimental analysis of the impact of contingent reinforcement on salespersons' performance behavior. *Journal of Applied Psychology, 66*, 314–323.

Lutz, W. (1989). *Doublespeak*. New York: Harper Perennial.

Lykken, D. T. (1981). *A tremor in the blood: Uses and abuses of the lie detector*. New York: McGraw-Hill.

Lykken, D. T., Bouchard, T. J., Jr., McGue, M., & Tellegen, A. (1993). Heritability of interests: A twin study. *Journal of Applied Psychology, 78*, 649–661.

Lykken, D. T., McGue, M., Tellegen, A., & Bouchard, T. J., Jr. (1992). Emergenesis: Genetic traits that may not run in families. *American Psychologist, 47*, 1565–1577.

Lynch, G., & Baudry, M. (1984). The biochemistry of memory: A new and specific hypothesis. *Science, 224*, 1057–1064.

Lynn, S. J., Rhue, J. W., & Weekes, J. R. (1990). Hypnotic involuntariness: A social cognitive analysis. *Psychological Review, 97*, 169–184.

Lyons, L. C., & Woods, P. J. (1991). The efficacy of rational-emotive therapy: A quantitative review of outcome research. *Clinical Psychology Review, 11*, 357–369.

Lytton, H., Romney, D. M. (1991). Parents' differential socialization of boys and girls: A meta-analysis. *Psychological Bulletin, 109*, 267–296.

Maccoby, E. E. (1980). *Social development: Psychological growth and the parent-child relationship*. New York: Harcourt Brace Jovanovich.

Maccoby, E. E. (1990). Gender and relationships: A developmental account. *American Psychologist, 45*, 513–520.

Maccoby, E. E., & Jacklin, C. N. (1974). *The psychology of sex differences*. Stanford, CA: Stanford University Press.

Maccoby, E. E., & Jacklin, C. N. (1987). Gender segregation in childhood. In H. W. Reese (Ed.), *Advances in child development and behavior* (Vol. 20, pp. 239–287).

MacCoun, R. J. (1993). Drugs and the law: A psychological analysis of drug prohibition. *Psychological Bulletin, 113*, 497–512.

Mackavey, W. R., Malley, J. E., & Stewart, A. J. (1991). Remembering autobiographically consequential experiences: Content analysis of psychologists' accounts of their lives. *Psychology and Aging, 6*, 50–59.

Mackie, D. M., & Worth, L. T. (1989). Processing deficits and the mediation of positive affect in persuasion. *Journal of Personality and Social Psychology, 57*, 27–40.

Mackie, D. M., Worth, L. T., & Asuncion, A. G. (1990). Processing of persuasive in-group messages. *Journal of Personality and Social Psychology, 58*, 812–822.

MacLeod, C. M. (1991). Half a century of research on the Stroop effect: An integrative review. *Psychological Bulletin, 109*, 163–203.

MacLeod-Morgan, C., & Lack, L. (1982). Hemispheric specificity: A physiological concomitant of hypnotizability. *Psychophysiology, 19*, 687–690.

Macmillan, M. B. (1986). A wonderful journey through skull and brains: The travels of Mr. Gage's tamping iron. *Brain and Cognition, 5*, 67–104.

MacNeilage, P. F., Studdert-Kennedy, M. G., & Lindblom, B. (1987). *Behavioral and Brain Sciences, 10*, 247–303.

MacQueen, G., Marshall, J., Perdue, M., Siegal, S., & Bienenstock, J. (1989). Pavlovian conditioning of rat mast cells to secrete rat mast cell protease II. *Science, 234*, 83–85.

Macrae, C. N., Milne, A. B., & Bodenhausen, G. V. (1994). Stereotypes as energy-saving devices: A peek inside the cognitive toolbox. *Journal of Personality and Social Psychology, 66*, 37–47.

Maddi, S. R., Bartone, P. T., & Puccetti, M. C. (1987). Stressful events are indeed a factor in physical illness: Reply to Schroeder and Costa (1984). *Journal of Personality and Social Psychology, 52*, 833–843.

Maddux, J. E. (1991). Self-efficacy. In C. R. Snyder & D. R. Forsyth (Eds.), *Handbook of social and clinical psychology: The health perspective* (pp. 57–78). New York: Pergamon Press.

Madigan, S., & O'Hara, R. (1992). Short-term memory at the turn of the century: Mary Whiton Calkins's memory research. *American Psychologist, 47*, 170–174.

Madrazo, I., Drucker-Colin, R., Diaz, V., Martinez-Mata, J., Torres, C., & Becerril, J. J. (1987). Open microsurgical autograft of adrenal medulla to the right caudate nucleus in two patients with intractable Parkinson's disease. *New England Journal of Medicine, 316*, 831–834.

Magnusson, D., & Endler, N. S. (Eds.). (1977). *Personality at the crossroads: Current issues in interactional psychology*. Hillsdale, NJ: Erlbaum.

Mahoney, M. J. (1991). *Human change processes*. New York: Basic Books.

Mahoney, M. J. (1993). Introduction to special section: Theoretical developments in the cognitive psychotherapies. *Journal of Consulting and Clinical Psychology, 61*, 187–193.

Mahowald, M. W., & Schenck, C. H. (1989). Narcolepsy. In G. Adelman (Ed.), *Neuroscience year: Supplement 1 to the Encyclopedia of Neuroscience*. Boston: Birkhauser.

Major, B., Carrington, P. I., & Carnivale, P. J. (1984). Physical attractiveness and self-esteem: Attributions for praise from an other-sex evaluator. *Personality and Social Psychology Bulletin, 10*, 43–50.

Major, B., Cozzarelli, C., Sciacchitano, A. M., Cooper, M. L., Testa, M., & Mueller, P. M. (1990). Perceived social support, self-efficacy, and adjustment to abortion. *Journal of Personality and Social Psychology, 59*, 452–463.

Major, B., & Konar, E. (1984). An investigation of sex differences in pay expectations and their possible causes. *Academy of Management Journal, 27*, 777–792.

Major, B., McFarlin, D. B., & Gagnon, D. (1984). Overworked and underpaid: On the nature of gender differences in personal entitlement. *Journal of Personality and Social Psychology, 47*, 1399–1412.

Major, B., Schmidlin, A. M., & Williams, L. (1990). Gender patterns in social touch: The impact of setting and age. *Journal of Personality and Social Psychology, 58*, 634–643.

Majors, R. (1991). Nonverbal behaviors and communication styles among African Americans. In R. Jones (Ed.), *Black psychology* (pp. 269–294). Berkeley, CA: Cobb & Henry.

Malamuth, N. M., & Check, J.V.P. (1981). The effects of mass media exposure on acceptance of violence against women: A field experiment. *Journal of Research in Personality, 15*, 436–446.

Malpass, R. S., & Devine, P. G. (1981). Eyewitness identification: Lineup instructions and the absence of the offender. *Journal of Applied Psychology, 66*, 482–489.

Mandler, G. (1980). Recognizing: The judgment of previous occurrence. *Psychological Review, 87*, 252–271.

Mann, J. M. (1992). AIDS—the second decade: A global perspective. *Journal of Infectious Diseases, 165*, 245–250.

Marcel, A. J. (1983). Conscious and unconscious perception: Experiments on visual masking and word recognition. *Cognitive Psychology, 15*, 197–237.

Mark, V. H., & Ervin, F. R. (1970). *Violence and the brain.* New York: Harper & Row.

Marks, D. F. (1986). Investigating the paranormal. *Nature, 320*, 119–124.

Marks, I. M. (1987). *Fears, phobias, and rituals: Panic, anxiety, and their disorders.* New York: Oxford University Press.

Markus, H. (1977). Self-schemata and processing information about the self. *Journal of Personality and Social Psychology, 35*, 63–78.

Markus, H., & Nurius, P. (1986). Possible selves. *American Psychologist, 41*, 954–969.

Markus, H. R., & Kitayama, S. (1991). Culture and the self: Implications for cognition, emotion, and motivation. *Psychological Review, 98*, 224–253.

Marsh, H. W., & Parker, J. W. (1984). Determinants of student self-concept: Is it better to be a relatively large fish in a small pond even if you don't learn to swim as well? *Journal of Personality and Social Psychology, 47*, 213–231.

Marsh, R. L., & Bower, G. H. (1993). Eliciting cryptomnesia: Unconscious plagiarism in a puzzle task. *Journal of Experimental Psychology: Learning, Memory, and Cognition, 19*, 673–688.

Marshall, D. A., & Moulton, D. G. (1981). Olfactory sensitivity to x-ionone in humans and dogs. *Chemical Senses, 6*, 53–61.

Martin, C. L. (1987). A ratio measure of sex stereotyping. *Journal of Personality and Social Psychology, 52*, 489–499.

Martin, C. L., Wood, C. H., & Little, J. K. (1990). The development of gender stereotype components. *Child Development, 61*, 1891–1904.

Martin, G., & Pear, J. (1992). *Behavior modification: What it is and how to do it* (4th ed.). Englewood Cliffs, NJ: Prentice-Hall.

Martin, J. H. (1991). Coding and processing of sensory information. In E. R. Kandel, J. H. Schwartz, & T. M. Jessell (Eds.), *Principles of neural science* (3rd ed., pp. 329–340). New York: Elsevier.

Martin, J. H., Brust, J.C.M., & Hilal, S. (1991). Imaging the living brain. In E. R. Kandel, J. H. Schwartz, & T. M. Jessell (Eds.), *Principles of neural science* (pp. 309–324).

Maser, J. D. (1985). List of phobias. In A. H. Tuma & J. D. Maser (Eds.), *Anxiety and the anxiety disorders.* Hillsdale, NJ: Erlbaum.

Maslach, C. (1982). *Burnout: The cost of caring.* Englewood Cliffs, NJ: Prentice-Hall.

Maslow, A. (1954). *Motivation and personality.* New York: Harper.

Maslow, A. (1968). *Toward a psychology of being.* New York: Van Nostrand.

Masters, W. H., & Johnson, V. E. (1966). *Human sexual response.* Boston: Little, Brown.

Matarazzo, J. D. (1983). The reliability of psychiatric and psychological diagnosis. *Clinical Psychology Review, 3*, 103–145.

Matarazzo, J. D. (1992). Psychological testing and assessment in the 21st century. *American Psychologist, 47*, 1007–1018.

Matsumoto, D., & Ekman, P. (1989). Japanese-American cultural differences in intensity ratings of facial expressions of emotion. *Motivation and Emotion, 13*, 143–157.

Matsumoto, D., Kudoh, T., Scherer, K., & Wallbott, H. (1988). Antecedents and reactions to emotions in the United States and Japan. *Journal of Cross-Cultural Psychology, 19*, 267–286.

Matthews, K. A. (1988). CHD and Type A behavior: Update on and alternative to the Booth-Kewley and Friedman quantitative review. *Psychological Bulletin, 104*, 373–380.

Maurer, D., & Maurer, C. (1988). *The world of the newborn.* New York: Basic Books.

Mauro, R., Sato, K., & Tucker, J. (1992). The role of appraisal in human emotions: A cross-cultural study. *Journal of Personality and Social Psychology, 62*, 301–317.

Maylor, E. A. (1993). Aging and forgetting in prospective and retrospective memory tasks. *Psychology and Aging, 8*, 420–428.

Mazur, A., Booth, A., & Dabbs, J. M., Jr. (1992). Testosterone and chess competition. *Social Psychology Quarterly, 55*, 70–77.

McAdams, D. P., Jackson, R. J., & Kirshnit, C. (1984). Looking, laughing, and smiling in dyads as a function of intimacy motivation and reciprocity. *Journal of Personality, 52*, 261–273.

McAndrew, F. T. (1993). *Environmental psychology.* Pacific Grove, CA: Brooks/Cole.

McCartney, K., Harris, M. J., & Bernieri, F. (1990). Growing up and growing apart: A developmental meta-analysis of twin studies. *Psychological Bulletin, 107*, 226–237.

McCaul, K. D., & Malott, J. (1984). Distraction and coping with pain. *Psychological Bulletin, 95*, 516–533.

McCauley, C. (1989). The nature of social influence in groupthink: Compliance and internalization. *Journal of Personality and Social Psychology, 57*, 250–260.

McClelland, D. C. (1985). *Human motivation.* Glenview, IL: Scott, Foresman.

McCloskey, M. (1983). Naive theories of motion. In D. Gentner & K. Stevens (Eds.), *Mental models.* Hillsdale, NJ: Erlbaum.

McCloskey, M., Wible, C. G., & Cohen, N. J. (1988). Is there a special flashbulb-memory mechanism? *Journal of Experimental Psychology: General, 117*, 171–181.

McCloskey, M., & Zaragoza, M. (1985). Misleading postevent information and memory for events: Arguments and evidence against memory impairment hypotheses. *Journal of Experimental Psychology, 114*, 3–18.

McCormack, K., & Gruzelier, J. (1993). Cerebral asymmetry and hypnosis: A signal detection analysis of divided field stimulation. *Journal of Abnormal Psychology, 102*, 352–357.

McCormick, D. A., & Thompson, R. F. (1984). Cerebellum: Essential involvement in the classically conditioned eyelid response. *Science, 223*, 296–299.

McCrae, R. R., & Costa, P. T., Jr. (1990). *Personality in adulthood.* New York: Guilford Press.

McCrae, R. R., & John, O. P. (1992). An introduction to the five-factor model and its applications. *Journal of Personality, 60*, 175–216.

McGaugh, J. L. (1990). Significance and remembrance: The role of neuromodulatory systems. *Psychological Science, 1*, 15–25.

McGhie, A., & Chapman, J. (1961). Disorders of attention and perception in early schizophrenia. *British Journal of Medical Psychology, 34*, 102–116.

McGinnis, A. L. (1987). *The power of optimism.* San Francisco: Harper & Row.

McGlashan, T. H., & Fenton, W. S. (1991). Classical subtypes for schizophrenia: Literature review for DSM-IV. *Schizophrenia Bulletin, 17*, 609–623.

McGlashan, T. H., & Fenton, W. S. (1992). The positive-negative distinction in schizophrenia: Review of natural history validators. *Archives of General Psychiatry, 49*, 63–72.

McGlone, J. (1980). Sex differences in human brain asymmetry: A critical survey. *The Behavioral and Brain Sciences, 3*, 215–263.

McGlynn, S. M., & Kaszniak, A. W. (1991). When metacognition fails: Impaired awareness of deficit in Alzheimer's disease. *Journal of Cognitive Neuroscience, 3*, 183–189.

McGue, M., Bacon, S., & Lykken, D. T. (1993). Personality stability and change in early adulthood: A behavioral genetic analysis. *Developmental Psychology, 29*, 96–109.

McGue, M., & Lykken, D. T. (1992). Genetic influence on risk of divorce. *Psychological Science, 3*, 368–373.

McGuire, A. M. (1994). Helping behaviors in the natural environment: Dimensions and correlates of helping. *Personality and Social Psychology Bulletin, 20*, 45–56.

McGuire, W. J. (1968). Personality and susceptibility to social influence. In E. F. Borgatta & W. W. Lambert (Eds.), *Handbook of personality theory and research.* Chicago, IL: Rand McNally.

McKey, R. H., Condeli, L., Granson, H., Barrett, B., McConkey, C., &

Plantz, M. (1985). *The impact of Head Start on children, families, and communities* (final report of the Head Start Evaluation, Synthesis and Utilization Project). Washington, DC: CSR.

McKim, W. A. (1991). *Drugs and behavior.* Engelwood Cliffs, NJ: Prentice-Hall.

McKinlay, J. B., McKinlay, S. M., & Brambilla, D. J. (1987). Health status and utilization behavior associated with menopause. *American Journal of Epidemiology, 125,* 110–121.

McKinlay, J. B., McKinlay, S. M., & Brambilla, D. J. (1987). The relative contributions of endocrine changes and social circumstances to depression in middle-aged women. *Journal of Health and Social Behavior, 28,* 345–363.

McNally, R. J. (1987). Preparedness and phobias: A review. *Psychological Bulletin, 101,* 283–303.

McNally, R. J. (1990). Psychological approaches to panic disorder: A review. *Psychological Bulletin, 108,* 403–419.

McNamara, T. P. (1992). Priming and the constraints it places on theories of memory and retrieval. *Psychological Review, 99,* 650–662.

McNamara, T. P. (1994). Theories of priming: II. Types of primes. *Journal of Experimental Psychology: Learning, Memory, and Cognition, 20,* 507–520.

McNeal, E. T., & Cimbolic, P. (1986). Antidepressants and biochemical theories of depression. *Psychological Bulletin, 99,* 361–374.

McNeil, D. (1970). *The acquisition of language: The study of developmental psycholinguistics.* New York: Harper & Row.

McWhorter, K. T. (1988). *Study and thinking skills in college.* Glenview, IL: Scott, Foresman.

Mead, M. (1928). *Coming of age in Samoa.* New York: Morrow.

Medin, D. L., & Ross, B. H. (1992). *Cognitive psychology.* Ft. Worth, TX: Harcourt Brace Jovanovich.

Mednick, S. A. (1962). The associative basis of the creative process. *Psychological Review, 69,* 220–232.

Meehl, P. E. (1962). Schizotaxia, schizotypy, schizophrenia. *American Psychologist, 17,* 827–838.

Meichenbaum, D. (1985). *Stress inoculation training.* New York: Pergamon.

Melton, G. (1992). Children as partners for justice: Next steps for developmentalists. *Monographs of the Society for Research in Child Development, 57*(5, Serial No. 229).

Meltzer, H. Y. (Ed.). (1987). *Psychopharmacology: The third generation of progress.* New York: Raven Press.

Meltzer, H. Y., & Stahl, S. M. (1976). The dopamine hypothesis of schizophrenia: A review. *Schizophrenia Bulletin, 2,* 19–76.

Meltzoff, A. N., & Moore, M. K. (1983). Imitation of facial and manual gestures by human neonates. *Child Development, 54,* 702–709.

Meltzoff, A. N., & Moore, M. K. (1989). Imitation in newborn infants: Exploring the range of gestures imitated and the underlying mechanisms. *Developmental Psychology, 25,* 954–962.

Meltzoff, A. N., & Moore, M. K. (1992). Early imitation within a functional framework: The importance of person identity, movement, and development. *Infant Behavior and Development, 15,* 479–505.

Melzack, R., & Wall, P. (1965). Pain mechanisms: A new theory. *Science, 150,* 971–979.

Melzack, R., & Wall, P. (1982). *The challenge of pain.* New York: Penguin Books.

Merikle, P. M., & Reingold, E. M. (1992). Measuring unconscious perceptual processes. In R. F. Bornstein & T. S. Pittman (Eds.), *Perception without awareness.* New York: Guilford Press.

Mesquita, B., & Frijda, N. H. (1992). Cultural variations in emotions: A review. *Psychological Bulletin, 112,* 179–204.

Messick, D. M., & Mackie, D. M. (1989). Intergroup relations. *Annual Review of Psychology, 40,* 51–81.

Metalsky, G. I., & Joiner, T. E. (1992). Vulnerability to depressive symptomatology: A prospective test of the diathesis-stress and causal mediation components of the hopelessness theory of depression. *Journal of Personality and Social Psychology, 63,* 667–675.

Metalsky, G. I., Joiner, T. E., Hardin, T. S., & Abramson, L. Y. (1993). Depressive reactions to failure in a naturalistic setting: A test of the hopelessness and self-esteem theories of depression. *Journal of Abnormal Psychology, 102,* 101–109.

Metcalfe, J., & Weibe, D. (1987). Intuition in insight and non-insight problem solving. *Memory and Cognition, 15,* 238–246.

Meyer, D. E., & Schvaneveldt, R. W. (1971). Facilitation in recognizing pairs of words: Evidence of a dependence between retrieval operations. *Journal of Experimental Psychology, 90,* 227–234.

Meyer, G. E., & Hilterbrand, K. (1984). Does it pay to be "Bashful"? The seven dwarfs and long-term memory. *American Journal of Psychology, 97,* 47–55.

Michelson, L. K., & Marchione, K. (1991). Behavioral, cognitive, and pharmacological treatments of panic disorder with agoraphobia: Critique and synthesis. *Journal of Consulting and Clinical Psychology, 59,* 100–114.

Middlebrooks, J. C., & Green, D. M. (1991). Sound localization by human listeners. *Annual Review of Psychology, 42,* 135–159.

Milgram, S. (1963). Behavioral study of obedience. *Journal of Abnormal and Social Psychology, 67,* 371–378.

Milgram, S. (1965). Some conditions of obedience and disobedience to authority. *Human Relations, 18,* 57–76.

Milgram, S. (1974). *Obedience to authority: An experimental view.* New York: Harper & Row.

Milgram, S., Bickman, L., & Berkowitz, L. (1969). Note on the drawing power of crowds of different size. *Journal of Personality and Social Psychology, 13,* 79–82.

Miller, A. G. (1986). *The obedience experiments: A case study of controversy in social science.* New York: Praeger.

Miller, A. G., Ashton, W., & Mishal, M. (1990). Beliefs concerning the features of constrained behavior: A basis for the fundamental attribution error. *Journal of Personality and Social Psychology, 59,* 635–650.

Miller, G. A. (1956). The magical number seven plus or minus two: Some limits on our capacity for processing information. *Psychological Review, 63,* 81–97.

Miller, I. J., & Reedy, F. E. (1990). Variations in human taste bud density and taste intensity perception. *Physiology and Behavior, 47,* 1213–1219.

Miller, J. G. (1984). Culture and the development of everyday social explanation. *Journal of Personality and Social Psychology, 46,* 961–978.

Miller, J. G., & Bersoff, D. M. (1992). Culture and moral judgment: How are conflicts between justice and interpersonal responsibilities resolved? *Journal of Personality and Social Psychology, 62,* 541–554.

Miller, M. E., & Bowers, K. S. (1993). Hypnotic analgesia: Dissociated experience or dissociated control? *Journal of Abnormal Psychology, 102,* 29–38.

Miller, N. E. (1969). Learning of visceral and glandular responses. *Science, 163,* 434–445.

Miller, N. E. (1985). The value of behavioral research on animals. *American Psychologist, 40,* 423–440.

Miller, P. A., & Eisenberg, N. (1988). The relation of empathy to aggressive and externalizing/antisocial behavior. *Psychological Bulletin, 103,* 324–344.

Miller, T. Q., Turner, C. W., Tindale, R. S., Posavac, E. J., & Dugon, B. L. (1991). Reasons for the trend toward null findings in research on Type A behavior. *Psychological Bulletin, 110,* 469–485.

Miller-Jones, D. (1989). Culture and testing. *American Psychologist, 44,* 360–366.

Millon, T. (1990). The disorders of personality. In L. A. Pervin (Ed.), *Handbook of personality theory and research* (pp. 339–370). New York: Guilford Press.

Mills, H. L., Agras, W. S., Barlow, D. H., & Mills, J. R. (1973). Compulsive rituals treated by response prevention. *Archives of General Psychiatry, 28,* 524–529.

Milner, B., Corkin, S., & Teuber, H. L. (1968). Further analysis of the hippocampal amnesic syndrome: 14-year follow-up study of H. M. *Neuropsychologica, 6,* 215–234.

Mineka, S., & Cook, M. (1993). Mechanisms involved in the observational conditioning of fear. *Journal of Experimental Psychology: General, 122,* 23–38.

Mischel, W. (1968). *Personality and assessment.* New York: Wiley.

Mischel, W. (1973). Toward a cognitive social-learning reconceptualization of personality. *Psychological Review, 80,* 252–283.

Mischel, W. (1990). Personality dispositions revisited and revised: A view after three decades. In L. A. Pervin (Ed.), *Handbook of personality theory and research* (pp. 111–134). New York: Guilford Press.

Mischel, W., Shoda, Y., & Rodriguez, M. L. (1989). Delay of gratification in children. *Science, 244,* 933–938.

Mita, T. H., Dermer, M., & Knight, J. (1977). Reversed facial images and the mere-exposure hypothesis. *Journal of Personality and Social Psychology, 35,* 597–601.

Mitchell, P. (1976). *Act of love: The killing of George Zygmanik.* New York: Knopf.

Moghaddam, F. M., Taylor, D. M., & Wright, S. C. (1993). *Social psychology in cross-cultural perspective.* New York: W. H. Freeman.

Moir, A., & Jessel, D. (1989). *Brain sex: The real difference between men and women.* New York: Dell.

Monaghan, E. P., & Glickman, S. E. (1992). Hormones and aggressive behavior. In J. B. Becker, S. M. Breedlove, & D. Crews (Eds.), *Behavioral endocrinology* (pp. 261–285). Cambridge, MA: MIT Press.

Moncher, M. S., Holden, G. W., & Trimble, J. E. (1990). Substance abuse among Native-American youth. *Journal of Consulting and Clinical Psychology, 58,* 408–415.

Monk, T. H. (1987). Coping with the stress of jet-lag. *Work & Stress, 1,* 163–166.

Monk, T. H. (1988). Coping with the stress of shift work. *Work & Stress, 2,* 169–172.

Montepare, J. M., & Lachman, M. E. (1989). "You're only as old as you feel": Self perceptions of age, fears of aging, and life satisfaction from adolescence to old age. *Psychology and Aging, 4,* 73–78.

Montepare, J. M., & McArthur, L. Z. (1988). Impressions of people created by age-related qualities of their gait. *Journal of Personality and Social Psychology, 55,* 547–556.

Moore, T. E. (1982). Subliminal advertising: What you see is what you get. *Journal of Marketing, 46,* 38–47.

Moran, G., & Cutler, B. L. (1991). The prejudicial impact of pretrial publicity. *Journal of Applied Social Psychology, 21,* 345–367.

Morawetz, D. (1989). Behavioral self-help treatment for insomnia: A controlled evaluation. *Behavior Therapy, 20,* 365–379.

Moray, N. (1959). Attention in dichotic listening: Affective cues and the influence of instructions. *Quarterly Journal of Experimental Psychology, 11,* 56–60.

Morelli, G. A., Rogoff, B., Oppenheim, D., & Goldsmith, D. (1992). Cultural variation in infants' sleeping arrangements: Questions of independence. *Developmental Psychology, 28,* 604–613.

Morokoff, P. J. (1988). Sexuality in perimenopausal and postmenopausal women. *Psychology of Women Quarterly, 12,* 489–511.

Morris, M. W., & Nisbett, R. E. (1993). Tools of the trade: Deductive schemas taught in psychology and philosophy. In R. E. Nisbett (Ed.), *Rules for reasoning* (pp. 228–256). Hillsdale, NJ: Erlbaum.

Morrison, A. M., & Von Glinow, M. A. (1990). Women and minorities in management. *American Psychologist, 45,* 200–208.

Morrison, D. C. (1988). Marine mammals join the navy. *Science, 242,* 1503–1504.

Morrison, D. M. (1985). Adolescent contraceptive behavior: A review. *Psychological Bulletin, 98,* 538–568.

Morrow, D., Leirer, V., Altieri, P., and Fitzsimmons, C. (1994). When expertise reduces age differences in performance. *Psychology and Aging, 9,* 134–148.

Morrow, J., & Nolen-Hoeksema, S. (1990). Effects of responses to depression on the remediation of depressive affect. *Journal of Personality and Social Psychology, 58,* 519–527.

Morton, J., & Johnson, M. H. (1991). CONSPEC and CONLERN: A two-process theory of infant face recognition. *Psychological Review, 98,* 164–181.

Morton, J., Johnson, M. H., & Maurer, D. (1990). On the reasons for newborns' responses to faces. *Infant Behavior and Development, 13,* 99–103.

Moscovici, S. (1985). Social influence and conformity. In G. Lindzey & E. Aronson (Eds.), *The handbook of social psychology* (3rd ed., pp. 347–412). New York: Random House.

Moscovici, S., Lage, E., & Naffrechoux, M. (1969). Influence of a consistent minority on the responses of a majority in a color perception task. *Sociometry, 32,* 365–380.

Moscovici, S., & Personnaz, B. (1991). Studies in social influence: VI. Is Lenin orange or red? Imagery and social influence. *European Journal of Social Psychology, 21,* 101–118.

Moscovici, S., & Zavalloni, M. (1969). The group as a polarizer of attitudes. *Journal of Personality and Social Psychology, 12,* 125–135.

Moskowitz, D. S. (1982). Coherence and cross-situational generality in personality: A new analysis of old problems. *Journal of Personality and Social Psychology, 43,* 754–768.

Moulton, J., Robinson, G. M., & Elias, C. (1978). Sex bias in language use: "Neutral pronouns that aren't." *American Psychologist, 33,* 1032–1036.

Mozell, M. M., Smith, B., Smith, P., Sullivan, R., & Swender, P. (1969). Nasal chemoreception in flavor identification. *Archives of Otolaryngology, 90,* 367–373.

Muehlenhard, C. L. (1988). Misinterpreted dating behaviors and the risk of date rape. *Journal of Social and Clinical Psychology, 6,* 20–37.

Mukherjee, S., Sackheim, H. A., & Schnur, D. B. (1994). Electroconvulsive therapy of acute manic episodes: A review of 50 years' experience. *American Journal of Psychiatry, 151,* 169–176.

Mukherjee, S., Shukla, S., Woodle, J., Rosen, A. M., & Olarte, S. (1983). Misdiagnosis of schizophrenia in bipolar patients: A multiethnic comparison. *American Journal of Psychiatry, 140,* 1571–1574.

Mulder, H. E., Van Olphen, A. F., Bosman, A., & Smoorenburg, G. F. (1992). Phoneme recognition by deaf individuals using the multichannel nucleus cochlear implant. *Acta Otolaryngology, 112,* 946–955.

Mullen, B. (1986). Atrocity as a function of lynch mob composition: A self-attention perspective. *Personality and Social Psychology Bulletin, 12,* 187–197.

Murray, H. A. (1938). *Explorations in personality.* New York: Oxford University Press.

Murray, H. A. (1943). *Thematic Apperception Test: Pictures and manual.* Cambridge, MA: Harvard University Press.

Murstein, B. L. (1986). *Paths to marriage.* Newbury Park, CA: Sage.

Mustillo, P. (1985). Binocular mechanisms mediating crossed and uncrossed stereopsis. *Psychological Bulletin, 97,* 187–201.

Mydans, S. (1990, January). For jurors, facts could not be sifted from fantasies. *New York Times,* p. A18.

Myers, D. G. (1992). *Well-being: How is happy—and why.* New York: Morrow.

Myers, D. G. (1993). *The pursuit of happiness*. New York: Avon.

Myers, D. G., & Bishop, G. D. (1970). Discussion effects on racial attitudes. *Science, 169*, 778–779.

Myers, D. G., & Lamm, H. (1976). The group polarization phenomenon. *Psychological Bulletin, 83*, 602–627.

Nadon, R., Hoyt, I. P., Register, P. A., & Kihlstrom, J. F. (1991). Absorption and hypnotizability: Context effects reexamined. *Journal of Personality and Social Psychology, 60*, 144–153.

Nathans, J., Piantanida, T. P., Eddy, R. L., Shows, T. B., & Hogness, D. S. (1986). Molecular genetics of inherited variation in human color vision. *Science, 232*, 203–210.

National Law Journal (1990, September 10). Rock group not liable for deaths, p. 33.

Nebes, R. D. (1990). The commissurotomized brain: Introduction. In R. D. Nebes & S. Corkin (Eds.), *Handbook of Neuropsychology* (Vol. 4). Amsterdam: Elsevier.

Neiberg, P., Marks, J. S., McLaren, N. M., & Remongton, P. (1985). The fetal tobacco syndrome. *Journal of the American Medical Association, 253*, 2998–2999.

Neill, S. R. (1982). Preschool design and child behavior. *Journal of Child Psychology and Psychiatry, 23*, 309–318.

Neisser, U. (1967). *Cognitive psychology*. New York: Appleton-Century-Crofts.

Neisser, U. (1981). John Dean's memory: A case study. *Cognition, 9*, 1–22.

Neisser, U., & Becklen, R. (1975). Selective looking: Attending to visually specified events. *Cognitive Psychology, 7*, 480–494.

Nelson, K. (1973). Structure and strategy in learning to talk. *Monographs of the Society for Research in Child Development, 38*(Whole No. 149).

Nemeroff, C. B. (1989). Clinical significance of psychoneuroendocrinology in psychiatry: Focus on the thyroid and adrenal. *Journal of Clinical Psychiatry, 50*, 13–20.

Neuberg, S. L. (1989). The goal of forming accurate impressions during social interactions: Attenuating the impact of negative expectancies. *Journal of Personality and Social Psychology, 56*, 374–386.

Neuberg, S. L., Judice, T. N., Virdin, L. M., & Carrillo, M. A. (1993). Perceiver self-presentational goals as moderators of expectancy influences: Ingratiation and the disconfirmation of negative expectancies. *Journal of Personality and Social Psychology, 64*, 409–420.

Neugarten, B. L. (1967, December). A new look at menopause. *Psychology Today*, pp. 42–45.

Neugarten, B. L. (1979). Time, age, and the life cycle. *American Journal of Psychiatry, 136*, 887–894.

Nevid, J. S., Lavi, B., & Primavera, L. H. (1987). Principal components analysis of therapeutic orientations of doctoral programs in clinical psychology. *Journal of Clinical Psychology, 43*, 723–729.

Nevin, J. A. (1988). Behavioral momentum and the partial reinforcement effect. *Psychological Bulletin, 103*, 44–56.

Newcomb, A. F., Bukowski, W. M., & Pattee, L. (1993). Children's peer relations: A meta-analytic review of popular, rejected, neglected, controversial, and average sociometric status. *Psychological Bulletin, 113*, 99–128.

Newcomb, M. D., & Bentler, P. M. (1989). Substance use and abuse among children and teenagers. *American Psychologist, 44*, 242–248.

Newcomb, T. M. (1961). *The acquaintance process*. New York: Holt, Rinehart & Winston.

Newcombe, F., & Ratcliff, G. (1990). Disorders of visuospatial analysis. In H. Goodglass & A. R. Damasio (Eds.), *Handbook of Neuropsychology* (Vol. 2). Amsterdam: Elsevier.

Newcombe, N., & Fox, N. A. (1994). Infantile amnesia: Through a glass darkly. *Child Development, 65*, 31–40.

Newcombe, N. S., & Baenninger, M. (1989). Biological change and cognitive ability in adolescence. In G. Adams, R. Montemayor, & T. Gullotta (Eds.), *Biology of adolescent behavior and development* (pp. 168–191). Newbury Park, CA: Sage.

Newell, A., Shaw, J. G., & Simon, H. A. (1958). Elements of a theory of human problem solving. *Psychological Review, 65*, 151–166.

Newell, A., & Simon, H. (1972). *Human problem solving*. Englewood Cliffs, NJ: Prentice-Hall.

Newmann, J. P. (1989). Aging and depression. *Psychology and Aging, 4*, 150–165.

Ng, S. H. (1990). Androcentric coding of *man* and *his* in memory by language users. *Journal of Experimental Social Psychology, 26*, 455–464.

Nicholls, J. G., Martin, A. R., & Wallace, B. G. (1992). *From neuron to brain*. Sunderland, MA: Sinauer.

Nickerson, R. S., & Adams, M. J. (1979). Long-term memory for a common object. *Cognitive Psychology, 11*, 287–307.

Nielson, S. L., & Sarason, I. G. (1981). Emotion, personality, and selective attention. *Journal of Personality and Social Psychology, 41*, 945–960.

Nijhawan, R. (1991). Three-dimensional Müller-Lyer illusion. *Perception and Psychophysics, 49*, 333–341.

Nimmons, D. (1994, March). Sex and the brain. *Discover*, pp. 64–71.

Nisbett, R. E., Fong, G. T., Lehman, D. R., & Cheng, P. W. (1987). Teaching reasoning. *Science, 238*, 625–631.

Nisbett, R. E., & Wilson, T. D. (1977). Telling more than we can know: Verbal reports on mental processes. *Psychological Review, 84*, 231–259.

Nolen-Hoeksema, S. (1990). *Sex differences in depression*. Stanford, CA: Stanford University Press.

Nolen-Hoeksema, S., Morrow, J., & Fredrickson, N. (1993). Response styles and the duration of episodes of depressed mood. *Journal of Abnormal Psychology, 102*, 20–28.

Norcross, J. C. (1991). Prescriptive matching in psychotherapy: An introduction. *Psychotherapy, 28*, 439–443.

Norton, G. R., Cox, B., & Malan, J. (1992). Nonclinical panickers: A critical review. *Clinical Psychology Review, 12*, 121–139.

O'Leary, A. (1990). Stress, emotion, and human immune function. *Psychological Bulletin, 108*, 363–382.

O'Leary, K. D., & Wilson, G. T. (1987). *Behavior therapy: Application and outcome*. Englewood Cliffs, NJ: Prentice-Hall.

Oakes, J. (1985). *Keeping track: How schools structure inequality*. New Haven, CT: Yale University Press.

Oetting, E. R., & Beauvais, F. (1990). Adolescent drug use: Findings of national and local surveys. *Journal of Consulting and Clinical Psychology, 58*, 385–394.

Offer, D. (1987). In defense of adolescents. *Journal of the American Medical Association, 257*, 3407–3408.

Offer, D., Ostrov, E., & Howard, I. (1981). *The adolescent: A psychological self-portrait*. New York: Basic Books.

Offer, D., & Schonert-Reichl, K. A. (1992). Debunking the myths of adolescence: Findings from recent research. *Journal of the American Academy of Child and Adolescent Psychiatry, 31*, 1003–1013.

Ogilvy, D. (1985). *Ogilvy on advertising*. New York: Vintage Books.

Ohman, A. (1986). Face the beast and fear the face: Animal and social fears as prototypes for evolutionary analyses of emotion. *Psychophysiology, 23*, 123–145.

Okagaki, L., and French, P. A. (1994). Effects of video game playing on measures of spatial performance: Gender effects in late adolescence. *Journal of Applied Developmental Psychology, 15*, 33–58.

Olds, J., & Milner, P. M. (1954). Positive reinforcement produced by electrical stimulation of septal area and other regions of the rat brain. *Journal of Comparative and Physiological Psychology, 47*, 419–427.

Oliver, M. B., & Hyde, J. S. (1993). Gender differences in sexuality: A meta-analysis. *Psychological Bulletin, 114*, 29–51.

Olness, K. (1993). Hypnosis: The power of attention. In D. Goleman & J. Gurin (Eds.), *Mind body medicine* (pp. 277–290). Yonkers, New York: Consumer Reports Books.

Olson, J. M. (1988). Misattribution, preparatory information, and speech anxiety. *Journal of Personality and Social Psychology, 54,* 758–767.

Olzak, S., & Nagel, J. (1986). *Competitive ethnic relations.* New York: Academic Press.

Ones, D. S., Viswesvaran, C., & Schmidt, F. L. (1993). Comprehensive meta-analysis of integrity test validities: Findings and implications for personnel selection and theories of job performance. *Journal of Applied Psychology, 78,* 679–703.

Orne, M. T., Dinges, D. F., & Orne, E. C. (1984). The differential diagnosis of multiple personality in the forensic court. *International Journal of Clinical and Experimental Hypnosis, 32,* 118–169.

Orne, M. T., & Evans, F. J. (1965). Social control in the psychological experiment: Antisocial behavior and hypnosis. *Journal of Personality and Social Psychology, 1,* 189–200.

Ornstein, R. E. (1972). *The psychology of consciousness.* San Francisco: W. H. Freeman.

Ornstein, R. E. (1978). The split and whole brain. *Human Nature, 1,* 76–83.

Ornstein, R., & Sobel, D. (1987). *The healing brain.* New York: Simon & Schuster.

Ost, L. G. (1989). One-session treatment for specific phobias. *Behavioral Research and Therapy, 27,* 1–7.

Ost, L.-G. (1992). Blood and injection phobia: Background and cognitive, physiological, and behavioral variables. *Journal of Abnormal Psychology, 101,* 68–74.

Ost, L.-G., Salkovskis, P. M., & Hellstrom, K. (1991). One-session therapist-directed exposure vs. self-exposure in the treatment of spider phobia. *Behavior Therapy, 22,* 407–422.

Ostrom, T. M., & Sedikides, C. (1992). Out-group homogeneity effects in natural and minimal groups. *Psychological Bulletin, 112,* 536–552.

Ottati, V. C., Riggle, E. J., Wyer, R. S., Schwarz, N., & Kuklinski, J. (1989). Cognitive and affective bases of opinion survey responses. *Journal of Personality and Social Psychology, 57,* 404–415.

P.A.S.E. v. *Hannon,* 506 F. Supp. 931 (N. D. Ill. 1980).

Packard, V. (1957). *The hidden persuaders.* New York: Pocket Books.

Paffenbarger, R. S., Jr., Hyde, R. T., Wing, A. L., & Hsieh, C. (1986). Physical activity, all-cause mortality, and longevity of college alumni. *New England Journal of Medicine, 314,* 605–613.

Paikoff, R. L., & Brooks-Gunn, J. (1991). Do parent-child relationships change during puberty? *Psychological Bulletin, 110,* 47–66.

Paivio, A. (1969). Mental imagery in associative learning and memory. *Psychological Review, 76,* 241–263.

Palfai, T., & Jankiewicz, H. (1991). *Drugs and human behavior.* Dubuque, IA: Wm. C. Brown.

Palmore, E. B. (1982). Predictors of the longevity difference: A 25-year follow-up. *The Gerontologist, 22,* 513–518.

Palmore, E. B., & Jeffers, F. C. (1971). *Predictions of the life span.* Lexington, MA: Heath.

Panskepp, J. (1986). The anatomy of emotions. In R. Plutchik & H. Kellerman (Eds.), *Emotion: Theory, research, and experience—Biological foundations of emotion* (Vol. 3, pp. 91–124). San Diego: Academic Press.

Panskepp, J. (1992). A critical role for "affective neuroscience" in resolving what is basic about basic emotions. *Psychological Review, 99,* 554–560.

Parke, R. D. (1981). *Fathers.* Cambridge, MA: Harvard University Press.

Parker, J. G., & Asher, S. R. (1987). Peer relations and later adjustment: Are low-accepted children "at risk"? *Psychological Bulletin, 102,* 357–389.

Parker, K., Hanson, R., & Hinsley, J. (1988). MMPI, Rorschach, and WAIS: A meta-analytic comparison of reliability, stability, and validity. *Psychological Bulletin, 103,* 367–373.

Parks, R. W., Zec, R. F., & Wilson, R. S. (Eds.). (1993). *Neuropsychology of Alzheimer's Disease and other dementias.* New York: Oxford University Press.

Parmelee, A. H., Jr., & Sigman, M. D. (1983). Perinatal brain development and behavior. In P. H. Mussen (Ed.), *Handbook of child psychology: Vol. 2. Infancy and developmental psychobiology.* New York: Wiley.

Parr, W. V., & Siegert, R. (1993). Adults' conceptions of everyday memory failures in others: Factors that mediate the effects of target age. *Psychology and Aging, 8,* 599–605.

Pascual-Leone, J. (1970). A mathematical model for the transition rule in Piaget's developmental stages. *Acta Psychologica, 32,* 301–345.

Passman, R. H. (1987). Attachments to inanimate objects: Are children who have security blankets insecure? *Journal of Consulting and Clinical Psychology, 55,* 825–830.

Patrick, C. J., Bradley, M. M., & Lang, P. J. (1993). Emotion in the criminal psychopath: Startle reflex modulation. *Journal of Abnormal Psychology, 102,* 82–92.

Patrick, C. J., & Iacono, W. G. (1991). Validity of the control question polygraph test: The problem of sampling bias. *Journal of Applied Psychology, 76,* 229–238.

Patterson, F., & Linden, E. (1981). *The education of Koko.* New York: Holt, Rinehart & Winston.

Patterson, M. L. (1983). *Nonverbal behavior: A functional perspective.* New York: Springer-Verlag.

Paulhus, D., Graf, P., & Van Selst, M. (1989). Attentional load increases the positivity of self-presentation. *Social Cognition, 7,* 389–400.

Paulos, J. A. (1988). *Innumeracy: Mathematical illiteracy and its consequences.* New York: Hill and Wang.

Paulus, P. B. (1988). *Prison crowding: A psychological perspective.* New York: Springer-Verlag.

Paunonen, S. V., Jackson, D. N., Trzebinski, J., & Fosterling, F. (1992). Personality structure across cultures: A multi-method evaluation. *Journal of Personality and Social Psychology, 62,* 447–456.

Pavlov, I. (1927). *Conditioned reflexes.* Oxford: Oxford University Press.

Pavot, W., & Diener, E. (1993). Review of the Satisfaction with Life Scale. *Psychological Assessment, 5,* 164–172.

Payne, J. W., Bettman, J. R., & Johnson, E. J. (1992). Behavioral decision research: A constructive processing approach. *Annual Review of Psychology, 43,* 87–131.

Pearce, J. M. (1987). A model for stimulus generalization in Pavlovian conditioning. *Psychological Review, 94,* 61–73.

Pelham, W. E. (1993). Pharmacotherapy for children with attention deficit hyperactivity disorder. *School Psychology Review, 22,* 199–227.

Pelham, W. E., Carlson, C. L., Sams, S. E., Vallano, G., et al. (1993). Separate and combined effects of methylphenidate and behavior modification on boys with attention deficit hyperactivity disorder in the classroom. *Journal of Consulting and Clinical Psychology, 61,* 506–515.

Penfield, W., & Roberts, L. (1959). *Speech and brain mechanisms.* Princeton, NJ: Princeton University Press.

Penfield, W., & Perot, P. (1963). The brain's record of auditory and visual experience. *Brain, 86,* 595–696.

Pennebaker, J. W. (1982). *The psychology of physical symptoms.* New York: Springer-Verlag.

Pennebaker, J. W. (1990). *Opening up: The healing power of confiding in others.* New York: Morrow.

Peplau, L. A., & Perlman, D. (Eds.). (1982). *Loneliness: A sourcebook of current theory, research and therapy.* New York: Wiley.

Pepperberg, I. M. (1991). A communicative approach to animal cognition: A study of the conceptual abilities of an African grey parrot. In C. A. Ristau (Ed.), *Cognitive ethology: The minds of other animals* (pp. 153–186). Hillsdale, NJ: Erlbaum.

Pepperberg, I. M. (1994). Numerical competence in an African gray parrot. *Journal of Comparative Psychology, 108,* 36–44.

Perdue, C. W., Dovidio, J. F., Gurtman, M. B., & Tyler, R. B. (1990). Us and them: Social categorization and the process of intergroup bias. *Journal of Personality and Social Psychology, 59,* 475–486.

Perlmutter, M. (1978). What is memory aging the aging of? *Developmental Psychology, 14,* 330–345.

Perlow, M. J., Freed, W. J., Hoffer, B. J., Seiger, A., Olson, L., & Wyatt, R. J. (1979). Brain grafts reduce motor abnormalities produced by destruction of nigrostriatal dopamine system. *Science, 204,* 643–646.

Perls, F. S. (1969). *Gestalt therapy verbatim.* Lafayette, CA: Real People Press.

Perls, F. S., Hefferline, R. F., & Goodman, P. (1951). *Gestalt therapy.* New York: Julian Press.

Perry, N. W., & Wrightsman, L. S. (1991). *The child witness: Legal issues and dilemmas.* Newbury Park, CA: Sage.

Persky, V. W., Kempthorne-Rawson, J., & Shekelle, R. B. (1987). Personality and risk of cancer: 20-year follow-up of the Western Electric Study. *Psychosomatic Medicine, 49,* 435–449.

Pert, C. B., & Snyder, S. H. (1973). Opiate receptor: Demonstration in nervous tissue. *Science, 179,* 1011–1014.

Petersen, A. C. (1985). Pubertal development as a cause of disturbance: Myths, realities, and unanswered questions. *Genetic, Social, and General Psychology Monographs, 111,* 205–232.

Petersen, A. C. (1988). Adolescent development. *Annual Review of Psychology, 39,* 583–607.

Peterson, C., Seligman, M. E. P., & Vaillant, G. E. (1988). Pessimistic explanatory style is a risk factor for physical illness: A thirty-five-year longitudinal study. *Journal of Personality and Social Psychology, 55,* 23–27.

Peterson, D., & Goodall, J. (1993). *Visions of Caliban.* Boston: Houghton Mifflin.

Peterson, L. R., & Peterson, M. J. (1959). Short-term retention of individual verbal items. *Journal of Experimental Psychology, 58,* 193–198.

Peterson, S. E., & Fiez, J. A. (1993). The processing of single words studied with positron emission tomography. *Annual Review of Neuroscience, 16,* 509–530.

Pettigrew, T. F., & Martin, J. (1987). Shaping the organizational context for black American inclusion. *Journal of Social Issues, 43,* 41–78.

Petty, M. M., Singleton, B., & Connell, D. W. (1992). An experimental evaluation of an organizational incentive plan in the electric utility industry. *Journal of Applied Psychology, 77,* 427–436.

Petty, R. E., & Cacioppo, J. T. (1986). *Communication and persuasion: Central and peripheral routes to attitude change.* New York: Springer-Verlag.

Petty, R. E., & Cacioppo, J. T. (1990). Involvement and persuasion: Tradition versus integration. *Psychological Bulletin, 107,* 367–374.

Petty, R. E., Cacioppo, J. T., & Goldman, R. (1981). Personal involvement as a determinant of argument-based persuasion. *Journal of Personality and Social Psychology, 41,* 847–855.

Pezdek, K., Whetstone, T., Reynolds, K., Askari, N., & Dougherty, T. (1989). Memory for real-world scenes: The role of consistency with schema expectation. *Journal of Experimental Psychology: Learning, Memory, and Cognition, 15,* 587–595.

Phares, E. J. (1976). *Locus of control in personality.* Morristown, NJ: General Learning Press.

Phelps, M. E., & Mazziotta, J. C. (1985). Positron-emission tomography: Human brain function and biochemistry. *Science, 228,* 799–809.

Phillips, A. P., & Dipboye, R. L. (1989). Correlational tests of predictions from a process model of the interview. *Journal of Applied Psychology, 74,* 41–52.

Phillips, D. P., & Feldman, K. A. (1973). A dip in deaths before ceremonial occasions: Some new relationships between social integration and mortality. *American Sociological Review, 38,* 678–696.

Phillips, D. P., Van Voorhees, C. A., & Ruth, T. E. (1992). The birthday: Lifeline or deadline? *Psychosomatic Medicine, 54,* 532–542.

Phinney, J. S. (1990). Ethnic identity in adolescents and adults: Review of research. *Psychological Bulletin, 108,* 499–514.

Piaget, J. (1932). *The moral judgment of the child.* New York: Harcourt, Brace & World.

Piaget, J. (1952). *The origins of intelligence.* New York: Norton. (Original work published 1936)

Piaget, J. (1952). *The origins of intelligence in children.* New York: International University Press. (Original work published 1936)

Piaget, J. (1965). *The moral judgment of the child.* New York: Free Press. (Original work published 1932)

Piaget, J. (1976). *The grasp of consciousness: Action and concept in the young child.* Cambridge, MA: Harvard University Press.

Piaget, J., & Inhelder, B. (1969). *The psychology of the child.* New York: Basic Books.

Piccione, C., Hilgard, E. R., & Zimbardo, P. G. (1989). On the degree of stability of measured hypnotizability over a 25-year period. *Journal of Personality and Social Psychology, 56,* 289–295.

Piliavin, J. A., Dovidio, J. F., Gaertner, S. S., & Clark, R. D., III. (1981). *Emergency intervention.* New York: Academic Press.

Pillemer, D. B., Picariello, M. L., & Pruett, J. C. (1994). Very long-term memories of a salient preschool event. *Applied Cognitive Psychology, 8,* 95–106.

Pines, A., & Aronson, E. (1988). *Career burnout: Causes and cures.* New York: Free Press.

Pinker, S. (1990). Language acquisition. In D. N. Osherson & H. Lasnik (Eds.), *Language.* Cambridge, MA: MIT Press.

Plomin, R. (1988). The nature and nurture of cognitive abilities. In R. J. Sternberg (Ed.), *Advances in the psychology of human intelligence* (Vol. 4, pp. 1–33). Hillsdale, NJ: Erlbaum.

Plomin, R. (1989). Environment and genes: Determinants of behavior. *American Psychologist, 44,* 105–111.

Plomin, R., et al. (1993). Genetic change and continuity from fourteen to twenty months: The MacArthur longitudinal twin study. *Child Development, 64,* 1354–1376.

Plomin, R., & McClearn, G. E. (Eds.). (1993). *Nature, nurture, and psychology.* Washington, DC: American Psychological Association.

Plomin, R., Reiss, D., Hetherington, E. M., & Howe, G. W. (1994). Nature and nurture: Genetic contributions to measures of the family environment. *Developmental Psychology, 30,* 32–43.

Plous, S. (1991). An attitude survey of animal rights activists. *Psychological Science, 2,* 194–196.

Plous, S. (1991). Biases in the assimilation of technological breakdowns: Do accidents make us safer? *Journal of Applied Social Psychology, 21,* 1058–1082.

Plutchik, R. (1980). *Emotion: A psychoevolutionary synthesis.* New York: Harper & Row.

Poincuré, H. (1929). *The foundations of science.* New York: Science House.

Poizner, H., Klima, E. S., & Bellugi, U. (1990). *What the hands reveal about the brain.* Cambridge, MA: MIT Press.

Poling, A., Schlinger, H. D., Jr., Starin, S., & Blakely, E. (1990). *Psychology: A behavioral overview.* New York: Plenum.

Poole, D. A., & White, L. T. (1991). Effects of question repetition on the eyewitness testimony of children and adults. *Developmental Psychology, 27,* 975–986.

Poole, G. D., & Craig, K. D. (1992). Judgments of genuine, suppressed, and faked facial expressions of pain. *Journal of Personality and Social Psychology, 63,* 797–805.

Pope, H. G., Jr., McElroy, S. L., Keck, P. E., Jr., & Hudson, J. I. (1991). Valproate in the treatment of acute mania. *Archives of*

General Psychiatry, 48, 62–68.

Pope, K. S., & Vetter, V. A. (1992). Ethical dilemmas encountered by members of the American Psychological Association: A national survey. *American Psychologist, 47,* 397–411.

Popkin, J. (1994, March 14). Tricks of the trade. *U.S. News and World Report,* pp. 48–52.

Porac, C., & Coren, S. (1981). *Lateral preferences and human behavior.* New York: Springer-Verlag.

Porter, D., & Neuringer, A. (1984). Music discrimination by pigeons. *Journal of Experimental Psychology: Animal Behavior Processes, 10,* 138–148.

Porter, R. H., Makin, J. W., Davis, L. B., & Christensen, K. M. (1992). Breast-fed infants respond to olfactory cues from their own mother and unfamiliar lactating females. *Infant Behavior and Development, 15,* 85–93.

Poulson, C. L., et al. (1991). Generalized vocal imitation in infants. *Journal of Experimental Child Psychology, 51,* 267–279.

Powers, D. E. (1986). Relations of test item characteristics to test preparation/test practice effects: A quantitative summary. *Psychological Bulletin, 100,* 67–77.

Powers, L. I., Hauser, S. T., & Kilner, L. A. (1989). Adolescent mental health. *American Psychologist, 44,* 200–208.

Pratkanis, A., & Aronson, E. (1992). *Age of propaganda: The everyday use and abuse of persuasion.* San Francisco: W. H. Freeman.

Premack, A., & Premack, D. (1983). *The mind of an ape.* New York: Norton.

Premack, D. (1971). Language in chimpanzee? *Science, 172,* 808–822.

Prentice-Dunn, S., & Rogers, R. W. (1989). Deindividuation and the self-regulation of behavior. In P. B. Paulus (Ed.), *Psychology of group influence* (2nd ed.). Hillsdale, NJ: Erlbaum.

Price, R. H. (1992). Psychosocial impact of job loss on individuals and families. *Current Directions in Psychological Science, 1,* 9–11.

Prioleau, L., Murdock, M., & Brody, N. (1983). An analysis of psychotherapy versus placebo studies. *Behavioral and Brain Sciences, 6,* 275–310.

Pritchard, R. D., Jones, S. D., Roth, P. L., Stuebing, K. K., & Ekeberg, S. E. (1988). Effects of group feedback, goal setting, and incentives on organizational productivity. *Journal of Applied Psychology, 73,* 337–358.

Privette, G. (1983). Peak experience, peak performance, and flow: A comparative analysis of positive human experiences. *Journal of Personality and Social Psychology, 45,* 1361–1368.

Purcell, P., & Stewart, L. (1990). Dick and Jane in 1989. *Sex Roles, 22,* 177–185.

Putnam, F. W., Guroff, J. J., Silberman, E. K., Barban, L., & Post, R. M. (1986). The clinical phenomenology of multiple personality disorder: 100 recent cases. *Journal of Clinical Psychiatry, 47,* 285–293.

Pyszczynski, T., & Greenberg, J. (1987). Self-regulatory preservation and the depressive self-focusing style: A self-awareness theory of reactive depression. *Psychological Bulletin, 201,* 122–138.

Quadrel, M. J., Fischhoff, B., & Davis, W. (1993). Adolescent (in)vulnerability. *American Psychologist, 48,* 102–116.

Quattrone, G. A. (1986). On the perception of a group's variability. In S. Worchel & W. G. Austin (Eds.), *Psychology of intergroup relations* (2nd. ed.). Chicago, IL: Nelson Hall.

Quattrone, G. A., & Jones, E. E. (1980). The perception of variability within ingroups and outgroups: Implications for the law of small numbers. *Journal of Personality and Social Psychology, 38,* 141–152.

Quinn, P. C., Burke, S., & Rush, A. (1993). Part-whole perception in early infancy: Evidence for perceptual grouping produced by lightness similarity. *Infant Behavior and Development, 16,* 19–42.

Rachman, S. J. (1990). *Fear and courage* (2nd ed.). San Francisco: W. H. Freeman.

Rachman, S., & Maser, J. D. (Eds.). (1988). *Panic: Psychological perspectives.* Hillsdale, NJ: Erlbaum.

Radford, J. (1990). *Child prodigies and exceptional early achievers.* New York: Free Press.

Rafaeli, A., & Klimoski, R. J. (1983). Predicting sales success through handwriting analysis: An evaluation of the effects of training and handwriting sample context. *Journal of Applied Psychology, 68,* 212–217.

Ragins, B. R., & Sundstrom, E. (1989). Gender and power in organizations: A longitudinal perspective. *Psychological Bulletin, 105,* 51–88.

Raichle, M. E. (1994). Images of the mind: Studies with modern imaging techniques. *Annual Review of Psychology, 45,* 333–356.

Rajaram, S., & Roediger, H. L., III. (1993). Direct comparisons of four implicit memory tests. *Journal of Experimental Psychology: Learning, Memory, and Cognition, 19,* 765–776.

Rajecki, D. W., Bledsoe, S. B., & Rasmussen, J. L. (1991). Successful personal ads: Gender differences and similarities in offers, stipulations, and outcomes. *Basic and Applied Social Psychology, 12,* 457–469.

Raloff, J. (1982). Noise can be hazardous to your health. *Science News, 121,* 377–381.

Ralph, M. R., Foster, R. G., Davis, F. C., & Menaker, M. (1990). Transplanted suprachiasmatic nucleus determines circadian period. *Science, 247,* 975–978.

Ramey, C. T., Bryant, D. M., Wasik, B. H., Sparling, J. J., Fendt, K. H., & LaVange, L. M. (1992). Infant health and development program for low weight, premature infants: Program elements, family participation, and child intelligence. *Pediatrics, 89,* 454–465.

Rapoport, J. L. (1989). *The boy who couldn't stop washing: The experience and treatment of obsessive-compulsive disorder.* New York: Plume.

Raskin, D. C. (1982, June). *Science,* pp. 24–27.

Raskin, D. C. (1986). The polygraph in 1986: Scientific, professional, and legal issues surrounding application and acceptance of polygraph evidence. *Utah Law Review,* 29–74.

Raskin, N. J. (1985). Client-centered therapy. In S. Lynn & J. Garske (Eds.), *Contemporary psychotherapies: Models and methods* (pp. 155–190). Columbus, OH: Charles E. Merrill.

Rasmussen, B. K., Jensen, R., Schroll, M., & Olesen, J. (1991). Epidemiology of headache in a general population—a prevalence study. *Journal of Clinical Epidemiology, 44,* 1147–1157.

Raven, J. C., Court, J. H., & Raven, J. (1985). *A manual for Raven's progressive matrices and vocabulary scales.* London: H. K. Lewis.

Raz, S., & Raz, N. (1990). Structural brain abnormalities in the major psychoses: A quantitative review of the evidence from computerized imaging. *Psychological Bulletin, 108,* 93–108.

Reber, A. S. (1985). *The Penguin dictionary of psychology.* New York: Viking.

Reber, A. S. (1993). *Implicit learning and tacit knowledge: An essay on the cognitive unconscious.* New York: Oxford University Press.

Rechtschaffen, A., Gilliland, M. A., Bergmann, B. M., & Winter, J. B. (1983). Physiological correlates of prolonged sleep deprivation in rats. *Science, 221,* 182–185.

Reed, C. F., & Krupinski, E. A. (1992). The target in the celestial (moon) illusion. *Journal of Experimental Psychology: Human Perception and Performance, 18,* 247–256.

Reed, T. E., & Jensen, A. R. (1992). Conduction velocity in a brain nerve pathway of normal adults correlates with intelligence level. *Intelligence, 16,* 259–272.

Regier, D. A., et al. (1988). One-month prevalence of mental disorders in the United States. *Archives of General Psychiatry, 45,* 977–986.

Regier, D. A., Narrow, W., Rae, D., Manderschied, R., Locke, B., & Goodwin, F. (1993). The de facto U. S. mental and addictive disorders service system: Epidemiologic catchment area prospective

1-year prevalence rates of disorders and services. *Archives of General Psychiatry, 50,* 85–94.

Reid, W. H., Dorr, D., Walker, J. I., & Bonner, J. W. (Eds.). (1986). *Unmasking the psychopath: Antisocial personality and related syndromes.* New York: Norton.

Reifman, A. S., Larrick, R. P., & Fein, S. (1991). Temper and temperature on the diamond: The heat-aggression relationship in major league baseball. *Personality and Social Psychology Bulletin, 17,* 580–585.

Reis, S. M. (1989). Reflections on policy affecting the education of gifted and talented students: Past and future perspectives. *American Psychologist, 44,* 399–408.

Reisenzein, R. (1983). The Schachter theory of emotion: Two decades later. *Psychological Bulletin, 94,* 239–264.

Reiser, M. (1980). *Handbook of investigative hypnosis.* Los Angeles: LEHI.

Reiser, M., & Nielson, M. (1980). Investigative hypnosis: A developing specialty. *American Journal of Clinical Hypnosis, 23,* 75–83.

Reissland, N. (1988). Neonatal imitation in the first hour of life: Observations in rural Nepal. *Developmental Psychology, 24,* 464–469.

Remley, A. (1988, October). The great parental value shift: From obedience to independence. *Psychology Today,* pp. 56–59.

Renault, E. M., Signoret, J. L., Debruille, B., Breton, F., & Bolgert, F. (1989). Brain potentials reveal covert facial recognition in prosopagnosia. *Neuropsychologia, 27,* 905–912.

Renzulli, J. S. (1986). The three-ring conception of giftedness: A developmental model for creative productivity. In R. J. Sternberg & J. E. Davidson (Eds.), *Conceptions of giftedness* (pp. 53–92). New York: Cambridge University Press.

Rescorla, R. A. (1968). Probability of shock in the presence and absence of CS in fear conditioning. *Journal of Comparative and Physiological Psychology, 66,* 1–5.

Rescorla, R. A. (1980). *Pavlovian second-order conditioning.* Hillsdale, NJ: Erlbaum.

Rescorla, R. A. (1987). A Pavlovian analysis of goal-directed behavior. *American Psychologist, 42,* 119–129.

Rescorla, R. A. (1988). Pavlovian conditioning: It's not what you think it is. *American Psychologist, 43,* 151–160.

Resnick, L. R. (1989). Developing mathematical knowledge. *American Psychologist, 44,* 162–169.

Resnick, S. M. (1992). Positron emission tomography in psychiatric illness. *Current Directions in Psychological Science, 1,* 92–98.

Rest, J. R. (1986). *Moral development: Advances in research and theory.* New York: Praeger.

Restak, R. M. (1988). *The mind.* New York: Bantam.

Reuman, D. A. (1989). How social comparison mediates the relation between ability-grouping practices and students' achievement expectancies in mathematics. *Journal of Educational Psychology, 81,* 178–189.

Rhodes, N., & Wood, W. (1992). Self-esteem and intelligence affect influenceability: The mediating role of message reception. *Psychological Bulletin, 111,* 156–171.

Rhodes, S. R. (1983). Age-related differences in work attitudes and behavior: A review and conceptual analysis. *Psychological Bulletin, 93,* 328–367.

Rhue, J. W., Lynn, S. J., & Kirsch, I. (Eds.). (1993). *Handbook of clinical hypnosis.* Washington, DC: American Psychological Association.

Rice, M. L. (1989). Children's language acquisition. *American Psychologist, 44,* 149–156.

Rice, M. L., Huston, A. C., Truglio, R., & Wright, J. (1990). Words from "Sesame Street": Learning vocabulary while viewing. *Developmental Psychology, 26,* 421–428.

Richardson, J.T.E., & Zucco, G. M. (1989). Cognition and olfaction: A review. *Psychological Bulletin, 105,* 352–360.

Richardson, T. M., & Benbow, C. P. (1990). Long-term effects of ac-

celeration on the social-emotional adjustment of mathematically precocious youths. *Journal of Educational Psychology, 82,* 464–470.

Riefer, D. M., & Rouder, J. N. (1992). A multinomial modeling analysis of the mnemonic benefits of bizarre imagery. *Memory and Cognition, 20,* 601–611.

Rips, L. J. (1975). Inductive judgments about natural categories. *Journal of Verbal Learning and Verbal Behavior, 14,* 665–681.

Ristau, C. A. (Ed.). (1991). *Cognitive ethology: The minds of other animals.* Hillsdale, NJ: Erlbaum.

Ritter, P. L., & Dornbusch, S. M. (1989, March). *Ethnic variation in family influences on academic achievement.* Paper presented at the American Educational Research Association Meeting, San Francisco.

Robins, C. J., & Hayes, A. M. (1993). An appraisal of cognitive therapy. *Journal of Consulting and Clinical Psychology, 61,* 205–214.

Robinson, I., Ziss, K., Ganza, B., Katz, S., & Robinson, E. (1991). Twenty years of the sexual revolution, 1965–1985: An update. *Journal of Marriage and the Family, 53,* 216–220.

Robinson, J. L., Kagan, J., Reznick, J. S., & Corley, R. (1992). The heritability of inhibited and uninhibited behavior: A twin study. *Developmental Psychology, 28,* 1030–1037.

Rochat, P. (1989). Object manipulation and exploration in 2- to 5-month-old infants. *Developmental Psychology, 25,* 871–884.

Rock, I. (1983). *The logic of perception.* Cambridge, MA: MIT Press.

Rock, I., & Palmer, S. (1990). The legacy of Gestalt psychology. *Scientific American,* 84–90.

Rodgers, J. E. (1992). *Psychosurgery: Damaging the brain to save the mind.* New York: HarperCollins.

Rodgers, J. L., & Rowe, D. C. (1993). Social contagion and adolescent sexual behavior: A developmental EMOSA model. *Psychological Review, 100,* 479–510.

Rodin, J. (1986). Aging and health: Effects of the sense of control. *Science, 233,* 1271–1276.

Roediger, H. L., III. (1990). Implicit memory: Retention without remembering. *American Psychologist, 45,* 1043–1056.

Roediger, H. L., III, & Crowder, R. G. (1976). A serial position effect in recall of United States presidents. *Bulletin of the Psychonomic Society, 8,* 275–278.

Roffwarg, H. P., Muzio, J. N., & Dement, W. C. (1966). Ontogenetic development of the human sleep-dream cycle. *Science, 152,* 604–619.

Rogers, C. R. (1951). *Client-centered therapy.* Boston: Houghton Mifflin.

Rogers, C. R. (1959). *On becoming a person.* Boston: Houghton Mifflin.

Rogers, C. R. (1963). Actualizing tendency in relation to "motives" and to consciousness. In M. Jones (Ed.), *Nebraska symposium on motivation.* Lincoln: University of Nebraska Press.

Rogers, C. R. (1970). *Carl Rogers on encounter groups.* New York: Harper & Row.

Rogers, C. R. (1974). In retrospect: Forty-six years. *American Psychologist, 29,* 115–123.

Rogers, P. (1993, February 15). How many gays are there? *Newsweek,* p. 46.

Rogers, R. (1988). *Clinical assessment of malingering and deception.* New York: Guilford Press.

Rogers, R., Gillis, J. R., Dickens, S. E., & Bagby, R. M. (1991). Standardized assessment of malingering: Validation of the structured interview of reported symptoms. *Psychological Assessment, 3,* 89–96.

Rogers, R. W. (1983). Cognitive and psychological processes in fear appeals and attitude change: A revised theory of protection motivation. In J. Cacioppo & R. Petty (Eds.), *Social psychophysiology: A sourcebook* (pp. 153–176). New York: Guilford Press.

Rogers, R. W., & Mewborn, R. C. (1976). Fear appeals and attitude change: Effects of a threat's noxiousness, probability of occurrence, and the efficacy of coping responses. *Journal of Personality and Social Psychology, 34,* 54–61.

Rogers, T. B., Kuiper, N. A., & Kirker, W. S. (1977). Self-reference and the encoding of personal information. *Journal of Personality and Social Psychology, 35,* 677–688.

Rogoff, B., & Morelli, G. (1989). Perspectives on children's development from cultural psychology. *American Psychologist, 44,* 343–348.

Romney, A. K., Brewer, D. D., & Batchelder, W. H. (1993). Predicting clustering from semantic structure. *Psychological Science, 4,* 28–34.

Rook, K. S., & Peplau, L. A. (1982). Perspectives on helping the lonely. In L. A. Peplau & D. Perlman (Eds.), *Loneliness: A sourcebook of current theory, research and therapy* (pp. 351–378). New York: Wiley.

Roper Reports (1989, May).

Rorschach, H. (1921). *Psychodiagnostik.* Bern: Bircher.

Rosch, E. (1973). On the internal structure of perceptual and semantic categories. In T. E. Moore (Ed.), *Cognitive development and the acquisition of language.* New York: Academic Press.

Rosch, E. (1975). Cognitive representations of semantic categories. *Journal of Experimental Psychology: General, 104,* 192–223.

Rosch, E. H., & Mervis, C. B. (1975). Family resemblances: Studies in the internal structure of categories. *Cognitive Psychology, 7,* 573–605.

Roseman, I. J., Spindel, M. S., & Jose, P. E. (1990). Appraisals of emotion-eliciting events: Testing a theory of discrete emotions. *Journal of Personality and Social Psychology, 59,* 899–915.

Rosen, R. C., & Ashton, A. K. (1993). Psychosexual drugs: Empirical status of the "new aphrodisiacs." *Archives of Sexual Behavior, 22,* 521–543.

Rosener, J. B. (1990). Ways women lead. *Harvard Business Review, 68,* 119–125.

Rosenfeld, A., & Stark, E. (1986, May). The prime of our lives. *Psychology Today,* pp. 62–72.

Rosenfield, P., Lambert, N. M., & Black, A. (1985). Desk arrangement effects on pupil classroom behavior. *Journal of Educational Psychology, 77,* 101–108.

Rosenhan, D. L. (1973). On being sane in insane places. *Science, 179,* 250–258.

Rosenman, R. H., Brand, R. J., Jenkins, C. D., Friedman, M., Strau, R., & Wurm, M. (1975). Coronary heart disease in the Western Collaborative Group Study: Final follow-up experience of $8\frac{1}{2}$ years. *Journal of the American Medical Association, 233,* 872–877.

Rosenstein, D., & Oster, H. (1988). Differential facial responses to four basic tastes in newborns. *Child Development, 59,* 1555–1568.

Rosenthal, N. E., et al. (1984). Seasonal affective disorder: A description of the syndrome and preliminary findings with light therapy. *Archives of General Psychiatry, 41,* 72–80.

Rosenthal, R. (1985). From unconscious experimenter bias to teacher expectancy effects. In J. B. Dusek, V. C. Hall, & W. J. Meyer (Eds.), *Teacher expectancies.* Hillsdale, NJ: Erlbaum.

Rosenthal, R. (1991). *Meta-analytic procedures for social research* (2nd ed.). Newbury Park, CA: Sage.

Rosenthal, R., Hall, J. A., DiMatteo, M. R., Rogers, P., & Archer, D. (1979). *Sensitivity to nonverbal communication: A profile approach to the measurement of individual differences.* Baltimore: Johns Hopkins University Press.

Rosenthal, R., & Jacobson, L. (1968). *Pygmalion in the classroom: Teacher expectation and pupils' intellectual development.* New York: Holt, Rinehart & Winston.

Rosenzweig, M. R. (1984). Experience, memory, and the brain. *American Psychologist, 39,* 365–376.

Rosnow, R. L., Rotheram-Borus, M. J., Ceci, S. J., Blanck, P. D., & Koocher, G. P. (1993). The institutional review board as a mirror of scientific and ethical standards. *American Psychologist, 48,* 821–826.

Ross, C. A. (1994). *The Osiris complex: Case studies in multiple personality disorder.* Toronto: University of Toronto Press.

Ross, C. A., Joshi, S., & Currie, R. (1990). Dissociative experiences in the general population. *American Journal of Psychiatry, 147,* 1547–1552.

Ross, C. A., Miller, S. D., Reagor, P., Bjornson, L., Fraser, G. A., & Anderson, G. (1990). Structured interview data on 102 cases of Multiple Personality Disorder from four centers. *American Journal of Psychiatry, 147,* 596–601.

Ross, D. F., Read, J. D., & Toglia, M. P. (Eds.). (1994). *Adult eyewitness testimony: Current trends and developments.* New York: Cambridge University Press.

Ross, G., Kagan, J., Zelazo, P., & Kotelchuck, M. (1975). Separation protest in infants in home and laboratory. *Developmental Psychology, 11,* 256–257.

Ross, L. (1977). The intuitive psychologist and his shortcomings: Distortions in the attribution process. In L. Berkowitz (Ed.), *Advances in experimental social psychology* (Vol. 10). New York: Academic Press.

Ross, L., Amabile, T. M., & Steinmetz, J. L. (1977). Social roles, social control, and biases in social-perception processes. *Journal of Personality and Social Psychology, 35,* 485–494.

Ross, M. (1989). The relation of implicit theories to the construction of personal histories. *Psychological Review, 96,* 341–357.

Ross, M., & Sicoly, F. (1979). Egocentric biases in availability and attribution. *Journal of Personality and Social Psychology, 37,* 322–336.

Ross, R. T., & LoLordo, V. M. (1987). Evaluation of the relation between Pavlovian occasion-setting and instrumental discriminative stimuli. *Journal of Experimental Psychology: Animal Behavior Processes, 13,* 3–16.

Roth, T., Roehrs, T., & Zorick, F. (1987). Sleep disorders. In G. Adelman (Ed.), *Encyclopedia of neuroscience.* Boston: Birkhauser.

Rotter, J. B. (1954). *Social learning and clinical psychology.* Englewood Cliffs, NJ: Prentice-Hall.

Rotter, J. B. (1966). Generalized expectancies for internal versus external control of reinforcement. *Psychological Monographs, 80*(Whole No. 609).

Rotter, J. B. (1990). Internal versus external control of reinforcement: A case history of a variable. *American Psychologist, 45,* 489–493.

Rotter, J. B., Chance, J. E., & Phares, E. J. (Eds.). (1972). *Applications of a social learning theory of personality.* New York: Holt, Rinehart & Winston.

Rousseau, D. L. (1992). Case studies in pathological science. *American Scientist, 80,* 54–63.

Rovee-Collier, C. (1988). The joy of kicking: Memories, motives, and mobiles. In P. Solomon, G. Goethals, C. Kelley, & B. Stephens (Eds.), *Memory: Interdisciplinary approaches.* New York: Springer-Verlag.

Rovee-Collier, C., Hankins, E., & Bhatt, R. (1992). Textons, visual pop-out effects, and object recognition in infancy. *Journal of Experimental Psychology: General, 121,* 435–445.

Rozee, P. D., & Van Boemel, G. V. (1989). The psychological effects of war trauma and abuse on older Cambodian refugee women. *Women and Therapy, 8,* 23–50.

Rozin, E. (1983). *Ethnic cuisine: The flavor-principle cookbook.* Brattleboro, VT: Stephen Greene Press.

Rozin, P., & Fallon, A. E. (1987). A perspective on disgust. *Psychological Review, 94,* 23–41.

Rubin, D. C. (Ed.). (1986). *Autobiographical memory.* Cambridge: Cambridge University Press.

Rubin, D. C., & Kozin, M. (1984). Vivid memories. *Cognition, 16,* 81–95.

Rubin, J. Z., Provenzano, F. J., & Luria, Z. (1974). The eye of the beholder: Parents' views on sex of newborns. *American Journal of*

Orthopsychiatry, 44, 512–519.

Ruble, D. N., & Brooks-Gunn, J. (1982). The experience of menarche. *Child Development, 53*, 1557–1566.

Rubonis, A. V., & Bickman, L. (1991). Psychological impairment in the wake of disaster: The disaster-psychopathology relationship. *Psychological Bulletin, 109*, 384–399.

Ruderman, A. J., & Besbeas, M. (1992). Psychological characteristics of dieters and bulimics. *Journal of Abnormal Psychology, 101*, 383–390.

Rule, B. G., Taylor, B. R., & Dobbs, A. R. (1987). Priming effects of heat on aggressive thoughts. *Social Cognition, 5*, 131–143.

Rumbaugh, D. M. (1977). *Language learning by a chimpanzee: The Lana project*. New York: Academic Press.

Rumelhart, D. E., & McClelland, J. L. (1986). On learning the past tenses of English verbs. In J. L. McClelland & D. E. Rumelhart (Eds.), *Parallel distributed processing: Explorations in the microstructure of cognition: Vol 2. Psychological and biological models* (pp. 216–271). Cambridge, MA: MIT Press.

Rushton, J. P. (1989). Genetic similarity, human altruism, and group selection. *Behavioral and Brain Sciences, 12*, 503–559.

Rushton, J. P., Brainerd, C. J., & Pressley, M. (1983). Behavioral development and construct validity: The principle of aggregation. *Psychological Bulletin, 94*, 18–38.

Rushton, J. P., Fulker, D. W., Neale, M. C., Nias, D.K.B., & Eysenck, H. J. (1986). Altruism and aggression: The heritability of individual differences. *Journal of Personality and Social Psychology, 50*, 1192–1198.

Russell, D., Peplau, L. A., & Cutrona, C. E. (1980). The revised UCLA Loneliness Scale: Concurrent and discriminant validity evidence. *Journal of Personality and Social Psychology, 39*, 472–480.

Russell, J. A. (1980). A circumplex model of affect. *Journal of Personality and Social Psychology, 39*, 1161–1178.

Russell, J. A. (1991). Culture and the categorization of emotions. *Psychological Bulletin, 110*, 426–450.

Russell, J. R. (1994). Is there universal recognition of emotion from facial expression? A review of cross-cultural studies. *Psychological Bulletin, 115*, 102–141.

Russell, M. J. (1976). Human olfactory communication. *Nature (London), 260*, 520–522.

Ryff, C. D. (1989). In the eye of the beholder: Views of psychological well-being among middle-aged and older adults. *Psychology and Aging, 4*, 195–210.

Saal, F. E., Johnson, C. B., & Weber, N. (1989). Friendly or sexy? Friendly or sex? It may depend on whom you ask. *Psychology of Women Quarterly, 13*, 263–276.

Sacco, W. P., & Dunn, V. K. (1990). Effect of actor depression on observer attributions: Existence and impact of negative attributions toward the depressed. *Journal of Personality and Social Psychology, 59*, 517–524.

Sachs, J. (1967). Recognition memory for syntactic and semantic aspects of connected discourse. *Perception and Psychophysics, 2*, 437–442.

Sack, R. L., Lewy, A. J., White, D. M., Singer, C. M., Fireman, M. J., & Vandiver, R. (1990). Morning vs. evening light treatment for winter depression: Evidence that the therapeutic effects of light are mediated by circadian phase shift. *Archives of General Psychiatry, 47*, 343–351.

Sackett, P. R., & DuBois, C. L. Z. (1991). Rater-ratee race effects on performance evaluation: Challenging meta-analytic conclusions. *Journal of Applied Psychology, 76*, 873–877.

Sackheim, H. A. (1988). Mechanisms of action of electroconvulsive therapy. In A. J. Francis & R. E. Hales (Eds.), *Review of Psychiatry* (Vol. 7). Washington, DC: American Psychiatric Press.

Sacks, O. (1983). *Awakenings*. New York: E. P. Dutton.

Sacks, O. (1985). *The man who mistook his wife for a hat and other clinical tales*. New York: Summit Books.

Sacks, O. (1993, May 10). A neurologist's notebook: To see and not to see. *The New Yorker*, 59–73.

Sagar, H. A., & Schofield, J. W. (1980). Racial and behavioral cues in black and white children's perceptions of ambiguously aggressive acts. *Journal of Personality and Social Psychology, 39*, 590–598.

Salthouse, T. A. (1984). Effects of age and skill in typing. *Journal of Experimental Psychology: General, 113*, 345–371.

Salthouse, T. A. (1991). Decomposing adult age differences in working memory. *Developmental Psychology, 27*, 763–776.

Salthouse, T. A. (1992). Why do adult age differences increase with task complexity? *Developmental Psychology, 28*, 905–918.

Sams, M., Hari, R., Rif, J., & Knuutila, J. (1993). The human auditory memory trace persists about 10 sec: Neuromagnetic evidence. *Journal of Cognitive Neuroscience, 5*, 363–370.

Sanchez, J. I., & Fernandez, D. M. (1993). Acculturative stress among Hispanics: A bidimensional model of ethnic identification. *Journal of Applied Social Psychology, 23*, 654–668.

Sanderson, W. C., DiNardo, P. A., Rapee, R. M., & Barlow, D. H. (1990). Syndrome comorbidity in patients diagnosed with a DSM-III-R anxiety disorder. *Journal of Abnormal Psychology, 99*, 308–312.

Sapir, E. (1941). *Language, culture, and personality: Essays in honor of Edward Sapir* (L. Sapir, Ed.). Menasha, WI: Sapir Memorial Publication Fund.

Sarbin, T. R. (1992). Accounting for "dissociative" actions without invoking mentalistic constructs. *Consciousness and Cognition, 1*, 54–58.

Savage-Rumbaugh, E. S. (1990). Language acquisition in a nonhuman species: Implications for the innateness debate. *Developmental Psychobiology, 23*, 599–620.

Savage-Rumbaugh, E. S., McDonald, K., Sevcik, R., Hopkins, W. D., & Rupert, E. (1986). Spontaneous symbol acquisition and communication use by pygmy chimpanzees. *Journal of Experimental Psychology: General, 115*, 211–235.

Savage-Rumbaugh, S., Murphy, J., Sevcik, R. A., Brakke, K. E., Williams, S. L., & Rumbaugh, D. M. (1993). Language comprehension in ape and child. *Monographs of the Society for Research in Child Development, 58*(3–4, Serial No. 233).

Saxe, L., Dougherty, D., & Cross, T. (1985). The validity of polygraph testing: Scientific analysis and public controversy. *American Psychologist, 38*, 355–366.

Scafidi, F. A., Field, T. M., Schanberg, S. M., Bauer, C. R., Tucci, K., Roberts, J., Morrow, C., & Kuhn, C. M. (1990). Massage stimulates growth in preterm infants: A replication. *Infant Behavior and Development, 13*, 167–188.

Scarr, S. (1986). *Mother care/other care*. New York: Basic Books.

Scarr, S., & McCartney, K. (1983). How people make their own environments: A theory of genotype -> environment effects. *Child Development, 54*, 424–435.

Scarr, S., & Weinberg, R. A. (1976). I.Q. test performance of black children adopted by white families. *American Psychologist, 31*, 726–739.

Scarr, S., & Weinberg, R. A. (1983). The Minnesota adoption studies: Genetic differences and malleability. *Child Development, 54*, 260–267.

Schab, F. R. (1990). Odors and the remembrance of things past. *Journal of Experimental Psychology: Learning, Memory, and Cognition, 16*, 648–655.

Schacter, D. L. (1986). Amnesia and crime: How much do we really know? *American Psychologist, 41*, 286–295.

Schacter, D. L. (1987). Implicit memory: History and current status. *Journal of Experimental Psychology: Learning, Memory, and Cognition, 13*, 501–518.

Schacter, D. L. (1992). Understanding implicit memory: A cognitive neuroscience approach. *American Psychologist, 47, 559–569.*

Schachter, S. (1964). The interaction of cognitive and physiological determinants of emotional state. In L. Berkowitz (Ed.), *Advances in experimental social psychology* (Vol. 1, pp. 49–80). New York: Academic Press.

Schachter, S., & Singer, J. E. (1962). Cognitive, social, and physiological determinants of emotional state. *Psychological Review, 69,* 379–399.

Schaie, K. W. (Ed.). (1983). *Longitudinal studies of adult psychological development.* New York: Guilford Press.

Schaie, K. W. (1989). Perceptual speed in adulthood: Cross-sectional and longitudinal studies. *Psychology and Aging, 4,* 443–453.

Schaie, K. W. (1994). The course of adult intellectual development. *American Psychologist, 49,* 304–313.

Schaie, K. W., & Willis, S. L. (1993). Age difference patterns of psychometric intelligence in adulthood: Generalizability within and across ability domains. *Psychology and Aging, 8,* 44–55.

Schaller, M., & Cialdini, R. B. (1988). The economics of empathic helping: Support for a mood management motive. *Journal of Experimental Social Psychology, 24,* 163–181.

Schanberg, S. M., & Field, T. M. (1987). Sensory deprivation stress and supplemental stimulation in the rat pup and preterm human neonate. *Child Development, 58,* 1431–1447.

Scheflin, A. W., & Shapiro, J. L. (1989). *Trance on trial.* New York: Guilford Press.

Scheier, M. F., & Carver, C. S. (1985). Optimism, coping, and health: Assessment and implications of generalized outcome expectancies. *Health Psychology, 4,* 219–247.

Scheier, M. F., & Carver, C. S. (1992). Effects of optimism on psychological and physical well-being: Theoretical overview and empirical update. *Cognitive Therapy and Research, 16,* 201–228.

Scherer, K. R., & Wallbott, H. G. (1994). Evidence for universality and cultural variation of differential emotion response patterning. *Journal of Personality and Social Psychology, 66,* 310–328.

Schiff, W. (1980). *Perception: An applied approach.* Boston: Houghton Mifflin.

Schiller, F. (1992). *Paul Broca.* New York: Oxford University Press.

Schlenker, B. R., Weigold, M. F., & Hallam, J. R. (1990). Self-serving attributions in social context: Effects of self-esteem and social pressure. *Journal of Personality and Social Psychology, 58,* 855–863.

Schmidt, F. L. (1992). What do data really mean? Research findings, meta-analysis, and cumulative knowledge in psychology. *American Psychologist, 47,* 1173–1181.

Schmidt, S. R. (1991). Can we have a distinctive theory of memory? *Memory and Cognition, 19,* 523–542.

Schnapf, J. L., Kraft, T. W., & Baylor, D. A. (1987). Spectral sensitivity of human cone photoreceptors. *Nature, 325,* 439–441.

Schneider, D. J., & Shiffrin, R. M. (1977). Controlled and automatic human information processing: I. Detection, search, and attention. *Psychological Review, 84,* 1–66.

Schneider, S. G., Taylor, S. E., Hammen, C., Kemeny, M. E., & Dudley, J. (1991). Factors influencing suicide intent in gay and bisexual suicide ideators: Differing models for men with and without human immunodeficiency virus. *Journal of Personality and Social Psychology, 61,* 776–788.

Schofield, J. W. (1982). *Black and white in school: Trust, tension, or tolerance?* New York: Praeger.

Schooler, J. W., & Engstler-Schooler, T. Y. (1990). Verbal overshadowing of visual memories: Some things are better left unsaid. *Cognitive Psychology, 17,* 36–71.

Schooler, J. W., Ohlsson, S., & Brooks, K. (1993). Thoughts beyond words: When language overshadows insight. *Journal of Experimental Psychology: General, 122,* 166–183.

Schor, J. B. (1991). *The overworked American: The unexpected decline of leisure.* New York: Basic Books.

Schretlen, D., Wilkins, S. S., Van Gorp, W. G., & Bobholz, J. H. (1992). Cross-validation of a psychological test battery to detect faked insanity. *Psychological Assessment, 4,* 77–83.

Schroeder, S. R., Schroeder, C. S., & Landesman, S. (1987). Psychological services in educational settings to persons with mental retardation. *American Psychologist, 42,* 805–807.

Schulz, R., Musa, D., Staszewski, J., & Siegler, R. S. (1994). The relationship between age and major league baseball performance: Implications for development. *Psychology and Aging, 9,* 274–286.

Schutte, N. S., Malouff, J. M., Post-Gorden, J. C., & Rodasta, A. L. (1988). Effects of playing videogames on children's aggressive and other behaviors. *Journal of Applied Social Psychology, 18,* 454–460.

Schwartz, A., & Schwartz, R. M. (1993). *Depression—Theories and treatments: Psychological, biological, and social perspectives.* New York: Columbia University Press.

Schwartz, B., & Reisberg, D. (1991). *Learning and memory.* New York: W. W. Norton.

Schwarz, J. R. (1981). *The Hillside strangler: A murderer's mind.* New York: New American Library.

Schwarz, N. (1990). Assessing frequency reports of mundane behaviors: Contribution of cognitive psychology to questionnaire constructions. In C. Hendrick & M. S. Clarke (Eds.), *Review of Personality and Social Psychology* (Vol. 11, pp. 98–119). Newbury Park, CA: Sage.

Schwarz, N., Bless, H., & Bohner, G. (1991). Mood and persuasion: Affective states influence the processing of persuasive communications. In M. P. Zanna (Ed.), *Advances in experimental social psychology* (Vol. 24). New York: Academic Press.

Scogin, F., Jamison, C., & Gochneaur, K. (1989). Comparative efficacy of cognitive and behavioral bibliotherapy for mildly and moderately depressed older adults. *Journal of Consulting and Clinical Psychology, 57,* 403–407.

Scott, L., & O'Hara, M. W. (1993). Self-discrepancies in clinically anxious and depressed university students. *Journal of Abnormal Psychology, 102,* 282–287.

Scoville, W. B., & Milner, B. (1957). Loss of recent memory after bilateral hippocampal lesions. *Journal of Neurology, Neurosurgery, and Psychiatry, 20,* 11–21.

Searle, J. R. (1992). *The rediscovery of the mind.* Cambridge, MA: MIT Press.

Sears, D. O., & Kinder, D. R. (1985). Whites' opposition to busing: On conceptualizing and operationalizing group conflict. *Journal of Personality and Social Psychology, 48,* 1141–1147.

Sedikides, C., & Ostrom, T. M. (Eds.). (1993). Perceptions of group variability. *Social Cognition, 11*(1).

Segall, M. H., Campbell, D. T., & Herskovitz, M. J. (1966). *The influence of culture on visual perception.* Indianapolis, IN: Bobbs-Merrill.

Segerberg, O. (1982). *Living to be 100: 1200 who did and how they did it.* New York: Charles Scribner's Sons.

Seidlitz, L., & Diener, E. (1993). Memory for positive versus negative events: Theories for the differences between happy and unhappy persons. *Journal of Personality and Social Psychology, 64,* 654–664.

Seligman, M.E.P. (1971). Phobias and preparedness. *Behavior Therapy, 2,* 307–320.

Seligman, M.E.P. (1975). *Helplessness: On depression, development, and death.* San Francisco: W. H. Freeman.

Seligman, M.E.P. (1990). *Learned optimism.* New York: Knopf.

Seligman, M.E.P. (1991). *Learned optimism.* New York: Alfred A. Knopf.

Selye, H. (1936). A syndrome produced by diverse nocuous agents. *Nature, 138,* 32.

Selye, H. (1976). *The stress of life.* New York: McGraw-Hill.

Semb, G. B., Ellis, J. A., & Araujo, J. (1993). Long-term memory for knowledge learned in school. *Journal of Educational Psychology, 85,* 305–316.

Sergent, J. (1983). The role of the input in visual hemispheric asymmetries. *Psychological Bulletin, 93,* 481–512.

Sergent, J. (1990). Furtive incursions into bicameral minds. *Brain, 113,* 537–568.

Shapiro, A. K. (1960). A contribution to a history of the placebo effect. *Behavioral Science, 5,* 109–135.

Shapley, R. (1990). Visual sensitivity and parallel retinocortical channels. *Annual Review of Psychology, 41,* 635–658.

Shaywitz, S. E., & Shaywitz, B. A. (1991). Introduction to the special series on attention deficit disorder. *Journal of Learning Disabilities, 24,* 68–71.

Shearn, D., Bergman, E., Hill, D., Abel, A., & Hinds, L. (1990). Facial coloration and temperature responses in blushing. *Psychophysiology, 27,* 687–693.

Shedler, J., & Block, J. (1990). Adolescent drug use and psychological health: A longitudinal inquiry. *American Psychologist, 45,* 612–630.

Sheehan, P. W., Statham, D., & Jamieson, G. A. (1991). Pseudomemory effects and their relationship to level of susceptibility to hypnosis and state instruction. *Journal of Personality and Social Psychology, 60,* 130–137.

Sheehan, P. W., & Tilden, J. (1983). Effects of suggestibility and hypnosis on accurate and distorted retrieval from memory. *Journal of Experimental Psychology: Human Learning and Memory, 9,* 283–293.

Sheehy, G. (1976). *Passages: Predictable crises of adult life.* New York: E. P. Dutton.

Sheldon, W. H. (1954). *Atlas of man: A guide for somatotyping the adult male of all ages.* New York: Harper & Row.

Shelton, R. C., & Weinberger, D. R. (1986). X-ray computerized tomography studies in schizophrenia: Review and synthesis. In H. A. Nasrallah & D. R. Weinberger (Eds.), *The neurology of schizophrenia.* Amsterdam: Elsevier.

Shepard, R. N. (1990). *Mind sights.* New York: W. H. Freeman.

Shepard, R. N., & Metzler, J. (1971). Mental rotation of three-dimensional objects. Science, 171, 701–703.

Sheppard, J. A. (1993). Productivity loss in performance groups: A motivation analysis. *Psychological Bulletin, 113,* 67–81.

Sherif, M. (1936). *The psychology of social norms.* New York: Harper.

Sherrod, D. (1989). The influence of gender on same-sex friendships. In C. Hendrick (Ed.), *Review of Personality and Social Psychology* (Vol. 10, pp. 164–186). Newbury Park, CA: Sage.

Sherry, D. F. (1992). Memory, the hippocampus, and natural selection: Studies of food-storing birds. In L. Squire & N. Butters (Eds.), *Neuropsychology of memory* (2nd ed., pp. 521–532). New York: Guilford Press.

Shiffrin, R. M. (1993). Short-term memory: A brief commentary. *Memory and Cognition, 21,* 193–197.

Shimamura, A. P. (1986). Priming effects in amnesia: Evidence for a dissociable memory function. *Quarterly Journal of Experimental Psychology, 38A,* 619–644.

Shneidman, E. (Ed.). (1984). *Death: Current perspectives.* Palo Alto, CA: Mayfield.

Shneidman, E. (1987, March). At the point of no return. *Psychology Today,* pp. 54–58.

Shneidman, E. (1989). The Indian summer of life: A preliminary study of septuagenarians. *American Psychologist, 44,* 684–694.

Shostrom, E. (1965). An inventory for the measurement of self-actualization. *Educational and psychological measurement, 24,* 207–218.

Shulgin, A. T. (1986). The background and chemistry of MDMA. *Journal of Psychoactive Drugs, 18,* 291–303.

Sidey, H. (1993, August 9). The flood: A broken heartland. *Time,* p. 28.

Siegel, J. M. (1990). Stressful life events and use of physician services among the elderly. *Journal of Personality and Social Psychology, 58,* 1081–1086.

Siegel, J. M., et al. (1991). Neuronal activity in narcolepsy: Identification of cataplexy-related cells in the medial medulla. *Science, 252,* 1315–1318.

Siegel, R. K. (1980). The psychology of life after death. *American Psychologist, 35,* 911–931.

Siegel, R. K. (1989). *Intoxication: Life in pursuit of artificial paradise.* New York: Dutton.

Siegler, R. S. (1991). *Children's thinking* (2nd ed.). Englewood Cliffs, NJ: Prentice-Hall.

Sigelman, L., & Welch, S. (1991). *Black Americans' views of racial inequality: The dream deferred.* New York: Cambridge University Press.

Silveira, J. (1971). *Incubation: The effect of interruption timing and length on problem solution and quality of problem processing.* Unpublished doctoral dissertation. University of Oregon, Eugene.

Silver, E., Cirincione, C., & Steadman, H. J. (1994). Demythologizing inaccurate perceptions of the insanity defense. *Law and Human Behavior, 18,* 63–70.

Silverberg, S. B., & Steinberg, L. (1990). Psychological well-being of parents with early adolescent children. *Developmental Psychology, 26,* 658–666.

Silverman, L., & Weinberger, J. (1985). Mommy and I are one: Implications for psychotherapy. *American Psychologist, 40,* 1296–1308.

Silverstein, A. B. (1990). Short forms of individual intelligence tests. *Psychological Assessment: A Journal of Consulting and Clinical Psychology, 2,* 3–11.

Silverstein, B., Perdue, L., & Kelly, E. (1986). The role of the mass media in promoting a thin standard of bodily attractiveness for women. *Sex Roles, 14,* 519–532.

Simmons, J. V. (1981). *Project sea hunt: A report on prototype development and tests.* Technical Report 746, Naval Ocean Systems Center, San Diego.

Simon, H. A. (1975). The functional equivalence of problem solving skills. *Cognitive Psychology, 7,* 268–288.

Simon, H. A. (1989). The scientist as a problem solver. In D. Klahr and K. Kotovsky (Eds.), *Complex information processing: The impact of Herbert Simon.* Hillsdale, NJ: Erlbaum.

Simon, H. A. (1991). Cognitive architectives and rational analysis: Comment, in K. VanLehn (Ed.), *Architectures for intelligence* (pp. 25–39). Hillsdale, NJ: Erlbaum.

Simon, H. B. (1991). Exercise and human immune function. In R. Ader, D. E. Felton, & N. Cohen (Eds.), *Psychoneuroimmunology* (2nd ed.), pp. 869–895. New York: Academic Press.

Simon, S. A., & Roper, S. D. (1993). *Mechanisms of taste transduction.* Boca Raton, FL: CRC Press.

Simonton, D. K. (1988). Age and outstanding achievement: What do we know after a century of research? *Psychological Bulletin, 104,* 251–267.

Simpson, G. B. (1989). Varieties of ambiguity: What are we seeking? In D. S. Gorfein (Ed.), *Resolving semantic ambiguity.* New York: Springer-Verlag.

Simpson, J. A. (1987). The dissolution of romantic relationships: Factors involved in relationship stability and emotional distress. *Journal of Personality and Social Psychology, 53,* 683–692.

Singer, J. L. (Ed.). (1990). *Repression and dissociation: Implications for personality theory, psychopathology, and health.* Chicago: University of Chicago Press.

Skinner, B. F. (1938). *The behavior of organisms.* New York: Appleton-Century-Crofts.

Skinner, B. F. (1948). "Superstition" in the pigeon. *Journal of Experimental Psychology, 38,* 168–172.

Skinner, B. F. (1948). *Walden two.* New York: Macmillan.

Skinner, B. F. (1956). A case history in scientific method. *American*

Psychologist, 11, 221–233.

Skinner, B. F. (1957). *Verbal behavior.* Englewood Cliffs, NJ: Prentice-Hall.

Skinner, B. F. (1957). *Verbal behavior.* New York: Appleton-Century-Crofts.

Skinner, B. F. (1959). A case history in scientific method. In S. Koch (Ed.), *Psychology: A study of a science* (Vol. 2, pp. 359–379). New York: McGraw-Hill.

Skinner, B. F. (1971). *Beyond freedom and dignity.* New York: Alfred A. Knopf.

Skinner, B. F. (1988). *The school of the future.* Paper presented at the annual meeting of the American Psychological Association, Atlanta, GA.

Skinner, B. F. (1990). Can psychology be a science of mind? *American Psychologist, 45,* 1206–1210.

Sklar, L. S., & Anisman, H. (1981). Stress and cancer. *Psychological Bulletin, 89,* 369–406.

Sladek, J. R., & Shoulson, I. (1988). Neural transplantation: A call for patience rather than patients. *Science, 240,* 1386–1388.

Slater, A., Mattock, A., & Brown, E. (1990). Size constancy at birth: Newborn infants' responses to retinal and real size. *Journal of Experimental Child Psychology, 49,* 314–322.

Slater, P.J.B., Eales, L. A., & Clayton, N. S. (1988). Song learning in zebra finches (Taeniopygia guttata): Progress and prospects. *Advances in the Study of Animal Behavior, 18,* 1–34.

Slavin, R. E. (1987). Ability grouping and student achievement in elementary schools: A best-evidence synthesis. *Review of Educational Research, 57,* 293–336.

Slawinski, E. B., Hartel, D. M., & Kline, D. W. (1993). Self-reported hearing problems in daily life throughout adulthood. *Psychology and Aging, 8,* 552–561.

Slobin, D. I. (1966). Grammatical transformations and sentence comprehension in childhood and adulthood. *Journal of Verbal Learning and Verbal Behavior, 5,* 219–227.

Slovic, P., Fischoff, B., & Lichtenstein, S. (1982). Facts versus fears: Understanding perceived risk. In D. Kahneman, P. Slovic, & A. Tversky (Eds.), *Judgment under uncertainty: Heuristics and biases* (pp. 463–489). New York: Cambridge University Press.

Small, S. A., Eastman, G., & Cornelius, S. (1988). Adolescent autonomy and parental stress. *Journal of Youth and Adolescence, 17,* 377–392.

Smetana, J. G. (1988). Concepts of self and social convention: Adolescents' and parents' reasoning about hypothetical and actual family conflicts. In M. R. Gunnar & W. A. Collins (Eds.), *Development during the transition to adolescence: Minnesota symposia on child psychology* (Vol. 21, pp. 79–122). Hillsdale, NJ: Erlbaum.

Smith, C. A., & Ellsworth, P. C. (1985). Patterns of cognitive appraisal in emotion. *Journal of Personality and Social Psychology, 48,* 813–838.

Smith, C. A., Haynes, K. N., Lazarus, R. S., & Pope, L. K. (1993). In search of the "hot" cognitions: Attributions, appraisals, and their relation to emotion. *Journal of Personality and Social Psychology, 65,* 916–929.

Smith, C. S., Reilly, C., & Midkiff, K. (1989). Evaluation of three circadian rhythm questionnaires with suggestions for an improved measure of morningness. *Journal of Applied Psychology, 74,* 728–738.

Smith, D. (1982). Trends in counseling and psychotherapy. *American Psychologist, 37,* 802–809.

Smith, E. E., Shoben, E. J., & Ripps, L. J. (1974). Structure and processes in semantic memory: A featural model for semantic decisions. *Psychological Review, 81,* 214–241.

Smith, M. C. (1983). Hypnotic memory enhancement of witnesses: Does it work? *Psychological Bulletin, 94,* 387–407.

Smith, M. L., Glass, G. V., & Miller, T. I. (1980). *The benefits of psychotherapy.* Baltimore: Johns Hopkins University Press.

Smith, R. F., Mattran, K. M., Kurkjian, M. F., & Kurtz, S. L. (1989). Alterations in offspring behavior induced by chronic prenatal cocaine dosing. *Neurotoxicology and Teratology, 11,* 35–38.

Smith, S. M. (1979). Remembering in and out of context. *Journal of Experimental Psychology: Human Learning and Memory, 5,* 460–471.

Smith, S. M., Brown, H. O., Toman, J.E.P., & Goodman, L. S. (1947). The lack of cerebral effects of d-Tubercuratine Anesthesiology, 8, 1–14.

Smith, T. W. (1992). Hostility and health: Current status of a psychosomatic hypothesis. *Health Psychology, 11,* 139–150.

Smith, V. L. (1991). Prototypes in the courtroom: Lay representations of legal concepts. *Journal of Personality and Social Psychology, 61,* 857–872.

Snarey, J. R. (1985). Cross-cultural universality of social-moral development: A critical review of Kohlbergian research. *Psychological Bulletin, 97,* 202–233.

Sno, H. N., & Linszen, D. H. (1990). The deja vu experience: Remembrance of things past? *American Journal of Psychiatry, 147,* 1587–1595.

Snodgrass, S. E. (1985). Women's intuition: The effect of subordinate roles on interpersonal sensitivity. *Journal of Personality and Social Psychology, 49,* 146–155.

Snyder, C. R., Higgins, R. L., & Stucky, R. J. (1983). *Excuses: Masquerades in search of grace.* New York: Wiley.

Snyder, M. (1987). *Public appearances/private realities: The psychology of self-monitoring.* New York: W. H. Freeman.

Snyder, M. (1993). Motivational foundations of behavioral confirmation. *Advances in Experimental Social Psychology, 25.*

Snyder, M., & DeBono, K. (1985). Appeals to image and claims about quality: Understanding the psychology of advertising. *Journal of Personality and Social Psychology, 49,* 586–597.

Snyder, M., & Gangestad, S. (1986). On the nature of self-monitoring: Matters of assessment, matters of validity. *Journal of Personality and Social Psychology, 51,* 125–139.

Snyder, M., & Ickes, W. (1985). Personality and social behavior. In G. Lindzey & E. Aronson (Eds.), *Handbook of social psychology* (3rd ed., Vol. II, pp. 883–948). Reading, MA: Addison-Wesley.

Snyder, M., Tanke, E. D., & Berscheid, E. (1977). Social perception and interpersonal behavior: On the self-fulfilling nature of social stereotypes. *Journal of Personality and Social Psychology, 35,* 656–666.

Snyder, S. H. (1992). Nitric oxide: First in a new class of neurotransmitters? *Science, 257,* 494–496.

Snyderman, M., & Rothman, S. (1987). Survey of expert opinion on intelligence and aptitude testing. *American Psychologist, 42,* 137–144.

Sokolov, E. M. (1963). Higher nervous functions: The orienting reflex. *Annual Review of Physiology, 25,* 545–580.

Solomon, P. R., Levine, E., Bein, T., & Pendlebury, W. W. (1991). Disruption of classical conditioning in patients with Alzheimer's disease. *Neurobiology of Aging, 12,* 283–287.

Solomon, R. L. (1980). The opponent-process theory of motivation. *American Psychologist, 35,* 691–712.

Sommer, R. (1967). Classroom ecology. *Journal of Applied Behavioral Science, 3,* 489–503.

Spangler, W. (1992). Validity of questionnaire and TAT measures of need for achievement: Two meta-analyses. *Psychological Bulletin, 112,* 140–154.

Spanos, N. P. (1994). Multiple identity enactments and multiple personality disorder: A sociocognitive perspective. *Psychology Bulletin, 116,* 143–165.

Spanos, N. P. (1986). Hypnotic behavior: A social-psychological interpretation of amnesia, analgesia, and "trance-logic." *Behavioral and Brain Sciences, 9,* 449–467.

Spanos, N. P., Burgess, C. A., Roncon, V., Wallace-Capretta, S., & Cross, P. (1993). Surreptitiously observed hypnotic responding in simulators and in skill-trained and untrained high hypnotizables. *Journal of Personality and Social Psychology, 65,* 391–398.

Spanos, N. P., & Katsanis, J. (1989). Effects of instructional set of non-volition during hypnotic and nonhypnotic analgesia. *Journal of Personality and Social Psychology, 56,* 182–188.

Spanos, N. P., Stenstrom, R. J., & Johnson, J. C. (1988). Hypnosis, placebo, and suggestion in the treatment of warts. *Psychosomatic Medicine, 50,* 245–260.

Spearman, C. (1904). General intelligence objectively determined and measured. *American Journal of Psychology, 15,* 201–293.

Sperling, G. (1960). The information available in brief visual presentations. *Psychological Monographs, 74*(Whole No. 11), 1–29.

Sperry, R. W. (1966). Brain bisection and consciousness. In J. Eccles (Ed.), *Brain and conscious experience.* New York: Springer-Verlag.

Sperry, R. W. (1968). Hemisphere deconnection and unity in conscious awareness. *American Psychologist, 23,* 723–733.

Sperry, R. W. (1982). Some effects of disconnecting the cerebral hemispheres. *Science, 217,* 1223–1226, 1250.

Sperry, R. W. (1993). The impact and promise of the cognitive revolution. *American Psychologist, 48,* 878–885.

Spiro, A., III., Schnurr, P. P., & Aldwin, C. M. (1994). Combat-related posttraumatic stress disorder symptoms in older men. *Psychology and Aging, 9,* 17–26.

Spitzer, R. L., Gibbon, M., Skodol, A. E., Williams, J. B., & First, M. B. (Eds.) (1994). *DSM-IV Casebook.* Washington, DC: American Psychiatric Press.

Spock, B. J. (1945). *The common sense book of child and baby care.* New York: Duell, Sloan, & Pearce.

Springer, S. P., & Deutsch, G. (1989). *Left brain, right brain* (3rd ed.). New York: W. H. Freeman.

Squire, L. R. (1992). Memory and the hippocampus: A synthesis from findings with rats, monkeys, and humans. *Psychological Review, 99,* 195–231.

Squire, L. R., & Butters, N. (Eds.). (1992). *Neuropsychology of memory* (2nd ed.). New York: Guilford Press.

Sroufe, L. A., & Jacobvitz, D. (1989). Diverging pathways, developmental transformations, multiple etiologies, and the problem of continuity in development. *Human Development, 32,* 196–203.

Staats, A. W., & Staats, C. K. (1958). Attitudes established by classical conditioning. *Journal of Abnormal and Social Psychology, 57,* 37–40.

Stangor, C., & Lange, J. E. (1994). Mental representations of social groups: Advances in understanding stereotypes and stereotyping. *Advances in Experimental Social Psychology, 26,* 357–416.

Stangor, C., Sullivan, L. A., & Ford, T. E. (1991). Affective and cognitive determinants of prejudice. *Social Cognition, 9,* 359–380.

Stanley, J. (1990, January 10). We need to know why women falter in math. *The Chronicle of Higher Education,* p. B4 (Letter to the editor)

Stanley, J. C., & Benbow, C. P. (1986). Youths who reason exceptionally well mathematically. In R. J. Sternberg & J. E. Davidson (Eds.), *Conceptions of giftedness* (pp. 361–387). New York: Cambridge University Press.

Stanley, J. C., Keating, D., & Fox, L. (Eds.). (1974). *Mathematical talent: Discovery, description, and development.* Baltimore: Johns Hopkins University Press.

Stapp, J., Tucker, A. M., & VandenBos, G. R. (1983). Census of psychological personnel. *American Psychologist, 40,* 1317–1351.

Stark, E. (1984, October). To sleep, perchance to dream. *Psychology Today,* p. 16.

Stark, E. (1986, October). Young, innocent, and pregnant. *Psychology Today,* pp. 28–35.

Staszewski, J. J. (1988). Skilled memory and expert mental calculation. In M.T.H. Chi, R. Blaser, & M. J. Farr (Eds.), *The nature of expertise* (pp. 71–128). Hillsdale, NJ: Erlbaum.

Stattin, H., & Magnusson, D. (1990). *Pubertal maturation in female development.* Hillsdale, NJ: Erlbaum.

Steblay, N. M. (1992). A meta-analytic review of the weapon-focus effect. *Law and Human Behavior, 16,* 413–424.

Steele, C. M. (1988). The psychology of self-affirmation: Sustaining the integrity of the self. In L. Berkowitz (Ed.), *Advances in experimental social psychology* (Vol. 21, pp. 261–302). New York: Academic Press.

Steele, C. M., & Josephs, R. A. (1990). Alcohol myopia: Its prized and dangerous effects. *American Psychologist, 45,* 921–933.

Steele, S. (1990). *The content of our character.* New York: St. Martin's Press.

Stein, B. E., & Meredith, M. A. (1993). *The merging of the senses.* Cambridge, MA: MIT Press.

Stein, J. H., & Reiser, L. W. (1994). A study of white middle-class adolescent boys' responses to "semenarche" (the first ejaculation). *Journal of Youth and Adolescence, 23,* 373–384.

Steinberg, L. (1987, September). Bound to bicker. *Psychology Today,* pp. 36–39.

Steinberg, L. (1989). Pubertal maturation and parent-adolescent distance: An evolutionary perspective. In G. Adams, R. Montemayor, & T. Gullotta (Eds.), *Biology of adolescent behavior and development.* Newbury Park, CA: Sage.

Steiner, J. (1979). Human facial expressions in response to taste and smell stimulation. In H. Reese & L. P. Lipsitt (Eds.), *Advances in child development and behavior* (Vol. 13, pp. 257–295). New York: Academic Press.

Stellar, E. (1954). The physiology of motivation. *Psychological Review, 61,* 5–22.

Stelmack, R. M. (1990). Biological bases of extraversion: Psychophysiological evidence. *Journal of Personality, 58,* 293–311.

Stephan, W. G. (1986). The effects of school desegregation: An evaluation 30 years after *Brown.* In M. J. Saks & L. Saxe (Eds.), *Advances in applied social psychology* (Vol. 3, pp. 181–206). Hillsdale, NJ: Erlbaum.

Stepper, S., & Strack, F. (1993). Proprioceptive determinants of emotional and nonemotional feelings. *Journal of Personality and Social Psychology, 64,* 211–220.

Sternbach, R. A. (1964). The effects of instructional sets of autonomic responsivity. *Psychophysiology, 1,* 67–72.

Sternberg, R. J. (1980). Sketch of a componential subtheory of human intelligence. *Behavioral and Brain Sciences, 3,* 573–584.

Sternberg, R. J. (1985). *Beyond IQ.* Cambridge, MA: Cambridge University Press.

Sternberg, R. J. (1988). *The triarchic mind: A new theory of human intelligence.* New York: Viking.

Sternberg, R. J. (Ed.). (1988). *The nature of creativity: Contemporary psychological perspectives.* New York: Cambridge University Press.

Sternberg, R. J. (Ed.). (1990). *Wisdom: Its nature, origins, and development.* New York: Cambridge University Press.

Sternberg, R. J., Conway, B. E., Ketron, J. L., & Bernstein, M. (1981). People's conceptions of intelligence. *Journal of Personality and Social Psychology, 41,* 37–55.

Sternberg, R. J., & Lubart, T. I. (1991). An investment theory of creativity and its development. *Human development, 34,* 1–31.

Sternberg, R. J., & Okagaki, L. (1989). Continuity and discontinuity in intellectual development are not a matter of "either-or." *Human Development, 32,* 158–166.

Sternberg, R. J., & Wagner, R. K. (Eds.). (1986). *Practical intelligence: Nature and origins of competence in the everyday world.* New York: Cambridge University Press.

Stevenson, H. W., Lee, S., & Stigler, J. (1986). Mathematics achievement of Chinese, Japanese, and American children. *Science, 231,* 693–699.

Stevenson, H. W., Lee, S., Chen, C., Stigler, J., Fan, L., & Ge, F. (1990). Mathematics achievement of children in China and the United States. *Child Development, 61,* 1053–1066.

Stewart, A. J., Sokol, M., Healy, J. M., & Chester, N. L. (1986). Longitudinal studies of psychological consequences of life changes in children and adults. *Journal of Personality and Social Psychology, 50,* 143–151.

Stewart, J. E., II. (1980). Defendant's attractiveness as a factor in the outcome of criminal trials: An observational study. *Journal of Applied Social Psychology, 10,* 348–361.

Stewart, W. F., Lipton, R. B., Celentano, D. D., & Reed, M. L. (1992). Prevalence of migraine headache in the United States: Relation to age, income, race, and other sociodemographic factors. *Journal of the American Medical Association, 267,* 84–89.

Stigler, J., Shweder, R. A., & Herdt, G. (Eds.). (1990). *Cultural psychology: Essays on comparative human development.* New York: Cambridge University Press.

Stiles, W. B., Shapiro, D. A., & Elliott, R. (1986). Are all psychotherapies equivalent? *American Psychologist, 41,* 165–180.

Stokols, D. (1972). On the distinction between density and crowding: Some implications for future research. *Psychological Review, 79,* 275–277.

Strack, F., Argyle, M., & Schwarz, N. (Eds.). (1991). *Subjective well-being.* London: Pergamon.

Strack, S., & Coyne, J. C. (1983). Social confirmation of dysphoria: Shared and private reactions to depression. *Journal of Personality and Social Psychology, 44,* 798–806.

Straube, E. R., & Oades, R. D. (1992). *Schizophrenia: Empirical research and findings.* San Diego: Academic Press.

Strauman, T. J. (1989). Self-discrepancies in clinical depression and social phobia: Cognitive structures that underly emotional disorders? *Journal of Abnormal Psychology, 98,* 5–14.

Strauman, T. J., & Higgins, E. T. (1987). Automatic activation of self-discrepancies and emotional syndromes: When cognitive structures influence affect. *Journal of Personality and Social Psychology, 53,* 1004–1014.

Strauman, T. J., Lemieux, A. M., & Coe, C. L. (1993). Self-discrepancy and natural killer cell activity: Immunological consequences of negative self-evaluation. *Journal of Personality and Social Psychology, 64,* 1042–1052.

Strauss, D. H., Spitzer, R. L., Muskin, P. R. (1990). Maladaptive denial of physical illness: A proposal for DSM-IV. *American Journal of Psychiatry, 147,* 1168–1172.

Streissguth, A. P., Barr, H. M., Sampson, P. D., Darby, B. L., & Martin, C. (1989). IQ at age 4 in relation to maternal alcohol use and smoking during pregnancy. *Developmental Psychology, 25,* 3–11.

Streri, A., & Pecheux, M. G. (1986). Tactual habituation and discrimination of form in infancy: A comparison with vision. *Child Development, 57,* 100–104.

Strichartz, A. F., & Burton, R. V. (1990). Lies and truth: A study of the development of the concept. *Child Development, 61,* 211–220.

Stricker, E. (1990). *Handbook of behavioral neurobiology: Volume 10: Neurobiology of food and water intake.* New York: Plenum.

Strickland, B. R. (1989). Internal-external control expectancies: From contingency to creativity. *American Psychologist, 44,* 1–12.

Stroop, J. R. (1935). Studies of interference in serial verbal reactions. *Journal of Experimental Psychology, 18,* 643–662.

Strube, M. J., & Werner, C. (1985). Relinquishment of control and the Type A behavior pattern. *Journal of Personality and Social Psychology, 48,* 688–701.

Struckman-Johnson, C. J., Gilliland, R. G., Struckman-Johnson, D. L., & North, T. C. (1990). The effects of fear of AIDS and gender on responses to fear-arousing condom advertisements. *Journal of Applied Social Psychology, 20,* 1396–1410.

Strupp, H. H. (1989). Psychotherapy: Can the practitioner learn from the researcher? *American Psychologist, 44,* 717–724.

Stuart, E. W., Shimp, T. A., & Engle, R. W. (1987). Classical conditioning of consumer attitudes: Four experiments in an advertising context. *Journal of Consumer Research, 14,* 334–349.

Subrahmanyan, K., and Greenfield, P. M. Effects of video game practice on spatial skills in girls and boys. *Journal of Applied Developmental Psychology, 15,* 13–32.

Sue, S., & Okazaki, S. (1990). Asian-American educational achievement: A phenomenon in search of an explanation. *American Psychologist, 45,* 913–920.

Sue, S., Smith, R., & Caldwell, C. (1973). Effects of inadmissible evidence on the decisions of simulated jurors: A moral dilemma. *Journal of Applied Social Psychology, 3,* 345–353.

Sullivan, R. M., Taborsky-Barbar, S., Mendoza, R., Itino, A., Leon, M., et al. (1991). Olfactory classical conditioning in neonates. *Pediatrics, 87,* 511–518.

Super, D. (1985). Career and life development. In D. Brown & L. Brooks (Eds.), *Career choice and development.* San Francisco: Jossey-Bass.

Suzuki, K. (1991). Moon illusion simulated in complete darkness: Planetarium experiment reexamined. *Perception and Psychophysics, 49,* 349–354.

Swann, W. B., Jr., & Ely, R. J. (1984). A battle of wills: Self-verification versus behavioral confirmation. *Journal of Personality and Social Psychology, 46,* 1287–1302.

Sweeney, P. D., Anderson, K., & Bailey, S. (1986). Attributional style in depression: A meta-analytic review. *Journal of Personality and Social Psychology, 50,* 974–991.

Swets, J. A. (1992). The science of choosing the right decision threshold in high stakes diagnostics. *American Psychologist, 47,* 522–532.

Swets, J. A., & Bjork, R. A. (1990). Enhancing human performance: An evaluation of "new age" techniques considered by the U.S. Army. *Psychological Science, 1,* 85–96.

Swim, J. K. (1994). Perceived versus meta-analytic effect sizes: An assessment of the accuracy of gender stereotypes. *Journal of Personality and Social Psychology, 66,* 21–36.

Swim, J. K., Borgida, E., Maruyama, G., & Myers, D. G. (1989). Joan McKay versus John McKay: Do gender stereotypes bias evaluations? *Psychological Bulletin, 105,* 409–429.

Switzer, J. Y. (1990). The impact of generic word choices: An empirical investigation of age- and sex-related differences. *Sex Roles, 22,* 69–82.

Szasz, T. (1961). *The myth of mental illness.* New York: Harper & Row.

Szasz, T. (1987). *Insanity: The idea and its consequences.* New York: Wiley.

Tajfel, H. (Ed.). (1982). *Social identity and intergroup relations.* London: Cambridge University Press.

Tajfel, H., Billig, M. G., Bundy, R. P., & Flament, C. (1971). Social categorization and intergroup behavior. *European Journal of Social Psychology, 1,* 149–178.

Takahashi, J. S., & Zatz, M. (1982). Regulation of circadian rhythmicity. *Science, 217,* 1104–1111.

Takeuchi, A. H., & Hulse, S. H. (1993). Absolute pitch. *Psychological Bulletin, 113,* 345–361.

Tannen, D. (1990). *You just don't understand: Women and men in conversation.* New York: Morrow.

Tartter, V. C. (1986). *Language Processes.* New York: Holt, Rinehart & Winston.

Tassinary, L. G., & Cacioppo, J. T. (1992). Unobservable facial actions and emotion. *Psychological Science, 3,* 28–33.

Tavris, C. (1992). *The mismeasure of woman.* New York: Simon & Schuster.

Taylor, C. B., Sheikh, J., Agras, W. S., Roth, W. T., Margraf, J., Ehlers, A., Maddock, R., & Gossard, D. (1986). Self-report of panic attacks: Agreement with heart rate changes. *American Journal of Psychiatry, 143,* 478–482.

Taylor, S. E. (1986). *Health psychology.* New York: Random House.

Taylor, S. E. (1989). *Positive illusions: Creative self-deception and the healthy mind.* New York: Basic Books.

Taylor, S. E. (1990). Health psychology: The science and the field. *American Psychologist, 45,* 40–50.

Taylor, S. E., & Brown, J. D. (1988). Illusion and well-being: A social psychological perspective on mental health. *Psychological Bulletin, 103,* 193–210.

Taylor, S. E., & Brown, J. D. (1994). Positive illusions and well-being revisited: Separating fact from fiction. *Psychological Bulletin, 116,* 21–27.

Taylor, S. E., Falke, R. L., Shoptaw, S. J., & Lichtman, R. R. (1986). Social support, social groups, and the cancer patient. *Journal of Consulting and Clinical Psychology, 54,* 608–615.

Taylor, S. E., & Fiske, S. T. (1978). Salience, attention, and attribution: Top of the head phenomena. *Advances in Experimental Social Psychology, 11,* 249–288.

Taylor, S. E., & Lobel, M. (1989). Social comparison activity under threat: Downward evaluation and upward contacts. *Psychological Review, 96,* 569–575.

Taylor, S. P., & Leonard, K. E. (1983). Alcohol and human physical aggression. In R. G. Geen & E. I. Donnerstein (Eds.), *Aggression: Theoretical and empirical reviews* (Vol. 2, pp. 77–101). New York: Academic Press.

Teas, D. C. (1989). Auditory physiology: Present trends. *Annual Review of Psychology, 40,* 405–429.

Tedeschi, J. T., Schlenker, B. R., & Bonoma, T. V. (1971). Cognitive dissonance: Private ratiocination or public spectacle? *American Psychologist, 26,* 685–695.

Teitelbaum, P., & Epstein, A. N. (1962). The lateral hypothalamic syndrome: Recovery of feeding and drinking after lateral hypothalamic lesions. *Psychological Review, 69,* 74–90.

Telch, M. J., Lucas, J. A., & Nelson, P. (1989). Nonclinical panic in college students: An investigation of prevalence and symptomatology. *Journal of Abnormal Psychology, 98,* 300–306.

Tellegen, A., Lykken, D. T., Bouchard, T. J., Jr., Wilcox, K. J., & Rich, S. (1988). Personality similarity in twins reared apart and together. *Journal of Personality and Social Psychology, 54,* 1031–1039.

Tennen, H., & Affleck, G. (1990). Blaming others for threatening events. *Psychological Bulletin, 108,* 209–232.

Terkel, S. (1992). *Race: How blacks and whites think and feel about the American obsession.* New York: New Press.

Terman, L. M. (1916). *The measurement of intelligence.* Boston: Houghton Mifflin.

Terman, M., Terman, J., Quitkin, F., McGrath, P., Stewart, J., & Rafferty, B. (1989). Light therapy for seasonal affective disorder: A review of efficacy. *Neuropsychopharmacology, 2,* 1–22.

Terrace, H. S. (1985). In the beginning was the "name." *American Psychologist, 40,* 1011–1028.

Terrace, H. S. (1986). *Nim: A chimpanzee who learned sign language.* New York: Columbia University Press.

Terrace, H. S., Petitto, L. A., Sanders, R. J., & Bever, T. G. (1979). Can an ape create a sentence? *Science, 206,* 891–902.

Tesser, A. (1993). The importance of heritability in psychological research: The case of attitudes. *Psychological Review, 100,* 129–142.

Tetlock, P. E., Peterson, R. S., McGuire, C., Chang, S., & Feld, P. (1992). Assessing political group dynamics: A test of the groupthink model. *Journal of Personality and Social Psychology, 63,* 403–425.

Tett, R. P., Jackson, D. N., & Rothstein, M. (1991). Personality measures as predictors of job performance: A meta-analytic review. *Personnel Psychology, 44,* 703–742.

Thach, W. T., Goodkin, H. P., & Keating, J. G. (1992). The cerebellum and the adaptive coordination of movement. *Annual Review of Neuroscience, 15,* 403–442.

Thal, L. J. (1992). Cholinomimetic therapy in Alzheimer's disease. In L. Squire & N. Butters (Eds.), *Neuropsychology of memory* (2nd ed., pp. 277–284). New York: Guilford Press.

Thatcher, R. W., Walker, R. A., & Giudice, S. (1986). Human cerebral hemispheres develop at different rates and different ages. *Science, 236,* 1110–1113.

The fetal tobacco syndrome. *Journal of the American Medical Association, 253,* 2998–2999.

Thibodeau, R., & Aronson, E. (1992). Taking a closer look: Reasserting the role of the self-concept in dissonance theory. *Personality and Social Psychology Bulletin.*

Thoman, E. B., & Ingersoll, E. W. (1993). Learning in premature infants. *Developmental Psychology, 29,* 692–700.

Thoman, E. B., Ingersoll, E. W., & Acebo, C. (1991). Premature infants seek rhythmic stimulation, and the experience facilitates neurobehavioral development. *Journal of Developmental and Behavioral Pediatrics, 12,* 11–18.

Thompson, J. G. (1988). *The psychobiology of emotions.* New York: Plenum.

Thompson, S. C. (1981). Will it hurt less if I can control it? A complex answer to a simple question. *Psychological Bulletin, 90,* 89–101.

Thorndike, E. L. (1898). Animal intelligence: An experimental study of the associative processes in animals. *Psychological Monographs, 2*(Whole No. 8).

Thorndike, E. L. (1911). *Animal intelligence: Experimental studies.* New York: Macmillan.

Thorndike, E. L., et al. (1921). Intelligence and its measurement: A symposium. *Journal of Educational Psychology, 12,* 123–247.

Thorne, B. (1986). Girls and boys together . . . but mostly apart: Gender arrangements in elementary schools. In W. W. Hartup & Z. Rubin (Eds.), *Relationships and development* (pp. 167–184). Hillsdale, NJ: Erlbaum.

Thornton, B., Hogate, L., Moirs, K., Pinette, M., & Presby, W. (1986). Physiological evidence for an arousal-based motivational bias in the defensive attribution of responsibility. *Journal of Experimental Social Psychology, 22,* 148–162.

Thurstone, L. L. (1938). *Primary mental abilities.* Chicago: University of Chicago Press.

Tice, D. M. (1991). Esteem protection or enhancement? Self-handicapping motives and attributions differ by trait self-esteem. *Journal of Personality and Social Psychology, 60,* 711–725.

Timberlake, W. (1993). Animal behavior: A continuing synthesis. *Annual Review of Psychology, 44,* 675–708.

Time (1990). Women: The road ahead. (Special Issue)

Time, June 27, 1994, p. 26.

Tinbergen, N. (1951). *The study of instinct.* New York: Oxford University Press.

Tobias, S. (1989, September). Tracked to fail. *Psychology Today,* pp. 54–60.

Tolman, E. C. (1948). Cognitive maps in rats and men. *Psychological Review, 55,* 189–208.

Tolman, E. C., & Honzik, C. H. (1930). Introduction and removal of reward and maze performance in rats. *University of California Publications in Psychology, 4,* 257–275.

Tomarken, A. J., Davidson, R. J., Wheeler, R. E., & Doss, R. C. (1992). Individual differences in anterior brain asymmetry and fundamental dimensions of emotion. *Journal of Personality and Social Psychology, 62,* 676–687.

Top, T. J. (1991). Sex bias in the evaluation of performance in the scientific, artistic, and literary professions: A review. *Sex Roles, 24,* 73–106.

Torrey, E. F. (1988). *Surviving schizophrenia: A family manual.* New York: Harper & Row.

Toufexis, A. (1989, June 12). Our violent kids. *Time,* pp. 52–58.

Toufexis, A. (1990, December 17). Drowsy America. *Time.* pp. 78–85.

Toufexis, A. (1991, August 15). Now hear this—if you can. *Time,* pp. 33–34.

Tourangeau, R., Rasinski, K. A., & D'Andrade, R. (1991). Attitude structure and belief accessibility. *Journal of Experimental Social Psychology, 27,* 48–75.

Townsend, B., Cotter, N., Van Compernolled, J. & White, R. L. (1987). Pitch perception of cochlear implant subjects. *Journal of the Acoustical Society of America, 82,* 106–114.

Trafimow, D., Triandis, H. C., & Goto, S. G. (1991). Some tests of the distinction between the private and collective self. *Journal of Personality and Social Psychology, 60,* 649–655.

Tranel, D., & Damasio, A. R. (1985). Knowledge without awareness: An autonomic index of facial recognition by prosopagnosics. *Science, 228,* 1453–1454.

Treisman, A., Viera, A., & Hayes, A. (1992). Automaticity and preattentive processes. *American Journal of Psychology, 105,* 341–362.

Triandis, H. C. (1989). The self and social behavior in differing cultural contexts. *Psychological Review, 96,* 506–520.

Triandis, H. C. (1994). *Culture and social behavior.* New York: McGraw-Hill.

Triandis, H. C., Bontempo, R., Villareal, M. J., Asai, M., & Lucca, N. (1988). Individualism and collectivism: Cross-cultural perspectives on self-ingroup relationships. *Journal of Personality and Social Psychology, 54,* 323–338.

Triplett, N. (1898). The dynamogenic factors in pacemaking and competition. *American Journal of Psychology, 9,* 507–533.

Trope, Y. (1986). Identification and inferential processes in dispositional attribution. *Psychological Review, 93,* 239–257.

Trotter, R. J. (1986, August). Three heads are better than one. *Psychology Today,* pp. 56–62.

Tsuang, M. T., & Faraone, S. V. (1990). *The genetics of mood disorders.* Baltimore, MD: Johns Hopkins University Press.

Tulving, E. (1983). *Elements of episodic memory.* Oxford: Oxford University Press.

Tulving, E., & Schacter, D. L. (1990). Priming and human memory systems. *Science, 247,* 301–306.

Turiel, E. (1983). *The development of social knowledge: Morality and convention.* Cambridge: Cambridge University Press.

Turk, D. C., & Salovey, P. (Eds.). (1988). *Reasoning, inference, and judgment in psychotherapy.* New York: Free Press.

Turkkan, J. S. (1989). Classical conditioning: The new hegemony. *Behavioral and Brain Sciences, 12,* 121–179.

Turnbull, C. M. (1961). *The forest people: A study of the Pygmies of the Congo.* New York: Clarion.

Turner, J. C. (1987). *Rediscovering the social group: A self-categorization theory.* Oxford: Basil Blackwell.

Turner, M. E., Pratkanis, A. R., Probasco, P., & Leve, C. (1992). Threat, cohesion, and group effectiveness: Testing a social identity maintenance perspective on groupthink. *Journal of Personality and Social Psychology, 63,* 781–796.

Turner, S. M., & Beidel, D. C. (1989). Social phobia: Clinical syndrome, diagnosis, and comorbidity. *Clinical Psychology Review, 9,* 3–18.

Tversky, A., & Kahneman, D. (1971). Belief in the law of small numbers. *Psychological Bulletin, 76,* 105–110.

Tversky, A., & Kahneman, D. (1973). Availability: A heuristic for judging frequency and probability. *Cognitive Psychology, 5,* 207–232.

Tversky, A., & Kahneman, D. (1981). The framing of decisions and the psychology of choice. *Science, 211,* 453–458.

Tversky, B., & Tuchin, M. (1989). A reconciliation of the evidence on eyewitness testimony: Comments on McCloskey and Zaragoza. *Journal of Experimental Psychology, 118,* 86–91.

Tyron, R. C. (1940). Genetic differences in maze learning in rats. *Yearbook of the National Society for Studies in Education, 39,* 111–119.

U.S. Bureau of the Census (1991). *World Population Profile.*

U.S. Department of Education (1990). *America's challenge: Accelerating academic achievement (1990).* Princeton, NJ: Educational Testing Service.

U.S. Department of Education (1993). *Adult literacy in America (1993).* Princeton, NJ: Educational Testing Service.

U.S. National Center for Health Statistics (1990). *Vital and health statistics,* Series 10.

Ucros, C. G. (1989). Mood state–dependent memory: A meta-analysis. *Cognition and Emotion, 3,* 139–167.

Underwood, B. J. (1957). Interference and forgetting. *Psychological Review, 64,* 49–60.

UNICEF (1990). *The state of the world's children.* New York: Oxford University Press.

Usher, J. A., & Neisser, U. (1993). Childhood amnesia and the beginnings of memory for four early life events. *Journal of Experimental Psychology: General, 122,* 155–165.

Vaillant, G. E. (1977). *Adaptation to life.* Boston: Little, Brown.

Valenstein, E. S. (Ed.). (1980). *The psychosurgery debate: Scientific, legal, and ethical perspectives.* San Francisco: W. H. Freeman.

Valenstein, E. S. (1986). *Great and desperate cures: The rise and decline of psychosurgery and other radical treatments for mental illness.* New York: Basic Books.

Vallone, R. P., Griffin, D. W., Lin, S., & Ross, L. (1990). Overconfident prediction of future actions and outcomes by self and others. *Journal of Personality and Social Psychology, 58,* 582–592.

Van Giffen, K., & Haith, M. M. (1984). Infant visual response to gestalt geometric forms. *Infant Behavior and Development, 7,* 335–346.

Van IJzendoorn, M. H., & Kroonenberg, P. M. (1988). Cross-cultural patterns of attachment: A meta-analysis of the Strange Situation. *Child Development, 59,* 147–156.

Verma, A., Hirsch, D. J., Glatt, C. E., Ronnett, G. V., & Snyder, S. H. (1993). Carbon monoxide: A putative neural messenger. *Science, 259,* 381–384.

Vernon, P. A. (1987). *Speed of information-processing and intelligence.* Norwood, NJ: Ablex.

Vernon, P. A., & Mori, M. (1992). Intelligence, reaction times, and peripheral nerve conduction velocity. *Intelligence, 16,* 273–288.

Vimal, R.L.P., Pokorny, J., & Smith, V. C. (1987). Appearance of steadily viewed lights. *Vision Research, 27,* 1309–1318.

Visintainer, M., Volpicelli, J., & Seligman, M. (1982). Tumor rejection in rats after inescapable or escapable shock. *Science, 216,* 437–439.

Vogel, D. A., Lake, M. A., Evans, S., & Karraker, K. H. (1991). Children's and adults' sex-stereotyped perceptions of infants. *Sex Roles, 24,* 605–616.

von Frisch, K. (1974). Decoding the language of the bee. *Science, 185,* 663–668.

Wade, M. G., & Whiting, H.T.A. (Eds.). (1986). *Motor development in children: Aspects of coordination and control.* Dordrecht, Holland: Martinus Nijhoff.

Wade, N. (1990). *Visual allusions: Pictures of perception.* Hillsdale, NJ: Erlbaum.

Wagenaar, W. A. (1988). *Paradoxes of gambling behavior.* Hillsdale, NJ: Erlbaum.

Wagner, H. L., MacDonald, C. J., & Manstead, A.S.R. (1986). Communication of individual emotions by spontaneous facial expressions. *Journal of Personality and Social Psychology, 50,* 737–743.

Wagstaff, G. F. (1981). *Hypnosis, compliance, and belief.* New York: St. Martin's Press.

Wald, G. (1964). The receptors of human color vision. *Science, 145,* 1007–1017.

Waldman, D. A., & Avolio, B. J. (1986). A meta-analysis of age differences in job performance. *Journal of Applied Psychology, 71,* 33–38.

Waldman, D. A., & Avolio, B. J. (1991). Race effects in performance evaluations: Controlling for ability, education, and experience. *Journal of Applied Psychology, 76,* 897–901.

Walk, R. D. (1981). *Perceptual development.* Monterey, CA: Brooks/Cole.

Walker, E., & Lewine, R. J. (1990). Prediction of adult-onset schizophrenia from childhood home movies of the patients. *American Journal of Psychiatry, 147,* 1052–1056.

Walker, L. J. (1984). Sex differences in the development of moral reasoning: A critical review. *Child Development, 55,* 677–691.

Walker, L. J. (1989). A longitudinal study of moral reasoning. *Child Development, 60,* 157–166.

Wallace, A. (1986). *The prodigy: A biography of William James Sidis, the world's greatest child prodigy.* London: Macmillan.

Wallace, W. P. (1965). Review of the historical, empirical, and theoretical status of the von Restorff phenomenon. *Psychological Bulletin, 63,* 410–424.

Walsh, J. (1981). A plenipotentiary for human intelligence. *Science, 214,* 640–641.

Walster, E., Aronson, V., Abrahams, D., & Rottman, L. (1966). Importance of physical attractiveness in dating behavior. *Journal of Personality and Social Psychology, 4,* 508–516.

Warchol, M. E., Lambert, P. R., Goldstein, B. J., Forge, A., & Corwin, J. T. (1993). Regenerative proliferation in inner ear sensory epithelia from adult guinea pigs and humans. *Science, 259,* 1619–1622.

Warga, C. (1988, September). Profile: Albert Ellis. *Psychology Today,* pp. 55–58.

Warr, P. (1992). Age and occupational well-being. *Psychology and Aging, 7,* 37–45.

Warrington, E. K., & Weiskrantz, L. (1970). Amnesic syndrome: Consolidation or retrieval? *Nature, 228,* 629–630.

Wason, P. C. (1960). On the failure to eliminate hypotheses in a conceptual task. *Quarterly Journal of Experimental Psychology, 12,* 129–140.

Wasserman, E. A. (1993). Comparative cognition: Beginning the second century of the study of animal intelligence. *Psychological Bulletin, 113,* 211–228.

Waterman, A. S. (1982). Identity development from adolescence to adulthood: An extension of theory and a review of research. *Developmental Psychology, 18,* 341–358.

Watkins, L. R., & Mayer, D. J. (1982). Organization of endogenous opiate and nonopiate pain control systems. *Science, 216,* 1185–1192.

Watkins, M. J., & Peynircioglu, Z. F. (1984). Determining perceived meaning during impression formation: Another look at the meaning change hypothesis. *Journal of Personality and Social Psychology, 46,* 1005–1016.

Watson, D., & Pennebaker, J. W. (1989). Health complaints, stress, and distress: Exploring the central role of negative affectivity. *Psychological Review, 96,* 234–254.

Watson, D. L., & Tharp, R. G. (1989). *Self-directed behavior: Self-modification for personal adjustment.* Pacific Grove, CA: Brooks/Cole.

Watson, J. B. (1913). Psychology as the behaviorist views it. *Psychological Review, 20,* 158–177.

Watson, J. B. (1925). *Behaviorism.* New York: Norton.

Watson, J. B. (1927). The myth of the unconscious. *Harper's, 155,* 502–508.

Watson, J. B., & Rayner, R. (1920). Conditioned emotional reactions. *Journal of Experimental Psychology, 3,* 1–14.

Watson, R. I., & Evans, R. B. (1991). *The great psychologists: A history of psychological thought.* New York: Harper Collins.

Weaver, C. A., III. (1993). Do you need a "flash" to form a flashbulb memory? *Journal of Experimental Psychology: General, 122,* 39–46.

Webb, W. B. (1992). *Sleep the gentle tyrant* (2nd ed.). Bolton, MA: Anker.

Weber, E. H. (1834). *De pulen, resorptione, auditu et tactu: Annotationes anatomicae et physiologicae.* Leipzig: Kohler.

Wechsler, D. (1939). *The measurement of adult intelligence.* Baltimore: Williams & Wilkins.

Wechsler, D. (1972). "Hold" and "don't hold" test. In S. M. Chown (Ed.), *Human aging.* New York: Penguin.

Wechsler, D. (1981). *Manual for the Wechsler Adult Intelligence Scale—Revised.* New York: Psychological Corporation.

Wegner, D. M. (1989). *White bears and other unwanted thoughts: Suppression, obsession, and the psychology of mental control.* New York: Viking.

Wegner, D. M. (1994). Ironic processes of mental control. *Psychological Review, 101,* 34–52.

Weil, A., & Rosen, W. (1993). *From chocolate to morphine: Everyday mind-altering drugs.* Boston: Houghton Mifflin.

Weil, A. T. (1974, July). Parapsychology: Andrew Weil's search for the true Geller: Part II. The letdown. *Psychology Today,* pp. 74–78, 82.

Weinberg, R. A. (1989). Intelligence and IQ: Landmark issues and great debates. *American Psychologist, 44,* 98–104.

Weinberg, R. A., Scarr, S., & Waldman, I. D. (1992). The Minnesota transracial adoption study: The follow-up of IQ test performance at adolescence. *Intelligence, 16,* 117–135.

Weinberger, H., Hiner, S. L., & Tierney, W. M. (1987). In support of hassles as a measure of stress in predicting health outcomes. *Journal of Behavioral Medicine, 10,* 481–500.

Weiner, B. (1985). An attributional theory of achievement motivation and emotion. *Psychological Review, 92,* 548–573.

Weiner, R. D., & Coffey, C. E. (1988). Indications for use of electroconvulsive therapy. In A. J. Francis & R. E. Hales (Eds.), *Review of Psychiatry* (Vol. 7). Washington, DC: American Psychiatric Press.

Weingartner, H., Grafman, J., Boutelle, W., Kaye, W., & Martin, P. R. (1983). Forms of memory failure. *Science, 221,* 380–382.

Weinstein, N. D. (1980). Unrealistic optimism about future life events. *Journal of Personality and Social Psychology, 39,* 806–820.

Weinstein, N. D. (1982). Unrealistic optimism about susceptibility to health problems. *Journal of Behavioral Medicine, 5,* 441–460.

Weinstein, S. (1968). Intensive and extensive aspects of tactile sensitivity as a function of body part, sex, and laterality. In D. R. Kenshalo (Ed.), *The skin senses* (pp. 195–218). Springfield, IL: Thomas.

Weisberg, R. W. (1986). *Creativity: Genius and other myths.* New York: W. H. Freeman.

Weisberg, R. W. (1992). Metacognition and insight during problem solving: Comment on Metcalfe. *Journal of Experimental Psychology: Learning, Memory, and Cognition, 18,* 426–431.

Weiskrantz, L. (1986). *Blindsight: A case study and implications.* Oxford: Clarendon Press.

Weiss, D. E. (1991). *The great divide.* New York: Simon & Schuster.

Weiss, D. E. (1991). *The great divide: How females and males really differ.* New York: Poseiden Press.

Weissberg, M. (1993). Multiple personality disorder and iatrogenesis: The cautionary tale of Anna O. *International Journal of Clinical and Experimental Hypnosis, 41,* 15–34.

Weisse, C. S. (1992). Depression and immunocompetence: A review of the literature. *Psychological Bulletin, 111,* 475–489.

Weisz, J. R., Suwanlert, S., Chaiyasit, W., Weiss, B., Achenbach, T. M., & Eastman, K. L. (1993). *Journal of Abnormal Psychology, 102,* 395–403.

Wells, G. L. (1993). What do we know about eyewitness identification? *American Psychologist, 48*, 553–571.

Wells, G. L., Lindsay, R.C.L., & Ferguson, T. J. (1979). Accuracy, confidence, and juror perceptions in eyewitness identification. *Journal of Applied Psychology, 64*, 440–448.

Wells, G. L., & Loftus, E. F. (Eds.). (1984). *Eyewitness testimony: Psychological perspectives.* New York: Cambridge University Press.

Wells, G. L., & Murray, D. M. (1984). Eyewitness confidence. In G. Wells & E. Loftus (Eds.), *Eyewitness testimony: Psychological perspectives* (pp. 155–170). New York: Cambridge University Press.

Wenk, G. L. (1989). An hypothesis on the role of glucose in the mechanism of action of cognitive enhancers. *Psychopharmacology, 99*, 431–438.

Werner, E. E. (1988). A cross-cultural perspective on infancy. *Journal of Cross-Cultural Psychology, 19*, 96–113.

Wernicke, C. (1874). *Das aphasische symptomenkomplex.* Breslau: Cohn und Weigart.

West, J. R. (Ed.). (1986). *Alcohol and brain development.* New York: Oxford University Press.

West, P.D.B., & Evans, E. F. (1990). Early detection of hearing damage in young listeners resulting from exposure to amplified music. *British Journal of Audiology, 24*, 89–103.

Westefeld, J. S., & Furr, S. R. (1987). Suicide and depression among college students. *Professional Psychology: Research and Practice, 18*, 119–123.

Westen, D. (1990). Psychoanalytic approaches to personality. In L. A. Pervin (Ed.), *Handbook of personality theory and research.* New York: Guilford Press.

Wheeler, L., & Miyake, K. (1992). Social comparison in everyday life. *Journal of Personality and Social Psychology, 62*, 760–773.

Whitaker, A., et al. (1990). Uncommon troubles in young people: Prevalence estimates of selected psychiatric disorders in a nonreferred adolescent population. *Archives of General Psychiatry, 47*, 487–496.

Whitam, F. L., Diamond, M., & Martin, J. (1993). Homosexual orientation in twins: A report on 61 pairs and three triplet sets. *Archives of Sexual Behavior, 22*, 187–206.

White, G. L., Fishbein, S., & Rutstein, J. (1981). Passionate love and misattribution of arousal. *Journal of Personality and Social Psychology, 41*, 52–62.

White, L., & Edwards, J. N. (1990). Emptying the nest and parental well-being: An analysis of national panel data. *American Sociological Review, 55*, 235–242.

White, L., Tursky, B., & Schwartz, G. E. (1985). *Placebo: Theory, research, and mechanisms.* New York: Guilford Press.

White, N. M., & Milner, P. M. (1992). The psychobiology of reinforcers. *Annual Review of Psychology, 43*, 443–471.

White, R. W. (1975). *Lives in progress* (3rd ed.). New York: Holt, Rinehart & Winston.

Whiting, B. B., & Edwards, C. P. (1988). *Children of different worlds.* Cambridge, MA: Harvard University Press.

Whiting, J.W.M., & Edwards, C. (1988). *Children of different worlds: The formation of social behavior.* Cambridge, MA: Harvard University Press.

Whitney, P. (1986). Processing category terms in context: Instantiations as inferences. *Memory and Cognition, 14*, 39–48.

Whorf, B. L. (1956). Science and linguistics. In J. B. Carroll (Ed.), *Language, thought, and reality: Selected writings of Benjamin Lee Whorf* (pp. 207–219). Cambridge, MA: MIT Press.

Wicker, A. W. (1969). Attitudes versus actions: The relationship between verbal and overt behavioral responses to attitude objects. *Journal of Social Issues, 25*(4), 41–78.

Wicklund, R. A. (1975). Objective self-awareness. In L. Berkowitz (Ed.), *Advances in experimental social psychology* (Vol 8, pp. 233–275). New York: Academic Press.

Widiger, T. A., Frances, A. J., Pincus, H. A., First, M. B., Ross, R., &

Davis, W. (Eds.) (1994). DSM-IV Sourcebook. Washington, DC: American Psychiatric Press.

Wiedenfeld, S. A., O'Leary, A., Bandura, A., Brown, S., Levine, S., & Raska, K. (1990). Impact of perceived self-efficacy in coping with stressors on coping with the immune system. *Journal of Personality and Social Psychology, 59*, 1082–1094.

Wiens, A. N., & Minustik, C. E. (1983). Treatment outcome and patient characteristics in an aversion therapy program for alcoholism. *American Psychologist, 38*, 1089–1096.

Wierzbicka, A. (1985). Different cultures, different languages, different speech acts. *Journal of Pragmatics, 9*, 145–178.

Wiggins, J. S., & Pincus, A. L. (1992). Personality: Structure and assessment. *Annual Review of Psychology, 43*, 473–504.

Wilder, D. A. (1986). Social categorization: Implications for creation and reduction of intergroup bias. In L. Berkowitz (Ed.), *Advances in experimental social psychology* (Vol. 19, pp. 291–355). New York: Academic Press.

Wilder, D. A., & Shapiro, P. (1991). Facilitation of outgroup stereotypes by enhanced ingroup identity. *Journal of Experimental Social Psychology, 27*, 431–452.

Williams, J. E., & Best, D. L. (1982). *Measuring sex stereotypes: A thirty-nation study.* Beverly Hills, CA: Sage.

Williams, J. E., & Best, D. L. (1990). *Sex and psyche: Gender and self viewed cross-culturally.* Newbury Park, CA: Sage.

Williams, K., Harkins, S., & Latané, B. (1981). Identifiability as a deterrent to social loafing: Two cheering experiments. *Journal of Personality and Social Psychology, 40*, 303–311.

Willis, S. L. (1990). Introduction to the special section on cognitive training in later adulthood. *Developmental Psychology, 26*, 875–878.

Wills, T. A. (Ed.). (1990). Social support in social and clinical psychology. *Journal of Social and Clinical Psychology, 9* (Special Issue)

Wilson, G. T., Rossiter, E., Kleinfield, E. I., & Lindholm, L. (1986). Cognitive-behavioral treatment of bulimia nervosa: A controlled evaluation. *Behavior Research and Therapy, 24*, 277–288.

Winger, G., Hofmann, F. G. & Woods, J. H. (1992). *A handbook on drug and alcohol abuse* (3rd. ed.). New York: Oxford University Press.

Winograd, E., & Neisser, U. (Eds.). (1992). *Affect and accuracy in recall: Studies of "flashbulb" memories.* New York: Cambridge University Press.

Wise, R. A., & Rompre, P. P. (1989). Brain dopamine and reward. *Annual Review of Psychology, 40*, 191–225.

Wittchen, H. U., Zhao, S., Kessler, R. C., & Eaton, W. W. (1994). DSM-III-R generalized anxiety disorder in the National Comorbidity Survey. *Archives of General Psychiatry, 51*, 355–364.

Witteman, P. A. (1990, April 30). Vietnam: 15 years later. *Time*, pp. 19–21.

Wolpe, J. (1958). *Psychotherapy by reciprocal inhibition.* Stanford, CA: Stanford University Press.

Wolpe, J. (1982). *The practice of behavior therapy* (3rd ed.). New York: Pergamon.

Wong, D. F., et al. (1986). Positron emission tomography reveals elevated D-2 dopamine receptors in drug-naive schizophrenics. *Science, 234*, 1558–1563.

Wood, J. V., Taylor, S. E., & Lichtman, R. R. (1985). Social comparison in adjustment to breast cancer. *Journal of Personality and Social Psychology, 49*, 1169–1183.

Wood, W., Wong, F. Y., & Chachere, J. G. (1991). Effects of media violence on viewers' aggression in unconstrained social interaction. *Psychological Bulletin, 109*, 371–383.

Woodhead, M. (1988). When psychology informs public policy: The case of early childhood intervention. *American Psychologist, 43*, 443–454.

Word, C. O., Zanna, M. P., & Cooper, J. (1974). The nonverbal mediation of self-fulfilling prophecies in interracial interaction. *Journal of Experimental Social Psychology, 10,* 109–120.

Wright, E. (1992). The original of E. G. Boring's "young girl/mother-in-law" drawing and its relation to the pattern of a joke. *Perception, 21,* 273–275.

Wright, J. W. (Ed.). (1993). *The Universal Almanac.* Kansas City, MO: Andrews & McMeel.

Wright, L. (1988). Type A behavior pattern and coronary artery disease: Quest for the active ingredients and the elusive mechanism. *American Psychologist, 43,* 2–14.

Wright, L., von Bussman, K., Friedman, A., Khoury, M., & Owens, F. (1990). Exaggerated social control and its relationship to the Type A behavior pattern. *Journal of Research in Personality, 24,* 258–269.

Wynn, K. (1992). Addition and subtraction by human infants. *Nature, 358,* 749–750.

Wynne, L. C. (Ed.). (1988). *The state of the art in family therapy research: Controversies and recommendations.* New York: Norton.

Wyrwicka, W., & Dobrzecka, C. (1960). Relationship between feeding and satiation centers of the hypothalamus. *Science, 132,* 805–806.

Yalom, I. D. (1989). *Love's executioner and other tales of psychotherapy.* New York: HarperCollins.

Yee, D. K., & Eccles, J. S. (1988). Parent perceptions and attributions for children's math achievement. *Sex Roles, 19,* 317–333.

Young, A. W., & De Haan, E.H.F. (1992). Face recognition and awareness after brain injury. In A. D. Milner & M. D. Rugg (Eds.), *The neuropsychology of consciousness.* London: Academic Press.

Young, K. T. (1990). American conceptions of infant development from 1955 to 1984: What the experts are telling parents. *Child Development, 61,* 17–28.

Young, T. (1802). On the theory of light and colors. *Philosophical Transactions of the Royal Society of London, 92,* 12–48.

Yuille, J. C., & Tollestrup, P. A. (1990). Some effects of alcohol on eyewitness memory. *Journal of Applied Psychology, 75,* 268–273.

Zahler, D., & Zahler, K. A. (1993). *Test your cultural literacy* (2nd ed.). New York: ARCO.

Zahn-Waxler, C., Radke-Yarrow, M., Wagner, E., & Chapman, M. (1992). Development of concern for others. *Developmental Psychology, 28,* 126–136.

Zajonc, R. B. (1965). Social facilitation. *Science, 149,* 269–274.

Zajonc, R. B. (1968). Attitudinal effects of mere exposure. *Journal of Personality and Social Psychology Monograph, 9* (2, part 2), 1–27.

Zajonc, R. B. (1976). Family configuration and intelligence. *Science, 192,* 227–236.

Zajonc, R. B. (1984). On the primacy of affect. *American Psychologist, 39,* 117–123.

Zajonc, R. B. (1986). The decline and rise of Scholastic Aptitude Scores: A prediction derived from the confluence model. *American Psychologist, 41,* 862–867.

Zajonc, R. B. (1993). Brain temperature and subjective emotional experience. In M. Lewis & J. M. Haviland (Eds.), *Handbook of emotions* (pp. 209–220). New York: Guilford Press.

Zajonc, R. B., Murphy, S. T., & Inglehart, M. (1989). Feeling and facial efference: Implications of the vascular theory of emotion. *Psychological Review, 96,* 395–416.

Zebrowitz, L. A., Kendall-Tackett, K., & Fafel, J. (1991a). The influence of children's facial maturity on parental expectations and punishment. *Journal of Experimental Child Psychology, 52,* 221–238.

Zebrowitz, L. A., & McDonald, S. M. (1991). The impact of litigants' babyfacedness and attractiveness on adjudications in small claims courts. *Law and Human Behavior,* 603–624.

Zebrowitz, L. A., Tenenbaum, D. R., & Goldstein, L. H. (1991b). The impact of job applicants' facial maturity, gender, and academic achievement on hiring recommendations. *Journal of Applied Social Psychology, 21,* 525–548.

Zec, R. F. (1993). Neuropsychological functioning in Alzheimer's disease. In R. W. Parks, R. F. Zec, & R. S. Wilson (Eds.), *Neuropsychology of Alzheimer's Disease and other dementias* (pp. 3–80). New York: Oxford University Press.

Zechmeister, E. B., & Johnson, J. E. (1992). *Critical thinking: A functional approach.* Belmont, CA: Wadsworth.

Zeki, S. (1992). The visual image in mind and brain. *Scientific American, 267,* 68–76.

Zentall, S. S., & Zentall, T. R. (1983). Optimal stimulation: A model of disordered activity and performance in normal and deviant children. *Psychological Bulletin, 94,* 446–471.

Zigler, E. (1987). Formal schooling for 4-year-olds? No. *American Psychologist, 42,* 254–260.

Zigler, E. F., & Berman, W. (1983). Discerning the future of early childhood education. *American Psychologist, 38,* 894–906.

Zillman, D. (1983). Transfer of excitation in emotional behavior. In J. Cacioppo and R. Petty (Eds.), *Social psychophysiology: A sourcebook* (pp. 215–240). New York: Guilford Press.

Zillman, D., & Bryant, J. (Eds.). (1989). *Pornography: Research advances and policy considerations.* Hillsdale, NJ: Erlbaum.

Zimbardo, P. G. (1970). The human choice: Individuation, reason, and order versus deindividuation, impulse, and chaos. In W. J. Arnold & D. Levine (Eds.), *Nebraska Symposium on Motivation: 1969* (Vol. 17, pp. 237–307). Lincoln: University of Nebraska Press.

Zimbardo, P. G. (1977). *Shyness.* New York: Jove.

Zimbardo, P. G. (1985, June). Laugh where we must, be candid where we can. *Psychology Today,* pp. 43–47.

Zimmerberg, B., and Gray, M. S. (1992). The effects of cocaine on maternal behaviors in the rat. *Physiology and Behavior, 52,* 379–384.

Zinbarg, R. E., Barlow, D. H., Brown, T. A., & Hertz, R. M. (1992). Cognitive-behavioral approaches to the nature and treatment of anxiety disorders. *Annual Review of Psychology, 43,* 235–267.

Zubin, J., & Spring, B. (1977). Vulnerability—A new view of schizophrenia. *Journal of Abnormal Psychology, 86,* 103–126.

Zuckerman, M. (1979). *Sensation seeking: Beyond the optimal level of arousal.* Hillsdale, NJ: Erlbaum.

Zuckerman, M. (1990). The psychophysiology of sensation seeking. *Journal of Personality, 58,* 313–345.

Zuckerman, M., DePaulo, B. M., & Rosenthal, R. (1981). Verbal and nonverbal communication of deception. *Advances in Experimental Social Psychology, 14,* 1–59.

Name Index

Subject Index

SUBJECT INDEX I-25

Problem solving (*con't*)
divergent thinking and, 426, 442
hyperactivity and, 608, 609
problem representation in, 258–259, 264, 290
strategies for, 259–264, 290
Procedural memory, 223, 224
Prodigies, 421–422
Productivity, 394–395
Progesterone, 372, 537, 542
Project Head Start, 428, 431–432
Projection, 567–568, 598
Projective tests, 570–571, 598
Prosopagnosia, 136, 139, 166, 232
Protolanguage, 283
Prototypes, 256–257, 290
Proximity, in perceptual grouping 111
Prozac, 676
Psychiatric social work, 647–648
Psychiatry, 647
"Psychic energy," 566, 649
"Psychic numbing," 573
Psychoactive drugs, 160–165, 167
antianxiety drugs as, 674–675
antidepressants as, 617, 625, 675–676, 681
antipsychotic drugs as, 636, 676–677, 681
defined, 161
hallucinogens as, 160, 164–165, 167
opiates as, 165, 167
sedatives as, 161–163, 167
stimulants as, 163–164, 167
as treatment approach, 674–677, 681
Psychoanalysis, 561–573, 596, 597–598, 605, 680
brief version of, 652
criticisms of, 572, 652
current perspectives on, 571–572
defined, 562
dream interpretation in, 148–149, 566–567, 649
free association in, 562, 570, 649, 651
hypnosis and, 154, 158, 562, 570
interpretation in, 651–652
personality and, 563–564, 566–568
projective tests in, 570–571
psychosexual development and, 564–566
resistance in, 562, 650, 651, 652
trait approach and, 595
transference in, 562, 650–651, 652
as treatment approach, 647–653, 668
variations on, 568–570
Psychoanalytic approach
to abnormality, 605
to depression, 626
to obsessive-compulsive disorder, 617
to phobic disorder, 615
Psychoeducation, 663, 681
Psycholinguistics, 19
Psychological dependence, 161, 167
Psychological disorder(s), 602–643
abnormal behavior and, 602–606, 640–641, 642
anxiety disorders as, 610–617, 642

bipolar disorder as, 629–631, 643
classification of, 606–610
comorbidity of, 639–640, 643
dissociative disorders as, 620–623, 642
mood disorders as, 623–629, 642–643
personality disorders as, 637–639, 643
schizophrenic disorders as, 631–637, 643
somatoform disorders as, 617–619, 642
See also Treatment, of psychological disorders
Psychological model, of abnormality, 605, 642
Psychology
applications of, 12–13, 33
areas of specialization, 10–11, 33
current status of, 30–32, 33
defined, 2, 32
ethics considerations in, 12, 26–30, 33
historical roots of, 3–10, 32
measures used in, 16–19, 33
research designs in, 19–26, 33
research settings in, 15–16, 33
scientific methods of, 9–10, 13, 15, 33
Psychology of Interpersonal Relations, The (Heider), 455
Psychoneuroimmunology (PNI), 41, 76, 708, 709, 721
Psychopaths, 638
Psychophysics, 82, 128
Psychophysiological disorders, 698
Psychosexual stages, 564–566, 572, 598
Psychosomatic symptoms, 618, 698
Psychosurgery, 57, 678–679, 681
Psychotherapist's Guide to Psychopharmacology, The (Gitlin), 674
Psychotherapy, 239, 562, 570, 648
defined, 647, 680
vs. drug therapies, 677
eclecticism of, 673–674
effectiveness of, 669–671, 681
key ingredients of, 672–673
Puberty, 372–374, 380–381, 404, 537
Public conformity, 486
Puluwat Islanders, 408
Punishment, 190, 207
as treatment approach, 659
unwanted side effects of, 194–195
Pupil, of eye, 87, 128
Purity
of lightwaves, 86
of soundwaves, 95
Puzzle box, 188, 189, 259
Pygmies, of Africa, 113, 119

Questionnaires, 576, 577, 581, 585, 589, 594

Race
IQ scores and, 416–418, 432–433, 443
life satisfaction and, 398–399
See also Discrimination, social; Prejudice; Racism
Race (Terkel), 531
Racism, 448, 452, 478, 530–535, 553
method of combating, 534–535

in workplace, 532–533
Radiation problem, 261, 262
Random assignment, 25, 33
Random samples, 20, 33
Rape, 504
Rapid eye movement (REM) sleep, 142–143, 166
alcohol and, 162
dreams and, 143, 147
sleep disturbances and, 151, 152
Rapid-smoking technique, 659
Rational-emotive therapy, 662–663, 681
Rationalization, 568, 573, 598
Reaction formation, 568, 598
Realistic conflict theory, 476–477, 479
Reality principle, 564, 598
Reasoning
development of, 355–356
formal logic and, 267–269, 289, 374
moral, 374, 377
Rebound anxiety, 674
Recall, 212, 223, 229–230, 231, 246. *See also* Retrieval
Recency effect, 219
Receptive field, 89
Receptors, neurotransmitter, 47, 48
Reciprocal determinism, 580–581, 598
Reciprocity, norm of, 508
Recognition, 229–231, 389
Reconstruction, of memories, 239–243
Reconstructive memory, theory of, 241
Recovery, following habituation, 341, 367
Recursion, 277
Reflection, 666
Reflexes
aging and, 386, 388
classical conditioning and, 185, 227
defined, 43, 76
in infancy, 173, 344, 367
orienting, 176
Reinforcement, 7, 189–203, 207
defined, 190
expectancy of, 575–576
motivation and, 202–203
negative vs. positive, 190
schedules of, 192–194
in social-learning theory, 575–576
as treatment approach, 659, 661
vicarious, 205
Rejection
depression and, 627
by peers, 365
Relaxation training, 613, 656, 660, 712–713
Reliability
of IQ tests, 414–415, 442
of MMPI-2, 591
of projective tests, 570, 571
of psychiatric diagnosis, 608–609, 610
Religion, 518, 520
Remembrance of Things Past (Proust), 233
REM sleep. *See* Rapid eye movement sleep
REM sleep behavior disorder, 152
Reminiscence peak, 244
Remote Associates Test, 426
Replication, of experiments, 25–26, 33

Credits *(continued from page A-10)*

sic Syndrome: Consolidation or Retrieval?" by E.K. Warrington & L. Weiskrantz. Reprinted with permission from *Nature, 228,* 629–630. Copyright © 1970 Macmillan Magazines Limited. **p. 236:** *Table 6.3* From Baddeley, A., *Human Memory: Theory and Practice.* Copyright © 1990 by Allyn and Bacon. Reprinted by permission. **p. 237:** *Figure 6.17* "Semantic Memory Content in Permastore: Fifty Years of Memory for Spanish Learned in School" from *Journal of Experimental Psychology: General, 113,* 1–35. Copyright © 1984 by the American Psychological Association. Reprinted by permission. *Figure 6.18* "Long-term Memory for a Common Object" by R.S. Nickerson and M.J. Adams from *Cognitive Psychology, vol. 11,* pp. 287–307. Copyright © 1979 by Academic Press. Reprinted by permission. **p. 238:** *Figure 6.19* "Oblivescence During Sleep and Waking" by J.G. Jendins & K.M. Dallenbach from *American Journal of Psychology, 35,* 605–612. Reprinted by permission. **p. 240:** Courtesy of William F. Brewer; originally appeared in *Cognitive Psychology.* **p. 241:** *Figure 6.21* Data from Loftus & Palmer, 1974 and Loftus & Loftus, 1976. Brehm, Sharon, and Saul M. Kassin, *Social Psychology, 2/e.* Copyright © 1993 by Houghton Mifflin Company. Used with permission. **p. 244:** *Figure 6.22* "Remembering Autobiographically Consequential Experiences: Content Analysis of Psychologists' Accounts of Their Lives" by W.R. Mackavey, J.E. Malley & A.J. Stewart from *Psychology and Aging, 6,* 50–59. Copyright © 1991 by the American Psychological Association. Reprinted by permission. **p. 245:** NASA/Science Source/Photo Researchers. **Chapter 7: p. 255:** *Figure 7.1* "A Personal Case History of Transient Anomia" by M. H. Ashcraft from *Brain and Language, 44,* 47–57. Copyright © 1993 by Academic Press, Inc. Reprinted by permission. **p. 256:** (left) © Frank Siteman/Rainbow; (center) © M. Antman/The Image Works; (right) © Dan McCoy/Rainbow. **p. 257:** © Bob Daemmrich/Stock Boston. **p. 258:** *Figure 7.2* "Imaginal Priming" by M. J. Intons-Peterson from *Journal of Experimental Psychology: Learning, Memory, and Cognition, 19,* 223–235. Copyright © 1993 by the American Psychological Association. Reprinted by permission. **p. 259:** *Figure 7.3* "Naive Theories of Motion" by M. McCloskey in *Mental Models* edited by D. Gentner & K. Stevens. Copyright © by Lawrence Erlbaum Associates, Inc. Reprinted by permission. **p. 259:** *Figure 7.4* "Naive Theories of Motion" by M. McCloskey in *Mental Models,* edited by D. Gentner & K. Stevens. Copyright © by Lawrence Erlbaum Associates, Inc. Reprinted by permission. **p. 261:** "*The radiation problem*" from "Analogical Problem Solving" by M.L. Gick and K.J. Holyoak from *Cognitive Psychology, vol. 12,* pp. 306–355. Copyright © 1980 by Academic Press. Reprinted by permission. **p. 263:** *Figure 7.6* From *Cognitive Psychology and Its Implications* by Anderson. Copyright © 1990 by W.H. Freeman and Company. Used with permission. **p. 264:** *Figure 7.7b* Source: Duncker, Karl (1945), "On Problem-Solving" trans. by L.S. Lees. *Psychological Monographs, 58,* No. 270. **p. 268:** *Figure 7.12* "On the Failure to Eliminate Hypotheses in a Conceptual Task" by P. C. Wason from *Quarterly Journal of Experimental Psychology.* Copyright © 1960 by Lawrence Erlbaum Associates, Ltd. Reprinted by permission of Quarterly Journal of Experimental Psychology. **p. 269:** *Figure 7.13* "The Elusive Thematic-Materials Effect in Wason's Selection Task" by R.A. Griggs & J.R. Cox from *British Journal of Psychology, 73,* 407–420. Reprinted by permission of The British Psychological Society and the author. *Figure 7.14* Morris et al "Tools of the Trade: Deductive Schemas Taught in Psychology and Philosophy" by M.W. Morris & R.E. Nisbett in *Rules for Reasoning* by R.E. Nisbett. Copyright © 1993 by Lawrence Erlbaum Associates, Inc. Reprinted by permission. **p. 271:** *Figure 7.15* "The Overconfidence Effect in Social Prediction" by D. Dunning et al. from *Journal of Personality and Social Psychology, 58,* 568–581. Copyright 1990 by the American Psychological Association. Reprinted by permission. **p. 273:** © Ron Lowery/Tony Stone Images. **p. 275:** (left) © Gay Bumgarner/Tony Stone Images; (right) © Gary Brettnacher/Tony Stone Images. **p. 276:** © Owen Franken/Stock Boston. **p. 280:** (top) © Michael Goldman/TIME Magazine; (bottom) Harris/Cartoonists & Writers Syndicate. **p. 282:** © Michael Nichols/Magnum Photos. **p. 284:** *Table 7.3* "Language Com-

prehension in Ape and Child" by S. Savage-Rumbaugh et al. from *Monographs of the Society for Research in Child Development, 58 (3–4, serial No.233).* Copyright © 1993 by The Society for Research in Child Development, Inc. **p. 285:** © Ben Blankenburg/Stock Boston. **p. 286:** *Figure 7.17* Based on "An Experimental Study of the Effect of Language on the Reproduction of Visually Perceived Form," by L. Carmichael et al. from *Journal of Experimental Psychology, 15,* 73–86. **Chapter 8: p. 297:** *Figure 8.4* "Individual Differences in Anterior Brain Asymmetry and Fundamental Dimensions of Emotion" by A.J. Tomarken, R.J. Davidson, R.E. Wheeler & R.C. Doss from *Journal of Personality and Social Psychology, 62,* 676–687. Copyright © 1992 by the American Psychological Association, Inc. Reprinted by permission. Photo © Joe McNally/Sygma. **p. 298:** © Chad Slattery/Tony Stone Images. **p. 299:** *Figure 8.6* "Autonomic Nervous System Activity Distinguished Among Emotions" by P. Ekman, R.W. Levenson & W.V. Friesen from *Science, 221,* 1208–1210. Copyright © 1983 by the AAAS. Reprinted by permission. **p. 302:** *Figure 8.7* Article by D.C. Raskin appearing in *Science,* June, p. 24–27. Copyright © 1982 by the AAAS. Reprinted by permission. **p. 303:** 6 emotion set, copyright Paul Ekman, 1975. **p. 304:** *Figure 8.8* "The Recognition of Threatening Facial Stimuli" by J. Aronoff, A.M. Barclay & L.A. Stevenson in *Journal of Personality and Social Psychology, 54,* p. 651. Copyright © 1988 by the American Psychological Association. Reprinted by permission. Photo courtesy of Dr. Carroll Izard. **p. 305:** © Allsport USA. **p. 305:** *Figure 8.9* Transfer of Excitation in Emotional Behavior" by D. Aillman in *Social Psychophysiology: A Sourcebook* edited by J. Cacioppo and R. Petty. Copyright © 1983 by Guilford Publications, Inc. Reprinted by permission. **p. 306:** © T. Clark/The Image Works. **p. 308:** *Figure 8.10* "Feeling and Facial Efference: Implications of the Vascular Theory of Emotion" by R. B. Zajonc, S.T. Murphy & M. Inglehart from *Psychological Review, 96,* 395–416. Copyright © 1989 by the American Psychological Association. Reprinted by permission. **p. 310:** © Steve Winter/Black Star. **p. 314:** *Figure 8.12 Three-Dimensional Model of Emotions* from *Emotion: A Psychoevolutionary Synthesis* by Robert Plutchik. Copyright © 1980 by Robert Plutchik. Reprinted by permission of HarperCollins Publishers, Inc. **p. 315:** *Figure 8.13* "A Circumplex Model of Affect" by J.A. Russell from *Journal of Personality and Social Psychology, 39,* p. 1169. Copyright © 1980 by the American Psychological Association. Reprinted by permission. Photos (left) © 1993 Mark Simon/Black Star; (right) © Bob Daemmrich/Stock Boston. **p. 316:** *Boxed figure* "Anxiety and Depression in Seasonal Affective Disorders" by S. Kasper and N.E. Rosenthal from *Anxiety and Depression: Distinct and Overlapping Features* edited by P. Kendall and D. Watson. Copyright © 1989 by Academic Press. Reprinted by permission. **p. 317:** *Table 8.3* "Prevalence of Seasonal Affective Disorder in Alaska" by J.M. Booker & C.J. Hellekson from *American Journal of Psychiatry, 149,* 1176–1182, 1992. Copyright © 1992, the American Psychiatric Associatrion. Reprinted by permission. Photo © B&C Alexander/Black Star. **p. 318:** *Figure 8.14* "The Opponent-Process Theory of Motivation" by R.L. Solomon from *American Psychologist, 35,* 694–695. Copyright © 1980 by the American Psychological Association. Reprinted by permission. **p. 319:** © Mark Downey. **p. 321:** © Kezar/Black Star. *Table 8.4* Diener et al "The Satisfaction with Life Scale" by E. Diener, R.A. Emmons, R.J. Larsen & S. Griffin from *Journal of Personality Assessment, 49,* p. 72. Copyright © 1984 by Lawrence Erlbaum Associates, Inc. Reprinted by permission. **Chapter 9: p. 334:** both © Michael Nichols/Magnum. **p. 336:** © Harry Benson. **p. 337:** *Figure 9.2* Diagram "Genetic Building Blocks" from *Time* Magazine, January 17, 1994. Copyright © 1994 TIME, Inc. Reprinted by permission. **p. 338:** all four by Lennart Nilsson, *A Child Is Born,* Dell Publishing Company. **p. 339:** Property of Anthony DeCasper; photographer Walter Salinger. **p. 341:** © J. Pavlovsky/Sygma. **p. 342:** © Joe McNally/Sygma. **p. 344:** *Figure 9.4* "Addition and Subtraction by Human Infants" by K. Wynn. Reprinted with permission from *Nature, 358,* p. 749. Copyright © 1992 Macmillan Magazines Limited. Photo © Joe McNally/Sygma. **p.345:** *Figure 9.6* "CONSPEC and CONLERN: A Two-Process Theory of Infant Face Recognition" by J. Morton & M.H. Johnson from *Psychological Review, 98,* p. 167. Copyright © 1991 by